Table II

O*NET™—SOC 5.1 Definitions
by Code Number

O*NET 5.1 Database Revision and all updates to Dictionary of Occupational Titles with O*NET™ Definitions
5th Edition

Volumes I-III

Table II

Published and for sale by:
CLAITOR'S PUBLISHING DIVISION
P.O. Box 261333, Baton Rouge, LA 70826-1333
800-274-1403 (In LA 225-344-0476)
Fax: 225-344-0480
Internet address:
e mail: claitors@claitors.com
World Wide Web: http://www.claitors.com

ISBN : 1-57980-979-0

Published and for sale by:
CLAITOR'S PUBLISHING DIVISION
P.O. Box 261333, Baton Rouge, LA 70826-1333
800-274-1403 (In LA 225-344-0476)
Fax: 225-344-0480
Internet address:
e mail: claitors@claitors.com
World Wide Web: http://www.claitors.com

*We acknowlege the input and assistance of the U. S. Department of Labor, since much of the following is extracted from their website at http://online.onetcenter.org.

Introduction

The New O*NET 5.0 Database

The O*NET 5.0 database represents a major milestone for the O*NET project. The major data collection underway has resulted in a significant update to the database. Highlights include:

- New and revised Task Statements for 455 O*NET-SOC occupations
- Addition of Task Statement ratings (importance and frequency) for 54 O*NET-SOC occupations
- Updated Abilities, Work Activities, Knowledge, Skills, and Work Context data for 54 occupations
- Addition of Training and Work Experience, and Education data for 54 occupations (not reflected in this Supplement as yet)
- Addition of Work Styles data for 54 occupations
- Addition of metadata to the file structure to specify source of data and date of update
- Addition of Emerging Task Statements
- Addition of Detailed Work Activities

With the November 2003 release of the enhanced O*NET 5.1 database, metadata is now included that will provide users with information that helps in evaluating the quality of the data and valid uses of the data.

Changes provided in Release 5.1

- New and Revised Task Statements (69 occupations)
- Updated Job Zones (54 occupations)

Database Errata: Changes made to the O*NET 5.0 database since its initial release (April 15, 2003) are documented in the O*NET Errata Sheet of June 17, 2003. The purpose of the errata sheet is to enable users of the 5.0 database to maintain consistency with the current database file. The errata sheet explains the changes made to the O*NET database, the reasons for the changes, and ways users may implement the same....

All of the above is incorporated in this Revision #2 of O*NET™ Database 5.0 to enable the user to be as current as possible. As the O*NET organization continues with Revisions 2, 3,4, 5, etc., at semi-annual to annual periods over the next contemplated five years until Revision is completed , we will keep pace with cumulative Revisions, each replacing the prior Revision, to maintain a current sourcebook for the user. Please register with us if you would like to receive these future Revisions, which will be available at moderate cost depending on size.

How to Use This Revision

1. Research the O*NET-SOC Code Number of your interest in Table II of basic volumes I-III.
2. Then go to the same number in this Revision #1 to see changes, if any. If Code Number is not listed in the proper numbering sequence, this means no changes to same in Revision #1 (changes to follow as future Revisions are released).

This material is mostly downloaded from the O*NET website at www.onetcenter.org, and the user is encouraged to go to this site for even further information. We express our appreciation and congratulations to the talented and hardworking O*NET organization for this giant step forward in the vocational field. Many thanks from all of us laboring in this arena for your "sea change" approach and improvements enabling us more capability to better serve the community!

-- Claitor's Publishing Division

11-1021.00 - General and Operations Managers

Plan, direct, or coordinate the operations of companies or public and private sector organizations. Duties and responsibilities include formulating policies, managing daily operations, and planning the use of materials and human resources, but are too diverse and general in nature to be classified in any one functional area of management or administration, such as personnel, purchasing, or administrative services. Includes owners and managers who head small business establishments whose duties are primarily managerial.

Tasks

1) Recommend locations for new facilities or oversee the remodeling of current facilities.

2) Oversee activities directly related to making products or providing services.

3) Establish and implement departmental policies, goals, objectives, and procedures, conferring with board members, organization officials, and staff members as necessary.

4) Monitor businesses and agencies to ensure that they efficiently and effectively provide needed services while staying within budgetary limits.

5) Plan and direct activities such as sales promotions, coordinating with other department heads as required.

6) Review financial statements, sales and activity reports, and other performance data to measure productivity and goal achievement and to determine areas needing cost reduction and program improvement.

7) Determine goods and services to be sold, and set prices and credit terms, based on forecasts of customer demand.

8) Direct and coordinate activities of businesses or departments concerned with the production, pricing, sales, and/or distribution of products.

9) Direct non-merchandising departments of businesses, such as advertising and purchasing.

10) Locate, select, and procure merchandise for resale, representing management in purchase negotiations.

11) Manage the movement of goods into and out of production facilities.

12) Plan store layouts, and design displays.

13) Perform sales floor work such as greeting and assisting customers, stocking shelves, and taking inventory.

14) Determine staffing requirements, and interview, hire and train new employees, or oversee those personnel processes.

15) Direct and coordinate organization's financial and budget activities to fund operations, maximize investments, and increase efficiency.

16) Develop and implement product marketing strategies including advertising campaigns and sales promotions.

11-2011.00 - Advertising and Promotions Managers

Plan and direct advertising policies and programs or produce collateral materials, such as posters, contests, coupons, or give-aways, to create extra interest in the purchase of a product or service for a department, an entire organization, or on an account basis.

Tasks

1) Confer with clients to provide marketing or technical advice.

2) Confer with department heads and/or staff to discuss topics such as contracts, selection of advertising media, or product to be advertised.

3) Monitor and analyze sales promotion results to determine cost effectiveness of promotion campaigns.

4) Coordinate with the media to disseminate advertising.

5) Provide presentation and product demonstration support during the introduction of new products and services to field staff and customers.

6) Gather and organize information to plan advertising campaigns.

7) Inspect layouts and advertising copy and edit scripts, audio and video tapes, and other promotional material for adherence to specifications.

8) Plan and execute advertising policies and strategies for organizations.

9) Prepare and negotiate advertising and sales contracts.

10) Identify and develop contacts for promotional campaigns and industry programs that meet identified buyer targets such as dealers, distributors, or consumers.

11) Plan and prepare advertising and promotional material to increase sales of products or services, working with customers, company officials, sales departments and advertising agencies.

12) Read trade journals and professional literature to stay informed on trends, innovations, and changes that affect media planning.

13) Formulate plans to extend business with established accounts and to transact business as agent for advertising accounts.

14) Direct, motivate, and monitor the mobilization of a campaign team to advance campaign goals.

15) Consult publications to learn about conventions and social functions and to organize prospect files for promotional purposes.

16) Represent company at trade association meetings to promote products.

17) Train and direct workers engaged in developing and producing advertisements.

18) Assemble and communicate with a strong, diverse coalition of organizations and/or public figures, securing their cooperation, support and action, to further campaign goals.

19) Contact organizations to explain services and facilities offered.

20) Direct and coordinate product research and development.

21) Prepare budgets and submit estimates for program costs as part of campaign plan development.

22) Track program budgets and expenses and campaign response rates to evaluate each campaign based on program objectives and industry norms.

23) Assist with annual budget development.

11-2021.00 - Marketing Managers

Determine the demand for products and services offered by a firm and its competitors and identify potential customers. Develop pricing strategies with the goal of maximizing the firm's profits or share of the market while ensuring the firm's customers are satisfied. Oversee product development or monitor trends that indicate the need for new products and services.

Tasks

1) Identify, develop, and evaluate marketing strategy, based on knowledge of establishment objectives, market characteristics, and cost and markup factors.

2) Develop pricing strategies, balancing firm objectives and customer satisfaction.

3) Direct the hiring, training, and performance evaluations of marketing and sales staff and oversee their daily activities.

4) Consult with product development personnel on product specifications such as design, color, and packaging.

5) Evaluate the financial aspects of product development, such as budgets, expenditures, research and development appropriations, and return-on-investment and profit-loss projections.

6) Compile lists describing product or service offerings.

7) Formulate, direct and coordinate marketing activities and policies to promote products and services, working with advertising and promotion managers.

8) Confer with legal staff to resolve problems, such as copyright infringement and royalty sharing with outside producers and distributors.

9) Use sales forecasting and strategic planning to ensure the sale and profitability of products, lines, or services, analyzing business developments and monitoring market trends.

10) Coordinate and participate in promotional activities and trade shows, working with developers, advertisers, and production managers, to market products and services.

11) Select products and accessories to be displayed at trade or special production shows.

12) Conduct economic and commercial surveys to identify potential markets for products and services.

13) Consult with buying personnel to gain advice regarding the types of products or services expected to be in demand.

14) Initiate market research studies and analyze their findings.

15) Advise business and other groups on local, national, and international factors affecting the buying and selling of products and services.

11-2022.00 - Sales Managers

Direct the actual distribution or movement of a product or service to the customer. Coordinate sales distribution by establishing sales territories, quotas, and goals and establish training programs for sales representatives. Analyze sales statistics gathered by staff to determine sales potential and inventory requirements and monitor the preferences of customers.

Tasks

1) Determine price schedules and discount rates.

2) Review operational records and reports to project sales and determine profitability.

3) Direct and coordinate activities involving sales of manufactured products, services, commodities, real estate or other subjects of sale.

4) Monitor customer preferences to determine focus of sales efforts.

5) Direct, coordinate, and review activities in sales and service accounting and record keeping, and in receiving and shipping operations.

6) Represent company at trade association meetings to promote products.

7) Advise dealers and distributors on policies and operating procedures to ensure functional effectiveness of business.

8) Confer or consult with department heads to plan advertising services and to secure information on equipment and customer specifications.

9) Prepare budgets and approve budget expenditures.

10) Confer with potential customers regarding equipment needs and advise customers on types of equipment to purchase.

11) Plan and direct staffing, training, and performance evaluations to develop and control sales and service programs.

12) Direct clerical staff to keep records of export correspondence, bid requests, and credit collections, and to maintain current information on tariffs, licenses, and restrictions.

13) Assess marketing potential of new and existing store locations, considering statistics and expenditures.

14) Oversee regional and local sales managers and their staffs.

15) Visit franchised dealers to stimulate interest in establishment or expansion of leasing programs.

16) Direct foreign sales and service outlets of an organization.

Knowledge	Knowledge Definitions
Mathematics	Knowledge of arithmetic, algebra, geometry, calculus, statistics, and their applications.
Sales and Marketing	Knowledge of principles and methods for showing, promoting, and selling products or services. This includes marketing strategy and tactics, product demonstration, sales techniques, and sales control systems.
Computers and Electronics	Knowledge of circuit boards, processors, chips, electronic equipment, and computer hardware and software, including applications and programming.
English Language	Knowledge of the structure and content of the English language including the meaning and spelling of words, rules of composition, and grammar.
Customer and Personal Service	Knowledge of principles and processes for providing customer and personal services. This includes customer needs assessment, meeting quality standards for services, and evaluation of customer satisfaction.
Administration and Management	Knowledge of business and management principles involved in strategic planning, resource allocation, human resources modeling, leadership technique, production methods, and coordination of people and resources.
Transportation	Knowledge of principles and methods for moving people or goods by air, rail, sea, or road, including the relative costs and benefits.
Clerical	Knowledge of administrative and clerical procedures and systems such as word processing, managing files and records, stenography and transcription, designing forms, and other office procedures and terminology.
Law and Government	Knowledge of laws, legal codes, court procedures, precedents, government regulations, executive orders, agency rules, and the democratic political process.
Communications and Media	Knowledge of media production, communication, and dissemination techniques and methods. This includes alternative ways to inform and entertain via written, oral, and visual media.
Personnel and Human Resources	Knowledge of principles and procedures for personnel recruitment, selection, training, compensation and benefits, labor relations and negotiation, and personnel information systems.
Education and Training	Knowledge of principles and methods for curriculum and training design, teaching and instruction for individuals and groups, and the measurement of training effects.
Economics and Accounting	Knowledge of economic and accounting principles and practices, the financial markets, banking and the analysis and reporting of financial data.
Engineering and Technology	Knowledge of the practical application of engineering science and technology. This includes applying principles, techniques, procedures, and equipment to the design and production of various goods and services.

Geography	Knowledge of principles and methods for describing the features of land, sea, and air masses, including their physical characteristics, locations, interrelationships, and distribution of plant, animal, and human life.
Building and Construction	Knowledge of materials, methods, and the tools involved in the construction or repair of houses, buildings, or other structures such as highways and roads.
Production and Processing	Knowledge of raw materials, production processes, quality control, costs, and other techniques for maximizing the effective manufacture and distribution of goods.
Mechanical	Knowledge of machines and tools, including their designs, uses, repair, and maintenance.
Design	Knowledge of design techniques, tools, and principles involved in production of precision technical plans, blueprints, drawings, and models.
Psychology	Knowledge of human behavior and performance; individual differences in ability, personality, and interests; learning and motivation; psychological research methods; and the assessment and treatment of behavioral and affective disorders.
Chemistry	Knowledge of the chemical composition, structure, and properties of substances and of the chemical processes and transformations that they undergo. This includes uses of chemicals and their interactions, danger signs, production techniques, and disposal methods.
Telecommunications	Knowledge of transmission, broadcasting, switching, control, and operation of telecommunications systems.
Food Production	Knowledge of techniques and equipment for planting, growing, and harvesting food products (both plant and animal) for consumption, including storage/handling techniques.
Physics	Knowledge and prediction of physical principles, laws, their interrelationships, and applications to understanding fluid, material, and atmospheric dynamics, and mechanical, electrical, atomic and sub-atomic structures and processes.
Public Safety and Security	Knowledge of relevant equipment, policies, procedures, and strategies to promote effective local, state, or national security operations for the protection of people, data, property, and institutions.
Biology	Knowledge of plant and animal organisms, their tissues, cells, functions, interdependencies, and interactions with each other and the environment.
Sociology and Anthropology	Knowledge of group behavior and dynamics, societal trends and influences, human migrations, ethnicity, cultures and their history and origins.
Foreign Language	Knowledge of the structure and content of a foreign (non-English) language including the meaning and spelling of words, rules of composition and grammar, and pronunciation.
Therapy and Counseling	Knowledge of principles, methods, and procedures for diagnosis, treatment, and rehabilitation of physical and mental dysfunctions, and for career counseling and guidance.
Philosophy and Theology	Knowledge of different philosophical systems and religions. This includes their basic principles, values, ethics, ways of thinking, customs, practices, and their impact on human culture.
Fine Arts	Knowledge of the theory and techniques required to compose, produce, and perform works of music, dance, visual arts, drama, and sculpture.
Medicine and Dentistry	Knowledge of the information and techniques needed to diagnose and treat human injuries, diseases, and deformities. This includes symptoms, treatment alternatives, drug properties and interactions, and preventive health-care measures.
History and Archeology	Knowledge of historical events and their causes, indicators, and effects on civilizations and cultures.

Skills	Skills Definitions
Active Listening	Giving full attention to what other people are saying, taking time to understand the points being made, asking questions as appropriate, and not interrupting at inappropriate times.
Speaking	Talking to others to convey information effectively.
Mathematics	Using mathematics to solve problems.
Time Management	Managing one's own time and the time of others.
Service Orientation	Actively looking for ways to help people.
Persuasion	Persuading others to change their minds or behavior.
Social Perceptiveness	Being aware of others' reactions and understanding why they react as they do.
Reading Comprehension	Understanding written sentences and paragraphs in work related documents.
Monitoring	Monitoring/Assessing performance of yourself, other individuals, or organizations to make improvements or take corrective action.
Active Learning	Understanding the implications of new information for both current and future problem-solving and decision-making.
Negotiation	Bringing others together and trying to reconcile differences.
Judgment and Decision Making	Considering the relative costs and benefits of potential actions to choose the most appropriate one.
Coordination	Adjusting actions in relation to others' actions.
Instructing	Teaching others how to do something.

Critical Thinking	Using logic and reasoning to identify the strengths and weaknesses of alternative solutions, conclusions or approaches to problems.
Management of Personnel Resources	Motivating, developing, and directing people as they work, identifying the best people for the job.
Complex Problem Solving	Identifying complex problems and reviewing related information to develop and evaluate options and implement solutions.
Writing	Communicating effectively in writing as appropriate for the needs of the audience.
Learning Strategies	Selecting and using training/instructional methods and procedures appropriate for the situation when learning or teaching new things.
Operations Analysis	Analyzing needs and product requirements to create a design.
Management of Financial Resources	Determining how money will be spent to get the work done, and accounting for these expenditures.
Troubleshooting	Determining causes of operating errors and deciding what to do about it.
Management of Material Resources	Obtaining and seeing to the appropriate use of equipment, facilities, and materials needed to do certain work.
Systems Evaluation	Identifying measures or indicators of system performance and the actions needed to improve or correct performance, relative to the goals of the system.
Science	Using scientific rules and methods to solve problems.
Systems Analysis	Determining how a system should work and how changes in conditions, operations, and the environment will affect outcomes.
Operation and Control	Controlling operations of equipment or systems.
Quality Control Analysis	Conducting tests and inspections of products, services, or processes to evaluate quality or performance.
Equipment Selection	Determining the kind of tools and equipment needed to do a job.
Equipment Maintenance	Performing routine maintenance on equipment and determining when and what kind of maintenance is needed.
Technology Design	Generating or adapting equipment and technology to serve user needs.
Operation Monitoring	Watching gauges, dials, or other indicators to make sure a machine is working properly.
Repairing	Repairing machines or systems using the needed tools.
Installation	Installing equipment, machines, wiring, or programs to meet specifications.
Programming	Writing computer programs for various purposes.

Ability	**Ability Definitions**
Oral Expression	The ability to communicate information and ideas in speaking so others will understand.
Speech Clarity	The ability to speak clearly so others can understand you.
Speech Recognition	The ability to identify and understand the speech of another person.
Oral Comprehension	The ability to listen to and understand information and ideas presented through spoken words and sentences.
Problem Sensitivity	The ability to tell when something is wrong or is likely to go wrong. It does not involve solving the problem, only recognizing there is a problem.
Written Comprehension	The ability to read and understand information and ideas presented in writing.
Originality	The ability to come up with unusual or clever ideas about a given topic or situation, or to develop creative ways to solve a problem.
Information Ordering	The ability to arrange things or actions in a certain order or pattern according to a specific rule or set of rules (e.g., patterns of numbers, letters, words, pictures, mathematical operations).
Inductive Reasoning	The ability to combine pieces of information to form general rules or conclusions (includes finding a relationship among seemingly unrelated events).
Deductive Reasoning	The ability to apply general rules to specific problems to produce answers that make sense.
Written Expression	The ability to communicate information and ideas in writing so others will understand.
Near Vision	The ability to see details at close range (within a few feet of the observer).
Fluency of Ideas	The ability to come up with a number of ideas about a topic (the number of ideas is important, not their quality, correctness, or creativity).
Category Flexibility	The ability to generate or use different sets of rules for combining or grouping things in different ways.
Mathematical Reasoning	The ability to choose the right mathematical methods or formulas to solve a problem.
Number Facility	The ability to add, subtract, multiply, or divide quickly and correctly.
Selective Attention	The ability to concentrate on a task over a period of time without being distracted.
Speed of Closure	The ability to quickly make sense of, combine, and organize information into meaningful patterns.

Finger Dexterity	The ability to make precisely coordinated movements of the fingers of one or both hands to grasp, manipulate, or assemble very small objects.
Time Sharing	The ability to shift back and forth between two or more activities or sources of information (such as speech, sounds, touch, or other sources).
Perceptual Speed	The ability to quickly and accurately compare similarities and differences among sets of letters, numbers, objects, pictures, or patterns. The things to be compared may be presented at the same time or one after the other. This ability also includes comparing a presented object with a remembered object.
Flexibility of Closure	The ability to identify or detect a known pattern (a figure, object, word, or sound) that is hidden in other distracting material.
Depth Perception	The ability to judge which of several objects is closer or farther away from you, or to judge the distance between you and an object.
Memorization	The ability to remember information such as words, numbers, pictures, and procedures.
Multilimb Coordination	The ability to coordinate two or more limbs (for example, two arms, two legs, or one leg and one arm) while sitting, standing, or lying down. It does not involve performing the activities while the whole body is in motion.
Static Strength	The ability to exert maximum muscle force to lift, push, pull, or carry objects.
Control Precision	The ability to quickly and repeatedly adjust the controls of a machine or a vehicle to exact positions.
Auditory Attention	The ability to focus on a single source of sound in the presence of other distracting sounds.
Stamina	The ability to exert yourself physically over long periods of time without getting winded or out of breath.
Far Vision	The ability to see details at a distance.
Trunk Strength	The ability to use your abdominal and lower back muscles to support part of the body repeatedly or continuously over time without 'giving out' or fatiguing.
Manual Dexterity	The ability to quickly move your hand, your hand together with your arm, or your two hands to grasp, manipulate, or assemble objects.
Gross Body Coordination	The ability to coordinate the movement of your arms, legs, and torso together when the whole body is in motion.
Speed of Limb Movement	The ability to quickly move the arms and legs.
Visualization	The ability to imagine how something will look after it is moved around or when its parts are moved or rearranged.
Arm-Hand Steadiness	The ability to keep your hand and arm steady while moving your arm or while holding your arm and hand in one position.
Visual Color Discrimination	The ability to match or detect differences between colors, including shades of color and brightness.
Extent Flexibility	The ability to bend, stretch, twist, or reach with your body, arms, and/or legs.
Hearing Sensitivity	The ability to detect or tell the differences between sounds that vary in pitch and loudness.
Dynamic Strength	The ability to exert muscle force repeatedly or continuously over time. This involves muscular endurance and resistance to muscle fatigue.
Gross Body Equilibrium	The ability to keep or regain your body balance or stay upright when in an unstable position.
Spatial Orientation	The ability to know your location in relation to the environment or to know where other objects are in relation to you.
Wrist-Finger Speed	The ability to make fast, simple, repeated movements of the fingers, hands, and wrists.
Sound Localization	The ability to tell the direction from which a sound originated.
Peripheral Vision	The ability to see objects or movement of objects to one's side when the eyes are looking ahead.
Glare Sensitivity	The ability to see objects in the presence of glare or bright lighting.
Rate Control	The ability to time your movements or the movement of a piece of equipment in anticipation of changes in the speed and/or direction of a moving object or scene.
Dynamic Flexibility	The ability to quickly and repeatedly bend, stretch, twist, or reach out with your body, arms, and/or legs.
Explosive Strength	The ability to use short bursts of muscle force to propel oneself (as in jumping or sprinting), or to throw an object.
Night Vision	The ability to see under low light conditions.
Reaction Time	The ability to quickly respond (with the hand, finger, or foot) to a signal (sound, light, picture) when it appears.
Response Orientation	The ability to choose quickly between two or more movements in response to two or more different signals (lights, sounds, pictures). It includes the speed with which the correct response is started with the hand, foot, or other body part.

Work_Activity	**Work_Activity Definitions**
Communicating with Persons Outside Organization	Communicating with people outside the organization, representing the organization to customers, the public, government, and other external sources. This information can be exchanged in person, in writing, or by telephone or e-mail.

Organizing, Planning, and Prioritizing Work	Developing specific goals and plans to prioritize, organize, and accomplish your work.
Making Decisions and Solving Problems	Analyzing information and evaluating results to choose the best solution and solve problems.
Communicating with Supervisors, Peers, or Subordin	Providing information to supervisors, co-workers, and subordinates by telephone, in written form, e-mail, or in person.
Interacting With Computers	Using computers and computer systems (including hardware and software) to program, write software, set up functions, enter data, or process information.
Establishing and Maintaining Interpersonal Relatio	Developing constructive and cooperative working relationships with others, and maintaining them over time.
Updating and Using Relevant Knowledge	Keeping up-to-date technically and applying new knowledge to your job.
Getting Information	Observing, receiving, and otherwise obtaining information from all relevant sources.
Identifying Objects, Actions, and Events	Identifying information by categorizing, estimating, recognizing differences or similarities, and detecting changes in circumstances or events.
Selling or Influencing Others	Convincing others to buy merchandise/goods or to otherwise change their minds or actions.
Developing Objectives and Strategies	Establishing long-range objectives and specifying the strategies and actions to achieve them.
Guiding, Directing, and Motivating Subordinates	Providing guidance and direction to subordinates, including setting performance standards and monitoring performance.
Analyzing Data or Information	Identifying the underlying principles, reasons, or facts of information by breaking down information or data into separate parts.
Performing for or Working Directly with the Public	Performing for people or dealing directly with the public. This includes serving customers in restaurants and stores, and receiving clients or guests.
Processing Information	Compiling, coding, categorizing, calculating, tabulating, auditing, or verifying information or data.
Coordinating the Work and Activities of Others	Getting members of a group to work together to accomplish tasks.
Thinking Creatively	Developing, designing, or creating new applications, ideas, relationships, systems, or products, including artistic contributions.
Scheduling Work and Activities	Scheduling events, programs, and activities, as well as the work of others.
Staffing Organizational Units	Recruiting, interviewing, selecting, hiring, and promoting employees in an organization.
Resolving Conflicts and Negotiating with Others	Handling complaints, settling disputes, and resolving grievances and conflicts, or otherwise negotiating with others.
Monitoring and Controlling Resources	Monitoring and controlling resources and overseeing the spending of money.
Training and Teaching Others	Identifying the educational needs of others, developing formal educational or training programs or classes, and teaching or instructing others.
Developing and Building Teams	Encouraging and building mutual trust, respect, and cooperation among team members.
Estimating the Quantifiable Characteristics of Pro	Estimating sizes, distances, and quantities; or determining time, costs, resources, or materials needed to perform a work activity.
Interpreting the Meaning of Information for Others	Translating or explaining what information means and how it can be used.
Coaching and Developing Others	Identifying the developmental needs of others and coaching, mentoring, or otherwise helping others to improve their knowledge or skills.
Judging the Qualities of Things, Services, or Peop	Assessing the value, importance, or quality of things or people.
Provide Consultation and Advice to Others	Providing guidance and expert advice to management or other groups on technical, systems-, or process-related topics.
Performing Administrative Activities	Performing day-to-day administrative tasks such as maintaining information files and processing paperwork.
Documenting/Recording Information	Entering, transcribing, recording, storing, or maintaining information in written or electronic/magnetic form.
Monitor Processes, Materials, or Surroundings	Monitoring and reviewing information from materials, events, or the environment, to detect or assess problems.
Inspecting Equipment, Structures, or Material	Inspecting equipment, structures, or materials to identify the cause of errors or other problems or defects.
Handling and Moving Objects	Using hands and arms in handling, installing, positioning, and moving materials, and manipulating things.
Evaluating Information to Determine Compliance wit	Using relevant information and individual judgment to determine whether events or processes comply with laws, regulations, or standards.
Assisting and Caring for Others	Providing personal assistance, medical attention, emotional support, or other personal care to others such as coworkers, customers, or patients.
Performing General Physical Activities	Performing physical activities that require considerable use of your arms and legs and moving your whole body, such as climbing, lifting, balancing, walking, stooping, and handling of materials.

Repairing and Maintaining Electronic Equipment	Servicing, repairing, calibrating, regulating, fine-tuning, or testing machines, devices, and equipment that operate primarily on the basis of electrical or electronic (not mechanical) principles.
Operating Vehicles, Mechanized Devices, or Equipme	Running, maneuvering, navigating, or driving vehicles or mechanized equipment, such as forklifts, passenger vehicles, aircraft, or water craft.
Controlling Machines and Processes	Using either control mechanisms or direct physical activity to operate machines or processes (not including computers or vehicles).
Drafting, Laying Out, and Specifying Technical Dev	Providing documentation, detailed instructions, drawings, or specifications to tell others about how devices, parts, equipment, or structures are to be fabricated, constructed, assembled, modified, maintained, or used.
Repairing and Maintaining Mechanical Equipment	Servicing, repairing, adjusting, and testing machines, devices, moving parts, and equipment that operate primarily on the basis of mechanical (not electronic) principles.

Work_Content	Work_Content Definitions
Telephone	How often do you have telephone conversations in this job?
Contact With Others	How much does this job require the worker to be in contact with others (face-to-face, by telephone, or otherwise) in order to perform it?
Electronic Mail	How often do you use electronic mail in this job?
Freedom to Make Decisions	How much decision making freedom, without supervision, does the job offer?
Frequency of Decision Making	How frequently is the worker required to make decisions that affect other people, the financial resources, and/or the image and reputation of the organization?
Structured versus Unstructured Work	To what extent is this job structured for the worker, rather than allowing the worker to determine tasks, priorities, and goals?
Letters and Memos	How often does the job require written letters and memos?
Work With Work Group or Team	How important is it to work with others in a group or team in this job?
Coordinate or Lead Others	How important is it to coordinate or lead others in accomplishing work activities in this job?
Deal With External Customers	How important is it to work with external customers or the public in this job?
Impact of Decisions on Co-workers or Company Resul	How do the decisions an employee makes impact the results of co-workers, clients or the company?
Indoors, Environmentally Controlled	How often does this job require working indoors in environmentally controlled conditions?
Time Pressure	How often does this job require the worker to meet strict deadlines?
Level of Competition	To what extent does this job require the worker to compete or to be aware of competitive pressures?
Importance of Being Exact or Accurate	How important is being very exact or highly accurate in performing this job?
Responsibility for Outcomes and Results	How responsible is the worker for work outcomes and results of other workers?
Face-to-Face Discussions	How often do you have to have face-to-face discussions with individuals or teams in this job?
In an Enclosed Vehicle or Equipment	How often does this job require working in a closed vehicle or equipment (e.g., car)?
Frequency of Conflict Situations	How often are there conflict situations the employee has to face in this job?
Spend Time Sitting	How much does this job require sitting?
Responsible for Others' Health and Safety	How much responsibility is there for the health and safety of others in this job?
Physical Proximity	To what extent does this job require the worker to perform job tasks in close physical proximity to other people?
Importance of Repeating Same Tasks	How important is repeating the same physical activities (e.g., key entry) or mental activities (e.g., checking entries in a ledger) over and over, without stopping, to performing this job?
Deal With Unpleasant or Angry People	How frequently does the worker have to deal with unpleasant, angry, or discourteous individuals as part of the job requirements?
Sounds, Noise Levels Are Distracting or Uncomforta	How often does this job require working exposed to sounds and noise levels that are distracting or uncomfortable?
Public Speaking	How often do you have to perform public speaking in this job?
Degree of Automation	How automated is the job?
Spend Time Walking and Running	How much does this job require walking and running?
Consequence of Error	How serious would the result usually be if the worker made a mistake that was not readily correctable?
Outdoors, Exposed to Weather	How often does this job require working outdoors, exposed to all weather conditions?
Indoors, Not Environmentally Controlled	How often does this job require working indoors in non-controlled environmental conditions (e.g., warehouse without heat)?
Spend Time Standing	How much does this job require standing?
Pace Determined by Speed of Equipment	How important is it to this job that the pace is determined by the speed of equipment or machinery? (This does not refer to keeping busy at all times on this job.)

4

Outdoors, Under Cover	How often does this job require working outdoors, under cover (e.g., structure with roof but no walls)?
Very Hot or Cold Temperatures	How often does this job require working in very hot (above 90 F degrees) or very cold (below 32 F degrees) temperatures?
Spend Time Using Your Hands to Handle, Control, or	How much does this job require using your hands to handle, control, or feel objects, tools or controls?
Extremely Bright or Inadequate Lighting	How often does this job require working in extremely bright or inadequate lighting conditions?
Exposed to Hazardous Equipment	How often does this job require exposure to hazardous equipment?
Wear Common Protective or Safety Equipment such as	How much does this job require wearing common protective or safety equipment such as safety shoes, glasses, gloves, hard hats or live jackets?
Exposed to Hazardous Conditions	How often does this job require exposure to hazardous conditions?
Exposed to Contaminants	How often does this job require working, exposed to contaminants (such as pollutants, gases, dust or odors)?
Cramped Work Space, Awkward Positions	How often does this job require working in cramped work spaces that requires getting into awkward positions?
Spend Time Bending or Twisting the Body	How much does this job require bending or twisting your body?
Spend Time Making Repetitive Motions	How much does this job require making repetitive motions?
Spend Time Kneeling, Crouching, Stooping, or Crawl	How much does this job require kneeling, crouching, stooping or crawling?
Wear Specialized Protective or Safety Equipment su	How much does this job require wearing specialized protective or safety equipment such as breathing apparatus, safety harness, full protection suits, or radiation protection?
Exposed to High Places	How often does this job require exposure to high places?
Spend Time Keeping or Regaining Balance	How much does this job require keeping or regaining your balance?
Spend Time Climbing Ladders, Scaffolds, or Poles	How much does this job require climbing ladders, scaffolds, or poles?
Exposed to Whole Body Vibration	How often does this job require exposure to whole body vibration (e.g., operate a jackhammer)?
Deal With Physically Aggressive People	How frequently does this job require the worker to deal with physical aggression of violent individuals?
In an Open Vehicle or Equipment	How often does this job require working in an open vehicle or equipment (e.g., tractor)?
Exposed to Minor Burns, Cuts, Bites, or Stings	How often does this job require exposure to minor burns, cuts, bites, or stings?
Exposed to Disease or Infections	How often does this job require exposure to disease/infections?
Exposed to Radiation	How often does this job require exposure to radiation?

Work_Styles	Work_Styles Definitions
Attention to Detail	Job requires being careful about detail and thorough in completing work tasks.
Integrity	Job requires being honest and ethical.
Self Control	Job requires maintaining composure, keeping emotions in check, controlling anger, and avoiding aggressive behavior, even in very difficult situations.
Analytical Thinking	Job requires analyzing information and using logic to address work-related issues and problems.
Concern for Others	Job requires being sensitive to others' needs and feelings and being understanding and helpful on the job.
Independence	Job requires developing one's own ways of doing things, guiding oneself with little or no supervision, and depending on oneself to get things done.
Cooperation	Job requires being pleasant with others on the job and displaying a good-natured, cooperative attitude.
Innovation	Job requires creativity and alternative thinking to develop new ideas for and answers to work-related problems.
Persistence	Job requires persistence in the face of obstacles.
Adaptability/Flexibility	Job requires being open to change (positive or negative) and to considerable variety in the workplace.
Dependability	Job requires being reliable, responsible, and dependable, and fulfilling obligations.
Initiative	Job requires a willingness to take on responsibilities and challenges.
Leadership	Job requires a willingness to lead, take charge, and offer opinions and direction.
Stress Tolerance	Job requires accepting criticism and dealing calmly and effectively with high stress situations.
Achievement/Effort	Job requires establishing and maintaining personally challenging achievement goals and exerting effort toward mastering tasks.
Social Orientation	Job requires preferring to work with others rather than alone, and being personally connected with others on the job.

Job Zone Component	Job Zone Component Definitions
Title	Job Zone Four: Considerable Preparation Needed
Overall Experience	A minimum of two to four years of work-related skill, knowledge, or experience is needed for these occupations. For example, an accountant must complete four years of college and work for several years in accounting to be considered qualified.
Job Training	Employees in these occupations usually need several years of work-related experience, on-the-job training, and/or vocational training.
Job Zone Examples	Many of these occupations involve coordinating, supervising, managing, or training others. Examples include accountants, chefs and head cooks, computer programmers, historians, pharmacists, and police detectives.
SVP Range	(7.0 to < 8.0)
Education	Most of these occupations require a four - year bachelor's degree, but some do not.

11-2031.00 - Public Relations Managers

Plan and direct public relations programs designed to create and maintain a favorable public image for employer or client; or if engaged in fundraising, plan and direct activities to solicit and maintain funds for special projects and nonprofit organizations.

Tasks

1) Observe and report on social, economic and political trends that might affect employers.

2) Assign, supervise and review the activities of public relations staff.

3) Direct activities of external agencies, establishments and departments that develop and implement communication strategies and information programs.

4) Evaluate advertising and promotion programs for compatibility with public relations efforts.

5) Facilitate consumer relations, or the relationship between parts of the company such as the managers and employees, or different branch offices.

6) Manage special events such as sponsorship of races, parties introducing new products, or other activities the firm supports in order to gain public attention through the media without advertising directly.

7) Identify main client groups and audiences and determine the best way to communicate publicity information to them.

8) Establish and maintain effective working relationships with local and municipal government officials and media representatives.

9) Confer with labor relations managers to develop internal communications that keep employees informed of company activities.

10) Produce films and other video products, regulate their distribution, and operate film library.

11) Manage in-house communication courses.

12) Establish goals for soliciting funds, develop policies for collection and safeguarding of contributions, and coordinate disbursement of funds.

13) Draft speeches for company executives, and arrange interviews and other forms of contact for them.

14) Develop and maintain the company's corporate image and identity, which includes the use of logos and signage.

15) Write interesting and effective press releases, prepare information for media kits and develop and maintain company internet or intranet web pages.

16) Maintain company archives.

17) Formulate policies and procedures related to public information programs, working with public relations executives.

18) Respond to requests for information about employers' activities or status.

11-3011.00 - Administrative Services Managers

Plan, direct, or coordinate supportive services of an organization, such as recordkeeping, mail distribution, telephone operator/receptionist, and other office support services. May oversee facilities planning and maintenance and custodial operations.

Tasks

1) Direct or coordinate the supportive services department of a business, agency, or organization.

5

2) Analyze internal processes and recommend and implement procedural or policy changes to improve operations, such as supply changes or the disposal of records.

3) Set goals and deadlines for the department.

4) Acquire, distribute and store supplies.

5) Monitor the facility to ensure that it remains safe, secure, and well maintained.

6) Hire and terminate clerical and administrative personnel.

7) Plan, administer and control budgets for contracts, equipment and supplies.

8) Conduct classes to teach procedures to staff.

9) Oversee the maintenance and repair of machinery, equipment, and electrical and mechanical systems.

10) Oversee construction and renovation projects to improve efficiency and to ensure that facilities meet environmental, health, and security standards, and comply with government regulations.

11) Dispose of, or oversee the disposal of, surplus or unclaimed property.

12) Participate in architectural and engineering planning and design, including space and installation management.

13) Manage leasing of facility space.

Knowledge	Knowledge Definitions
Clerical	Knowledge of administrative and clerical procedures and systems such as word processing, managing files and records, stenography and transcription, designing forms, and other office procedures and terminology.
Administration and Management	Knowledge of business and management principles involved in strategic planning, resource allocation, human resources modeling, leadership technique, production methods, and coordination of people and resources.
Customer and Personal Service	Knowledge of principles and processes for providing customer and personal services. This includes customer needs assessment, meeting quality standards for services, and evaluation of customer satisfaction.
Personnel and Human Resources	Knowledge of principles and procedures for personnel recruitment, selection, training, compensation and benefits, labor relations and negotiation, and personnel information systems.
English Language	Knowledge of the structure and content of the English language including the meaning and spelling of words, rules of composition, and grammar.
Law and Government	Knowledge of laws, legal codes, court procedures, precedents, government regulations, executive orders, agency rules, and the democratic political process.
Mathematics	Knowledge of arithmetic, algebra, geometry, calculus, statistics, and their applications.
Economics and Accounting	Knowledge of economic and accounting principles and practices, the financial markets, banking and the analysis and reporting of financial data.
Public Safety and Security	Knowledge of relevant equipment, policies, procedures, and strategies to promote effective local, state, or national security operations for the protection of people, data, property, and institutions.
Communications and Media	Knowledge of media production, communication, and dissemination techniques and methods. This includes alternative ways to inform and entertain via written, oral, and visual media.
Computers and Electronics	Knowledge of circuit boards, processors, chips, electronic equipment, and computer hardware and software, including applications and programming.
Production and Processing	Knowledge of raw materials, production processes, quality control, costs, and other techniques for maximizing the effective manufacture and distribution of goods.
Education and Training	Knowledge of principles and methods for curriculum and training design, teaching and instruction for individuals and groups, and the measurement of training effects.
Transportation	Knowledge of principles and methods for moving people or goods by air, rail, sea, or road, including the relative costs and benefits.
Psychology	Knowledge of human behavior and performance; individual differences in ability, personality, and interests; learning and motivation; psychological research methods; and the assessment and treatment of behavioral and affective disorders.
Sales and Marketing	Knowledge of principles and methods for showing, promoting, and selling products or services. This includes marketing strategy and tactics, product demonstration, sales techniques, and sales control systems.
Sociology and Anthropology	Knowledge of group behavior and dynamics, societal trends and influences, human migrations, ethnicity, cultures and their history and origins.
Engineering and Technology	Knowledge of the practical application of engineering science and technology. This includes applying principles, techniques, procedures, and equipment to the design and production of various goods and services.
Telecommunications	Knowledge of transmission, broadcasting, switching, control, and operation of telecommunications systems.
Mechanical	Knowledge of machines and tools, including their designs, uses, repair, and maintenance.
Food Production	Knowledge of techniques and equipment for planting, growing, and harvesting food products (both plant and animal) for consumption, including storage/handling techniques.
Chemistry	Knowledge of the chemical composition, structure, and properties of substances and of the chemical processes and transformations that they undergo. This includes uses of chemicals and their interactions, danger signs, production techniques, and disposal methods.
Therapy and Counseling	Knowledge of principles, methods, and procedures for diagnosis, treatment, and rehabilitation of physical and mental dysfunctions, and for career counseling and guidance.
Foreign Language	Knowledge of the structure and content of a foreign (non-English) language including the meaning and spelling of words, rules of composition and grammar, and pronunciation.
Medicine and Dentistry	Knowledge of the information and techniques needed to diagnose and treat human injuries, diseases, and deformities. This includes symptoms, treatment alternatives, drug properties and interactions, and preventive health-care measures.
Physics	Knowledge and prediction of physical principles, laws, their interrelationships, and applications to understanding fluid, material, and atmospheric dynamics, and mechanical, electrical, atomic and sub-atomic structures and processes.
Philosophy and Theology	Knowledge of different philosophical systems and religions. This includes their basic principles, values, ethics, ways of thinking, customs, practices, and their impact on human culture.
Geography	Knowledge of principles and methods for describing the features of land, sea, and air masses, including their physical characteristics, locations, interrelationships, and distribution of plant, animal, and human life.
Design	Knowledge of design techniques, tools, and principles involved in production of precision technical plans, blueprints, drawings, and models.
Building and Construction	Knowledge of materials, methods, and the tools involved in the construction or repair of houses, buildings, or other structures such as highways and roads.
History and Archeology	Knowledge of historical events and their causes, indicators, and effects on civilizations and cultures.
Biology	Knowledge of plant and animal organisms, their tissues, cells, functions, interdependencies, and interactions with each other and the environment.
Fine Arts	Knowledge of the theory and techniques required to compose, produce, and perform works of music, dance, visual arts, drama, and sculpture.

Skills	Skills Definitions
Social Perceptiveness	Being aware of others' reactions and understanding why they react as they do.
Time Management	Managing one's own time and the time of others.
Reading Comprehension	Understanding written sentences and paragraphs in work related documents.
Coordination	Adjusting actions in relation to others' actions.
Service Orientation	Actively looking for ways to help people.
Active Listening	Giving full attention to what other people are saying, taking time to understand the points being made, asking questions as appropriate, and not interrupting at inappropriate times.
Active Learning	Understanding the implications of new information for both current and future problem-solving and decision-making.
Instructing	Teaching others how to do something.
Writing	Communicating effectively in writing as appropriate for the needs of the audience.
Speaking	Talking to others to convey information effectively.
Monitoring	Monitoring/Assessing performance of yourself, other individuals, or organizations to make improvements or take corrective action.
Critical Thinking	Using logic and reasoning to identify the strengths and weaknesses of alternative solutions, conclusions or approaches to problems.
Management of Personnel Resources	Motivating, developing, and directing people as they work, identifying the best people for the job.
Management of Financial Resources	Determining how money will be spent to get the work done, and accounting for these expenditures.
Judgment and Decision Making	Considering the relative costs and benefits of potential actions to choose the most appropriate one.
Mathematics	Using mathematics to solve problems.
Complex Problem Solving	Identifying complex problems and reviewing related information to develop and evaluate options and implement solutions.
Learning Strategies	Selecting and using training/instructional methods and procedures appropriate for the situation when learning or teaching new things.
Operation and Control	Controlling operations of equipment or systems.

Negotiation	Bringing others together and trying to reconcile differences.
Persuasion	Persuading others to change their minds or behavior.
Management of Material Resources	Obtaining and seeing to the appropriate use of equipment, facilities, and materials needed to do certain work.
Systems Evaluation	Identifying measures or indicators of system performance and the actions needed to improve or correct performance, relative to the goals of the system.
Operations Analysis	Analyzing needs and product requirements to create a design
Systems Analysis	Determining how a system should work and how changes in conditions, operations, and the environment will affect outcomes.
Operation Monitoring	Watching gauges, dials, or other indicators to make sure a machine is working properly.
Equipment Selection	Determining the kind of tools and equipment needed to do a job.
Troubleshooting	Determining causes of operating errors and deciding what to do about it.
Programming	Writing computer programs for various purposes.
Quality Control Analysis	Conducting tests and inspections of products, services, or processes to evaluate quality or performance.
Equipment Maintenance	Performing routine maintenance on equipment and determining when and what kind of maintenance is needed.
Technology Design	Generating or adapting equipment and technology to serve user needs.
Science	Using scientific rules and methods to solve problems.
Repairing	Repairing machines or systems using the needed tools.
Installation	Installing equipment, machines, wiring, or programs to meet specifications.

Ability	Ability Definitions
Oral Comprehension	The ability to listen to and understand information and ideas presented through spoken words and sentences.
Oral Expression	The ability to communicate information and ideas in speaking so others will understand.
Written Expression	The ability to communicate information and ideas in writing so others will understand.
Speech Clarity	The ability to speak clearly so others can understand you.
Written Comprehension	The ability to read and understand information and ideas presented in writing.
Speech Recognition	The ability to identify and understand the speech of another person.
Problem Sensitivity	The ability to tell when something is wrong or is likely to go wrong. It does not involve solving the problem, only recognizing there is a problem.
Information Ordering	The ability to arrange things or actions in a certain order or pattern according to a specific rule or set of rules (e.g., patterns of numbers, letters, words, pictures, mathematical operations).
Near Vision	The ability to see details at close range (within a few feet of the observer).
Inductive Reasoning	The ability to combine pieces of information to form general rules or conclusions (includes finding a relationship among seemingly unrelated events).
Deductive Reasoning	The ability to apply general rules to specific problems to produce answers that make sense.
Selective Attention	The ability to concentrate on a task over a period of time without being distracted.
Category Flexibility	The ability to generate or use different sets of rules for combining or grouping things in different ways.
Originality	The ability to come up with unusual or clever ideas about a given topic or situation, or to develop creative ways to solve a problem.
Finger Dexterity	The ability to make precisely coordinated movements of the fingers of one or both hands to grasp, manipulate, or assemble very small objects.
Far Vision	The ability to see details at a distance.
Number Facility	The ability to add, subtract, multiply, or divide quickly and correctly.
Fluency of Ideas	The ability to come up with a number of ideas about a topic (the number of ideas is important, not their quality, correctness, or creativity).
Time Sharing	The ability to shift back and forth between two or more activities or sources of information (such as speech, sounds, touch, or other sources).
Memorization	The ability to remember information such as words, numbers, pictures, and procedures.
Mathematical Reasoning	The ability to choose the right mathematical methods or formulas to solve a problem.
Trunk Strength	The ability to use your abdominal and lower back muscles to support part of the body repeatedly or continuously over time without 'giving out' or fatiguing.
Flexibility of Closure	The ability to identify or detect a known pattern (a figure, object, word, or sound) that is hidden in other distracting material.
Speed of Closure	The ability to quickly make sense of, combine, and organize information into meaningful patterns.

Perceptual Speed	The ability to quickly and accurately compare similarities and differences among sets of letters, numbers, objects, pictures, or patterns. The things to be compared may be presented at the same time or one after the other. This ability also includes comparing a presented object with a remembered object.
Auditory Attention	The ability to focus on a single source of sound in the presence of other distracting sounds.
Visualization	The ability to imagine how something will look after it is moved around or when its parts are moved or rearranged.
Depth Perception	The ability to judge which of several objects is closer or farther away from you, or to judge the distance between you and an object.
Manual Dexterity	The ability to quickly move your hand, your hand together with your arm, or your two hands to grasp, manipulate, or assemble objects.
Multilimb Coordination	The ability to coordinate two or more limbs (for example, two arms, two legs, or one leg and one arm) while sitting, standing, or lying down. It does not involve performing the activities while the whole body is in motion.
Control Precision	The ability to quickly and repeatedly adjust the controls of a machine or a vehicle to exact positions.
Hearing Sensitivity	The ability to detect or tell the differences between sounds that vary in pitch and loudness.
Arm-Hand Steadiness	The ability to keep your hand and arm steady while moving your arm or while holding your arm and hand in one position.
Visual Color Discrimination	The ability to match or detect differences between colors, including shades of color and brightness.
Spatial Orientation	The ability to know your location in relation to the environment or to know where other objects are in relation to you.
Static Strength	The ability to exert maximum muscle force to lift, push, pull, or carry objects.
Extent Flexibility	The ability to bend, stretch, twist, or reach with your body, arms, and/or legs.
Stamina	The ability to exert yourself physically over long periods of time without getting winded or out of breath.
Wrist-Finger Speed	The ability to make fast, simple, repeated movements of the fingers, hands, and wrists.
Response Orientation	The ability to choose quickly between two or more movements in response to two or more different signals (lights, sounds, pictures). It includes the speed with which the correct response is started with the hand, foot, or other body part.
Reaction Time	The ability to quickly respond (with the hand, finger, or foot) to a signal (sound, light, picture) when it appears.
Explosive Strength	The ability to use short bursts of muscle force to propel oneself (as in jumping or sprinting), or to throw an object.
Dynamic Strength	The ability to exert muscle force repeatedly or continuously over time. This involves muscular endurance and resistance to muscle fatigue.
Dynamic Flexibility	The ability to quickly and repeatedly bend, stretch, twist, or reach out with your body, arms, and/or legs.
Gross Body Coordination	The ability to coordinate the movement of your arms, legs, and torso together when the whole body is in motion.
Gross Body Equilibrium	The ability to keep or regain your body balance or stay upright when in an unstable position.
Glare Sensitivity	The ability to see objects in the presence of glare or bright lighting.
Speed of Limb Movement	The ability to quickly move the arms and legs.
Sound Localization	The ability to tell the direction from which a sound originated.
Rate Control	The ability to time your movements or the movement of a piece of equipment in anticipation of changes in the speed and/or direction of a moving object or scene.
Peripheral Vision	The ability to see objects or movement of objects to one's side when the eyes are looking ahead.
Night Vision	The ability to see under low light conditions.

Work_Activity	Work_Activity Definitions
Getting Information	Observing, receiving, and otherwise obtaining information from all relevant sources.
Making Decisions and Solving Problems	Analyzing information and evaluating results to choose the best solution and solve problems.
Communicating with Supervisors, Peers, or Subordin	Providing information to supervisors, co-workers, and subordinates by telephone, in written form, e-mail, or in person.
Communicating with Persons Outside Organization	Communicating with people outside the organization, representing the organization to customers, the public, government, and other external sources. This information can be exchanged in person, in writing, or by telephone or e-mail.
Organizing, Planning, and Prioritizing Work	Developing specific goals and plans to prioritize, organize, and accomplish your work.
Performing for or Working Directly with the Public	Performing for people or dealing directly with the public. This includes serving customers in restaurants and stores, and receiving clients or guests.
Performing Administrative Activities	Performing day-to-day administrative tasks such as maintaining information files and processing paperwork.

Establishing and Maintaining Interpersonal Relatio	Developing constructive and cooperative working relationships with others, and maintaining them over time.
Interacting With Computers	Using computers and computer systems (including hardware and software) to program, write software, set up functions, enter data, or process information.
Documenting/Recording Information	Entering, transcribing, recording, storing, or maintaining information in written or electronic/magnetic form.
Identifying Objects, Actions, and Events	Identifying information by categorizing, estimating, recognizing differences or similarities, and detecting changes in circumstances or events.
Analyzing Data or Information	Identifying the underlying principles, reasons, or facts of information by breaking down information or data into separate parts.
Judging the Qualities of Things, Services, or Peop	Assessing the value, importance, or quality of things or people.
Resolving Conflicts and Negotiating with Others	Handling complaints, settling disputes, and resolving grievances and conflicts, or otherwise negotiating with others.
Monitoring and Controlling Resources	Monitoring and controlling resources and overseeing the spending of money.
Evaluating Information to Determine Compliance wit	Using relevant information and individual judgment to determine whether events or processes comply with laws, regulations, or standards.
Thinking Creatively	Developing, designing, or creating new applications, ideas, relationships, systems, or products, including artistic contributions.
Processing Information	Compiling, coding, categorizing, calculating, tabulating, auditing, or verifying information or data.
Coordinating the Work and Activities of Others	Getting members of a group to work together to accomplish tasks.
Scheduling Work and Activities	Scheduling events, programs, and activities, as well as the work of others.
Updating and Using Relevant Knowledge	Keeping up-to-date technically and applying new knowledge to your job.
Interpreting the Meaning of Information for Others	Translating or explaining what information means and how it can be used.
Provide Consultation and Advice to Others	Providing guidance and expert advice to management or other groups on technical, systems-, or process-related topics.
Monitor Processes, Materials, or Surroundings	Monitoring and reviewing information from materials, events, or the environment, to detect or assess problems.
Coaching and Developing Others	Identifying the developmental needs of others and coaching, mentoring, or otherwise helping others to improve their knowledge or skills.
Assisting and Caring for Others	Providing personal assistance, medical attention, emotional support, or other personal care to others such as coworkers, customers, or patients.
Developing Objectives and Strategies	Establishing long-range objectives and specifying the strategies and actions to achieve them.
Staffing Organizational Units	Recruiting, interviewing, selecting, hiring, and promoting employees in an organization.
Inspecting Equipment, Structures, or Material	Inspecting equipment, structures, or materials to identify the cause of errors or other problems or defects.
Guiding, Directing, and Motivating Subordinates	Providing guidance and direction to subordinates, including setting performance standards and monitoring performance.
Training and Teaching Others	Identifying the educational needs of others, developing formal educational or training programs or classes, and teaching or instructing others.
Developing and Building Teams	Encouraging and building mutual trust, respect, and cooperation among team members.
Selling or Influencing Others	Convincing others to buy merchandise/goods or to otherwise change their minds or actions.
Estimating the Quantifiable Characteristics of Pro	Estimating sizes, distances, and quantities; or determining time, costs, resources, or materials needed to perform a work activity.
Performing General Physical Activities	Performing physical activities that require considerable use of your arms and legs and moving your whole body, such as climbing, lifting, balancing, walking, stooping, and handling of materials.
Handling and Moving Objects	Using hands and arms in handling, installing, positioning, and moving materials, and manipulating things.
Operating Vehicles, Mechanized Devices, or Equipme	Running, maneuvering, navigating, or driving vehicles or mechanized equipment, such as forklifts, passenger vehicles, aircraft, or water craft.
Controlling Machines and Processes	Using either control mechanisms or direct physical activity to operate machines or processes (not including computers or vehicles).
Repairing and Maintaining Mechanical Equipment	Servicing, repairing, adjusting, and testing machines, devices, moving parts, and equipment that operate primarily on the basis of mechanical (not electronic) principles.
Drafting, Laying Out, and Specifying Technical Dev	Providing documentation, detailed instructions, drawings, or specifications to tell others about how devices, parts, equipment, or structures are to be fabricated, constructed, assembled, modified, maintained, or used.

Repairing and Maintaining Electronic Equipment	Servicing, repairing, calibrating, regulating, fine-tuning, or testing machines, devices, and equipment that operate primarily on the basis of electrical or electronic (not mechanical) principles.

Work_Content	Work_Content Definitions
Telephone	How often do you have telephone conversations in this job?
Face-to-Face Discussions	How often do you have to have face-to-face discussions with individuals or teams in this job?
Contact With Others	How much does the job require the worker to be in contact with others (face-to-face, by telephone, or otherwise) in order to perform it?
Letters and Memos	How often does the job require written letters and memos?
Structured versus Unstructured Work	To what extent is this job structured for the worker, rather than allowing the worker to determine tasks, priorities, and goals?
Electronic Mail	How often do you use electronic mail in this job?
Work With Work Group or Team	How important is it to work with others in a group or team in this job?
Freedom to Make Decisions	How much decision making freedom, without supervision, does the job offer?
Coordinate or Lead Others	How important is it to coordinate or lead others in accomplishing work activities in this job?
Frequency of Decision Making	How frequently is the worker required to make decisions that affect other people, the financial resources, and/or the image and reputation of the organization?
Responsibility for Outcomes and Results	How responsible is the worker for work outcomes and results of other workers?
Indoors, Environmentally Controlled	How often does this job require working indoors in environmentally controlled conditions?
Deal With External Customers	How important is it to work with external customers or the public in this job?
Impact of Decisions on Co-workers or Company Resul	How do the decisions an employee makes impact the results of co-workers, clients or the company?
Responsible for Others' Health and Safety	How much responsibility is there for the health and safety of others in this job?
Importance of Being Exact or Accurate	How important is being very exact or highly accurate in performing this job?
Time Pressure	How often does this job require the worker to meet strict deadlines?
Deal With Unpleasant or Angry People	How frequently does the worker have to deal with unpleasant, angry, or discourteous individuals as part of the job requirements?
Importance of Repeating Same Tasks	How important is repeating the same physical activities (e.g., key entry) or mental activities (e.g., checking entries in a ledger) over and over, without stopping, to performing this job?
Frequency of Conflict Situations	How often are there conflict situations the employee has to face in this job?
Spend Time Standing	How much does this job require standing?
Consequence of Error	How serious would the result usually be if the worker made a mistake that was not readily correctable?
Degree of Automation	How automated is the job?
Spend Time Sitting	How much does this job require sitting?
Spend Time Using Your Hands to Handle, Control, or	How much does this job require using your hands to handle, control, or feel objects, tools or controls?
Sounds, Noise Levels Are Distracting or Uncomforta	How often does this job require working exposed to sounds and noise levels that are distracting or uncomfortable?
Spend Time Making Repetitive Motions	How much does this job require making repetitive motions?
Exposed to Contaminants	How often does this job require working exposed to contaminants (such as pollutants, gases, dust or odors)?
In an Enclosed Vehicle or Equipment	How often does this job require working in a closed vehicle or equipment (e.g., car)?
Physical Proximity	To what extent does this job require the worker to perform job tasks in close physical proximity to other people?
Spend Time Walking and Running	How much does this job require walking and running?
Outdoors, Exposed to Weather	How often does this job require working outdoors, exposed to all weather conditions?
Level of Competition	To what extent does this job require the worker to compete or to be aware of competitive pressures?
Public Speaking	How often do you have to perform public speaking in this job?
Spend Time Bending or Twisting the Body	How much does this job require bending or twisting your body?
Wear Common Protective or Safety Equipment such as	How much does this job require wearing common protective or safety equipment such as safety shoes, glasses, gloves, hard hats or live jackets?
Deal With Physically Aggressive People	How frequently does this job require the worker to deal with physical aggression of violent individuals?
Very Hot or Cold Temperatures	How often does this job require working in very hot (above 90 F degrees) or very cold (below 32 F degrees) temperatures?
Exposed to Disease or Infections	How often does this job require exposure to disease/infections?

Cramped Work Space, Awkward Positions	How often does this job require working in cramped work spaces that requires getting into awkward positions?
Spend Time Kneeling, Crouching, Stooping, or Crawl	How much does this job require kneeling, crouching, stooping or crawling?
Exposed to Minor Burns, Cuts, Bites, or Stings	How often does this job require exposure to minor burns, cuts, bites, or stings?
Spend Time Climbing Ladders, Scaffolds, or Poles	How much does this job require climbing ladders, scaffolds, or poles?
Exposed to Hazardous Conditions	How often does this job require exposure to hazardous conditions?
In an Open Vehicle or Equipment	How often does this job require working in an open vehicle or equipment (e.g., tractor)?
Exposed to Hazardous Equipment	How often does this job require exposure to hazardous equipment?
Indoors, Not Environmentally Controlled	How often does this job require working indoors in non-controlled environmental conditions (e.g., warehouse without heat)?
Extremely Bright or Inadequate Lighting	How often does this job require working in extremely bright or inadequate lighting conditions?
Pace Determined by Speed of Equipment	How important is it to this job that the pace is determined by the speed of equipment or machinery? (This does not refer to keeping busy at all times on this job.)
Exposed to High Places	How often does this job require exposure to high places?
Exposed to Radiation	How often does this job require exposure to radiation?
Outdoors, Under Cover	How often does this job require working outdoors, under cover (e.g., structure with roof but no walls)?
Wear Specialized Protective or Safety Equipment su	How much does this job require wearing specialized protective or safety equipment such as breathing apparatus, safety harness, full protection suits, or radiation protection?
Spend Time Keeping or Regaining Balance	How much does this job require keeping or regaining your balance?
Exposed to Whole Body Vibration	How often does this job require exposure to whole body vibration (e.g., operate a jackhammer)?

Work_Styles	Work_Styles Definitions
Integrity	Job requires being honest and ethical.
Dependability	Job requires being reliable, responsible, and dependable, and fulfilling obligations.
Leadership	Job requires a willingness to lead, take charge, and offer opinions and direction.
Independence	Job requires developing one's own ways of doing things, guiding oneself with little or no supervision, and depending on oneself to get things done.
Attention to Detail	Job requires being careful about detail and thorough in completing work tasks.
Self Control	Job requires maintaining composure, keeping emotions in check, controlling anger, and avoiding aggressive behavior, even in very difficult situations.
Cooperation	Job requires being pleasant with others on the job and displaying a good-natured, cooperative attitude.
Social Orientation	Job requires preferring to work with others rather than alone, and being personally connected with others on the job.
Concern for Others	Job requires being sensitive to others' needs and feelings and being understanding and helpful on the job.
Adaptability/Flexibility	Job requires being open to change (positive or negative) and to considerable variety in the workplace.
Stress Tolerance	Job requires accepting criticism and dealing calmly and effectively with high stress situations.
Analytical Thinking	Job requires analyzing information and using logic to address work-related issues and problems.
Initiative	Job requires a willingness to take on responsibilities and challenges.
Innovation	Job requires creativity and alternative thinking to develop new ideas for and answers to work-related problems.
Persistence	Job requires persistence in the face of obstacles.
Achievement/Effort	Job requires establishing and maintaining personally challenging achievement goals and exerting effort toward mastering tasks.

Job Zone Component	Job Zone Component Definitions
Title	Job Zone Four: Considerable Preparation Needed
Overall Experience	A minimum of two to four years of work-related skill, knowledge, or experience is needed for these occupations. For example, an accountant must complete four years of college and work for several years in accounting to be considered qualified.
Job Training	Employees in these occupations usually need several years of work-related experience, on-the-job training, and/or vocational training.

Job Zone Examples	Many of these occupations involve coordinating, supervising, managing, or training others. Examples include accountants, chefs and head cooks, computer programmers, historians, pharmacists, and police detectives.
SVP Range	(7.0 to < 8.0)
Education	Most of these occupations require a four - year bachelor's degree, but some do not.

11-3021.00 - Computer and Information Systems Managers

Plan, direct, or coordinate activities in such fields as electronic data processing, information systems, systems analysis, and computer programming.

Tasks

1) Develop and interpret organizational goals, policies, and procedures.

2) Assign and review the work of systems analysts, programmers, and other computer-related workers.

3) Consult with users, management, vendors, and technicians to assess computing needs and system requirements.

4) Develop computer information resources, providing for data security and control, strategic computing, and disaster recovery.

5) Evaluate the organization's technology use and needs and recommend improvements, such as hardware and software upgrades.

6) Review and approve all systems charts and programs prior to their implementation.

7) Control operational budget and expenditures.

8) Evaluate data processing proposals to assess project feasibility and requirements.

9) Manage backup, security and user help systems.

10) Meet with department heads, managers, supervisors, vendors, and others, to solicit cooperation and resolve problems.

11) Prepare and review operational reports or project progress reports.

12) Purchase necessary equipment.

13) Review project plans in order to plan and coordinate project activity.

14) Stay abreast of advances in technology.

15) Recruit, hire, train and supervise staff, and/or participate in staffing decisions.

11-3031.01 - Treasurers, Controllers, and Chief Financial Officers

Plan, direct, and coordinate the financial activities of an organization at the highest level of management. Includes financial reserve officers.

Tasks

1) Prepare and file annual tax returns, or prepare financial information so that outside accountants can complete tax returns.

2) Receive cash and checks, and deposit funds.

3) Monitor and evaluate the performance of accounting and other financial staff; recommend and implement personnel actions such as promotions and dismissals.

4) Develop and maintain relationships with banking, insurance, and non-organizational accounting personnel in order to facilitate financial activities.

5) Monitor financial activities and details such as reserve levels to ensure that all legal and regulatory requirements are met.

6) Analyze the financial details of past, present, and expected operations in order to identify development opportunities and areas where improvement is needed.

7) Perform tax planning work.

8) Evaluate needs for procurement of funds and investment of surpluses, and make appropriate recommendations.

9) Lead staff training and development in budgeting and financial management areas.

10) Maintain current knowledge of organizational policies and procedures, federal and state policies and directives, and current accounting standards.

11) Receive and record requests for disbursements; authorize disbursements in accordance with policies and procedures.

12) Determine depreciation rates to apply to capitalized items, and advise management on actions regarding the purchase, lease, or disposal of such items.

13) Delegate authority for the receipt, disbursement, banking, protection, and custody of funds, securities, and financial instruments.

14) Advise management on short-term and long-term financial objectives, policies, and actions.

15) Prepare or direct preparation of financial statements. business activity reports, financial position forecasts, annual budgets, and/or reports required by regulatory agencies.

16) Develop internal control policies. guidelines. and procedures for activities such as budget administration, cash and credit management. and accounting.

17) Supervise employees performing financial reporting. accounting. billing, collections. payroll, and budgeting duties.

18) Compute, withhold, and account for all payroll deductions.

19) Conduct or coordinate audits of company accounts and financial transactions to ensure compliance with state and federal requirements and statutes.

20) Coordinate and direct the financial planning, budgeting, procurement, or investment activities of all or part of an organization.

11-3040.00 - Human Resources Managers

Plan, direct, and coordinate human resource management activities of an organization to maximize the strategic use of human resources and maintain functions such as employee compensation, recruitment, personnel policies, and regulatory compliance.

Tasks

1) Allocate human resources, ensuring appropriate matches between personnel.

2) Analyze training needs to design employee development. language training and health and safety programs.

3) Advise managers on organizational policy matters such as equal employment opportunity and sexual harassment, and recommend needed changes.

4) Develop, administer and evaluate applicant tests.

5) Identify staff vacancies and recruit, interview and select applicants.

6) Maintain records and compile statistical reports concerning personnel-related data such as hires, transfers, performance appraisals, and absenteeism rates.

7) Oversee the evaluation, classification and rating of occupations and job positions.

8) Administer compensation, benefits and performance management systems, and safety and recreation programs.

9) Analyze statistical data and reports to identify and determine causes of personnel problems and develop recommendations for improvement of organization's personnel policies and practices.

10) Conduct exit interviews to identify reasons for employee termination.

11) Plan and conduct new employee orientation to foster positive attitude toward organizational objectives.

12) Prepare personnel forecast to project employment needs.

13) Investigate and report on industrial accidents for insurance carriers.

14) Perform difficult staffing duties, including dealing with understaffing, refereeing disputes, firing employees, and administering disciplinary procedures.

15) Prepare and follow budgets for personnel operations.

16) Study legislation, arbitration decisions, and collective bargaining contracts to assess industry trends.

17) Provide current and prospective employees with information about policies, job duties, working conditions, wages, opportunities for promotion and employee benefits

18) Provide terminated employees with outplacement or relocation assistance.

19) Serve as a link between management and employees by handling questions, interpreting and administering contracts and helping resolve work-related problems.

20) Develop and/or administer special projects in areas such as pay equity, savings bond programs, day-care, and employee awards.

21) Represent organization at personnel-related hearings and investigations.

22) Contract with vendors to provide employee services, such as food service, transportation, or relocation service.

23) Plan, organize, direct, control or coordinate the personnel, training, or labor relations activities of an organization

24) Negotiate bargaining agreements and help interpret labor contracts.

25) Analyze and modify compensation and benefits policies to establish competitive programs and ensure compliance with legal requirements.

11-3041.00 - Compensation and Benefits Managers

Plan, direct, or coordinate compensation and benefits activities and staff of an organization.

Tasks

1) Plan, direct. supervise, and coordinate work activities of subordinates and staff relating to employment. compensation. labor relations, and employee relations.

2) Administer, direct, and review employee benefit programs, including the integration of benefit programs following mergers and acquisitions.

3) Analyze statistical data and reports to identify and determine causes of personnel problems and develop recommendations for improvement of organization's personnel policies and practices.

4) Develop methods to improve employment policies, processes, and practices. and recommend changes to management.

5) Direct preparation and distribution of written and verbal information to inform employees of benefits, compensation, and personnel policies.

6) Identify and implement benefits to increase the quality of life for employees, by working with brokers and researching benefits issues.

7) Analyze compensation policies, government regulations, and prevailing wage rates to develop competitive compensation plan.

8) Manage the design and development of tools to assist employees in benefits selection, and to guide managers through compensation decisions.

9) Plan and conduct new employee orientations to foster positive attitude toward organizational objectives.

10) Design, evaluate and modify benefits policies to ensure that programs are current, competitive and in compliance with legal requirements.

11) Fulfill all reporting requirements of all relevant government rules and regulations, including the Employee Retirement Income Security Act (ERISA).

12) Negotiate bargaining agreements.

13) Prepare budgets for personnel operations.

14) Conduct exit interviews to identify reasons for employee termination.

15) Investigate and report on industrial accidents for insurance carriers.

16) Advise management on such matters as equal employment opportunity, sexual harassment and discrimination.

17) Prepare personnel forecasts to project employment needs.

18) Resolve labor disputes and grievances.

19) Study legislation, arbitration decisions, and collective bargaining contracts to assess industry trends.

20) Contract with vendors to provide employee services, such as food services, transportation, or relocation service.

21) Represent organization at personnel-related hearings and investigations.

22) Formulate policies, procedures and programs for recruitment, testing, placement, classification, orientation, benefits and compensation, and labor and industrial relations.

23) Prepare detailed job descriptions and classification systems and define job levels and families, in partnership with other managers.

24) Maintain records and compile statistical reports concerning personnel-related data such as hires, transfers, performance appraisals, and absenteeism rates.

11-3042.00 - Training and Development Managers

Plan, direct, or coordinate the training and development activities and staff of an organization.

Tasks

1) Develop testing and evaluation procedures.

2) Analyze training needs to develop new training programs or modify and improve existing programs.

3) Conduct or arrange for ongoing technical training and personal development classes for staff members.

4) Conduct orientation sessions and arrange on-the-job training for new hires.

5) Confer with management and conduct surveys to identify training needs based on projected production processes, changes, and other factors.

6) Develop and organize training manuals, multimedia visual aids. and other educational materials.

7) Coordinate established courses with technical and professional courses provided by community schools and designate training procedures.

8) Review and evaluate training and apprenticeship programs for compliance with government standards.

10

9) Evaluate instructor performance and the effectiveness of training programs, providing recommendations for improvement.

10) Prepare training budget for department or organization.

11) Plan, develop, and provide training and staff development programs, using knowledge of the effectiveness of methods such as classroom training, demonstrations, on-the-job training, meetings, conferences, and workshops.

11-3051.00 - Industrial Production Managers

Plan, direct, or coordinate the work activities and resources necessary for manufacturing products in accordance with cost, quality, and quantity specifications.

Tasks

1) Review processing schedules and production orders to make decisions concerning inventory requirements, staffing requirements, work procedures, and duty assignments, considering budgetary limitations and time constraints.

2) Direct and coordinate production, processing, distribution, and marketing activities of industrial organization.

3) Hire, train, evaluate, and discharge staff, and resolve personnel grievances.

4) Develop and implement production tracking and quality control systems, analyzing production, quality control, maintenance, and other operational reports, to detect production problems.

5) Coordinate and recommend procedures for facility and equipment maintenance or modification, including the replacement of machines.

6) Set and monitor product standards, examining samples of raw products or directing testing during processing, to ensure finished products are of prescribed quality.

7) Develop budgets and approve expenditures for supplies, materials, and human resources, ensuring that materials, labor and equipment are used efficiently to meet production targets.

8) Institute employee suggestion or involvement programs.

9) Prepare and maintain production reports and personnel records.

10) Maintain current knowledge of the quality control field, relying on current literature pertaining to materials use, technological advances, and statistical studies.

11) Initiate and coordinate inventory and cost control programs.

12) Review plans and confer with research and support staff to develop new products and processes.

13) Negotiate materials prices with suppliers.

Knowledge / Knowledge Definitions

Knowledge	Knowledge Definitions
Production and Processing	Knowledge of raw materials, production processes, quality control, costs, and other techniques for maximizing the effective manufacture and distribution of goods.
Administration and Management	Knowledge of business and management principles involved in strategic planning, resource allocation, human resources modeling, leadership technique, production methods, and coordination of people and resources.
Mathematics	Knowledge of arithmetic, algebra, geometry, calculus, statistics, and their applications.
Education and Training	Knowledge of principles and methods for curriculum and training design, teaching and instruction for individuals and groups, and the measurement of training effects.
Mechanical	Knowledge of machines and tools, including their designs, uses, repair, and maintenance.
Personnel and Human Resources	Knowledge of principles and procedures for personnel recruitment, selection, training, compensation and benefits, labor relations and negotiation, and personnel information systems.
English Language	Knowledge of the structure and content of the English language including the meaning and spelling of words, rules of composition, and grammar.
Customer and Personal Service	Knowledge of principles and processes for providing customer and personal services. This includes customer needs assessment, meeting quality standards for services, and evaluation of customer satisfaction.
Engineering and Technology	Knowledge of the practical application of engineering science and technology. This includes applying principles, techniques, procedures, and equipment to the design and production of various goods and services.
Design	Knowledge of design techniques, tools, and principles involved in production of precision technical plans, blueprints, drawings, and models.
Psychology	Knowledge of human behavior and performance; individual differences in ability, personality, and interests; learning and motivation; psychological research methods; and the assessment and treatment of behavioral and affective disorders.
Sales and Marketing	Knowledge of principles and methods for showing, promoting, and selling products or services. This includes marketing strategy and tactics, product demonstration, sales techniques, and sales control systems.
Economics and Accounting	Knowledge of economic and accounting principles and practices, the financial markets, banking and the analysis and reporting of financial data.
Clerical	Knowledge of administrative and clerical procedures and systems such as word processing, managing files and records, stenography and transcription, designing forms, and other office procedures and terminology.
Public Safety and Security	Knowledge of relevant equipment, policies, procedures, and strategies to promote effective local, state, or national security operations for the protection of people, data, property, and institutions.
Transportation	Knowledge of principles and methods for moving people or goods by air, rail, sea, or road, including the relative costs and benefits.
Chemistry	Knowledge of the chemical composition, structure, and properties of substances and of the chemical processes and transformations that they undergo. This includes uses of chemicals and their interactions, danger signs, production techniques, and disposal methods.
Law and Government	Knowledge of laws, legal codes, court procedures, precedents, government regulations, executive orders, agency rules, and the democratic political process.
Computers and Electronics	Knowledge of circuit boards, processors, chips, electronic equipment, and computer hardware and software, including applications and programming.
Communications and Media	Knowledge of media production, communication, and dissemination techniques and methods. This includes alternative ways to inform and entertain via written, oral, and visual media.
Physics	Knowledge and prediction of physical principles, laws, their interrelationships, and applications to understanding fluid, material, and atmospheric dynamics, and mechanical, electrical, atomic and sub-atomic structures and processes.
Telecommunications	Knowledge of transmission, broadcasting, switching, control, and operation of telecommunications systems.
Building and Construction	Knowledge of materials, methods, and the tools involved in the construction or repair of houses, buildings, or other structures such as highways and roads.
Food Production	Knowledge of techniques and equipment for planting, growing, and harvesting food products (both plant and animal) for consumption, including storage/handling techniques.
Geography	Knowledge of principles and methods for describing the features of land, sea, and air masses, including their physical characteristics, locations, interrelationships, and distribution of plant, animal, and human life.
Sociology and Anthropology	Knowledge of group behavior and dynamics, societal trends and influences, human migrations, ethnicity, cultures and their history and origins.
Therapy and Counseling	Knowledge of principles, methods, and procedures for diagnosis, treatment, and rehabilitation of physical and mental dysfunctions, and for career counseling and guidance.
Biology	Knowledge of plant and animal organisms, their tissues, cells, functions, interdependencies, and interactions with each other and the environment.
Foreign Language	Knowledge of the structure and content of a foreign (non-English) language including the meaning and spelling of words, rules of composition and grammar, and pronunciation.
Medicine and Dentistry	Knowledge of the information and techniques needed to diagnose and treat human injuries, diseases, and deformities. This includes symptoms, treatment alternatives, drug properties and interactions, and preventive health-care measures.
Philosophy and Theology	Knowledge of different philosophical systems and religions. This includes their basic principles, values, ethics, ways of thinking, customs, practices, and their impact on human culture.
History and Archeology	Knowledge of historical events and their causes, indicators, and effects on civilizations and cultures.
Fine Arts	Knowledge of the theory and techniques required to compose, produce, and perform works of music, dance, visual arts, drama, and sculpture.

Skills / Skills Definitions

Skills	Skills Definitions
Active Listening	Giving full attention to what other people are saying, taking time to understand the points being made, asking questions as appropriate, and not interrupting at inappropriate times.
Judgment and Decision Making	Considering the relative costs and benefits of potential actions to choose the most appropriate one.
Critical Thinking	Using logic and reasoning to identify the strengths and weaknesses of alternative solutions, conclusions or approaches to problems.
Reading Comprehension	Understanding written sentences and paragraphs in work related documents.

Management of Personnel Resources	Motivating, developing, and directing people as they work, identifying the best people for the job.
Coordination	Adjusting actions in relation to others' actions.
Monitoring	Monitoring/Assessing performance of yourself, other individuals, or organizations to make improvements or take corrective action.
Time Management	Managing one's own time and the time of others.
Complex Problem Solving	Identifying complex problems and reviewing related information to develop and evaluate options and implement solutions.
Speaking	Talking to others to convey information effectively.
Instructing	Teaching others how to do something.
Quality Control Analysis	Conducting tests and inspections of products, services, or processes to evaluate quality or performance.
Management of Material Resources	Obtaining and seeing to the appropriate use of equipment, facilities, and materials needed to do certain work.
Equipment Selection	Determining the kind of tools and equipment needed to do a job.
Persuasion	Persuading others to change their minds or behavior.
Operations Analysis	Analyzing needs and product requirements to create a design.
Active Learning	Understanding the implications of new information for both current and future problem-solving and decision-making.
Social Perceptiveness	Being aware of others' reactions and understanding why they react as they do.
Mathematics	Using mathematics to solve problems.
Systems Evaluation	Identifying measures or indicators of system performance and the actions needed to improve or correct performance, relative to the goals of the system.
Writing	Communicating effectively in writing as appropriate for the needs of the audience.
Learning Strategies	Selecting and using training/instructional methods and procedures appropriate for the situation when learning or teaching new things.
Systems Analysis	Determining how a system should work and how changes in conditions, operations, and the environment will affect outcomes.
Service Orientation	Actively looking for ways to help people.
Negotiation	Bringing others together and trying to reconcile differences.
Troubleshooting	Determining causes of operating errors and deciding what to do about it.
Management of Financial Resources	Determining how money will be spent to get the work done, and accounting for these expenditures.
Operation and Control	Controlling operations of equipment or systems.
Operation Monitoring	Watching gauges, dials, or other indicators to make sure a machine is working properly.
Equipment Maintenance	Performing routine maintenance on equipment and determining when and what kind of maintenance is needed.
Technology Design	Generating or adapting equipment and technology to serve user needs.
Science	Using scientific rules and methods to solve problems.
Repairing	Repairing machines or systems using the needed tools.
Installation	Installing equipment, machines, wiring, or programs to meet specifications.
Programming	Writing computer programs for various purposes.

Ability	**Ability Definitions**
Oral Comprehension	The ability to listen to and understand information and ideas presented through spoken words and sentences.
Oral Expression	The ability to communicate information and ideas in speaking so others will understand.
Written Comprehension	The ability to read and understand information and ideas presented in writing.
Inductive Reasoning	The ability to combine pieces of information to form general rules or conclusions (includes finding a relationship among seemingly unrelated events).
Problem Sensitivity	The ability to tell when something is wrong or is likely to go wrong. It does not involve solving the problem, only recognizing there is a problem.
Deductive Reasoning	The ability to apply general rules to specific problems to produce answers that make sense.
Speech Clarity	The ability to speak clearly so others can understand you.
Information Ordering	The ability to arrange things or actions in a certain order or pattern according to a specific rule or set of rules (e.g., patterns of numbers, letters, words, pictures, mathematical operations).
Speech Recognition	The ability to identify and understand the speech of another person.
Near Vision	The ability to see details at close range (within a few feet of the observer).
Written Expression	The ability to communicate information and ideas in writing so others will understand.
Perceptual Speed	The ability to quickly and accurately compare similarities and differences among sets of letters, numbers, objects, pictures, or patterns. The things to be compared may be presented at the same time or one after the other. This ability also includes comparing a presented object with a remembered object.

Category Flexibility	The ability to generate or use different sets of rules for combining or grouping things in different ways.
Originality	The ability to come up with unusual or clever ideas about a given topic or situation, or to develop creative ways to solve a problem.
Mathematical Reasoning	The ability to choose the right mathematical methods or formulas to solve a problem.
Far Vision	The ability to see details at a distance.
Selective Attention	The ability to concentrate on a task over a period of time without being distracted.
Visualization	The ability to imagine how something will look after it is moved around or when its parts are moved or rearranged.
Flexibility of Closure	The ability to identify or detect a known pattern (a figure, object, word, or sound) that is hidden in other distracting material.
Number Facility	The ability to add, subtract, multiply, or divide quickly and correctly.
Fluency of Ideas	The ability to come up with a number of ideas about a topic (the number of ideas is important, not their quality, correctness, or creativity).
Speed of Closure	The ability to quickly make sense of, combine, and organize information into meaningful patterns.
Memorization	The ability to remember information such as words, numbers, pictures, and procedures.
Time Sharing	The ability to shift back and forth between two or more activities or sources of information (such as speech, sounds, touch, or other sources).
Finger Dexterity	The ability to make precisely coordinated movements of the fingers of one or both hands to grasp, manipulate, or assemble very small objects.
Depth Perception	The ability to judge which of several objects is closer or farther away from you, or to judge the distance between you and an object.
Auditory Attention	The ability to focus on a single source of sound in the presence of other distracting sounds.
Trunk Strength	The ability to use your abdominal and lower back muscles to support part of the body repeatedly or continuously over time without 'giving out' or fatiguing.
Hearing Sensitivity	The ability to detect or tell the differences between sounds that vary in pitch and loudness.
Control Precision	The ability to quickly and repeatedly adjust the controls of a machine or a vehicle to exact positions.
Arm-Hand Steadiness	The ability to keep your hand and arm steady while moving your arm or while holding your arm and hand in one position.
Visual Color Discrimination	The ability to match or detect differences between colors, including shades of color and brightness.
Multilimb Coordination	The ability to coordinate two or more limbs (for example, two arms, two legs, or one leg and one arm) while sitting, standing, or lying down. It does not involve performing the activities while the whole body is in motion.
Manual Dexterity	The ability to quickly move your hand, your hand together with your arm, or your two hands to grasp, manipulate, or assemble objects.
Reaction Time	The ability to quickly respond (with the hand, finger, or foot) to a signal (sound, light, picture) when it appears.
Wrist-Finger Speed	The ability to make fast, simple, repeated movements of the fingers, hands, and wrists.
Response Orientation	The ability to choose quickly between two or more movements in response to two or more different signals (lights, sounds, pictures). It includes the speed with which the correct response is started with the hand, foot, or other body part.
Gross Body Coordination	The ability to coordinate the movement of your arms, legs, and torso together when the whole body is in motion.
Rate Control	The ability to time your movements or the movement of a piece of equipment in anticipation of changes in the speed and/or direction of a moving object or scene.
Dynamic Strength	The ability to exert muscle force repeatedly or continuously over time. This involves muscular endurance and resistance to muscle fatigue.
Stamina	The ability to exert yourself physically over long periods of time without getting winded or out of breath.
Static Strength	The ability to exert maximum muscle force to lift, push, pull, or carry objects.
Extent Flexibility	The ability to bend, stretch, twist, or reach with your body, arms, and/or legs.
Gross Body Equilibrium	The ability to keep or regain your body balance or stay upright when in an unstable position.
Spatial Orientation	The ability to know your location in relation to the environment or to know where other objects are in relation to you.
Speed of Limb Movement	The ability to quickly move the arms and legs.
Peripheral Vision	The ability to see objects or movement of objects to one's side when the eyes are looking ahead.
Glare Sensitivity	The ability to see objects in the presence of glare or bright lighting.
Explosive Strength	The ability to use short bursts of muscle force to propel oneself (as in jumping or sprinting), or to throw an object.

Term	Definition
Dynamic Flexibility	The ability to quickly and repeatedly bend, stretch, twist, or reach out with your body, arms, and/or legs.
Night Vision	The ability to see under low light conditions.
Sound Localization	The ability to tell the direction from which a sound originated.

Work_Activity — Work_Activity Definitions

Work_Activity	Definition
Getting Information	Observing, receiving, and otherwise obtaining information from all relevant sources.
Communicating with Supervisors, Peers, or Subordin	Providing information to supervisors, co-workers, and subordinates by telephone, in written form, e-mail, or in person.
Making Decisions and Solving Problems	Analyzing information and evaluating results to choose the best solution and solve problems.
Guiding, Directing, and Motivating Subordinates	Providing guidance and direction to subordinates, including setting performance standards and monitoring performance.
Coordinating the Work and Activities of Others	Getting members of a group to work together to accomplish tasks.
Organizing, Planning, and Prioritizing Work	Developing specific goals and plans to prioritize, organize, and accomplish your work.
Scheduling Work and Activities	Scheduling events, programs, and activities, as well as the work of others.
Identifying Objects, Actions, and Events	Identifying information by categorizing, estimating, recognizing differences or similarities, and detecting changes in circumstances or events.
Inspecting Equipment, Structures, or Material	Inspecting equipment, structures, or materials to identify the cause of errors or other problems or defects.
Monitor Processes, Materials, or Surroundings	Monitoring and reviewing information from materials, events, or the environment, to detect or assess problems.
Interacting With Computers	Using computers and computer systems (including hardware and software) to program, write software, set up functions, enter data, or process information.
Coaching and Developing Others	Identifying the developmental needs of others and coaching, mentoring, or otherwise helping others to improve their knowledge or skills.
Analyzing Data or Information	Identifying the underlying principles, reasons, or facts of information by breaking down information or data into separate parts.
Monitoring and Controlling Resources	Monitoring and controlling resources and overseeing the spending of money.
Training and Teaching Others	Identifying the educational needs of others, developing formal educational or training programs or classes, and teaching or instructing others.
Establishing and Maintaining Interpersonal Relatio	Developing constructive and cooperative working relationships with others, and maintaining them over time.
Judging the Qualities of Things, Services, or Peop	Assessing the value, importance, or quality of things or people.
Developing and Building Teams	Encouraging and building mutual trust, respect, and cooperation among team members.
Resolving Conflicts and Negotiating with Others	Handling complaints, settling disputes, and resolving grievances and conflicts, or otherwise negotiating with others.
Evaluating Information to Determine Compliance wit	Using relevant information and individual judgment to determine whether events or processes comply with laws, regulations, or standards.
Updating and Using Relevant Knowledge	Keeping up-to-date technically and applying new knowledge to your job.
Controlling Machines and Processes	Using either control mechanisms or direct physical activity to operate machines or processes (not including computers or vehicles).
Thinking Creatively	Developing, designing, or creating new applications, ideas, relationships, systems, or products, including artistic contributions.
Provide Consultation and Advice to Others	Providing guidance and expert advice to management or other groups on technical, systems-, or process-related topics.
Estimating the Quantifiable Characteristics of Pro	Estimating sizes, distances, and quantities; or determining time, costs, resources, or materials needed to perform a work activity.
Documenting/Recording Information	Entering, transcribing, recording, storing, or maintaining information in written or electronic/magnetic form.
Interpreting the Meaning of Information for Others	Translating or explaining what information means and how it can be used.
Processing Information	Compiling, coding, categorizing, calculating, tabulating, auditing, or verifying information or data.
Developing Objectives and Strategies	Establishing long-range objectives and specifying the strategies and actions to achieve them.
Performing Administrative Activities	Performing day-to-day administrative tasks such as maintaining information files and processing paperwork.
Performing General Physical Activities	Performing physical activities that require considerable use of your arms and legs and moving your whole body, such as climbing, lifting, balancing, walking, stooping, and handling of materials.
Staffing Organizational Units	Recruiting, interviewing, selecting, hiring, and promoting employees in an organization.

Term	Definition
Selling or Influencing Others	Convincing others to buy merchandise/goods or to otherwise change their minds or actions.
Communicating with Persons Outside Organization	Communicating with people outside the organization, representing the organization to customers, the public, government, and other external sources. This information can be exchanged in person, in writing, or by telephone or e-mail.
Repairing and Maintaining Mechanical Equipment	Servicing, repairing, adjusting, and testing machines, devices, moving parts, and equipment that operate primarily on the basis of mechanical (not electronic) principles.
Assisting and Caring for Others	Providing personal assistance, medical attention, emotional support, or other personal care to others such as coworkers, customers, or patients.
Repairing and Maintaining Electronic Equipment	Servicing, repairing, calibrating, regulating, fine-tuning, or testing machines, devices, and equipment that operate primarily on the basis of electrical or electronic (not mechanical) principles.
Drafting, Laying Out, and Specifying Technical Dev	Providing documentation, detailed instructions, drawings, or specifications to tell others about how devices, parts, equipment, or structures are to be fabricated, constructed, assembled, modified, maintained, or used.
Handling and Moving Objects	Using hands and arms in handling, installing, positioning, and moving materials, and manipulating things.
Performing for or Working Directly with the Public	Performing for people or dealing directly with the public. This includes serving customers in restaurants and stores, and receiving clients or guests.
Operating Vehicles, Mechanized Devices, or Equipme	Running, maneuvering, navigating, or driving vehicles or mechanized equipment, such as forklifts, passenger vehicles, aircraft, or water craft.

Work_Content — Work_Content Definitions

Work_Content	Definition
Face-to-Face Discussions	How often do you have to have face-to-face discussions with individuals or teams in this job?
Telephone	How often do you have telephone conversations in this job?
Freedom to Make Decisions	How much decision making freedom, without supervision, does the job offer?
Contact With Others	How much does this job require the worker to be in contact with others (face-to-face, by telephone, or otherwise) in order to perform it?
Structured versus Unstructured Work	To what extent is this job structured for the worker, rather than allowing the worker to determine tasks, priorities, and goals?
Responsibility for Outcomes and Results	How responsible is the worker for work outcomes and results of other workers?
Work With Work Group or Team	How important is it to work with others in a group or team in this job?
Electronic Mail	How often do you use electronic mail in this job?
Indoors, Environmentally Controlled	How often does this job require working indoors in environmentally controlled conditions?
Coordinate or Lead Others	How important is it to coordinate or lead others in accomplishing work activities in this job?
Frequency of Decision Making	How frequently is the worker required to make decisions that affect other people, the financial resources, and/or the image and reputation of the organization?
Time Pressure	How often does this job require the worker to meet strict deadlines?
Impact of Decisions on Co-workers or Company Resul	How do the decisions an employee makes impact the results of co-workers, clients or the company?
Importance of Being Exact or Accurate	How important is being very exact or highly accurate in performing this job?
Responsible for Others' Health and Safety	How much responsibility is there for the health and safety of others in this job?
Letters and Memos	How often does the job require written letters and memos?
Wear Common Protective or Safety Equipment such as	How much does this job require wearing common protective or safety equipment such as safety shoes, glasses, gloves, hard hats or live jackets?
Level of Competition	To what extent does this job require the worker to compete or to be aware of competitive pressures?
Spend Time Sitting	How much does this job require sitting?
Deal With External Customers	How important is it to work with external customers or the public in this job?
Frequency of Conflict Situations	How often are there conflict situations the employee has to face in this job?
Deal With Unpleasant or Angry People	How frequently does the worker have to deal with unpleasant, angry, or discourteous individuals as part of the job requirements?
Importance of Repeating Same Tasks	How important is repeating the same physical activities (e.g., key entry) or mental activities (e.g., checking entries in a ledger) over and over, without stopping, to performing this job?
Physical Proximity	To what extent does this job require the worker to perform job tasks in close physical proximity to other people?
Sounds, Noise Levels Are Distracting or Uncomforta	How often does this job require working exposed to sounds and noise levels that are distracting or uncomfortable?
Indoors, Not Environmentally Controlled	How often does this job require working indoors in non-controlled environmental conditions (e.g., warehouse without heat)?

Exposed to Contaminants	How often does this job require working exposed to contaminants (such as pollutants, gases, dust or odors)?
Consequence of Error	How serious would the result usually be if the worker made a mistake that was not readily correctable?
Spend Time Standing	How much does this job require standing?
Exposed to Hazardous Equipment	How often does this job require exposure to hazardous equipment?
In an Enclosed Vehicle or Equipment	How often does this job require working in a closed vehicle or equipment (e.g., car)?
Public Speaking	How often do you have to perform public speaking in this job?
Spend Time Walking and Running	How much does this job require walking and running?
Spend Time Using Your Hands to Handle, Control, or	How much does this job require using your hands to handle, control, or feel objects, tools or controls?
Exposed to Minor Burns, Cuts, Bites, or Stings	How often does this job require exposure to minor burns, cuts, bites, or stings?
Outdoors, Exposed to Weather	How often does this job require working outdoors, exposed to all weather conditions?
Degree of Automation	How automated is the job?
Exposed to Hazardous Conditions	How often does this job require exposure to hazardous conditions?
Outdoors, Under Cover	How often does this job require working outdoors, under cover (e.g., structure with roof but no walls)?
Very Hot or Cold Temperatures	How often does this job require working in very hot (above 90 F degrees) or very cold (below 32 F degrees) temperatures?
Extremely Bright or Inadequate Lighting	How often does this job require working in extremely bright or inadequate lighting conditions?
Pace Determined by Speed of Equipment	How important is it to this job that the pace is determined by the speed of equipment or machinery? (This does not refer to keeping busy at all times on this job.)
Spend Time Making Repetitive Motions	How much does this job require making repetitive motions?
Spend Time Bending or Twisting the Body	How much does this job require bending or twisting your body?
Spend Time Keeping or Regaining Balance	How much does this job require keeping or regaining your balance?
Exposed to High Places	How often does this job require exposure to high places?
In an Open Vehicle or Equipment	How often does this job require working in an open vehicle or equipment (e.g., tractor)?
Exposed to Whole Body Vibration	How often does this job require exposure to whole body vibration (e.g., operate a jackhammer)?
Spend Time Kneeling, Crouching, Stooping, or Crawl	How much does this job require kneeling, crouching, stooping or crawling?
Deal With Physically Aggressive People	How frequently does this job require the worker to deal with physical aggression of violent individuals?
Spend Time Climbing Ladders, Scaffolds, or Poles	How much does this job require climbing ladders, scaffolds, or poles?
Cramped Work Space, Awkward Work Positions	How often does this job require working in cramped work spaces that requires getting into awkward positions?
Wear Specialized Protective or Safety Equipment su	How much does this job require wearing specialized protective or safety equipment such as breathing apparatus, safety harness, full protection suits, or radiation protection?
Exposed to Radiation	How often does this job require exposure to radiation?
Exposed to Disease or Infections	How often does this job require exposure to disease/infections?

Work_Styles	Work_Styles Definitions
Leadership	Job requires a willingness to lead, take charge, and offer opinions and direction.
Attention to Detail	Job requires being careful about detail and thorough in completing work tasks.
Integrity	Job requires being honest and ethical.
Adaptability/Flexibility	Job requires being open to change (positive or negative) and to considerable variety in the workplace.
Initiative	Job requires a willingness to take on responsibilities and challenges.
Dependability	Job requires being reliable, responsible, and dependable, and fulfilling obligations.
Self Control	Job requires maintaining composure, keeping emotions in check, controlling anger, and avoiding aggressive behavior, even in very difficult situations.
Stress Tolerance	Job requires accepting criticism and dealing calmly and effectively with high stress situations.
Cooperation	Job requires being pleasant with others on the job and displaying a good-natured, cooperative attitude.
Independence	Job requires developing one's own ways of doing things, guiding oneself with little or no supervision, and depending on oneself to get things done.
Achievement/Effort	Job requires establishing and maintaining personally challenging achievement goals and exerting effort toward mastering tasks.
Persistence	Job requires persistence in the face of obstacles.

Concern for Others	Job requires being sensitive to others' needs and feelings and being understanding and helpful on the job.
Analytical Thinking	Job requires analyzing information and using logic to address work-related issues and problems.
Innovation	Job requires creativity and alternative thinking to develop new ideas for and answers to work-related problems.
Social Orientation	Job requires preferring to work with others rather than alone, and being personally connected with others on the job.

Job Zone Component	Job Zone Component Definitions
Title	Job Zone Four: Considerable Preparation Needed
Overall Experience	A minimum of two to four years of work-related skill, knowledge, or experience is needed for these occupations. For example, an accountant must complete four years of college and work for several years in accounting to be considered qualified.
Job Training	Employees in these occupations usually need several years of work-related experience, on-the-job training, and/or vocational training.
Job Zone Examples	Many of these occupations involve coordinating, supervising, managing, or training others. Examples include accountants, chefs and head cooks, computer programmers, historians, pharmacists, and police detectives.
SVP Range	(7.0 to < 8.0)
Education	Most of these occupations require a four - year bachelor's degree, but some do not.

11-3061.00 - Purchasing Managers

Plan, direct, or coordinate the activities of buyers, purchasing officers, and related workers involved in purchasing materials, products, and services.

Tasks

1) Develop and implement purchasing and contract management instructions, policies, and procedures.

2) Interview and hire staff, and oversee staff training.

3) Participate in the development of specifications for equipment, products or substitute materials.

4) Arrange for disposal of surplus materials.

5) Prepare reports regarding market conditions and merchandise costs.

6) Resolve vendor or contractor grievances, and claims against suppliers.

7) Analyze market and delivery systems in order to assess present and future material availability.

8) Review purchase order claims and contracts for conformance to company policy.

9) Administer on-line purchasing systems.

10) Control purchasing department budgets.

11) Review, evaluate, and approve specifications for issuing and awarding bids.

12) Represent companies in negotiating contracts and formulating policies with suppliers.

13) Prepare bid awards requiring board approval.

14) Prepare and process requisitions and purchase orders for supplies and equipment.

15) Maintain records of goods ordered and received.

16) Locate vendors of materials, equipment or supplies, and interview them in order to determine product availability and terms of sales.

11-3071.01 - Transportation Managers

Plan, direct, and coordinate the transportation operations within an organization or the activities of organizations that provide transportation services.

Tasks

1) Collaborate with other managers and staff members in order to formulate and implement policies, procedures, goals, and objectives.

2) Recommend or authorize capital expenditures for acquisition of new equipment or property in order to increase efficiency and services of operations department.

3) Serve as contact persons for all workers within assigned territories.

4) Direct activities related to dispatching, routing, and tracking transportation vehicles, such as aircraft and railroad cars.

5) Analyze expenditures and other financial information in order to develop plans, policies, and budgets for increasing profits and improving services.

6) Conduct employee training sessions on subjects such as hazardous material handling, employee orientation, quality improvement and computer use.

7) Supervise workers assigning tariff classifications and preparing billing.

8) Promote safe work activities by conducting safety audits, attending company safety meetings, and meeting with individual staff members.

9) Direct and coordinate, through subordinates, activities of operations department in order to obtain use of equipment, facilities, and human resources.

10) Direct procurement processes, including equipment research and testing, vendor contracts, and requisitions approval.

11) Monitor operations to ensure that staff members comply with administrative policies and procedures, safety rules, union contracts, and government regulations.

12) Monitor spending to ensure that expenses are consistent with approved budgets.

13) Plan, organize and manage the work of subordinate staff to ensure that the work is accomplished in a manner consistent with organizational requirements.

14) Prepare management recommendations, such as proposed fee and tariff increases or schedule changes.

15) Implement schedule and policy changes.

16) Direct activities of staff performing repairs and maintenance to equipment, vehicles, and facilities.

17) Set operations policies and standards, including determination of safety procedures for the handling of dangerous goods.

18) Provide administrative and technical assistance to those receiving transportation-related grants.

19) Promote public transportation issues at state and local levels, by representing the organization before commissions or regulatory bodies during rate increase hearings.

20) Participate in union contract negotiations and settlements of grievances.

21) Direct investigations to verify and resolve customer or shipper complaints.

22) Conduct investigations in cooperation with government agencies to determine causes of transportation accidents and to improve safety procedures.

23) Develop criteria, application instructions, procedural manuals, and contracts for federal and state public transportation programs.

11-3071.02 - Storage and Distribution Managers

Plan, direct, and coordinate the storage and distribution operations within an organization or the activities of organizations that are engaged in storing and distributing materials and products.

Tasks

1) Participate in setting transportation and service rates.

2) Negotiate with carriers, warehouse operators and insurance company representatives for services and preferential rates.

3) Issue shipping instructions and provide routing information to ensure that delivery times and locations are coordinated.

4) Inspect physical conditions of warehouses, vehicle fleets and equipment, and order testing, maintenance, repair, or replacement as necessary.

5) Examine invoices and shipping manifests for conformity to tariff and customs regulations.

6) Evaluate freight costs and the inventory costs associated with transit times in order to ensure that costs are appropriate.

7) Confer with department heads to coordinate warehouse activities, such as production, sales, records control, and purchasing.

8) Advise sales and billing departments of transportation charges for customers' accounts.

9) Plan, develop, and implement warehouse safety and security programs and activities.

10) Develop and document standard and emergency operating procedures for receiving, handling, storing, shipping, or salvaging products or materials.

11) Interview, select, and train warehouse and supervisory personnel.

12) Schedule and monitor air or surface pickup, delivery, or distribution of products or materials.

13) Prepare or direct preparation of correspondence, reports, and operations, maintenance, and safety manuals.

14) Arrange for storage facilities when required.

15) Develop and implement plans for facility modification or expansion, such as equipment purchase or changes in space allocation or structural design.

16) Track and trace goods while they are en route to their destinations, expediting orders when necessary.

17) Arrange for necessary shipping documentation, and contact customs officials in order to effect release of shipments.

18) Supervise the activities of workers engaged in receiving, storing, testing, and shipping products or materials.

19) Examine products or materials in order to estimate quantities or weight and type of container required for storage or transport.

20) Respond to customers' or shippers' questions and complaints regarding storage and distribution services.

21) Review invoices, work orders, consumption reports, and demand forecasts in order to estimate peak delivery periods and to issue work assignments.

22) Prepare and manage departmental budgets.

11-9021.00 - Construction Managers

Plan, direct, coordinate, or budget, usually through subordinate supervisory personnel, activities concerned with the construction and maintenance of structures, facilities, and systems. Participate in the conceptual development of a construction project and oversee its organization, scheduling, and implementation.

Tasks

1) Requisition supplies and materials to complete construction projects.

2) Obtain all necessary permits and licenses.

3) Schedule the project in logical steps and budget time required to meet deadlines.

4) Determine labor requirements and dispatch workers to construction sites.

5) Take actions to deal with the results of delays, bad weather, or emergencies at construction site.

6) Prepare contracts and negotiate revisions, changes and additions to contractual agreements with architects, consultants, clients, suppliers and subcontractors.

7) Investigate damage, accidents, or delays at construction sites, to ensure that proper procedures are being carried out.

8) Inspect and review projects to monitor compliance with building and safety codes, and other regulations.

9) Direct acquisition of land for construction projects.

10) Interpret and explain plans and contract terms to administrative staff, workers, and clients, representing the owner or developer.

11) Study job specifications to determine appropriate construction methods.

12) Select, contract, and oversee workers who complete specific pieces of the project, such as painting or plumbing.

13) Confer with supervisory personnel, owners, contractors, and design professionals to discuss and resolve matters such as work procedures, complaints, and construction problems.

14) Prepare and submit budget estimates and progress and cost tracking reports.

15) Plan, organize, and direct activities concerned with the construction and maintenance of structures, facilities, and systems.

16) Develop and implement quality control programs.

17) Evaluate construction methods and determine cost-effectiveness of plans, using computers.

11-9031.00 - Education Administrators, Preschool and Child Care Center/Program

Plan, direct, or coordinate the academic and nonacademic activities of preschool and child care centers or programs.

Tasks

1) Determine the scope of educational program offerings, and prepare drafts of program schedules and descriptions, in order to estimate staffing and facility requirements.

2) Organize and direct committees of specialists, volunteers, and staff to provide technical and advisory assistance for programs.

3) Write articles, manuals, and other publications, and assist in the distribution of promotional literature about programs and facilities.

4) Confer with parents and staff to discuss educational activities and policies, and students' behavioral or learning problems.

5) Set educational standards and goals, and help establish policies, procedures, and programs to carry them out.

6) Plan, direct, and monitor instructional methods and content of educational, vocational, or student activity programs.

7) Review and evaluate new and current programs to determine their efficiency, effectiveness, and compliance with state, local, and federal regulations; recommend any necessary modifications.

8) Prepare and maintain attendance, activity, planning, accounting, or personnel reports and records for officials and agencies, or direct preparation and maintenance activities.

9) Prepare and submit budget requests or grant proposals to solicit program funding.

10) Direct and coordinate activities of teachers or administrators at daycare centers, schools, public agencies, and/or institutions.

11) Review and interpret government codes, and develop procedures to meet codes and to ensure facility safety, security, and maintenance.

12) Monitor students' progress, and provide students and teachers with assistance in resolving any problems.

13) Determine allocations of funds for staff, supplies, materials, and equipment, and authorize purchases.

14) Recruit, hire, train, and evaluate primary and supplemental staff, and recommend personnel actions for programs and services.

15) Inform businesses, community groups, and governmental agencies about educational needs, available programs, and program policies.

16) Teach classes or courses, and/or provide direct care to children.

11-9032.00 - Education Administrators, Elementary and Secondary School

Plan, direct, or coordinate the academic, clerical, or auxiliary activities of public or private elementary or secondary level schools.

Tasks

1) Direct and coordinate activities of teachers, administrators, and support staff at schools, public agencies, and institutions.

2) Teach classes or courses to students.

3) Set educational standards and goals, and help establish policies and procedures to carry them out.

4) Organize and direct committees of specialists, volunteers, and staff to provide technical and advisory assistance for programs.

5) Develop partnerships with businesses, communities, and other organizations to help meet identified educational needs and to provide school-to-work programs.

6) Advocate for new schools to be built, or for existing facilities to be repaired or remodeled.

7) Collaborate with teachers to develop and maintain curriculum standards, develop mission statements, and set performance goals and objectives.

8) Observe teaching methods and examine learning materials in order to evaluate and standardize curricula and teaching techniques, and to determine areas where improvement is needed.

9) Determine the scope of educational program offerings, and prepare drafts of course schedules and descriptions in order to estimate staffing and facility requirements.

10) Establish, coordinate, and oversee particular programs across school districts, such as programs to evaluate student academic achievement.

11) Direct and coordinate school maintenance services and the use of school facilities.

12) Confer with parents and staff to discuss educational activities, policies, and student behavioral or learning problems.

13) Recruit, hire, train, and evaluate primary and supplemental staff.

14) Enforce discipline and attendance rules.

15) Counsel and provide guidance to students regarding personal, academic, vocational, or behavioral issues.

16) Determine allocations of funds for staff, supplies, materials, and equipment, and authorize purchases.

17) Write articles, manuals, and other publications, and assist in the distribution of promotional literature about facilities and programs.

18) Review and approve new programs, or recommend modifications to existing programs, submitting program proposals for school board approval as necessary.

19) Review and interpret government codes, and develop programs to ensure adherence to codes and facility safety, security, and maintenance.

20) Recommend personnel actions related to programs and services.

21) Prepare, maintain, or oversee the preparation/maintenance of attendance, activity, planning, or personnel reports and records.

22) Prepare and submit budget requests and recommendations, or grant proposals to solicit program funding.

23) Plan and develop instructional methods and content for educational, vocational, or student activity programs.

24) Collect and analyze survey data, regulatory information, and data on demographic and employment trends to forecast enrollment patterns and curriculum change needs.

11-9033.00 - Education Administrators, Postsecondary

Plan, direct, or coordinate research, instructional, student administration and services, and other educational activities at postsecondary institutions, including universities, colleges, and junior and community colleges.

Tasks

1) Direct and participate in institutional fundraising activities, and encourage alumni participation in such activities.

2) Determine course schedules, and coordinate teaching assignments and room assignments in order to ensure optimum use of buildings and equipment.

3) Direct scholarship, fellowship, and loan programs, performing activities such as selecting recipients and distributing aid.

4) Coordinate the production and dissemination of university publications such as course catalogs and class schedules.

5) Review student misconduct reports requiring disciplinary action, and counsel students regarding such reports.

6) Supervise coaches.

7) Teach courses within their department.

8) Audit the financial status of student organizations and facility accounts.

9) Provide assistance to faculty and staff in duties such as teaching classes, conducting orientation programs, issuing transcripts, and scheduling events.

10) Direct activities of administrative departments such as admissions, registration, and career services.

11) Recruit, hire, train, and terminate departmental personnel.

12) Plan, administer, and control budgets, maintain financial records, and produce financial reports.

13) Negotiate with foundation and industry representatives on issues such as securing loans and determining construction costs and materials.

14) Review registration statistics, and consult with faculty officials to develop registration policies.

15) Direct, coordinate, and evaluate the activities of personnel engaged in administering academic institutions, departments, and/or alumni organizations.

16) Represent institutions at community and campus events, in meetings with other institution personnel, and during accreditation processes.

17) Participate in student recruitment, selection, and admission, making admissions recommendations when required to do so.

18) Assess and collect tuition and fees.

19) Establish operational policies and procedures and make any necessary modifications, based on analysis of operations, demographics, and other research information.

20) Appoint individuals to faculty positions, and evaluate their performance.

21) Confer with other academic staff to explain and formulate admission requirements and course credit policies.

22) Develop curricula, and recommend curricula revisions and additions.

23) Participate in faculty and college committee activities.

24) Consult with government regulatory and licensing agencies in order to ensure the institution's conformance with applicable standards.

11-9041.00 - Engineering Managers

Plan, direct, or coordinate activities in such fields as architecture and engineering or research and development in these fields.

Tasks

1) Analyze technology, resource needs, and market demand, to plan and assess the feasibility of projects.

2) Confer with management, production, and marketing staff to discuss project specifications

and procedures.

3) Coordinate and direct projects, making detailed plans to accomplish goals and directing the integration of technical activities.

4) Direct, review, and approve product design and changes.

5) Prepare budgets, bids, and contracts, and direct the negotiation of research contracts.

6) Consult or negotiate with clients to prepare project specifications.

7) Recruit employees; assign, direct, and evaluate their work; and oversee the development and maintenance of staff competence.

8) Develop and implement policies, standards and procedures for the engineering and technical work performed in the department, service, laboratory or firm.

9) Perform administrative functions such as reviewing and writing reports, approving expenditures, enforcing rules, and making decisions about the purchase of materials or services.

10) Present and explain proposals, reports, and findings to clients.

11) Review and recommend or approve contracts and cost estimates.

12) Direct the engineering of water control, treatment, and distribution projects.

13) Plan and direct oil field development, gas and oil production, and geothermal drilling.

14) Plan and direct the installation, testing, operation, maintenance, and repair of facilities and equipment.

15) Administer highway planning, construction, and maintenance.

16) Plan, direct, and coordinate survey work with other staff activities, certifying survey work, and writing land legal descriptions.

17) Set scientific and technical goals within broad outlines provided by top management.

11-9051.00 - Food Service Managers

Plan, direct, or coordinate activities of an organization or department that serves food and beverages.

Tasks

1) Monitor compliance with health and fire regulations regarding food preparation and serving, and building maintenance in lodging and dining facilities.

2) Plan menus and food utilization based on anticipated number of guests, nutritional value, palatability, popularity, and costs.

3) Organize and direct worker training programs, resolve personnel problems, hire new staff, and evaluate employee performance in dining and lodging facilities.

4) Greet guests, escort them to their seats, and present them with menus and wine lists.

5) Take dining reservations.

6) Schedule use of facilities or catering services for events such as banquets or receptions, and negotiate details of arrangements with clients.

7) Schedule staff hours and assign duties.

8) Schedule and receive food and beverage deliveries, checking delivery contents in order to verify product quality and quantity.

9) Review work procedures and operational problems in order to determine ways to improve service, performance, and/or safety.

10) Record the number, type, and cost of items sold in order to determine which items may be unpopular or less profitable.

11) Perform some food preparation or service tasks such as cooking, clearing tables, and serving food and drinks when necessary.

12) Monitor food preparation methods, portion sizes, and garnishing and presentation of food in order to ensure that food is prepared and presented in an acceptable manner.

13) Coordinate assignments of cooking personnel in order to ensure economical use of food and timely preparation.

14) Keep records required by government agencies regarding sanitation, and food subsidies when appropriate.

15) Estimate food, liquor, wine, and other beverage consumption in order to anticipate amounts to be purchased or requisitioned.

16) Establish standards for personnel performance and customer service.

17) Assess staffing needs, and recruit staff using methods such as newspaper advertisements or attendance at job fairs.

18) Create specialty dishes and develop recipes to be used in dining facilities.

19) Establish and enforce nutritional standards for dining establishments based on accepted industry standards.

20) Investigate and resolve complaints regarding food quality, service, or accommodations.

21) Monitor budgets and payroll records, and review financial transactions in order to ensure that expenditures are authorized and budgeted.

22) Test cooked food by tasting and smelling it in order to ensure palatability and flavor conformity.

23) Monitor employee and patron activities in order to ensure liquor regulations are obeyed.

24) Arrange for equipment maintenance and repairs, and coordinate a variety of services such as waste removal and pest control.

25) Order and purchase equipment and supplies.

26) Review menus and analyze recipes in order to determine labor and overhead costs, and assign prices to menu items.

11-9061.00 - Funeral Directors

Perform various tasks to arrange and direct funeral services, such as coordinating transportation of body to mortuary for embalming, interviewing family or other authorized person to arrange details, selecting pallbearers, procuring official for religious rites, and providing transportation for mourners.

Tasks

1) Close caskets and lead funeral corteges to churches or burial sites.

2) Consult with families and/or friends of the deceased to arrange funeral details such as obituary notice wording, casket selection, and plans for services.

3) Contact cemeteries to schedule the opening and closing of graves.

4) Discuss and negotiate pre-arranged funerals with clients.

5) Obtain information needed to complete legal documents such as death certificates and burial permits.

6) Arrange for clergy members to perform needed services.

7) Arrange for pallbearers, and inform pallbearers and honorary groups of their duties.

8) Provide or arrange transportation between sites for the remains, mourners, pallbearers, clergy, and flowers.

9) Oversee the preparation and care of the remains of people who have died.

10) Direct preparations and shipment of bodies for out-of-state burial.

11) Inform survivors of benefits for which they may be eligible.

12) Maintain financial records, order merchandise, and prepare accounts.

13) Manage funeral home operations, including hiring and supervising embalmers, funeral attendants, and other staff.

14) Perform embalming duties as necessary.

15) Plan, schedule and coordinate funerals, burials, and cremations, arranging such details as the time and place of services.

16) Plan placement of caskets at funeral sites, and place and adjust lights, fixtures, and floral displays.

17) Offer counsel and comfort to bereaved families and friends.

18) Provide information on funeral service options, products, and merchandise, and maintain a casket display area.

11-9071.00 - Gaming Managers

Plan, organize, direct, control, or coordinate gaming operations in a casino. Formulate gaming policies for their area of responsibility.

Tasks

1) Review operational expenses, budget estimates, betting accounts, and collection reports for accuracy.

2) Circulate among gaming tables to ensure that operations are conducted properly, that dealers follow house rules, and that players are not cheating.

3) Record, collect, and pay off bets, issuing receipts as necessary.

4) Notify board attendants of table vacancies so that waiting patrons can play.

5) Establish policies on issues such as the type of gambling offered and the odds, the extension of credit, and the serving of food and beverages.

6) Direct workers compiling summary sheets that show wager amounts and payoffs for races and events.

7) Train new workers and evaluate their performance.

8) Direct the distribution of complimentary hotel rooms, meals, and other discounts or free

items given to players based on their length of play and betting totals.

9) Interview and hire workers.

10) Track supplies of money to tables, and perform any required paperwork.

11) Maintain familiarity with all games used at a facility, as well as strategies and tricks employed in those games.

12) Set and maintain a bank and table limit for each game.

13) Prepare work schedules and station assignments, and keep attendance records.

14) Remove suspected cheaters, such as card counters and other players who may have systems that shift the odds of winning to their favor.

15) Monitor credit extended to players.

16) Resolve customer complaints regarding problems such as payout errors.

17) Monitor staffing levels to ensure that games and tables are adequately staffed for each shift, arranging for staff rotations and breaks, and locating substitute employees as necessary.

11-9081.00 - Lodging Managers

Plan, direct, or coordinate activities of an organization or department that provides lodging and other accommodations.

Tasks

1) Organize and coordinate the work of staff and convention personnel for meetings to be held at a particular facility.

2) Show, rent, or assign accommodations.

3) Participate in financial activities such as the setting of room rates, the establishment of budgets, and the allocation of funds to departments.

4) Provide assistance to staff members by performing activities such as inspecting rooms, setting tables and doing laundry.

5) Prepare required paperwork pertaining to departmental functions.

6) Answer inquiries pertaining to hotel policies and services, and resolve occupants' complaints.

7) Receive and process advance registration payments, send out letters of confirmation, and return checks when registrations cannot be accepted.

8) Purchase supplies, and arrange for outside services, such as deliveries, laundry, maintenance and repair, and trash collection.

9) Assign duties to workers, and schedule shifts.

10) Interview and hire applicants.

11) Perform marketing and public relations activities.

12) Develop and implement policies and procedures for the operation of a department or establishment.

13) Inspect guest rooms, public areas, and grounds for cleanliness and appearance.

14) Observe and monitor staff performance in order to ensure efficient operations and adherence to facility's policies and procedures.

15) Arrange telephone answering services, deliver mail and packages, and answer questions regarding locations for eating and entertainment.

16) Train staff members in their duties.

17) Manage and maintain temporary or permanent lodging facilities.

18) Greet and register guests.

19) Collect payments, and record data pertaining to funds and expenditures.

20) Coordinate front-office activities of hotels or motels, and resolve problems.

21) Confer and cooperate with other managers in order to ensure coordination of hotel activities.

22) Meet with clients in order to schedule and plan details of conventions, banquets, receptions and other functions.

11-9111.00 - Medical and Health Services Managers

Plan, direct, or coordinate medicine and health services in hospitals, clinics, managed care organizations, public health agencies, or similar organizations.

Tasks

1) Establish work schedules and assignments for staff, according to workload, space and equipment availability.

2) Direct or conduct recruitment, hiring and training of personnel.

3) Develop and implement organizational policies and procedures for the facility or medical unit.

4) Prepare activity reports to inform management of the status and implementation plans of programs, services, and quality initiatives.

5) Establish objectives and evaluative or operational criteria for units they manage.

6) Conduct and administer fiscal operations, including accounting, planning budgets, authorizing expenditures, establishing rates for services, and coordinating financial reporting.

7) Maintain awareness of advances in medicine, computerized diagnostic and treatment equipment, data processing technology, government regulations, health insurance changes, and financing options.

8) Manage change in integrated health care delivery systems, such as work restructuring, technological innovations, and shifts in the focus of care.

9) Maintain communication between governing boards, medical staff, and department heads by attending board meetings and coordinating interdepartmental functioning.

10) Monitor the use of diagnostic services, inpatient beds, facilities, and staff to ensure effective use of resources and assess the need for additional staff, equipment, and services.

11) Review and analyze facility activities and data to aid planning and cash and risk management and to improve service utilization.

12) Consult with medical, business, and community groups to discuss service problems, respond to community needs, enhance public relations, coordinate activities and plans, and promote health programs.

13) Plan, implement and administer programs and services in a health care or medical facility, including personnel administration, training, and coordination of medical, nursing and physical plant staff.

14) Develop and maintain computerized record management systems to store and process data, such as personnel activities and information, and to produce reports.

15) Develop instructional materials and conduct in-service and community-based educational programs.

16) Inspect facilities and recommend building or equipment modifications to ensure emergency readiness and compliance to access, safety, and sanitation regulations.

17) Develop or expand and implement medical programs or health services that promote research, rehabilitation, and community health.

Knowledge	Knowledge Definitions
Customer and Personal Service	Knowledge of principles and processes for providing customer and personal services. This includes customer needs assessment, meeting quality standards for services, and evaluation of customer satisfaction.
Administration and Management	Knowledge of business and management principles involved in strategic planning, resource allocation, human resources modeling, leadership technique, production methods, and coordination of people and resources.
Personnel and Human Resources	Knowledge of principles and procedures for personnel recruitment, selection, training, compensation and benefits, labor relations and negotiation, and personnel information systems.
English Language	Knowledge of the structure and content of the English language including the meaning and spelling of words, rules of composition, and grammar.
Medicine and Dentistry	Knowledge of the information and techniques needed to diagnose and treat human injuries, diseases, and deformities. This includes symptoms, treatment alternatives, drug properties and interactions, and preventive health-care measures.
Public Safety and Security	Knowledge of relevant equipment, policies, procedures, and strategies to promote effective local, state, or national security operations for the protection of people, data, property, and institutions.
Computers and Electronics	Knowledge of circuit boards, processors, chips, electronic equipment, and computer hardware and software, including applications and programming.
Education and Training	Knowledge of principles and methods for curriculum and training design, teaching and instruction for individuals and groups, and the measurement of training effects.
Law and Government	Knowledge of laws, legal codes, court procedures, precedents, government regulations, executive orders, agency rules, and the democratic political process.
Therapy and Counseling	Knowledge of principles, methods, and procedures for diagnosis, treatment, and rehabilitation of physical and mental dysfunctions, and for career counseling and guidance.
Psychology	Knowledge of human behavior and performance; individual differences in ability, personality, and interests; learning and motivation; psychological research methods; and the assessment and treatment of behavioral and affective disorders.
Mathematics	Knowledge of arithmetic, algebra, geometry, calculus, statistics, and their applications.

Communications and Media	Knowledge of media production, communication, and dissemination techniques and methods. This includes alternative ways to inform and entertain via written, oral, and visual media.
Production and Processing	Knowledge of raw materials, production processes, quality control, costs, and other techniques for maximizing the effective manufacture and distribution of goods.
Economics and Accounting	Knowledge of economic and accounting principles and practices, the financial markets, banking and the analysis and reporting of financial data.
Sociology and Anthropology	Knowledge of group behavior and dynamics, societal trends and influences, human migrations, ethnicity, cultures and their history and origins.
Philosophy and Theology	Knowledge of different philosophical systems and religions. This includes their basic principles, values, ethics, ways of thinking, customs, practices, and their impact on human culture.
Sales and Marketing	Knowledge of principles and methods for showing, promoting, and selling products or services. This includes marketing strategy and tactics, product demonstration, sales techniques, and sales control systems.
Telecommunications	Knowledge of transmission, broadcasting, switching, control, and operation of telecommunications systems.
Chemistry	Knowledge of the chemical composition, structure, and properties of substances and of the chemical processes and transformations that they undergo. This includes uses of chemicals and their interactions, danger signs, production techniques, and disposal methods.
Clerical	Knowledge of administrative and clerical procedures and systems such as word processing, managing files and records, stenography and transcription, designing forms, and other office procedures and terminology.
Biology	Knowledge of plant and animal organisms, their tissues, cells, functions, interdependencies, and interactions with each other and the environment.
Physics	Knowledge and prediction of physical principles, laws, their interrelationships, and applications to understanding fluid, material, and atmospheric dynamics, and mechanical, electrical, atomic and sub-atomic structures and processes.
Building and Construction	Knowledge of materials, methods, and the tools involved in the construction or repair of houses, buildings, or other structures such as highways and roads.
Engineering and Technology	Knowledge of the practical application of engineering science and technology. This includes applying principles, techniques, procedures, and equipment to the design and production of various goods and services.
Design	Knowledge of design techniques, tools, and principles involved in production of precision technical plans, blueprints, drawings, and models.
Food Production	Knowledge of techniques and equipment for planting, growing, and harvesting food products (both plant and animal) for consumption, including storage/handling techniques.
Foreign Language	Knowledge of the structure and content of a foreign (non-English) language including the meaning and spelling of words, rules of composition and grammar, and pronunciation.
Transportation	Knowledge of principles and methods for moving people or goods by air, rail, sea, or road, including the relative costs and benefits.
History and Archeology	Knowledge of historical events and their causes, indicators, and effects on civilizations and cultures.
Mechanical	Knowledge of machines and tools, including their designs, uses, repair, and maintenance.
Fine Arts	Knowledge of the theory and techniques required to compose, produce, and perform works of music, dance, visual arts, drama, and sculpture.
Geography	Knowledge of principles and methods for describing the features of land, sea, and air masses, including their physical characteristics, locations, interrelationships, and distribution of plant, animal, and human life.

Skills	**Skills Definitions**
Active Listening	Giving full attention to what other people are saying, taking time to understand the points being made, asking questions as appropriate, and not interrupting at inappropriate times.
Reading Comprehension	Understanding written sentences and paragraphs in work related documents.
Critical Thinking	Using logic and reasoning to identify the strengths and weaknesses of alternative solutions, conclusions or approaches to problems.
Speaking	Talking to others to convey information effectively.
Monitoring	Monitoring/Assessing performance of yourself, other individuals, or organizations to make improvements or take corrective action.
Time Management	Managing one's own time and the time of others.
Judgment and Decision Making	Considering the relative costs and benefits of potential actions to choose the most appropriate one.
Service Orientation	Actively looking for ways to help people.

Writing	Communicating effectively in writing as appropriate for the needs of the audience.
Active Learning	Understanding the implications of new information for both current and future problem-solving and decision-making.
Management of Personnel Resources	Motivating, developing, and directing people as they work, identifying the best people for the job.
Coordination	Adjusting actions in relation to others' actions.
Social Perceptiveness	Being aware of others' reactions and understanding why they react as they do.
Learning Strategies	Selecting and using training/instructional methods and procedures appropriate for the situation when learning or teaching new things.
Persuasion	Persuading others to change their minds or behavior.
Instructing	Teaching others how to do something.
Complex Problem Solving	Identifying complex problems and reviewing related information to develop and evaluate options and implement solutions.
Management of Financial Resources	Determining how money will be spent to get the work done, and accounting for these expenditures.
Operations Analysis	Analyzing needs and product requirements to create a design.
Systems Evaluation	Identifying measures or indicators of system performance and the actions needed to improve or correct performance, relative to the goals of the system.
Quality Control Analysis	Conducting tests and inspections of products, services, or processes to evaluate quality or performance.
Management of Material Resources	Obtaining and seeing to the appropriate use of equipment, facilities, and materials needed to do certain work.
Equipment Selection	Determining the kind of tools and equipment needed to do a job.
Mathematics	Using mathematics to solve problems.
Negotiation	Bringing others together and trying to reconcile differences.
Troubleshooting	Determining causes of operating errors and deciding what to do about it.
Systems Analysis	Determining how a system should work and how changes in conditions, operations, and the environment will affect outcomes.
Science	Using scientific rules and methods to solve problems.
Operation Monitoring	Watching gauges, dials, or other indicators to make sure a machine is working properly.
Technology Design	Generating or adapting equipment and technology to serve user needs.
Operation and Control	Controlling operations of equipment or systems.
Equipment Maintenance	Performing routine maintenance on equipment and determining when and what kind of maintenance is needed.
Programming	Writing computer programs for various purposes.
Installation	Installing equipment, machines, wiring, or programs to meet specifications.
Repairing	Repairing machines or systems using the needed tools.

Ability	**Ability Definitions**
Oral Comprehension	The ability to listen to and understand information and ideas presented through spoken words and sentences.
Inductive Reasoning	The ability to combine pieces of information to form general rules or conclusions (includes finding a relationship among seemingly unrelated events).
Problem Sensitivity	The ability to tell when something is wrong or is likely to go wrong. It does not involve solving the problem, only recognizing there is a problem.
Oral Expression	The ability to communicate information and ideas in speaking so others will understand.
Written Comprehension	The ability to read and understand information and ideas presented in writing.
Deductive Reasoning	The ability to apply general rules to specific problems to produce answers that make sense.
Written Expression	The ability to communicate information and ideas in writing so others will understand.
Information Ordering	The ability to arrange things or actions in a certain order or pattern according to a specific rule or set of rules (e.g., patterns of numbers, letters, words, pictures, mathematical operations).
Speech Recognition	The ability to identify and understand the speech of another person.
Speech Clarity	The ability to speak clearly so others can understand you.
Near Vision	The ability to see details at close range (within a few feet of the observer).
Category Flexibility	The ability to generate or use different sets of rules for combining or grouping things in different ways.
Mathematical Reasoning	The ability to choose the right mathematical methods or formulas to solve a problem.
Originality	The ability to come up with unusual or clever ideas about a given topic or situation, or to develop creative ways to solve a problem.
Time Sharing	The ability to shift back and forth between two or more activities or sources of information (such as speech, sounds, touch, or other sources).

Selective Attention	The ability to concentrate on a task over a period of time without being distracted.
Perceptual Speed	The ability to quickly and accurately compare similarities and differences among sets of letters, numbers, objects, pictures, or patterns. The things to be compared may be presented at the same time or one after the other. This ability also includes comparing a presented object with a remembered object.
Fluency of Ideas	The ability to come up with a number of ideas about a topic (the number of ideas is important, not their quality, correctness, or creativity).
Flexibility of Closure	The ability to identify or detect a known pattern (a figure, object, word, or sound) that is hidden in other distracting material.
Far Vision	The ability to see details at a distance.
Number Facility	The ability to add, subtract, multiply, or divide quickly and correctly.
Speed of Closure	The ability to quickly make sense of, combine, and organize information into meaningful patterns.
Memorization	The ability to remember information such as words, numbers, pictures, and procedures.
Visualization	The ability to imagine how something will look after it is moved around or when its parts are moved or rearranged.
Trunk Strength	The ability to use your abdominal and lower back muscles to support part of the body repeatedly or continuously over time without 'giving out' or fatiguing.
Depth Perception	The ability to judge which of several objects is closer or farther away from you, or to judge the distance between you and an object.
Finger Dexterity	The ability to make precisely coordinated movements of the fingers of one or both hands to grasp, manipulate, or assemble very small objects.
Auditory Attention	The ability to focus on a single source of sound in the presence of other distracting sounds.
Hearing Sensitivity	The ability to detect or tell the differences between sounds that vary in pitch and loudness.
Manual Dexterity	The ability to quickly move your hand, your hand together with your arm, or your two hands to grasp, manipulate, or assemble objects.
Gross Body Coordination	The ability to coordinate the movement of your arms, legs, and torso together when the whole body is in motion.
Control Precision	The ability to quickly and repeatedly adjust the controls of a machine or a vehicle to exact positions.
Visual Color Discrimination	The ability to match or detect differences between colors, including shades of color and brightness.
Stamina	The ability to exert yourself physically over long periods of time without getting winded or out of breath.
Speed of Limb Movement	The ability to quickly move the arms and legs.
Arm-Hand Steadiness	The ability to keep your hand and arm steady while moving your arm or while holding your arm and hand in one position.
Wrist-Finger Speed	The ability to make fast, simple, repeated movements of the fingers, hands, and wrists.
Spatial Orientation	The ability to know your location in relation to the environment or to know where other objects are in relation to you.
Extent Flexibility	The ability to bend, stretch, twist, or reach with your body, arms, and/or legs.
Dynamic Flexibility	The ability to quickly and repeatedly bend, stretch, twist, or reach out with your body, arms, and/or legs.
Explosive Strength	The ability to use short bursts of muscle force to propel oneself (as in jumping or sprinting), or to throw an object.
Sound Localization	The ability to tell the direction from which a sound originated.
Glare Sensitivity	The ability to see objects in the presence of glare or bright lighting.
Night Vision	The ability to see under low light conditions.
Peripheral Vision	The ability to see objects or movement of objects to one's side when the eyes are looking ahead.
Gross Body Equilibrium	The ability to keep or regain your body balance or stay upright when in an unstable position.
Response Orientation	The ability to choose quickly between two or more movements in response to two or more different signals (lights, sounds, pictures). It includes the speed with which the correct response is started with the hand, foot, or other body part.
Multilimb Coordination	The ability to coordinate two or more limbs (for example, two arms, two legs, or one leg and one arm) while sitting, standing, or lying down. It does not involve performing the activities while the whole body is in motion.
Static Strength	The ability to exert maximum muscle force to lift, push, pull, or carry objects.
Rate Control	The ability to time your movements or the movement of a piece of equipment in anticipation of changes in the speed and/or direction of a moving object or scene.
Dynamic Strength	The ability to exert muscle force repeatedly or continuously over time. This involves muscular endurance and resistance to muscle fatigue.
Reaction Time	The ability to quickly respond (with the hand, finger, or foot) to a signal (sound, light, picture) when it appears.

Work_Activity	Work_Activity Definitions
Establishing and Maintaining Interpersonal Relatio	Developing constructive and cooperative working relationships with others, and maintaining them over time.
Making Decisions and Solving Problems	Analyzing information and evaluating results to choose the best solution and solve problems.
Monitor Processes, Materials, or Surroundings	Monitoring and reviewing information from materials, events, or the environment, to detect or assess problems.
Coordinating the Work and Activities of Others	Getting members of a group to work together to accomplish tasks.
Communicating with Supervisors, Peers, or Subordin	Providing information to supervisors, co-workers, and subordinates by telephone, in written form, e-mail, or in person.
Evaluating Information to Determine Compliance wit	Using relevant information and individual judgment to determine whether events or processes comply with laws, regulations, or standards.
Analyzing Data or Information	Identifying the underlying principles, reasons, or facts of information by breaking down information or data into separate parts.
Updating and Using Relevant Knowledge	Keeping up-to-date technically and applying new knowledge to your job.
Monitoring and Controlling Resources	Monitoring and controlling resources and overseeing the spending of money.
Resolving Conflicts and Negotiating with Others	Handling complaints, settling disputes, and resolving grievances and conflicts, or otherwise negotiating with others.
Staffing Organizational Units	Recruiting, interviewing, selecting, hiring, and promoting employees in an organization.
Guiding, Directing, and Motivating Subordinates	Providing guidance and direction to subordinates, including setting performance standards and monitoring performance.
Getting Information	Observing, receiving, and otherwise obtaining information from all relevant sources.
Organizing, Planning, and Prioritizing Work	Developing specific goals and plans to prioritize, organize, and accomplish your work.
Developing and Building Teams	Encouraging and building mutual trust, respect, and cooperation among team members.
Documenting/Recording Information	Entering, transcribing, recording, storing, or maintaining information in written or electronic/magnetic form.
Interacting With Computers	Using computers and computer systems (including hardware and software) to program, write software, set up functions, enter data, or process information.
Processing Information	Compiling, coding, categorizing, calculating, tabulating, auditing, or verifying information or data.
Developing Objectives and Strategies	Establishing long-range objectives and specifying the strategies and actions to achieve them.
Performing Administrative Activities	Performing day-to-day administrative tasks such as maintaining information files and processing paperwork.
Identifying Objects, Actions, and Events	Identifying information by categorizing, estimating, recognizing differences or similarities, and detecting changes in circumstances or events.
Communicating with Persons Outside Organization	Communicating with people outside the organization, representing the organization to customers, the public, government, and other external sources. This information can be exchanged in person, in writing, or by telephone or e-mail.
Thinking Creatively	Developing, designing, or creating new applications, ideas, relationships, systems, or products, including artistic contributions.
Scheduling Work and Activities	Scheduling events, programs, and activities, as well as the work of others.
Judging the Qualities of Things, Services, or Peop	Assessing the value, importance, or quality of things or people.
Provide Consultation and Advice to Others	Providing guidance and expert advice to management or other groups on technical, systems-, or process-related topics.
Selling or Influencing Others	Convincing others to buy merchandise/goods or to otherwise change their minds or actions.
Estimating the Quantifiable Characteristics of Pro	Estimating sizes, distances, and quantities; or determining time, costs, resources, or materials needed to perform a work activity.
Coaching and Developing Others	Identifying the developmental needs of others and coaching, mentoring, or otherwise helping others to improve their knowledge or skills.
Inspecting Equipment, Structures, or Material	Inspecting equipment, structures, or materials to identify the cause of errors or other problems or defects.
Training and Teaching Others	Identifying the educational needs of others, developing formal educational or training programs or classes, and teaching or instructing others.
Assisting and Caring for Others	Providing personal assistance, medical attention, emotional support, or other personal care to others such as coworkers, customers, or patients.
Interpreting the Meaning of Information for Others	Translating or explaining what information means and how it can be used.
Performing General Physical Activities	Performing physical activities that require considerable use of your arms and legs and moving your whole body, such as climbing, lifting, balancing, walking, stooping, and handling of materials.

Performing for or Working Directly with the Public	Performing for people or dealing directly with the public. This includes serving customers in restaurants and stores, and receiving clients or guests.
Handling and Moving Objects	Using hands and arms in handling, installing, positioning, and moving materials, and manipulating things.
Controlling Machines and Processes	Using either control mechanisms or direct physical activity to operate machines or processes (not including computers or vehicles).
Repairing and Maintaining Electronic Equipment	Servicing, repairing, calibrating, regulating, fine-tuning, or testing machines, devices, and equipment that operate primarily on the basis of electrical or electronic (not mechanical) principles.
Operating Vehicles, Mechanized Devices, or Equipme	Running, maneuvering, navigating, or driving vehicles or mechanized equipment, such as forklifts, passenger vehicles, aircraft, or water craft.
Repairing and Maintaining Mechanical Equipment	Servicing, repairing, adjusting, and testing machines, devices, moving parts, and equipment that operate primarily on the basis of mechanical (not electronic) principles.
Drafting, Laying Out, and Specifying Technical Dev	Providing documentation, detailed instructions, drawings, or specifications to tell others about how devices, parts, equipment, or structures are to be fabricated, constructed, assembled, modified, maintained, or used.

Work_Content	Work_Content Definitions
Telephone	How often do you have telephone conversations in this job?
Face-to-Face Discussions	How often do you have to have face-to-face discussions with individuals or teams in this job?
Contact With Others	How much does this job require the worker to be in contact with others (face-to-face, by telephone, or otherwise) in order to perform it?
Structured versus Unstructured Work	To what extent is this job structured for the worker, rather than allowing the worker to determine tasks, priorities, and goals?
Indoors, Environmentally Controlled	How often does this job require working indoors in environmentally controlled conditions?
Frequency of Decision Making	How frequently is the worker required to make decisions that affect other people, the financial resources, and/or the image and reputation of the organization?
Coordinate or Lead Others	How important is it to coordinate or lead others in accomplishing work activities in this job?
Freedom to Make Decisions	How much decision making freedom, without supervision, does the job offer?
Work With Work Group or Team	How important is it to work with others in a group or team in this job?
Impact of Decisions on Co-workers or Company Resul	How do the decisions an employee makes impact the results of co-workers, clients or the company?
Importance of Being Exact or Accurate	How important is being very exact or highly accurate in performing this job?
Time Pressure	How often does this job require the worker to meet strict deadlines?
Responsibility for Outcomes and Results	How responsible is the worker for work outcomes and results of other workers?
Frequency of Conflict Situations	How often are there conflict situations the employee has to face in this job?
Letters and Memos	How often does the job require written letters and memos?
Deal With External Customers	How important is it to work with external customers or the public in this job?
Deal With Unpleasant or Angry People	How frequently does the worker have to deal with unpleasant, angry, or discourteous individuals as part of the job requirements?
Exposed to Disease or Infections	How often does this job require exposure to disease/infections?
Responsible for Others' Health and Safety	How much responsibility is there for the health and safety of others in this job?
Physical Proximity	To what extent does this job require the worker to perform job tasks in close physical proximity to other people?
Electronic Mail	How often do you use electronic mail in this job?
Level of Competition	To what extent does this job require the worker to compete or to be aware of competitive pressures?
Spend Time Sitting	How much does this job require sitting?
Sounds, Noise Levels Are Distracting or Uncomforta	How often does this job require working exposed to sounds and noise levels that are distracting or uncomfortable?
Wear Common Protective or Safety Equipment such as	How much does this job require wearing common protective or safety equipment such as safety shoes, glasses, gloves, hard hats or live jackets?
Spend Time Walking and Running	How much does this job require walking and running?
Exposed to Radiation	How often does this job require exposure to radiation?
Spend Time Using Your Hands to Handle, Control, or	How much does this job require using your hands to handle, control, or feel objects, tools or controls?
Spend Time Standing	How much does this job require standing?
Importance of Repeating Same Tasks	How important is repeating the same physical activities (e.g., key entry) or mental activities (e.g., checking entries in a ledger) over and over, without stopping, to performing this job?

Consequence of Error	How serious would the result usually be if the worker made a mistake that was not readily correctable?
Degree of Automation	How automated is the job?
Exposed to Contaminants	How often does this job require working exposed to contaminants (such as pollutants, gases, dust or odors)?
Wear Specialized Protective or Safety Equipment su	How much does this job require wearing specialized protective or safety equipment such as breathing apparatus, safety harness, full protection suits, or radiation protection?
Deal With Physically Aggressive People	How frequently does this job require the worker to deal with physical aggression of violent individuals?
Spend Time Bending or Twisting the Body	How much does this job require bending or twisting your body?
Spend Time Making Repetitive Motions	How much does this job require making repetitive motions?
Public Speaking	How often do you have to perform public speaking in this job?
Spend Time Kneeling, Crouching, Stooping, or Crawl	How much does this job require kneeling, crouching, stooping or crawling?
Extremely Bright or Inadequate Lighting	How often does this job require working in extremely bright or inadequate lighting conditions?
Indoors, Not Environmentally Controlled	How often does this job require working indoors in non-controlled environmental conditions (e.g., warehouse without heat)?
Exposed to Minor Burns, Cuts, Bites, or Stings	How often does this job require exposure to minor burns, cuts, bites, or stings?
In an Enclosed Vehicle or Equipment	How often does this job require working in a closed vehicle or equipment (e.g., car)?
Outdoors, Exposed to Weather	How often does this job require working outdoors, exposed to all weather conditions?
Very Hot or Cold Temperatures	How often does this job require working in very hot (above 90 F degrees) or very cold (below 32 F degrees) temperatures?
Pace Determined by Speed of Equipment	How important is it to this job that the pace is determined by the speed of equipment or machinery? (This does not refer to keeping busy at all times on this job.)
Exposed to Hazardous Conditions	How often does this job require exposure to hazardous conditions?
Spend Time Keeping or Regaining Balance	How much does this job require keeping or regaining your balance?
Cramped Work Space, Awkward Positions	How often does this job require working in cramped work spaces that requires getting into awkward positions?
Exposed to Hazardous Equipment	How often does this job require exposure to hazardous equipment?
Outdoors, Under Cover	How often does this job require working outdoors, under cover (e.g., structure with roof but no walls)?
Exposed to High Places	How often does this job require exposure to high places?
Exposed to Whole Body Vibration	How often does this job require exposure to whole body vibration (e.g., operate a jackhammer)?
In an Open Vehicle or Equipment	How often does this job require working in an open vehicle or equipment (e.g., tractor)?
Spend Time Climbing Ladders, Scaffolds, or Poles	How much does this job require climbing ladders, scaffolds, or poles?

Work_Styles	Work_Styles Definitions
Attention to Detail	Job requires being careful about detail and thorough in completing work tasks.
Leadership	Job requires a willingness to lead, take charge, and offer opinions and direction.
Dependability	Job requires being reliable, responsible, and dependable, and fulfilling obligations.
Integrity	Job requires being honest and ethical.
Adaptability/Flexibility	Job requires being open to change (positive or negative) and to considerable variety in the workplace.
Cooperation	Job requires being pleasant with others on the job and displaying a good-natured, cooperative attitude.
Self Control	Job requires maintaining composure, keeping emotions in check, controlling anger, and avoiding aggressive behavior, even in very difficult situations.
Concern for Others	Job requires being sensitive to others' needs and feelings and being understanding and helpful on the job.
Independence	Job requires developing one's own ways of doing things, guiding oneself with little or no supervision, and depending on oneself to get things done.
Social Orientation	Job requires preferring to work with others rather than alone, and being personally connected with others on the job.
Initiative	Job requires a willingness to take on responsibilities and challenges.
Stress Tolerance	Job requires accepting criticism and dealing calmly and effectively with high stress situations.
Persistence	Job requires persistence in the face of obstacles.
Achievement/Effort	Job requires establishing and maintaining personally challenging achievement goals and exerting effort toward mastering tasks.
Innovation	Job requires creativity and alternative thinking to develop new ideas for and answers to work-related problems.

11-9121.00 - Natural Sciences Managers

Analytical Thinking	Job requires analyzing information and using logic to address work-related issues and problems.

Job Zone Component	Job Zone Component Definitions
Title	Job Zone Five: Extensive Preparation Needed
Overall Experience	Extensive skill. knowledge. and experience are needed for these occupations. Many require more than five years of experience. For example, surgeons must complete four years of college and an additional five to seven years of specialized medical training to be able to do their job.
Job Training	Employees may need some on-the-job training, but most of these occupations assume that the person will already have the required skills. knowledge. work-related experience, and/or training.
Job Zone Examples	These occupations often involve coordinating, training, supervising, or managing the activities of others to accomplish goals. Very advanced communication and organizational skills are required. Examples include athletic trainers, lawyers, managing editors, physicists, social psychologists, and surgeons.
SVP Range	(8.0 and above)
Education	A bachelor's degree is the minimum formal education required for these occupations. However, many also require graduate school. For example, they may require a master's degree, and some require a Ph.D., M.D., or J.D. (law degree).

11-9121.00 - Natural Sciences Managers

Plan, direct, or coordinate activities in such fields as life sciences, physical sciences. mathematics, statistics, and research and development in these fields.

Tasks

1) Advise and assist in obtaining patents or meeting other legal requirements.

2) Provide for stewardship of plant and animal resources and habitats, studying land use, monitoring animal populations and/or providing shelter, resources, and medical treatment for animals.

3) Confer with scientists, engineers, regulators, and others, to plan and review projects, and to provide technical assistance.

4) Design and coordinate successive phases of problem analysis, solution proposals, and testing.

5) Develop and implement policies, standards and procedures for the architectural, scientific and technical work performed, to ensure regulatory compliance and operations enhancement.

6) Prepare project proposals.

7) Make presentations at professional meetings to further knowledge in the field.

8) Develop client relationships and communicate with clients to explain proposals, present research findings, establish specifications or discuss project status.

9) Determine scientific and technical goals within broad outlines provided by top management and make detailed plans to accomplish these goals.

10) Conduct own research in field of expertise.

11) Develop innovative technology and train staff for its implementation.

12) Hire, supervise and evaluate engineers, technicians, researchers and other staff.

13) Prepare and administer budget, approve and review expenditures, and prepare financial reports.

14) Recruit personnel and oversee the development and maintenance of staff competence.

15) Review project activities, and prepare and review research, testing, and operational reports.

11-9131.00 - Postmasters and Mail Superintendents

Direct and coordinate operational, administrative, management, and supportive services of a U.S. post office; or coordinate activities of workers engaged in postal and related work in assigned post office.

Tasks

1) Direct and coordinate operational, management, and supportive services of one or a number of postal facilities.

2) Hire and train employees, and evaluate their performance.

3) Select and train postmasters and managers of associate postal units.

4) Negotiate labor disputes.

5) Issue and cash money orders.

6) Inform the public of available services, and of postal laws and regulations.

7) Resolve customer complaints.

8) Prepare and submit detailed and summary reports of post office activities to designated supervisors.

9) Organize and supervise activities such as the processing of incoming and outgoing mail.

10) Prepare employee work schedules.

11) Confer with suppliers to obtain bids for proposed purchases and to requisition supplies: disburse funds according to federal regulations.

11-9141.00 - Property, Real Estate, and Community Association Managers

Plan, direct, or coordinate selling, buying, leasing, or governance activities of commercial, industrial, or residential real estate properties.

Tasks

1) Investigate complaints. disturbances and violations, and resolve problems, following management rules and regulations.

2) Maintain records of sales. rental or usage activity, special permits issued, maintenance and operating costs, or property availability.

3) Manage and oversee operations, maintenance, administration, and improvement of commercial, industrial, or residential properties.

4) Market vacant space to prospective tenants through leasing agents, advertising, or other methods.

5) Meet with prospective tenants to show properties, explain terms of occupancy, and provide information about local areas.

6) Negotiate the sale, lease, or development of property, and complete or review appropriate documents and forms.

7) Confer regularly with community association members to ensure their needs are being met.

8) Prepare and administer contracts for provision of property services such as cleaning, maintenance, and security services.

9) Act as liaisons between on-site managers or tenants and owners.

10) Purchase building and maintenance supplies, equipment, or furniture.

11) Direct collection of monthly assessments, rental fees, and deposits and payment of insurance premiums, mortgage, taxes, and incurred operating expenses.

12) Clean common areas, change light bulbs, and make minor property repairs.

13) Direct and coordinate the activities of staff and contract personnel, and evaluate their performance.

14) Maintain contact with insurance carriers, fire and police departments, and other agencies to ensure protection and compliance with codes and regulations.

15) Meet with boards of directors and committees to discuss and resolve legal and environmental issues or disputes between neighbors.

16) Meet with clients to negotiate management and service contracts, determine priorities, and discuss the financial and operational status of properties.

17) Review rents to ensure that they are in line with rental markets.

18) Solicit and analyze bids from contractors for repairs, renovations, and maintenance.

19) Contract with architectural firms to draw up detailed plans for new structures.

20) Negotiate short- and long-term loans to finance construction and ownership of structures.

21) Negotiate with government leaders, businesses, special interest representatives, and utility companies to gain support for new projects and to eliminate potential obstacles.

22) Plan, schedule, and coordinate general maintenance, major repairs, and remodeling or construction projects for commercial or residential properties.

23) Analyze information on property values, taxes, zoning, population growth, and traffic volume and patterns in order to determine if properties should be acquired.

24) Determine and certify the eligibility of prospective tenants, following government regulations.

25) Prepare detailed budgets and financial reports for properties.

26) Inspect grounds, facilities, and equipment routinely to determine necessity of repairs or maintenance.

11-9151.00 - Social and Community Service Managers

Plan, organize, or coordinate the activities of a social service program or community outreach organization. Oversee the program or organization's budget and policies regarding participant involvement, program requirements, and benefits. Work may involve directing social workers, counselors, or probation officers.

Tasks

1) Evaluate the work of staff and volunteers in order to ensure that programs are of appropriate quality and that resources are used effectively.

2) Recruit, interview, and hire or sign up volunteers and staff.

3) Prepare and maintain records and reports, such as budgets, personnel records, or training manuals.

4) Plan and administer budgets for programs, equipment and support services.

5) Participate in the determination of organizational policies regarding such issues as participant eligibility, program requirements, and program benefits.

6) Research and analyze member or community needs in order to determine program directions and goals.

7) Establish and oversee administrative procedures to meet objectives set by boards of directors or senior management.

8) Establish and maintain relationships with other agencies and organizations in community in order to meet community needs and to ensure that services are not duplicated.

9) Direct fund-raising activities and the preparation of public relations materials.

10) Speak to community groups to explain and interpret agency purposes, programs, and policies.

11) Act as consultants to agency staff and other community programs regarding the interpretation of program-related federal, state, and county regulations and policies.

12) Represent organizations in relations with governmental and media institutions.

13) Direct activities of professional and technical staff members and volunteers.

14) Analyze proposed legislation, regulations, or rule changes in order to determine how agency services could be impacted.

13-1022.00 - Wholesale and Retail Buyers, Except Farm Products

Buy merchandise or commodities, other than farm products, for resale to consumers at the wholesale or retail level, including both durable and nondurable goods. Analyze past buying trends, sales records, price, and quality of merchandise to determine value and yield. Select, order, and authorize payment for merchandise according to contractual agreements. May conduct meetings with sales personnel and introduce new products.

Tasks

1) Negotiate prices, discount terms and transportation arrangements for merchandise.

2) Interview and work closely with vendors to obtain and develop desired products.

3) Authorize payment of invoices or return of merchandise.

4) Analyze and monitor sales records, trends and economic conditions to anticipate consumer buying patterns and determine what the company will sell and how much inventory is needed.

5) Confer with sales and purchasing personnel to obtain information about customer needs and preferences.

6) Conduct staff meetings with sales personnel to introduce new merchandise.

7) Set or recommend mark-up rates, mark-down rates, and selling prices for merchandise.

8) Inspect merchandise or products to determine value or yield.

9) Consult with store or merchandise managers about budget and goods to be purchased.

10) Use computers to organize and locate inventory, and operate spreadsheet and word processing software.

11) Monitor competitors' sales activities by following their advertisements in newspapers and other media.

12) Determine which products should be featured in advertising, the advertising medium to be used, and when the ads should be run.

13) Train and supervise sales and clerical staff.

14) Provide clerks with information to print on price tags, such as price, mark-ups or mark-downs, manufacturer number, season code, and style number.

15) Manage the department for which they buy.

Knowledge

Knowledge	Knowledge Definitions
Sales and Marketing	Knowledge of principles and methods for showing, promoting, and selling products or services. This includes marketing strategy and tactics, product demonstration, sales techniques, and sales control systems.
Customer and Personal Service	Knowledge of principles and processes for providing customer and personal services. This includes customer needs assessment, meeting quality standards for services, and evaluation of customer satisfaction.
Economics and Accounting	Knowledge of economic and accounting principles and practices, the financial markets, banking and the analysis and reporting of financial data.
English Language	Knowledge of the structure and content of the English language including the meaning and spelling of words, rules of composition, and grammar.
Clerical	Knowledge of administrative and clerical procedures and systems such as word processing, managing files and records, stenography and transcription, designing forms, and other office procedures and terminology.
Administration and Management	Knowledge of business and management principles involved in strategic planning, resource allocation, human resources modeling, leadership technique, production methods, and coordination of people and resources.
Mathematics	Knowledge of arithmetic, algebra, geometry, calculus, statistics, and their applications.
Transportation	Knowledge of principles and methods for moving people or goods by air, rail, sea, or road, including the relative costs and benefits.
Computers and Electronics	Knowledge of circuit boards, processors, chips, electronic equipment, and computer hardware and software, including applications and programming.
Communications and Media	Knowledge of media production, communication, and dissemination techniques and methods. This includes alternative ways to inform and entertain via written, oral, and visual media.
Telecommunications	Knowledge of transmission, broadcasting, switching, control, and operation of telecommunications systems.
Education and Training	Knowledge of principles and methods for curriculum and training design, teaching and instruction for individuals and groups, and the measurement of training effects.
Production and Processing	Knowledge of raw materials, production processes, quality control, costs, and other techniques for maximizing the effective manufacture and distribution of goods.
Building and Construction	Knowledge of materials, methods, and the tools involved in the construction or repair of houses, buildings, or other structures such as highways and roads.
Personnel and Human Resources	Knowledge of principles and procedures for personnel recruitment, selection, training, compensation and benefits, labor relations and negotiation, and personnel information systems.
Psychology	Knowledge of human behavior and performance; individual differences in ability, personality, and interests; learning and motivation; psychological research methods; and the assessment and treatment of behavioral and affective disorders.
Law and Government	Knowledge of laws, legal codes, court procedures, precedents, government regulations, executive orders, agency rules, and the democratic political process.
Public Safety and Security	Knowledge of relevant equipment, policies, procedures, and strategies to promote effective local, state, or national security operations for the protection of people, data, property, and institutions.
Mechanical	Knowledge of machines and tools, including their designs, uses, repair, and maintenance.
Design	Knowledge of design techniques, tools, and principles involved in production of precision technical plans, blueprints, drawings, and models.
Geography	Knowledge of principles and methods for describing the features of land, sea, and air masses, including their physical characteristics, locations, interrelationships, and distribution of plant, animal, and human life.
Chemistry	Knowledge of the chemical composition, structure, and properties of substances and of the chemical processes and transformations that they undergo. This includes uses of chemicals and their interactions, danger signs, production techniques, and disposal methods.
Sociology and Anthropology	Knowledge of group behavior and dynamics, societal trends and influences, human migrations, ethnicity, cultures and their history and origins.
Engineering and Technology	Knowledge of the practical application of engineering science and technology. This includes applying principles, techniques, procedures, and equipment to the design and production of various goods and services.
Physics	Knowledge and prediction of physical principles, laws, their interrelationships, and applications to understanding fluid, material, and atmospheric dynamics, and mechanical, electrical, atomic and sub-atomic structures and processes.
Foreign Language	Knowledge of the structure and content of a foreign (non-English) language including the meaning and spelling of words, rules of composition and grammar, and pronunciation.
Fine Arts	Knowledge of the theory and techniques required to compose, produce, and perform works of music, dance, visual arts, drama, and sculpture.

Biology	Knowledge of plant and animal organisms, their tissues, cells, functions, interdependencies, and interactions with each other and the environment.		

Biology	Knowledge of plant and animal organisms, their tissues, cells, functions, interdependencies, and interactions with each other and the environment.
Therapy and Counseling	Knowledge of principles, methods, and procedures for diagnosis, treatment, and rehabilitation of physical and mental dysfunctions, and for career counseling and guidance.
Philosophy and Theology	Knowledge of different philosophical systems and religions. This includes their basic principles, values, ethics, ways of thinking, customs, practices, and their impact on human culture.
Medicine and Dentistry	Knowledge of the information and techniques needed to diagnose and treat human injuries, diseases, and deformities. This includes symptoms, treatment alternatives, drug properties and interactions, and preventive health-care measures.
History and Archeology	Knowledge of historical events and their causes, indicators, and effects on civilizations and cultures.
Food Production	Knowledge of techniques and equipment for planting, growing, and harvesting food products (both plant and animal) for consumption, including storage/handling techniques.

Skills	**Skills Definitions**
Active Listening	Giving full attention to what other people are saying, taking time to understand the points being made, asking questions as appropriate, and not interrupting at inappropriate times.
Speaking	Talking to others to convey information effectively.
Reading Comprehension	Understanding written sentences and paragraphs in work related documents.
Critical Thinking	Using logic and reasoning to identify the strengths and weaknesses of alternative solutions, conclusions or approaches to problems.
Time Management	Managing one's own time and the time of others.
Service Orientation	Actively looking for ways to help people.
Judgment and Decision Making	Considering the relative costs and benefits of potential actions to choose the most appropriate one.
Mathematics	Using mathematics to solve problems.
Instructing	Teaching others how to do something.
Management of Material Resources	Obtaining and seeing to the appropriate use of equipment, facilities, and materials needed to do certain work.
Management of Financial Resources	Determining how money will be spent to get the work done, and accounting for these expenditures.
Coordination	Adjusting actions in relation to others' actions.
Writing	Communicating effectively in writing as appropriate for the needs of the audience.
Monitoring	Monitoring/Assessing performance of yourself, other individuals, or organizations to make improvements or take corrective action.
Quality Control Analysis	Conducting tests and inspections of products, services, or processes to evaluate quality or performance.
Social Perceptiveness	Being aware of others' reactions and understanding why they react as they do.
Operations Analysis	Analyzing needs and product requirements to create a design.
Active Learning	Understanding the implications of new information for both current and future problem-solving and decision-making.
Negotiation	Bringing others together and trying to reconcile differences.
Learning Strategies	Selecting and using training/instructional methods and procedures appropriate for the situation when learning or teaching new things.
Management of Personnel Resources	Motivating, developing, and directing people as they work, identifying the best people for the job.
Equipment Selection	Determining the kind of tools and equipment needed to do a job.
Persuasion	Persuading others to change their minds or behavior.
Complex Problem Solving	Identifying complex problems and reviewing related information to develop and evaluate options and implement solutions.
Troubleshooting	Determining causes of operating errors and deciding what to do about it.
Operation and Control	Controlling operations of equipment or systems.
Systems Evaluation	Identifying measures or indicators of system performance and the actions needed to improve or correct performance, relative to the goals of the system.
Installation	Installing equipment, machines, wiring, or programs to meet specifications.
Technology Design	Generating or adapting equipment and technology to serve user needs.
Systems Analysis	Determining how a system should work and how changes in conditions, operations, and the environment will affect outcomes.
Operation Monitoring	Watching gauges, dials, or other indicators to make sure a machine is working properly.
Equipment Maintenance	Performing routine maintenance on equipment and determining when and what kind of maintenance is needed.
Repairing	Repairing machines or systems using the needed tools.
Science	Using scientific rules and methods to solve problems.
Programming	Writing computer programs for various purposes.

Ability	**Ability Definitions**
Oral Expression	The ability to communicate information and ideas in speaking so others will understand.
Oral Comprehension	The ability to listen to and understand information and ideas presented through spoken words and sentences.
Written Comprehension	The ability to read and understand information and ideas presented in writing.
Speech Clarity	The ability to speak clearly so others can understand you.
Inductive Reasoning	The ability to combine pieces of information to form general rules or conclusions (includes finding a relationship among seemingly unrelated events).
Speech Recognition	The ability to identify and understand the speech of another person.
Problem Sensitivity	The ability to tell when something is wrong or is likely to go wrong. It does not involve solving the problem, only recognizing there is a problem.
Deductive Reasoning	The ability to apply general rules to specific problems to produce answers that make sense.
Mathematical Reasoning	The ability to choose the right mathematical methods or formulas to solve a problem.
Near Vision	The ability to see details at close range (within a few feet of the observer).
Information Ordering	The ability to arrange things or actions in a certain order or pattern according to a specific rule or set of rules (e.g., patterns of numbers, letters, words, pictures, mathematical operations).
Category Flexibility	The ability to generate or use different sets of rules for combining or grouping things in different ways.
Fluency of Ideas	The ability to come up with a number of ideas about a topic (the number of ideas is important, not their quality, correctness, or creativity).
Written Expression	The ability to communicate information and ideas in writing so others will understand.
Flexibility of Closure	The ability to identify or detect a known pattern (a figure, object, word, or sound) that is hidden in other distracting material.
Selective Attention	The ability to concentrate on a task over a period of time without being distracted.
Number Facility	The ability to add, subtract, multiply, or divide quickly and correctly.
Originality	The ability to come up with unusual or clever ideas about a given topic or situation, or to develop creative ways to solve a problem.
Speed of Closure	The ability to quickly make sense of, combine, and organize information into meaningful patterns.
Time Sharing	The ability to shift back and forth between two or more activities or sources of information (such as speech, sounds, touch, or other sources).
Perceptual Speed	The ability to quickly and accurately compare similarities and differences among sets of letters, numbers, objects, pictures, or patterns. The things to be compared may be presented at the same time or one after the other. This ability also includes comparing a presented object with a remembered object.
Far Vision	The ability to see details at a distance.
Memorization	The ability to remember information such as words, numbers, pictures, and procedures.
Arm-Hand Steadiness	The ability to keep your hand and arm steady while moving your arm or while holding your arm and hand in one position.
Auditory Attention	The ability to focus on a single source of sound in the presence of other distracting sounds.
Visual Color Discrimination	The ability to match or detect differences between colors, including shades of color and brightness.
Visualization	The ability to imagine how something will look after it is moved around or when its parts are moved or rearranged.
Finger Dexterity	The ability to make precisely coordinated movements of the fingers of one or both hands to grasp, manipulate, or assemble very small objects.
Manual Dexterity	The ability to quickly move your hand, your hand together with your arm, or your two hands to grasp, manipulate, or assemble objects.
Control Precision	The ability to quickly and repeatedly adjust the controls of a machine or a vehicle to exact positions.
Static Strength	The ability to exert maximum muscle force to lift, push, pull, or carry objects.
Depth Perception	The ability to judge which of several objects is closer or farther away from you, or to judge the distance between you and an object.
Trunk Strength	The ability to use your abdominal and lower back muscles to support part of the body repeatedly or continuously over time without 'giving out' or fatiguing.
Extent Flexibility	The ability to bend, stretch, twist, or reach with your body, arms, and/or legs.
Dynamic Strength	The ability to exert muscle force repeatedly or continuously over time. This involves muscular endurance and resistance to muscle fatigue.

Hearing Sensitivity	The ability to detect or tell the differences between sounds that vary in pitch and loudness.
Multilimb Coordination	The ability to coordinate two or more limbs (for example, two arms, two legs, or one leg and one arm) while sitting, standing, or lying down. It does not involve performing the activities while the whole body is in motion.
Gross Body Equilibrium	The ability to keep or regain your body balance or stay upright when in an unstable position.
Stamina	The ability to exert yourself physically over long periods of time without getting winded or out of breath.
Gross Body Coordination	The ability to coordinate the movement of your arms, legs, and torso together when the whole body is in motion.
Wrist-Finger Speed	The ability to make fast, simple, repeated movements of the fingers, hands, and wrists.
Glare Sensitivity	The ability to see objects in the presence of glare or bright lighting.
Spatial Orientation	The ability to know your location in relation to the environment or to know where other objects are in relation to you.
Sound Localization	The ability to tell the direction from which a sound originated.
Peripheral Vision	The ability to see objects or movement of objects to one's side when the eyes are looking ahead.
Dynamic Flexibility	The ability to quickly and repeatedly bend, stretch, twist, or reach out with your body, arms, and/or legs.
Rate Control	The ability to time your movements or the movement of a piece of equipment in anticipation of changes in the speed and/or direction of a moving object or scene.
Explosive Strength	The ability to use short bursts of muscle force to propel oneself (as in jumping or sprinting), or to throw an object.
Response Orientation	The ability to choose quickly between two or more movements in response to two or more different signals (lights, sounds, pictures). It includes the speed with which the correct response is started with the hand, foot, or other body part.
Night Vision	The ability to see under low light conditions.
Speed of Limb Movement	The ability to quickly move the arms and legs.
Reaction Time	The ability to quickly respond (with the hand, finger, or foot) to a signal (sound, light, picture) when it appears.

Work_Activity	Work_Activity Definitions
Selling or Influencing Others	Convincing others to buy merchandise/goods or to otherwise change their minds or actions.
Establishing and Maintaining Interpersonal Relatio	Developing constructive and cooperative working relationships with others, and maintaining them over time.
Updating and Using Relevant Knowledge	Keeping up-to-date technically and applying new knowledge to your job.
Organizing, Planning, and Prioritizing Work	Developing specific goals and plans to prioritize, organize, and accomplish your work.
Thinking Creatively	Developing, designing, or creating new applications, ideas, relationships, systems, or products, including artistic contributions.
Resolving Conflicts and Negotiating with Others	Handling complaints, settling disputes, and resolving grievances and conflicts, or otherwise negotiating with others.
Judging the Qualities of Things, Services, or Peop	Assessing the value, importance, or quality of things or people.
Estimating the Quantifiable Characteristics of Pro	Estimating sizes, distances, and quantities; or determining time, costs, resources, or materials needed to perform a work activity.
Making Decisions and Solving Problems	Analyzing information and evaluating results to choose the best solution and solve problems.
Performing for or Working Directly with the Public	Performing for people or dealing directly with the public. This includes serving customers in restaurants and stores, and receiving clients or guests.
Communicating with Supervisors, Peers, or Subordin	Providing information to supervisors, co-workers, and subordinates by telephone, in written form, e-mail, or in person.
Communicating with Persons Outside Organization	Communicating with people outside the organization, representing the organization to customers, the public, government, and other external sources. This information can be exchanged in person, in writing, or by telephone or e-mail.
Performing Administrative Activities	Performing day-to-day administrative tasks such as maintaining information files and processing paperwork.
Scheduling Work and Activities	Scheduling events, programs, and activities, as well as the work of others.
Interacting With Computers	Using computers and computer systems (including hardware and software) to program, write software, set up functions, enter data, or process information.
Getting Information	Observing, receiving, and otherwise obtaining information from all relevant sources.
Processing Information	Compiling, coding, categorizing, calculating, tabulating, auditing, or verifying information or data.
Developing Objectives and Strategies	Establishing long-range objectives and specifying the strategies and actions to achieve them.
Training and Teaching Others	Identifying the educational needs of others, developing formal educational or training programs or classes, and teaching or instructing others.

Guiding, Directing, and Motivating Subordinates	Providing guidance and direction to subordinates, including setting performance standards and monitoring performance.
Developing and Building Teams	Encouraging and building mutual trust, respect, and cooperation among team members.
Interpreting the Meaning of Information for Others	Translating or explaining what information means and how it can be used.
Monitor Processes, Materials, or Surroundings	Monitoring and reviewing information from materials, events, or the environment, to detect or assess problems.
Coordinating the Work and Activities of Others	Getting members of a group to work together to accomplish tasks.
Coaching and Developing Others	Identifying the developmental needs of others and coaching, mentoring, or otherwise helping others to improve their knowledge or skills.
Performing General Physical Activities	Performing physical activities that require considerable use of your arms and legs and moving your whole body, such as climbing, lifting, balancing, walking, stooping, and handling of materials.
Handling and Moving Objects	Using hands and arms in handling, installing, positioning, and moving materials, and manipulating things.
Inspecting Equipment, Structures, or Material	Inspecting equipment, structures, or materials to identify the cause of errors or other problems or defects.
Monitoring and Controlling Resources	Monitoring and controlling resources and overseeing the spending of money.
Identifying Objects, Actions, and Events	Identifying information by categorizing, estimating, recognizing differences or similarities, and detecting changes in circumstances or events.
Assisting and Caring for Others	Providing personal assistance, medical attention, emotional support, or other personal care to others such as coworkers, customers, or patients.
Analyzing Data or Information	Identifying the underlying principles, reasons, or facts of information by breaking down information or data into separate parts.
Provide Consultation and Advice to Others	Providing guidance and expert advice to management or other groups on technical, systems-, or process-related topics.
Evaluating Information to Determine Compliance wit	Using relevant information and individual judgment to determine whether events or processes comply with laws, regulations, or standards.
Staffing Organizational Units	Recruiting, interviewing, selecting, hiring, and promoting employees in an organization.
Controlling Machines and Processes	Using either control mechanisms or direct physical activity to operate machines or processes (not including computers or vehicles).
Repairing and Maintaining Mechanical Equipment	Servicing, repairing, adjusting, and testing machines, devices, moving parts, and equipment that operate primarily on the basis of mechanical (not electronic) principles.
Documenting/Recording Information	Entering, transcribing, recording, storing, or maintaining information in written or electronic/magnetic form.
Repairing and Maintaining Electronic Equipment	Servicing, repairing, calibrating, regulating, fine-tuning, or testing machines, devices, and equipment that operate primarily on the basis of electrical or electronic (not mechanical) principles.
Drafting, Laying Out, and Specifying Technical Dev	Providing documentation, detailed instructions, drawings, or specifications to tell others about how devices, parts, equipment, or structures are to be fabricated, constructed, assembled, modified, maintained, or used.
Operating Vehicles, Mechanized Devices, or Equipme	Running, maneuvering, navigating, or driving vehicles or mechanized equipment, such as forklifts, passenger vehicles, aircraft, or water craft.

Work_Content	Work_Content Definitions
Telephone	How often do you have telephone conversations in this job?
Contact With Others	How much does this job require the worker to be in contact with others (face-to-face, by telephone, or otherwise) in order to perform it?
Importance of Being Exact or Accurate	How important is being very exact or highly accurate in performing this job?
Freedom to Make Decisions	How much decision making freedom, without supervision, does the job offer?
Indoors, Environmentally Controlled	How often does this job require working indoors in environmentally controlled conditions?
Importance of Repeating Same Tasks	How important is repeating the same physical activities (e.g., key entry) or mental activities (e.g., checking entries in a ledger) over and over, without stopping, to performing this job?
Spend Time Sitting	How much does this job require sitting?
Face-to-Face Discussions	How often do you have to have face-to-face discussions with individuals or teams in this job?
Time Pressure	How often does this job require the worker to meet strict deadlines?
Electronic Mail	How often do you use electronic mail in this job?
Spend Time Making Repetitive Motions	How much does this job require making repetitive motions?
Deal With Unpleasant or Angry People	How frequently does the worker have to deal with unpleasant, angry, or discourteous individuals as part of the job requirements?

Frequency of Decision Making	How frequently is the worker required to make decisions that affect other people, the financial resources, and/or the image and reputation of the organization?
Letters and Memos	How often does the job require written letters and memos?
Deal With External Customers	How important is it to work with external customers or the public in this job?
Work With Work Group or Team	How important is it to work with others in a group or team in this job?
Physical Proximity	To what extent does this job require the worker to perform job tasks in close physical proximity to other people?
Frequency of Conflict Situations	How often are there conflict situations the employee has to face in this job?
Structured versus Unstructured Work	To what extent is this job structured for the worker, rather than allowing the worker to determine tasks, priorities, and goals?
Impact of Decisions on Co-workers or Company Resul	How do the decisions an employee makes impact the results of co-workers, clients or the company?
Level of Competition	To what extent does this job require the worker to compete or to be aware of competitive pressures?
Coordinate or Lead Others	How important is it to coordinate or lead others in accomplishing work activities in this job?
Degree of Automation	How automated is the job?
Spend Time Using Your Hands to Handle, Control, or	How much does this job require using your hands to handle, control, or feel objects, tools or controls?
Sounds, Noise Levels Are Distracting or Uncomforta	How often does this job require working exposed to sounds and noise levels that are distracting or uncomfortable?
Consequence of Error	How serious would the result usually be if the worker made a mistake that was not readily correctable?
Spend Time Standing	How much does this job require standing?
Responsibility for Outcomes and Results	How responsible is the worker for work outcomes and results of other workers?
Pace Determined by Speed of Equipment	How important is it to this job that the pace is determined by the speed of equipment or machinery? (This does not refer to keeping busy at all times on this job.)
Responsible for Others' Health and Safety	How much responsibility is there for the health and safety of others in this job?
Exposed to Contaminants	How often does this job require working exposed to contaminants (such as pollutants, gases, dust or odors)?
Spend Time Walking and Running	How much does this job require walking and running?
Spend Time Kneeling, Crouching, Stooping, or Crawl	How much does this job require kneeling, crouching, stooping or crawling?
Spend Time Climbing Ladders, Scaffolds, or Poles	How much does this job require climbing ladders, scaffolds, or poles?
Outdoors, Under Cover	How often does this job require working outdoors, under cover (e.g., structure with roof but no walls)?
Exposed to High Places	How often does this job require exposure to high places?
Public Speaking	How often do you have to perform public speaking in this job?
Indoors, Not Environmentally Controlled	How often does this job require working indoors in non-controlled environmental conditions (e.g., warehouse without heat)?
Exposed to Hazardous Equipment	How often does this job require exposure to hazardous equipment?
Outdoors, Exposed to Weather	How often does this job require working outdoors, exposed to all weather conditions?
Spend Time Bending or Twisting the Body	How much does this job require bending or twisting your body?
In an Enclosed Vehicle or Equipment	How often does this job require working in a closed vehicle or equipment (e.g., car)?
Deal With Physically Aggressive People	How frequently does this job require the worker to deal with physical aggression of violent individuals?
Very Hot or Cold Temperatures	How often does this job require working in very hot (above 90 F degrees) or very cold (below 32 F degrees) temperatures?
Wear Common Protective or Safety Equipment such as	How much does this job require wearing common protective or safety equipment such as safety shoes, glasses, gloves, hard hats or live jackets?
Exposed to Minor Burns, Cuts, Bites, or Stings	How often does this job require exposure to minor burns, cuts, bites, or stings?
In an Open Vehicle or Equipment	How often does this job require working in an open vehicle or equipment (e.g., tractor)?
Cramped Work Space, Awkward Positions	How often does this job require working in cramped work spaces that requires getting into awkward positions?
Exposed to Disease or Infections	How often does this job require exposure to disease/infections?
Extremely Bright or Inadequate Lighting	How often does this job require working in extremely bright or inadequate lighting conditions?
Exposed to Hazardous Conditions	How often does this job require exposure to hazardous conditions?
Spend Time Keeping or Regaining Balance	How much does this job require keeping or regaining your balance?
Wear Specialized Protective or Safety Equipment su	How much does this job require wearing specialized protective or safety equipment such as breathing apparatus, safety harness, full protection suits, or radiation protection?

Exposed to Radiation	How often does this job require exposure to radiation?
Exposed to Whole Body Vibration	How often does this job require exposure to whole body vibration (e.g., operate a jackhammer)?

Work_Styles	**Work_Styles Definitions**
Dependability	Job requires being reliable, responsible, and dependable, and fulfilling obligations.
Integrity	Job requires being honest and ethical.
Cooperation	Job requires being pleasant with others on the job and displaying a good-natured, cooperative attitude.
Attention to Detail	Job requires being careful about detail and thorough in completing work tasks.
Persistence	Job requires persistence in the face of obstacles.
Stress Tolerance	Job requires accepting criticism and dealing calmly and effectively with high stress situations.
Initiative	Job requires a willingness to take on responsibilities and challenges.
Achievement/Effort	Job requires establishing and maintaining personally challenging achievement goals and exerting effort toward mastering tasks.
Self Control	Job requires maintaining composure, keeping emotions in check, controlling anger, and avoiding aggressive behavior, even in very difficult situations.
Adaptability/Flexibility	Job requires being open to change (positive or negative) and to considerable variety in the workplace.
Concern for Others	Job requires being sensitive to others' needs and feelings and being understanding and helpful on the job.
Leadership	Job requires a willingness to lead, take charge, and offer opinions and direction.
Independence	Job requires developing one's own ways of doing things, guiding oneself with little or no supervision, and depending on oneself to get things done.
Innovation	Job requires creativity and alternative thinking to develop new ideas for and answers to work-related problems.
Analytical Thinking	Job requires analyzing information and using logic to address work-related issues and problems.
Social Orientation	Job requires preferring to work with others rather than alone, and being personally connected with others on the job.

Job Zone Component	**Job Zone Component Definitions**
Title	Job Zone Three: Medium Preparation Needed
Overall Experience	Previous work-related skill, knowledge, or experience is required for these occupations. For example, an electrician must have completed three or four years of apprenticeship or several years of vocational training, and often must have passed a licensing exam, in order to perform the job.
Job Training	Employees in these occupations usually need one or two years of training involving both on-the-job experience and informal training with experienced workers.
Job Zone Examples	These occupations usually involve using communication and organizational skills to coordinate, supervise, manage, or train others to accomplish goals. Examples include dental assistants, electricians, fish and game wardens, legal secretaries, personnel recruiters, and recreation workers.
SVP Range	(6.0 to < 7.0)
Education	Most occupations in this zone require training in vocational schools, related on-the-job experience, or an associate's degree. Some may require a bachelor's degree.

13-1023.00 - Purchasing Agents, Except Wholesale, Retail, and Farm Products

Purchase machinery, equipment, tools, parts, supplies, or services necessary for the operation of an establishment. Purchase raw or semi-finished materials for manufacturing.

Tasks

1) Evaluate and monitor contract performance to ensure compliance with contractual obligations and to determine need for changes.

2) Study sales records and inventory levels of current stock to develop strategic purchasing programs that facilitate employee access to supplies.

3) Negotiate leases of land and rights-of-way.

4) Formulate policies and procedures for bid proposals and procurement of goods and services.

5) Negotiate, or renegotiate, and administer contracts with suppliers, vendors, and other representatives.

6) Confer with staff, users, and vendors to discuss defective or unacceptable goods or services and determine corrective action.

7) Write and review product specifications, maintaining a working technical knowledge of the goods or services to be purchased.

8) Research and evaluate suppliers based on price, quality, selection, service, support, availability, reliability, production and distribution capabilities, and the supplier's reputation and history.

9) Arrange the payment of duty and freight charges.

10) Review catalogs, industry periodicals, directories, trade journals, and Internet sites, and consult with other department personnel to locate necessary goods and services.

11) Analyze price proposals, financial reports, and other data and information to determine reasonable prices.

12) Hire, train and/or supervise purchasing clerks, buyers, and expediters.

13) Monitor and follow applicable laws and regulations.

14) Monitor changes affecting supply and demand, tracking market conditions, price trends, or futures markets.

15) Purchase the highest quality merchandise at the lowest possible price and in correct amounts.

16) Prepare purchase orders, solicit bid proposals and review requisitions for goods and services.

17) Monitor shipments to ensure that goods come in on time, and in the event of problems trace shipments and follow up undelivered goods.

18) Maintain and review computerized or manual records of items purchased, costs, delivery, product performance, and inventories.

19) Attend meetings, trade shows, conferences, conventions and seminars to network with people in other purchasing departments.

13-1031.01 - Claims Examiners, Property and Casualty Insurance

Review settled insurance claims to determine that payments and settlements have been made in accordance with company practices and procedures. Report overpayments, underpayments, and other irregularities. Confer with legal counsel on claims requiring litigation.

Tasks

1) Conduct detailed bill reviews to implement sound litigation management and expense control.

2) Prepare reports to be submitted to company's data processing department.

3) Adjust reserves and provide reserve recommendations to ensure reserving activities consistent with corporate policies.

4) Supervise claims adjusters to ensure that adjusters have followed proper methods.

5) Resolve complex, severe exposure claims, using high service oriented file handling.

6) Report overpayments, underpayments, and other irregularities.

7) Present cases and participate in their discussion at claim committee meetings.

8) Pay and process claims within designated authority level.

9) Investigate, evaluate and settle claims, applying technical knowledge and human relations skills to effect fair and prompt disposal of cases and to contribute to a reduced loss ratio.

10) Examine claims investigated by insurance adjusters, further investigating questionable claims to determine whether to authorize payments.

11) Contact and/or interview claimants, doctors, medical specialists, or employers to get additional information.

12) Confer with legal counsel on claims requiring litigation.

13) Communicate with reinsurance brokers to obtain information necessary for processing claims.

14) Maintain claim files, such as records of settled claims and an inventory of claims requiring detailed analysis.

15) Enter claim payments, reserves and new claims on computer system, inputting concise yet sufficient file documentation.

13-1031.02 - Insurance Adjusters, Examiners, and Investigators

Investigate, analyze, and determine the extent of insurance company's liability concerning personal, casualty, or property loss or damages, and attempt to effect settlement with claimants. Correspond with or interview medical specialists, agents, witnesses, or claimants to compile information. Calculate benefit payments and approve payment of claims within a certain monetary limit.

13-1031.01 - Claims Examiners, Property and Casualty Insurance

Tasks

1) Obtain credit information from banks and other credit services.

2) Refer questionable claims to investigator or claims adjuster for investigation or settlement.

3) Prepare report of findings of investigation.

4) Collect evidence to support contested claims in court.

5) Examine claims form and other records to determine insurance coverage.

6) Examine titles to property to determine validity and act as company agent in transactions with property owners.

7) Negotiate claim settlements and recommend litigation when settlement cannot be negotiated.

8) Analyze information gathered by investigation and report findings and recommendations.

9) Interview or correspond with claimant and witnesses, consult police and hospital records, and inspect property damage to determine extent of liability.

10) Communicate with former associates to verify employment record and to obtain background information regarding persons or businesses applying for credit.

11) Interview or correspond with agents and claimants to correct errors or omissions and to investigate questionable claims.

13-1032.00 - Insurance Appraisers, Auto Damage

Appraise automobile or other vehicle damage to determine cost of repair for insurance claim settlement and seek agreement with automotive repair shop on cost of repair. Prepare insurance forms to indicate repair cost or cost estimates and recommendations.

Tasks

1) Review repair-cost estimates with automobile-repair shop to secure agreement on cost of repairs.

2) Arrange to have damage appraised by another appraiser to resolve disagreement with shop on repair cost.

3) Estimate parts and labor to repair damage, using standard automotive labor and parts-cost manuals and knowledge of automotive repair.

4) Prepare insurance forms to indicate repair-cost estimates and recommendations.

5) Examine damaged vehicle to determine extent of structural, body, mechanical, electrical, or interior damage.

6) Determine salvage value on total-loss vehicle.

13-1051.00 - Cost Estimators

Prepare cost estimates for product manufacturing, construction projects, or services to aid management in bidding on or determining price of product or service. May specialize according to particular service performed or type of product manufactured.

Tasks

1) Consult with clients, vendors, personnel in other departments or construction foremen to discuss and formulate estimates and resolve issues.

2) Confer with engineers, architects, owners, contractors and subcontractors on changes and adjustments to cost estimates.

3) Prepare and maintain a directory of suppliers, contractors and subcontractors.

4) Prepare estimates for use in selecting vendors or subcontractors.

5) Prepare estimates used by management for purposes such as planning, organizing, and scheduling work.

6) Analyze blueprints and other documentation to prepare time, cost, materials, and labor estimates.

7) Review material and labor requirements, to decide whether it is more cost-effective to produce or purchase components.

8) Prepare cost and expenditure statements and other necessary documentation at regular intervals for the duration of the project.

9) Conduct special studies to develop and establish standard hour and related cost data or to effect cost reduction.

10) Set up cost monitoring and reporting systems and procedures.

11) Establish and maintain tendering process, and conduct negotiations.

12) Visit site and record information about access, drainage and topography, and availability of services such as water and electricity.

Knowledge	Knowledge Definitions
Mathematics	Knowledge of arithmetic, algebra, geometry, calculus, statistics, and their applications.
Administration and Management	Knowledge of business and management principles involved in strategic planning, resource allocation, human resources modeling, leadership technique, production methods, and coordination of people and resources.
English Language	Knowledge of the structure and content of the English language including the meaning and spelling of words, rules of composition, and grammar.
Customer and Personal Service	Knowledge of principles and processes for providing customer and personal services. This includes customer needs assessment, meeting quality standards for services, and evaluation of customer satisfaction.
Production and Processing	Knowledge of raw materials, production processes, quality control, costs, and other techniques for maximizing the effective manufacture and distribution of goods.
Clerical	Knowledge of administrative and clerical procedures and systems such as word processing, managing files and records, stenography and transcription, designing forms, and other office procedures and terminology.
Economics and Accounting	Knowledge of economic and accounting principles and practices, the financial markets, banking and the analysis and reporting of financial data.
Sales and Marketing	Knowledge of principles and methods for showing, promoting, and selling products or services. This includes marketing strategy and tactics, product demonstration, sales techniques, and sales control systems.
Personnel and Human Resources	Knowledge of principles and procedures for personnel recruitment, selection, training, compensation and benefits, labor relations and negotiation, and personnel information systems.
Education and Training	Knowledge of principles and methods for curriculum and training design, teaching and instruction for individuals and groups, and the measurement of training effects.
Communications and Media	Knowledge of media production, communication, and dissemination techniques and methods. This includes alternative ways to inform and entertain via written, oral, and visual media.
Building and Construction	Knowledge of materials, methods, and the tools involved in the construction or repair of houses, buildings, or other structures such as highways and roads.
Computers and Electronics	Knowledge of circuit boards, processors, chips, electronic equipment, and computer hardware and software, including applications and programming.
Law and Government	Knowledge of laws, legal codes, court procedures, precedents, government regulations, executive orders, agency rules, and the democratic political process.
Design	Knowledge of design techniques, tools, and principles involved in production of precision technical plans, blueprints, drawings, and models.
Public Safety and Security	Knowledge of relevant equipment, policies, procedures, and strategies to promote effective local, state, or national security operations for the protection of people, data, property, and institutions.
Engineering and Technology	Knowledge of the practical application of engineering science and technology. This includes applying principles, techniques, procedures, and equipment to the design and production of various goods and services.
Transportation	Knowledge of principles and methods for moving people or goods by air, rail, sea, or road, including the relative costs and benefits.
Mechanical	Knowledge of machines and tools, including their designs, uses, repair, and maintenance.
Chemistry	Knowledge of the chemical composition, structure, and properties of substances and of the chemical processes and transformations that they undergo. This includes uses of chemicals and their interactions, danger signs, production techniques, and disposal methods.
Physics	Knowledge and prediction of physical principles, laws, their interrelationships, and applications to understanding fluid, material, and atmospheric dynamics, and mechanical, electrical, atomic and sub- atomic structures and processes.
Telecommunications	Knowledge of transmission, broadcasting, switching, control, and operation of telecommunications systems.
Psychology	Knowledge of human behavior and performance; individual differences in ability, personality, and interests; learning and motivation; psychological research methods; and the assessment and treatment of behavioral and affective disorders.
Geography	Knowledge of principles and methods for describing the features of land, sea, and air masses, including their physical characteristics, locations, interrelationships, and distribution of plant, animal, and human life.
History and Archeology	Knowledge of historical events and their causes, indicators, and effects on civilizations and cultures.
Foreign Language	Knowledge of the structure and content of a foreign (non-English) language including the meaning and spelling of words, rules of composition and grammar, and pronunciation.
Medicine and Dentistry	Knowledge of the information and techniques needed to diagnose and treat human injuries, diseases, and deformities. This includes symptoms, treatment alternatives, drug properties and interactions, and preventive health-care measures.
Therapy and Counseling	Knowledge of principles, methods, and procedures for diagnosis, treatment, and rehabilitation of physical and mental dysfunctions, and for career counseling and guidance.
Philosophy and Theology	Knowledge of different philosophical systems and religions. This includes their basic principles, values, ethics, ways of thinking, customs, practices, and their impact on human culture.
Biology	Knowledge of plant and animal organisms, their tissues, cells, functions, interdependencies, and interactions with each other and the environment.
Sociology and Anthropology	Knowledge of group behavior and dynamics, societal trends and influences, human migrations, ethnicity, cultures and their history and origins.
Food Production	Knowledge of techniques and equipment for planting, growing, and harvesting food products (both plant and animal) for consumption, including storage/handling techniques.
Fine Arts	Knowledge of the theory and techniques required to compose, produce, and perform works of music, dance, visual arts, drama, and sculpture.

Skills	Skills Definitions
Active Listening	Giving full attention to what other people are saying, taking time to understand the points being made, asking questions as appropriate, and not interrupting at inappropriate times.
Reading Comprehension	Understanding written sentences and paragraphs in work related documents.
Mathematics	Using mathematics to solve problems.
Time Management	Managing one's own time and the time of others.
Writing	Communicating effectively in writing as appropriate for the needs of the audience.
Management of Personnel Resources	Motivating, developing, and directing people as they work, identifying the best people for the job.
Critical Thinking	Using logic and reasoning to identify the strengths and weaknesses of alternative solutions, conclusions or approaches to problems.
Active Learning	Understanding the implications of new information for both current and future problem-solving and decision-making.
Speaking	Talking to others to convey information effectively.
Equipment Selection	Determining the kind of tools and equipment needed to do a job.
Complex Problem Solving	Identifying complex problems and reviewing related information to develop and evaluate options and implement solutions.
Coordination	Adjusting actions in relation to others' actions.
Social Perceptiveness	Being aware of others' reactions and understanding why they react as they do.
Judgment and Decision Making	Considering the relative costs and benefits of potential actions to choose the most appropriate one.
Monitoring	Monitoring/Assessing performance of yourself, other individuals, or organizations to make improvements or take corrective action.
Negotiation	Bringing others together and trying to reconcile differences.
Instructing	Teaching others how to do something.
Management of Financial Resources	Determining how money will be spent to get the work done, and accounting for these expenditures.
Learning Strategies	Selecting and using training/instructional methods and procedures appropriate for the situation when learning or teaching new things.
Quality Control Analysis	Conducting tests and inspections of products, services, or processes to evaluate quality or performance.
Service Orientation	Actively looking for ways to help people.
Persuasion	Persuading others to change their minds or behavior.
Operations Analysis	Analyzing needs and product requirements to create a design.
Technology Design	Generating or adapting equipment and technology to serve user needs.
Management of Material Resources	Obtaining and seeing to the appropriate use of equipment, facilities, and materials needed to do certain work.
Troubleshooting	Determining causes of operating errors and deciding what to do about it.
Installation	Installing equipment, machines, wiring, or programs to meet specifications.
Science	Using scientific rules and methods to solve problems.
Operation Monitoring	Watching gauges, dials, or other indicators to make sure a machine is working properly.
Equipment Maintenance	Performing routine maintenance on equipment and determining when and what kind of maintenance is needed.
Systems Evaluation	Identifying measures or indicators of system performance and the actions needed to improve or correct performance, relative to the goals of the system.

Operation and Control	Controlling operations of equipment or systems.
Systems Analysis	Determining how a system should work and how changes in conditions, operations, and the environment will affect outcomes.
Repairing	Repairing machines or systems using the needed tools.
Programming	Writing computer programs for various purposes.

Ability	**Ability Definitions**
Oral Comprehension	The ability to listen to and understand information and ideas presented through spoken words and sentences.
Oral Expression	The ability to communicate information and ideas in speaking so others will understand.
Information Ordering	The ability to arrange things or actions in a certain order or pattern according to a specific rule or set of rules (e.g., patterns of numbers, letters, words, pictures, mathematical operations).
Near Vision	The ability to see details at close range (within a few feet of the observer).
Speech Recognition	The ability to identify and understand the speech of another person.
Deductive Reasoning	The ability to apply general rules to specific problems to produce answers that make sense.
Written Comprehension	The ability to read and understand information and ideas presented in writing.
Inductive Reasoning	The ability to combine pieces of information to form general rules or conclusions (includes finding a relationship among seemingly unrelated events).
Speech Clarity	The ability to speak clearly so others can understand you.
Mathematical Reasoning	The ability to choose the right mathematical methods or formulas to solve a problem.
Problem Sensitivity	The ability to tell when something is wrong or is likely to go wrong. It does not involve solving the problem, only recognizing there is a problem.
Written Expression	The ability to communicate information and ideas in writing so others will understand.
Category Flexibility	The ability to generate or use different sets of rules for combining or grouping things in different ways.
Number Facility	The ability to add, subtract, multiply, or divide quickly and correctly.
Originality	The ability to come up with unusual or clever ideas about a given topic or situation, or to develop creative ways to solve a problem.
Fluency of Ideas	The ability to come up with a number of ideas about a topic (the number of ideas is important, not their quality, correctness, or creativity).
Selective Attention	The ability to concentrate on a task over a period of time without being distracted.
Visualization	The ability to imagine how something will look after it is moved around or when its parts are moved or rearranged.
Flexibility of Closure	The ability to identify or detect a known pattern (a figure, object, word, or sound) that is hidden in other distracting material.
Memorization	The ability to remember information such as words, numbers, pictures, and procedures.
Far Vision	The ability to see details at a distance.
Perceptual Speed	The ability to quickly and accurately compare similarities and differences among sets of letters, numbers, objects, pictures, or patterns. The things to be compared may be presented at the same time or one after the other. This ability also includes comparing a presented object with a remembered object.
Speed of Closure	The ability to quickly make sense of, combine, and organize information into meaningful patterns.
Time Sharing	The ability to shift back and forth between two or more activities or sources of information (such as speech, sounds, touch, or other sources).
Depth Perception	The ability to judge which of several objects is closer or farther away from you, or to judge the distance between you and an object.
Trunk Strength	The ability to use your abdominal and lower back muscles to support part of the body repeatedly or continuously over time without 'giving out' or fatiguing.
Finger Dexterity	The ability to make precisely coordinated movements of the fingers of one or both hands to grasp, manipulate, or assemble very small objects.
Auditory Attention	The ability to focus on a single source of sound in the presence of other distracting sounds.
Reaction Time	The ability to quickly respond (with the hand, finger, or foot) to a signal (sound, light, picture) when it appears.
Multilimb Coordination	The ability to coordinate two or more limbs (for example, two arms, two legs, or one leg and one arm) while sitting, standing, or lying down. It does not involve performing the activities while the whole body is in motion.
Control Precision	The ability to quickly and repeatedly adjust the controls of a machine or a vehicle to exact positions.
Visual Color Discrimination	The ability to match or detect differences between colors, including shades of color and brightness.

Hearing Sensitivity	The ability to detect or tell the differences between sounds that vary in pitch and loudness.
Wrist-Finger Speed	The ability to make fast, simple, repeated movements of the fingers, hands, and wrists.
Spatial Orientation	The ability to know your location in relation to the environment or to know where other objects are in relation to you.
Manual Dexterity	The ability to quickly move your hand, your hand together with your arm, or your two hands to grasp, manipulate, or assemble objects.
Sound Localization	The ability to tell the direction from which a sound originated.
Arm-Hand Steadiness	The ability to keep your hand and arm steady while moving your arm or while holding your arm and hand in one position.
Gross Body Coordination	The ability to coordinate the movement of your arms, legs, and torso together when the whole body is in motion.
Response Orientation	The ability to choose quickly between two or more movements in response to two or more different signals (lights, sounds, pictures). It includes the speed with which the correct response is started with the hand, foot, or other body part.
Peripheral Vision	The ability to see objects or movement of objects to one's side when the eyes are looking ahead.
Gross Body Equilibrium	The ability to keep or regain your body balance or stay upright when in an unstable position.
Night Vision	The ability to see under low light conditions.
Static Strength	The ability to exert maximum muscle force to lift, push, pull, or carry objects.
Rate Control	The ability to time your movements or the movement of a piece of equipment in anticipation of changes in the speed and/or direction of a moving object or scene.
Speed of Limb Movement	The ability to quickly move the arms and legs.
Explosive Strength	The ability to use short bursts of muscle force to propel oneself (as in jumping or sprinting), or to throw an object.
Dynamic Strength	The ability to exert muscle force repeatedly or continuously over time. This involves muscular endurance and resistance to muscle fatigue.
Stamina	The ability to exert yourself physically over long periods of time without getting winded or out of breath.
Extent Flexibility	The ability to bend, stretch, twist, or reach with your body, arms, and/or legs.
Glare Sensitivity	The ability to see objects in the presence of glare or bright lighting.
Dynamic Flexibility	The ability to quickly and repeatedly bend, stretch, twist, or reach out with your body, arms, and/or legs.

Work_Activity	**Work_Activity Definitions**
Communicating with Persons Outside Organization	Communicating with people outside the organization, representing the organization to customers, the public, government, and other external sources. This information can be exchanged in person, in writing, or by telephone or e-mail.
Scheduling Work and Activities	Scheduling events, programs, and activities, as well as the work of others.
Communicating with Supervisors, Peers, or Subordin	Providing information to supervisors, co-workers, and subordinates by telephone, in written form, e-mail, or in person.
Getting Information	Observing, receiving, and otherwise obtaining information from all relevant sources.
Establishing and Maintaining Interpersonal Relatio	Developing constructive and cooperative working relationships with others, and maintaining them over time.
Estimating the Quantifiable Characteristics of Pro	Estimating sizes, distances, and quantities; or determining time, costs, resources, or materials needed to perform a work activity.
Performing for or Working Directly with the Public	Performing for people or dealing directly with the public. This includes serving customers in restaurants and stores, and receiving clients or guests.
Coordinating the Work and Activities of Others	Getting members of a group to work together to accomplish tasks.
Making Decisions and Solving Problems	Analyzing information and evaluating results to choose the best solution and solve problems.
Organizing, Planning, and Prioritizing Work	Developing specific goals and plans to prioritize, organize, and accomplish your work.
Resolving Conflicts and Negotiating with Others	Handling complaints, settling disputes, and resolving grievances and conflicts, or otherwise negotiating with others.
Selling or Influencing Others	Convincing others to buy merchandise/goods or to otherwise change their minds or actions.
Thinking Creatively	Developing, designing, or creating new applications, ideas, relationships, systems, or products, including artistic contributions.
Developing and Building Teams	Encouraging and building mutual trust, respect, and cooperation among team members.
Identifying Objects, Actions, and Events	Identifying information by categorizing, estimating, recognizing differences or similarities, and detecting changes in circumstances or events.
Evaluating Information to Determine Compliance wit	Using relevant information and individual judgment to determine whether events or processes comply with laws, regulations, or standards.

Interacting With Computers	Using computers and computer systems (including hardware and software) to program, write software, set up functions, enter data, or process information.
Updating and Using Relevant Knowledge	Keeping up-to-date technically and applying new knowledge to your job.
Performing Administrative Activities	Performing day-to-day administrative tasks such as maintaining information files and processing paperwork.
Monitor Processes, Materials, or Surroundings	Monitoring and reviewing information from materials, events, or the environment, to detect or assess problems.
Inspecting Equipment, Structures, or Material	Inspecting equipment, structures, or materials to identify the cause of errors or other problems or defects.
Judging the Qualities of Things, Services, or Peop	Assessing the value, importance, or quality of things or people.
Drafting, Laying Out, and Specifying Technical Dev	Providing documentation, detailed instructions, drawings, or specifications to tell others about how devices, parts, equipment, or structures are to be fabricated, constructed, assembled, modified, maintained, or used.
Processing Information	Compiling, coding, categorizing, calculating, tabulating, auditing, or verifying information or data.
Developing Objectives and Strategies	Establishing long-range objectives and specifying the strategies and actions to achieve them.
Guiding, Directing, and Motivating Subordinates	Providing guidance and direction to subordinates, including setting performance standards and monitoring performance.
Interpreting the Meaning of Information for Others	Translating or explaining what information means and how it can be used.
Coaching and Developing Others	Identifying the developmental needs of others and coaching, mentoring, or otherwise helping others to improve their knowledge or skills.
Documenting/Recording Information	Entering, transcribing, recording, storing, or maintaining information in written or electronic/magnetic form.
Monitoring and Controlling Resources	Monitoring and controlling resources and overseeing the spending of money.
Analyzing Data or Information	Identifying the underlying principles, reasons, or facts of information by breaking down information or data into separate parts.
Provide Consultation and Advice to Others	Providing guidance and expert advice to management or other groups on technical, systems-, or process-related topics.
Staffing Organizational Units	Recruiting, interviewing, selecting, hiring, and promoting employees in an organization.
Training and Teaching Others	Identifying the educational needs of others, developing formal educational or training programs or classes, and teaching or instructing others.
Operating Vehicles, Mechanized Devices, or Equipme	Running, maneuvering, navigating, or driving vehicles or mechanized equipment, such as forklifts, passenger vehicles, aircraft, or water craft.
Assisting and Caring for Others	Providing personal assistance, medical attention, emotional support, or other personal care to others such as coworkers, customers, or patients.
Performing General Physical Activities	Performing physical activities that require considerable use of your arms and legs and moving your whole body, such as climbing, lifting, balancing, walking, stooping, and handling of materials.
Handling and Moving Objects	Using hands and arms in handling, installing, positioning, and moving materials, and manipulating things.
Repairing and Maintaining Mechanical Equipment	Servicing, repairing, adjusting, and testing machines, devices, moving parts, and equipment that operate primarily on the basis of mechanical (not electronic) principles.
Controlling Machines and Processes	Using either control mechanisms or direct physical activity to operate machines or processes (not including computers or vehicles).
Repairing and Maintaining Electronic Equipment	Servicing, repairing, calibrating, regulating, fine-tuning, or testing machines, devices, and equipment that operate primarily on the basis of electrical or electronic (not mechanical) principles.

Work_Content	**Work_Content Definitions**
Face-to-Face Discussions	How often do you have to have face-to-face discussions with individuals or teams in this job?
Telephone	How often do you have telephone conversations in this job?
Freedom to Make Decisions	How much decision making freedom, without supervision, does the job offer?
Structured versus Unstructured Work	To what extent is this job structured for the worker, rather than allowing the worker to determine tasks, priorities, and goals?
Impact of Decisions on Co-workers or Company Resul	How do the decisions an employee makes impact the results of co-workers, clients or the company?
Contact With Others	How much does this job require the worker to be in contact with others (face-to-face, by telephone, or otherwise) in order to perform it?
Work With Work Group or Team	How important is it to work with others in a group or team in this job?
Importance of Being Exact or Accurate	How important is being very exact or highly accurate in performing this job?

Frequency of Decision Making	How frequently is the worker required to make decisions that affect other people, the financial resources, and/or the image and reputation of the organization?
Time Pressure	How often does this job require the worker to meet strict deadlines?
Coordinate or Lead Others	How important is it to coordinate or lead others in accomplishing work activities in this job?
Deal With External Customers	How important is it to work with external customers or the public in this job?
Responsibility for Outcomes and Results	How responsible is the worker for work outcomes and results of other workers?
Indoors, Environmentally Controlled	How often does this job require working indoors in environmentally controlled conditions?
Electronic Mail	How often do you use electronic mail in this job?
Frequency of Conflict Situations	How often are there conflict situations the employee has to face in this job?
Letters and Memos	How often does the job require written letters and memos?
Responsible for Others' Health and Safety	How much responsibility is there for the health and safety of others in this job?
Consequence of Error	How serious would the result usually be if the worker made a mistake that was not readily correctable?
Level of Competition	To what extent does this job require the worker to compete or to be aware of competitive pressures?
In an Enclosed Vehicle or Equipment	How often does this job require working in a closed vehicle or equipment (e.g., car)?
Physical Proximity	To what extent does this job require the worker to perform job tasks in close physical proximity to other people?
Spend Time Sitting	How much does this job require sitting?
Importance of Repeating Same Tasks	How important is repeating the same physical activities (e.g., key entry) or mental activities (e.g., checking entries in a ledger) over and over, without stopping, to performing this job?
Exposed to Contaminants	How often does this job require working exposed to contaminants (such as pollutants, gases, dust or odors)?
Deal With Unpleasant or Angry People	How frequently does the worker have to deal with unpleasant, angry, or discourteous individuals as part of the job requirements?
Indoors, Not Environmentally Controlled	How often does this job require working indoors in non-controlled environmental conditions (e.g., warehouse without heat)?
Outdoors, Exposed to Weather	How often does this job require working outdoors, exposed to all weather conditions?
Exposed to Hazardous Equipment	How often does this job require exposure to hazardous equipment?
Spend Time Standing	How much does this job require standing?
Very Hot or Cold Temperatures	How often does this job require working in very hot (above 90 F degrees) or very cold (below 32 F degrees) temperatures?
Sounds, Noise Levels Are Distracting or Uncomforta	How often does this job require working exposed to sounds and noise levels that are distracting or uncomfortable?
Spend Time Using Your Hands to Handle, Control, or	How much does this job require using your hands to handle, control, or feel objects, tools or controls?
Wear Common Protective or Safety Equipment such as	How much does this job require wearing common protective or safety equipment such as safety shoes, glasses, gloves, hard hats or live jackets?
Outdoors, Under Cover	How often does this job require working outdoors, under cover (e.g., structure with roof but no walls)?
Degree of Automation	How automated is the job?
Spend Time Making Repetitive Motions	How much does this job require making repetitive motions?
Exposed to Minor Burns, Cuts, Bites, or Stings	How often does this job require exposure to minor burns, cuts, bites, or stings?
Spend Time Walking and Running	How much does this job require walking and running?
Public Speaking	How often do you have to perform public speaking in this job?
Exposed to High Places	How often does this job require exposure to high places?
Spend Time Kneeling, Crouching, Stooping, or Crawl	How much does this job require kneeling, crouching, stooping, or crawling?
Extremely Bright or Inadequate Lighting	How often does this job require working in extremely bright or inadequate lighting conditions?
Pace Determined by Speed of Equipment	How important is it to this job that the pace is determined by the speed of equipment or machinery? (This does not refer to keeping busy at all times on this job.)
Exposed to Hazardous Conditions	How often does this job require exposure to hazardous conditions?
Spend Time Bending or Twisting the Body	How much does this job require bending or twisting your body?
Spend Time Climbing Ladders, Scaffolds, or Poles	How much does this job require climbing ladders, scaffolds, or poles?
Cramped Work Space, Awkward Positions	How often does this job require working in cramped work spaces that requires getting into awkward positions?
Deal With Physically Aggressive People	How frequently does this job require the worker to deal with physical aggression of violent individuals?
Spend Time Keeping or Regaining Balance	How much does this job require keeping or regaining your balance?

30

O*NET™–SOC Definitions by Code Number 5.1 Supp.

In an Open Vehicle or Equipment	How often does this job require working in an open vehicle or equipment (e.g., tractor)?
Exposed to Whole Body Vibration	How often does this job require exposure to whole body vibration (e.g., operate a jackhammer)?
Wear Specialized Protective or Safety Equipment su	How much does this job require wearing specialized protective or safety equipment such as breathing apparatus, safety harness, full protection suits, or radiation protection?
Exposed to Disease or Infections	How often does this job require exposure to disease/infections?
Exposed to Radiation	How often does this job require exposure to radiation?

Work_Styles	Work_Styles Definitions
Attention to Detail	Job requires being careful about detail and thorough in completing work tasks.
Dependability	Job requires being reliable, responsible, and dependable, and fulfilling obligations.
Integrity	Job requires being honest and ethical.
Cooperation	Job requires being pleasant with others on the job and displaying a good-natured, cooperative attitude.
Concern for Others	Job requires being sensitive to others' needs and feelings and being understanding and helpful on the job.
Independence	Job requires developing one's own ways of doing things, guiding oneself with little or no supervision, and depending on oneself to get things done.
Self Control	Job requires maintaining composure, keeping emotions in check, controlling anger, and avoiding aggressive behavior, even in very difficult situations.
Analytical Thinking	Job requires analyzing information and using logic to address work-related issues and problems.
Stress Tolerance	Job requires accepting criticism and dealing calmly and effectively with high stress situations.
Adaptability/Flexibility	Job requires being open to change (positive or negative) and to considerable variety in the workplace.
Innovation	Job requires creativity and alternative thinking to develop new ideas for and answers to work-related problems.
Leadership	Job requires a willingness to lead, take charge, and offer opinions and direction.
Initiative	Job requires a willingness to take on responsibilities and challenges.
Persistence	Job requires persistence in the face of obstacles.
Social Orientation	Job requires preferring to work with others rather than alone, and being personally connected with others on the job.
Achievement/Effort	Job requires establishing and maintaining personally challenging achievement goals and exerting effort toward mastering tasks.

Job Zone Component	Job Zone Component Definitions
Title	Job Zone Four: Considerable Preparation Needed
Overall Experience	A minimum of two to four years of work-related skill, knowledge, or experience is needed for these occupations. For example, an accountant must complete four years of college and work for several years in accounting to be considered qualified.
Job Training	Employees in these occupations usually need several years of work-related experience, on-the-job training, and/or vocational training.
Job Zone Examples	Many of these occupations involve coordinating, supervising, managing, or training others. Examples include accountants, chefs and head cooks, computer programmers, historians, pharmacists, and police detectives.
SVP Range	(7.0 to < 8.0)
Education	Most of these occupations require a four-year bachelor's degree, but some do not.

13-1061.00 - Emergency Management Specialists

Coordinate disaster response or crisis management activities, provide disaster preparedness training, and prepare emergency plans and procedures for natural (e.g., hurricanes, floods, earthquakes), wartime, or technological (e.g., nuclear power plant emergencies, hazardous materials spills) disasters or hostage situations.

Tasks

1) Develop instructional materials for the public, and make presentations to citizens' groups in order to provide information on emergency plans and their implementation process.

2) Develop and implement training procedures and strategies for radiological protection, detection, and decontamination.

3) Attend meetings, conferences, and workshops related to emergency management in order to learn new information and to develop working relationships with other emergency management specialists.

13-1061.00 - Emergency Management Specialists

4) Apply for federal funding for emergency management related needs; administer such grants and report on their progress.

5) Study emergency plans used elsewhere in order to gather information for plan development.

6) Review emergency plans of individual organizations such as medical facilities in order to ensure their adequacy.

7) Consult with officials of local and area governments, schools, hospitals, and other institutions in order to determine their needs and capabilities in the event of a natural disaster or other emergency.

8) Conduct surveys to determine the types of emergency-related needs that will need to be addressed in disaster planning, or provide technical support to others conducting such surveys.

9) Train local groups in the preparation of long-term plans that are compatible with federal and state plans.

10) Keep informed of federal, state and local regulations affecting emergency plans, and ensure that plans adhere to these regulations.

11) Keep informed of activities or changes that could affect the likelihood of an emergency, as well as those that could affect response efforts and details of plan implementation.

12) Inspect facilities and equipment such as emergency management centers and communications equipment in order to determine their operational and functional capabilities in emergency situations.

13) Develop and perform tests and evaluations of emergency management plans in accordance with state and federal regulations.

14) Develop and maintain liaisons with municipalities, county departments, and similar entities in order to facilitate plan development, response effort coordination, and exchanges of personnel and equipment.

15) Collaborate with other officials in order to prepare and analyze damage assessments following disasters or emergencies.

16) Coordinate disaster response or crisis management activities such as ordering evacuations, opening public shelters, and implementing special needs plans and programs.

17) Propose alteration of emergency response procedures based on regulatory changes, technological changes, or knowledge gained from outcomes of previous emergency situations.

18) Prepare plans that outline operating procedures to be used in response to disasters/emergencies such as hurricanes, nuclear accidents, and terrorist attacks, and in recovery from these events.

19) Prepare emergency situation status reports that describe response and recovery efforts, needs, and preliminary damage assessments.

20) Design and administer emergency/disaster preparedness training courses that teach people how to effectively respond to major emergencies and disasters.

21) Provide communities with assistance in applying for federal funding for emergency management facilities, radiological instrumentation, and other related items.

22) Inventory and distribute nuclear, biological, and chemical detection and contamination equipment, providing instruction in its maintenance and use.

13-1071.01 - Employment Interviewers, Private or Public Employment Service

Interview job applicants in employment office and refer them to prospective employers for consideration. Search application files, notify selected applicants of job openings, and refer qualified applicants to prospective employers. Contact employers to verify referral results. Record and evaluate various pertinent data.

Tasks

1) Select qualified applicants or refer them to employers, according to organization policy.

2) Instruct job applicants in presenting a positive image by providing help with resume writing, personal appearance, and interview techniques.

3) Refer applicants to services such as vocational counseling, literacy or language instruction, transportation assistance, vocational training and child care.

4) Evaluate selection and testing techniques by conducting research or follow-up activities and conferring with management and supervisory personnel.

5) Conduct workshops and demonstrate the use of job listings to assist applicants with skill building.

6) Administer assessment tests to identify skill building needs.

7) Search for and recruit applicants for open positions through campus job fairs and advertisements.

8) Perform reference and background checks on applicants.

9) Inform applicants of job openings and details such as duties and responsibilities, compensation, benefits, schedules, working conditions, and promotion opportunities.

10) Hire workers and place them with employers needing temporary help.

11) Contact employers to solicit orders for job vacancies. determining their requirements and recording relevant data such as job descriptions.

12) Conduct or arrange for skill, intelligence, or psychological testing of applicants and current employees.

13) Provide background information on organizations with which interviews are scheduled.

14) Maintain records of applicants not selected for employment.

15) Review employment applications and job orders to match applicants with job requirements. using manual or computerized file searches.

13-1071.02 - Personnel Recruiters

Seek out, interview. and screen applicants to fill existing and future job openings and promote career opportunities within an organization.

Tasks

1) Maintain current knowledge of Equal Employment Opportunity (EEO) and affirmative action guidelines and laws, such as the Americans with Disabilities Act.

2) Arrange for interviews and provide travel arrangements as necessary.

3) Contact applicants to inform them of employment possibilities, consideration. and selection.

4) Hire applicants and authorize paperwork assigning them to positions.

5) Prepare and maintain employment records.

6) Project yearly recruitment expenditures for budgetary consideration and control.

7) Serve on selection and examination boards to evaluate applicants according to test scores. contacting promising candidates for interviews.

8) Supervise personnel clerks performing filing, typing and record-keeping duties.

9) Advise management on organizing, preparing, and implementing recruiting and retention programs.

10) Address civic and social groups and attend conferences to disseminate information concerning possible job openings and career opportunities.

11) Screen and refer applicants to hiring personnel in the organization, making hiring recommendations when appropriate.

12) Perform searches for qualified candidates according to relevant job criteria, using computer databases, networking, Internet recruiting resources, cold calls, media, recruiting firms, and employee referrals.

13) Recruit applicants for open positions, arranging job fairs with college campus representatives.

14) Evaluate recruitment and selection criteria to ensure conformance to professional, statistical, and testing standards, recommending revision as needed.

15) Interview applicants to obtain information on work history, training, education, and job skills.

16) Inform potential applicants about facilities, operations, benefits, and job or career opportunities in organizations.

17) Advise managers and employees on staffing policies and procedures.

18) Review and evaluate applicant qualifications or eligibility for specified licensing. according to established guidelines and designated licensing codes.

19) Conduct reference and background checks on applicants.

13-1072.00 - Compensation, Benefits, and Job Analysis Specialists

Conduct programs of compensation and benefits and job analysis for employer. May specialize in specific areas, such as position classification and pension programs.

Tasks

1) Evaluate job positions, determining classification, exempt or non-exempt status, and salary.

2) Develop, implement, administer and evaluate personnel and labor relations programs. including performance appraisal, affirmative action and employment equity programs.

3) Analyze organizational, occupational, and industrial data to facilitate organizational functions and provide technical information to business, industry, and government.

4) Prepare occupational classifications, job descriptions and salary scales.

5) Administer employee insurance, pension and savings plans, working with insurance brokers and plan carriers.

6) Plan and develop curricula and materials for training programs and conduct training.

7) Provide advice on the resolution of classification and salary complaints.

8) Research employee benefit and health and safety practices and recommend changes or modifications to existing policies.

9) Speak at conferences and events to promote apprenticeships and related training programs.

10) Observe. interview, and survey employees and conduct focus group meetings to collect job. organizational, and occupational information.

11) Advise managers and employees on state and federal employment regulations, collective agreements, benefit and compensation policies, personnel procedures and classification programs.

12) Prepare reports, such as organization and flow charts, and career path reports, to summarize job analysis and evaluation and compensation analysis information.

13) Consult with or serve as a technical liaison between business, industry, government, and union officials.

14) Review occupational data on Alien Employment Certification Applications to determine the appropriate occupational title and code, and provide local offices with information about immigration and occupations.

15) Ensure company compliance with federal and state laws, including reporting requirements.

16) Prepare research results for publication in form of journals, books, manuals, and film.

17) Assess need for and develop job analysis instruments and materials.

18) Negotiate collective agreements on behalf of employers or workers, and mediate labor disputes and grievances.

19) Research job and worker requirements, structural and functional relationships among jobs and occupations, and occupational trends.

20) Advise staff of individuals' qualifications.

21) Assist in preparing and maintaining personnel records and handbooks.

22) Work with the Department of Labor and promote its use with employers.

23) Perform multifactor data and cost analyses that may be used in areas such as support of collective bargaining agreements.

13-1073.00 - Training and Development Specialists

Conduct training and development programs for employees.

Tasks

1) Keep up with developments in area of expertise by reading current journals, books and magazine articles.

2) Assess training needs through surveys, interviews with employees, focus groups, and/or consultation with managers, instructors or customer representatives.

3) Present information, using a variety of instructional techniques and formats such as role playing, simulations, team exercises, group discussions, videos and lectures.

4) Organize and develop, or obtain, training procedure manuals and guides and course materials such as handouts and visual materials.

5) Monitor, evaluate and record training activities and program effectiveness.

6) Develop alternative training methods if expected improvements are not seen.

7) Evaluate training materials prepared by instructors, such as outlines, text, and handouts.

8) Offer specific training programs to help workers maintain or improve job skills.

9) Coordinate recruitment and placement of training program participants.

10) Schedule classes based on availability of classrooms, equipment, and instructors.

11) Design, plan, organize and direct orientation and training for employees or customers of industrial or commercial establishment.

12) Select and assign instructors to conduct training.

13) Monitor training costs to ensure budget is not exceeded, and prepare budget reports to justify expenditures.

14) Screen, hire, and assign workers to positions based on qualifications.

15) Supervise instructors, evaluate instructor performance, and refer instructors to classes for skill development.

16) Devise programs to develop executive potential among employees in lower-level positions.

17) Negotiate contracts with clients, including desired training outcomes, fees and expenses.

18) Refer trainees to employer relations representatives, to locations offering job placement assistance, or to appropriate social services agencies if warranted.

Knowledge	Knowledge Definitions
Customer and Personal Service	Knowledge of principles and processes for providing customer and personal services. This includes customer needs assessment, meeting quality standards for services, and evaluation of customer satisfaction.
Personnel and Human Resources	Knowledge of principles and procedures for personnel recruitment, selection, training, compensation and benefits, labor relations and negotiation, and personnel information systems.
Education and Training	Knowledge of principles and methods for curriculum and training design, teaching and instruction for individuals and groups, and the measurement of training effects.
Clerical	Knowledge of administrative and clerical procedures and systems such as word processing, managing files and records, stenography and transcription, designing forms, and other office procedures and terminology.
English Language	Knowledge of the structure and content of the English language including the meaning and spelling of words, rules of composition, and grammar.
Psychology	Knowledge of human behavior and performance; individual differences in ability, personality, and interests; learning and motivation; psychological research methods; and the assessment and treatment of behavioral and affective disorders.
Administration and Management	Knowledge of business and management principles involved in strategic planning, resource allocation, human resources modeling, leadership technique, production methods, and coordination of people and resources.
Computers and Electronics	Knowledge of circuit boards, processors, chips, electronic equipment, and computer hardware and software, including applications and programming.
Public Safety and Security	Knowledge of relevant equipment, policies, procedures, and strategies to promote effective local, state, or national security operations for the protection of people, data, property, and institutions.
Communications and Media	Knowledge of media production, communication, and dissemination techniques and methods. This includes alternative ways to inform and entertain via written, oral, and visual media.
Sociology and Anthropology	Knowledge of group behavior and dynamics, societal trends and influences, human migrations, ethnicity, cultures and their history and origins.
Law and Government	Knowledge of laws, legal codes, court procedures, precedents, government regulations, executive orders, agency rules, and the democratic political process.
Therapy and Counseling	Knowledge of principles, methods, and procedures for diagnosis, treatment, and rehabilitation of physical and mental dysfunctions, and for career counseling and guidance.
Mathematics	Knowledge of arithmetic, algebra, geometry, calculus, statistics, and their applications.
Medicine and Dentistry	Knowledge of the information and techniques needed to diagnose and treat human injuries, diseases, and deformities. This includes symptoms, treatment alternatives, drug properties and interactions, and preventive health-care measures.
Sales and Marketing	Knowledge of principles and methods for showing, promoting, and selling products or services. This includes marketing strategy and tactics, product demonstration, sales techniques, and sales control systems.
Economics and Accounting	Knowledge of economic and accounting principles and practices, the financial markets, banking and the analysis and reporting of financial data.
Telecommunications	Knowledge of transmission, broadcasting, switching, control, and operation of telecommunications systems.
Philosophy and Theology	Knowledge of different philosophical systems and religions. This includes their basic principles, values, ethics, ways of thinking, customs, practices, and their impact on human culture.
Foreign Language	Knowledge of the structure and content of a foreign (non-English) language including the meaning and spelling of words, rules of composition and grammar, and pronunciation.
Mechanical	Knowledge of machines and tools, including their designs, uses, repair, and maintenance.
Transportation	Knowledge of principles and methods for moving people or goods by air, rail, sea, or road, including the relative costs and benefits.
Engineering and Technology	Knowledge of the practical application of engineering science and technology. This includes applying principles, techniques, procedures, and equipment to the design and production of various goods and services.
Biology	Knowledge of plant and animal organisms, their tissues, cells, functions, interdependencies, and interactions with each other and the environment.
Design	Knowledge of design techniques, tools, and principles involved in production of precision technical plans, blueprints, drawings, and models.
Physics	Knowledge and prediction of physical principles, laws, their interrelationships, and applications to understanding fluid, material, and atmospheric dynamics, and mechanical, electrical, atomic and sub-atomic structures and processes.
History and Archeology	Knowledge of historical events and their causes, indicators, and effects on civilizations and cultures.
Chemistry	Knowledge of the chemical composition, structure, and properties of substances and of the chemical processes and transformations that they undergo. This includes uses of chemicals and their interactions, danger signs, production techniques, and disposal methods.
Production and Processing	Knowledge of raw materials, production processes, quality control, costs, and other techniques for maximizing the effective manufacture and distribution of goods.
Fine Arts	Knowledge of the theory and techniques required to compose, produce, and perform works of music, dance, visual arts, drama, and sculpture.
Geography	Knowledge of principles and methods for describing the features of land, sea, and air masses, including their physical characteristics, locations, interrelationships, and distribution of plant, animal, and human life.
Food Production	Knowledge of techniques and equipment for planting, growing, and harvesting food products (both plant and animal) for consumption, including storage/handling techniques.
Building and Construction	Knowledge of materials, methods, and the tools involved in the construction or repair of houses, buildings, or other structures such as highways and roads.

Skills	Skills Definitions
Active Listening	Giving full attention to what other people are saying, taking time to understand the points being made, asking questions as appropriate, and not interrupting at inappropriate times.
Speaking	Talking to others to convey information effectively.
Time Management	Managing one's own time and the time of others.
Writing	Communicating effectively in writing as appropriate for the needs of the audience.
Reading Comprehension	Understanding written sentences and paragraphs in work related documents.
Critical Thinking	Using logic and reasoning to identify the strengths and weaknesses of alternative solutions, conclusions or approaches to problems.
Instructing	Teaching others how to do something.
Learning Strategies	Selecting and using training/instructional methods and procedures appropriate for the situation when learning or teaching new things.
Service Orientation	Actively looking for ways to help people.
Active Learning	Understanding the implications of new information for both current and future problem-solving and decision-making.
Monitoring	Monitoring/Assessing performance of yourself, other individuals, or organizations to make improvements or take corrective action.
Coordination	Adjusting actions in relation to others' actions.
Social Perceptiveness	Being aware of others' reactions and understanding why they react as they do.
Persuasion	Persuading others to change their minds or behavior.
Mathematics	Using mathematics to solve problems.
Judgment and Decision Making	Considering the relative costs and benefits of potential actions to choose the most appropriate one.
Management of Personnel Resources	Motivating, developing, and directing people as they work, identifying the best people for the job.
Complex Problem Solving	Identifying complex problems and reviewing related information to develop and evaluate options and implement solutions.
Negotiation	Bringing others together and trying to reconcile differences.
Quality Control Analysis	Conducting tests and inspections of products, services, or processes to evaluate quality or performance.
Equipment Maintenance	Performing routine maintenance on equipment and determining when and what kind of maintenance is needed.
Operations Analysis	Analyzing needs and product requirements to create a design.
Management of Material Resources	Obtaining and seeing to the appropriate use of equipment, facilities, and materials needed to do certain work.
Equipment Selection	Determining the kind of tools and equipment needed to do a job.
Science	Using scientific rules and methods to solve problems.
Systems Evaluation	Identifying measures or indicators of system performance and the actions needed to improve or correct performance, relative to the goals of the system.
Troubleshooting	Determining causes of operating errors and deciding what to do about it.
Installation	Installing equipment, machines, wiring, or programs to meet specifications.
Technology Design	Generating or adapting equipment and technology to serve user needs.
Management of Financial Resources	Determining how money will be spent to get the work done, and accounting for these expenditures.

Repairing	Repairing machines or systems using the needed tools.
Systems Analysis	Determining how a system should work and how changes in conditions, operations, and the environment will affect outcomes.
Operation and Control	Controlling operations of equipment or systems.
Operation Monitoring	Watching gauges, dials, or other indicators to make sure a machine is working properly.
Programming	Writing computer programs for various purposes.

Ability	Ability Definitions
Oral Expression	The ability to communicate information and ideas in speaking so others will understand.
Speech Clarity	The ability to speak clearly so others can understand you.
Oral Comprehension	The ability to listen to and understand information and ideas presented through spoken words and sentences.
Written Comprehension	The ability to read and understand information and ideas presented in writing.
Deductive Reasoning	The ability to apply general rules to specific problems to produce answers that make sense.
Written Expression	The ability to communicate information and ideas in writing so others will understand.
Originality	The ability to come up with unusual or clever ideas about a given topic or situation, or to develop creative ways to solve a problem.
Speech Recognition	The ability to identify and understand the speech of another person.
Near Vision	The ability to see details at close range (within a few feet of the observer).
Problem Sensitivity	The ability to tell when something is wrong or is likely to go wrong. It does not involve solving the problem, only recognizing there is a problem.
Information Ordering	The ability to arrange things or actions in a certain order or pattern according to a specific rule or set of rules (e.g., patterns of numbers, letters, words, pictures, mathematical operations).
Category Flexibility	The ability to generate or use different sets of rules for combining or grouping things in different ways.
Inductive Reasoning	The ability to combine pieces of information to form general rules or conclusions (includes finding a relationship among seemingly unrelated events).
Fluency of Ideas	The ability to come up with a number of ideas about a topic (the number of ideas is important, not their quality, correctness, or creativity).
Selective Attention	The ability to concentrate on a task over a period of time without being distracted.
Time Sharing	The ability to shift back and forth between two or more activities or sources of information (such as speech, sounds, touch, or other sources).
Memorization	The ability to remember information such as words, numbers, pictures, and procedures.
Flexibility of Closure	The ability to identify or detect a known pattern (a figure, object, word, or sound) that is hidden in other distracting material.
Far Vision	The ability to see details at a distance.
Finger Dexterity	The ability to make precisely coordinated movements of the fingers of one or both hands to grasp, manipulate, or assemble very small objects.
Auditory Attention	The ability to focus on a single source of sound in the presence of other distracting sounds.
Speed of Closure	The ability to quickly make sense of, combine, and organize information into meaningful patterns.
Trunk Strength	The ability to use your abdominal and lower back muscles to support part of the body repeatedly or continuously over time without 'giving out' or fatiguing.
Depth Perception	The ability to judge which of several objects is closer or farther away from you, or to judge the distance between you and an object.
Mathematical Reasoning	The ability to choose the right mathematical methods or formulas to solve a problem.
Perceptual Speed	The ability to quickly and accurately compare similarities and differences among sets of letters, numbers, objects, pictures, or patterns. The things to be compared may be presented at the same time or one after the other. This ability also includes comparing a presented object with a remembered object.
Visualization	The ability to imagine how something will look after it is moved around or when its parts are moved or rearranged.
Number Facility	The ability to add, subtract, multiply, or divide quickly and correctly.
Extent Flexibility	The ability to bend, stretch, twist, or reach with your body, arms, and/or legs.
Control Precision	The ability to quickly and repeatedly adjust the controls of a machine or a vehicle to exact positions.
Gross Body Coordination	The ability to coordinate the movement of your arms, legs, and torso together when the whole body is in motion.
Stamina	The ability to exert yourself physically over long periods of time without getting winded or out of breath.

Multilimb Coordination	The ability to coordinate two or more limbs (for example, two arms, two legs, or one leg and one arm) while sitting, standing, or lying down. It does not involve performing the activities while the whole body is in motion.
Manual Dexterity	The ability to quickly move your hand, your hand together with your arm, or your two hands to grasp, manipulate, or assemble objects.
Arm-Hand Steadiness	The ability to keep your hand and arm steady while moving your arm or while holding your arm and hand in one position.
Visual Color Discrimination	The ability to match or detect differences between colors, including shades of color and brightness.
Hearing Sensitivity	The ability to detect or tell the differences between sounds that vary in pitch and loudness.
Speed of Limb Movement	The ability to quickly move the arms and legs.
Wrist-Finger Speed	The ability to make fast, simple, repeated movements of the fingers, hands, and wrists.
Night Vision	The ability to see under low light conditions.
Sound Localization	The ability to tell the direction from which a sound originated.
Glare Sensitivity	The ability to see objects in the presence of glare or bright lighting.
Peripheral Vision	The ability to see objects or movement of objects to one's side when the eyes are looking ahead.
Rate Control	The ability to time your movements or the movement of a piece of equipment in anticipation of changes in the speed and/or direction of a moving object or scene.
Response Orientation	The ability to choose quickly between two or more movements in response to two or more different signals (lights, sounds, pictures). It includes the speed with which the correct response is started with the hand, foot, or other body part.
Reaction Time	The ability to quickly respond (with the hand, finger, or foot) to a signal (sound, light, picture) when it appears.
Gross Body Equilibrium	The ability to keep or regain your body balance or stay upright when in an unstable position.
Spatial Orientation	The ability to know your location in relation to the environment or to know where other objects are in relation to you.
Explosive Strength	The ability to use short bursts of muscle force to propel oneself (as in jumping or sprinting), or to throw an object.
Dynamic Strength	The ability to exert muscle force repeatedly or continuously over time. This involves muscular endurance and resistance to muscle fatigue.
Dynamic Flexibility	The ability to quickly and repeatedly bend, stretch, twist, or reach out with your body, arms, and/or legs.
Static Strength	The ability to exert maximum muscle force to lift, push, pull, or carry objects.

Work_Activity	Work_Activity Definitions
Communicating with Supervisors, Peers, or Subordin	Providing information to supervisors, co-workers, and subordinates by telephone, in written form, e-mail, or in person.
Getting Information	Observing, receiving, and otherwise obtaining information from all relevant sources.
Training and Teaching Others	Identifying the educational needs of others, developing formal educational or training programs or classes, and teaching or instructing others.
Organizing, Planning, and Prioritizing Work	Developing specific goals and plans to prioritize, organize, and accomplish your work.
Developing Objectives and Strategies	Establishing long-range objectives and specifying the strategies and actions to achieve them.
Interacting With Computers	Using computers and computer systems (including hardware and software) to program, write software, set up functions, enter data, or process information.
Making Decisions and Solving Problems	Analyzing information and evaluating results to choose the best solution and solve problems.
Updating and Using Relevant Knowledge	Keeping up-to-date technically and applying new knowledge to your job.
Performing for or Working Directly with the Public	Performing for people or dealing directly with the public. This includes serving customers in restaurants and stores, and receiving clients or guests.
Establishing and Maintaining Interpersonal Relatio	Developing constructive and cooperative working relationships with others, and maintaining them over time.
Developing and Building Teams	Encouraging and building mutual trust, respect, and cooperation among team members.
Evaluating Information to Determine Compliance wit	Using relevant information and individual judgment to determine whether events or processes comply with laws, regulations, or standards.
Coaching and Developing Others	Identifying the developmental needs of others and coaching, mentoring, or otherwise helping others to improve their knowledge or skills.
Processing Information	Compiling, coding, categorizing, calculating, tabulating, auditing, or verifying information or data.
Judging the Qualities of Things, Services, or Peop	Assessing the value, importance, or quality of things or people.
Scheduling Work and Activities	Scheduling events, programs, and activities, as well as the work of others.

Coordinating the Work and Activities of Others	Getting members of a group to work together to accomplish tasks.
Analyzing Data or Information	Identifying the underlying principles, reasons, or facts of information by breaking down information or data into separate parts.
Thinking Creatively	Developing, designing, or creating new applications, ideas, relationships, systems, or products, including artistic contributions.
Identifying Objects, Actions, and Events	Identifying information by categorizing, estimating, recognizing differences or similarities, and detecting changes in circumstances or events.
Communicating with Persons Outside Organization	Communicating with people outside the organization, representing the organization to customers, the public, government, and other external sources. This information can be exchanged in person, in writing, or by telephone or e-mail.
Provide Consultation and Advice to Others	Providing guidance and expert advice to management or other groups on technical, systems-, or process-related topics.
Interpreting the Meaning of Information for Others	Translating or explaining what information means and how it can be used.
Guiding, Directing, and Motivating Subordinates	Providing guidance and direction to subordinates, including setting performance standards and monitoring performance.
Documenting/Recording Information	Entering, transcribing, recording, storing, or maintaining information in written or electronic/magnetic form.
Monitor Processes, Materials, or Surroundings	Monitoring and reviewing information from materials, events, or the environment, to detect or assess problems.
Estimating the Quantifiable Characteristics of Pro	Estimating sizes, distances, and quantities; or determining time, costs, resources, or materials needed to perform a work activity.
Performing Administrative Activities	Performing day-to-day administrative tasks such as maintaining information files and processing paperwork.
Assisting and Caring for Others	Providing personal assistance, medical attention, emotional support, or other personal care to others such as coworkers, customers, or patients.
Selling or Influencing Others	Convincing others to buy merchandise/goods or to otherwise change their minds or actions.
Inspecting Equipment, Structures, or Material	Inspecting equipment, structures, or materials to identify the cause of errors or other problems or defects.
Resolving Conflicts and Negotiating with Others	Handling complaints, settling disputes, and resolving grievances and conflicts, or otherwise negotiating with others.
Monitoring and Controlling Resources	Monitoring and controlling resources and overseeing the spending of money.
Staffing Organizational Units	Recruiting, interviewing, selecting, hiring, and promoting employees in an organization.
Handling and Moving Objects	Using hands and arms in handling, installing, positioning, and moving materials, and manipulating things.
Controlling Machines and Processes	Using either control mechanisms or direct physical activity to operate machines or processes (not including computers or vehicles).
Performing General Physical Activities	Performing physical activities that require considerable use of your arms and legs and moving your whole body, such as climbing, lifting, balancing, walking, stooping, and handling of materials.
Operating Vehicles, Mechanized Devices, or Equipme	Running, maneuvering, navigating, or driving vehicles or mechanized equipment, such as forklifts, passenger vehicles, aircraft, or water craft.
Repairing and Maintaining Electronic Equipment	Servicing, repairing, calibrating, regulating, fine-tuning, or testing machines, devices, and equipment that operate primarily on the basis of electrical or electronic (not mechanical) principles.
Repairing and Maintaining Mechanical Equipment	Servicing, repairing, adjusting, and testing machines, devices, moving parts, and equipment that operate primarily on the basis of mechanical (not electronic) principles.
Drafting, Laying Out, and Specifying Technical Dev	Providing documentation, detailed instructions, drawings, or specifications to tell others about how devices, parts, equipment, or structures are to be fabricated, constructed, assembled, modified, maintained, or used.

Work_Content	Work_Content Definitions
Telephone	How often do you have telephone conversations in this job?
Electronic Mail	How often do you use electronic mail in this job?
Freedom to Make Decisions	How much decision making freedom, without supervision, does the job offer?
Face-to-Face Discussions	How often do you have to have face-to-face discussions with individuals or teams in this job?
Indoors, Environmentally Controlled	How often does this job require working indoors in environmentally controlled conditions?
Coordinate or Lead Others	How important is it to coordinate or lead others in accomplishing work activities in this job?
Deal With External Customers	How important is it to work with external customers or the public in this job?
Letters and Memos	How often does the job require written letters and memos?
Importance of Being Exact or Accurate	How important is being very exact or highly accurate in performing this job?

Contact With Others	How much does this job require the worker to be in contact with others (face-to-face, by telephone, or otherwise) in order to perform it?
Impact of Decisions on Co-workers or Company Resul	How do the decisions an employee makes impact the results of co-workers, clients or the company?
Public Speaking	How often do you have to perform public speaking in this job?
Structured versus Unstructured Work	To what extent is this job structured for the worker, rather than allowing the worker to determine tasks, priorities, and goals?
Work With Work Group or Team	How important is it to work with others in a group or team in this job?
Physical Proximity	To what extent does this job require the worker to perform job tasks in close physical proximity to other people?
Frequency of Decision Making	How frequently is the worker required to make decisions that affect other people, the financial resources, and/or the image and reputation of the organization?
Time Pressure	How often does this job require the worker to meet strict deadlines?
In an Enclosed Vehicle or Equipment	How often does this job require working in a closed vehicle or equipment (e.g., car)?
Spend Time Standing	How much does this job require standing?
Deal-With Unpleasant or Angry People	How frequently does the worker have to deal with unpleasant, angry, or discourteous individuals as part of the job requirements?
Sounds, Noise Levels Are Distracting or Uncomforta	How often does this job require working exposed to sounds and noise levels that are distracting or uncomfortable?
Spend Time Making Repetitive Motions	How much does this job require making repetitive motions?
Degree of Automation	How automated is the job?
Spend Time Sitting	How much does this job require sitting?
Importance of Repeating Same Tasks	How important is repeating the same physical activities (e.g., key entry) or mental activities (e.g., checking entries in a ledger) over and over, without stopping, to performing this job?
Consequence of Error	How serious would the result usually be if the worker made a mistake that was not readily correctable?
Spend Time Using Your Hands to Handle, Control, or	How much does this job require using your hands to handle, control, or feel objects, tools or controls?
Frequency of Conflict Situations	How often are there conflict situations the employee has to face in this job?
Responsibility for Outcomes and Results	How responsible is the worker for work outcomes and results of other workers?
Cramped Work Space, Awkward Positions	How often does this job require working in cramped work spaces that requires getting into awkward positions?
Spend Time Walking and Running	How much does this job require walking and running?
Responsible for Others' Health and Safety	How much responsibility is there for the health and safety of others in this job?
Level of Competition	To what extent does this job require the worker to compete or to be aware of competitive pressures?
Exposed to Contaminants	How often does this job require working exposed to contaminants (such as pollutants, gases, dust or odors)?
Exposed to Disease or Infections	How often does this job require exposure to disease/infections?
Wear Common Protective or Safety Equipment such as	How much does this job require wearing common protective or safety equipment such as safety shoes, glasses, gloves, hard hats or live jackets?
Exposed to Radiation	How often does this job require exposure to radiation?
Wear Specialized Protective or Safety Equipment su	How much does this job require wearing specialized protective or safety equipment such as breathing apparatus, safety harness, full protection suits, or radiation protection?
Deal With Physically Aggressive People	How frequently does this job require the worker to deal with physical aggression of violent individuals?
Spend Time Bending or Twisting the Body	How much does this job require bending or twisting your body?
Very Hot or Cold Temperatures	How often does this job require working in very hot (above 90 F degrees) or very cold (below 32 F degrees) temperatures?
Outdoors, Exposed to Weather	How often does this job require working outdoors, exposed to all weather conditions?
Pace Determined by Speed of Equipment	How important is it to this job that the pace is determined by the speed of equipment or machinery? (This does not refer to keeping busy at all times on this job.)
Outdoors, Under Cover	How often does this job require working outdoors, under cover (e.g., structure with roof but no walls)?
Spend Time Kneeling, Crouching, Stooping, or Crawl	How much does this job require kneeling, crouching, stooping, or crawling?
Extremely Bright or Inadequate Lighting	How often does this job require working in extremely bright or inadequate lighting conditions?
Exposed to Minor Burns, Cuts, Bites, or Stings	How often does this job require exposure to minor burns, cuts, bites, or stings?
Exposed to Hazardous Conditions	How often does this job require exposure to hazardous conditions?
Indoors, Not Environmentally Controlled	How often does this job require working indoors in non-controlled environmental conditions (e.g., warehouse without heat)?

35

Spend Time Climbing Ladders, Scaffolds, or Poles	How much does this job require climbing ladders, scaffolds, or poles?
Exposed to High Places	How often does this job require exposure to high places?
Exposed to Hazardous Equipment	How often does this job require exposure to hazardous equipment?
Spend Time Keeping or Regaining Balance	How much does this job require keeping or regaining your balance?
In an Open Vehicle or Equipment	How often does this job require working in an open vehicle or equipment (e.g., tractor)?
Exposed to Whole Body Vibration	How often does this job require exposure to whole body vibration (e.g., operate a jackhammer)?

Work_Styles	Work_Styles Definitions
Integrity	Job requires being honest and ethical.
Dependability	Job requires being reliable, responsible, and dependable, and fulfilling obligations.
Cooperation	Job requires being pleasant with others on the job and displaying a good-natured, cooperative attitude.
Concern for Others	Job requires being sensitive to others' needs and feelings and being understanding and helpful on the job.
Stress Tolerance	Job requires accepting criticism and dealing calmly and effectively with high stress situations.
Social Orientation	Job requires preferring to work with others rather than alone, and being personally connected with others on the job.
Self Control	Job requires maintaining composure, keeping emotions in check, controlling anger, and avoiding aggressive behavior, even in very difficult situations.
Adaptability/Flexibility	Job requires being open to change (positive or negative) and to considerable variety in the workplace.
Attention to Detail	Job requires being careful about detail and thorough in completing work tasks.
Leadership	Job requires a willingness to lead, take charge, and offer opinions and direction.
Initiative	Job requires a willingness to take on responsibilities and challenges.
Independence	Job requires developing one's own ways of doing things, guiding oneself with little or no supervision, and depending on oneself to get things done.
Analytical Thinking	Job requires analyzing information and using logic to address work-related issues and problems.
Persistence	Job requires persistence in the face of obstacles.
Achievement/Effort	Job requires establishing and maintaining personally challenging achievement goals and exerting effort toward mastering tasks.
Innovation	Job requires creativity and alternative thinking to develop new ideas for and answers to work-related problems.

Job Zone Component	Job Zone Component Definitions
Title	Job Zone Four: Considerable Preparation Needed
Overall Experience	A minimum of two to four years of work-related skill, knowledge, or experience is needed for these occupations. For example, an accountant must complete four years of college and work for several years in accounting to be considered qualified.
Job Training	Employees in these occupations usually need several years of work-related experience, on-the-job training, and/or vocational training.
Job Zone Examples	Many of these occupations involve coordinating, supervising, managing, or training others. Examples include accountants, chefs and head cooks, computer programmers, historians, pharmacists, and police detectives.
SVP Range	(7.0 to < 8.0)
Education	Most of these occupations require a four - year bachelor's degree, but some do not.

13-1081.00 - Logisticians

Analyze and coordinate the logistical functions of a firm or organization. Responsible for the entire life cycle of a product, including acquisition, distribution, internal allocation, delivery, and final disposal of resources.

Tasks

1) Develop proposals that include documentation for estimates.

2) Collaborate with other departments as necessary to meet customer requirements, to take advantage of sales opportunities or, in the case of shortages, to minimize negative impacts on a business.

3) Stay informed of logistics technology advances, and apply appropriate technology in order to improve logistics processes.

4) Report project plans, progress, and results.

5) Direct and support the compilation and analysis of technical source data necessary for product development.

6) Redesign the movement of goods in order to maximize value and minimize costs.

7) Provide project management services, including the provision and analysis of technical data.

8) Plan, organize, and execute logistics support activities such as maintenance planning, repair analysis, and test equipment recommendations.

9) Manage the logistical aspects of product life cycles, including coordination or provisioning of samples, and the minimization of obsolescence.

10) Participate in the assessment and review of design alternatives and design change proposal impacts.

11) Direct team activities, establishing task priorities, scheduling and tracking work assignments, providing guidance, and ensuring the availability of resources.

12) Perform system life-cycle cost analysis, and develop component studies.

13) Protect and control proprietary materials.

14) Explain proposed solutions to customers, management, or other interested parties through written proposals and oral presentations.

15) Maintain and develop positive business relationships with a customer's key personnel involved in or directly relevant to a logistics activity.

16) Manage subcontractor activities, reviewing proposals, developing performance specifications, and serving as liaisons between subcontractors and organizations.

17) Support the development of training materials and technical manuals.

18) Develop and implement technical project management tools such as plans, schedules, and responsibility and compliance matrices.

19) Review logistics performance with customers against targets, benchmarks and service agreements.

20) Develop an understanding of customers' needs, and take actions to ensure that such needs are met.

13-1111.00 - Management Analysts

Conduct organizational studies and evaluations, design systems and procedures, conduct work simplifications and measurement studies, and prepare operations and procedures manuals to assist management in operating more efficiently and effectively. Includes program analysts and management consultants.

Tasks

1) Confer with personnel concerned to ensure successful functioning of newly implemented systems or procedures.

2) Design, evaluate, recommend, and approve changes of forms and reports.

3) Recommend purchase of storage equipment, and design area layout to locate equipment in space available.

4) Plan study of work problems and procedures, such as organizational change, communications, information flow, integrated production methods, inventory control, or cost analysis.

5) Gather and organize information on problems or procedures.

6) Review forms and reports, and confer with management and users about format, distribution, and purpose, and to identify problems and improvements.

7) Interview personnel and conduct on-site observation to ascertain unit functions, work performed, and methods, equipment, and personnel used.

8) Develop and implement records management program for filing, protection, and retrieval of records, and assure compliance with program.

9) Analyze data gathered and develop solutions or alternative methods of proceeding.

10) Prepare manuals and train workers in use of new forms, reports, procedures or equipment, according to organizational policy.

13-1121.00 - Meeting and Convention Planners

Coordinate activities of staff and convention personnel to make arrangements for group meetings and conventions.

Tasks

1) Evaluate and select providers of services according to customer requirements.

2) Maintain records of event aspects, including financial details.

3) Obtain permits from fire and health departments to erect displays and exhibits and serve food at events.

4) Coordinate services for events, such as accommodation and transportation for participants, facilities, catering, signage, displays, special needs requirements, printing and event security.

5) Organize registration of event participants.

6) Read trade publications, attend seminars, and consult with other meeting professionals in order to keep abreast of meeting management standards and trends.

7) Monitor event activities in order to ensure compliance with applicable regulations and laws, satisfaction of participants, and resolution of any problems that arise.

8) Negotiate contracts with such service providers and suppliers as hotels, convention centers, and speakers.

9) Consult with customers in order to determine objectives and requirements for events such as meetings, conferences, and conventions.

10) Arrange the availability of audio-visual equipment, transportation, displays, and other event needs.

11) Design and implement efforts to publicize events and promote sponsorships.

12) Conduct post-event evaluations in order to determine how future events could be improved.

13) Develop event topics and choose featured speakers.

14) Hire, train, and supervise volunteers and support staff required for events.

15) Plan and develop programs, agendas, budgets, and services according to customer requirements.

16) Confer with staff at a chosen event site in order to coordinate details.

17) Meet with sponsors and organizing committees in order to plan scope and format of events, to establish and monitor budgets, and to review administrative procedures and event progress.

18) Promote conference, convention and trades show services by performing tasks such as meeting with professional and trade associations, and producing brochures and other publications.

19) Direct administrative details such as financial operations, dissemination of promotional materials, and responses to inquiries.

20) Inspect event facilities in order to ensure that they conform to customer requirements.

13-2011.01 - Accountants

Analyze financial information and prepare financial reports to determine or maintain record of assets, liabilities, profit and loss, tax liability, or other financial activities within an organization.

Tasks

1) Establish tables of accounts, and assign entries to proper accounts.

2) Develop, implement, modify, and document record keeping and accounting systems, making use of current computer technology.

3) Survey operations to ascertain accounting needs and to recommend, develop, and maintain solutions to business and financial problems.

4) Report to management regarding the finances of establishment.

5) Compute taxes owed and prepare tax returns, ensuring compliance with payment, reporting and other tax requirements.

6) Analyze business operations, trends, costs, revenues, financial commitments, and obligations, to project future revenues and expenses or to provide advice.

7) Develop, maintain, and analyze budgets, preparing periodic reports that compare budgeted costs to actual costs.

8) Prepare forms and manuals for accounting and bookkeeping personnel, and direct their work activities.

9) Appraise, evaluate, and inventory real property and equipment, recording information such as the property's description, value, and location.

10) Advise management about issues such as resource utilization, tax strategies, and the assumptions underlying budget forecasts.

11) Advise clients in areas such as compensation, employee health care benefits, the design of accounting and data processing systems, and long-range tax and estate plans.

12) Provide internal and external auditing services for businesses and individuals.

13) Investigate bankruptcies and other complex financial transactions and prepare reports summarizing the findings.

14) Represent clients before taxing authorities and provide support during litigation involving financial issues.

15) Maintain and examine the records of government agencies.

16) Serve as bankruptcy trustees and business valuators.

17) Work as Internal Revenue Service agents.

Knowledge	Knowledge Definitions
Mathematics	Knowledge of arithmetic, algebra, geometry, calculus, statistics, and their applications.
Economics and Accounting	Knowledge of economic and accounting principles and practices, the financial markets, banking and the analysis and reporting of financial data.
English Language	Knowledge of the structure and content of the English language including the meaning and spelling of words, rules of composition, and grammar.
Customer and Personal Service	Knowledge of principles and processes for providing customer and personal services. This includes customer needs assessment, meeting quality standards for services, and evaluation of customer satisfaction.
Computers and Electronics	Knowledge of circuit boards, processors, chips, electronic equipment, and computer hardware and software, including applications and programming.
Law and Government	Knowledge of laws, legal codes, court procedures, precedents, government regulations, executive orders, agency rules, and the democratic political process.
Clerical	Knowledge of administrative and clerical procedures and systems such as word processing, managing files and records, stenography and transcription, designing forms, and other office procedures and terminology.
Personnel and Human Resources	Knowledge of principles and procedures for personnel recruitment, selection, training, compensation and benefits, labor relations and negotiation, and personnel information systems.
Administration and Management	Knowledge of business and management principles involved in strategic planning, resource allocation, human resources modeling, leadership technique, production methods, and coordination of people and resources.
Production and Processing	Knowledge of raw materials, production processes, quality control, costs, and other techniques for maximizing the effective manufacture and distribution of goods.
Education and Training	Knowledge of principles and methods for curriculum and training design, teaching and instruction for individuals and groups, and the measurement of training effects.
Public Safety and Security	Knowledge of relevant equipment, policies, procedures, and strategies to promote effective local, state, or national security operations for the protection of people, data, property, and institutions.
Telecommunications	Knowledge of transmission, broadcasting, switching, control, and operation of telecommunications systems.
Communications and Media	Knowledge of media production, communication, and dissemination techniques and methods. This includes alternative ways to inform and entertain via written, oral, and visual media.
Engineering and Technology	Knowledge of the practical application of engineering science and technology. This includes applying principles, techniques, procedures, and equipment to the design and production of various goods and services.
Sales and Marketing	Knowledge of principles and methods for showing, promoting, and selling products or services. This includes marketing strategy and tactics, product demonstration, sales techniques, and sales control systems.
Psychology	Knowledge of human behavior and performance; individual differences in ability, personality, and interests; learning and motivation; psychological research methods; and the assessment and treatment of behavioral and affective disorders.
Foreign Language	Knowledge of the structure and content of a foreign (non-English) language including the meaning and spelling of words, rules of composition and grammar, and pronunciation.
Transportation	Knowledge of principles and methods for moving people or goods by air, rail, sea, or road, including the relative costs and benefits.
Sociology and Anthropology	Knowledge of group behavior and dynamics, societal trends and influences, human migrations, ethnicity, cultures and their history and origins.
Building and Construction	Knowledge of materials, methods, and the tools involved in the construction or repair of houses, buildings, or other structures such as highways and roads.
Philosophy and Theology	Knowledge of different philosophical systems and religions. This includes their basic principles, values, ethics, ways of thinking, customs, practices, and their impact on human culture.
Design	Knowledge of design techniques, tools, and principles involved in production of precision technical plans, blueprints, drawings, and models.
Therapy and Counseling	Knowledge of principles, methods, and procedures for diagnosis, treatment, and rehabilitation of physical and mental dysfunctions, and for career counseling and guidance.

Geography	Knowledge of principles and methods for describing the features of land, sea, and air masses, including their physical characteristics, locations, interrelationships, and distribution of plant, animal, and human life.
Medicine and Dentistry	Knowledge of the information and techniques needed to diagnose and treat human injuries, diseases, and deformities. This includes symptoms, treatment alternatives, drug properties and interactions, and preventive health-care measures.
Food Production	Knowledge of techniques and equipment for planting, growing, and harvesting food products (both plant and animal) for consumption, including storage/handling techniques.
Mechanical	Knowledge of machines and tools, including their designs, uses, repair, and maintenance.
Physics	Knowledge and prediction of physical principles, laws, their interrelationships, and applications to understanding fluid, material, and atmospheric dynamics, and mechanical, electrical, atomic and sub- atomic structures and processes.
Chemistry	Knowledge of the chemical composition, structure, and properties of substances and of the chemical processes and transformations that they undergo. This includes uses of chemicals and their interactions, danger signs, production techniques, and disposal methods.
History and Archeology	Knowledge of historical events and their causes, indicators, and effects on civilizations and cultures.
Biology	Knowledge of plant and animal organisms, their tissues, cells, functions, interdependencies, and interactions with each other and the environment.
Fine Arts	Knowledge of the theory and techniques required to compose, produce, and perform works of music, dance, visual arts, drama, and sculpture.

Skills	Skills Definitions
Mathematics	Using mathematics to solve problems.
Active Listening	Giving full attention to what other people are saying, taking time to understand the points being made, asking questions as appropriate, and not interrupting at inappropriate times.
Critical Thinking	Using logic and reasoning to identify the strengths and weaknesses of alternative solutions, conclusions or approaches to problems.
Monitoring	Monitoring/Assessing performance of yourself, other individuals, or organizations to make improvements or take corrective action.
Judgment and Decision Making	Considering the relative costs and benefits of potential actions to choose the most appropriate one.
Active Learning	Understanding the implications of new information for both current and future problem-solving and decision-making.
Reading Comprehension	Understanding written sentences and paragraphs in work related documents.
Systems Analysis	Determining how a system should work and how changes in conditions, operations, and the environment will affect outcomes.
Systems Evaluation	Identifying measures or indicators of system performance and the actions needed to improve or correct performance, relative to the goals of the system.
Coordination	Adjusting actions in relation to others' actions.
Management of Financial Resources	Determining how money will be spent to get the work done, and accounting for these expenditures.
Time Management	Managing one's own time and the time of others.
Social Perceptiveness	Being aware of others' reactions and understanding why they react as they do.
Operations Analysis	Analyzing needs and product requirements to create a design.
Speaking	Talking to others to convey information effectively.
Complex Problem Solving	Identifying complex problems and reviewing related information to develop and evaluate options and implement solutions.
Learning Strategies	Selecting and using training/instructional methods and procedures appropriate for the situation when learning or teaching new things.
Writing	Communicating effectively in writing as appropriate for the needs of the audience.
Troubleshooting	Determining causes of operating errors and deciding what to do about it.
Service Orientation	Actively looking for ways to help people.
Instructing	Teaching others how to do something.
Persuasion	Persuading others to change their minds or behavior.
Negotiation	Bringing others together and trying to reconcile differences.
Quality Control Analysis	Conducting tests and inspections of products, services, or processes to evaluate quality or performance.
Equipment Selection	Determining the kind of tools and equipment needed to do a job.
Operation Monitoring	Watching gauges, dials, or other indicators to make sure a machine is working properly.
Programming	Writing computer programs for various purposes.
Management of Material Resources	Obtaining and seeing to the appropriate use of equipment, facilities, and materials needed to do certain work.

Management of Personnel Resources	Motivating, developing, and directing people as they work, identifying the best people for the job.
Operation and Control	Controlling operations of equipment or systems.
Equipment Maintenance	Performing routine maintenance on equipment and determining when and what kind of maintenance is needed.
Technology Design	Generating or adapting equipment and technology to serve user needs.
Installation	Installing equipment, machines, wiring, or programs to meet specifications.
Science	Using scientific rules and methods to solve problems.
Repairing	Repairing machines or systems using the needed tools.

Ability	Ability Definitions
Problem Sensitivity	The ability to tell when something is wrong or is likely to go wrong. It does not involve solving the problem, only recognizing there is a problem.
Deductive Reasoning	The ability to apply general rules to specific problems to produce answers that make sense.
Oral Expression	The ability to communicate information and ideas in speaking so others will understand.
Information Ordering	The ability to arrange things or actions in a certain order or pattern according to a specific rule or set of rules (e.g., patterns of numbers, letters, words, pictures, mathematical operations).
Written Expression	The ability to communicate information and ideas in writing so others will understand.
Mathematical Reasoning	The ability to choose the right mathematical methods or formulas to solve a problem.
Written Comprehension	The ability to read and understand information and ideas presented in writing.
Near Vision	The ability to see details at close range (within a few feet of the observer).
Inductive Reasoning	The ability to combine pieces of information to form general rules or conclusions (includes finding a relationship among seemingly unrelated events).
Speech Clarity	The ability to speak clearly so others can understand you.
Speech Recognition	The ability to identify and understand the speech of another person.
Oral Comprehension	The ability to listen to and understand information and ideas presented through spoken words and sentences.
Number Facility	The ability to add, subtract, multiply, or divide quickly and correctly.
Selective Attention	The ability to concentrate on a task over a period of time without being distracted.
Flexibility of Closure	The ability to identify or detect a known pattern (a figure, object, word, or sound) that is hidden in other distracting material.
Perceptual Speed	The ability to quickly and accurately compare similarities and differences among sets of letters, numbers, objects, pictures, or patterns. The things to be compared may be presented at the same time or one after the other. This ability also includes comparing a presented object with a remembered object.
Category Flexibility	The ability to generate or use different sets of rules for combining or grouping things in different ways.
Finger Dexterity	The ability to make precisely coordinated movements of the fingers of one or both hands to grasp, manipulate, or assemble very small objects.
Speed of Closure	The ability to quickly make sense of, combine, and organize information into meaningful patterns.
Originality	The ability to come up with unusual or clever ideas about a given topic or situation, or to develop creative ways to solve a problem.
Memorization	The ability to remember information such as words, numbers, pictures, and procedures.
Fluency of Ideas	The ability to come up with a number of ideas about a topic (the number of ideas is important, not their quality, correctness, or creativity).
Far Vision	The ability to see details at a distance.
Time Sharing	The ability to shift back and forth between two or more activities or sources of information (such as speech, sounds, touch, or other sources).
Visualization	The ability to imagine how something will look after it is moved around or when its parts are moved or rearranged.
Trunk Strength	The ability to use your abdominal and lower back muscles to support part of the body repeatedly or continuously over time without 'giving out' or fatiguing.
Depth Perception	The ability to judge which of several objects is closer or farther away from you, or to judge the distance between you and an object.
Visual Color Discrimination	The ability to match or detect differences between colors, including shades of color and brightness.
Hearing Sensitivity	The ability to detect or tell the differences between sounds that vary in pitch and loudness.
Manual Dexterity	The ability to quickly move your hand, your hand together with your arm, or your two hands to grasp, manipulate, or assemble objects.

Wrist-Finger Speed	The ability to make fast, simple, repeated movements of the fingers, hands, and wrists.
Auditory Attention	The ability to focus on a single source of sound in the presence of other distracting sounds.
Arm-Hand Steadiness	The ability to keep your hand and arm steady while moving your arm or while holding your arm and hand in one position.
Control Precision	The ability to quickly and repeatedly adjust the controls of a machine or a vehicle to exact positions.
Extent Flexibility	The ability to bend, stretch, twist, or reach with your body, arms, and/or legs.
Stamina	The ability to exert yourself physically over long periods of time without getting winded or out of breath.
Dynamic Strength	The ability to exert muscle force repeatedly or continuously over time. This involves muscular endurance and resistance to muscle fatigue.
Static Strength	The ability to exert maximum muscle force to lift, push, pull, or carry objects.
Glare Sensitivity	The ability to see objects in the presence of glare or bright lighting.
Reaction Time	The ability to quickly respond (with the hand, finger, or foot) to a signal (sound, light, picture) when it appears.
Speed of Limb Movement	The ability to quickly move the arms and legs.
Gross Body Coordination	The ability to coordinate the movement of your arms, legs, and torso together when the whole body is in motion.
Explosive Strength	The ability to use short bursts of muscle force to propel oneself (as in jumping or sprinting), or to throw an object.
Multilimb Coordination	The ability to coordinate two or more limbs (for example, two arms, two legs, or one leg and one arm) while sitting, standing, or lying down. It does not involve performing the activities while the whole body is in motion.
Spatial Orientation	The ability to know your location in relation to the environment or to know where other objects are in relation to you.
Response Orientation	The ability to choose quickly between two or more movements in response to two or more different signals (lights, sounds, pictures). It includes the speed with which the correct response is started with the hand, foot, or other body part.
Sound Localization	The ability to tell the direction from which a sound originated.
Gross Body Equilibrium	The ability to keep or regain your body balance or stay upright when in an unstable position.
Night Vision	The ability to see under low light conditions.
Peripheral Vision	The ability to see objects or movement of objects to one's side when the eyes are looking ahead.
Rate Control	The ability to time your movements or the movement of a piece of equipment in anticipation of changes in the speed and/or direction of a moving object or scene.
Dynamic Flexibility	The ability to quickly and repeatedly bend, stretch, twist, or reach out with your body, arms, and/or legs.

Work_Activity	Work_Activity Definitions
Interacting With Computers	Using computers and computer systems (including hardware and software) to program, write software, set up functions, enter data, or process information.
Analyzing Data or Information	Identifying the underlying principles, reasons, or facts of information by breaking down information or data into separate parts.
Processing Information	Compiling, coding, categorizing, calculating, tabulating, auditing, or verifying information or data.
Getting Information	Observing, receiving, and otherwise obtaining information from all relevant sources.
Documenting/Recording Information	Entering, transcribing, recording, storing, or maintaining information in written or electronic/magnetic form.
Establishing and Maintaining Interpersonal Relatio	Developing constructive and cooperative working relationships with others, and maintaining them over time.
Organizing, Planning, and Prioritizing Work	Developing specific goals and plans to prioritize, organize, and accomplish your work.
Communicating with Supervisors, Peers, or Subordin	Providing information to supervisors, co-workers, and subordinates by telephone, in written form, e-mail, or in person.
Making Decisions and Solving Problems	Analyzing information and evaluating results to choose the best solution and solve problems.
Interpreting the Meaning of Information for Others	Translating or explaining what information means and how it can be used.
Evaluating Information to Determine Compliance wit	Using relevant information and individual judgment to determine whether events or processes comply with laws, regulations, or standards.
Updating and Using Relevant Knowledge	Keeping up-to-date technically and applying new knowledge to your job.
Communicating with Persons Outside Organization	Communicating with people outside the organization, representing the organization to customers, the public, government, and other external sources. This information can be exchanged in person, in writing, or by telephone or e-mail.
Identifying Objects, Actions, and Events	Identifying information by categorizing, estimating, recognizing differences or similarities, and detecting changes in circumstances or events.

Developing Objectives and Strategies	Establishing long-range objectives and specifying the strategies and actions to achieve them.
Thinking Creatively	Developing, designing, or creating new applications, ideas, relationships, systems, or products, including artistic contributions.
Developing and Building Teams	Encouraging and building mutual trust, respect, and cooperation among team members.
Coordinating the Work and Activities of Others	Getting members of a group to work together to accomplish tasks.
Performing Administrative Activities	Performing day-to-day administrative tasks such as maintaining information files and processing paperwork.
Monitoring and Controlling Resources	Monitoring and controlling resources and overseeing the spending of money.
Guiding, Directing, and Motivating Subordinates	Providing guidance and direction to subordinates, including setting performance standards and monitoring performance.
Scheduling Work and Activities	Scheduling events, programs, and activities, as well as the work of others.
Estimating the Quantifiable Characteristics of Pro	Estimating sizes, distances, and quantities; or determining time, costs, resources, or materials needed to perform a work activity.
Resolving Conflicts and Negotiating with Others	Handling complaints, settling disputes, and resolving grievances and conflicts, or otherwise negotiating with others.
Training and Teaching Others	Identifying the educational needs of others, developing formal educational or training programs or classes, and teaching or instructing others.
Coaching and Developing Others	Identifying the developmental needs of others and coaching, mentoring, or otherwise helping others to improve their knowledge or skills.
Provide Consultation and Advice to Others	Providing guidance and expert advice to management or other groups on technical, systems-, or process-related topics.
Staffing Organizational Units	Recruiting, interviewing, selecting, hiring, and promoting employees in an organization.
Judging the Qualities of Things, Services, or Peop	Assessing the value, importance, or quality of things or people.
Assisting and Caring for Others	Providing personal assistance, medical attention, emotional support, or other personal care to others such as coworkers, customers, or patients.
Selling or Influencing Others	Convincing others to buy merchandise/goods or to otherwise change their minds or actions.
Controlling Machines and Processes	Using either control mechanisms or direct physical activity to operate machines or processes (not including computers or vehicles).
Monitor Processes, Materials, or Surroundings	Monitoring and reviewing information from materials, events, or the environment, to detect or assess problems.
Handling and Moving Objects	Using hands and arms in handling, installing, positioning, and moving materials, and manipulating things.
Performing General Physical Activities	Performing physical activities that require considerable use of your arms and legs and moving your whole body, such as climbing, lifting, balancing, walking, stooping, and handling of materials.
Performing for or Working Directly with the Public	Performing for people or dealing directly with the public. This includes serving customers in restaurants and stores, and receiving clients or guests.
Operating Vehicles, Mechanized Devices, or Equipme	Running, maneuvering, navigating, or driving vehicles or mechanized equipment, such as forklifts, passenger vehicles, aircraft, or water craft.
Inspecting Equipment, Structures, or Material	Inspecting equipment, structures, or materials to identify the cause of errors or other problems or defects.
Repairing and Maintaining Electronic Equipment	Servicing, repairing, calibrating, regulating, fine-tuning, or testing machines, devices, and equipment that operate primarily on the basis of electrical or electronic (not mechanical) principles.
Drafting, Laying Out, and Specifying Technical Dev	Providing documentation, detailed instructions, drawings, or specifications to tell others about how devices, parts, equipment, or structures are to be fabricated, constructed, assembled, modified, maintained, or used.
Repairing and Maintaining Mechanical Equipment	Servicing, repairing, adjusting, and testing machines, devices, moving parts, and equipment that operate primarily on the basis of mechanical (not electronic) principles.

Work_Content	Work_Content Definitions
Telephone	How often do you have telephone conversations in this job?
Electronic Mail	How often do you use electronic mail in this job?
Indoors, Environmentally Controlled	How often does this job require working indoors in environmentally controlled conditions?
Face-to-Face Discussions	How often do you have to have face-to-face discussions with individuals or teams in this job?
Structured versus Unstructured Work	To what extent is this job structured for the worker rather than allowing the worker to determine tasks, priorities, and goals?
Spend Time Sitting	How much does this job require sitting?
Freedom to Make Decisions	How much decision making freedom, without supervision, does the job offer?
Importance of Being Exact or Accurate	How important is being very exact or highly accurate in performing this job?

Work With Work Group or Team	How important is it to work with others in a group or team in this job?
Letters and Memos	How often does the job require written letters and memos?
Contact With Others	How much does this job require the worker to be in contact with others (face-to-face, by telephone, or otherwise) in order to perform it?
Degree of Automation	How automated is the job?
Importance of Repeating Same Tasks	How important is repeating the same physical activities (e.g., key entry) or mental activities (e.g., checking entries in a ledger) over and over, without stopping, to performing this job?
Impact of Decisions on Co-workers or Company Resul	How do the decisions an employee makes impact the results of co-workers, clients or the company?
Time Pressure	How often does this job require the worker to meet strict deadlines?
Frequency of Decision Making	How frequently is the worker required to make decisions that affect other people, the financial resources, and/or the image and reputation of the organization?
Physical Proximity	To what extent does this job require the worker to perform job tasks in close physical proximity to other people?
Spend Time Making Repetitive Motions	How much does this job require making repetitive motions?
Responsibility for Outcomes and Results	How responsible is the worker for work outcomes and results of other workers?
Deal With Unpleasant or Angry People	How frequently does the worker have to deal with unpleasant, angry, or discourteous individuals as part of the job requirements?
Level of Competition	To what extent does this job require the worker to compete or to be aware of competitive pressures?
Deal With External Customers	How important is it to work with external customers or the public in this job?
Coordinate or Lead Others	How important is it to coordinate or lead others in accomplishing work activities in this job?
Spend Time Using Your Hands to Handle, Control, or	How much does this job require using your hands to handle, control, or feel objects, tools or controls?
Spend Time Standing	How much does this job require standing?
Frequency of Conflict Situations	How often are there conflict situations the employee has to face in this job?
Responsible for Others' Health and Safety	How much responsibility is there for the health and safety of others in this job?
Consequence of Error	How serious would the result usually be if the worker made a mistake that was not readily correctable?
Spend Time Walking and Running	How much does this job require walking and running?
Sounds, Noise Levels Are Distracting or Uncomforta	How often does this job require working exposed to sounds and noise levels that are distracting or uncomfortable?
Very Hot or Cold Temperatures	How often does this job require working in very hot (above 90 F degrees) or very cold (below 32 F degrees) temperatures?
In an Enclosed Vehicle or Equipment	How often does this job require working in a closed vehicle or equipment (e.g., car)?
Public Speaking	How often do you have to perform public speaking in this job?
Exposed to Minor Burns, Cuts, Bites, or Stings	How often does this job require exposure to minor burns, cuts, bites, or stings?
Spend Time Kneeling, Crouching, Stooping, or Crawl	How much does this job require kneeling, crouching, stooping, or crawling?
Extremely Bright or Inadequate Lighting	How often does this job require working in extremely bright or inadequate lighting conditions?
Spend Time Bending or Twisting the Body	How much does this job require bending or twisting your body?
Exposed to Contaminants	How often does this job require working exposed to contaminants (such as pollutants, gases, dust or odors)?
Exposed to High Places	How often does this job require exposure to high places?
Outdoors, Exposed to Weather	How often does this job require working outdoors, exposed to all weather conditions?
Deal With Physically Aggressive People	How frequently does this job require the worker to deal with physical aggression of violent individuals?
Indoors, Not Environmentally Controlled	How often does this job require working indoors in non-controlled environmental conditions (e.g., warehouse without heat)?
Wear Common Protective or Safety Equipment such as	How much does this job require wearing common protective or safety equipment such as safety shoes, glasses, gloves, hard hats or life jackets?
Outdoors, Under Cover	How often does this job require working outdoors, under cover (e.g., structure with roof but no walls)?
Spend Time Climbing Ladders, Scaffolds, or Poles	How much does this job require climbing ladders, scaffolds, or poles?
Spend Time Keeping or Regaining Balance	How much does this job require keeping or regaining your balance?
Cramped Work Space, Awkward Positions	How often does this job require working in cramped work spaces that requires getting into awkward positions?
Exposed to Hazardous Conditions	How often does this job require exposure to hazardous conditions?

Exposed to Disease or Infections	How often does this job require exposure to disease/infections?
Exposed to Radiation	How often does this job require exposure to radiation?
Exposed to Hazardous Equipment	How often does this job require exposure to hazardous equipment?
Wear Specialized Protective or Safety Equipment su	How much does this job require wearing specialized protective or safety equipment such as breathing apparatus, safety harness, full protection suits, or radiation protection?
Pace Determined by Speed of Equipment	How important is it to this job that the pace is determined by the speed of equipment or machinery? (This does not refer to keeping busy at all times on this job.)
In an Open Vehicle or Equipment	How often does this job require working in an open vehicle or equipment (e.g., tractor)?
Exposed to Whole Body Vibration	How often does this job require exposure to whole body vibration (e.g., operate a jackhammer)?

Work_Styles	Work_Styles Definitions
Attention to Detail	Job requires being careful about detail and thorough in completing work tasks.
Dependability	Job requires being reliable, responsible, and dependable, and fulfilling obligations.
Integrity	Job requires being honest and ethical.
Analytical Thinking	Job requires analyzing information and using logic to address work-related issues and problems.
Stress Tolerance	Job requires accepting criticism and dealing calmly and effectively with high stress situations.
Cooperation	Job requires being pleasant with others on the job and displaying a good-natured, cooperative attitude.
Achievement/Effort	Job requires establishing and maintaining personally challenging achievement goals and exerting effort toward mastering tasks.
Adaptability/Flexibility	Job requires being open to change (positive or negative) and to considerable variety in the workplace.
Independence	Job requires developing one's own ways of doing things, guiding oneself with little or no supervision, and depending on oneself to get things done.
Self Control	Job requires maintaining composure, keeping emotions in check, controlling anger, and avoiding aggressive behavior, even in very difficult situations.
Persistence	Job requires persistence in the face of obstacles.
Concern for Others	Job requires being sensitive to others' needs and feelings and being understanding and helpful on the job.
Initiative	Job requires a willingness to take on responsibilities and challenges.
Leadership	Job requires a willingness to lead, take charge, and offer opinions and direction.
Innovation	Job requires creativity and alternative thinking to develop new ideas for and answers to work-related problems.
Social Orientation	Job requires preferring to work with others rather than alone, and being personally connected with others on the job.

Job Zone Component	Job Zone Component Definitions
Title	Job Zone Four: Considerable Preparation Needed
Overall Experience	A minimum of two to four years of work-related skill, knowledge, or experience is needed for these occupations. For example, an accountant must complete four years of college and work for several years in accounting to be considered qualified.
Job Training	Employees in these occupations usually need several years of work-related experience, on-the-job training, and/or vocational training.
Job Zone Examples	Many of these occupations involve coordinating, supervising, managing, or training others. Examples include accountants, chefs and head cooks, computer programmers, historians, pharmacists, and police detectives.
SVP Range	(7.0 to < 8.0)
Education	Most of these occupations require a four - year bachelor's degree, but some do not.

13-2011.02 - Auditors

Examine and analyze accounting records to determine financial status of establishment and prepare financial reports concerning operating procedures.

Tasks

1) Confer with company officials about financial and regulatory matters.

2) Collect and analyze data to detect deficient controls, duplicated effort, extravagance, fraud, or non-compliance with laws, regulations, and management policies.

3) Prepare, analyze, and verify annual reports, financial statements, and other records, using accepted accounting and statistical procedures to assess financial condition and facilitate financial planning.

4) Examine whether the organization's objectives are reflected in its management activities, and whether employees understand the objectives.

5) Review taxpayer accounts, and conduct audits on-site, by correspondence. or by summoning taxpayer to office.

6) Produce up-to-the-minute information. using internal computer systems. to allow management to base decisions on actual, not historical, data.

7) Examine records, tax returns. and related documents pertaining to settlement of decedent's estate.

8) Examine records and interview workers to ensure recording of transactions and compliance with laws and regulations.

9) Evaluate taxpayer finances to determine tax liability, using knowledge of interest and discount rates, annuities, valuation of stocks and bonds, and amortization valuation of depletable assets.

10) Examine inventory to verify journal and ledger entries.

11) Examine and evaluate financial and information systems. recommending controls to ensure system reliability and data integrity.

12) Inspect account books and accounting systems for efficiency, effectiveness. and use of accepted accounting procedures to record transactions.

13) Inspect cash on hand, notes receivable and payable, negotiable securities, and canceled checks to confirm records are accurate.

14) Prepare detailed reports on audit findings.

15) Report to management about asset utilization and audit results, and recommend changes in operations and financial activities.

16) Audit payroll and personnel records to determine unemployment insurance premiums, workers' compensation coverage, liabilities, and compliance with tax laws.

17) Supervise auditing of establishments, and determine scope of investigation required.

18) Conduct pre-implementation audits to determine if systems and programs under development will work as planned.

19) Review data about material assets, net worth, liabilities, capital stock, surplus, income, and expenditures.

13-2021.01 - Assessors

Appraise real and personal property to determine its fair value. May assess taxes in accordance with prescribed schedules.

Tasks

1) Approve applications for property tax exemptions or deductions.

2) Calculate tax bills for properties by multiplying assessed values by jurisdiction tax rates.

3) Maintain familiarity with aspects of local real estate markets.

4) Determine taxability and value of properties, using methods such as field inspection, structural measurement, calculation, sales analysis, market trend studies, and income and expense analysis.

5) Serve on assessment review boards.

6) Review information about transfers of property to ensure its accuracy, checking basic information on buyers, sellers, and sales prices and making corrections as necessary.

7) Provide sales analyses to be used for equalization of school aid.

8) Conduct regular reviews of property within jurisdictions in order to determine changes in property due to construction or demolition.

9) Explain assessed values to property owners and defend appealed assessments at public hearings.

10) Establish uniform and equitable systems for assessing all classes and kinds of property.

11) Analyze trends in sales prices. construction costs, and rents, in order to assess property values and/or determine the accuracy of assessments.

12) Complete and maintain assessment rolls that show the assessed values and status of all property in a municipality.

13) Inspect new construction and major improvements to existing structures in order to determine values.

14) Inspect properties, considering factors such as market value, location, and building or replacement costs to determine appraisal value.

15) Issue notices of assessments and taxes.

16) Identify the ownership of each piece of taxable property.

17) Write and submit appraisal and tax reports for public record.

18) Prepare and maintain current data on each parcel assessed, including maps of boundaries, inventories of land and structures, property characteristics, and any applicable exemptions.

13-2021.02 - Appraisers, Real Estate

Appraise real property to determine its value for purchase. sales, investment, mortgage, or loan purposes.

Tasks

1) Prepare written reports that estimate property values. outline methods by which the estimations were made, and meet appraisal standards.

2) Search public records for transactions such as sales, leases, and assessments.

3) Obtain county land values and sales information about nearby properties in order to aid in establishment of property values.

4) Testify in court as to the value of a piece of real estate property.

5) Interview persons familiar with properties and immediate surroundings, such as contractors, home owners, and realtors, in order to obtain pertinent information.

6) Photograph interiors and exteriors of properties in order to assist in estimating property value, substantiate findings, and complete appraisal reports.

7) Check building codes and zoning bylaws in order to determine any effects on the properties being appraised.

8) Compute final estimation of property values, taking into account such factors as depreciation, replacement costs, value comparisons of similar properties, and income potential.

9) Inspect properties to evaluate construction, condition, special features, and functional design, and to take property measurements.

10) Examine the type and location of nearby services such as shopping centers, schools. parks, and other neighborhood features in order to evaluate their impact on property values.

11) Evaluate land and neighborhoods where properties are situated, considering locations and trends or impending changes that could influence future values.

12) Estimate building replacement costs using building valuation manuals and professional cost estimators.

13) Draw land diagrams that will be used in appraisal reports to support findings.

14) Verify legal descriptions of properties by comparing them to county records.

13-2031.00 - Budget Analysts

Examine budget estimates for completeness, accuracy, and conformance with procedures and regulations. Analyze budgeting and accounting reports for the purpose of maintaining expenditure controls.

Tasks

1) Direct the preparation of regular and special budget reports.

2) Compile and analyze accounting records and other data to determine the financial resources required to implement a program.

3) Examine budget estimates for completeness, accuracy, and conformance with procedures and regulations.

4) Interpret budget directives and establish policies for carrying out directives.

5) Review operating budgets to analyze trends affecting budget needs.

6) Consult with managers to ensure that budget adjustments are made in accordance with program changes.

7) Match appropriations for specific programs with appropriations for broader programs, including items for emergency funds.

8) Provide advice and technical assistance with cost analysis, fiscal allocation, and budget preparation.

9) Seek new ways to improve efficiency and increase profits.

10) Testify before examining and fund-granting authorities, clarifying and promoting the proposed budgets.

11) Analyze monthly department budgeting and accounting reports to maintain expenditure controls.

12) Perform cost-benefits analyses to compare operating programs, review financial requests, and explore alternative financing methods.

13-2041.00 - Credit Analysts

Analyze current credit data and financial statements of individuals or firms to determine the degree of risk involved in extending credit or lending money. Prepare reports with this credit information for use in decision-making.

Tasks

1) Analyze financial data such as income growth, quality of management, and market share to determine expected profitability of loans.

2) Review individual or commercial customer files to identify and select delinquent accounts for collection.

3) Consult with customers to resolve complaints and verify financial and credit transactions.

4) Prepare reports that include the degree of risk involved in extending credit or lending money.

5) Generate financial ratios, using computer programs, to evaluate customers' financial status.

6) Evaluate customer records and recommend payment plans based on earnings, savings data, payment history, and purchase activity.

7) Compare liquidity, profitability, and credit histories of establishments being evaluated with those of similar establishments in the same industries and geographic locations.

8) Confer with credit association and other business representatives to exchange credit information.

9) Analyze credit data and financial statements to determine the degree of risk involved in extending credit or lending money.

13-2051.00 - Financial Analysts

Conduct quantitative analyses of information affecting investment programs of public or private institutions.

Tasks

1) Collaborate with investment bankers to attract new corporate clients to securities firms.

2) Analyze financial information to produce forecasts of business, industry, and economic conditions for use in making investment decisions.

3) Determine the prices at which securities should be syndicated and offered to the public.

4) Monitor fundamental economic, industrial, and corporate developments through the analysis of information obtained from financial publications and services, investment banking firms, government agencies, trade publications, company sources, and personal interviews.

5) Maintain knowledge and stay abreast of developments in the fields of industrial technology, business, finance, and economic theory.

6) Present oral and written reports on general economic trends, individual corporations, and entire industries.

7) Interpret data affecting investment programs, such as price, yield, stability, future trends in investment risks, and economic influences.

8) Recommend investments and investment timing to companies, investment firm staff, or the investing public.

9) Assemble spreadsheets and draw charts and graphs used to illustrate technical reports, using computer.

10) Evaluate and compare the relative quality of various securities in a given industry.

11) Contact brokers and purchase investments for companies, according to company policy.

13-2053.00 - Insurance Underwriters

Review individual applications for insurance to evaluate degree of risk involved and determine acceptance of applications.

Tasks

1) Maintains records of performance reports for future reference.

2) Evaluates and approves selection of vendors by study of past performance and new advertisements.

3) Examine documents to determine degree of risk from such factors as applicant financial standing and value and condition of property.

4) Decline excessive risks.

5) Write to field representatives, medical personnel, and others to obtain further information, quote rates, or explain company underwriting policies.

6) Decrease value of policy when risk is substandard and specify applicable endorsements or apply rating to ensure safe profitable distribution of risks, using reference materials.

7) Authorize reinsurance of policy when risk is high.

8) Directs research and development programs to improve

9) Writes technical reports and other documentation, such as handbooks and bulletins, for use by engineering staff, management, and customers.

10) Reviews performance reports and documentation from customers and field engineers, and inspects malfunctioning or damaged products to determine problem.

11) Plans and coordinates activities concerned with investigating and resolving customers reports of technical problems with aircraft or aerospace vehicles.

12) Review company records to determine amount of insurance in force on single risk or group of closely related risks.

13-2061.00 - Financial Examiners

Enforce or ensure compliance with laws and regulations governing financial and securities institutions and financial and real estate transactions. May examine, verify correctness of, or establish authenticity of records.

Tasks

1) Evaluate data processing applications for institutions under examination in order to develop recommendations for coordinating existing systems with examination procedures.

2) Train other examiners in the financial examination process.

3) Review and analyze new, proposed, or revised laws, regulations, policies, and procedures in order to interpret their meaning and determine their impact.

4) Plan, supervise, and review work of assigned subordinates.

5) Examine the minutes of meetings of directors, stockholders and committees in order to investigate the specific authority extended at various levels of management.

6) Investigate activities of institutions in order to enforce laws and regulations and to ensure legality of transactions and operations or financial solvency.

7) Direct and participate in formal and informal meetings with bank directors, trustees, senior management, counsels, outside accountants and consultants in order to gather information and discuss findings.

8) Establish guidelines for procedures and policies that comply with new and revised regulations, and direct their implementation.

9) Prepare reports, exhibits and other supporting schedules that detail an institution's safety and soundness, compliance with laws and regulations, and recommended solutions to questionable financial conditions.

10) Confer with officials of real estate, securities, or financial institution industries in order to exchange views and discuss issues or pending cases.

11) Recommend actions to ensure compliance with laws and regulations, or to protect solvency of institutions.

12) Resolve problems concerning the overall financial integrity of banking institutions including loan investment portfolios, capital, earnings, and specific or large troubled accounts.

13) Review audit reports of internal and external auditors in order to monitor adequacy of scope of reports or to discover specific weaknesses in internal routines.

14) Review balance sheets, operating income and expense accounts, and loan documentation in order to confirm institution assets and liabilities.

15) Verify and inspect cash reserves, assigned collateral, and bank-owned securities in order to check internal control procedures.

13-2071.00 - Loan Counselors

Provide guidance to prospective loan applicants who have problems qualifying for traditional loans. Guidance may include determining the best type of loan and explaining loan requirements or restrictions.

Tasks

1) Confer with underwriters to resolve mortgage application problems.

2) Petition courts to transfer titles and deeds of collateral to banks.

3) Review billing for accuracy.

4) Supervise loan personnel.

5) Open accounts for clients and disburse funds from clients' accounts to creditors.

6) Interview applicants and request specified information for loan applications.

7) Check loan agreements to ensure that they are complete and accurate, according to policies.

8) Approve loans within specified limits.

9) Refer loans to loan committees for approval.

10) Match students' needs and eligibility with available financial aid programs in order to provide informed recommendations.

11) Analyze applicants' financial status, credit, and property evaluations to determine feasibility of granting loans.

12) Arrange for maintenance and liquidation of delinquent properties.

13) Submit applications to credit analysts for verification and recommendation.

14) Locate debtors using post office directories, utility services account listings, and mailing lists.

15) Calculate amount of debt and funds available in order to plan methods of payoff and to estimate time for debt liquidation.

16) Assist in selection of financial award candidates, using electronic databases to certify loan eligibility.

17) Authorize and sign mail collection letters.

18) Review accounts to determine write-offs for collection agencies.

19) Compare data on student aid applications with eligibility requirements of assistance programs.

20) Maintain current knowledge of credit regulations.

21) Contact borrowers with delinquent accounts to obtain payment in full or to negotiate repayment plans.

22) Maintain and review account records, updating and recategorizing them according to status changes.

23) Counsel clients on personal and family financial problems, such as excessive spending and borrowing of funds.

24) Establish payment priorities according to credit terms and interest rates in order to reduce clients' overall costs.

25) Inform individuals and groups about the financial assistance available to college or university students.

26) Contact creditors to explain clients' financial situations and to arrange for payment adjustments so that payments are feasible for clients and agreeable to creditors.

27) Analyze potential loan markets to find opportunities to promote loans and financial services.

13-2072.00 - Loan Officers

Evaluate, authorize, or recommend approval of commercial, real estate, or credit loans. Advise borrowers on financial status and methods of payments. Includes mortgage loan officers and agents, collection analysts, loan servicing officers, and loan underwriters.

Tasks

1) Supervise loan personnel.

2) Obtain and compile copies of loan applicants' credit histories, corporate financial statements, and other financial information.

3) Submit applications to credit analysts for verification and recommendation.

4) Petition courts to transfer titles and deeds of collateral to banks.

5) Approve loans within specified limits, and refer loan applications outside those limits to management for approval.

6) Analyze potential loan markets and develop referral networks in order to locate prospects for loans.

7) Arrange for maintenance and liquidation of delinquent properties.

8) Provide special services such as investment banking for clients with more specialized needs.

9) Analyze applicants' financial status, credit, and property evaluations to determine feasibility of granting loans.

10) Interview, hire, and train new employees.

11) Stay abreast of new types of loans and other financial services and products in order to better meet customers' needs.

12) Meet with applicants to obtain information for loan applications and to answer questions about the process.

13) Prepare reports to send to customers whose accounts are delinquent, and forward irreconcilable accounts for collector action.

14) Confer with underwriters to aid in resolving mortgage application problems.

15) Review loan agreements to ensure that they are complete and accurate according to policy.

16) Handle customer complaints and take appropriate action to resolve them.

17) Negotiate payment arrangements with customers who have delinquent loans.

18) Set credit policies, credit lines, procedures and standards in conjunction with senior managers.

19) Review and update credit and loan files.

20) Market bank products to individuals and firms, promoting bank services that may meet customers' needs.

21) Explain to customers the different types of loans and credit options that are available, as well as the terms of those services.

22) Work with clients to identify their financial goals and to find ways of reaching those goals.

13-2081.00 - Tax Examiners, Collectors, and Revenue Agents

Determine tax liability or collect taxes from individuals or business firms according to prescribed laws and regulations.

Tasks

1) Enter tax return information into computers for processing.

2) Send notices to taxpayers when accounts are delinquent.

3) Check tax forms in order to verify that names and taxpayer identification numbers are correct, that computations have been performed correctly, and that amounts match those on supporting documentation.

4) Collect taxes from individuals or businesses according to prescribed laws and regulations.

5) Request that the state or federal revenue service prepare a return on a taxpayer's behalf in cases where taxes have not been filed.

6) Recommend criminal prosecutions and/or civil penalties.

7) Prepare briefs, and assist in searching and seizing records in order to prepare charges and documentation for court cases.

8) Install systems of recording costs or other financial and budgetary data or provide advice on such systems, based on examination of current financial records.

9) Direct service of legal documents, such as subpoenas, warrants, notices of assessment and garnishments.

10) Notify taxpayers of any overpayment or underpayment, and either issue a refund or request further payment.

11) Examine and analyze tax assets and liabilities in order to determine resolution of delinquent tax problems.

12) Review filed tax returns in order to determine whether claimed tax credits and deductions are allowed by law.

13) Confer with taxpayers or their representatives in order to discuss the issues, laws, and regulations involved in returns, and to resolve problems with returns.

14) Secure a taxpayer's agreement to discharge a tax assessment, or submit contested determinations to other administrative or judicial conferees for appeals hearings.

15) Maintain records for each case, including contacts, telephone numbers, and actions taken.

16) Contact taxpayers by mail or telephone in order to address discrepancies and to request supporting documentation.

17) Examine accounting systems and records in order to determine whether accounting methods used were appropriate and in compliance with statutory provisions.

18) Impose payment deadlines on delinquent taxpayers and monitor payments in order to ensure that deadlines are met.

19) Investigate claims of inability to pay taxes by researching court information for the status of liens, mortgages, or financial statements, or by locating assets through third parties.

20) Maintain knowledge of tax code changes, and of accounting procedures and theory in order to properly evaluate financial information.

21) Conduct independent field audits and investigations of income tax returns in order to verify information and/or to amend tax liabilities.

22) Process individual and corporate income tax returns, and sales and excise tax returns.

23) Participate in informal appeals hearings on contested cases from other agents.

24) Review selected tax returns in order to determine the nature and extent of audits to be performed on them.

25) Determine appropriate methods of debt settlement, such as offers of compromise, wage garnishment, or seizure and sale of property.

13-2082.00 - Tax Preparers

15-1021.00 - Computer Programmers

Prepare tax returns for individuals or small businesses but do not have the background or responsibilities of an accredited or certified public accountant.

Tasks

1) Check data input or verify totals on forms prepared by others to detect errors in arithmetic, data entry, or procedures.

2) Consult tax law handbooks or bulletins in order to determine procedures for preparation of atypical returns.

3) Furnish taxpayers with sufficient information and advice in order to ensure correct tax form completion.

4) Calculate form preparation fees according to return complexity and processing time required.

5) Prepare or assist in preparing simple to complex tax returns for individuals or small businesses.

6) Compute taxes owed or overpaid, using adding machines or personal computers, and complete entries on forms, following tax form instructions and tax tables.

7) Use all appropriate adjustments, deductions, and credits to keep clients' taxes to a minimum.

8) Review financial records such as income statements and documentation of expenditures in order to determine forms needed to prepare tax returns.

15-1021.00 - Computer Programmers

Convert project specifications and statements of problems and procedures to detailed logical flow charts for coding into computer language. Develop and write computer programs to store, locate, and retrieve specific documents, data, and information. May program web sites.

Tasks

1) Write, update, and maintain computer programs or software packages to handle specific jobs, such as tracking inventory, storing or retrieving data, or controlling other equipment.

2) Compile and write documentation of program development and subsequent revisions, inserting comments in the coded instructions so others can understand the program.

3) Train subordinates in programming and program coding.

4) Conduct trial runs of programs and software applications to be sure they will produce the desired information and that the instructions are correct.

5) Consult with managerial, engineering, and technical personnel to clarify program intent, identify problems, and suggest changes.

6) Perform or direct revision, repair, or expansion of existing programs to increase operating efficiency or adapt to new requirements.

7) Perform systems analysis and programming tasks to maintain and control the use of computer systems software as a systems programmer.

8) Write, analyze, review, and rewrite programs, using workflow chart and diagram, and applying knowledge of computer capabilities, subject matter, and symbolic logic.

9) Assign, coordinate, and review work and activities of programming personnel.

10) Collaborate with computer manufacturers and other users to develop new programming methods.

11) Consult with and assist computer operators or system analysts to define and resolve problems in running computer programs.

12) Write or contribute to instructions or manuals to guide end users.

13) Investigate whether networks, workstations, the central processing unit of the system, and/or peripheral equipment are responding to a program's instructions.

14) Prepare detailed workflow charts and diagrams that describe input, output, and logical operation, and convert them into a series of instructions coded in a computer language.

15-1031.00 - Computer Software Engineers, Applications

Develop, create, and modify general computer applications software or specialized utility programs. Analyze user needs and develop software solutions. Design software or customize software for client use with the aim of optimizing operational efficiency. May analyze and design databases within an application area, working individually or coordinating database development as part of a team.

Tasks

1) Design, develop and modify software systems, using scientific analysis and mathematical models to predict and measure outcome and consequences of design.

2) Develop and direct software system testing and validation procedures, programming, and documentation.

3) Obtain and evaluate information on factors such as reporting formats required, costs, and security needs to determine hardware configuration.

4) Store, retrieve, and manipulate data for analysis of system capabilities and requirements.

5) Consult with customers about software system design and maintenance.

6) Recommend purchase of equipment to control dust, temperature, and humidity in area of system installation.

7) Specify power supply requirements and configuration.

8) Supervise the work of programmers, technologists and technicians and other engineering and scientific personnel.

9) Analyze user needs and software requirements to determine feasibility of design within time and cost constraints.

10) Coordinate software system installation and monitor equipment functioning to ensure specifications are met.

11) Confer with systems analysts, engineers, programmers and others to design system and to obtain information on project limitations and capabilities, performance requirements and interfaces.

12) Train users to use new or modified equipment.

13) Modify existing software to correct errors, allow it to adapt to new hardware, or to improve its performance.

14) Analyze information to determine, recommend, and plan computer specifications and layouts, and peripheral equipment modifications.

15-1032.00 - Computer Software Engineers, Systems Software

Research, design, develop, and test operating systems-level software, compilers, and network distribution software for medical, industrial, military, communications, aerospace, business, scientific, and general computing applications. Set operational specifications and formulate and analyze software requirements. Apply principles and techniques of computer science, engineering, and mathematical analysis.

Tasks

1) Train users to use new or modified equipment.

2) Supervise and assign work to programmers, designers, technologists and technicians and other engineering and scientific personnel.

3) Specify power supply requirements and configuration.

4) Recommend purchase of equipment to control dust, temperature, and humidity in area of system installation.

5) Advise customer about, or perform, maintenance of software system.

6) Store, retrieve, and manipulate data for analysis of system capabilities and requirements.

7) Design and develop software systems, using scientific analysis and mathematical models to predict and measure outcome and consequences of design.

8) Consult with engineering staff to evaluate interface between hardware and software, develop specifications and performance requirements and resolve customer problems.

9) Direct software programming and development of documentation.

10) Evaluate factors such as reporting formats required, cost constraints, and need for security restrictions to determine hardware configuration.

11) Modify existing software to correct errors, to adapt it to new hardware or to upgrade interfaces and improve performance.

12) Prepare reports and correspondence concerning project specifications, activities and status.

13) Consult with customers and/or other departments on project status, proposals and technical issues such as software system design and maintenance.

14) Analyze information to determine, recommend and plan installation of a new system or modification of an existing system.

15) Coordinate installation of software system.

16) Confer with data processing and project managers to obtain information on limitations and capabilities for data processing projects.

17) Utilize microcontrollers to develop control signals, implement control algorithms and measure process variables such as temperatures, pressures and positions.

18) Monitor functioning of equipment to ensure system operates in conformance with specifications.

15-1041.00 - Computer Support Specialists

44

Provide technical assistance to computer system users. Answer questions or resolve computer problems for clients in person, via telephone or from remote location. May provide assistance concerning the use of computer hardware and software, including printing, installation, word processing, electronic mail, and operating systems.

Tasks

1) Modify and customize commercial programs for internal needs.

2) Read technical manuals, confer with users, and conduct computer diagnostics to investigate and resolve problems and to provide technical assistance and support.

3) Read trade magazines and technical manuals, and attend conferences and seminars to maintain knowledge of hardware and software.

4) Refer major hardware or software problems or defective products to vendors or technicians for service.

5) Conduct office automation feasibility studies, including workflow analysis, space design, and cost comparison analysis.

6) Confer with staff, users, and management to establish requirements for new systems or modifications.

7) Install and perform minor repairs to hardware, software, and peripheral equipment, following design or installation specifications.

8) Prepare evaluations of software or hardware, and recommend improvements or upgrades.

9) Answer users' inquiries regarding computer software and hardware operation to resolve problems.

10) Set up equipment for employee use, performing or ensuring proper installation of cable, operating systems, and appropriate software.

11) Enter commands and observe system functioning to verify correct operations and detect errors.

12) Inspect equipment and read order sheets to prepare for delivery to users.

13) Supervise and coordinate workers engaged in problem-solving, monitoring, and installing data communication equipment and software.

14) Develop training materials and procedures, and/or train users in the proper use of hardware and software.

15) Maintain record of daily data communication transactions, problems and remedial action taken, and installation activities.

15-1051.00 - Computer Systems Analysts

Analyze science, engineering, business, and all other data processing problems for application to electronic data processing systems. Analyze user requirements, procedures, and problems to automate or improve existing systems and review computer system capabilities, workflow, and scheduling limitations. May analyze or recommend commercially available software. May supervise computer programmers.

Tasks

1) Develop, document and revise system design procedures, test procedures, and quality standards.

2) Expand or modify system to serve new purposes or improve work flow.

3) Interview or survey workers, observe job performance and/or perform the job in order to determine what information is processed and how it is processed.

4) Provide staff and users with assistance solving computer related problems, such as malfunctions and program problems.

5) Recommend new equipment or software packages.

6) Review and analyze computer printouts and performance indicators to locate code problems, and correct errors by correcting codes.

7) Specify inputs accessed by the system and plan the distribution and use of the results.

8) Define the goals of the system and devise flow charts and diagrams describing logical operational steps of programs.

9) Use object-oriented programming languages, as well as client/server applications development processes and multimedia and Internet technology.

10) Confer with clients regarding the nature of the information processing or computation needs a computer program is to address.

11) Supervise computer programmers or other systems analysts or serve as project leaders for particular systems projects.

12) Coordinate and link the computer systems within an organization to increase compatibility and so information can be shared.

13) Prepare cost-benefit and return-on-investment analyses to aid in decisions on system implementation.

14) Read manuals, periodicals, and technical reports to learn how to develop programs that

meet staff and user requirements.

15) Utilize the computer in the analysis and solution of business problems such as development of integrated production and inventory control and cost analysis systems.

16) Assess the usefulness of pre-developed application packages and adapt them to a user environment.

17) Analyze information processing or computation needs and plan and design computer systems, using techniques such as structured analysis, data modeling and information engineering.

18) Determine computer software or hardware needed to set up or alter system.

19) Train staff and users to work with computer systems and programs.

20) Test, maintain, and monitor computer programs and systems, including coordinating the installation of computer programs and systems.

15-1061.00 - Database Administrators

Coordinate changes to computer databases, test and implement the database applying knowledge of database management systems. May plan, coordinate, and implement security measures to safeguard computer databases.

Tasks

1) Train users and answer questions.

2) Identify and evaluate industry trends in database systems to serve as a source of information and advice for upper management.

3) Develop methods for integrating different products so they work properly together, such as customizing commercial databases to fit specific needs.

4) Write and code logical and physical database descriptions and specify identifiers of database to management system or direct others in coding descriptions.

5) Specify users and user access levels for each segment of database.

6) Review project requests describing database user needs to estimate time and cost required to accomplish project.

7) Revise company definition of data as defined in data dictionary.

8) Approve, schedule, plan, and supervise the installation and testing of new products and improvements to computer systems, such as the installation of new databases.

9) Plan, coordinate and implement security measures to safeguard information in computer files against accidental or unauthorized damage, modification or disclosure.

10) Modify existing databases and database management systems or direct programmers and analysts to make changes.

11) Establish and calculate optimum values for database parameters, using manuals and calculator.

12) Develop standards and guidelines to guide the use and acquisition of software and to protect vulnerable information.

13) Select and enter codes to monitor database performance and to create production database.

14) Work as part of a project team to coordinate database development and determine project scope and limitations.

15) Develop data model describing data elements and how they are used, following procedures and using pen, template or computer software.

16) Review workflow charts developed by programmer analyst to understand tasks computer will perform, such as updating records.

17) Test programs or databases, correct errors and make necessary modifications.

15-1071.00 - Network and Computer Systems Administrators

Install, configure, and support an organization's local area network (LAN), wide area network (WAN), and Internet system or a segment of a network system. Maintain network hardware and software. Monitor network to ensure network availability to all system users and perform necessary maintenance to support network availability. May supervise other network support and client server specialists and plan, coordinate, and implement network security measures.

Tasks

1) Analyze equipment performance records in order to determine the need for repair or replacement.

2) Maintain and administer computer networks and related computing environments, including computer hardware, systems software, applications software, and all configurations.

3) Operate master consoles in order to monitor the performance of computer systems and

networks, and to coordinate computer network access and use.

4) Perform routine network startup and shutdown procedures, and maintain control records.

5) Plan, coordinate, and implement network security measures in order to protect data, software, and hardware.

6) Diagnose hardware and software problems, and replace defective components.

7) Train people in computer system use.

8) Confer with network users about how to solve existing system problems.

9) Monitor network performance in order to determine whether adjustments need to be made, and to determine where changes will need to be made in the future.

10) Design, configure, and test computer hardware, networking software and operating system software.

11) Maintain logs related to network functions, as well as maintenance and repair records.

12) Recommend changes to improve systems and network configurations, and determine hardware or software requirements related to such changes.

13) Research new technology, and implement it or recommend its implementation.

14) Maintain an inventory of parts for emergency repairs.

15) Load computer tapes and disks, and install software and printer paper or forms.

16) Gather data pertaining to customer needs, and use the information to identify, predict, interpret, and evaluate system and network requirements.

17) Coordinate with vendors and with company personnel in order to facilitate purchases.

15-1071.01 - Computer Security Specialists

Plan, coordinate, and implement security measures for information systems to regulate access to computer data files and prevent unauthorized modification, destruction, or disclosure of information.

Tasks

1) Coordinate implementation of computer system plan with establishment personnel and outside vendors.

2) Train users and promote security awareness to ensure system security and to improve server and network efficiency.

3) Confer with users to discuss issues such as computer data access needs, security violations, and programming changes.

4) Review violations of computer security procedures and discuss procedures with violators to ensure violations are not repeated.

5) Perform risk assessments and execute tests of data processing system to ensure functioning of data processing activities and security measures.

6) Monitor current reports of computer viruses to determine when to update virus protection systems.

7) Encrypt data transmissions and erect firewalls to conceal confidential information as it is being transmitted and to keep out tainted digital transfers.

8) Document computer security and emergency measures policies, procedures, and tests.

9) Develop plans to safeguard computer files against accidental or unauthorized modification, destruction, or disclosure and to meet emergency data processing needs.

10) Maintain permanent fleet cryptologic and carry-on direct support systems required in special land, sea surface and subsurface operations.

11) Monitor use of data files and regulate access to safeguard information in computer files.

15-1081.00 - Network Systems and Data Communications Analysts

Analyze, design, test, and evaluate network systems, such as local area networks (LAN), wide area networks (WAN), Internet, intranet, and other data communications systems. Perform network modeling, analysis, and planning. Research and recommend network and data communications hardware and software. Includes telecommunications specialists who deal with the interfacing of computer and communications equipment. May supervise computer programmers.

Tasks

1) Train users in use of equipment.

2) Assist users to diagnose and solve data communication problems.

3) Develop and write procedures for installation, use, and troubleshooting of communications hardware and software.

4) Adapt and modify existing software to meet specific needs.

5) Visit vendors, attend conferences or training and study technical journals to keep up with changes in technology.

6) Design and implement network configurations, network architecture (including hardware and software technology, site locations, and integration of technologies), and systems.

7) Set up user accounts, regulating and monitoring file access to ensure confidentiality and proper use.

8) Read technical manuals and brochures to determine which equipment meets establishment requirements.

9) Identify areas of operation that need upgraded equipment such as modems, fiber optic cables, and telephone wires.

10) Consult customers, visit workplaces or conduct surveys to determine present and future user needs.

11) Monitor system performance and provide security measures, troubleshooting and maintenance as needed.

12) Maintain needed files by adding and deleting files on the network server and backing up files to guarantee their safety in the event of problems with the network.

13) Maintain the peripherals, such as printers, that are connected to the network.

14) Work with other engineers, systems analysts, programmers, technicians, scientists and top-level managers in the design, testing and evaluation of systems.

15-2011.00 - Actuaries

Analyze statistical data, such as mortality, accident, sickness, disability, and retirement rates and construct probability tables to forecast risk and liability for payment of future benefits. May ascertain premium rates required and cash reserves necessary to ensure payment of future benefits.

Tasks

1) Design, review and help administer insurance, annuity and pension plans, determining financial soundness and calculating premiums.

2) Ascertain premium rates required and cash reserves and liabilities necessary to ensure payment of future benefits.

3) Manage credit and help price corporate security offerings.

4) Determine equitable basis for distributing surplus earnings under participating insurance and annuity contracts in mutual companies.

5) Testify before public agencies on proposed legislation affecting businesses.

6) Provide expertise to help financial institutions manage risks and maximize returns associated with investment products or credit offerings.

7) Provide advice to clients on a contract basis, working as a consultant.

8) Testify in court as expert witness or to provide legal evidence on matters such as the value of potential lifetime earnings of a person who is disabled or killed in an accident.

9) Collaborate with programmers, underwriters, accounts, claims experts, and senior management to help companies develop plans for new lines of business or improving existing business.

10) Determine policy contract provisions for each type of insurance.

11) Explain changes in contract provisions to customers.

12) Determine or help determine company policy, and explain complex technical matters to company executives, government officials, shareholders, policyholders, and/or the public.

13) Construct probability tables for events such as fires, natural disasters, and unemployment, based on analysis of statistical data and other pertinent information.

15-2021.00 - Mathematicians

Conduct research in fundamental mathematics or in application of mathematical techniques to science, management, and other fields. Solve or direct solutions to problems in various fields by mathematical methods.

Tasks

1) Assemble sets of assumptions and explore the consequences of each set.

2) Develop new principles, and new relationships between existing mathematical principles, to advance mathematical science.

3) Maintain knowledge in the field by reading professional journals, talking with other mathematicians, and attending professional conferences.

4) Address the relationships of quantities, magnitudes, and forms through the use of numbers

and symbols.

5) Conduct research to extend mathematical knowledge in traditional areas, such as algebra, geometry, probability, and logic.

6) Apply mathematical theories and techniques to the solution of practical problems in business, engineering, or the sciences.

7) Design, analyze, and decipher encryption systems designed to transmit military, political, financial, or law-enforcement-related information in code.

15-2041.00 - Statisticians

Engage in the development of mathematical theory or apply statistical theory and methods to collect, organize, interpret, and summarize numerical data to provide usable information. May specialize in fields, such as bio-statistics, agricultural statistics, business statistics, economic statistics, or other fields.

Tasks

1) Supervise and provide instructions for workers collecting and tabulating data.

2) Prepare data for processing by organizing information, checking for any inaccuracies, and adjusting and weighting the raw data.

3) Develop an understanding of fields to which statistical methods are to be applied in order to determine whether methods and results are appropriate.

4) Report results of statistical analyses, including information in the form of graphs, charts, and tables.

5) Plan data collection methods for specific projects, and determine the types and sizes of sample groups to be used.

6) Evaluate the statistical methods and procedures used to obtain data in order to ensure validity, applicability, efficiency, and accuracy.

7) Evaluate sources of information in order to determine any limitations in terms of reliability or usability.

8) Process large amounts of data for statistical modeling and graphic analysis, using computers.

9) Adapt statistical methods in order to solve specific problems in many fields, such as economics, biology and engineering.

10) Apply sampling techniques or utilize complete enumeration bases in order to determine and define groups to be surveyed.

11) Design research projects that apply valid scientific techniques and utilize information obtained from baselines or historical data in order to structure uncompromised and efficient analyses.

12) Develop and test experimental designs, sampling techniques, and analytical methods.

13) Examine theories, such as those of probability and inference in order to discover mathematical bases for new or improved methods of obtaining and evaluating numerical data.

14) Analyze and interpret statistical data in order to identify significant differences in relationships among sources of information.

15-2091.00 - Mathematical Technicians

Apply standardized mathematical formulas, principles, and methodology to technological problems in engineering and physical sciences in relation to specific industrial and research objectives, processes, equipment, and products.

Tasks

1) Reduce raw data to meaningful terms, using the most practical and accurate combination and sequence of computational methods.

2) Translate data into numbers, equations, flow charts, graphs, or other forms.

3) Apply standardized mathematical formulas, principles, and methodology to the solution of technological problems involving engineering or physical science.

4) Modify standard formulas so that they conform to project needs and data processing methods.

5) Process data for analysis, using computers.

17-1011.00 - Architects, Except Landscape and Naval

Plan and design structures, such as private residences, office buildings, theaters, factories, and other structural property.

Tasks

1) Prepare information regarding design, structure specifications, materials, color, equipment, estimated costs, and construction time.

2) Consult with client to determine functional and spatial requirements of structure.

3) Conduct periodic on-site observation of work during construction to monitor compliance with plans.

4) Direct activities of workers engaged in preparing drawings and specification documents.

5) Prepare scale drawings.

6) Integrate engineering element into unified design.

7) Prepare contract documents for building contractors.

8) Represent client in obtaining bids and awarding construction contracts.

9) Administer construction contracts.

10) Prepare operating and maintenance manuals, studies, and reports.

Knowledge	Knowledge Definitions
Building and Construction	Knowledge of materials, methods, and the tools involved in the construction or repair of houses, buildings, or other structures such as highways and roads.
Design	Knowledge of design techniques, tools, and principles involved in production of precision technical plans, blueprints, drawings, and models.
Engineering and Technology	Knowledge of the practical application of engineering science and technology. This includes applying principles, techniques, procedures, and equipment to the design and production of various goods and services.
English Language	Knowledge of the structure and content of the English language including the meaning and spelling of words, rules of composition, and grammar.
Mathematics	Knowledge of arithmetic, algebra, geometry, calculus, statistics, and their applications.
Administration and Management	Knowledge of business and management principles involved in strategic planning, resource allocation, human resources modeling, leadership technique, production methods, and coordination of people and resources.
Computers and Electronics	Knowledge of circuit boards, processors, chips, electronic equipment, and computer hardware and software, including applications and programming.
Customer and Personal Service	Knowledge of principles and processes for providing customer and personal services. This includes customer needs assessment, meeting quality standards for services, and evaluation of customer satisfaction.
Public Safety and Security	Knowledge of relevant equipment, policies, procedures, and strategies to promote effective local, state, or national security operations for the protection of people, data, property, and institutions.
Law and Government	Knowledge of laws, legal codes, court procedures, precedents, government regulations, executive orders, agency rules, and the democratic political process.
Clerical	Knowledge of administrative and clerical procedures and systems such as word processing, managing files and records, stenography and transcription, designing forms, and other office procedures and terminology.
Sales and Marketing	Knowledge of principles and methods for showing, promoting, and selling products or services. This includes marketing strategy and tactics, product demonstration, sales techniques, and sales control systems.
Mechanical	Knowledge of machines and tools, including their designs, uses, repair, and maintenance.
Communications and Media	Knowledge of media production, communication, and dissemination techniques and methods. This includes alternative ways to inform and entertain via written, oral, and visual media.
Economics and Accounting	Knowledge of economic and accounting principles and practices, the financial markets, banking and the analysis and reporting of financial data.
Education and Training	Knowledge of principles and methods for curriculum and training design, teaching and instruction for individuals and groups, and the measurement of training effects.
Physics	Knowledge and prediction of physical principles, laws, their interrelationships, and applications to understanding fluid, material, and atmospheric dynamics, and mechanical, electrical, atomic and sub-atomic structures and processes.
Fine Arts	Knowledge of the theory and techniques required to compose, produce, and perform works of music, dance, visual arts, drama, and sculpture.
Production and Processing	Knowledge of raw materials, production processes, quality control, costs, and other techniques for maximizing the effective manufacture and distribution of goods.
Telecommunications	Knowledge of transmission, broadcasting, switching, control, and operation of telecommunications systems.

Personnel and Human Resources	Knowledge of principles and procedures for personnel recruitment, selection. training. compensation and benefits. labor relations and negotiation. and personnel information systems.
Geography	Knowledge of principles and methods for describing the features of land, sea, and air masses. including their physical characteristics. locations, interrelationships, and distribution of plant. animal. and human life.
History and Archeology	Knowledge of historical events and their causes. indicators. and effects on civilizations and cultures.
Psychology	Knowledge of human behavior and performance; individual differences in ability. personality. and interests: learning and motivation; psychological research methods; and the assessment and treatment of behavioral and affective disorders.
Chemistry	Knowledge of the chemical composition. structure, and properties of substances and of the chemical processes and transformations that they undergo. This includes uses of chemicals and their interactions. danger signs. production techniques, and disposal methods.
Sociology and Anthropology	Knowledge of group behavior and dynamics. societal trends and influences. human migrations, ethnicity, cultures and their history and origins.
Transportation	Knowledge of principles and methods for moving people or goods by air, rail, sea, or road, including the relative costs and benefits.
Biology	Knowledge of plant and animal organisms, their tissues, cells, functions, interdependencies, and interactions with each other and the environment.
Philosophy and Theology	Knowledge of different philosophical systems and religions. This includes their basic principles, values, ethics, ways of thinking, customs, practices, and their impact on human culture.
Foreign Language	Knowledge of the structure and content of a foreign (non-English) language including the meaning and spelling of words, rules of composition and grammar, and pronunciation.
Medicine and Dentistry	Knowledge of the information and techniques needed to diagnose and treat human injuries, diseases, and deformities. This includes symptoms, treatment alternatives, drug properties and interactions, and preventive health-care measures.
Therapy and Counseling	Knowledge of principles, methods, and procedures for diagnosis, treatment, and rehabilitation of physical and mental dysfunctions, and for career counseling and guidance.
Food Production	Knowledge of techniques and equipment for planting, growing, and harvesting food products (both plant and animal) for consumption, including storage/handling techniques.

Skills	Skills Definitions
Active Listening	Giving full attention to what other people are saying, taking time to understand the points being made, asking questions as appropriate, and not interrupting at inappropriate times.
Critical Thinking	Using logic and reasoning to identify the strengths and weaknesses of alternative solutions, conclusions or approaches to problems.
Complex Problem Solving	Identifying complex problems and reviewing related information to develop and evaluate options and implement solutions.
Time Management	Managing one's own time and the time of others.
Reading Comprehension	Understanding written sentences and paragraphs in work related documents.
Management of Personnel Resources	Motivating, developing, and directing people as they work, identifying the best people for the job.
Coordination	Adjusting actions in relation to others' actions.
Writing	Communicating effectively in writing as appropriate for the needs of the audience.
Speaking	Talking to others to convey information effectively.
Operations Analysis	Analyzing needs and product requirements to create a design.
Active Learning	Understanding the implications of new information for both current and future problem-solving and decision-making.
Judgment and Decision Making	Considering the relative costs and benefits of potential actions to choose the most appropriate one.
Mathematics	Using mathematics to solve problems.
Monitoring	Monitoring/Assessing performance of yourself, other individuals, or organizations to make improvements or take corrective action.
Persuasion	Persuading others to change their minds or behavior.
Management of Financial Resources	Determining how money will be spent to get the work done, and accounting for these expenditures.
Quality Control Analysis	Conducting tests and inspections of products, services, or processes to evaluate quality or performance.
Negotiation	Bringing others together and trying to reconcile differences.
Instructing	Teaching others how to do something.
Learning Strategies	Selecting and using training/instructional methods and procedures appropriate for the situation when learning or teaching new things.
Social Perceptiveness	Being aware of others' reactions and understanding why they react as they do.

Troubleshooting	Determining causes of operating errors and deciding what to do about it.
Service Orientation	Actively looking for ways to help people.
Science	Using scientific rules and methods to solve problems.
Technology Design	Generating or adapting equipment and technology to serve user needs.
Systems Evaluation	Identifying measures or indicators of system performance and the actions needed to improve or correct performance. relative to the goals of the system.
Management of Material Resources	Obtaining and seeing to the appropriate use of equipment. facilities. and materials needed to do certain work.
Equipment Selection	Determining the kind of tools and equipment needed to do a job.
Systems Analysis	Determining how a system should work and how changes in conditions, operations, and the environment will affect outcomes.
Repairing	Repairing machines or systems using the needed tools.
Operation and Control	Controlling operations of equipment or systems.
Installation	Installing equipment, machines, wiring, or programs to meet specifications.
Equipment Maintenance	Performing routine maintenance on equipment and determining when and what kind of maintenance is needed.
Operation Monitoring	Watching gauges, dials, or other indicators to make sure a machine is working properly.
Programming	Writing computer programs for various purposes.

Ability	Ability Definitions
Oral Comprehension	The ability to listen to and understand information and ideas presented through spoken words and sentences.
Oral Expression	The ability to communicate information and ideas in speaking so others will understand.
Problem Sensitivity	The ability to tell when something is wrong or is likely to go wrong. It does not involve solving the problem, only recognizing there is a problem.
Near Vision	The ability to see details at close range (within a few feet of the observer).
Speech Clarity	The ability to speak clearly so others can understand you.
Information Ordering	The ability to arrange things or actions in a certain order or pattern according to a specific rule or set of rules (e.g., patterns of numbers, letters, words, pictures, mathematical operations).
Written Expression	The ability to communicate information and ideas in writing so others will understand.
Visualization	The ability to imagine how something will look after it is moved around or when its parts are moved or rearranged.
Deductive Reasoning	The ability to apply general rules to specific problems to produce answers that make sense.
Speech Recognition	The ability to identify and understand the speech of another person.
Written Comprehension	The ability to read and understand information and ideas presented in writing.
Originality	The ability to come up with unusual or clever ideas about a given topic or situation, or to develop creative ways to solve a problem.
Category Flexibility	The ability to generate or use different sets of rules for combining or grouping things in different ways.
Fluency of Ideas	The ability to come up with a number of ideas about a topic (the number of ideas is important, not their quality, correctness, or creativity).
Inductive Reasoning	The ability to combine pieces of information to form general rules or conclusions (includes finding a relationship among seemingly unrelated events).
Selective Attention	The ability to concentrate on a task over a period of time without being distracted.
Finger Dexterity	The ability to make precisely coordinated movements of the fingers of one or both hands to grasp, manipulate, or assemble very small objects.
Arm-Hand Steadiness	The ability to keep your hand and arm steady while moving your arm or while holding your arm and hand in one position.
Far Vision	The ability to see details at a distance.
Visual Color Discrimination	The ability to match or detect differences between colors, including shades of color and brightness.
Mathematical Reasoning	The ability to choose the right mathematical methods or formulas to solve a problem.
Depth Perception	The ability to judge which of several objects is closer or farther away from you, or to judge the distance between you and an object.
Flexibility of Closure	The ability to identify or detect a known pattern (a figure, object, word, or sound) that is hidden in other distracting material.
Memorization	The ability to remember information such as words, numbers, pictures, and procedures.
Manual Dexterity	The ability to quickly move your hand, your hand together with your arm, or your two hands to grasp, manipulate, or assemble objects.

Control Precision	The ability to quickly and repeatedly adjust the controls of a machine or a vehicle to exact positions.
Number Facility	The ability to add, subtract, multiply, or divide quickly and correctly.
Time Sharing	The ability to shift back and forth between two or more activities or sources of information (such as speech, sounds, touch, or other sources).
Auditory Attention	The ability to focus on a single source of sound in the presence of other distracting sounds.
Speed of Closure	The ability to quickly make sense of, combine, and organize information into meaningful patterns.
Perceptual Speed	The ability to quickly and accurately compare similarities and differences among sets of letters, numbers, objects, pictures, or patterns. The things to be compared may be presented at the same time or one after the other. This ability also includes comparing a presented object with a remembered object.
Multilimb Coordination	The ability to coordinate two or more limbs (for example, two arms, two legs, or one leg and one arm) while sitting, standing, or lying down. It does not involve performing the activities while the whole body is in motion.
Hearing Sensitivity	The ability to detect or tell the differences between sounds that vary in pitch and loudness.
Trunk Strength	The ability to use your abdominal and lower back muscles to support part of the body repeatedly or continuously over time without 'giving out' or fatiguing.
Spatial Orientation	The ability to know your location in relation to the environment or to know where other objects are in relation to you.
Wrist-Finger Speed	The ability to make fast, simple, repeated movements of the fingers, hands, and wrists.
Extent Flexibility	The ability to bend, stretch, twist, or reach with your body, arms, and/or legs.
Static Strength	The ability to exert maximum muscle force to lift, push, pull, or carry objects.
Sound Localization	The ability to tell the direction from which a sound originated.
Glare Sensitivity	The ability to see objects in the presence of glare or bright lighting.
Night Vision	The ability to see under low light conditions.
Speed of Limb Movement	The ability to quickly move the arms and legs.
Peripheral Vision	The ability to see objects or movement of objects to one's side when the eyes are looking ahead.
Response Orientation	The ability to choose quickly between two or more movements in response to two or more different signals (lights, sounds, pictures). It includes the speed with which the correct response is started with the hand, foot, or other body part.
Dynamic Flexibility	The ability to quickly and repeatedly bend, stretch, twist, or reach out with your body, arms, and/or legs.
Reaction Time	The ability to quickly respond (with the hand, finger, or foot) to a signal (sound, light, picture) when it appears.
Explosive Strength	The ability to use short bursts of muscle force to propel oneself (as in jumping or sprinting), or to throw an object.
Stamina	The ability to exert yourself physically over long periods of time without getting winded or out of breath.
Gross Body Coordination	The ability to coordinate the movement of your arms, legs, and torso together when the whole body is in motion.
Rate Control	The ability to time your movements or the movement of a piece of equipment in anticipation of changes in the speed and/or direction of a moving object or scene.
Dynamic Strength	The ability to exert muscle force repeatedly or continuously over time. This involves muscular endurance and resistance to muscle fatigue.
Gross Body Equilibrium	The ability to keep or regain your body balance or stay upright when in an unstable position.

Work_Activity	**Work_Activity Definitions**
Interacting With Computers	Using computers and computer systems (including hardware and software) to program, write software, set up functions, enter data, or process information.
Thinking Creatively	Developing, designing, or creating new applications, ideas, relationships, systems, or products, including artistic contributions.
Making Decisions and Solving Problems	Analyzing information and evaluating results to choose the best solution and solve problems.
Drafting, Laying Out, and Specifying Technical Dev	Providing documentation, detailed instructions, drawings, or specifications to tell others about how devices, parts, equipment, or structures are to be fabricated, constructed, assembled, modified, maintained, or used.
Organizing, Planning, and Prioritizing Work	Developing specific goals and plans to prioritize, organize, and accomplish your work.
Communicating with Supervisors, Peers, or Subordin	Providing information to supervisors, co-workers, and subordinates by telephone, in written form, e-mail, or in person.
Communicating with Persons Outside Organization	Communicating with people outside the organization, representing the organization to customers, the public, government, and other external sources. This information can be exchanged in person, in writing, or by telephone or e-mail.

Updating and Using Relevant Knowledge	Keeping up-to-date technically and applying new knowledge to your job.
Getting Information	Observing, receiving, and otherwise obtaining information from all relevant sources.
Evaluating Information to Determine Compliance wit	Using relevant information and individual judgment to determine whether events or processes comply with laws, regulations, or standards.
Coordinating the Work and Activities of Others	Getting members of a group to work together to accomplish tasks.
Identifying Objects, Actions, and Events	Identifying information by categorizing, estimating, recognizing differences or similarities, and detecting changes in circumstances or events.
Establishing and Maintaining Interpersonal Relatio	Developing constructive and cooperative working relationships with others, and maintaining them over time.
Developing and Building Teams	Encouraging and building mutual trust, respect, and cooperation among team members.
Scheduling Work and Activities	Scheduling events, programs, and activities, as well as the work of others.
Analyzing Data or Information	Identifying the underlying principles, reasons, or facts of information by breaking down information or data into separate parts.
Monitor Processes, Materials, or Surroundings	Monitoring and reviewing information from materials, events, or the environment, to detect or assess problems.
Judging the Qualities of Things, Services, or Peop	Assessing the value, importance, or quality of things or people.
Documenting/Recording Information	Entering, transcribing, recording, storing, or maintaining information in written or electronic/magnetic form.
Performing Administrative Activities	Performing day-to-day administrative tasks such as maintaining information files and processing paperwork.
Interpreting the Meaning of Information for Others	Translating or explaining what information means and how it can be used.
Inspecting Equipment, Structures, or Material	Inspecting equipment, structures, or materials to identify the cause of errors or other problems or defects.
Processing Information	Compiling, coding, categorizing, calculating, tabulating, auditing, or verifying information or data.
Monitoring and Controlling Resources	Monitoring and controlling resources and overseeing the spending of money.
Resolving Conflicts and Negotiating with Others	Handling complaints, settling disputes, and resolving grievances and conflicts, or otherwise negotiating with others.
Developing Objectives and Strategies	Establishing long-range objectives and specifying the strategies and actions to achieve them.
Coaching and Developing Others	Identifying the developmental needs of others and coaching, mentoring, or otherwise helping others to improve their knowledge or skills.
Provide Consultation and Advice to Others	Providing guidance and expert advice to management or other groups on technical, systems-, or process-related topics.
Guiding, Directing, and Motivating Subordinates	Providing guidance and direction to subordinates, including setting performance standards and monitoring performance.
Performing for or Working Directly with the Public	Performing for people or dealing directly with the public. This includes serving customers in restaurants and stores, and receiving clients or guests.
Training and Teaching Others	Identifying the educational needs of others, developing formal educational or training programs or classes, and teaching or instructing others.
Estimating the Quantifiable Characteristics of Pro	Estimating sizes, distances, and quantities; or determining time, costs, resources, or materials needed to perform a work activity.
Selling or Influencing Others	Convincing others to buy merchandise/goods or to otherwise change their minds or actions.
Controlling Machines and Processes	Using either control mechanisms or direct physical activity to operate machines or processes (not including computers or vehicles).
Staffing Organizational Units	Recruiting, interviewing, selecting, hiring, and promoting employees in an organization.
Repairing and Maintaining Electronic Equipment	Servicing, repairing, calibrating, regulating, fine-tuning, or testing machines, devices, and equipment that operate primarily on the basis of electrical or electronic (not mechanical) principles.
Assisting and Caring for Others	Providing personal assistance, medical attention, emotional support, or other personal care to others such as coworkers, customers, or patients.
Performing General Physical Activities	Performing physical activities that require considerable use of your arms and legs and moving your whole body, such as climbing, lifting, balancing, walking, stooping, and handling of materials.
Handling and Moving Objects	Using hands and arms in handling, installing, positioning, and moving materials, and manipulating things.
Operating Vehicles, Mechanized Devices, or Equipme	Running, maneuvering, navigating, or driving vehicles or mechanized equipment, such as forklifts, passenger vehicles, aircraft, or water craft.
Repairing and Maintaining Mechanical Equipment	Servicing, repairing, adjusting, and testing machines, devices, moving parts, and equipment that operate primarily on the basis of mechanical (not electronic) principles.

Work_Content	Work_Content Definitions
Telephone	How often do you have telephone conversations in this job?
Face-to-Face Discussions	How often do you have to have face-to-face discussions with individuals or teams in this job?
Freedom to Make Decisions	How much decision making freedom, without supervision, does the job offer?
Letters and Memos	How often does the job require written letters and memos?
Work With Work Group or Team	How important is it to work with others in a group or team in this job?
Structured versus Unstructured Work	To what extent is this job structured for the worker, rather than allowing the worker to determine tasks, priorities, and goals?
Importance of Being Exact or Accurate	How important is being very exact or highly accurate in performing this job?
Contact With Others	How much does this job require the worker to be in contact with others (face-to-face, by telephone, or otherwise) in order to perform it?
Indoors, Environmentally Controlled	How often does this job require working indoors in environmentally controlled conditions?
Electronic Mail	How often do you use electronic mail in this job?
Frequency of Decision Making	How frequently is the worker required to make decisions that affect other people, the financial resources, and/or the image and reputation of the organization?
Coordinate or Lead Others	How important is it to coordinate or lead others in accomplishing work activities in this job?
Impact of Decisions on Co-workers or Company Resul	How do the decisions an employee makes impact the results of co-workers, clients or the company?
Spend Time Sitting	How much does this job require sitting?
Level of Competition	To what extent does this job require the worker to compete or to be aware of competitive pressures?
Responsibility for Outcomes and Results	How responsible is the worker for work outcomes and results of other workers?
Time Pressure	How often does this job require the worker to meet strict deadlines?
Importance of Repeating Same Tasks	How important is repeating the same physical activities (e.g., key entry) or mental activities (e.g., checking entries in a ledger) over and over, without stopping, to performing this job?
Physical Proximity	To what extent does this job require the worker to perform job tasks in close physical proximity to other people?
Deal With External Customers	How important is it to work with external customers or the public in this job?
Consequence of Error	How serious would the result usually be if the worker made a mistake that was not readily correctable?
In an Enclosed Vehicle or Equipment	How often does this job require working in a closed vehicle or equipment (e.g., car)?
Spend Time Using Your Hands to Handle, Control, or	How much does this job require using your hands to handle, control, or feel objects, tools or controls?
Frequency of Conflict Situations	How often are there conflict situations the employee has to face in this job?
Spend Time Making Repetitive Motions	How much does this job require making repetitive motions?
Outdoors, Exposed to Weather	How often does this job require working outdoors, exposed to all weather conditions?
Sounds, Noise Levels Are Distracting or Uncomforta	How often does this job require working exposed to sounds and noise levels that are distracting or uncomfortable?
Indoors, Not Environmentally Controlled	How often does this job require working indoors in non-controlled environmental conditions (e.g., warehouse without heat)?
Responsible for Others' Health and Safety	How much responsibility is there for the health and safety of others in this job?
Degree of Automation	How automated is the job?
Deal With Unpleasant or Angry People	How frequently does the worker have to deal with unpleasant, angry, or discourteous individuals as part of the job requirements?
Extremely Bright or Inadequate Lighting	How often does this job require working in extremely bright or inadequate lighting conditions?
Wear Common Protective or Safety Equipment such as	How much does this job require wearing common protective or safety equipment such as safety shoes, glasses, gloves, hard hats or live jackets?
Public Speaking	How often do you have to perform public speaking in this job?
Spend Time Standing	How much does this job require standing?
Very Hot or Cold Temperatures	How often does this job require working in very hot (above 90 F degrees) or very cold (below 32 F degrees) temperatures?
Outdoors, Under Cover	How often does this job require working outdoors, under cover (e.g., structure with roof but no walls)?
Exposed to Contaminants	How often does this job require working exposed to contaminants (such as pollutants, gases, dust or odors)?
Spend Time Walking and Running	How much does this job require walking and running?
Exposed to High Places	How often does this job require exposure to high places?
Spend Time Bending or Twisting the Body	How much does this job require bending or twisting your body?
Cramped Work Space, Awkward Positions	How often does this job require working in cramped work spaces that requires getting into awkward positions?
Spend Time Kneeling, Crouching, Stooping, or Crawl	How much does this job require kneeling, crouching, stooping, or crawling?
Exposed to Hazardous Equipment	How often does this job require exposure to hazardous equipment?
Spend Time Climbing Ladders, Scaffolds, or Poles	How much does this job require climbing ladders, scaffolds, or poles?
Exposed to Hazardous Conditions	How often does this job require exposure to hazardous conditions?
Pace Determined by Speed of Equipment	How important is it to this job that the pace is determined by the speed of equipment or machinery? (This does not refer to keeping busy at all times on this job.)
Deal With Physically Aggressive People	How frequently does this job require the worker to deal with physical aggression of violent individuals?
Exposed to Disease or Infections	How often does this job require exposure to disease/infections?
Exposed to Minor Burns, Cuts, Bites, or Stings	How often does this job require exposure to minor burns, cuts, bites, or stings?
Spend Time Keeping or Regaining Balance	How much does this job require keeping or regaining your balance?
Wear Specialized Protective or Safety Equipment su	How much does this job require wearing specialized protective or safety equipment such as breathing apparatus, safety harness, full protection suits, or radiation protection?
Exposed to Whole Body Vibration	How often does this job require exposure to whole body vibration (e.g., operate a jackhammer)?
Exposed to Radiation	How often does this job require exposure to radiation?
In an Open Vehicle or Equipment	How often does this job require working in an open vehicle or equipment (e.g., tractor)?

Work_Styles	Work_Styles Definitions
Attention to Detail	Job requires being careful about detail and thorough in completing work tasks.
Dependability	Job requires being reliable, responsible, and dependable, and fulfilling obligations.
Analytical Thinking	Job requires analyzing information and using logic to address work-related issues and problems.
Innovation	Job requires creativity and alternative thinking to develop new ideas for and answers to work-related problems.
Initiative	Job requires a willingness to take on responsibilities and challenges.
Stress Tolerance	Job requires accepting criticism and dealing calmly and effectively with high stress situations.
Integrity	Job requires being honest and ethical.
Cooperation	Job requires being pleasant with others on the job and displaying a good-natured, cooperative attitude.
Leadership	Job requires a willingness to lead, take charge, and offer opinions and direction.
Adaptability/Flexibility	Job requires being open to change (positive or negative) and to considerable variety in the workplace.
Achievement/Effort	Job requires establishing and maintaining personally challenging achievement goals and exerting effort toward mastering tasks.
Persistence	Job requires persistence in the face of obstacles.
Self Control	Job requires maintaining composure, keeping emotions in check, controlling anger, and avoiding aggressive behavior, even in very difficult situations.
Independence	Job requires developing one's own ways of doing things, guiding oneself with little or no supervision, and depending on oneself to get things done.
Concern for Others	Job requires being sensitive to others' needs and feelings and being understanding and helpful on the job.
Social Orientation	Job requires preferring to work with others rather than alone, and being personally connected with others on the job.

Job Zone Component	Job Zone Component Definitions
Title	Job Zone Five: Extensive Preparation Needed
Overall Experience	Extensive skill, knowledge, and experience are needed for these occupations. Many require more than five years of experience. For example, surgeons must complete four years of college and an additional five to seven years of specialized medical training to be able to do their job.
Job Training	Employees may need some on-the-job training, but most of these occupations assume that the person will already have the required skills, knowledge, work-related experience, and/or training.
Job Zone Examples	These occupations often involve coordinating, training, supervising, or managing the activities of others to accomplish goals. Very advanced communication and organizational skills are required. Examples include athletic trainers, lawyers, managing editors, phyicists, social psychologists, and surgeons.
SVP Range	(8.0 and above)

Education	A bachelor's degree is the minimum formal education required for these occupations. However. many also require graduate school. For example, they may require a master's degree. and some require a Ph.D., M.D., or J.D. (law degree).

17-1012.00 - Landscape Architects

Plan and design land areas for such projects as parks and other recreational facilities. airports. highways, hospitals, schools, land subdivisions, and commercial, industrial. and residential sites.

Tasks

1) Compile and analyze data on conditions, such as location, drainage. and location of structures for environmental reports and landscaping plans.

2) Prepare site plans, specifications, and cost estimates for land development. coordinating arrangement of existing and proposed land features and structures.

3) Confer with clients, engineering personnel, and architects on overall program.

Knowledge	Knowledge Definitions
Design	Knowledge of design techniques, tools, and principles involved in production of precision technical plans, blueprints. drawings. and models.
Building and Construction	Knowledge of materials, methods, and the tools involved in the construction or repair of houses, buildings. or other structures such as highways and roads.
Administration and Management	Knowledge of business and management principles involved in strategic planning, resource allocation, human resources modeling, leadership technique, production methods. and coordination of people and resources.
Engineering and Technology	Knowledge of the practical application of engineering science and technology. This includes applying principles. techniques, procedures, and equipment to the design and production of various goods and services.
Computers and Electronics	Knowledge of circuit boards, processors, chips, electronic equipment, and computer hardware and software, including applications and programming.
Mathematics	Knowledge of arithmetic, algebra, geometry, calculus, statistics, and their applications.
Geography	Knowledge of principles and methods for describing the features of land, sea, and air masses, including their physical characteristics, locations, interrelationships, and distribution of plant, animal, and human life.
English Language	Knowledge of the structure and content of the English language including the meaning and spelling of words, rules of composition, and grammar.
Sales and Marketing	Knowledge of principles and methods for showing, promoting, and selling products or services. This includes marketing strategy and tactics, product demonstration, sales techniques, and sales control systems.
Public Safety and Security	Knowledge of relevant equipment, policies, procedures, and strategies to promote effective local, state, or national security operations for the protection of people, data, property, and institutions.
Law and Government	Knowledge of laws, legal codes, court procedures, precedents, government regulations, executive orders, agency rules, and the democratic political process.
Biology	Knowledge of plant and animal organisms, their tissues, cells, functions, interdependencies, and interactions with each other and the environment.
Fine Arts	Knowledge of the theory and techniques required to compose, produce, and perform works of music, dance, visual arts, drama, and sculpture.
Customer and Personal Service	Knowledge of principles and processes for providing customer and personal services. This includes customer needs assessment, meeting quality standards for services, and evaluation of customer satisfaction.
Clerical	Knowledge of administrative and clerical procedures and systems such as word processing, managing files and records, stenography and transcription, designing forms, and other office procedures and terminology.
Communications and Media	Knowledge of media production, communication, and dissemination techniques and methods. This includes alternative ways to inform and entertain via written, oral, and visual media.
Transportation	Knowledge of principles and methods for moving people or goods by air, rail, sea, or road, including the relative costs and benefits.
Education and Training	Knowledge of principles and methods for curriculum and training design, teaching and instruction for individuals and groups, and the measurement of training effects.

Personnel and Human Resources	Knowledge of principles and procedures for personnel recruitment. selection. training. compensation and benefits, labor relations and negotiation, and personnel information systems.
Physics	Knowledge and prediction of physical principles, laws, their interrelationships. and applications to understanding fluid, material. and atmospheric dynamics, and mechanical, electrical, atomic and sub- atomic structures and processes.
Psychology	Knowledge of human behavior and performance; individual differences in ability. personality, and interests; learning and motivation; psychological research methods; and the assessment and treatment of behavioral and affective disorders.
History and Archeology	Knowledge of historical events and their causes, indicators, and effects on civilizations and cultures.
Production and Processing	Knowledge of raw materials, production processes, quality control, costs, and other techniques for maximizing the effective manufacture and distribution of goods.
Economics and Accounting	Knowledge of economic and accounting principles and practices. the financial markets, banking and the analysis and reporting of financial data.
Telecommunications	Knowledge of transmission, broadcasting, switching, control, and operation of telecommunications systems.
Chemistry	Knowledge of the chemical composition, structure, and properties of substances and of the chemical processes and transformations that they undergo. This includes uses of chemicals and their interactions, danger signs, production techniques, and disposal methods.
Sociology and Anthropology	Knowledge of group behavior and dynamics, societal trends and influences, human migrations, ethnicity, cultures and their history and origins.
Mechanical	Knowledge of machines and tools, including their designs, uses, repair, and maintenance.
Philosophy and Theology	Knowledge of different philosophical systems and religions. This includes their basic principles, values, ethics, ways of thinking, customs, practices, and their impact on human culture.
Therapy and Counseling	Knowledge of principles, methods, and procedures for diagnosis, treatment, and rehabilitation of physical and mental dysfunctions, and for career counseling and guidance.
Foreign Language	Knowledge of the structure and content of a foreign (non-English) language including the meaning and spelling of words, rules of composition and grammar, and pronunciation.
Food Production	Knowledge of techniques and equipment for planting, growing, and harvesting food products (both plant and animal) for consumption, including storage/handling techniques.
Medicine and Dentistry	Knowledge of the information and techniques needed to diagnose and treat human injuries, diseases, and deformities. This includes symptoms, treatment alternatives, drug properties and interactions, and preventive health-care measures.

Skills	Skills Definitions
Time Management	Managing one's own time and the time of others.
Coordination	Adjusting actions in relation to others' actions.
Active Listening	Giving full attention to what other people are saying, taking time to understand the points being made, asking questions as appropriate, and not interrupting at inappropriate times.
Reading Comprehension	Understanding written sentences and paragraphs in work related documents.
Judgment and Decision Making	Considering the relative costs and benefits of potential actions to choose the most appropriate one.
Critical Thinking	Using logic and reasoning to identify the strengths and weaknesses of alternative solutions, conclusions or approaches to problems.
Active Learning	Understanding the implications of new information for both current and future problem-solving and decision-making.
Writing	Communicating effectively in writing as appropriate for the needs of the audience.
Complex Problem Solving	Identifying complex problems and reviewing related information to develop and evaluate options and implement solutions.
Mathematics	Using mathematics to solve problems.
Operations Analysis	Analyzing needs and product requirements to create a design.
Speaking	Talking to others to convey information effectively.
Monitoring	Monitoring/Assessing performance of yourself, other individuals, or organizations to make improvements or take corrective action.
Social Perceptiveness	Being aware of others' reactions and understanding why they react as they do.
Management of Financial Resources	Determining how money will be spent to get the work done, and accounting for these expenditures.
Management of Personnel Resources	Motivating. developing, and directing people as they work, identifying the best people for the job.
Negotiation	Bringing others together and trying to reconcile differences.
Instructing	Teaching others how to do something.
Persuasion	Persuading others to change their minds or behavior.
Service Orientation	Actively looking for ways to help people.

Learning Strategies	Selecting and using training/instructional methods and procedures appropriate for the situation when learning or teaching new things.
Technology Design	Generating or adapting equipment and technology to serve user needs.
Science	Using scientific rules and methods to solve problems.
Equipment Selection	Determining the kind of tools and equipment needed to do a job.
Systems Evaluation	Identifying measures or indicators of system performance and the actions needed to improve or correct performance, relative to the goals of the system.
Troubleshooting	Determining causes of operating errors and deciding what to do about it.
Quality Control Analysis	Conducting tests and inspections of products, services, or processes to evaluate quality or performance.
Management of Material Resources	Obtaining and seeing to the appropriate use of equipment, facilities, and materials needed to do certain work.
Systems Analysis	Determining how a system should work and how changes in conditions, operations, and the environment will affect outcomes.
Equipment Maintenance	Performing routine maintenance on equipment and determining when and what kind of maintenance is needed.
Operation and Control	Controlling operations of equipment or systems.
Repairing	Repairing machines or systems using the needed tools.
Installation	Installing equipment, machines, wiring, or programs to meet specifications.
Programming	Writing computer programs for various purposes.
Operation Monitoring	Watching gauges, dials, or other indicators to make sure a machine is working properly.

Ability	Ability Definitions
Oral Comprehension	The ability to listen to and understand information and ideas presented through spoken words and sentences.
Written Expression	The ability to communicate information and ideas in writing so others will understand.
Oral Expression	The ability to communicate information and ideas in speaking so others will understand.
Originality	The ability to come up with unusual or clever ideas about a given topic or situation, or to develop creative ways to solve a problem.
Fluency of Ideas	The ability to come up with a number of ideas about a topic (the number of ideas is important, not their quality, correctness, or creativity).
Written Comprehension	The ability to read and understand information and ideas presented in writing.
Visualization	The ability to imagine how something will look after it is moved around or when its parts are moved or rearranged.
Information Ordering	The ability to arrange things or actions in a certain order or pattern according to a specific rule or set of rules (e.g., patterns of numbers, letters, words, pictures, mathematical operations).
Deductive Reasoning	The ability to apply general rules to specific problems to produce answers that make sense.
Inductive Reasoning	The ability to combine pieces of information to form general rules or conclusions (includes finding a relationship among seemingly unrelated events).
Speech Clarity	The ability to speak clearly so others can understand you.
Problem Sensitivity	The ability to tell when something is wrong or is likely to go wrong. It does not involve solving the problem, only recognizing there is a problem.
Category Flexibility	The ability to generate or use different sets of rules for combining or grouping things in different ways.
Speech Recognition	The ability to identify and understand the speech of another person.
Near Vision	The ability to see details at close range (within a few feet of the observer).
Far Vision	The ability to see details at a distance.
Mathematical Reasoning	The ability to choose the right mathematical methods or formulas to solve a problem.
Selective Attention	The ability to concentrate on a task over a period of time without being distracted.
Perceptual Speed	The ability to quickly and accurately compare similarities and differences among sets of letters, numbers, objects, pictures, or patterns. The things to be compared may be presented at the same time or one after the other. This ability also includes comparing a presented object with a remembered object.
Flexibility of Closure	The ability to identify or detect a known pattern (a figure, object, word, or sound) that is hidden in other distracting material.
Time Sharing	The ability to shift back and forth between two or more activities or sources of information (such as speech, sounds, touch, or other sources).
Speed of Closure	The ability to quickly make sense of, combine, and organize information into meaningful patterns.

Depth Perception	The ability to judge which of several objects is closer or farther away from you, or to judge the distance between you and an object.
Visual Color Discrimination	The ability to match or detect differences between colors, including shades of color and brightness.
Number Facility	The ability to add, subtract, multiply, or divide quickly and correctly.
Finger Dexterity	The ability to make precisely coordinated movements of the fingers of one or both hands to grasp, manipulate, or assemble very small objects.
Memorization	The ability to remember information such as words, numbers, pictures, and procedures.
Control Precision	The ability to quickly and repeatedly adjust the controls of a machine or a vehicle to exact positions.
Arm-Hand Steadiness	The ability to keep your hand and arm steady while moving your arm or while holding your arm and hand in one position.
Auditory Attention	The ability to focus on a single source of sound in the presence of other distracting sounds.
Multilimb Coordination	The ability to coordinate two or more limbs (for example, two arms, two legs, or one leg and one arm) while sitting, standing, or lying down. It does not involve performing the activities while the whole body is in motion.
Manual Dexterity	The ability to quickly move your hand, your hand together with your arm, or your two hands to grasp, manipulate, or assemble objects.
Hearing Sensitivity	The ability to detect or tell the differences between sounds that vary in pitch and loudness.
Glare Sensitivity	The ability to see objects in the presence of glare or bright lighting.
Reaction Time	The ability to quickly respond (with the hand, finger, or foot) to a signal (sound, light, picture) when it appears.
Gross Body Equilibrium	The ability to keep or regain your body balance or stay upright when in an unstable position.
Spatial Orientation	The ability to know your location in relation to the environment or to know where other objects are in relation to you.
Trunk Strength	The ability to use your abdominal and lower back muscles to support part of the body repeatedly or continuously over time without 'giving out' or fatiguing.
Extent Flexibility	The ability to bend, stretch, twist, or reach with your body, arms, and/or legs.
Gross Body Coordination	The ability to coordinate the movement of your arms, legs, and torso together when the whole body is in motion.
Peripheral Vision	The ability to see objects or movement of objects to one's side when the eyes are looking ahead.
Dynamic Strength	The ability to exert muscle force repeatedly or continuously over time. This involves muscular endurance and resistance to muscle fatigue.
Speed of Limb Movement	The ability to quickly move the arms and legs.
Wrist-Finger Speed	The ability to make fast, simple, repeated movements of the fingers, hands, and wrists.
Explosive Strength	The ability to use short bursts of muscle force to propel oneself (as in jumping or sprinting), or to throw an object.
Response Orientation	The ability to choose quickly between two or more movements in response to two or more different signals (lights, sounds, pictures). It includes the speed with which the correct response is started with the hand, foot, or other body part.
Static Strength	The ability to exert maximum muscle force to lift, push, pull, or carry objects.
Stamina	The ability to exert yourself physically over long periods of time without getting winded or out of breath.
Rate Control	The ability to time your movements or the movement of a piece of equipment in anticipation of changes in the speed and/or direction of a moving object or scene.
Night Vision	The ability to see under low light conditions.
Dynamic Flexibility	The ability to quickly and repeatedly bend, stretch, twist, or reach out with your body, arms, and/or legs.
Sound Localization	The ability to tell the direction from which a sound originated.

Work_Activity	Work_Activity Definitions
Thinking Creatively	Developing, designing, or creating new applications, ideas, relationships, systems, or products, including artistic contributions.
Making Decisions and Solving Problems	Analyzing information and evaluating results to choose the best solution and solve problems.
Drafting, Laying Out, and Specifying Technical Dev	Providing documentation, detailed instructions, drawings, or specifications to tell others about how devices, parts, equipment, or structures are to be fabricated, constructed, assembled, modified, maintained, or used.
Getting Information	Observing, receiving, and otherwise obtaining information from all relevant sources.
Communicating with Persons Outside Organization	Communicating with people outside the organization, representing the organization to customers, the public, government, and other external sources. This information can be exchanged in person, in writing, or by telephone or e-mail.

Communicating with Supervisors, Peers, or Subordin	Providing information to supervisors, co-workers, and subordinates by telephone, in written form, e-mail, or in person.
Identifying Objects, Actions, and Events	Identifying information by categorizing, estimating, recognizing differences or similarities, and detecting changes in circumstances or events.
Organizing, Planning, and Prioritizing Work	Developing specific goals and plans to prioritize, organize, and accomplish your work.
Establishing and Maintaining Interpersonal Relatio	Developing constructive and cooperative working relationships with others, and maintaining them over time.
Performing for or Working Directly with the Public	Performing for people or dealing directly with the public. This includes serving customers in restaurants and stores, and receiving clients or guests.
Evaluating Information to Determine Compliance wit	Using relevant information and individual judgment to determine whether events or processes comply with laws, regulations, or standards.
Updating and Using Relevant Knowledge	Keeping up-to-date technically and applying new knowledge to your job.
Scheduling Work and Activities	Scheduling events, programs, and activities, as well as the work of others.
Coordinating the Work and Activities of Others	Getting members of a group to work together to accomplish tasks.
Interacting With Computers	Using computers and computer systems (including hardware and software) to program, write software, set up functions, enter data, or process information.
Provide Consultation and Advice to Others	Providing guidance and expert advice to management or other groups on technical, systems-, or process-related topics.
Inspecting Equipment, Structures, or Material	Inspecting equipment, structures, or materials to identify the cause of errors or other problems or defects.
Developing and Building Teams	Encouraging and building mutual trust, respect, and cooperation among team members.
Monitor Processes, Materials, or Surroundings	Monitoring and reviewing information from materials, events, or the environment, to detect or assess problems.
Judging the Qualities of Things, Services, or Peop	Assessing the value, importance, or quality of things or people.
Analyzing Data or Information	Identifying the underlying principles, reasons, or facts of information by breaking down information or data into separate parts.
Resolving Conflicts and Negotiating with Others	Handling complaints, settling disputes, and resolving grievances and conflicts, or otherwise negotiating with others.
Developing Objectives and Strategies	Establishing long-range objectives and specifying the strategies and actions to achieve them.
Processing Information	Compiling, coding, categorizing, calculating, tabulating, auditing, or verifying information or data.
Training and Teaching Others	Identifying the educational needs of others, developing formal educational or training programs or classes, and teaching or instructing others.
Guiding, Directing, and Motivating Subordinates	Providing guidance and direction to subordinates, including setting performance standards and monitoring performance.
Estimating the Quantifiable Characteristics of Pro	Estimating sizes, distances, and quantities; or determining time, costs, resources, or materials needed to perform a work activity.
Performing Administrative Activities	Performing day-to-day administrative tasks such as maintaining information files and processing paperwork.
Interpreting the Meaning of Information for Others	Translating or explaining what information means and how it can be used.
Selling or Influencing Others	Convincing others to buy merchandise/goods or to otherwise change their minds or actions.
Documenting/Recording Information	Entering, transcribing, recording, storing, or maintaining information in written or electronic/magnetic form.
Monitoring and Controlling Resources	Monitoring and controlling resources and overseeing the spending of money.
Coaching and Developing Others	Identifying the developmental needs of others and coaching, mentoring, or otherwise helping others to improve their knowledge or skills.
Staffing Organizational Units	Recruiting, interviewing, selecting, hiring, and promoting employees in an organization.
Handling and Moving Objects	Using hands and arms in handling, installing, positioning, and moving materials, and manipulating things.
Operating Vehicles, Mechanized Devices, or Equipme	Running, maneuvering, navigating, or driving vehicles or mechanized equipment, such as forklifts, passenger vehicles, aircraft, or water craft.
Assisting and Caring for Others	Providing personal assistance, medical attention, emotional support, or other personal care to others such as coworkers, customers, or patients.
Repairing and Maintaining Mechanical Equipment	Servicing, repairing, adjusting, and testing machines, devices, moving parts, and equipment that operate primarily on the basis of mechanical (not electronic) principles.
Repairing and Maintaining Electronic Equipment	Servicing, repairing, calibrating, regulating, fine-tuning, or testing machines, devices, and equipment that operate primarily on the basis of electrical or electronic (not mechanical) principles.
Performing General Physical Activities	Performing physical activities that require considerable use of your arms and legs and moving your whole body, such as climbing, lifting, balancing, walking, stooping, and handling of materials.
Controlling Machines and Processes	Using either control mechanisms or direct physical activity to operate machines or processes (not including computers or vehicles).

Work_Content	Work_Content Definitions
Face-to-Face Discussions	How often do you have to have face-to-face discussions with individuals or teams in this job?
Telephone	How often do you have telephone conversations in this job?
Contact With Others	How much does this job require the worker to be in contact with others (face-to-face, by telephone, or otherwise) in order to perform it?
Importance of Being Exact or Accurate	How important is being very exact or highly accurate in performing this job?
Indoors, Environmentally Controlled	How often does this job require working indoors in environmentally controlled conditions?
Letters and Memos	How often does the job require written letters and memos?
Coordinate or Lead Others	How important is it to coordinate or lead others in accomplishing work activities in this job?
Structured versus Unstructured Work	To what extent is this job structured for the worker, rather than allowing the worker to determine tasks, priorities, and goals?
Freedom to Make Decisions	How much decision making freedom, without supervision, does the job offer?
Time Pressure	How often does this job require the worker to meet strict deadlines?
Frequency of Decision Making	How frequently is the worker required to make decisions that affect other people, the financial resources, and/or the image and reputation of the organization?
Responsibility for Outcomes and Results	How responsible is the worker for work outcomes and results of other workers?
Deal With External Customers	How important is it to work with external customers or the public in this job?
Electronic Mail	How often do you use electronic mail in this job?
Impact of Decisions on Co-workers or Company Resul	How do the decisions an employee makes impact the results of co-workers, clients or the company?
Level of Competition	To what extent does this job require the worker to compete or to be aware of competitive pressures?
Work With Work Group or Team	How important is it to work with others in a group or team in this job?
In an Enclosed Vehicle or Equipment	How often does this job require working in a closed vehicle or equipment (e.g., car)?
Consequence of Error	How serious would the result usually be if the worker made a mistake that was not readily correctable?
Outdoors, Exposed to Weather	How often does this job require working outdoors, exposed to all weather conditions?
Responsible for Others' Health and Safety	How much responsibility is there for the health and safety of others in this job?
Spend Time Sitting	How much does this job require sitting?
Frequency of Conflict Situations	How often are there conflict situations the employee has to face in this job?
Physical Proximity	To what extent does this job require the worker to perform job tasks in close physical proximity to other people?
Very Hot or Cold Temperatures	How often does this job require working in very hot (above 90 F degrees) or very cold (below 32 F degrees) temperatures?
Indoors, Not Environmentally Controlled	How often does this job require working indoors in non-controlled environmental conditions (e.g., warehouse without heat)?
Deal With Unpleasant or Angry People	How frequently does the worker have to deal with unpleasant, angry, or discourteous individuals as part of the job requirements?
Exposed to Minor Burns, Cuts, Bites, or Stings	How often does this job require exposure to minor burns, cuts, bites, or stings?
Exposed to Hazardous Equipment	How often does this job require exposure to hazardous equipment?
Sounds, Noise Levels Are Distracting or Uncomforta	How often does this job require working exposed to sounds and noise levels that are distracting or uncomfortable?
Importance of Repeating Same Tasks	How important is repeating the same physical activities (e.g., key entry) or mental activities (e.g., checking entries in a ledger) over and over, without stopping, to performing this job?
Exposed to Hazardous Conditions	How often does this job require exposure to hazardous conditions?
Outdoors, Under Cover	How often does this job require working outdoors, under cover (e.g., structure with roof but no walls)?
Extremely Bright or Inadequate Lighting	How often does this job require working in extremely bright or inadequate lighting conditions?
Exposed to High Places	How often does this job require exposure to high places?
Spend Time Using Your Hands to Handle, Control, or	How much does this job require using your hands to handle, control, or feel objects, tools or controls?
Spend Time Standing	How much does this job require standing?
Public Speaking	How often do you have to perform public speaking in this job?

Spend Time Making Repetitive Motions	How much does this job require making repetitive motions?
Cramped Work Space, Awkward Positions	How often does this job require working in cramped work spaces that requires getting into awkward positions?
Wear Common Protective or Safety Equipment such as	How much does this job require wearing common protective or safety equipment such as safety shoes, glasses, gloves, hard hats or live jackets?
Spend Time Walking and Running	How much does this job require walking and running?
Exposed to Contaminants	How often does this job require working exposed to contaminants (such as pollutants, gases, dust or odors)?
Degree of Automation	How automated is the job?
Wear Specialized Protective or Safety Equipment su	How much does this job require wearing specialized protective or safety equipment such as breathing apparatus, safety harness, full protection suits, or radiation protection?
Spend Time Bending or Twisting the Body	How much does this job require bending or twisting your body?
Spend Time Kneeling, Crouching, Stooping, or Crawl	How much does this job require kneeling, crouching, stooping or crawling?
Spend Time Keeping or Regaining Balance	How much does this job require keeping or regaining your balance?
Spend Time Climbing Ladders, Scaffolds, or Poles	How much does this job require climbing ladders, scaffolds, or poles?
In an Open Vehicle or Equipment	How often does this job require working in an open vehicle or equipment (e.g., tractor)?
Deal With Physically Aggressive People	How frequently does this job require the worker to deal with physical aggression of violent individuals?
Pace Determined by Speed of Equipment	How important is it to this job that the pace is determined by the speed of equipment or machinery? (This does not refer to keeping busy at all times on this job.)
Exposed to Radiation	How often does this job require exposure to radiation?
Exposed to Whole Body Vibration	How often does this job require exposure to whole body vibration (e.g., operate a jackhammer)?
Exposed to Disease or Infections	How often does this job require exposure to disease/infections?

Work_Styles	Work_Styles Definitions
Attention to Detail	Job requires being careful about detail and thorough in completing work tasks.
Dependability	Job requires being reliable, responsible, and dependable, and fulfilling obligations.
Stress Tolerance	Job requires accepting criticism and dealing calmly and effectively with high stress situations.
Innovation	Job requires creativity and alternative thinking to develop new ideas for and answers to work-related problems.
Independence	Job requires developing one's own ways of doing things, guiding oneself with little or no supervision, and depending on oneself to get things done.
Leadership	Job requires a willingness to lead, take charge, and offer opinions and direction.
Persistence	Job requires persistence in the face of obstacles.
Analytical Thinking	Job requires analyzing information and using logic to address work-related issues and problems.
Integrity	Job requires being honest and ethical.
Cooperation	Job requires being pleasant with others on the job and displaying a good-natured, cooperative attitude.
Adaptability/Flexibility	Job requires being open to change (positive or negative) and to considerable variety in the workplace.
Initiative	Job requires a willingness to take on responsibilities and challenges.
Achievement/Effort	Job requires establishing and maintaining personally challenging achievement goals and exerting effort toward mastering tasks.
Self Control	Job requires maintaining composure, keeping emotions in check, controlling anger, and avoiding aggressive behavior, even in very difficult situations.
Social Orientation	Job requires preferring to work with others rather than alone, and being personally connected with others on the job.
Concern for Others	Job requires being sensitive to others' needs and feelings and being understanding and helpful on the job.

Job Zone Component	Job Zone Component Definitions
Title	Job Zone Four: Considerable Preparation Needed
Overall Experience	A minimum of two to four years of work-related skill, knowledge, or experience is needed for these occupations. For example, an accountant must complete four years of college and work for several years in accounting to be considered qualified.
Job Training	Employees in these occupations usually need several years of work-related experience, on-the-job training, and/or vocational training.

Job Zone Examples	Many of these occupations involve coordinating, supervising, managing, or training others. Examples include accountants, chefs and head cooks, computer programmers, historians, pharmacists, and police detectives.
SVP Range	(7.0 to < 8.0)
Education	Most of these occupations require a four - year bachelor's degree, but some do not.

17-1021.00 - Cartographers and Photogrammetrists

Collect, analyze, and interpret geographic information provided by geodetic surveys, aerial photographs, and satellite data. Research, study, and prepare maps and other spatial data in digital or graphic form for legal, social, political, educational, and design purposes. May work with Geographic Information Systems (GIS). May design and evaluate algorithms, data structures, and user interfaces for GIS and mapping systems.

Tasks

1) Identify, scale, and orient geodetic points, elevations, and other planimetric or topographic features, applying standard mathematical formulas.

2) Build and update digital databases.

3) Inspect final compositions in order to ensure completeness and accuracy.

4) Revise existing maps and charts, making all necessary corrections and adjustments.

5) Determine guidelines that specify which source material is acceptable for use.

6) Compile data required for map preparation, including aerial photographs, survey notes, records, reports, and original maps.

7) Delineate aerial photographic detail, such as control points, hydrography, topography, and cultural features, using precision stereoplotting apparatus or drafting instruments.

8) Prepare and alter trace maps, charts, tables, detailed drawings, and three-dimensional optical models of terrain, using stereoscopic plotting and computer graphics equipment.

9) Travel over photographed areas in order to observe, identify, record, and verify all relevant features.

10) Study legal records in order to establish boundaries of local, national, and international properties.

11) Collect information about specific features of the Earth, using aerial photography and other digital remote sensing techniques.

12) Examine and analyze data from ground surveys, reports, aerial photographs, and satellite images in order to prepare topographic maps, aerial-photograph mosaics, and related charts.

13) Determine map content and layout, as well as production specifications such as scale, size, projection, and colors, and direct production in order to ensure that specifications are followed.

17-1022.00 - Surveyors

Make exact measurements and determine property boundaries. Provide data relevant to the shape, contour, gravitation, location, elevation, or dimension of land or land features on or near the earth's surface for engineering, mapmaking, mining, land evaluation, construction, and other purposes.

Tasks

1) Train assistants and helpers, and direct their work in such activities as performing surveys or drafting maps.

2) Develop criteria for the design and modification of survey instruments.

3) Analyze survey objectives and specifications in order to prepare survey proposals or to direct others in survey proposal preparation.

4) Conduct research in surveying and mapping methods, using knowledge of techniques of photogrammetric map compilation and electronic data processing.

5) Determine longitudes and latitudes of important features and boundaries in survey areas, using theodolites, transits, levels, and satellite-based global positioning systems (GPS).

6) Compute geodetic measurements and interpret survey data in order to determine positions, shapes, and elevations of geomorphic and topographic features.

7) Direct or conduct surveys in order to establish legal boundaries for properties, based on legal deeds and titles.

8) Locate and mark sites selected for geophysical prospecting activities, such as efforts to locate petroleum or other mineral products.

9) Verify the accuracy of survey data, including measurements and calculations conducted at survey sites.

10) Calculate heights, depths, relative positions, property lines, and other characteristics of

terrain.

11) Search legal records, survey records, and land titles in order to obtain information about property boundaries in areas to be surveyed.

12) Direct aerial surveys of specified geographical areas.

13) Determine specifications for photographic equipment to be used for aerial photography, as well as altitudes from which to photograph terrain.

14) Plan and conduct ground surveys designed to establish baselines, elevations, and other geodetic measurements.

15) Prepare and maintain sketches, maps, reports, and legal descriptions of surveys in order to describe, certify, and assume liability for work performed.

16) Record the results of surveys, including the shape, contour, location, elevation, and dimensions of land or land features.

17) Write descriptions of property boundary surveys for use in deeds, leases, or other legal documents.

18) Adjust surveying instruments in order to maintain their accuracy.

19) Develop criteria for survey methods and procedures.

20) Establish fixed points for use in making maps, using geodetic and engineering instruments.

21) Coordinate findings with the work of engineering and architectural personnel, clients, and others concerned with projects.

22) Prepare or supervise preparation of all data, charts, plots, maps, records, and documents related to surveys.

17-2011.00 - Aerospace Engineers

Perform a variety of engineering work in designing, constructing, and testing aircraft, missiles, and spacecraft. May conduct basic and applied research to evaluate adaptability of materials and equipment to aircraft design and manufacture. May recommend improvements in testing equipment and techniques.

Tasks

1) Plan and coordinate activities concerned with investigating and resolving customers' reports of technical problems with aircraft or aerospace vehicles.

2) Formulate conceptual design of aeronautical or aerospace products or systems to meet customer requirements.

3) Plan and conduct experimental, environmental, operational and stress tests on models and prototypes of aircraft and aerospace systems and equipment.

4) Evaluate product data and design from inspections and reports for conformance to engineering principles, customer requirements, and quality standards.

5) Direct and coordinate activities of engineering or technical personnel designing, fabricating, modifying, or testing of aircraft or aerospace products.

6) Develop design criteria for aeronautical or aerospace products or systems, including testing methods, production costs, quality standards, and completion dates.

7) Review performance reports and documentation from customers and field engineers, and inspect malfunctioning or damaged products to determine problem.

8) Analyze project requests and proposals and engineering data to determine feasibility, productibility, cost, and production time of aerospace or aeronautical product.

9) Maintain records of performance reports for future reference.

10) Direct research and development programs.

11) Formulate mathematical models or other methods of computer analysis to develop, evaluate, or modify design according to customer engineering requirements.

12) Write technical reports and other documentation, such as handbooks and bulletins, for use by engineering staff, management, and customers.

17-2021.00 - Agricultural Engineers

Apply knowledge of engineering technology and biological science to agricultural problems concerned with power and machinery, electrification, structures, soil and water conservation, and processing of agricultural products.

Tasks

1) Plan and direct construction of rural electric-power distribution systems, and irrigation, drainage, and flood control systems for soil and water conservation.

2) Supervise food processing or manufacturing plant operations.

3) Design structures for crop storage, animal shelter and loading, and animal and crop

processing, and supervise their construction.

4) Design and supervise environmental and land reclamation projects in agriculture and related industries.

5) Test agricultural machinery and equipment to ensure adequate performance.

6) Prepare reports, sketches, working drawings, specifications, proposals, and budgets for proposed sites or systems.

7) Visit sites to observe environmental problems, to consult with contractors, and/or to monitor construction activities.

8) Meet with clients, such as district or regional councils, farmers, and developers, to discuss their needs.

9) Discuss plans with clients, contractors, consultants, and other engineers so that they can be evaluated and necessary changes made.

10) Conduct educational programs that provide farmers or farm cooperative members with information that can help them improve agricultural productivity.

11) Design agricultural machinery components and equipment, using computer-aided design technology.

12) Design sensing, measuring, and recording devices, and other instrumentation used to study plant or animal life.

13) Provide advice on water quality and issues related to pollution management, river control, and ground and surface water resources.

17-2031.00 - Biomedical Engineers

Apply knowledge of engineering, biology, and biomechanical principles to the design, development, and evaluation of biological and health systems and products, such as artificial organs, prostheses, instrumentation, medical information systems, and health management and care delivery systems.

Tasks

1) Evaluate the safety, efficiency, and effectiveness of biomedical equipment.

2) Install, adjust, maintain, and/or repair biomedical equipment.

3) Advise and assist in the application of instrumentation in clinical environments.

4) Develop new applications for energy sources, such as using nuclear power for biomedical implants.

5) Research new materials to be used for products such as implanted artificial organs.

6) Adapt or design computer hardware or software for medical science uses.

7) Advise hospital administrators on the planning, acquisition, and use of medical equipment.

8) Design and deliver technology to assist people with disabilities.

9) Diagnose and interpret bioelectric data, using signal processing techniques.

10) Design and develop medical diagnostic and clinical instrumentation, equipment, and procedures, utilizing the principles of engineering and bio-behavioral sciences.

11) Analyze new medical procedures in order to forecast likely outcomes.

12) Conduct research, along with life scientists, chemists, and medical scientists, on the engineering aspects of the biological systems of humans and animals.

13) Teach biomedical engineering, or disseminate knowledge about field through writing or consulting.

17-2041.00 - Chemical Engineers

Design chemical plant equipment and devise processes for manufacturing chemicals and products, such as gasoline, synthetic rubber, plastics, detergents, cement, paper, and pulp, by applying principles and technology of chemistry, physics, and engineering.

Tasks

1) Conduct research to develop new and improved chemical manufacturing processes.

2) Design measurement and control systems for chemical plants based on data collected in laboratory experiments and in pilot plant operations.

3) Determine most effective arrangement of operations, such as mixing, crushing, heat transfer, distillation, and drying.

4) Perform laboratory studies of steps in manufacture of new product and test proposed process in small scale operation (pilot plant).

5) Perform tests throughout stages of production to determine degree of control over variables, including temperature, density, specific gravity, and pressure.

6) Develop safety procedures to be employed by workers operating equipment or working in

close proximity to on-going chemical reactions.

7) Prepare estimate of production costs and production progress reports for management.

8) Direct activities of workers who operate or who are engaged in constructing and improving absorption, evaporation, or electromagnetic equipment.

9) Develop processes to separate components of liquids or gases or generate electrical currents, using controlled chemical processes.

17-2051.00 - Civil Engineers

Perform engineering duties in planning, designing, and overseeing construction and maintenance of building structures, and facilities, such as roads, railroads, airports, bridges, harbors, channels, dams, irrigation projects, pipelines, power plants, water and sewage systems, and waste disposal units. Includes architectural, structural, traffic, ocean, and geo-technical engineers.

Tasks

1) Plan and design transportation or hydraulic systems and structures, following construction and government standards, using design software and drawing tools.

2) Compute load and grade requirements, water flow rates, and material stress factors to determine design specifications.

3) Inspect project sites to monitor progress and ensure conformance to design specifications and safety or sanitation standards.

4) Provide technical advice regarding design, construction, or program modifications and structural repairs to industrial and managerial personnel.

5) Test soils and materials to determine the adequacy and strength of foundations, concrete, asphalt, or steel.

6) Direct or participate in surveying to lay out installations and establish reference points, grades, and elevations to guide construction.

7) Direct construction, operations, and maintenance activities at project site.

8) Prepare or present public reports, such as bid proposals, deeds, environmental impact statements, and property and right-of-way descriptions.

9) Conduct studies of traffic patterns or environmental conditions to identify engineering problems and assess the potential impact of projects.

10) Analyze survey reports, maps, drawings, blueprints, aerial photography, and other topographical or geologic data to plan projects.

Knowledge	Knowledge Definitions
Engineering and Technology	Knowledge of the practical application of engineering science and technology. This includes applying principles, techniques, procedures, and equipment to the design and production of various goods and services.
Design	Knowledge of design techniques, tools, and principles involved in production of precision technical plans, blueprints, drawings, and models.
Mathematics	Knowledge of arithmetic, algebra, geometry, calculus, statistics, and their applications.
Building and Construction	Knowledge of materials, methods, and the tools involved in the construction or repair of houses, buildings, or other structures such as highways and roads.
English Language	Knowledge of the structure and content of the English language including the meaning and spelling of words, rules of composition, and grammar.
Customer and Personal Service	Knowledge of principles and processes for providing customer and personal services. This includes customer needs assessment, meeting quality standards for services, and evaluation of customer satisfaction.
Administration and Management	Knowledge of business and management principles involved in strategic planning, resource allocation, human resources modeling, leadership technique, production methods, and coordination of people and resources.
Transportation	Knowledge of principles and methods for moving people or goods by air, rail, sea, or road, including the relative costs and benefits.
Public Safety and Security	Knowledge of relevant equipment, policies, procedures, and strategies to promote effective local, state, or national security operations for the protection of people, data, property, and institutions.
Computers and Electronics	Knowledge of circuit boards, processors, chips, electronic equipment, and computer hardware and software, including applications and programming.
Personnel and Human Resources	Knowledge of principles and procedures for personnel recruitment, selection, training, compensation and benefits, labor relations and negotiation, and personnel information systems.

Law and Government	Knowledge of laws, legal codes, court procedures, precedents, government regulations, executive orders, agency rules, and the democratic political process.
Economics and Accounting	Knowledge of economic and accounting principles and practices, the financial markets, banking and the analysis and reporting of financial data.
Clerical	Knowledge of administrative and clerical procedures and systems such as word processing, managing files and records, stenography and transcription, designing forms, and other office procedures and terminology.
Physics	Knowledge and prediction of physical principles, laws, their interrelationships, and applications to understanding fluid, material, and atmospheric dynamics, and mechanical, electrical, atomic and sub-atomic structures and processes.
Education and Training	Knowledge of principles and methods for curriculum and training design, teaching and instruction for individuals and groups, and the measurement of training effects.
Sales and Marketing	Knowledge of principles and methods for showing, promoting, and selling products or services. This includes marketing strategy and tactics, product demonstration, sales techniques, and sales control systems.
Geography	Knowledge of principles and methods for describing the features of land, sea, and air masses, including their physical characteristics, locations, interrelationships, and distribution of plant, animal, and human life.
Psychology	Knowledge of human behavior and performance; individual differences in ability, personality, and interests; learning and motivation; psychological research methods; and the assessment and treatment of behavioral and affective disorders.
Mechanical	Knowledge of machines and tools, including their designs, uses, repair, and maintenance.
Communications and Media	Knowledge of media production, communication, and dissemination techniques and methods. This includes alternative ways to inform and entertain via written, oral, and visual media.
Production and Processing	Knowledge of raw materials, production processes, quality control, costs, and other techniques for maximizing the effective manufacture and distribution of goods.
Biology	Knowledge of plant and animal organisms, their tissues, cells, functions, interdependencies, and interactions with each other and the environment.
Chemistry	Knowledge of the chemical composition, structure, and properties of substances and of the chemical processes and transformations that they undergo. This includes uses of chemicals and their interactions, danger signs, production techniques, and disposal methods.
Telecommunications	Knowledge of transmission, broadcasting, switching, control, and operation of telecommunications systems.
Sociology and Anthropology	Knowledge of group behavior and dynamics, societal trends and influences, human migrations, ethnicity, cultures and their history and origins.
History and Archeology	Knowledge of historical events and their causes, indicators, and effects on civilizations and cultures.
Therapy and Counseling	Knowledge of principles, methods, and procedures for diagnosis, treatment, and rehabilitation of physical and mental dysfunctions, and for career counseling and guidance.
Philosophy and Theology	Knowledge of different philosophical systems and religions. This includes their basic principles, values, ethics, ways of thinking, customs, practices, and their impact on human culture.
Foreign Language	Knowledge of the structure and content of a foreign (non-English) language including the meaning and spelling of words, rules of composition and grammar, and pronunciation.
Medicine and Dentistry	Knowledge of the information and techniques needed to diagnose and treat human injuries, diseases, and deformities. This includes symptoms, treatment alternatives, drug properties and interactions, and preventive health-care measures.
Food Production	Knowledge of techniques and equipment for planting, growing, and harvesting food products (both plant and animal) for consumption, including storage/handling techniques.
Fine Arts	Knowledge of the theory and techniques required to compose, produce, and perform works of music, dance, visual arts, drama, and sculpture.

Skills	Skills Definitions
Mathematics	Using mathematics to solve problems.
Critical Thinking	Using logic and reasoning to identify the strengths and weaknesses of alternative solutions, conclusions or approaches to problems.
Science	Using scientific rules and methods to solve problems.
Active Listening	Giving full attention to what other people are saying, taking time to understand the points being made, asking questions as appropriate, and not interrupting at inappropriate times.
Reading Comprehension	Understanding written sentences and paragraphs in work related documents.
Active Learning	Understanding the implications of new information for both current and future problem-solving and decision-making.

Complex Problem Solving	Identifying complex problems and reviewing related information to develop and evaluate options and implement solutions.
Monitoring	Monitoring/Assessing performance of yourself, other individuals, or organizations to make improvements or take corrective action.
Negotiation	Bringing others together and trying to reconcile differences.
Judgment and Decision Making	Considering the relative costs and benefits of potential actions to choose the most appropriate one.
Writing	Communicating effectively in writing as appropriate for the needs of the audience.
Coordination	Adjusting actions in relation to others' actions.
Time Management	Managing one's own time and the time of others.
Operations Analysis	Analyzing needs and product requirements to create a design.
Social Perceptiveness	Being aware of others' reactions and understanding why they react as they do.
Service Orientation	Actively looking for ways to help people.
Persuasion	Persuading others to change their minds or behavior.
Speaking	Talking to others to convey information effectively.
Instructing	Teaching others how to do something.
Technology Design	Generating or adapting equipment and technology to serve user needs.
Learning Strategies	Selecting and using training/instructional methods and procedures appropriate for the situation when learning or teaching new things.
Equipment Selection	Determining the kind of tools and equipment needed to do a job.
Quality Control Analysis	Conducting tests and inspections of products, services, or processes to evaluate quality or performance.
Troubleshooting	Determining causes of operating errors and deciding what to do about it.
Management of Personnel Resources	Motivating, developing, and directing people as they work, identifying the best people for the job.
Systems Evaluation	Identifying measures or indicators of system performance and the actions needed to improve or correct performance, relative to the goals of the system.
Systems Analysis	Determining how a system should work and how changes in conditions, operations, and the environment will affect outcomes.
Operation and Control	Controlling operations of equipment or systems.
Management of Financial Resources	Determining how money will be spent to get the work done, and accounting for these expenditures.
Installation	Installing equipment, machines, wiring, or programs to meet specifications.
Operation Monitoring	Watching gauges, dials, or other indicators to make sure a machine is working properly.
Programming	Writing computer programs for various purposes.
Management of Material Resources	Obtaining and seeing to the appropriate use of equipment, facilities, and materials needed to do certain work.
Equipment Maintenance	Performing routine maintenance on equipment and determining when and what kind of maintenance is needed.
Repairing	Repairing machines or systems using the needed tools.

Ability

Ability Definitions

Problem Sensitivity	The ability to tell when something is wrong or is likely to go wrong. It does not involve solving the problem, only recognizing there is a problem.
Oral Expression	The ability to communicate information and ideas in speaking so others will understand.
Deductive Reasoning	The ability to apply general rules to specific problems to produce answers that make sense.
Written Comprehension	The ability to read and understand information and ideas presented in writing.
Oral Comprehension	The ability to listen to and understand information and ideas presented through spoken words and sentences.
Near Vision	The ability to see details at close range (within a few feet of the observer).
Information Ordering	The ability to arrange things or actions in a certain order or pattern according to a specific rule or set of rules (e.g., patterns of numbers, letters, words, pictures, mathematical operations).
Visualization	The ability to imagine how something will look after it is moved around or when its parts are moved or rearranged.
Speech Clarity	The ability to speak clearly so others can understand you.
Originality	The ability to come up with unusual or clever ideas about a given topic or situation, or to develop creative ways to solve a problem.
Inductive Reasoning	The ability to combine pieces of information to form general rules or conclusions (includes finding a relationship among seemingly unrelated events).
Fluency of Ideas	The ability to come up with a number of ideas about a topic (the number of ideas is important, not their quality, correctness, or creativity).
Speech Recognition	The ability to identify and understand the speech of another person.

Written Expression	The ability to communicate information and ideas in writing so others will understand.
Mathematical Reasoning	The ability to choose the right mathematical methods or formulas to solve a problem.
Selective Attention	The ability to concentrate on a task over a period of time without being distracted.
Category Flexibility	The ability to generate or use different sets of rules for combining or grouping things in different ways.
Flexibility of Closure	The ability to identify or detect a known pattern (a figure, object, word, or sound) that is hidden in other distracting material.
Far Vision	The ability to see details at a distance.
Depth Perception	The ability to judge which of several objects is closer or farther away from you, or to judge the distance between you and an object.
Finger Dexterity	The ability to make precisely coordinated movements of the fingers of one or both hands to grasp, manipulate, or assemble very small objects.
Speed of Closure	The ability to quickly make sense of, combine, and organize information into meaningful patterns.
Visual Color Discrimination	The ability to match or detect differences between colors, including shades of color and brightness.
Number Facility	The ability to add, subtract, multiply, or divide quickly and correctly.
Control Precision	The ability to quickly and repeatedly adjust the controls of a machine or a vehicle to exact positions.
Multilimb Coordination	The ability to coordinate two or more limbs (for example, two arms, two legs, or one leg and one arm) while sitting, standing, or lying down. It does not involve performing the activities while the whole body is in motion.
Time Sharing	The ability to shift back and forth between two or more activities or sources of information (such as speech, sounds, touch, or other sources).
Memorization	The ability to remember information such as words, numbers, pictures, and procedures.
Perceptual Speed	The ability to quickly and accurately compare similarities and differences among sets of letters, numbers, objects, pictures, or patterns. The things to be compared may be presented at the same time or one after the other. This ability also includes comparing a presented object with a remembered object.
Arm-Hand Steadiness	The ability to keep your hand and arm steady while moving your arm or while holding your arm and hand in one position.
Auditory Attention	The ability to focus on a single source of sound in the presence of other distracting sounds.
Manual Dexterity	The ability to quickly move your hand, your hand together with your arm, or your two hands to grasp, manipulate, or assemble objects.
Hearing Sensitivity	The ability to detect or tell the differences between sounds that vary in pitch and loudness.
Spatial Orientation	The ability to know your location in relation to the environment or to know where other objects are in relation to you.
Reaction Time	The ability to quickly respond (with the hand, finger, or foot) to a signal (sound, light, picture) when it appears.
Trunk Strength	The ability to use your abdominal and lower back muscles to support part of the body repeatedly or continuously over time without 'giving out' or fatiguing.
Peripheral Vision	The ability to see objects or movement of objects to one's side when the eyes are looking ahead.
Extent Flexibility	The ability to bend, stretch, twist, or reach with your body, arms, and/or legs.
Wrist-Finger Speed	The ability to make fast, simple, repeated movements of the fingers, hands, and wrists.
Stamina	The ability to exert yourself physically over long periods of time without getting winded or out of breath.
Dynamic Strength	The ability to exert muscle force repeatedly or continuously over time. This involves muscular endurance and resistance to muscle fatigue.
Gross Body Coordination	The ability to coordinate the movement of your arms, legs, and torso together when the whole body is in motion.
Response Orientation	The ability to choose quickly between two or more movements in response to two or more different signals (lights, sounds, pictures). It includes the speed with which the correct response is started with the hand, foot, or other body part.
Static Strength	The ability to exert maximum muscle force to lift, push, pull, or carry objects.
Dynamic Flexibility	The ability to quickly and repeatedly bend, stretch, twist, or reach out with your body, arms, and/or legs.
Gross Body Equilibrium	The ability to keep or regain your body balance or stay upright when in an unstable position.
Sound Localization	The ability to tell the direction from which a sound originated.
Rate Control	The ability to time your movements or the movement of a piece of equipment in anticipation of changes in the speed and/or direction of a moving object or scene.
Speed of Limb Movement	The ability to quickly move the arms and legs.
Night Vision	The ability to see under low light conditions.

Explosive Strength	The ability to use short bursts of muscle force to propel oneself (as in jumping or sprinting), or to throw an object.
Glare Sensitivity	The ability to see objects in the presence of glare or bright lighting.

Work_Activity	Work_Activity Definitions
Drafting, Laying Out, and Specifying Technical Dev	Providing documentation, detailed instructions, drawings, or specifications to tell others about how devices, parts, equipment, or structures are to be fabricated, constructed, assembled, modified, maintained, or used.
Making Decisions and Solving Problems	Analyzing information and evaluating results to choose the best solution and solve problems.
Interacting With Computers	Using computers and computer systems (including hardware and software) to program, write software, set up functions, enter data, or process information.
Communicating with Supervisors, Peers, or Subordin	Providing information to supervisors, co-workers, and subordinates by telephone, in written form, e-mail, or in person.
Documenting/Recording Information	Entering, transcribing, recording, storing, or maintaining information in written or electronic/magnetic form.
Thinking Creatively	Developing, designing, or creating new applications, ideas, relationships, systems, or products, including artistic contributions.
Organizing, Planning, and Prioritizing Work	Developing specific goals and plans to prioritize, organize, and accomplish your work.
Getting Information	Observing, receiving, and otherwise obtaining information from all relevant sources.
Estimating the Quantifiable Characteristics of Pro	Estimating sizes, distances, and quantities; or determining time, costs, resources, or materials needed to perform a work activity.
Analyzing Data or Information	Identifying the underlying principles, reasons, or facts of information by breaking down information or data into separate parts.
Interpreting the Meaning of Information for Others	Translating or explaining what information means and how it can be used.
Scheduling Work and Activities	Scheduling events, programs, and activities, as well as the work of others.
Evaluating Information to Determine Compliance wit	Using relevant information and individual judgment to determine whether events or processes comply with laws, regulations, or standards.
Updating and Using Relevant Knowledge	Keeping up-to-date technically and applying new knowledge to your job.
Communicating with Persons Outside Organization	Communicating with people outside the organization, representing the organization to customers, the public, government, and other external sources. This information can be exchanged in person, in writing, or by telephone or e-mail.
Judging the Qualities of Things, Services, or Peop	Assessing the value, importance, or quality of things or people.
Developing and Building Teams	Encouraging and building mutual trust, respect, and cooperation among team members.
Resolving Conflicts and Negotiating with Others	Handling complaints, settling disputes, and resolving grievances and conflicts, or otherwise negotiating with others.
Establishing and Maintaining Interpersonal Relatio	Developing constructive and cooperative working relationships with others, and maintaining them over time.
Processing Information	Compiling, coding, categorizing, calculating, tabulating, auditing, or verifying information or data.
Monitor Processes, Materials, or Surroundings	Monitoring and reviewing information from materials, events, or the environment, to detect or assess problems.
Performing for or Working Directly with the Public	Performing for people or dealing directly with the public. This includes serving customers in restaurants and stores, and receiving clients or guests.
Inspecting Equipment, Structures, or Material	Inspecting equipment, structures, or materials to identify the cause of errors or other problems or defects.
Identifying Objects, Actions, and Events	Identifying information by categorizing, estimating, recognizing differences or similarities, and detecting changes in circumstances or events.
Coordinating the Work and Activities of Others	Getting members of a group to work together to accomplish tasks.
Coaching and Developing Others	Identifying the developmental needs of others and coaching, mentoring, or otherwise helping others to improve their knowledge or skills.
Selling or Influencing Others	Convincing others to buy merchandise/goods or to otherwise change their minds or actions.
Training and Teaching Others	Identifying the educational needs of others, developing formal educational or training programs or classes, and teaching or instructing others.
Monitoring and Controlling Resources	Monitoring and controlling resources and overseeing the spending of money.
Developing Objectives and Strategies	Establishing long-range objectives and specifying the strategies and actions to achieve them.
Provide Consultation and Advice to Others	Providing guidance and expert advice to management or other groups on technical, systems-, or process-related topics.

Guiding, Directing, and Motivating Subordinates	Providing guidance and direction to subordinates, including setting performance standards and monitoring performance.
Performing Administrative Activities	Performing day-to-day administrative tasks such as maintaining information files and processing paperwork.
Staffing Organizational Units	Recruiting, interviewing, selecting, hiring, and promoting employees in an organization.
Assisting and Caring for Others	Providing personal assistance, medical attention, emotional support, or other personal care to others such as coworkers, customers, or patients.
Repairing and Maintaining Electronic Equipment	Servicing, repairing, calibrating, regulating, fine-tuning, or testing machines, devices, and equipment that operate primarily on the basis of electrical or electronic (not mechanical) principles.
Operating Vehicles, Mechanized Devices, or Equipme	Running, maneuvering, navigating, or driving vehicles or mechanized equipment, such as forklifts, passenger vehicles, aircraft, or water craft.
Performing General Physical Activities	Performing physical activities that require considerable use of your arms and legs and moving your whole body, such as climbing, lifting, balancing, walking, stooping, and handling of materials.
Repairing and Maintaining Mechanical Equipment	Servicing, repairing, adjusting, and testing machines, devices, moving parts, and equipment that operate primarily on the basis of mechanical (not electronic) principles.
Controlling Machines and Processes	Using either control mechanisms or direct physical activity to operate machines or processes (not including computers or vehicles).
Handling and Moving Objects	Using hands and arms in handling, installing, positioning, and moving materials, and manipulating things.

Work_Content	Work_Content Definitions
Telephone	How often do you have telephone conversations in this job?
Freedom to Make Decisions	How much decision making freedom, without supervision, does the job offer?
Face-to-Face Discussions	How often do you have to have face-to-face discussions with individuals or teams in this job?
Importance of Being Exact or Accurate	How important is being very exact or highly accurate in performing this job?
Letters and Memos	How often does the job require written letters and memos?
In an Enclosed Vehicle or Equipment	How often does this job require working in a closed vehicle or equipment (e.g., car)?
Responsibility for Outcomes and Results	How responsible is the worker for work outcomes and results of other workers?
Structured versus Unstructured Work	To what extent is this job structured for the worker, rather than allowing the worker to determine tasks, priorities, and goals?
Impact of Decisions on Co-workers or Company Resul	How do the decisions an employee makes impact the results of co-workers, clients or the company?
Spend Time Sitting	How much does this job require sitting?
Outdoors, Exposed to Weather	How often does this job require working outdoors, exposed to all weather conditions?
Frequency of Conflict Situations	How often are there conflict situations the employee has to face in this job?
Indoors, Environmentally Controlled	How often does this job require working indoors in environmentally controlled conditions?
Coordinate or Lead Others	How important is it to coordinate or lead others in accomplishing work activities in this job?
Frequency of Decision Making	How frequently is the worker required to make decisions that affect other people, the financial resources, and/or the image and reputation of the organization?
Work With Work Group or Team	How important is it to work with others in a group or team in this job?
Deal With External Customers	How important is it to work with external customers or the public in this job?
Exposed to Contaminants	How often does this job require working exposed to contaminants (such as pollutants, gases, dust or odors)?
Very Hot or Cold Temperatures	How often does this job require working in very hot (above 90 F degrees) or very cold (below 32 F degrees) temperatures?
Indoors, Not Environmentally Controlled	How often does this job require working indoors in non-controlled environmental conditions (e.g., warehouse without heat)?
Contact With Others	How much does this job require the worker to be in contact with others (face-to-face, by telephone, or otherwise) in order to perform it?
Time Pressure	How often does this job require the worker to meet strict deadlines?
Exposed to Hazardous Equipment	How often does this job require exposure to hazardous equipment?
Consequence of Error	How serious would the result usually be if the worker made a mistake that was not readily correctable?
Deal With Unpleasant or Angry People	How frequently does the worker have to deal with unpleasant, angry, or discourteous individuals as part of the job requirements?
Level of Competition	To what extent does this job require the worker to compete or to be aware of competitive pressures?

Sounds, Noise Levels Are Distracting or Uncomforta	How often does this job require working exposed to sounds and noise levels that are distracting or uncomfortable?
Electronic Mail	How often do you use electronic mail in this job?
Wear Common Protective or Safety Equipment such as	How much does this job require wearing common protective or safety equipment such as safety shoes, glasses, gloves, hard hats or live jackets?
Physical Proximity	To what extent does this job require the worker to perform job tasks in close physical proximity to other people?
Spend Time Standing	How much does this job require standing?
Importance of Repeating Same Tasks	How important is repeating the same physical activities (e.g., key entry) or mental activities (e.g., checking entries in a ledger) over and over, without stopping, to performing this job?
Public Speaking	How often do you have to perform public speaking in this job?
Responsible for Others' Health and Safety	How much responsibility is there for the health and safety of others in this job?
Spend Time Using Your Hands to Handle, Control, or	How much does this job require using your hands to handle, control, or feel objects, tools or controls?
Spend Time Walking and Running	How much does this job require walking and running?
Outdoors, Under Cover	How often does this job require working outdoors, under cover (e.g., structure with roof but no walls)?
Exposed to Hazardous Conditions	How often does this job require exposure to hazardous conditions?
Cramped Work Space, Awkward Positions	How often does this job require working in cramped work spaces that requires getting into awkward positions?
Spend Time Making Repetitive Motions	How much does this job require making repetitive motions?
Exposed to Radiation	How often does this job require exposure to radiation?
Exposed to Minor Burns, Cuts, Bites, or Stings	How often does this job require exposure to minor burns, cuts, bites, or stings?
Degree of Automation	How automated is the job?
Exposed to Disease or Infections	How often does this job require exposure to disease/infections?
Spend Time Bending or Twisting the Body	How much does this job require bending or twisting your body?
Extremely Bright or Inadequate Lighting	How often does this job require working in extremely bright or inadequate lighting conditions?
Pace Determined by Speed of Equipment	How important is it to this job that the pace is determined by the speed of equipment or machinery? (This does not refer to keeping busy at all times on this job.)
Deal With Physically Aggressive People	How frequently does this job require the worker to deal with physical aggression of violent individuals?
Exposed to High Places	How often does this job require exposure to high places?
Spend Time Kneeling, Crouching, Stooping, or Crawl	How much does this job require kneeling, crouching, stooping or crawling?
Wear Specialized Protective or Safety Equipment su	How much does this job require wearing specialized protective or safety equipment such as breathing apparatus, safety harness, full protection suits, or radiation protection?
Spend Time Climbing Ladders, Scaffolds, or Poles	How much does this job require climbing ladders, scaffolds, or poles?
Spend Time Keeping or Regaining Balance	How much does this job require keeping or regaining your balance?
Exposed to Whole Body Vibration	How often does this job require exposure to whole body vibration (e.g., operate a jackhammer)?
In an Open Vehicle or Equipment	How often does this job require working in an open vehicle or equipment (e.g., tractor)?

Work_Styles	Work_Styles Definitions
Dependability	Job requires being reliable, responsible, and dependable, and fulfilling obligations.
Integrity	Job requires being honest and ethical.
Attention to Detail	Job requires being careful about detail and thorough in completing work tasks.
Initiative	Job requires a willingness to take on responsibilities and challenges.
Analytical Thinking	Job requires analyzing information and using logic to address work-related issues and problems.
Leadership	Job requires a willingness to lead, take charge, and offer opinions and direction.
Self Control	Job requires maintaining composure, keeping emotions in check, controlling anger, and avoiding aggressive behavior, even in very difficult situations.
Persistence	Job requires persistence in the face of obstacles.
Achievement/Effort	Job requires establishing and maintaining personally challenging achievement goals and exerting effort toward mastering tasks.
Stress Tolerance	Job requires accepting criticism and dealing calmly and effectively with high stress situations.
Cooperation	Job requires being pleasant with others on the job and displaying a good-natured, cooperative attitude.

Independence	Job requires developing one's own ways of doing things, guiding oneself with little or no supervision, and depending on oneself to get things done.
Adaptability/Flexibility	Job requires being open to change (positive or negative) and to considerable variety in the workplace.
Social Orientation	Job requires preferring to work with others rather than alone, and being personally connected with others on the job.
Innovation	Job requires creativity and alternative thinking to develop new ideas for and answers to work-related problems.
Concern for Others	Job requires being sensitive to others' needs and feelings and being understanding and helpful on the job.

Job Zone Component	Job Zone Component Definitions
Title	Job Zone Four: Considerable Preparation Needed
Overall Experience	A minimum of two to four years of work-related skill, knowledge, or experience is needed for these occupations. For example, an accountant must complete four years of college and work for several years in accounting to be considered qualified.
Job Training	Employees in these occupations usually need several years of work-related experience, on-the-job training, and/or vocational training.
Job Zone Examples	Many of these occupations involve coordinating, supervising, managing, or training others. Examples include accountants, chefs and head cooks, computer programmers, historians, pharmacists, and police detectives.
SVP Range	(7.0 to < 8.0)
Education	Most of these occupations require a four-year bachelor's degree, but some do not.

17-2061.00 - Computer Hardware Engineers

Research, design, develop, and test computer or computer-related equipment for commercial, industrial, military, or scientific use. May supervise the manufacturing and installation of computer or computer-related equipment and components.

Tasks

1) Specify power supply requirements and configuration, drawing on system performance expectations and design specifications.

2) Update knowledge and skills to keep up with rapid advancements in computer technology.

3) Select hardware and material, assuring compliance with specifications and product requirements.

4) Recommend purchase of equipment to control dust, temperature, and humidity in area of system installation.

5) Provide training and support to system designers and users.

6) Provide technical support to designers, marketing and sales departments, suppliers, engineers and other team members throughout the product development and implementation process.

7) Direct technicians, engineering designers or other technical support personnel as needed.

8) Store, retrieve, and manipulate data for analysis of system capabilities and requirements.

9) Monitor functioning of equipment and make necessary modifications to ensure system operates in conformance with specifications.

10) Evaluate factors such as reporting formats required, cost constraints, and need for security restrictions to determine hardware configuration.

11) Design and develop computer hardware and support peripherals, including central processing units (CPUs), support logic, microprocessors, custom integrated circuits, and printers and disk drives.

12) Confer with engineering staff and consult specifications to evaluate interface between hardware and software and operational and performance requirements of overall system.

13) Analyze user needs and recommend appropriate hardware.

14) Test and verify hardware and support peripherals to ensure that they meet specifications and requirements, analyzing and recording test data.

15) Analyze information to determine, recommend, and plan layout, including type of computers and peripheral equipment modifications.

16) Write detailed functional specifications that document the hardware development process and support hardware introduction.

17) Assemble and modify existing pieces of equipment to meet special needs.

17-2071.00 - Electrical Engineers

Design, develop, test, or supervise the manufacturing and installation of electrical equipment, components, or systems for commercial, industrial, military, or scientific use.

Tasks

1) Compile data and write reports regarding existing and potential engineering studies and projects.

2) Conduct field surveys and study maps, graphs, diagrams, and other data to identify and correct power system problems.

3) Develop budgets, estimating labor, material, and construction costs.

4) Investigate customer or public complaints, determine nature and extent of problem, and recommend remedial measures.

5) Inspect completed installations and observe operations, to ensure conformance to design and equipment specifications and compliance with operational and safety standards.

6) Prepare specifications for purchase of materials and equipment.

7) Perform detailed calculations to compute and establish manufacturing, construction, and installation standards and specifications.

8) Collect data relating to commercial and residential development, population, and power system interconnection to determine operating efficiency of electrical systems.

9) Operate computer-assisted engineering and design software and equipment to perform engineering tasks.

10) Prepare and study technical drawings, specifications of electrical systems, and topographical maps to ensure that installation and operations conform to standards and customer requirements.

11) Assist in developing capital project programs for new equipment and major repairs.

12) Oversee project production efforts to assure projects are completed satisfactorily, on time and within budget.

13) Confer with engineers, customers, and others to discuss existing or potential engineering projects and products.

14) Plan layout of electric power generating plants and distribution lines and stations.

15) Design, implement, maintain, and improve electrical instruments, equipment, facilities, components, products, and systems for commercial, industrial, and domestic purposes.

16) Supervise and train project team members as necessary.

17) Direct and coordinate manufacturing, construction, installation, maintenance, support, documentation, and testing activities to ensure compliance with specifications, codes, and customer requirements.

18) Investigate and test vendors' and competitors' products.

17-2072.00 - Electronics Engineers, Except Computer

Research, design, develop, and test electronic components and systems for commercial, industrial, military, or scientific use utilizing knowledge of electronic theory and materials properties. Design electronic circuits and components for use in fields such as telecommunications, aerospace guidance and propulsion control, acoustics, or instruments and controls.

Tasks

1) Develop and perform operational, maintenance, and testing procedures for electronic products, components, equipment, and systems.

2) Direct and coordinate activities concerned with manufacture, construction, installation, maintenance, operation, and modification of electronic equipment, products, and systems.

3) Evaluate operational systems, prototypes and proposals and recommend repair or design modifications based on factors such as environment, service, cost, and system capabilities.

4) Inspect electronic equipment, instruments, products, and systems to ensure conformance to specifications, safety standards, and applicable codes and regulations.

5) Plan and develop applications and modifications for electronic properties used in components, products, and systems, to improve technical performance.

6) Plan and implement research, methodology, and procedures to apply principles of electronic theory to engineering projects.

7) Operate computer-assisted engineering and design software and equipment to perform engineering tasks.

8) Prepare engineering sketches and specifications for construction, relocation, and installation of equipment, facilities, products, and systems.

9) Provide technical support and instruction to staff and customers regarding equipment standards, and help solve specific, difficult in-service engineering problems.

10) Prepare, review, and maintain maintenance schedules, design documentation and operational reports and charts.

11) Review and evaluate work of others, inside and outside the organization, to ensure effectiveness, technical adequacy and compatibility in the resolution of complex engineering problems.

12) Review or prepare budget and cost estimates for equipment, construction, and installation

projects, and control expenditures.

13) Prepare documentation containing information such as confidential descriptions and specifications of proprietary hardware and software, product development and introduction schedules, product costs, and information about product performance weaknesses.

14) Prepare necessary criteria, procedures, reports, and plans for successful conduct of the program/project with consideration given to site preparation, facility validation, installation, quality assurance and testing.

15) Represent employer at conferences, meetings, boards, panels, committees, and working groups to present, explain, and defend findings and recommendations, negotiate compromises and agreements and exchange information.

16) Determine material and equipment needs and order supplies.

17) Analyze system requirements, capacity, cost, and customer needs to determine feasibility of project and develop system plan.

18) Confer with engineers, customers, vendors and others to discuss existing and potential engineering projects or products.

17-2081.00 - Environmental Engineers

Design, plan, or perform engineering duties in the prevention, control, and remediation of environmental health hazards utilizing various engineering disciplines. Work may include waste treatment, site remediation, or pollution control technology.

Tasks

1) Develop proposed project objectives and targets, and report to management on progress in attaining them.

2) Request bids from suppliers or consultants.

3) Monitor progress of environmental improvement programs.

4) Inspect industrial and municipal facilities and programs in order to evaluate operational effectiveness and ensure compliance with environmental regulations.

5) Inform company employees and other interested parties of environmental issues.

6) Provide environmental engineering assistance in network analysis, regulatory analysis, and planning or reviewing database development.

7) Provide technical-level support for environmental remediation and litigation projects, including remediation system design and determination of regulatory applicability.

8) Serve as liaison with federal, state, and local agencies and officials on issues pertaining to solid and hazardous waste program requirements.

9) Assess, sort, characterize, and pack known and unknown materials.

10) Coordinate and manage environmental protection programs and projects, assigning and evaluating work.

11) Develop site-specific health and safety protocols, such as spill contingency plans and methods for loading and transporting waste.

12) Develop and present environmental compliance training or orientation sessions.

13) Design systems, processes, and equipment for control, management, and remediation of water, air, and soil quality.

14) Develop, implement, and manage plans and programs related to conservation and management of natural resources.

15) Maintain, write, and revise quality-assurance documentation and procedures.

16) Obtain, update, and maintain plans, permits, and standard operating procedures.

17) Prepare hazardous waste manifests and land disposal restriction notifications.

18) Provide administrative support for projects by collecting data, providing project documentation, training staff, and performing other general administrative duties.

19) Serve on teams conducting multimedia inspections at complex facilities, providing assistance with planning, quality assurance, safety inspection protocols, and sampling.

20) Advise industries and government agencies about environmental policies and standards.

21) Advise corporations and government agencies of procedures to follow in cleaning up contaminated sites in order to protect people and the environment.

22) Prepare, review, and update environmental investigation and recommendation reports.

23) Collaborate with environmental scientists, planners, hazardous waste technicians, engineers, and other specialists, and experts in law and business to address environmental problems.

24) Assess the existing or potential environmental impact of land use projects on air, water, and land.

17-2112.00 - Industrial Engineers

Design, develop, test, and evaluate integrated systems for managing industrial production processes including human work factors, quality control, inventory control, logistics and material flow, cost analysis, and production coordination.

Tasks

1) Implement methods and procedures for disposition of discrepant material and defective or damaged parts, and assess cost and responsibility.

2) Develop manufacturing methods, labor utilization standards, and cost analysis systems to promote efficient staff and facility utilization.

3) Recommend methods for improving utilization of personnel, material, and utilities.

4) Plan and establish sequence of operations to fabricate and assemble parts or products and to promote efficient utilization.

5) Confer with vendors, staff, and management personnel regarding purchases, procedures, product specifications, manufacturing capabilities, and project status.

6) Review production schedules, engineering specifications, orders, and related information to obtain knowledge of manufacturing methods, procedures, and activities.

7) Draft and design layout of equipment, materials, and workspace to illustrate maximum efficiency, using drafting tools and computer.

8) Analyze statistical data and product specifications to determine standards and establish quality and reliability objectives of finished product.

9) Record or oversee recording of information to ensure currency of engineering drawings and documentation of production problems.

10) Direct workers engaged in product measurement, inspection, and testing activities to ensure quality control and reliability.

11) Estimate production cost and effect of product design changes for management review, action, and control.

12) Communicate with management and user personnel to develop production and design standards.

13) Coordinate quality control objectives and activities to resolve production problems, maximize product reliability, and minimize cost.

14) Apply statistical methods and perform mathematical calculations to determine manufacturing processes, staff requirements, and production standards.

15) Formulate sampling procedures and designs and develop forms and instructions for recording, evaluating, and reporting quality and reliability data.

16) Schedule deliveries based on production forecasts, material substitutions, storage and handling facilities, and maintenance requirements.

17) Study operations sequence, material flow, functional statements, organization charts, and project information to determine worker functions and responsibilities.

18) Complete production reports, purchase orders, and material, tool, and equipment lists.

19) Evaluate precision and accuracy of production and testing equipment and engineering drawings to formulate corrective action plan.

17-2121.01 - Marine Engineers

Design, develop, and take responsibility for the installation of ship machinery and related equipment including propulsion machines and power supply systems.

Tasks

1) Maintain records of engineering department activities, including expense records and details of equipment maintenance and repairs.

2) Evaluate operation of marine equipment during acceptance testing and shakedown cruises.

3) Design and oversee testing, installation, and repair of marine apparatus and equipment.

4) Determine conditions under which tests are to be conducted, as well as sequences and phases of test operations.

5) Conduct analytical, environmental, operational, or performance studies in order to develop designs for products, such as marine engines, equipment, and structures.

6) Prepare, or direct the preparation of, product or system layouts and detailed drawings and schematics.

7) Maintain contact with, and formulate reports for, contractors and clients in order to ensure completion of work at minimum cost.

8) Supervise other engineers and crewmembers, and train them for routine and emergency duties.

9) Schedule machine overhauls and the servicing of electrical, heating, ventilation, refrigeration, water, and sewage systems.

10) Procure materials needed to repair marine equipment and machinery.

11) Perform monitoring activities in order to ensure that ships comply with international

regulations and standards for life saving equipment and pollution preventatives.

12) Confer with research personnel in order to clarify or resolve problems, and to develop or modify designs.

13) Check, test, and maintain automatic controls and alarm systems.

14) Act as liaisons between ships' captains and shore personnel in order to ensure that schedules and budgets are maintained, and that ships are operated safely and efficiently.

15) Investigate and observe tests on machinery and equipment for compliance with standards.

16) Coordinate activities with regulatory bodies in order to ensure repairs and alterations are at minimum cost, consistent with safety.

17) Analyze data in order to determine feasibility of product proposals.

18) Review work requests, and compare them with previous work completed on ships in order to ensure that costs are economically sound.

19) Maintain and coordinate repair of marine machinery and equipment for installation on vessels.

20) Inspect marine equipment and machinery in order to draw up work requests and job specifications.

21) Prepare plans, estimates, design and construction schedules, and contract specifications, including any special provisions.

22) Prepare technical reports for use by engineering, management, or sales personnel.

17-2121.02 - Marine Architects

Design and oversee construction and repair of marine craft and floating structures such as ships, barges, tugs, dredges, submarines, torpedoes, floats, and buoys. May confer with marine engineers.

Tasks

1) Evaluate performance of craft during dock and sea trials to determine design changes and conformance with national and international standards.

2) Confer with marine engineering personnel to establish arrangement of boiler room equipment and propulsion machinery, heating and ventilating systems, refrigeration equipment, piping, and other functional equipment.

3) Oversee construction and testing of prototype in model basin and develop sectional and waterline curves of hull to establish center of gravity, ideal hull form, and buoyancy and stability data.

4) Study design proposals and specifications to establish basic characteristics of craft, such as size, weight, speed, propulsion, displacement, and draft.

5) Design complete hull and superstructure according to specifications and test data, in conformity with standards of safety, efficiency, and economy.

17-2131.00 - Materials Engineers

Evaluate materials and develop machinery and processes to manufacture materials for use in products that must meet specialized design and performance specifications. Develop new uses for known materials. Includes those working with composite materials or specializing in one type of material, such as graphite, metal and metal alloys, ceramics and glass, plastics and polymers, and naturally occurring materials.

Tasks

1) Monitor material performance and evaluate material deterioration.

2) Teach in colleges and universities.

3) Evaluate technical specifications and economic factors relating to process or product design objectives.

4) Supervise the work of technologists, technicians and other engineers and scientists.

5) Remove metals from ores, and refine and alloy them to obtain useful metal.

6) Perform managerial functions such as preparing proposals and budgets, analyzing labor costs, and writing reports.

7) Modify properties of metal alloys, using thermal and mechanical treatments.

8) Plan and evaluate new projects, consulting with other engineers and corporate executives as necessary.

9) Design processing plants and equipment.

10) Sell and service metal products.

11) Supervise production and testing processes in industrial settings such as metal refining facilities, smelting or foundry operations, or non-metallic materials production operations.

12) Review new product plans and make recommendations for material selection based on design objectives, such as strength, weight, heat resistance, electrical conductivity, and cost.

13) Determine appropriate methods for fabricating and joining materials.

14) Plan and implement laboratory operations for the purpose of developing material and fabrication procedures that meet cost, product specification, and performance standards.

15) Replicate the characteristics of materials and their components with computers.

16) Conduct or supervise tests on raw materials or finished products in order to ensure their quality.

17) Analyze product failure data and laboratory test results in order to determine causes of problems and develop solutions.

18) Design and direct the testing and/or control of processing procedures.

19) Solve problems in a number of engineering fields, such as mechanical, chemical, electrical, civil, nuclear and aerospace.

20) Guide technical staff engaged in developing materials for specific uses in projected products or devices.

21) Write for technical magazines, journals, and trade association publications.

17-2141.00 - Mechanical Engineers

Perform engineering duties in planning and designing tools, engines, machines, and other mechanically functioning equipment. Oversee installation, operation, maintenance, and repair of such equipment as centralized heat, gas, water, and steam systems.

Tasks

1) Oversee installation, operation, maintenance, and repair to ensure that machines and equipment are installed and functioning according to specifications.

2) Investigate equipment failures and difficulties to diagnose faulty operation, and to make recommendations to maintenance crew.

3) Establish and coordinate the maintenance and safety procedures, service schedule, and supply of materials required to maintain machines and equipment in the prescribed condition.

4) Provide feedback to design engineers on customer problems and needs.

5) Research and analyze customer design proposals, specifications, manuals, and other data to evaluate the feasibility, cost, and maintenance requirements of designs or applications.

6) Assist drafters in developing the structural design of products, using drafting tools or computer-assisted design/drafting equipment and software.

7) Design test control apparatus and equipment and develop procedures for testing products.

8) Conduct research that tests and analyzes the feasibility, design, operation and performance of equipment, components and systems.

9) Confer with engineers and other personnel to implement operating procedures, resolve system malfunctions, and provide technical information.

10) Develop, coordinate, and monitor all aspects of production, including selection of manufacturing methods, fabrication, and operation of product designs.

11) Solicit new business and provide technical customer service.

12) Estimate costs and submit bids for engineering, construction, or extraction projects, and prepare contract documents.

13) Write performance requirements for product development or engineering projects.

14) Study industrial processes to determine where and how application of equipment can be made.

15) Research, design, evaluate, install, operate, and maintain mechanical products, equipment, systems and processes to meet requirements, applying knowledge of engineering principles.

16) Perform personnel functions, such as supervision of production workers, technicians, technologists and other engineers, and design of evaluation programs.

17) Develop and test models of alternate designs and processing methods to assess feasibility, operating condition effects, possible new applications and necessity of modification.

18) Specify system components or direct modification of products to ensure conformance with engineering design and performance specifications.

19) Read and interpret blueprints, technical drawings, schematics, and computer-generated reports.

20) Recommend design modifications to eliminate machine or system malfunctions.

17-2151.00 - Mining and Geological Engineers, Including Mining Safety Engineers

Determine the location and plan the extraction of coal, metallic ores, nonmetallic minerals, and building materials, such as stone and gravel. Work involves conducting preliminary surveys of deposits or undeveloped mines and planning their development; examining deposits or mines to determine whether they can be worked at a profit; making geological and topographical surveys; evolving methods of mining best suited to character, type, and size of deposits; and supervising mining operations.

Tasks

1) Inspect mining areas for unsafe structures, equipment, and working conditions.

2) Implement and coordinate mine safety programs, including the design and maintenance of protective and rescue equipment and safety devices.

3) Design, implement, and monitor the development of mines, facilities, systems, and equipment.

4) Devise solutions to problems of land reclamation and water and air pollution, such as methods of storing excavated soil and returning exhausted mine sites to natural states.

5) Examine maps, deposits, drilling locations, and/or mines in order to determine the location, size, accessibility, contents, value, and potential profitability of mineral, oil, and gas deposits.

6) Evaluate data in order to develop new mining products, equipment, or processes.

7) Supervise and coordinate the work of technicians, technologists, survey personnel, engineers, scientists and other mine personnel.

8) Monitor mine production rates in order to assess operational effectiveness.

9) Lay out, direct, and supervise mine construction operations, such as the construction of shafts and tunnels.

10) Prepare schedules, reports, and estimates of the costs involved in developing and operating mines.

11) Select locations and plan underground or surface mining operations, specifying processes, labor usage, and equipment that will result in safe, economical, and environmentally sound extraction of minerals and ores.

12) Select or develop mineral location, extraction, and production methods, based on factors such as safety, cost, and deposit characteristics.

13) Conduct or direct mining experiments in order to test or prove research findings.

14) Select or devise materials-handling methods and equipment to transport ore, waste materials, and mineral products efficiently and economically.

15) Design, develop, and implement computer applications for use in mining operations such as mine design, modeling, or mapping; or for monitoring mine conditions.

16) Test air to detect toxic gases and recommend measures to remove them, such as installation of ventilation shafts.

17) Design mining and mineral treatment equipment and machinery in collaboration with other engineering specialists.

17-2161.00 - Nuclear Engineers

Conduct research on nuclear engineering problems or apply principles and theory of nuclear science to problems concerned with release, control, and utilization of nuclear energy and nuclear waste disposal.

Tasks

1) Formulate equations that describe phenomena occurring during fission of nuclear fuels, and develop research models based on the equations.

2) Analyze available data and consult with other scientists in order to determine parameters of experimentation and suitability of analytical models.

3) Recommend preventive measures to be taken in the handling of nuclear technology, based on data obtained from operations monitoring or from evaluation of test results.

4) Design and oversee construction and operation of nuclear reactors and power plants and nuclear fuels reprocessing and reclamation systems.

5) Design and develop nuclear equipment such as reactor cores, radiation shielding, and associated instrumentation and control mechanisms.

6) Conduct tests of nuclear fuel behavior and cycles and performance of nuclear machinery and equipment, in order to optimize performance of existing plants.

7) Design and direct nuclear research projects in order to discover facts, to test or modify theoretical models, or to develop new theoretical models or new uses for current models.

8) Monitor nuclear facility operations in order to identify any design, construction, or operation practices that violate safety regulations and laws or that could jeopardize the safety of operations.

9) Develop new medical scanning technologies.

10) Direct operating and maintenance activities of operational nuclear power plants in order to ensure efficiency and conformity to safety standards.

11) Initiate corrective actions and/or order plant shutdowns in emergency situations.

12) Prepare construction project proposals that include cost estimates, and discuss proposals

with interested parties such as vendors, contractors, and nuclear facility review boards.

13) Write operational instructions to be used in nuclear plant operation and nuclear fuel and waste handling and disposal.

14) Design and develop nuclear weapons.

15) Synthesize analyses of test results, and use the results to prepare technical reports of findings and recommendations.

16) Examine accidents in order to obtain data that can be used to design preventive measures.

17) Perform experiments that will provide information about acceptable methods of nuclear material usage, nuclear fuel reclamation, and waste disposal.

17-2171.00 - Petroleum Engineers

Devise methods to improve oil and gas well production and determine the need for new or modified tool designs. Oversee drilling and offer technical advice to achieve economical and satisfactory progress.

Tasks

1) Simulate reservoir performance for different recovery techniques, using computer models.

2) Specify and supervise well modification and stimulation programs, in order to maximize oil and gas recovery.

3) Supervise the removal of drilling equipment, the removal of any waste, and the safe return of land to structural stability when wells or pockets are exhausted.

4) Take samples in order to assess the amount and quality of oil, the depth at which resources lie, and the equipment needed to properly extract them.

5) Write technical reports for engineering and management personnel.

6) Develop plans for oil and gas field drilling, and for product recovery and treatment.

7) Conduct engineering research experiments in order to improve or modify mining and oil machinery and operations.

8) Test machinery and equipment in order to ensure that it is safe and conforms to performance specifications.

9) Maintain records of drilling and production operations.

10) Inspect oil and gas wells in order to determine that installations are completed.

11) Design or modify mining and oil field machinery and tools, applying engineering principles.

12) Design and implement environmental controls on oil and gas operations.

13) Coordinate the installation, maintenance, and operation of mining and oil field equipment.

14) Assign work to staff in order to obtain maximum utilization of personnel.

15) Assess costs and estimate the production capabilities and economic value of oil and gas wells, in order to evaluate the economic viability of potential drilling sites.

16) Interpret drilling and testing information for personnel.

17) Evaluate findings in order to develop, design, or test equipment or processes.

18) Coordinate activities of workers engaged in research, planning, and development.

19) Assist engineering and other personnel to solve operating problems.

20) Analyze data in order to recommend placement of wells and supplementary processes to enhance production.

21) Monitor production rates, and plan rework processes in order to improve production.

22) Direct and monitor the completion and evaluation of wells, well testing, and well surveys.

17-3011.01 - Architectural Drafters

Prepare detailed drawings of architectural designs and plans for buildings and structures according to specifications provided by architect.

Tasks

1) Obtain and assemble data to complete architectural designs, visiting job sites to compile measurements as necessary.

2) Analyze building codes, by-laws, space and site requirements, and other technical documents and reports to determine their effect on architectural designs.

3) Coordinate structural, electrical and mechanical designs and determine a method of presentation in order to graphically represent building plans.

4) Draw rough and detailed scale plans for foundations, buildings and structures, based on preliminary concepts, sketches, engineering calculations, specification sheets and other data.

5) Lay out and plan interior room arrangements for commercial buildings, using computer-assisted drafting (CAD) equipment and software.

6) Create freehand drawings and lettering to accompany drawings.

7) Check dimensions of materials to be used and assign numbers to lists of materials.

8) Prepare colored drawings of landscape and interior designs for presentation to client.

9) Determine procedures and instructions to be followed, according to design specifications and quantity of required materials.

10) Represent architect on construction site, ensuring builder compliance with design specifications and advising on design corrections, under architect's supervision.

11) Supervise, coordinate, and inspect the work of draftspersons, technicians, and technologists on construction projects.

12) Reproduce drawings on copy machines or trace copies of plans and drawings, using transparent paper or cloth, ink, pencil, and standard drafting instruments.

13) Analyze technical implications of architect's design concept, calculating weights, volumes, and stress factors.

14) Prepare cost estimates, contracts, bidding documents and technical reports for specific projects under an architect's supervision.

15) Build landscape, architectural and display models.

16) Calculate heat loss and gain of buildings and structures to determine required equipment specifications, following standard procedures.

Knowledge	Knowledge Definitions
Design	Knowledge of design techniques, tools, and principles involved in production of precision technical plans, blueprints, drawings, and models.
Building and Construction	Knowledge of materials, methods, and the tools involved in the construction or repair of houses, buildings, or other structures such as highways and roads.
Mathematics	Knowledge of arithmetic, algebra, geometry, calculus, statistics, and their applications.
Computers and Electronics	Knowledge of circuit boards, processors, chips, electronic equipment, and computer hardware and software, including applications and programming.
English Language	Knowledge of the structure and content of the English language including the meaning and spelling of words, rules of composition, and grammar.
Engineering and Technology	Knowledge of the practical application of engineering science and technology. This includes applying principles, techniques, procedures, and equipment to the design and production of various goods and services.
Customer and Personal Service	Knowledge of principles and processes for providing customer and personal services. This includes customer needs assessment, meeting quality standards for services, and evaluation of customer satisfaction.
Public Safety and Security	Knowledge of relevant equipment, policies, procedures, and strategies to promote effective local, state, or national security operations for the protection of people, data, property, and institutions.
Administration and Management	Knowledge of business and management principles involved in strategic planning, resource allocation, human resources modeling, leadership technique, production methods, and coordination of people and resources.
Law and Government	Knowledge of laws, legal codes, court procedures, precedents, government regulations, executive orders, agency rules, and the democratic political process.
Physics	Knowledge and prediction of physical principles, laws, their interrelationships, and applications to understanding fluid, material, and atmospheric dynamics, and mechanical, electrical, atomic and sub- atomic structures and processes.
Production and Processing	Knowledge of raw materials, production processes, quality control, costs, and other techniques for maximizing the effective manufacture and distribution of goods.
Clerical	Knowledge of administrative and clerical procedures and systems such as word processing, managing files and records, stenography and transcription, designing forms, and other office procedures and terminology.
Mechanical	Knowledge of machines and tools, including their designs, uses, repair, and maintenance.
Psychology	Knowledge of human behavior and performance; individual differences in ability, personality, and interests; learning and motivation; psychological research methods; and the assessment and treatment of behavioral and affective disorders.
Geography	Knowledge of principles and methods for describing the features of land, sea, and air masses, including their physical characteristics, locations, interrelationships, and distribution of plant, animal, and human life.
Education and Training	Knowledge of principles and methods for curriculum and training design, teaching and instruction for individuals and groups, and the measurement of training effects.

Sales and Marketing	Knowledge of principles and methods for showing, promoting, and selling products or services. This includes marketing strategy and tactics, product demonstration, sales techniques, and sales control systems.
Fine Arts	Knowledge of the theory and techniques required to compose, produce, and perform works of music, dance, visual arts, drama, and sculpture.
Telecommunications	Knowledge of transmission, broadcasting, switching, control, and operation of telecommunications systems.
History and Archeology	Knowledge of historical events and their causes, indicators, and effects on civilizations and cultures.
Communications and Media	Knowledge of media production, communication, and dissemination techniques and methods. This includes alternative ways to inform and entertain via written, oral, and visual media.
Personnel and Human Resources	Knowledge of principles and procedures for personnel recruitment, selection, training, compensation and benefits, labor relations and negotiation, and personnel information systems.
Sociology and Anthropology	Knowledge of group behavior and dynamics, societal trends and influences, human migrations, ethnicity, cultures and their history and origins.
Economics and Accounting	Knowledge of economic and accounting principles and practices, the financial markets, banking and the analysis and reporting of financial data.
Transportation	Knowledge of principles and methods for moving people or goods by air, rail, sea, or road, including the relative costs and benefits.
Philosophy and Theology	Knowledge of different philosophical systems and religions. This includes their basic principles, values, ethics, ways of thinking, customs, practices, and their impact on human culture.
Foreign Language	Knowledge of the structure and content of a foreign (non-English) language including the meaning and spelling of words, rules of composition and grammar, and pronunciation.
Chemistry	Knowledge of the chemical composition, structure, and properties of substances and of the chemical processes and transformations that they undergo. This includes uses of chemicals and their interactions, danger signs, production techniques, and disposal methods.
Therapy and Counseling	Knowledge of principles, methods, and procedures for diagnosis, treatment, and rehabilitation of physical and mental dysfunctions, and for career counseling and guidance.
Medicine and Dentistry	Knowledge of the information and techniques needed to diagnose and treat human injuries, diseases, and deformities. This includes symptoms, treatment alternatives, drug properties and interactions, and preventive health-care measures.
Food Production	Knowledge of techniques and equipment for planting, growing, and harvesting food products (both plant and animal) for consumption, including storage/handling techniques.
Biology	Knowledge of plant and animal organisms, their tissues, cells, functions, interdependencies, and interactions with each other and the environment.

Skills — Skills Definitions

Active Listening	Giving full attention to what other people are saying, taking time to understand the points being made, asking questions as appropriate, and not interrupting at inappropriate times.
Coordination	Adjusting actions in relation to others' actions.
Active Learning	Understanding the implications of new information for both current and future problem-solving and decision-making.
Complex Problem Solving	Identifying complex problems and reviewing related information to develop and evaluate options and implement solutions.
Mathematics	Using mathematics to solve problems.
Reading Comprehension	Understanding written sentences and paragraphs in work related documents.
Critical Thinking	Using logic and reasoning to identify the strengths and weaknesses of alternative solutions, conclusions or approaches to problems.
Operations Analysis	Analyzing needs and product requirements to create a design.
Time Management	Managing one's own time and the time of others.
Speaking	Talking to others to convey information effectively.
Instructing	Teaching others how to do something.
Monitoring	Monitoring/Assessing performance of yourself, other individuals, or organizations to make improvements or take corrective action.
Learning Strategies	Selecting and using training/instructional methods and procedures appropriate for the situation when learning or teaching new things.
Technology Design	Generating or adapting equipment and technology to serve user needs.
Writing	Communicating effectively in writing as appropriate for the needs of the audience.
Social Perceptiveness	Being aware of others' reactions and understanding why they react as they do.
Service Orientation	Actively looking for ways to help people.

Persuasion	Persuading others to change their minds or behavior.
Quality Control Analysis	Conducting tests and inspections of products, services, or processes to evaluate quality or performance.
Science	Using scientific rules and methods to solve problems.
Judgment and Decision Making	Considering the relative costs and benefits of potential actions to choose the most appropriate one.
Equipment Selection	Determining the kind of tools and equipment needed to do a job.
Negotiation	Bringing others together and trying to reconcile differences.
Systems Evaluation	Identifying measures or indicators of system performance and the actions needed to improve or correct performance, relative to the goals of the system.
Systems Analysis	Determining how a system should work and how changes in conditions, operations, and the environment will affect outcomes.
Management of Personnel Resources	Motivating, developing, and directing people as they work, identifying the best people for the job.
Troubleshooting	Determining causes of operating errors and deciding what to do about it.
Management of Financial Resources	Determining how money will be spent to get the work done, and accounting for these expenditures.
Installation	Installing equipment, machines, wiring, or programs to meet specifications.
Programming	Writing computer programs for various purposes.
Management of Material Resources	Obtaining and seeing to the appropriate use of equipment, facilities, and materials needed to do certain work.
Operation and Control	Controlling operations of equipment or systems.
Operation Monitoring	Watching gauges, dials, or other indicators to make sure a machine is working properly.
Equipment Maintenance	Performing routine maintenance on equipment and determining when and what kind of maintenance is needed.
Repairing	Repairing machines or systems using the needed tools.

Ability — Ability Definitions

Visualization	The ability to imagine how something will look after it is moved around or when its parts are moved or rearranged.
Deductive Reasoning	The ability to apply general rules to specific problems to produce answers that make sense.
Information Ordering	The ability to arrange things or actions in a certain order or pattern according to a specific rule or set of rules (e.g., patterns of numbers, letters, words, pictures, mathematical operations).
Near Vision	The ability to see details at close range (within a few feet of the observer).
Inductive Reasoning	The ability to combine pieces of information to form general rules or conclusions (includes finding a relationship among seemingly unrelated events).
Finger Dexterity	The ability to make precisely coordinated movements of the fingers of one or both hands to grasp, manipulate, or assemble very small objects.
Oral Comprehension	The ability to listen to and understand information and ideas presented through spoken words and sentences.
Written Comprehension	The ability to read and understand information and ideas presented in writing.
Arm-Hand Steadiness	The ability to keep your hand and arm steady while moving your arm or while holding your arm and hand in one position.
Problem Sensitivity	The ability to tell when something is wrong or is likely to go wrong. It does not involve solving the problem, only recognizing there is a problem.
Originality	The ability to come up with unusual or clever ideas about a given topic or situation, or to develop creative ways to solve a problem.
Oral Expression	The ability to communicate information and ideas in speaking so others will understand.
Written Expression	The ability to communicate information and ideas in writing so others will understand.
Selective Attention	The ability to concentrate on a task over a period of time without being distracted.
Speech Clarity	The ability to speak clearly so others can understand you.
Mathematical Reasoning	The ability to choose the right mathematical methods or formulas to solve a problem.
Category Flexibility	The ability to generate or use different sets of rules for combining or grouping things in different ways.
Fluency of Ideas	The ability to come up with a number of ideas about a topic (the number of ideas is important, not their quality, correctness, or creativity).
Visual Color Discrimination	The ability to match or detect differences between colors, including shades of color and brightness.
Speech Recognition	The ability to identify and understand the speech of another person.
Manual Dexterity	The ability to quickly move your hand, your hand together with your arm, or your two hands to grasp, manipulate, or assemble objects.
Far Vision	The ability to see details at a distance.

Depth Perception	The ability to judge which of several objects is closer or farther away from you, or to judge the distance between you and an object.
Flexibility of Closure	The ability to identify or detect a known pattern (a figure, object, word, or sound) that is hidden in other distracting material.
Memorization	The ability to remember information such as words, numbers, pictures, and procedures.
Speed of Closure	The ability to quickly make sense of, combine, and organize information into meaningful patterns.
Control Precision	The ability to quickly and repeatedly adjust the controls of a machine or a vehicle to exact positions.
Number Facility	The ability to add, subtract, multiply, or divide quickly and correctly.
Perceptual Speed	The ability to quickly and accurately compare similarities and differences among sets of letters, numbers, objects, pictures, or patterns. The things to be compared may be presented at the same time or one after the other. This ability also includes comparing a presented object with a remembered object.
Time Sharing	The ability to shift back and forth between two or more activities or sources of information (such as speech, sounds, touch, or other sources).
Auditory Attention	The ability to focus on a single source of sound in the presence of other distracting sounds.
Multilimb Coordination	The ability to coordinate two or more limbs (for example, two arms, two legs, or one leg and one arm) while sitting, standing, or lying down. It does not involve performing the activities while the whole body is in motion.
Wrist-Finger Speed	The ability to make fast, simple, repeated movements of the fingers, hands, and wrists.
Spatial Orientation	The ability to know your location in relation to the environment or to know where other objects are in relation to you.
Trunk Strength	The ability to use your abdominal and lower back muscles to support part of the body repeatedly or continuously over time without 'giving out' or fatiguing.
Hearing Sensitivity	The ability to detect or tell the differences between sounds that vary in pitch and loudness.
Reaction Time	The ability to quickly respond (with the hand, finger, or foot) to a signal (sound, light, picture) when it appears.
Response Orientation	The ability to choose quickly between two or more movements in response to two or more different signals (lights, sounds, pictures). It includes the speed with which the correct response is started with the hand, foot, or other body part.
Rate Control	The ability to time your movements or the movement of a piece of equipment in anticipation of changes in the speed and/or direction of a moving object or scene.
Extent Flexibility	The ability to bend, stretch, twist, or reach with your body, arms, and/or legs.
Night Vision	The ability to see under low light conditions.
Gross Body Equilibrium	The ability to keep or regain your body balance or stay upright when in an unstable position.
Static Strength	The ability to exert maximum muscle force to lift, push, pull, or carry objects.
Gross Body Coordination	The ability to coordinate the movement of your arms, legs, and torso together when the whole body is in motion.
Dynamic Flexibility	The ability to quickly and repeatedly bend, stretch, twist, or reach out with your body, arms, and/or legs.
Stamina	The ability to exert yourself physically over long periods of time without getting winded or out of breath.
Explosive Strength	The ability to use short bursts of muscle force to propel oneself (as in jumping or sprinting), or to throw an object.
Speed of Limb Movement	The ability to quickly move the arms and legs.
Peripheral Vision	The ability to see objects or movement of objects to one's side when the eyes are looking ahead.
Glare Sensitivity	The ability to see objects in the presence of glare or bright lighting.
Sound Localization	The ability to tell the direction from which a sound originated.
Dynamic Strength	The ability to exert muscle force repeatedly or continuously over time. This involves muscular endurance and resistance to muscle fatigue.

Work_Activity	Work_Activity Definitions
Interacting With Computers	Using computers and computer systems (including hardware and software) to program, write software, set up functions, enter data, or process information.
Drafting, Laying Out, and Specifying Technical Dev	Providing documentation, detailed instructions, drawings, or specifications to tell others about how devices, parts, equipment, or structures are to be fabricated, constructed, assembled, modified, maintained, or used.
Getting Information	Observing, receiving, and otherwise obtaining information from all relevant sources.
Thinking Creatively	Developing, designing, or creating new applications, ideas, relationships, systems, or products, including artistic contributions.

Estimating the Quantifiable Characteristics of Pro	Estimating sizes, distances, and quantities; or determining time, costs, resources, or materials needed to perform a work activity.
Evaluating Information to Determine Compliance wit	Using relevant information and individual judgment to determine whether events or processes comply with laws, regulations, or standards.
Identifying Objects, Actions, and Events	Identifying information by categorizing, estimating, recognizing differences or similarities, and detecting changes in circumstances or events.
Making Decisions and Solving Problems	Analyzing information and evaluating results to choose the best solution and solve problems.
Organizing, Planning, and Prioritizing Work	Developing specific goals and plans to prioritize, organize, and accomplish your work.
Establishing and Maintaining Interpersonal Relatio	Developing constructive and cooperative working relationships with others, and maintaining them over time.
Communicating with Persons Outside Organization	Communicating with people outside the organization, representing the organization to customers, the public, government, and other external sources. This information can be exchanged in person, in writing, or by telephone or e-mail.
Updating and Using Relevant Knowledge	Keeping up-to-date technically and applying new knowledge to your job.
Communicating with Supervisors, Peers, or Subordin	Providing information to supervisors, co-workers, and subordinates by telephone, in written form, e-mail, or in person.
Analyzing Data or Information	Identifying the underlying principles, reasons, or facts of information by breaking down information or data into separate parts.
Processing Information	Compiling, coding, categorizing, calculating, tabulating, auditing, or verifying information or data.
Interpreting the Meaning of Information for Others	Translating or explaining what information means and how it can be used.
Monitor Processes, Materials, or Surroundings	Monitoring and reviewing information from materials, events, or the environment, to detect or assess problems.
Coordinating the Work and Activities of Others	Getting members of a group to work together to accomplish tasks.
Documenting/Recording Information	Entering, transcribing, recording, storing, or maintaining information in written or electronic/magnetic form.
Inspecting Equipment, Structures, or Material	Inspecting equipment, structures, or materials to identify the cause of errors or other problems or defects.
Scheduling Work and Activities	Scheduling events, programs, and activities, as well as the work of others.
Judging the Qualities of Things, Services, or Peop	Assessing the value, importance, or quality of things or people.
Controlling Machines and Processes	Using either control mechanisms or direct physical activity to operate machines or processes (not including computers or vehicles).
Performing Administrative Activities	Performing day-to-day administrative tasks such as maintaining information files and processing paperwork.
Resolving Conflicts and Negotiating with Others	Handling complaints, settling disputes, and resolving grievances and conflicts, or otherwise negotiating with others.
Provide Consultation and Advice to Others	Providing guidance and expert advice to management or other groups on technical, systems-, or process-related topics.
Developing and Building Teams	Encouraging and building mutual trust, respect, and cooperation among team members.
Developing Objectives and Strategies	Establishing long-range objectives and specifying the strategies and actions to achieve them.
Selling or Influencing Others	Convincing others to buy merchandise/goods or to otherwise change their minds or actions.
Training and Teaching Others	Identifying the educational needs of others, developing formal educational or training programs or classes, and teaching or instructing others.
Guiding, Directing, and Motivating Subordinates	Providing guidance and direction to subordinates, including setting performance standards and monitoring performance.
Monitoring and Controlling Resources	Monitoring and controlling resources and overseeing the spending of money.
Performing for or Working Directly with the Public	Performing for people or dealing directly with the public. This includes serving customers in restaurants and stores, and receiving clients or guests.
Assisting and Caring for Others	Providing personal assistance, medical attention, emotional support, or other personal care to others such as coworkers, customers, or patients.
Repairing and Maintaining Electronic Equipment	Servicing, repairing, calibrating, regulating, fine-tuning, or testing machines, devices, and equipment that operate primarily on the basis of electrical or electronic (not mechanical) principles.
Performing General Physical Activities	Performing physical activities that require considerable use of your arms and legs and moving your whole body, such as climbing, lifting, balancing, walking, stooping, and handling of materials.
Handling and Moving Objects	Using hands and arms in handling, installing, positioning, and moving materials, and manipulating things.
Coaching and Developing Others	Identifying the developmental needs of others and coaching, mentoring, or otherwise helping others to improve their knowledge or skills.

65

Staffing Organizational Units	Recruiting, interviewing, selecting, hiring, and promoting employees in an organization.
Operating Vehicles, Mechanized Devices, or Equipme	Running, maneuvering, navigating, or driving vehicles or mechanized equipment, such as forklifts, passenger vehicles, aircraft, or water craft.
Repairing and Maintaining Mechanical Equipment	Servicing, repairing, adjusting, and testing machines, devices, moving parts, and equipment that operate primarily on the basis of mechanical (not electronic) principles.

Work_Content	Work_Content Definitions
Indoors, Environmentally Controlled	How often does this job require working indoors in environmentally controlled conditions?
Importance of Being Exact or Accurate	How important is being very exact or highly accurate in performing this job?
Face-to-Face Discussions	How often do you have to have face-to-face discussions with individuals or teams in this job?
Work With Work Group or Team	How important is it to work with others in a group or team in this job?
Letters and Memos	How often does the job require written letters and memos?
Spend Time Sitting	How much does this job require sitting?
Electronic Mail	How often do you use electronic mail in this job?
Telephone	How often do you have telephone conversations in this job?
Contact With Others	How much does this job require the worker to be in contact with others (face-to-face, by telephone, or otherwise) in order to perform it?
Importance of Repeating Same Tasks	How important is repeating the same physical activities (e.g., key entry) or mental activities (e.g., checking entries in a ledger) over and over, without stopping, to performing this job?
Spend Time Using Your Hands to Handle, Control, or	How much does this job require using your hands to handle, control, or feel objects, tools or controls?
Structured versus Unstructured Work	To what extent is this job structured for the worker, rather than allowing the worker to determine tasks, priorities, and goals?
Freedom to Make Decisions	How much decision making freedom, without supervision, does the job offer?
Time Pressure	How often does this job require the worker to meet strict deadlines?
Sounds, Noise Levels Are Distracting or Uncomforta	How often does this job require working exposed to sounds and noise levels that are distracting or uncomfortable?
Spend Time Making Repetitive Motions	How much does this job require making repetitive motions?
Physical Proximity	To what extent does this job require the worker to perform job tasks in close physical proximity to other people?
Coordinate or Lead Others	How important is it to coordinate or lead others in accomplishing work activities in this job?
Deal With External Customers	How important is it to work with external customers or the public in this job?
Frequency of Conflict Situations	How often are there conflict situations the employee has to face in this job?
Level of Competition	To what extent does this job require the worker to compete or to be aware of competitive pressures?
Frequency of Decision Making	How frequently is the worker required to make decisions that affect other people, the financial resources, and/or the image and reputation of the organization?
Consequence of Error	How serious would the result usually be if the worker made a mistake that was not readily correctable?
Impact of Decisions on Co-workers or Company Resul	How do the decisions an employee makes impact the results of co-workers, clients or the company?
Deal With Unpleasant or Angry People	How frequently does the worker have to deal with unpleasant, angry, or discourteous individuals as part of the job requirements?
Responsibility for Outcomes and Results	How responsible is the worker for work outcomes and results of other workers?
Degree of Automation	How automated is the job?
Outdoors, Exposed to Weather	How often does this job require working outdoors, exposed to all weather conditions?
Public Speaking	How often do you have to perform public speaking in this job?
Spend Time Standing	How much does this job require standing?
Indoors, Not Environmentally Controlled	How often does this job require working indoors in non-controlled environmental conditions (e.g., warehouse without heat)?
Exposed to Hazardous Equipment	How often does this job require exposure to hazardous equipment?
Spend Time Walking and Running	How much does this job require walking and running?
Pace Determined by Speed of Equipment	How important is it to this job that the pace is determined by the speed of equipment or machinery? (This does not refer to keeping busy at all times on this job.)
Exposed to Contaminants	How often does this job require working exposed to contaminants (such as pollutants, gases, dust or odors)?
Exposed to High Places	How often does this job require exposure to high places?
Outdoors, Under Cover	How often does this job require working outdoors, under cover (e.g., structure with roof but no walls)?

Very Hot or Cold Temperatures	How often does this job require working in very hot (above 90 F degrees) or very cold (below 32 F degrees) temperatures?
In an Enclosed Vehicle or Equipment	How often does this job require working in a closed vehicle or equipment (e.g., car)?
Responsible for Others' Health and Safety	How much responsibility is there for the health and safety of others in this job?
Exposed to Hazardous Conditions	How often does this job require exposure to hazardous conditions?
Wear Common Protective or Safety Equipment such as	How much does this job require wearing common protective or safety equipment such as safety shoes, glasses, gloves, hard hats or live jackets?
Extremely Bright or Inadequate Lighting	How often does this job require working in extremely bright or inadequate lighting conditions?
Spend Time Bending or Twisting the Body	How much does this job require bending or twisting your body?
Spend Time Kneeling, Crouching, Stooping, or Crawl	How much does this job require kneeling, crouching, stooping, or crawling?
Spend Time Climbing Ladders, Scaffolds, or Poles	How much does this job require climbing ladders, scaffolds, or poles?
Exposed to Minor Burns, Cuts, Bites, or Stings	How often does this job require exposure to minor burns, cuts, bites, or stings?
Cramped Work Space, Awkward Positions	How often does this job require working in cramped work spaces that requires getting into awkward positions?
Deal With Physically Aggressive People	How frequently does this job require the worker to deal with physical aggression of violent individuals?
Spend Time Keeping or Regaining Balance	How much does this job require keeping or regaining your balance?
Wear Specialized Protective or Safety Equipment su	How much does this job require wearing specialized protective or safety equipment such as breathing apparatus, safety harness, full protection suits, or radiation protection?
In an Open Vehicle or Equipment	How often does this job require working in an open vehicle or equipment (e.g., tractor)?
Exposed to Disease or Infections	How often does this job require exposure to disease/infections?
Exposed to Radiation	How often does this job require exposure to radiation?
Exposed to Whole Body Vibration	How often does this job require exposure to whole body vibration (e.g., operate a jackhammer)?

Work_Styles	Work_Styles Definitions
Attention to Detail	Job requires being careful about detail and thorough in completing work tasks.
Dependability	Job requires being reliable, responsible, and dependable, and fulfilling obligations.
Stress Tolerance	Job requires accepting criticism and dealing calmly and effectively with high stress situations.
Cooperation	Job requires being pleasant with others on the job and displaying a good-natured, cooperative attitude.
Adaptability/Flexibility	Job requires being open to change (positive or negative) and to considerable variety in the workplace.
Analytical Thinking	Job requires analyzing information and using logic to address work-related issues and problems.
Integrity	Job requires being honest and ethical.
Concern for Others	Job requires being sensitive to others' needs and feelings and being understanding and helpful on the job.
Initiative	Job requires a willingness to take on responsibilities and challenges.
Self Control	Job requires maintaining composure, keeping emotions in check, controlling anger, and avoiding aggressive behavior, even in very difficult situations.
Achievement/Effort	Job requires establishing and maintaining personally challenging achievement goals and exerting effort toward mastering tasks.
Innovation	Job requires creativity and alternative thinking to develop new ideas for and answers to work-related problems.
Independence	Job requires developing one's own ways of doing things, guiding oneself with little or no supervision, and depending on oneself to get things done.
Persistence	Job requires persistence in the face of obstacles.
Leadership	Job requires a willingness to lead, take charge, and offer opinions and direction.
Social Orientation	Job requires preferring to work with others rather than alone, and being personally connected with others on the job.

Job Zone Component	Job Zone Component Definitions
Title	Job Zone Three: Medium Preparation Needed
Overall Experience	Previous work-related skill, knowledge, or experience is required for these occupations. For example, an electrician must have completed three or four years of apprenticeship or several years of vocational training, and often must have passed a licensing exam, in order to perform the job.

Job Training	Employees in these occupations usually need one or two years of training involving both on-the-job experience and informal training with experienced workers.
Job Zone Examples	These occupations usually involve using communication and organizational skills to coordinate, supervise, manage, or train others to accomplish goals. Examples include dental assistants, electricians, fish and game wardens, legal secretaries, personnel recruiters, and recreation workers.
SVP Range	(6.0 to < 7.0)
Education	Most occupations in this zone require training in vocational schools, related on-the-job experience, or an associate's degree. Some may require a bachelor's degree.

17-3011.02 - Civil Drafters

Prepare drawings and topographical and relief maps used in civil engineering projects, such as highways, bridges, pipelines, flood control projects, and water and sewerage control systems.

Tasks

1) Supervise or conduct field surveys, inspections or technical investigations to obtain data required to revise construction drawings.

2) Produce drawings using computer assisted drafting systems (CAD) or drafting machines or by hand using compasses, dividers, protractors, triangles and other drafting devices.

3) Correlate, interpret, and modify data obtained from topographical surveys, well logs, and geophysical prospecting reports.

4) Finish and duplicate drawings and documentation packages, according to required mediums and specifications for reproduction, using blueprinting, photography, or other duplicating methods.

5) Review rough sketches, drawings, specifications, and other engineering data received from civil engineers to ensure that they conform to design concepts.

6) Calculate excavation tonnage and prepare graphs and fill-hauling diagrams for use in earth-moving operations.

7) Calculate weights, volumes, and stress factors and their implications for technical aspects of designs.

8) Determine the order of work and method of presentation, such as orthographic or isometric drawing.

9) Explain drawings to production or construction teams and provide adjustments as necessary.

10) Locate and identify symbols located on topographical surveys to denote geological and geophysical formations or oil field installations.

11) Plot characteristics of boreholes for oil and gas wells from photographic subsurface survey recordings and other data, representing depth, degree and direction of inclination.

12) Determine quality, cost, strength and quantity of required materials, and enter figures on materials lists.

13) Supervise and train other technologists, technicians and drafters.

14) Draft plans and detailed drawings for structures, installations, and construction projects such as highways, sewage disposal systems, and dikes, working from sketches or notes.

17-3012.01 - Electronic Drafters

Draw wiring diagrams, circuit board assembly diagrams, schematics, and layout drawings used for manufacture, installation, and repair of electronic equipment.

Tasks

1) Key and program specified commands and engineering specifications into computer system to change functions and test final layout.

2) Supervise and coordinate work activities of workers engaged in drafting, designing layouts, assembling, and testing printed circuit boards.

3) Compare logic element configuration on display screen with engineering schematics and calculate figures to convert, redesign, and modify element.

4) Consult with engineers to discuss and interpret design concepts, and determine requirements of detailed working drawings.

5) Draft detail and assembly drawings of design components, circuitry and printed circuit boards, using computer-assisted equipment or standard drafting techniques and devices.

6) Examine electronic schematics and supporting documents to develop, compute, and verify specifications for drafting data, such as configuration of parts, dimensions, and tolerances.

7) Plot electrical test points on layout sheets, and draw schematics for wiring test fixture heads to frames.

8) Review work orders and procedural manuals and confer with vendors and design staff to resolve problems and modify design.

9) Copy drawings of printed circuit board fabrication, using print machine or blueprinting procedure.

10) Generate computer tapes of final layout design to produce layered photo masks and photo plotting design onto film.

11) Review blueprints to determine customer requirements and consult with assembler regarding schematics, wiring procedures, and conductor paths.

12) Train students to use drafting machines and to prepare schematic diagrams, block diagrams, control drawings, logic diagrams, integrated circuit drawings, and interconnection diagrams.

13) Locate files relating to specified design project in database library, load program into computer, and record completed job data.

17-3012.02 - Electrical Drafters

Develop specifications and instructions for installation of voltage transformers, overhead or underground cables, and related electrical equipment used to conduct electrical energy from transmission lines or high-voltage distribution lines to consumers.

Tasks

1) Draft working drawings, wiring diagrams, wiring connection specifications or cross-sections of underground cables, as required for instructions to installation crew.

2) Assemble documentation packages and produce drawing sets which are then checked by an engineer or an architect.

3) Use computer-aided drafting equipment and/or conventional drafting stations, technical handbooks, tables, calculators, and traditional drafting tools such as boards, pencils, protractors, and T-squares.

4) Measure factors that affect installation and arrangement of equipment, such as distances to be spanned by wire and cable.

5) Write technical reports and draw charts that display statistics and data.

6) Supervise and train other technologists, technicians and drafters.

7) Review completed construction drawings and cost estimates for accuracy and conformity to standards and regulations.

8) Explain drawings to production or construction teams and provide adjustments as necessary.

9) Determine the order of work and the method of presentation, such as orthographic or isometric drawing.

10) Visit proposed installation sites and draw rough sketches of location.

11) Draw master sketches to scale showing relation of proposed installations to existing facilities and exact specifications and dimensions.

12) Confer with engineering staff and other personnel to resolve problems.

13) Prepare and interpret specifications, calculating weights, volumes, and stress factors.

14) Study work order requests to determine type of service, such as lighting or power, demanded by installation.

17-3013.00 - Mechanical Drafters

Prepare detailed working diagrams of machinery and mechanical devices, including dimensions, fastening methods, and other engineering information.

Tasks

1) Lay out, draw, and reproduce illustrations for reference manuals and technical publications to describe operation and maintenance of mechanical systems.

2) Check dimensions of materials to be used and assign numbers to the materials.

3) Design scale or full-size blueprints of specialty items, such as furniture and automobile body or chassis components.

4) Lay out and draw schematic, orthographic, or angle views to depict functional relationships of components, assemblies, systems, and machines.

5) Position instructions and comments onto drawings.

6) Review and analyze specifications, sketches, drawings, ideas, and related data to assess factors affecting component designs and the procedures and instructions to be followed.

7) Confer with customer representatives to review schematics and answer questions pertaining to installation of systems.

8) Draw freehand sketches of designs, trace finished drawings onto designated paper for the

reproduction of blueprints, and reproduce working drawings on copy machines.

9) Modify and revise designs to correct operating deficiencies or to reduce production problems.

10) Shade or color drawings to clarify and emphasize details and dimensions and eliminate background, using ink, crayon, airbrush, and overlays.

11) Supervise and train other drafters, technologists, and technicians.

12) Develop detailed design drawings and specifications for mechanical equipment, dies/tools, and controls, using computer-assisted drafting (CAD) equipment.

13) Compute mathematical formulas to develop and design detailed specifications for components or machinery, using computer-assisted equipment.

17-3021.00 - Aerospace Engineering and Operations Technicians

Operate, install, calibrate, and maintain integrated computer/communications systems consoles, simulators, and other data acquisition, test, and measurement instruments and equipment to launch, track, position, and evaluate air and space vehicles. May record and interpret test data.

Tasks

1) Record and interpret test data on parts, assemblies, and mechanisms.

2) Adjust, repair or replace faulty components of test setups and equipment.

3) Inspect, diagnose, maintain, and operate test setups and equipment to detect malfunctions.

4) Confer with engineering personnel regarding details and implications of test procedures and results.

5) Finish vehicle instrumentation and deinstrumentation.

6) Exchange cooling system components in various vehicles.

7) Operate and calibrate computer systems and devices to comply with test requirements and to perform data acquisition and analysis.

8) Test aircraft systems under simulated operational conditions, performing systems readiness tests and pre- and post-operational checkouts, to establish design or fabrication parameters.

9) Identify required data, data acquisition plans and test parameters, setting up equipment to conform to these specifications.

10) Fabricate and install parts and systems to be tested in test equipment, using hand tools, power tools, and test instruments.

17-3022.00 - Civil Engineering Technicians

Apply theory and principles of civil engineering in planning, designing, and overseeing construction and maintenance of structures and facilities under the direction of engineering staff or physical scientists.

Tasks

1) Analyze proposed site factors and design maps, graphs, tracings, and diagrams to illustrate findings.

2) Respond to public suggestions and complaints.

3) Evaluate facility to determine suitability for occupancy and square footage availability.

4) Conduct materials test and analysis, using tools and equipment, and applying engineering knowledge.

5) Calculate dimensions, square footage, profile and component specifications, and material quantities, using calculator or computer.

6) Draft detailed dimensional drawings and design layouts for projects and to ensure conformance to specifications.

7) Develop plans and estimate costs for installation of systems, utilization of facilities, or construction of structures.

8) Prepare reports and document project activities and data.

9) Plan and conduct field surveys to locate new sites and analyze details of project sites.

10) Inspect project site and evaluate contractor work to detect design malfunctions and ensure conformance to design specifications and applicable codes.

11) Read and review project blueprints and structural specifications to determine dimensions of structure or system and material requirements.

12) Confer with supervisor to determine project details, such as plan preparation, acceptance testing, and evaluation of field conditions.

17-3023.01 - Electronics Engineering Technicians

Lay out, build, test, troubleshoot, repair, and modify developmental and production electronic components, parts, equipment, and systems, such as computer equipment, missile control instrumentation, electron tubes, test equipment, and machine tool numerical controls, applying principles and theories of electronics, electrical circuitry, engineering mathematics, electronic and electrical testing, and physics. Usually work under direction of engineering staff.

Tasks

1) Write reports and record data on testing techniques, laboratory equipment, and specifications to assist engineers.

2) Maintain working knowledge of state-of-the-art tools, software, etc., through reading and/or attending conferences, workshops or other training.

3) Read blueprints, wiring diagrams, schematic drawings, and engineering instructions for assembling electronics units, applying knowledge of electronic theory and components.

4) Provide user applications and engineering support and recommendations for new and existing equipment with regard to installation, upgrades and enhancement.

5) Provide customer support and education, working with users to identify needs, determine sources of problems and to provide information on product use.

6) Write computer or microprocessor software programs.

7) Research equipment and component needs, sources, competitive prices, delivery times and ongoing operational costs.

8) Perform preventative maintenance and calibration of equipment and systems.

9) Fabricate parts, such as coils, terminal boards, and chassis, using bench lathes, drills, or other machine tools.

10) Procure parts and maintain inventory and related documentation.

11) Maintain system logs and manuals to document testing and operation of equipment.

12) Survey satellite receival sites for proper signal level and provide technical assistance in dish location and installation, transporting dishes as necessary.

13) Build prototypes from rough sketches or plans.

14) Develop and upgrade preventative maintenance procedures for components, equipment, parts and systems.

15) Assemble, test, and maintain circuitry or electronic components according to engineering instructions, technical manuals, and knowledge of electronics, using hand and power tools.

16) Adjust and replace defective or improperly functioning circuitry and electronics components, using hand tools and soldering iron.

17) Design basic circuitry and draft sketches for clarification of details and design documentation under engineers' direction, using drafting instruments and computer aided design equipment.

18) Identify and resolve equipment malfunctions, working with manufacturers and field representatives as necessary to procure replacement parts.

17-3023.03 - Electrical Engineering Technicians

Apply electrical theory and related knowledge to test and modify developmental or operational electrical machinery and electrical control equipment and circuitry in industrial or commercial plants and laboratories. Usually work under direction of engineering staff.

Tasks

1) Install and maintain electrical control systems and solid state equipment.

2) Build, calibrate, maintain, troubleshoot and repair electrical instruments or testing equipment.

3) Collaborate with electrical engineers and other personnel to identify, define, and solve developmental problems.

4) Modify electrical prototypes, parts, assemblies, and systems to correct functional deviations.

5) Plan method and sequence of operations for developing and testing experimental electronic and electrical equipment.

6) Analyze and interpret test information to resolve design-related problems.

7) Set up and operate test equipment to evaluate performance of developmental parts, assemblies, or systems under simulated operating conditions, and record results.

8) Draw or modify diagrams and write engineering specifications to clarify design details and functional criteria of experimental electronics units.

9) Perform supervisory duties such as recommending work assignments, approving leaves and completing performance evaluations.

10) Prepare project cost and work-time estimates.

11) Review existing electrical engineering criteria to identify necessary revisions, deletions or amendments to outdated material.

12) Prepare contracts and initiate, review and coordinate modifications to contract specifications and plans throughout the construction process.

13) Visit construction sites to observe conditions impacting design and to identify solutions to technical design problems involving electrical systems equipment that arise during construction.

14) Write commissioning procedures for electrical installations.

15) Plan, schedule and monitor work of support personnel to assist supervisor.

16) Evaluate engineering proposals, shop drawings and design comments for sound electrical engineering practice and conformance with established safety and design criteria, and recommend approval or disapproval.

17) Assemble electrical and electronic systems and prototypes according to engineering data and knowledge of electrical principles, using hand tools and measuring instruments.

18) Conduct inspections for quality control and assurance programs, reporting findings and recommendations.

17-3025.00 - Environmental Engineering Technicians

Apply theory and principles of environmental engineering to modify, test, and operate equipment and devices used in the prevention, control, and remediation of environmental pollution, including waste treatment and site remediation. May assist in the development of environmental pollution remediation devices under direction of engineer.

Tasks

1) Inspect facilities to monitor compliance with regulations governing substances such as asbestos, lead, and wastewater.

2) Maintain process parameters and evaluate process anomalies.

3) Work with customers to assess the environmental impact of proposed construction and to develop pollution prevention programs.

4) Obtain product information, identify vendors and suppliers, and order materials and equipment to maintain inventory.

5) Receive, set up, test, and decontaminate equipment.

6) Arrange for the disposal of lead, asbestos and other hazardous materials.

7) Assist in the cleanup of hazardous material spills.

8) Develop work plans, including writing specifications and establishing material, manpower and facilities needs.

9) Conduct pollution surveys, collecting and analyzing samples such as air and ground water.

10) Perform laboratory work such as logging numerical and visual observations, preparing and packaging samples, recording test results, and performing photo documentation.

11) Perform environmental quality work in field and office settings.

12) Oversee support staff.

13) Perform statistical analysis and correction of air and/or water pollution data submitted by industry and other agencies.

14) Produce environmental assessment reports, tabulating data and preparing charts, graphs and sketches.

15) Provide technical engineering support in the planning of projects, such as wastewater treatment plants, to ensure compliance with environmental regulations and policies

16) Review technical documents to ensure completeness and conformance to requirements.

17) Improve chemical processes to reduce toxic emissions.

18) Review work plans to schedule activities.

19) Manage Government Impact Card purchases with environmental laboratories to support customers' projects.

17-3026.00 - Industrial Engineering Technicians

Apply engineering theory and principles to problems of industrial layout or manufacturing production, usually under the direction of engineering staff. May study and record time, motion, method, and speed involved in performance of production, maintenance, clerical, and other worker operations for such purposes as establishing standard production rates or improving efficiency.

Tasks

1) Observe worker using equipment to verify that equipment is being operated and maintained according to quality assurance standards.

2) Evaluate data and write reports to validate or indicate deviations from existing standards.

3) Recommend revision to methods of operation, material handling, equipment layout, or other changes to increase production or improve standards.

4) Prepare charts, graphs, and diagrams to illustrate workflow, routing, floor layouts, material handling, and machine utilization.

5) Study time, motion, methods, and speed involved in maintenance, production, and other operations to establish standard production rate and improve efficiency.

6) Record test data, applying statistical quality control procedures.

7) Aid in planning work assignments in accordance with worker performance, machine capacity, production schedules, and anticipated delays.

8) Interpret engineering drawings, schematic diagrams, or formulas and confer with management or engineering staff to determine quality and reliability standards.

9) Read worker logs, product processing sheets, and specification sheets, to verify that records adhere to quality assurance specifications.

10) Compile and evaluate statistical data to determine and maintain quality and reliability of products.

11) Select products for tests at specified stages in production process, and test products for performance characteristics and adherence to specifications.

12) Observe workers operating equipment or performing tasks to determine time involved and fatigue rate, using timing devices.

13) Recommend modifications to existing quality or production standards to achieve optimum quality within limits of equipment capability.

17-3027.00 - Mechanical Engineering Technicians

Apply theory and principles of mechanical engineering to modify, develop, and test machinery and equipment under direction of engineering staff or physical scientists.

Tasks

1) Review project instructions and blueprints to ascertain test specifications, procedures, and objectives, and test nature of technical problems, such as redesign.

2) Set up prototype and test apparatus and operate test controlling equipment to observe and record prototype test results.

3) Review project instructions and specifications to identify, modify and plan requirements fabrication, assembly and testing.

4) Test equipment, using test devices attached to generator, voltage regulator, or other electrical parts, such as generators or spark plugs.

5) Prepare parts sketches and write work orders and purchase requests to be furnished by outside contractors.

6) Estimate cost factors, including labor and material for purchased and fabricated parts and costs for assembly, testing, and installing.

7) Record test procedures and results, numerical and graphical data, and recommendations for changes in product or test methods.

8) Devise, fabricate, and assemble new or modified mechanical components for products, such as industrial machinery or equipment, and measuring instruments.

9) Set up and conduct tests of complete units and components under operational conditions to investigate proposals for improving equipment performance.

10) Confer with technicians and submit reports of test results to engineering department and recommend design or material changes.

11) Draft detail drawing or sketch for drafting room completion or to request parts fabrication by machine, sheet or wood shops.

12) Calculate required capacities for equipment of proposed system to obtain specified performance and submit data to engineering personnel for approval.

13) Discuss changes in design, method of manufacture and assembly, and drafting techniques and procedures with staff and coordinate corrections.

14) Analyze test results in relation to design or rated specifications and test objectives, and modify or adjust equipment to meet specifications.

15) Read dials and meters to determine amperage, voltage, electrical output and input at specific operating temperature to analyze parts performance.

16) Operate drill press, grinders, engine lathe, or other machines to modify parts tested or to fabricate experimental parts for testing.

17) Inspect lines and figures for clarity and return erroneous drawings to designer for correction.

17-3031.01 - Surveying Technicians

Adjust and operate surveying instruments, such as the theodolite and electronic distance-measuring equipment. and compile notes, make sketches and enter data into computers.

Tasks

1) Position and hold the vertical rods, or targets, that theodolite operators use for sighting in order to measure angles, distances, and elevations.

2) Place and hold measuring tapes when electronic distance-measuring equipment is not used.

3) Perform calculations to determine earth curvature corrections, atmospheric impacts on measurements, traverse closures and adjustments, azimuths, level runs, and placement of markers.

4) Lay out grids, and determine horizontal and vertical controls.

5) Record survey measurements and descriptive data, using notes, drawings, sketches, and inked tracings.

6) Adjust and operate surveying instruments such as prisms, theodolites, and electronic distance-measuring equipment.

7) Prepare topographic and contour maps of land surveyed, including site features and other relevant information such as charts, drawings, and survey notes.

8) Compile information necessary to stake projects for construction, using engineering plans.

9) Perform manual labor, such as cutting brush for lines, carrying stakes, rebar, and other heavy items, and stacking rods.

10) Conduct surveys to ascertain the locations of natural features and human-made structures on the Earth's surface, underground, and underwater, using electronic distance-measuring equipment and other surveying instruments.

11) Search for section corners, property irons, and survey points.

12) Maintain equipment and vehicles used by surveying crews.

13) Direct and supervise work of subordinate members of surveying parties.

14) Compare survey computations with applicable standards in order to determine adequacy of data.

15) Collect information needed to carry out new surveys, using source maps, previous survey data, photographs, computer records, and other relevant information.

16) Operate and manage land-information computer systems, performing tasks such as storing data, making inquiries, and producing plots and reports.

17) Provide assistance in the development of methods and procedures for conducting field surveys.

18) Set out and recover stakes, marks, and other monumentation.

17-3031.02 - Mapping Technicians

Calculate mapmaking information from field notes, and draw and verify accuracy of topographical maps.

Tasks

1) Trim, align, and join prints in order to form photographic mosaics, maintaining scaled distances between reference points.

2) Redraw and correct maps, such as revising parcel maps to reflect tax code area changes, using information from official records and surveys.

3) Monitor mapping work and the updating of maps in order to ensure accuracy, the inclusion of new and/or changed information, and compliance with rules and regulations.

4) Lay out and match aerial photographs in sequences in which they were taken, and identify any areas missing from photographs.

5) Form three-dimensional images of aerial photographs taken from different locations, using mathematical techniques and plotting instruments.

6) Compute and measure scaled distances between reference points in order to establish relative positions of adjoining prints and enable the creation of photographic mosaics.

7) Compare topographical features and contour lines with images from aerial photographs, old maps, and other reference materials in order to verify the accuracy of their identification.

8) Calculate latitudes, longitudes, angles, areas, and other information for mapmaking, using survey field notes and reference tables.

9) Complete detailed source and method notes detailing the location of routine and complex land parcels.

10) Analyze aerial photographs in order to detect and interpret significant military, industrial, resource, or topographical data.

11) Check all layers of maps in order to ensure accuracy, identifying and marking errors and making corrections.

12) Answer questions and provide information to the public and to staff members regarding assessment maps, surveys, boundaries, easements, property ownership, roads, zoning, and similar matters.

13) Produce and update overlay maps in order to show information boundaries, water locations, and topographic features on various base maps and at different scales.

14) Research resources such as survey maps and legal descriptions in order to verify property lines and to obtain information needed for mapping.

15) Identify, research, and resolve anomalies in legal land descriptions, referring issues to title and survey experts as appropriate.

16) Identify and compile database information in order to create maps in response to requests.

17) Enter GPS data, legal deeds, field notes, and land survey reports into GIS workstations so that information can be transformed into graphic land descriptions, such as maps and drawings.

18) Create survey description pages and historical records related to the mapping activities and specifications of section plats.

19) Determine scales, line sizes, and colors to be used for hard copies of computerized maps, using plotters.

20) Train staff members in duties such as tax mapping, the use of computerized mapping equipment, and the interpretation of source documents.

21) Produce representations of surface and mineral ownership layers, by interpreting legal survey plans.

22) Trace contours and topographic details in order to generate maps that denote specific land and property locations and geographic attributes.

23) Research and combine existing property information in order to describe property boundaries in relation to adjacent properties, taking into account parcel splits, combinations, and land boundary adjustments.

19-1012.00 - Food Scientists and Technologists

Use chemistry, microbiology, engineering, and other sciences to study the principles underlying the processing and deterioration of foods; analyze food content to determine levels of vitamins, fat, sugar, and protein; discover new food sources; research ways to make processed foods safe, palatable, and healthful; and apply food science knowledge to determine best ways to process, package, preserve, store, and distribute food.

Tasks

1) Develop new or improved ways of preserving, processing, packaging, storing, and delivering foods, using knowledge of chemistry, microbiology, and other sciences.

2) Search for substitutes for harmful or undesirable additives, such as nitrites.

3) Study the structure and composition of food, or the changes foods undergo in storage and processing.

4) Confer with process engineers, plant operators, flavor experts, and packaging and marketing specialists in order to resolve problems in product development.

5) Evaluate food processing and storage operations, and assist in the development of quality assurance programs for such operations.

6) Inspect food processing areas in order to ensure compliance with government regulations and standards for sanitation, safety, quality, and waste management standards.

7) Demonstrate products to clients.

8) Test new products for flavor, texture, color, nutritional content, and adherence to government and industry standards.

9) Check raw ingredients for maturity or stability for processing, and finished products for safety, quality and nutritional value.

10) Develop food standards and production specifications, safety and sanitary regulations, and waste management and water supply specifications.

19-1020.01 - Biologists

Research or study basic principles of plant and animal life, such as origin, relationship, development, anatomy, and functions.

Tasks

1) Communicate test results to state and federal representatives and general public.

2) Program and use computers to store, process and analyze data.

3) Collect and analyze biological data about relationships among and between organisms and

their environment.

4) Develop and maintain liaisons and effective working relations with groups and individuals, agencies, and the public to encourage cooperative management strategies or to develop information and interpret findings.

5) Study aquatic plants and animals and environmental conditions affecting them, such as radioactivity or pollution.

6) Identify, classify, and study structure, behavior, ecology, physiology, nutrition, culture, and distribution of plant and animal species.

7) Prepare environmental impact reports for industry, government, or publication.

8) Measure salinity, acidity, light, oxygen content, and other physical conditions of water to determine their relationship to aquatic life.

9) Study basic principles of plant and animal life, such as origin, relationship, development, anatomy, and functions.

10) Study and manage wild animal populations.

11) Supervise biological technicians and technologists and other scientists.

12) Prepare requests for proposals or statements of work.

13) Develop methods and apparatus for securing representative plant, animal, aquatic, or soil samples.

14) Study reactions of plants, animals, and marine species to parasites.

15) Plan and administer biological research programs for government, research firms, medical industries, or manufacturing firms.

16) Review reports such as those relating to land use classifications and recreational development for accuracy and adequacy.

17) Prepare plans for management of renewable resources.

18) Research environmental effects of present and potential uses of land and water areas, determining methods of improving environmental conditions or such outputs as crop yields.

19) Cultivate, breed, and grow aquatic life, such as lobsters, clams, or fish.

20) Develop pest management and control measures, and conduct risk assessments related to pest exclusion, using scientific methods.

21) Teach, supervise students and perform research at universities and colleges.

Knowledge	Knowledge Definitions
Biology	Knowledge of plant and animal organisms, their tissues, cells, functions, interdependencies, and interactions with each other and the environment.
Law and Government	Knowledge of laws, legal codes, court procedures, precedents, government regulations, executive orders, agency rules, and the democratic political process.
Chemistry	Knowledge of the chemical composition, structure, and properties of substances and of the chemical processes and transformations that they undergo. This includes uses of chemicals and their interactions, danger signs, production techniques, and disposal methods.
English Language	Knowledge of the structure and content of the English language including the meaning and spelling of words, rules of composition, and grammar.
Computers and Electronics	Knowledge of circuit boards, processors, chips, electronic equipment, and computer hardware and software, including applications and programming.
Customer and Personal Service	Knowledge of principles and processes for providing customer and personal services. This includes customer needs assessment, meeting quality standards for services, and evaluation of customer satisfaction.
Public Safety and Security	Knowledge of relevant equipment, policies, procedures, and strategies to promote effective local, state, or national security operations for the protection of people, data, property, and institutions.
Mathematics	Knowledge of arithmetic, algebra, geometry, calculus, statistics, and their applications.
Geography	Knowledge of principles and methods for describing the features of land, sea, and air masses, including their physical characteristics, locations, interrelationships, and distribution of plant, animal, and human life.
Engineering and Technology	Knowledge of the practical application of engineering science and technology. This includes applying principles, techniques, procedures, and equipment to the design and production of various goods and services.
Clerical	Knowledge of administrative and clerical procedures and systems such as word processing, managing files and records, stenography and transcription, designing forms, and other office procedures and terminology.
Administration and Management	Knowledge of business and management principles involved in strategic planning, resource allocation, human resources modeling, leadership technique, production methods, and coordination of people and resources.
Education and Training	Knowledge of principles and methods for curriculum and training design, teaching and instruction for individuals and groups, and the measurement of training effects.
Communications and Media	Knowledge of media production, communication, and dissemination techniques and methods. This includes alternative ways to inform and entertain via written, oral, and visual media.
Physics	Knowledge and prediction of physical principles, laws, their interrelationships, and applications to understanding fluid, material, and atmospheric dynamics, and mechanical, electrical, atomic and sub-atomic structures and processes.
Mechanical	Knowledge of machines and tools, including their designs, uses, repair, and maintenance.
Design	Knowledge of design techniques, tools, and principles involved in production of precision technical plans, blueprints, drawings, and models.
Transportation	Knowledge of principles and methods for moving people or goods by air, rail, sea, or road, including the relative costs and benefits.
Medicine and Dentistry	Knowledge of the information and techniques needed to diagnose and treat human injuries, diseases, and deformities. This includes symptoms, treatment alternatives, drug properties and interactions, and preventive health-care measures.
Building and Construction	Knowledge of materials, methods, and the tools involved in the construction or repair of houses, buildings, or other structures such as highways and roads.
Psychology	Knowledge of human behavior and performance; individual differences in ability, personality, and interests; learning and motivation; psychological research methods; and the assessment and treatment of behavioral and affective disorders.
History and Archeology	Knowledge of historical events and their causes, indicators, and effects on civilizations and cultures.
Personnel and Human Resources	Knowledge of principles and procedures for personnel recruitment, selection, training, compensation and benefits, labor relations and negotiation, and personnel information systems.
Telecommunications	Knowledge of transmission, broadcasting, switching, control, and operation of telecommunications systems.
Economics and Accounting	Knowledge of economic and accounting principles and practices, the financial markets, banking and the analysis and reporting of financial data.
Production and Processing	Knowledge of raw materials, production processes, quality control, costs, and other techniques for maximizing the effective manufacture and distribution of goods.
Sales and Marketing	Knowledge of principles and methods for showing, promoting, and selling products or services. This includes marketing strategy and tactics, product demonstration, sales techniques, and sales control systems.
Foreign Language	Knowledge of the structure and content of a foreign (non-English) language including the meaning and spelling of words, rules of composition and grammar, and pronunciation.
Therapy and Counseling	Knowledge of principles, methods, and procedures for diagnosis, treatment, and rehabilitation of physical and mental dysfunctions, and for career counseling and guidance.
Philosophy and Theology	Knowledge of different philosophical systems and religions. This includes their basic principles, values, ethics, ways of thinking, customs, practices, and their impact on human culture.
Sociology and Anthropology	Knowledge of group behavior and dynamics, societal trends and influences, human migrations, ethnicity, cultures and their history and origins.
Food Production	Knowledge of techniques and equipment for planting, growing, and harvesting food products (both plant and animal) for consumption, including storage/handling techniques.
Fine Arts	Knowledge of the theory and techniques required to compose, produce, and perform works of music, dance, visual arts, drama, and sculpture.

Skills	Skills Definitions
Science	Using scientific rules and methods to solve problems.
Reading Comprehension	Understanding written sentences and paragraphs in work related documents.
Time Management	Managing one's own time and the time of others.
Judgment and Decision Making	Considering the relative costs and benefits of potential actions to choose the most appropriate one.
Critical Thinking	Using logic and reasoning to identify the strengths and weaknesses of alternative solutions, conclusions or approaches to problems.
Active Listening	Giving full attention to what other people are saying, taking time to understand the points being made, asking questions as appropriate, and not interrupting at inappropriate times.
Writing	Communicating effectively in writing as appropriate for the needs of the audience.
Active Learning	Understanding the implications of new information for both current and future problem-solving and decision-making.

Complex Problem Solving	Identifying complex problems and reviewing related information to develop and evaluate options and implement solutions.
Equipment Selection	Determining the kind of tools and equipment needed to do a job.
Persuasion	Persuading others to change their minds or behavior.
Management of Material Resources	Obtaining and seeing to the appropriate use of equipment, facilities, and materials needed to do certain work.
Negotiation	Bringing others together and trying to reconcile differences.
Management of Financial Resources	Determining how money will be spent to get the work done, and accounting for these expenditures.
Coordination	Adjusting actions in relation to others' actions.
Monitoring	Monitoring/Assessing performance of yourself, other individuals, or organizations to make improvements or take corrective action.
Mathematics	Using mathematics to solve problems.
Management of Personnel Resources	Motivating, developing, and directing people as they work, identifying the best people for the job.
Speaking	Talking to others to convey information effectively.
Learning Strategies	Selecting and using training/instructional methods and procedures appropriate for the situation when learning or teaching new things.
Social Perceptiveness	Being aware of others' reactions and understanding why they react as they do.
Instructing	Teaching others how to do something.
Service Orientation	Actively looking for ways to help people.
Troubleshooting	Determining causes of operating errors and deciding what to do about it.
Quality Control Analysis	Conducting tests and inspections of products, services, or processes to evaluate quality or performance.
Operations Analysis	Analyzing needs and product requirements to create a design.
Systems Evaluation	Identifying measures or indicators of system performance and the actions needed to improve or correct performance, relative to the goals of the system.
Systems Analysis	Determining how a system should work and how changes in conditions, operations, and the environment will affect outcomes.
Equipment Maintenance	Performing routine maintenance on equipment and determining when and what kind of maintenance is needed.
Technology Design	Generating or adapting equipment and technology to serve user needs.
Operation Monitoring	Watching gauges, dials, or other indicators to make sure a machine is working properly.
Operation and Control	Controlling operations of equipment or systems.
Installation	Installing equipment, machines, wiring, or programs to meet specifications.
Repairing	Repairing machines or systems using the needed tools.
Programming	Writing computer programs for various purposes.

Ability	Ability Definitions
Oral Expression	The ability to communicate information and ideas in speaking so others will understand.
Inductive Reasoning	The ability to combine pieces of information to form general rules or conclusions (includes finding a relationship among seemingly unrelated events).
Near Vision	The ability to see details at close range (within a few feet of the observer).
Written Expression	The ability to communicate information and ideas in writing so others will understand.
Written Comprehension	The ability to read and understand information and ideas presented in writing.
Speech Clarity	The ability to speak clearly so others can understand you.
Information Ordering	The ability to arrange things or actions in a certain order or pattern according to a specific rule or set of rules (e.g., patterns of numbers, letters, words, pictures, mathematical operations).
Category Flexibility	The ability to generate or use different sets of rules for combining or grouping things in different ways.
Oral Comprehension	The ability to listen to and understand information and ideas presented through spoken words and sentences.
Problem Sensitivity	The ability to tell when something is wrong or is likely to go wrong. It does not involve solving the problem, only recognizing there is a problem.
Speech Recognition	The ability to identify and understand the speech of another person.
Deductive Reasoning	The ability to apply general rules to specific problems to produce answers that make sense.
Flexibility of Closure	The ability to identify or detect a known pattern (a figure, object, word, or sound) that is hidden in other distracting material.
Mathematical Reasoning	The ability to choose the right mathematical methods or formulas to solve a problem.
Finger Dexterity	The ability to make precisely coordinated movements of the fingers of one or both hands to grasp, manipulate, or assemble very small objects.

Selective Attention	The ability to concentrate on a task over a period of time without being distracted.
Auditory Attention	The ability to focus on a single source of sound in the presence of other distracting sounds.
Originality	The ability to come up with unusual or clever ideas about a given topic or situation, or to develop creative ways to solve a problem.
Fluency of Ideas	The ability to come up with a number of ideas about a topic (the number of ideas is important, not their quality, correctness, or creativity).
Visual Color Discrimination	The ability to match or detect differences between colors, including shades of color and brightness.
Perceptual Speed	The ability to quickly and accurately compare similarities and differences among sets of letters, numbers, objects, pictures, or patterns. The things to be compared may be presented at the same time or one after the other. This ability also includes comparing a presented object with a remembered object.
Speed of Closure	The ability to quickly make sense of, combine, and organize information into meaningful patterns.
Memorization	The ability to remember information such as words, numbers, pictures, and procedures.
Number Facility	The ability to add, subtract, multiply, or divide quickly and correctly.
Time Sharing	The ability to shift back and forth between two or more activities or sources of information (such as speech, sounds, touch, or other sources).
Far Vision	The ability to see details at a distance.
Multilimb Coordination	The ability to coordinate two or more limbs (for example, two arms, two legs, or one leg and one arm) while sitting, standing, or lying down. It does not involve performing the activities while the whole body is in motion.
Control Precision	The ability to quickly and repeatedly adjust the controls of a machine or a vehicle to exact positions.
Visualization	The ability to imagine how something will look after it is moved around or when its parts are moved or rearranged.
Depth Perception	The ability to judge which of several objects is closer or farther away from you, or to judge the distance between you and an object.
Arm-Hand Steadiness	The ability to keep your hand and arm steady while moving your arm or while holding your arm and hand in one position.
Hearing Sensitivity	The ability to detect or tell the differences between sounds that vary in pitch and loudness.
Trunk Strength	The ability to use your abdominal and lower back muscles to support part of the body repeatedly or continuously over time without 'giving out' or fatiguing.
Manual Dexterity	The ability to quickly move your hand, your hand together with your arm, or your two hands to grasp, manipulate, or assemble objects.
Spatial Orientation	The ability to know your location in relation to the environment or to know where other objects are in relation to you.
Static Strength	The ability to exert maximum muscle force to lift, push, pull, or carry objects.
Response Orientation	The ability to choose quickly between two or more movements in response to two or more different signals (lights, sounds, pictures). It includes the speed with which the correct response is started with the hand, foot, or other body part.
Night Vision	The ability to see under low light conditions.
Peripheral Vision	The ability to see objects or movement of objects to one's side when the eyes are looking ahead.
Reaction Time	The ability to quickly respond (with the hand, finger, or foot) to a signal (sound, light, picture) when it appears.
Wrist-Finger Speed	The ability to make fast, simple, repeated movements of the fingers, hands, and wrists.
Dynamic Strength	The ability to exert muscle force repeatedly or continuously over time. This involves muscular endurance and resistance to muscle fatigue.
Gross Body Equilibrium	The ability to keep or regain your body balance or stay upright when in an unstable position.
Glare Sensitivity	The ability to see objects in the presence of glare or bright lighting.
Extent Flexibility	The ability to bend, stretch, twist, or reach with your body, arms, and/or legs.
Sound Localization	The ability to tell the direction from which a sound originated.
Dynamic Flexibility	The ability to quickly and repeatedly bend, stretch, twist, or reach out with your body, arms, and/or legs.
Stamina	The ability to exert yourself physically over long periods of time without getting winded or out of breath.
Speed of Limb Movement	The ability to quickly move the arms and legs.
Rate Control	The ability to time your movements or the movement of a piece of equipment in anticipation of changes in the speed and/or direction of a moving object or scene.
Gross Body Coordination	The ability to coordinate the movement of your arms, legs, and torso together when the whole body is in motion.
Explosive Strength	The ability to use short bursts of muscle force to propel oneself (as in jumping or sprinting), or to throw an object.

Work_Activity	Work_Activity Definitions
Getting Information	Observing, receiving, and otherwise obtaining information from all relevant sources.
Interacting With Computers	Using computers and computer systems (including hardware and software) to program, write software, set up functions, enter data, or process information.
Documenting/Recording Information	Entering, transcribing, recording, storing, or maintaining information in written or electronic/magnetic form.
Identifying Objects, Actions, and Events	Identifying information by categorizing, estimating, recognizing differences or similarities, and detecting changes in circumstances or events.
Processing Information	Compiling, coding, categorizing, calculating, tabulating, auditing, or verifying information or data.
Monitor Processes, Materials, or Surroundings	Monitoring and reviewing information from materials, events, or the environment, to detect or assess problems.
Updating and Using Relevant Knowledge	Keeping up-to-date technically and applying new knowledge to your job.
Evaluating Information to Determine Compliance wit	Using relevant information and individual judgment to determine whether events or processes comply with laws, regulations, or standards.
Interpreting the Meaning of Information for Others	Translating or explaining what information means and how it can be used.
Organizing, Planning, and Prioritizing Work	Developing specific goals and plans to prioritize, organize, and accomplish your work.
Communicating with Supervisors, Peers, or Subordin	Providing information to supervisors, co-workers, and subordinates by telephone, in written form, e-mail, or in person.
Establishing and Maintaining Interpersonal Relatio	Developing constructive and cooperative working relationships with others, and maintaining them over time.
Analyzing Data or Information	Identifying the underlying principles, reasons, or facts of information by breaking down information or data into separate parts.
Making Decisions and Solving Problems	Analyzing information and evaluating results to choose the best solution and solve problems.
Communicating with Persons Outside Organization	Communicating with people outside the organization, representing the organization to customers, the public, government, and other external sources. This information can be exchanged in person, in writing, or by telephone or e-mail.
Thinking Creatively	Developing, designing, or creating new applications, ideas, relationships, systems, or products, including artistic contributions.
Performing for or Working Directly with the Public	Performing for people or dealing directly with the public. This includes serving customers in restaurants and stores, and receiving clients or guests.
Judging the Qualities of Things, Services, or Peop	Assessing the value, importance, or quality of things or people.
Provide Consultation and Advice to Others	Providing guidance and expert advice to management or other groups on technical, systems-, or process-related topics.
Resolving Conflicts and Negotiating with Others	Handling complaints, settling disputes, and resolving grievances and conflicts, or otherwise negotiating with others.
Scheduling Work and Activities	Scheduling events, programs, and activities, as well as the work of others.
Controlling Machines and Processes	Using either control mechanisms or direct physical activity to operate machines or processes (not including computers or vehicles).
Repairing and Maintaining Electronic Equipment	Servicing, repairing, calibrating, regulating, fine-tuning, or testing machines, devices, and equipment that operate primarily on the basis of electrical or electronic (not mechanical) principles.
Inspecting Equipment, Structures, or Material	Inspecting equipment, structures, or materials to identify the cause of errors or other problems or defects.
Operating Vehicles, Mechanized Devices, or Equipme	Running, maneuvering, navigating, or driving vehicles or mechanized equipment, such as forklifts, passenger vehicles, aircraft, or water craft.
Performing General Physical Activities	Performing physical activities that require considerable use of your arms and legs and moving your whole body, such as climbing, lifting, balancing, walking, stooping, and handling of materials.
Handling and Moving Objects	Using hands and arms in handling, installing, positioning, and moving materials, and manipulating things.
Developing Objectives and Strategies	Establishing long-range objectives and specifying the strategies and actions to achieve them.
Selling or Influencing Others	Convincing others to buy merchandise/goods or to otherwise change their minds or actions.
Coaching and Developing Others	Identifying the developmental needs of others and coaching, mentoring, or otherwise helping others to improve their knowledge or skills.
Performing Administrative Activities	Performing day-to-day administrative tasks such as maintaining information files and processing paperwork.
Estimating the Quantifiable Characteristics of Pro	Estimating sizes, distances, and quantities; or determining time, costs, resources, or materials needed to perform a work activity.
Training and Teaching Others	Identifying the educational needs of others, developing formal educational or training programs or classes, and teaching or instructing others.
Repairing and Maintaining Mechanical Equipment	Servicing, repairing, adjusting, and testing machines, devices, moving parts, and equipment that operate primarily on the basis of mechanical (not electronic) principles.
Coordinating the Work and Activities of Others	Getting members of a group to work together to accomplish tasks.
Assisting and Caring for Others	Providing personal assistance, medical attention, emotional support, or other personal care to others such as coworkers, customers, or patients.
Developing and Building Teams	Encouraging and building mutual trust, respect, and cooperation among team members.
Guiding, Directing, and Motivating Subordinates	Providing guidance and direction to subordinates, including setting performance standards and monitoring performance.
Monitoring and Controlling Resources	Monitoring and controlling resources and overseeing the spending of money.
Drafting, Laying Out, and Specifying Technical Dev	Providing documentation, detailed instructions, drawings, or specifications to tell others about how devices, parts, equipment, or structures are to be fabricated, constructed, assembled, modified, maintained, or used.
Staffing Organizational Units	Recruiting, interviewing, selecting, hiring, and promoting employees in an organization.

Work_Content	Work_Content Definitions
Face-to-Face Discussions	How often do you have to have face-to-face discussions with individuals or teams in this job?
Telephone	How often do you have telephone conversations in this job?
Electronic Mail	How often do you use electronic mail in this job?
Indoors, Environmentally Controlled	How often does this job require working indoors in environmentally controlled conditions?
Spend Time Sitting	How much does this job require sitting?
Sounds, Noise Levels Are Distracting or Uncomforta	How often does this job require working exposed to sounds and noise levels that are distracting or uncomfortable?
Importance of Being Exact or Accurate	How important is being very exact or highly accurate in performing this job?
Work With Work Group or Team	How important is it to work with others in a group or team in this job?
Letters and Memos	How often does the job require written letters and memos?
Structured versus Unstructured Work	To what extent is this job structured for the worker, rather than allowing the worker to determine tasks, priorities, and goals?
Contact With Others	How much does this job require the worker to be in contact with others (face-to-face, by telephone, or otherwise) in order to perform it?
In an Enclosed Vehicle or Equipment	How often does this job require working in a closed vehicle or equipment (e.g., car)?
Outdoors, Exposed to Weather	How often does this job require working outdoors, exposed to all weather conditions?
Physical Proximity	To what extent does this job require the worker to perform job tasks in close physical proximity to other people?
Freedom to Make Decisions	How much decision making freedom, without supervision, does the job offer?
Impact of Decisions on Co-workers or Company Resul	How do the decisions an employee makes impact the results of co-workers, clients or the company?
Deal With External Customers	How important is it to work with external customers or the public in this job?
Responsibility for Outcomes and Results	How responsible is the worker for work outcomes and results of other workers?
Time Pressure	How often does this job require the worker to meet strict deadlines?
Frequency of Decision Making	How frequently is the worker required to make decisions that affect other people, the financial resources, and/or the image and reputation of the organization?
Consequence of Error	How serious would the result usually be if the worker made a mistake that was not readily correctable?
Coordinate or Lead Others	How important is it to coordinate or lead others in accomplishing work activities in this job?
Wear Common Protective or Safety Equipment such as	How much does this job require wearing common protective or safety equipment such as safety shoes, glasses, gloves, hard hats or live jackets?
Exposed to Hazardous Conditions	How often does this job require exposure to hazardous conditions?
Level of Competition	To what extent does this job require the worker to compete or to be aware of competitive pressures?
Deal With Unpleasant or Angry People	How frequently does the worker have to deal with unpleasant, angry, or discourteous individuals as part of the job requirements?
Exposed to Contaminants	How often does this job require working exposed to contaminants (such as pollutants, gases, dust or odors)?
Public Speaking	How often do you have to perform public speaking in this job?
Responsible for Others' Health and Safety	How much responsibility is there for the health and safety of others in this job?
Very Hot or Cold Temperatures	How often does this job require working in very hot (above 90 F degrees) or very cold (below 32 F degrees) temperatures?

73

Extremely Bright or Inadequate Lighting	How often does this job require working in extremely bright or inadequate lighting conditions?
Spend Time Walking and Running	How much does this job require walking and running?
Exposed to Minor Burns, Cuts. Bites, or Stings	How often does this job require exposure to minor burns. cuts. bites, or stings?
Exposed to Hazardous Equipment	How often does this job require exposure to hazardous equipment?
In an Open Vehicle or Equipment	How often does this job require working in an open vehicle or equipment (e.g., tractor)?
Exposed to Whole Body Vibration	How often does this job require exposure to whole body vibration (e.g., operate a jackhammer)?
Importance of Repeating Same Tasks	How important is repeating the same physical activities (e.g.. key entry) or mental activities (e.g., checking entries in a ledger) over and over, without stopping, to performing this job?
Frequency of Conflict Situations	How often are there conflict situations the employee has to face in this job?
Indoors, Not Environmentally Controlled	How often does this job require working indoors in non-controlled environmental conditions (e.g., warehouse without heat)?
Spend Time Making Repetitive Motions	How much does this job require making repetitive motions?
Spend Time Standing	How much does this job require standing?
Spend Time Using Your Hands to Handle, Control, or	How much does this job require using your hands to handle. control, or feel objects. tools or controls?
Exposed to Disease or Infections	How often does this job require exposure to disease/infections?
Spend Time Kneeling, Crouching, Stooping, or Crawl	How much does this job require kneeling, crouching. stooping or crawling?
Spend Time Bending or Twisting the Body	How much does this job require bending or twisting your body?
Cramped Work Space, Awkward Positions	How often does this job require working in cramped work spaces that requires getting into awkward positions?
Outdoors, Under Cover	How often does this job require working outdoors. under cover (e.g., structure with roof but no walls)?
Spend Time Keeping or Regaining Balance	How much does this job require keeping or regaining your balance?
Degree of Automation	How automated is the job?
Exposed to High Places	How often does this job require exposure to high places?
Deal With Physically Aggressive People	How frequently does this job require the worker to deal with physical aggression of violent individuals?
Spend Time Climbing Ladders, Scaffolds, or Poles	How much does this job require climbing ladders, scaffolds, or poles?
Wear Specialized Protective or Safety Equipment su	How much does this job require wearing specialized protective or safety equipment such as breathing apparatus, safety harness, full protection suits, or radiation protection?
Pace Determined by Speed of Equipment	How important is it to this job that the pace is determined by the speed of equipment or machinery? (This does not refer to keeping busy at all times on this job.)
Exposed to Radiation	How often does this job require exposure to radiation?

Work_Styles	Work_Styles Definitions
Attention to Detail	Job requires being careful about detail and thorough in completing work tasks.
Analytical Thinking	Job requires analyzing information and using logic to address work-related issues and problems.
Integrity	Job requires being honest and ethical.
Cooperation	Job requires being pleasant with others on the job and displaying a good-natured, cooperative attitude.
Dependability	Job requires being reliable, responsible, and dependable, and fulfilling obligations.
Stress Tolerance	Job requires accepting criticism and dealing calmly and effectively with high stress situations.
Initiative	Job requires a willingness to take on responsibilities and challenges.
Persistence	Job requires persistence in the face of obstacles.
Independence	Job requires developing one's own ways of doing things, guiding oneself with little or no supervision, and depending on oneself to get things done.
Achievement/Effort	Job requires establishing and maintaining personally challenging achievement goals and exerting effort toward mastering tasks.
Leadership	Job requires a willingness to lead, take charge, and offer opinions and direction.
Self Control	Job requires maintaining composure, keeping emotions in check, controlling anger, and avoiding aggressive behavior, even in very difficult situations.
Adaptability/Flexibility	Job requires being open to change (positive or negative) and to considerable variety in the workplace.
Concern for Others	Job requires being sensitive to others' needs and feelings and being understanding and helpful on the job.

Innovation	Job requires creativity and alternative thinking to develop new ideas for and answers to work-related problems.
Social Orientation	Job requires preferring to work with others rather than alone, and being personally connected with others on the job.

Job Zone Component	Job Zone Component Definitions
Title	Job Zone Five: Extensive Preparation Needed
Overall Experience	Extensive skill, knowledge, and experience are needed for these occupations. Many require more than five years of experience. For example, surgeons must complete four years of college and an additional five to seven years of specialized medical training to be able to do their job.
Job Training	Employees may need some on-the-job training, but most of these occupations assume that the person will already have the required skills, knowledge, work-related experience, and/or training.
Job Zone Examples	These occupations often involve coordinating, training, supervising, or managing the activities of others to accomplish goals. Very advanced communication and organizational skills are required. Examples include athletic trainers, lawyers, managing editors, phyicists, social psychologists, and surgeons.
SVP Range	(8.0 and above)
Education	A bachelor's degree is the minimum formal education required for these occupations. However, many also require graduate school. For example, they may require a master's degree, and some require a Ph.D., M.D., or J.D. (law degree).

19-1022.00 - Microbiologists

Investigate the growth, structure, development, and other characteristics of microscopic organisms, such as bacteria, algae, or fungi. Includes medical microbiologists who study the relationship between organisms and disease or the effects of antibiotics on microorganisms.

Tasks

1) Conduct chemical analyses of substances, such as acids, alcohols, and enzymes.

2) Research use of bacteria and microorganisms to develop vitamins, antibiotics, amino acids, grain alcohol, sugars, and polymers.

3) Prepare technical reports and recommendations based upon research outcomes.

4) Perform tests on water, food and the environment to detect harmful microorganisms and to obtain information about sources of pollution and contamination.

5) Observe action of microorganisms upon living tissues of plants, higher animals, and other microorganisms, and on dead organic matter.

6) Isolate and make cultures of bacteria or other microorganisms in prescribed media, controlling moisture, aeration, temperature, and nutrition.

7) Examine physiological, morphological, and cultural characteristics, using microscope, to identify and classify microorganisms in human, water, and food specimens.

8) Supervise biological technologists and technicians and other scientists.

9) Develop new products and new methods of food and pharmaceutical supply preservation.

10) Study growth, structure, development, and general characteristics of bacteria and other microorganisms to understand their relationship to human, plant, and animal health.

11) Use a variety of specialized equipment such as electron microscopes, gas chromatographs and high pressure liquid chromatographs, electrophoresis units, thermocyclers, fluorescence activated cell sorters and phosphoimagers.

12) Isolate and tend microorganisms that break down pollutants or produce alternate sources of energy.

13) Conduct research to address agricultural issues such as increasing crop yield, combating crop damage and determining the effects of microorganisms on soil and agricultural products and insect control.

14) Investigate the relationship between organisms and disease, including the control of epidemics and the effects of antibiotics on microorganisms.

15) Study the structure and function of human, animal and plant tissues, cells, pathogens and toxins.

16) Provide laboratory services for health departments, for community environmental health programs and for physicians needing information for diagnosis and treatment.

19-1023.00 - Zoologists and Wildlife Biologists

Study the origins, behavior, diseases, genetics, and life processes of animals and wildlife. May specialize in wildlife research and management, including the collection and analysis of biological data to determine the environmental effects of present and potential use of land and water areas.

Tasks

1) Coordinate preventive programs to control the outbreak of wildlife diseases.

2) Study animals in their natural habitats, assessing effects of environment and industry on animals, interpreting findings and recommending alternative operating conditions for industry.

3) Study characteristics of animals such as origin, interrelationships, classification, life histories and diseases, development, genetics, and distribution.

4) Collect and dissect animal specimens and examine specimens under microscope.

5) Inventory or estimate plant and wildlife populations.

6) Organize and conduct experimental studies with live animals in controlled or natural surroundings.

7) Prepare collections of preserved specimens or microscopic slides for species identification and study of development or disease.

8) Design zoo education programs.

9) Oversee the care and distribution of zoo animals, working with curators and zoo directors to determine the best way to contain animals, maintain their habitats and manage facilities.

10) Perform administrative duties such as fundraising, public relations, budgeting, and supervision of zoo staff.

11) Procure animals for zoo exhibition and locate mates for them.

12) Disseminate information by writing reports and scientific papers or journal articles, and by making presentations and giving talks for schools, clubs, interest groups and park interpretive programs.

13) Make recommendations on management systems and planning for wildlife populations and habitat, consulting with stakeholders and the public at large to explore options.

14) Raise specimens for study and observation or for use in experiments.

19-1031.01 - Soil Conservationists

Plan and develop coordinated practices for soil erosion control, soil and water conservation, and sound land use.

Tasks

1) Compute design specifications for implementation of conservation practices, using survey and field information technical guides, engineering manuals, and calculator.

2) Manage field offices and involve staff in cooperative ventures.

3) Analyze results of investigations to determine measures needed to maintain or restore proper soil management.

4) Develop, conduct and/or participate in surveys, studies and investigations of various land uses, gathering information for use in developing corrective action plans.

5) Monitor projects during and after construction to ensure projects conform to design specifications.

6) Plan soil management and conservation practices, such as crop rotation, reforestation, permanent vegetation, contour plowing, or terracing, to maintain soil and conserve water.

7) Compile and interpret wetland biodata to determine extent and type of wetland and to aid in program formulation.

8) Compute cost estimates of different conservation practices based on needs of land users, maintenance requirements and life expectancy of practices.

9) Review grant applications and make funding recommendations.

10) Initiate, schedule and conduct annual audits and compliance checks of program implementation by local government.

11) Provide information, knowledge, expertise, and training to government agencies at all levels to solve water and soil management problems and to assure coordination of resource protection activities.

12) Participate on work teams to plan, develop, and implement water and land management programs and policies.

13) Apply principles of specialized fields of science, such as agronomy, soil science, forestry, or agriculture, to achieve conservation objectives.

14) Visit areas affected by erosion problems to seek sources and solutions.

15) Review proposed wetland restoration easements and provide technical recommendations.

16) Review annual reports of counties, conservation districts, and watershed management organizations, certifying compliance with mandated reporting requirements.

17) Review and approve amendments to comprehensive local water plans and conservation district plans.

18) Develop and maintain working relationships with local government staff and board members.

19) Respond to complaints and questions on wetland jurisdiction, providing information and clarification.

20) Provide access to programs and training to assist in completion of government groundwater protection plans.

21) Conduct fact-finding and mediation sessions among government units, landowners, and other agencies in order to resolve disputes.

22) Advise land users such as farmers and ranchers on conservation plans, problems and alternative solutions, and provide technical and planning assistance.

23) Survey property to mark locations and measurements, using surveying instruments.

24) Revisit land users to view implemented land use practices and plans.

19-1031.02 - Range Managers

Research or study range land management practices to provide sustained production of forage, livestock, and wildlife.

Tasks

1) Study forage plants and their growth requirements to determine varieties best suited to particular range.

2) Regulate grazing, and help ranchers plan and organize grazing systems in order to manage, improve and protect rangelands and maximize their use.

3) Maintain soil stability and vegetation for non-grazing uses, such as wildlife habitats and outdoor recreation.

4) Develop methods for protecting range from fire and rodent damage and for controlling poisonous plants.

5) Develop technical standards and specifications used to manage, protect and improve the natural resources of range lands and related grazing lands.

6) Develop new and improved instruments and techniques for activities such as range reseeding.

7) Study grazing patterns to determine number and kind of livestock that can be most profitably grazed and to determine the best grazing seasons.

8) Manage private livestock operations.

9) Study rangeland management practices and research range problems to provide sustained production of forage, livestock, and wildlife.

10) Tailor conservation plans to landowners' goals, such as livestock support, wildlife, or recreation.

11) Measure and assess vegetation resources for biological assessment companies, environmental impact statements, and rangeland monitoring programs.

12) Mediate agreements among rangeland users and preservationists as to appropriate land use and management.

13) Offer advice to rangeland users on water management, forage production methods, and control of brush.

14) Plan and implement revegetation of disturbed sites.

15) Plan and direct construction and maintenance of range improvements such as fencing, corrals, stock-watering reservoirs and soil-erosion control structures.

19-1031.03 - Park Naturalists

Plan, develop, and conduct programs to inform public of historical, natural, and scientific features of national, state, or local park.

Tasks

1) Take photographs and motion pictures for use in lectures and publications and to develop displays.

2) Construct historical, scientific, and nature visitor-center displays.

3) Interview specialists in desired fields to obtain and develop data for park information programs.

4) Conduct field trips to point out scientific, historic, and natural features of parks, forests, historic sites or other attractions.

5) Plan and develop audiovisual devices for public programs.

6) Prepare and present illustrated lectures and interpretive talks about park features.

7) Provide visitor services by explaining regulations; answering visitor requests, needs and complaints; and providing information about the park and surrounding areas.

8) Research stories regarding the area's natural history or environment.

9) Plan, organize and direct activities of seasonal staff members.

10) Perform routine maintenance on park structures.

11) Prepare brochures and write newspaper articles.

12) Survey park to determine forest conditions and distribution and abundance of fauna and flora.

13) Assist with operations of general facilities, such as visitor centers.

14) Perform emergency duties to protect human life, government property, and natural features of park.

15) Compile and maintain official park photographic and information files.

19-1032.00 - Foresters

Manage forested lands for economic, recreational, and conservation purposes. May inventory the type, amount, and location of standing timber, appraise the timber's worth, negotiate the purchase, and draw up contracts for procurement. May determine how to conserve wildlife habitats, creek beds, water quality, and soil stability, and how best to comply with environmental regulations. May devise plans for planting and growing new trees, monitor trees for healthy growth, and determine the best time for harvesting. Develop forest management plans for public and privately-owned forested lands.

Tasks

1) Direct, and participate in, forest-fire suppression.

2) Establish short- and long-term plans for management of forest lands and forest resources.

3) Supervise activities of other forestry workers.

4) Plan and implement projects for conservation of wildlife habitats and soil and water quality.

5) Plan and direct forest surveys and related studies and prepare reports and recommendations.

6) Choose and prepare sites for new trees, using controlled burning, bulldozers, or herbicides to clear weeds, brush, and logging debris.

7) Plan and supervise forestry projects, such as determining the type, number and placement of trees to be planted, managing tree nurseries, thinning forest and monitoring growth of new seedlings.

8) Analyze effect of forest conditions on tree growth rates and tree species prevalence and the yield, duration, seed production, growth viability, and germination of different species.

9) Perform inspections of forests or forest nurseries.

10) Monitor forest-cleared lands to ensure that they are reclaimed to their most suitable end use.

11) Conduct public educational programs on forest care and conservation.

12) Map forest area soils and vegetation to estimate the amount of standing timber and future value and growth.

13) Negotiate terms and conditions of agreements and contracts for forest harvesting, forest management and leasing of forest lands.

14) Determine methods of cutting and removing timber with minimum waste and environmental damage.

15) Study different tree species' classification, life history, light and soil requirements, adaptation to new environmental conditions and resistance to disease and insects.

16) Monitor wildlife populations and assess the impacts of forest operations on population and habitats.

17) Plan cutting programs and manage timber sales from harvested areas, assisting companies to achieve production goals.

18) Plan and direct construction and maintenance of recreation facilities, fire towers, trails, roads and bridges, ensuring that they comply with guidelines and regulations set for forested public lands.

19) Develop techniques for measuring and identifying trees.

20) Provide advice and recommendations, as a consultant on forestry issues, to private woodlot owners, firefighters, government agencies or to companies.

21) Subcontract with loggers or pulpwood cutters for tree removal and to aid in road layout.

22) Develop new techniques for wood or residue use.

23) Procure timber from private landowners.

24) Contact local forest owners and gain permission to take inventory of the type, amount, and location of all standing timber on the property.

Knowledge	Knowledge Definitions
Biology	Knowledge of plant and animal organisms, their tissues, cells, functions, interdependencies, and interactions with each other and the environment.
English Language	Knowledge of the structure and content of the English language including the meaning and spelling of words, rules of composition, and grammar.
Mathematics	Knowledge of arithmetic, algebra, geometry, calculus, statistics, and their applications.
Administration and Management	Knowledge of business and management principles involved in strategic planning, resource allocation, human resources modeling, leadership technique, production methods, and coordination of people and resources.
Computers and Electronics	Knowledge of circuit boards, processors, chips, electronic equipment, and computer hardware and software, including applications and programming.
Geography	Knowledge of principles and methods for describing the features of land, sea, and air masses, including their physical characteristics, locations, interrelationships, and distribution of plant, animal, and human life.
Customer and Personal Service	Knowledge of principles and processes for providing customer and personal services. This includes customer needs assessment, meeting quality standards for services, and evaluation of customer satisfaction.
Law and Government	Knowledge of laws, legal codes, court procedures, precedents, government regulations, executive orders, agency rules, and the democratic political process.
Education and Training	Knowledge of principles and methods for curriculum and training design, teaching and instruction for individuals and groups, and the measurement of training effects.
Communications and Media	Knowledge of media production, communication, and dissemination techniques and methods. This includes alternative ways to inform and entertain via written, oral, and visual media.
Mechanical	Knowledge of machines and tools, including their designs, uses, repair, and maintenance.
Psychology	Knowledge of human behavior and performance; individual differences in ability, personality, and interests; learning and motivation; psychological research methods; and the assessment and treatment of behavioral and affective disorders.
Clerical	Knowledge of administrative and clerical procedures and systems such as word processing, managing files and records, stenography and transcription, designing forms, and other office procedures and terminology.
Public Safety and Security	Knowledge of relevant equipment, policies, procedures, and strategies to promote effective local, state, or national security operations for the protection of people, data, property, and institutions.
Chemistry	Knowledge of the chemical composition, structure, and properties of substances and of the chemical processes and transformations that they undergo. This includes uses of chemicals and their interactions, danger signs, production techniques, and disposal methods.
Building and Construction	Knowledge of materials, methods, and the tools involved in the construction or repair of houses, buildings, or other structures such as highways and roads.
Transportation	Knowledge of principles and methods for moving people or goods by air, rail, sea, or road, including the relative costs and benefits.
Personnel and Human Resources	Knowledge of principles and procedures for personnel recruitment, selection, training, compensation and benefits, labor relations and negotiation, and personnel information systems.
Telecommunications	Knowledge of transmission, broadcasting, switching, control, and operation of telecommunications systems.
Physics	Knowledge and prediction of physical principles, laws, their interrelationships, and applications to understanding fluid, material, and atmospheric dynamics, and mechanical, electrical, atomic and sub-atomic structures and processes.
Engineering and Technology	Knowledge of the practical application of engineering science and technology. This includes applying principles, techniques, procedures, and equipment to the design and production of various goods and services.
Design	Knowledge of design techniques, tools, and principles involved in production of precision technical plans, blueprints, drawings, and models.
Production and Processing	Knowledge of raw materials, production processes, quality control, costs, and other techniques for maximizing the effective manufacture and distribution of goods.
Economics and Accounting	Knowledge of economic and accounting principles and practices, the financial markets, banking and the analysis and reporting of financial data.
Sales and Marketing	Knowledge of principles and methods for showing, promoting, and selling products or services. This includes marketing strategy and tactics, product demonstration, sales techniques, and sales control systems.
Sociology and Anthropology	Knowledge of group behavior and dynamics, societal trends and influences, human migrations, ethnicity, cultures and their history and origins.
History and Archeology	Knowledge of historical events and their causes, indicators, and effects on civilizations and cultures.

Philosophy and Theology	Knowledge of different philosophical systems and religions. This includes their basic principles, values, ethics, ways of thinking, customs, practices, and their impact on human culture.
Therapy and Counseling	Knowledge of principles, methods, and procedures for diagnosis, treatment, and rehabilitation of physical and mental dysfunctions, and for career counseling and guidance.
Foreign Language	Knowledge of the structure and content of a foreign (non-English) language including the meaning and spelling of words, rules of composition and grammar, and pronunciation.
Food Production	Knowledge of techniques and equipment for planting, growing, and harvesting food products (both plant and animal) for consumption, including storage/handling techniques.
Medicine and Dentistry	Knowledge of the information and techniques needed to diagnose and treat human injuries, diseases, and deformities. This includes symptoms, treatment alternatives, drug properties and interactions, and preventive health-care measures.
Fine Arts	Knowledge of the theory and techniques required to compose, produce, and perform works of music, dance, visual arts, drama, and sculpture.

Skills	Skills Definitions
Time Management	Managing one's own time and the time of others.
Coordination	Adjusting actions in relation to others' actions.
Science	Using scientific rules and methods to solve problems.
Critical Thinking	Using logic and reasoning to identify the strengths and weaknesses of alternative solutions, conclusions or approaches to problems.
Reading Comprehension	Understanding written sentences and paragraphs in work related documents.
Active Listening	Giving full attention to what other people are saying, taking time to understand the points being made, asking questions as appropriate, and not interrupting at inappropriate times.
Active Learning	Understanding the implications of new information for both current and future problem-solving and decision-making.
Mathematics	Using mathematics to solve problems.
Speaking	Talking to others to convey information effectively.
Management of Financial Resources	Determining how money will be spent to get the work done, and accounting for these expenditures.
Writing	Communicating effectively in writing as appropriate for the needs of the audience.
Operations Analysis	Analyzing needs and product requirements to create a design.
Judgment and Decision Making	Considering the relative costs and benefits of potential actions to choose the most appropriate one.
Complex Problem Solving	Identifying complex problems and reviewing related information to develop and evaluate options and implement solutions.
Quality Control Analysis	Conducting tests and inspections of products, services, or processes to evaluate quality or performance.
Equipment Selection	Determining the kind of tools and equipment needed to do a job.
Monitoring	Monitoring/Assessing performance of yourself, other individuals, or organizations to make improvements or take corrective action.
Instructing	Teaching others how to do something.
Social Perceptiveness	Being aware of others' reactions and understanding why they react as they do.
Management of Personnel Resources	Motivating, developing, and directing people as they work, identifying the best people for the job.
Service Orientation	Actively looking for ways to help people.
Persuasion	Persuading others to change their minds or behavior.
Learning Strategies	Selecting and using training/instructional methods and procedures appropriate for the situation when learning or teaching new things.
Troubleshooting	Determining causes of operating errors and deciding what to do about it.
Systems Analysis	Determining how a system should work and how changes in conditions, operations, and the environment will affect outcomes.
Negotiation	Bringing others together and trying to reconcile differences.
Operation Monitoring	Watching gauges, dials, or other indicators to make sure a machine is working properly.
Management of Material Resources	Obtaining and seeing to the appropriate use of equipment, facilities, and materials needed to do certain work.
Programming	Writing computer programs for various purposes.
Systems Evaluation	Identifying measures or indicators of system performance and the actions needed to improve or correct performance, relative to the goals of the system.
Operation and Control	Controlling operations of equipment or systems.
Equipment Maintenance	Performing routine maintenance on equipment and determining when and what kind of maintenance is needed.
Technology Design	Generating or adapting equipment and technology to serve user needs.
Repairing	Repairing machines or systems using the needed tools.
Installation	Installing equipment, machines, wiring, or programs to meet specifications.

Ability	Ability Definitions
Oral Expression	The ability to communicate information and ideas in speaking so others will understand.
Deductive Reasoning	The ability to apply general rules to specific problems to produce answers that make sense.
Oral Comprehension	The ability to listen to and understand information and ideas presented through spoken words and sentences.
Problem Sensitivity	The ability to tell when something is wrong or is likely to go wrong. It does not involve solving the problem, only recognizing there is a problem.
Written Comprehension	The ability to read and understand information and ideas presented in writing.
Category Flexibility	The ability to generate or use different sets of rules for combining or grouping things in different ways.
Inductive Reasoning	The ability to combine pieces of information to form general rules or conclusions (includes finding a relationship among seemingly unrelated events).
Speech Clarity	The ability to speak clearly so others can understand you.
Near Vision	The ability to see details at close range (within a few feet of the observer).
Originality	The ability to come up with unusual or clever ideas about a given topic or situation, or to develop creative ways to solve a problem.
Speech Recognition	The ability to identify and understand the speech of another person.
Information Ordering	The ability to arrange things or actions in a certain order or pattern according to a specific rule or set of rules (e.g., patterns of numbers, letters, words, pictures, mathematical operations).
Written Expression	The ability to communicate information and ideas in writing so others will understand.
Far Vision	The ability to see details at a distance.
Fluency of Ideas	The ability to come up with a number of ideas about a topic (the number of ideas is important, not their quality, correctness, or creativity).
Spatial Orientation	The ability to know your location in relation to the environment or to know where other objects are in relation to you.
Static Strength	The ability to exert maximum muscle force to lift, push, pull, or carry objects.
Time Sharing	The ability to shift back and forth between two or more activities or sources of information (such as speech, sounds, touch, or other sources).
Selective Attention	The ability to concentrate on a task over a period of time without being distracted.
Flexibility of Closure	The ability to identify or detect a known pattern (a figure, object, word, or sound) that is hidden in other distracting material.
Visualization	The ability to imagine how something will look after it is moved around or when its parts are moved or rearranged.
Multilimb Coordination	The ability to coordinate two or more limbs (for example, two arms, two legs, or one leg and one arm) while sitting, standing, or lying down. It does not involve performing the activities while the whole body is in motion.
Speed of Closure	The ability to quickly make sense of, combine, and organize information into meaningful patterns.
Depth Perception	The ability to judge which of several objects is closer or farther away from you, or to judge the distance between you and an object.
Mathematical Reasoning	The ability to choose the right mathematical methods or formulas to solve a problem.
Trunk Strength	The ability to use your abdominal and lower back muscles to support part of the body repeatedly or continuously over time without 'giving out' or fatiguing.
Dynamic Strength	The ability to exert muscle force repeatedly or continuously over time. This involves muscular endurance and resistance to muscle fatigue.
Finger Dexterity	The ability to make precisely coordinated movements of the fingers of one or both hands to grasp, manipulate, or assemble very small objects.
Control Precision	The ability to quickly and repeatedly adjust the controls of a machine or a vehicle to exact positions.
Visual Color Discrimination	The ability to match or detect differences between colors, including shades of color and brightness.
Arm-Hand Steadiness	The ability to keep your hand and arm steady while moving your arm or while holding your arm and hand in one position.
Reaction Time	The ability to quickly respond (with the hand, finger, or foot) to a signal (sound, light, picture) when it appears.
Memorization	The ability to remember information such as words, numbers, pictures, and procedures.
Perceptual Speed	The ability to quickly and accurately compare similarities and differences among sets of letters, numbers, objects, pictures, or patterns. The things to be compared may be presented at the same time or one after the other. This ability also includes comparing a presented object with a remembered object.

Auditory Attention	The ability to focus on a single source of sound in the presence of other distracting sounds.
Stamina	The ability to exert yourself physically over long periods of time without getting winded or out of breath.
Number Facility	The ability to add, subtract, multiply, or divide quickly and correctly.
Gross Body Coordination	The ability to coordinate the movement of your arms, legs, and torso together when the whole body is in motion.
Manual Dexterity	The ability to quickly move your hand, your hand together with your arm, or your two hands to grasp, manipulate, or assemble objects.
Peripheral Vision	The ability to see objects or movement of objects to one's side when the eyes are looking ahead.
Glare Sensitivity	The ability to see objects in the presence of glare or bright lighting.
Extent Flexibility	The ability to bend, stretch, twist, or reach with your body, arms, and/or legs.
Night Vision	The ability to see under low light conditions.
Speed of Limb Movement	The ability to quickly move the arms and legs.
Response Orientation	The ability to choose quickly between two or more movements in response to two or more different signals (lights, sounds, pictures). It includes the speed with which the correct response is started with the hand, foot, or other body part.
Gross Body Equilibrium	The ability to keep or regain your body balance or stay upright when in an unstable position.
Wrist-Finger Speed	The ability to make fast, simple, repeated movements of the fingers, hands, and wrists.
Rate Control	The ability to time your movements or the movement of a piece of equipment in anticipation of changes in the speed and/or direction of a moving object or scene.
Hearing Sensitivity	The ability to detect or tell the differences between sounds that vary in pitch and loudness.
Sound Localization	The ability to tell the direction from which a sound originated.
Dynamic Flexibility	The ability to quickly and repeatedly bend, stretch, twist, or reach out with your body, arms, and/or legs.
Explosive Strength	The ability to use short bursts of muscle force to propel oneself (as in jumping or sprinting), or to throw an object.

Work_Activity	Work_Activity Definitions
Documenting/Recording Information	Entering, transcribing, recording, storing, or maintaining information in written or electronic/magnetic form.
Organizing, Planning, and Prioritizing Work	Developing specific goals and plans to prioritize, organize, and accomplish your work.
Making Decisions and Solving Problems	Analyzing information and evaluating results to choose the best solution and solve problems.
Monitor Processes, Materials, or Surroundings	Monitoring and reviewing information from materials, events, or the environment, to detect or assess problems.
Communicating with Supervisors, Peers, or Subordin	Providing information to supervisors, co-workers, and subordinates by telephone, in written form, e-mail, or in person.
Communicating with Persons Outside Organization	Communicating with people outside the organization, representing the organization to customers, the public, government, and other external sources. This information can be exchanged in person, in writing, or by telephone or e-mail.
Processing Information	Compiling, coding, categorizing, calculating, tabulating, auditing, or verifying information or data.
Performing for or Working Directly with the Public	Performing for people or dealing directly with the public. This includes serving customers in restaurants and stores, and receiving clients or guests.
Getting Information	Observing, receiving, and otherwise obtaining information from all relevant sources.
Evaluating Information to Determine Compliance wit	Using relevant information and individual judgment to determine whether events or processes comply with laws, regulations, or standards.
Performing General Physical Activities	Performing physical activities that require considerable use of your arms and legs and moving your whole body, such as climbing, lifting, balancing, walking, stooping, and handling of materials.
Scheduling Work and Activities	Scheduling events, programs, and activities, as well as the work of others.
Analyzing Data or Information	Identifying the underlying principles, reasons, or facts of information by breaking down information or data into separate parts.
Resolving Conflicts and Negotiating with Others	Handling complaints, settling disputes, and resolving grievances and conflicts, or otherwise negotiating with others.
Interacting With Computers	Using computers and computer systems (including hardware and software) to program, write software, set up functions, enter data, or process information.
Identifying Objects, Actions, and Events	Identifying information by categorizing, estimating, recognizing differences or similarities, and detecting changes in circumstances or events.
Thinking Creatively	Developing, designing, or creating new applications, ideas, relationships, systems, or products, including artistic contributions.

Coordinating the Work and Activities of Others	Getting members of a group to work together to accomplish tasks.
Developing Objectives and Strategies	Establishing long-range objectives and specifying the strategies and actions to achieve them.
Establishing and Maintaining Interpersonal Relatio	Developing constructive and cooperative working relationships with others, and maintaining them over time.
Operating Vehicles, Mechanized Devices, or Equipme	Running, maneuvering, navigating, or driving vehicles or mechanized equipment, such as forklifts, passenger vehicles, aircraft, or water craft.
Estimating the Quantifiable Characteristics of Pro	Estimating sizes, distances, and quantities; or determining time, costs, resources, or materials needed to perform a work activity.
Updating and Using Relevant Knowledge	Keeping up-to-date technically and applying new knowledge to your job.
Judging the Qualities of Things, Services, or Peop	Assessing the value, importance, or quality of things or people.
Developing and Building Teams	Encouraging and building mutual trust, respect, and cooperation among team members.
Selling or Influencing Others	Convincing others to buy merchandise/goods or to otherwise change their minds or actions.
Controlling Machines and Processes	Using either control mechanisms or direct physical activity to operate machines or processes (not including computers or vehicles).
Provide Consultation and Advice to Others	Providing guidance and expert advice to management or other groups on technical, systems-, or process-related topics.
Interpreting the Meaning of Information for Others	Translating or explaining what information means and how it can be used.
Guiding, Directing, and Motivating Subordinates	Providing guidance and direction to subordinates, including setting performance standards and monitoring performance.
Training and Teaching Others	Identifying the educational needs of others, developing formal educational or training programs or classes, and teaching or instructing others.
Handling and Moving Objects	Using hands and arms in handling, installing, positioning, and moving materials, and manipulating things.
Monitoring and Controlling Resources	Monitoring and controlling resources and overseeing the spending of money.
Drafting, Laying Out, and Specifying Technical Dev	Providing documentation, detailed instructions, drawings, or specifications to tell others about how devices, parts, equipment, or structures are to be fabricated, constructed, assembled, modified, maintained, or used.
Assisting and Caring for Others	Providing personal assistance, medical attention, emotional support, or other personal care to others such as coworkers, customers, or patients.
Inspecting Equipment, Structures, or Material	Inspecting equipment, structures, or materials to identify the cause of errors or other problems or defects.
Performing Administrative Activities	Performing day-to-day administrative tasks such as maintaining information files and processing paperwork.
Coaching and Developing Others	Identifying the developmental needs of others and coaching, mentoring, or otherwise helping others to improve their knowledge or skills.
Repairing and Maintaining Mechanical Equipment	Servicing, repairing, adjusting, and testing machines, devices, moving parts, and equipment that operate primarily on the basis of mechanical (not electronic) principles.
Repairing and Maintaining Electronic Equipment	Servicing, repairing, calibrating, regulating, fine-tuning, or testing machines, devices, and equipment that operate primarily on the basis of electrical or electronic (not mechanical) principles.
Staffing Organizational Units	Recruiting, interviewing, selecting, hiring, and promoting employees in an organization.

Work_Content	Work_Content Definitions
Freedom to Make Decisions	How much decision making freedom, without supervision, does the job offer?
Electronic Mail	How often do you use electronic mail in this job?
Telephone	How often do you have telephone conversations in this job?
Structured versus Unstructured Work	To what extent is this job structured for the worker, rather than allowing the worker to determine tasks, priorities, and goals?
Face-to-Face Discussions	How often do you have to have face-to-face discussions with individuals or teams in this job?
Frequency of Decision Making	How frequently is the worker required to make decisions that affect other people, the financial resources, and/or the image and reputation of the organization?
Responsibility for Outcomes and Results	How responsible is the worker for work outcomes and results of other workers?
Work With Work Group or Team	How important is it to work with others in a group or team in this job?
Coordinate or Lead Others	How important is it to coordinate or lead others in accomplishing work activities in this job?
Impact of Decisions on Co-workers or Company Resul	How do the decisions an employee makes impact the results of co-workers, clients or the company?
Responsible for Others' Health and Safety	How much responsibility is there for the health and safety of others in this job?

Indoors, Environmentally Controlled	How often does this job require working indoors in environmentally controlled conditions?
In an Enclosed Vehicle or Equipment	How often does this job require working in a closed vehicle or equipment (e.g., car)?
Consequence of Error	How serious would the result usually be if the worker made a mistake that was not readily correctable?
Contact With Others	How much does this job require the worker to be in contact with others (face-to-face, by telephone, or otherwise) in order to perform it?
Letters and Memos	How often does the job require written letters and memos?
Level of Competition	To what extent does this job require the worker to compete or to be aware of competitive pressures?
Importance of Being Exact or Accurate	How important is being very exact or highly accurate in performing this job?
Deal With External Customers	How important is it to work with external customers or the public in this job?
Spend Time Sitting	How much does this job require sitting?
Outdoors, Exposed to Weather	How often does this job require working outdoors, exposed to all weather conditions?
Indoors, Not Environmentally Controlled	How often does this job require working indoors in non-controlled environmental conditions (e.g., warehouse without heat)?
Sounds, Noise Levels Are Distracting or Uncomforta	How often does this job require working exposed to sounds and noise levels that are distracting or uncomfortable?
Time Pressure	How often does this job require the worker to meet strict deadlines?
Wear Common Protective or Safety Equipment such as	How much does this job require wearing common protective or safety equipment such as safety shoes, glasses, gloves, hard hats or live jackets?
Importance of Repeating Same Tasks	How important is repeating the same physical activities (e.g., key entry) or mental activities (e.g., checking entries in a ledger) over and over, without stopping, to performing this job?
Exposed to Hazardous Equipment	How often does this job require exposure to hazardous equipment?
Exposed to Contaminants	How often does this job require working exposed to contaminants (such as pollutants, gases, dust or odors)?
Frequency of Conflict Situations	How often are there conflict situations the employee has to face in this job?
Very Hot or Cold Temperatures	How often does this job require working in very hot (above 90 F degrees) or very cold (below 32 F degrees) temperatures?
Deal With Unpleasant or Angry People	How frequently does the worker have to deal with unpleasant, angry, or discourteous individuals as part of the job requirements?
Exposed to Minor Burns, Cuts, Bites, or Stings	How often does this job require exposure to minor burns, cuts, bites, or stings?
Spend Time Making Repetitive Motions	How much does this job require making repetitive motions?
Spend Time Standing	How much does this job require standing?
Spend Time Walking and Running	How much does this job require walking and running?
Physical Proximity	To what extent does this job require the worker to perform job tasks in close physical proximity to other people?
Public Speaking	How often do you have to perform public speaking in this job?
Degree of Automation	How automated is the job?
Extremely Bright or Inadequate Lighting	How often does this job require working in extremely bright or inadequate lighting conditions?
Exposed to Hazardous Conditions	How often does this job require exposure to hazardous conditions?
Spend Time Using Your Hands to Handle, Control, or	How much does this job require using your hands to handle, control, or feel objects, tools or controls?
Spend Time Bending or Twisting the Body	How much does this job require bending or twisting your body?
Spend Time Keeping or Regaining Balance	How much does this job require keeping or regaining your balance?
Exposed to High Places	How often does this job require exposure to high places?
Spend Time Kneeling, Crouching, Stooping, or Crawl	How much does this job require kneeling, crouching, stooping or crawling?
Deal With Physically Aggressive People	How frequently does this job require the worker to deal with physical aggression of violent individuals?
Outdoors, Under Cover	How often does this job require working outdoors, under cover (e.g., structure with roof but no walls)?
Wear Specialized Protective or Safety Equipment su	How much does this job require wearing specialized protective or safety equipment such as breathing apparatus, safety harness, full protection suits, or radiation protection?
Cramped Work Space, Awkward Positions	How often does this job require working in cramped work spaces that requires getting into awkward positions?
In an Open Vehicle or Equipment	How often does this job require working in an open vehicle or equipment (e.g., tractor)?
Exposed to Whole Body Vibration	How often does this job require exposure to whole body vibration (e.g., operate a jackhammer)?
Spend Time Climbing Ladders, Scaffolds, or Poles	How much does this job require climbing ladders, scaffolds, or poles?
Exposed to Radiation	How often does this job require exposure to radiation?

Exposed to Disease or Infections	How often does this job require exposure to disease/infections?
Pace Determined by Speed of Equipment	How important is it to this job that the pace is determined by the speed of equipment or machinery? (This does not refer to keeping busy at all times on this job.)

Work_Styles	Work_Styles Definitions
Cooperation	Job requires being pleasant with others on the job and displaying a good-natured, cooperative attitude.
Independence	Job requires developing one's own ways of doing things, guiding oneself with little or no supervision, and depending on oneself to get things done.
Dependability	Job requires being reliable, responsible, and dependable, and fulfilling obligations.
Integrity	Job requires being honest and ethical.
Initiative	Job requires a willingness to take on responsibilities and challenges.
Attention to Detail	Job requires being careful about detail and thorough in completing work tasks.
Persistence	Job requires persistence in the face of obstacles.
Self Control	Job requires maintaining composure, keeping emotions in check, controlling anger, and avoiding aggressive behavior, even in very difficult situations.
Adaptability/Flexibility	Job requires being open to change (positive or negative) and to considerable variety in the workplace.
Concern for Others	Job requires being sensitive to others' needs and feelings and being understanding and helpful on the job.
Analytical Thinking	Job requires analyzing information and using logic to address work-related issues and problems.
Achievement/Effort	Job requires establishing and maintaining personally challenging achievement goals and exerting effort toward mastering tasks.
Innovation	Job requires creativity and alternative thinking to develop new ideas for and answers to work-related problems.
Leadership	Job requires a willingness to lead, take charge, and offer opinions and direction.
Social Orientation	Job requires preferring to work with others rather than alone, and being personally connected with others on the job.
Stress Tolerance	Job requires accepting criticism and dealing calmly and effectively with high stress situations.

Job Zone Component	Job Zone Component Definitions
Title	Job Zone Four: Considerable Preparation Needed
Overall Experience	A minimum of two to four years of work-related skill, knowledge, or experience is needed for these occupations. For example, an accountant must complete four years of college and work for several years in accounting to be considered qualified.
Job Training	Employees in these occupations usually need several years of work-related experience, on-the-job training, and/or vocational training.
Job Zone Examples	Many of these occupations involve coordinating, supervising, managing, or training others. Examples include accountants, chefs and head cooks, computer programmers, historians, pharmacists, and police detectives.
SVP Range	(7.0 to < 8.0)
Education	Most of these occupations require a four-year bachelor's degree, but some do not.

19-1041.00 - Epidemiologists

Investigate and describe the determinants and distribution of disease, disability, and other health outcomes and develop the means for prevention and control.

Tasks

1) Plan and direct studies to investigate human or animal disease, preventive methods, and treatments for disease.

2) Conduct research to develop methodologies, instrumentation and procedures for medical application, analyzing data and presenting findings.

3) Investigate diseases or parasites to determine cause and risk factors, progress, life cycle, or mode of transmission.

4) Provide expertise in the design, management and evaluation of study protocols and health status questionnaires, sample selection and analysis.

5) Prepare and analyze samples to study effects of drugs, gases, pesticides, or microorganisms on cell structure and tissue.

6) Plan, administer and evaluate health safety standards and programs to improve public health, conferring with health department, industry personnel, physicians and others.

7) Oversee public health programs, including statistical analysis, health care planning, surveillance systems, and public health improvement.

8) Consult with and advise physicians. educators, researchers, government health officials and others regarding medical applications of sciences. such as physics, biology, and chemistry.

9) Supervise professional. technical and clerical personnel.

10) Identify and analyze public health issues related to foodborne parasitic diseases and their impact on public policies or scientific studies or surveys.

11) Teach principles of medicine and medical and laboratory procedures to physicians, residents, students. and technicians.

19-1042.00 - Medical Scientists, Except Epidemiologists

Conduct research dealing with the understanding of human diseases and the improvement of human health. Engage in clinical investigation or other research, production, technical writing, or related activities.

Tasks

1) Conduct research to develop methodologies, instrumentation and procedures for medical application, analyzing data and presenting findings.

2) Evaluate effects of drugs, gases, pesticides, parasites, and microorganisms at various levels.

3) Follow strict safety procedures when handling toxic materials to avoid contamination.

4) Plan and direct studies to investigate human or animal disease, preventive methods, and treatments for disease.

5) Confer with health department. industry personnel, physicians, and others to develop health safety standards and public health improvement programs.

6) Study animal and human health and physiological processes.

7) Consult with and advise physicians, educators, researchers, and others regarding medical applications of physics, biology, and chemistry.

8) Teach principles of medicine and medical and laboratory procedures to physicians, residents, students, and technicians.

9) Use equipment such as atomic absorption spectrometers, electron microscopes, flow cytometers and chromatography systems.

10) Prepare and analyze organ, tissue and cell samples to identify toxicity, bacteria, or microorganisms, or to study cell structure.

11) Investigate cause, progress, life cycle, or mode of transmission of diseases or parasites.

19-2012.00 - Physicists

Conduct research into the phases of physical phenomena, develop theories and laws on the basis of observation and experiments, and devise methods to apply laws and theories to industry and other fields.

Tasks

1) Design computer simulations to model physical data so that it can be better understood.

2) Develop manufacturing, assembly, and fabrication processes of lasers, masers, infrared, and other light-emitting and light-sensitive devices.

3) Observe the structure and properties of matter, and the transformation and propagation of energy, using equipment such as masers, lasers, and telescopes, in order to explore and identify the basic principles governing these phenomena.

4) Perform complex calculations as part of the analysis and evaluation of data, using computers.

5) Report experimental results by writing papers for scientific journals or by presenting information at scientific conferences.

6) Collaborate with other scientists in the design, development, and testing of experimental, industrial, or medical equipment, instrumentation, and procedures.

7) Conduct application evaluations and analyze results in order to determine commercial, industrial, scientific. medical, military, or other uses for electro-optical devices.

8) Teach physics to students.

9) Advise authorities of procedures to be followed in radiation incidents or hazards, and assist in civil defense planning.

10) Conduct research pertaining to potential environmental impacts of atomic energy-related industrial development in order to determine licensing qualifications.

11) Develop standards of permissible concentrations of radioisotopes in liquids and gases.

12) Direct testing and monitoring of contamination of radioactive equipment, and recording of personnel and plant area radiation exposure data.

13) Describe and express observations and conclusions in mathematical terms.

14) Develop theories and laws on the basis of observation and experiments. and apply these theories and laws to problems in areas such as nuclear energy. optics, and aerospace technology.

15) Analyze data from research conducted to detect and measure physical phenomena.

19-2031.00 - Chemists

Conduct qualitative and quantitative chemical analyses or chemical experiments in laboratories for quality or process control or to develop new products or knowledge.

Tasks

1) Confer with scientists and engineers to conduct analyses of research projects. interpret test results, or develop nonstandard tests.

2) Prepare test solutions, compounds, and reagents for laboratory personnel to conduct test.

3) Write technical papers and reports; and prepare standards and specifications for processes, facilities, products, and tests.

4) Analyze organic and inorganic compounds to determine chemical and physical properties, composition, structure, relationships, and reactions, utilizing chromatography. spectroscopy, and spectrophotometry techniques.

5) Study effects of various methods of processing, preserving. and packaging on composition and properties of foods.

6) Compile and analyze test information to determine process or equipment operating efficiency and to diagnose malfunctions.

7) Direct, coordinate, and advise personnel in test procedures for analyzing components and physical properties of materials.

8) Develop, improve, and customize products, equipment, formulas. processes, and analytical methods.

19-2032.00 - Materials Scientists

Research and study the structures and chemical properties of various natural and manmade materials, including metals, alloys, rubber, ceramics, semiconductors, polymers, and glass. Determine ways to strengthen or combine materials or develop new materials with new or specific properties for use in a variety of products and applications.

Tasks

1) Test metals in order to determine whether they meet specifications of mechanical strength, strength-weight ratio, ductility, magnetic and electrical properties, and resistance to abrasion, corrosion, heat and cold.

2) Study the nature, structure and physical properties of metals and their alloys, and their responses to applied forces.

3) Conduct research into the structures and properties of materials, such as metals, alloys, polymers, and ceramics in order to obtain information that could be used to develop new products or enhance existing ones.

4) Determine ways to strengthen or combine materials, or develop new materials with new or specific properties for use in a variety of products and applications.

5) Devise testing methods to evaluate the effects of various conditions on particular materials.

6) Prepare reports of materials study findings for the use of other scientists and requestors.

7) Test material samples for tolerance under tension, compression and shear, to determine the cause of metal failures.

8) Research methods of processing, forming, and firing materials in order to develop such products as ceramic fillings for teeth, unbreakable dinner plates, and telescope lenses.

9) Confer with customers in order to determine how materials can be tailored to suit their needs.

10) Monitor production processes in order to ensure that equipment is used efficiently and that projects are completed within appropriate time frames and budgets.

11) Receive molten metal from smelters, and further alloy and refine it in oxygen. open-hearth or other kinds of furnaces.

12) Visit suppliers of materials or users of products in order to gather specific information.

13) Test individual parts and products in order to ensure that manufacturer and governmental quality and safety standards are met.

14) Teach in colleges and universities.

15) Recommend materials for reliable performance in various environments.

19-2041.00 - Environmental Scientists and Specialists,

Including Health

Conduct research or perform investigation for the purpose of identifying, abating, or eliminating sources of pollutants or hazards that affect either the environment or the health of the population. Utilizing knowledge of various scientific disciplines may collect, synthesize, study, report, and take action based on data derived from measurements or observations of air, food, soil, water, and other sources.

Tasks

1) Conduct environmental audits and inspections, and investigations of violations.

2) Design and direct studies to obtain technical environmental information about planned projects.

3) Analyze data to determine validity, quality, and scientific significance, and to interpret correlations between human activities and environmental effects.

4) Determine data collection methods to be employed in research projects and surveys.

5) Conduct applied research on topics such as waste control and treatment and pollution control methods.

6) Develop methods to minimize the impact of production processes on the environment, based on the study and assessment of industrial production, environmental legislation, and physical, biological, and social environments.

7) Investigate and report on accidents affecting the environment.

8) Provide technical guidance, support, and oversight to environmental programs, industry, and the public.

9) Prepare charts or graphs from data samples, and provide summary information on the environmental relevance of the data.

10) Evaluate violations or problems discovered during inspections in order to determine appropriate regulatory actions or to provide advice on the development and prosecution of regulatory cases.

11) Review and implement environmental technical standards, guidelines, policies, and formal regulations that meet all appropriate requirements.

12) Provide advice on proper standards and regulations and the development of policies, strategies, and codes of practice for environmental management.

13) Research sources of pollution to determine their effects on the environment and to develop theories or methods of pollution abatement or control.

14) Communicate scientific and technical information through oral briefings, written documents, workshops, conferences, and public hearings.

15) Develop programs designed to obtain the most productive, non-damaging use of land.

16) Monitor effects of pollution and land degradation, and recommend means of prevention or control.

17) Supervise environmental technologists and technicians.

18) Develop the technical portions of legal documents, administrative orders, or consent decrees.

19) Collect, synthesize, and analyze data derived from pollution emission measurements, atmospheric monitoring, meteorological and mineralogical information, and soil or water samples.

20) Plan and develop research models using knowledge of mathematical and statistical concepts.

19-2042.01 - Geologists

Study composition, structure, and history of the earth's crust; examine rocks, minerals, and fossil remains to identify and determine the sequence of processes affecting the development of the earth; apply knowledge of chemistry, physics, biology, and mathematics to explain these phenomena and to help locate mineral and petroleum deposits and underground water resources; prepare geologic reports and maps; and interpret research data to recommend further action for study.

Tasks

1) Develop applied software for the analysis and interpretation of geological data.

2) Assess ground and surface water movement in order to provide advice regarding issues such as waste management, route and site selection, and the restoration of contaminated sites.

3) Identify risks for natural disasters such as mud slides, earthquakes, and volcanic eruptions, and provide advice on ways in which potential damage can be mitigated.

4) Investigate the composition, structure, and history of the Earth's crust through the collection, examination, measurement, and classification of soils, minerals, rocks, and fossil remains.

5) Measure characteristics of the Earth, such as gravity and magnetic fields, using equipment such as seismographs, gravimeters, torsion balances, and magnetometers.

6) Plan and conduct geological, geochemical, and geophysical field studies and surveys; sample collection; and drilling and testing programs used to collect data for research and/or application.

7) Test industrial diamonds and abrasives, soil, or rocks in order to determine their geological characteristics, using optical, x-ray, heat, acid, and precision instruments.

8) Advise construction firms and government agencies on dam and road construction, foundation design, and land use and resource management.

9) Analyze and interpret geological, geochemical, and geophysical information from sources such as survey data, well logs, boreholes, and aerial photos.

10) Develop instruments for geological work, such as diamond tools and dies, jeweled bearings, and grinding laps and wheels.

11) Inspect construction projects in order to analyze engineering problems, applying geological knowledge and using test equipment and drilling machinery.

12) Locate and estimate probable natural gas, oil, and mineral ore deposits and underground water resources, using aerial photographs, charts, and research and survey results.

13) Prepare geological maps, cross-sectional diagrams, charts, and reports concerning mineral extraction, land use, and resource management, using results of field work and laboratory research.

14) Communicate geological findings by writing research papers, participating in conferences, and/or teaching geological science at universities.

15) Conduct geological and geophysical studies to provide information for use in regional development, site selection, and the development of public works projects.

19-3011.00 - Economists

Conduct research, prepare reports, or formulate plans to aid in solution of economic problems arising from production and distribution of goods and services. May collect and process economic and statistical data using econometric and sampling techniques.

Tasks

1) Forecast production and consumption of renewable resources and supply, consumption and depletion of non-renewable resources.

2) Formulate recommendations, policies, or plans to solve economic problems or to interpret markets.

3) Compile, analyze, and report data to explain economic phenomena and forecast market trends, applying mathematical models and statistical techniques.

4) Develop economic guidelines and standards and prepare points of view used in forecasting trends and formulating economic policy.

5) Supervise research projects and students' study projects.

6) Testify at regulatory or legislative hearings concerning the estimated effects of changes in legislation or public policy and present recommendations based on cost-benefit analyses.

7) Teach theories, principles, and methods of economics.

8) Provide advice and consultation on economic relationships to businesses, public and private agencies, and other employers.

19-3021.00 - Market Research Analysts

Research market conditions in local, regional, or national areas to determine potential sales of a product or service. May gather information on competitors, prices, sales, and methods of marketing and distribution. May use survey results to create a marketing campaign based on regional preferences and buying habits.

Tasks

1) Develop and implement procedures for identifying advertising needs.

2) Conduct research on consumer opinions and marketing strategies, collaborating with marketing professionals, statisticians, pollsters, and other professionals.

3) Devise and evaluate methods and procedures for collecting data (such as surveys, opinion polls, or questionnaires), or arrange to obtain existing data.

4) Gather data on competitors and analyze their prices, sales, and method of marketing and distribution.

5) Monitor industry statistics and follow trends in trade literature.

6) Prepare reports of findings, illustrating data graphically and translating complex findings into written text.

7) Attend staff conferences to provide management with information and proposals concerning the promotion, distribution, design, and pricing of company products or services.

8) Direct trained survey interviewers.

9) Seek and provide information to help companies determine their position in the marketplace.

10) Collect and analyze data on customer demographics, preferences, needs, and buying habits to identify potential markets and factors affecting product demand.

11) Measure the effectiveness of marketing, advertising, and communications programs and strategies.

12) Forecast and track marketing and sales trends, analyzing collected data.

19-3022.00 - Survey Researchers

Design or conduct surveys. May supervise interviewers who conduct the survey in person or over the telephone. May present survey results to client.

Tasks

1) Support, plan, and coordinate operations for single or multiple surveys.

2) Consult with clients in order to identify survey needs and any specific requirements, such as special samples.

3) Prepare and present summaries and analyses of survey data, including tables, graphs, and fact sheets that describe survey techniques and results.

4) Conduct surveys and collect data, using methods such as interviews, questionnaires, focus groups, market analysis surveys, public opinion polls, literature reviews, and file reviews.

5) Determine and specify details of survey projects, including sources of information, procedures to be used, and the design of survey instruments and materials.

6) Direct and review the work of staff members, including survey support staff and interviewers who gather survey data.

7) Write training manuals to be used by survey interviewers.

8) Analyze data from surveys, old records, and/or case studies, using statistical software programs.

9) Produce documentation of the questionnaire development process, data collection methods, sampling designs, and decisions related to sample statistical weighting.

10) Conduct research in order to gather information about survey topics.

11) Hire and train recruiters and data collectors.

12) Collaborate with other researchers in the planning, implementation, and evaluation of surveys.

13) Review, classify, and record survey data in preparation for computer analysis.

14) Direct updates and changes in survey implementation and methods.

19-3031.01 - Educational Psychologists

Investigate processes of learning and teaching and develop psychological principles and techniques applicable to educational problems.

Tasks

1) Refer students and their families to appropriate community agencies for medical, vocational, or social services.

2) Provide educational programs on topics such as classroom management, teaching strategies, or parenting skills.

3) Provide consultation to parents, teachers, administrators, and others on topics such as learning styles and behavior modification techniques.

4) Promote an understanding of child development and its relationship to learning and behavior.

5) Assess an individual child's needs, limitations, and potential, using observation, review of school records, and consultation with parents and school personnel.

6) Design classes and programs to meet the needs of special students.

7) Report any pertinent information to the proper authorities in cases of child endangerment, neglect, or abuse.

8) Collaborate with other educational professionals to develop teaching strategies and school programs.

9) Initiate and direct efforts to foster tolerance, understanding, and appreciation of diversity in school communities.

10) Conduct research to generate new knowledge that can be used to address learning and behavior issues.

11) Counsel children and families to help solve conflicts and problems in learning and

adjustment.

12) Compile and interpret students' test results, along with information from teachers and parents, in order to diagnose conditions, and to help assess eligibility for special services.

13) Select, administer, and score psychological tests.

14) Serve as a resource to help families and schools deal with crises, such as separation and loss.

15) Attend workshops, seminars, and/or professional meetings in order to remain informed of new developments in school psychology.

16) Develop individualized educational plans in collaboration with teachers and other staff members.

17) Maintain student records, including special education reports, confidential records, records of services provided, and behavioral data.

19-3032.00 - Industrial-Organizational Psychologists

Apply principles of psychology to personnel, administration, management, sales, and marketing problems. Activities may include policy planning; employee screening, training and development; and organizational development and analysis. May work with management to reorganize the work setting to improve worker productivity.

Tasks

1) Facilitate organizational development and change.

2) Develop and implement employee selection and placement programs.

3) Conduct research studies of physical work environments, organizational structures, communication systems, group interactions, morale, and motivation in order to assess organizational functioning.

4) Analyze job requirements and content in order to establish criteria for classification, selection, training, and other related personnel functions.

5) Formulate and implement training programs, applying principles of learning and individual differences.

6) Assess employee performance.

7) Analyze data, using statistical methods and applications, in order to evaluate the outcomes and effectiveness of workplace programs.

8) Observe and interview workers in order to obtain information about the physical, mental, and educational requirements of jobs as well as information about aspects such as job satisfaction.

9) Advise management concerning personnel, managerial, and marketing policies and practices and their potential effects on organizational effectiveness and efficiency.

10) Counsel workers about job and career-related issues.

11) Participate in mediation and dispute resolution.

12) Study consumers' reactions to new products and package designs, and to advertising efforts, using surveys and tests.

13) Write reports on research findings and implications in order to contribute to general knowledge and to suggest potential changes in organizational functioning.

14) Develop interview techniques, rating scales, and psychological tests used to assess skills, abilities, and interests for the purpose of employee selection, placement, and promotion.

15) Study organizational effectiveness, productivity, and efficiency, including the nature of workplace supervision and leadership.

19-3051.00 - Urban and Regional Planners

Develop comprehensive plans and programs for use of land and physical facilities of local jurisdictions, such as towns, cities, counties, and metropolitan areas.

Tasks

1) Discuss with planning officials the purpose of land use projects such as transportation, conservation, residential, commercial, industrial, and community use.

2) Conduct field investigations, surveys, impact studies or other research in order to compile and analyze data on economic, social, regulatory and physical factors affecting land use.

3) Keep informed about economic and legal issues involved in zoning codes, building codes, and environmental regulations.

4) Assess the feasibility of proposals and identify necessary changes.

5) Determine the effects of regulatory limitations on projects.

6) Create, prepare, or requisition graphic and narrative reports on land use data, including land area maps overlaid with geographic variables such as population density.

7) Hold public meetings and confer with government, social scientists, lawyers, developers, the public, and special interest groups to formulate and develop land use or community plans.

8) Coordinate work with economic consultants and architects during the formulation of plans and the design of large pieces of infrastructure.

9) Design, promote and administer government plans and policies affecting land use, zoning, public utilities, community facilities, housing, and transportation.

10) Recommend approval, denial or conditional approval of proposals.

11) Mediate community disputes and assist in developing alternative plans and recommendations for programs or projects.

12) Review and evaluate environmental impact reports pertaining to private and public planning projects and programs.

13) Investigate property availability.

14) Supervise and coordinate the work of urban planning technicians and technologists.

Knowledge	Knowledge Definitions
Design	Knowledge of design techniques, tools, and principles involved in production of precision technical plans, blueprints, drawings, and models.
Customer and Personal Service	Knowledge of principles and processes for providing customer and personal services. This includes customer needs assessment, meeting quality standards for services, and evaluation of customer satisfaction.
English Language	Knowledge of the structure and content of the English language including the meaning and spelling of words, rules of composition, and grammar.
Law and Government	Knowledge of laws, legal codes, court procedures, precedents, government regulations, executive orders, agency rules, and the democratic political process.
Building and Construction	Knowledge of materials, methods, and the tools involved in the construction or repair of houses, buildings, or other structures such as highways and roads.
Administration and Management	Knowledge of business and management principles involved in strategic planning, resource allocation, human resources modeling, leadership technique, production methods, and coordination of people and resources.
Geography	Knowledge of principles and methods for describing the features of land, sea, and air masses, including their physical characteristics, locations, interrelationships, and distribution of plant, animal, and human life.
Computers and Electronics	Knowledge of circuit boards, processors, chips, electronic equipment, and computer hardware and software, including applications and programming.
Mathematics	Knowledge of arithmetic, algebra, geometry, calculus, statistics, and their applications.
Clerical	Knowledge of administrative and clerical procedures and systems such as word processing, managing files and records, stenography and transcription, designing forms, and other office procedures and terminology.
Engineering and Technology	Knowledge of the practical application of engineering science and technology. This includes applying principles, techniques, procedures, and equipment to the design and production of various goods and services.
Personnel and Human Resources	Knowledge of principles and procedures for personnel recruitment, selection, training, compensation and benefits, labor relations and negotiation, and personnel information systems.
Economics and Accounting	Knowledge of economic and accounting principles and practices, the financial markets, banking and the analysis and reporting of financial data.
Transportation	Knowledge of principles and methods for moving people or goods by air, rail, sea, or road, including the relative costs and benefits.
Communications and Media	Knowledge of media production, communication, and dissemination techniques and methods. This includes alternative ways to inform and entertain via written, oral, and visual media.
History and Archeology	Knowledge of historical events and their causes, indicators, and effects on civilizations and cultures.
Sales and Marketing	Knowledge of principles and methods for showing, promoting, and selling products or services. This includes marketing strategy and tactics, product demonstration, sales techniques, and sales control systems.
Education and Training	Knowledge of principles and methods for curriculum and training design, teaching and instruction for individuals and groups, and the measurement of training effects.
Public Safety and Security	Knowledge of relevant equipment, policies, procedures, and strategies to promote effective local, state, or national security operations for the protection of people, data, property, and institutions.
Psychology	Knowledge of human behavior and performance; individual differences in ability, personality, and interests; learning and motivation; psychological research methods; and the assessment and treatment of behavioral and affective disorders.

Sociology and Anthropology	Knowledge of group behavior and dynamics, societal trends and influences, human migrations, ethnicity, cultures and their history and origins.
Telecommunications	Knowledge of transmission, broadcasting, switching, control, and operation of telecommunications systems.
Mechanical	Knowledge of machines and tools, including their designs, uses, repair, and maintenance.
Production and Processing	Knowledge of raw materials, production processes, quality control, costs, and other techniques for maximizing the effective manufacture and distribution of goods.
Biology	Knowledge of plant and animal organisms, their tissues, cells, functions, interdependencies, and interactions with each other and the environment.
Therapy and Counseling	Knowledge of principles, methods, and procedures for diagnosis, treatment, and rehabilitation of physical and mental dysfunctions, and for career counseling and guidance.
Philosophy and Theology	Knowledge of different philosophical systems and religions. This includes their basic principles, values, ethics, ways of thinking, customs, practices, and their impact on human culture.
Chemistry	Knowledge of the chemical composition, structure, and properties of substances and of the chemical processes and transformations that they undergo. This includes uses of chemicals and their interactions, danger signs, production techniques, and disposal methods.
Foreign Language	Knowledge of the structure and content of a foreign (non-English) language including the meaning and spelling of words, rules of composition and grammar, and pronunciation.
Medicine and Dentistry	Knowledge of the information and techniques needed to diagnose and treat human injuries, diseases, and deformities. This includes symptoms, treatment alternatives, drug properties and interactions, and preventive health-care measures.
Fine Arts	Knowledge of the theory and techniques required to compose, produce, and perform works of music, dance, visual arts, drama, and sculpture.
Physics	Knowledge and prediction of physical principles, laws, their interrelationships, and applications to understanding fluid, material, and atmospheric dynamics, and mechanical, electrical, atomic and sub-atomic structures and processes.
Food Production	Knowledge of techniques and equipment for planting, growing, and harvesting food products (both plant and animal) for consumption, including storage/handling techniques.

Skills	Skills Definitions
Writing	Communicating effectively in writing as appropriate for the needs of the audience.
Active Listening	Giving full attention to what other people are saying, taking time to understand the points being made, asking questions as appropriate, and not interrupting at inappropriate times.
Reading Comprehension	Understanding written sentences and paragraphs in work related documents.
Critical Thinking	Using logic and reasoning to identify the strengths and weaknesses of alternative solutions, conclusions or approaches to problems.
Time Management	Managing one's own time and the time of others.
Speaking	Talking to others to convey information effectively.
Judgment and Decision Making	Considering the relative costs and benefits of potential actions to choose the most appropriate one.
Complex Problem Solving	Identifying complex problems and reviewing related information to develop and evaluate options and implement solutions.
Service Orientation	Actively looking for ways to help people.
Coordination	Adjusting actions in relation to others' actions.
Social Perceptiveness	Being aware of others' reactions and understanding why they react as they do.
Active Learning	Understanding the implications of new information for both current and future problem-solving and decision-making.
Monitoring	Monitoring/Assessing performance of yourself, other individuals, or organizations to make improvements or take corrective action.
Persuasion	Persuading others to change their minds or behavior.
Learning Strategies	Selecting and using training/instructional methods and procedures appropriate for the situation when learning or teaching new things.
Mathematics	Using mathematics to solve problems.
Negotiation	Bringing others together and trying to reconcile differences.
Instructing	Teaching others how to do something.
Management of Personnel Resources	Motivating, developing, and directing people as they work, identifying the best people for the job.
Operations Analysis	Analyzing needs and product requirements to create a design.
Management of Financial Resources	Determining how money will be spent to get the work done, and accounting for these expenditures.
Science	Using scientific rules and methods to solve problems.
Systems Evaluation	Identifying measures or indicators of system performance and the actions needed to improve or correct performance, relative to the goals of the system.

Equipment Selection	Determining the kind of tools and equipment needed to do a job.
Quality Control Analysis	Conducting tests and inspections of products, services, or processes to evaluate quality or performance.
Management of Material Resources	Obtaining and seeing to the appropriate use of equipment, facilities, and materials needed to do certain work.
Systems Analysis	Determining how a system should work and how changes in conditions, operations, and the environment will affect outcomes.
Operation and Control	Controlling operations of equipment or systems.
Technology Design	Generating or adapting equipment and technology to serve user needs.
Troubleshooting	Determining causes of operating errors and deciding what to do about it.
Programming	Writing computer programs for various purposes.
Equipment Maintenance	Performing routine maintenance on equipment and determining when and what kind of maintenance is needed.
Installation	Installing equipment, machines, wiring, or programs to meet specifications.
Operation Monitoring	Watching gauges, dials, or other indicators to make sure a machine is working properly.
Repairing	Repairing machines or systems using the needed tools.

Ability	**Ability Definitions**
Oral Comprehension	The ability to listen to and understand information and ideas presented through spoken words and sentences.
Written Comprehension	The ability to read and understand information and ideas presented in writing.
Deductive Reasoning	The ability to apply general rules to specific problems to produce answers that make sense.
Inductive Reasoning	The ability to combine pieces of information to form general rules or conclusions (includes finding a relationship among seemingly unrelated events).
Written Expression	The ability to communicate information and ideas in writing so others will understand.
Oral Expression	The ability to communicate information and ideas in speaking so others will understand.
Problem Sensitivity	The ability to tell when something is wrong or is likely to go wrong. It does not involve solving the problem, only recognizing there is a problem.
Information Ordering	The ability to arrange things or actions in a certain order or pattern according to a specific rule or set of rules (e.g., patterns of numbers, letters, words, pictures, mathematical operations).
Speech Clarity	The ability to speak clearly so others can understand you.
Near Vision	The ability to see details at close range (within a few feet of the observer).
Category Flexibility	The ability to generate or use different sets of rules for combining or grouping things in different ways.
Speech Recognition	The ability to identify and understand the speech of another person.
Originality	The ability to come up with unusual or clever ideas about a given topic or situation, or to develop creative ways to solve a problem.
Fluency of Ideas	The ability to come up with a number of ideas about a topic (the number of ideas is important, not their quality, correctness, or creativity).
Visualization	The ability to imagine how something will look after it is moved around or when its parts are moved or rearranged.
Selective Attention	The ability to concentrate on a task over a period of time without being distracted.
Flexibility of Closure	The ability to identify or detect a known pattern (a figure, object, word, or sound) that is hidden in other distracting material.
Far Vision	The ability to see details at a distance.
Time Sharing	The ability to shift back and forth between two or more activities or sources of information (such as speech, sounds, touch, or other sources).
Speed of Closure	The ability to quickly make sense of, combine, and organize information into meaningful patterns.
Mathematical Reasoning	The ability to choose the right mathematical methods or formulas to solve a problem.
Finger Dexterity	The ability to make precisely coordinated movements of the fingers of one or both hands to grasp, manipulate, or assemble very small objects.
Depth Perception	The ability to judge which of several objects is closer or farther away from you, or to judge the distance between you and an object.
Perceptual Speed	The ability to quickly and accurately compare similarities and differences among sets of letters, numbers, objects, pictures, or patterns. The things to be compared may be presented at the same time or one after the other. This ability also includes comparing a presented object with a remembered object.
Number Facility	The ability to add, subtract, multiply, or divide quickly and correctly.

Memorization	The ability to remember information such as words, numbers, pictures, and procedures.
Visual Color Discrimination	The ability to match or detect differences between colors, including shades of color and brightness.
Control Precision	The ability to quickly and repeatedly adjust the controls of a machine or a vehicle to exact positions.
Multilimb Coordination	The ability to coordinate two or more limbs (for example, two arms, two legs, or one leg and one arm) while sitting, standing, or lying down. It does not involve performing the activities while the whole body is in motion.
Arm-Hand Steadiness	The ability to keep your hand and arm steady while moving your arm or while holding your arm and hand in one position.
Auditory Attention	The ability to focus on a single source of sound in the presence of other distracting sounds.
Stamina	The ability to exert yourself physically over long periods of time without getting winded or out of breath.
Gross Body Coordination	The ability to coordinate the movement of your arms, legs, and torso together when the whole body is in motion.
Manual Dexterity	The ability to quickly move your hand, your hand together with your arm, or your two hands to grasp, manipulate, or assemble objects.
Glare Sensitivity	The ability to see objects in the presence of glare or bright lighting.
Speed of Limb Movement	The ability to quickly move the arms and legs.
Hearing Sensitivity	The ability to detect or tell the differences between sounds that vary in pitch and loudness.
Trunk Strength	The ability to use your abdominal and lower back muscles to support part of the body repeatedly or continuously over time without 'giving out' or fatiguing.
Extent Flexibility	The ability to bend, stretch, twist, or reach with your body, arms, and/or legs.
Spatial Orientation	The ability to know your location in relation to the environment or to know where other objects are in relation to you.
Wrist-Finger Speed	The ability to make fast, simple, repeated movements of the fingers, hands, and wrists.
Explosive Strength	The ability to use short bursts of muscle force to propel oneself (as in jumping or sprinting), or to throw an object.
Rate Control	The ability to time your movements or the movement of a piece of equipment in anticipation of changes in the speed and/or direction of a moving object or scene.
Dynamic Flexibility	The ability to quickly and repeatedly bend, stretch, twist, or reach out with your body, arms, and/or legs.
Sound Localization	The ability to tell the direction from which a sound originated.
Reaction Time	The ability to quickly respond (with the hand, finger, or foot) to a signal (sound, light, picture) when it appears.
Static Strength	The ability to exert maximum muscle force to lift, push, pull, or carry objects.
Response Orientation	The ability to choose quickly between two or more movements in response to two or more different signals (lights, sounds, pictures). It includes the speed with which the correct response is started with the hand, foot, or other body part.
Night Vision	The ability to see under low light conditions.
Gross Body Equilibrium	The ability to keep or regain your body balance or stay upright when in an unstable position.
Dynamic Strength	The ability to exert muscle force repeatedly or continuously over time. This involves muscular endurance and resistance to muscle fatigue.
Peripheral Vision	The ability to see objects or movement of objects to one's side when the eyes are looking ahead.

Work_Activity	**Work_Activity Definitions**
Communicating with Persons Outside Organization	Communicating with people outside the organization, representing the organization to customers, the public, government, and other external sources. This information can be exchanged in person, in writing, or by telephone or e-mail.
Getting Information	Observing, receiving, and otherwise obtaining information from all relevant sources.
Evaluating Information to Determine Compliance wit	Using relevant information and individual judgment to determine whether events or processes comply with laws, regulations, or standards.
Performing for or Working Directly with the Public	Performing for people or dealing directly with the public. This includes serving customers in restaurants and stores, and receiving clients or guests.
Making Decisions and Solving Problems	Analyzing information and evaluating results to choose the best solution and solve problems.
Communicating with Supervisors, Peers, or Subordin	Providing information to supervisors, co-workers, and subordinates by telephone, in written form, e-mail, or in person.
Establishing and Maintaining Interpersonal Relatio	Developing constructive and cooperative working relationships with others, and maintaining them over time.
Analyzing Data or Information	Identifying the underlying principles, reasons, or facts of information by breaking down information or data into separate parts.

		Work_Content	Work_Content Definitions
Processing Information	Compiling, coding, categorizing, calculating, tabulating, auditing, or verifying information or data.	Telephone	How often do you have telephone conversations in this job?
Organizing, Planning, and Prioritizing Work	Developing specific goals and plans to prioritize, organize, and accomplish your work.	Electronic Mail	How often do you use electronic mail in this job?
Developing Objectives and Strategies	Establishing long-range objectives and specifying the strategies and actions to achieve them.	Face-to-Face Discussions	How often do you have to have face-to-face discussions with individuals or teams in this job?
Interacting With Computers	Using computers and computer systems (including hardware and software) to program, write software, set up functions, enter data, or process information.	Contact With Others	How much does this job require the worker to be in contact with others (face-to-face, by telephone, or otherwise) in order to perform it?
Updating and Using Relevant Knowledge	Keeping up-to-date technically and applying new knowledge to your job.	Letters and Memos	How often does the job require written letters and memos?
Interpreting the Meaning of Information for Others	Translating or explaining what information means and how it can be used.	Indoors, Environmentally Controlled	How often does this job require working indoors in environmentally controlled conditions?
Identifying Objects, Actions, and Events	Identifying information by categorizing, estimating, recognizing differences or similarities, and detecting changes in circumstances or events.	Deal With External Customers	How important is it to work with external customers or the public in this job?
		Spend Time Sitting	How much does this job require sitting?
Thinking Creatively	Developing, designing, or creating new applications, ideas, relationships, systems, or products, including artistic contributions.	Coordinate or Lead Others	How important is it to coordinate or lead others in accomplishing work activities in this job?
Resolving Conflicts and Negotiating with Others	Handling complaints, settling disputes, and resolving grievances and conflicts, or otherwise negotiating with others.	Frequency of Decision Making	How frequently is the worker required to make decisions that affect other people, the financial resources, and/or the image and reputation of the organization?
Provide Consultation and Advice to Others	Providing guidance and expert advice to management or other groups on technical, systems-, or process-related topics.	Structured versus Unstructured Work	To what extent is this job structured for the worker, rather than allowing the worker to determine tasks, priorities, and goals?
Scheduling Work and Activities	Scheduling events, programs, and activities, as well as the work of others.	Impact of Decisions on Co-workers or Company Resul	How do the decisions an employee makes impact the results of co-workers, clients or the company?
Performing Administrative Activities	Performing day-to-day administrative tasks such as maintaining information files and processing paperwork.	Deal With Unpleasant or Angry People	How frequently does the worker have to deal with unpleasant, angry, or discourteous individuals as part of the job requirements?
Documenting/Recording Information	Entering, transcribing, recording, storing, or maintaining information in written or electronic/magnetic form.	Work With Work Group or Team	How important is it to work with others in a group or team in this job?
Coordinating the Work and Activities of Others	Getting members of a group to work together to accomplish tasks.	Freedom to Make Decisions	How much decision making freedom, without supervision, does the job offer?
Monitor Processes, Materials, or Surroundings	Monitoring and reviewing information from materials, events, or the environment, to detect or assess problems.	Time Pressure	How often does this job require the worker to meet strict deadlines?
Estimating the Quantifiable Characteristics of Pro	Estimating sizes, distances, and quantities; or determining time, costs, resources, or materials needed to perform a work activity.	Frequency of Conflict Situations	How often are there conflict situations the employee has to face in this job?
Developing and Building Teams	Encouraging and building mutual trust, respect, and cooperation among team members.	Responsibility for Outcomes and Results	How responsible is the worker for work outcomes and results of other workers?
Judging the Qualities of Things, Services, or Peop	Assessing the value, importance, or quality of things or people.	Importance of Being Exact or Accurate	How important is being very exact or highly accurate in performing this job?
Training and Teaching Others	Identifying the educational needs of others, developing formal educational or training programs or classes, and teaching or instructing others.	Spend Time Using Your Hands to Handle, Control, or	How much does this job require using your hands to handle, control, or feel objects, tools or controls?
		Public Speaking	How often do you have to perform public speaking in this job?
Assisting and Caring for Others	Providing personal assistance, medical attention, emotional support, or other personal care to others such as coworkers, customers, or patients.	Spend Time Making Repetitive Motions	How much does this job require making repetitive motions?
Coaching and Developing Others	Identifying the developmental needs of others and coaching, mentoring, or otherwise helping others to improve their knowledge or skills.	Sounds, Noise Levels Are Distracting or Uncomforta	How often does this job require working exposed to sounds and noise levels that are distracting or uncomfortable?
Guiding, Directing, and Motivating Subordinates	Providing guidance and direction to subordinates, including setting performance standards and monitoring performance.	In an Enclosed Vehicle or Equipment	How often does this job require working in a closed vehicle or equipment (e.g., car)?
Monitoring and Controlling Resources	Monitoring and controlling resources and overseeing the spending of money.	Extremely Bright or Inadequate Lighting	How often does this job require working in extremely bright or inadequate lighting conditions?
Selling or Influencing Others	Convincing others to buy merchandise/goods or to otherwise change their minds or actions.	Spend Time Bending or Twisting the Body	How much does this job require bending or twisting your body?
Staffing Organizational Units	Recruiting, interviewing, selecting, hiring, and promoting employees in an organization.	Importance of Repeating Same Tasks	How important is repeating the same physical activities (e.g., key entry) or mental activities (e.g., checking entries in a ledger) over and over, without stopping, to performing this job?
Operating Vehicles, Mechanized Devices, or Equipme	Running, maneuvering, navigating, or driving vehicles or mechanized equipment, such as forklifts, passenger vehicles, aircraft, or water craft.	Spend Time Walking and Running	How much does this job require walking and running?
Performing General Physical Activities	Performing physical activities that require considerable use of your arms and legs and moving your whole body, such as climbing, lifting, balancing, walking, stooping, and handling of materials.	Level of Competition	To what extent does this job require the worker to compete or to be aware of competitive pressures?
Inspecting Equipment, Structures, or Material	Inspecting equipment, structures, or materials to identify the cause of errors or other problems or defects.	Exposed to Contaminants	How often does this job require working exposed to contaminants (such as pollutants, gases, dust or odors)?
Drafting, Laying Out, and Specifying Technical Dev	Providing documentation, detailed instructions, drawings, or specifications to tell others about how devices, parts, equipment, or structures are to be fabricated, constructed, assembled, modified, maintained, or used.	Outdoors, Exposed to Weather	How often does this job require working outdoors, exposed to all weather conditions?
		Responsible for Others' Health and Safety	How much responsibility is there for the health and safety of others in this job?
Handling and Moving Objects	Using hands and arms in handling, installing, positioning, and moving materials, and manipulating things.	Consequence of Error	How serious would the result usually be if the worker made a mistake that was not readily correctable?
Controlling Machines and Processes	Using either control mechanisms or direct physical activity to operate machines or processes (not including computers or vehicles).	Degree of Automation	How automated is the job?
		Physical Proximity	To what extent does this job require the worker to perform job tasks in close physical proximity to other people?
Repairing and Maintaining Electronic Equipment	Servicing, repairing, calibrating, regulating, fine-tuning, or testing machines, devices, and equipment that operate primarily on the basis of electrical or electronic (not mechanical) principles.	Spend Time Standing	How much does this job require standing?
		Indoors, Not Environmentally Controlled	How often does this job require working indoors in non-controlled environmental conditions (e.g., warehouse without heat)?
Repairing and Maintaining Mechanical Equipment	Servicing, repairing, adjusting, and testing machines, devices, moving parts, and equipment that operate primarily on the basis of mechanical (not electronic) principles.	Cramped Work Space, Awkward Positions	How often does this job require working in cramped work spaces that requires getting into awkward positions?
		Spend Time Kneeling, Crouching, Stooping, or Crawl	How much does this job require kneeling, crouching, stooping, or crawling?
		Deal With Physically Aggressive People	How frequently does this job require the worker to deal with physical aggression of violent individuals?
		Very Hot or Cold Temperatures	How often does this job require working in very hot (above 90 F degrees) or very cold (below 32 F degrees) temperatures?

Wear Common Protective or Safety Equipment such as	How much does this job require wearing common protective or safety equipment such as safety shoes. glasses. gloves. hard hats or live jackets?
Outdoors. Under Cover	How often does this job require working outdoors. under cover (e.g., structure with roof but no walls)?
Exposed to Hazardous Conditions	How often does this job require exposure to hazardous conditions?
Spend Time Climbing Ladders. Scaffolds, or Poles	How much does this job require climbing ladders. scaffolds, or poles?
Exposed to Minor Burns. Cuts. Bites. or Stings	How often does this job require exposure to minor burns. cuts. bites. or stings?
Spend Time Keeping or Regaining Balance	How much does this job require keeping or regaining your balance?
Exposed to Hazardous Equipment	How often does this job require exposure to hazardous equipment?
Pace Determined by Speed of Equipment	How important is it to this job that the pace is determined by the speed of equipment or machinery? (This does not refer to keeping busy at all times on this job.)
Exposed to High Places	How often does this job require exposure to high places?
Exposed to Whole Body Vibration	How often does this job require exposure to whole body vibration (e.g.. operate a jackhammer)?
Exposed to Disease or Infections	How often does this job require exposure to disease/infections?
Wear Specialized Protective or Safety Equipment su	How much does this job require wearing specialized protective or safety equipment such as breathing apparatus. safety harness, full protection suits, or radiation protection?
In an Open Vehicle or Equipment	How often does this job require working in an open vehicle or equipment (e.g., tractor)?
Exposed to Radiation	How often does this job require exposure to radiation?

Work_Styles	Work_Styles Definitions
Integrity	Job requires being honest and ethical.
Attention to Detail	Job requires being careful about detail and thorough in completing work tasks.
Initiative	Job requires a willingness to take on responsibilities and challenges.
Self Control	Job requires maintaining composure, keeping emotions in check, controlling anger, and avoiding aggressive behavior, even in very difficult situations.
Dependability	Job requires being reliable, responsible, and dependable, and fulfilling obligations.
Cooperation	Job requires being pleasant with others on the job and displaying a good-natured, cooperative attitude.
Analytical Thinking	Job requires analyzing information and using logic to address work-related issues and problems.
Stress Tolerance	Job requires accepting criticism and dealing calmly and effectively with high stress situations.
Concern for Others	Job requires being sensitive to others' needs and feelings and being understanding and helpful on the job.
Persistence	Job requires persistence in the face of obstacles.
Adaptability/Flexibility	Job requires being open to change (positive or negative) and to considerable variety in the workplace.
Leadership	Job requires a willingness to lead, take charge, and offer opinions and direction.
Innovation	Job requires creativity and alternative thinking to develop new ideas for and answers to work-related problems.
Social Orientation	Job requires preferring to work with others rather than alone, and being personally connected with others on the job.
Independence	Job requires developing one's own ways of doing things, guiding oneself with little or no supervision, and depending on oneself to get things done.
Achievement/Effort	Job requires establishing and maintaining personally challenging achievement goals and exerting effort toward mastering tasks.

Job Zone Component	Job Zone Component Definitions
Title	Job Zone Four: Considerable Preparation Needed
Overall Experience	A minimum of two to four years of work-related skill, knowledge, or experience is needed for these occupations. For example, an accountant must complete four years of college and work for several years in accounting to be considered qualified.
Job Training	Employees in these occupations usually need several years of work-related experience, on-the-job training, and/or vocational training.
Job Zone Examples	Many of these occupations involve coordinating, supervising, managing, or training others. Examples include accountants, chefs and head cooks, computer programmers, historians, pharmacists, and police detectives.
SVP Range	(7.0 to < 8.0)
Education	Most of these occupations require a four-year bachelor's degree, but some do not.

19-3091.01 - Anthropologists

Research or study the origins and physical. social. and cultural development and behavior of humans and the cultures and organizations they have created.

Tasks

1) Formulate general rules that describe how cultures and societies develop and behave.

2) Study linguistics. chemistry. nutrition. or behavioral science in order to apply those disciplines' methodologies to the study of culture.

3) Write about and present research findings.

4) Compare the customs, values, and social patterns of different cultures.

5) Advise government agencies and private organizations on matters such as the concerns of different groups and cultures.

6) Observe and measure bodily variations and physical attributes in different human groups.

7) Teach anthropology.

8) Study the origin and physical. social. or cultural development of humans, including physical attributes, cultural traditions, possessions. beliefs, languages, and settlement patterns.

9) Examine museum collections of human fossils to determine how they fit into evolutionary theory.

10) Study specific groups in the field, observing and interviewing members to obtain information about topics such as group and family relationships and activities.

11) Gather and analyze artifacts and skeletal remains in order to increase knowledge of ancient cultures.

19-3091.02 - Archeologists

Conduct research to reconstruct record of past human life and culture from human remains, artifacts, architectural features, and structures recovered through excavation, underwater recovery, or other means of discovery.

Tasks

1) Lead field training sites and train field staff, students, and volunteers in excavation methods.

2) Describe artifacts' physical properties or attributes, such as the materials from which artifacts are made, and their size, shape, function, and decoration.

3) Clean, restore, and preserve artifacts.

4) Collect artifacts made of stone, bone, metal. and other materials, placing them in bags and marking them to show where they were found.

5) Compare findings from one site with archeological data from other sites to find similarities or differences.

6) Consult site reports, existing artifacts, and topographic maps to identify archaeological sites.

7) Record the exact locations and conditions of artifacts uncovered in diggings or surveys, using drawings and photographs as necessary.

8) Research, survey, and assess sites of past societies and cultures in search of answers to specific research questions.

9) Study objects and structures recovered by excavation to identify, date, and/or authenticate them, and to interpret their significance.

10) Teach archaeology at colleges and universities.

11) Assess archaeological sites for resource management, development, or conservation purposes, and recommend methods for site protection.

12) Develop and test theories concerning the origin and development of past cultures.

13) Write, present, and publish reports that record site history, methodology and artifact analysis results, along with recommendations for conserving and interpreting findings.

14) Create artifact typologies to organize and make sense of past material cultures.

19-3092.00 - Geographers

Study nature and use of areas of earth's surface. relating and interpreting interactions of physical and cultural phenomena. Conduct research on physical aspects of a region. including land forms, climates, soils, plants and animals. and conduct research on the spatial implications of human activities within a given area, including social characteristics, economic activities, and political organization. as well as researching interdependence between regions at scales ranging from local to global.

86

Tasks

1) Provide consulting services in fields including resource development and management. business location and market area analysis, environmental hazards, regional cultural history. and urban social planning.

2) Write and present reports of research findings.

3) Collect data on physical characteristics of specified areas, such as geological formations. climates, and vegetation. using surveying or meteorological equipment.

4) Gather and compile geographic data from sources including censuses, field observations. satellite imagery, aerial photographs, and existing maps.

5) Conduct fieldwork at outdoor sites.

6) Develop, operate. and maintain geographical information (GIS) computer systems, including hardware, software, plotters, digitizers, printers, and video cameras.

7) Provide geographical information systems support to the private and public sectors.

8) Study the economic. political, and cultural characteristics of a specific region's population.

9) Teach geography.

10) Analyze geographic distributions of physical and cultural phenomena on local, regional. continental, and global scales.

11) Create and modify maps, graphs, and diagrams, using geographical information software and related equipment, and principles of cartography such as coordinate systems, longitude. latitude, elevation, topography, and map scales.

19-3093.00 - Historians

Research, analyze, record, and interpret the past as recorded in sources, such as government and institutional records, newspapers and other periodicals, photographs, interviews, films. and unpublished manuscripts, such as personal diaries and letters.

Tasks

1) Advise or consult with individuals and institutions regarding issues such as the historical authenticity of materials or the customs of a specific historical period.

2) Conduct historical research, and publish or present findings and theories.

3) Trace historical development in a particular field, such as social, cultural, political, or diplomatic history.

4) Research the history of a particular country or region, or of a specific time period.

5) Organize information for publication and for other means of dissemination, such as use in CD-ROMs or Internet sites.

6) Organize data, and analyze and interpret its authenticity and relative significance.

7) Coordinate activities of workers engaged in cataloging and filing materials.

8) Recommend actions related to historical art, such as which items to add to a collection or which items to display in an exhibit.

9) Gather historical data from sources such as archives, court records, diaries, news files, and photographs, as well as collect data sources such as books, pamphlets, and periodicals.

10) Translate or request translation of reference materials.

11) Present historical accounts in terms of individuals or social, ethnic, political, economic, or geographic groupings.

12) Prepare publications and exhibits, or review those prepared by others in order to ensure their historical accuracy.

13) Interview people in order to gather information about historical events, and to record oral histories.

14) Teach and conduct research in colleges, universities, museums, and other research agencies and schools.

15) Edit historical society publications.

16) Speak to various groups, organizations, and clubs in order to promote the aims and activities of historical societies.

17) Determine which topics to research, or pursue research topics specified by clients or employers.

18) Conduct historical research as a basis for the identification, conservation, and reconstruction of historic places and materials.

19) Research and prepare manuscripts in support of public programming and the development of exhibits at historic sites, museums, libraries, and archives.

19-4011.01 - Agricultural Technicians

Set up and maintain laboratory and collect and record data to assist scientist in biology or

related agricultural science experiments.

Tasks

1) Respond to inquiries and requests from the public that do not require specialized scientific knowledge or expertise.

2) Measure or weigh ingredients used in testing or for purposes such as animal feed.

3) Prepare data summaries, reports, and analyses that include results. charts, and graphs in order to document research findings and results.

4) Collect samples from crops or animals so testing can be performed.

5) Examine animals and specimens in order to determine the presence of diseases or other problems.

6) Adjust testing equipment, and prepare culture media, following standard procedures.

7) Conduct insect and plant disease surveys.

8) Transplant trees, vegetables, and/or horticultural plants.

9) Plant seeds in specified areas, and count the resulting plants in order to determine the percentage of seeds that germinated.

10) Maintain and repair agricultural facilities, equipment, and tools in order to ensure operational readiness, safety, and cleanliness.

11) Record data pertaining to experimentation, research, and animal care.

12) Provide food and water to livestock and laboratory animals, and record details of their food consumption.

13) Supervise and train agricultural technicians and farm laborers.

14) Provide routine animal care such as taking and recording body measurements, applying identification, and assisting in the birthing process.

15) Conduct inspections of apiaries in order to locate diseases and destroy contaminated bees and hives.

16) Prepare and present agricultural demonstrations.

17) Set up laboratory or field equipment, and prepare sites for testing.

18) Receive and prepare laboratory samples for analysis. following proper protocols in order to ensure that they will be stored, prepared, and disposed of efficiently and effectively.

19) Perform crop production duties such as tilling, hoeing, pruning, weeding, and harvesting crops.

20) Operate farm machinery including tractors, plows, mowers, combines, balers, sprayers, earthmoving equipment, and trucks.

21) Measure and mark plot areas; and plow, disc, level, and otherwise prepare land for cultivated crops, orchards and vineyards.

22) Devise cultural methods and environmental controls for plants for which guidelines are sketchy or nonexistent.

23) Perform general nursery duties such as propagating standard varieties of plant materials, collecting and germinating seeds, maintaining cuttings of plants, and controlling environmental conditions.

24) Operate laboratory equipment such as spectrometers, nitrogen determination apparatus, air samplers, centrifuges, and PH meters in order to perform tests.

19-4011.02 - Food Science Technicians

Perform standardized qualitative and quantitative tests to determine physical or chemical properties of food or beverage products.

Tasks

1) Record and compile test results, and prepare graphs, charts, and reports.

2) Provide assistance to food scientists and technologists in research and development, production technology, and quality control.

3) Order supplies needed to maintain inventories in laboratories or in storage facilities of food or beverage processing plants.

4) Mix, blend, or cultivate ingredients in order to make reagents or to manufacture food or beverage products.

5) Measure, test, and weigh bottles, cans, and other containers in order to ensure hardness, strength, and dimensions that meet specifications.

6) Examine chemical and biological samples in order to identify cell structures, and to locate bacteria, or extraneous material, using microscope.

7) Conduct standardized tests on food, beverages, additives, and preservatives in order to ensure compliance with standards and regulations regarding factors such as color, texture, and nutrients.

8) Compute moisture or salt content, percentages of ingredients, formulas, or other product

19-4021.00 - Biological Technicians

factors, using mathematical and chemical procedures.

9) Analyze test results to classify products, or compare results with standard tables.

10) Clean and sterilize laboratory equipment.

11) Prepare slides and incubate slides with cell cultures.

19-4021.00 - Biological Technicians

Assist biological and medical scientists in laboratories. Set up, operate, and maintain laboratory instruments and equipment, monitor experiments, make observations, and calculate and record results. May analyze organic substances, such as blood, food, and drugs.

Tasks

1) Feed livestock and laboratory animals.

2) Conduct or supervise operational programs such as fish hatcheries, greenhouses and livestock production programs.

3) Participate in the research, development, and manufacturing of medicinal and pharmaceutical preparations.

4) Keep detailed logs of all work-related activities.

5) Set up, adjust, calibrate, clean, maintain, and troubleshoot laboratory and field equipment.

6) Provide technical support and services for scientists and engineers working in fields such as agriculture, environmental science, resource management, biology, and health sciences.

7) Isolate, identify and prepare specimens for examination.

8) Measure or weigh compounds and solutions for use in testing or animal feed.

9) Examine animals and specimens to detect the presence of disease or other problems.

10) Conduct standardized biological, microbiological and biochemical tests and laboratory analyses to evaluate the quantity or quality of physical or chemical substances in food and other products.

11) Conduct, or assist in conducting, research, including the collection of information and samples, such as blood, water, soil, plants and animals.

12) Clean, maintain and prepare supplies and work areas.

13) Analyze experimental data and interpret results to write reports and summaries of findings.

14) Monitor and observe experiments, recording production and test data for evaluation by research personnel.

15) Use computers, computer-interfaced equipment, robotics and high-technology industrial applications to perform work duties.

19-4031.00 - Chemical Technicians

Conduct chemical and physical laboratory tests to assist scientists in making qualitative and quantitative analyses of solids, liquids, and gaseous materials for purposes, such as research and development of new products or processes, quality control, maintenance of environmental standards, and other work involving experimental, theoretical, or practical application of chemistry and related sciences.

Tasks

1) Set up and conduct chemical experiments, tests, and analyses using techniques such as chromatography, spectroscopy, physical and chemical separation techniques, and microscopy.

2) Monitor product quality to ensure compliance to standards and specifications.

3) Compile and interpret results of tests and analyses.

4) Maintain, clean, and sterilize laboratory instruments and equipment.

5) Provide technical support and assistance to chemists and engineers.

6) Write technical reports or prepare graphs and charts to document experimental results.

7) Conduct chemical and physical laboratory tests to assist scientists in making qualitative and quantitative analyses of solids, liquids, and gaseous materials.

8) Order and inventory materials in order to maintain supplies.

9) Operate experimental pilot plants, assisting with experimental design.

10) Develop and conduct programs of sampling and analysis to maintain quality standards of raw materials, chemical intermediates, and products.

11) Direct or monitor other workers producing chemical products.

12) Prepare chemical solutions for products and processes following standardized formulas, or create experimental formulas.

13) Develop new chemical engineering processes or production techniques.

19-4041.01 - Geological Data Technicians

Measure, record, and evaluate geological data, using sonic, electronic, electrical, seismic, or gravity-measuring instruments to prospect for oil or gas. May collect and evaluate core samples and cuttings.

Tasks

1) Collect samples and cuttings, using equipment and hand tools.

2) Evaluate and interpret core samples and cuttings, and other geological data used in prospecting for oil or gas.

3) Measure geological characteristics used in prospecting for oil or gas, using measuring instruments.

4) Record readings in order to compile data used in prospecting for oil or gas.

5) Operate and adjust equipment and apparatus used to obtain geological data.

6) Read and study reports in order to compile information and data for geological and geophysical prospecting.

7) Interview individuals, and research public databases in order to obtain information

8) Plan and direct activities of workers who operate equipment to collect data.

9) Diagnose and repair malfunctioning instruments and equipment, using manufacturers' manuals and hand tools.

10) Develop and design packing materials and handling procedures for shipping of objects.

11) Prepare and attach packing instructions to shipping containers.

12) Supervise oil, water, and gas well drilling activities.

13) Set up, or direct set-up of instruments used to collect geological data.

14) Prepare notes, sketches, geological maps and cross-sections.

15) Assemble, maintain, and distribute information for library or record systems.

19-4041.02 - Geological Sample Test Technicians

Test and analyze geological samples, crude oil, or petroleum products to detect presence of petroleum, gas, or mineral deposits indicating potential for exploration and production, or to determine physical and chemical properties to ensure that products meet quality standards.

Tasks

1) Supervise well exploration and drilling activities, and well completions.

2) Adjust and repair testing, electrical, and mechanical equipment and devices.

3) Inspect engines for wear and defective parts, using equipment and measuring devices.

4) Participate in the evaluation of possible mining locations.

5) Participate in geological, geophysical, geochemical, hydrographic or oceanographic surveys, prospecting field trips, exploratory drilling, well logging or underground mine survey programs.

6) Assess the environmental impacts of development projects on subsurface materials.

7) Compile and record testing and operational data for review and further analysis.

8) Prepare, transcribe, and/or analyze seismic, gravimetric, well log or other geophysical and survey data.

9) Plot information from aerial photographs, well logs, section descriptions, and other databases.

10) Assemble, operate, and maintain field and laboratory testing, measuring, and mechanical equipment, working as part of a crew when required.

11) Collaborate with hydro-geologists in order to evaluate groundwater and well circulation.

12) Prepare notes, sketches, geological maps, and cross sections.

13) Collect and prepare solid and fluid samples for analysis.

19-4051.01 - Nuclear Equipment Operation Technicians

Operate equipment used for the release, control, and utilization of nuclear energy to assist scientists in laboratory and production activities.

Tasks

1) Warn maintenance workers of radiation hazards, and direct workers to vacate hazardous areas.

2) Write summaries of activities and record experimental data, such as accelerator performance. systems status, particle beam specification and beam conditions obtained.

3) Communicate with accelerator maintenance personnel in order to ensure readiness of support systems. such as vacuum, water cooling, and radiofrequency power sources.

4) Diagnose routine problems affecting accelerator performance.

5) Direct the work of accelerator support service personnel.

6) Disassemble, clean, and decontaminate hot cells and reactor parts during maintenance shutdowns, using slave manipulators, cranes, and hand tools.

7) Set up and operate machines to cut fuel elements to size to fit into shielding boxes or to polish test pieces, following blueprints and other specifications and using extension tools.

8) Submit computations to supervisors for review.

9) Transfer capsules of experimental materials to and from tubes, chambers, or tunnels leading to reactor cores, using slave manipulators or extension tools.

10) Set control panel switches, according to standard procedures, in order to route electric power from sources and direct particle beams through injector units.

11) Perform testing, maintenance, repair, and upgrading of accelerator systems.

12) Adjust controls of equipment in order to control particle beam movement, pulse rates, energy and intensity, or radiation, according to specifications.

13) Collaborate with accelerator and beamline physicists in order to make experimental measurements.

14) Review experiment schedules in order to determine specifications, such as subatomic particle energy, intensity, and repetition rate parameters.

15) Calculate equipment operating factors, such as radiation times, dosages, temperatures, gamma intensities, and pressures, using standard formulas and conversion tables.

16) Clear personnel from particle beam areas before operations begin.

17) Control laboratory compounding equipment enclosed in protective hot cells in order to prepare radioisotopes and other radioactive materials.

18) Follow policies and procedures for radiation workers in order to ensure personnel safety.

19) Install instrumentation leads in reactor cores in order to measure operating temperatures and pressures, according to mockups, blueprints, and diagrams.

20) Monitor instruments, gauges, and recording devices in control rooms during operation of equipment, under direction of nuclear experimenters.

21) Notify experimenters in target control rooms when particle beam parameters meet specifications.

22) Position fuel elements in geometric configurations around tubes in reactors or gamma facilities, according to radiation intensity specifications, using slave manipulators or extension tools.

23) Modify, devise, and maintain equipment used in operations.

19-4051.02 - Nuclear Monitoring Technicians

Collect and test samples to monitor results of nuclear experiments and contamination of humans, facilities, and environment.

Tasks

1) Set up equipment that automatically detects area radiation deviations, and test detection equipment in order to ensure its accuracy.

2) Observe projected photographs to locate particle tracks and events, and compile lists of events from particle detectors.

3) Confer with scientists directing projects in order to determine significant events to monitor during tests.

4) Decontaminate objects by cleaning with soap or solvents or by abrading with wire brushes, buffing wheels, or sandblasting machines.

5) Enter data into computers in order to record characteristics of nuclear events and locating coordinates of particles.

6) Place radioactive waste, such as sweepings and broken sample bottles, into containers for disposal.

7) Collect samples of air, water, gases, and solids in order to determine radioactivity levels of contamination.

8) Scan photographic emulsions exposed to direct radiation in order to compute track properties from standard formulas, using microscopes with scales and protractors.

9) Determine intensities and types of radiation in work areas, equipment, and materials, using radiation detectors and other instruments.

10) Weigh and mix decontamination chemical solutions in tanks, and immerse objects in solutions for specified times, using hoists.

11) Determine or recommend radioactive decontamination procedures, according to the size

and nature of equipment and the degree of contamination.

12) Monitor personnel in order to determine the amounts and intensities of radiation exposure.

13) Calculate safe radiation exposure times for personnel, using plant contamination readings and prescribed safe levels of radiation.

14) Inform supervisors when individual exposures or area radiation levels approach maximum permissible limits.

15) Prepare reports describing contamination tests. material and equipment decontaminated, and methods used in decontamination processes.

16) Operate manipulators from outside cells to move specimens into and out of shielded containers, to remove specimens from cells, or to place specimens on benches or equipment work stations.

17) Place irradiated nuclear fuel materials in environmental chambers for testing, and observe reactions through cell windows.

18) Provide initial response to abnormal events and to alarms from radiation monitoring equipment.

19) Instruct personnel in radiation safety procedures, and demonstrate use of protective clothing and equipment.

20) Test materials' physical, chemical, or metallurgical properties, using equipment such as tensile testers, hardness testers. metallographic units, micrometers, and gauges.

21) Set up and operate machines that cut, lap, and polish test pieces, following blueprints, x-ray negatives, and sketches.

22) Immerse samples in chemical compounds in order to prepare them for testing.

19-4061.00 - Social Science Research Assistants

Assist social scientists in laboratory, survey, and other social research. May perform publication activities, laboratory analysis, quality control, or data management. Normally these individuals work under the direct supervision of a social scientist and assist in those activities which are more routine.

Tasks

1) Conduct internet-based and library research.

2) Supervise the work of survey interviewers.

3) Track laboratory supplies, and expenses such as participant reimbursement.

4) Prepare tables, graphs, fact sheets, and written reports summarizing research results.

5) Develop and implement research quality control procedures.

6) Perform descriptive and multivariate statistical analyses of data, using computer software.

7) Code data in preparation for computer entry.

8) Present research findings to groups of people.

9) Obtain informed consent of research subjects and/or their guardians.

10) Prepare, manipulate, and manage extensive databases.

11) Provide assistance in the design of survey instruments such as questionnaires.

12) Collect specimens such as blood samples, as required by research projects.

13) Provide assistance with the preparation of project-related reports, manuscripts, and presentations.

14) Recruit and schedule research participants.

15) Edit and submit protocols and other required research documentation.

16) Perform needs assessments and/or consult with clients in order to determine the types of research and information that are required.

17) Screen potential subjects in order to determine their suitability as study participants.

18) Design and create special programs for tasks such as statistical analysis and data entry and cleaning.

19) Allocate and manage laboratory space and resources.

20) Verify the accuracy and validity of data entered in databases; correct any errors.

21) Track research participants, and perform any necessary followup tasks.

22) Perform data entry and other clerical work as required for project completion.

19-4061.01 - City Planning Aides

Compile data from various sources, such as maps, reports, and field and file investigations, for use by city planner in making planning studies.

19-4091.00 - Environmental Science and Protection Technicians, Including Health

Tasks

1) Conduct interviews, surveys and site inspections concerning factors that affect land usage, such as zoning, traffic flow and housing.

2) Serve as a liaison between planning department and other departments and agencies.

3) Provide and process zoning and project permits and applications

4) Prepare reports, using statistics, charts, and graphs, to illustrate planning studies in areas such as population, land use, or zoning.

5) Perform code enforcement tasks.

6) Inspect sites and review plans for minor development permit applications.

7) Research, compile, analyze and organize information from maps, reports, investigations, and books for use in reports and special projects.

8) Prepare, maintain and update files and records, including land use data and statistics.

9) Prepare, develop and maintain maps and databases.

10) Participate in and support team planning efforts.

11) Perform clerical duties such as composing, typing and proofreading documents, scheduling appointments and meetings, handling mail and posting public notices.

19-4091.00 - Environmental Science and Protection Technicians, Including Health

Performs laboratory and field tests to monitor the environment and investigate sources of pollution, including those that affect health. Under direction of an environmental scientist or specialist, may collect samples of gases, soil, water, and other materials for testing and take corrective actions as assigned.

Tasks

1) Calibrate microscopes and test instruments.

2) Determine amounts and kinds of chemicals to use in destroying harmful organisms and removing impurities from purification systems.

3) Develop testing procedures, and direct activities of workers in laboratory.

4) Record test data and prepare reports, summaries, and charts that interpret test results.

5) Discuss test results and analyses with customers.

6) Maintain files such as hazardous waste databases, chemical usage data, personnel exposure information and diagrams showing equipment locations.

7) Collect samples of gases, soils, water, industrial wastewater, and asbestos products to conduct tests on pollutant levels and identify sources of pollution.

8) Perform statistical analysis of environmental data.

9) Provide information and technical and program assistance to government representatives, employers and the general public on the issues of public health, environmental protection or workplace safety.

10) Distribute permits, closure plans and cleanup plans.

11) Conduct standardized tests to ensure materials and supplies used throughout power supply systems meet processing and safety specifications.

12) Develop and implement programs for monitoring of environmental pollution and radiation.

13) Prepare samples or photomicrographs for testing and analysis.

14) Make recommendations to control or eliminate unsafe conditions at workplaces or public facilities.

15) Inspect workplaces to ensure the absence of health and safety hazards such as high noise levels, radiation or potential lighting hazards.

16) Inspect sanitary conditions at public facilities.

17) Examine and analyze material for presence and concentration of contaminants such as asbestos, using variety of microscopes.

18) Calculate amount of pollutant in samples or compute air pollution or gas flow in industrial processes, using chemical and mathematical formulas.

19) Set up equipment or stations to monitor and collect pollutants from sites, such as smoke stacks, manufacturing plants, or mechanical equipment.

20) Respond to and investigate hazardous conditions or spills, or outbreaks of disease or food poisoning, collecting samples for analysis.

21) Initiate procedures to close down or fine establishments violating environmental and/or health regulations.

19-4092.00 - Forensic Science Technicians

Collect, identify, classify, and analyze physical evidence related to criminal investigations. Perform tests on weapons or substances, such as fiber, hair, and tissue to determine significance to investigation. May testify as expert witnesses on evidence or crime laboratory techniques. May serve as specialists in area of expertise, such as ballistics, fingerprinting, handwriting, or biochemistry.

Tasks

1) Reconstruct crime scenes in order to determine relationships among pieces of evidence.

2) Examine firearms in order to determine mechanical condition and legal status, performing restoration work on damaged firearms in order to obtain information such as serial numbers.

3) Operate and maintain laboratory equipment and apparatus.

4) Testify in court about investigative and analytical methods and findings.

5) Perform polygraph examination by explaining tests to subjects, attaching equipment to measure physiological responses, questioning subjects, and recording and interpreting subsequent machine readouts.

6) Examine physical evidence such as hair, fiber, wood or soil residues in order to obtain information about its source and composition.

7) Test race horses and racing dogs for substances that may affect their performances.

8) Interpret the pharmacological effects of a drug or a combination of drugs on an individual.

9) Visit morgues, examine scenes of crimes, or contact other sources in order to obtain evidence or information to be used in investigations.

10) Prepare solutions, reagents, and sample formulations needed for laboratory work.

11) Analyze gunshot residue and bullet paths in order to determine how shootings occurred.

12) Identify and quantify drugs and poisons found in biological fluids and tissues, in foods, and at crime scenes.

13) Collect evidence from crime scenes, storing it in conditions that preserve its integrity.

14) Interpret laboratory findings and test results in order to identify and classify substances, materials, and other evidence collected at crime scenes.

15) Compare objects such as tools with impression marks in order to determine whether a specific object is responsible for a specific mark.

16) Analyze handwritten and machine-produced textual evidence to decipher altered or obliterated text or to determine authorship, age, and/or source.

17) Confer with ballistics, fingerprinting, handwriting, documents, electronics, medical, chemical, or metallurgical experts concerning evidence and its interpretation.

18) Determine types of bullets used in shooting and if fired from a specific weapon.

19) Examine DNA samples to determine if they match other samples.

20) Collect impressions of dust from surfaces in order to obtain and identify fingerprints.

21) Analyze and classify biological fluids using DNA typing or serological techniques.

19-4093.00 - Forest and Conservation Technicians

Compile data pertaining to size, content, condition, and other characteristics of forest tracts, under direction of foresters; train and lead forest workers in forest propagation, fire prevention and suppression. May assist conservation scientists in managing, improving, and protecting rangelands and wildlife habitats, and help provide technical assistance regarding the conservation of soil, water, and related natural resources.

Tasks

1) Provide forestry education and general information, advice, and recommendations to woodlot owners, community organizations, and the general public.

2) Manage forest protection activities, including fire control, fire crew training, and coordination of fire detection and public education programs.

3) Issue fire permits, timber permits and other forest use licenses.

4) Perform reforestation (forest renewal), including nursery and silviculture operations, site preparation, seeding and tree planting programs, cone collection, and tree improvement.

5) Develop and maintain computer databases.

6) Survey, measure, and map access roads and forest areas such as burns, cut-over areas, experimental plots, and timber sales sections.

7) Provide technical support to forestry research programs in areas such as tree improvement, seed orchard operations, insect and disease surveys, or experimental forestry and forest engineering research.

8) Provide information about, and enforce, regulations such as those concerning environmental protection, resource utilization, fire safety and accident prevention.

9) Plan and supervise construction of access routes and forest roads.

10) Measure distances, clean site-lines, and record data to help survey crews.

11) Keep records of the amount and condition of logs taken to mills.

12) Install gauges, stream flow recorders, and soil moisture measuring instruments, and collect and record data from them to assist with watershed analysis.

13) Train and lead forest and conservation workers in seasonal activities, such as planting tree seedlings, putting out forest fires and maintaining recreational facilities.

14) Patrol park or forest areas to protect resources and prevent damage.

15) Supervise forest nursery operations, timber harvesting, land use activities such as livestock grazing, and disease or insect control programs.

16) Select and mark trees for thinning or logging, drawing detailed plans that include access roads.

17) Inspect trees and collect samples of plants, seeds, foliage, bark and roots to locate insect and disease damage.

18) Conduct laboratory or field experiments with plants, animals, insects, diseases and soils.

19) Monitor activities of logging companies and contractors.

21-1011.00 - Substance Abuse and Behavioral Disorder Counselors

Counsel and advise individuals with alcohol, tobacco, drug, or other problems, such as gambling and eating disorders. May counsel individuals, families, or groups or engage in prevention programs.

Tasks

1) Follow progress of discharged patients in order to determine effectiveness of treatments.

2) Develop, implement, and evaluate public education, prevention, and health promotion programs, working in collaboration with organizations, institutions and communities.

3) Counsel family members to assist them in understanding, dealing with, and supporting clients or patients.

4) Confer with family members or others close to clients in order to keep them informed of treatment planning and progress.

5) Coordinate counseling efforts with mental health professionals and other health professionals such as doctors, nurses, and social workers.

6) Act as liaisons between clients and medical staff.

7) Complete and maintain accurate records and reports regarding the patients' histories and progress, services provided, and other required information.

8) Instruct others in program methods, procedures, and functions.

9) Plan and implement follow-up and aftercare programs for clients to be discharged from treatment programs.

10) Coordinate activities with courts, probation officers, community services and other post-treatment agencies.

11) Modify treatment plans to comply with changes in client status.

12) Interview clients, review records, and confer with other professionals in order to evaluate individuals' mental and physical condition, and to determine their suitability for participation in a specific program.

13) Develop client treatment plans based on research, clinical experience, and client histories.

14) Counsel clients and patients, individually and in group sessions, to assist in overcoming dependencies, adjusting to life, and making changes.

15) Attend training sessions in order to increase knowledge and skills.

16) Supervise and direct other workers providing services to clients or patients.

17) Provide clients or family members with information about addiction issues and about available services and programs, making appropriate referrals when necessary.

18) Review and evaluate clients' progress in relation to measurable goals described in treatment and care plans.

19) Conduct chemical dependency program orientation sessions.

20) Intervene as advocate for clients or patients in order to resolve emergency problems in crisis situations.

21-1012.00 - Educational, Vocational, and School Counselors

Counsel individuals and provide group educational and vocational guidance services.

Tasks

1) Provide information to businesses regarding human resource and employment issues.

2) Provide special services such as alcohol and drug prevention programs, and classes that teach students to handle conflicts without resorting to violence.

3) Attend staff meetings, and serve on committees as required.

4) Confer with parents or guardians, teachers, other counselors, and administrators to resolve students' behavioral, academic, and other problems.

5) Review transcripts to ensure that students meet graduation or college entrance requirements, and write letters of recommendation.

6) Enforce all administration policies and rules governing students.

7) Establish and supervise peer counseling and peer tutoring programs.

8) Provide disabled students with assistive devices, supportive technology, and assistance accessing facilities such as restrooms.

9) Attend professional meetings, educational conferences, and teacher training workshops, in order to maintain and improve professional competence.

10) Meet with other professionals to discuss individual students' needs and progress.

11) Maintain accurate and complete student records as required by laws, district policies, and administrative regulations.

12) Compile and study occupational, educational, and economic information to assist counselees in determining and carrying out vocational and educational objectives.

13) Observe children during classroom and play activities to gain additional information about them.

14) Assess needs for assistance such as rehabilitation, financial aid, or additional vocational training, and refer clients to the appropriate services.

15) Provide crisis intervention to students when difficult situations occur at schools.

16) Prepare students for later educational experiences by encouraging them to explore learning opportunities and to persevere with challenging tasks.

17) Prepare reports on students and activities as required by administration.

18) Plan and promote career and employment-related programs such as work-experience programs.

19) Plan and conduct orientation programs and group conferences to promote the adjustment of individuals to new life experiences such as starting college.

20) Observe and evaluate students' performance, behavior, social development, and physical health.

21) Meet with parents and guardians to discuss their children's progress, and to determine their priorities for their children and their resource needs.

22) Instruct individuals in career development techniques such as job search and application strategies, resume writing, and interview skills.

23) Interview clients to obtain information about employment history, educational background, and career goals, and to identify barriers to employment.

24) Encourage students and/or parents to seek additional assistance from mental health professionals when necessary.

25) Refer students to degree programs based on interests, aptitudes, or educational assessments.

26) Teach classes and present self-help or information sessions on subjects related to education and career planning.

27) Conduct follow-up interviews with counselees to determine if their needs have been met.

28) Identify cases involving domestic abuse or other family problems affecting students' development.

29) Address community groups, faculty, and staff members to explain available counseling services.

30) Collaborate with teachers and administrators in the development, evaluation, and revision of school programs.

31) Perform administrative duties such as hall and cafeteria monitoring, and bus loading and unloading.

32) Provide information for teachers and staff members involved in helping students or graduates identify and pursue employment opportunities.

33) Refer qualified counselees to employers or employment services for job placement.

34) Counsel individuals to help them understand and overcome personal, social, or behavioral problems affecting their educational or vocational situations.

35) Counsel students regarding educational issues such as course and program selection, class scheduling, school adjustment, truancy, study habits, and career planning.

36) Evaluate individuals' abilities, interests, and personality characteristics using tests, records, interviews, and professional sources.

37) Sponsor extracurricular activities such as clubs, student organizations, and academic contests.

38) Provide students with information on such topics as college degree programs and admission requirements, financial aid opportunities, trade and technical schools, and apprenticeship programs.

21-1013.00 - Marriage and Family Therapists

Diagnose and treat mental and emotional disorders, whether cognitive, affective, or behavioral, within the context of marriage and family systems. Apply psychotherapeutic and family systems theories and techniques in the delivery of professional services to individuals, couples, and families for the purpose of treating such diagnosed nervous and mental disorders.

Tasks

1) Provide family counseling and treatment services to inmates participating in substance abuse programs.

2) Encourage individuals and family members to develop and use skills and strategies for confronting their problems in a constructive manner.

3) Provide public education and consultation to other professionals or groups regarding counseling services, issues and methods.

4) Develop and implement individualized treatment plans addressing family relationship problems.

5) Maintain case files that include activities, progress notes, evaluations, and recommendations.

6) Counsel clients on concerns such as unsatisfactory relationships, divorce and separation, child rearing, home management, and financial difficulties.

7) Collect information about clients, using techniques such as testing, interviewing, discussion, and observation.

8) Follow up on results of counseling programs and clients' adjustments in order to determine effectiveness of programs.

9) Confer with clients in order to develop plans for post-treatment activities.

10) Write evaluations of parents and children for use by courts deciding divorce and custody cases, testifying in court if necessary.

11) Contact doctors, schools, social workers, juvenile counselors, law enforcement personnel and others to gather information in order to make recommendations to courts for the resolution of child custody or visitation disputes.

12) Supervise other counselors, social service staff and assistants.

13) Provide instructions to clients on how to obtain help with legal, financial, and other personal issues.

14) Ask questions that will help clients identify their feelings and behaviors.

15) Confer with other counselors in order to analyze individual cases and to coordinate counseling services.

21-1014.00 - Mental Health Counselors

Counsel with emphasis on prevention. Work with individuals and groups to promote optimum mental health. May help individuals deal with addictions and substance abuse; family, parenting, and marital problems; suicide; stress management; problems with self-esteem; and issues associated with aging and mental and emotional health.

Tasks

1) Monitor clients' use of medications.

2) Evaluate clients' physical or mental condition based on review of client information.

3) Evaluate the effectiveness of counseling programs and clients' progress in resolving identified problems and moving towards defined objectives.

4) Guide clients in the development of skills and strategies for dealing with their problems.

5) Run workshops and courses about mental health issues.

6) Maintain confidentiality of records relating to clients' treatment.

7) Prepare and maintain all required treatment records and reports.

8) Plan and conduct programs to prevent substance abuse or improve community health and counseling services.

9) Learn about new developments in their field by reading professional literature, attending courses and seminars, and establishing and maintaining contact with other social service agencies.

10) Counsel clients and patients, individually and in group sessions, to assist in overcoming dependencies, adjusting to life, and making changes.

11) Collaborate with other staff members to perform clinical assessments and develop treatment plans.

12) Supervise other counselors, social service staff, and assistants.

13) Counsel family members to assist them in understanding, dealing with, and supporting

clients or patients.

14) Refer patients, clients, or family members to community resources or to specialists as necessary.

15) Develop and implement treatment plans based on clinical experience and knowledge.

16) Modify treatment activities and approaches as needed in order to comply with changes in clients' status.

17) Encourage clients to express their feelings and discuss what is happening in their lives, and help them to develop insight into themselves and their relationships.

18) Act as client advocates in order to coordinate required services or to resolve emergency problems in crisis situations.

19) Plan, organize and lead structured programs of counseling, work, study, recreation and social activities for clients.

20) Collect information about clients through interviews, observation, and tests.

21) Gather information about community mental health needs and resources that could be used in conjunction with therapy.

22) Discuss with individual patients their plans for life after leaving therapy.

21-1021.00 - Child, Family, and School Social Workers

Provide social services and assistance to improve the social and psychological functioning of children and their families and to maximize the family well-being and the academic functioning of children. May assist single parents, arrange adoptions, and find foster homes for abandoned or abused children. In schools, they address such problems as teenage pregnancy, misbehavior, and truancy. May also advise teachers on how to deal with problem children.

Tasks

1) Develop and review service plans in consultation with clients, and perform follow-ups assessing the quantity and quality of services provided.

2) Refer clients to community resources for services such as job placement, debt counseling, legal aid, housing, medical treatment, or financial assistance, and provide concrete information, such as where to go and how to apply.

3) Counsel individuals, groups, families, or communities regarding issues including mental health, poverty, unemployment, substance abuse, physical abuse, rehabilitation, social adjustment, child care, and/or medical care.

4) Arrange for medical, psychiatric, and other tests that may disclose causes of difficulties and indicate remedial measures.

5) Collect supplementary information needed to assist client, such as employment records, medical records, or school reports.

6) Maintain case history records and prepare reports.

7) Provide, find, or arrange for support services, such as child care, homemaker service, prenatal care, substance abuse treatment, job training, counseling, or parenting classes, to prevent more serious problems from developing.

8) Consult with parents, teachers, and other school personnel to determine causes of problems such as truancy and misbehavior, and to implement solutions.

9) Counsel parents with child rearing problems, interviewing the child and family to determine whether further action is required.

10) Address legal issues, such as child abuse and discipline, assisting with hearings and providing testimony to inform custody arrangements.

11) Counsel students whose behavior, school progress, or mental or physical impairment indicate a need for assistance, diagnosing students' problems and arranging for needed services.

12) Serve as liaisons between students, homes, schools, family services, child guidance clinics, courts, protective services, doctors, and other contacts, to help children who face problems such as disabilities, abuse, or poverty.

13) Serve on policymaking committees, assist in community development, and assist client groups by lobbying for solutions to problems.

14) Lead group counseling sessions that provide support in such areas as grief, stress, or chemical dependency.

15) Place children in foster or adoptive homes, institutions, or medical treatment centers.

16) Determine clients' eligibility for financial assistance.

17) Recommend temporary foster care and advise foster or adoptive parents.

18) Evaluate personal characteristics and home conditions of foster home or adoption applicants.

19) Supervise other social workers.

20) Conduct social research.

21) Work in child and adolescent residential institutions.

22) Administer welfare programs.

Knowledge	Knowledge Definitions
Psychology	Knowledge of human behavior and performance; individual differences in ability, personality, and interests; learning and motivation; psychological research methods; and the assessment and treatment of behavioral and affective disorders.
Therapy and Counseling	Knowledge of principles, methods, and procedures for diagnosis, treatment, and rehabilitation of physical and mental dysfunctions, and for career counseling and guidance.
Customer and Personal Service	Knowledge of principles and processes for providing customer and personal services. This includes customer needs assessment, meeting quality standards for services, and evaluation of customer satisfaction.
Sociology and Anthropology	Knowledge of group behavior and dynamics, societal trends and influences, human migrations, ethnicity, cultures and their history and origins.
English Language	Knowledge of the structure and content of the English language including the meaning and spelling of words, rules of composition, and grammar.
Law and Government	Knowledge of laws, legal codes, court procedures, precedents, government regulations, executive orders, agency rules, and the democratic political process.
Computers and Electronics	Knowledge of circuit boards, processors, chips, electronic equipment, and computer hardware and software, including applications and programming.
Education and Training	Knowledge of principles and methods for curriculum and training design, teaching and instruction for individuals and groups, and the measurement of training effects.
Clerical	Knowledge of administrative and clerical procedures and systems such as word processing, managing files and records, stenography and transcription, designing forms, and other office procedures and terminology.
Public Safety and Security	Knowledge of relevant equipment, policies, procedures, and strategies to promote effective local, state, or national security operations for the protection of people, data, property, and institutions.
Philosophy and Theology	Knowledge of different philosophical systems and religions. This includes their basic principles, values, ethics, ways of thinking, customs, practices, and their impact on human culture.
Communications and Media	Knowledge of media production, communication, and dissemination techniques and methods. This includes alternative ways to inform and entertain via written, oral, and visual media.
Administration and Management	Knowledge of business and management principles involved in strategic planning, resource allocation, human resources modeling, leadership technique, production methods, and coordination of people and resources.
Transportation	Knowledge of principles and methods for moving people or goods by air, rail, sea, or road, including the relative costs and benefits.
Telecommunications	Knowledge of transmission, broadcasting, switching, control, and operation of telecommunications systems.
Personnel and Human Resources	Knowledge of principles and procedures for personnel recruitment, selection, training, compensation and benefits, labor relations and negotiation, and personnel information systems.
Mathematics	Knowledge of arithmetic, algebra, geometry, calculus, statistics, and their applications.
Medicine and Dentistry	Knowledge of the information and techniques needed to diagnose and treat human injuries, diseases, and deformities. This includes symptoms, treatment alternatives, drug properties and interactions, and preventive health-care measures.
Geography	Knowledge of principles and methods for describing the features of land, sea, and air masses, including their physical characteristics, locations, interrelationships, and distribution of plant, animal, and human life.
Foreign Language	Knowledge of the structure and content of a foreign (non-English) language including the meaning and spelling of words, rules of composition and grammar, and pronunciation.
Biology	Knowledge of plant and animal organisms, their tissues, cells, functions, interdependencies, and interactions with each other and the environment.
Economics and Accounting	Knowledge of economic and accounting principles and practices, the financial markets, banking and the analysis and reporting of financial data.
History and Archeology	Knowledge of historical events and their causes, indicators, and effects on civilizations and cultures.
Sales and Marketing	Knowledge of principles and methods for showing, promoting, and selling products or services. This includes marketing strategy and tactics, product demonstration, sales techniques, and sales control systems.
Production and Processing	Knowledge of raw materials, production processes, quality control, costs, and other techniques for maximizing the effective manufacture and distribution of goods.
Chemistry	Knowledge of the chemical composition, structure, and properties of substances and of the chemical processes and transformations that they undergo. This includes uses of chemicals and their interactions, danger signs, production techniques, and disposal methods.
Mechanical	Knowledge of machines and tools, including their designs, uses, repair, and maintenance.
Fine Arts	Knowledge of the theory and techniques required to compose, produce, and perform works of music, dance, visual arts, drama, and sculpture.
Design	Knowledge of design techniques, tools, and principles involved in production of precision technical plans, blueprints, drawings, and models.
Physics	Knowledge and prediction of physical principles, laws, their interrelationships, and applications to understanding fluid, material, and atmospheric dynamics, and mechanical, electrical, atomic and sub-atomic structures and processes.
Building and Construction	Knowledge of materials, methods, and the tools involved in the construction or repair of houses, buildings, or other structures such as highways and roads.
Engineering and Technology	Knowledge of the practical application of engineering science and technology. This includes applying principles, techniques, procedures, and equipment to the design and production of various goods and services.
Food Production	Knowledge of techniques and equipment for planting, growing, and harvesting food products (both plant and animal) for consumption, including storage/handling techniques.

Skills	Skills Definitions
Speaking	Talking to others to convey information effectively.
Active Listening	Giving full attention to what other people are saying, taking time to understand the points being made, asking questions as appropriate, and not interrupting at inappropriate times.
Monitoring	Monitoring/Assessing performance of yourself, other individuals, or organizations to make improvements or take corrective action.
Social Perceptiveness	Being aware of others' reactions and understanding why they react as they do.
Service Orientation	Actively looking for ways to help people.
Reading Comprehension	Understanding written sentences and paragraphs in work related documents.
Active Learning	Understanding the implications of new information for both current and future problem-solving and decision-making.
Writing	Communicating effectively in writing as appropriate for the needs of the audience.
Critical Thinking	Using logic and reasoning to identify the strengths and weaknesses of alternative solutions, conclusions or approaches to problems.
Judgment and Decision Making	Considering the relative costs and benefits of potential actions to choose the most appropriate one.
Coordination	Adjusting actions in relation to others' actions.
Time Management	Managing one's own time and the time of others.
Negotiation	Bringing others together and trying to reconcile differences.
Persuasion	Persuading others to change their minds or behavior.
Learning Strategies	Selecting and using training/instructional methods and procedures appropriate for the situation when learning or teaching new things.
Complex Problem Solving	Identifying complex problems and reviewing related information to develop and evaluate options and implement solutions.
Instructing	Teaching others how to do something.
Management of Personnel Resources	Motivating, developing, and directing people as they work, identifying the best people for the job.
Mathematics	Using mathematics to solve problems.
Systems Evaluation	Identifying measures or indicators of system performance and the actions needed to improve or correct performance, relative to the goals of the system.
Science	Using scientific rules and methods to solve problems.
Operations Analysis	Analyzing needs and product requirements to create a design.
Management of Financial Resources	Determining how money will be spent to get the work done, and accounting for these expenditures.
Systems Analysis	Determining how a system should work and how changes in conditions, operations, and the environment will affect outcomes.
Quality Control Analysis	Conducting tests and inspections of products, services, or processes to evaluate quality or performance.
Troubleshooting	Determining causes of operating errors and deciding what to do about it.
Equipment Selection	Determining the kind of tools and equipment needed to do a job.
Management of Material Resources	Obtaining and seeing to the appropriate use of equipment, facilities, and materials needed to do certain work.
Technology Design	Generating or adapting equipment and technology to serve user needs.
Operation and Control	Controlling operations of equipment or systems.

Repairing	Repairing machines or systems using the needed tools.
Operation Monitoring	Watching gauges. dials. or other indicators to make sure a machine is working properly.
Programming	Writing computer programs for various purposes.
Installation	Installing equipment. machines. wiring. or programs to meet specifications.
Equipment Maintenance	Performing routine maintenance on equipment and determining when and what kind of maintenance is needed.

Ability	Ability Definitions
Oral Comprehension	The ability to listen to and understand information and ideas presented through spoken words and sentences.
Oral Expression	The ability to communicate information and ideas in speaking so others will understand.
Problem Sensitivity	The ability to tell when something is wrong or is likely to go wrong. It does not involve solving the problem, only recognizing there is a problem.
Speech Clarity	The ability to speak clearly so others can understand you.
Speech Recognition	The ability to identify and understand the speech of another person.
Inductive Reasoning	The ability to combine pieces of information to form general rules or conclusions (includes finding a relationship among seemingly unrelated events).
Written Expression	The ability to communicate information and ideas in writing so others will understand.
Near Vision	The ability to see details at close range (within a few feet of the observer).
Written Comprehension	The ability to read and understand information and ideas presented in writing.
Deductive Reasoning	The ability to apply general rules to specific problems to produce answers that make sense.
Selective Attention	The ability to concentrate on a task over a period of time without being distracted.
Originality	The ability to come up with unusual or clever ideas about a given topic or situation, or to develop creative ways to solve a problem.
Fluency of Ideas	The ability to come up with a number of ideas about a topic (the number of ideas is important, not their quality, correctness, or creativity).
Information Ordering	The ability to arrange things or actions in a certain order or pattern according to a specific rule or set of rules (e.g., patterns of numbers, letters, words, pictures, mathematical operations).
Category Flexibility	The ability to generate or use different sets of rules for combining or grouping things in different ways.
Speed of Closure	The ability to quickly make sense of, combine, and organize information into meaningful patterns.
Flexibility of Closure	The ability to identify or detect a known pattern (a figure, object, word, or sound) that is hidden in other distracting material.
Time Sharing	The ability to shift back and forth between two or more activities or sources of information (such as speech, sounds, touch, or other sources).
Finger Dexterity	The ability to make precisely coordinated movements of the fingers of one or both hands to grasp, manipulate, or assemble very small objects.
Trunk Strength	The ability to use your abdominal and lower back muscles to support part of the body repeatedly or continuously over time without 'giving out' or fatiguing.
Auditory Attention	The ability to focus on a single source of sound in the presence of other distracting sounds.
Memorization	The ability to remember information such as words, numbers, pictures, and procedures.
Depth Perception	The ability to judge which of several objects is closer or farther away from you, or to judge the distance between you and an object.
Far Vision	The ability to see details at a distance.
Multilimb Coordination	The ability to coordinate two or more limbs (for example, two arms, two legs, or one leg and one arm) while sitting, standing, or lying down. It does not involve performing the activities while the whole body is in motion.
Control Precision	The ability to quickly and repeatedly adjust the controls of a machine or a vehicle to exact positions.
Perceptual Speed	The ability to quickly and accurately compare similarities and differences among sets of letters, numbers, objects, pictures, or patterns. The things to be compared may be presented at the same time or one after the other. This ability also includes comparing a presented object with a remembered object.
Mathematical Reasoning	The ability to choose the right mathematical methods or formulas to solve a problem.
Number Facility	The ability to add, subtract, multiply, or divide quickly and correctly.
Visualization	The ability to imagine how something will look after it is moved around or when its parts are moved or rearranged.
Hearing Sensitivity	The ability to detect or tell the differences between sounds that vary in pitch and loudness.

Visual Color Discrimination	The ability to match or detect differences between colors. including shades of color and brightness.
Wrist-Finger Speed	The ability to make fast, simple, repeated movements of the fingers, hands, and wrists.
Night Vision	The ability to see under low light conditions.
Dynamic Flexibility	The ability to quickly and repeatedly bend, stretch. twist. or reach out with your body, arms, and/or legs.
Gross Body Coordination	The ability to coordinate the movement of your arms. legs. and torso together when the whole body is in motion.
Reaction Time	The ability to quickly respond (with the hand. finger. or foot) to a signal (sound, light, picture) when it appears.
Spatial Orientation	The ability to know your location in relation to the environment or to know where other objects are in relation to you.
Manual Dexterity	The ability to quickly move your hand, your hand together with your arm, or your two hands to grasp, manipulate, or assemble objects.
Speed of Limb Movement	The ability to quickly move the arms and legs.
Static Strength	The ability to exert maximum muscle force to lift, push. pull. or carry objects.
Explosive Strength	The ability to use short bursts of muscle force to propel oneself (as in jumping or sprinting), or to throw an object.
Dynamic Strength	The ability to exert muscle force repeatedly or continuously over time. This involves muscular endurance and resistance to muscle fatigue.
Extent Flexibility	The ability to bend, stretch, twist, or reach with your body, arms, and/or legs.
Peripheral Vision	The ability to see objects or movement of objects to one's side when the eyes are looking ahead.
Arm-Hand Steadiness	The ability to keep your hand and arm steady while moving your arm or while holding your arm and hand in one position.
Rate Control	The ability to time your movements or the movement of a piece of equipment in anticipation of changes in the speed and/or direction of a moving object or scene.
Glare Sensitivity	The ability to see objects in the presence of glare or bright lighting.
Response Orientation	The ability to choose quickly between two or more movements in response to two or more different signals (lights, sounds, pictures). It includes the speed with which the correct response is started with the hand, foot, or other body part.
Gross Body Equilibrium	The ability to keep or regain your body balance or stay upright when in an unstable position.
Sound Localization	The ability to tell the direction from which a sound originated.
Stamina	The ability to exert yourself physically over long periods of time without getting winded or out of breath.

Work_Activity	Work_Activity Definitions
Communicating with Supervisors, Peers, or Subordin	Providing information to supervisors, co-workers, and subordinates by telephone, in written form, e-mail, or in person.
Making Decisions and Solving Problems	Analyzing information and evaluating results to choose the best solution and solve problems.
Getting Information	Observing, receiving, and otherwise obtaining information from all relevant sources.
Communicating with Persons Outside Organization	Communicating with people outside the organization, representing the organization to customers, the public, government, and other external sources. This information can be exchanged in person, in writing, or by telephone or e-mail.
Establishing and Maintaining Interpersonal Relatio	Developing constructive and cooperative working relationships with others, and maintaining them over time.
Evaluating Information to Determine Compliance wit	Using relevant information and individual judgment to determine whether events or processes comply with laws, regulations, or standards.
Organizing, Planning, and Prioritizing Work	Developing specific goals and plans to prioritize, organize, and accomplish your work.
Assisting and Caring for Others	Providing personal assistance, medical attention, emotional support, or other personal care to others such as coworkers, customers, or patients.
Documenting/Recording Information	Entering, transcribing, recording, storing, or maintaining information in written or electronic/magnetic form.
Resolving Conflicts and Negotiating with Others	Handling complaints, settling disputes, and resolving grievances and conflicts, or otherwise negotiating with others.
Coordinating the Work and Activities of Others	Getting members of a group to work together to accomplish tasks.
Developing and Building Teams	Encouraging and building mutual trust, respect, and cooperation among team members.
Training and Teaching Others	Identifying the educational needs of others, developing formal educational or training programs or classes, and teaching or instructing others.
Developing Objectives and Strategies	Establishing long-range objectives and specifying the strategies and actions to achieve them.
Scheduling Work and Activities	Scheduling events, programs, and activities, as well as the work of others.
Performing Administrative Activities	Performing day-to-day administrative tasks such as maintaining information files and processing paperwork.

Coaching and Developing Others	Identifying the developmental needs of others and coaching, mentoring, or otherwise helping others to improve their knowledge or skills.
Interacting With Computers	Using computers and computer systems (including hardware and software) to program, write software, set up functions, enter data, or process information.
Thinking Creatively	Developing, designing, or creating new applications, ideas, relationships, systems, or products, including artistic contributions.
Judging the Qualities of Things, Services, or Peop	Assessing the value, importance, or quality of things or people.
Updating and Using Relevant Knowledge	Keeping up-to-date technically and applying new knowledge to your job.
Identifying Objects, Actions, and Events	Identifying information by categorizing, estimating, recognizing differences or similarities, and detecting changes in circumstances or events.
Guiding, Directing, and Motivating Subordinates	Providing guidance and direction to subordinates, including setting performance standards and monitoring performance.
Performing for or Working Directly with the Public	Performing for people or dealing directly with the public. This includes serving customers in restaurants and stores, and receiving clients or guests.
Processing Information	Compiling, coding, categorizing, calculating, tabulating, auditing, or verifying information or data.
Monitor Processes, Materials, or Surroundings	Monitoring and reviewing information from materials, events, or the environment, to detect or assess problems.
Interpreting the Meaning of Information for Others	Translating or explaining what information means and how it can be used.
Staffing Organizational Units	Recruiting, interviewing, selecting, hiring, and promoting employees in an organization.
Provide Consultation and Advice to Others	Providing guidance and expert advice to management or other groups on technical, systems-, or process-related topics.
Monitoring and Controlling Resources	Monitoring and controlling resources and overseeing the spending of money.
Analyzing Data or Information	Identifying the underlying principles, reasons, or facts of information by breaking down information or data into separate parts.
Selling or Influencing Others	Convincing others to buy merchandise/goods or to otherwise change their minds or actions.
Operating Vehicles, Mechanized Devices, or Equipme	Running, maneuvering, navigating, or driving vehicles or mechanized equipment, such as forklifts, passenger vehicles, aircraft, or water craft.
Performing General Physical Activities	Performing physical activities that require considerable use of your arms and legs and moving your whole body, such as climbing, lifting, balancing, walking, stooping, and handling of materials.
Estimating the Quantifiable Characteristics of Pro	Estimating sizes, distances, and quantities; or determining time, costs, resources, or materials needed to perform a work activity.
Inspecting Equipment, Structures, or Material	Inspecting equipment, structures, or materials to identify the cause of errors or other problems or defects.
Controlling Machines and Processes	Using either control mechanisms or direct physical activity to operate machines or processes (not including computers or vehicles).
Handling and Moving Objects	Using hands and arms in handling, installing, positioning, and moving materials, and manipulating things.
Drafting, Laying Out, and Specifying Technical Dev	Providing documentation, detailed instructions, drawings, or specifications to tell others about how devices, parts, equipment, or structures are to be fabricated, constructed, assembled, modified, maintained, or used.
Repairing and Maintaining Electronic Equipment	Servicing, repairing, calibrating, regulating, fine-tuning, or testing machines, devices, and equipment that operate primarily on the basis of electrical or electronic (not mechanical) principles.
Repairing and Maintaining Mechanical Equipment	Servicing, repairing, adjusting, and testing machines, devices, moving parts, and equipment that operate primarily on the basis of mechanical (not electronic) principles.

Work_Content	Work_Content Definitions
Telephone	How often do you have telephone conversations in this job?
Face-to-Face Discussions	How often do you have to have face-to-face discussions with individuals or teams in this job?
Contact With Others	How much does this job require the worker to be in contact with others (face-to-face, by telephone, or otherwise) in order to perform it?
Freedom to Make Decisions	How much decision making freedom, without supervision, does the job offer?
Structured versus Unstructured Work	To what extent is this job structured for the worker, rather than allowing the worker to determine tasks, priorities, and goals?
Deal With External Customers	How important is it to work with external customers or the public in this job?
Work With Work Group or Team	How important is it to work with others in a group or team in this job?
Letters and Memos	How often does the job require written letters and memos?

Impact of Decisions on Co-workers or Company Resul	How do the decisions an employee makes impact the results of co-workers, clients or the company?
Importance of Being Exact or Accurate	How important is being very exact or highly accurate in performing this job?
Frequency of Decision Making	How frequently is the worker required to make decisions that affect other people, the financial resources, and/or the image and reputation of the organization?
Indoors, Environmentally Controlled	How often does this job require working indoors in environmentally controlled conditions?
Time Pressure	How often does this job require the worker to meet strict deadlines?
Spend Time Sitting	How much does this job require sitting?
Electronic Mail	How often do you use electronic mail in this job?
Coordinate or Lead Others	How important is it to coordinate or lead others in accomplishing work activities in this job?
In an Enclosed Vehicle or Equipment	How often does this job require working in a closed vehicle or equipment (e.g., car)?
Physical Proximity	To what extent does this job require the worker to perform job tasks in close physical proximity to other people?
Deal With Unpleasant or Angry People	How frequently does the worker have to deal with unpleasant, angry, or discourteous individuals as part of the job requirements?
Frequency of Conflict Situations	How often are there conflict situations the employee has to face in this job?
Consequence of Error	How serious would the result usually be if the worker made a mistake that was not readily correctable?
Sounds, Noise Levels Are Distracting or Uncomforta	How often does this job require working exposed to sounds and noise levels that are distracting or uncomfortable?
Responsibility for Outcomes and Results	How responsible is the worker for work outcomes and results of other workers?
Outdoors, Exposed to Weather	How often does this job require working outdoors, exposed to all weather conditions?
Spend Time Standing	How much does this job require standing?
Degree of Automation	How automated is the job?
Responsible for Others' Health and Safety	How much responsibility is there for the health and safety of others in this job?
Exposed to Disease or Infections	How often does this job require exposure to disease/infections?
Level of Competition	To what extent does this job require the worker to compete or to be aware of competitive pressures?
Public Speaking	How often do you have to perform public speaking in this job?
Spend Time Walking and Running	How much does this job require walking and running?
Deal With Physically Aggressive People	How frequently does this job require the worker to deal with physical aggression of violent individuals?
Exposed to Contaminants	How often does this job require working exposed to contaminants (such as pollutants, gases, dust or odors)?
Spend Time Using Your Hands to Handle, Control, or	How much does this job require using your hands to handle, control, or feel objects, tools or controls?
Importance of Repeating Same Tasks	How important is repeating the same physical activities (e.g., key entry) or mental activities (e.g., checking entries in a ledger) over and over, without stopping, to performing this job?
Indoors, Not Environmentally Controlled	How often does this job require working indoors in non-controlled environmental conditions (e.g., warehouse without heat)?
Spend Time Making Repetitive Motions	How much does this job require making repetitive motions?
Wear Common Protective or Safety Equipment such as	How much does this job require wearing common protective or safety equipment such as safety shoes, glasses, gloves, hard hats or live jackets?
Very Hot or Cold Temperatures	How often does this job require working in very hot (above 90 F degrees) or very cold (below 32 F degrees) temperatures?
Pace Determined by Speed of Equipment	How important is it to this job that the pace is determined by the speed of equipment or machinery? (This does not refer to keeping busy at all times on this job.)
Exposed to Minor Burns, Cuts, Bites, or Stings	How often does this job require exposure to minor burns, cuts, bites, or stings?
Spend Time Bending or Twisting the Body	How much does this job require bending or twisting your body?
Outdoors, Under Cover	How often does this job require working outdoors, under cover (e.g., structure with roof but no walls)?
Extremely Bright or Inadequate Lighting	How often does this job require working in extremely bright or inadequate lighting conditions?
Spend Time Kneeling, Crouching, Stooping, or Crawl	How much does this job require kneeling, crouching, stooping, or crawling?
Cramped Work Space, Awkward Positions	How often does this job require working in cramped work spaces that requires getting into awkward positions?
Spend Time Climbing Ladders, Scaffolds, or Poles	How much does this job require climbing ladders, scaffolds, or poles?
Exposed to Hazardous Equipment	How often does this job require exposure to hazardous equipment?

In an Open Vehicle or Equipment	How often does this job require working in an open vehicle or equipment (e.g., tractor)?
Exposed to Hazardous Conditions	How often does this job require exposure to hazardous conditions?
Exposed to Radiation	How often does this job require exposure to radiation?
Spend Time Keeping or Regaining Balance	How much does this job require keeping or regaining your balance?
Wear Specialized Protective or Safety Equipment su	How much does this job require wearing specialized protective or safety equipment such as breathing apparatus, safety harness, full protection suits, or radiation protection?
Exposed to High Places	How often does this job require exposure to high places?
Exposed to Whole Body Vibration	How often does this job require exposure to whole body vibration (e.g., operate a jackhammer)?

Work_Styles	Work_Styles Definitions
Integrity	Job requires being honest and ethical.
Concern for Others	Job requires being sensitive to others' needs and feelings and being understanding and helpful on the job.
Stress Tolerance	Job requires accepting criticism and dealing calmly and effectively with high stress situations.
Cooperation	Job requires being pleasant with others on the job and displaying a good-natured, cooperative attitude.
Self Control	Job requires maintaining composure, keeping emotions in check, controlling anger, and avoiding aggressive behavior, even in very difficult situations.
Initiative	Job requires a willingness to take on responsibilities and challenges.
Dependability	Job requires being reliable, responsible, and dependable, and fulfilling obligations.
Adaptability/Flexibility	Job requires being open to change (positive or negative) and to considerable variety in the workplace.
Social Orientation	Job requires preferring to work with others rather than alone, and being personally connected with others on the job.
Persistence	Job requires persistence in the face of obstacles.
Attention to Detail	Job requires being careful about detail and thorough in completing work tasks.
Achievement/Effort	Job requires establishing and maintaining personally challenging achievement goals and exerting effort toward mastering tasks.
Independence	Job requires developing one's own ways of doing things, guiding oneself with little or no supervision, and depending on oneself to get things done.
Leadership	Job requires a willingness to lead, take charge, and offer opinions and direction.
Analytical Thinking	Job requires analyzing information and using logic to address work-related issues and problems.
Innovation	Job requires creativity and alternative thinking to develop new ideas for and answers to work-related problems.

Job Zone Component	Job Zone Component Definitions
Title	Job Zone Five: Extensive Preparation Needed
	Extensive skill, knowledge, and experience are needed for these occupations. Many require more than five years of experience.
Overall Experience	For example, surgeons must complete four years of college and an additional five to seven years of specialized medical training to be able to do their job.
Job Training	Employees may need some on-the-job training, but most of these occupations assume that the person will already have the required skills, knowledge, work-related experience, and/or training.
Job Zone Examples	These occupations often involve coordinating, training, supervising, or managing the activities of others to accomplish goals. Very advanced communication and organizational skills are required. Examples include athletic trainers, lawyers, managing editors, physicists, social psychologists, and surgeons.
SVP Range	(8.0 and above)
Education	A bachelor's degree is the minimum formal education required for these occupations. However, many also require graduate school. For example, they may require a master's degree, and some require a Ph.D., M.D., or J.D. (law degree).

21-1022.00 - Medical and Public Health Social Workers

Provide persons, families, or vulnerable populations with the psychosocial support needed to cope with chronic, acute, or terminal illnesses, such as Alzheimer's, cancer, or AIDS. Services include advising family caregivers, providing patient education and counseling, and making necessary referrals for other social services.

Tasks

1) Advocate for clients or patients to resolve crises.

2) Identify environmental impediments to client or patient progress through interviews and review of patient records.

3) Modify treatment plans to comply with changes in clients' status.

4) Refer patient, client, or family to community resources to assist in recovery from mental or physical illness and to provide access to services such as financial assistance, legal aid, housing, job placement or education.

5) Utilize consultation data and social work experience to plan and coordinate client or patient care and rehabilitation, following through to ensure service efficacy.

6) Counsel clients and patients in individual and group sessions to help them overcome dependencies, recover from illness, and adjust to life.

7) Monitor, evaluate, and record client progress according to measurable goals described in treatment and care plan.

8) Organize support groups or counsel family members to assist them in understanding, dealing with, and supporting the client or patient.

9) Investigate child abuse or neglect cases and take authorized protective action when necessary.

10) Plan and conduct programs to combat social problems, prevent substance abuse, or improve community health and counseling services.

11) Develop or advise on social policy and assist in community development.

12) Supervise and direct other workers providing services to clients or patients.

13) Oversee Medicaid- and Medicare-related paperwork and record-keeping in hospitals.

14) Conduct social research to advance knowledge in the social work field.

Knowledge	Knowledge Definitions
Psychology	Knowledge of human behavior and performance; individual differences in ability, personality, and interests; learning and motivation; psychological research methods; and the assessment and treatment of behavioral and affective disorders.
Customer and Personal Service	Knowledge of principles and processes for providing customer and personal services. This includes customer needs assessment, meeting quality standards for services, and evaluation of customer satisfaction.
Therapy and Counseling	Knowledge of principles, methods, and procedures for diagnosis, treatment, and rehabilitation of physical and mental dysfunctions, and for career counseling and guidance.
English Language	Knowledge of the structure and content of the English language including the meaning and spelling of words, rules of composition, and grammar.
Sociology and Anthropology	Knowledge of group behavior and dynamics, societal trends and influences, human migrations, ethnicity, cultures and their history and origins.
Education and Training	Knowledge of principles and methods for curriculum and training design, teaching and instruction for individuals and groups, and the measurement of training effects.
Philosophy and Theology	Knowledge of different philosophical systems and religions. This includes their basic principles, values, ethics, ways of thinking, customs, practices, and their impact on human culture.
Medicine and Dentistry	Knowledge of the information and techniques needed to diagnose and treat human injuries, diseases, and deformities. This includes symptoms, treatment alternatives, drug properties and interactions, and preventive health-care measures.
Law and Government	Knowledge of laws, legal codes, court procedures, precedents, government regulations, executive orders, agency rules, and the democratic political process.
Personnel and Human Resources	Knowledge of principles and procedures for personnel recruitment, selection, training, compensation and benefits, labor relations and negotiation, and personnel information systems.
Clerical	Knowledge of administrative and clerical procedures and systems such as word processing, managing files and records, stenography and transcription, designing forms, and other office procedures and terminology.
Administration and Management	Knowledge of business and management principles involved in strategic planning, resource allocation, human resources modeling, leadership technique, production methods, and coordination of people and resources.
Mathematics	Knowledge of arithmetic, algebra, geometry, calculus, statistics, and their applications.
Computers and Electronics	Knowledge of circuit boards, processors, chips, electronic equipment, and computer hardware and software, including applications and programming.
Transportation	Knowledge of principles and methods for moving people or goods by air, rail, sea, or road, including the relative costs and benefits.
Public Safety and Security	Knowledge of relevant equipment, policies, procedures, and strategies to promote effective local, state, or national security operations for the protection of people, data, property, and institutions.

Biology	Knowledge of plant and animal organisms, their tissues. cells. functions, interdependencies, and interactions with each other and the environment.
Communications and Media	Knowledge of media production, communication, and dissemination techniques and methods. This includes alternative ways to inform and entertain via written, oral, and visual media.
Chemistry	Knowledge of the chemical composition, structure, and properties of substances and of the chemical processes and transformations that they undergo. This includes uses of chemicals and their interactions. danger signs, production techniques, and disposal methods.
Physics	Knowledge and prediction of physical principles. laws, their interrelationships, and applications to understanding fluid, material, and atmospheric dynamics, and mechanical, electrical, atomic and sub- atomic structures and processes.
Sales and Marketing	Knowledge of principles and methods for showing, promoting, and selling products or services. This includes marketing strategy and tactics. product demonstration, sales techniques, and sales control systems.
History and Archeology	Knowledge of historical events and their causes, indicators, and effects on civilizations and cultures.
Production and Processing	Knowledge of raw materials, production processes, quality control, costs, and other techniques for maximizing the effective manufacture and distribution of goods.
Telecommunications	Knowledge of transmission, broadcasting, switching, control, and operation of telecommunications systems.
Geography	Knowledge of principles and methods for describing the features of land, sea, and air masses, including their physical characteristics, locations, interrelationships, and distribution of plant, animal, and human life.
Mechanical	Knowledge of machines and tools, including their designs, uses, repair, and maintenance.
Foreign Language	Knowledge of the structure and content of a foreign (non-English) language including the meaning and spelling of words, rules of composition and grammar, and pronunciation.
Engineering and Technology	Knowledge of the practical application of engineering science and technology. This includes applying principles, techniques, procedures, and equipment to the design and production of various goods and services.
Economics and Accounting	Knowledge of economic and accounting principles and practices, the financial markets, banking and the analysis and reporting of financial data.
Fine Arts	Knowledge of the theory and techniques required to compose, produce, and perform works of music, dance, visual arts, drama, and sculpture.
Building and Construction	Knowledge of materials, methods, and the tools involved in the construction or repair of houses, buildings, or other structures such as highways and roads.
Design	Knowledge of design techniques, tools, and principles involved in production of precision technical plans, blueprints, drawings, and models.
Food Production	Knowledge of techniques and equipment for planting, growing, and harvesting food products (both plant and animal) for consumption, including storage/handling techniques.

Skills	Skills Definitions
Active Listening	Giving full attention to what other people are saying, taking time to understand the points being made, asking questions as appropriate, and not interrupting at inappropriate times.
Writing	Communicating effectively in writing as appropriate for the needs of the audience.
Reading Comprehension	Understanding written sentences and paragraphs in work related documents.
Social Perceptiveness	Being aware of others' reactions and understanding why they react as they do.
Speaking	Talking to others to convey information effectively.
Critical Thinking	Using logic and reasoning to identify the strengths and weaknesses of alternative solutions, conclusions or approaches to problems.
Coordination	Adjusting actions in relation to others' actions.
Time Management	Managing one's own time and the time of others.
Service Orientation	Actively looking for ways to help people.
Active Learning	Understanding the implications of new information for both current and future problem-solving and decision-making.
Judgment and Decision Making	Considering the relative costs and benefits of potential actions to choose the most appropriate one.
Complex Problem Solving	Identifying complex problems and reviewing related information to develop and evaluate options and implement solutions.
Negotiation	Bringing others together and trying to reconcile differences.
Monitoring	Monitoring/Assessing performance of yourself, other individuals, or organizations to make improvements or take corrective action.

Learning Strategies	Selecting and using training/instructional methods and procedures appropriate for the situation when learning or teaching new things.
Instructing	Teaching others how to do something.
Persuasion	Persuading others to change their minds or behavior.
Systems Analysis	Determining how a system should work and how changes in conditions. operations. and the environment will affect outcomes.
Management of Personnel Resources	Motivating. developing, and directing people as they work. identifying the best people for the job.
Systems Evaluation	Identifying measures or indicators of system performance and the actions needed to improve or correct performance, relative to the goals of the system.
Quality Control Analysis	Conducting tests and inspections of products, services, or processes to evaluate quality or performance.
Troubleshooting	Determining causes of operating errors and deciding what to do about it.
Science	Using scientific rules and methods to solve problems.
Operations Analysis	Analyzing needs and product requirements to create a design.
Management of Financial Resources	Determining how money will be spent to get the work done, and accounting for these expenditures.
Mathematics	Using mathematics to solve problems.
Equipment Selection	Determining the kind of tools and equipment needed to do a job.
Technology Design	Generating or adapting equipment and technology to serve user needs.
Operation Monitoring	Watching gauges, dials, or other indicators to make sure a machine is working properly.
Management of Material Resources	Obtaining and seeing to the appropriate use of equipment, facilities, and materials needed to do certain work.
Operation and Control	Controlling operations of equipment or systems.
Installation	Installing equipment, machines. wiring, or programs to meet specifications.
Programming	Writing computer programs for various purposes.
Repairing	Repairing machines or systems using the needed tools.
Equipment Maintenance	Performing routine maintenance on equipment and determining when and what kind of maintenance is needed.

Ability	Ability Definitions
Oral Comprehension	The ability to listen to and understand information and ideas presented through spoken words and sentences.
Oral Expression	The ability to communicate information and ideas in speaking so others will understand.
Problem Sensitivity	The ability to tell when something is wrong or is likely to go wrong. It does not involve solving the problem, only recognizing there is a problem.
Inductive Reasoning	The ability to combine pieces of information to form general rules or conclusions (includes finding a relationship among seemingly unrelated events).
Deductive Reasoning	The ability to apply general rules to specific problems to produce answers that make sense.
Speech Clarity	The ability to speak clearly so others can understand you.
Speech Recognition	The ability to identify and understand the speech of another person.
Written Comprehension	The ability to read and understand information and ideas presented in writing.
Written Expression	The ability to communicate information and ideas in writing so others will understand.
Near Vision	The ability to see details at close range (within a few feet of the observer).
Speed of Closure	The ability to quickly make sense of, combine, and organize information into meaningful patterns.
Category Flexibility	The ability to generate or use different sets of rules for combining or grouping things in different ways.
Flexibility of Closure	The ability to identify or detect a known pattern (a figure, object, word, or sound) that is hidden in other distracting material.
Information Ordering	The ability to arrange things or actions in a certain order or pattern according to a specific rule or set of rules (e.g., patterns of numbers, letters, words, pictures, mathematical operations).
Selective Attention	The ability to concentrate on a task over a period of time without being distracted.
Fluency of Ideas	The ability to come up with a number of ideas about a topic (the number of ideas is important, not their quality, correctness, or creativity).
Originality	The ability to come up with unusual or clever ideas about a given topic or situation, or to develop creative ways to solve a problem.
Time Sharing	The ability to shift back and forth between two or more activities or sources of information (such as speech, sounds, touch, or other sources).
Far Vision	The ability to see details at a distance.
Finger Dexterity	The ability to make precisely coordinated movements of the fingers of one or both hands to grasp, manipulate, or assemble very small objects.

97

Memorization	The ability to remember information such as words, numbers, pictures, and procedures.
Auditory Attention	The ability to focus on a single source of sound in the presence of other distracting sounds.
Perceptual Speed	The ability to quickly and accurately compare similarities and differences among sets of letters, numbers, objects, pictures, or patterns. The things to be compared may be presented at the same time or one after the other. This ability also includes comparing a presented object with a remembered object.
Visual Color Discrimination	The ability to match or detect differences between colors, including shades of color and brightness.
Hearing Sensitivity	The ability to detect or tell the differences between sounds that vary in pitch and loudness.
Response Orientation	The ability to choose quickly between two or more movements in response to two or more different signals (lights, sounds, pictures). It includes the speed with which the correct response is started with the hand, foot, or other body part.
Mathematical Reasoning	The ability to choose the right mathematical methods or formulas to solve a problem.
Reaction Time	The ability to quickly respond (with the hand, finger, or foot) to a signal (sound, light, picture) when it appears.
Number Facility	The ability to add, subtract, multiply, or divide quickly and correctly.
Stamina	The ability to exert yourself physically over long periods of time without getting winded or out of breath.
Visualization	The ability to imagine how something will look after it is moved around or when its parts are moved or rearranged.
Static Strength	The ability to exert maximum muscle force to lift, push, pull, or carry objects.
Gross Body Equilibrium	The ability to keep or regain your body balance or stay upright when in an unstable position.
Gross Body Coordination	The ability to coordinate the movement of your arms, legs, and torso together when the whole body is in motion.
Explosive Strength	The ability to use short bursts of muscle force to propel oneself (as in jumping or sprinting), or to throw an object.
Trunk Strength	The ability to use your abdominal and lower back muscles to support part of the body repeatedly or continuously over time without 'giving out' or fatiguing.
Extent Flexibility	The ability to bend, stretch, twist, or reach with your body, arms, and/or legs.
Spatial Orientation	The ability to know your location in relation to the environment or to know where other objects are in relation to you.
Multilimb Coordination	The ability to coordinate two or more limbs (for example, two arms, two legs, or one leg and one arm) while sitting, standing, or lying down. It does not involve performing the activities while the whole body is in motion.
Rate Control	The ability to time your movements or the movement of a piece of equipment in anticipation of changes in the speed and/or direction of a moving object or scene.
Night Vision	The ability to see under low light conditions.
Manual Dexterity	The ability to quickly move your hand, your hand together with your arm, or your two hands to grasp, manipulate, or assemble objects.
Control Precision	The ability to quickly and repeatedly adjust the controls of a machine or a vehicle to exact positions.
Arm-Hand Steadiness	The ability to keep your hand and arm steady while moving your arm or while holding your arm and hand in one position.
Dynamic Flexibility	The ability to quickly and repeatedly bend, stretch, twist, or reach out with your body, arms, and/or legs.
Speed of Limb Movement	The ability to quickly move the arms and legs.
Dynamic Strength	The ability to exert muscle force repeatedly or continuously over time. This involves muscular endurance and resistance to muscle fatigue.
Wrist-Finger Speed	The ability to make fast, simple, repeated movements of the fingers, hands, and wrists.
Sound Localization	The ability to tell the direction from which a sound originated.
Peripheral Vision	The ability to see objects or movement of objects to one's side when the eyes are looking ahead.
Depth Perception	The ability to judge which of several objects is closer or farther away from you, or to judge the distance between you and an object.
Glare Sensitivity	The ability to see objects in the presence of glare or bright lighting.

Work_Activity	Work_Activity Definitions
Getting Information	Observing, receiving, and otherwise obtaining information from all relevant sources.
Making Decisions and Solving Problems	Analyzing information and evaluating results to choose the best solution and solve problems.
Establishing and Maintaining Interpersonal Relatio	Developing constructive and cooperative working relationships with others, and maintaining them over time.
Identifying Objects, Actions, and Events	Identifying information by categorizing, estimating, recognizing differences or similarities, and detecting changes in circumstances or events.

Assisting and Caring for Others	Providing personal assistance, medical attention, emotional support, or other personal care to others such as coworkers, customers, or patients.
Documenting/Recording Information	Entering, transcribing, recording, storing, or maintaining information in written or electronic/magnetic form.
Communicating with Supervisors, Peers, or Subordin	Providing information to supervisors, co-workers, and subordinates by telephone, in written form, e-mail, or in person.
Updating and Using Relevant Knowledge	Keeping up-to-date technically and applying new knowledge to your job.
Performing for or Working Directly with the Public	Performing for people or dealing directly with the public. This includes serving customers in restaurants and stores, and receiving clients or guests.
Organizing, Planning, and Prioritizing Work	Developing specific goals and plans to prioritize, organize, and accomplish your work.
Judging the Qualities of Things, Services, or Peop	Assessing the value, importance, or quality of things or people.
Communicating with Persons Outside Organization	Communicating with people outside the organization, representing the organization to customers, the public, government, and other external sources. This information can be exchanged in person, in writing, or by telephone or e-mail.
Interacting With Computers	Using computers and computer systems (including hardware and software) to program, write software, set up functions, enter data, or process information.
Resolving Conflicts and Negotiating with Others	Handling complaints, settling disputes, and resolving grievances and conflicts, or otherwise negotiating with others.
Interpreting the Meaning of Information for Others	Translating or explaining what information means and how it can be used.
Thinking Creatively	Developing, designing, or creating new applications, ideas, relationships, systems, or products, including artistic contributions.
Developing and Building Teams	Encouraging and building mutual trust, respect, and cooperation among team members.
Developing Objectives and Strategies	Establishing long-range objectives and specifying the strategies and actions to achieve them.
Processing Information	Compiling, coding, categorizing, calculating, tabulating, auditing, or verifying information or data.
Analyzing Data or Information	Identifying the underlying principles, reasons, or facts of information by breaking down information or data into separate parts.
Training and Teaching Others	Identifying the educational needs of others, developing formal educational or training programs or classes, and teaching or instructing others.
Provide Consultation and Advice to Others	Providing guidance and expert advice to management or other groups on technical, systems-, or process-related topics.
Evaluating Information to Determine Compliance wit	Using relevant information and individual judgment to determine whether events or processes comply with laws, regulations, or standards.
Monitor Processes, Materials, or Surroundings	Monitoring and reviewing information from materials, events, or the environment, to detect or assess problems.
Coaching and Developing Others	Identifying the developmental needs of others and coaching, mentoring, or otherwise helping others to improve their knowledge or skills.
Performing Administrative Activities	Performing day-to-day administrative tasks such as maintaining information files and processing paperwork.
Scheduling Work and Activities	Scheduling events, programs, and activities, as well as the work of others.
Coordinating the Work and Activities of Others	Getting members of a group to work together to accomplish tasks.
Selling or Influencing Others	Convincing others to buy merchandise/goods or to otherwise change their minds or actions.
Guiding, Directing, and Motivating Subordinates	Providing guidance and direction to subordinates, including setting performance standards and monitoring performance.
Performing General Physical Activities	Performing physical activities that require considerable use of your arms and legs and moving your whole body, such as climbing, lifting, balancing, walking, stooping, and handling of materials.
Monitoring and Controlling Resources	Monitoring and controlling resources and overseeing the spending of money.
Staffing Organizational Units	Recruiting, interviewing, selecting, hiring, and promoting employees in an organization.
Estimating the Quantifiable Characteristics of Pro	Estimating sizes, distances, and quantities; or determining time, costs, resources, or materials needed to perform a work activity.
Operating Vehicles, Mechanized Devices, or Equipme	Running, maneuvering, navigating, or driving vehicles or mechanized equipment, such as forklifts, passenger vehicles, aircraft, or water craft.
Handling and Moving Objects	Using hands and arms in handling, installing, positioning, and moving materials, and manipulating things.
Controlling Machines and Processes	Using either control mechanisms or direct physical activity to operate machines or processes (not including computers or vehicles).
Inspecting Equipment, Structures, or Material	Inspecting equipment, structures, or materials to identify the cause of errors or other problems or defects.

98

Repairing and Maintaining Electronic Equipment	Servicing, repairing, calibrating, regulating, fine-tuning, or testing machines, devices, and equipment that operate primarily on the basis of electrical or electronic (not mechanical) principles.
Drafting, Laying Out, and Specifying Technical Dev	Providing documentation, detailed instructions, drawings, or specifications to tell others about how devices, parts, equipment, or structures are to be fabricated, constructed, assembled, modified, maintained, or used.
Repairing and Maintaining Mechanical Equipment	Servicing, repairing, adjusting, and testing machines, devices, moving parts, and equipment that operate primarily on the basis of mechanical (not electronic) principles.

Work_Content	Work_Content Definitions
Telephone	How often do you have telephone conversations in this job?
Face-to-Face Discussions	How often do you have to have face-to-face discussions with individuals or teams in this job?
Contact With Others	How much does this job require the worker to be in contact with others (face-to-face, by telephone, or otherwise) in order to perform it?
Work With Work Group or Team	How important is it to work with others in a group or team in this job?
Indoors, Environmentally Controlled	How often does this job require working indoors in environmentally controlled conditions?
Frequency of Decision Making	How frequently is the worker required to make decisions that affect other people, the financial resources, and/or the image and reputation of the organization?
Physical Proximity	To what extent does this job require the worker to perform job tasks in close physical proximity to other people?
Freedom to Make Decisions	How much decision making freedom, without supervision, does the job offer?
Structured versus Unstructured Work	To what extent is this job structured for the worker, rather than allowing the worker to determine tasks, priorities, and goals?
Exposed to Disease or Infections	How often does this job require exposure to disease/infections?
Impact of Decisions on Co-workers or Company Resul	How do the decisions an employee makes impact the results of co-workers, clients or the company?
Letters and Memos	How often does the job require written letters and memos?
Frequency of Conflict Situations	How often are there conflict situations the employee has to face in this job?
Deal With Unpleasant or Angry People	How frequently does the worker have to deal with unpleasant, angry, or discourteous individuals as part of the job requirements?
Electronic Mail	How often do you use electronic mail in this job?
Time Pressure	How often does this job require the worker to meet strict deadlines?
Deal With External Customers	How important is it to work with external customers or the public in this job?
Coordinate or Lead Others	How important is it to coordinate or lead others in accomplishing work activities in this job?
Spend Time Sitting	How much does this job require sitting?
Sounds, Noise Levels Are Distracting or Uncomforta	How often does this job require working exposed to sounds and noise levels that are distracting or uncomfortable?
Importance of Being Exact or Accurate	How important is being very exact or highly accurate in performing this job?
Deal With Physically Aggressive People	How frequently does this job require the worker to deal with physical aggression of violent individuals?
Consequence of Error	How serious would the result usually be if the worker made a mistake that was not readily correctable?
Level of Competition	To what extent does this job require the worker to compete or to be aware of competitive pressures?
Exposed to Contaminants	How often does this job require working exposed to contaminants (such as pollutants, gases, dust or odors)?
Responsible for Others' Health and Safety	How much responsibility is there for the health and safety of others in this job?
Spend Time Standing	How much does this job require standing?
Extremely Bright or Inadequate Lighting	How often does this job require working in extremely bright or inadequate lighting conditions?
Spend Time Walking and Running	How much does this job require walking and running?
Responsibility for Outcomes and Results	How responsible is the worker for work outcomes and results of other workers?
Importance of Repeating Same Tasks	How important is repeating the same physical activities (e.g., key entry) or mental activities (e.g., checking entries in a ledger) over and over, without stopping, to performing this job?
Spend Time Making Repetitive Motions	How much does this job require making repetitive motions?
Wear Common Protective or Safety Equipment such as	How much does this job require wearing common protective or safety equipment such as safety shoes, glasses, gloves, hard hats or live jackets?
Public Speaking	How often do you have to perform public speaking in this job?
Cramped Work Space, Awkward Positions	How often does this job require working in cramped work spaces that requires getting into awkward positions?
Spend Time Bending or Twisting the Body	How much does this job require bending or twisting your body?

Spend Time Kneeling, Crouching, Stooping, or Crawl	How much does this job require kneeling, crouching, stooping or crawling?
Spend Time Using Your Hands to Handle, Control, or	How much does this job require using your hands to handle, control, or feel objects, tools or controls?
Exposed to Minor Burns, Cuts, Bites, or Stings	How often does this job require exposure to minor burns, cuts, bites, or stings?
Degree of Automation	How automated is the job?
Wear Specialized Protective or Safety Equipment su	How much does this job require wearing specialized protective or safety equipment such as breathing apparatus, safety harness, full protection suits, or radiation protection?
In an Enclosed Vehicle or Equipment	How often does this job require working in a closed vehicle or equipment (e.g., car)?
Exposed to Radiation	How often does this job require exposure to radiation?
Very Hot or Cold Temperatures	How often does this job require working in very hot (above 90 F degrees) or very cold (below 32 F degrees) temperatures?
Indoors, Not Environmentally Controlled	How often does this job require working indoors in non-controlled environmental conditions (e.g., warehouse without heat)?
Outdoors, Exposed to Weather	How often does this job require working outdoors, exposed to all weather conditions?
Exposed to Hazardous Conditions	How often does this job require exposure to hazardous conditions?
Spend Time Keeping or Regaining Balance	How much does this job require keeping or regaining your balance?
Outdoors, Under Cover	How often does this job require working outdoors, under cover (e.g., structure with roof but no walls)?
Pace Determined by Speed of Equipment	How important is it to this job that the pace is determined by the speed of equipment or machinery? (This does not refer to keeping busy at all times on this job.)
Exposed to Whole Body Vibration	How often does this job require exposure to whole body vibration (e.g., operate a jackhammer)?
Exposed to Hazardous Equipment	How often does this job require exposure to hazardous equipment?
In an Open Vehicle or Equipment	How often does this job require working in an open vehicle or equipment (e.g., tractor)?
Exposed to High Places	How often does this job require exposure to high places?
Spend Time Climbing Ladders, Scaffolds, or Poles	How much does this job require climbing ladders, scaffolds, or poles?

Work_Styles	Work_Styles Definitions
Dependability	Job requires being reliable, responsible, and dependable, and fulfilling obligations.
Integrity	Job requires being honest and ethical.
Concern for Others	Job requires being sensitive to others' needs and feelings and being understanding and helpful on the job.
Persistence	Job requires persistence in the face of obstacles.
Self Control	Job requires maintaining composure, keeping emotions in check, controlling anger, and avoiding aggressive behavior, even in very difficult situations.
Cooperation	Job requires being pleasant with others on the job and displaying a good-natured, cooperative attitude.
Initiative	Job requires a willingness to take on responsibilities and challenges.
Attention to Detail	Job requires being careful about detail and thorough in completing work tasks.
Adaptability/Flexibility	Job requires being open to change (positive or negative) and to considerable variety in the workplace.
Stress Tolerance	Job requires accepting criticism and dealing calmly and effectively with high stress situations.
Independence	Job requires developing one's own ways of doing things, guiding oneself with little or no supervision, and depending on oneself to get things done.
Achievement/Effort	Job requires establishing and maintaining personally challenging achievement goals and exerting effort toward mastering tasks.
Innovation	Job requires creativity and alternative thinking to develop new ideas for and answers to work-related problems.
Social Orientation	Job requires preferring to work with others rather than alone, and being personally connected with others on the job.
Analytical Thinking	Job requires analyzing information and using logic to address work-related issues and problems.
Leadership	Job requires a willingness to lead, take charge, and offer opinions and direction.

Job Zone Component	Job Zone Component Definitions
Title	Job Zone Five: Extensive Preparation Needed Extensive skill, knowledge, and experience are needed for these occupations. Many require more than five years of experience.
Overall Experience	For example, surgeons must complete four years of college and an additional five to seven years of specialized medical training to be able to do their job.

Job Training	Employees may need some on-the-job training, but most of these occupations assume that the person will already have the required skills, knowledge, work-related experience, and/or training.
Job Zone Examples	These occupations often involve coordinating, training, supervising, or managing the activities of others to accomplish goals. Very advanced communication and organizational skills are required. Examples include athletic trainers, lawyers, managing editors, physicists, social psychologists, and surgeons.
SVP Range	(8.0 and above)
Education	A bachelor's degree is the minimum formal education required for these occupations. However, many also require graduate school. For example, they may require a master's degree, and some require a Ph.D., M.D., or J.D. (law degree).

21-1023.00 - Mental Health and Substance Abuse Social Workers

Assess and treat individuals with mental, emotional, or substance abuse problems, including abuse of alcohol, tobacco, and/or other drugs. Activities may include individual and group therapy, crisis intervention, case management, client advocacy, prevention, and education.

Tasks

1) Interview clients, review records, and confer with other professionals to evaluate mental or physical condition of client or patient.

2) Monitor, evaluate, and record client progress with respect to treatment goals.

3) Modify treatment plans according to changes in client status.

4) Counsel clients in individual and group sessions to assist them in dealing with substance abuse, mental and physical illness, poverty, unemployment, or physical abuse.

5) Collaborate with counselors, physicians, and nurses to plan and coordinate treatment, drawing on social work experience and patient needs.

6) Refer patient, client, or family to community resources for housing or treatment to assist in recovery from mental or physical illness, following through to ensure service efficacy.

7) Plan and conduct programs to prevent substance abuse, to combat social problems, or to improve health and counseling services in community.

8) Supervise and direct other workers who provide services to clients or patients.

9) Develop or advise on social policy and assist in community development.

10) Conduct social research to advance knowledge in the social work field.

Knowledge	Knowledge Definitions
Psychology	Knowledge of human behavior and performance; individual differences in ability, personality, and interests; learning and motivation; psychological research methods; and the assessment and treatment of behavioral and affective disorders.
Therapy and Counseling	Knowledge of principles, methods, and procedures for diagnosis, treatment, and rehabilitation of physical and mental dysfunctions, and for career counseling and guidance.
Customer and Personal Service	Knowledge of principles and processes for providing customer and personal services. This includes customer needs assessment, meeting quality standards for services, and evaluation of customer satisfaction.
Sociology and Anthropology	Knowledge of group behavior and dynamics, societal trends and influences, human migrations, ethnicity, cultures and their history and origins.
English Language	Knowledge of the structure and content of the English language including the meaning and spelling of words, rules of composition, and grammar.
Administration and Management	Knowledge of business and management principles involved in strategic planning, resource allocation, human resources modeling, leadership technique, production methods, and coordination of people and resources.
Personnel and Human Resources	Knowledge of principles and procedures for personnel recruitment, selection, training, compensation and benefits, labor relations and negotiation, and personnel information systems.
Education and Training	Knowledge of principles and methods for curriculum and training design, teaching and instruction for individuals and groups, and the measurement of training effects.
Medicine and Dentistry	Knowledge of the information and techniques needed to diagnose and treat human injuries, diseases, and deformities. This includes symptoms, treatment alternatives, drug properties and interactions, and preventive health-care measures.
Communications and Media	Knowledge of media production, communication, and dissemination techniques and methods. This includes alternative ways to inform and entertain via written, oral, and visual media.
Telecommunications	Knowledge of transmission, broadcasting, switching, control, and operation of telecommunications systems.

Clerical	Knowledge of administrative and clerical procedures and systems such as word processing, managing files and records, stenography and transcription, designing forms, and other office procedures and terminology.
Philosophy and Theology	Knowledge of different philosophical systems and religions. This includes their basic principles, values, ethics, ways of thinking, customs, practices, and their impact on human culture.
Law and Government	Knowledge of laws, legal codes, court procedures, precedents, government regulations, executive orders, agency rules, and the democratic political process.
Public Safety and Security	Knowledge of relevant equipment, policies, procedures, and strategies to promote effective local, state, or national security operations for the protection of people, data, property, and institutions.
Transportation	Knowledge of principles and methods for moving people or goods by air, rail, sea, or road, including the relative costs and benefits.
Mathematics	Knowledge of arithmetic, algebra, geometry, calculus, statistics, and their applications.
Computers and Electronics	Knowledge of circuit boards, processors, chips, electronic equipment, and computer hardware and software, including applications and programming.
Sales and Marketing	Knowledge of principles and methods for showing, promoting, and selling products or services. This includes marketing strategy and tactics, product demonstration, sales techniques, and sales control systems.
Biology	Knowledge of plant and animal organisms, their tissues, cells, functions, interdependencies, and interactions with each other and the environment.
Economics and Accounting	Knowledge of economic and accounting principles and practices, the financial markets, banking and the analysis and reporting of financial data.
Chemistry	Knowledge of the chemical composition, structure, and properties of substances and of the chemical processes and transformations that they undergo. This includes uses of chemicals and their interactions, danger signs, production techniques, and disposal methods.
History and Archeology	Knowledge of historical events and their causes, indicators, and effects on civilizations and cultures.
Foreign Language	Knowledge of the structure and content of a foreign (non-English) language including the meaning and spelling of words, rules of composition and grammar, and pronunciation.
Fine Arts	Knowledge of the theory and techniques required to compose, produce, and perform works of music, dance, visual arts, drama, and sculpture.
Geography	Knowledge of principles and methods for describing the features of land, sea, and air masses, including their physical characteristics, locations, interrelationships, and distribution of plant, animal, and human life.
Mechanical	Knowledge of machines and tools, including their designs, uses, repair, and maintenance.
Food Production	Knowledge of techniques and equipment for planting, growing, and harvesting food products (both plant and animal) for consumption, including storage/handling techniques.
Engineering and Technology	Knowledge of the practical application of engineering science and technology. This includes applying principles, techniques, procedures, and equipment to the design and production of various goods and services.
Production and Processing	Knowledge of raw materials, production processes, quality control, costs, and other techniques for maximizing the effective manufacture and distribution of goods.
Design	Knowledge of design techniques, tools, and principles involved in production of precision technical plans, blueprints, drawings, and models.
Building and Construction	Knowledge of materials, methods, and the tools involved in the construction or repair of houses, buildings, or other structures such as highways and roads.
Physics	Knowledge and prediction of physical principles, laws, their interrelationships, and applications to understanding fluid, material, and atmospheric dynamics, and mechanical, electrical, atomic and sub-atomic structures and processes.

Skills	Skills Definitions
Active Listening	Giving full attention to what other people are saying, taking time to understand the points being made, asking questions as appropriate, and not interrupting at inappropriate times.
Social Perceptiveness	Being aware of others' reactions and understanding why they react as they do.
Critical Thinking	Using logic and reasoning to identify the strengths and weaknesses of alternative solutions, conclusions or approaches to problems.
Speaking	Talking to others to convey information effectively.
Writing	Communicating effectively in writing as appropriate for the needs of the audience.

Reading Comprehension	Understanding written sentences and paragraphs in work related documents.
Active Learning	Understanding the implications of new information for both current and future problem-solving and decision-making.
Coordination	Adjusting actions in relation to others' actions.
Service Orientation	Actively looking for ways to help people.
Judgment and Decision Making	Considering the relative costs and benefits of potential actions to choose the most appropriate one.
Time Management	Managing one's own time and the time of others.
Monitoring	Monitoring/Assessing performance of yourself, other individuals, or organizations to make improvements or take corrective action.
Complex Problem Solving	Identifying complex problems and reviewing related information to develop and evaluate options and implement solutions.
Negotiation	Bringing others together and trying to reconcile differences.
Instructing	Teaching others how to do something.
Learning Strategies	Selecting and using training/instructional methods and procedures appropriate for the situation when learning or teaching new things.
Persuasion	Persuading others to change their minds or behavior.
Systems Evaluation	Identifying measures or indicators of system performance and the actions needed to improve or correct performance, relative to the goals of the system.
Systems Analysis	Determining how a system should work and how changes in conditions, operations, and the environment will affect outcomes.
Quality Control Analysis	Conducting tests and inspections of products, services, or processes to evaluate quality or performance.
Management of Financial Resources	Determining how money will be spent to get the work done, and accounting for these expenditures.
Management of Personnel Resources	Motivating, developing, and directing people as they work, identifying the best people for the job.
Troubleshooting	Determining causes of operating errors and deciding what to do about it.
Science	Using scientific rules and methods to solve problems.
Operations Analysis	Analyzing needs and product requirements to create a design.
Management of Material Resources	Obtaining and seeing to the appropriate use of equipment, facilities, and materials needed to do certain work.
Operation and Control	Controlling operations of equipment or systems.
Equipment Selection	Determining the kind of tools and equipment needed to do a job.
Mathematics	Using mathematics to solve problems.
Operation Monitoring	Watching gauges, dials, or other indicators to make sure a machine is working properly.
Technology Design	Generating or adapting equipment and technology to serve user needs.
Installation	Installing equipment, machines, wiring, or programs to meet specifications.
Repairing	Repairing machines or systems using the needed tools.
Programming	Writing computer programs for various purposes.
Equipment Maintenance	Performing routine maintenance on equipment and determining when and what kind of maintenance is needed.

Ability	Ability Definitions
Oral Expression	The ability to communicate information and ideas in speaking so others will understand.
Oral Comprehension	The ability to listen to and understand information and ideas presented through spoken words and sentences.
Speech Clarity	The ability to speak clearly so others can understand you.
Problem Sensitivity	The ability to tell when something is wrong or is likely to go wrong. It does not involve solving the problem, only recognizing there is a problem.
Inductive Reasoning	The ability to combine pieces of information to form general rules or conclusions (includes finding a relationship among seemingly unrelated events).
Written Comprehension	The ability to read and understand information and ideas presented in writing.
Speech Recognition	The ability to identify and understand the speech of another person.
Selective Attention	The ability to concentrate on a task over a period of time without being distracted.
Written Expression	The ability to communicate information and ideas in writing so others will understand.
Deductive Reasoning	The ability to apply general rules to specific problems to produce answers that make sense.
Near Vision	The ability to see details at close range (within a few feet of the observer).
Originality	The ability to come up with unusual or clever ideas about a given topic or situation, or to develop creative ways to solve a problem.
Information Ordering	The ability to arrange things or actions in a certain order or pattern according to a specific rule or set of rules (e.g., patterns of numbers, letters, words, pictures, mathematical operations).

Flexibility of Closure	The ability to identify or detect a known pattern (a figure, object, word, or sound) that is hidden in other distracting material.
Fluency of Ideas	The ability to come up with a number of ideas about a topic (the number of ideas is important, not their quality, correctness, or creativity).
Category Flexibility	The ability to generate or use different sets of rules for combining or grouping things in different ways.
Auditory Attention	The ability to focus on a single source of sound in the presence of other distracting sounds.
Time Sharing	The ability to shift back and forth between two or more activities or sources of information (such as speech, sounds, touch, or other sources).
Speed of Closure	The ability to quickly make sense of, combine, and organize information into meaningful patterns.
Finger Dexterity	The ability to make precisely coordinated movements of the fingers of one or both hands to grasp, manipulate, or assemble very small objects.
Memorization	The ability to remember information such as words, numbers, pictures, and procedures.
Response Orientation	The ability to choose quickly between two or more movements in response to two or more different signals (lights, sounds, pictures). It includes the speed with which the correct response is started with the hand, foot, or other body part.
Static Strength	The ability to exert maximum muscle force to lift, push, pull, or carry objects.
Far Vision	The ability to see details at a distance.
Gross Body Coordination	The ability to coordinate the movement of your arms, legs, and torso together when the whole body is in motion.
Perceptual Speed	The ability to quickly and accurately compare similarities and differences among sets of letters, numbers, objects, pictures, or patterns. The things to be compared may be presented at the same time or one after the other. This ability also includes comparing a presented object with a remembered object.
Reaction Time	The ability to quickly respond (with the hand, finger, or foot) to a signal (sound, light, picture) when it appears.
Mathematical Reasoning	The ability to choose the right mathematical methods or formulas to solve a problem.
Explosive Strength	The ability to use short bursts of muscle force to propel oneself (as in jumping or sprinting), or to throw an object.
Stamina	The ability to exert yourself physically over long periods of time without getting winded or out of breath.
Visualization	The ability to imagine how something will look after it is moved around or when its parts are moved or rearranged.
Gross Body Equilibrium	The ability to keep or regain your body balance or stay upright when in an unstable position.
Number Facility	The ability to add, subtract, multiply, or divide quickly and correctly.
Trunk Strength	The ability to use your abdominal and lower back muscles to support part of the body repeatedly or continuously over time without 'giving out' or fatiguing.
Hearing Sensitivity	The ability to detect or tell the differences between sounds that vary in pitch and loudness.
Visual Color Discrimination	The ability to match or detect differences between colors, including shades of color and brightness.
Wrist-Finger Speed	The ability to make fast, simple, repeated movements of the fingers, hands, and wrists.
Rate Control	The ability to time your movements or the movement of a piece of equipment in anticipation of changes in the speed and/or direction of a moving object or scene.
Extent Flexibility	The ability to bend, stretch, twist, or reach with your body, arms, and/or legs.
Night Vision	The ability to see under low light conditions.
Spatial Orientation	The ability to know your location in relation to the environment or to know where other objects are in relation to you.
Speed of Limb Movement	The ability to quickly move the arms and legs.
Dynamic Strength	The ability to exert muscle force repeatedly or continuously over time. This involves muscular endurance and resistance to muscle fatigue.
Dynamic Flexibility	The ability to quickly and repeatedly bend, stretch, twist, or reach out with your body, arms, and/or legs.
Control Precision	The ability to quickly and repeatedly adjust the controls of a machine or a vehicle to exact positions.
Manual Dexterity	The ability to quickly move your hand, your hand together with your arm, or your two hands to grasp, manipulate, or assemble objects.
Arm-Hand Steadiness	The ability to keep your hand and arm steady while moving your arm or while holding your arm and hand in one position.
Peripheral Vision	The ability to see objects or movement of objects to one's side when the eyes are looking ahead.
Depth Perception	The ability to judge which of several objects is closer or farther away from you, or to judge the distance between you and an object.
Glare Sensitivity	The ability to see objects in the presence of glare or bright lighting.
Sound Localization	The ability to tell the direction from which a sound originated.

Multilimb Coordination	The ability to coordinate two or more limbs (for example, two arms, two legs, or one leg and one arm) while sitting, standing, or lying down. It does not involve performing the activities while the whole body is in motion.

Work_Activity	Work_Activity Definitions
Establishing and Maintaining Interpersonal Relatio	Developing constructive and cooperative working relationships with others, and maintaining them over time.
Getting Information	Observing, receiving, and otherwise obtaining information from all relevant sources.
Assisting and Caring for Others	Providing personal assistance, medical attention, emotional support, or other personal care to others such as coworkers, customers, or patients.
Performing for or Working Directly with the Public	Performing for people or dealing directly with the public. This includes serving customers in restaurants and stores, and receiving clients or guests.
Communicating with Supervisors, Peers, or Subordin	Providing information to supervisors, co-workers, and subordinates by telephone, in written form, e-mail, or in person.
Documenting/Recording Information	Entering, transcribing, recording, storing, or maintaining information in written or electronic/magnetic form.
Judging the Qualities of Things, Services, or Peop	Assessing the value, importance, or quality of things or people.
Making Decisions and Solving Problems	Analyzing information and evaluating results to choose the best solution and solve problems.
Communicating with Persons Outside Organization	Communicating with people outside the organization, representing the organization to customers, the public, government, and other external sources. This information can be exchanged in person, in writing, or by telephone or e-mail.
Identifying Objects, Actions, and Events	Identifying information by categorizing, estimating, recognizing differences or similarities, and detecting changes in circumstances or events.
Resolving Conflicts and Negotiating with Others	Handling complaints, settling disputes, and resolving grievances and conflicts, or otherwise negotiating with others.
Updating and Using Relevant Knowledge	Keeping up-to-date technically and applying new knowledge to your job.
Training and Teaching Others	Identifying the educational needs of others, developing formal educational or training programs or classes, and teaching or instructing others.
Organizing, Planning, and Prioritizing Work	Developing specific goals and plans to prioritize, organize, and accomplish your work.
Provide Consultation and Advice to Others	Providing guidance and expert advice to management or other groups on technical, systems-, or process-related topics.
Interpreting the Meaning of Information for Others	Translating or explaining what information means and how it can be used.
Thinking Creatively	Developing, designing, or creating new applications, ideas, relationships, systems, or products, including artistic contributions.
Selling or Influencing Others	Convincing others to buy merchandise/goods or to otherwise change their minds or actions.
Evaluating Information to Determine Compliance wit	Using relevant information and individual judgment to determine whether events or processes comply with laws, regulations, or standards.
Coaching and Developing Others	Identifying the developmental needs of others and coaching, mentoring, or otherwise helping others to improve their knowledge or skills.
Developing and Building Teams	Encouraging and building mutual trust, respect, and cooperation among team members.
Developing Objectives and Strategies	Establishing long-range objectives and specifying the strategies and actions to achieve them.
Scheduling Work and Activities	Scheduling events, programs, and activities, as well as the work of others.
Processing Information	Compiling, coding, categorizing, calculating, tabulating, auditing, or verifying information or data.
Monitor Processes, Materials, or Surroundings	Monitoring and reviewing information from materials, events, or the environment, to detect or assess problems.
Performing Administrative Activities	Performing day-to-day administrative tasks such as maintaining information files and processing paperwork.
Analyzing Data or Information	Identifying the underlying principles, reasons, or facts of information by breaking down information or data into separate parts.
Coordinating the Work and Activities of Others	Getting members of a group to work together to accomplish tasks.
Interacting With Computers	Using computers and computer systems (including hardware and software) to program, write software, set up functions, enter data, or process information.
Guiding, Directing, and Motivating Subordinates	Providing guidance and direction to subordinates, including setting performance standards and monitoring performance.
Estimating the Quantifiable Characteristics of Pro	Estimating sizes, distances, and quantities; or determining time, costs, resources, or materials needed to perform a work activity.
Monitoring and Controlling Resources	Monitoring and controlling resources and overseeing the spending of money.

Staffing Organizational Units	Recruiting, interviewing, selecting, hiring, and promoting employees in an organization.
Operating Vehicles, Mechanized Devices, or Equipme	Running, maneuvering, navigating, or driving vehicles or mechanized equipment, such as forklifts, passenger vehicles, aircraft, or water craft.
Inspecting Equipment, Structures, or Material	Inspecting equipment, structures, or materials to identify the cause of errors or other problems or defects.
Performing General Physical Activities	Performing physical activities that require considerable use of your arms and legs and moving your whole body, such as climbing, lifting, balancing, walking, stooping, and handling of materials.
Handling and Moving Objects	Using hands and arms in handling, installing, positioning, and moving materials, and manipulating things.
Controlling Machines and Processes	Using either control mechanisms or direct physical activity to operate machines or processes (not including computers or vehicles).
Repairing and Maintaining Electronic Equipment	Servicing, repairing, calibrating, regulating, fine-tuning, or testing machines, devices, and equipment that operate primarily on the basis of electrical or electronic (not mechanical) principles.
Drafting, Laying Out, and Specifying Technical Dev	Providing documentation, detailed instructions, drawings, or specifications to tell others about how devices, parts, equipment, or structures are to be fabricated, constructed, assembled, modified, maintained, or used.
Repairing and Maintaining Mechanical Equipment	Servicing, repairing, adjusting, and testing machines, devices, moving parts, and equipment that operate primarily on the basis of mechanical (not electronic) principles.

Work_Content	Work_Content Definitions
Face-to-Face Discussions	How often do you have to have face-to-face discussions with individuals or teams in this job?
Telephone	How often do you have telephone conversations in this job?
Contact With Others	How much does this job require the worker to be in contact with others (face-to-face, by telephone, or otherwise) in order to perform it?
Letters and Memos	How often does the job require written letters and memos?
Frequency of Conflict Situations	How often are there conflict situations the employee has to face in this job?
Freedom to Make Decisions	How much decision making freedom, without supervision, does the job offer?
Frequency of Decision Making	How frequently is the worker required to make decisions that affect other people, the financial resources, and/or the image and reputation of the organization?
Deal With Unpleasant or Angry People	How frequently does the worker have to deal with unpleasant, angry, or discourteous individuals as part of the job requirements?
Work With Work Group or Team	How important is it to work with others in a group or team in this job?
Time Pressure	How often does this job require the worker to meet strict deadlines?
Deal With External Customers	How important is it to work with external customers or the public in this job?
Coordinate or Lead Others	How important is it to coordinate or lead others in accomplishing work activities in this job?
Importance of Being Exact or Accurate	How important is being very exact or highly accurate in performing this job?
Spend Time Sitting	How much does this job require sitting?
Structured versus Unstructured Work	To what extent is this job structured for the worker, rather than allowing the worker to determine tasks, priorities, and goals?
Indoors, Environmentally Controlled	How often does this job require working indoors in environmentally controlled conditions?
Sounds, Noise Levels Are Distracting or Uncomforta	How often does this job require working exposed to sounds and noise levels that are distracting or uncomfortable?
Physical Proximity	To what extent does this job require the worker to perform job tasks in close physical proximity to other people?
Deal With Physically Aggressive People	How frequently does this job require the worker to deal with physical aggression of violent individuals?
Impact of Decisions on Co-workers or Company Resul	How do the decisions an employee makes impact the results of co-workers, clients or the company?
Electronic Mail	How often do you use electronic mail in this job?
Responsible for Others' Health and Safety	How much responsibility is there for the health and safety of others in this job?
Responsibility for Outcomes and Results	How responsible is the worker for work outcomes and results of other workers?
Exposed to Disease or Infections	How often does this job require exposure to disease/infections?
Level of Competition	To what extent does this job require the worker to compete or to be aware of competitive pressures?
Importance of Repeating Same Tasks	How important is repeating the same physical activities (e.g., key entry) or mental activities (e.g., checking entries in a ledger) over and over, without stopping, to performing this job?
Consequence of Error	How serious would the result usually be if the worker made a mistake that was not readily correctable?

In an Enclosed Vehicle or Equipment	How often does this job require working in a closed vehicle or equipment (e.g., car)?
Spend Time Standing	How much does this job require standing?
Spend Time Walking and Running	How much does this job require walking and running?
Public Speaking	How often do you have to perform public speaking in this job?
Degree of Automation	How automated is the job?
Exposed to Minor Burns. Cuts, Bites, or Stings	How often does this job require exposure to minor burns, cuts, bites, or stings?
Outdoors, Exposed to Weather	How often does this job require working outdoors, exposed to all weather conditions?
Exposed to Contaminants	How often does this job require working exposed to contaminants (such as pollutants, gases, dust or odors)?
Spend Time Making Repetitive Motions	How much does this job require making repetitive motions?
Indoors, Not Environmentally Controlled	How often does this job require working indoors in non-controlled environmental conditions (e.g., warehouse without heat)?
Extremely Bright or Inadequate Lighting	How often does this job require working in extremely bright or inadequate lighting conditions?
Spend Time Using Your Hands to Handle, Control, or	How much does this job require using your hands to handle, control, or feel objects, tools or controls?
Spend Time Kneeling, Crouching, Stooping, or Crawl	How much does this job require kneeling, crouching, stooping or crawling?
Spend Time Bending or Twisting the Body	How much does this job require bending or twisting your body?
Wear Common Protective or Safety Equipment such as	How much does this job require wearing common protective or safety equipment such as safety shoes, glasses, gloves, hard hats or live jackets?
Very Hot or Cold Temperatures	How often does this job require working in very hot (above 90 F degrees) or very cold (below 32 F degrees) temperatures?
Outdoors, Under Cover	How often does this job require working outdoors, under cover (e.g., structure with roof but no walls)?
Cramped Work Space, Awkward Positions	How often does this job require working in cramped work spaces that requires getting into awkward positions?
Pace Determined by Speed of Equipment	How important is it to this job that the pace is determined by the speed of equipment or machinery? (This does not refer to keeping busy at all times on this job.)
Exposed to Hazardous Conditions	How often does this job require exposure to hazardous conditions?
Spend Time Climbing Ladders, Scaffolds, or Poles	How much does this job require climbing ladders, scaffolds, or poles?
In an Open Vehicle or Equipment	How often does this job require working in an open vehicle or equipment (e.g., tractor)?
Spend Time Keeping or Regaining Balance	How much does this job require keeping or regaining your balance?
Exposed to Radiation	How often does this job require exposure to radiation?
Exposed to Hazardous Equipment	How often does this job require exposure to hazardous equipment?
Wear Specialized Protective or Safety Equipment su	How much does this job require wearing specialized protective or safety equipment such as breathing apparatus, safety harness, full protection suits, or radiation protection?
Exposed to High Places	How often does this job require exposure to high places?
Exposed to Whole Body Vibration	How often does this job require exposure to whole body vibration (e.g., operate a jackhammer)?

Work_Styles	Work_Styles Definitions
Concern for Others	Job requires being sensitive to others' needs and feelings and being understanding and helpful on the job.
Integrity	Job requires being honest and ethical.
Self Control	Job requires maintaining composure, keeping emotions in check, controlling anger, and avoiding aggressive behavior, even in very difficult situations.
Dependability	Job requires being reliable, responsible, and dependable, and fulfilling obligations.
Cooperation	Job requires being pleasant with others on the job and displaying a good-natured, cooperative attitude.
Adaptability/Flexibility	Job requires being open to change (positive or negative) and to considerable variety in the workplace.
Stress Tolerance	Job requires accepting criticism and dealing calmly and effectively with high stress situations.
Attention to Detail	Job requires being careful about detail and thorough in completing work tasks.
Independence	Job requires developing one's own ways of doing things, guiding oneself with little or no supervision, and depending on oneself to get things done.
Social Orientation	Job requires preferring to work with others rather than alone, and being personally connected with others on the job.
Initiative	Job requires a willingness to take on responsibilities and challenges.
Analytical Thinking	Job requires analyzing information and using logic to address work-related issues and problems.

Leadership	Job requires a willingness to lead, take charge, and offer opinions and direction.
Persistence	Job requires persistence in the face of obstacles.
Innovation	Job requires creativity and alternative thinking to develop new ideas for and answers to work-related problems.
Achievement/Effort	Job requires establishing and maintaining personally challenging achievement goals and exerting effort toward mastering tasks.

Job Zone Component	Job Zone Component Definitions
Title	Job Zone Five: Extensive Preparation Needed Extensive skill, knowledge, and experience are needed for these occupations. Many require more than five years of experience.
Overall Experience	For example, surgeons must complete four years of college and an additional five to seven years of specialized medical training to be able to do their job.
Job Training	Employees may need some on-the-job training, but most of these occupations assume that the person will already have the required skills, knowledge, work-related experience, and/or training.
Job Zone Examples	These occupations often involve coordinating, training, supervising, or managing the activities of others to accomplish goals. Very advanced communication and organizational skills are required. Examples include athletic trainers, lawyers, managing editors, physicists, social psychologists, and surgeons.
SVP Range	(8.0 and above)
Education	A bachelor's degree is the minimum formal education required for these occupations. However, many also require graduate school. For example, they may require a master's degree, and some require a Ph.D., M.D., or J.D. (law degree).

21-1092.00 - Probation Officers and Correctional Treatment Specialists

Provide social services to assist in rehabilitation of law offenders in custody or on probation or parole. Make recommendations for actions involving formulation of rehabilitation plan and treatment of offender, including conditional release and education and employment stipulations.

Tasks

1) Investigate alleged parole violations, using interviews, surveillance, and search and seizure.

2) Arrange for post-release services such as employment, housing, counseling, education, and social activities.

3) Assess the suitability of penitentiary inmates for release under parole and statutory release programs, and submit recommendations to parole boards.

4) Conduct prehearing and presentencing investigations, and testify in court regarding offenders' backgrounds and recommended sentences and sentencing conditions.

5) Develop liaisons and networks with other parole officers, community agencies, staff in correctional institutions, psychiatric facilities and after-care agencies in order to make plans for helping offenders with life adjustments.

6) Provide offenders or inmates with assistance in matters concerning detainers, sentences in other jurisdictions, writs, and applications for social assistance.

7) Gather information about offenders' backgrounds by talking to offenders, their families and friends, and other people who have relevant information.

8) Write reports describing offenders' progress.

9) Interview probationers and parolees regularly to evaluate their progress in accomplishing goals and maintaining the terms specified in their probation contracts and rehabilitation plans.

10) Develop and prepare packets containing information about social service agencies and assistance organizations and programs that might be useful for inmates or offenders.

11) Prepare and maintain case folder for each assigned inmate or offender.

12) Recommend remedial action or initiate court action when terms of probation or parole are not complied with.

13) Discuss with offenders how such issues as drug and alcohol abuse, and anger management problems might have played roles in their criminal behavior.

14) Recommend appropriate penitentiary for initial placement of an offender.

15) Develop rehabilitation programs for assigned offenders or inmates, establishing rules of conduct, goals, and objectives.

16) Arrange for medical, mental health, or substance abuse treatment services according to individual needs and/or court orders.

17) Inform offenders or inmates of requirements of conditional release, such as office visits, restitution payments, or educational and employment stipulations.

18) Participate in decisions about whether cases should go before courts and which court should hear them.

21-1093.00 - Social and Human Service Assistants

19) Identify and approve work placements for offenders with community service sentences.

21-1093.00 - Social and Human Service Assistants

Assist professionals from a wide variety of fields, such as psychology, rehabilitation, or social work, to provide client services, as well as support for families. May assist clients in identifying available benefits and social and community services and help clients obtain them. May assist social workers with developing, organizing, and conducting programs to prevent and resolve problems relevant to substance abuse, human relationships, rehabilitation, or adult daycare.

Tasks

1) Oversee day-to-day group activities of residents in institution.

2) Submit to and review reports and problems with superior.

3) Inform tenants of facilities, such as laundries and playgrounds.

4) Demonstrate use and care of equipment for tenant use.

5) Transport and accompany clients to shopping area and to appointments, using automobile.

6) Assist in planning of food budget, utilizing charts and sample budgets.

7) Observe and discuss meal preparation and suggest alternate methods of food preparation.

8) Observe clients' food selections and recommend alternate economical and nutritional food choices.

9) Interview individuals and family members to compile information on social, educational, criminal, institutional, or drug history.

10) Meet with youth groups to acquaint them with consequences of delinquent acts.

11) Visit individuals in homes or attend group meetings to provide information on agency services, requirements and procedures.

12) Explain rules established by owner or management, such as sanitation and maintenance requirements, and parking regulations.

13) Advise clients regarding food stamps, child care, food, money management, sanitation, and housekeeping.

14) Keep records and prepare reports for owner or management concerning visits with clients.

15) Provide information on and refer individuals to public or private agencies and community services for assistance.

16) Assist clients with preparation of forms, such as tax or rent forms.

17) Assist in locating housing for displaced individuals.

18) Care for children in client's home during client's appointments.

19) Monitor free, supplementary meal program to ensure cleanliness of facility and that eligibility guidelines are met for persons receiving meals.

21-2011.00 - Clergy

Conduct religious worship and perform other spiritual functions associated with beliefs and practices of religious faith or denomination. Provide spiritual and moral guidance and assistance to members.

Tasks

1) Prepare and deliver sermons and other talks.

2) Administer religious rites or ordinances.

3) Collaborate with committees and individuals to address financial and administrative issues pertaining to congregations.

4) Organize and engage in interfaith, community, civic, educational, and recreational activities sponsored by or related to their religion.

5) Devise ways in which congregation membership can be expanded.

6) Refer people to community support services, psychologists, and/or doctors as necessary.

7) Prepare people for participation in religious ceremonies.

8) Plan and lead religious education programs for their congregations.

9) Pray and promote spirituality.

10) Visit people in homes, hospitals, and prisons to provide them with comfort and support.

11) Instruct people who seek conversion to a particular faith.

12) Participate in fundraising activities to support congregation activities and facilities.

13) Train leaders of church, community, and youth groups.

14) Share information about religious issues by writing articles, giving speeches, or teaching.

15) Respond to requests for assistance during emergencies or crises.

16) Conduct special ceremonies such as weddings, funerals, and confirmations.

17) Study and interpret religious laws, doctrines, and/or traditions.

18) Counsel individuals and groups concerning their spiritual, emotional, and personal needs.

19) Organize and lead regular religious services.

20) Read from sacred texts such as the Bible, Torah, or Koran.

23-1011.00 - Lawyers

Represent clients in criminal and civil litigation and other legal proceedings, draw up legal documents, and manage or advise clients on legal transactions. May specialize in a single area or may practice broadly in many areas of law.

Tasks

1) Advise clients concerning business transactions, claim liability, advisability of prosecuting or defending lawsuits, or legal rights and obligations.

2) Prepare legal briefs and opinions, and file appeals in state and federal courts of appeal.

3) Perform administrative and management functions related to the practice of law.

4) Supervise legal assistants.

5) Select jurors, argue motions, meet with judges and question witnesses during the course of a trial.

6) Search for and examine public and other legal records to write opinions or establish ownership.

7) Represent clients in court or before government agencies.

8) Probate wills and represent and advise executors and administrators of estates.

9) Work as law school faculty member or administrator.

10) Analyze the probable outcomes of cases, using knowledge of legal precedents.

11) Present evidence to defend clients or prosecute defendants in criminal or civil litigation.

12) Confer with colleagues with specialties in appropriate areas of legal issue to establish and verify bases for legal proceedings.

13) Prepare and draft legal documents, such as wills, deeds, patent applications, mortgages, leases, and contracts.

14) Negotiate settlements of civil disputes.

15) Interpret laws, rulings and regulations for individuals and businesses.

16) Examine legal data to determine advisability of defending or prosecuting lawsuit.

17) Help develop federal and state programs, draft and interpret laws and legislation, and establish enforcement procedures.

18) Work in environmental law, representing public interest groups, waste disposal companies, or construction firms in their dealings with state and federal agencies.

19) Present and summarize cases to judges and juries.

20) Gather evidence to formulate defense or to initiate legal actions, by such means as interviewing clients and witnesses to ascertain the facts of a case.

21) Study Constitution, statutes, decisions, regulations, and ordinances of quasi-judicial bodies to determine ramifications for cases.

22) Evaluate findings and develop strategies and arguments in preparation for presentation of cases.

23-1021.00 - Administrative Law Judges, Adjudicators, and Hearing Officers

Conduct hearings to decide or recommend decisions on claims concerning government programs or other government-related matters and prepare decisions. Determine penalties or the existence and the amount of liability, or recommend the acceptance or rejection of claims, or compromise settlements.

Tasks

1) Recommend the acceptance or rejection of claims or compromise settlements according to laws, regulations, policies, and precedent decisions.

2) Conduct studies of appeals procedures in field agencies to ensure adherence to legal requirements and to facilitate determination of cases.

3) Review and evaluate data on documents such as claim applications, birth or death certificates, and physician or employer records.

4) Research and analyze laws, regulations, policies, and precedent decisions to prepare for

hearings and to determine conclusions.

5) Prepare written opinions and decisions.

6) Issue subpoenas and administer oaths in preparation for formal hearings.

7) Explain to claimants how they can appeal rulings that go against them.

8) Determine existence and amount of liability, according to current laws, administrative and judicial precedents, and available evidence.

9) Confer with individuals or organizations involved in cases in order to obtain relevant information.

10) Conduct hearings to review and decide claims regarding issues such as social program eligibility, environmental protection, and enforcement of health and safety regulations.

11) Authorize payment of valid claims and determine method of payment.

12) Monitor and direct the activities of trials and hearings to ensure that they are conducted fairly and that courts administer justice while safeguarding the legal rights of all involved parties.

23-1023.00 - Judges, Magistrate Judges, and Magistrates

Arbitrate, advise, adjudicate, or administer justice in a court of law. May sentence defendant in criminal cases according to government statutes. May determine liability of defendant in civil cases. May issue marriage licenses and perform wedding ceremonies.

Tasks

1) Settle disputes between opposing attorneys.

2) Write decisions on cases.

3) Participate in judicial tribunals to help resolve disputes.

4) Sentence defendants in criminal cases, on conviction by jury, according to applicable government statutes.

5) Research legal issues and write opinions on the issues.

6) Supervise other judges, court officers, and the court's administrative staff.

7) Preside over hearings and listen to allegations made by plaintiffs to determine whether the evidence supports the charges.

8) Instruct juries on applicable laws, direct juries to deduce the facts from the evidence presented, and hear their verdicts.

9) Impose restrictions upon parties in civil cases until trials can be held.

10) Grant divorces and divide assets between spouses.

11) Monitor proceedings to ensure that all applicable rules and procedures are followed.

12) Conduct preliminary hearings to decide issues such as whether there is reasonable and probable cause to hold defendants in felony cases.

13) Award compensation for damages to litigants in civil cases in relation to findings by juries or by the court.

14) Advise attorneys, juries, litigants, and court personnel regarding conduct, issues, and proceedings.

15) Rule on custody and access disputes, and enforce court orders regarding custody and support of children.

16) Read documents on pleadings and motions to ascertain facts and issues.

17) Perform wedding ceremonies.

18) Interpret and enforce rules of procedure or establish new rules in situations where there are no procedures already established by law.

23-2011.00 - Paralegals and Legal Assistants

Assist lawyers by researching legal precedent, investigating facts, or preparing legal documents. Conduct research to support a legal proceeding, to formulate a defense, or to initiate legal action.

Tasks

1) Keep and monitor legal volumes to ensure that law library is up-to-date.

2) Call upon witnesses to testify at hearing.

3) Answer questions regarding legal issues pertaining to civil service hearings.

4) Gather and analyze research data, such as statutes, decisions, and legal articles, codes, and documents.

5) Investigate facts and law of cases to determine causes of action and to prepare cases.

6) Appraise and inventory real and personal property for estate planning.

7) Prepare legal documents, including briefs, pleadings, appeals, wills, contracts, and real estate closing statements.

8) Direct and coordinate law office activity, including delivery of subpoenas.

9) Present arguments and evidence to support appeal at appeal hearing.

10) Prepare affidavits or other documents, maintain document file, and file pleadings with court clerk.

23-2091.00 - Court Reporters

Use verbatim methods and equipment to capture, store, retrieve, and transcribe pretrial and trial proceedings or other information. Includes stenocaptioners who operate computerized stenographic captioning equipment to provide captions of live or prerecorded broadcasts for hearing-impaired viewers.

Tasks

1) Record symbols on computer disks or CD-ROM, then translate and display them as text in computer-aided transcription process.

2) Provide transcripts of proceedings upon request of judges, lawyers, or the public.

3) Record verbatim proceedings of courts, legislative assemblies, committee meetings, and other proceedings, using computerized recording equipment, electronic stenograph machines, or stenomasks.

4) Ask speakers to clarify inaudible statements.

5) Transcribe recorded proceedings in accordance with established formats.

6) Verify accuracy of transcripts by checking copies against original records of proceedings and accuracy of rulings by checking with judges.

7) Caption news, emergency broadcasts, sporting events, and other programming for television networks or cable stations.

8) File and store shorthand notes of court session.

9) Record depositions and other proceedings for attorneys.

10) Take notes in shorthand or use a stenotype or shorthand machine that prints letters on a paper tape.

11) Respond to requests during court sessions to read portions of the proceedings already recorded.

23-2092.00 - Law Clerks

Assist lawyers or judges by researching or preparing legal documents. May meet with clients or assist lawyers and judges in court.

Tasks

1) Review and file pleadings, petitions and other documents relevant to court actions.

2) Prepare real estate closing statements and assist in closing process.

3) Search patent files to ascertain originality of patent applications.

4) Serve copies of pleas to opposing counsel.

5) Arrange transportation and accommodation for witnesses and jurors, if required.

6) Research and analyze law sources to prepare drafts of briefs or arguments for review, approval, and use by attorney.

7) Search for and study legal documents to investigate facts and law of cases, to determine causes of action and to prepare cases.

8) Store, catalog, and maintain currency of legal volumes.

9) Communicate and arbitrate disputes between parties.

10) Appraise and inventory real and personal property for estate planning.

11) Deliver or direct delivery of subpoenas to witnesses and parties to action.

23-2093.00 - Title Examiners, Abstractors, and Searchers

Search real estate records, examine titles, or summarize pertinent legal or insurance details for a variety of purposes. May compile lists of mortgages, contracts, and other instruments pertaining to titles by searching public and private records for law firms, real estate agencies, or title insurance companies.

25-1011.00 - Business Teachers, Postsecondary

Tasks

1) Verify accuracy and completeness of land-related documents accepted for registration; prepare rejection notices when documents are not acceptable.

2) Read search requests in order to ascertain types of title evidence required and to obtain descriptions of properties and names of involved parties.

3) Prepare reports describing any title encumbrances encountered during searching activities, and outlining actions needed to clear titles.

4) Copy or summarize recorded documents, such as mortgages, trust deeds, and contracts, that affect property titles.

5) Enter into record-keeping systems appropriate data needed to create new title records or update existing ones.

6) Examine documentation such as mortgages, liens, judgments, easements, plat books, maps, contracts, and agreements in order to verify factors such as properties' legal descriptions, ownership, or restrictions.

7) Examine individual titles in order to determine if restrictions, such as delinquent taxes, will affect titles and limit property use.

8) Obtain maps or drawings delineating properties from company title plants, county surveyors, and/or assessors' offices.

9) Prepare lists of all legal instruments applying to a specific piece of land and the buildings on it.

10) Confer with realtors, lending institution personnel, buyers, sellers, contractors, surveyors, and courthouse personnel in order to exchange title-related information or to resolve problems.

11) Prepare and issue title commitments and title insurance policies based on information compiled from title searches.

12) Retrieve and examine real estate closing files for accuracy and to ensure that information included is recorded and executed according to regulations.

13) Summarize pertinent legal or insurance details, or sections of statutes or case law from reference books so that they can be used in examinations, or as proofs or ready reference.

14) Direct activities of workers who search records and examine titles, assigning, scheduling, and evaluating work, and providing technical guidance as necessary.

15) Determine whether land-related documents can be registered under the relevant legislation such as the Land Titles Act.

16) Assess fees related to registration of property-related documents.

25-1011.00 - Business Teachers, Postsecondary

Teach courses in business administration and management, such as accounting, finance, human resources, labor relations, marketing, and operations research.

Tasks

1) Collaborate with colleagues to address teaching and research issues.

2) Conduct research in a particular field of knowledge, and publish findings in professional journals, books, and/or electronic media.

3) Participate in student recruitment, registration, and placement activities.

4) Perform administrative duties such as serving as department head.

5) Write grant proposals to procure external research funding.

6) Serve on academic or administrative committees that deal with institutional policies, departmental matters, and academic issues.

7) Supervise undergraduate and/or graduate teaching, internship, and research work.

8) Prepare and deliver lectures to undergraduate and/or graduate students on topics such as financial accounting, principles of marketing, and operations management.

9) Act as advisers to student organizations.

10) Provide professional consulting services to government and/or industry.

11) Select and obtain materials and supplies such as textbooks.

12) Prepare course materials such as syllabi, homework assignments, and handouts.

13) Plan, evaluate, and revise curricula, course content, and course materials and methods of instruction.

14) Maintain student attendance records, grades, and other required records.

15) Compile bibliographies of specialized materials for outside reading assignments.

16) Evaluate and grade students' class work, assignments, and papers.

17) Keep abreast of developments in their field by reading current literature, talking with colleagues, and participating in professional organizations and conferences.

18) Initiate, facilitate, and moderate classroom discussions.

19) Collaborate with members of the business community to improve programs, to develop

new programs, and to provide student access to learning opportunities such as internships.

20) Participate in campus and community events.

21) Maintain regularly scheduled office hours in order to advise and assist students.

22) Compile, administer, and grade examinations, or assign this work to others.

25-1021.00 - Computer Science Teachers, Postsecondary

Teach courses in computer science. May specialize in a field of computer science, such as the design and function of computers or operations and research analysis.

Tasks

1) Keep abreast of developments in their field by reading current literature, talking with colleagues, and participating in professional conferences.

2) Perform administrative duties such as serving as department head.

3) Collaborate with colleagues to address teaching and research issues.

4) Act as advisers to student organizations.

5) Supervise undergraduate and/or graduate teaching, internship, and research work.

6) Supervise students' laboratory work.

7) Select and obtain materials and supplies such as textbooks and laboratory equipment.

8) Prepare course materials such as syllabi, homework assignments, and handouts.

9) Plan, evaluate, and revise curricula, course content, and course materials and methods of instruction.

10) Participate in student recruitment, registration, and placement activities.

11) Initiate, facilitate, and moderate classroom discussions.

12) Compile bibliographies of specialized materials for outside reading assignments.

13) Compile, administer, and grade examinations, or assign this work to others.

14) Maintain student attendance records, grades, and other required records.

15) Conduct research in a particular field of knowledge, and publish findings in professional journals, books, and/or electronic media.

16) Advise students on academic and vocational curricula, and on career issues.

17) Participate in campus and community events.

18) Evaluate and grade students' class work, laboratory work, assignments, and papers.

19) Provide professional consulting services to government and/or industry.

20) Serve on academic or administrative committees that deal with institutional policies, departmental matters, and academic issues.

21) Write grant proposals to procure external research funding.

22) Prepare and deliver lectures to undergraduate and/or graduate students on topics such as programming, data structures, and software design.

23) Direct research of other teachers or of graduate students working for advanced academic degrees.

25-1022.00 - Mathematical Science Teachers, Postsecondary

Teach courses pertaining to mathematical concepts, statistics, and actuarial science and to the application of original and standardized mathematical techniques in solving specific problems and situations.

Tasks

1) Prepare course materials such as syllabi, homework assignments, and handouts.

2) Evaluate and grade students' class work, assignments, and papers.

3) Compile, administer, and grade examinations, or assign this work to others.

4) Advise students on academic and vocational curricula, and on career issues.

5) Prepare and deliver lectures to undergraduate and/or graduate students on topics such as linear algebra, differential equations, and discrete mathematics.

6) Write grant proposals to procure external research funding.

7) Plan, evaluate, and revise curricula, course content, and course materials and methods of instruction.

8) Maintain student attendance records, grades, and other required records.

9) Serve on academic or administrative committees that deal with institutional policies, departmental matters, and academic issues.

10) Select and obtain materials and supplies such as textbooks.

11) Keep abreast of developments in their field by reading current literature, talking with colleagues, and participating in professional conferences.

12) Provide professional consulting services to government and/or industry.

13) Act as advisers to student organizations.

14) Compile bibliographies of specialized materials for outside reading assignments.

15) Collaborate with colleagues to address teaching and research issues.

16) Conduct research in a particular field of knowledge, and publish findings in books, professional journals, and/or electronic media.

17) Participate in campus and community events.

18) Participate in student recruitment, registration, and placement activities.

19) Initiate, facilitate, and moderate classroom discussions.

20) Supervise undergraduate and/or graduate teaching, internship, and research work.

21) Maintain regularly scheduled office hours in order to advise and assist students.

25-1031.00 - Architecture Teachers, Postsecondary

Teach courses in architecture and architectural design, such as architectural environmental design, interior architecture/design, and landscape architecture.

Tasks

1) Maintain student attendance records, grades, and other required records.

2) Plan, evaluate, and revise curricula, course content, and course materials and methods of instruction.

3) Prepare course materials such as syllabi, homework assignments, and handouts.

4) Supervise undergraduate and/or graduate teaching, internship, and research work.

5) Collaborate with colleagues to address teaching and research issues.

6) Conduct research in a particular field of knowledge, and publish findings in professional journals, books, and/or electronic media.

7) Participate in campus and community events.

8) Initiate, facilitate, and moderate classroom discussions.

9) Provide professional consulting services to government and/or industry.

10) Act as advisers to student organizations.

11) Serve on academic or administrative committees that deal with institutional policies, departmental matters, and academic issues.

12) Participate in student recruitment, registration, and placement activities.

13) Maintain regularly scheduled office hours in order to advise and assist students.

14) Compile bibliographies of specialized materials for outside reading assignments.

15) Compile, administer, and grade examinations, or assign this work to others.

16) Advise students on academic and vocational curricula, and on career issues.

17) Prepare and deliver lectures to undergraduate and/or graduate students on topics such as architectural design methods, aesthetics and design, and structures and materials.

18) Evaluate and grade students' work, including work performed in design studios.

19) Perform administrative duties such as serving as department head.

20) Select and obtain materials and supplies such as textbooks and laboratory equipment.

21) Keep abreast of developments in their field by reading current literature, talking with colleagues, and participating in professional conferences.

25-1032.00 - Engineering Teachers, Postsecondary

Teach courses pertaining to the application of physical laws and principles of engineering for the development of machines, materials, instruments, processes, and services. Includes teachers of subjects, such as chemical, civil, electrical, industrial, mechanical, mineral, and petroleum engineering. Includes both teachers primarily engaged in teaching and those who do a combination of both teaching and research.

Tasks

1) Supervise students' laboratory work.

2) Keep abreast of developments in their field by reading current literature, talking with colleagues, and participating in professional conferences.

3) Act as advisers to student organizations.

4) Evaluate and grade students' class work, laboratory work, assignments, and papers.

5) Compile, administer, and grade examinations, or assign this work to others.

6) Supervise undergraduate and/or graduate teaching, internship, and research work.

7) Prepare and deliver lectures to undergraduate and/or graduate students on topics such as mechanics, hydraulics, and robotics.

8) Advise students on academic and vocational curricula, and on career issues.

9) Write grant proposals to procure external research funding.

10) Select and obtain materials and supplies such as textbooks and laboratory equipment.

11) Compile bibliographies of specialized materials for outside reading assignments.

12) Initiate, facilitate, and moderate class discussions.

13) Maintain regularly scheduled office hours in order to advise and assist students.

14) Prepare course materials such as syllabi, homework assignments, and handouts.

15) Participate in student recruitment, registration, and placement activities.

16) Plan, evaluate, and revise curricula, course content, and course materials and methods of instruction.

17) Participate in campus and community events.

18) Perform administrative duties such as serving as department head.

19) Serve on academic or administrative committees that deal with institutional policies, departmental matters, and academic issues.

20) Maintain student attendance records, grades, and other required records.

21) Conduct research in a particular field of knowledge, and publish findings in professional journals, books, and/or electronic media.

22) Provide professional consulting services to government and/or industry.

25-1041.00 - Agricultural Sciences Teachers, Postsecondary

Teach courses in the agricultural sciences. Includes teachers of agronomy, dairy sciences, fisheries management, horticultural sciences, poultry sciences, range management, and agricultural soil conservation.

Tasks

1) Compile bibliographies of specialized materials for outside reading assignments.

2) Keep abreast of developments in their field by reading current literature, talking with colleagues, and participating in professional conferences.

3) Plan, evaluate, and revise curricula, course content, and course materials and methods of instruction.

4) Evaluate and grade students' class work, laboratory work, assignments, and papers.

5) Maintain regularly scheduled office hours in order to advise and assist students.

6) Initiate, facilitate, and moderate classroom discussions.

7) Compile, administer, and grade examinations, or assign this work to others.

8) Advise students on academic and vocational curricula, and on career issues.

9) Prepare and deliver lectures to undergraduate and/or graduate students on topics such as crop production, plant genetics, and soil chemistry.

10) Supervise laboratory sessions and field work, and coordinate laboratory operations.

11) Collaborate with colleagues to address teaching and research issues.

12) Supervise undergraduate and/or graduate teaching, internship, and research work.

13) Maintain student attendance records, grades, and other required records.

14) Prepare course materials such as syllabi, homework assignments, and handouts.

15) Write grant proposals to procure external research funding.

16) Serve on academic or administrative committees that deal with institutional policies, departmental matters, and academic issues.

17) Conduct research in a particular field of knowledge, and publish findings in professional journals, books, and/or electronic media.

18) Perform administrative duties such as serving as department head.

19) Participate in student recruitment, registration, and placement activities.

20) Participate in campus and community events.

21) Provide professional consulting services to government and/or industry.

22) Select and obtain materials and supplies such as textbooks and laboratory equipment.

25-1042.00 - Biological Science Teachers, Postsecondary

Teach courses in biological sciences.

Tasks

1) Provide professional consulting services to government and/or industry.

2) Select and obtain materials and supplies such as textbooks and laboratory equipment.

3) Prepare course materials such as syllabi, homework assignments, and handouts.

4) Maintain student attendance records, grades, and other required records.

5) Evaluate and grade students' class work, laboratory work, assignments, and papers.

6) Keep abreast of developments in their field by reading current literature, talking with colleagues, and participating in professional conferences.

7) Prepare and deliver lectures to undergraduate and/or graduate students on topics such as molecular biology, marine biology, and botany.

8) Advise students on academic and vocational curricula, and on career issues.

9) Compile bibliographies of specialized materials for outside reading assignments.

10) Write grant proposals to procure external research funding.

11) Participate in student recruitment, registration, and placement activities.

12) Compile, administer, and grade examinations, or assign this work to others.

13) Supervise undergraduate and/or graduate teaching, internship, and research work.

14) Maintain regularly scheduled office hours in order to advise and assist students.

15) Supervise students' laboratory work.

16) Serve on academic or administrative committees that deal with institutional policies, departmental matters, and academic issues.

17) Conduct research in a particular field of knowledge, and publish findings in professional journals, books, and/or electronic media.

18) Collaborate with colleagues to address teaching and research issues.

19) Participate in campus and community events.

20) Act as advisers to student organizations.

21) Plan, evaluate, and revise curricula, course content, and course materials and methods of instruction.

22) Perform administrative duties such as serving as department head.

25-1043.00 - Forestry and Conservation Science Teachers, Postsecondary

Teach courses in environmental and conservation science.

Tasks

1) Participate in campus and community events.

2) Initiate, facilitate, and moderate classroom discussions.

3) Keep abreast of developments in their field by reading current literature, talking with colleagues, and participating in professional conferences.

4) Maintain regularly scheduled office hours in order to advise and assist students.

5) Maintain student attendance records, grades, and other required records.

6) Prepare course materials such as syllabi, homework assignments, and handouts.

7) Supervise undergraduate and/or graduate teaching, internship, and research work.

8) Compile bibliographies of specialized materials for outside reading assignments.

9) Act as advisers to student organizations.

10) Collaborate with colleagues to address teaching and research issues.

11) Supervise students' laboratory and/or field work.

12) Plan, evaluate, and revise curricula, course content, and course materials and methods of instruction.

13) Evaluate and grade students' class work, assignments, and papers.

14) Prepare and deliver lectures to undergraduate and/or graduate students on topics such as forest resource policy, forest pathology, and mapping.

15) Advise students on academic and vocational curricula, and on career issues.

16) Compile, administer, and grade examinations, or assign this work to others.

17) Write grant proposals to procure external research funding.

18) Serve on academic or administrative committees that deal with institutional policies, departmental matters, and academic issues.

19) Provide professional consulting services to government and/or industry.

20) Perform administrative duties such as serving as department head.

21) Participate in student recruitment, registration, and placement activities.

22) Conduct research in a particular field of knowledge, and publish findings in books, professional journals, and/or electronic media.

25-1051.00 - Atmospheric, Earth, Marine, and Space Sciences Teachers, Postsecondary

Teach courses in the physical sciences, except chemistry and physics.

Tasks

1) Supervise undergraduate and/or graduate teaching, internship, and research work.

2) Maintain student attendance records, grades, and other required records.

3) Prepare course materials such as syllabi, homework assignments, and handouts.

4) Select and obtain materials and supplies such as textbooks and laboratory equipment.

5) Supervise laboratory work and field work.

6) Compile, administer, and grade examinations, or assign this work to others.

7) Prepare and deliver lectures to undergraduate and/or graduate students on topics such as structural geology, micrometeorology, and atmospheric thermodynamics.

8) Keep abreast of developments in their field by reading current literature, talking with colleagues, and participating in professional conferences.

9) Compile bibliographies of specialized materials for outside reading assignments.

10) Participate in student recruitment, registration, and placement activities.

11) Advise students on academic and vocational curricula, and on career issues.

12) Provide professional consulting services to government and/or industry.

13) Serve on academic or administrative committees that deal with institutional policies, departmental matters, and academic issues.

14) Write grant proposals to procure external research funding.

15) Plan, evaluate, and revise curricula, course content, and course materials and methods of instruction.

16) Perform administrative duties such as serving as department head.

17) Initiate, facilitate, and moderate classroom discussions.

18) Collaborate with colleagues to address teaching and research issues.

19) Participate in campus and community events.

20) Evaluate and grade students' class work, assignments, and papers.

21) Act as advisers to student organizations.

22) Conduct research in a particular field of knowledge, and publish findings in professional journals, books, and/or electronic media.

25-1052.00 - Chemistry Teachers, Postsecondary

Teach courses pertaining to the chemical and physical properties and compositional changes of substances. Work may include instruction in the methods of qualitative and quantitative chemical analysis. Includes both teachers primarily engaged in teaching, and those who do a combination of both teaching and research.

Tasks

1) Act as advisers to student organizations.

2) Compile bibliographies of specialized materials for outside reading assignments.

3) Maintain student attendance records, grades, and other required records.

4) Compile, administer, and grade examinations, or assign this work to others.

5) Keep abreast of developments in their field by reading current literature, talking with colleagues, and participating in professional conferences.

6) Provide professional consulting services to government and/or industry.

7) Maintain regularly scheduled office hours in order to advise and assist students.

8) Prepare and submit required reports related to instruction.

9) Advise students on academic and vocational curricula, and on career issues.

10) Prepare and deliver lectures to undergraduate and/or graduate students on topics such as organic chemistry, analytical chemistry, and chemical separation.

11) Conduct research in a particular field of knowledge, and publish findings in professional journals, books and/or electronic media.

12) Write grant proposals to procure external research funding.

13) Provide professional consulting services to government and/or industry.

14) Plan, evaluate, and revise curricula, course content, and course materials and methods of instruction.

15) Evaluate and grade students' class work, laboratory performance, assignments, and papers.

16) Serve on academic or administrative committees that deal with institutional policies, departmental matters, and academic issues.

17) Perform administrative duties such as serving as department head.

18) Participate in campus and community events.

19) Collaborate with colleagues to address teaching and research issues.

20) Participate in student recruitment, registration, and placement activities.

21) Supervise students' laboratory work.

22) Prepare course materials such as syllabi, homework assignments, and handouts.

23) Perform administrative duties such as serving as a department head.

24) Select and obtain materials and supplies such as textbooks and laboratory equipment.

25) Supervise undergraduate and/or graduate teaching, internship, and research work.

25-1053.00 - Environmental Science Teachers, Postsecondary

Teach courses in environmental science.

Tasks

1) Advise students on academic and vocational curricula, and on career issues.

2) Compile, administer, and grade examinations, or assign this work to others.

3) Compile bibliographies of specialized materials for outside reading assignments.

4) Plan, evaluate, and revise curricula, course content, and course materials and methods of instruction.

5) Initiate, facilitate, and moderate classroom discussions.

6) Maintain regularly scheduled office hours in order to advise and assist students.

7) Evaluate and grade students' class work, laboratory work, assignments, and papers.

8) Supervise students' laboratory and field work.

9) Act as advisers to student organizations.

10) Keep abreast of developments in their field by reading current literature, talking with colleagues, and participating in professional conferences.

11) Prepare course materials such as syllabi, homework assignments, and handouts.

12) Perform administrative duties such as serving as department head.

13) Prepare and deliver lectures to undergraduate and/or graduate students on topics such as hazardous waste management, industrial safety, and environmental toxicology.

14) Supervise undergraduate and/or graduate teaching, internship, and research work.

15) Conduct research in a particular field of knowledge, and publish findings in professional journals, books, and/or electronic media.

16) Provide professional consulting services to government and/or industry.

17) Serve on academic or administrative committees that deal with institutional policies, departmental matters, and academic issues.

18) Write grant proposals to procure external research funding.

19) Participate in campus and community events.

20) Collaborate with colleagues to address teaching and research issues.

21) Maintain student attendance records, grades, and other required records.

22) Participate in student recruitment, registration, and placement activities.

25-1054.00 - Physics Teachers, Postsecondary

Teach courses pertaining to the laws of matter and energy. Includes both teachers primarily engaged in teaching and those who do a combination of both teaching and research.

Tasks

1) Keep abreast of developments in their field by reading current literature, talking with colleagues, and participating in professional conferences.

2) Evaluate and grade students' class work, laboratory work, assignments, and papers.

25-1053.00 - Environmental Science Teachers, Postsecondary

3) Maintain student attendance records, grades, and other required records.

4) Write grant proposals to procure external research funding.

5) Maintain regularly scheduled office hours in order to advise and assist students.

6) Initiate, facilitate, and moderate classroom discussions.

7) Serve on academic or administrative committees that deal with institutional policies, departmental matters, and academic issues.

8) Plan, evaluate, and revise curricula, course content, and course materials and methods of instruction.

9) Provide professional consulting services to government and/or industry.

10) Conduct research in a particular field of knowledge, and publish findings in professional journals, books, and/or electronic media.

11) Perform administrative duties such as serving as department head.

12) Compile, administer, and grade examinations, or assign this work to others.

13) Select and obtain materials and supplies such as textbooks and laboratory equipment.

14) Participate in student recruitment, registration, and placement activities.

15) Prepare and deliver lectures to undergraduate and/or graduate students on topics such as quantum mechanics, particle physics, and optics.

16) Advise students on academic and vocational curricula, and on career issues.

17) Participate in campus and community events.

18) Collaborate with colleagues to address teaching and research issues.

19) Act as advisers to student organizations.

20) Supervise undergraduate and/or graduate teaching, internship, and research work.

21) Supervise students' laboratory work.

22) Compile bibliographies of specialized materials for outside reading assignments.

25-1061.00 - Anthropology and Archeology Teachers, Postsecondary

Teach courses in anthropology or archeology.

Tasks

1) Provide professional consulting services to government and/or industry.

2) Write grant proposals to procure external research funding.

3) Maintain regularly scheduled office hours in order to advise and assist students.

4) Select and obtain materials and supplies such as textbooks and laboratory equipment.

5) Collaborate with colleagues to address teaching and research issues.

6) Supervise students' laboratory or field work.

7) Prepare course materials such as syllabi, homework assignments, and handouts.

8) Supervise undergraduate and/or graduate teaching, internship, and research work.

9) Serve on academic or administrative committees that deal with institutional policies, departmental matters, and academic issues.

10) Act as advisers to student organizations.

11) Keep abreast of developments in their field by reading current literature, talking with colleagues, and participating in professional conferences.

12) Participate in campus and community events.

13) Maintain student attendance records, grades, and other required records.

14) Participate in student recruitment, registration, and placement activities.

15) Plan, evaluate, and revise curricula, course content, and course materials and methods of instruction.

16) Initiate, facilitate, and moderate classroom discussions.

17) Compile bibliographies of specialized materials for outside reading assignments.

18) Compile, administer, and grade examinations, or assign this work to others.

19) Advise students on academic and vocational curricula, career issues, and laboratory and field research.

20) Prepare and deliver lectures to undergraduate and/or graduate students on topics such as research methods, urban anthropology, and language and culture.

21) Evaluate and grade students' class work, assignments, and papers.

22) Perform administrative duties such as serving as department head.

25-1062.00 - Area, Ethnic, and Cultural Studies Teachers,

Postsecondary

Teach courses pertaining to the culture and development of an area (e.g., Latin America), an ethnic group, or any other group (e.g., women's studies, urban affairs).

Tasks

1) Keep abreast of developments in their field by reading current literature, talking with colleagues, and participating in professional conferences.

2) Act as advisers to student organizations.

3) Serve on academic or administrative committees that deal with institutional policies, departmental matters, and academic issues.

4) Select and obtain materials and supplies such as textbooks.

5) Prepare course materials such as syllabi, homework assignments, and handouts.

6) Plan, evaluate, and revise curricula, course content, and course materials and methods of instruction.

7) Compile bibliographies of specialized materials for outside reading assignments.

8) Initiate, facilitate, and moderate classroom discussions.

9) Participate in campus and community events.

10) Maintain regularly scheduled office hours in order to advise and assist students.

11) Conduct research in a particular field of knowledge, and publish findings in professional journals, books, and/or electronic media.

12) Maintain student attendance records, grades, and other required records.

13) Evaluate and grade students' class work, assignments, and papers.

14) Compile, administer, and grade examinations, or assign this work to others.

15) Incorporate experiential/site visit components into courses.

16) Participate in student recruitment, registration, and placement activities.

17) Provide professional consulting services to government and/or industry.

18) Advise students on academic and vocational curricula, and on career issues.

19) Write grant proposals to procure external research funding.

20) Collaborate with colleagues to address teaching and research issues.

21) Prepare and deliver lectures to undergraduate and/or graduate students on topics such as race and ethnic relations, gender studies, and cross-cultural perspectives.

22) Perform administrative duties such as serving as department head.

25-1063.00 - Economics Teachers, Postsecondary

Teach courses in economics.

Tasks

1) Participate in student recruitment, registration, and placement activities.

2) Compile, administer, and grade examinations, or assign this work to others.

3) Compile bibliographies of specialized materials for outside reading assignments.

4) Participate in campus and community events.

5) Serve on academic or administrative committees that deal with institutional policies, departmental matters, and academic issues.

6) Maintain student attendance records, grades, and other required records.

7) Collaborate with colleagues to address teaching and research issues.

8) Advise students on academic and vocational curricula, and on career issues.

9) Prepare and deliver lectures to undergraduate and/or graduate students on topics such as econometrics, price theory, and macroeconomics.

10) Plan, evaluate, and revise curricula, course content, and course materials and methods of instruction.

11) Perform administrative duties such as serving as department head.

12) Select and obtain materials and supplies such as textbooks.

13) Evaluate and grade students' class work, assignments, and papers.

14) Prepare course materials such as syllabi, homework assignments, and handouts.

15) Supervise undergraduate and/or graduate teaching, internship, and research work.

16) Act as advisers to student organizations.

17) Provide professional consulting services to government and/or industry.

18) Conduct research in a particular field of knowledge, and publish findings in professional journals, books, and/or electronic media.

19) Maintain regularly scheduled office hours in order to advise and assist students.

20) Keep abreast of developments in their field by reading current literature, talking with colleagues, and participating in professional conferences.

21) Initiate, facilitate, and moderate classroom discussions.

25-1064.00 - Geography Teachers, Postsecondary

Teach courses in geography.

Tasks

1) Write grant proposals to procure external research funding.

2) Perform spatial analysis and modeling, using geographic information system techniques.

3) Plan, evaluate, and revise curricula, course content, and course materials and methods of instruction.

4) Collaborate with colleagues to address teaching and research issues.

5) Supervise undergraduate and/or graduate teaching, internship, and research work.

6) Maintain geographic information systems laboratories, performing duties such as updating software.

7) Act as advisers to student organizations.

8) Prepare course materials such as syllabi, homework assignments, and handouts.

9) Compile, administer, and grade examinations, or assign this work to others.

10) Supervise students' laboratory and field work.

11) Compile bibliographies of specialized materials for outside reading assignments.

12) Serve on academic or administrative committees that deal with institutional policies, departmental matters, and academic issues.

13) Keep abreast of developments in their field by reading current literature, talking with colleagues, and participating in professional conferences.

14) Conduct research in a particular field of knowledge, and publish findings in professional journals, books, and/or electronic media.

15) Prepare and deliver lectures to undergraduate and/or graduate students on topics such as urbanization, environmental systems, and cultural geography.

16) Evaluate and grade students' class work, assignments, and papers.

17) Participate in campus and community events.

18) Participate in student recruitment, registration, and placement activities.

19) Initiate, facilitate, and moderate classroom discussions.

20) Maintain regularly scheduled office hours in order to advise and assist students.

21) Provide professional consulting services to government and/or industry.

22) Maintain student attendance records, grades, and other required records.

23) Perform administrative duties such as serving as department head.

24) Advise students on academic and vocational curricula, and on career issues.

25-1065.00 - Political Science Teachers, Postsecondary

Teach courses in political science, international affairs, and international relations.

Tasks

1) Prepare course materials such as syllabi, homework assignments, and handouts.

2) Plan, evaluate, and revise curricula, course content, and course materials and methods of instruction.

3) Maintain student attendance records, grades, and other required records.

4) Maintain regularly scheduled office hours in order to advise and assist students.

5) Keep abreast of developments in their field by reading current literature, talking with colleagues, and participating in professional conferences.

6) Prepare and deliver lectures to undergraduate and/or graduate students on topics such as classical political thought, international relations, and democracy and citizenship.

7) Conduct research in a particular field of knowledge, and publish findings in professional journals, books, and/or electronic media.

8) Participate in student recruitment, registration, and placement activities.

9) Provide professional consulting services to government and/or industry.

10) Serve on academic or administrative committees that deal with institutional policies, departmental matters, and academic issues.

11) Initiate, facilitate, and moderate classroom discussions.

12) Evaluate and grade students' class work, assignments, and papers.

13) Compile, administer, and grade examinations, or assign this work to others.

14) Write grant proposals to procure external research funding.

15) Select and obtain materials and supplies such as textbooks.

16) Supervise undergraduate and/or graduate teaching, internship, and research work.

17) Act as advisers to student organizations.

18) Collaborate with colleagues to address teaching and research issues.

19) Participate in campus and community events.

20) Advise students on academic and vocational curricula, and on career issues.

21) Compile bibliographies of specialized materials for outside reading assignments.

25-1066.00 - Psychology Teachers, Postsecondary

Teach courses in psychology, such as child, clinical, and developmental psychology, and psychological counseling.

Tasks

1) Participate in student recruitment, registration, and placement activities.

2) Evaluate and grade students' class work, laboratory work, assignments, and papers.

3) Maintain student attendance records, grades, and other required records.

4) Supervise undergraduate and/or graduate teaching, internship, and research work.

5) Prepare and deliver lectures to undergraduate and/or graduate students on topics such as abnormal psychology, cognitive processes, and work motivation.

6) Compile, administer, and grade examinations, or assign this work to others.

7) Initiate, facilitate, and moderate classroom discussions.

8) Keep abreast of developments in their field by reading current literature, talking with colleagues, and participating in professional conferences.

9) Collaborate with colleagues to address teaching and research issues.

10) Maintain regularly scheduled office hours in order to advise and assist students.

11) Prepare course materials such as syllabi, homework assignments, and handouts.

12) Compile bibliographies of specialized materials for outside reading assignments.

13) Conduct research in a particular field of knowledge, and publish findings in professional journals, books, and/or electronic media.

14) Select and obtain materials and supplies such as textbooks.

15) Advise students on academic and vocational curricula, and on career issues.

16) Plan, evaluate, and revise curricula, course content, and course materials and methods of instruction.

17) Serve on academic or administrative committees that deal with institutional policies, departmental matters, and academic issues.

18) Provide professional consulting services to government and/or industry.

19) Perform administrative duties such as serving as department head.

20) Supervise students' laboratory work.

21) Participate in campus and community events.

22) Write grant proposals to procure external research funding.

25-1067.00 - Sociology Teachers, Postsecondary

Teach courses in sociology.

Tasks

1) Plan, evaluate, and revise curricula, course content, and course materials and methods of instruction.

2) Participate in campus and community events.

3) Perform administrative duties such as serving as department head.

4) Prepare and deliver lectures to undergraduate and/or graduate students on topics such as

race and ethnic relations, measurement and data collection, and workplace social relations.

5) Maintain student attendance records, grades, and other required records.

6) Prepare course materials such as syllabi, homework assignments, and handouts.

7) Conduct research in a particular field of knowledge, and publish findings in professional journals, books, and/or electronic media.

8) Keep abreast of developments in their field by reading current literature, talking with colleagues, and participating in professional conferences.

9) Initiate, facilitate, and moderate classroom discussions.

10) Select and obtain materials and supplies such as textbooks and laboratory equipment.

11) Compile, administer, and grade examinations, or assign this work to others.

12) Advise students on academic and vocational curricula, and on career issues.

13) Compile bibliographies of specialized materials for outside reading assignments.

14) Participate in student recruitment, registration, and placement activities.

15) Maintain regularly scheduled office hours in order to advise and assist students.

16) Write grant proposals to procure external research funding.

17) Supervise students' laboratory and field work.

18) Provide professional consulting services to government and/or industry.

19) Evaluate and grade students' class work, assignments, and papers.

20) Supervise undergraduate and/or graduate teaching, internship, and research work.

21) Act as advisers to student organizations.

22) Collaborate with colleagues to address teaching and research issues.

25-1071.00 - Health Specialties Teachers, Postsecondary

Teach courses in health specialties, such as veterinary medicine, dentistry, pharmacy, therapy, laboratory technology, and public health.

Tasks

1) Act as advisers to student organizations.

2) Write grant proposals to procure external research funding.

3) Provide professional consulting services to government and/or industry.

4) Participate in student recruitment, registration, and placement activities.

5) Participate in campus and community events.

6) Conduct research in a particular field of knowledge, and publish findings in professional journals, books, and/or electronic media.

7) Perform administrative duties such as serving as department head.

8) Prepare course materials such as syllabi, homework assignments, and handouts.

9) Plan, evaluate, and revise curricula, course content, and course materials and methods of instruction.

10) Collaborate with colleagues to address teaching and research issues.

11) Advise students on academic and vocational curricula, and on career issues.

12) Supervise laboratory sessions.

13) Select and obtain materials and supplies such as textbooks and laboratory equipment.

14) Evaluate and grade students' class work, assignments, and papers.

15) Maintain student attendance records, grades, and other required records.

16) Supervise undergraduate and/or graduate teaching, internship, and research work.

17) Keep abreast of developments in their field by reading current literature, talking with colleagues, and participating in professional conferences.

18) Initiate, facilitate, and moderate classroom discussions.

19) Prepare and deliver lectures to undergraduate and/or graduate students on topics such as public health, stress management, and worksite health promotion.

20) Compile bibliographies of specialized materials for outside reading assignments.

21) Compile, administer, and grade examinations, or assign this work to others.

22) Maintain regularly scheduled office hours in order to advise and assist students.

25-1072.00 - Nursing Instructors and Teachers, Postsecondary

Demonstrate and teach patient care in classroom and clinical units to nursing students. Includes both teachers primarily engaged in teaching and those who do a combination of both teaching and research.

Tasks

1) Initiate, facilitate, and moderate classroom discussions.

2) Coordinate training programs with area universities, clinics, hospitals, health agencies, and/or vocational schools.

3) Keep abreast of developments in their field by reading current literature, talking with colleagues, and participating in professional conferences.

4) Maintain regularly scheduled office hours in order to advise and assist students.

5) Maintain student attendance records, grades, and other required records.

6) Plan, evaluate, and revise curricula, course content, and course materials and methods of instruction.

7) Write grant proposals to procure external research funding.

8) Assess clinical education needs, and patient and client teaching needs, utilizing a variety of methods.

9) Conduct research in a particular field of knowledge, and publish findings in professional journals, books, and/or electronic media.

10) Advise students on academic and vocational curricula, and on career issues.

11) Evaluate and grade students' class work, laboratory and clinic work, assignments, and papers.

12) Act as advisers to student organizations.

13) Prepare and deliver lectures to undergraduate and/or graduate students on topics such as pharmacology, mental health nursing, and community health care practices.

14) Perform administrative duties such as serving as department head.

15) Demonstrate patient care in clinical units of hospitals.

16) Select and obtain materials and supplies such as textbooks and laboratory equipment.

17) Participate in student recruitment, registration, and placement activities.

18) Supervise students' laboratory and clinical work.

19) Provide professional consulting services to government and/or industry.

20) Serve on academic or administrative committees that deal with institutional policies, departmental matters, and academic issues.

21) Participate in campus and community events.

22) Supervise undergraduate and/or graduate teaching, internship, and research work.

23) Compile, administer, and grade examinations, or assign this work to others.

24) Compile bibliographies of specialized materials for outside reading assignments.

25) Prepare course materials such as syllabi, homework assignments, and handouts.

25-1081.00 - Education Teachers, Postsecondary

Teach courses pertaining to education, such as counseling, curriculum, guidance, instruction, teacher education, and teaching English as a second language.

Tasks

1) Collaborate with colleagues to address teaching and research issues.

2) Conduct research in a particular field of knowledge, and publish findings in professional journals, books, and/or electronic media.

3) Participate in campus and community events.

4) Participate in student recruitment, registration, and placement activities.

5) Provide professional consulting services to government and/or industry.

6) Serve on academic or administrative committees that deal with institutional policies, departmental matters, and academic issues.

7) Write grant proposals to procure external research funding.

8) Act as advisers to student organizations.

9) Maintain student attendance records, grades, and other required records.

10) Plan, evaluate, and revise curricula, course content, and course materials and methods of instruction.

11) Advise and instruct teachers employed in school systems, by providing activities such as in-service seminars.

12) Advise students on academic and vocational curricula, and on career issues.

13) Supervise students' fieldwork, internship, and research work.

14) Evaluate and grade students' class work, assignments, and papers.

15) Prepare and deliver lectures to undergraduate and/or graduate students on topics such as children's literature, learning and development, and reading instruction.

16) Compile, administer, and grade examinations, or assign this work to others.

17) Compile bibliographies of specialized materials for outside reading assignments.

18) Initiate, facilitate, and moderate classroom discussions.

19) Keep abreast of developments in their field by reading current literature, talking with colleagues, and participating in professional conferences.

20) Maintain regularly scheduled office hours in order to advise and assist students.

21) Select and obtain materials and supplies such as textbooks.

22) Prepare course materials such as syllabi, homework assignments, and handouts.

25-1082.00 - Library Science Teachers, Postsecondary

Teach courses in library science.

Tasks

1) Participate in campus and community events.

2) Keep abreast of developments in their field by reading current literature, talking with colleagues, and participating in professional conferences.

3) Maintain regularly scheduled office hours in order to advise and assist students.

4) Maintain student attendance records, grades, and other required records.

5) Prepare course materials such as syllabi, homework assignments, and handouts.

6) Select and obtain materials and supplies such as textbooks.

7) Compile, administer, and grade examinations, or assign this work to others.

8) Supervise undergraduate and/or graduate teaching, internship, and research work.

9) Compile bibliographies of specialized materials for outside reading assignments.

10) Act as advisers to student organizations.

11) Collaborate with colleagues to address teaching and research issues.

12) Serve on academic or administrative committees that deal with institutional policies, departmental matters, and academic issues.

13) Advise students on academic and vocational curricula, and on career issues.

14) Prepare and deliver lectures to undergraduate and/or graduate students on topics such as collection development, archival methods, and indexing and abstracting.

15) Evaluate and grade students' class work, assignments, and papers.

16) Conduct research in a particular field of knowledge, and publish findings in professional journals, books, and/or electronic media.

17) Write grant proposals to procure external research funding.

18) Participate in student recruitment, registration, and placement activities.

19) Perform administrative duties such as serving as department head.

20) Initiate, facilitate, and moderate classroom discussions.

21) Provide professional consulting services to government and/or industry.

25-1111.00 - Criminal Justice and Law Enforcement Teachers, Postsecondary

Teach courses in criminal justice, corrections, and law enforcement administration.

Tasks

1) Plan, evaluate, and revise curricula, course content, and course materials and methods of instruction.

2) Select and obtain materials and supplies such as textbooks.

3) Maintain student attendance records, grades, and other required records.

4) Provide professional consulting services to government and/or industry.

5) Collaborate with colleagues to address teaching and research issues.

6) Act as advisers to student organizations.

7) Prepare course materials such as syllabi, homework assignments, and handouts.

8) Perform administrative duties such as serving as department head.

9) Supervise undergraduate and/or graduate teaching, internship, and research work.

10) Prepare and deliver lectures to undergraduate and/or graduate students on topics such as

criminal law, defensive policing, and investigation techniques.

11) Compile bibliographies of specialized materials for outside reading assignments.

12) Advise students on academic and vocational curricula, and on career issues.

13) Compile, administer, and grade examinations, or assign this work to others.

14) Conduct research in a particular field of knowledge, and publish findings in professional journals, books, and/or electronic media.

15) Participate in campus and community events.

16) Participate in student recruitment, registration, and placement activities.

17) Keep abreast of developments in their field by reading current literature, talking with colleagues, and participating in professional conferences.

18) Evaluate and grade students' class work, assignments, and papers.

19) Write grant proposals to procure external research funding.

20) Serve on academic or administrative committees that deal with institutional policies, departmental matters, and academic issues.

21) Maintain regularly scheduled office hours in order to advise and assist students.

25-1112.00 - Law Teachers, Postsecondary

Teach courses in law.

Tasks

1) Evaluate and grade students' class work, assignments, papers, and oral presentations.

2) Prepare and deliver lectures to undergraduate and/or graduate students on topics such as civil procedure, contracts, and torts.

3) Advise students on academic and vocational curricula, and on career issues.

4) Assign cases for students to hear and try.

5) Maintain student attendance records, grades, and other required records.

6) Keep abreast of developments in their field by reading current literature, talking with colleagues, and participating in professional conferences.

7) Maintain regularly scheduled office hours in order to advise and assist students.

8) Compile, administer, and grade examinations, or assign this work to others.

9) Select and obtain materials and supplies such as textbooks.

10) Perform administrative duties such as serving as department head.

11) Write grant proposals to procure external research funding.

12) Collaborate with colleagues to address teaching and research issues.

13) Plan, evaluate, and revise curricula, course content, and course materials and methods of instruction.

14) Compile bibliographies of specialized materials for outside reading assignments.

15) Act as advisers to student organizations.

16) Conduct research in a particular field of knowledge, and publish findings in professional journals, books, and/or electronic media.

17) Participate in campus and community events.

18) Participate in student recruitment, registration, and placement activities.

19) Provide professional consulting services to government and/or industry.

20) Supervise undergraduate and/or graduate teaching, internship, and research work.

21) Initiate, facilitate, and moderate classroom discussions.

22) Serve on academic or administrative committees that deal with institutional policies, departmental matters, and academic issues.

25-1113.00 - Social Work Teachers, Postsecondary

Teach courses in social work.

Tasks

1) Keep abreast of developments in their field by reading current literature, talking with colleagues, and participating in professional conferences.

2) Serve on academic or administrative committees that deal with institutional policies, departmental matters, and academic issues.

3) Provide professional consulting services to government and/or industry.

4) Perform administrative duties such as serving as department head.

5) Participate in student recruitment, registration, and placement activities.

6) Participate in campus and community events.

7) Conduct research in a particular field of knowledge, and publish findings in professional journals, books, and/or electronic media.

8) Compile, administer, and grade examinations, or assign this work to others.

9) Act as advisers to student organizations.

10) Write grant proposals to procure external research funding.

11) Advise students on academic and vocational curricula, and on career issues.

12) Initiate, facilitate, and moderate classroom discussions.

13) Supervise undergraduate and/or graduate teaching, internship, and research work.

14) Prepare and deliver lectures to undergraduate and/or graduate students on topics such as family behavior, child and adolescent mental health, and social intervention evaluation.

15) Evaluate and grade students' class work, assignments, and papers.

16) Collaborate with colleagues, and with community agencies, in order to address teaching and research issues.

17) Maintain regularly scheduled office hours in order to advise and assist students.

18) Maintain student attendance records, grades, and other required records.

19) Plan, evaluate, and revise curricula, course content, and course materials and methods of instruction.

20) Prepare course materials such as syllabi, homework assignments, and handouts.

21) Select and obtain materials and supplies such as textbooks and laboratory equipment.

22) Supervise students' laboratory and field work.

25-1121.00 - Art, Drama, and Music Teachers, Postsecondary

Teach courses in drama, music, and the arts including fine and applied art, such as painting and sculpture, or design and crafts.

Tasks

1) Provide professional consulting services to government and/or industry.

2) Perform administrative duties such as serving as department head.

3) Participate in student recruitment, registration, and placement activities.

4) Participate in campus and community events.

5) Display students' work in schools, galleries, and exhibitions.

6) Keep students informed of community events such as plays and concerts.

7) Conduct research in a particular field of knowledge, and publish findings in professional journals, books, and/or electronic media.

8) Collaborate with colleagues to address teaching and research issues.

9) Organize performance groups, and direct their rehearsals.

10) Advise students on academic and vocational curricula, and on career issues.

11) Prepare and deliver lectures to undergraduate and/or graduate students on topics such as acting techniques, fundamentals of music, and art history.

12) Supervise undergraduate and/or graduate teaching, internship, and research work.

13) Act as advisers to student organizations.

14) Explain and demonstrate artistic techniques.

15) Initiate, facilitate, and moderate classroom discussions.

16) Compile bibliographies of specialized materials for outside reading assignments.

17) Compile, administer, and grade examinations, or assign this work to others.

18) Keep abreast of developments in their field by reading current literature, talking with colleagues, and participating in professional conferences.

19) Maintain regularly scheduled office hours in order to advise and assist students.

20) Maintain student attendance records, grades, and other required records.

21) Write grant proposals to procure external research funding.

22) Prepare course materials such as syllabi, homework assignments, and handouts.

23) Prepare students for performances, exams, or assessments.

24) Select and obtain materials and supplies such as textbooks and performance pieces.

25) Serve on academic or administrative committees that deal with institutional policies, departmental matters, and academic issues.

26) Plan, evaluate, and revise curricula, course content, and course materials and methods of instruction.

25-1122.00 - Communications Teachers, Postsecondary

Teach courses in communications, such as organizational communications, public relations, radio/television broadcasting, and journalism.

Tasks

1) Plan, evaluate, and revise curricula, course content, and course materials and methods of instruction.

2) Prepare course materials such as syllabi, homework assignments, and handouts.

3) Select and obtain materials and supplies such as textbooks.

4) Act as advisers to student organizations.

5) Write grant proposals to procure external research funding.

6) Provide professional consulting services to government and/or industry.

7) Participate in student recruitment, registration, and placement activities.

8) Compile, administer, and grade examinations, or assign this work to others.

9) Compile bibliographies of specialized materials for outside reading assignments.

10) Serve on academic or administrative committees that deal with institutional policies, departmental matters, and academic issues.

11) Prepare and deliver lectures to undergraduate and/or graduate students on topics such as public speaking, media criticism, and oral traditions.

12) Perform administrative duties such as serving as department head.

13) Participate in campus and community events.

14) Evaluate and grade students' class work, assignments, and papers.

15) Collaborate with colleagues to address teaching and research issues.

16) Conduct research in a particular field of knowledge, and publish findings in professional journals, books, and/or electronic media.

17) Advise students on academic and vocational curricula, and on career issues.

18) Maintain regularly scheduled office hours in order to advise and assist students.

19) Keep abreast of developments in their field by reading current literature, talking with colleagues, and participating in professional conferences.

20) Initiate, facilitate, and moderate classroom discussions.

21) Maintain student attendance records, grades, and other required records.

25-1123.00 - English Language and Literature Teachers, Postsecondary

Teach courses in English language and literature, including linguistics and comparative literature.

Tasks

1) Collaborate with colleagues to address teaching and research issues.

2) Supervise undergraduate and/or graduate teaching, internship, and research work.

3) Provide assistance to students in college writing centers.

4) Act as advisers to student organizations.

5) Conduct research in a particular field of knowledge, and publish findings in professional journals, books, and/or electronic media.

6) Participate in campus and community events.

7) Participate in student recruitment, registration, and placement activities.

8) Prepare course materials such as syllabi, homework assignments, and handouts.

9) Advise students on academic and vocational curricula, and on career issues.

10) Perform administrative duties such as serving as department head.

11) Compile, administer, and grade examinations, or assign this work to others.

12) Plan, evaluate, and revise curricula, course content, and course materials and methods of instruction.

13) Compile bibliographies of specialized materials for outside reading assignments.

14) Evaluate and grade students' class work, assignments, and papers.

15) Provide professional consulting services to government and/or industry.

16) Recruit, train, and supervise student writing instructors.

17) Serve on academic or administrative committees that deal with institutional policies, departmental matters, and academic issues.

18) Write grant proposals to procure external research funding.

19) Initiate, facilitate, and moderate classroom discussions.

20) Keep abreast of developments in their field by reading current literature, talking with colleagues, and participating in professional conferences.

21) Maintain student attendance records, grades, and other required records.

22) Maintain regularly scheduled office hours in order to advise and assist students.

23) Select and obtain materials and supplies such as textbooks.

25-1124.00 - Foreign Language and Literature Teachers, Postsecondary

Teach courses in foreign (i.e., other than English) languages and literature.

Tasks

1) Collaborate with colleagues to address teaching and research issues.

2) Act as advisers to student organizations.

3) Select and obtain materials and supplies such as textbooks.

4) Plan, evaluate, and revise curricula, course content, and course materials and methods of instruction.

5) Maintain student attendance records, grades, and other required records.

6) Maintain regularly scheduled office hours in order to advise and assist students.

7) Prepare course materials such as syllabi, homework assignments, and handouts.

8) Supervise undergraduate and/or graduate teaching, internship, and research work.

9) Participate in campus and community events.

10) Write grant proposals to procure external research funding.

11) Serve on academic or administrative committees that deal with institutional policies, departmental matters, and academic issues.

12) Participate in student recruitment, registration, and placement activities.

13) Provide professional consulting services to government and/or industry.

14) Perform administrative duties such as serving as department head.

15) Evaluate and grade students' class work, assignments, and papers.

16) Initiate, facilitate, and moderate classroom discussions.

17) Compile bibliographies of specialized materials for outside reading assignments.

18) Compile, administer, and grade examinations, or assign this work to others.

19) Keep abreast of developments in their field by reading current literature, talking with colleagues, and participating in professional organizations and activities.

20) Prepare and deliver lectures to undergraduate and/or graduate students on topics such as how to speak and write a foreign language, and the cultural aspects of areas where a particular language is used.

21) Advise students on academic and vocational curricula, and on career issues.

25-1125.00 - History Teachers, Postsecondary

Teach courses in human history and historiography.

Tasks

1) Compile, administer, and grade examinations, or assign this work to others.

2) Select and obtain materials and supplies such as textbooks.

3) Advise students on academic and vocational curricula, and on career issues.

4) Conduct research in a particular field of knowledge, and publish findings in professional journals, books, and/or electronic media.

5) Collaborate with colleagues to address teaching and research issues.

6) Evaluate and grade students' class work, assignments, and papers.

7) Act as advisers to student organizations.

8) Prepare course materials such as syllabi, homework assignments, and handouts.

9) Compile bibliographies of specialized materials for outside reading assignments.

10) Write grant proposals to procure external research funding.

11) Participate in student recruitment, registration, and placement activities.

12) Initiate, facilitate, and moderate classroom discussions.

13) Perform administrative duties such as serving as department head.

14) Plan, evaluate, and revise curricula, course content, and course materials and methods of instruction.

15) Maintain student attendance records, grades, and other required records.

16) Maintain regularly scheduled office hours in order to advise and assist students.

17) Prepare and deliver lectures to undergraduate and/or graduate students on topics such as ancient history, postwar civilizations, and the history of third-world countries.

18) Participate in campus and community events.

19) Serve on academic or administrative committees that deal with institutional policies, departmental matters, and academic issues.

20) Provide professional consulting services to government, educational institutions, and/or industry.

21) Keep abreast of developments in their field by reading current literature, talking with colleagues, and participating in professional conferences.

25-1126.00 - Philosophy and Religion Teachers, Postsecondary

Teach courses in philosophy, religion, and theology.

Tasks

1) Select and obtain materials and supplies such as textbooks.

2) Prepare course materials such as syllabi, homework assignments, and handouts.

3) Evaluate and grade students' class work, assignments, and papers.

4) Advise students on academic and vocational curricula, and on career issues.

5) Prepare and deliver lectures to undergraduate and/or graduate students on topics such as ethics, logic, and contemporary religious thought.

6) Perform administrative duties such as serving as department head.

7) Conduct research in a particular field of knowledge, and publish findings in professional journals, books, and/or electronic media.

8) Act as advisers to student organizations.

9) Supervise undergraduate and/or graduate teaching, internship, and research work.

10) Collaborate with colleagues to address teaching and research issues.

11) Serve on academic or administrative committees that deal with institutional policies, departmental matters, and academic issues.

12) Provide professional consulting services to government and/or industry.

13) Keep abreast of developments in their field by reading current literature, talking with colleagues, and participating in professional conferences.

14) Maintain regularly scheduled office hours in order to advise and assist students.

15) Initiate, facilitate, and moderate classroom discussions.

16) Compile bibliographies of specialized materials for outside reading assignments.

17) Participate in campus and community events.

18) Compile, administer, and grade examinations, or assign this work to others.

19) Write grant proposals to procure external research funding.

20) Maintain student attendance records, grades, and other required records.

21) Plan, evaluate, and revise curricula, course content, and course materials and methods of instruction.

25-1191.00 - Graduate Teaching Assistants

Assist department chairperson, faculty members, or other professional staff members in college or university by performing teaching or teaching-related duties, such as teaching lower level courses, developing teaching materials, preparing and giving examinations, and grading examinations or papers. Graduate assistants must be enrolled in a graduate school program. Graduate assistants who primarily perform non-teaching duties, such as laboratory research, should be reported in the occupational category related to the work performed.

Tasks

1) Provide instructors with assistance in the use of audiovisual equipment.

2) Develop teaching materials such as syllabi, visual aids, answer keys, supplementary notes, and course websites.

3) Teach undergraduate level courses.

4) Copy and distribute classroom materials.

25-1126.00 - Philosophy and Religion Teachers, Postsecondary

5) Provide assistance to library staff in maintaining library collections.

6) Lead discussion sections, tutorials, and laboratory sections.

7) Evaluate and grade examinations, assignments, and papers, and record grades.

8) Schedule and maintain regular office hours to meet with students.

9) Order or obtain materials needed for classes.

10) Attend lectures given by the instructor whom they are assisting.

11) Arrange for supervisors to conduct teaching observations; meet with supervisors to receive feedback about teaching performance.

12) Return assignments to students in accordance with established deadlines.

13) Meet with supervisors to discuss students' grades, and to complete required grade-related paperwork.

14) Prepare and proctor examinations.

15) Demonstrate use of laboratory equipment, and enforce laboratory rules.

16) Inform students of the procedures for completing and submitting class work such as lab reports.

17) Assist faculty members or staff with student conferences.

18) Provide assistance to faculty members or staff with laboratory or field research.

19) Notify instructors of errors or problems with assignments.

25-1192.00 - Home Economics Teachers, Postsecondary

Teach courses in child care, family relations, finance, nutrition, and related subjects as pertaining to home management.

Tasks

1) Prepare course materials such as syllabi, homework assignments, and handouts.

2) Select and obtain materials and supplies such as textbooks.

3) Evaluate and grade students' class work, laboratory work, projects, assignments, and papers.

4) Prepare and deliver lectures to undergraduate and/or graduate students on topics such as food science, nutrition, and child care.

5) Advise students on academic and vocational curricula, and on career issues.

6) Compile bibliographies of specialized materials for outside reading assignments.

7) Maintain regularly scheduled office hours in order to advise and assist students.

8) Supervise undergraduate and/or graduate teaching, internship, and research work.

9) Act as advisers to student organizations.

10) Compile, administer, and grade examinations, or assign this work to others.

11) Collaborate with colleagues to address teaching and research issues.

12) Keep abreast of developments in their field by reading current literature, talking with colleagues, and participating in professional conferences.

13) Conduct research in a particular field of knowledge, and publish findings in professional journals, books, and/or electronic media.

14) Provide professional consulting services to government and/or industry.

15) Maintain student attendance records, grades, and other required records.

16) Participate in student recruitment, registration, and placement activities.

17) Participate in campus and community events.

18) Plan, evaluate, and revise curricula, course content, and course materials and methods of instruction.

19) Initiate, facilitate, and moderate classroom discussions.

20) Serve on academic or administrative committees that deal with institutional policies, departmental matters, and academic issues.

21) Perform administrative duties such as serving as department head.

25-1193.00 - Recreation and Fitness Studies Teachers, Postsecondary

Teach courses pertaining to recreation, leisure, and fitness studies, including exercise physiology and facilities management.

Tasks

1) Collaborate with colleagues to address teaching and research issues.

2) Conduct research in a particular field of knowledge, and publish findings in professional journals, books, and/or electronic media.

3) Participate in campus and community events.

4) Perform administrative duties such as serving as department heads.

5) Supervise undergraduate and/or graduate teaching, internship, and research work.

6) Participate in student recruitment, registration, and placement activities.

7) Serve on academic or administrative committees that deal with institutional policies, departmental matters, and academic issues.

8) Maintain regularly scheduled office hours in order to advise and assist students.

9) Select and obtain materials and supplies such as textbooks.

10) Maintain student attendance records, grades, and other required records.

11) Prepare and deliver lectures to undergraduate and/or graduate students on topics such as anatomy, therapeutic recreation, and conditioning theory.

12) Advise students on academic and vocational curricula, and on career issues.

13) Write grant proposals to procure external research funding.

14) Provide professional consulting services to government and/or industry.

15) Initiate, facilitate, and moderate classroom discussions.

16) Evaluate and grade students' class work, assignments, and papers.

17) Keep abreast of developments in their field by reading current literature, talking with colleagues, and participating in professional conferences.

18) Prepare students to act as sports coaches.

19) Compile bibliographies of specialized materials for outside reading assignments.

20) Plan, evaluate, and revise curricula, course content, and course materials and methods of instruction.

21) Prepare course materials such as syllabi, homework assignments, and handouts.

22) Compile, administer, and grade examinations, or assign this work to others.

25-1194.00 - Vocational Education Teachers Postsecondary

Teach or instruct vocational or occupational subjects at the postsecondary level (but at less than the baccalaureate) to students who have graduated or left high school. Includes correspondence school instructors; industrial, commercial and government training instructors; and adult education teachers and instructors who prepare persons to operate industrial machinery and equipment and transportation and communications equipment. Teaching may take place in public or private schools whose primary business is education or in a school associated with an organization whose primary business is other than education.

Tasks

1) Participate in conferences, seminars, and training sessions to keep abreast of developments in the field; and integrate relevant information into training programs.

2) Supervise independent or group projects, field placements, laboratory work, or other training.

3) Serve on faculty and school committees concerned with budgeting, curriculum revision, and course and diploma requirements.

4) Prepare reports and maintain records such as student grades, attendance rolls, and training activity details.

5) Arrange for lectures by experts in designated fields.

6) Advise students on course selection, career decisions, and other academic and vocational concerns.

7) Review enrollment applications, and correspond with applicants to obtain additional information.

8) Prepare outlines of instructional programs and training schedules, and establish course goals.

9) Integrate academic and vocational curricula so that students can obtain a variety of skills.

10) Determine training needs of students or workers.

11) Administer oral, written, or performance tests in order to measure progress, and to evaluate training effectiveness.

12) Present lectures and conduct discussions to increase students' knowledge and competence, using visual aids such as graphs, charts, videotapes, and slides.

13) Conduct on-the-job training, classes, or training sessions to teach and demonstrate principles, techniques, procedures, and/or methods of designated subjects.

14) Observe and evaluate students' work to determine progress, provide feedback, and make

suggestions for improvement.

15) Supervise and monitor students' use of tools and equipment.

16) Provide individualized instruction and tutorial and/or remedial instruction.

17) Select and assemble books, materials, supplies, and equipment for training, courses, or projects.

18) Develop curricula, and plan course content and methods of instruction.

25-2011.00 - Preschool Teachers, Except Special Education

Instruct children (normally up to 5 years of age) in activities designed to promote social, physical, and intellectual growth needed for primary school in preschool, day care center, or other child development facility. May be required to hold State certification.

Tasks

1) Supervise, evaluate, and plan assignments for teacher assistants and volunteers.

2) Arrange indoor and outdoor space to facilitate creative play, motor-skill activities, and safety.

3) Assimilate arriving children to the school environment by greeting them, helping them remove outerwear, and selecting activities of interest to them.

4) Enforce all administration policies and rules governing students.

5) Collaborate with other teachers and administrators in the development, evaluation, and revision of preschool programs.

6) Serve meals and snacks in accordance with nutritional guidelines.

7) Teach proper eating habits and personal hygiene.

8) Administer tests to help determine children's developmental levels, needs, and potential.

9) Attend professional meetings, educational conferences, and teacher training workshops in order to maintain and improve professional competence.

10) Organize and label materials, and display students' work in a manner appropriate for their ages and perceptual skills.

11) Select, store, order, issue, and inventory classroom equipment, materials, and supplies.

12) Perform administrative duties such as hall and cafeteria monitoring, and bus loading and unloading.

13) Teach basic skills such as color, shape, number and letter recognition, personal hygiene, and social skills.

14) Read books to entire classes or to small groups.

15) Meet with other professionals to discuss individual students' needs and progress.

16) Plan and supervise class projects, field trips, visits by guests, or other experiential activities, and guide students in learning from those activities.

17) Prepare and implement remedial programs for students requiring extra help.

18) Attend to children's basic needs by feeding them, dressing them, and changing their diapers.

19) Attend staff meetings, and serve on committees as required.

20) Confer with other staff members to plan and schedule lessons promoting learning, following approved curricula.

21) Adapt teaching methods and instructional materials to meet students' varying needs and interests.

22) Meet with parents and guardians to discuss their children's progress and needs, determine their priorities for their children, and suggest ways that they can promote learning and development.

23) Maintain accurate and complete student records as required by laws, district policies, and administrative regulations.

24) Identify children showing signs of emotional, developmental, or health-related problems, and discuss them with supervisors, parents or guardians, and child development specialists.

25) Establish and enforce rules for behavior, and procedures for maintaining order.

26) Provide a variety of materials and resources for children to explore, manipulate and use, both in learning activities and in imaginative play.

27) Demonstrate activities to children.

28) Prepare reports on students and activities as required by administration.

29) Establish clear objectives for all lessons, units, and projects, and communicate those objectives to children.

30) Organize and lead activities designed to promote physical, mental and social development, such as games, arts and crafts, music, storytelling, and field trips.

31) Plan and conduct activities for a balanced program of instruction, demonstration, and work time that provides students with opportunities to observe, question, and investigate.

32) Prepare materials and classrooms for class activities.

33) Observe and evaluate children's performance, behavior, social development, and physical health.

25-2012.00 - Kindergarten Teachers, Except Special Education

Teach elemental natural and social science, personal hygiene, music, art, and literature to children from 4 to 6 years old. Promote physical, mental, and social development. May be required to hold State certification.

Tasks

1) Prepare and implement remedial programs for students requiring extra help.

2) Prepare children for later grades by encouraging them to explore learning opportunities and to persevere with challenging tasks.

3) Perform administrative duties such as assisting in school libraries, hall and cafeteria monitoring, and bus loading and unloading.

4) Prepare for assigned classes, and show written evidence of preparation upon request of immediate supervisors.

5) Prepare objectives and outlines for courses of study, following curriculum guidelines or requirements of states and schools.

6) Provide disabled students with assistive devices, supportive technology, and assistance accessing facilities such as restrooms.

7) Provide a variety of materials and resources for children to explore, manipulate, and use, both in learning activities and in imaginative play.

8) Plan and supervise class projects, field trips, visits by guests, or other experiential activities, and guide students in learning from those activities.

9) Involve parent volunteers and older students in children's activities, in order to facilitate involvement in focused, complex play.

10) Attend staff meetings, and serve on committees as required.

11) Observe and evaluate children's performance, behavior, social development, and physical health.

12) Collaborate with other teachers and administrators in the development, evaluation, and revision of kindergarten programs.

13) Plan and conduct activities for a balanced program of instruction, demonstration, and work time that provides students with opportunities to observe, question, and investigate.

14) Organize and lead activities designed to promote physical, mental, and social development such as games, arts and crafts, music, and storytelling.

15) Organize and label materials and display children's work in a manner appropriate for their sizes and perceptual skills.

16) Meet with other professionals to discuss individual students' needs and progress.

17) Use computers, audiovisual aids, and other equipment and materials to supplement presentations.

18) Prepare materials, classrooms, and other indoor and outdoor spaces to facilitate creative play, learning and motor-skill activities, and safety.

19) Guide and counsel students with adjustment and/or academic problems, or special academic interests.

20) Establish and enforce rules for behavior, and policies and procedures to maintain order among students.

21) Confer with parents or guardians, other teachers, counselors, and administrators to resolve students' behavioral and academic problems.

22) Confer with other staff members to plan and schedule lessons promoting learning, following approved curricula.

23) Read books to entire classes or to small groups.

24) Assimilate arriving children to the school environment by greeting them, helping them remove outerwear, and selecting activities of interest to them.

25) Meet with parents and guardians to discuss their children's progress, and to determine their priorities for their children and their resource needs.

26) Establish clear objectives for all lessons, units, and projects, and communicate those objectives to children.

27) Attend professional meetings, educational conferences, and teacher training workshops in order to maintain and improve professional competence.

28) Teach basic skills such as color, shape, number and letter recognition, personal hygiene, and social skills.

29) Identify children showing signs of emotional, developmental, or health-related problems, and discuss them with supervisors, parents or guardians, and child development specialists.

30) Instruct and monitor students in the use and care of equipment and materials, in order to prevent injuries and damage.

31) Supervise, evaluate, and plan assignments for teacher assistants and volunteers.

32) Prepare, administer, and grade tests and assignments to evaluate children's progress.

33) Administer standardized ability and achievement tests, and interpret results to determine children's developmental levels and needs.

34) Maintain accurate and complete student records, and prepare reports on children and activities, as required by laws, district policies, and administrative regulations.

35) Instruct students individually and in groups, adapting teaching methods to meet students' varying needs and interests.

36) Demonstrate activities to children.

25-2021.00 - Elementary School Teachers, Except Special Education

Teach pupils in public or private schools at the elementary level basic academic, social, and other formative skills.

Tasks

1) Adapt teaching methods and instructional materials to meet students' varying needs and interests.

2) Provide a variety of materials and resources for children to explore, manipulate and use, both in learning activities and in imaginative play.

3) Use computers, audiovisual aids, and other equipment and materials to supplement presentations.

4) Sponsor extracurricular activities such as clubs, student organizations, and academic contests.

5) Select, store, order, issue, and inventory classroom equipment, materials, and supplies.

6) Provide disabled students with assistive devices, supportive technology, and assistance accessing facilities such as restrooms.

7) Perform administrative duties such as assisting in school libraries, hall and cafeteria monitoring, and bus loading and unloading.

8) Involve parent volunteers and older students in children's activities, in order to facilitate involvement in focused, complex play.

9) Organize and lead activities designed to promote physical, mental and social development, such as games, arts and crafts, music, and storytelling.

10) Attend staff meetings, and serve on committees as required.

11) Read books to entire classes or small groups.

12) Confer with other staff members to plan and schedule lessons promoting learning, following approved curricula.

13) Prepare, administer, and grade tests and assignments in order to evaluate students' progress.

14) Prepare materials and classrooms for class activities.

15) Establish clear objectives for all lessons, units, and projects, and communicate those objectives to students.

16) Attend professional meetings, educational conferences, and teacher training workshops in order to maintain and improve professional competence.

17) Assign and grade class work and homework.

18) Confer with parents or guardians, teachers, counselors, and administrators in order to resolve students' behavioral and academic problems.

19) Guide and counsel students with adjustment and/or academic problems, or special academic interests.

20) Establish and enforce rules for behavior and procedures for maintaining order among the students for whom they are responsible.

21) Maintain accurate and complete student records as required by laws, district policies, and administrative regulations.

22) Prepare and implement remedial programs for students requiring extra help.

23) Meet with other professionals to discuss individual students' needs and progress.

24) Meet with parents and guardians to discuss their children's progress, and to determine their priorities for their children and their resource needs.

25) Observe and evaluate students' performance, behavior, social development, and physical health.

26) Supervise, evaluate, and plan assignments for teacher assistants and volunteers.

27) Enforce administration policies and rules governing students.

28) Collaborate with other teachers and administrators in the development, evaluation, and revision of elementary school programs.

29) Plan and supervise class projects, field trips, visits by guest speakers or other experiential

activities, and guide students in learning from those activities.

30) Prepare for assigned classes, and show written evidence of preparation upon request of immediate supervisors.

31) Plan and conduct activities for a balanced program of instruction, demonstration, and work time that provides students with opportunities to observe, question, and investigate.

32) Organize and label materials, and display students' work.

33) Administer standardized ability and achievement tests, and interpret results to determine student strengths and areas of need.

34) Prepare students for later grades by encouraging them to explore learning opportunities and to persevere with challenging tasks.

35) Prepare objectives and outlines for courses of study, following curriculum guidelines or requirements of states and schools.

36) Instruct and monitor students in the use and care of equipment and materials, in order to prevent injuries and damage.

37) Prepare reports on students and activities as required by administration.

25-2022.00 - Middle School Teachers, Except Special and Vocational Education

Teach students in public or private schools in one or more subjects at the middle, intermediate, or junior high level, which falls between elementary and senior high school as defined by applicable State laws and regulations.

Tasks

1) Instruct through lectures, discussions, and demonstrations in one or more subjects such as English, mathematics, or social studies.

2) Prepare, administer, and grade tests and assignments in order to evaluate students' progress.

3) Assign lessons and correct homework.

4) Adapt teaching methods and instructional materials to meet students' varying needs and interests.

5) Confer with parents or guardians, other teachers, counselors, and administrators in order to resolve students' behavioral and academic problems.

6) Establish clear objectives for all lessons, units, and projects, and communicate these objectives to students.

7) Establish and enforce rules for behavior and procedures for maintaining order among the students for whom they are responsible.

8) Plan and conduct activities for a balanced program of instruction, demonstration, and work time that provides students with opportunities to observe, question, and investigate.

9) Instruct and monitor students in the use and care of equipment and materials, in order to prevent injury and damage.

10) Maintain accurate, complete, and correct student records as required by laws, district policies, and administrative regulations.

11) Prepare for assigned classes, and show written evidence of preparation upon request of immediate supervisors.

12) Meet with parents and guardians to discuss their children's progress, and to determine their priorities for their children and their resource needs.

13) Confer with other staff members to plan and schedule lessons promoting learning, following approved curricula.

14) Meet with other professionals to discuss individual students' needs and progress.

15) Prepare materials and classrooms for class activities.

16) Observe and evaluate students' performance, behavior, social development, and physical health.

17) Plan and supervise class projects, field trips, visits by guest speakers or other experiential activities, and guide students in learning from such activities.

18) Prepare and implement remedial programs for students requiring extra help.

19) Administer standardized ability and achievement tests, and interpret results to determine student strengths and areas of need.

20) Enforce all administration policies and rules governing students.

21) Use computers, audiovisual aids, and other equipment and materials to supplement presentations.

22) Prepare objectives and outlines for courses of study, following curriculum guidelines or requirements of states and schools.

23) Prepare reports on students and activities as required by administration.

24) Organize and supervise games and other recreational activities to promote physical, mental, and social development.

25) Supervise, evaluate, and plan assignments for teacher assistants and volunteers.

26) Select, store, order, issue, and inventory classroom equipment, materials, and supplies.

27) Attend professional meetings, educational conferences, and teacher training workshops in order to maintain and improve professional competence.

28) Attend staff meetings, and serve on staff committees as required.

29) Prepare students for later grades by encouraging them to explore learning opportunities and to persevere with challenging tasks.

30) Collaborate with other teachers and administrators in the development, evaluation, and revision of middle school programs.

31) Perform administrative duties such as assisting in school libraries, hall and cafeteria monitoring, and bus loading and unloading.

32) Provide disabled students with assistive devices, supportive technology, and assistance accessing facilities such as restrooms.

33) Sponsor extracurricular activities such as clubs, student organizations, and academic contests.

34) Organize and label materials, and display students' work.

25-2023.00 - Vocational Education Teachers, Middle School

Teach or instruct vocational or occupational subjects at the middle school level.

Tasks

1) Instruct and monitor students in the use and care of equipment and materials, in order to prevent injuries and damage.

2) Prepare and implement remedial programs for students requiring extra help.

3) Establish clear objectives for all lessons, units, and projects, and communicate those objectives to students.

4) Attend staff meetings, and serve on committees as required.

5) Select, store, order, issue, and inventory classroom equipment, materials, and supplies.

6) Assign and grade class work and homework.

7) Maintain accurate and complete student records as required by laws, district policies, and administrative regulations.

8) Use computers, audiovisual aids, and other equipment and materials to supplement presentations.

9) Sponsor extracurricular activities such as clubs, student organizations, and academic contests.

10) Guide and counsel students with adjustment and/or academic problems, or special academic interests.

11) Prepare materials and classrooms for class activities.

12) Meet with other professionals to discuss individual students' needs and progress.

13) Prepare reports on students and activities as required by administration.

14) Observe and evaluate students' performance, behavior, social development, and physical health.

15) Enforce all administration policies and rules governing students.

16) Attend professional meetings, educational conferences, and teacher training workshops in order to maintain and improve professional competence.

17) Prepare students for later educational experiences by encouraging them to explore learning opportunities and to persevere with challenging tasks.

18) Meet with parents and guardians to discuss their children's progress, and to determine their priorities for their children and their resource needs.

19) Collaborate with other teachers and administrators in the development, evaluation, and revision of middle school programs.

20) Establish and enforce rules for behavior and procedures for maintaining order among the students for whom they are responsible.

21) Confer with parents or guardians, other teachers, counselors, and administrators in order to resolve students' behavioral and academic problems.

22) Plan and conduct activities for a balanced program of instruction, demonstration, and work time that provides students with opportunities to observe, question, and investigate.

23) Confer with other staff members to plan and schedule lessons promoting learning, following approved curricula.

24) Adapt teaching methods and instructional materials to meet students' varying needs and interests.

25) Plan and supervise class projects, field trips, visits by guest speakers or other experiential activities, and guide students in learning from those activities.

26) Prepare objectives and outlines for courses of study, following curriculum guidelines or

requirements of states and schools.

27) Provide disabled students with assistive devices, supportive technology, and assistance accessing facilities such as restrooms.

28) Prepare for assigned classes, and show written evidence of preparation upon request of immediate supervisors.

29) Prepare, administer, and grade tests and assignments to evaluate students⊦ progress.

30) Perform administrative duties such as assisting in school libraries, hall and cafeteria monitoring, and bus loading and unloading.

25-2031.00 - Secondary School Teachers, Except Special and Vocational Education

Instruct students in secondary public or private schools in one or more subjects at the secondary level, such as English, mathematics, or social studies. May be designated according to subject matter specialty, such as typing instructors, commercial teachers, or English teachers.

Tasks

1) Perform administrative duties such as assisting in school libraries, hall and cafeteria monitoring, and bus loading and unloading.

2) Assign and grade class work and homework.

3) Instruct and monitor students in the use and care of equipment and materials, in order to prevent injuries and damage.

4) Adapt teaching methods and instructional materials to meet students⊦ varying needs and interests.

5) Confer with other staff members to plan and schedule lessons promoting learning, following approved curricula.

6) Confer with parents or guardians, other teachers, counselors, and administrators in order to resolve students⊦ behavioral and academic problems.

7) Maintain accurate and complete student records as required by laws, district policies, and administrative regulations.

8) Prepare, administer, and grade tests and assignments to evaluate students⊦ progress.

9) Instruct through lectures, discussions, and demonstrations in one or more subjects such as English, mathematics, or social studies.

10) Establish clear objectives for all lessons, units, and projects, and communicate those objectives to students.

11) Prepare and implement remedial programs for students requiring extra help.

12) Administer standardized ability and achievement tests, and interpret results to determine students' strengths and areas of need.

13) Attend staff meetings, and serve on committees as required.

14) Attend professional meetings, educational conferences, and teacher training workshops in order to maintain and improve professional competence.

15) Enforce all administration policies and rules governing students.

16) Collaborate with other teachers and administrators in the development, evaluation, and revision of secondary school programs.

17) Prepare objectives and outlines for courses of study, following curriculum guidelines or requirements of states and schools.

18) Guide and counsel students with adjustment and/or academic problems, or special academic interests.

19) Meet with parents and guardians to discuss their children⊦s progress, and to determine their priorities for their children and their resource needs.

20) Meet with other professionals to discuss individual students' needs and progress.

21) Observe and evaluate students⊦ performance, behavior, social development, and physical health.

22) Prepare materials and classrooms for class activities.

23) Plan and supervise class projects, field trips, visits by guest speakers, or other experiential activities, and guide students in learning from those activities.

24) Sponsor extracurricular activities such as clubs, student organizations, and academic contests.

25) Use computers, audiovisual aids, and other equipment and materials to supplement presentations.

26) Prepare reports on students and activities as required by administration.

27) Prepare students for later grades by encouraging them to explore learning opportunities and to persevere with challenging tasks.

28) Establish and enforce rules for behavior and procedures for maintaining order among the students for whom they are responsible.

29) Provide disabled students with assistive devices, supportive technology, and assistance accessing facilities such as restrooms.

30) Select, store, order, issue, and inventory classroom equipment, materials, and supplies.

31) Plan and conduct activities for a balanced program of instruction, demonstration, and work time that provides students with opportunities to observe, question, and investigate.

25-2032.00 - Vocational Education Teachers, Secondary School

Teach or instruct vocational or occupational subjects at the secondary school level.

Tasks

1) Assign and grade class work and homework.

2) Prepare students for later grades by encouraging them to explore learning opportunities and to persevere with challenging tasks.

3) Prepare objectives and outlines for courses of study, following curriculum guidelines or requirements of states and schools.

4) Prepare materials and classroom for class activities.

5) Observe and evaluate students⊦ performance, behavior, social development, and physical health.

6) Plan and conduct activities for a balanced program of instruction, demonstration, and work time that provides students with opportunities to observe, question, and investigate.

7) Confer with other staff members to plan and schedule lessons promoting learning, following approved curricula.

8) Confer with parents or guardians, other teachers, counselors, and administrators in order to resolve students⊦ behavioral and academic problems.

9) Use computers, audiovisual aids, and other equipment and materials to supplement presentations.

10) Enforce all administration policies and rules governing students.

11) Meet with parents and guardians to discuss their children⊦s progress, and to determine their priorities for their children and their resource needs.

12) Prepare, administer, and grade tests and assignments in order to evaluate students⊦ progress.

13) Attend professional meetings, educational conferences, and teacher training workshops in order to maintain and improve professional competence.

14) Establish and enforce rules for behavior and procedures for maintaining order among the students for whom they are responsible.

15) Establish clear objectives for all lessons, units, and projects, and communicate those objectives to students.

16) Guide and counsel students with adjustment and/or academic problems, or special academic interests.

17) Instruct and monitor students the in use and care of equipment and materials, in order to prevent injury and damage.

18) Maintain accurate and complete student records as required by law, district policy, and administrative regulations.

19) Meet with other professionals to discuss individual students' needs and progress.

20) Prepare reports on students and activities as required by administration.

21) Attend staff meetings, and serve on committees as required.

22) Perform administrative duties such as assisting in school libraries, hall and cafeteria monitoring, and bus loading and unloading.

23) Keep informed about trends in education and subject matter specialties.

24) Sponsor extracurricular activities such as clubs, student organizations, and academic contests.

25) Instruct students individually and in groups, using various teaching methods such as lectures, discussions, and demonstrations.

26) Plan and supervise work-experience programs in businesses, industrial shops, and school laboratories.

27) Plan and supervise class projects, field trips, visits by guest speakers or other experiential activities, and guide students in learning from those activities.

28) Instruct students in the knowledge and skills required in a specific occupation or occupational field, using a systematic plan of lectures, discussions, audiovisual presentations, and laboratory, shop and field studies.

29) Select, order, store, issue, and inventory classroom equipment, materials, and supplies.

30) Provide disabled students with assistive devices, supportive technology, and assistance accessing facilities such as restrooms.

31) Prepare and implement remedial programs for students requiring extra help.

25-2041.00 - Special Education Teachers, Preschool, Kindergarten, and Elementary School

32) Collaborate with other teachers and administrators in the development, evaluation, and revision of secondary school programs.

25-2041.00 - Special Education Teachers, Preschool, Kindergarten, and Elementary School

Teach elementary and preschool school subjects to educationally and physically handicapped students. Includes teachers who specialize and work with audibly and visually handicapped students and those who teach basic academic and life processes skills to the mentally impaired.

Tasks

1) Supervise, evaluate, and plan assignments for teacher assistants and volunteers.

2) Perform administrative duties such as assisting in school libraries, hall and cafeteria monitoring, and bus loading and unloading.

3) Provide interpretation and transcription of regular classroom materials through Braille and sign language.

4) Teach students personal development skills such as goal setting, independence, and self-advocacy.

5) Attend professional meetings, educational conferences, and teacher training workshops in order to maintain and improve professional competence.

6) Attend staff meetings, and serve on committees as required.

7) Collaborate with other teachers and administrators in the development, evaluation, and revision of preschool, kindergarten, or elementary school programs.

8) Monitor teachers and teacher assistants to ensure that they adhere to inclusive special education program requirements.

9) Select, store, order, issue, and inventory classroom equipment, materials, and supplies.

10) Prepare students for later grades by encouraging them to explore learning opportunities and to persevere with challenging tasks.

11) Meet with parents and guardians to discuss their children's progress, and to determine their priorities for their children and their resource needs.

12) Use computers, audiovisual aids, and other equipment and materials to supplement presentations.

13) Prepare, administer, and grade tests and assignments to evaluate students' progress.

14) Visit schools to tutor students with sensory impairments, and to consult with teachers regarding students' special needs.

15) Prepare objectives and outlines for courses of study, following curriculum guidelines or requirements of states and schools.

16) Prepare classrooms for class activities and provide a variety of materials and resources for children to explore, manipulate, and use, both in learning activities and imaginative play.

17) Instruct and monitor students in the use and care of equipment and materials, in order to prevent injuries and damage.

18) Maintain accurate and complete student records, and prepare reports on children and activities, as required by laws, district policies, and administrative regulations.

19) Meet with parents to provide guidance in using community resources, and to teach skills for dealing with students' impairments.

20) Observe and evaluate students' performance, behavior, social development, and physical health.

21) Organize and label materials, and display students' work in a manner appropriate for their eye levels and perceptual skills.

22) Organize and supervise games and other recreational activities to promote physical, mental, and social development.

23) Plan and supervise class projects, field trips, visits by guest speakers, or other experiential activities, and guide students in learning from those activities.

24) Guide and counsel students with adjustment and/or academic problems, or special academic interests.

25) Confer with other staff members to plan and schedule lessons promoting learning, following approved curricula.

26) Prepare for assigned classes, and show written evidence of preparation upon request of immediate supervisors.

27) Administer standardized ability and achievement tests, and interpret results to determine students' strengths and areas of need.

28) Plan and conduct activities for a balanced program of instruction, demonstration, and work time that provides students with opportunities to observe, question, and investigate.

29) Establish clear objectives for all lessons, units, and projects, and communicate those objectives to students.

30) Establish and enforce rules for behavior and policies and procedures to maintain order

among the students for whom they are responsible.

31) Employ special educational strategies and techniques during instruction to improve the development of sensory- and perceptual-motor skills, language, cognition, and memory.

32) Coordinate placement of students with special needs into mainstream classes.

33) Confer with parents or guardians, teachers, counselors, and administrators in order to resolve students' behavioral and academic problems.

34) Develop and implement strategies to meet the needs of students with a variety of handicapping conditions.

35) Instruct students in daily living skills required for independent maintenance and self-sufficiency, such as hygiene, safety, and food preparation.

36) Confer with parents, administrators, testing specialists, social workers, and professionals to develop individual educational plans designed to promote students' educational, physical, and social development.

37) Modify the general education curriculum for special-needs students based upon a variety of instructional techniques and technologies.

38) Instruct students in academic subjects, using a variety of techniques such as phonetics, multisensory learning, and repetition, in order to reinforce learning and to meet students' varying needs and interests.

39) Teach socially acceptable behavior, employing techniques such as behavior modification and positive reinforcement.

25-2042.00 - Special Education Teachers, Middle School

Teach middle school subjects to educationally and physically handicapped students. Includes teachers who specialize and work with audibly and visually handicapped students and those who teach basic academic and life processes skills to the mentally impaired.

Tasks

1) Provide additional instruction in vocational areas.

2) Prepare objectives and outlines for courses of study, following curriculum guidelines or requirements of states and schools.

3) Prepare for assigned classes, and show written evidence of preparation upon request of immediate supervisors.

4) Establish clear objectives for all lessons, units, and projects, and communicate those objectives to students.

5) Prepare materials and classrooms for class activities.

6) Administer standardized ability and achievement tests, and interpret results to determine students' strengths and areas of need.

7) Attend professional meetings, educational conferences, and teacher training workshops in order to maintain and improve professional competence.

8) Attend staff meetings, and serve on committees as required.

9) Provide interpretation and transcription of regular classroom materials through Braille and sign language.

10) Provide assistive devices, supportive technology, and assistance accessing facilities such as restrooms.

11) Prepare, administer, and grade tests and assignments to evaluate students' progress.

12) Sponsor extracurricular activities such as clubs, student organizations, and academic contests.

13) Use computers, audiovisual aids, and other equipment and materials to supplement presentations.

14) Visit schools to tutor students with sensory impairments, and to consult with teachers regarding students' special needs.

15) Organize and label materials, and display students' work.

16) Modify the general education curriculum for special-needs students based upon a variety of instructional techniques and instructional technology.

17) Establish and enforce rules for behavior and policies and procedures to maintain order among students.

18) Confer with parents or guardians, other teachers, counselors, and administrators in order to resolve students' behavioral and academic problems.

19) Coordinate placement of students with special needs into mainstream classes.

20) Teach students personal development skills such as goal setting, independence, and self-advocacy.

21) Organize and supervise games and other recreational activities to promote physical, mental, and social development.

22) Perform administrative duties such as assisting in school libraries, hall and cafeteria monitoring, and bus loading and unloading.

23) Plan and conduct activities for a balanced program of instruction, demonstration, and work time that provides students with opportunities to observe, question, and investigate.

24) Guide and counsel students with adjustment and/or academic problems, or special academic interests.

25) Maintain accurate and complete student records, and prepare reports on children and activities, as required by laws, district policies, and administrative regulations.

26) Employ special educational strategies and techniques during instruction to improve the development of sensory- and perceptual-motor skills, language, cognition, and memory.

27) Meet with parents and guardians to discuss their children's progress, and to determine their priorities for their children and their resource needs.

28) Instruct and monitor students in the use and care of equipment and materials, in order to prevent injuries and damage.

29) Confer with other staff members to plan and schedule lessons promoting learning, following approved curricula.

30) Develop and implement strategies to meet the needs of students with a variety of handicapping conditions.

31) Monitor teachers and teacher assistants to ensure that they adhere to inclusive special education program requirements.

32) Supervise, evaluate, and plan assignments for teacher assistants and volunteers.

33) Observe and evaluate students' performance, behavior, social development, and physical health.

34) Teach socially acceptable behavior, employing techniques such as behavior modification and positive reinforcement.

35) Meet with parents and guardians to provide guidance in using community resources, and to teach skills for dealing with students' impairments.

36) Confer with parents, administrators, testing specialists, social workers, and professionals to develop individual educational plans designed to promote students' educational, physical, and social development.

37) Instruct through lectures, discussions, and demonstrations in one or more subjects such as English, mathematics, or social studies.

38) Instruct students in daily living skills required for independent maintenance and self-sufficiency, such as hygiene, safety, and food preparation.

39) Plan and supervise class projects, field trips, visits by guest speakers, or other experiential activities, and guide students in learning from those activities.

25-2043.00 - Special Education Teachers, Secondary School

Teach secondary school subjects to educationally and physically handicapped students. Includes teachers who specialize and work with audibly and visually handicapped students and those who teach basic academic and life processes skills to the mentally impaired.

Tasks

1) Teach personal development skills such as goal setting, independence, and self-advocacy.

2) Confer with parents, administrators, testing specialists, social workers, and professionals to develop individual educational plans designed to promote students' educational, physical, and social development.

3) Administer standardized ability and achievement tests, and interpret results to determine students' strengths and areas of need.

4) Teach socially acceptable behavior, employing techniques such as behavior modification and positive reinforcement.

5) Modify the general education curriculum for special-needs students, based upon a variety of instructional techniques and technologies.

6) Prepare objectives and outlines for courses of study, following curriculum guidelines or requirements of states and schools.

7) Attend staff meetings, and serve on committees as required.

8) Attend professional meetings, educational conferences, and teacher training workshops to maintain and improve professional competence.

9) Prepare students for later grades by encouraging them to explore learning opportunities and to persevere with challenging tasks.

10) Prepare materials and classrooms for class activities.

11) Collaborate with other teachers and administrators in the development, evaluation, and revision of secondary school programs.

12) Instruct through lectures, discussions, and demonstrations in one or more subjects such as English, mathematics, or social studies.

13) Coordinate placement of students with special needs into mainstream classes.

14) Use computers, audiovisual aids, and other equipment and materials to supplement presentations.

15) Establish and enforce rules for behavior and policies and procedures to maintain order among students.

16) Prepare, administer, and grade tests and assignments to evaluate students' progress.

17) Guide and counsel students with adjustment and/or academic problems, or special academic interests.

18) Develop and implement strategies to meet the needs of students with a variety of handicapping conditions.

19) Meet with other professionals to discuss individual students' needs and progress.

20) Employ special educational strategies and techniques during instruction to improve the development of sensory- and perceptual-motor skills, language, cognition, and memory.

21) Confer with other staff members to plan and schedule lessons promoting learning, following approved curricula.

22) Confer with parents or guardians, other teachers, counselors, and administrators in order to resolve students' behavioral and academic problems.

23) Observe and evaluate students' performance, behavior, social development, and physical health.

24) Meet with parents and guardians to discuss their children's progress, and to determine their priorities for their children and their resource needs.

25) Plan and supervise class projects, field trips, visits by guest speakers, or other experiential activities, and guide students in learning from those activities.

26) Prepare for assigned classes, and show written evidence of preparation upon request of immediate supervisors.

27) Monitor teachers and teacher assistants to ensure that they adhere to inclusive special education program requirements.

28) Perform administrative duties such as assisting in school libraries, hall and cafeteria monitoring, and bus loading and unloading.

29) Provide additional instruction in vocational areas.

30) Visit schools to tutor students with sensory impairments, and to consult with teachers regarding students' special needs.

31) Select, store, order, issue, and inventory classroom equipment, materials, and supplies.

32) Sponsor extracurricular activities such as clubs, student organizations, and academic contests.

33) Plan and conduct activities for a balanced program of instruction, demonstration, and work time that provides students with opportunities to observe, question, and investigate.

34) Provide assistive devices, supportive technology, and assistance accessing facilities such as restrooms.

35) Meet with parents and guardians to provide guidance in using community resources, and to teach skills for dealing with students' impairments.

36) Instruct students in daily living skills required for independent maintenance and self-sufficiency, such as hygiene, safety, and food preparation.

37) Maintain accurate and complete student records, and prepare reports on children and activities, as required by laws, district policies, and administrative regulations.

38) Establish clear objectives for all lessons, units, and projects, and communicate those objectives to students.

39) Instruct and monitor students in the use and care of equipment and materials, in order to prevent injuries and damage.

25-3011.00 - Adult Literacy, Remedial Education, and GED Teachers and Instructors

Teach or instruct out-of-school youths and adults in remedial education classes, preparatory classes for the General Educational Development test, literacy, or English as a Second Language. Teaching may or may not take place in a traditional educational institution.

Tasks

1) Guide and counsel students with adjustment and/or academic problems, or special academic interests.

2) Meet with other professionals to discuss individual students' needs and progress.

3) Observe and evaluate students' work to determine progress and make suggestions for improvement.

4) Observe students to determine qualifications, limitations, abilities, interests, and other individual characteristics.

5) Maintain accurate and complete student records as required by laws or administrative policies.

6) Attend staff meetings, and serve on committees as required.

7) Prepare and administer written, oral, and performance tests, and issue grades in accordance

121

with performance.

8) Establish and enforce rules for behavior and procedures for maintaining order among the students for whom they are responsible.

9) Prepare for assigned classes, and show written evidence of preparation upon request of immediate supervisors.

10) Conduct classes, workshops, and demonstrations to teach principles, techniques, or methods in subjects such as basic English language skills, life skills, and workforce entry skills.

11) Prepare objectives and outlines for courses of study, following curriculum guidelines or requirements of states and schools.

12) Prepare reports on students and activities as required by administration.

13) Prepare students for further education by encouraging them to explore learning opportunities and to persevere with challenging tasks.

14) Provide information, guidance, and preparation for the General Equivalency Diploma (GED) examination.

15) Review instructional content, methods, and student evaluations to assess strengths and weaknesses, and to develop recommendations for course revision, development, or elimination.

16) Advise students on internships, prospective employers, and job placement services.

17) Attend professional meetings, conferences, and workshops in order to maintain and improve professional competence.

18) Prepare and implement remedial programs for students requiring extra help.

19) Register, orient, and assess new students according to standards and procedures.

20) Confer with leaders of government and community groups to coordinate student training or to find opportunities for students to fulfill curriculum requirements.

21) Select and schedule class times to ensure maximum attendance.

22) Plan and conduct activities for a balanced program of instruction, demonstration, and work time that provides students with opportunities to observe, question, and investigate.

23) Provide disabled students with assistive devices, supportive technology, and assistance accessing facilities such as restrooms.

24) Enforce administration policies and rules governing students.

25) Observe and evaluate the performance of other instructors.

26) Select, order, and issue books, materials, and supplies for courses or projects.

27) Train and assist tutors and community literacy volunteers.

28) Write grants to obtain program funding.

29) Write instructional articles on designated subjects.

30) Instruct students individually and in groups, using various teaching methods such as lectures, discussions, and demonstrations.

31) Participate in publicity planning, community awareness efforts, and student recruitment.

32) Assign and grade class work and homework.

33) Adapt teaching methods and instructional materials to meet students' varying needs, abilities, and interests.

34) Plan and supervise class projects, field trips, visits by guest speakers, contests, or other experiential activities, and guide students in learning from those activities.

35) Use computers, audiovisual aids, and other equipment and materials to supplement presentations.

36) Collaborate with other teachers and professionals in the development of instructional programs.

37) Establish clear objectives for all lessons, units, and projects, and communicate those objectives to students.

38) Confer with other staff members to plan and schedule lessons that promote learning, following approved curricula.

25-3021.00 - Self-Enrichment Education Teachers

Teach or instruct courses other than those that normally lead to an occupational objective or degree. Courses may include self-improvement, nonvocational, and nonacademic subjects. Teaching may or may not take place in a traditional educational institution.

Tasks

1) Confer with other teachers and professionals to plan and schedule lessons promoting learning and development.

2) Monitor students' performance in order to make suggestions for improvement, and to ensure that they satisfy course standards, training requirements, and objectives.

3) Attend professional meetings, conferences, and workshops in order to maintain and

improve professional competence.

4) Prepare and implement remedial programs for students requiring extra help.

5) Plan and conduct activities for a balanced program of instruction, demonstration, and work time that provides students with opportunities to observe, question, and investigate.

6) Assign and grade class work and homework.

7) Write instructional articles on designated subjects.

8) Maintain accurate and complete student records as required by administrative policy.

9) Instruct and monitor students in use and care of equipment and materials, in order to prevent injury and damage.

10) Enforce policies and rules governing students.

11) Plan and supervise class projects, field trips, visits by guest speakers, contests, or other experiential activities, and guide students in learning from those activities.

12) Meet with parents and guardians to discuss their children's progress, and to determine their priorities for their children.

13) Use computers, audiovisual aids, and other equipment and materials to supplement presentations.

14) Establish clear objectives for all lessons, units, and projects, and communicate those objectives to students.

15) Prepare instructional program objectives, outlines, and lesson plans.

16) Instruct students individually and in groups, using various teaching methods such as lectures, discussions, and demonstrations.

17) Prepare students for further development by encouraging them to explore learning opportunities and to persevere with challenging tasks.

18) Adapt teaching methods and instructional materials to meet students' varying needs and interests.

19) Review instructional content, methods, and student evaluations in order to assess strengths and weaknesses, and to develop recommendations for course revision, development, or elimination.

20) Select, order, and issue books, materials, and supplies for courses or projects.

21) Observe students to determine qualifications, limitations, abilities, interests, and other individual characteristics.

22) Schedule class times to ensure maximum attendance.

23) Organize and supervise games and other recreational activities to promote physical, mental, and social development.

24) Observe and evaluate the performance of other instructors.

25) Conduct classes, workshops, and demonstrations, and provide individual instruction to teach topics and skills such as cooking, dancing, writing, physical fitness, photography, personal finance, and flying.

26) Attend staff meetings, and serve on committees as required.

27) Meet with other instructors to discuss individual students and their progress.

28) Participate in publicity planning and student recruitment.

29) Prepare materials and classrooms for class activities.

25-4011.00 - Archivists

Appraise, edit, and direct safekeeping of permanent records and historically valuable documents. Participate in research activities based on archival materials.

Tasks

1) Locate new materials and direct their acquisition and display.

2) Authenticate and appraise historical documents and archival materials.

3) Specialize in an area of history or technology, researching topics or items relevant to collections to determine what should be retained or acquired.

4) Direct activities of workers who assist in arranging, cataloguing, exhibiting and maintaining collections of valuable materials.

5) Organize archival records and develop classification systems to facilitate access to archival materials.

6) Prepare archival records, such as document descriptions, to allow easy access to information.

7) Preserve records, documents, and objects, copying records to film, videotape, audiotape, disk, or computer formats as necessary.

8) Research and record the origins and historical significance of archival materials.

9) Select and edit documents for publication and display, applying knowledge of subject, literary expression, and presentation techniques.

10) Coordinate educational and public outreach programs, such as tours, workshops, lectures, and classes.

11) Establish and administer policy guidelines concerning public access and use of materials.

12) Provide reference services and assistance for users needing archival materials.

25-4012.00 - Curators

Administer affairs of museum and conduct research programs. Direct instructional, research, and public service activities of institution.

Tasks

1) Attend meetings, conventions, and civic events to promote use of institution's services, to seek financing, and to maintain community alliances.

2) Conduct or organize tours, workshops, and instructional sessions to acquaint individuals with an institution's facilities and materials.

3) Develop and maintain an institution's registration, cataloging, and basic record-keeping systems, using computer databases.

4) Confer with the board of directors to formulate and interpret policies, to determine budget requirements, and to plan overall operations.

5) Inspect premises to assess the need for repairs and to ensure that climate and pest-control issues are addressed.

6) Negotiate and authorize purchase, sale, exchange, or loan of collections.

7) Plan and organize the acquisition, storage, and exhibition of collections and related materials, including the selection of exhibition themes and designs.

8) Plan and conduct special research projects in area of interest or expertise.

9) Schedule events, and organize details including refreshment, entertainment, decorations, and the collection of any fees.

10) Train and supervise curatorial, fiscal, technical, research, and clerical staff, as well as volunteers or interns.

11) Arrange insurance coverage for objects on loan or for special exhibits, and recommend changes in coverage for the entire collection.

12) Establish specifications for reproductions and oversee their manufacture, or select items from commercially available replica sources.

13) Provide information from the institution's holdings to other curators and to the public.

14) Write and review grant proposals, journal articles, institutional reports, and publicity materials.

25-4013.00 - Museum Technicians and Conservators

Prepare specimens, such as fossils, skeletal parts, lace, and textiles, for museum collection and exhibits. May restore documents or install, arrange, and exhibit materials.

Tasks

1) Notify superior when restoration of artifacts requires outside experts.

2) Prepare reports on the operation of conservation laboratories, documenting the condition of artifacts, treatment options, and the methods of preservation and repair used.

3) Preserve or direct preservation of objects, using plaster, resin, sealants, hardeners, and shellac.

4) Supervise and work with volunteers.

5) Present public programs and tours.

6) Recommend preservation procedures, such as control of temperature and humidity, to curatorial and building staff.

7) Specialize in particular materials or types of object, such as documents and books, paintings, decorative arts, textiles, metals, or architectural materials.

8) Build, repair, and install wooden steps, scaffolds, and walkways to gain access to or permit improved view of exhibited equipment.

9) Clean objects, such as paper, textiles, wood, metal, glass, rock, pottery, and furniture, using cleansers, solvents, soap solutions, and polishes.

10) Study object documentation or conduct standard chemical and physical tests to ascertain the object's age, composition, original appearance, need for treatment or restoration, and appropriate preservation method.

11) Cut and weld metal sections in reconstruction or renovation of exterior structural sections and accessories of exhibits.

12) Perform tests and examinations to establish storage and conservation requirements,

policies, and procedures.

13) Estimate cost of restoration work.

14) Direct and supervise curatorial and technical staff in the handling, mounting, care, and storage of art objects.

15) Construct skeletal mounts of fossils, replicas of archaeological artifacts, or duplicate specimens, using a variety of materials and hand tools.

16) Classify and assign registration numbers to artifacts, and supervise inventory control.

17) Coordinate exhibit installations, assisting with design, constructing displays, dioramas, display cases, and models, and ensuring the availability of necessary materials.

18) Determine whether objects need repair and choose the safest and most effective method of repair.

19) Install, arrange, assemble, and prepare artifacts for exhibition, ensuring the artifacts' safety, reporting their status and condition, and identifying and correcting any problems with the set-up.

20) Plan and conduct research to develop and improve methods of restoring and preserving specimens.

21) Repair, restore and reassemble artifacts, designing and fabricating missing or broken parts, to restore them to their original appearance and prevent deterioration.

22) Prepare artifacts for storage and shipping.

25-4021.00 - Librarians

Administer libraries and perform related library services. Work in a variety of settings, including public libraries, schools, colleges and universities, museums, corporations, government agencies, law firms, non-profit organizations, and healthcare providers. Tasks may include selecting, acquiring, cataloguing, classifying, circulating, and maintaining library materials; and furnishing reference, bibliographical, and readers' advisory services. May perform in-depth, strategic research, and synthesize, analyze, edit, and filter information. May set up or work with databases and information systems to catalogue and access information.

Tasks

1) Review and evaluate resource material, such as book reviews and catalogs, in order to select and order print, audiovisual, and electronic resources.

2) Supervise budgeting, planning, and personnel activities.

3) Compile lists of overdue materials, and notify borrowers that their materials are overdue.

4) Organize collections of books, publications, documents, audiovisual aids, and other reference materials for convenient access.

5) Develop and index databases that provide information for library users.

6) Explain use of library facilities, resources, equipment, and services, and provide information about library policies.

7) Develop information access aids such as indexes and annotated bibliographies, web pages, electronic pathfinders, and on-line tutorials.

8) Perform public relations work for the library, such as giving televised book reviews and community talks.

9) Design information storage and retrieval systems, and develop procedures for collecting, organizing, interpreting, and classifying information.

10) Plan and participate in fundraising drives.

11) Keep records of circulation and materials.

12) Plan and deliver client-centered programs and services such as special services for corporate clients, storytelling for children, newsletters, or programs for special groups.

13) Evaluate materials to determine outdated or unused items to be discarded.

14) Search standard reference materials, including on-line sources and the Internet, in order to answer patrons' reference questions.

15) Develop library policies and procedures.

16) Compile lists of books, periodicals, articles, and audiovisual materials on particular subjects.

17) Collect and organize books, pamphlets, manuscripts, and other materials in specific fields, such as rare books, genealogy, or music.

18) Code, classify, and catalog books, publications, films, audiovisual aids, and other library materials based on subject matter or standard library classification systems.

19) Assemble and arrange display materials.

20) Arrange for interlibrary loans of materials not available in a particular library.

21) Analyze patrons' requests to determine needed information, and assist in furnishing or locating that information.

22) Locate unusual or unique information in response to specific requests.

23) Write proposals for research or project grants.

24) Negotiate contracts for library services, materials, and equipment.

25) Provide input into the architectural planning of library facilities.

26) Respond to customer complaints, taking action as necessary.

27) Check books in and out of the library.

28) Confer with teachers, parents, and community organizations to develop, plan, and conduct programs in reading, viewing, and communication skills.

29) Teach library patrons to search for information using databases.

25-4031.00 - Library Technicians

Assist librarians by helping readers in the use of library catalogs, databases, and indexes to locate books and other materials; and by answering questions that require only brief consultation of standard reference. Compile records; sort and shelve books; remove or repair damaged books; register patrons; check materials in and out of the circulation process. Replace materials in shelving area (stacks) or files. Includes bookmobile drivers who operate bookmobiles or light trucks that pull trailers to specific locations on a predetermined schedule and assist with providing services in mobile libraries.

Tasks

1) Review subject matter of materials to be classified, and select classification numbers and headings according to classification systems.

2) Conduct reference searches, using printed materials and in-house and online databases.

3) File catalog cards according to system used.

4) Collect fines, and respond to complaints about fines.

5) Sort books, publications, and other items according to procedure and return them to shelves, files, or other designated storage areas.

6) Design posters and special displays to promote use of library facilities or specific reading programs at libraries.

7) Send out notices about lost or overdue books.

8) Prepare order slips for materials to be acquired, checking prices and figuring costs.

9) Compile and maintain records relating to circulation, materials, and equipment.

10) Prepare volumes for binding.

11) Enter and update patrons' records on computers.

12) Retrieve information from central databases for storage in a library's computer.

13) Reserve, circulate, renew, and discharge books and other materials.

14) Drive bookmobiles or light trucks with book trailers to specific locations at predetermined times in order to provide library service to patrons.

15) Guide patrons in finding and using library resources, including reference materials, audiovisual equipment, computers, and electronic resources.

16) Design, customize, and maintain databases, web pages, and local area networks.

17) Deliver and retrieve items throughout the library by hand or using pushcart.

18) Operate and maintain audiovisual equipment such as projectors, tape recorders, and videocassette recorders.

19) Issue identification cards to borrowers.

20) Process interlibrary loans for patrons.

21) Organize and maintain periodicals and reference materials.

22) Answer routine reference inquiries, and refer patrons needing further assistance to librarians.

23) Process print and non-print library materials to prepare them for inclusion in library collections.

24) Provide assistance to teachers and students by locating materials and helping to complete special projects.

25) Take actions to halt disruption of library activities by problem patrons.

26) Compose explanatory summaries of contents of books and other reference materials.

27) Conduct children's programs and other specialized programs such as library tours.

28) Compile bibliographies and prepare abstracts on subjects of interest to particular organizations or groups.

29) Collaborate with archivists to arrange for the safe storage of historical records and documents.

30) Verify bibliographical data for materials, including author, title, publisher, publication date, and edition.

31) Train other staff, volunteers and/or student assistants, and schedule and supervise their work.

25-9011.00 - Audio-Visual Collections Specialists

Prepare, plan, and operate audio-visual teaching aids for use in education. May record, catalogue, and file audio-visual materials.

Tasks

1) Construct and position properties, sets, lighting equipment, and other equipment.

2) Direct and coordinate activities of assistants and other personnel during production.

3) Develop preproduction ideas and incorporate them into outlines, scripts, story boards, and graphics.

4) Locate and secure settings, properties, effects, and other production necessities.

5) Set up, adjust, and operate audiovisual equipment such as cameras, film and slide projectors, and recording equipment, for meetings, events, classes, seminars and video conferences.

6) Plan and prepare audiovisual teaching aids and methods for use in school systems.

7) Produce rough and finished graphics and graphic designs.

8) Maintain hardware and software, including computers, scanners, color copiers, and color laser printers.

9) Instruct users in the selection, use, and design of audiovisual materials, and assist them in the preparation of instructional materials and the rehearsal of presentations.

10) Acquire, catalog, and maintain collections of audiovisual material such as films, video- and audio-tapes, photographs, and software programs.

11) Develop manuals, texts, workbooks, or related materials for use in conjunction with production materials.

12) Determine formats, approaches, content, levels, and mediums necessary to meet production objectives effectively and within budgetary constraints.

13) Narrate presentations and productions.

14) Confer with teachers in order to select course materials and to determine which training aids are best suited to particular grade levels.

15) Perform simple maintenance tasks such as cleaning monitors and lenses and changing batteries and light bulbs.

16) Offer presentations and workshops on the role of multimedia in effective presentations.

25-9031.00 - Instructional Coordinators

Develop instructional material, coordinate educational content, and incorporate current technology in specialized fields that provide guidelines to educators and instructors for developing curricula and conducting courses.

Tasks

1) Research, evaluate, and prepare recommendations on curricula, instructional methods, and materials for school systems.

2) Update the content of educational programs to ensure that students are being trained with equipment and processes that are technologically current.

3) Coordinate activities of workers engaged in cataloging, distributing, and maintaining educational materials and equipment in curriculum libraries and laboratories.

4) Prepare grant proposals, budgets, and program policies and goals, or assist in their preparation.

5) Develop instructional materials to be used by educators and instructors.

6) Organize production and design of curriculum materials.

7) Advise teaching and administrative staff in curriculum development, use of materials and equipment, and implementation of state and federal programs and procedures.

8) Develop classroom-based and distance learning training courses, using needs assessments and skill level analyses.

9) Recommend, order, or authorize purchase of instructional materials, supplies, equipment, and visual aids designed to meet student educational needs and district standards.

10) Advise and teach students.

11) Conduct or participate in workshops, committees, and conferences designed to promote the intellectual, social, and physical welfare of students.

12) Inspect instructional equipment to determine if repairs are needed; authorize necessary repairs.

13) Plan and conduct teacher training programs and conferences dealing with new classroom procedures, instructional materials and equipment, and teaching aids.

14) Address public audiences to explain program objectives and to elicit support.

15) Interpret and enforce provisions of state education codes, and rules and regulations of state education boards.

16) Observe work of teaching staff in order to evaluate performance, and to recommend changes that could strengthen teaching skills.

17) Prepare or approve manuals, guidelines, and reports on state educational policies and practices for distribution to school districts.

18) Confer with members of educational committees and advisory groups to obtain knowledge of subject areas, and to relate curriculum materials to specific subjects, individual student needs, and occupational areas.

25-9041.00 - Teacher Assistants

Perform duties that are instructional in nature or deliver direct services to students or parents. Serve in a position for which a teacher or another professional has ultimate responsibility for the design and implementation of educational programs and services.

Tasks

1) Operate and maintain audiovisual equipment.

2) Supervise students in classrooms, halls, cafeterias, school yards, and gymnasiums, or on field trips.

3) Monitor classroom viewing of live or recorded courses transmitted by communication satellites.

4) Distribute tests and homework assignments, and collect them when they are completed.

5) Prepare lesson materials, bulletin board displays, exhibits, equipment, and demonstrations.

6) Maintain computers in classrooms and laboratories, and assist students with hardware and software use.

7) Present subject matter to students under the direction and guidance of teachers, using lectures, discussions, or supervised role-playing methods.

8) Assist in bus loading and unloading.

9) Assist librarians in school libraries.

10) Attend staff meetings, and serve on committees as required.

11) Collect money from students for school-related projects.

12) Tutor and assist children individually or in small groups in order to help them master assignments and to reinforce learning concepts presented by teachers.

13) Discuss assigned duties with classroom teachers in order to coordinate instructional efforts.

14) Requisition and stock teaching materials and supplies.

15) Carry out therapeutic regimens such as behavior modification and personal development programs, under the supervision of special education instructors, psychologists, or speech-language pathologists.

16) Conduct demonstrations to teach such skills as sports, dancing, and handicrafts.

17) Plan, prepare, and develop various teaching aids such as bibliographies, charts, and graphs.

18) Provide extra assistance to students with special needs, such as non-English-speaking students or those with physical and mental disabilities.

19) Type, file, and duplicate materials.

20) Use computers, audiovisual aids, and other equipment and materials to supplement presentations.

21) Take class attendance, and maintain attendance records.

22) Prepare lesson outlines and plans in assigned subject areas, and submit outlines to teachers for review.

23) Provide disabled students with assistive devices, supportive technology, and assistance accessing facilities such as restrooms.

24) Organize and supervise games and other recreational activities to promote physical, mental, and social development.

25) Laminate teaching materials to increase their durability under repeated use.

26) Observe students' performance, and record relevant data to assess progress.

27) Instruct and monitor students in the use and care of equipment and materials, in order to prevent injuries and damage.

28) Grade homework and tests, and compute and record results, using answer sheets or electronic marking devices.

29) Enforce administration policies and rules governing students.

30) Participate in teacher-parent conferences regarding students' progress or problems.

31) Organize and label materials, and display students' work in a manner appropriate for their eye levels and perceptual skills.

27-1011.00 - Art Directors

Formulate design concepts and presentation approaches, and direct workers engaged in art work, layout design, and copy writing for visual communications media, such as magazines, books, newspapers, and packaging.

Tasks

1) Confer with creative, art, copy-writing, or production department heads to discuss client requirements and presentation concepts, and to coordinate creative activities.

2) Create custom illustrations or other graphic elements.

3) Review and approve proofs of printed copy and art and copy materials developed by staff members.

4) Review illustrative material to determine if it conforms to standards and specifications.

5) Present final layouts to clients for approval.

6) Work with creative directors to develop design solutions.

7) Confer with clients to determine objectives, budget, background information, and presentation approaches, styles, and techniques.

8) Mark up, paste, and complete layouts, and write typography instructions to prepare materials for typesetting or printing.

9) Hire, train and direct staff members who develop design concepts into art layouts or who prepare layouts for printing.

10) Manage own accounts and projects, working within budget and scheduling requirements.

11) Attend photo shoots and printing sessions to ensure that the products needed are obtained.

12) Negotiate with printers and estimators to determine what services will be performed.

13) Prepare detailed storyboards showing sequence and timing of story development for television production.

14) Conceptualize and help design interfaces for multimedia games, products and devices.

Knowledge	Knowledge Definitions
Design	Knowledge of design techniques, tools, and principles involved in production of precision technical plans, blueprints, drawings, and models.
Administration and Management	Knowledge of business and management principles involved in strategic planning, resource allocation, human resources modeling, leadership technique, production methods, and coordination of people and resources.
Computers and Electronics	Knowledge of circuit boards, processors, chips, electronic equipment, and computer hardware and software, including applications and programming.
Customer and Personal Service	Knowledge of principles and processes for providing customer and personal services. This includes customer needs assessment, meeting quality standards for services, and evaluation of customer satisfaction.
Production and Processing	Knowledge of raw materials, production processes, quality control, costs, and other techniques for maximizing the effective manufacture and distribution of goods.
Communications and Media	Knowledge of media production, communication, and dissemination techniques and methods. This includes alternative ways to inform and entertain via written, oral, and visual media.
Fine Arts	Knowledge of the theory and techniques required to compose, produce, and perform works of music, dance, visual arts, drama, and sculpture.
English Language	Knowledge of the structure and content of the English language including the meaning and spelling of words, rules of composition, and grammar.
Sales and Marketing	Knowledge of principles and methods for showing, promoting, and selling products or services. This includes marketing strategy and tactics, product demonstration, sales techniques, and sales control systems.
Education and Training	Knowledge of principles and methods for curriculum and training design, teaching and instruction for individuals and groups, and the measurement of training effects.
Engineering and Technology	Knowledge of the practical application of engineering science and technology. This includes applying principles, techniques, procedures, and equipment to the design and production of various goods and services.
Personnel and Human Resources	Knowledge of principles and procedures for personnel recruitment, selection, training, compensation and benefits, labor relations and negotiation, and personnel information systems.
Psychology	Knowledge of human behavior and performance; individual differences in ability, personality, and interests; learning and motivation; psychological research methods; and the assessment and treatment of behavioral and affective disorders.
Telecommunications	Knowledge of transmission, broadcasting, switching, control, and operation of telecommunications systems.

Mathematics	Knowledge of arithmetic, algebra, geometry, calculus, statistics, and their applications.
Clerical	Knowledge of administrative and clerical procedures and systems such as word processing, managing files and records, stenography and transcription, designing forms, and other office procedures and terminology.
Geography	Knowledge of principles and methods for describing the features of land, sea, and air masses, including their physical characteristics, locations, interrelationships, and distribution of plant, animal, and human life.
Sociology and Anthropology	Knowledge of group behavior and dynamics, societal trends and influences, human migrations, ethnicity, cultures and their history and origins.
History and Archeology	Knowledge of historical events and their causes, indicators, and effects on civilizations and cultures.
Mechanical	Knowledge of machines and tools, including their designs, uses, repair, and maintenance.
Economics and Accounting	Knowledge of economic and accounting principles and practices, the financial markets, banking and the analysis and reporting of financial data.
Law and Government	Knowledge of laws, legal codes, court procedures, precedents, government regulations, executive orders, agency rules, and the democratic political process.
Therapy and Counseling	Knowledge of principles, methods, and procedures for diagnosis, treatment, and rehabilitation of physical and mental dysfunctions, and for career counseling and guidance.
Foreign Language	Knowledge of the structure and content of a foreign (non-English) language including the meaning and spelling of words, rules of composition and grammar, and pronunciation.
Public Safety and Security	Knowledge of relevant equipment, policies, procedures, and strategies to promote effective local, state, or national security operations for the protection of people, data, property, and institutions.
Philosophy and Theology	Knowledge of different philosophical systems and religions. This includes their basic principles, values, ethics, ways of thinking, customs, practices, and their impact on human culture.
Transportation	Knowledge of principles and methods for moving people or goods by air, rail, sea, or road, including the relative costs and benefits.
Building and Construction	Knowledge of materials, methods, and the tools involved in the construction or repair of houses, buildings, or other structures such as highways and roads.
Chemistry	Knowledge of the chemical composition, structure, and properties of substances and of the chemical processes and transformations that they undergo. This includes uses of chemicals and their interactions, danger signs, production techniques, and disposal methods.
Physics	Knowledge and prediction of physical principles, laws, their interrelationships, and applications to understanding fluid, material, and atmospheric dynamics, and mechanical, electrical, atomic and sub- atomic structures and processes.
Food Production	Knowledge of techniques and equipment for planting, growing, and harvesting food products (both plant and animal) for consumption, including storage/handling techniques.
Medicine and Dentistry	Knowledge of the information and techniques needed to diagnose and treat human injuries, diseases, and deformities. This includes symptoms, treatment alternatives, drug properties and interactions, and preventive health-care measures.
Biology	Knowledge of plant and animal organisms, their tissues, cells, functions, interdependencies, and interactions with each other and the environment.

Skills	Skills Definitions
Active Listening	Giving full attention to what other people are saying, taking time to understand the points being made, asking questions as appropriate, and not interrupting at inappropriate times.
Time Management	Managing one's own time and the time of others.
Reading Comprehension	Understanding written sentences and paragraphs in work related documents.
Critical Thinking	Using logic and reasoning to identify the strengths and weaknesses of alternative solutions, conclusions or approaches to problems.
Coordination	Adjusting actions in relation to others' actions.
Speaking	Talking to others to convey information effectively.
Judgment and Decision Making	Considering the relative costs and benefits of potential actions to choose the most appropriate one.
Active Learning	Understanding the implications of new information for both current and future problem-solving and decision-making.
Negotiation	Bringing others together and trying to reconcile differences.
Persuasion	Persuading others to change their minds or behavior.
Complex Problem Solving	Identifying complex problems and reviewing related information to develop and evaluate options and implement solutions.
Instructing	Teaching others how to do something.
Operations Analysis	Analyzing needs and product requirements to create a design.

Equipment Selection	Determining the kind of tools and equipment needed to do a job.
Writing	Communicating effectively in writing as appropriate for the needs of the audience.
Social Perceptiveness	Being aware of others' reactions and understanding why they react as they do.
Learning Strategies	Selecting and using training/instructional methods and procedures appropriate for the situation when learning or teaching new things.
Monitoring	Monitoring/Assessing performance of yourself, other individuals, or organizations to make improvements or take corrective action.
Management of Financial Resources	Determining how money will be spent to get the work done, and accounting for these expenditures.
Management of Personnel Resources	Motivating, developing, and directing people as they work, identifying the best people for the job.
Mathematics	Using mathematics to solve problems.
Service Orientation	Actively looking for ways to help people.
Quality Control Analysis	Conducting tests and inspections of products, services, or processes to evaluate quality or performance.
Management of Material Resources	Obtaining and seeing to the appropriate use of equipment, facilities, and materials needed to do certain work.
Systems Evaluation	Identifying measures or indicators of system performance and the actions needed to improve or correct performance, relative to the goals of the system.
Technology Design	Generating or adapting equipment and technology to serve user needs.
Troubleshooting	Determining causes of operating errors and deciding what to do about it.
Operation and Control	Controlling operations of equipment or systems.
Equipment Maintenance	Performing routine maintenance on equipment and determining when and what kind of maintenance is needed.
Installation	Installing equipment, machines, wiring, or programs to meet specifications.
Science	Using scientific rules and methods to solve problems.
Systems Analysis	Determining how a system should work and how changes in conditions, operations, and the environment will affect outcomes.
Operation Monitoring	Watching gauges, dials, or other indicators to make sure a machine is working properly.
Repairing	Repairing machines or systems using the needed tools.
Programming	Writing computer programs for various purposes.

Ability	Ability Definitions
Originality	The ability to come up with unusual or clever ideas about a given topic or situation, or to develop creative ways to solve a problem.
Oral Comprehension	The ability to listen to and understand information and ideas presented through spoken words and sentences.
Fluency of Ideas	The ability to come up with a number of ideas about a topic (the number of ideas is important, not their quality, correctness, or creativity).
Oral Expression	The ability to communicate information and ideas in speaking so others will understand.
Near Vision	The ability to see details at close range (within a few feet of the observer).
Written Comprehension	The ability to read and understand information and ideas presented in writing.
Problem Sensitivity	The ability to tell when something is wrong or is likely to go wrong. It does not involve solving the problem, only recognizing there is a problem.
Inductive Reasoning	The ability to combine pieces of information to form general rules or conclusions (includes finding a relationship among seemingly unrelated events).
Speech Clarity	The ability to speak clearly so others can understand you.
Visualization	The ability to imagine how something will look after it is moved around or when its parts are moved or rearranged.
Information Ordering	The ability to arrange things or actions in a certain order or pattern according to a specific rule or set of rules (e.g., patterns of numbers, letters, words, pictures, mathematical operations).
Written Expression	The ability to communicate information and ideas in writing so others will understand.
Speech Recognition	The ability to identify and understand the speech of another person.
Deductive Reasoning	The ability to apply general rules to specific problems to produce answers that make sense.
Category Flexibility	The ability to generate or use different sets of rules for combining or grouping things in different ways.
Visual Color Discrimination	The ability to match or detect differences between colors, including shades of color and brightness.
Selective Attention	The ability to concentrate on a task over a period of time without being distracted.
Speed of Closure	The ability to quickly make sense of, combine, and organize information into meaningful patterns.
Far Vision	The ability to see details at a distance.

Time Sharing	The ability to shift back and forth between two or more activities or sources of information (such as speech, sounds, touch, or other sources).
Finger Dexterity	The ability to make precisely coordinated movements of the fingers of one or both hands to grasp, manipulate, or assemble very small objects.
Mathematical Reasoning	The ability to choose the right mathematical methods or formulas to solve a problem.
Flexibility of Closure	The ability to identify or detect a known pattern (a figure, object, word, or sound) that is hidden in other distracting material.
Memorization	The ability to remember information such as words, numbers, pictures, and procedures.
Perceptual Speed	The ability to quickly and accurately compare similarities and differences among sets of letters, numbers, objects, pictures, or patterns. The things to be compared may be presented at the same time or one after the other. This ability also includes comparing a presented object with a remembered object.
Arm-Hand Steadiness	The ability to keep your hand and arm steady while moving your arm or while holding your arm and hand in one position.
Manual Dexterity	The ability to quickly move your hand, your hand together with your arm, or your two hands to grasp, manipulate, or assemble objects.
Number Facility	The ability to add, subtract, multiply, or divide quickly and correctly.
Auditory Attention	The ability to focus on a single source of sound in the presence of other distracting sounds.
Depth Perception	The ability to judge which of several objects is closer or farther away from you, or to judge the distance between you and an object.
Control Precision	The ability to quickly and repeatedly adjust the controls of a machine or a vehicle to exact positions.
Hearing Sensitivity	The ability to detect or tell the differences between sounds that vary in pitch and loudness.
Multilimb Coordination	The ability to coordinate two or more limbs (for example, two arms, two legs, or one leg and one arm) while sitting, standing, or lying down. It does not involve performing the activities while the whole body is in motion.
Trunk Strength	The ability to use your abdominal and lower back muscles to support part of the body repeatedly or continuously over time without 'giving out' or fatiguing.
Wrist-Finger Speed	The ability to make fast, simple, repeated movements of the fingers, hands, and wrists.
Extent Flexibility	The ability to bend, stretch, twist, or reach with your body, arms, and/or legs.
Glare Sensitivity	The ability to see objects in the presence of glare or bright lighting.
Gross Body Coordination	The ability to coordinate the movement of your arms, legs, and torso together when the whole body is in motion.
Spatial Orientation	The ability to know your location in relation to the environment or to know where other objects are in relation to you.
Response Orientation	The ability to choose quickly between two or more movements in response to two or more different signals (lights, sounds, pictures). It includes the speed with which the correct response is started with the hand, foot, or other body part.
Rate Control	The ability to time your movements or the movement of a piece of equipment in anticipation of changes in the speed and/or direction of a moving object or scene.
Speed of Limb Movement	The ability to quickly move the arms and legs.
Explosive Strength	The ability to use short bursts of muscle force to propel oneself (as in jumping or sprinting), or to throw an object.
Dynamic Strength	The ability to exert muscle force repeatedly or continuously over time. This involves muscular endurance and resistance to muscle fatigue.
Stamina	The ability to exert yourself physically over long periods of time without getting winded or out of breath.
Gross Body Equilibrium	The ability to keep or regain your body balance or stay upright when in an unstable position.
Sound Localization	The ability to tell the direction from which a sound originated.
Night Vision	The ability to see under low light conditions.
Peripheral Vision	The ability to see objects or movement of objects to one's side when the eyes are looking ahead.
Static Strength	The ability to exert maximum muscle force to lift, push, pull, or carry objects.
Dynamic Flexibility	The ability to quickly and repeatedly bend, stretch, twist, or reach out with your body, arms, and/or legs.
Reaction Time	The ability to quickly respond (with the hand, finger, or foot) to a signal (sound, light, picture) when it appears.

Work_Activity	**Work_Activity Definitions**
Thinking Creatively	Developing, designing, or creating new applications, ideas, relationships, systems, or products, including artistic contributions.
Interacting With Computers	Using computers and computer systems (including hardware and software) to program, write software, set up functions, enter data, or process information.
Making Decisions and Solving Problems	Analyzing information and evaluating results to choose the best solution and solve problems.
Communicating with Supervisors, Peers, or Subordin	Providing information to supervisors, co-workers, and subordinates by telephone, in written form, e-mail, or in person.
Updating and Using Relevant Knowledge	Keeping up-to-date technically and applying new knowledge to your job.
Getting Information	Observing, receiving, and otherwise obtaining information from all relevant sources.
Establishing and Maintaining Interpersonal Relatio	Developing constructive and cooperative working relationships with others, and maintaining them over time.
Organizing, Planning, and Prioritizing Work	Developing specific goals and plans to prioritize, organize, and accomplish your work.
Interpreting the Meaning of Information for Others	Translating or explaining what information means and how it can be used.
Guiding, Directing, and Motivating Subordinates	Providing guidance and direction to subordinates, including setting performance standards and monitoring performance.
Provide Consultation and Advice to Others	Providing guidance and expert advice to management or other groups on technical, systems-, or process-related topics.
Coordinating the Work and Activities of Others	Getting members of a group to work together to accomplish tasks.
Identifying Objects, Actions, and Events	Identifying information by categorizing, estimating, recognizing differences or similarities, and detecting changes in circumstances or events.
Judging the Qualities of Things, Services, or Peop	Assessing the value, importance, or quality of things or people.
Communicating with Persons Outside Organization	Communicating with people outside the organization, representing the organization to customers, the public, government, and other external sources. This information can be exchanged in person, in writing, or by telephone or e-mail.
Scheduling Work and Activities	Scheduling events, programs, and activities, as well as the work of others.
Developing Objectives and Strategies	Establishing long-range objectives and specifying the strategies and actions to achieve them.
Estimating the Quantifiable Characteristics of Pro	Estimating sizes, distances, and quantities; or determining time, costs, resources, or materials needed to perform a work activity.
Analyzing Data or Information	Identifying the underlying principles, reasons, or facts of information by breaking down information or data into separate parts.
Documenting/Recording Information	Entering, transcribing, recording, storing, or maintaining information in written or electronic/magnetic form.
Performing Administrative Activities	Performing day-to-day administrative tasks such as maintaining information files and processing paperwork.
Processing Information	Compiling, coding, categorizing, calculating, tabulating, auditing, or verifying information or data.
Training and Teaching Others	Identifying the educational needs of others, developing formal educational or training programs or classes, and teaching or instructing others.
Monitoring and Controlling Resources	Monitoring and controlling resources and overseeing the spending of money.
Resolving Conflicts and Negotiating with Others	Handling complaints, settling disputes, and resolving grievances and conflicts, or otherwise negotiating with others.
Coaching and Developing Others	Identifying the developmental needs of others and coaching, mentoring, or otherwise helping others to improve their knowledge or skills.
Selling or Influencing Others	Convincing others to buy merchandise/goods or to otherwise change their minds or actions.
Evaluating Information to Determine Compliance wit	Using relevant information and individual judgment to determine whether events or processes comply with laws, regulations, or standards.
Assisting and Caring for Others	Providing personal assistance, medical attention, emotional support, or other personal care to others such as coworkers, customers, or patients.
Developing and Building Teams	Encouraging and building mutual trust, respect, and cooperation among team members.
Monitor Processes, Materials, or Surroundings	Monitoring and reviewing information from materials, events, or the environment, to detect or assess problems.
Performing for or Working Directly with the Public	Performing for people or dealing directly with the public. This includes serving customers in restaurants and stores, and receiving clients or guests.
Repairing and Maintaining Mechanical Equipment	Servicing, repairing, adjusting, and testing machines, devices, moving parts, and equipment that operate primarily on the basis of mechanical (not electronic) principles.
Repairing and Maintaining Electronic Equipment	Servicing, repairing, calibrating, regulating, fine-tuning, or testing machines, devices, and equipment that operate primarily on the basis of electrical or electronic (not mechanical) principles.
Controlling Machines and Processes	Using either control mechanisms or direct physical activity to operate machines or processes (not including computers or vehicles).

127

Performing General Physical Activities	Performing physical activities that require considerable use of your arms and legs and moving your whole body, such as climbing, lifting, balancing, walking, stooping, and handling of materials.
Handling and Moving Objects	Using hands and arms in handling, installing, positioning, and moving materials, and manipulating things.
Inspecting Equipment, Structures, or Material	Inspecting equipment, structures, or materials to identify the cause of errors or other problems or defects.
Drafting, Laying Out, and Specifying Technical Dev	Providing documentation, detailed instructions, drawings, or specifications to tell others about how devices, parts, equipment, or structures are to be fabricated, constructed, assembled, modified, maintained, or used.
Staffing Organizational Units	Recruiting, interviewing, selecting, hiring, and promoting employees in an organization.
Operating Vehicles, Mechanized Devices, or Equipme	Running, maneuvering, navigating, or driving vehicles or mechanized equipment, such as forklifts, passenger vehicles, aircraft, or water craft.

Work_Content	Work_Content Definitions
Telephone	How often do you have telephone conversations in this job?
Electronic Mail	How often do you use electronic mail in this job?
Face-to-Face Discussions	How often do you have to have face-to-face discussions with individuals or teams in this job?
Contact With Others	How much does this job require the worker to be in contact with others (face-to-face, by telephone, or otherwise) in order to perform it?
Indoors, Environmentally Controlled	How often does this job require working indoors in environmentally controlled conditions?
Work With Work Group or Team	How important is it to work with others in a group or team in this job?
Time Pressure	How often does this job require the worker to meet strict deadlines?
Freedom to Make Decisions	How much decision making freedom, without supervision, does the job offer?
Importance of Being Exact or Accurate	How important is being very exact or highly accurate in performing this job?
Coordinate or Lead Others	How important is it to coordinate or lead others in accomplishing work activities in this job?
Spend Time Sitting	How much does this job require sitting?
Structured versus Unstructured Work	To what extent is this job structured for the worker, rather than allowing the worker to determine tasks, priorities, and goals?
Responsibility for Outcomes and Results	How responsible is the worker for work outcomes and results of other workers?
Deal With External Customers	How important is it to work with external customers or the public in this job?
Frequency of Decision Making	How frequently is the worker required to make decisions that affect other people, the financial resources, and/or the image and reputation of the organization?
Impact of Decisions on Co-workers or Company Resul	How do the decisions an employee makes impact the results of co-workers, clients or the company?
Frequency of Conflict Situations	How often are there conflict situations the employee has to face in this job?
Spend Time Making Repetitive Motions	How much does this job require making repetitive motions?
Spend Time Using Your Hands to Handle, Control, or	How much does this job require using your hands to handle, control, or feel objects, tools or controls?
Physical Proximity	To what extent does this job require the worker to perform job tasks in close physical proximity to other people?
Deal With Unpleasant or Angry People	How frequently does the worker have to deal with unpleasant, angry, or discourteous individuals as part of the job requirements?
Letters and Memos	How often does the job require written letters and memos?
Level of Competition	To what extent does this job require the worker to compete or to be aware of competitive pressures?
Sounds, Noise Levels Are Distracting or Uncomforta	How often does this job require working exposed to sounds and noise levels that are distracting or uncomfortable?
Consequence of Error	How serious would the result usually be if the worker made a mistake that was not readily correctable?
Public Speaking	How often do you have to perform public speaking in this job?
Importance of Repeating Same Tasks	How important is repeating the same physical activities (e.g., key entry) or mental activities (e.g., checking entries in a ledger) over and over, without stopping, to performing this job?
Degree of Automation	How automated is the job?
Responsible for Others' Health and Safety	How much responsibility is there for the health and safety of others in this job?
Spend Time Standing	How much does this job require standing?
Spend Time Walking and Running	How much does this job require walking and running?
Pace Determined by Speed of Equipment	How important is it to this job that the pace is determined by the speed of equipment or machinery? (This does not refer to keeping busy at all times on this job.)
Exposed to Contaminants	How often does this job require working exposed to contaminants (such as pollutants, gases, dust or odors)?

Extremely Bright or Inadequate Lighting	How often does this job require working in extremely bright or inadequate lighting conditions?
In an Enclosed Vehicle or Equipment	How often does this job require working in a closed vehicle or equipment (e.g., car)?
Exposed to Hazardous Conditions	How often does this job require exposure to hazardous conditions?
Spend Time Bending or Twisting the Body	How much does this job require bending or twisting your body?
Outdoors, Exposed to Weather	How often does this job require working outdoors, exposed to all weather conditions?
Indoors, Not Environmentally Controlled	How often does this job require working indoors in non-controlled environmental conditions (e.g., warehouse without heat)?
Spend Time Kneeling, Crouching, Stooping, or Crawl	How much does this job require kneeling, crouching, stooping or crawling?
Spend Time Climbing Ladders, Scaffolds, or Poles	How much does this job require climbing ladders, scaffolds, or poles?
Cramped Work Space, Awkward Positions	How often does this job require working in cramped work spaces that requires getting into awkward positions?
Outdoors, Under Cover	How often does this job require working outdoors, under cover (e.g., structure with roof but no walls)?
Wear Common Protective or Safety Equipment such as	How much does this job require wearing common protective or safety equipment such as safety shoes, glasses, gloves, hard hats or live jackets?
Exposed to Minor Burns, Cuts, Bites, or Stings	How often does this job require exposure to minor burns, cuts, bites, or stings?
Exposed to Disease or Infections	How often does this job require exposure to disease/infections?
Very Hot or Cold Temperatures	How often does this job require working in very hot (above 90 F degrees) or very cold (below 32 F degrees) temperatures?
Spend Time Keeping or Regaining Balance	How much does this job require keeping or regaining your balance?
Exposed to High Places	How often does this job require exposure to high places?
Exposed to Hazardous Equipment	How often does this job require exposure to hazardous equipment?
Deal With Physically Aggressive People	How frequently does this job require the worker to deal with physical aggression of violent individuals?
Wear Specialized Protective or Safety Equipment su	How much does this job require wearing specialized protective or safety equipment such as breathing apparatus, safety harness, full protection suits, or radiation protection?
Exposed to Radiation	How often does this job require exposure to radiation?
In an Open Vehicle or Equipment	How often does this job require working in an open vehicle or equipment (e.g., tractor)?
Exposed to Whole Body Vibration	How often does this job require exposure to whole body vibration (e.g., operate a jackhammer)?

Work_Styles	Work_Styles Definitions
Dependability	Job requires being reliable, responsible, and dependable, and fulfilling obligations.
Attention to Detail	Job requires being careful about detail and thorough in completing work tasks.
Adaptability/Flexibility	Job requires being open to change (positive or negative) and to considerable variety in the workplace.
Integrity	Job requires being honest and ethical.
Achievement/Effort	Job requires establishing and maintaining personally challenging achievement goals and exerting effort toward mastering tasks.
Stress Tolerance	Job requires accepting criticism and dealing calmly and effectively with high stress situations.
Cooperation	Job requires being pleasant with others on the job and displaying a good-natured, cooperative attitude.
Initiative	Job requires a willingness to take on responsibilities and challenges.
Innovation	Job requires creativity and alternative thinking to develop new ideas for and answers to work-related problems.
Leadership	Job requires a willingness to lead, take charge, and offer opinions and direction.
Persistence	Job requires persistence in the face of obstacles.
Analytical Thinking	Job requires analyzing information and using logic to address work-related issues and problems.
Concern for Others	Job requires being sensitive to others' needs and feelings and being understanding and helpful on the job.
Self Control	Job requires maintaining composure, keeping emotions in check, controlling anger, and avoiding aggressive behavior, even in very difficult situations.
Independence	Job requires developing one's own ways of doing things, guiding oneself with little or no supervision, and depending on oneself to get things done.
Social Orientation	Job requires preferring to work with others rather than alone, and being personally connected with others on the job.

Job Zone Component	Job Zone Component Definitions
Title	Job Zone Four: Considerable Preparation Needed
Overall Experience	A minimum of two to four years of work-related skill, knowledge, or experience is needed for these occupations. For example, an accountant must complete four years of college and work for several years in accounting to be considered qualified.
Job Training	Employees in these occupations usually need several years of work-related experience, on-the-job training, and/or vocational training.
Job Zone Examples	Many of these occupations involve coordinating, supervising, managing, or training others. Examples include accountants, chefs and head cooks, computer programmers, historians, pharmacists, and police detectives.
SVP Range	(7.0 to < 8.0)
Education	Most of these occupations require a four-year bachelor's degree, but some do not.

27-1014.00 - Multi-Media Artists and Animators

Create special effects, animation, or other visual images using film, video, computers, or other electronic tools and media for use in products or creations, such as computer games, movies, music videos, and commercials.

Tasks

1) Assemble, typeset, scan and produce digital camera-ready art or film negatives and printer's proofs.

2) Use models to simulate the behavior of animated objects in the finished sequence.

3) Create two-dimensional and three-dimensional images depicting objects in motion or illustrating a process, using computer animation or modeling programs.

4) Create pen-and-paper images to be scanned, edited, colored, textured or animated by computer.

5) Create basic designs, drawings, and illustrations for product labels, cartons, direct mail, or television.

6) Apply story development, directing, cinematography, and editing to animation to create storyboards that show the flow of the animation and map out key scenes and characters.

7) Participate in design and production of multimedia campaigns, handling budgeting and scheduling, and assisting with such responsibilities as production coordination, background design and progress tracking.

8) Develop briefings, brochures, multimedia presentations, web pages, promotional products, technical illustrations, and computer artwork for use in products, technical manuals, literature, newsletters and slide shows.

9) Make objects or characters appear lifelike by manipulating light, color, texture, shadow, and transparency, and/or manipulating static images to give the illusion of motion.

10) Implement and maintain configuration control systems.

11) Script, plan, and create animated narrative sequences under tight deadlines, using computer software and hand drawing techniques.

12) Convert real objects to animated objects through modeling, using techniques such as optical scanning.

13) Create and install special effects as required by the script, mixing chemicals and fabricating needed parts from wood, metal, plaster, and clay.

27-1021.00 - Commercial and Industrial Designers

Develop and design manufactured products, such as cars, home appliances, and children's toys. Combine artistic talent with research on product use, marketing, and materials to create the most functional and appealing product design.

Tasks

1) Research production specifications, costs, production materials and manufacturing methods, and provide cost estimates and itemized production requirements.

2) Modify and refine designs, using working models, to conform with customer specifications, production limitations, or changes in design trends.

3) Participate in new product planning or market research, including studying the potential need for new products.

4) Investigate product characteristics such as the product's safety and handling qualities, its market appeal, how efficiently it can be produced, and ways of distributing, using and maintaining it.

5) Develop manufacturing procedures and monitor the manufacture of their designs in a factory to improve operations and product quality.

6) Develop industrial standards and regulatory guidelines.

7) Coordinate the look and function of product lines.

8) Direct and coordinate the fabrication of models or samples and the drafting of working drawings and specification sheets from sketches.

9) Read publications, attend showings, and study competing products and design styles and motifs to obtain perspective and generate design concepts.

10) Supervise assistants' work throughout the design process.

11) Fabricate models or samples in paper, wood, glass, fabric, plastic, metal, or other materials, using hand and/or power tools.

12) Evaluate feasibility of design ideas, based on factors such as appearance, safety, function, serviceability, budget, production costs/methods, and market characteristics.

13) Advise corporations on issues involving corporate image projects or problems.

14) Prepare sketches of ideas, detailed drawings, illustrations, artwork, and/or blueprints, using drafting instruments, paints and brushes, or computer-aided design equipment.

15) Design graphic material for use as ornamentation, illustration, or advertising on manufactured materials and packaging or containers.

16) Present designs and reports to customers or design committees for approval, and discuss need for modification.

27-1023.00 - Floral Designers

Design, cut, and arrange live, dried, or artificial flowers and foliage.

Tasks

1) Unpack stock as it comes into the shop.

2) Order and purchase flowers and supplies from wholesalers and growers.

3) Water plants, and cut, condition, and clean flowers and foliage for storage.

4) Trim material and arrange bouquets, wreaths, terrariums, and other items using trimmers, shapers, wire, pins, floral tape, foam, and other materials.

5) Select flora and foliage for arrangements, working with numerous combinations to synthesize and develop new creations.

6) Decorate or supervise the decoration of buildings, halls, churches, or other facilities for parties, weddings and other occasions.

7) Confer with clients regarding price and type of arrangement desired and the date, time, and place of delivery

8) Perform general cleaning duties in the store to ensure the shop is clean and tidy.

9) Grow flowers for use in arrangements or for sale in shop.

10) Wrap and price completed arrangements.

11) Perform office and retail service duties such as keeping financial records, serving customers, answering telephones, selling giftware items and receiving payment.

12) Create and change in-store and window displays, designs, and looks to enhance a shop's image.

13) Inform customers about the care, maintenance, and handling of various flowers and foliage, indoor plants, and other items.

14) Conduct classes or demonstrations, or train other workers.

27-1024.00 - Graphic Designers

Design or create graphics to meet specific commercial or promotional needs, such as packaging, displays, or logos. May use a variety of mediums to achieve artistic or decorative effects.

Tasks

1) Determine size and arrangement of illustrative material and copy, and select style and size of type.

2) Create designs, concepts, and sample layouts based on knowledge of layout principles and esthetic design concepts.

3) Develop graphics and layouts for product illustrations, company logos, and Internet websites.

4) Use computer software to generate new images.

5) Draw and print charts, graphs, illustrations, and other artwork, using computer.

6) Mark up, paste, and assemble final layouts to prepare layouts for printer.

7) Review final layouts and suggest improvements as needed.

129

8) Confer with clients to discuss and determine layout design.

9) Prepare illustrations or rough sketches of material, discussing them with clients and/or supervisors and making necessary changes.

10) Study illustrations and photographs to plan presentation of materials, products, or services.

11) Prepare notes and instructions for workers who assemble and prepare final layouts for printing.

12) Produce still and animated graphics for on-air and taped portions of television news broadcasts, using electronic video equipment.

13) Develop negatives and prints to produce layout photographs, using negative and print developing equipment and tools.

14) Photograph layouts, using camera, to make layout prints for supervisors or clients.

Knowledge	Knowledge Definitions
Computers and Electronics	Knowledge of circuit boards, processors, chips, electronic equipment, and computer hardware and software, including applications and programming.
English Language	Knowledge of the structure and content of the English language including the meaning and spelling of words, rules of composition, and grammar.
Communications and Media	Knowledge of media production, communication, and dissemination techniques and methods. This includes alternative ways to inform and entertain via written, oral, and visual media.
Design	Knowledge of design techniques, tools, and principles involved in production of precision technical plans, blueprints, drawings, and models.
Customer and Personal Service	Knowledge of principles and processes for providing customer and personal services. This includes customer needs assessment, meeting quality standards for services, and evaluation of customer satisfaction.
Sales and Marketing	Knowledge of principles and methods for showing, promoting, and selling products or services. This includes marketing strategy and tactics, product demonstration, sales techniques, and sales control systems.
Fine Arts	Knowledge of the theory and techniques required to compose, produce, and perform works of music, dance, visual arts, drama, and sculpture.
Production and Processing	Knowledge of raw materials, production processes, quality control, costs, and other techniques for maximizing the effective manufacture and distribution of goods.
Mathematics	Knowledge of arithmetic, algebra, geometry, calculus, statistics, and their applications.
Psychology	Knowledge of human behavior and performance; individual differences in ability, personality, and interests; learning and motivation; psychological research methods; and the assessment and treatment of behavioral and affective disorders.
Engineering and Technology	Knowledge of the practical application of engineering science and technology. This includes applying principles, techniques, procedures, and equipment to the design and production of various goods and services.
Clerical	Knowledge of administrative and clerical procedures and systems such as word processing, managing files and records, stenography and transcription, designing forms, and other office procedures and terminology.
Sociology and Anthropology	Knowledge of group behavior and dynamics, societal trends and influences, human migrations, ethnicity, cultures and their history and origins.
Administration and Management	Knowledge of business and management principles involved in strategic planning, resource allocation, human resources modeling, leadership technique, production methods, and coordination of people and resources.
Geography	Knowledge of principles and methods for describing the features of land, sea, and air masses, including their physical characteristics, locations, interrelationships, and distribution of plant, animal, and human life.
Personnel and Human Resources	Knowledge of principles and procedures for personnel recruitment, selection, training, compensation and benefits, labor relations and negotiation, and personnel information systems.
Mechanical	Knowledge of machines and tools, including their designs, uses, repair, and maintenance.
Education and Training	Knowledge of principles and methods for curriculum and training design, teaching and instruction for individuals and groups, and the measurement of training effects.
Economics and Accounting	Knowledge of economic and accounting principles and practices, the financial markets, banking and the analysis and reporting of financial data.
Philosophy and Theology	Knowledge of different philosophical systems and religions. This includes their basic principles, values, ethics, ways of thinking, customs, practices, and their impact on human culture.
Telecommunications	Knowledge of transmission, broadcasting, switching, control, and operation of telecommunications systems.
Law and Government	Knowledge of laws, legal codes, court procedures, precedents, government regulations, executive orders, agency rules, and the democratic political process.
History and Archeology	Knowledge of historical events and their causes, indicators, and effects on civilizations and cultures.
Physics	Knowledge and prediction of physical principles, laws, their interrelationships, and applications to understanding fluid, material, and atmospheric dynamics, and mechanical, electrical, atomic and sub-atomic structures and processes.
Public Safety and Security	Knowledge of relevant equipment, policies, procedures, and strategies to promote effective local, state, or national security operations for the protection of people, data, property, and institutions.
Building and Construction	Knowledge of materials, methods, and the tools involved in the construction or repair of houses, buildings, or other structures such as highways and roads.
Foreign Language	Knowledge of the structure and content of a foreign (non-English) language including the meaning and spelling of words, rules of composition and grammar, and pronunciation.
Transportation	Knowledge of principles and methods for moving people or goods by air, rail, sea, or road, including the relative costs and benefits.
Chemistry	Knowledge of the chemical composition, structure, and properties of substances and of the chemical processes and transformations that they undergo. This includes uses of chemicals and their interactions, danger signs, production techniques, and disposal methods.
Medicine and Dentistry	Knowledge of the information and techniques needed to diagnose and treat human injuries, diseases, and deformities. This includes symptoms, treatment alternatives, drug properties and interactions, and preventive health-care measures.
Therapy and Counseling	Knowledge of principles, methods, and procedures for diagnosis, treatment, and rehabilitation of physical and mental dysfunctions, and for career counseling and guidance.
Biology	Knowledge of plant and animal organisms, their tissues, cells, functions, interdependencies, and interactions with each other and the environment.
Food Production	Knowledge of techniques and equipment for planting, growing, and harvesting food products (both plant and animal) for consumption, including storage/handling techniques.

Skills	Skills Definitions
Time Management	Managing one's own time and the time of others.
Coordination	Adjusting actions in relation to others' actions.
Active Listening	Giving full attention to what other people are saying, taking time to understand the points being made, asking questions as appropriate, and not interrupting at inappropriate times.
Judgment and Decision Making	Considering the relative costs and benefits of potential actions to choose the most appropriate one.
Active Learning	Understanding the implications of new information for both current and future problem-solving and decision-making.
Critical Thinking	Using logic and reasoning to identify the strengths and weaknesses of alternative solutions, conclusions or approaches to problems.
Complex Problem Solving	Identifying complex problems and reviewing related information to develop and evaluate options and implement solutions.
Reading Comprehension	Understanding written sentences and paragraphs in work related documents.
Monitoring	Monitoring/Assessing performance of yourself, other individuals, or organizations to make improvements or take corrective action.
Social Perceptiveness	Being aware of others' reactions and understanding why they react as they do.
Troubleshooting	Determining causes of operating errors and deciding what to do about it.
Learning Strategies	Selecting and using training/instructional methods and procedures appropriate for the situation when learning or teaching new things.
Persuasion	Persuading others to change their minds or behavior.
Speaking	Talking to others to convey information effectively.
Operations Analysis	Analyzing needs and product requirements to create a design.
Equipment Selection	Determining the kind of tools and equipment needed to do a job.
Instructing	Teaching others how to do something.
Writing	Communicating effectively in writing as appropriate for the needs of the audience.
Quality Control Analysis	Conducting tests and inspections of products, services, or processes to evaluate quality or performance.
Service Orientation	Actively looking for ways to help people.
Operation and Control	Controlling operations of equipment or systems.
Equipment Maintenance	Performing routine maintenance on equipment and determining when and what kind of maintenance is needed.
Technology Design	Generating or adapting equipment and technology to serve user needs.

Negotiation	Bringing others together and trying to reconcile differences.
Systems Evaluation	Identifying measures or indicators of system performance and the actions needed to improve or correct performance, relative to the goals of the system.
Mathematics	Using mathematics to solve problems.
Management of Material Resources	Obtaining and seeing to the appropriate use of equipment, facilities, and materials needed to do certain work.
Installation	Installing equipment, machines, wiring, or programs to meet specifications.
Management of Personnel Resources	Motivating, developing, and directing people as they work, identifying the best people for the job.
Management of Financial Resources	Determining how money will be spent to get the work done, and accounting for these expenditures.
Systems Analysis	Determining how a system should work and how changes in conditions, operations, and the environment will affect outcomes.
Operation Monitoring	Watching gauges, dials, or other indicators to make sure a machine is working properly.
Repairing	Repairing machines or systems using the needed tools.
Science	Using scientific rules and methods to solve problems.
Programming	Writing computer programs for various purposes.

Ability	**Ability Definitions**
Originality	The ability to come up with unusual or clever ideas about a given topic or situation, or to develop creative ways to solve a problem.
Fluency of Ideas	The ability to come up with a number of ideas about a topic (the number of ideas is important, not their quality, correctness, or creativity).
Near Vision	The ability to see details at close range (within a few feet of the observer).
Visualization	The ability to imagine how something will look after it is moved around or when its parts are moved or rearranged.
Speech Recognition	The ability to identify and understand the speech of another person.
Oral Comprehension	The ability to listen to and understand information and ideas presented through spoken words and sentences.
Speech Clarity	The ability to speak clearly so others can understand you.
Inductive Reasoning	The ability to combine pieces of information to form general rules or conclusions (includes finding a relationship among seemingly unrelated events).
Visual Color Discrimination	The ability to match or detect differences between colors, including shades of color and brightness.
Category Flexibility	The ability to generate or use different sets of rules for combining or grouping things in different ways.
Information Ordering	The ability to arrange things or actions in a certain order or pattern according to a specific rule or set of rules (e.g., patterns of numbers, letters, words, pictures, mathematical operations).
Oral Expression	The ability to communicate information and ideas in speaking so others will understand.
Selective Attention	The ability to concentrate on a task over a period of time without being distracted.
Written Comprehension	The ability to read and understand information and ideas presented in writing.
Finger Dexterity	The ability to make precisely coordinated movements of the fingers of one or both hands to grasp, manipulate, or assemble very small objects.
Deductive Reasoning	The ability to apply general rules to specific problems to produce answers that make sense.
Problem Sensitivity	The ability to tell when something is wrong or is likely to go wrong. It does not involve solving the problem, only recognizing there is a problem.
Written Expression	The ability to communicate information and ideas in writing so others will understand.
Arm-Hand Steadiness	The ability to keep your hand and arm steady while moving your arm or while holding your arm and hand in one position.
Manual Dexterity	The ability to quickly move your hand, your hand together with your arm, or your two hands to grasp, manipulate, or assemble objects.
Far Vision	The ability to see details at a distance.
Speed of Closure	The ability to quickly make sense of, combine, and organize information into meaningful patterns.
Perceptual Speed	The ability to quickly and accurately compare similarities and differences among sets of letters, numbers, objects, pictures, or patterns. The things to be compared may be presented at the same time or one after the other. This ability also includes comparing a presented object with a remembered object.
Flexibility of Closure	The ability to identify or detect a known pattern (a figure, object, word, or sound) that is hidden in other distracting material.
Time Sharing	The ability to shift back and forth between two or more activities or sources of information (such as speech, sounds, touch, or other sources).
Control Precision	The ability to quickly and repeatedly adjust the controls of a machine or a vehicle to exact positions.

Memorization	The ability to remember information such as words, numbers, pictures, and procedures.
Auditory Attention	The ability to focus on a single source of sound in the presence of other distracting sounds.
Hearing Sensitivity	The ability to detect or tell the differences between sounds that vary in pitch and loudness.
Mathematical Reasoning	The ability to choose the right mathematical methods or formulas to solve a problem.
Wrist-Finger Speed	The ability to make fast, simple, repeated movements of the fingers, hands, and wrists.
Trunk Strength	The ability to use your abdominal and lower back muscles to support part of the body repeatedly or continuously over time without 'giving out' or fatiguing.
Multilimb Coordination	The ability to coordinate two or more limbs (for example, two arms, two legs, or one leg and one arm) while sitting, standing, or lying down. It does not involve performing the activities while the whole body is in motion.
Depth Perception	The ability to judge which of several objects is closer or farther away from you, or to judge the distance between you and an object.
Dynamic Strength	The ability to exert muscle force repeatedly or continuously over time. This involves muscular endurance and resistance to muscle fatigue.
Reaction Time	The ability to quickly respond (with the hand, finger, or foot) to a signal (sound, light, picture) when it appears.
Spatial Orientation	The ability to know your location in relation to the environment or to know where other objects are in relation to you.
Dynamic Flexibility	The ability to quickly and repeatedly bend, stretch, twist, or reach out with your body, arms, and/or legs.
Extent Flexibility	The ability to bend, stretch, twist, or reach with your body, arms, and/or legs.
Stamina	The ability to exert yourself physically over long periods of time without getting winded or out of breath.
Gross Body Coordination	The ability to coordinate the movement of your arms, legs, and torso together when the whole body is in motion.
Static Strength	The ability to exert maximum muscle force to lift, push, pull, or carry objects.
Speed of Limb Movement	The ability to quickly move the arms and legs.
Peripheral Vision	The ability to see objects or movement of objects to one's side when the eyes are looking ahead.
Response Orientation	The ability to choose quickly between two or more movements in response to two or more different signals (lights, sounds, pictures). It includes the speed with which the correct response is started with the hand, foot, or other body part.
Number Facility	The ability to add, subtract, multiply, or divide quickly and correctly.
Gross Body Equilibrium	The ability to keep or regain your body balance or stay upright when in an unstable position.
Glare Sensitivity	The ability to see objects in the presence of glare or bright lighting.
Sound Localization	The ability to tell the direction from which a sound originated.
Night Vision	The ability to see under low light conditions.
Explosive Strength	The ability to use short bursts of muscle force to propel oneself (as in jumping or sprinting), or to throw an object.
Rate Control	The ability to time your movements or the movement of a piece of equipment in anticipation of changes in the speed and/or direction of a moving object or scene.

Work_Activity	**Work_Activity Definitions**
Thinking Creatively	Developing, designing, or creating new applications, ideas, relationships, systems, or products, including artistic contributions.
Interacting With Computers	Using computers and computer systems (including hardware and software) to program, write software, set up functions, enter data, or process information.
Getting Information	Observing, receiving, and otherwise obtaining information from all relevant sources.
Making Decisions and Solving Problems	Analyzing information and evaluating results to choose the best solution and solve problems.
Updating and Using Relevant Knowledge	Keeping up-to-date technically and applying new knowledge to your job.
Establishing and Maintaining Interpersonal Relatio	Developing constructive and cooperative working relationships with others, and maintaining them over time.
Communicating with Supervisors, Peers, or Subordin	Providing information to supervisors, co-workers, and subordinates by telephone, in written form, e-mail, or in person.
Organizing, Planning, and Prioritizing Work	Developing specific goals and plans to prioritize, organize, and accomplish your work.
Communicating with Persons Outside Organization	Communicating with people outside the organization, representing the organization to customers, the public, government, and other external sources. This information can be exchanged in person, in writing, or by telephone or e-mail.

Work_Content	Work_Content Definitions
Identifying Objects, Actions, and Events	Identifying information by categorizing, estimating, recognizing differences or similarities, and detecting changes in circumstances or events.
Scheduling Work and Activities	Scheduling events, programs, and activities, as well as the work of others.
Drafting, Laying Out, and Specifying Technical Dev	Providing documentation, detailed instructions, drawings, or specifications to tell others about how devices, parts, equipment, or structures are to be fabricated, constructed, assembled, modified, maintained, or used.
Selling or Influencing Others	Convincing others to buy merchandise/goods or to otherwise change their minds or actions.
Documenting/Recording Information	Entering, transcribing, recording, storing, or maintaining information in written or electronic/magnetic form.
Resolving Conflicts and Negotiating with Others	Handling complaints, settling disputes, and resolving grievances and conflicts, or otherwise negotiating with others.
Interpreting the Meaning of Information for Others	Translating or explaining what information means and how it can be used.
Estimating the Quantifiable Characteristics of Pro	Estimating sizes, distances, and quantities; or determining time, costs, resources, or materials needed to perform a work activity.
Judging the Qualities of Things, Services, or Peop	Assessing the value, importance, or quality of things or people.
Controlling Machines and Processes	Using either control mechanisms or direct physical activity to operate machines or processes (not including computers or vehicles).
Performing Administrative Activities	Performing day-to-day administrative tasks such as maintaining information files and processing paperwork.
Provide Consultation and Advice to Others	Providing guidance and expert advice to management or other groups on technical, systems-, or process-related topics.
Inspecting Equipment, Structures, or Material	Inspecting equipment, structures, or materials to identify the cause of errors or other problems or defects.
Performing for or Working Directly with the Public	Performing for people or dealing directly with the public. This includes serving customers in restaurants and stores, and receiving clients or guests.
Processing Information	Compiling, coding, categorizing, calculating, tabulating, auditing, or verifying information or data.
Repairing and Maintaining Electronic Equipment	Servicing, repairing, calibrating, regulating, fine-tuning, or testing machines, devices, and equipment that operate primarily on the basis of electrical or electronic (not mechanical) principles.
Monitor Processes, Materials, or Surroundings	Monitoring and reviewing information from materials, events, or the environment, to detect or assess problems.
Handling and Moving Objects	Using hands and arms in handling, installing, positioning, and moving materials, and manipulating things.
Performing General Physical Activities	Performing physical activities that require considerable use of your arms and legs and moving your whole body, such as climbing, lifting, balancing, walking, stooping, and handling of materials.
Evaluating Information to Determine Compliance wit	Using relevant information and individual judgment to determine whether events or processes comply with laws, regulations, or standards.
Developing Objectives and Strategies	Establishing long-range objectives and specifying the strategies and actions to achieve them.
Monitoring and Controlling Resources	Monitoring and controlling resources and overseeing the spending of money.
Coordinating the Work and Activities of Others	Getting members of a group to work together to accomplish tasks.
Assisting and Caring for Others	Providing personal assistance, medical attention, emotional support, or other personal care to others such as coworkers, customers, or patients.
Operating Vehicles, Mechanized Devices, or Equipme	Running, maneuvering, navigating, or driving vehicles or mechanized equipment, such as forklifts, passenger vehicles, aircraft, or water craft.
Analyzing Data or Information	Identifying the underlying principles, reasons, or facts of information by breaking down information or data into separate parts.
Developing and Building Teams	Encouraging and building mutual trust, respect, and cooperation among team members.
Training and Teaching Others	Identifying the educational needs of others, developing formal educational or training programs or classes, and teaching or instructing others.
Coaching and Developing Others	Identifying the developmental needs of others and coaching, mentoring, or otherwise helping others to improve their knowledge or skills.
Repairing and Maintaining Mechanical Equipment	Servicing, repairing, adjusting, and testing machines, devices, moving parts, and equipment that operate primarily on the basis of mechanical (not electronic) principles.
Guiding, Directing, and Motivating Subordinates	Providing guidance and direction to subordinates, including setting performance standards and monitoring performance.
Staffing Organizational Units	Recruiting, interviewing, selecting, hiring, and promoting employees in an organization.

Electronic Mail	How often do you use electronic mail in this job?
Spend Time Sitting	How much does this job require sitting?
Face-to-Face Discussions	How often do you have to have face-to-face discussions with individuals or teams in this job?
Importance of Being Exact or Accurate	How important is being very exact or highly accurate in performing this job?
Contact With Others	How much does this job require the worker to be in contact with others (face-to-face, by telephone, or otherwise) in order to perform it?
Time Pressure	How often does this job require the worker to meet strict deadlines?
Indoors, Environmentally Controlled	How often does this job require working indoors in environmentally controlled conditions?
Work With Work Group or Team	How important is it to work with others in a group or team in this job?
Structured versus Unstructured Work	To what extent is this job structured for the worker, rather than allowing the worker to determine tasks, priorities, and goals?
Spend Time Making Repetitive Motions	How much does this job require making repetitive motions?
Freedom to Make Decisions	How much decision making freedom, without supervision, does the job offer?
Telephone	How often do you have telephone conversations in this job?
Importance of Repeating Same Tasks	How important is repeating the same physical activities (e.g., key entry) or mental activities (e.g., checking entries in a ledger) over and over, without stopping, to performing this job?
Spend Time Using Your Hands to Handle, Control, or	How much does this job require using your hands to handle, control, or feel objects, tools or controls?
Frequency of Decision Making	How frequently is the worker required to make decisions that affect other people, the financial resources, and/or the image and reputation of the organization?
Impact of Decisions on Co-workers or Company Resul	How do the decisions an employee makes impact the results of co-workers, clients or the company?
Letters and Memos	How often does the job require written letters and memos?
Coordinate or Lead Others	How important is it to coordinate or lead others in accomplishing work activities in this job?
Physical Proximity	To what extent does this job require the worker to perform job tasks in close physical proximity to other people?
Frequency of Conflict Situations	How often are there conflict situations the employee has to face in this job?
Responsibility for Outcomes and Results	How responsible is the worker for work outcomes and results of other workers?
Degree of Automation	How automated is the job?
Consequence of Error	How serious would the result usually be if the worker made a mistake that was not readily correctable?
Sounds, Noise Levels Are Distracting or Uncomforta	How often does this job require working exposed to sounds and noise levels that are distracting or uncomfortable?
Deal With External Customers	How important is it to work with external customers or the public in this job?
Level of Competition	To what extent does this job require the worker to compete or to be aware of competitive pressures?
Deal With Unpleasant or Angry People	How frequently does the worker have to deal with unpleasant, angry, or discourteous individuals as part of the job requirements?
Pace Determined by Speed of Equipment	How important is it to this job that the pace is determined by the speed of equipment or machinery? (This does not refer to keeping busy at all times on this job.)
Exposed to Contaminants	How often does this job require working exposed to contaminants (such as pollutants, gases, dust or odors)?
Responsible for Others' Health and Safety	How much responsibility is there for the health and safety of others in this job?
Public Speaking	How often do you have to perform public speaking in this job?
Spend Time Walking and Running	How much does this job require walking and running?
Spend Time Standing	How much does this job require standing?
Very Hot or Cold Temperatures	How often does this job require working in very hot (above 90 F degrees) or very cold (below 32 F degrees) temperatures?
Cramped Work Space, Awkward Positions	How often does this job require working in cramped work spaces that requires getting into awkward positions?
Spend Time Bending or Twisting the Body	How much does this job require bending or twisting your body?
In an Enclosed Vehicle or Equipment	How often does this job require working in a closed vehicle or equipment (e.g., car)?
Extremely Bright or Inadequate Lighting	How often does this job require working in extremely bright or inadequate lighting conditions?
Spend Time Kneeling, Crouching, Stooping, or Crawl	How much does this job require kneeling, crouching, stooping or crawling?
Wear Common Protective or Safety Equipment such as	How much does this job require wearing common protective or safety equipment such as safety shoes, glasses, gloves, hard hats or live jackets?
Deal With Physically Aggressive People	How frequently does this job require the worker to deal with physical aggression of violent individuals?

Exposed to Hazardous Equipment	How often does this job require exposure to hazardous equipment?
Exposed to Minor Burns, Cuts, Bites, or Stings	How often does this job require exposure to minor burns, cuts, bites, or stings?
Indoors, Not Environmentally Controlled	How often does this job require working indoors in non-controlled environmental conditions (e.g., warehouse without heat)?
Outdoors, Exposed to Weather	How often does this job require working outdoors, exposed to all weather conditions?
Exposed to Hazardous Conditions	How often does this job require exposure to hazardous conditions?
Outdoors, Under Cover	How often does this job require working outdoors, under cover (e.g., structure with roof but no walls)?
Spend Time Climbing Ladders, Scaffolds, or Poles	How much does this job require climbing ladders, scaffolds, or poles?
Spend Time Keeping or Regaining Balance	How much does this job require keeping or regaining your balance?
In an Open Vehicle or Equipment	How often does this job require working in an open vehicle or equipment (e.g., tractor)?
Exposed to High Places	How often does this job require exposure to high places?
Exposed to Disease or Infections	How often does this job require exposure to disease/infections?
Wear Specialized Protective or Safety Equipment su	How much does this job require wearing specialized protective or safety equipment such as breathing apparatus, safety harness, full protection suits, or radiation protection?
Exposed to Radiation	How often does this job require exposure to radiation?
Exposed to Whole Body Vibration	How often does this job require exposure to whole body vibration (e.g., operate a jackhammer)?

Work_Styles	Work_Styles Definitions
Attention to Detail	Job requires being careful about detail and thorough in completing work tasks.
Dependability	Job requires being reliable, responsible, and dependable, and fulfilling obligations.
Cooperation	Job requires being pleasant with others on the job and displaying a good-natured, cooperative attitude.
Innovation	Job requires creativity and alternative thinking to develop new ideas for and answers to work-related problems.
Adaptability/Flexibility	Job requires being open to change (positive or negative) and to considerable variety in the workplace.
Stress Tolerance	Job requires accepting criticism and dealing calmly and effectively with high stress situations.
Analytical Thinking	Job requires analyzing information and using logic to address work-related issues and problems.
Achievement/Effort	Job requires establishing and maintaining personally challenging achievement goals and exerting effort toward mastering tasks.
Persistence	Job requires persistence in the face of obstacles.
Independence	Job requires developing one's own ways of doing things, guiding oneself with little or no supervision, and depending on oneself to get things done.
Initiative	Job requires a willingness to take on responsibilities and challenges.
Self Control	Job requires maintaining composure, keeping emotions in check, controlling anger, and avoiding aggressive behavior, even in very difficult situations.
Concern for Others	Job requires being sensitive to others' needs and feelings and being understanding and helpful on the job.
Integrity	Job requires being honest and ethical.
Leadership	Job requires a willingness to lead, take charge, and offer opinions and direction.
Social Orientation	Job requires preferring to work with others rather than alone, and being personally connected with others on the job.

Job Zone Component	Job Zone Component Definitions
Title	Job Zone Four: Considerable Preparation Needed
Overall Experience	A minimum of two to four years of work-related skill, knowledge, or experience is needed for these occupations. For example, an accountant must complete four years of college and work for several years in accounting to be considered qualified.
Job Training	Employees in these occupations usually need several years of work-related experience, on-the-job training, and/or vocational training.
Job Zone Examples	Many of these occupations involve coordinating, supervising, managing, or training others. Examples include accountants, chefs and head cooks, computer programmers, historians, pharmacists, and police detectives.
SVP Range	(7.0 to < 8.0)
Education	Most of these occupations require a four-year bachelor's degree, but some do not.

27-1025.00 - Interior Designers

27-1025.00 - Interior Designers

Plan, design, and furnish interiors of residential, commercial, or industrial buildings. Formulate design which is practical, aesthetic, and conducive to intended purposes, such as raising productivity, selling merchandise, or improving life style. May specialize in a particular field, style, or phase of interior design.

Tasks

1) Subcontract fabrication, installation, and arrangement of carpeting, fixtures, accessories, draperies, paint and wall coverings, art work, furniture, and related items.

2) Advise client on interior design factors, such as space planning, layout and utilization of furnishings and equipment, and color coordination.

3) Formulate environmental plan to be practical, esthetic, and conducive to intended purposes, such as raising productivity or selling merchandise.

4) Confer with client to determine factors affecting planning interior environments, such as budget, architectural preferences, and purpose and function.

5) Select or design, and purchase furnishings, art works, and accessories.

6) Plan and design interior environments for boats, planes, buses, trains, and other enclosed spaces.

7) Estimate material requirements and costs, and present design to client for approval.

27-1026.00 - Merchandise Displayers and Window Trimmers

Plan and erect commercial displays, such as those in windows and interiors of retail stores and at trade exhibitions.

Tasks

1) Take photographs of displays and signage.

2) Use computers to produce signage.

3) Collaborate with others to obtain products and other display items.

4) Plan and erect commercial displays to entice and appeal to customers.

5) Select themes, lighting, colors, and props to be used.

6) Prepare sketches, floor plans or models of proposed displays.

7) Instruct sales staff in color-coordination of clothing racks and counter displays.

8) Maintain props and mannequins, inspecting them for imperfections and applying preservative coatings as necessary.

9) Arrange properties, furniture, merchandise, backdrops, and other accessories, as shown in prepared sketches.

10) Attend training sessions and corporate planning meetings to obtain new ideas for product launches.

11) Cut out designs on cardboard, hardboard, and plywood, according to motif of event.

12) Install decorations such as flags, banners, festive lights, and bunting on or in building, street, exhibit hall, or booth.

13) Install booths, exhibits, displays, carpets, and drapes, as guided by floor plan of building and specifications.

14) Dress mannequins for displays.

15) Store, pack, and maintain records of props and display items.

16) Develop ideas or plans for merchandise displays or window decorations.

17) Consult with advertising and sales staff to determine type of merchandise to be featured and time and place for each display.

18) Construct or assemble displays and display components from fabric, glass, paper, and plastic, using hand tools and woodworking power tools, according to specifications.

19) Change or rotate window displays, interior display areas, and signage to reflect changes in inventory or promotion.

20) Obtain plans from display designers or display managers, and discuss their implementation with clients or supervisors.

21) Create and enhance mannequin faces by mixing and applying paint and attaching measured eyelash strips, using artist's brush, airbrush, pins, ruler, and scissors.

27-1027.00 - Set and Exhibit Designers

Design special exhibits and movie, television, and theater sets. May study scripts, confer with directors, and conduct research to determine appropriate architectural styles.

Tasks

1) Design and build scale models of set designs, or miniature sets used in filming backgrounds or special effects.

2) Coordinate the transportation of sets that are built off-site, and coordinate their setup at the site of use.

3) Incorporate security systems into exhibit layouts.

4) Arrange for outside contractors to construct exhibit structures.

5) Plan for location-specific issues such as space limitations, traffic flow patterns, and safety concerns.

6) Submit plans for approval, and adapt plans to serve intended purposes, or to conform to budget or fabrication restrictions.

7) Select set props such as furniture, pictures, lamps, and rugs.

8) Research architectural and stylistic elements appropriate to the time period to be depicted, consulting experts for information as necessary.

9) Attend rehearsals and production meetings in order to obtain and share information related to sets.

10) Read scripts in order to determine location, set, and design requirements.

11) Confer with clients and staff in order to gather information about exhibit space, proposed themes and content, timelines, budgets, materials, and/or promotion requirements.

12) Confer with conservators in order to determine how to handle an exhibit's environmental aspects, such as lighting, temperature, and humidity, so that objects will be protected and exhibits will be enhanced.

13) Prepare preliminary renderings of proposed exhibits, including detailed construction, layout, and material specifications, and diagrams relating to aspects such as special effects and/or lighting.

14) Provide supportive materials for exhibits and displays, such as press kits and advertising, posters, brochures, catalogues, and invitations and publicity notices.

15) Assign staff to complete design ideas and prepare sketches, illustrations, and detailed drawings of sets, or graphics and animation.

16) Coordinate the removal of sets, props, and exhibits after productions or events are complete.

17) Select and purchase lumber and hardware necessary for set construction.

18) Prepare rough drafts and scale working drawings of sets, including floor plans, scenery, and properties to be constructed.

19) Estimate set- or exhibit-related costs including materials, construction, and rental of props or locations.

20) Design and produce displays and materials that can be used to decorate windows, interior displays, or event locations such as streets and fairgrounds.

21) Inspect installed exhibits for conformance to specifications, and satisfactory operation of special effects components.

22) Develop set designs based on evaluation of scripts, budgets, research information, and available locations.

23) Direct and coordinate construction, erection, or decoration activities in order to ensure that sets or exhibits meet design, budget, and schedule requirements.

24) Examine objects to be included in exhibits in order to plan where and how to display them.

25) Observe sets during rehearsals in order to ensure that set elements do not interfere with performance aspects such as cast movement and camera angles.

26) Collaborate with those in charge of lighting and sound so that those production aspects can be coordinated with set designs or exhibit layouts.

27-2011.00 - Actors

Play parts in stage, television, radio, video, or motion picture productions for entertainment, information, or instruction. Interpret serious or comic role by speech, gesture, and body movement to entertain or inform audience. May dance and sing.

Tasks

1) Tell jokes, perform comic dances, songs and skits, impersonate mannerisms and voices of others, contort face, and use other devices to amuse audiences.

2) Work with other crewmembers responsible for lighting, costumes, makeup, and props.

3) Write original or adapted material for dramas, comedies, puppet shows, narration, or other performances.

4) Work closely with directors, other actors, and playwrights to find the interpretation most suited to the role.

5) Dress in comical clown costumes and makeup, and perform comedy routines to entertain audiences.

6) Introduce performances and performers in order to stimulate excitement and coordinate smooth transition of acts during events.

7) Study and rehearse roles from scripts in order to interpret, learn and memorize lines, stunts, and cues as directed.

8) Collaborate with other actors as part of an ensemble.

9) Construct puppets and ventriloquist dummies, and sew accessory clothing, using hand tools and machines.

10) Promote productions using means such as interviews about plays or movies.

11) Manipulate strings, wires, rods, or fingers to animate puppets or dummies in synchronization with talking, singing, or recorded programs.

12) Prepare and perform action stunts for motion picture, television, or stage productions.

13) Sing and/or dance during dramatic or comedic performances.

14) Attend auditions and casting calls in order to audition for roles.

15) Learn about characters in scripts and their relationships to each other in order to develop role interpretations.

16) Perform humorous and serious interpretations of emotions, actions, and situations, using body movements, facial expressions, and gestures.

17) Portray and interpret roles, using speech, gestures, and body movements in order to entertain, inform, or instruct radio, film, television, or live audiences.

18) Perform original and stock tricks of illusion to entertain and mystify audiences, occasionally including audience members as participants.

27-2012.01 - Producers

Plan and coordinate various aspects of radio, television, stage, or motion picture production, such as selecting script, coordinating writing, directing and editing, and arranging financing.

Tasks

1) Determine and direct the content of radio programming.

2) Write and submit proposals to bid on contracts for projects.

3) Compose and edit scripts, or provide screenwriters with story outlines from which scripts can be written.

4) Resolve personnel problems that arise during the production process by acting as liaisons between dissenting parties when necessary.

5) Plan and coordinate the production of musical recordings, selecting music and directing performers.

6) Perform management activities such as budgeting, scheduling, planning, and marketing.

7) Negotiate contracts with artistic personnel, often in accordance with collective bargaining agreements.

8) Monitor post-production processes in order to ensure accurate completion of all details.

9) Hire directors, principal cast members, and key production staff members.

10) Determine production size, content, and budget, establishing details such as production schedules and management policies.

11) Coordinate the activities of writers, directors, managers, and other personnel throughout the production process.

12) Select plays, scripts, books, or ideas to be produced.

13) Conduct meetings with staff to discuss production progress and to ensure production objectives are attained.

14) Produce shows for special occasions, such as holidays or testimonials.

15) Arrange financing for productions.

16) Develop marketing plans for finished products, collaborating with sales associates to supervise product distribution.

17) Distribute residual payments to artists.

18) Maintain knowledge of minimum wages and working conditions established by unions and/or associations of actors and technicians.

19) Negotiate with parties including independent producers, and the distributors and broadcasters who will be handling completed productions.

20) Obtain rights to scripts, or to such items as existing video footage.

21) Perform administrative duties such as preparing operational reports, distributing rehearsal call sheets and script copies, and arranging for rehearsal quarters.

22) Review film, recordings, or rehearsals to ensure conformance to production and broadcast standards.

23) Edit and write news stories from information collected by reporters.

24) Repay investors when completed projects begin to generate revenue.

27-2012.02 - Directors- Stage, Motion Pictures, Television, and Radio

Interpret script, conduct rehearsals, and direct activities of cast and technical crew for stage, motion pictures, television, or radio programs.

Tasks

1) Introduce plays, and meet with audiences after shows in order to explain how the play was interpreted.

2) Promote and market productions by giving interviews, participating in talk shows, and making other public appearances.

3) Choose settings and locations for films and determine how scenes will be shot in these settings.

4) Select plays or scripts for production, and determine how material should be interpreted and performed.

5) Perform producers' duties such as securing financial backing, establishing and administering budgets, and recruiting cast and crew.

6) Collaborate with producers in order to hire crewmembers such as art directors, cinematographers, and costumer designers.

7) Communicate to actors the approach, characterization, and movement needed for each scene in such a way that rehearsals and takes are minimized.

8) Confer with stage managers in order to arrange schedules for rehearsals, costume fittings, and sound/light development.

9) Confer with technical directors, managers, crew members, and writers to discuss details of production, such as photography, script, music, sets, and costumes.

10) Consult with writers, producers, and/or actors about script changes, or workshop scripts, through rehearsal with writers and actors to create final drafts.

11) Plan details such as framing, composition, camera movement, sound, and actor movement for each shot or scene.

12) Direct live broadcasts, films and recordings, or non-broadcast programming for public entertainment or education.

13) Hold auditions for parts and/or negotiate contracts with actors determined suitable for specific roles, working in conjunction with producers.

14) Review film daily in order to check on work in progress and to plan for future filming.

15) Study and research scripts in order to determine how they should be directed.

16) Supervise and coordinate the work of camera, lighting, design, and sound crewmembers.

17) Collaborate with film and sound editors during the post-production process as films are edited and soundtracks are added.

18) Compile cue words and phrases, and cue announcers, cast members, and technicians during performances.

19) Compile scripts, program notes, and other material related to productions.

20) Create and approve storyboards in conjunction with art directors.

21) Cut and edit film or tape in order to integrate component parts into desired sequences.

22) Identify and approve equipment and elements required for productions, such as scenery, lights, props, costumes, choreography, and music.

23) Interpret stage-set diagrams to determine stage layouts, and supervise placement of equipment and scenery.

27-2012.03 - Program Directors

Direct and coordinate activities of personnel engaged in preparation of radio or television station program schedules and programs, such as sports or news.

Tasks

1) Cue announcers, actors, performers, and guests.

2) Confer with directors and production staff to discuss issues such as production and casting problems, budgets, policies, and news coverage.

3) Perform personnel duties such as hiring staff and evaluating work performance.

4) Develop ideas for programs and features that a station could produce.

5) Operate and maintain on-air and production audio equipment.

6) Prepare copy and edit tape so that material is ready for broadcasting.

7) Read news, read and/or record public service and promotional announcements, and otherwise participate as a member of an on-air shift as required.

8) Review information about programs and schedules in order to ensure accuracy and provide such information to local media outlets as necessary.

9) Check completed program logs for accuracy and conformance with FCC rules and regulations, and resolve program log inaccuracies.

10) Act as a liaison between talent and directors, providing information that performers/guests need to prepare for appearances, and communicating relevant information from guests, performers, or staff to directors.

11) Select, acquire, and maintain programs, music, films, and other needed materials, and obtain legal clearances for their use as necessary.

12) Develop promotions for current programs and specials.

13) Monitor network transmissions for advisories concerning daily program schedules, program content, special feeds, and/or program changes.

14) Monitor and review programming in order to ensure that schedules are met, guidelines are adhered to, and performances are of adequate quality.

15) Evaluate new and existing programming for suitability and in order to assess the need for changes, using information such as audience surveys and feedback.

16) Establish work schedules and assign work to staff members.

17) Develop budgets for programming and broadcasting activities, and monitor expenditures to ensure that they remain within budgetary limits.

18) Plan and schedule programming and event coverage based on broadcast length, time availability, and other factors such as community needs, ratings data, and viewer demographics.

19) Participate in the planning and execution of fundraising activities.

20) Conduct interviews for broadcasts.

21) Direct and coordinate activities of personnel engaged in broadcast news, sports, or programming.

22) Coordinate activities between departments, such as news and programming.

27-2012.04 - Talent Directors

Audition and interview performers to select most appropriate talent for parts in stage, television, radio, or motion picture productions.

Tasks

1) Maintain talent files that include information such as performers' specialties, past performances, and availability.

2) Hire and supervise workers who help locate people with specified attributes and talents.

3) Review performer information such as photos, resumes, voice tapes, videos, and union membership, in order to decide whom to audition for parts.

4) Serve as liaisons between directors, actors, and agents.

5) Negotiate contract agreements with performers, with agents, or between performers and agents or production companies.

6) Locate performers or extras for crowd and background scenes, and stand-ins or photo doubles for actors, by direct contact or through agents.

7) Contact agents and actors in order to provide notification of audition and performance opportunities and to set up audition times.

8) Audition and interview performers in order to match their attributes to specific roles or to increase the pool of available acting talent.

9) Attend or view productions in order to maintain knowledge of available actors.

10) Arrange for and/or design screen tests or auditions for prospective performers.

11) Prepare actors for auditions by providing scripts and information about roles and casting requirements.

12) Select performers for roles or submit lists of suitable performers to producers or directors for final selection.

27-2012.05 - Technical Directors/Managers

Coordinate activities of technical departments, such as taping, editing, engineering, and maintenance, to produce radio or television programs.

Tasks

1) Schedule use of studio and editing facilities for producers and engineering and maintenance staff.

2) Set up and execute video transitions and special effects such as fades, dissolves, cuts, keys, and supers, using computers to manipulate pictures as necessary.

3) Switch between video sources in a studio or on multi-camera remotes, using equipment such as switchers, video slide projectors, and video effects generators.

4) Act as liaisons between engineering and production departments.

5) Discuss filter options, lens choices, and the visual effects of objects being filmed with photography directors and video operators.

6) Operate equipment to produce programs or broadcast live programs from remote locations.

7) Test equipment in order to ensure proper operation.

8) Confer with operations directors in order to formulate and maintain fair and attainable technical policies for programs.

9) Direct technical aspects of newscasts and other productions, checking and switching between video sources, and taking responsibility for the on-air product, including camera shots and graphics.

10) Monitor broadcasts in order to ensure that programs conform to station or network policies and regulations.

11) Follow instructions from production managers and directors during productions, such as commands for camera cuts, effects, graphics, and takes.

12) Train workers in use of equipment such as switchers, cameras, monitors, microphones, and lights.

13) Observe pictures through monitors, and direct camera and video staff concerning shading and composition.

14) Supervise and assign duties to workers engaged in technical control and production of radio and television programs.

27-2022.00 - Coaches and Scouts

Instruct or coach groups or individuals in the fundamentals of sports. Demonstrate techniques and methods of participation. May evaluate athletes' strengths and weaknesses as possible recruits or to improve the athletes' technique to prepare them for competition. Those required to hold teaching degrees should be reported in the appropriate teaching category.

Tasks

1) Negotiate with professional athletes or their representatives in order to obtain services and arrange contracts.

2) Adjust coaching techniques based on the strengths and weaknesses of athletes.

3) Provide training direction, encouragement, and motivation in order to prepare athletes for games, competitive events, and/or tours.

4) Keep abreast of changing rules, techniques, technologies, and philosophies relevant to their sport.

5) Plan, organize, and conduct practice sessions.

6) Arrange and conduct sports-related activities such as training camps, skill-improvement courses, clinics, and/or pre-season try-outs.

7) Develop and arrange competition schedules and programs.

8) Keep records of athlete, team, and opposing team performance.

9) Explain and demonstrate the use of sports and training equipment, such as trampolines or weights.

10) Serve as organizer, leader, instructor, or referee for outdoor and indoor games, such as volleyball, football, and soccer.

11) Plan strategies and choose team members for individual games and/or sports seasons.

12) Perform activities that support a team or a specific sport, such as meeting with media representatives and appearing at fundraising events.

13) Plan and direct physical conditioning programs that will enable athletes to achieve maximum performance.

14) Analyze the strengths and weaknesses of opposing teams in order to develop game strategies.

15) Explain and enforce safety rules and regulations.

16) File scouting reports that detail player assessments, provide recommendations on athlete recruitment, and identify locations and individuals to be targeted for future recruitment efforts.

17) Identify and recruit potential athletes, arranging and offering incentives such as athletic scholarships.

18) Instruct individuals or groups in sports rules, game strategies, and performance principles such as specific ways of moving the body, hands, and/or feet in order to achieve desired results.

19) Evaluate athletes' skills, and review performance records, in order to determine their fitness and potential in a particular area of athletics.

20) Select, acquire, store, and issue equipment and other materials as necessary.

27-2023.00 - Umpires, Referees, and Other Sports Officials

Officiate at competitive athletic or sporting events. Detect infractions of rules and decide penalties according to established regulations.

Tasks

1) Verify credentials of participants in sporting events, and make other qualifying determinations such as starting order or handicap number.

2) Start races and competitions.

3) Teach and explain the rules and regulations governing a specific sport.

4) Research and study players and teams in order to anticipate issues that might arise in future engagements.

5) Report to regulating organizations regarding sporting activities, complaints made, and actions taken or needed such as fines or other disciplinary actions.

6) Compile scores and other athletic records.

7) Verify scoring calculations before competition winners are announced.

8) Resolve claims of rule infractions or complaints by participants and assess any necessary penalties, according to regulations.

9) Confer with other sporting officials, coaches, players, and facility managers in order to provide information, coordinate activities, and discuss problems.

10) Keep track of event times, including race times and elapsed time during game segments, starting or stopping play when necessary.

11) Inspect sporting equipment and/or examine participants in order to ensure compliance with event and safety regulations.

12) Direct participants to assigned areas such as starting blocks or penalty areas.

13) Officiate at sporting events, games, or competitions, to maintain standards of play and to ensure that game rules are observed.

14) Signal participants or other officials to make them aware of infractions or to otherwise regulate play or competition.

27-2031.00 - Dancers

Perform dances. May also sing or act.

Tasks

1) Devise and choreograph dance for self or others.

2) Attend costume fittings, photography sessions, and makeup calls associated with dance performances.

3) Collaborate with choreographers in order to refine or modify dance steps.

4) Develop self-understanding of physical capabilities and limitations, and choose dance styles accordingly.

5) Perform classical, modern, or acrobatic dances in productions, expressing stories, rhythm, and sound with their bodies.

6) Study and practice dance moves required in roles.

7) Audition for dance roles or for membership in dance companies.

8) Monitor the field of dance to remain aware of current trends and innovations.

9) Teach dance students.

10) Train, exercise, and attend dance classes to maintain high levels of technical proficiency, physical ability, and physical fitness.

11) Perform in productions, singing or acting in addition to dancing, if required.

12) Coordinate dancing with that of partners or dance ensembles.

27-3011.00 - Radio and Television Announcers

Talk on radio or television. May interview guests, act as master of ceremonies, read news flashes, identify station by giving call letters, or announce song title and artist.

Tasks

1) Interview show guests about their lives, their work, or topics of current interest.

2) Identify stations, and introduce or close shows, using memorized or read scripts, and/or ad-libs.

3) Coordinate games, contests, or other on-air competitions, performing such duties as asking questions and awarding prizes.

4) Comment on music and other matters, such as weather or traffic conditions.

5) Announce musical selections, station breaks, commercials, or public service information, and accept requests from listening audience.

6) Read news flashes to inform audiences of important events.

7) Keep daily program logs to provide information on all elements aired during broadcast, such as musical selections and station promotions.

8) Attend press conferences in order to gather information for broadcast.

9) Study background information in order to prepare for programs or interviews.

10) Make promotional appearances at public or private events in order to represent their employers.

11) Record commercials for later broadcast.

12) Moderate panels or discussion shows on topics such as current affairs, art, or education.

13) Operate control consoles.

14) Locate guests to appear on talk or interview shows.

15) Give network cues permitting selected stations to receive programs.

16) Discuss various topics over the telephone with viewers or listeners.

17) Select program content, in conjunction with producers and assistants, based on factors such as program specialties, audience tastes, or requests from the public.

18) Provide commentary and conduct interviews during sporting events, parades, conventions, and other events.

19) Prepare and deliver news, sports, and/or weather reports, gathering and rewriting material so that it will convey required information and fit specific time slots.

20) Host civic, charitable, or promotional events that are broadcast over television or radio.

27-3012.00 - Public Address System and Other Announcers

Make announcements over loud speaker at sporting or other public events. May act as master of ceremonies or disc jockey at weddings, parties, clubs, or other gathering places.

Tasks

1) Greet attendees and serve as masters of ceremonies at banquets, store openings, and other events.

2) Furnish information concerning plays to scoreboard operators.

3) Study the layout of an event venue in order to be able to give accurate directions in the event of an emergency.

4) Preview any music intended to be broadcast over the public address system.

5) Announce programs and player substitutions or other changes to patrons.

6) Provide running commentaries of event activities, such as play-by-play descriptions, or explanations of official decisions.

7) Meet with event directors in order to review schedules and exchange information about details, such as national anthem performers and starting lineups.

8) Improvise commentary on items of interest, such as background and history of an event or past records of participants.

9) Learn to pronounce the names of players, coaches, institutional personnel, officials, and other individuals involved in an event.

10) Instruct and calm crowds during emergencies.

11) Inform patrons of coming events at a specific venue.

12) Review and announce crowd control procedures before the beginning of each event.

13) Read prepared scripts describing acts or tricks presented during performances.

27-3021.00 - Broadcast News Analysts

Analyze, interpret, and broadcast news received from various sources.

Tasks

1) Present news stories, and introduce in-depth videotaped segments or live transmissions from on-the-scene reporters.

2) Examine news items of local, national, and international significance in order to determine topics to address, or obtain assignments from editorial staff members.

3) Select material most pertinent to presentation, and organize this material into appropriate

formats.

4) Coordinate and serve as an anchor on news broadcast programs.

5) Edit news material to ensure that it fits within available time or space.

6) Write commentaries, columns, or scripts, using computers.

7) Analyze and interpret news and information received from various sources in order to be able to broadcast the information.

27-3022.00 - Reporters and Correspondents

Collect and analyze facts about newsworthy events by interview, investigation, or observation. Report and write stories for newspaper, news magazine, radio, or television.

Tasks

1) Write reviews of literary, musical, and other artwork based on knowledge, judgment, and experience.

2) Transmit news stories or reporting information from remote locations, using equipment such as satellite phones, telephones, fax machines, or modems.

3) Research and report on specialized fields such as medicine, science and technology, politics, foreign affairs, sports, arts, consumer affairs, business, religion, crime, or education.

4) Present live or recorded commentary via broadcast media.

5) Photograph or videotape news events, or request that a photographer be assigned to provide such coverage.

6) Revise work in order to meet editorial approval or to fit time or space requirements.

7) Edit or assist in editing videos for broadcast.

8) Investigate breaking news developments such as disasters, crimes, and human interest stories.

9) Determine a story's emphasis, length, and format, and organize material accordingly.

10) Report and write news stories for publication or broadcast, describing the background and details of events.

11) Write columns, editorials, commentaries, or reviews that interpret events or offer opinions.

12) Arrange interviews with people who can provide information about a particular story.

13) Receive assignments or evaluate leads and tips in order to develop story ideas.

14) Research and analyze background information related to stories in order to be able to provide complete and accurate information.

15) Review and evaluate notes taken about event aspects in order to isolate pertinent facts and details.

16) Review copy and correct errors in content, grammar, and punctuation, following prescribed editorial style and formatting guidelines.

17) Discuss issues with editors in order to establish priorities and positions.

18) Gather information about events through research, interviews, experience, and attendance at political, news, sports, artistic, social, and other functions.

19) Develop ideas and material for columns or commentaries by analyzing and interpreting news, current issues, and personal experiences.

20) Check reference materials such as books, news files, and public records in order to obtain relevant facts.

27-3031.00 - Public Relations Specialists

Engage in promoting or creating good will for individuals, groups, or organizations by writing or selecting favorable publicity material and releasing it through various communications media. May prepare and arrange displays, and make speeches.

Tasks

1) Respond to requests for information from the media or designate another appropriate spokesperson or information source.

2) Plan and conduct market and public opinion research to test products or determine potential for product success, communicating results to client or management.

3) Consult with advertising agencies or staff to arrange promotional campaigns in all types of media for products, organizations, or individuals.

4) Plan and direct development and communication of informational programs to maintain favorable public and stockholder perceptions of an organization's accomplishments and agenda.

5) Prepare or edit organizational publications for internal and external audiences, including

employee newsletters and stockholders' reports.

6) Confer with other managers to identify trends and key group interests and concerns or to provide advice on business decisions.

7) Confer with production and support personnel to produce or coordinate production of advertisements and promotions.

8) Prepare and deliver speeches to further public relations objectives.

9) Purchase advertising space and time as required to promote client's product or agenda.

10) Coach client representatives in effective communication with the public and with employees.

11) Arrange public appearances, lectures, contests, or exhibits for clients to increase product and service awareness and to promote goodwill.

12) Study the objectives, promotional policies and needs of organizations to develop public relations strategies that will influence public opinion or promote ideas, products and services.

27-3041.00 - Editors

Perform variety of editorial duties, such as laying out, indexing, and revising content of written materials, in preparation for final publication.

Tasks

1) Arrange for copyright permissions.

2) Prepare, rewrite and edit copy to improve readability, or supervise others who do this work.

3) Meet frequently with artists, typesetters, layout personnel, marketing directors, and production managers to discuss projects and resolve problems.

4) Select local, state, national, and international news items received from wire services, based on assessment of items' significance and interest value.

5) Verify facts, dates, and statistics, using standard reference sources.

6) Make manuscript acceptance or revision recommendations to the publisher.

7) Direct the policies and departments of newspapers, magazines and other publishing establishments.

8) Read material to determine index items and arrange them alphabetically or topically, indicating page or chapter location.

9) Read, evaluate and edit manuscripts or other materials submitted for publication and confer with authors regarding changes in content, style or organization, or publication.

10) Read copy or proof to detect and correct errors in spelling, punctuation, and syntax.

11) Confer with management and editorial staff members regarding placement and emphasis of developing news stories.

12) Monitor news-gathering operations to ensure utilization of all news sources, such as press releases, telephone contacts, radio, television, wire services, and other reporters.

13) Oversee publication production, including artwork, layout, computer typesetting, and printing, ensuring adherence to deadlines and budget requirements.

14) Plan the contents of publications according to the publication's style, editorial policy, and publishing requirements.

15) Interview and hire writers and reporters or negotiate contracts, royalties, and payments for authors or freelancers.

16) Develop story or content ideas, considering reader or audience appeal.

17) Review and approve proofs submitted by composing room prior to publication production.

18) Assign topics, events and stories to individual writers or reporters for coverage.

19) Supervise and coordinate work of reporters and other editors.

27-3042.00 - Technical Writers

Write technical materials, such as equipment manuals, appendices, or operating and maintenance instructions. May assist in layout work.

Tasks

1) Observe production, developmental, and experimental activities to determine operating procedure and detail.

2) Confer with customer representatives, vendors, plant executives, or publisher to establish technical specifications and to determine subject material to be developed for publication.

3) Draw sketches to illustrate specified materials or assembly sequence.

4) Maintain records and files of work and revisions.

5) Select photographs, drawings, sketches, diagrams, and charts to illustrate material.

6) Organize material and complete writing assignment according to set standards regarding order, clarity, conciseness, style, and terminology.

7) Edit, standardize, or make changes to material prepared by other writers or establishment personnel.

8) Review manufacturer's and trade catalogs, drawings and other data relative to operation, maintenance, and service of equipment.

9) Interview production and engineering personnel and read journals and other material to become familiar with product technologies and production methods.

10) Assist in laying out material for publication.

11) Review published materials and recommend revisions or changes in scope, format, content, and methods of reproduction and binding.

12) Analyze developments in specific field to determine need for revisions in previously published materials and development of new material.

13) Study drawings, specifications, mockups, and product samples to integrate and delineate technology, operating procedure, and production sequence and detail.

27-3043.04 - Copy Writers

Write advertising copy for use by publication or broadcast media to promote sale of goods and services.

Tasks

1) Write to customers in their terms and on their level so that the advertiser's sales message is more readily received.

2) Write articles, bulletins, sales letters, speeches, and other related informative, marketing and promotional material.

3) Write advertising copy for use by publication, broadcast or internet media to promote the sale of goods and services.

4) Vary language and tone of messages based on product and medium.

5) Invent names for products and write the slogans that appear on packaging, brochures and other promotional material.

6) Consult with sales, media and marketing representatives to obtain information on product or service and discuss style and length of advertising copy.

7) Review advertising trends, consumer surveys, and other data regarding marketing of goods and services to determine the best way to promote products.

8) Edit or rewrite existing copy as necessary, and submit copy for approval by supervisor.

9) Present drafts and ideas to clients.

10) Conduct research and interviews to determine which of a product's selling features should be promoted.

11) Discuss with the client the product, advertising themes and methods, and any changes that should be made in advertising copy.

27-4011.00 - Audio and Video Equipment Technicians

Set up or set up and operate audio and video equipment including microphones, sound speakers, video screens, projectors, video monitors, recording equipment, connecting wires and cables, sound and mixing boards, and related electronic equipment for concerts, sports events, meetings and conventions, presentations, and news conferences. May also set up and operate associated spotlights and other custom lighting systems.

Tasks

1) Control the lights and sound of events, such as live concerts, before and after performances, and during intermissions.

2) Design layouts of audio and video equipment, and perform upgrades and maintenance.

3) Diagnose and resolve media system problems in classrooms.

4) Install, adjust, and operate electronic equipment used to record, edit, and transmit radio and television programs, cable programs, and motion pictures.

5) Maintain inventories of audio and video tapes and related supplies.

6) Meet with directors and senior members of camera crews to discuss assignments and determine filming sequences, camera movements, and picture composition.

7) Mix and regulate sound inputs and feeds, or coordinate audio feeds with television pictures.

8) Monitor incoming and outgoing pictures and sound feeds to ensure quality, and notify directors of any possible problems.

9) Compress, digitize, duplicate, and store audio and video data.

10) Switch sources of video input from one camera or studio to another, from film to live programming, or from network to local programming.

11) Develop manuals, texts, workbooks, or related materials for use in conjunction with production materials or for training.

12) Organize and maintain compliance, license, and warranty information related to audio and video facilities.

13) Conduct training sessions on selection, use, and design of audiovisual materials and on operation of presentation equipment.

14) Construct and position properties, sets, lighting equipment, and other equipment.

15) Determine formats, approaches, content, levels, and mediums to effectively meet objectives within budgetary constraints, utilizing research, knowledge, and training.

16) Plan and develop pre-production ideas into outlines, scripts, story boards, and graphics, using own ideas or specifications of assignments.

17) Direct and coordinate activities of assistants and other personnel during production.

18) Inform users of audio and videotaping service policies and procedures.

19) Obtain, set up, and load videotapes for scheduled productions or broadcasts.

20) Record and label contents of exposed film.

21) Notify supervisors when major equipment repairs are needed.

22) Locate and secure settings, properties, effects, and other production necessities.

23) Perform narration of productions, or present announcements.

24) Record and edit audio material such as movie soundtracks, using audio recording and editing equipment.

25) Edit videotapes by erasing and removing portions of programs and adding video and/or sound as required.

26) Produce rough and finished graphics and graphic designs.

27) Obtain and preview musical performance programs prior to events in order to become familiar with the order and approximate times of pieces.

27-4012.00 - Broadcast Technicians

Set up, operate, and maintain the electronic equipment used to transmit radio and television programs. Control audio equipment to regulate volume level and quality of sound during radio and television broadcasts. Operate radio transmitter to broadcast radio and television programs.

Tasks

1) Align antennae with receiving dishes in order to obtain the clearest signal for transmission of broadcasts from field locations.

2) Set up and operate portable field transmission equipment outside the studio.

3) Discuss production requirements with clients.

4) Give technical directions to other personnel during filming.

5) Maintain programming logs, as required by station management and the Federal Communications Commission.

6) Organize recording sessions, and prepare areas such as radio booths and television stations for recording.

7) Perform preventive and minor equipment maintenance, using hand tools.

8) Monitor strength, clarity, and reliability of incoming and outgoing signals, and adjust equipment as necessary to maintain quality broadcasts.

9) Design and modify equipment to employer specifications.

10) Edit broadcast material electronically, using computers.

11) Produce educational and training films and videotapes by performing activities such as selecting equipment and preparing scripts.

12) Control audio equipment in order to regulate the volume and sound quality during radio and television broadcasts.

13) Determine the number, type, and approximate location of microphones needed for best sound recording or transmission quality, and position them appropriately.

14) Substitute programs in cases where signals fail.

15) Schedule programming, and/or read television programming logs in order to determine which programs are to be recorded or aired.

16) Instruct trainees in how to use television production equipment, how to film events, and how to copy/edit graphics or sound onto videotape.

17) Report equipment problems, and ensure that repairs are made; make emergency repairs to equipment when necessary and possible.

18) Record sound onto tape or film for radio or television, checking its quality and making adjustments where necessary.

19) Prepare reports outlining past and future programs, including content.

20) Regulate the fidelity, brightness, and contrast of video transmissions, using video console control panels.

21) Preview scheduled programs to ensure that signals are functioning and programs are ready for transmission.

22) Select sources from which programming will be received, or through which programming will be transmitted.

27-4013.00 - Radio Operators

Receive and transmit communications using radiotelegraph or radiotelephone equipment in accordance with government regulations. May repair equipment.

Tasks

1) Monitor emergency frequencies in order to detect distress calls and respond by dispatching emergency equipment.

2) Set up antennas and mobile communication units during military field exercises.

3) Conduct periodic equipment inspections and routine tests in order to ensure that operations standards are met.

4) Broadcast weather reports and warnings.

5) Examine and operate new equipment prior to installation in order to ensure that it performs properly.

6) Turn controls or throw switches in order to activate power, adjust voice volume and modulation, and set transmitters on specified frequencies.

7) Send, receive, and interpret coded messages.

8) Operate sound-recording equipment in order to record signals and preserve broadcasts for purposes such as analysis by intelligence personnel.

9) Repair radio equipment as necessary, using electronic testing equipment, hand tools, and power tools.

10) Communicate with receiving operators in order to exchange transmission instructions.

11) Review applicable regulations regarding radio communications, and report violations.

12) Determine and obtain bearings of sources from which signals originate, using direction-finding procedures and equipment.

13) Maintain station logs of messages transmitted and received for activities such as flight testing and fire locations.

14) Coordinate radio-related aspects of locating and contacting airplanes and ships that are missing or in distress.

27-4014.00 - Sound Engineering Technicians

Operate machines and equipment to record, synchronize, mix, or reproduce music, voices, or sound effects in sporting arenas, theater productions, recording studios, or movie and video productions.

Tasks

1) Prepare for recording sessions by performing activities such as selecting and setting up microphones.

2) Keep logs of recordings.

3) Create musical instrument digital interface programs for music projects, commercials or film post-production.

4) Set up, test, and adjust recording equipment for recording sessions and live performances; tear down equipment after event completion.

5) Synchronize and equalize prerecorded dialogue, music, and sound effects with visual action of motion pictures or television productions, using control consoles.

6) Reproduce and duplicate sound recordings from original recording media, using sound editing and duplication equipment.

7) Regulate volume level and sound quality during recording sessions, using control consoles.

8) Record speech, music, and other sounds on recording media, using recording equipment.

9) Confer with producers, performers, and others in order to determine and achieve the desired sound for a production such as a musical recording or a film.

10) Separate instruments, vocals, and other sounds, then combine sounds later during the mixing or post-production stage.

11) Mix and edit voices, music, and taped sound effects for live performances and for prerecorded events, using sound mixing boards.

27-4031.00 - Camera Operators, Television, Video, and Motion Picture

Operate television, video, or motion picture camera to photograph images or scenes for various purposes, such as TV broadcasts, advertising, video production, or motion pictures.

Tasks

1) Select and assemble cameras, accessories, equipment, and film stock to be used during filming, using knowledge of filming techniques, requirements, and computations.

2) Read charts and compute ratios to determine variables such as lighting, shutter angles, filter factors, and camera distances.

3) Reload camera magazines with fresh raw film stock.

4) Operate zoom lenses, changing images according to specifications and rehearsal instructions.

5) Adjust positions and controls of cameras, printers, and related equipment in order to change focus, exposure, and lighting.

6) Operate television or motion picture cameras to record scenes for television broadcasts, advertising, or motion pictures.

7) Confer with directors, sound and lighting technicians, electricians, and other crew members to discuss assignments and determine filming sequences, desired effects, camera movements, and lighting requirements.

8) Receive raw film stock, and maintain film inventories.

9) Observe sets or locations for potential problems and to determine filming and lighting requirements.

10) Read and analyze work orders and specifications to determine locations of subject material, work procedures, sequences of operations, and machine setups.

11) Instruct camera operators regarding camera setups, angles, distances, movement, and variables and cues for starting and stopping filming.

12) Prepare slates that describe the scenes being filmed.

13) Compose and frame each shot, applying the technical aspects of light, lenses, film, filters, and camera settings in order to achieve the effects sought by directors.

14) Label and record contents of exposed film, and note details on report forms.

15) Gather and edit raw footage on location to send to television affiliates for broadcast, using electronic news-gathering or film-production equipment.

16) View films to resolve problems of exposure control, subject and camera movement, changes in subject distance, and related variables.

17) Use cameras in any of several different camera mounts such as stationary, track-mounted, or crane-mounted.

18) Test, clean, and maintain equipment to ensure proper working condition.

19) Set up cameras, optical printers, and related equipment to produce photographs and special effects.

27-4032.00 - Film and Video Editors

Edit motion picture soundtracks, film, and video.

Tasks

1) Trim film segments to specified lengths, and reassemble segments in sequences that present stories with maximum effect.

2) Collaborate with music editors to select appropriate passages of music and develop production scores.

3) Set up and operate computer editing systems, electronic titling systems, video switching equipment, and digital video effects units in order to produce a final product.

4) Develop post-production models for films.

5) Discuss the sound requirements of pictures with sound effects editors.

6) Estimate how long audiences watching comedies will laugh at each gag line or situation, in order to space scenes appropriately.

7) Program computerized graphic effects.

8) Record needed sounds, or obtain them from sound effects libraries.

9) Select and combine the most effective shots of each scene in order to form a logical and smoothly running story.

10) Conduct film screenings for directors and members of production staffs.

11) Cut shot sequences to different angles at specific points in scenes, making each individual cut as fluid and seamless as possible.

12) Review assembled films or edited videotapes on screens or monitors in order to determine if corrections are necessary.

13) Confer with producers and directors concerning layout or editing approaches needed to increase dramatic or entertainment value of productions.

14) Verify key numbers and time codes on materials.

15) Study scripts to become familiar with production concepts and requirements.

16) Determine the specific audio and visual effects and music necessary to complete films.

17) Edit films and videotapes to insert music, dialogue, and sound effects, to arrange films into sequences, and to correct errors, using editing equipment.

18) Mark frames where a particular shot or piece of sound is to begin or end.

19) Organize and string together raw footage into a continuous whole according to scripts and/or the instructions of directors and producers.

20) Piece sounds together to develop film soundtracks.

21) Review footage sequence by sequence in order to become familiar with it before assembling it into a final product.

22) Manipulate plot, score, sound, and graphics to make the parts into a continuous whole, working closely with people in audio, visual, music, optical and/or special effects departments.

29-1011.00 - Chiropractors

Adjust spinal column and other articulations of the body to correct abnormalities of the human body believed to be caused by interference with the nervous system. Examine patient to determine nature and extent of disorder. Manipulate spine or other involved area. May utilize supplementary measures, such as exercise, rest, water, light, heat, and nutritional therapy.

Tasks

1) Counsel patients about nutrition, exercise, sleeping habits, stress management, and other matters.

2) Consult with and refer patients to appropriate health practitioners when necessary.

3) Advise patients about recommended courses of treatment.

4) Obtain and record patients' medical histories.

5) Maintain accurate case histories of patients.

6) Perform a series of manual adjustments to the spine, or other articulations of the body, in order to correct the musculoskeletal system.

7) Evaluate the functioning of the neuromuscularskeletal system and the spine using systems of chiropractic diagnosis.

8) Analyze x-rays in order to locate the sources of patients' difficulties and to rule out fractures or diseases as sources of problems.

9) Diagnose health problems by reviewing patients' health and medical histories; questioning, observing and examining patients; and interpreting x-rays.

10) Suggest and apply the use of supports such as straps, tapes, bandages, and braces if necessary.

29-1021.00 - Dentists, General

Diagnose and treat diseases, injuries, and malformations of teeth and gums and related oral structures. May treat diseases of nerve, pulp, and other dental tissues affecting vitality of teeth.

Tasks

1) Perform oral and periodontal surgery on the jaw or mouth.

2) Apply fluoride and sealants to teeth.

3) Examine teeth, gums, and related tissues, using dental instruments, x-rays, and other diagnostic equipment, to evaluate dental health, diagnose diseases or abnormalities, and plan appropriate treatments.

4) Use air turbine and hand instruments, dental appliances and surgical implements.

5) Write prescriptions for antibiotics and other medications.

6) Produce and evaluate dental health educational materials.

7) Plan, organize, and maintain dental health programs.

8) Manage business, employing and supervising staff and handling paperwork and insurance claims.

9) Use masks, gloves and safety glasses to protect themselves and their patients from infectious diseases.

10) Analyze and evaluate dental needs to determine changes and trends in patterns of dental disease.

11) Formulate plan of treatment for patient's teeth and mouth tissue.

12) Treat exposure of pulp by pulp capping, removal of pulp from pulp chamber, or root canal, using dental instruments.

13) Advise and instruct patients regarding preventive dental care, the causes and treatment of dental problems, and oral health care services.

14) Fill pulp chamber and canal with endodontic materials.

15) Bleach, clean or polish teeth to restore natural color.

16) Diagnose and treat diseases, injuries, and malformations of teeth, gums and related oral structures, and provide preventive and corrective services.

17) Eliminate irritating margins of fillings and correct occlusions, using dental instruments.

18) Design, make, and fit prosthodontic appliances such as space maintainers, bridges, and dentures, or write fabrication instructions or prescriptions for denturists and dental technicians.

19) Administer anesthetics to limit the amount of pain experienced by patients during procedures.

29-1022.00 - Oral and Maxillofacial Surgeons

Perform surgery on mouth, jaws, and related head and neck structure to execute difficult and multiple extractions of teeth, to remove tumors and other abnormal growths, to correct abnormal jaw relations by mandibular or maxillary revision, to prepare mouth for insertion of dental prosthesis, or to treat fractured jaws.

Tasks

1) Administer general and local anesthetics.

2) Treat problems affecting the oral mucosa such as mouth ulcers and infections.

3) Collaborate with other professionals such as restorative dentists and orthodontists in order to plan treatment.

4) Perform surgery to prepare the mouth for dental implants, and to aid in the regeneration of deficient bone and gum tissues.

5) Remove impacted, damaged, and non-restorable teeth.

6) Evaluate the position of the wisdom teeth in order to determine whether problems exist currently or might occur in the future.

7) Treat infections of the oral cavity, salivary glands, jaws, and neck.

8) Treat snoring problems, using laser surgery.

9) Provide emergency treatment of facial injuries including facial lacerations, intra-oral lacerations, and fractured facial bones.

10) Perform minor cosmetic procedures such as chin and cheek-bone enhancements, and minor facial rejuvenation procedures including the use of Botox and laser technology.

11) Perform surgery on the mouth and jaws in order to treat conditions such as cleft lip and palate and jaw growth problems.

12) Restore form and function by moving skin, bone, nerves, and other tissues from other parts of the body in order to reconstruct the jaws and face.

29-1023.00 - Orthodontists

Examine, diagnose, and treat dental malocclusions and oral cavity anomalies. Design and fabricate appliances to realign teeth and jaws to produce and maintain normal function and to improve appearance.

Tasks

1) Prepare diagnostic and treatment records.

2) Study diagnostic records such as medical/dental histories, plaster models of the teeth, photos of a patient's face and teeth, and X-rays in order to develop patient treatment plans.

3) Examine patients in order to assess abnormalities of jaw development, tooth position, and other dental-facial structures.

4) Instruct dental officers and technical assistants in orthodontic procedures and techniques.

5) Provide patients with proposed treatment plans and cost estimates.

6) Design and fabricate appliances, such as space maintainers, retainers, and labial and lingual arch wires.

7) Adjust dental appliances periodically in order to produce and maintain normal function.

8) Fit dental appliances in patients' mouths in order to alter the position and relationship of teeth and jaws, and to realign teeth.

9) Diagnose teeth and jaw or other dental-facial abnormalities.

29-1024.00 - Prosthodontists

Construct oral prostheses to replace missing teeth and other oral structures to correct natural and acquired deformation of mouth and jaws, to restore and maintain oral function, such as chewing and speaking, and to improve appearance.

Tasks

1) Place veneers onto teeth in order to conceal defects.

2) Use bonding technology on the surface of the teeth in order to change tooth shape or to close gaps.

3) Restore function and aesthetics to traumatic injury victims, or to individuals with diseases or birth defects.

4) Treat facial pain and jaw joint problems.

5) Repair, reline, and/or rebase dentures.

6) Replace missing teeth and associated oral structures with permanent fixtures, such as crowns and bridges, or removable fixtures, such as dentures.

7) Measure and take impressions of patients' jaws and teeth in order to determine the shape and size of dental prostheses, using face bows, dental articulators, recording devices, and other materials.

8) Fit prostheses to patients, making any necessary adjustments and modifications.

9) Collaborate with general dentists, specialists, and other health professionals in order to develop solutions to dental and oral health concerns.

10) Design and fabricate dental prostheses, or supervise dental technicians and laboratory bench workers who construct the devices.

29-1031.00 - Dietitians and Nutritionists

Plan and conduct food service or nutritional programs to assist in the promotion of health and control of disease. May supervise activities of a department providing quantity food services, counsel individuals, or conduct nutritional research.

Tasks

1) Assess nutritional needs, diet restrictions and current health plans to develop and implement dietary-care plans and provide nutritional counseling.

2) Counsel individuals and groups on basic rules of good nutrition, healthy eating habits, and nutrition monitoring to improve their quality of life.

3) Consult with physicians and health care personnel to determine nutritional needs and diet restrictions of patient or client.

4) Develop curriculum and prepare manuals, visual aids, course outlines, and other materials used in teaching.

5) Inspect meals served for conformance to prescribed diets and standards of palatability and appearance.

6) Develop policies for food service or nutritional programs to assist in health promotion and disease control.

7) Coordinate recipe development and standardization and develop new menus for independent food service operations.

8) Monitor food service operations to ensure conformance to nutritional, safety, sanitation and quality standards.

9) Coordinate diet counseling services.

10) Test new food products and equipment.

11) Plan and conduct training programs in dietetics, nutrition, and institutional management and administration for medical students, health-care personnel and the general public.

12) Manage quantity food service departments or clinical and community nutrition services.

13) Organize, develop, analyze, test, and prepare special meals such as low-fat, low-cholesterol and chemical-free meals.

14) Advise food service managers and organizations on sanitation, safety procedures, menu development, budgeting, and planning to assist with the establishment, operation, and evaluation of food service facilities and nutrition programs.

15) Purchase food in accordance with health and safety codes.

16) Select. train and supervise workers who plan, prepare and serve meals.

17) Prepare and administer budgets for food, equipment and supplies.

18) Plan, conduct, and evaluate dietary, nutritional, and epidemiological research.

19) Make recommendations regarding public policy, such as nutrition labeling, food fortification, and nutrition standards for school programs.

20) Plan and prepare grant proposals to request program funding.

21) Write research reports and other publications to document and communicate research findings.

22) Confer with design, building, and equipment personnel to plan for construction and remodeling of food service units.

Knowledge	Knowledge Definitions
Education and Training	Knowledge of principles and methods for curriculum and training design, teaching and instruction for individuals and groups, and the measurement of training effects.
Customer and Personal Service	Knowledge of principles and processes for providing customer and personal services. This includes customer needs assessment, meeting quality standards for services, and evaluation of customer satisfaction.
English Language	Knowledge of the structure and content of the English language including the meaning and spelling of words, rules of composition, and grammar.
Medicine and Dentistry	Knowledge of the information and techniques needed to diagnose and treat human injuries, diseases, and deformities. This includes symptoms, treatment alternatives, drug properties and interactions, and preventive health-care measures.
Psychology	Knowledge of human behavior and performance; individual differences in ability, personality, and interests; learning and motivation; psychological research methods; and the assessment and treatment of behavioral and affective disorders.
Therapy and Counseling	Knowledge of principles, methods, and procedures for diagnosis, treatment, and rehabilitation of physical and mental dysfunctions, and for career counseling and guidance.
Mathematics	Knowledge of arithmetic, algebra, geometry, calculus, statistics, and their applications.
Food Production	Knowledge of techniques and equipment for planting, growing, and harvesting food products (both plant and animal) for consumption, including storage/handling techniques.
Sociology and Anthropology	Knowledge of group behavior and dynamics, societal trends and influences, human migrations, ethnicity, cultures and their history and origins.
Computers and Electronics	Knowledge of circuit boards, processors, chips, electronic equipment, and computer hardware and software, including applications and programming.
Chemistry	Knowledge of the chemical composition, structure, and properties of substances and of the chemical processes and transformations that they undergo. This includes uses of chemicals and their interactions, danger signs, production techniques, and disposal methods.
Administration and Management	Knowledge of business and management principles involved in strategic planning, resource allocation, human resources modeling, leadership technique, production methods, and coordination of people and resources.
Clerical	Knowledge of administrative and clerical procedures and systems such as word processing, managing files and records, stenography and transcription, designing forms, and other office procedures and terminology.
Biology	Knowledge of plant and animal organisms, their tissues, cells, functions, interdependencies, and interactions with each other and the environment.
Communications and Media	Knowledge of media production, communication, and dissemination techniques and methods. This includes alternative ways to inform and entertain via written, oral, and visual media.
Law and Government	Knowledge of laws, legal codes, court procedures, precedents, government regulations, executive orders, agency rules, and the democratic political process.
Public Safety and Security	Knowledge of relevant equipment, policies, procedures, and strategies to promote effective local, state, or national security operations for the protection of people, data, property, and institutions.
Personnel and Human Resources	Knowledge of principles and procedures for personnel recruitment, selection, training, compensation and benefits, labor relations and negotiation, and personnel information systems.
Economics and Accounting	Knowledge of economic and accounting principles and practices, the financial markets, banking and the analysis and reporting of financial data.
Telecommunications	Knowledge of transmission, broadcasting, switching, control, and operation of telecommunications systems.

Philosophy and Theology	Knowledge of different philosophical systems and religions. This includes their basic principles, values, ethics, ways of thinking, customs, practices, and their impact on human culture.
Transportation	Knowledge of principles and methods for moving people or goods by air, rail, sea, or road, including the relative costs and benefits.
Sales and Marketing	Knowledge of principles and methods for showing, promoting, and selling products or services. This includes marketing strategy and tactics, product demonstration, sales techniques, and sales control systems.
Foreign Language	Knowledge of the structure and content of a foreign (non-English) language including the meaning and spelling of words, rules of composition and grammar, and pronunciation.
Production and Processing	Knowledge of raw materials, production processes, quality control, costs, and other techniques for maximizing the effective manufacture and distribution of goods.
Engineering and Technology	Knowledge of the practical application of engineering science and technology. This includes applying principles, techniques, procedures, and equipment to the design and production of various goods and services.
Fine Arts	Knowledge of the theory and techniques required to compose, produce, and perform works of music, dance, visual arts, drama, and sculpture.
History and Archeology	Knowledge of historical events and their causes, indicators, and effects on civilizations and cultures.
Geography	Knowledge of principles and methods for describing the features of land, sea, and air masses, including their physical characteristics, locations, interrelationships, and distribution of plant, animal, and human life.
Mechanical	Knowledge of machines and tools, including their designs, uses, repair, and maintenance.
Design	Knowledge of design techniques, tools, and principles involved in production of precision technical plans, blueprints, drawings, and models.
Physics	Knowledge and prediction of physical principles, laws, their interrelationships, and applications to understanding fluid, material, and atmospheric dynamics, and mechanical, electrical, atomic and sub-atomic structures and processes.
Building and Construction	Knowledge of materials, methods, and the tools involved in the construction or repair of houses, buildings, or other structures such as highways and roads.

Skills	Skills Definitions
Active Listening	Giving full attention to what other people are saying, taking time to understand the points being made, asking questions as appropriate, and not interrupting at inappropriate times.
Reading Comprehension	Understanding written sentences and paragraphs in work related documents.
Instructing	Teaching others how to do something.
Speaking	Talking to others to convey information effectively.
Writing	Communicating effectively in writing as appropriate for the needs of the audience.
Time Management	Managing one's own time and the time of others.
Critical Thinking	Using logic and reasoning to identify the strengths and weaknesses of alternative solutions, conclusions or approaches to problems.
Active Learning	Understanding the implications of new information for both current and future problem-solving and decision-making.
Judgment and Decision Making	Considering the relative costs and benefits of potential actions to choose the most appropriate one.
Social Perceptiveness	Being aware of others' reactions and understanding why they react as they do.
Science	Using scientific rules and methods to solve problems.
Service Orientation	Actively looking for ways to help people.
Coordination	Adjusting actions in relation to others' actions.
Learning Strategies	Selecting and using training/instructional methods and procedures appropriate for the situation when learning or teaching new things.
Monitoring	Monitoring/Assessing performance of yourself, other individuals, or organizations to make improvements or take corrective action.
Complex Problem Solving	Identifying complex problems and reviewing related information to develop and evaluate options and implement solutions.
Persuasion	Persuading others to change their minds or behavior.
Mathematics	Using mathematics to solve problems.
Quality Control Analysis	Conducting tests and inspections of products, services, or processes to evaluate quality or performance.
Negotiation	Bringing others together and trying to reconcile differences.
Management of Personnel Resources	Motivating, developing, and directing people as they work, identifying the best people for the job.
Systems Evaluation	Identifying measures or indicators of system performance and the actions needed to improve or correct performance, relative to the goals of the system.

Systems Analysis	Determining how a system should work and how changes in conditions, operations, and the environment will affect outcomes.
Troubleshooting	Determining causes of operating errors and deciding what to do about it.
Management of Financial Resources	Determining how money will be spent to get the work done, and accounting for these expenditures.
Equipment Selection	Determining the kind of tools and equipment needed to do a job.
Management of Material Resources	Obtaining and seeing to the appropriate use of equipment, facilities, and materials needed to do certain work.
Operations Analysis	Analyzing needs and product requirements to create a design.
Operation Monitoring	Watching gauges, dials, or other indicators to make sure a machine is working properly.
Equipment Maintenance	Performing routine maintenance on equipment and determining when and what kind of maintenance is needed.
Operation and Control	Controlling operations of equipment or systems.
Repairing	Repairing machines or systems using the needed tools.
Installation	Installing equipment, machines, wiring, or programs to meet specifications.
Technology Design	Generating or adapting equipment and technology to serve user needs.
Programming	Writing computer programs for various purposes.

Ability	**Ability Definitions**
Written Comprehension	The ability to read and understand information and ideas presented in writing.
Oral Expression	The ability to communicate information and ideas in speaking so others will understand.
Problem Sensitivity	The ability to tell when something is wrong or is likely to go wrong. It does not involve solving the problem, only recognizing there is a problem.
Speech Clarity	The ability to speak clearly so others can understand you.
Oral Comprehension	The ability to listen to and understand information and ideas presented through spoken words and sentences.
Deductive Reasoning	The ability to apply general rules to specific problems to produce answers that make sense.
Inductive Reasoning	The ability to combine pieces of information to form general rules or conclusions (includes finding a relationship among seemingly unrelated events).
Near Vision	The ability to see details at close range (within a few feet of the observer).
Written Expression	The ability to communicate information and ideas in writing so others will understand.
Speech Recognition	The ability to identify and understand the speech of another person.
Category Flexibility	The ability to generate or use different sets of rules for combining or grouping things in different ways.
Fluency of Ideas	The ability to come up with a number of ideas about a topic (the number of ideas is important, not their quality, correctness, or creativity).
Information Ordering	The ability to arrange things or actions in a certain order or pattern according to a specific rule or set of rules (e.g., patterns of numbers, letters, words, pictures, mathematical operations).
Originality	The ability to come up with unusual or clever ideas about a given topic or situation, or to develop creative ways to solve a problem.
Selective Attention	The ability to concentrate on a task over a period of time without being distracted.
Flexibility of Closure	The ability to identify or detect a known pattern (a figure, object, word, or sound) that is hidden in other distracting material.
Mathematical Reasoning	The ability to choose the right mathematical methods or formulas to solve a problem.
Perceptual Speed	The ability to quickly and accurately compare similarities and differences among sets of letters, numbers, objects, pictures, or patterns. The things to be compared may be presented at the same time or one after the other. This ability also includes comparing a presented object with a remembered object.
Far Vision	The ability to see details at a distance.
Visual Color Discrimination	The ability to match or detect differences between colors, including shades of color and brightness.
Memorization	The ability to remember information such as words, numbers, pictures, and procedures.
Speed of Closure	The ability to quickly make sense of, combine, and organize information into meaningful patterns.
Visualization	The ability to imagine how something will look after it is moved around or when its parts are moved or rearranged.
Time Sharing	The ability to shift back and forth between two or more activities or sources of information (such as speech, sounds, touch, or other sources).
Number Facility	The ability to add, subtract, multiply, or divide quickly and correctly.

Trunk Strength	The ability to use your abdominal and lower back muscles to support part of the body repeatedly or continuously over time without 'giving out' or fatiguing.
Finger Dexterity	The ability to make precisely coordinated movements of the fingers of one or both hands to grasp, manipulate, or assemble very small objects.
Auditory Attention	The ability to focus on a single source of sound in the presence of other distracting sounds.
Hearing Sensitivity	The ability to detect or tell the differences between sounds that vary in pitch and loudness.
Wrist-Finger Speed	The ability to make fast, simple, repeated movements of the fingers, hands, and wrists.
Reaction Time	The ability to quickly respond (with the hand, finger, or foot) to a signal (sound, light, picture) when it appears.
Peripheral Vision	The ability to see objects or movement of objects to one's side when the eyes are looking ahead.
Extent Flexibility	The ability to bend, stretch, twist, or reach with your body, arms, and/or legs.
Manual Dexterity	The ability to quickly move your hand, your hand together with your arm, or your two hands to grasp, manipulate, or assemble objects.
Night Vision	The ability to see under low light conditions.
Gross Body Equilibrium	The ability to keep or regain your body balance or stay upright when in an unstable position.
Gross Body Coordination	The ability to coordinate the movement of your arms, legs, and torso together when the whole body is in motion.
Depth Perception	The ability to judge which of several objects is closer or farther away from you, or to judge the distance between you and an object.
Sound Localization	The ability to tell the direction from which a sound originated.
Control Precision	The ability to quickly and repeatedly adjust the controls of a machine or a vehicle to exact positions.
Spatial Orientation	The ability to know your location in relation to the environment or to know where other objects are in relation to you.
Multilimb Coordination	The ability to coordinate two or more limbs (for example, two arms, two legs, or one leg and one arm) while sitting, standing, or lying down. It does not involve performing the activities while the whole body is in motion.
Stamina	The ability to exert yourself physically over long periods of time without getting winded or out of breath.
Dynamic Flexibility	The ability to quickly and repeatedly bend, stretch, twist, or reach out with your body, arms, and/or legs.
Response Orientation	The ability to choose quickly between two or more movements in response to two or more different signals (lights, sounds, pictures). It includes the speed with which the correct response is started with the hand, foot, or other body part.
Rate Control	The ability to time your movements or the movement of a piece of equipment in anticipation of changes in the speed and/or direction of a moving object or scene.
Speed of Limb Movement	The ability to quickly move the arms and legs.
Static Strength	The ability to exert maximum muscle force to lift, push, pull, or carry objects.
Explosive Strength	The ability to use short bursts of muscle force to propel oneself (as in jumping or sprinting), or to throw an object.
Dynamic Strength	The ability to exert muscle force repeatedly or continuously over time. This involves muscular endurance and resistance to muscle fatigue.
Arm-Hand Steadiness	The ability to keep your hand and arm steady while moving your arm or while holding your arm and hand in one position.
Glare Sensitivity	The ability to see objects in the presence of glare or bright lighting.

Work_Activity	**Work_Activity Definitions**
Interpreting the Meaning of Information for Others	Translating or explaining what information means and how it can be used.
Documenting/Recording Information	Entering, transcribing, recording, storing, or maintaining information in written or electronic/magnetic form.
Updating and Using Relevant Knowledge	Keeping up-to-date technically and applying new knowledge to your job.
Analyzing Data or Information	Identifying the underlying principles, reasons, or facts of information by breaking down information or data into separate parts.
Getting Information	Observing, receiving, and otherwise obtaining information from all relevant sources.
Communicating with Supervisors, Peers, or Subordin	Providing information to supervisors, co-workers, and subordinates by telephone, in written form, e-mail, or in person.
Making Decisions and Solving Problems	Analyzing information and evaluating results to choose the best solution and solve problems.
Interacting With Computers	Using computers and computer systems (including hardware and software) to program, write software, set up functions, enter data, or process information.
Assisting and Caring for Others	Providing personal assistance, medical attention, emotional support, or other personal care to others such as coworkers, customers, or patients.

Identifying Objects, Actions, and Events	Identifying information by categorizing, estimating, recognizing differences or similarities, and detecting changes in circumstances or events.
Organizing, Planning, and Prioritizing Work	Developing specific goals and plans to prioritize, organize, and accomplish your work.
Processing Information	Compiling, coding, categorizing, calculating, tabulating, auditing, or verifying information or data.
Provide Consultation and Advice to Others	Providing guidance and expert advice to management or other groups on technical, systems-, or process-related topics.
Training and Teaching Others	Identifying the educational needs of others, developing formal educational or training programs or classes, and teaching or instructing others.
Judging the Qualities of Things, Services, or Peop	Assessing the value, importance, or quality of things or people.
Establishing and Maintaining Interpersonal Relatio	Developing constructive and cooperative working relationships with others, and maintaining them over time.
Selling or Influencing Others	Convincing others to buy merchandise/goods or to otherwise change their minds or actions.
Developing and Building Teams	Encouraging and building mutual trust, respect, and cooperation among team members.
Monitor Processes, Materials, or Surroundings	Monitoring and reviewing information from materials, events, or the environment, to detect or assess problems.
Evaluating Information to Determine Compliance wit	Using relevant information and individual judgment to determine whether events or processes comply with laws, regulations, or standards.
Thinking Creatively	Developing, designing, or creating new applications, ideas, relationships, systems, or products, including artistic contributions.
Communicating with Persons Outside Organization	Communicating with people outside the organization, representing the organization to customers, the public, government, and other external sources. This information can be exchanged in person, in writing, or by telephone or e-mail.
Performing for or Working Directly with the Public	Performing for people or dealing directly with the public. This includes serving customers in restaurants and stores, and receiving clients or guests.
Coordinating the Work and Activities of Others	Getting members of a group to work together to accomplish tasks.
Monitoring and Controlling Resources	Monitoring and controlling resources and overseeing the spending of money.
Performing Administrative Activities	Performing day-to-day administrative tasks such as maintaining information files and processing paperwork.
Developing Objectives and Strategies	Establishing long-range objectives and specifying the strategies and actions to achieve them.
Coaching and Developing Others	Identifying the developmental needs of others and coaching, mentoring, or otherwise helping others to improve their knowledge or skills.
Scheduling Work and Activities	Scheduling events, programs, and activities, as well as the work of others.
Guiding, Directing, and Motivating Subordinates	Providing guidance and direction to subordinates, including setting performance standards and monitoring performance.
Estimating the Quantifiable Characteristics of Pro	Estimating sizes, distances, and quantities; or determining time, costs, resources, or materials needed to perform a work activity.
Inspecting Equipment, Structures, or Material	Inspecting equipment, structures, or materials to identify the cause of errors or other problems or defects.
Resolving Conflicts and Negotiating with Others	Handling complaints, settling disputes, and resolving grievances and conflicts, or otherwise negotiating with others.
Performing General Physical Activities	Performing physical activities that require considerable use of your arms and legs and moving your whole body, such as climbing, lifting, balancing, walking, stooping, and handling of materials.
Staffing Organizational Units	Recruiting, interviewing, selecting, hiring, and promoting employees in an organization.
Handling and Moving Objects	Using hands and arms in handling, installing, positioning, and moving materials, and manipulating things.
Controlling Machines and Processes	Using either control mechanisms or direct physical activity to operate machines or processes (not including computers or vehicles).
Operating Vehicles, Mechanized Devices, or Equipme	Running, maneuvering, navigating, or driving vehicles or mechanized equipment, such as forklifts, passenger vehicles, aircraft, or water craft.
Repairing and Maintaining Mechanical Equipment	Servicing, repairing, adjusting, and testing machines, devices, moving parts, and equipment that operate primarily on the basis of mechanical (not electronic) principles.
Repairing and Maintaining Electronic Equipment	Servicing, repairing, calibrating, regulating, fine-tuning, or testing machines, devices, and equipment that operate primarily on the basis of electrical or electronic (not mechanical) principles.
Drafting, Laying Out, and Specifying Technical Dev	Providing documentation, detailed instructions, drawings, or specifications to tell others about how devices, parts, equipment, or structures are to be fabricated, constructed, assembled, modified, maintained, or used.

Work_Content	Work_Content Definitions
Freedom to Make Decisions	How much decision making freedom, without supervision, does the job offer?
Structured versus Unstructured Work	To what extent is this job structured for the worker, rather than allowing the worker to determine tasks, priorities, and goals?
Frequency of Decision Making	How frequently is the worker required to make decisions that affect other people, the financial resources, and/or the image and reputation of the organization?
Face-to-Face Discussions	How often do you have to have face-to-face discussions with individuals or teams in this job?
Contact With Others	How much does this job require the worker to be in contact with others (face-to-face, by telephone, or otherwise) in order to perform it?
Impact of Decisions on Co-workers or Company Resul	How do the decisions an employee makes impact the results of co-workers, clients or the company?
Telephone	How often do you have telephone conversations in this job?
Indoors, Environmentally Controlled	How often does this job require working indoors in environmentally controlled conditions?
Spend Time Sitting	How much does this job require sitting?
Work With Work Group or Team	How important is it to work with others in a group or team in this job?
Time Pressure	How often does this job require the worker to meet strict deadlines?
Importance of Being Exact or Accurate	How important is being very exact or highly accurate in performing this job?
Spend Time Standing	How much does this job require standing?
Physical Proximity	To what extent does this job require the worker to perform job tasks in close physical proximity to other people?
Wear Common Protective or Safety Equipment such as	How much does this job require wearing common protective or safety equipment such as safety shoes, glasses, gloves, hard hats or live jackets?
Deal With External Customers	How important is it to work with external customers or the public in this job?
Letters and Memos	How often does the job require written letters and memos?
Deal With Unpleasant or Angry People	How frequently does the worker have to deal with unpleasant, angry, or discourteous individuals as part of the job requirements?
Electronic Mail	How often do you use electronic mail in this job?
Coordinate or Lead Others	How important is it to coordinate or lead others in accomplishing work activities in this job?
Frequency of Conflict Situations	How often are there conflict situations the employee has to face in this job?
Responsibility for Outcomes and Results	How responsible is the worker for work outcomes and results of other workers?
Spend Time Walking and Running	How much does this job require walking and running?
Exposed to Disease or Infections	How often does this job require exposure to disease/infections?
Indoors, Not Environmentally Controlled	How often does this job require working indoors in non-controlled environmental conditions (e.g., warehouse without heat)?
Responsible for Others' Health and Safety	How much responsibility is there for the health and safety of others in this job?
In an Enclosed Vehicle or Equipment	How often does this job require working in a closed vehicle or equipment (e.g., car)?
Sounds, Noise Levels Are Distracting or Uncomforta	How often does this job require working exposed to sounds and noise levels that are distracting or uncomfortable?
Level of Competition	To what extent does this job require the worker to compete or to be aware of competitive pressures?
Exposed to Minor Burns, Cuts, Bites, or Stings	How often does this job require exposure to minor burns, cuts, bites, or stings?
Deal With Physically Aggressive People	How frequently does this job require the worker to deal with physical aggression of violent individuals?
Spend Time Making Repetitive Motions	How much does this job require making repetitive motions?
Very Hot or Cold Temperatures	How often does this job require working in very hot (above 90 F degrees) or very cold (below 32 F degrees) temperatures?
Public Speaking	How often do you have to perform public speaking in this job?
Importance of Repeating Same Tasks	How important is repeating the same physical activities (e.g., key entry) or mental activities (e.g., checking entries in a ledger) over and over, without stopping, to performing this job?
Exposed to Contaminants	How often does this job require working exposed to contaminants (such as pollutants, gases, dust or odors)?
Consequence of Error	How serious would the result usually be if the worker made a mistake that was not readily correctable?
Spend Time Using Your Hands to Handle, Control, or	How much does this job require using your hands to handle, control, or feel objects, tools or controls?
Spend Time Kneeling, Crouching, Stooping, or Crawl	How much does this job require kneeling, crouching, stooping or crawling?
Spend Time Bending or Twisting the Body	How much does this job require bending or twisting your body?

Outdoors, Exposed to Weather	How often does this job require working outdoors, exposed to all weather conditions?
Degree of Automation	How automated is the job?
Cramped Work Space, Awkward Positions	How often does this job require working in cramped work spaces that requires getting into awkward positions?
Exposed to Hazardous Conditions	How often does this job require exposure to hazardous conditions?
Extremely Bright or Inadequate Lighting	How often does this job require working in extremely bright or inadequate lighting conditions?
Wear Specialized Protective or Safety Equipment su	How much does this job require wearing specialized protective or safety equipment such as breathing apparatus, safety harness, full protection suits, or radiation protection?
Exposed to Radiation	How often does this job require exposure to radiation?
Exposed to Hazardous Equipment	How often does this job require exposure to hazardous equipment?
Pace Determined by Speed of Equipment	How important is it to this job that the pace is determined by the speed of equipment or machinery? (This does not refer to keeping busy at all times on this job.)
In an Open Vehicle or Equipment	How often does this job require working in an open vehicle or equipment (e.g., tractor)?
Outdoors, Under Cover	How often does this job require working outdoors, under cover (e.g., structure with roof but no walls)?
Exposed to Whole Body Vibration	How often does this job require exposure to whole body vibration (e.g., operate a jackhammer)?
Exposed to High Places	How often does this job require exposure to high places?
Spend Time Keeping or Regaining Balance	How much does this job require keeping or regaining your balance?
Spend Time Climbing Ladders, Scaffolds, or Poles	How much does this job require climbing ladders, scaffolds, or poles?

Work_Styles

Work_Styles	Work_Styles Definitions
Integrity	Job requires being honest and ethical.
Concern for Others	Job requires being sensitive to others' needs and feelings and being understanding and helpful on the job.
Dependability	Job requires being reliable, responsible, and dependable, and fulfilling obligations.
Cooperation	Job requires being pleasant with others on the job and displaying a good-natured, cooperative attitude.
Independence	Job requires developing one's own ways of doing things, guiding oneself with little or no supervision, and depending on oneself to get things done.
Attention to Detail	Job requires being careful about detail and thorough in completing work tasks.
Self Control	Job requires maintaining composure, keeping emotions in check, controlling anger, and avoiding aggressive behavior, even in very difficult situations.
Adaptability/Flexibility	Job requires being open to change (positive or negative) and to considerable variety in the workplace.
Achievement/Effort	Job requires establishing and maintaining personally challenging achievement goals and exerting effort toward mastering tasks.
Initiative	Job requires a willingness to take on responsibilities and challenges.
Social Orientation	Job requires preferring to work with others rather than alone, and being personally connected with others on the job.
Stress Tolerance	Job requires accepting criticism and dealing calmly and effectively with high stress situations.
Persistence	Job requires persistence in the face of obstacles.
Analytical Thinking	Job requires analyzing information and using logic to address work-related issues and problems.
Leadership	Job requires a willingness to lead, take charge, and offer opinions and direction.
Innovation	Job requires creativity and alternative thinking to develop new ideas for and answers to work-related problems.

Job Zone Component

Job Zone Component	Job Zone Component Definitions
Title	Job Zone Five: Extensive Preparation Needed Extensive skill, knowledge, and experience are needed for these occupations. Many require more than five years of experience.
Overall Experience	For example, surgeons must complete four years of college and an additional five to seven years of specialized medical training to be able to do their job.
Job Training	Employees may need some on-the-job training, but most of these occupations assume that the person will already have the required skills, knowledge, work-related experience, and/or training.
Job Zone Examples	These occupations often involve coordinating, training, supervising, or managing the activities of others to accomplish goals. Very advanced communication and organizational skills are required. Examples include athletic trainers, lawyers, managing editors, phyicists, social psychologists, and surgeons.
SVP Range	(8.0 and above)

Education	A bachelor's degree is the minimum formal education required for these occupations. However, many also require graduate school. For example, they may require a master's degree, and some require a Ph.D., M.D., or J.D. (law degree).

29-1041.00 - Optometrists

Diagnose, manage, and treat conditions and diseases of the human eye and visual system. Examine eyes and visual system, diagnose problems or impairments, prescribe corrective lenses, and provide treatment. May prescribe therapeutic drugs to treat specific eye conditions.

Tasks

1) Analyze test results and develop a treatment plan.

2) Prescribe medications to treat eye diseases if state laws permit.

3) Prescribe therapeutic procedures to correct or conserve vision.

4) Provide patients undergoing eye surgeries, such as cataract and laser vision correction, with pre- and post-operative care.

5) Remove foreign bodies from the eye.

6) Provide vision therapy and low vision rehabilitation.

7) Examine eyes, using observation, instruments and pharmaceutical agents, to determine visual acuity and perception, focus and coordination and to diagnose diseases and other abnormalities such as glaucoma or color blindness.

8) Consult with and refer patients to ophthalmologist or other health care practitioner if additional medical treatment is determined necessary.

9) Educate and counsel patients on contact lens care, visual hygiene, lighting arrangements and safety factors.

Knowledge	Knowledge Definitions
Medicine and Dentistry	Knowledge of the information and techniques needed to diagnose and treat human injuries, diseases, and deformities. This includes symptoms, treatment alternatives, drug properties and interactions, and preventive health-care measures.
Customer and Personal Service	Knowledge of principles and processes for providing customer and personal services. This includes customer needs assessment, meeting quality standards for services, and evaluation of customer satisfaction.
English Language	Knowledge of the structure and content of the English language including the meaning and spelling of words, rules of composition, and grammar.
Biology	Knowledge of plant and animal organisms, their tissues, cells, functions, interdependencies, and interactions with each other and the environment.
Mathematics	Knowledge of arithmetic, algebra, geometry, calculus, statistics, and their applications.
Economics and Accounting	Knowledge of economic and accounting principles and practices, the financial markets, banking and the analysis and reporting of financial data.
Administration and Management	Knowledge of business and management principles involved in strategic planning, resource allocation, human resources modeling, leadership technique, production methods, and coordination of people and resources.
Psychology	Knowledge of human behavior and performance; individual differences in ability, personality, and interests; learning and motivation; psychological research methods; and the assessment and treatment of behavioral and affective disorders.
Sales and Marketing	Knowledge of principles and methods for showing, promoting, and selling products or services. This includes marketing strategy and tactics, product demonstration, sales techniques, and sales control systems.
Personnel and Human Resources	Knowledge of principles and procedures for personnel recruitment, selection, training, compensation and benefits, labor relations and negotiation, and personnel information systems.
Clerical	Knowledge of administrative and clerical procedures and systems such as word processing, managing files and records, stenography and transcription, designing forms, and other office procedures and terminology.
Education and Training	Knowledge of principles and methods for curriculum and training design, teaching and instruction for individuals and groups, and the measurement of training effects.
Chemistry	Knowledge of the chemical composition, structure, and properties of substances and of the chemical processes and transformations that they undergo. This includes uses of chemicals and their interactions, danger signs, production techniques, and disposal methods.

Production and Processing	Knowledge of raw materials, production processes, quality control, costs, and other techniques for maximizing the effective manufacture and distribution of goods.	Social Perceptiveness	Being aware of others' reactions and understanding why they react as they do.
Physics	Knowledge and prediction of physical principles, laws, their interrelationships, and applications to understanding fluid, material, and atmospheric dynamics, and mechanical, electrical, atomic and sub-atomic structures and processes.	Time Management	Managing one's own time and the time of others.
		Equipment Selection	Determining the kind of tools and equipment needed to do a job.
Therapy and Counseling	Knowledge of principles, methods, and procedures for diagnosis, treatment, and rehabilitation of physical and mental dysfunctions, and for career counseling and guidance.	Management of Personnel Resources	Motivating, developing, and directing people as they work, identifying the best people for the job.
Computers and Electronics	Knowledge of circuit boards, processors, chips, electronic equipment, and computer hardware and software, including applications and programming.	Writing	Communicating effectively in writing as appropriate for the needs of the audience.
Law and Government	Knowledge of laws, legal codes, court procedures, precedents, government regulations, executive orders, agency rules, and the democratic political process.	Learning Strategies	Selecting and using training/instructional methods and procedures appropriate for the situation when learning or teaching new things.
Engineering and Technology	Knowledge of the practical application of engineering science and technology. This includes applying principles, techniques, procedures, and equipment to the design and production of various goods and services.	Monitoring	Monitoring/Assessing performance of yourself, other individuals, or organizations to make improvements or take corrective action.
Sociology and Anthropology	Knowledge of group behavior and dynamics, societal trends and influences, human migrations, ethnicity, cultures and their history and origins.	Troubleshooting	Determining causes of operating errors and deciding what to do about it.
Telecommunications	Knowledge of transmission, broadcasting, switching, control, and operation of telecommunications systems.	Negotiation	Bringing others together and trying to reconcile differences.
Communications and Media	Knowledge of media production, communication, and dissemination techniques and methods. This includes alternative ways to inform and entertain via written, oral, and visual media.	Quality Control Analysis	Conducting tests and inspections of products, services, or processes to evaluate quality or performance.
		Operation and Control	Controlling operations of equipment or systems.
Foreign Language	Knowledge of the structure and content of a foreign (non-English) language including the meaning and spelling of words, rules of composition and grammar, and pronunciation.	Systems Evaluation	Identifying measures or indicators of system performance and the actions needed to improve or correct performance, relative to the goals of the system.
Public Safety and Security	Knowledge of relevant equipment, policies, procedures, and strategies to promote effective local, state, or national security operations for the protection of people, data, property, and institutions.	Operation Monitoring	Watching gauges, dials, or other indicators to make sure a machine is working properly.
		Management of Material Resources	Obtaining and seeing to the appropriate use of equipment, facilities, and materials needed to do certain work.
Design	Knowledge of design techniques, tools, and principles involved in production of precision technical plans, blueprints, drawings, and models.	Operations Analysis	Analyzing needs and product requirements to create a design.
		Management of Financial Resources	Determining how money will be spent to get the work done, and accounting for these expenditures.
Mechanical	Knowledge of machines and tools, including their designs, uses, repair, and maintenance.	Equipment Maintenance	Performing routine maintenance on equipment and determining when and what kind of maintenance is needed.
Transportation	Knowledge of principles and methods for moving people or goods by air, rail, sea, or road, including the relative costs and benefits.	Technology Design	Generating or adapting equipment and technology to serve user needs.
Philosophy and Theology	Knowledge of different philosophical systems and religions. This includes their basic principles, values, ethics, ways of thinking, customs, practices, and their impact on human culture.	Installation	Installing equipment, machines, wiring, or programs to meet specifications.
Geography	Knowledge of principles and methods for describing the features of land, sea, and air masses, including their physical characteristics, locations, interrelationships, and distribution of plant, animal, and human life.	Systems Analysis	Determining how a system should work and how changes in conditions, operations, and the environment will affect outcomes.
History and Archeology	Knowledge of historical events and their causes, indicators, and effects on civilizations and cultures.	Repairing	Repairing machines or systems using the needed tools.
		Programming	Writing computer programs for various purposes.
Building and Construction	Knowledge of materials, methods, and the tools involved in the construction or repair of houses, buildings, or other structures such as highways and roads.	**Ability**	**Ability Definitions**
Fine Arts	Knowledge of the theory and techniques required to compose, produce, and perform works of music, dance, visual arts, drama, and sculpture.	Oral Expression	The ability to communicate information and ideas in speaking so others will understand.
Food Production	Knowledge of techniques and equipment for planting, growing, and harvesting food products (both plant and animal) for consumption, including storage/handling techniques.	Problem Sensitivity	The ability to tell when something is wrong or is likely to go wrong. It does not involve solving the problem, only recognizing there is a problem.
Skills	**Skills Definitions**	Arm-Hand Steadiness	The ability to keep your hand and arm steady while moving your arm or while holding your arm and hand in one position.
Active Listening	Giving full attention to what other people are saying, taking time to understand the points being made, asking questions as appropriate, and not interrupting at inappropriate times.	Oral Comprehension	The ability to listen to and understand information and ideas presented through spoken words and sentences.
		Near Vision	The ability to see details at close range (within a few feet of the observer).
Reading Comprehension	Understanding written sentences and paragraphs in work related documents.	Inductive Reasoning	The ability to combine pieces of information to form general rules or conclusions (includes finding a relationship among seemingly unrelated events).
Critical Thinking	Using logic and reasoning to identify the strengths and weaknesses of alternative solutions, conclusions or approaches to problems.	Speech Recognition	The ability to identify and understand the speech of another person.
Judgment and Decision Making	Considering the relative costs and benefits of potential actions to choose the most appropriate one.	Speech Clarity	The ability to speak clearly so others can understand you.
Science	Using scientific rules and methods to solve problems.	Manual Dexterity	The ability to quickly move your hand, your hand together with your arm, or your two hands to grasp, manipulate, or assemble objects.
Service Orientation	Actively looking for ways to help people.		
Speaking	Talking to others to convey information effectively.	Finger Dexterity	The ability to make precisely coordinated movements of the fingers of one or both hands to grasp, manipulate, or assemble very small objects.
Complex Problem Solving	Identifying complex problems and reviewing related information to develop and evaluate options and implement solutions.	Written Comprehension	The ability to read and understand information and ideas presented in writing.
Instructing	Teaching others how to do something.	Control Precision	The ability to quickly and repeatedly adjust the controls of a machine or a vehicle to exact positions.
Mathematics	Using mathematics to solve problems.	Deductive Reasoning	The ability to apply general rules to specific problems to produce answers that make sense.
Active Learning	Understanding the implications of new information for both current and future problem-solving and decision-making.	Written Expression	The ability to communicate information and ideas in writing so others will understand.
Coordination	Adjusting actions in relation to others' actions.	Flexibility of Closure	The ability to identify or detect a known pattern (a figure, object, word, or sound) that is hidden in other distracting material.
Persuasion	Persuading others to change their minds or behavior.	Information Ordering	The ability to arrange things or actions in a certain order or pattern according to a specific rule or set of rules (e.g., patterns of numbers, letters, words, pictures, mathematical operations).
		Visual Color Discrimination	The ability to match or detect differences between colors, including shades of color and brightness.

Multilimb Coordination	The ability to coordinate two or more limbs (for example, two arms, two legs, or one leg and one arm) while sitting, standing, or lying down. It does not involve performing the activities while the whole body is in motion.
Speed of Closure	The ability to quickly make sense of, combine, and organize information into meaningful patterns.
Category Flexibility	The ability to generate or use different sets of rules for combining or grouping things in different ways.
Selective Attention	The ability to concentrate on a task over a period of time without being distracted.
Far Vision	The ability to see details at a distance.
Depth Perception	The ability to judge which of several objects is closer or farther away from you, or to judge the distance between you and an object.
Originality	The ability to come up with unusual or clever ideas about a given topic or situation, or to develop creative ways to solve a problem.
Perceptual Speed	The ability to quickly and accurately compare similarities and differences among sets of letters, numbers, objects, pictures, or patterns. The things to be compared may be presented at the same time or one after the other. This ability also includes comparing a presented object with a remembered object.
Memorization	The ability to remember information such as words, numbers, pictures, and procedures.
Number Facility	The ability to add, subtract, multiply, or divide quickly and correctly.
Trunk Strength	The ability to use your abdominal and lower back muscles to support part of the body repeatedly or continuously over time without 'giving out' or fatiguing.
Visualization	The ability to imagine how something will look after it is moved around or when its parts are moved or rearranged.
Time Sharing	The ability to shift back and forth between two or more activities or sources of information (such as speech, sounds, touch, or other sources).
Fluency of Ideas	The ability to come up with a number of ideas about a topic (the number of ideas is important, not their quality, correctness, or creativity).
Mathematical Reasoning	The ability to choose the right mathematical methods or formulas to solve a problem.
Wrist-Finger Speed	The ability to make fast, simple, repeated movements of the fingers, hands, and wrists.
Rate Control	The ability to time your movements or the movement of a piece of equipment in anticipation of changes in the speed and/or direction of a moving object or scene.
Reaction Time	The ability to quickly respond (with the hand, finger, or foot) to a signal (sound, light, picture) when it appears.
Spatial Orientation	The ability to know your location in relation to the environment or to know where other objects are in relation to you.
Response Orientation	The ability to choose quickly between two or more movements in response to two or more different signals (lights, sounds, pictures). It includes the speed with which the correct response is started with the hand, foot, or other body part.
Auditory Attention	The ability to focus on a single source of sound in the presence of other distracting sounds.
Hearing Sensitivity	The ability to detect or tell the differences between sounds that vary in pitch and loudness.
Night Vision	The ability to see under low light conditions.
Extent Flexibility	The ability to bend, stretch, twist, or reach with your body, arms, and/or legs.
Static Strength	The ability to exert maximum muscle force to lift, push, pull, or carry objects.
Sound Localization	The ability to tell the direction from which a sound originated.
Explosive Strength	The ability to use short bursts of muscle force to propel oneself (as in jumping or sprinting), or to throw an object.
Glare Sensitivity	The ability to see objects in the presence of glare or bright lighting.
Speed of Limb Movement	The ability to quickly move the arms and legs.
Dynamic Strength	The ability to exert muscle force repeatedly or continuously over time. This involves muscular endurance and resistance to muscle fatigue.
Dynamic Flexibility	The ability to quickly and repeatedly bend, stretch, twist, or reach out with your body, arms, and/or legs.
Gross Body Coordination	The ability to coordinate the movement of your arms, legs, and torso together when the whole body is in motion.
Gross Body Equilibrium	The ability to keep or regain your body balance or stay upright when in an unstable position.
Peripheral Vision	The ability to see objects or movement of objects to one's side when the eyes are looking ahead.
Stamina	The ability to exert yourself physically over long periods of time without getting winded or out of breath.

Work_Activity	Work_Activity Definitions
Making Decisions and Solving Problems	Analyzing information and evaluating results to choose the best solution and solve problems.

Performing for or Working Directly with the Public	Performing for people or dealing directly with the public. This includes serving customers in restaurants and stores, and receiving clients or guests.
Updating and Using Relevant Knowledge	Keeping up-to-date technically and applying new knowledge to your job.
Establishing and Maintaining Interpersonal Relatio	Developing constructive and cooperative working relationships with others, and maintaining them over time.
Processing Information	Compiling, coding, categorizing, calculating, tabulating, auditing, or verifying information or data.
Evaluating Information to Determine Compliance wit	Using relevant information and individual judgment to determine whether events or processes comply with laws, regulations, or standards.
Organizing, Planning, and Prioritizing Work	Developing specific goals and plans to prioritize, organize, and accomplish your work.
Getting Information	Observing, receiving, and otherwise obtaining information from all relevant sources.
Assisting and Caring for Others	Providing personal assistance, medical attention, emotional support, or other personal care to others such as coworkers, customers, or patients.
Scheduling Work and Activities	Scheduling events, programs, and activities, as well as the work of others.
Communicating with Supervisors, Peers, or Subordin	Providing information to supervisors, co-workers, and subordinates by telephone, in written form, e-mail, or in person.
Resolving Conflicts and Negotiating with Others	Handling complaints, settling disputes, and resolving grievances and conflicts, or otherwise negotiating with others.
Selling or Influencing Others	Convincing others to buy merchandise/goods or to otherwise change their minds or actions.
Training and Teaching Others	Identifying the educational needs of others, developing formal educational or training programs or classes, and teaching or instructing others.
Interpreting the Meaning of Information for Others	Translating or explaining what information means and how it can be used.
Documenting/Recording Information	Entering, transcribing, recording, storing, or maintaining information in written or electronic/magnetic form.
Provide Consultation and Advice to Others	Providing guidance and expert advice to management or other groups on technical, systems-, or process-related topics.
Performing Administrative Activities	Performing day-to-day administrative tasks such as maintaining information files and processing paperwork.
Identifying Objects, Actions, and Events	Identifying information by categorizing, estimating, recognizing differences or similarities, and detecting changes in circumstances or events.
Handling and Moving Objects	Using hands and arms in handling, installing, positioning, and moving materials, and manipulating things.
Analyzing Data or Information	Identifying the underlying principles, reasons, or facts of information by breaking down information or data into separate parts.
Interacting With Computers	Using computers and computer systems (including hardware and software) to program, write software, set up functions, enter data, or process information.
Coaching and Developing Others	Identifying the developmental needs of others and coaching, mentoring, or otherwise helping others to improve their knowledge or skills.
Judging the Qualities of Things, Services, or Peop	Assessing the value, importance, or quality of things or people.
Guiding, Directing, and Motivating Subordinates	Providing guidance and direction to subordinates, including setting performance standards and monitoring performance.
Monitor Processes, Materials, or Surroundings	Monitoring and reviewing information from materials, events, or the environment, to detect or assess problems.
Controlling Machines and Processes	Using either control mechanisms or direct physical activity to operate machines or processes (not including computers or vehicles).
Thinking Creatively	Developing, designing, or creating new applications, ideas, relationships, systems, or products, including artistic contributions.
Coordinating the Work and Activities of Others	Getting members of a group to work together to accomplish tasks.
Developing and Building Teams	Encouraging and building mutual trust, respect, and cooperation among team members.
Developing Objectives and Strategies	Establishing long-range objectives and specifying the strategies and actions to achieve them.
Inspecting Equipment, Structures, or Material	Inspecting equipment, structures, or materials to identify the cause of errors or other problems or defects.
Staffing Organizational Units	Recruiting, interviewing, selecting, hiring, and promoting employees in an organization.
Estimating the Quantifiable Characteristics of Pro	Estimating sizes, distances, and quantities; or determining time, costs, resources, or materials needed to perform a work activity.
Monitoring and Controlling Resources	Monitoring and controlling resources and overseeing the spending of money.
Communicating with Persons Outside Organization	Communicating with people outside the organization, representing the organization to customers, the public, government, and other external sources. This information can be exchanged in person, in writing, or by telephone or e-mail.

147

Performing General Physical Activities	Performing physical activities that require considerable use of your arms and legs and moving your whole body, such as climbing, lifting, balancing, walking, stooping, and handling of materials.
Repairing and Maintaining Electronic Equipment	Servicing, repairing, calibrating, regulating, fine-tuning, or testing machines, devices, and equipment that operate primarily on the basis of electrical or electronic (not mechanical) principles.
Repairing and Maintaining Mechanical Equipment	Servicing, repairing, adjusting, and testing machines, devices, moving parts, and equipment that operate primarily on the basis of mechanical (not electronic) principles.
Operating Vehicles, Mechanized Devices, or Equipme	Running, maneuvering, navigating, or driving vehicles or mechanized equipment, such as forklifts, passenger vehicles, aircraft, or water craft.
Drafting, Laying Out, and Specifying Technical Dev	Providing documentation, detailed instructions, drawings, or specifications to tell others about how devices, parts, equipment, or structures are to be fabricated, constructed, assembled, modified, maintained, or used.

Work_Content	Work_Content Definitions
Freedom to Make Decisions	How much decision making freedom, without supervision, does the job offer?
Face-to-Face Discussions	How often do you have to have face-to-face discussions with individuals or teams in this job?
Physical Proximity	To what extent does this job require the worker to perform job tasks in close physical proximity to other people?
Contact With Others	How much does this job require the worker to be in contact with others (face-to-face, by telephone, or otherwise) in order to perform it?
Indoors, Environmentally Controlled	How often does this job require working indoors in environmentally controlled conditions?
Structured versus Unstructured Work	To what extent is this job structured for the worker, rather than allowing the worker to determine tasks, priorities, and goals?
Deal With External Customers	How important is it to work with external customers or the public in this job?
Telephone	How often do you have telephone conversations in this job?
Importance of Being Exact or Accurate	How important is being very exact or highly accurate in performing this job?
Frequency of Decision Making	How frequently is the worker required to make decisions that affect other people, the financial resources, and/or the image and reputation of the organization?
Impact of Decisions on Co-workers or Company Resul	How do the decisions an employee makes impact the results of co-workers, clients or the company?
Work With Work Group or Team	How important is it to work with others in a group or team in this job?
Exposed to Disease or Infections	How often does this job require exposure to disease/infections?
Spend Time Using Your Hands to Handle, Control, or	How much does this job require using your hands to handle, control, or feel objects, tools or controls?
Time Pressure	How often does this job require the worker to meet strict deadlines?
Responsibility for Outcomes and Results	How responsible is the worker for work outcomes and results of other workers?
Letters and Memos	How often does the job require written letters and memos?
Responsible for Others' Health and Safety	How much responsibility is there for the health and safety of others in this job?
Level of Competition	To what extent does this job require the worker to compete or to be aware of competitive pressures?
Spend Time Making Repetitive Motions	How much does this job require making repetitive motions?
Consequence of Error	How serious would the result usually be if the worker made a mistake that was not readily correctable?
Coordinate or Lead Others	How important is it to coordinate or lead others in accomplishing work activities in this job?
Frequency of Conflict Situations	How often are there conflict situations the employee has to face in this job?
Spend Time Sitting	How much does this job require sitting?
Deal With Unpleasant or Angry People	How frequently does the worker have to deal with unpleasant, angry, or discourteous individuals as part of the job requirements?
Spend Time Standing	How much does this job require standing?
Electronic Mail	How often do you use electronic mail in this job?
Importance of Repeating Same Tasks	How important is repeating the same physical activities (e.g., key entry) or mental activities (e.g., checking entries in a ledger) over and over, without stopping, to performing this job?
Degree of Automation	How automated is the job?
Spend Time Bending or Twisting the Body	How much does this job require bending or twisting your body?
Wear Common Protective or Safety Equipment such as	How much does this job require wearing common protective or safety equipment such as safety shoes, glasses, gloves, hard hats or live jackets?
Spend Time Walking and Running	How much does this job require walking and running?

Exposed to Contaminants	How often does this job require working exposed to contaminants (such as pollutants, gases, dust or odors)?
Public Speaking	How often do you have to perform public speaking in this job?
Deal With Physically Aggressive People	How frequently does this job require the worker to deal with physical aggression of violent individuals?
Extremely Bright or Inadequate Lighting	How often does this job require working in extremely bright or inadequate lighting conditions?
Sounds, Noise Levels Are Distracting or Uncomforta	How often does this job require working exposed to sounds and noise levels that are distracting or uncomfortable?
Exposed to Minor Burns, Cuts, Bites, or Stings	How often does this job require exposure to minor burns, cuts, bites, or stings?
Exposed to Hazardous Conditions	How often does this job require exposure to hazardous conditions?
Cramped Work Space, Awkward Positions	How often does this job require working in cramped work spaces that requires getting into awkward positions?
Spend Time Kneeling, Crouching, Stooping, or Crawl	How much does this job require kneeling, crouching, stooping or crawling?
Wear Specialized Protective or Safety Equipment su	How much does this job require wearing specialized protective or safety equipment such as breathing apparatus, safety harness, full protection suits, or radiation protection?
Spend Time Keeping or Regaining Balance	How much does this job require keeping or regaining your balance?
Pace Determined by Speed of Equipment	How important is it to this job that the pace is determined by the speed of equipment or machinery? (This does not refer to keeping busy at all times on this job.)
Indoors, Not Environmentally Controlled	How often does this job require working indoors in non-controlled environmental conditions (e.g., warehouse without heat)?
Spend Time Climbing Ladders, Scaffolds, or Poles	How much does this job require climbing ladders, scaffolds, or poles?
Very Hot or Cold Temperatures	How often does this job require working in very hot (above 90 F degrees) or very cold (below 32 F degrees) temperatures?
In an Enclosed Vehicle or Equipment	How often does this job require working in a closed vehicle or equipment (e.g., car)?
Outdoors, Exposed to Weather	How often does this job require working outdoors, exposed to all weather conditions?
In an Open Vehicle or Equipment	How often does this job require working in an open vehicle or equipment (e.g., tractor)?
Exposed to Whole Body Vibration	How often does this job require exposure to whole body vibration (e.g., operate a jackhammer)?
Exposed to Radiation	How often does this job require exposure to radiation?
Exposed to High Places	How often does this job require exposure to high places?
Exposed to Hazardous Equipment	How often does this job require exposure to hazardous equipment?
Outdoors, Under Cover	How often does this job require working outdoors, under cover (e.g., structure with roof but no walls)?

Work_Styles	Work_Styles Definitions
Attention to Detail	Job requires being careful about detail and thorough in completing work tasks.
Concern for Others	Job requires being sensitive to others' needs and feelings and being understanding and helpful on the job.
Integrity	Job requires being honest and ethical.
Dependability	Job requires being reliable, responsible, and dependable, and fulfilling obligations.
Cooperation	Job requires being pleasant with others on the job and displaying a good-natured, cooperative attitude.
Self Control	Job requires maintaining composure, keeping emotions in check, controlling anger, and avoiding aggressive behavior, even in very difficult situations.
Analytical Thinking	Job requires analyzing information and using logic to address work-related issues and problems.
Stress Tolerance	Job requires accepting criticism and dealing calmly and effectively with high stress situations.
Adaptability/Flexibility	Job requires being open to change (positive or negative) and to considerable variety in the workplace.
Initiative	Job requires a willingness to take on responsibilities and challenges.
Independence	Job requires developing one's own ways of doing things, guiding oneself with little or no supervision, and depending on oneself to get things done.
Achievement/Effort	Job requires establishing and maintaining personally challenging achievement goals and exerting effort toward mastering tasks.
Persistence	Job requires persistence in the face of obstacles.
Leadership	Job requires a willingness to lead, take charge, and offer opinions and direction.
Social Orientation	Job requires preferring to work with others rather than alone, and being personally connected with others on the job.
Innovation	Job requires creativity and alternative thinking to develop new ideas for and answers to work-related problems.

Job Zone Component	Job Zone Component Definitions
Title	Job Zone Five: Extensive Preparation Needed
	Extensive skill, knowledge, and experience are needed for these occupations. Many require more than five years of experience.
Overall Experience	For example, surgeons must complete four years of college and an additional five to seven years of specialized medical training to be able to do their job.
Job Training	Employees may need some on-the-job training, but most of these occupations assume that the person will already have the required skills, knowledge, work-related experience, and/or training.
Job Zone Examples	These occupations often involve coordinating, training, supervising, or managing the activities of others to accomplish goals. Very advanced communication and organizational skills are required. Examples include athletic trainers, lawyers, managing editors, phyicists, social psychologists, and surgeons.
SVP Range	(8.0 and above)
Education	A bachelor's degree is the minimum formal education required for these occupations. However, many also require graduate school. For example, they may require a master's degree, and some require a Ph.D., M.D., or J.D. (law degree).

29-1051.00 - Pharmacists

Compound and dispense medications following prescriptions issued by physicians, dentists, or other authorized medical practitioners.

Tasks

1) Order and purchase pharmaceutical supplies, medical supplies, and drugs, maintaining stock and storing and handling it properly.

2) Compound radioactive substances and reagents to prepare radiopharmaceuticals, following radiopharmacy laboratory procedures.

3) Offer health promotion and prevention activities, for example, training people to use devices such as blood pressure or diabetes monitors.

4) Review prescriptions to assure accuracy, to ascertain the needed ingredients, and to evaluate their suitability.

5) Plan, implement, and maintain procedures for mixing, packaging, and labeling pharmaceuticals, according to policy and legal requirements, to ensure quality, security, and proper disposal.

6) Provide information and advice regarding drug interactions, side effects, dosage and proper medication storage.

7) Refer patients to other health professionals and agencies when appropriate.

8) Work for pharmaceutical firms in production, marketing, quality control, or sales.

9) Work in hospitals, clinics, or for HMOs, dispensing prescriptions, serving as a medical team consultants, or specializing in specific drug therapy areas such as oncology or nuclear pharmacotherapy.

10) Provide specialized services to help patients manage conditions such as diabetes, asthma, smoking cessation, or high blood pressure.

11) Manage pharmacy operations, hiring and supervising staff, performing administrative duties, and buying and selling non-pharmaceutical merchandise.

12) Analyze prescribing trends to monitor patient compliance and to prevent excessive usage or harmful interactions.

13) Maintain records, such as pharmacy files, patient profiles, charge system files, inventories, control records for radioactive nuclei, and registries of poisons, narcotics, and controlled drugs.

14) Publish educational information for other pharmacists, doctors, and/or patients.

15) Assay radiopharmaceuticals, verify rates of disintegration, and calculate the volume required to produce the desired results, to ensure proper dosages.

16) Assess the identity, strength and purity of medications.

17) Compound and dispense medications as prescribed by doctors and dentists, by calculating, weighing, measuring, and mixing ingredients, or oversee these activities.

18) Prepare sterile solutions and infusions for use in surgical procedures, emergency rooms, or patients' homes.

19) Advise customers on the selection of medication brands, medical equipment and health-care supplies.

20) Collaborate with other health care professionals to plan, monitor, review, and evaluate the quality and effectiveness of drugs and drug regimens, providing advice on drug applications and characteristics.

21) Research and develop drug products and drug therapies, such as radiopharmaceuticals or therapies for psychiatric disorders.

29-1061.00 - Anesthesiologists

Administer anesthetics during surgery or other medical procedures.

Tasks

1) Manage anesthesiological services, coordinating them with other medical activities and formulating plans and procedures.

2) Instruct individuals and groups on ways to preserve health and prevent disease.

3) Provide medical care and consultation in many settings, prescribing medication and treatment and referring patients for surgery.

4) Provide and maintain life support and airway management, and help prepare patients for emergency surgery.

5) Position patient on operating table to maximize patient comfort and surgical accessibility.

6) Order laboratory tests, x-rays and other diagnostic procedures

7) Conduct medical research to aid in controlling and curing disease, to investigate new medications, and to develop and test new medical techniques.

8) Inform students and staff of types and methods of anesthesia administration, signs of complications, and emergency methods to counteract reactions.

9) Coordinate and direct work of nurses, medical technicians and other health care providers.

10) Record type and amount of anesthesia and patient condition throughout procedure.

11) Examine patient, obtain medical history and use diagnostic tests to determine risk during surgical, obstetrical, and other medical procedures.

12) Confer with other medical professionals to determine type and method of anesthetic or sedation to render patient insensible to pain.

13) Diagnose illnesses, using examinations, tests and reports.

14) Decide when patients have recovered or stabilized enough to be sent to another room or ward or to be sent home following outpatient surgery.

15) Monitor patient before, during, and after anesthesia and counteract adverse reactions or complications.

16) Coordinate administration of anesthetics with surgeons during operation.

17) Schedule and maintain use of surgical suite, including operating, wash-up, waiting rooms and anesthetic and sterilizing equipment.

29-1062.00 - Family and General Practitioners

Diagnose, treat, and help prevent diseases and injuries that commonly occur in the general population.

Tasks

1) Order, perform and interpret tests, and analyze records, reports and examination information to diagnose patients' condition.

2) Refer patients to medical specialists or other practitioners when necessary.

3) Conduct research to study anatomy and develop or test medications, treatments, or procedures to prevent or control disease or injury.

4) Coordinate work with nurses, social workers, rehabilitation therapists, pharmacists, psychologists and other health care providers.

5) Deliver babies.

6) Operate on patients to remove, repair, or improve functioning of diseased or injured body parts and systems.

7) Plan, implement, or administer health programs or standards in hospital, business, or community for information, prevention, or treatment of injury or illness.

8) Prepare reports for government or management of birth, death, and disease statistics, workforce evaluations, or medical status of individuals.

9) Monitor the patients' conditions and progress and re-evaluate treatments as necessary.

10) Direct and coordinate activities of nurses, students, assistants, specialists, therapists, and other medical staff.

11) Explain procedures and discuss test results or prescribed treatments with patients.

12) Prescribe or administer treatment, therapy, medication, vaccination, and other specialized medical care to treat or prevent illness, disease, or injury.

13) Collect, record, and maintain patient information, such as medical history, reports, and examination results.

29-1063.00 - Internists, General

149

Diagnose and provide non-surgical treatment of diseases and injuries of internal organ systems. Provide care mainly for adults who have a wide range of problems associated with the internal organs.

Tasks

1) Collect, record, and maintain patient information, such as medical history, reports, and examination results.

2) Make diagnoses when different illnesses occur together or in situations where the diagnosis may be obscure.

3) Advise patients and community members concerning diet, activity, hygiene, and disease prevention.

4) Explain procedures and discuss test results or prescribed treatments with patients.

5) Prescribe or administer medication, therapy, and other specialized medical care to treat or prevent illness, disease, or injury.

6) Advise surgeon of a patient's risk status and recommend appropriate intervention to minimize risk.

7) Provide and manage long-term, comprehensive medical care, including diagnosis and non-surgical treatment of diseases, for adult patients in an office or hospital.

8) Prepare government or organizational reports on birth, death, and disease statistics, workforce evaluations, or the medical status of individuals.

9) Treat internal disorders, such as hypertension, heart disease, diabetes, and problems of the lung, brain, kidney, and gastrointestinal tract.

10) Immunize patients to protect them from preventable diseases.

11) Plan, implement, or administer health programs in hospitals, businesses, or communities for prevention and treatment of injuries or illnesses.

12) Provide consulting services to other doctors caring for patients with special or difficult problems.

13) Operate on patients to remove, repair, or improve functioning of diseased or injured body parts and systems.

14) Analyze records, reports, test results, or examination information to diagnose medical condition of patient.

15) Direct and coordinate activities of nurses, students, assistants, specialists, therapists, and other medical staff.

16) Conduct research to develop or test medications, treatments, or procedures to prevent or control disease or injury

17) Manage and treat common health problems, such as infections, influenza and pneumonia, as well as serious, chronic, and complex illnesses, in adolescents, adults, and the elderly.

18) Refer patient to medical specialist or other practitioner when necessary.

29-1064.00 - Obstetricians and Gynecologists

Diagnose, treat, and help prevent diseases of women, especially those affecting the reproductive system and the process of childbirth.

Tasks

1) Monitor patients' condition and progress and re-evaluate treatments as necessary.

2) Prescribe or administer therapy, medication, and other specialized medical care to treat or prevent illness, disease, or injury.

3) Advise patients and community members concerning diet, activity, hygiene, and disease prevention.

4) Analyze records, reports, test results, or examination information to diagnose medical condition of patient.

5) Care for and treat women during prenatal, natal and post-natal periods.

6) Consult with, or provide consulting services to, other physicians.

7) Conduct research to develop or test medications, treatments, or procedures to prevent or control disease or injury.

8) Collect, record, and maintain patient information, such as medical histories, reports, and examination results.

9) Refer patient to medical specialist or other practitioner when necessary.

10) Plan, implement, or administer health programs in hospitals, businesses, or communities for prevention and treatment of injuries or illnesses.

11) Perform cesarean sections or other surgical procedures as needed to preserve patients' health and deliver babies safely

12) Explain procedures and discuss test results or prescribed treatments with patients.

13) Treat diseases of female organs.

14) Direct and coordinate activities of nurses, students, assistants, specialists, therapists, and other medical staff.

29-1065.00 - Pediatricians, General

Diagnose, treat, and help prevent children's diseases and injuries.

Tasks

1) Examine patients or order, perform and interpret diagnostic tests to obtain information on medical condition and determine diagnosis.

2) Explain procedures and discuss test results or prescribed treatments with patients and parents or guardians.

3) Monitor patients' condition and progress and re-evaluate treatments as necessary.

4) Prescribe or administer treatment, therapy, medication, vaccination, and other specialized medical care to treat or prevent illness, disease, or injury in infants and children.

5) Treat children who have minor illnesses, acute and chronic health problems, and growth and development concerns.

6) Conduct research to study anatomy and develop or test medications, treatments, or procedures to prevent, or control disease or injury.

7) Operate on patients to remove, repair, or improve functioning of diseased or injured body parts and systems.

8) Direct and coordinate activities of nurses, students, assistants, specialists, therapists, and other medical staff.

9) Plan and execute medical care programs to aid in the mental and physical growth and development of children and adolescents.

10) Advise patients, parents or guardians and community members concerning diet, activity, hygiene, and disease prevention.

11) Plan, implement, or administer health programs or standards in hospital, business, or community for information, prevention, or treatment of injury or illness.

12) Examine children regularly to assess their growth and development.

13) Prepare reports for government or management of birth, death, and disease statistics, workforce evaluations, or medical status of individuals.

14) Provide consulting services to other physicians.

15) Refer patient to medical specialist or other practitioner when necessary.

29-1066.00 - Psychiatrists

Diagnose, treat, and help prevent disorders of the mind.

Tasks

1) Prescribe, direct, and administer psychotherapeutic treatments or medications to treat mental, emotional, or behavioral disorders.

2) Advise and inform guardians, relatives, and significant others of patients' conditions and treatment.

3) Teach, conduct research, and publish findings to increase understanding of mental, emotional, and behavioral states and disorders.

4) Counsel outpatients and other patients during office visits.

5) Prepare and submit case reports and summaries to government and mental health agencies.

6) Analyze and evaluate patient data and test or examination findings to diagnose nature and extent of mental disorder.

7) Gather and maintain patient information and records, including social and medical history obtained from patients, relatives, and other professionals.

8) Review and evaluate treatment procedures and outcomes of other psychiatrists and medical professionals.

9) Serve on committees to promote and maintain community mental health services and delivery systems.

10) Collaborate with physicians, psychologists, social workers, psychiatric nurses, or other professionals to discuss treatment plans and progress.

11) Design individualized care plans, using a variety of treatments.

29-1067.00 - Surgeons

Treat diseases, injuries, and deformities by invasive methods, such as manual manipulation or by using instruments and appliances.

Tasks

1) Direct and coordinate activities of nurses, assistants, specialists, residents and other medical staff.

2) Examine instruments, equipment, and operating room to ensure sterility.

3) Conduct research to develop and test surgical techniques that can improve operating procedures and outcomes.

4) Follow established surgical techniques during the operation.

5) Operate on patients to correct deformities, repair injuries, prevent and treat diseases, or improve or restore patients' functions.

6) Prepare case histories.

7) Provide consultation and surgical assistance to other physicians and surgeons.

8) Diagnose bodily disorders and orthopedic conditions and provide treatments, such as medicines and surgeries, in clinics, hospital wards, and operating rooms.

9) Manage surgery services, including planning, scheduling and coordination, determination of procedures, and procurement of supplies and equipment.

10) Analyze patient's medical history, medication allergies, physical condition, and examination results to verify operation's necessity and to determine best procedure.

11) Refer patient to medical specialist or other practitioners when necessary.

12) Prescribe preoperative and postoperative treatments and procedures, such as sedatives, diets, antibiotics, and preparation and treatment of the patient's operative area.

29-1071.00 - Physician Assistants

Provide healthcare services typically performed by a physician, under the supervision of a physician. Conduct complete physicals, provide treatment, and counsel patients. May, in some cases, prescribe medication. Must graduate from an accredited educational program for physician assistants.

Tasks

1) Make tentative diagnoses and decisions about management and treatment of patients.

2) Order medical and laboratory supplies and equipment.

3) Instruct and counsel patients about prescribed therapeutic regimens, normal growth and development, family planning, emotional problems of daily living, and health maintenance.

4) Prescribe therapy or medication with physician approval.

5) Supervise and coordinate activities of technicians and technical assistants.

6) Visit and observe patients on hospital rounds or house calls, updating charts, ordering therapy, and reporting back to physician.

7) Provide physicians with assistance during surgery or complicated medical procedures.

8) Obtain, compile and record patient medical data, including health history, progress notes and results of physical examination.

9) Interpret diagnostic test results for deviations from normal.

10) Examine patients to obtain information about their physical condition.

11) Administer or order diagnostic tests, such as x-ray, electrocardiogram, and laboratory tests.

29-1081.00 - Podiatrists

Diagnose and treat diseases and deformities of the human foot.

Tasks

1) Make and fit prosthetic appliances.

2) Perform administrative duties such as hiring employees, ordering supplies, and keeping records.

3) Educate the public about the benefits of foot care through techniques such as speaking engagements, advertising, and other forums.

4) Treat deformities using mechanical methods, such as whirlpool or paraffin baths, and electrical methods, such as short wave and low voltage currents.

5) Treat conditions such as corns, calluses, ingrown nails, tumors, shortened tendons, bunions, cysts, and abscesses by surgical methods.

6) Treat bone, muscle, and joint disorders affecting the feet.

7) Prescribe medications, corrective devices, physical therapy, or surgery.

8) Diagnose diseases and deformities of the foot using medical histories, physical examinations, x-rays, and laboratory test results.

9) Correct deformities by means of plaster casts and strapping.

10) Refer patients to physicians when symptoms indicative of systemic disorders, such as arthritis or diabetes, are observed in feet and legs.

29-1111.00 - Registered Nurses

Assess patient health problems and needs, develop and implement nursing care plans, and maintain medical records. Administer nursing care to ill, injured, convalescent, or disabled patients. May advise patients on health maintenance and disease prevention or provide case management. Licensing or registration required. Includes advance practice nurses such as: nurse practitioners, clinical nurse specialists, certified nurse midwives, and certified registered nurse anesthetists. Advanced practice nursing is practiced by RNs who have specialized formal, post-basic education and who function in highly autonomous and specialized roles.

Tasks

1) Prescribe or recommend drugs, medical devices or other forms of treatment, such as physical therapy, inhalation therapy, or related therapeutic procedures.

2) Provide or arrange for training/instruction of auxiliary personnel or students.

3) Contract independently to render nursing care, usually to one patient, in hospital or private home.

4) Work with individuals, groups, and families to plan and implement programs designed to improve the overall health of communities.

5) Perform physical examinations, make tentative diagnoses, and treat patients en route to hospitals or at disaster site triage centers.

6) Refer students or patients to specialized health resources or community agencies furnishing assistance.

7) Inform physician of patient's condition during anesthesia.

8) Record patients' medical information and vital signs.

9) Direct and coordinate infection control programs, advising and consulting with specified personnel about necessary precautions.

10) Deliver infants and provide prenatal and postpartum care and treatment under obstetrician's supervision.

11) Direct and supervise less skilled nursing/health care personnel, or supervise a particular unit on one shift.

12) Administer local, inhalation, intravenous, and other anesthetics.

13) Conduct specified laboratory tests.

14) Perform administrative and managerial functions, such as taking responsibility for a unit's staff, budget, planning, and long-range goals.

15) Consult with institutions or associations regarding issues and concerns relevant to the practice and profession of nursing.

16) Hand items to surgeons during operations.

17) Assess the needs of individuals, families and/or communities, including assessment of individuals home and/or work environments to identify potential health or safety problems.

18) Provide health care, first aid, immunizations and assistance in convalescence and rehabilitation in locations such as schools, hospitals, and industry.

19) Prepare rooms, sterile instruments, equipment and supplies, and ensure that stock of supplies is maintained.

20) Prepare patients for, and assist with, examinations and treatments.

21) Consult and coordinate with health care team members to assess, plan, implement and evaluate patient care plans.

22) Monitor, record and report symptoms and changes in patients' conditions.

23) Monitor all aspects of patient care, including diet and physical activity.

24) Modify patient treatment plans as indicated by patients' responses and conditions.

25) Maintain accurate, detailed reports and records.

26) Observe nurses and visit patients to ensure that proper nursing care is provided.

27) Instruct individuals, families and other groups on topics such as health education, disease prevention and childbirth, and develop health improvement programs.

28) Order, interpret, and evaluate diagnostic tests to identify and assess patient's condition.

29-1121.00 - Audiologists

29-1122.00 - Occupational Therapists

Assess and treat persons with hearing and related disorders. May fit hearing aids and provide auditory training. May perform research related to hearing problems.

Tasks

1) Fit and tune cochlear implants, providing rehabilitation for adjustment to listening with implant amplification systems.

2) Work with multi-disciplinary teams to assess and rehabilitate recipients of implanted hearing devices.

3) Advise educators or other medical staff on speech or hearing topics.

4) Instruct clients, parents, teachers, or employers in how to avoid behavior patterns that lead to miscommunication.

5) Educate and supervise audiology students and health care personnel.

6) Administer hearing or speech/language evaluations, tests, or examinations to patients to collect information on type and degree of impairment, using specialized instruments and electronic equipment.

7) Monitor clients' progress and discharge them from treatment when goals have been attained.

8) Maintain client records at all stages, including initial evaluation and discharge.

9) Counsel and instruct clients in techniques to improve hearing or speech impairment, including sign language or lip-reading.

10) Examine and clean patients' ear canals.

11) Evaluate hearing and speech/language disorders to determine diagnoses and courses of treatment.

12) Participate in conferences or training to update or share knowledge of new hearing or speech disorder treatment methods or technologies.

13) Plan and conduct treatment programs for clients' hearing or speech problems, consulting with physicians, nurses, psychologists, and other health care personnel as necessary.

14) Recommend assistive devices according to clients' needs or nature of impairments.

15) Refer clients to additional medical or educational services if needed.

16) Fit and dispense assistive devices, such as hearing aids.

17) Develop and supervise hearing screening programs.

18) Conduct or direct research on hearing or speech topics and report findings to help in the development of procedures, technology, or treatments.

29-1122.00 - Occupational Therapists

Assess, plan, organize, and participate in rehabilitative programs that help restore vocational, homemaking, and daily living skills, as well as general independence, to disabled persons.

Tasks

1) Plan, organize, and conduct occupational therapy programs in hospital, institutional, or community settings to help rehabilitate those impaired because of illness, injury or psychological or developmental problems.

2) Provide training and supervision in therapy techniques and objectives for students and nurses and other medical staff.

3) Lay out materials such as puzzles, scissors and eating utensils for use in therapy, and clean and repair these tools after therapy sessions.

4) Develop and participate in health promotion programs, group activities, or discussions to promote client health, facilitate social adjustment, alleviate stress, and prevent physical or mental disability.

5) Plan and implement programs and social activities to help patients learn work and school skills and adjust to handicaps.

6) Help clients improve decision making, abstract reasoning, memory, sequencing, coordination and perceptual skills, using computer programs.

7) Advise on health risks in the workplace and on health-related transition to retirement.

8) Conduct research in occupational therapy.

9) Provide patients with assistance in locating and holding jobs.

10) Consult with rehabilitation team to select activity programs and coordinate occupational therapy with other therapeutic activities.

11) Recommend changes in patients' work or living environments, consistent with their needs and capabilities.

12) Complete and maintain necessary records.

13) Design and create, or requisition, special supplies and equipment, such as splints, braces and computer-aided adaptive equipment.

14) Test and evaluate patients' physical and mental abilities and analyze medical data to determine realistic rehabilitation goals for patients.

15) Evaluate patients' progress and prepare reports that detail progress.

Knowledge	Knowledge Definitions
Therapy and Counseling	Knowledge of principles, methods, and procedures for diagnosis, treatment, and rehabilitation of physical and mental dysfunctions, and for career counseling and guidance.
Psychology	Knowledge of human behavior and performance; individual differences in ability, personality, and interests; learning and motivation; psychological research methods; and the assessment and treatment of behavioral and affective disorders.
Customer and Personal Service	Knowledge of principles and processes for providing customer and personal services. This includes customer needs assessment, meeting quality standards for services, and evaluation of customer satisfaction.
English Language	Knowledge of the structure and content of the English language including the meaning and spelling of words, rules of composition, and grammar.
Education and Training	Knowledge of principles and methods for curriculum and training design, teaching and instruction for individuals and groups, and the measurement of training effects.
Medicine and Dentistry	Knowledge of the information and techniques needed to diagnose and treat human injuries, diseases, and deformities. This includes symptoms, treatment alternatives, drug properties and interactions, and preventive health-care measures.
Biology	Knowledge of plant and animal organisms, their tissues, cells, functions, interdependencies, and interactions with each other and the environment.
Sociology and Anthropology	Knowledge of group behavior and dynamics, societal trends and influences, human migrations, ethnicity, cultures and their history and origins.
Public Safety and Security	Knowledge of relevant equipment, policies, procedures, and strategies to promote effective local, state, or national security operations for the protection of people, data, property, and institutions.
Computers and Electronics	Knowledge of circuit boards, processors, chips, electronic equipment, and computer hardware and software, including applications and programming.
Administration and Management	Knowledge of business and management principles involved in strategic planning, resource allocation, human resources modeling, leadership technique, production methods, and coordination of people and resources.
Clerical	Knowledge of administrative and clerical procedures and systems such as word processing, managing files and records, stenography and transcription, designing forms, and other office procedures and terminology.
Sales and Marketing	Knowledge of principles and methods for showing, promoting, and selling products or services. This includes marketing strategy and tactics, product demonstration, sales techniques, and sales control systems.
Communications and Media	Knowledge of media production, communication, and dissemination techniques and methods. This includes alternative ways to inform and entertain via written, oral, and visual media.
Physics	Knowledge and prediction of physical principles, laws, their interrelationships, and applications to understanding fluid, material, and atmospheric dynamics, and mechanical, electrical, atomic and sub-atomic structures and processes.
Law and Government	Knowledge of laws, legal codes, court procedures, precedents, government regulations, executive orders, agency rules, and the democratic political process.
Personnel and Human Resources	Knowledge of principles and procedures for personnel recruitment, selection, training, compensation and benefits, labor relations and negotiation, and personnel information systems.
Telecommunications	Knowledge of transmission, broadcasting, switching, control, and operation of telecommunications systems.
Mathematics	Knowledge of arithmetic, algebra, geometry, calculus, statistics, and their applications.
Philosophy and Theology	Knowledge of different philosophical systems and religions. This includes their basic principles, values, ethics, ways of thinking, customs, practices, and their impact on human culture.
Engineering and Technology	Knowledge of the practical application of engineering science and technology. This includes applying principles, techniques, procedures, and equipment to the design and production of various goods and services.
Chemistry	Knowledge of the chemical composition, structure, and properties of substances and of the chemical processes and transformations that they undergo. This includes uses of chemicals and their interactions, danger signs, production techniques, and disposal methods.
Foreign Language	Knowledge of the structure and content of a foreign (non-English) language including the meaning and spelling of words, rules of composition and grammar, and pronunciation.

Design	Knowledge of design techniques, tools, and principles involved in production of precision technical plans, blueprints, drawings, and models.
Mechanical	Knowledge of machines and tools, including their designs, uses, repair, and maintenance.
Transportation	Knowledge of principles and methods for moving people or goods by air, rail, sea, or road, including the relative costs and benefits.
Production and Processing	Knowledge of raw materials, production processes, quality control, costs, and other techniques for maximizing the effective manufacture and distribution of goods.
Economics and Accounting	Knowledge of economic and accounting principles and practices, the financial markets, banking and the analysis and reporting of financial data.
Geography	Knowledge of principles and methods for describing the features of land, sea, and air masses, including their physical characteristics, locations, interrelationships, and distribution of plant, animal, and human life.
Building and Construction	Knowledge of materials, methods, and the tools involved in the construction or repair of houses, buildings, or other structures such as highways and roads.
History and Archeology	Knowledge of historical events and their causes, indicators, and effects on civilizations and cultures.
Fine Arts	Knowledge of the theory and techniques required to compose, produce, and perform works of music, dance, visual arts, drama, and sculpture.
Food Production	Knowledge of techniques and equipment for planting, growing, and harvesting food products (both plant and animal) for consumption, including storage/handling techniques.

Skills	Skills Definitions
Active Listening	Giving full attention to what other people are saying, taking time to understand the points being made, asking questions as appropriate, and not interrupting at inappropriate times.
Reading Comprehension	Understanding written sentences and paragraphs in work related documents.
Service Orientation	Actively looking for ways to help people.
Writing	Communicating effectively in writing as appropriate for the needs of the audience.
Speaking	Talking to others to convey information effectively.
Instructing	Teaching others how to do something.
Social Perceptiveness	Being aware of others' reactions and understanding why they react as they do.
Time Management	Managing one's own time and the time of others.
Critical Thinking	Using logic and reasoning to identify the strengths and weaknesses of alternative solutions, conclusions or approaches to problems.
Active Learning	Understanding the implications of new information for both current and future problem-solving and decision-making.
Coordination	Adjusting actions in relation to others' actions.
Learning Strategies	Selecting and using training/instructional methods and procedures appropriate for the situation when learning or teaching new things.
Monitoring	Monitoring/Assessing performance of yourself, other individuals, or organizations to make improvements or take corrective action.
Science	Using scientific rules and methods to solve problems.
Complex Problem Solving	Identifying complex problems and reviewing related information to develop and evaluate options and implement solutions.
Judgment and Decision Making	Considering the relative costs and benefits of potential actions to choose the most appropriate one.
Persuasion	Persuading others to change their minds or behavior.
Equipment Selection	Determining the kind of tools and equipment needed to do a job.
Technology Design	Generating or adapting equipment and technology to serve user needs.
Negotiation	Bringing others together and trying to reconcile differences.
Management of Personnel Resources	Motivating, developing, and directing people as they work, identifying the best people for the job.
Quality Control Analysis	Conducting tests and inspections of products, services, or processes to evaluate quality or performance.
Mathematics	Using mathematics to solve problems.
Troubleshooting	Determining causes of operating errors and deciding what to do about it.
Management of Material Resources	Obtaining and seeing to the appropriate use of equipment, facilities, and materials needed to do certain work.
Management of Financial Resources	Determining how money will be spent to get the work done, and accounting for these expenditures.
Operations Analysis	Analyzing needs and product requirements to create a design.
Systems Evaluation	Identifying measures or indicators of system performance and the actions needed to improve or correct performance, relative to the goals of the system.
Operation and Control	Controlling operations of equipment or systems.

Equipment Maintenance	Performing routine maintenance on equipment and determining when and what kind of maintenance is needed.
Repairing	Repairing machines or systems using the needed tools.
Systems Analysis	Determining how a system should work and how changes in conditions, operations, and the environment will affect outcomes.
Operation Monitoring	Watching gauges, dials, or other indicators to make sure a machine is working properly.
Installation	Installing equipment, machines, wiring, or programs to meet specifications.
Programming	Writing computer programs for various purposes.

Ability	Ability Definitions
Oral Comprehension	The ability to listen to and understand information and ideas presented through spoken words and sentences.
Oral Expression	The ability to communicate information and ideas in speaking so others will understand.
Written Expression	The ability to communicate information and ideas in writing so others will understand.
Problem Sensitivity	The ability to tell when something is wrong or is likely to go wrong. It does not involve solving the problem, only recognizing there is a problem.
Inductive Reasoning	The ability to combine pieces of information to form general rules or conclusions (includes finding a relationship among seemingly unrelated events).
Deductive Reasoning	The ability to apply general rules to specific problems to produce answers that make sense.
Information Ordering	The ability to arrange things or actions in a certain order or pattern according to a specific rule or set of rules (e.g., patterns of numbers, letters, words, pictures, mathematical operations).
Speech Recognition	The ability to identify and understand the speech of another person.
Speech Clarity	The ability to speak clearly so others can understand you.
Written Comprehension	The ability to read and understand information and ideas presented in writing.
Near Vision	The ability to see details at close range (within a few feet of the observer).
Category Flexibility	The ability to generate or use different sets of rules for combining or grouping things in different ways.
Time Sharing	The ability to shift back and forth between two or more activities or sources of information (such as speech, sounds, touch, or other sources).
Originality	The ability to come up with unusual or clever ideas about a given topic or situation, or to develop creative ways to solve a problem.
Selective Attention	The ability to concentrate on a task over a period of time without being distracted.
Finger Dexterity	The ability to make precisely coordinated movements of the fingers of one or both hands to grasp, manipulate, or assemble very small objects.
Fluency of Ideas	The ability to come up with a number of ideas about a topic (the number of ideas is important, not their quality, correctness, or creativity).
Flexibility of Closure	The ability to identify or detect a known pattern (a figure, object, word, or sound) that is hidden in other distracting material.
Speed of Closure	The ability to quickly make sense of, combine, and organize information into meaningful patterns.
Trunk Strength	The ability to use your abdominal and lower back muscles to support part of the body repeatedly or continuously over time without 'giving out' or fatiguing.
Far Vision	The ability to see details at a distance.
Multilimb Coordination	The ability to coordinate two or more limbs (for example, two arms, two legs, or one leg and one arm) while sitting, standing, or lying down. It does not involve performing the activities while the whole body is in motion.
Visualization	The ability to imagine how something will look after it is moved around or when its parts are moved or rearranged.
Manual Dexterity	The ability to quickly move your hand, your hand together with your arm, or your two hands to grasp, manipulate, or assemble objects.
Arm-Hand Steadiness	The ability to keep your hand and arm steady while moving your arm or while holding your arm and hand in one position.
Perceptual Speed	The ability to quickly and accurately compare similarities and differences among sets of letters, numbers, objects, pictures, or patterns. The things to be compared may be presented at the same time or one after the other. This ability also includes comparing a presented object with a remembered object.
Memorization	The ability to remember information such as words, numbers, pictures, and procedures.
Visual Color Discrimination	The ability to match or detect differences between colors, including shades of color and brightness.
Extent Flexibility	The ability to bend, stretch, twist, or reach with your body, arms, and/or legs.

Mathematical Reasoning	The ability to choose the right mathematical methods or formulas to solve a problem.
Stamina	The ability to exert yourself physically over long periods of time without getting winded or out of breath.
Static Strength	The ability to exert maximum muscle force to lift, push, pull, or carry objects.
Hearing Sensitivity	The ability to detect or tell the differences between sounds that vary in pitch and loudness.
Dynamic Strength	The ability to exert muscle force repeatedly or continuously over time. This involves muscular endurance and resistance to muscle fatigue.
Number Facility	The ability to add, subtract, multiply, or divide quickly and correctly.
Gross Body Coordination	The ability to coordinate the movement of your arms, legs, and torso together when the whole body is in motion.
Depth Perception	The ability to judge which of several objects is closer or farther away from you, or to judge the distance between you and an object.
Auditory Attention	The ability to focus on a single source of sound in the presence of other distracting sounds.
Control Precision	The ability to quickly and repeatedly adjust the controls of a machine or a vehicle to exact positions.
Gross Body Equilibrium	The ability to keep or regain your body balance or stay upright when in an unstable position.
Spatial Orientation	The ability to know your location in relation to the environment or to know where other objects are in relation to you.
Explosive Strength	The ability to use short bursts of muscle force to propel oneself (as in jumping or sprinting), or to throw an object.
Response Orientation	The ability to choose quickly between two or more movements in response to two or more different signals (lights, sounds, pictures). It includes the speed with which the correct response is started with the hand, foot, or other body part.
Peripheral Vision	The ability to see objects or movement of objects to one's side when the eyes are looking ahead.
Night Vision	The ability to see under low light conditions.
Rate Control	The ability to time your movements or the movement of a piece of equipment in anticipation of changes in the speed and/or direction of a moving object or scene.
Reaction Time	The ability to quickly respond (with the hand, finger, or foot) to a signal (sound, light, picture) when it appears.
Wrist-Finger Speed	The ability to make fast, simple, repeated movements of the fingers, hands, and wrists.
Speed of Limb Movement	The ability to quickly move the arms and legs.
Dynamic Flexibility	The ability to quickly and repeatedly bend, stretch, twist, or reach out with your body, arms, and/or legs.
Glare Sensitivity	The ability to see objects in the presence of glare or bright lighting.
Sound Localization	The ability to tell the direction from which a sound originated.

Work_Activity	**Work_Activity Definitions**
Getting Information	Observing, receiving, and otherwise obtaining information from all relevant sources.
Establishing and Maintaining Interpersonal Relatio	Developing constructive and cooperative working relationships with others, and maintaining them over time.
Documenting/Recording Information	Entering, transcribing, recording, storing, or maintaining information in written or electronic/magnetic form.
Assisting and Caring for Others	Providing personal assistance, medical attention, emotional support, or other personal care to others such as coworkers, customers, or patients.
Developing Objectives and Strategies	Establishing long-range objectives and specifying the strategies and actions to achieve them.
Performing General Physical Activities	Performing physical activities that require considerable use of your arms and legs and moving your whole body, such as climbing, lifting, balancing, walking, stooping, and handling of materials.
Training and Teaching Others	Identifying the educational needs of others, developing formal educational or training programs or classes, and teaching or instructing others.
Making Decisions and Solving Problems	Analyzing information and evaluating results to choose the best solution and solve problems.
Communicating with Supervisors, Peers, or Subordin	Providing information to supervisors, co-workers, and subordinates by telephone, in written form, e-mail, or in person.
Updating and Using Relevant Knowledge	Keeping up-to-date technically and applying new knowledge to your job.
Organizing, Planning, and Prioritizing Work	Developing specific goals and plans to prioritize, organize, and accomplish your work.
Developing and Building Teams	Encouraging and building mutual trust, respect, and cooperation among team members.
Monitor Processes, Materials, or Surroundings	Monitoring and reviewing information from materials, events, or the environment, to detect or assess problems.

Coaching and Developing Others	Identifying the developmental needs of others and coaching, mentoring, or otherwise helping others to improve their knowledge or skills.
Interpreting the Meaning of Information for Others	Translating or explaining what information means and how it can be used.
Identifying Objects, Actions, and Events	Identifying information by categorizing, estimating, recognizing differences or similarities, and detecting changes in circumstances or events.
Performing for or Working Directly with the Public	Performing for people or dealing directly with the public. This includes serving customers in restaurants and stores, and receiving clients or guests.
Handling and Moving Objects	Using hands and arms in handling, installing, positioning, and moving materials, and manipulating things.
Analyzing Data or Information	Identifying the underlying principles, reasons, or facts of information by breaking down information or data into separate parts.
Thinking Creatively	Developing, designing, or creating new applications, ideas, relationships, systems, or products, including artistic contributions.
Evaluating Information to Determine Compliance wit	Using relevant information and individual judgment to determine whether events or processes comply with laws, regulations, or standards.
Resolving Conflicts and Negotiating with Others	Handling complaints, settling disputes, and resolving grievances and conflicts, or otherwise negotiating with others.
Judging the Qualities of Things, Services, or Peop	Assessing the value, importance, or quality of things or people.
Coordinating the Work and Activities of Others	Getting members of a group to work together to accomplish tasks.
Inspecting Equipment, Structures, or Material	Inspecting equipment, structures, or materials to identify the cause of errors or other problems or defects.
Provide Consultation and Advice to Others	Providing guidance and expert advice to management or other groups on technical, systems-, or process-related topics.
Communicating with Persons Outside Organization	Communicating with people outside the organization, representing the organization to customers, the public, government, and other external sources. This information can be exchanged in person, in writing, or by telephone or e-mail.
Performing Administrative Activities	Performing day-to-day administrative tasks such as maintaining information files and processing paperwork.
Guiding, Directing, and Motivating Subordinates	Providing guidance and direction to subordinates, including setting performance standards and monitoring performance.
Estimating the Quantifiable Characteristics of Pro	Estimating sizes, distances, and quantities; or determining time, costs, resources, or materials needed to perform a work activity.
Scheduling Work and Activities	Scheduling events, programs, and activities, as well as the work of others.
Processing Information	Compiling, coding, categorizing, calculating, tabulating, auditing, or verifying information or data.
Interacting With Computers	Using computers and computer systems (including hardware and software) to program, write software, set up functions, enter data, or process information.
Staffing Organizational Units	Recruiting, interviewing, selecting, hiring, and promoting employees in an organization.
Controlling Machines and Processes	Using either control mechanisms or direct physical activity to operate machines or processes (not including computers or vehicles).
Monitoring and Controlling Resources	Monitoring and controlling resources and overseeing the spending of money.
Selling or Influencing Others	Convincing others to buy merchandise/goods or to otherwise change their minds or actions.
Operating Vehicles, Mechanized Devices, or Equipme	Running, maneuvering, navigating, or driving vehicles or mechanized equipment, such as forklifts, passenger vehicles, aircraft, or water craft.
Repairing and Maintaining Mechanical Equipment	Servicing, repairing, adjusting, and testing machines, devices, moving parts, and equipment that operate primarily on the basis of mechanical (not electronic) principles.
Drafting, Laying Out, and Specifying Technical Dev	Providing documentation, detailed instructions, drawings, or specifications to tell others about how devices, parts, equipment, or structures are to be fabricated, constructed, assembled, modified, maintained, or used.
Repairing and Maintaining Electronic Equipment	Servicing, repairing, calibrating, regulating, fine-tuning, or testing machines, devices, and equipment that operate primarily on the basis of electrical or electronic (not mechanical) principles.

Work_Content	**Work_Content Definitions**
Face-to-Face Discussions	How often do you have to have face-to-face discussions with individuals or teams in this job?
Contact With Others	How much does this job require the worker to be in contact with others (face-to-face, by telephone, or otherwise) in order to perform it?
Structured versus Unstructured Work	To what extent is this job structured for the worker, rather than allowing the worker to determine tasks, priorities, and goals?
Freedom to Make Decisions	How much decision making freedom, without supervision, does the job offer?

Physical Proximity	To what extent does this job require the worker to perform job tasks in close physical proximity to other people?
Frequency of Decision Making	How frequently is the worker required to make decisions that affect other people, the financial resources, and/or the image and reputation of the organization?
Work With Work Group or Team	How important is it to work with others in a group or team in this job?
Telephone	How often do you have telephone conversations in this job?
Indoors, Environmentally Controlled	How often does this job require working indoors in environmentally controlled conditions?
Letters and Memos	How often does the job require written letters and memos?
Exposed to Disease or Infections	How often does this job require exposure to disease/infections?
Time Pressure	How often does this job require the worker to meet strict deadlines?
Coordinate or Lead Others	How important is it to coordinate or lead others in accomplishing work activities in this job?
Impact of Decisions on Co-workers or Company Resul	How do the decisions an employee makes impact the results of co-workers, clients or the company?
Importance of Being Exact or Accurate	How important is being very exact or highly accurate in performing this job?
Deal With External Customers	How important is it to work with external customers or the public in this job?
Spend Time Standing	How much does this job require standing?
Deal With Unpleasant or Angry People	How frequently does the worker have to deal with unpleasant, angry, or discourteous individuals as part of the job requirements?
Responsible for Others' Health and Safety	How much responsibility is there for the health and safety of others in this job?
Wear Common Protective or Safety Equipment such as	How much does this job require wearing common protective or safety equipment such as safety shoes, glasses, gloves, hard hats or live jackets?
Level of Competition	To what extent does this job require the worker to compete or to be aware of competitive pressures?
Frequency of Conflict Situations	How often are there conflict situations the employee has to face in this job?
Spend Time Using Your Hands to Handle, Control, or	How much does this job require using your hands to handle, control, or feel objects, tools or controls?
Consequence of Error	How serious would the result usually be if the worker made a mistake that was not readily correctable?
Spend Time Sitting	How much does this job require sitting?
Responsibility for Outcomes and Results	How responsible is the worker for work outcomes and results of other workers?
Spend Time Walking and Running	How much does this job require walking and running?
Sounds, Noise Levels Are Distracting or Uncomforta	How often does this job require working exposed to sounds and noise levels that are distracting or uncomfortable?
In an Enclosed Vehicle or Equipment	How often does this job require working in a closed vehicle or equipment (e.g., car)?
Spend Time Bending or Twisting the Body	How much does this job require bending or twisting your body?
Electronic Mail	How often do you use electronic mail in this job?
Exposed to Contaminants	How often does this job require working exposed to contaminants (such as pollutants, gases, dust or odors)?
Cramped Work Space, Awkward Positions	How often does this job require working in cramped work spaces that requires getting into awkward positions?
Spend Time Kneeling, Crouching, Stooping, or Crawl	How much does this job require kneeling, crouching, stooping or crawling?
Deal With Physically Aggressive People	How frequently does this job require the worker to deal with physical aggression of violent individuals?
Spend Time Making Repetitive Motions	How much does this job require making repetitive motions?
Public Speaking	How often do you have to perform public speaking in this job?
Importance of Repeating Same Tasks	How important is repeating the same physical activities (e.g., key entry) or mental activities (e.g., checking entries in a ledger) over and over, without stopping, to performing this job?
Exposed to Minor Burns, Cuts, Bites, or Stings	How often does this job require exposure to minor burns, cuts, bites, or stings?
Degree of Automation	How automated is the job?
Spend Time Keeping or Regaining Balance	How much does this job require keeping or regaining your balance?
Indoors, Not Environmentally Controlled	How often does this job require working indoors in non-controlled environmental conditions (e.g., warehouse without heat)?
Wear Specialized Protective or Safety Equipment su	How much does this job require wearing specialized protective or safety equipment such as breathing apparatus, safety harness, full protection suits, or radiation protection?
Outdoors, Exposed to Weather	How often does this job require working outdoors, exposed to all weather conditions?
Extremely Bright or Inadequate Lighting	How often does this job require working in extremely bright or inadequate lighting conditions?
Very Hot or Cold Temperatures	How often does this job require working in very hot (above 90 F degrees) or very cold (below 32 F degrees) temperatures?

Exposed to Radiation	How often does this job require exposure to radiation?
Spend Time Climbing Ladders, Scaffolds, or Poles	How much does this job require climbing ladders, scaffolds, or poles?
Exposed to Hazardous Equipment	How often does this job require exposure to hazardous equipment?
Outdoors, Under Cover	How often does this job require working outdoors, under cover (e.g., structure with roof but no walls)?
Exposed to Hazardous Conditions	How often does this job require exposure to hazardous conditions?
Exposed to High Places	How often does this job require exposure to high places?
Exposed to Whole Body Vibration	How often does this job require exposure to whole body vibration (e.g., operate a jackhammer)?
In an Open Vehicle or Equipment	How often does this job require working in an open vehicle or equipment (e.g., tractor)?
Pace Determined by Speed of Equipment	How important is it to this job that the pace is determined by the speed of equipment or machinery? (This does not refer to keeping busy at all times on this job.)

Work_Styles	Work_Styles Definitions
Concern for Others	Job requires being sensitive to others' needs and feelings and being understanding and helpful on the job.
Adaptability/Flexibility	Job requires being open to change (positive or negative) and to considerable variety in the workplace.
Integrity	Job requires being honest and ethical.
Cooperation	Job requires being pleasant with others on the job and displaying a good-natured, cooperative attitude.
Dependability	Job requires being reliable, responsible, and dependable, and fulfilling obligations.
Self Control	Job requires maintaining composure, keeping emotions in check, controlling anger, and avoiding aggressive behavior, even in very difficult situations.
Stress Tolerance	Job requires accepting criticism and dealing calmly and effectively with high stress situations.
Social Orientation	Job requires preferring to work with others rather than alone, and being personally connected with others on the job.
Innovation	Job requires creativity and alternative thinking to develop new ideas for and answers to work-related problems.
Attention to Detail	Job requires being careful about detail and thorough in completing work tasks.
Initiative	Job requires a willingness to take on responsibilities and challenges.
Persistence	Job requires persistence in the face of obstacles.
Independence	Job requires developing one's own ways of doing things, guiding oneself with little or no supervision, and depending on oneself to get things done.
Analytical Thinking	Job requires analyzing information and using logic to address work-related issues and problems.
Achievement/Effort	Job requires establishing and maintaining personally challenging achievement goals and exerting effort toward mastering tasks.
Leadership	Job requires a willingness to lead, take charge, and offer opinions and direction.

Job Zone Component	Job Zone Component Definitions
Title	Job Zone Four: Considerable Preparation Needed
Overall Experience	A minimum of two to four years of work-related skill, knowledge, or experience is needed for these occupations. For example, an accountant must complete four years of college and work for several years in accounting to be considered qualified.
Job Training	Employees in these occupations usually need several years of work-related experience, on-the-job training, and/or vocational training.
Job Zone Examples	Many of these occupations involve coordinating, supervising, managing, or training others. Examples include accountants, chefs and head cooks, computer programmers, historians, pharmacists, and police detectives.
SVP Range	(7.0 to < 8.0)
Education	Most of these occupations require a four - year bachelor's degree, but some do not.

29-1123.00 - Physical Therapists

Assess, plan, organize, and participate in rehabilitative programs that improve mobility, relieve pain, increase strength, and decrease or prevent deformity of patients suffering from disease or injury.

Tasks

1) Refer clients to community resources and services.

2) Provide information to the patient about the proposed intervention, its material risks and

expected benefits and any reasonable alternatives.

3) Inform the patient when diagnosis reveals findings outside their scope and refer to an appropriate practitioner.

4) Teach physical therapy students as well as those in other health professions.

5) Direct and supervise supportive personnel, assessing their competence, delegating specific tasks to them and establishing channels of communication.

6) Evaluate, fit, and adjust prosthetic and orthotic devices and recommend modification to orthotist.

7) Obtain patients' informed consent to proposed interventions.

8) Direct group rehabilitation activities.

9) Conduct and support research and apply research findings to practice.

10) Participate in community and community agency activities and help to formulate public policy.

11) Construct, maintain and repair medical supportive devices.

12) Provide educational information about physical therapy and physical therapists, injury prevention, ergonomics and ways to promote health.

13) Plan, prepare and carry out individually designed programs of physical treatment to maintain, improve or restore physical functioning, alleviate pain and prevent physical dysfunction in patients.

14) Instruct patient and family in treatment procedures to be continued at home.

15) Confer with the patient, medical practitioners and appropriate others to plan, implement and assess the intervention program.

16) Discharge patient from physical therapy when goals or projected outcomes have been attained and provide for appropriate followup care or referrals.

17) Review physician's referral and patient's medical records to help determine diagnosis and physical therapy treatment required.

18) Evaluate effects of treatment at various stages and adjust treatments to achieve maximum benefit.

19) Administer manual exercises, massage and/or traction to help relieve pain, increase the patient's strength, and decrease or prevent deformity and crippling.

20) Identify and document goals, anticipated progress and plans for reevaluation.

21) Perform and document an initial exam, evaluating the data to identify problems and determine a diagnosis prior to intervention.

22) Record prognosis, treatment, response, and progress in patient's chart or enter information into computer.

23) Test and measure patient's strength, motor development and function, sensory perception, functional capacity, and respiratory and circulatory efficiency and record data.

Knowledge	Knowledge Definitions
Medicine and Dentistry	Knowledge of the information and techniques needed to diagnose and treat human injuries, diseases, and deformities. This includes symptoms, treatment alternatives, drug properties and interactions, and preventive health-care measures.
Therapy and Counseling	Knowledge of principles, methods, and procedures for diagnosis, treatment, and rehabilitation of physical and mental dysfunctions, and for career counseling and guidance.
Customer and Personal Service	Knowledge of principles and processes for providing customer and personal services. This includes customer needs assessment, meeting quality standards for services, and evaluation of customer satisfaction.
Education and Training	Knowledge of principles and methods for curriculum and training design, teaching and instruction for individuals and groups, and the measurement of training effects.
Biology	Knowledge of plant and animal organisms, their tissues, cells, functions, interdependencies, and interactions with each other and the environment.
Psychology	Knowledge of human behavior and performance; individual differences in ability, personality, and interests; learning and motivation; psychological research methods; and the assessment and treatment of behavioral and affective disorders.
English Language	Knowledge of the structure and content of the English language including the meaning and spelling of words, rules of composition, and grammar.
Sociology and Anthropology	Knowledge of group behavior and dynamics, societal trends and influences, human migrations, ethnicity, cultures and their history and origins.
Physics	Knowledge and prediction of physical principles, laws, their interrelationships, and applications to understanding fluid, material, and atmospheric dynamics, and mechanical, electrical, atomic and sub- atomic structures and processes.
Communications and Media	Knowledge of media production, communication, and dissemination techniques and methods. This includes alternative ways to inform and entertain via written, oral, and visual media.

Law and Government	Knowledge of laws, legal codes, court procedures, precedents, government regulations, executive orders, agency rules, and the democratic political process.
Administration and Management	Knowledge of business and management principles involved in strategic planning, resource allocation, human resources modeling, leadership technique, production methods, and coordination of people and resources.
Computers and Electronics	Knowledge of circuit boards, processors, chips, electronic equipment, and computer hardware and software, including applications and programming.
Public Safety and Security	Knowledge of relevant equipment, policies, procedures, and strategies to promote effective local, state, or national security operations for the protection of people, data, property, and institutions.
Chemistry	Knowledge of the chemical composition, structure, and properties of substances and of the chemical processes and transformations that they undergo. This includes uses of chemicals and their interactions, danger signs, production techniques, and disposal methods.
Mathematics	Knowledge of arithmetic, algebra, geometry, calculus, statistics, and their applications.
Personnel and Human Resources	Knowledge of principles and procedures for personnel recruitment, selection, training, compensation and benefits, labor relations and negotiation, and personnel information systems.
Telecommunications	Knowledge of transmission, broadcasting, switching, control, and operation of telecommunications systems.
Clerical	Knowledge of administrative and clerical procedures and systems such as word processing, managing files and records, stenography and transcription, designing forms, and other office procedures and terminology.
Foreign Language	Knowledge of the structure and content of a foreign (non-English) language including the meaning and spelling of words, rules of composition and grammar, and pronunciation.
Sales and Marketing	Knowledge of principles and methods for showing, promoting, and selling products or services. This includes marketing strategy and tactics, product demonstration, sales techniques, and sales control systems.
Mechanical	Knowledge of machines and tools, including their designs, uses, repair, and maintenance.
Philosophy and Theology	Knowledge of different philosophical systems and religions. This includes their basic principles, values, ethics, ways of thinking, customs, practices, and their impact on human culture.
Transportation	Knowledge of principles and methods for moving people or goods by air, rail, sea, or road, including the relative costs and benefits.
Economics and Accounting	Knowledge of economic and accounting principles and practices, the financial markets, banking and the analysis and reporting of financial data.
Engineering and Technology	Knowledge of the practical application of engineering science and technology. This includes applying principles, techniques, procedures, and equipment to the design and production of various goods and services.
Geography	Knowledge of principles and methods for describing the features of land, sea, and air masses, including their physical characteristics, locations, interrelationships, and distribution of plant, animal, and human life.
Production and Processing	Knowledge of raw materials, production processes, quality control, costs, and other techniques for maximizing the effective manufacture and distribution of goods.
Fine Arts	Knowledge of the theory and techniques required to compose, produce, and perform works of music, dance, visual arts, drama, and sculpture.
Design	Knowledge of design techniques, tools, and principles involved in production of precision technical plans, blueprints, drawings, and models.
History and Archeology	Knowledge of historical events and their causes, indicators, and effects on civilizations and cultures.
Building and Construction	Knowledge of materials, methods, and the tools involved in the construction or repair of houses, buildings, or other structures such as highways and roads.
Food Production	Knowledge of techniques and equipment for planting, growing, and harvesting food products (both plant and animal) for consumption, including storage/handling techniques.

Skills	Skills Definitions
Active Listening	Giving full attention to what other people are saying, taking time to understand the points being made, asking questions as appropriate, and not interrupting at inappropriate times.
Instructing	Teaching others how to do something.
Time Management	Managing one's own time and the time of others.
Speaking	Talking to others to convey information effectively.
Critical Thinking	Using logic and reasoning to identify the strengths and weaknesses of alternative solutions, conclusions or approaches to problems.

Learning Strategies	Selecting and using training/instructional methods and procedures appropriate for the situation when learning or teaching new things.
Science	Using scientific rules and methods to solve problems.
Active Learning	Understanding the implications of new information for both current and future problem-solving and decision-making.
Monitoring	Monitoring/Assessing performance of yourself, other individuals, or organizations to make improvements or take corrective action.
Reading Comprehension	Understanding written sentences and paragraphs in work related documents.
Service Orientation	Actively looking for ways to help people.
Writing	Communicating effectively in writing as appropriate for the needs of the audience.
Judgment and Decision Making	Considering the relative costs and benefits of potential actions to choose the most appropriate one.
Complex Problem Solving	Identifying complex problems and reviewing related information to develop and evaluate options and implement solutions.
Coordination	Adjusting actions in relation to others' actions.
Social Perceptiveness	Being aware of others' reactions and understanding why they react as they do.
Equipment Selection	Determining the kind of tools and equipment needed to do a job.
Persuasion	Persuading others to change their minds or behavior.
Management of Personnel Resources	Motivating, developing, and directing people as they work, identifying the best people for the job.
Negotiation	Bringing others together and trying to reconcile differences.
Quality Control Analysis	Conducting tests and inspections of products, services, or processes to evaluate quality or performance.
Troubleshooting	Determining causes of operating errors and deciding what to do about it.
Technology Design	Generating or adapting equipment and technology to serve user needs.
Operations Analysis	Analyzing needs and product requirements to create a design.
Operation and Control	Controlling operations of equipment or systems.
Mathematics	Using mathematics to solve problems.
Operation Monitoring	Watching gauges, dials, or other indicators to make sure a machine is working properly.
Management of Financial Resources	Determining how money will be spent to get the work done, and accounting for these expenditures.
Management of Material Resources	Obtaining and seeing to the appropriate use of equipment, facilities, and materials needed to do certain work.
Equipment Maintenance	Performing routine maintenance on equipment and determining when and what kind of maintenance is needed.
Systems Evaluation	Identifying measures or indicators of system performance and the actions needed to improve or correct performance, relative to the goals of the system.
Repairing	Repairing machines or systems using the needed tools.
Systems Analysis	Determining how a system should work and how changes in conditions, operations, and the environment will affect outcomes.
Installation	Installing equipment, machines, wiring, or programs to meet specifications.
Programming	Writing computer programs for various purposes.

Ability	Ability Definitions
Oral Expression	The ability to communicate information and ideas in speaking so others will understand.
Oral Comprehension	The ability to listen to and understand information and ideas presented through spoken words and sentences.
Inductive Reasoning	The ability to combine pieces of information to form general rules or conclusions (includes finding a relationship among seemingly unrelated events).
Problem Sensitivity	The ability to tell when something is wrong or is likely to go wrong. It does not involve solving the problem, only recognizing there is a problem.
Written Comprehension	The ability to read and understand information and ideas presented in writing.
Written Expression	The ability to communicate information and ideas in writing so others will understand.
Deductive Reasoning	The ability to apply general rules to specific problems to produce answers that make sense.
Information Ordering	The ability to arrange things or actions in a certain order or pattern according to a specific rule or set of rules (e.g., patterns of numbers, letters, words, pictures, mathematical operations).
Trunk Strength	The ability to use your abdominal and lower back muscles to support part of the body repeatedly or continuously over time without 'giving out' or fatiguing.
Speech Clarity	The ability to speak clearly so others can understand you.
Near Vision	The ability to see details at close range (within a few feet of the observer).
Finger Dexterity	The ability to make precisely coordinated movements of the fingers of one or both hands to grasp, manipulate, or assemble very small objects.

Speech Recognition	The ability to identify and understand the speech of another person.
Static Strength	The ability to exert maximum muscle force to lift, push, pull, or carry objects.
Category Flexibility	The ability to generate or use different sets of rules for combining or grouping things in different ways.
Manual Dexterity	The ability to quickly move your hand, your hand together with your arm, or your two hands to grasp, manipulate, or assemble objects.
Multilimb Coordination	The ability to coordinate two or more limbs (for example, two arms, two legs, or one leg and one arm) while sitting, standing, or lying down. It does not involve performing the activities while the whole body is in motion.
Selective Attention	The ability to concentrate on a task over a period of time without being distracted.
Arm-Hand Steadiness	The ability to keep your hand and arm steady while moving your arm or while holding your arm and hand in one position.
Speed of Closure	The ability to quickly make sense of, combine, and organize information into meaningful patterns.
Stamina	The ability to exert yourself physically over long periods of time without getting winded or out of breath.
Time Sharing	The ability to shift back and forth between two or more activities or sources of information (such as speech, sounds, touch, or other sources).
Dynamic Strength	The ability to exert muscle force repeatedly or continuously over time. This involves muscular endurance and resistance to muscle fatigue.
Extent Flexibility	The ability to bend, stretch, twist, or reach with your body, arms, and/or legs.
Flexibility of Closure	The ability to identify or detect a known pattern (a figure, object, word, or sound) that is hidden in other distracting material.
Perceptual Speed	The ability to quickly and accurately compare similarities and differences among sets of letters, numbers, objects, pictures, or patterns. The things to be compared may be presented at the same time or one after the other. This ability also includes comparing a presented object with a remembered object.
Fluency of Ideas	The ability to come up with a number of ideas about a topic (the number of ideas is important, not their quality, correctness, or creativity).
Originality	The ability to come up with unusual or clever ideas about a given topic or situation, or to develop creative ways to solve a problem.
Far Vision	The ability to see details at a distance.
Gross Body Coordination	The ability to coordinate the movement of your arms, legs, and torso together when the whole body is in motion.
Memorization	The ability to remember information such as words, numbers, pictures, and procedures.
Control Precision	The ability to quickly and repeatedly adjust the controls of a machine or a vehicle to exact positions.
Speed of Limb Movement	The ability to quickly move the arms and legs.
Depth Perception	The ability to judge which of several objects is closer or farther away from you, or to judge the distance between you and an object.
Gross Body Equilibrium	The ability to keep or regain your body balance or stay upright when in an unstable position.
Mathematical Reasoning	The ability to choose the right mathematical methods or formulas to solve a problem.
Visualization	The ability to imagine how something will look after it is moved around or when its parts are moved or rearranged.
Auditory Attention	The ability to focus on a single source of sound in the presence of other distracting sounds.
Hearing Sensitivity	The ability to detect or tell the differences between sounds that vary in pitch and loudness.
Visual Color Discrimination	The ability to match or detect differences between colors, including shades of color and brightness.
Number Facility	The ability to add, subtract, multiply, or divide quickly and correctly.
Wrist-Finger Speed	The ability to make fast, simple, repeated movements of the fingers, hands, and wrists.
Rate Control	The ability to time your movements or the movement of a piece of equipment in anticipation of changes in the speed and/or direction of a moving object or scene.
Dynamic Flexibility	The ability to quickly and repeatedly bend, stretch, twist, or reach out with your body, arms, and/or legs.
Response Orientation	The ability to choose quickly between two or more movements in response to two or more different signals (lights, sounds, pictures). It includes the speed with which the correct response is started with the hand, foot, or other body part.
Reaction Time	The ability to quickly respond (with the hand, finger, or foot) to a signal (sound, light, picture) when it appears.
Night Vision	The ability to see under low light conditions.
Peripheral Vision	The ability to see objects or movement of objects to one's side when the eyes are looking ahead.
Sound Localization	The ability to tell the direction from which a sound originated.

Glare Sensitivity	The ability to see objects in the presence of glare or bright lighting.
Explosive Strength	The ability to use short bursts of muscle force to propel oneself (as in jumping or sprinting), or to throw an object.
Spatial Orientation	The ability to know your location in relation to the environment or to know where other objects are in relation to you.

Work_Activity	Work_Activity Definitions
Assisting and Caring for Others	Providing personal assistance, medical attention, emotional support, or other personal care to others such as coworkers, customers, or patients.
Getting Information	Observing, receiving, and otherwise obtaining information from all relevant sources.
Establishing and Maintaining Interpersonal Relatio	Developing constructive and cooperative working relationships with others, and maintaining them over time.
Making Decisions and Solving Problems	Analyzing information and evaluating results to choose the best solution and solve problems.
Identifying Objects, Actions, and Events	Identifying information by categorizing, estimating, recognizing differences or similarities, and detecting changes in circumstances or events.
Communicating with Supervisors, Peers, or Subordin	Providing information to supervisors, co-workers, and subordinates by telephone, in written form, e-mail, or in person.
Updating and Using Relevant Knowledge	Keeping up-to-date technically and applying new knowledge to your job.
Analyzing Data or Information	Identifying the underlying principles, reasons, or facts of information by breaking down information or data into separate parts.
Organizing, Planning, and Prioritizing Work	Developing specific goals and plans to prioritize, organize, and accomplish your work.
Performing General Physical Activities	Performing physical activities that require considerable use of your arms and legs and moving your whole body, such as climbing, lifting, balancing, walking, stooping, and handling of materials.
Documenting/Recording Information	Entering, transcribing, recording, storing, or maintaining information in written or electronic/magnetic form.
Monitor Processes, Materials, or Surroundings	Monitoring and reviewing information from materials, events, or the environment, to detect or assess problems.
Handling and Moving Objects	Using hands and arms in handling, installing, positioning, and moving materials, and manipulating things.
Developing Objectives and Strategies	Establishing long-range objectives and specifying the strategies and actions to achieve them.
Judging the Qualities of Things, Services, or Peop	Assessing the value, importance, or quality of things or people.
Performing for or Working Directly with the Public	Performing for people or dealing directly with the public. This includes serving customers in restaurants and stores, and receiving clients or guests.
Developing and Building Teams	Encouraging and building mutual trust, respect, and cooperation among team members.
Evaluating Information to Determine Compliance wit	Using relevant information and individual judgment to determine whether events or processes comply with laws, regulations, or standards.
Interpreting the Meaning of Information for Others	Translating or explaining what information means and how it can be used.
Estimating the Quantifiable Characteristics of Pro	Estimating sizes, distances, and quantities; or determining time, costs, resources, or materials needed to perform a work activity.
Scheduling Work and Activities	Scheduling events, programs, and activities, as well as the work of others.
Coordinating the Work and Activities of Others	Getting members of a group to work together to accomplish tasks.
Guiding, Directing, and Motivating Subordinates	Providing guidance and direction to subordinates, including setting performance standards and monitoring performance.
Processing Information	Compiling, coding, categorizing, calculating, tabulating, auditing, or verifying information or data.
Resolving Conflicts and Negotiating with Others	Handling complaints, settling disputes, and resolving grievances and conflicts, or otherwise negotiating with others.
Thinking Creatively	Developing, designing, or creating new applications, ideas, relationships, systems, or products, including artistic contributions.
Provide Consultation and Advice to Others	Providing guidance and expert advice to management or other groups on technical, systems-, or process-related topics.
Training and Teaching Others	Identifying the educational needs of others, developing formal educational or training programs or classes, and teaching or instructing others.
Communicating with Persons Outside • Organization	Communicating with people outside the organization, representing the organization to customers, the public, government, and other external sources. This information can be exchanged in person, in writing, or by telephone or e-mail.
Performing Administrative Activities	Performing day-to-day administrative tasks such as maintaining information files and processing paperwork.
Inspecting Equipment, Structures, or Material	Inspecting equipment, structures, or materials to identify the cause of errors or other problems or defects.

Coaching and Developing Others	Identifying the developmental needs of others and coaching, mentoring, or otherwise helping others to improve their knowledge or skills.
Interacting With Computers	Using computers and computer systems (including hardware and software) to program, write software, set up functions, enter data, or process information.
Controlling Machines and Processes	Using either control mechanisms or direct physical activity to operate machines or processes (not including computers or vehicles).
Monitoring and Controlling Resources	Monitoring and controlling resources and overseeing the spending of money.
Selling or Influencing Others	Convincing others to buy merchandise/goods or to otherwise change their minds or actions.
Staffing Organizational Units	Recruiting, interviewing, selecting, hiring, and promoting employees in an organization.
Operating Vehicles, Mechanized Devices, or Equipme	Running, maneuvering, navigating, or driving vehicles or mechanized equipment, such as forklifts, passenger vehicles, aircraft, or water craft.
Drafting, Laying Out, and Specifying Technical Dev	Providing documentation, detailed instructions, drawings, or specifications to tell others about how devices, parts, equipment, or structures are to be fabricated, constructed, assembled, modified, maintained, or used.
Repairing and Maintaining Mechanical Equipment	Servicing, repairing, adjusting, and testing machines, devices, moving parts, and equipment that operate primarily on the basis of mechanical (not electronic) principles.
Repairing and Maintaining Electronic Equipment	Servicing, repairing, calibrating, regulating, fine-tuning, or testing machines, devices, and equipment that operate primarily on the basis of electrical or electronic (not mechanical) principles.

Work_Content	Work_Content Definitions
Indoors, Environmentally Controlled	How often does this job require working indoors in environmentally controlled conditions?
Contact With Others	How much does this job require the worker to be in contact with others (face-to-face, by telephone, or otherwise) in order to perform it?
Physical Proximity	To what extent does this job require the worker to perform job tasks in close physical proximity to other people?
Face-to-Face Discussions	How often do you have to have face-to-face discussions with individuals or teams in this job?
Telephone	How often do you have telephone conversations in this job?
Structured versus Unstructured Work	To what extent is this job structured for the worker, rather than allowing the worker to determine tasks, priorities, and goals?
Freedom to Make Decisions	How much decision making freedom, without supervision, does the job offer?
Frequency of Decision Making	How frequently is the worker required to make decisions that affect other people, the financial resources, and/or the image and reputation of the organization?
Work With Work Group or Team	How important is it to work with others in a group or team in this job?
Spend Time Standing	How much does this job require standing?
Exposed to Disease or Infections	How often does this job require exposure to disease/infections?
Impact of Decisions on Co-workers or Company Resul	How do the decisions an employee makes impact the results of co-workers, clients or the company?
Coordinate or Lead Others	How important is it to coordinate or lead others in accomplishing work activities in this job?
Importance of Being Exact or Accurate	How important is being very exact or highly accurate in performing this job?
Deal With External Customers	How important is it to work with external customers or the public in this job?
Letters and Memos	How often does the job require written letters and memos?
Responsible for Others' Health and Safety	How much responsibility is there for the health and safety of others in this job?
Level of Competition	To what extent does this job require the worker to compete or to be aware of competitive pressures?
Wear Common Protective or Safety Equipment such as	How much does this job require wearing common protective or safety equipment such as safety shoes, glasses, gloves, hard hats or live jackets?
Time Pressure	How often does this job require the worker to meet strict deadlines?
Consequence of Error	How serious would the result usually be if the worker made a mistake that was not readily correctable?
Spend Time Bending or Twisting the Body	How much does this job require bending or twisting your body?
Deal With Unpleasant or Angry People	How frequently does the worker have to deal with unpleasant, angry, or discourteous individuals as part of the job requirements?
Exposed to Contaminants	How often does this job require working exposed to contaminants (such as pollutants, gases, dust or odors)?
Spend Time Walking and Running	How much does this job require walking and running?
Cramped Work Space, Awkward Positions	How often does this job require working in cramped work spaces that requires getting into awkward positions?

Responsibility for Outcomes and Results	How responsible is the worker for work outcomes and results of other workers?
Frequency of Conflict Situations	How often are there conflict situations the employee has to face in this job?
Importance of Repeating Same Tasks	How important is repeating the same physical activities (e.g., key entry) or mental activities (e.g., checking entries in a ledger) over and over, without stopping, to performing this job?
Spend Time Using Your Hands to Handle, Control, or	How much does this job require using your hands to handle, control, or feel objects, tools or controls?
Spend Time Kneeling, Crouching, Stooping, or Crawl	How much does this job require kneeling, crouching, stooping or crawling?
Spend Time Keeping or Regaining Balance	How much does this job require keeping or regaining your balance?
Spend Time Making Repetitive Motions	How much does this job require making repetitive motions?
Sounds, Noise Levels Are Distracting or Uncomforta	How often does this job require working exposed to sounds and noise levels that are distracting or uncomfortable?
Wear Specialized Protective or Safety Equipment su	How much does this job require wearing specialized protective or safety equipment such as breathing apparatus, safety harness, full protection suits, or radiation protection?
In an Enclosed Vehicle or Equipment	How often does this job require working in a closed vehicle or equipment (e.g., car)?
Electronic Mail	How often do you use electronic mail in this job?
Spend Time Sitting	How much does this job require sitting?
Exposed to Minor Burns, Cuts, Bites, or Stings	How often does this job require exposure to minor burns, cuts, bites, or stings?
Public Speaking	How often do you have to perform public speaking in this job?
Indoors, Not Environmentally Controlled	How often does this job require working indoors in non-controlled environmental conditions (e.g., warehouse without heat)?
Extremely Bright or Inadequate Lighting	How often does this job require working in extremely bright or inadequate lighting conditions?
Deal With Physically Aggressive People	How frequently does this job require the worker to deal with physical aggression of violent individuals?
Degree of Automation	How automated is the job?
Exposed to Hazardous Conditions	How often does this job require exposure to hazardous conditions?
Very Hot or Cold Temperatures	How often does this job require working in very hot (above 90 F degrees) or very cold (below 32 F degrees) temperatures?
Exposed to Radiation	How often does this job require exposure to radiation?
Exposed to Hazardous Equipment	How often does this job require exposure to hazardous equipment?
Outdoors, Exposed to Weather	How often does this job require working outdoors, exposed to all weather conditions?
Outdoors, Under Cover	How often does this job require working outdoors, under cover (e.g., structure with roof but no walls)?
Pace Determined by Speed of Equipment	How important is it to this job that the pace is determined by the speed of equipment or machinery? (This does not refer to keeping busy at all times on this job.)
Exposed to Whole Body Vibration	How often does this job require exposure to whole body vibration (e.g., operate a jackhammer)?
In an Open Vehicle or Equipment	How often does this job require working in an open vehicle or equipment (e.g., tractor)?
Exposed to High Places	How often does this job require exposure to high places?
Spend Time Climbing Ladders, Scaffolds, or Poles	How much does this job require climbing ladders, scaffolds, or poles?

Work_Styles	Work_Styles Definitions
Concern for Others	Job requires being sensitive to others' needs and feelings and being understanding and helpful on the job.
Integrity	Job requires being honest and ethical.
Dependability	Job requires being reliable, responsible, and dependable, and fulfilling obligations.
Cooperation	Job requires being pleasant with others on the job and displaying a good-natured, cooperative attitude.
Self Control	Job requires maintaining composure, keeping emotions in check, controlling anger, and avoiding aggressive behavior, even in very difficult situations.
Independence	Job requires developing one's own ways of doing things, guiding oneself with little or no supervision, and depending on oneself to get things done.
Social Orientation	Job requires preferring to work with others rather than alone, and being personally connected with others on the job.
Adaptability/Flexibility	Job requires being open to change (positive or negative) and to considerable variety in the workplace.
Initiative	Job requires a willingness to take on responsibilities and challenges.
Leadership	Job requires a willingness to lead, take charge, and offer opinions and direction.
Attention to Detail	Job requires being careful about detail and thorough in completing work tasks.

Stress Tolerance	Job requires accepting criticism and dealing calmly and effectively with high stress situations.
Achievement/Effort	Job requires establishing and maintaining personally challenging achievement goals and exerting effort toward mastering tasks.
Analytical Thinking	Job requires analyzing information and using logic to address work-related issues and problems.
Persistence	Job requires persistence in the face of obstacles.
Innovation	Job requires creativity and alternative thinking to develop new ideas for and answers to work-related problems.

Job Zone Component	Job Zone Component Definitions
Title	Job Zone Five: Extensive Preparation Needed
Overall Experience	Extensive skill, knowledge, and experience are needed for these occupations. Many require more than five years of experience. For example, surgeons must complete four years of college and an additional five to seven years of specialized medical training to be able to do their job.
Job Training	Employees may need some on-the-job training, but most of these occupations assume that the person will already have the required skills, knowledge, work-related experience, and/or training.
Job Zone Examples	These occupations often involve coordinating, training, supervising, or managing the activities of others to accomplish goals. Very advanced communication and organizational skills are required. Examples include athletic trainers, lawyers, managing editors, physicists, social psychologists, and surgeons.
SVP Range	(8.0 and above)
Education	A bachelor's degree is the minimum formal education required for these occupations. However, many also require graduate school. For example, they may require a master's degree, and some require a Ph.D., M.D., or J.D. (law degree).

29-1124.00 - Radiation Therapists

Provide radiation therapy to patients as prescribed by a radiologist according to established practices and standards. Duties may include reviewing prescription and diagnosis; acting as liaison with physician and supportive care personnel; preparing equipment, such as immobilization, treatment, and protection devices; and maintaining records, reports, and files. May assist in dosimetry procedures and tumor localization.

Tasks

1) Observe and reassure patients during treatment and report unusual reactions to physician or turn equipment off if unexpected adverse reactions occur.

2) Maintain records, reports and files as required, including such information as radiation dosages, equipment settings and patients' reactions.

3) Help physicians, radiation oncologists and clinical physicists to prepare physical and technical aspects of radiation treatment plans, using information about patient condition and anatomy.

4) Enter data into computer and set controls to operate and adjust equipment and regulate dosage.

5) Check radiation therapy equipment to ensure proper operation.

6) Calculate actual treatment dosages delivered during each session.

7) Assist in the preparation of sealed radioactive materials, such as cobalt, radium, cesium and isotopes, for use in radiation treatments.

8) Follow principles of radiation protection for patient, self, and others.

9) Prepare and construct equipment, such as immobilization, treatment, and protection devices.

10) Conduct most treatment sessions independently, in accordance with the long-term treatment plan and under the general direction of the patient's physician.

11) Review prescription, diagnosis, patient chart, and identification.

12) Train and supervise student or subordinate radiotherapy technologists.

13) Act as liaison with physicist and supportive care personnel.

14) Check for side effects such as skin irritation, nausea and hair loss to assess patients' reaction to treatment.

15) Educate, prepare and reassure patients and their families by answering questions, providing physical assistance, and reinforcing physicians' advice regarding treatment reactions and post-treatment care.

16) Implement appropriate follow-up care plans.

17) Provide assistance to other health-care personnel during dosimetry procedures and tumor localization.

18) Photograph treated area of patient and process film.

19) Store, sterilize, or prepare the special applicators containing the radioactive substance

implanted by the physician.

20) Position patients for treatment with accuracy according to prescription.

29-1125.00 - Recreational Therapists

Plan, direct, or coordinate medically-approved recreation programs for patients in hospitals, nursing homes, or other institutions. Activities include sports, trips, dramatics, social activities, and arts and crafts. May assess a patient condition and recommend appropriate recreational activity.

Tasks

1) Instruct patient in activities and techniques, such as sports, dance, music, art or relaxation techniques, designed to meet their specific physical or psychological needs.

2) Develop treatment plan to meet needs of patient, based on needs assessment, patient interests and objectives of therapy.

3) Confer with members of treatment team to plan and evaluate therapy programs.

4) Prepare and submit reports and charts to treatment team to reflect patients' reactions and evidence of progress or regression.

5) Plan, organize, direct and participate in treatment programs and activities to facilitate patients' rehabilitation, help them integrate into the community and prevent further medical problems.

6) Conduct therapy sessions to improve patients' mental and physical well-being.

7) Obtain information from medical records, medical staff, family members and the patients themselves to assess patients' capabilities, needs and interests.

8) Observe, analyze, and record patients' participation, reactions, and progress during treatment sessions, modifying treatment programs as needed.

9) Counsel and encourage patients to develop leisure activities.

Knowledge	Knowledge Definitions
Psychology	Knowledge of human behavior and performance; individual differences in ability, personality, and interests; learning and motivation; psychological research methods; and the assessment and treatment of behavioral and affective disorders.
Therapy and Counseling	Knowledge of principles, methods, and procedures for diagnosis, treatment, and rehabilitation of physical and mental dysfunctions, and for career counseling and guidance.
Customer and Personal Service	Knowledge of principles and processes for providing customer and personal services. This includes customer needs assessment, meeting quality standards for services, and evaluation of customer satisfaction.
Sociology and Anthropology	Knowledge of group behavior and dynamics, societal trends and influences, human migrations, ethnicity, cultures and their history and origins.
Education and Training	Knowledge of principles and methods for curriculum and training design, teaching and instruction for individuals and groups, and the measurement of training effects.
English Language	Knowledge of the structure and content of the English language including the meaning and spelling of words, rules of composition, and grammar.
Fine Arts	Knowledge of the theory and techniques required to compose, produce, and perform works of music, dance, visual arts, drama, and sculpture.
Medicine and Dentistry	Knowledge of the information and techniques needed to diagnose and treat human injuries, diseases, and deformities. This includes symptoms, treatment alternatives, drug properties and interactions, and preventive health-care measures.
Administration and Management	Knowledge of business and management principles involved in strategic planning, resource allocation, human resources modeling, leadership technique, production methods, and coordination of people and resources.
Public Safety and Security	Knowledge of relevant equipment, policies, procedures, and strategies to promote effective local, state, or national security operations for the protection of people, data, property, and institutions.
Transportation	Knowledge of principles and methods for moving people or goods by air, rail, sea, or road, including the relative costs and benefits.
Law and Government	Knowledge of laws, legal codes, court procedures, precedents, government regulations, executive orders, agency rules, and the democratic political process.
Communications and Media	Knowledge of media production, communication, and dissemination techniques and methods. This includes alternative ways to inform and entertain via written, oral, and visual media.
Mathematics	Knowledge of arithmetic, algebra, geometry, calculus, statistics, and their applications.
Philosophy and Theology	Knowledge of different philosophical systems and religions. This includes their basic principles, values, ethics, ways of thinking, customs, practices, and their impact on human culture.
Clerical	Knowledge of administrative and clerical procedures and systems such as word processing, managing files and records, stenography and transcription, designing forms, and other office procedures and terminology.
Computers and Electronics	Knowledge of circuit boards, processors, chips, electronic equipment, and computer hardware and software, including applications and programming.
Personnel and Human Resources	Knowledge of principles and procedures for personnel recruitment, selection, training, compensation and benefits, labor relations and negotiation, and personnel information systems.
Biology	Knowledge of plant and animal organisms, their tissues, cells, functions, interdependencies, and interactions with each other and the environment.
Telecommunications	Knowledge of transmission, broadcasting, switching, control, and operation of telecommunications systems.
Food Production	Knowledge of techniques and equipment for planting, growing, and harvesting food products (both plant and animal) for consumption, including storage/handling techniques.
Geography	Knowledge of principles and methods for describing the features of land, sea, and air masses, including their physical characteristics, locations, interrelationships, and distribution of plant, animal, and human life.
History and Archeology	Knowledge of historical events and their causes, indicators, and effects on civilizations and cultures.
Economics and Accounting	Knowledge of economic and accounting principles and practices, the financial markets, banking and the analysis and reporting of financial data.
Sales and Marketing	Knowledge of principles and methods for showing, promoting, and selling products or services. This includes marketing strategy and tactics, product demonstration, sales techniques, and sales control systems.
Physics	Knowledge and prediction of physical principles, laws, their interrelationships, and applications to understanding fluid, material, and atmospheric dynamics, and mechanical, electrical, atomic and sub- atomic structures and processes.
Production and Processing	Knowledge of raw materials, production processes, quality control, costs, and other techniques for maximizing the effective manufacture and distribution of goods.
Foreign Language	Knowledge of the structure and content of a foreign (non-English) language including the meaning and spelling of words, rules of composition and grammar, and pronunciation.
Mechanical	Knowledge of machines and tools, including their designs, uses, repair, and maintenance.
Design	Knowledge of design techniques, tools, and principles involved in production of precision technical plans, blueprints, drawings, and models.
Chemistry	Knowledge of the chemical composition, structure, and properties of substances and of the chemical processes and transformations that they undergo. This includes uses of chemicals and their interactions, danger signs, production techniques, and disposal methods.
Building and Construction	Knowledge of materials, methods, and the tools involved in the construction or repair of houses, buildings, or other structures such as highways and roads.
Engineering and Technology	Knowledge of the practical application of engineering science and technology. This includes applying principles, techniques, procedures, and equipment to the design and production of various goods and services.

Skills	Skills Definitions
Social Perceptiveness	Being aware of others' reactions and understanding why they react as they do.
Active Listening	Giving full attention to what other people are saying, taking time to understand the points being made, asking questions as appropriate, and not interrupting at inappropriate times.
Writing	Communicating effectively in writing as appropriate for the needs of the audience.
Speaking	Talking to others to convey information effectively.
Reading Comprehension	Understanding written sentences and paragraphs in work related documents.
Monitoring	Monitoring/Assessing performance of yourself, other individuals, or organizations to make improvements or take corrective action.
Service Orientation	Actively looking for ways to help people.
Coordination	Adjusting actions in relation to others' actions.
Time Management	Managing one's own time and the time of others.
Learning Strategies	Selecting and using training/instructional methods and procedures appropriate for the situation when learning or teaching new things.
Persuasion	Persuading others to change their minds or behavior.
Instructing	Teaching others how to do something.

160

Critical Thinking	Using logic and reasoning to identify the strengths and weaknesses of alternative solutions, conclusions or approaches to problems.
Active Learning	Understanding the implications of new information for both current and future problem-solving and decision-making.
Judgment and Decision Making	Considering the relative costs and benefits of potential actions to choose the most appropriate one.
Negotiation	Bringing others together and trying to reconcile differences.
Complex Problem Solving	Identifying complex problems and reviewing related information to develop and evaluate options and implement solutions.
Management of Personnel Resources	Motivating, developing, and directing people as they work, identifying the best people for the job.
Management of Financial Resources	Determining how money will be spent to get the work done, and accounting for these expenditures.
Systems Evaluation	Identifying measures or indicators of system performance and the actions needed to improve or correct performance, relative to the goals of the system.
Equipment Selection	Determining the kind of tools and equipment needed to do a job.
Operations Analysis	Analyzing needs and product requirements to create a design.
Management of Material Resources	Obtaining and seeing to the appropriate use of equipment, facilities, and materials needed to do certain work.
Quality Control Analysis	Conducting tests and inspections of products, services, or processes to evaluate quality or performance.
Technology Design	Generating or adapting equipment and technology to serve user needs.
Mathematics	Using mathematics to solve problems.
Systems Analysis	Determining how a system should work and how changes in conditions, operations, and the environment will affect outcomes.
Troubleshooting	Determining causes of operating errors and deciding what to do about it.
Operation and Control	Controlling operations of equipment or systems.
Science	Using scientific rules and methods to solve problems.
Repairing	Repairing machines or systems using the needed tools.
Equipment Maintenance	Performing routine maintenance on equipment and determining when and what kind of maintenance is needed.
Operation Monitoring	Watching gauges, dials, or other indicators to make sure a machine is working properly.
Programming	Writing computer programs for various purposes.
Installation	Installing equipment, machines, wiring, or programs to meet specifications.

Ability	Ability Definitions
Oral Expression	The ability to communicate information and ideas in speaking so others will understand.
Oral Comprehension	The ability to listen to and understand information and ideas presented through spoken words and sentences.
Inductive Reasoning	The ability to combine pieces of information to form general rules or conclusions (includes finding a relationship among seemingly unrelated events).
Speech Clarity	The ability to speak clearly so others can understand you.
Problem Sensitivity	The ability to tell when something is wrong or is likely to go wrong. It does not involve solving the problem, only recognizing there is a problem.
Near Vision	The ability to see details at close range (within a few feet of the observer).
Written Expression	The ability to communicate information and ideas in writing so others will understand.
Originality	The ability to come up with unusual or clever ideas about a given topic or situation, or to develop creative ways to solve a problem.
Deductive Reasoning	The ability to apply general rules to specific problems to produce answers that make sense.
Speech Recognition	The ability to identify and understand the speech of another person.
Written Comprehension	The ability to read and understand information and ideas presented in writing.
Fluency of Ideas	The ability to come up with a number of ideas about a topic (the number of ideas is important, not their quality, correctness, or creativity).
Information Ordering	The ability to arrange things or actions in a certain order or pattern according to a specific rule or set of rules (e.g., patterns of numbers, letters, words, pictures, mathematical operations).
Selective Attention	The ability to concentrate on a task over a period of time without being distracted.
Gross Body Coordination	The ability to coordinate the movement of your arms, legs, and torso together when the whole body is in motion.
Time Sharing	The ability to shift back and forth between two or more activities or sources of information (such as speech, sounds, touch, or other sources).
Static Strength	The ability to exert maximum muscle force to lift, push, pull, or carry objects.

Stamina	The ability to exert yourself physically over long periods of time without getting winded or out of breath.
Flexibility of Closure	The ability to identify or detect a known pattern (a figure, object, word, or sound) that is hidden in other distracting material.
Multilimb Coordination	The ability to coordinate two or more limbs (for example, two arms, two legs, or one leg and one arm) while sitting, standing, or lying down. It does not involve performing the activities while the whole body is in motion.
Far Vision	The ability to see details at a distance.
Trunk Strength	The ability to use your abdominal and lower back muscles to support part of the body repeatedly or continuously over time without 'giving out' or fatiguing.
Category Flexibility	The ability to generate or use different sets of rules for combining or grouping things in different ways.
Finger Dexterity	The ability to make precisely coordinated movements of the fingers of one or both hands to grasp, manipulate, or assemble very small objects.
Manual Dexterity	The ability to quickly move your hand, your hand together with your arm, or your two hands to grasp, manipulate, or assemble objects.
Visualization	The ability to imagine how something will look after it is moved around or when its parts are moved or rearranged.
Reaction Time	The ability to quickly respond (with the hand, finger, or foot) to a signal (sound, light, picture) when it appears.
Gross Body Equilibrium	The ability to keep or regain your body balance or stay upright when in an unstable position.
Memorization	The ability to remember information such as words, numbers, pictures, and procedures.
Auditory Attention	The ability to focus on a single source of sound in the presence of other distracting sounds.
Dynamic Strength	The ability to exert muscle force repeatedly or continuously over time. This involves muscular endurance and resistance to muscle fatigue.
Arm-Hand Steadiness	The ability to keep your hand and arm steady while moving your arm or while holding your arm and hand in one position.
Speed of Closure	The ability to quickly make sense of, combine, and organize information into meaningful patterns.
Depth Perception	The ability to judge which of several objects is closer or farther away from you, or to judge the distance between you and an object.
Perceptual Speed	The ability to quickly and accurately compare similarities and differences among sets of letters, numbers, objects, pictures, or patterns. The things to be compared may be presented at the same time or one after the other. This ability also includes comparing a presented object with a remembered object.
Speed of Limb Movement	The ability to quickly move the arms and legs.
Response Orientation	The ability to choose quickly between two or more movements in response to two or more different signals (lights, sounds, pictures). It includes the speed with which the correct response is started with the hand, foot, or other body part.
Extent Flexibility	The ability to bend, stretch, twist, or reach with your body, arms, and/or legs.
Explosive Strength	The ability to use short bursts of muscle force to propel oneself (as in jumping or sprinting), or to throw an object.
Hearing Sensitivity	The ability to detect or tell the differences between sounds that vary in pitch and loudness.
Control Precision	The ability to quickly and repeatedly adjust the controls of a machine or a vehicle to exact positions.
Number Facility	The ability to add, subtract, multiply, or divide quickly and correctly.
Visual Color Discrimination	The ability to match or detect differences between colors, including shades of color and brightness.
Mathematical Reasoning	The ability to choose the right mathematical methods or formulas to solve a problem.
Rate Control	The ability to time your movements or the movement of a piece of equipment in anticipation of changes in the speed and/or direction of a moving object or scene.
Glare Sensitivity	The ability to see objects in the presence of glare or bright lighting.
Wrist-Finger Speed	The ability to make fast, simple, repeated movements of the fingers, hands, and wrists.
Peripheral Vision	The ability to see objects or movement of objects to one's side when the eyes are looking ahead.
Dynamic Flexibility	The ability to quickly and repeatedly bend, stretch, twist, or reach out with your body, arms, and/or legs.
Sound Localization	The ability to tell the direction from which a sound originated.
Night Vision	The ability to see under low light conditions.
Spatial Orientation	The ability to know your location in relation to the environment or to know where other objects are in relation to you.

Work_Activity	Work_Activity Definitions
Assisting and Caring for Others	Providing personal assistance, medical attention, emotional support, or other personal care to others such as coworkers, customers, or patients.

Scheduling Work and Activities	Scheduling events, programs, and activities, as well as the work of others.
Getting Information	Observing, receiving, and otherwise obtaining information from all relevant sources.
Thinking Creatively	Developing, designing, or creating new applications, ideas, relationships, systems, or products, including artistic contributions.
Monitor Processes, Materials, or Surroundings	Monitoring and reviewing information from materials, events, or the environment, to detect or assess problems.
Organizing, Planning, and Prioritizing Work	Developing specific goals and plans to prioritize, organize, and accomplish your work.
Identifying Objects, Actions, and Events	Identifying information by categorizing, estimating, recognizing differences or similarities, and detecting changes in circumstances or events.
Communicating with Supervisors, Peers, or Subordin	Providing information to supervisors, co-workers, and subordinates by telephone, in written form, e-mail, or in person.
Making Decisions and Solving Problems	Analyzing information and evaluating results to choose the best solution and solve problems.
Documenting/Recording Information	Entering, transcribing, recording, storing, or maintaining information in written or electronic/magnetic form.
Performing General Physical Activities	Performing physical activities that require considerable use of your arms and legs and moving your whole body, such as climbing, lifting, balancing, walking, stooping, and handling of materials.
Establishing and Maintaining Interpersonal Relatio	Developing constructive and cooperative working relationships with others, and maintaining them over time.
Evaluating Information to Determine Compliance wit	Using relevant information and individual judgment to determine whether events or processes comply with laws, regulations, or standards.
Updating and Using Relevant Knowledge	Keeping up-to-date technically and applying new knowledge to your job.
Inspecting Equipment, Structures, or Material	Inspecting equipment, structures, or materials to identify the cause of errors or other problems or defects.
Coordinating the Work and Activities of Others	Getting members of a group to work together to accomplish tasks.
Judging the Qualities of Things, Services, or Peop	Assessing the value, importance, or quality of things or people.
Communicating with Persons Outside Organization	Communicating with people outside the organization, representing the organization to customers, the public, government, and other external sources. This information can be exchanged in person, in writing, or by telephone or e-mail.
Monitoring and Controlling Resources	Monitoring and controlling resources and overseeing the spending of money.
Interacting With Computers	Using computers and computer systems (including hardware and software) to program, write software, set up functions, enter data, or process information.
Processing Information	Compiling, coding, categorizing, calculating, tabulating, auditing, or verifying information or data.
Performing Administrative Activities	Performing day-to-day administrative tasks such as maintaining information files and processing paperwork.
Developing and Building Teams	Encouraging and building mutual trust, respect, and cooperation among team members.
Resolving Conflicts and Negotiating with Others	Handling complaints, settling disputes, and resolving grievances and conflicts, or otherwise negotiating with others.
Training and Teaching Others	Identifying the educational needs of others, developing formal educational or training programs or classes, and teaching or instructing others.
Estimating the Quantifiable Characteristics of Pro	Estimating sizes, distances, and quantities; or determining time, costs, resources, or materials needed to perform a work activity.
Analyzing Data or Information	Identifying the underlying principles, reasons, or facts of information by breaking down information or data into separate parts.
Developing Objectives and Strategies	Establishing long-range objectives and specifying the strategies and actions to achieve them.
Coaching and Developing Others	Identifying the developmental needs of others and coaching, mentoring, or otherwise helping others to improve their knowledge or skills.
Handling and Moving Objects	Using hands and arms in handling, installing, positioning, and moving materials, and manipulating things.
Guiding, Directing, and Motivating Subordinates	Providing guidance and direction to subordinates, including setting performance standards and monitoring performance.
Interpreting the Meaning of Information for Others	Translating or explaining what information means and how it can be used.
Provide Consultation and Advice to Others	Providing guidance and expert advice to management or other groups on technical, systems-, or process-related topics.
Operating Vehicles, Mechanized Devices, or Equipme	Running, maneuvering, navigating, or driving vehicles or mechanized equipment, such as forklifts, passenger vehicles, aircraft, or water craft.
Performing for or Working Directly with the Public	Performing for people or dealing directly with the public. This includes serving customers in restaurants and stores, and receiving clients or guests.

Selling or Influencing Others	Convincing others to buy merchandise/goods or to otherwise change their minds or actions.
Staffing Organizational Units	Recruiting, interviewing, selecting, hiring, and promoting employees in an organization.
Controlling Machines and Processes	Using either control mechanisms or direct physical activity to operate machines or processes (not including computers or vehicles).
Drafting, Laying Out, and Specifying Technical Dev	Providing documentation, detailed instructions, drawings, or specifications to tell others about how devices, parts, equipment, or structures are to be fabricated, constructed, assembled, modified, maintained, or used.
Repairing and Maintaining Electronic Equipment	Servicing, repairing, calibrating, regulating, fine-tuning, or testing machines, devices, and equipment that operate primarily on the basis of electrical or electronic (not mechanical) principles.
Repairing and Maintaining Mechanical Equipment	Servicing, repairing, adjusting, and testing machines, devices, moving parts, and equipment that operate primarily on the basis of mechanical (not electronic) principles.

Work_Content	Work_Content Definitions
Face-to-Face Discussions	How often do you have to have face-to-face discussions with individuals or teams in this job?
Work With Work Group or Team	How important is it to work with others in a group or team in this job?
Contact With Others	How much does this job require the worker to be in contact with others (face-to-face, by telephone, or otherwise) in order to perform it?
Physical Proximity	To what extent does this job require the worker to perform job tasks in close physical proximity to other people?
Deal With Physically Aggressive People	How frequently does this job require the worker to deal with physical aggression of violent individuals?
Structured versus Unstructured Work	To what extent is this job structured for the worker, rather than allowing the worker to determine tasks, priorities, and goals?
Freedom to Make Decisions	How much decision making freedom, without supervision, does the job offer?
Telephone	How often do you have telephone conversations in this job?
Exposed to Disease or Infections	How often does this job require exposure to disease/infections?
Time Pressure	How often does this job require the worker to meet strict deadlines?
Coordinate or Lead Others	How important is it to coordinate or lead others in accomplishing work activities in this job?
Frequency of Decision Making	How frequently is the worker required to make decisions that affect other people, the financial resources, and/or the image and reputation of the organization?
Electronic Mail	How often do you use electronic mail in this job?
Responsible for Others' Health and Safety	How much responsibility is there for the health and safety of others in this job?
Deal With Unpleasant or Angry People	How frequently does the worker have to deal with unpleasant, angry, or discourteous individuals as part of the job requirements?
Impact of Decisions on Co-workers or Company Resul	How do the decisions an employee makes impact the results of co-workers, clients or the company?
Importance of Being Exact or Accurate	How important is being very exact or highly accurate in performing this job?
Frequency of Conflict Situations	How often are there conflict situations the employee has to face in this job?
Deal With External Customers	How important is it to work with external customers or the public in this job?
Spend Time Standing	How much does this job require standing?
Indoors, Environmentally Controlled	How often does this job require working indoors in environmentally controlled conditions?
Letters and Memos	How often does the job require written letters and memos?
Consequence of Error	How serious would the result usually be if the worker made a mistake that was not readily correctable?
Importance of Repeating Same Tasks	How important is repeating the same physical activities (e.g., key entry) or mental activities (e.g., checking entries in a ledger) over and over, without stopping, to performing this job?
Sounds, Noise Levels Are Distracting or Uncomforta	How often does this job require working exposed to sounds and noise levels that are distracting or uncomfortable?
Exposed to Contaminants	How often does this job require working exposed to contaminants (such as pollutants, gases, dust or odors)?
In an Enclosed Vehicle or Equipment	How often does this job require working in a closed vehicle or equipment (e.g., car)?
Public Speaking	How often do you have to perform public speaking in this job?
Outdoors, Exposed to Weather	How often does this job require working outdoors, exposed to all weather conditions?
Spend Time Walking and Running	How much does this job require walking and running?
Exposed to Minor Burns, Cuts, Bites, or Stings	How often does this job require exposure to minor burns, cuts, bites, or stings?
Responsibility for Outcomes and Results	How responsible is the worker for work outcomes and results of other workers?

162

Level of Competition	To what extent does this job require the worker to compete or to be aware of competitive pressures?
Degree of Automation	How automated is the job?
Spend Time Bending or Twisting the Body	How much does this job require bending or twisting your body?
Spend Time Making Repetitive Motions	How much does this job require making repetitive motions?
Wear Common Protective or Safety Equipment such as	How much does this job require wearing common protective or safety equipment such as safety shoes, glasses, gloves, hard hats or live jackets?
Spend Time Sitting	How much does this job require sitting?
Spend Time Using Your Hands to Handle, Control, or	How much does this job require using your hands to handle, control, or feel objects, tools or controls?
Extremely Bright or Inadequate Lighting	How often does this job require working in extremely bright or inadequate lighting conditions?
Very Hot or Cold Temperatures	How often does this job require working in very hot (above 90 F degrees) or very cold (below 32 F degrees) temperatures?
Cramped Work Space, Awkward Positions	How often does this job require working in cramped work spaces that requires getting into awkward positions?
Exposed to Hazardous Conditions	How often does this job require exposure to hazardous conditions?
Indoors, Not Environmentally Controlled	How often does this job require working indoors in non-controlled environmental conditions (e.g., warehouse without heat)?
Spend Time Kneeling, Crouching, Stooping, or Crawl	How much does this job require kneeling, crouching, stooping or crawling?
Spend Time Keeping or Regaining Balance	How much does this job require keeping or regaining your balance?
Outdoors, Under Cover	How often does this job require working outdoors, under cover (e.g., structure with roof but no walls)?
In an Open Vehicle or Equipment	How often does this job require working in an open vehicle or equipment (e.g., tractor)?
Spend Time Climbing Ladders, Scaffolds, or Poles	How much does this job require climbing ladders, scaffolds, or poles?
Exposed to Radiation	How often does this job require exposure to radiation?
Wear Specialized Protective or Safety Equipment su	How much does this job require wearing specialized protective or safety equipment such as breathing apparatus, safety harness, full protection suits, or radiation protection?
Exposed to High Places	How often does this job require exposure to high places?
Exposed to Hazardous Equipment	How often does this job require exposure to hazardous equipment?
Pace Determined by Speed of Equipment	How important is it to this job that the pace is determined by the speed of equipment or machinery? (This does not refer to keeping busy at all times on this job.)
Exposed to Whole Body Vibration	How often does this job require exposure to whole body vibration (e.g., operate a jackhammer)?

Work_Styles	Work_Styles Definitions
Concern for Others	Job requires being sensitive to others' needs and feelings and being understanding and helpful on the job.
Self Control	Job requires maintaining composure, keeping emotions in check, controlling anger, and avoiding aggressive behavior, even in very difficult situations.
Cooperation	Job requires being pleasant with others on the job and displaying a good-natured, cooperative attitude.
Integrity	Job requires being honest and ethical.
Adaptability/Flexibility	Job requires being open to change (positive or negative) and to considerable variety in the workplace.
Dependability	Job requires being reliable, responsible, and dependable, and fulfilling obligations.
Social Orientation	Job requires preferring to work with others rather than alone, and being personally connected with others on the job.
Innovation	Job requires creativity and alternative thinking to develop new ideas for and answers to work-related problems.
Stress Tolerance	Job requires accepting criticism and dealing calmly and effectively with high stress situations.
Leadership	Job requires a willingness to lead, take charge, and offer opinions and direction.
Attention to Detail	Job requires being careful about detail and thorough in completing work tasks.
Initiative	Job requires a willingness to take on responsibilities and challenges.
Independence	Job requires developing one's own ways of doing things, guiding oneself with little or no supervision, and depending on oneself to get things done.
Achievement/Effort	Job requires establishing and maintaining personally challenging achievement goals and exerting effort toward mastering tasks.
Persistence	Job requires persistence in the face of obstacles.
Analytical Thinking	Job requires analyzing information and using logic to address work-related issues and problems.

Job Zone Component	Job Zone Component Definitions
Title	Job Zone Four: Considerable Preparation Needed
Overall Experience	A minimum of two to four years of work-related skill, knowledge, or experience is needed for these occupations. For example, an accountant must complete four years of college and work for several years in accounting to be considered qualified.
Job Training	Employees in these occupations usually need several years of work-related experience, on-the-job training, and/or vocational training.
Job Zone Examples	Many of these occupations involve coordinating, supervising, managing, or training others. Examples include accountants, chefs and head cooks, computer programmers, historians, pharmacists, and police detectives.
SVP Range	(7.0 to < 8.0)
Education	Most of these occupations require a four - year bachelor's degree, but some do not.

29-1126.00 - Respiratory Therapists

Assess, treat, and care for patients with breathing disorders. Assume primary responsibility for all respiratory care modalities, including the supervision of respiratory therapy technicians. Initiate and conduct therapeutic procedures; maintain patient records; and select, assemble, check, and operate equipment.

Tasks

1) Enforce safety rules and ensure careful adherence to physicians' orders.

2) Determine requirements for treatment, such as type, method and duration of therapy, precautions to be taken, and medication and dosages, compatible with physicians' orders.

3) Work as part of a team of physicians, nurses and other health care professionals to manage patient care.

4) Set up and operate devices such as mechanical ventilators, therapeutic gas administration apparatus, environmental control systems, and aerosol generators, following specified parameters of treatment.

5) Provide emergency care, including artificial respiration, external cardiac massage and assistance with cardiopulmonary resuscitation.

6) Teach, train, supervise, and utilize the assistance of students, respiratory therapy technicians, and assistants.

7) Inspect, clean, test and maintain respiratory therapy equipment to ensure equipment is functioning safely and efficiently, ordering repairs when necessary.

8) Monitor patient's physiological responses to therapy, such as vital signs, arterial blood gases, and blood chemistry changes, and consult with physician if adverse reactions occur.

9) Perform bronchopulmonary drainage and assist or instruct patients in performance of breathing exercises.

10) Read prescription, measure arterial blood gases, and review patient information to assess patient condition.

11) Conduct tests, such as electrocardiograms, stress testing, and lung capacity tests, to evaluate patients' cardiopulmonary functions.

12) Relay blood analysis results to a physician.

13) Make emergency visits to resolve equipment problems.

14) Use a variety of testing techniques to assist doctors in cardiac and pulmonary research and to diagnose disorders.

15) Perform pulmonary function and adjust equipment to obtain optimum results in therapy.

16) Educate patients and their families about their conditions and teach appropriate disease management techniques, such as breathing exercises and the use of medications and respiratory equipment.

17) Maintain charts that contain patients' pertinent identification and therapy information.

18) Explain treatment procedures to patients to gain cooperation and allay fears.

Knowledge	Knowledge Definitions
Medicine and Dentistry	Knowledge of the information and techniques needed to diagnose and treat human injuries, diseases, and deformities. This includes symptoms, treatment alternatives, drug properties and interactions, and preventive health-care measures.
Customer and Personal Service	Knowledge of principles and processes for providing customer and personal services. This includes customer needs assessment, meeting quality standards for services, and evaluation of customer satisfaction.
Psychology	Knowledge of human behavior and performance; individual differences in ability, personality, and interests; learning and motivation; psychological research methods; and the assessment and treatment of behavioral and affective disorders.

Education and Training	Knowledge of principles and methods for curriculum and training design. teaching and instruction for individuals and groups, and the measurement of training effects.
English Language	Knowledge of the structure and content of the English language including the meaning and spelling of words, rules of composition. and grammar.
Chemistry	Knowledge of the chemical composition, structure, and properties of substances and of the chemical processes and transformations that they undergo. This includes uses of chemicals and their interactions. danger signs, production techniques. and disposal methods.
Biology	Knowledge of plant and animal organisms, their tissues, cells, functions, interdependencies, and interactions with each other and the environment.
Mechanical	Knowledge of machines and tools, including their designs, uses, repair. and maintenance.
Mathematics	Knowledge of arithmetic. algebra, geometry, calculus, statistics, and their applications.
Physics	Knowledge and prediction of physical principles, laws, their interrelationships. and applications to understanding fluid, material, and atmospheric dynamics, and mechanical, electrical, atomic and sub- atomic structures and processes.
Computers and Electronics	Knowledge of circuit boards, processors, chips, electronic equipment, and computer hardware and software, including applications and programming.
Clerical	Knowledge of administrative and clerical procedures and systems such as word processing, managing files and records, stenography and transcription, designing forms, and other office procedures and terminology.
Therapy and Counseling	Knowledge of principles. methods, and procedures for diagnosis, treatment. and rehabilitation of physical and mental dysfunctions, and for career counseling and guidance.
Personnel and Human Resources	Knowledge of principles and procedures for personnel recruitment. selection, training, compensation and benefits, labor relations and negotiation, and personnel information systems.
Administration and Management	Knowledge of business and management principles involved in strategic planning. resource allocation, human resources modeling, leadership technique, production methods, and coordination of people and resources.
Law and Government	Knowledge of laws, legal codes, court procedures, precedents, government regulations, executive orders, agency rules, and the democratic political process.
Public Safety and Security	Knowledge of relevant equipment, policies, procedures, and strategies to promote effective local, state, or national security operations for the protection of people, data, property, and institutions.
Engineering and Technology	Knowledge of the practical application of engineering science and technology. This includes applying principles, techniques, procedures, and equipment to the design and production of various goods and services.
Philosophy and Theology	Knowledge of different philosophical systems and religions. This includes their basic principles, values, ethics, ways of thinking, customs, practices, and their impact on human culture.
Communications and Media	Knowledge of media production, communication, and dissemination techniques and methods. This includes alternative ways to inform and entertain via written, oral, and visual media.
Sociology and Anthropology	Knowledge of group behavior and dynamics, societal trends and influences, human migrations, ethnicity, cultures and their history and origins.
Telecommunications	Knowledge of transmission, broadcasting, switching, control, and operation of telecommunications systems.
Production and Processing	Knowledge of raw materials, production processes, quality control, costs, and other techniques for maximizing the effective manufacture and distribution of goods.
Foreign Language	Knowledge of the structure and content of a foreign (non-English) language including the meaning and spelling of words, rules of composition and grammar, and pronunciation.
Sales and Marketing	Knowledge of principles and methods for showing, promoting, and selling products or services. This includes marketing strategy and tactics, product demonstration, sales techniques, and sales control systems.
Transportation	Knowledge of principles and methods for moving people or goods by air, rail, sea, or road, including the relative costs and benefits.
History and Archeology	Knowledge of historical events and their causes, indicators, and effects on civilizations and cultures.
Economics and Accounting	Knowledge of economic and accounting principles and practices, the financial markets, banking and the analysis and reporting of financial data.
Geography	Knowledge of principles and methods for describing the features of land, sea, and air masses, including their physical characteristics. locations, interrelationships, and distribution of plant, animal, and human life.

Design	Knowledge of design techniques, tools, and principles involved in production of precision technical plans. blueprints, drawings. and models.
Building and Construction	Knowledge of materials, methods, and the tools involved in the construction or repair of houses, buildings. or other structures such as highways and roads.
Food Production	Knowledge of techniques and equipment for planting, growing. and harvesting food products (both plant and animal) for consumption, including storage/handling techniques.
Fine Arts	Knowledge of the theory and techniques required to compose. produce, and perform works of music, dance, visual arts. drama, and sculpture.

Skills	Skills Definitions
Active Listening	Giving full attention to what other people are saying, taking time to understand the points being made. asking questions as appropriate, and not interrupting at inappropriate times.
Instructing	Teaching others how to do something.
Reading Comprehension	Understanding written sentences and paragraphs in work related documents.
Critical Thinking	Using logic and reasoning to identify the strengths and weaknesses of alternative solutions. conclusions or approaches to problems.
Monitoring	Monitoring/Assessing performance of yourself, other individuals, or organizations to make improvements or take corrective action.
Time Management	Managing one's own time and the time of others.
Speaking	Talking to others to convey information effectively.
Operation Monitoring	Watching gauges, dials, or other indicators to make sure a machine is working properly.
Active Learning	Understanding the implications of new information for both current and future problem-solving and decision-making.
Troubleshooting	Determining causes of operating errors and deciding what to do about it.
Writing	Communicating effectively in writing as appropriate for the needs of the audience.
Service Orientation	Actively looking for ways to help people.
Science	Using scientific rules and methods to solve problems.
Mathematics	Using mathematics to solve problems.
Complex Problem Solving	Identifying complex problems and reviewing related information to develop and evaluate options and implement solutions.
Learning Strategies	Selecting and using training/instructional methods and procedures appropriate for the situation when learning or teaching new things.
Coordination	Adjusting actions in relation to others' actions.
Quality Control Analysis	Conducting tests and inspections of products, services, or processes to evaluate quality or performance.
Judgment and Decision Making	Considering the relative costs and benefits of potential actions to choose the most appropriate one.
Social Perceptiveness	Being aware of others' reactions and understanding why they react as they do.
Persuasion	Persuading others to change their minds or behavior.
Equipment Selection	Determining the kind of tools and equipment needed to do a job.
Equipment Maintenance	Performing routine maintenance on equipment and determining when and what kind of maintenance is needed.
Operation and Control	Controlling operations of equipment or systems.
Negotiation	Bringing others together and trying to reconcile differences.
Repairing	Repairing machines or systems using the needed tools.
Management of Material Resources	Obtaining and seeing to the appropriate use of equipment, facilities, and materials needed to do certain work.
Systems Evaluation	Identifying measures or indicators of system performance and the actions needed to improve or correct performance, relative to the goals of the system.
Systems Analysis	Determining how a system should work and how changes in conditions, operations, and the environment will affect outcomes.
Management of Personnel Resources	Motivating, developing, and directing people as they work, identifying the best people for the job.
Technology Design	Generating or adapting equipment and technology to serve user needs.
Installation	Installing equipment, machines, wiring, or programs to meet specifications.
Operations Analysis	Analyzing needs and product requirements to create a design.
Management of Financial Resources	Determining how money will be spent to get the work done, and accounting for these expenditures.
Programming	Writing computer programs for various purposes.

Ability	Ability Definitions
Oral Expression	The ability to communicate information and ideas in speaking so others will understand.
Oral Comprehension	The ability to listen to and understand information and ideas presented through spoken words and sentences.

Problem Sensitivity	The ability to tell when something is wrong or is likely to go wrong. It does not involve solving the problem, only recognizing there is a problem.
Speech Clarity	The ability to speak clearly so others can understand you.
Speech Recognition	The ability to identify and understand the speech of another person.
Inductive Reasoning	The ability to combine pieces of information to form general rules or conclusions (includes finding a relationship among seemingly unrelated events).
Information Ordering	The ability to arrange things or actions in a certain order or pattern according to a specific rule or set of rules (e.g., patterns of numbers, letters, words, pictures, mathematical operations).
Near Vision	The ability to see details at close range (within a few feet of the observer).
Written Comprehension	The ability to read and understand information and ideas presented in writing.
Deductive Reasoning	The ability to apply general rules to specific problems to produce answers that make sense.
Finger Dexterity	The ability to make precisely coordinated movements of the fingers of one or both hands to grasp, manipulate, or assemble very small objects.
Flexibility of Closure	The ability to identify or detect a known pattern (a figure, object, word, or sound) that is hidden in other distracting material.
Selective Attention	The ability to concentrate on a task over a period of time without being distracted.
Speed of Closure	The ability to quickly make sense of, combine, and organize information into meaningful patterns.
Category Flexibility	The ability to generate or use different sets of rules for combining or grouping things in different ways.
Control Precision	The ability to quickly and repeatedly adjust the controls of a machine or a vehicle to exact positions.
Trunk Strength	The ability to use your abdominal and lower back muscles to support part of the body repeatedly or continuously over time without 'giving out' or fatiguing.
Arm-Hand Steadiness	The ability to keep your hand and arm steady while moving your arm or while holding your arm and hand in one position.
Manual Dexterity	The ability to quickly move your hand, your hand together with your arm, or your two hands to grasp, manipulate, or assemble objects.
Written Expression	The ability to communicate information and ideas in writing so others will understand.
Perceptual Speed	The ability to quickly and accurately compare similarities and differences among sets of letters, numbers, objects, pictures, or patterns. The things to be compared may be presented at the same time or one after the other. This ability also includes comparing a presented object with a remembered object.
Hearing Sensitivity	The ability to detect or tell the differences between sounds that vary in pitch and loudness.
Memorization	The ability to remember information such as words, numbers, pictures, and procedures.
Multilimb Coordination	The ability to coordinate two or more limbs (for example, two arms, two legs, or one leg and one arm) while sitting, standing, or lying down. It does not involve performing the activities while the whole body is in motion.
Auditory Attention	The ability to focus on a single source of sound in the presence of other distracting sounds.
Time Sharing	The ability to shift back and forth between two or more activities or sources of information (such as speech, sounds, touch, or other sources).
Visual Color Discrimination	The ability to match or detect differences between colors, including shades of color and brightness.
Far Vision	The ability to see details at a distance.
Originality	The ability to come up with unusual or clever ideas about a given topic or situation, or to develop creative ways to solve a problem.
Static Strength	The ability to exert maximum muscle force to lift, push, pull, or carry objects.
Reaction Time	The ability to quickly respond (with the hand, finger, or foot) to a signal (sound, light, picture) when it appears.
Response Orientation	The ability to choose quickly between two or more movements in response to two or more different signals (lights, sounds, pictures). It includes the speed with which the correct response is started with the hand, foot, or other body part.
Fluency of Ideas	The ability to come up with a number of ideas about a topic (the number of ideas is important, not their quality, correctness, or creativity).
Visualization	The ability to imagine how something will look after it is moved around or when its parts are moved or rearranged.
Dynamic Strength	The ability to exert muscle force repeatedly or continuously over time. This involves muscular endurance and resistance to muscle fatigue.
Rate Control	The ability to time your movements or the movement of a piece of equipment in anticipation of changes in the speed and/or direction of a moving object or scene.

Depth Perception	The ability to judge which of several objects is closer or farther away from you, or to judge the distance between you and an object.
Number Facility	The ability to add, subtract, multiply, or divide quickly and correctly.
Stamina	The ability to exert yourself physically over long periods of time without getting winded or out of breath.
Gross Body Coordination	The ability to coordinate the movement of your arms, legs, and torso together when the whole body is in motion.
Extent Flexibility	The ability to bend, stretch, twist, or reach with your body, arms, and/or legs.
Wrist-Finger Speed	The ability to make fast, simple, repeated movements of the fingers, hands, and wrists.
Speed of Limb Movement	The ability to quickly move the arms and legs.
Mathematical Reasoning	The ability to choose the right mathematical methods or formulas to solve a problem.
Gross Body Equilibrium	The ability to keep or regain your body balance or stay upright when in an unstable position.
Spatial Orientation	The ability to know your location in relation to the environment or to know where other objects are in relation to you.
Sound Localization	The ability to tell the direction from which a sound originated.
Dynamic Flexibility	The ability to quickly and repeatedly bend, stretch, twist, or reach out with your body, arms, and/or legs.
Peripheral Vision	The ability to see objects or movement of objects to one's side when the eyes are looking ahead.
Explosive Strength	The ability to use short bursts of muscle force to propel oneself (as in jumping or sprinting), or to throw an object.
Glare Sensitivity	The ability to see objects in the presence of glare or bright lighting.
Night Vision	The ability to see under low light conditions.

Work_Activity	Work_Activity Definitions
Assisting and Caring for Others	Providing personal assistance, medical attention, emotional support, or other personal care to others such as coworkers, customers, or patients.
Documenting/Recording Information	Entering, transcribing, recording, storing, or maintaining information in written or electronic/magnetic form.
Communicating with Supervisors, Peers, or Subordin	Providing information to supervisors, co-workers, and subordinates by telephone, in written form, e-mail, or in person.
Getting Information	Observing, receiving, and otherwise obtaining information from all relevant sources.
Organizing, Planning, and Prioritizing Work	Developing specific goals and plans to prioritize, organize, and accomplish your work.
Identifying Objects, Actions, and Events	Identifying information by categorizing, estimating, recognizing differences or similarities, and detecting changes in circumstances or events.
Monitor Processes, Materials, or Surroundings	Monitoring and reviewing information from materials, events, or the environment, to detect or assess problems.
Making Decisions and Solving Problems	Analyzing information and evaluating results to choose the best solution and solve problems.
Updating and Using Relevant Knowledge	Keeping up-to-date technically and applying new knowledge to your job.
Establishing and Maintaining Interpersonal Relatio	Developing constructive and cooperative working relationships with others, and maintaining them over time.
Training and Teaching Others	Identifying the educational needs of others, developing formal educational or training programs or classes, and teaching or instructing others.
Communicating with Persons Outside Organization	Communicating with people outside the organization, representing the organization to customers, the public, government, and other external sources. This information can be exchanged in person, in writing, or by telephone or e-mail.
Inspecting Equipment, Structures, or Material	Inspecting equipment, structures, or materials to identify the cause of errors or other problems or defects.
Interacting With Computers	Using computers and computer systems (including hardware and software) to program, write software, set up functions, enter data, or process information.
Analyzing Data or Information	Identifying the underlying principles, reasons, or facts of information by breaking down information or data into separate parts.
Developing and Building Teams	Encouraging and building mutual trust, respect, and cooperation among team members.
Evaluating Information to Determine Compliance wit	Using relevant information and individual judgment to determine whether events or processes comply with laws, regulations, or standards.
Performing for or Working Directly with the Public	Performing for people or dealing directly with the public. This includes serving customers in restaurants and stores, and receiving clients or guests.
Processing Information	Compiling, coding, categorizing, calculating, tabulating, auditing, or verifying information or data.
Interpreting the Meaning of Information for Others	Translating or explaining what information means and how it can be used.

Controlling Machines and Processes	Using either control mechanisms or direct physical activity to operate machines or processes (not including computers or vehicles).
Coordinating the Work and Activities of Others	Getting members of a group to work together to accomplish tasks.
Judging the Qualities of Things, Services, or Peop	Assessing the value, importance, or quality of things or people.
Guiding, Directing, and Motivating Subordinates	Providing guidance and direction to subordinates, including setting performance standards and monitoring performance.
Resolving Conflicts and Negotiating with Others	Handling complaints, settling disputes, and resolving grievances and conflicts, or otherwise negotiating with others.
Scheduling Work and Activities	Scheduling events, programs, and activities, as well as the work of others.
Performing General Physical Activities	Performing physical activities that require considerable use of your arms and legs and moving your whole body, such as climbing, lifting, balancing, walking, stooping, and handling of materials.
Coaching and Developing Others	Identifying the developmental needs of others and coaching, mentoring, or otherwise helping others to improve their knowledge or skills.
Handling and Moving Objects	Using hands and arms in handling, installing, positioning, and moving materials, and manipulating things.
Developing Objectives and Strategies	Establishing long-range objectives and specifying the strategies and actions to achieve them.
Provide Consultation and Advice to Others	Providing guidance and expert advice to management or other groups on technical, systems-, or process-related topics.
Thinking Creatively	Developing, designing, or creating new applications, ideas, relationships, systems, or products, including artistic contributions.
Estimating the Quantifiable Characteristics of Pro	Estimating sizes, distances, and quantities; or determining time, costs, resources, or materials needed to perform a work activity.
Repairing and Maintaining Electronic Equipment	Servicing, repairing, calibrating, regulating, fine-tuning, or testing machines, devices, and equipment that operate primarily on the basis of electrical or electronic (not mechanical) principles.
Performing Administrative Activities	Performing day-to-day administrative tasks such as maintaining information files and processing paperwork.
Operating Vehicles, Mechanized Devices, or Equipme	Running, maneuvering, navigating, or driving vehicles or mechanized equipment, such as forklifts, passenger vehicles, aircraft, or water craft.
Selling or Influencing Others	Convincing others to buy merchandise/goods or to otherwise change their minds or actions.
Staffing Organizational Units	Recruiting, interviewing, selecting, hiring, and promoting employees in an organization.
Drafting, Laying Out, and Specifying Technical Dev	Providing documentation, detailed instructions, drawings, or specifications to tell others about how devices, parts, equipment, or structures are to be fabricated, constructed, assembled, modified, maintained, or used.
Repairing and Maintaining Mechanical Equipment	Servicing, repairing, adjusting, and testing machines, devices, moving parts, and equipment that operate primarily on the basis of mechanical (not electronic) principles.
Monitoring and Controlling Resources	Monitoring and controlling resources and overseeing the spending of money.

Work_Content

Work_Content	Work_Content Definitions
Face-to-Face Discussions	How often do you have to have face-to-face discussions with individuals or teams on this job?
Contact With Others	How much does this job require the worker to be in contact with others (face-to-face, by telephone, or otherwise) in order to perform it?
Physical Proximity	To what extent does this job require the worker to perform job tasks in close physical proximity to other people?
Indoors, Environmentally Controlled	How often does this job require working indoors in environmentally controlled conditions?
Exposed to Disease or Infections	How often does this job require exposure to disease/infections?
Telephone	How often do you have telephone conversations in this job?
Work With Work Group or Team	How important is it to work with others in a group or team in this job?
Wear Common Protective or Safety Equipment such as	How much does this job require wearing common protective or safety equipment such as safety shoes, glasses, gloves, hard hats or live jackets?
Impact of Decisions on Co-workers or Company Resul	How do the decisions an employee makes impact the results of co-workers, clients or the company?
Structured versus Unstructured Work	To what extent is this job structured for the worker, rather than allowing the worker to determine tasks, priorities, and goals?
Freedom to Make Decisions	How much decision making freedom, without supervision, does the job offer?
Importance of Being Exact or Accurate	How important is being very exact or highly accurate in performing this job?
Deal With Unpleasant or Angry People	How frequently does the worker have to deal with unpleasant, angry, or discourteous individuals as part of the job requirements?

Spend Time Standing	How much does this job require standing?
Consequence of Error	How serious would the result usually be if the worker made a mistake that was not readily correctable?
Frequency of Decision Making	How frequently is the worker required to make decisions that affect other people, the financial resources, and/or the image and reputation of the organization?
Deal With External Customers	How important is it to work with external customers or the public in this job?
Responsibility for Outcomes and Results	How responsible is the worker for work outcomes and results of other workers?
Coordinate or Lead Others	How important is it to coordinate or lead others in accomplishing work activities in this job?
Frequency of Conflict Situations	How often are there conflict situations the employee has to face in this job?
Spend Time Making Repetitive Motions	How much does this job require making repetitive motions?
Spend Time Using Your Hands to Handle, Control, or	How much does this job require using your hands to handle, control, or feel objects, tools or controls?
Spend Time Walking and Running	How much does this job require walking and running?
Letters and Memos	How often does the job require written letters and memos?
Spend Time Sitting	How much does this job require sitting?
Level of Competition	To what extent does this job require the worker to compete or to be aware of competitive pressures?
Electronic Mail	How often do you use electronic mail in this job?
Exposed to Radiation	How often does this job require exposure to radiation?
Time Pressure	How often does this job require the worker to meet strict deadlines?
Responsible for Others' Health and Safety	How much responsibility is there for the health and safety of others in this job?
Exposed to Hazardous Conditions	How often does this job require exposure to hazardous conditions?
Exposed to Minor Burns, Cuts, Bites, or Stings	How often does this job require exposure to minor burns, cuts, bites, or stings?
Sounds, Noise Levels Are Distracting or Uncomforta	How often does this job require working exposed to sounds and noise levels that are distracting or uncomfortable?
Importance of Repeating Same Tasks	How important is repeating the same physical activities (e.g., key entry) or mental activities (e.g., checking entries in a ledger) over and over, without stopping, to performing this job?
Cramped Work Space, Awkward Positions	How often does this job require working in cramped work spaces that requires getting into awkward positions?
Wear Specialized Protective or Safety Equipment su	How much does this job require wearing specialized protective or safety equipment such as breathing apparatus, safety harness, full protection suits, or radiation protection?
Exposed to Contaminants	How often does this job require working exposed to contaminants (such as pollutants, gases, dust or odors)?
Degree of Automation	How automated is the job?
Deal With Physically Aggressive People	How frequently does this job require the worker to deal with physical aggression of violent individuals?
Spend Time Bending or Twisting the Body	How much does this job require bending or twisting your body?
Spend Time Kneeling, Crouching, Stooping, or Crawl	How much does this job require kneeling, crouching, stooping, or crawling?
Pace Determined by Speed of Equipment	How important is it to this job that the pace is determined by the speed of equipment or machinery? (This does not refer to keeping busy at all times on this job.)
Public Speaking	How often do you have to perform public speaking in this job?
Outdoors, Exposed to Weather	How often does this job require working outdoors, exposed to all weather conditions?
Spend Time Keeping or Regaining Balance	How much does this job require keeping or regaining your balance?
Exposed to Whole Body Vibration	How often does this job require exposure to whole body vibration (e.g., operate a jackhammer)?
In an Enclosed Vehicle or Equipment	How often does this job require working in a closed vehicle or equipment (e.g., car)?
Exposed to Hazardous Equipment	How often does this job require exposure to hazardous equipment?
Outdoors, Under Cover	How often does this job require working outdoors, under cover (e.g., structure with roof but no walls)?
Indoors, Not Environmentally Controlled	How often does this job require working indoors in non-controlled environmental conditions (e.g., warehouse without heat)?
Very Hot or Cold Temperatures	How often does this job require working in very hot (above 90 F degrees) or very cold (below 32 F degrees) temperatures?
Extremely Bright or Inadequate Lighting	How often does this job require working in extremely bright or inadequate lighting conditions?
Spend Time Climbing Ladders, Scaffolds, or Poles	How much does this job require climbing ladders, scaffolds, or poles?
Exposed to High Places	How often does this job require exposure to high places?
In an Open Vehicle or Equipment	How often does this job require working in an open vehicle or equipment (e.g., tractor)?

Work_Styles	Work_Styles Definitions
Dependability	Job requires being reliable, responsible, and dependable, and fulfilling obligations.
Integrity	Job requires being honest and ethical.
Self Control	Job requires maintaining composure, keeping emotions in check, controlling anger, and avoiding aggressive behavior, even in very difficult situations.
Concern for Others	Job requires being sensitive to others' needs and feelings and being understanding and helpful on the job.
Attention to Detail	Job requires being careful about detail and thorough in completing work tasks.
Cooperation	Job requires being pleasant with others on the job and displaying a good-natured, cooperative attitude.
Stress Tolerance	Job requires accepting criticism and dealing calmly and effectively with high stress situations.
Analytical Thinking	Job requires analyzing information and using logic to address work-related issues and problems.
Independence	Job requires developing one's own ways of doing things, guiding oneself with little or no supervision, and depending on oneself to get things done.
Adaptability/Flexibility	Job requires being open to change (positive or negative) and to considerable variety in the workplace.
Achievement/Effort	Job requires establishing and maintaining personally challenging achievement goals and exerting effort toward mastering tasks.
Persistence	Job requires persistence in the face of obstacles.
Social Orientation	Job requires preferring to work with others rather than alone, and being personally connected with others on the job.
Initiative	Job requires a willingness to take on responsibilities and challenges.
Leadership	Job requires a willingness to lead, take charge, and offer opinions and direction.
Innovation	Job requires creativity and alternative thinking to develop new ideas for and answers to work-related problems.

Job Zone Component	Job Zone Component Definitions
Title	Job Zone Three: Medium Preparation Needed
Overall Experience	Previous work-related skill, knowledge, or experience is required for these occupations. For example, an electrician must have completed three or four years of apprenticeship or several years of vocational training, and often must have passed a licensing exam, in order to perform the job.
Job Training	Employees in these occupations usually need one or two years of training involving both on-the-job experience and informal training with experienced workers.
Job Zone Examples	These occupations usually involve using communication and organizational skills to coordinate, supervise, manage, or train others to accomplish goals. Examples include dental assistants, electricians, fish and game wardens, legal secretaries, personnel recruiters, and recreation workers.
SVP Range	(6.0 to < 7.0)
Education	Most occupations in this zone require training in vocational schools, related on-the-job experience, or an associate's degree. Some may require a bachelor's degree.

29-1127.00 - Speech-Language Pathologists

Assess and treat persons with speech, language, voice, and fluency disorders. May select alternative communication systems and teach their use. May perform research related to speech and language problems.

Tasks

1) Communicate with non-speaking students, using sign language or computer technology.

2) Record information on the initial evaluation, treatment, progress, and discharge of clients.

3) Administer hearing or speech/language evaluations, tests, or examinations to patients to collect information on type and degree of impairments, using written and oral tests and special instruments.

4) Evaluate hearing and speech/language test results and medical or background information to diagnose and plan treatment for speech, language, fluency, voice, and swallowing disorders.

5) Instruct clients in techniques for more effective communication, including sign language, lip reading, and voice improvement.

6) Develop speech exercise programs to reduce disabilities.

7) Monitor patients' progress and adjust treatments accordingly.

8) Design, develop, and employ alternative diagnostic or communication devices and strategies.

9) Refer clients to additional medical or educational services if needed.

10) Develop and implement treatment plans for problems such as stuttering, delayed language, swallowing disorders, and inappropriate pitch or harsh voice problems, based on own assessments and recommendations of physicians, psychologists, and social workers.

11) Conduct or direct research on speech or hearing topics, and report findings for use in developing procedures, technologies, or treatments.

12) Consult with and advise educators or medical staff on speech or hearing topics such as communication strategies and speech and language stimulation.

13) Develop individual or group programs in schools to deal with speech or language problems.

14) Instruct patients and family members in strategies to cope with or avoid communication-related misunderstandings.

15) Participate in conferences or training, or publish research results, to share knowledge of new hearing or speech disorder treatment methods or technologies.

16) Provide communication instruction to dialect speakers or students with limited English proficiency.

17) Use computer applications to identify and assist with communication disabilities.

18) Conduct lessons and direct educational or therapeutic games to assist teachers dealing with speech problems.

29-1131.00 - Veterinarians

Diagnose and treat diseases and dysfunctions of animals. May engage in a particular function, such as research and development, consultation, administration, technical writing, sale or production of commercial products, or rendering of technical services to commercial firms or other organizations. Includes veterinarians who inspect livestock.

Tasks

1) Direct activities concerned with the feeding, care, and housing of laboratory animals to ensure compliance with laboratory regulations.

2) Euthanize animals.

3) Treat sick or injured animals by prescribing medication, setting bones, dressing wounds, or performing surgery.

4) Collect body tissue, feces, blood, urine, or other body fluids for examination and analysis.

5) Advise animal owners regarding sanitary measures, feeding, and general care necessary to promote health of animals.

6) Conduct postmortem studies and analyses to determine the causes of animals' deaths.

7) Exchange information with zoos and aquariums concerning care, transfer, sale, or trade of animals in order to maintain species inventories.

8) Enforce government regulations in disease control and food production by performing such tasks as inspecting meat packing plants, and inspecting food animals before and after slaughter.

9) Inspect animal housing facilities to determine their cleanliness and adequacy.

10) Monitor scientific research programs to ensure compliance with regulations governing humane and ethical treatment of animals.

11) Perform administrative duties such as scheduling appointments, accepting payments from clients, and maintaining business records.

12) Plan and execute animal nutrition and reproduction programs.

13) Research diseases to which animals could be susceptible.

14) Determine the effects of drug therapies, antibiotics, or new surgical techniques by testing them on animals.

15) Educate the public about diseases that can be spread from animals to humans.

16) Drive mobile clinic vans to farms so that health problems can be treated and/or prevented.

17) Provide care to a wide range of animals or specialize in a particular species, such as horses or exotic birds.

18) Teach in colleges of veterinary medicine.

19) Train and supervise workers who handle and care for animals.

20) Direct the overall operations of animal hospitals, clinics, or mobile services to farms.

21) Specialize in a particular type of treatment such as dentistry, pathology, nutrition, surgery, microbiology, or internal medicine.

22) Operate diagnostic equipment such as radiographic and ultrasound equipment, and interpret the resulting images.

23) Inspect and test horses, sheep, poultry, and other animals to detect the presence of communicable diseases.

24) Inoculate animals against various diseases such as rabies and distemper.

25) Examine animals to detect and determine the nature of diseases or injuries.

167

29-2011.00 - Medical and Clinical Laboratory Technologists

Perform complex medical laboratory tests for diagnosis, treatment, and prevention of disease. May train or supervise staff.

Tasks

1) Study blood samples to determine the number of cells and their morphology, as well as the blood group, type and compatibility for transfusion purposes, using microscopic technique.

2) Analyze laboratory findings to check the accuracy of the results.

3) Set up, clean, and maintain laboratory equipment.

4) Analyze samples of biological material for chemical content or reaction.

5) Conduct chemical analysis of body fluids, including blood, urine, and spinal fluid, to determine presence of normal and abnormal components.

6) Cultivate, isolate, and assist in identifying microbial organisms, and perform various tests on these microorganisms.

7) Enter data from analysis of medical tests and clinical results into computer for storage.

8) Harvest cell cultures at optimum time based on knowledge of cell cycle differences and culture conditions.

9) Conduct medical research under direction of microbiologist or biochemist.

10) Operate, calibrate and maintain equipment used in quantitative and qualitative analysis, such as spectrophotometers, calorimeters, flame photometers, and computer-controlled analyzers.

11) Prepare slide of cell culture to identify chromosomes, view and photograph slide under photo-microscope, and print picture.

12) Provide technical information about test results to physicians, family members and researchers.

13) Select and prepare specimen and media for cell culture, using aseptic technique and knowledge of medium components and cell requirements.

14) Cut images of chromosomes from photograph and identify and arrange them in numbered pairs on karyotype chart, using standard practices.

15) Develop, standardize, evaluate, and modify procedures, techniques and tests used in the analysis of specimens and in medical laboratory experiments.

16) Establish and monitor programs to ensure the accuracy of laboratory results.

17) Supervise, train, and direct lab assistants, medical and clinical laboratory technicians and technologists, and other medical laboratory workers engaged in laboratory testing.

18) Obtain, cut, stain, and mount biological material on slides for microscopic study and diagnosis, following standard laboratory procedures.

29-2012.00 - Medical and Clinical Laboratory Technicians

Perform routine medical laboratory tests for the diagnosis, treatment, and prevention of disease. May work under the supervision of a medical technologist.

Tasks

1) Inoculate fertilized eggs, broths, or other bacteriological media with organisms.

2) Prepare standard volumetric solutions and reagents to be combined with samples, following standardized formulas or experimental procedures.

3) Conduct chemical analyses of body fluids, such as blood and urine, using microscope or automatic analyzer to detect abnormalities or diseases, and enter findings into computer.

4) Consult with a pathologist to determine a final diagnosis when abnormal cells are found.

5) Cut, stain and mount tissue samples for examination by pathologists.

6) Examine cells stained with dye to locate abnormalities.

7) Analyze the results of tests and experiments to ensure conformity to specifications, using special mechanical and electrical devices.

8) Obtain specimens, cultivating, isolating and identifying microorganisms for analysis.

9) Prepare vaccines and serums by standard laboratory methods, testing for virus inactivity and sterility.

10) Perform medical research to further control and cure disease.

11) Set up, adjust, maintain and clean medical laboratory equipment.

12) Collect blood or tissue samples from patients, observing principles of asepsis to obtain blood sample.

13) Test raw materials, processes and finished products to determine quality and quantity of materials or characteristics of a substance.

14) Conduct blood tests for transfusion purposes and perform blood counts.

15) Supervise and instruct other technicians and laboratory assistants.

29-2021.00 - Dental Hygienists

Clean teeth and examine oral areas, head, and neck for signs of oral disease. May educate patients on oral hygiene, take and develop X-rays, or apply fluoride or sealants.

Tasks

1) Provide clinical services and health education to improve and maintain oral health of school children.

2) Feel lymph nodes under patient's chin to detect swelling or tenderness that could indicate presence of oral cancer.

3) Examine gums, using probes, to locate periodontal recessed gums and signs of gum disease.

4) Chart conditions of decay and disease for diagnosis and treatment by dentist.

5) Feel and visually examine gums for sores and signs of disease.

6) Remove excess cement from coronal surfaces of teeth.

7) Make impressions for study casts.

8) Administer local anesthetic agents.

9) Remove sutures and dressings.

10) Conduct dental health clinics for community groups to augment services of dentist.

11) Place and remove rubber dams, matrices, and temporary restorations.

12) Place, carve, and finish amalgam restorations.

13) Clean calcareous deposits, accretions, and stains from teeth and beneath margins of gums, using dental instruments.

14) Apply fluorides and other cavity preventing agents to arrest dental decay.

Knowledge	Knowledge Definitions
Medicine and Dentistry	Knowledge of the information and techniques needed to diagnose and treat human injuries, diseases, and deformities. This includes symptoms, treatment alternatives, drug properties and interactions, and preventive health-care measures.
Customer and Personal Service	Knowledge of principles and processes for providing customer and personal services. This includes customer needs assessment, meeting quality standards for services, and evaluation of customer satisfaction.
Biology	Knowledge of plant and animal organisms, their tissues, cells, functions, interdependencies, and interactions with each other and the environment.
Education and Training	Knowledge of principles and methods for curriculum and training design, teaching and instruction for individuals and groups, and the measurement of training effects.
English Language	Knowledge of the structure and content of the English language including the meaning and spelling of words, rules of composition, and grammar.
Psychology	Knowledge of human behavior and performance; individual differences in ability, personality, and interests; learning and motivation; psychological research methods; and the assessment and treatment of behavioral and affective disorders.
Sales and Marketing	Knowledge of principles and methods for showing, promoting, and selling products or services. This includes marketing strategy and tactics, product demonstration, sales techniques, and sales control systems.
Public Safety and Security	Knowledge of relevant equipment, policies, procedures, and strategies to promote effective local, state, or national security operations for the protection of people, data, property, and institutions.
Production and Processing	Knowledge of raw materials, production processes, quality control, costs, and other techniques for maximizing the effective manufacture and distribution of goods.
Law and Government	Knowledge of laws, legal codes, court procedures, precedents, government regulations, executive orders, agency rules, and the democratic political process.
Chemistry	Knowledge of the chemical composition, structure, and properties of substances and of the chemical processes and transformations that they undergo. This includes uses of chemicals and their interactions, danger signs, production techniques, and disposal methods.
Therapy and Counseling	Knowledge of principles, methods, and procedures for diagnosis, treatment, and rehabilitation of physical and mental dysfunctions, and for career counseling and guidance.

Computers and Electronics	Knowledge of circuit boards. processors, chips, electronic equipment. and computer hardware and software, including applications and programming.
Clerical	Knowledge of administrative and clerical procedures and systems such as word processing, managing files and records, stenography and transcription, designing forms, and other office procedures and terminology.
Administration and Management	Knowledge of business and management principles involved in strategic planning. resource allocation, human resources modeling, leadership technique. production methods. and coordination of people and resources.
Personnel and Human Resources	Knowledge of principles and procedures for personnel recruitment, selection. training. compensation and benefits, labor relations and negotiation, and personnel information systems.
Sociology and Anthropology	Knowledge of group behavior and dynamics, societal trends and influences, human migrations. ethnicity, cultures and their history and origins.
Mechanical	Knowledge of machines and tools, including their designs, uses, repair, and maintenance.
Communications and Media	Knowledge of media production, communication, and dissemination techniques and methods. This includes alternative ways to inform and entertain via written, oral, and visual media.
Mathematics	Knowledge of arithmetic, algebra, geometry, calculus, statistics, and their applications.
Philosophy and Theology	Knowledge of different philosophical systems and religions. This includes their basic principles, values, ethics, ways of thinking, customs, practices, and their impact on human culture.
Engineering and Technology	Knowledge of the practical application of engineering science and technology. This includes applying principles, techniques, procedures, and equipment to the design and production of various goods and services.
Telecommunications	Knowledge of transmission, broadcasting, switching, control, and operation of telecommunications systems.
Economics and Accounting	Knowledge of economic and accounting principles and practices, the financial markets, banking and the analysis and reporting of financial data.
Physics	Knowledge and prediction of physical principles, laws, their interrelationships, and applications to understanding fluid, material, and atmospheric dynamics, and mechanical, electrical, atomic and sub- atomic structures and processes.
History and Archeology	Knowledge of historical events and their causes, indicators, and effects on civilizations and cultures.
Building and Construction	Knowledge of materials, methods, and the tools involved in the construction or repair of houses, buildings, or other structures such as highways and roads.
Design	Knowledge of design techniques, tools, and principles involved in production of precision technical plans, blueprints, drawings, and models.
Foreign Language	Knowledge of the structure and content of a foreign (non-English) language including the meaning and spelling of words, rules of composition and grammar, and pronunciation.
Transportation	Knowledge of principles and methods for moving people or goods by air, rail, sea, or road, including the relative costs and benefits.
Fine Arts	Knowledge of the theory and techniques required to compose, produce, and perform works of music, dance, visual arts, drama, and sculpture.
Food Production	Knowledge of techniques and equipment for planting, growing, and harvesting food products (both plant and animal) for consumption, including storage/handling techniques.
Geography	Knowledge of principles and methods for describing the features of land, sea, and air masses, including their physical characteristics, locations, interrelationships, and distribution of plant, animal, and human life.

Skills	**Skills Definitions**
Active Listening	Giving full attention to what other people are saying, taking time to understand the points being made, asking questions as appropriate, and not interrupting at inappropriate times.
Speaking	Talking to others to convey information effectively.
Reading Comprehension	Understanding written sentences and paragraphs in work related documents.
Active Learning	Understanding the implications of new information for both current and future problem-solving and decision-making.
Time Management	Managing one's own time and the time of others.
Social Perceptiveness	Being aware of others' reactions and understanding why they react as they do.
Critical Thinking	Using logic and reasoning to identify the strengths and weaknesses of alternative solutions, conclusions or approaches to problems.
Coordination	Adjusting actions in relation to others' actions.
Instructing	Teaching others how to do something.
Writing	Communicating effectively in writing as appropriate for the needs of the audience.

Equipment Selection	Determining the kind of tools and equipment needed to do a job.
Science	Using scientific rules and methods to solve problems.
Learning Strategies	Selecting and using training/instructional methods and procedures appropriate for the situation when learning or teaching new things.
Persuasion	Persuading others to change their minds or behavior.
Service Orientation	Actively looking for ways to help people.
Judgment and Decision Making	Considering the relative costs and benefits of potential actions to choose the most appropriate one.
Monitoring	Monitoring/Assessing performance of yourself, other individuals, or organizations to make improvements or take corrective action.
Complex Problem Solving	Identifying complex problems and reviewing related information to develop and evaluate options and implement solutions.
Equipment Maintenance	Performing routine maintenance on equipment and determining when and what kind of maintenance is needed.
Troubleshooting	Determining causes of operating errors and deciding what to do about it.
Negotiation	Bringing others together and trying to reconcile differences.
Operation and Control	Controlling operations of equipment or systems.
Operation Monitoring	Watching gauges, dials, or other indicators to make sure a machine is working properly.
Mathematics	Using mathematics to solve problems.
Operations Analysis	Analyzing needs and product requirements to create a design.
Management of Material Resources	Obtaining and seeing to the appropriate use of equipment, facilities, and materials needed to do certain work.
Quality Control Analysis	Conducting tests and inspections of products, services, or processes to evaluate quality or performance.
Technology Design	Generating or adapting equipment and technology to serve user needs.
Systems Evaluation	Identifying measures or indicators of system performance and the actions needed to improve or correct performance, relative to the goals of the system.
Installation	Installing equipment, machines, wiring, or programs to meet specifications.
Management of Personnel Resources	Motivating, developing, and directing people as they work, identifying the best people for the job.
Repairing	Repairing machines or systems using the needed tools.
Management of Financial Resources	Determining how money will be spent to get the work done, and accounting for these expenditures.
Systems Analysis	Determining how a system should work and how changes in conditions, operations, and the environment will affect outcomes.
Programming	Writing computer programs for various purposes.

Ability	**Ability Definitions**
Near Vision	The ability to see details at close range (within a few feet of the observer).
Finger Dexterity	The ability to make precisely coordinated movements of the fingers of one or both hands to grasp, manipulate, or assemble very small objects.
Manual Dexterity	The ability to quickly move your hand, your hand together with your arm, or your two hands to grasp, manipulate, or assemble objects.
Problem Sensitivity	The ability to tell when something is wrong or is likely to go wrong. It does not involve solving the problem, only recognizing there is a problem.
Arm-Hand Steadiness	The ability to keep your hand and arm steady while moving your arm or while holding your arm and hand in one position.
Control Precision	The ability to quickly and repeatedly adjust the controls of a machine or a vehicle to exact positions.
Oral Expression	The ability to communicate information and ideas in speaking so others will understand.
Speech Clarity	The ability to speak clearly so others can understand you.
Selective Attention	The ability to concentrate on a task over a period of time without being distracted.
Inductive Reasoning	The ability to combine pieces of information to form general rules or conclusions (includes finding a relationship among seemingly unrelated events).
Oral Comprehension	The ability to listen to and understand information and ideas presented through spoken words and sentences.
Extent Flexibility	The ability to bend, stretch, twist, or reach with your body, arms, and/or legs.
Multilimb Coordination	The ability to coordinate two or more limbs (for example, two arms, two legs, or one leg and one arm) while sitting, standing, or lying down. It does not involve performing the activities while the whole body is in motion.
Deductive Reasoning	The ability to apply general rules to specific problems to produce answers that make sense.
Visual Color Discrimination	The ability to match or detect differences between colors, including shades of color and brightness.

Information Ordering	The ability to arrange things or actions in a certain order or pattern according to a specific rule or set of rules (e.g., patterns of numbers, letters, words, pictures, mathematical operations).
Written Comprehension	The ability to read and understand information and ideas presented in writing.
Speech Recognition	The ability to identify and understand the speech of another person.
Flexibility of Closure	The ability to identify or detect a known pattern (a figure, object, word, or sound) that is hidden in other distracting material.
Written Expression	The ability to communicate information and ideas in writing so others will understand.
Category Flexibility	The ability to generate or use different sets of rules for combining or grouping things in different ways.
Trunk Strength	The ability to use your abdominal and lower back muscles to support part of the body repeatedly or continuously over time without 'giving out' or fatiguing.
Speed of Closure	The ability to quickly make sense of, combine, and organize information into meaningful patterns.
Time Sharing	The ability to shift back and forth between two or more activities or sources of information (such as speech, sounds, touch, or other sources).
Memorization	The ability to remember information such as words, numbers, pictures, and procedures.
Depth Perception	The ability to judge which of several objects is closer or farther away from you, or to judge the distance between you and an object.
Perceptual Speed	The ability to quickly and accurately compare similarities and differences among sets of letters, numbers, objects, pictures, or patterns. The things to be compared may be presented at the same time or one after the other. This ability also includes comparing a presented object with a remembered object.
Originality	The ability to come up with unusual or clever ideas about a given topic or situation, or to develop creative ways to solve a problem.
Far Vision	The ability to see details at a distance.
Hearing Sensitivity	The ability to detect or tell the differences between sounds that vary in pitch and loudness.
Static Strength	The ability to exert maximum muscle force to lift, push, pull, or carry objects.
Visualization	The ability to imagine how something will look after it is moved around or when its parts are moved or rearranged.
Fluency of Ideas	The ability to come up with a number of ideas about a topic (the number of ideas is important, not their quality, correctness, or creativity).
Dynamic Strength	The ability to exert muscle force repeatedly or continuously over time. This involves muscular endurance and resistance to muscle fatigue.
Rate Control	The ability to time your movements or the movement of a piece of equipment in anticipation of changes in the speed and/or direction of a moving object or scene.
Response Orientation	The ability to choose quickly between two or more movements in response to two or more different signals (lights, sounds, pictures). It includes the speed with which the correct response is started with the hand, foot, or other body part.
Stamina	The ability to exert yourself physically over long periods of time without getting winded or out of breath.
Wrist-Finger Speed	The ability to make fast, simple, repeated movements of the fingers, hands, and wrists.
Auditory Attention	The ability to focus on a single source of sound in the presence of other distracting sounds.
Gross Body Equilibrium	The ability to keep or regain your body balance or stay upright when in an unstable position.
Reaction Time	The ability to quickly respond (with the hand, finger, or foot) to a signal (sound, light, picture) when it appears.
Gross Body Coordination	The ability to coordinate the movement of your arms, legs, and torso together when the whole body is in motion.
Spatial Orientation	The ability to know your location in relation to the environment or to know where other objects are in relation to you.
Mathematical Reasoning	The ability to choose the right mathematical methods or formulas to solve a problem.
Dynamic Flexibility	The ability to quickly and repeatedly bend, stretch, twist, or reach out with your body, arms, and/or legs.
Number Facility	The ability to add, subtract, multiply, or divide quickly and correctly.
Speed of Limb Movement	The ability to quickly move the arms and legs.
Glare Sensitivity	The ability to see objects in the presence of glare or bright lighting.
Night Vision	The ability to see under low light conditions.
Sound Localization	The ability to tell the direction from which a sound originated.
Peripheral Vision	The ability to see objects or movement of objects to one's side when the eyes are looking ahead.
Explosive Strength	The ability to use short bursts of muscle force to propel oneself (as in jumping or sprinting), or to throw an object.

Work_Activity	Work_Activity Definitions
Assisting and Caring for Others	Providing personal assistance, medical attention, emotional support, or other personal care to others such as coworkers, customers, or patients.
Getting Information	Observing, receiving, and otherwise obtaining information from all relevant sources.
Updating and Using Relevant Knowledge	Keeping up-to-date technically and applying new knowledge to your job.
Identifying Objects, Actions, and Events	Identifying information by categorizing, estimating, recognizing differences or similarities, and detecting changes in circumstances or events.
Performing for or Working Directly with the Public	Performing for people or dealing directly with the public. This includes serving customers in restaurants and stores, and receiving clients or guests.
Establishing and Maintaining Interpersonal Relatio	Developing constructive and cooperative working relationships with others, and maintaining them over time.
Interpreting the Meaning of Information for Others	Translating or explaining what information means and how it can be used.
Documenting/Recording Information	Entering, transcribing, recording, storing, or maintaining information in written or electronic/magnetic form.
Making Decisions and Solving Problems	Analyzing information and evaluating results to choose the best solution and solve problems.
Communicating with Supervisors, Peers, or Subordin	Providing information to supervisors, co-workers, and subordinates by telephone, in written form, e-mail, or in person.
Judging the Qualities of Things, Services, or Peop	Assessing the value, importance, or quality of things or people.
Organizing, Planning, and Prioritizing Work	Developing specific goals and plans to prioritize, organize, and accomplish your work.
Coaching and Developing Others	Identifying the developmental needs of others and coaching, mentoring, or otherwise helping others to improve their knowledge or skills.
Performing Administrative Activities	Performing day-to-day administrative tasks such as maintaining information files and processing paperwork.
Coordinating the Work and Activities of Others	Getting members of a group to work together to accomplish tasks.
Training and Teaching Others	Identifying the educational needs of others, developing formal educational or training programs or classes, and teaching or instructing others.
Developing and Building Teams	Encouraging and building mutual trust, respect, and cooperation among team members.
Monitor Processes, Materials, or Surroundings	Monitoring and reviewing information from materials, events, or the environment, to detect or assess problems.
Handling and Moving Objects	Using hands and arms in handling, installing, positioning, and moving materials, and manipulating things.
Selling or Influencing Others	Convincing others to buy merchandise/goods or to otherwise change their minds or actions.
Inspecting Equipment, Structures, or Material	Inspecting equipment, structures, or materials to identify the cause of errors or other problems or defects.
Scheduling Work and Activities	Scheduling events, programs, and activities, as well as the work of others.
Communicating with Persons Outside Organization	Communicating with people outside the organization, representing the organization to customers, the public, government, and other external sources. This information can be exchanged in person, in writing, or by telephone or e-mail.
Interacting With Computers	Using computers and computer systems (including hardware and software) to program, write software, set up functions, enter data, or process information.
Evaluating Information to Determine Compliance wit	Using relevant information and individual judgment to determine whether events or processes comply with laws, regulations, or standards.
Analyzing Data or Information	Identifying the underlying principles, reasons, or facts of information by breaking down information or data into separate parts.
Performing General Physical Activities	Performing physical activities that require considerable use of your arms and legs and moving your whole body, such as climbing, lifting, balancing, walking, stooping, and handling of materials.
Processing Information	Compiling, coding, categorizing, calculating, tabulating, auditing, or verifying information or data.
Guiding, Directing, and Motivating Subordinates	Providing guidance and direction to subordinates, including setting performance standards and monitoring performance.
Resolving Conflicts and Negotiating with Others	Handling complaints, settling disputes, and resolving grievances and conflicts, or otherwise negotiating with others.
Developing Objectives and Strategies	Establishing long-range objectives and specifying the strategies and actions to achieve them.
Provide Consultation and Advice to Others	Providing guidance and expert advice to management or other groups on technical, systems-, or process-related topics.
Controlling Machines and Processes	Using either control mechanisms or direct physical activity to operate machines or processes (not including computers or vehicles).

Estimating the Quantifiable Characteristics of Pro — Estimating sizes, distances, and quantities; or determining time. costs, resources, or materials needed to perform a work activity.

Thinking Creatively — Developing, designing, or creating new applications, ideas, relationships, systems, or products, including artistic contributions.

Repairing and Maintaining Electronic Equipment — Servicing, repairing, calibrating, regulating, fine-tuning, or testing machines, devices, and equipment that operate primarily on the basis of electrical or electronic (not mechanical) principles.

Repairing and Maintaining Mechanical Equipment — Servicing, repairing, adjusting, and testing machines, devices, moving parts, and equipment that operate primarily on the basis of mechanical (not electronic) principles.

Monitoring and Controlling Resources — Monitoring and controlling resources and overseeing the spending of money.

Staffing Organizational Units — Recruiting, interviewing, selecting, hiring, and promoting employees in an organization.

Drafting, Laying Out, and Specifying Technical Dev — Providing documentation, detailed instructions, drawings, or specifications to tell others about how devices, parts, equipment, or structures are to be fabricated, constructed, assembled, modified, maintained, or used.

Operating Vehicles, Mechanized Devices, or Equipme — Running, maneuvering, navigating, or driving vehicles or mechanized equipment, such as forklifts, passenger vehicles, aircraft, or water craft.

Work_Content — Work_Content Definitions

Contact With Others — How much does this job require the worker to be in contact with others (face-to-face, by telephone, or otherwise) in order to perform it?

Wear Common Protective or Safety Equipment such as — How much does this job require wearing common protective or safety equipment such as safety shoes, glasses, gloves, hard hats or live jackets?

Spend Time Using Your Hands to Handle, Control, or — How much does this job require using your hands to handle, control, or feel objects, tools or controls?

Physical Proximity — To what extent does this job require the worker to perform job tasks in close physical proximity to other people?

Work With Work Group or Team — How important is it to work with others in a group or team in this job?

Spend Time Sitting — How much does this job require sitting?

Spend Time Making Repetitive Motions — How much does this job require making repetitive motions?

Exposed to Disease or Infections — How often does this job require exposure to disease/infections?

Importance of Being Exact or Accurate — How important is being very exact or highly accurate in performing this job?

Frequency of Decision Making — How frequently is the worker required to make decisions that affect other people, the financial resources, and/or the image and reputation of the organization?

Impact of Decisions on Co-workers or Company Resul — How do the decisions an employee makes impact the results of co-workers, clients or the company?

Face-to-Face Discussions — How often do you have to have face-to-face discussions with individuals or teams in this job?

Structured versus Unstructured Work — To what extent is this job structured for the worker, rather than allowing the worker to determine tasks, priorities, and goals?

Freedom to Make Decisions — How much decision making freedom, without supervision, does the job offer?

Deal With External Customers — How important is it to work with external customers or the public in this job?

Telephone — How often do you have telephone conversations in this job?

Indoors, Environmentally Controlled — How often does this job require working indoors in environmentally controlled conditions?

Exposed to Radiation — How often does this job require exposure to radiation?

Spend Time Bending or Twisting the Body — How much does this job require bending or twisting your body?

Importance of Repeating Same Tasks — How important is repeating the same physical activities (e.g., key entry) or mental activities (e.g., checking entries in a ledger) over and over, without stopping, to performing this job?

Responsible for Others' Health and Safety — How much responsibility is there for the health and safety of others in this job?

Exposed to Contaminants — How often does this job require working exposed to contaminants (such as pollutants, gases, dust or odors)?

Consequence of Error — How serious would the result usually be if the worker made a mistake that was not readily correctable?

Letters and Memos — How often does the job require written letters and memos?

Coordinate or Lead Others — How important is it to coordinate or lead others in accomplishing work activities in this job?

Exposed to Hazardous Conditions — How often does this job require exposure to hazardous conditions?

Deal With Unpleasant or Angry People — How frequently does the worker have to deal with unpleasant, angry, or discourteous individuals as part of the job requirements?

Time Pressure — How often does this job require the worker to meet strict deadlines?

Frequency of Conflict Situations — How often are there conflict situations the employee has to face in this job?

Level of Competition — To what extent does this job require the worker to compete or to be aware of competitive pressures?

Sounds. Noise Levels Are Distracting or Uncomforta — How often does this job require working exposed to sounds and noise levels that are distracting or uncomfortable?

Spend Time Standing — How much does this job require standing?

Responsibility for Outcomes and Results — How responsible is the worker for work outcomes and results of other workers?

Exposed to Minor Burns, Cuts, Bites, or Stings — How often does this job require exposure to minor burns, cuts, bites, or stings?

Cramped Work Space, Awkward Positions — How often does this job require working in cramped work spaces that requires getting into awkward positions?

Degree of Automation — How automated is the job?

Wear Specialized Protective or Safety Equipment su — How much does this job require wearing specialized protective or safety equipment such as breathing apparatus, safety harness, full protection suits, or radiation protection?

Spend Time Walking and Running — How much does this job require walking and running?

Exposed to Hazardous Equipment — How often does this job require exposure to hazardous equipment?

Indoors, Not Environmentally Controlled — How often does this job require working indoors in non-controlled environmental conditions (e.g., warehouse without heat)?

Public Speaking — How often do you have to perform public speaking in this job?

Pace Determined by Speed of Equipment — How important is it to this job that the pace is determined by the speed of equipment or machinery? (This does not refer to keeping busy at all times on this job.)

Spend Time Keeping or Regaining Balance — How much does this job require keeping or regaining your balance?

Spend Time Kneeling, Crouching, Stooping, or Crawl — How much does this job require kneeling, crouching, stooping or crawling?

Electronic Mail — How often do you use electronic mail in this job?

Deal With Physically Aggressive People — How frequently does this job require the worker to deal with physical aggression of violent individuals?

Extremely Bright or Inadequate Lighting — How often does this job require working in extremely bright or inadequate lighting conditions?

Very Hot or Cold Temperatures — How often does this job require working in very hot (above 90 F degrees) or very cold (below 32 F degrees) temperatures?

Outdoors, Exposed to Weather — How often does this job require working outdoors, exposed to all weather conditions?

In an Enclosed Vehicle or Equipment — How often does this job require working in a closed vehicle or equipment (e.g., car)?

Exposed to Whole Body Vibration — How often does this job require exposure to whole body vibration (e.g., operate a jackhammer)?

Outdoors, Under Cover — How often does this job require working outdoors, under cover (e.g., structure with roof but no walls)?

Spend Time Climbing Ladders, Scaffolds, or Poles — How much does this job require climbing ladders, scaffolds, or poles?

In an Open Vehicle or Equipment — How often does this job require working in an open vehicle or equipment (e.g., tractor)?

Exposed to High Places — How often does this job require exposure to high places?

Work_Styles — Work_Styles Definitions

Dependability — Job requires being reliable, responsible, and dependable, and fulfilling obligations.

Cooperation — Job requires being pleasant with others on the job and displaying a good-natured, cooperative attitude.

Attention to Detail — Job requires being careful about detail and thorough in completing work tasks.

Concern for Others — Job requires being sensitive to others' needs and feelings and being understanding and helpful on the job.

Independence — Job requires developing one's own ways of doing things, guiding oneself with little or no supervision, and depending on oneself to get things done.

Integrity — Job requires being honest and ethical.

Self Control — Job requires maintaining composure, keeping emotions in check, controlling anger, and avoiding aggressive behavior, even in very difficult situations.

Stress Tolerance — Job requires accepting criticism and dealing calmly and effectively with high stress situations.

Initiative — Job requires a willingness to take on responsibilities and challenges.

Achievement/Effort — Job requires establishing and maintaining personally challenging achievement goals and exerting effort toward mastering tasks.

Social Orientation — Job requires preferring to work with others rather than alone, and being personally connected with others on the job.

Adaptability/Flexibility — Job requires being open to change (positive or negative) and to considerable variety in the workplace.

Persistence — Job requires persistence in the face of obstacles.

Analytical Thinking — Job requires analyzing information and using logic to address work-related issues and problems.

| Innovation | Job requires creativity and alternative thinking to develop new ideas for and answers to work-related problems. |
| Leadership | Job requires a willingness to lead, take charge, and offer opinions and direction. |

Job Zone Component	**Job Zone Component Definitions**
Title	Job Zone Three: Medium Preparation Needed
Overall Experience	Previous work-related skill, knowledge, or experience is required for these occupations. For example, an electrician must have completed three or four years of apprenticeship or several years of vocational training, and often must have passed a licensing exam, in order to perform the job.
Job Training	Employees in these occupations usually need one or two years of training involving both on-the-job experience and informal training with experienced workers.
Job Zone Examples	These occupations usually involve using communication and organizational skills to coordinate, supervise, manage, or train others to accomplish goals. Examples include dental assistants, electricians, fish and game wardens, legal secretaries, personnel recruiters, and recreation workers.
SVP Range	(6.0 to < 7.0)
Education	Most occupations in this zone require training in vocational schools, related on-the-job experience, or an associate's degree. Some may require a bachelor's degree.

29-2031.00 - Cardiovascular Technologists and Technicians

Conduct tests on pulmonary or cardiovascular systems of patients for diagnostic purposes. May conduct or assist in electrocardiograms, cardiac catheterizations, pulmonary-functions, lung capacity, and similar tests.

Tasks

1) Observe gauges, recorder, and video screens of data analysis system during imaging of cardiovascular system.

2) Compare measurements of heart wall thickness and chamber sizes to standard norms to identify abnormalities.

3) Assist physicians in diagnosis and treatment of cardiac and peripheral vascular treatments, for example, assisting with balloon angioplasties to treat blood vessel blockages.

4) Assess cardiac physiology and calculate valve areas from blood flow velocity measurements.

5) Adjust equipment and controls according to physicians' orders or established protocol.

6) Conduct electrocardiogram, phonocardiogram, echocardiogram, stress testing, and other cardiovascular tests to record patients' cardiac activity, using specialized electronic test equipment, recording devices, and laboratory instruments.

7) Explain testing procedures to patient to obtain cooperation and reduce anxiety.

8) Activate fluoroscope and camera to produce images used to guide catheter through cardiovascular system.

9) Monitor patients' comfort and safety during tests, alerting physicians to abnormalities or changes in patient responses.

10) Inject contrast medium into patients' blood vessels.

11) Prepare reports of diagnostic procedures for interpretation by physician.

12) Check, test, and maintain cardiology equipment, making minor repairs when necessary, to ensure proper operation.

13) Supervise and train other cardiology technologists and students.

14) Obtain and record patient identification, medical history and test results.

15) Conduct tests of pulmonary system, using spirometer and other respiratory testing equipment.

16) Enter factors such as amount and quality of radiation beam, and filming sequence, into computer.

17) Monitor patients' blood pressure and heart rate using electrocardiogram (EKG) equipment during diagnostic and therapeutic procedures in order to notify the physician if something appears wrong.

18) Attach electrodes to the patients' chests, arms, and legs, connect electrodes to leads from the electrocardiogram (EKG) machine, and operate the EKG machine to obtain a reading.

19) Observe ultrasound display screen and listen to signals to record vascular information such as blood pressure, limb volume changes, oxygen saturation and cerebral circulation.

20) Operate diagnostic imaging equipment to produce contrast enhanced radiographs of heart and cardiovascular system.

21) Reprogram pacemakers according to required standards.

29-2032.00 - Diagnostic Medical Sonographers

Produce ultrasonic recordings of internal organs for use by physicians.

Tasks

1) Obtain and record accurate patient history, including prior test results and information from physical examinations.

2) Coordinate work with physicians and other health-care team members, including providing assistance during invasive procedures.

3) Record and store suitable images, using camera unit connected to the ultrasound equipment.

4) Maintain stock and supplies, preparing supplies for special examinations and ordering supplies when necessary.

5) Process and code film from procedures and complete appropriate documentation.

6) Maintain records that include patient information, sonographs and interpretations, files of correspondence, publications and regulations, and quality assurance records (e.g., pathology, biopsy, post-operative reports).

7) Perform clerical duties such as scheduling exams and special procedures, keeping records and archiving computerized images.

8) Supervise and train students and other medical sonographers.

9) Perform legal and ethical duties including preparing safety and accident reports, obtaining written consent from patient to perform invasive procedures, and reporting symptoms of abuse and neglect.

10) Load and unload film cassettes used to record images from procedures.

11) Perform medical procedures such as administering oxygen, inserting and removing airways, taking vital signs, and giving emergency treatment such as first aid or cardiopulmonary resuscitation.

12) Provide sonogram and oral or written summary of technical findings to physician for use in medical diagnosis.

13) Observe and care for patients throughout examinations to ensure their safety and comfort.

14) Decide which images to include, looking for differences between healthy and pathological areas.

15) Observe screen during scan to ensure that image produced is satisfactory for diagnostic purposes, making adjustments to equipment as required.

16) Determine whether scope of exam should be extended, based on findings.

17) Prepare patient for exam by explaining procedure, transferring them to ultrasound table, scrubbing skin and applying gel, and positioning them properly.

18) Select appropriate equipment settings and adjust patient positions to obtain the best sites and angles.

19) Operate ultrasound equipment to produce and record images of the motion, shape and composition of blood, organs, tissues and bodily masses such as fluid accumulations.

Knowledge	**Knowledge Definitions**
Medicine and Dentistry	Knowledge of the information and techniques needed to diagnose and treat human injuries, diseases, and deformities. This includes symptoms, treatment alternatives, drug properties and interactions, and preventive health-care measures.
English Language	Knowledge of the structure and content of the English language including the meaning and spelling of words, rules of composition, and grammar.
Customer and Personal Service	Knowledge of principles and processes for providing customer and personal services. This includes customer needs assessment, meeting quality standards for services, and evaluation of customer satisfaction.
Education and Training	Knowledge of principles and methods for curriculum and training design, teaching and instruction for individuals and groups, and the measurement of training effects.
Physics	Knowledge and prediction of physical principles, laws, their interrelationships, and applications to understanding fluid, material, and atmospheric dynamics, and mechanical, electrical, atomic and sub-atomic structures and processes.
Biology	Knowledge of plant and animal organisms, their tissues, cells, functions, interdependencies, and interactions with each other and the environment.
Clerical	Knowledge of administrative and clerical procedures and systems such as word processing, managing files and records, stenography and transcription, designing forms, and other office procedures and terminology.
Computers and Electronics	Knowledge of circuit boards, processors, chips, electronic equipment, and computer hardware and software, including applications and programming.
Mathematics	Knowledge of arithmetic, algebra, geometry, calculus, statistics, and their applications.

Therapy and Counseling	Knowledge of principles, methods, and procedures for diagnosis. treatment, and rehabilitation of physical and mental dysfunctions, and for career counseling and guidance.
Administration and Management	Knowledge of business and management principles involved in strategic planning, resource allocation, human resources modeling, leadership technique, production methods, and coordination of people and resources.
Psychology	Knowledge of human behavior and performance; individual differences in ability, personality, and interests; learning and motivation; psychological research methods; and the assessment and treatment of behavioral and affective disorders.
Personnel and Human Resources	Knowledge of principles and procedures for personnel recruitment, selection, training, compensation and benefits, labor relations and negotiation, and personnel information systems.
Engineering and Technology	Knowledge of the practical application of engineering science and technology. This includes applying principles, techniques, procedures, and equipment to the design and production of various goods and services.
Chemistry	Knowledge of the chemical composition, structure, and properties of substances and of the chemical processes and transformations that they undergo. This includes uses of chemicals and their interactions, danger signs, production techniques, and disposal methods.
Communications and Media	Knowledge of media production, communication, and dissemination techniques and methods. This includes alternative ways to inform and entertain via written, oral, and visual media.
Public Safety and Security	Knowledge of relevant equipment, policies, procedures, and strategies to promote effective local, state, or national security operations for the protection of people, data, property, and institutions.
Law and Government	Knowledge of laws, legal codes, court procedures, precedents, government regulations, executive orders, agency rules, and the democratic political process.
Telecommunications	Knowledge of transmission, broadcasting, switching, control, and operation of telecommunications systems.
Mechanical	Knowledge of machines and tools, including their designs, uses, repair, and maintenance.
Philosophy and Theology	Knowledge of different philosophical systems and religions. This includes their basic principles, values, ethics, ways of thinking, customs, practices, and their impact on human culture.
Sociology and Anthropology	Knowledge of group behavior and dynamics, societal trends and influences, human migrations, ethnicity, cultures and their history and origins.
Foreign Language	Knowledge of the structure and content of a foreign (non-English) language including the meaning and spelling of words, rules of composition and grammar, and pronunciation.
Design	Knowledge of design techniques, tools, and principles involved in production of precision technical plans, blueprints, drawings, and models.
Production and Processing	Knowledge of raw materials, production processes, quality control, costs, and other techniques for maximizing the effective manufacture and distribution of goods.
Sales and Marketing	Knowledge of principles and methods for showing, promoting, and selling products or services. This includes marketing strategy and tactics, product demonstration, sales techniques, and sales control systems.
Economics and Accounting	Knowledge of economic and accounting principles and practices, the financial markets, banking and the analysis and reporting of financial data.
Transportation	Knowledge of principles and methods for moving people or goods by air, rail, sea, or road, including the relative costs and benefits.
Building and Construction	Knowledge of materials, methods, and the tools involved in the construction or repair of houses, buildings, or other structures such as highways and roads.
History and Archeology	Knowledge of historical events and their causes, indicators, and effects on civilizations and cultures.
Fine Arts	Knowledge of the theory and techniques required to compose, produce, and perform works of music, dance, visual arts, drama, and sculpture.
Geography	Knowledge of principles and methods for describing the features of land, sea, and air masses, including their physical characteristics, locations, interrelationships, and distribution of plant, animal, and human life.
Food Production	Knowledge of techniques and equipment for planting, growing, and harvesting food products (both plant and animal) for consumption, including storage/handling techniques.

Skills	Skills Definitions
Active Listening	Giving full attention to what other people are saying, taking time to understand the points being made, asking questions as appropriate, and not interrupting at inappropriate times.
Reading Comprehension	Understanding written sentences and paragraphs in work related documents.

Social Perceptiveness	Being aware of others' reactions and understanding why they react as they do.
Speaking	Talking to others to convey information effectively.
Critical Thinking	Using logic and reasoning to identify the strengths and weaknesses of alternative solutions, conclusions or approaches to problems.
Active Learning	Understanding the implications of new information for both current and future problem-solving and decision-making.
Learning Strategies	Selecting and using training/instructional methods and procedures appropriate for the situation when learning or teaching new things.
Instructing	Teaching others how to do something.
Coordination	Adjusting actions in relation to others' actions.
Service Orientation	Actively looking for ways to help people.
Writing	Communicating effectively in writing as appropriate for the needs of the audience.
Operation and Control	Controlling operations of equipment or systems.
Science	Using scientific rules and methods to solve problems.
Time Management	Managing one's own time and the time of others.
Monitoring	Monitoring/Assessing performance of yourself, other individuals, or organizations to make improvements or take corrective action.
Judgment and Decision Making	Considering the relative costs and benefits of potential actions to choose the most appropriate one.
Equipment Selection	Determining the kind of tools and equipment needed to do a job.
Mathematics	Using mathematics to solve problems.
Quality Control Analysis	Conducting tests and inspections of products, services, or processes to evaluate quality or performance.
Troubleshooting	Determining causes of operating errors and deciding what to do about it.
Management of Material Resources	Obtaining and seeing to the appropriate use of equipment, facilities, and materials needed to do certain work.
Equipment Maintenance	Performing routine maintenance on equipment and determining when and what kind of maintenance is needed.
Operation Monitoring	Watching gauges, dials, or other indicators to make sure a machine is working properly.
Complex Problem Solving	Identifying complex problems and reviewing related information to develop and evaluate options and implement solutions.
Systems Evaluation	Identifying measures or indicators of system performance and the actions needed to improve or correct performance, relative to the goals of the system.
Systems Analysis	Determining how a system should work and how changes in conditions, operations, and the environment will affect outcomes.
Management of Personnel Resources	Motivating, developing, and directing people as they work, identifying the best people for the job.
Persuasion	Persuading others to change their minds or behavior.
Technology Design	Generating or adapting equipment and technology to serve user needs.
Operations Analysis	Analyzing needs and product requirements to create a design.
Negotiation	Bringing others together and trying to reconcile differences.
Installation	Installing equipment, machines, wiring, or programs to meet specifications.
Management of Financial Resources	Determining how money will be spent to get the work done, and accounting for these expenditures.
Repairing	Repairing machines or systems using the needed tools.
Programming	Writing computer programs for various purposes.

Ability	Ability Definitions
Oral Expression	The ability to communicate information and ideas in speaking so others will understand.
Problem Sensitivity	The ability to tell when something is wrong or is likely to go wrong. It does not involve solving the problem, only recognizing there is a problem.
Oral Comprehension	The ability to listen to and understand information and ideas presented through spoken words and sentences.
Near Vision	The ability to see details at close range (within a few feet of the observer).
Speech Clarity	The ability to speak clearly so others can understand you.
Written Expression	The ability to communicate information and ideas in writing so others will understand.
Speech Recognition	The ability to identify and understand the speech of another person.
Inductive Reasoning	The ability to combine pieces of information to form general rules or conclusions (includes finding a relationship among seemingly unrelated events).
Control Precision	The ability to quickly and repeatedly adjust the controls of a machine or a vehicle to exact positions.
Flexibility of Closure	The ability to identify or detect a known pattern (a figure, object, word, or sound) that is hidden in other distracting material.
Written Comprehension	The ability to read and understand information and ideas presented in writing.

Deductive Reasoning	The ability to apply general rules to specific problems to produce answers that make sense.
Finger Dexterity	The ability to make precisely coordinated movements of the fingers of one or both hands to grasp, manipulate, or assemble very small objects.
Perceptual Speed	The ability to quickly and accurately compare similarities and differences among sets of letters, numbers, objects, pictures, or patterns. The things to be compared may be presented at the same time or one after the other. This ability also includes comparing a presented object with a remembered object.
Arm-Hand Steadiness	The ability to keep your hand and arm steady while moving your arm or while holding your arm and hand in one position.
Manual Dexterity	The ability to quickly move your hand, your hand together with your arm, or your two hands to grasp, manipulate, or assemble objects.
Speed of Closure	The ability to quickly make sense of, combine, and organize information into meaningful patterns.
Extent Flexibility	The ability to bend, stretch, twist, or reach with your body, arms, and/or legs.
Multilimb Coordination	The ability to coordinate two or more limbs (for example, two arms, two legs, or one leg and one arm) while sitting, standing, or lying down. It does not involve performing the activities while the whole body is in motion.
Information Ordering	The ability to arrange things or actions in a certain order or pattern according to a specific rule or set of rules (e.g., patterns of numbers, letters, words, pictures, mathematical operations).
Selective Attention	The ability to concentrate on a task over a period of time without being distracted.
Response Orientation	The ability to choose quickly between two or more movements in response to two or more different signals (lights, sounds, pictures). It includes the speed with which the correct response is started with the hand, foot, or other body part.
Visual Color Discrimination	The ability to match or detect differences between colors, including shades of color and brightness.
Category Flexibility	The ability to generate or use different sets of rules for combining or grouping things in different ways.
Time Sharing	The ability to shift back and forth between two or more activities or sources of information (such as speech, sounds, touch, or other sources).
Wrist-Finger Speed	The ability to make fast, simple, repeated movements of the fingers, hands, and wrists.
Visualization	The ability to imagine how something will look after it is moved around or when its parts are moved or rearranged.
Reaction Time	The ability to quickly respond (with the hand, finger, or foot) to a signal (sound, light, picture) when it appears.
Depth Perception	The ability to judge which of several objects is closer or farther away from you, or to judge the distance between you and an object.
Far Vision	The ability to see details at a distance.
Trunk Strength	The ability to use your abdominal and lower back muscles to support part of the body repeatedly or continuously over time without 'giving out' or fatiguing.
Static Strength	The ability to exert maximum muscle force to lift, push, pull, or carry objects.
Fluency of Ideas	The ability to come up with a number of ideas about a topic (the number of ideas is important, not their quality, correctness, or creativity).
Originality	The ability to come up with unusual or clever ideas about a given topic or situation, or to develop creative ways to solve a problem.
Rate Control	The ability to time your movements or the movement of a piece of equipment in anticipation of changes in the speed and/or direction of a moving object or scene.
Hearing Sensitivity	The ability to detect or tell the differences between sounds that vary in pitch and loudness.
Mathematical Reasoning	The ability to choose the right mathematical methods or formulas to solve a problem.
Auditory Attention	The ability to focus on a single source of sound in the presence of other distracting sounds.
Gross Body Coordination	The ability to coordinate the movement of your arms, legs, and torso together when the whole body is in motion.
Stamina	The ability to exert yourself physically over long periods of time without getting winded or out of breath.
Memorization	The ability to remember information such as words, numbers, pictures, and procedures.
Speed of Limb Movement	The ability to quickly move the arms and legs.
Gross Body Equilibrium	The ability to keep or regain your body balance or stay upright when in an unstable position.
Dynamic Strength	The ability to exert muscle force repeatedly or continuously over time. This involves muscular endurance and resistance to muscle fatigue.
Explosive Strength	The ability to use short bursts of muscle force to propel oneself (as in jumping or sprinting), or to throw an object.
Number Facility	The ability to add, subtract, multiply, or divide quickly and correctly.

Spatial Orientation	The ability to know your location in relation to the environment or to know where other objects are in relation to you.
Sound Localization	The ability to tell the direction from which a sound originated.
Dynamic Flexibility	The ability to quickly and repeatedly bend, stretch, twist, or reach out with your body, arms, and/or legs.
Night Vision	The ability to see under low light conditions.
Peripheral Vision	The ability to see objects or movement of objects to one's side when the eyes are looking ahead.
Glare Sensitivity	The ability to see objects in the presence of glare or bright lighting.

Work_Activity	**Work_Activity Definitions**
Assisting and Caring for Others	Providing personal assistance, medical attention, emotional support, or other personal care to others such as coworkers, customers, or patients.
Documenting/Recording Information	Entering, transcribing, recording, storing, or maintaining information in written or electronic/magnetic form.
Getting Information	Observing, receiving, and otherwise obtaining information from all relevant sources.
Identifying Objects, Actions, and Events	Identifying information by categorizing, estimating, recognizing differences or similarities, and detecting changes in circumstances or events.
Establishing and Maintaining Interpersonal Relatio	Developing constructive and cooperative working relationships with others, and maintaining them over time.
Communicating with Supervisors, Peers, or Subordin	Providing information to supervisors, co-workers, and subordinates by telephone, in written form, e-mail, or in person.
Interacting With Computers	Using computers and computer systems (including hardware and software) to program, write software, set up functions, enter data, or process information.
Controlling Machines and Processes	Using either control mechanisms or direct physical activity to operate machines or processes (not including computers or vehicles).
Making Decisions and Solving Problems	Analyzing information and evaluating results to choose the best solution and solve problems.
Resolving Conflicts and Negotiating with Others	Handling complaints, settling disputes, and resolving grievances and conflicts, or otherwise negotiating with others.
Interpreting the Meaning of Information for Others	Translating or explaining what information means and how it can be used.
Monitor Processes, Materials, or Surroundings	Monitoring and reviewing information from materials, events, or the environment, to detect or assess problems.
Performing for or Working Directly with the Public	Performing for people or dealing directly with the public. This includes serving customers in restaurants and stores, and receiving clients or guests.
Handling and Moving Objects	Using hands and arms in handling, installing, positioning, and moving materials, and manipulating things.
Organizing, Planning, and Prioritizing Work	Developing specific goals and plans to prioritize, organize, and accomplish your work.
Updating and Using Relevant Knowledge	Keeping up-to-date technically and applying new knowledge to your job.
Estimating the Quantifiable Characteristics of Pro	Estimating sizes, distances, and quantities; or determining time, costs, resources, or materials needed to perform a work activity.
Performing General Physical Activities	Performing physical activities that require considerable use of your arms and legs and moving your whole body, such as climbing, lifting, balancing, walking, stooping, and handling of materials.
Analyzing Data or Information	Identifying the underlying principles, reasons, or facts of information by breaking down information or data into separate parts.
Evaluating Information to Determine Compliance wit	Using relevant information and individual judgment to determine whether events or processes comply with laws, regulations, or standards.
Inspecting Equipment, Structures, or Material	Inspecting equipment, structures, or materials to identify the cause of errors or other problems or defects.
Training and Teaching Others	Identifying the educational needs of others, developing formal educational or training programs or classes, and teaching or instructing others.
Communicating with Persons Outside Organization	Communicating with people outside the organization, representing the organization to customers, the public, government, and other external sources. This information can be exchanged in person, in writing, or by telephone or e-mail.
Developing and Building Teams	Encouraging and building mutual trust, respect, and cooperation among team members.
Coordinating the Work and Activities of Others	Getting members of a group to work together to accomplish tasks.
Performing Administrative Activities	Performing day-to-day administrative tasks such as maintaining information files and processing paperwork.
Judging the Qualities of Things, Services, or Peop	Assessing the value, importance, or quality of things or people.
Scheduling Work and Activities	Scheduling events, programs, and activities, as well as the work of others.

Processing Information	Compiling, coding, categorizing, calculating, tabulating, auditing, or verifying information or data.
Thinking Creatively	Developing, designing, or creating new applications, ideas, relationships, systems, or products, including artistic contributions.
Repairing and Maintaining Mechanical Equipment	Servicing, repairing, adjusting, and testing machines, devices, moving parts, and equipment that operate primarily on the basis of mechanical (not electronic) principles.
Coaching and Developing Others	Identifying the developmental needs of others and coaching, mentoring, or otherwise helping others to improve their knowledge or skills.
Guiding, Directing, and Motivating Subordinates	Providing guidance and direction to subordinates, including setting performance standards and monitoring performance.
Developing Objectives and Strategies	Establishing long-range objectives and specifying the strategies and actions to achieve them.
Provide Consultation and Advice to Others	Providing guidance and expert advice to management or other groups on technical, systems-, or process-related topics.
Repairing and Maintaining Electronic Equipment	Servicing, repairing, calibrating, regulating, fine-tuning, or testing machines, devices, and equipment that operate primarily on the basis of electrical or electronic (not mechanical) principles.
Monitoring and Controlling Resources	Monitoring and controlling resources and overseeing the spending of money.
Staffing Organizational Units	Recruiting, interviewing, selecting, hiring, and promoting employees in an organization.
Operating Vehicles, Mechanized Devices, or Equipme	Running, maneuvering, navigating, or driving vehicles or mechanized equipment, such as forklifts, passenger vehicles, aircraft, or water craft.
Drafting, Laying Out, and Specifying Technical Dev	Providing documentation, detailed instructions, drawings, or specifications to tell others about how devices, parts, equipment, or structures are to be fabricated, constructed, assembled, modified, maintained, or used.
Selling or Influencing Others	Convincing others to buy merchandise/goods or to otherwise change their minds or actions.

Work_Content	Work_Content Definitions
Spend Time Using Your Hands to Handle, Control, or	How much does this job require using your hands to handle, control, or feel objects, tools or controls?
Importance of Being Exact or Accurate	How important is being very exact or highly accurate in performing this job?
Contact With Others	How much does this job require the worker to be in contact with others (face-to-face, by telephone, or otherwise) in order to perform it?
Exposed to Disease or Infections	How often does this job require exposure to disease/infections?
Indoors, Environmentally Controlled	How often does this job require working indoors in environmentally controlled conditions?
Face-to-Face Discussions	How often do you have to have face-to-face discussions with individuals or teams in this job?
Physical Proximity	To what extent does this job require the worker to perform job tasks in close physical proximity to other people?
Telephone	How often do you have telephone conversations in this job?
Spend Time Making Repetitive Motions	How much does this job require making repetitive motions?
Frequency of Decision Making	How frequently is the worker required to make decisions that affect other people, the financial resources, and/or the image and reputation of the organization?
Time Pressure	How often does this job require the worker to meet strict deadlines?
Work With Work Group or Team	How important is it to work with others in a group or team in this job?
Structured versus Unstructured Work	To what extent is this job structured for the worker, rather than allowing the worker to determine tasks, priorities, and goals?
Impact of Decisions on Co-workers or Company Resul	How do the decisions an employee makes impact the results of co-workers, clients or the company?
Deal With External Customers	How important is it to work with external customers or the public in this job?
Freedom to Make Decisions	How much decision making freedom, without supervision, does the job offer?
Importance of Repeating Same Tasks	How important is repeating the same physical activities (e.g., key entry) or mental activities (e.g., checking entries in a ledger) over and over, without stopping, to performing this job?
Deal With Unpleasant or Angry People	How frequently does the worker have to deal with unpleasant, angry, or discourteous individuals as part of the job requirements?
Spend Time Bending or Twisting the Body	How much does this job require bending or twisting your body?
Responsible for Others' Health and Safety	How much responsibility is there for the health and safety of others in this job?
Level of Competition	To what extent does this job require the worker to compete or to be aware of competitive pressures?
Cramped Work Space, Awkward Positions	How often does this job require working in cramped work spaces that requires getting into awkward positions?

Consequence of Error	How serious would the result usually be if the worker made a mistake that was not readily correctable?
Spend Time Sitting	How much does this job require sitting?
Sounds, Noise Levels Are Distracting or Uncomforta	How often does this job require working exposed to sounds and noise levels that are distracting or uncomfortable?
Wear Common Protective or Safety Equipment such as	How much does this job require wearing common protective or safety equipment such as safety shoes, glasses, gloves, hard hats or live jackets?
Coordinate or Lead Others	How important is it to coordinate or lead others in accomplishing work activities in this job?
Exposed to Contaminants	How often does this job require working exposed to contaminants (such as pollutants, gases, dust or odors)?
Responsibility for Outcomes and Results	How responsible is the worker for work outcomes and results of other workers?
Spend Time Standing	How much does this job require standing?
Frequency of Conflict Situations	How often are there conflict situations the employee has to face in this job?
Spend Time Walking and Running	How much does this job require walking and running?
Deal With Physically Aggressive People	How frequently does this job require the worker to deal with physical aggression of violent individuals?
Exposed to Hazardous Conditions	How often does this job require exposure to hazardous conditions?
Letters and Memos	How often does the job require written letters and memos?
Exposed to Radiation	How often does this job require exposure to radiation?
Extremely Bright or Inadequate Lighting	How often does this job require working in extremely bright or inadequate lighting conditions?
Pace Determined by Speed of Equipment	How important is it to this job that the pace is determined by the speed of equipment or machinery? (This does not refer to keeping busy at all times on this job.)
Wear Specialized Protective or Safety Equipment su	How much does this job require wearing specialized protective or safety equipment such as breathing apparatus, safety harness, full protection suits, or radiation protection?
Electronic Mail	How often do you use electronic mail in this job?
Degree of Automation	How automated is the job?
Public Speaking	How often do you have to perform public speaking in this job?
Spend Time Keeping or Regaining Balance	How much does this job require keeping or regaining your balance?
Spend Time Kneeling, Crouching, Stooping, or Crawl	How much does this job require kneeling, crouching, stooping, or crawling?
In an Enclosed Vehicle or Equipment	How often does this job require working in a closed vehicle or equipment (e.g., car)?
Exposed to Minor Burns, Cuts, Bites, or Stings	How often does this job require exposure to minor burns, cuts, bites, or stings?
Exposed to Hazardous Equipment	How often does this job require exposure to hazardous equipment?
Very Hot or Cold Temperatures	How often does this job require working in very hot (above 90 F degrees) or very cold (below 32 F degrees) temperatures?
Spend Time Climbing Ladders, Scaffolds, or Poles	How much does this job require climbing ladders, scaffolds, or poles?
Indoors, Not Environmentally Controlled	How often does this job require working indoors in non-controlled environmental conditions (e.g., warehouse without heat)?
Outdoors, Under Cover	How often does this job require working outdoors, under cover (e.g., structure with roof but no walls)?
Exposed to Whole Body Vibration	How often does this job require exposure to whole body vibration (e.g., operate a jackhammer)?
Outdoors, Exposed to Weather	How often does this job require working outdoors, exposed to all weather conditions?
Exposed to High Places	How often does this job require exposure to high places?
In an Open Vehicle or Equipment	How often does this job require working in an open vehicle or equipment (e.g., tractor)?

Work_Styles	Work_Styles Definitions
Attention to Detail	Job requires being careful about detail and thorough in completing work tasks.
Integrity	Job requires being honest and ethical.
Dependability	Job requires being reliable, responsible, and dependable, and fulfilling obligations.
Concern for Others	Job requires being sensitive to others' needs and feelings and being understanding and helpful on the job.
Self Control	Job requires maintaining composure, keeping emotions in check, controlling anger, and avoiding aggressive behavior, even in very difficult situations.
Analytical Thinking	Job requires analyzing information and using logic to address work-related issues and problems.
Independence	Job requires developing one's own ways of doing things, guiding oneself with little or no supervision, and depending on oneself to get things done.
Cooperation	Job requires being pleasant with others on the job and displaying a good-natured, cooperative attitude.
Initiative	Job requires a willingness to take on responsibilities and challenges.

Persistence	Job requires persistence in the face of obstacles.
Stress Tolerance	Job requires accepting criticism and dealing calmly and effectively with high stress situations.
Adaptability/Flexibility	Job requires being open to change (positive or negative) and to considerable variety in the workplace.
Achievement/Effort	Job requires establishing and maintaining personally challenging achievement goals and exerting effort toward mastering tasks.
Social Orientation	Job requires preferring to work with others rather than alone, and being personally connected with others on the job.
Innovation	Job requires creativity and alternative thinking to develop new ideas for and answers to work-related problems.
Leadership	Job requires a willingness to lead, take charge, and offer opinions and direction.

Job Zone Component	Job Zone Component Definitions
Title	Job Zone Three: Medium Preparation Needed
Overall Experience	Previous work-related skill, knowledge, or experience is required for these occupations. For example, an electrician must have completed three or four years of apprenticeship or several years of vocational training, and often must have passed a licensing exam, in order to perform the job.
Job Training	Employees in these occupations usually need one or two years of training involving both on-the-job experience and informal training with experienced workers.
Job Zone Examples	These occupations usually involve using communication and organizational skills to coordinate, supervise, manage, or train others to accomplish goals. Examples include dental assistants, electricians, fish and game wardens, legal secretaries, personnel recruiters, and recreation workers.
SVP Range	(6.0 to < 7.0)
Education	Most occupations in this zone require training in vocational schools, related on-the-job experience, or an associate's degree. Some may require a bachelor's degree.

29-2033.00 - Nuclear Medicine Technologists

Prepare, administer, and measure radioactive isotopes in therapeutic, diagnostic, and tracer studies utilizing a variety of radioisotope equipment. Prepare stock solutions of radioactive materials and calculate doses to be administered by radiologists. Subject patients to radiation. Execute blood volume, red cell survival, and fat absorption studies following standard laboratory techniques.

Tasks

1) Dispose of radioactive materials and store radiopharmaceuticals, following radiation safety procedures.

2) Process cardiac function studies, using computer.

3) Maintain and calibrate radioisotope and laboratory equipment.

4) Gather information on patients' illnesses and medical history to guide the choice of diagnostic procedures for therapy.

5) Develop treatment procedures for nuclear medicine treatment programs.

6) Administer radiopharmaceuticals or radiation to patients to detect or treat diseases, using radioisotope equipment, under direction of physician.

7) Produce a computer-generated or film image for interpretation by a physician.

8) Measure glandular activity, blood volume, red cell survival, and radioactivity of patient, using scanners, Geiger counters, scintillometers, and other laboratory equipment.

9) Prepare stock radiopharmaceuticals, adhering to safety standards that minimize radiation exposure to workers and patients.

10) Position radiation fields, radiation beams, and patient to allow for most effective treatment of patient's disease, using computer.

11) Explain test procedures and safety precautions to patients and provide them with assistance during test procedures.

12) Detect and map radiopharmaceuticals in patients' bodies, using a camera to produce photographic or computer images.

13) Calculate, measure and record radiation dosage or radiopharmaceuticals received, used and disposed, using computer and following physician's prescription.

14) Add radioactive substances to biological specimens, such as blood, urine and feces, to determine therapeutic drug or hormone levels.

15) Record and process results of procedures.

29-2034.01 - Radiologic Technologists

Take X-rays and CAT scans or administer nonradioactive materials into patient's blood stream for diagnostic purposes. Includes technologists who specialize in other modalities, such as computed tomography, ultrasound, and magnetic resonance.

Tasks

1) Set up examination rooms, ensuring that all necessary equipment is ready.

2) Review and evaluate developed x-rays, video tape, or computer generated information to determine if images are satisfactory for diagnostic purposes.

3) Position and immobilize patient on examining table.

4) Monitor patients' conditions and reactions, reporting abnormal signs to physician.

5) Take thorough and accurate patient medical histories.

6) Use radiation safety measures and protection devices to comply with government regulations and to ensure safety of patients and staff.

7) Explain procedures and observe patients to ensure safety and comfort during scan.

8) Position imaging equipment and adjust controls to set exposure time and distance, according to specification of examination.

9) Monitor video display of area being scanned and adjust density or contrast to improve picture quality.

10) Operate or oversee operation of radiologic and magnetic imaging equipment to produce images of the body for diagnostic purposes.

11) Key commands and data into computer to document and specify scan sequences, adjust transmitters and receivers, or photograph certain images.

12) Remove and process film.

13) Prepare and administer oral or injected contrast media to patients.

14) Provide assistance with such tasks as dressing and changing to seriously ill, injured, or disabled patients.

15) Demonstrate new equipment, procedures, and techniques to staff, and provide technical assistance.

16) Record, process and maintain patient data and treatment records, and prepare reports.

17) Measure thickness of section to be radiographed, using instruments similar to measuring tapes.

18) Assign duties to radiologic staff to maintain patient flows and achieve production goals.

19) Perform scheduled maintenance and minor emergency repairs on radiographic equipment.

20) Collaborate with other medical team members, such as physicians and nurses, to conduct angiography or special vascular procedures.

21) Operate fluoroscope to aid physician to view and guide wire or catheter through blood vessels to area of interest.

22) Perform administrative duties such as developing departmental operating budget, coordinating purchases of supplies and equipment and preparing work schedules.

23) Move ultrasound scanner over patient's body and watch pattern produced on video screen.

Knowledge	Knowledge Definitions
Customer and Personal Service	Knowledge of principles and processes for providing customer and personal services. This includes customer needs assessment, meeting quality standards for services, and evaluation of customer satisfaction.
Medicine and Dentistry	Knowledge of the information and techniques needed to diagnose and treat human injuries, diseases, and deformities. This includes symptoms, treatment alternatives, drug properties and interactions, and preventive health-care measures.
Physics	Knowledge and prediction of physical principles, laws, their interrelationships, and applications to understanding fluid, material, and atmospheric dynamics, and mechanical, electrical, atomic and sub-atomic structures and processes.
Psychology	Knowledge of human behavior and performance; individual differences in ability, personality, and interests; learning and motivation; psychological research methods; and the assessment and treatment of behavioral and affective disorders.
English Language	Knowledge of the structure and content of the English language including the meaning and spelling of words, rules of composition, and grammar.
Computers and Electronics	Knowledge of circuit boards, processors, chips, electronic equipment, and computer hardware and software, including applications and programming.
Mathematics	Knowledge of arithmetic, algebra, geometry, calculus, statistics, and their applications.
Biology	Knowledge of plant and animal organisms, their tissues, cells, functions, interdependencies, and interactions with each other and the environment.

Chemistry	Knowledge of the chemical composition. structure. and properties of substances and of the chemical processes and transformations that they undergo. This includes uses of chemicals and their interactions, danger signs, production techniques, and disposal methods.
Public Safety and Security	Knowledge of relevant equipment. policies. procedures, and strategies to promote effective local. state. or national security operations for the protection of people. data. property. and institutions.
Clerical	Knowledge of administrative and clerical procedures and systems such as word processing. managing files and records. stenography and transcription, designing forms, and other office procedures and terminology.
Education and Training	Knowledge of principles and methods for curriculum and training design, teaching and instruction for individuals and groups, and the measurement of training effects.
Administration and Management	Knowledge of business and management principles involved in strategic planning, resource allocation. human resources modeling, leadership technique. production methods, and coordination of people and resources.
Mechanical	Knowledge of machines and tools. including their designs. uses, repair, and maintenance.
Engineering and Technology	Knowledge of the practical application of engineering science and technology. This includes applying principles, techniques, procedures, and equipment to the design and production of various goods and services.
Therapy and Counseling	Knowledge of principles, methods. and procedures for diagnosis, treatment, and rehabilitation of physical and mental dysfunctions, and for career counseling and guidance.
Foreign Language	Knowledge of the structure and content of a foreign (non-English) language including the meaning and spelling of words, rules of composition and grammar, and pronunciation.
Personnel and Human Resources	Knowledge of principles and procedures for personnel recruitment, selection, training, compensation and benefits, labor relations and negotiation, and personnel information systems.
Production and Processing	Knowledge of raw materials, production processes, quality control, costs, and other techniques for maximizing the effective manufacture and distribution of goods.
Sociology and Anthropology	Knowledge of group behavior and dynamics, societal trends and influences, human migrations, ethnicity, cultures and their history and origins.
Law and Government	Knowledge of laws, legal codes, court procedures, precedents, government regulations, executive orders, agency rules, and the democratic political process.
Communications and Media	Knowledge of media production, communication, and dissemination techniques and methods. This includes alternative ways to inform and entertain via written, oral, and visual media.
Telecommunications	Knowledge of transmission, broadcasting, switching, control, and operation of telecommunications systems.
Economics and Accounting	Knowledge of economic and accounting principles and practices, the financial markets, banking and the analysis and reporting of financial data.
Sales and Marketing	Knowledge of principles and methods for showing, promoting, and selling products or services. This includes marketing strategy and tactics, product demonstration, sales techniques, and sales control systems.
Design	Knowledge of design techniques, tools, and principles involved in production of precision technical plans, blueprints, drawings. and models.
Philosophy and Theology	Knowledge of different philosophical systems and religions. This includes their basic principles, values, ethics, ways of thinking, customs, practices, and their impact on human culture.
Transportation	Knowledge of principles and methods for moving people or goods by air, rail, sea, or road, including the relative costs and benefits.
History and Archeology	Knowledge of historical events and their causes, indicators, and effects on civilizations and cultures.
Geography	Knowledge of principles and methods for describing the features of land, sea, and air masses, including their physical characteristics, locations, interrelationships, and distribution of plant, animal, and human life.
Fine Arts	Knowledge of the theory and techniques required to compose, produce, and perform works of music, dance, visual arts, drama, and sculpture.
Building and Construction	Knowledge of materials, methods, and the tools involved in the construction or repair of houses, buildings, or other structures such as highways and roads.
Food Production	Knowledge of techniques and equipment for planting, growing, and harvesting food products (both plant and animal) for consumption, including storage/handling techniques.

Skills   **Skills Definitions**

Active Listening	Giving full attention to what other people are saying, taking time to understand the points being made, asking questions as appropriate, and not interrupting at inappropriate times.
Speaking	Talking to others to convey information effectively.
Reading Comprehension	Understanding written sentences and paragraphs in work related documents.
Time Management	Managing one's own time and the time of others.
Critical Thinking	Using logic and reasoning to identify the strengths and weaknesses of alternative solutions, conclusions or approaches to problems.
Instructing	Teaching others how to do something.
Coordination	Adjusting actions in relation to others' actions.
Social Perceptiveness	Being aware of others' reactions and understanding why they react as they do.
Monitoring	Monitoring/Assessing performance of yourself, other individuals, or organizations to make improvements or take corrective action.
Active Learning	Understanding the implications of new information for both current and future problem-solving and decision-making.
Service Orientation	Actively looking for ways to help people.
Learning Strategies	Selecting and using training/instructional methods and procedures appropriate for the situation when learning or teaching new things.
Operation Monitoring	Watching gauges, dials, or other indicators to make sure a machine is working properly.
Troubleshooting	Determining causes of operating errors and deciding what to do about it.
Writing	Communicating effectively in writing as appropriate for the needs of the audience.
Quality Control Analysis	Conducting tests and inspections of products, services, or processes to evaluate quality or performance.
Mathematics	Using mathematics to solve problems.
Operation and Control	Controlling operations of equipment or systems.
Equipment Selection	Determining the kind of tools and equipment needed to do a job.
Science	Using scientific rules and methods to solve problems.
Systems Evaluation	Identifying measures or indicators of system performance and the actions needed to improve or correct performance, relative to the goals of the system.
Equipment Maintenance	Performing routine maintenance on equipment and determining when and what kind of maintenance is needed.
Persuasion	Persuading others to change their minds or behavior.
Judgment and Decision Making	Considering the relative costs and benefits of potential actions to choose the most appropriate one.
Complex Problem Solving	Identifying complex problems and reviewing related information to develop and evaluate options and implement solutions.
Negotiation	Bringing others together and trying to reconcile differences.
Systems Analysis	Determining how a system should work and how changes in conditions, operations, and the environment will affect outcomes.
Management of Personnel Resources	Motivating, developing, and directing people as they work, identifying the best people for the job.
Management of Material Resources	Obtaining and seeing to the appropriate use of equipment, facilities, and materials needed to do certain work.
Operations Analysis	Analyzing needs and product requirements to create a design.
Technology Design	Generating or adapting equipment and technology to serve user needs.
Repairing	Repairing machines or systems using the needed tools.
Programming	Writing computer programs for various purposes.
Installation	Installing equipment, machines, wiring, or programs to meet specifications.
Management of Financial Resources	Determining how money will be spent to get the work done, and accounting for these expenditures.

Ability   **Ability Definitions**

Near Vision	The ability to see details at close range (within a few feet of the observer).
Oral Comprehension	The ability to listen to and understand information and ideas presented through spoken words and sentences.
Problem Sensitivity	The ability to tell when something is wrong or is likely to go wrong. It does not involve solving the problem, only recognizing there is a problem.
Oral Expression	The ability to communicate information and ideas in speaking so others will understand.
Speech Clarity	The ability to speak clearly so others can understand you.
Inductive Reasoning	The ability to combine pieces of information to form general rules or conclusions (includes finding a relationship among seemingly unrelated events).
Control Precision	The ability to quickly and repeatedly adjust the controls of a machine or a vehicle to exact positions.
Speech Recognition	The ability to identify and understand the speech of another person.

Deductive Reasoning	The ability to apply general rules to specific problems to produce answers that make sense.
Written Expression	The ability to communicate information and ideas in writing so others will understand.
Finger Dexterity	The ability to make precisely coordinated movements of the fingers of one or both hands to grasp, manipulate, or assemble very small objects.
Arm-Hand Steadiness	The ability to keep your hand and arm steady while moving your arm or while holding your arm and hand in one position.
Flexibility of Closure	The ability to identify or detect a known pattern (a figure, object, word, or sound) that is hidden in other distracting material.
Written Comprehension	The ability to read and understand information and ideas presented in writing.
Information Ordering	The ability to arrange things or actions in a certain order or pattern according to a specific rule or set of rules (e.g., patterns of numbers, letters, words, pictures, mathematical operations).
Far Vision	The ability to see details at a distance.
Perceptual Speed	The ability to quickly and accurately compare similarities and differences among sets of letters, numbers, objects, pictures, or patterns. The things to be compared may be presented at the same time or one after the other. This ability also includes comparing a presented object with a remembered object.
Multilimb Coordination	The ability to coordinate two or more limbs (for example, two arms, two legs, or one leg and one arm) while sitting, standing, or lying down. It does not involve performing the activities while the whole body is in motion.
Manual Dexterity	The ability to quickly move your hand, your hand together with your arm, or your two hands to grasp, manipulate, or assemble objects.
Visual Color Discrimination	The ability to match or detect differences between colors, including shades of color and brightness.
Speed of Closure	The ability to quickly make sense of, combine, and organize information into meaningful patterns.
Selective Attention	The ability to concentrate on a task over a period of time without being distracted.
Depth Perception	The ability to judge which of several objects is closer or farther away from you, or to judge the distance between you and an object.
Category Flexibility	The ability to generate or use different sets of rules for combining or grouping things in different ways.
Time Sharing	The ability to shift back and forth between two or more activities or sources of information (such as speech, sounds, touch, or other sources).
Visualization	The ability to imagine how something will look after it is moved around or when its parts are moved or rearranged.
Mathematical Reasoning	The ability to choose the right mathematical methods or formulas to solve a problem.
Originality	The ability to come up with unusual or clever ideas about a given topic or situation, or to develop creative ways to solve a problem.
Reaction Time	The ability to quickly respond (with the hand, finger, or foot) to a signal (sound, light, picture) when it appears.
Extent Flexibility	The ability to bend, stretch, twist, or reach with your body, arms, and/or legs.
Fluency of Ideas	The ability to come up with a number of ideas about a topic (the number of ideas is important, not their quality, correctness, or creativity).
Rate Control	The ability to time your movements or the movement of a piece of equipment in anticipation of changes in the speed and/or direction of a moving object or scene.
Memorization	The ability to remember information such as words, numbers, pictures, and procedures.
Trunk Strength	The ability to use your abdominal and lower back muscles to support part of the body repeatedly or continuously over time without 'giving out' or fatiguing.
Hearing Sensitivity	The ability to detect or tell the differences between sounds that vary in pitch and loudness.
Static Strength	The ability to exert maximum muscle force to lift, push, pull, or carry objects.
Auditory Attention	The ability to focus on a single source of sound in the presence of other distracting sounds.
Stamina	The ability to exert yourself physically over long periods of time without getting winded or out of breath.
Number Facility	The ability to add, subtract, multiply, or divide quickly and correctly.
Response Orientation	The ability to choose quickly between two or more movements in response to two or more different signals (lights, sounds, pictures). It includes the speed with which the correct response is started with the hand, foot, or other body part.
Gross Body Coordination	The ability to coordinate the movement of your arms, legs, and torso together when the whole body is in motion.
Wrist-Finger Speed	The ability to make fast, simple, repeated movements of the fingers, hands, and wrists.

Dynamic Strength	The ability to exert muscle force repeatedly or continuously over time. This involves muscular endurance and resistance to muscle fatigue.
Gross Body Equilibrium	The ability to keep or regain your body balance or stay upright when in an unstable position.
Speed of Limb Movement	The ability to quickly move the arms and legs.
Spatial Orientation	The ability to know your location in relation to the environment or to know where other objects are in relation to you.
Sound Localization	The ability to tell the direction from which a sound originated.
Peripheral Vision	The ability to see objects or movement of objects to one's side when the eyes are looking ahead.
Explosive Strength	The ability to use short bursts of muscle force to propel oneself (as in jumping or sprinting), or to throw an object.
Night Vision	The ability to see under low light conditions.
Dynamic Flexibility	The ability to quickly and repeatedly bend, stretch, twist, or reach out with your body, arms, and/or legs.
Glare Sensitivity	The ability to see objects in the presence of glare or bright lighting.

Work_Activity	Work_Activity Definitions
Assisting and Caring for Others	Providing personal assistance, medical attention, emotional support, or other personal care to others such as coworkers, customers, or patients.
Performing for or Working Directly with the Public	Performing for people or dealing directly with the public. This includes serving customers in restaurants and stores, and receiving clients or guests.
Documenting/Recording Information	Entering, transcribing, recording, storing, or maintaining information in written or electronic/magnetic form.
Communicating with Supervisors, Peers, or Subordin	Providing information to supervisors, co-workers, and subordinates by telephone, in written form, e-mail, or in person.
Interacting With Computers	Using computers and computer systems (including hardware and software) to program, write software, set up functions, enter data, or process information.
Handling and Moving Objects	Using hands and arms in handling, installing, positioning, and moving materials, and manipulating things.
Identifying Objects, Actions, and Events	Identifying information by categorizing, estimating, recognizing differences or similarities, and detecting changes in circumstances or events.
Establishing and Maintaining Interpersonal Relatio	Developing constructive and cooperative working relationships with others, and maintaining them over time.
Getting Information	Observing, receiving, and otherwise obtaining information from all relevant sources.
Performing General Physical Activities	Performing physical activities that require considerable use of your arms and legs and moving your whole body, such as climbing, lifting, balancing, walking, stooping, and handling of materials.
Updating and Using Relevant Knowledge	Keeping up-to-date technically and applying new knowledge to your job.
Controlling Machines and Processes	Using either control mechanisms or direct physical activity to operate machines or processes (not including computers or vehicles).
Making Decisions and Solving Problems	Analyzing information and evaluating results to choose the best solution and solve problems.
Inspecting Equipment, Structures, or Material	Inspecting equipment, structures, or materials to identify the cause of errors or other problems or defects.
Monitor Processes, Materials, or Surroundings	Monitoring and reviewing information from materials, events, or the environment, to detect or assess problems.
Coaching and Developing Others	Identifying the developmental needs of others and coaching, mentoring, or otherwise helping others to improve their knowledge or skills.
Training and Teaching Others	Identifying the educational needs of others, developing formal educational or training programs or classes, and teaching or instructing others.
Processing Information	Compiling, coding, categorizing, calculating, tabulating, auditing, or verifying information or data.
Organizing, Planning, and Prioritizing Work	Developing specific goals and plans to prioritize, organize, and accomplish your work.
Evaluating Information to Determine Compliance wit	Using relevant information and individual judgment to determine whether events or processes comply with laws, regulations, or standards.
Interpreting the Meaning of Information for Others	Translating or explaining what information means and how it can be used.
Thinking Creatively	Developing, designing, or creating new applications, ideas, relationships, systems, or products, including artistic contributions.
Developing and Building Teams	Encouraging and building mutual trust, respect, and cooperation among team members.
Estimating the Quantifiable Characteristics of Pro	Estimating sizes, distances, and quantities; or determining time, costs, resources, or materials needed to perform a work activity.
Coordinating the Work and Activities of Others	Getting members of a group to work together to accomplish tasks.

Resolving Conflicts and Negotiating with Others	Handling complaints, settling disputes, and resolving grievances and conflicts, or otherwise negotiating with others.
Communicating with Persons Outside Organization	Communicating with people outside the organization, representing the organization to customers, the public, government, and other external sources. This information can be exchanged in person, in writing, or by telephone or e-mail.
Repairing and Maintaining Electronic Equipment	Servicing, repairing, calibrating, regulating, fine-tuning, or testing machines, devices, and equipment that operate primarily on the basis of electrical or electronic (not mechanical) principles.
Analyzing Data or Information	Identifying the underlying principles, reasons, or facts of information by breaking down information or data into separate parts.
Developing Objectives and Strategies	Establishing long-range objectives and specifying the strategies and actions to achieve them.
Judging the Qualities of Things, Services, or Peop	Assessing the value, importance, or quality of things or people.
Performing Administrative Activities	Performing day-to-day administrative tasks such as maintaining information files and processing paperwork.
Scheduling Work and Activities	Scheduling events, programs, and activities, as well as the work of others.
Operating Vehicles, Mechanized Devices, or Equipme	Running, maneuvering, navigating, or driving vehicles or mechanized equipment, such as forklifts, passenger vehicles, aircraft, or water craft.
Guiding, Directing, and Motivating Subordinates	Providing guidance and direction to subordinates, including setting performance standards and monitoring performance.
Provide Consultation and Advice to Others	Providing guidance and expert advice to management or other groups on technical, systems-, or process-related topics.
Selling or Influencing Others	Convincing others to buy merchandise/goods or to otherwise change their minds or actions.
Drafting, Laying Out, and Specifying Technical Dev	Providing documentation, detailed instructions, drawings, or specifications to tell others about how devices, parts, equipment, or structures are to be fabricated, constructed, assembled, modified, maintained, or used.
Repairing and Maintaining Mechanical Equipment	Servicing, repairing, adjusting, and testing machines, devices, moving parts, and equipment that operate primarily on the basis of mechanical (not electronic) principles.
Monitoring and Controlling Resources	Monitoring and controlling resources and overseeing the spending of money.
Staffing Organizational Units	Recruiting, interviewing, selecting, hiring, and promoting employees in an organization.

Work_Content	**Work_Content Definitions**
Exposed to Disease or Infections	How often does this job require exposure to disease/infections?
Indoors, Environmentally Controlled	How often does this job require working indoors in environmentally controlled conditions?
Telephone	How often do you have telephone conversations in this job?
Face-to-Face Discussions	How often do you have to have face-to-face discussions with individuals or teams in this job?
Contact With Others	How much does this job require the worker to be in contact with others (face-to-face, by telephone, or otherwise) in order to perform it?
Deal With External Customers	How important is it to work with external customers or the public in this job?
Work With Work Group or Team	How important is it to work with others in a group or team in this job?
Freedom to Make Decisions	How much decision making freedom, without supervision, does the job offer?
Importance of Being Exact or Accurate	How important is being very exact or highly accurate in performing this job?
Impact of Decisions on Co-workers or Company Resul	How do the decisions an employee makes impact the results of co-workers, clients or the company?
Frequency of Decision Making	How frequently is the worker required to make decisions that affect other people, the financial resources, and/or the image and reputation of the organization?
Physical Proximity	To what extent does this job require the worker to perform job tasks in close physical proximity to other people?
Importance of Repeating Same Tasks	How important is repeating the same physical activities (e.g., key entry) or mental activities (e.g., checking entries in a ledger) over and over, without stopping, to performing this job?
Spend Time Using Your Hands to Handle, Control, or	How much does this job require using your hands to handle, control, or feel objects, tools or controls?
Structured versus Unstructured Work	To what extent is this job structured for the worker, rather than allowing the worker to determine tasks, priorities, and goals?
Responsible for Others' Health and Safety	How much responsibility is there for the health and safety of others in this job?
Deal With Unpleasant or Angry People	How frequently does the worker have to deal with unpleasant, angry, or discourteous individuals as part of the job requirements?
Coordinate or Lead Others	How important is it to coordinate or lead others in accomplishing work activities in this job?

Consequence of Error	How serious would the result usually be if the worker made a mistake that was not readily correctable?
Spend Time Standing	How much does this job require standing?
Spend Time Making Repetitive Motions	How much does this job require making repetitive motions?
Spend Time Walking and Running	How much does this job require walking and running?
Time Pressure	How often does this job require the worker to meet strict deadlines?
Exposed to Contaminants	How often does this job require working exposed to contaminants (such as pollutants, gases, dust or odors)?
Exposed to Radiation	How often does this job require exposure to radiation?
Sounds, Noise Levels Are Distracting or Uncomforta	How often does this job require working exposed to sounds and noise levels that are distracting or uncomfortable?
Wear Specialized Protective or Safety Equipment su	How much does this job require wearing specialized protective or safety equipment such as breathing apparatus, safety harness, full protection suits, or radiation protection?
Cramped Work Space, Awkward Positions	How often does this job require working in cramped work spaces that requires getting into awkward positions?
Frequency of Conflict Situations	How often are there conflict situations the employee has to face in this job?
Responsibility for Outcomes and Results	How responsible is the worker for work outcomes and results of other workers?
Letters and Memos	How often does the job require written letters and memos?
Spend Time Sitting	How much does this job require sitting?
Degree of Automation	How automated is the job?
Pace Determined by Speed of Equipment	How important is it to this job that the pace is determined by the speed of equipment or machinery? (This does not refer to keeping busy at all times on this job.)
Level of Competition	To what extent does this job require the worker to compete or to be aware of competitive pressures?
Spend Time Bending or Twisting the Body	How much does this job require bending or twisting your body?
Electronic Mail	How often do you use electronic mail in this job?
Wear Common Protective or Safety Equipment such as	How much does this job require wearing common protective or safety equipment such as safety shoes, glasses, gloves, hard hats or live jackets?
Deal With Physically Aggressive People	How frequently does this job require the worker to deal with physical aggression of violent individuals?
Exposed to Hazardous Conditions	How often does this job require exposure to hazardous conditions?
Outdoors, Exposed to Weather	How often does this job require working outdoors, exposed to all weather conditions?
Spend Time Kneeling, Crouching, Stooping, or Crawl	How much does this job require kneeling, crouching, stooping or crawling?
Extremely Bright or Inadequate Lighting	How often does this job require working in extremely bright or inadequate lighting conditions?
Indoors, Not Environmentally Controlled	How often does this job require working indoors in non-controlled environmental conditions (e.g., warehouse without heat)?
Exposed to Hazardous Equipment	How often does this job require exposure to hazardous equipment?
Very Hot or Cold Temperatures	How often does this job require working in very hot (above 90 F degrees) or very cold (below 32 F degrees) temperatures?
Exposed to Minor Burns, Cuts, Bites, or Stings	How often does this job require exposure to minor burns, cuts, bites, or stings?
In an Enclosed Vehicle or Equipment	How often does this job require working in a closed vehicle or equipment (e.g., car)?
Outdoors, Under Cover	How often does this job require working outdoors, under cover (e.g., structure with roof but no walls)?
Public Speaking	How often do you have to perform public speaking in this job?
Spend Time Keeping or Regaining Balance	How much does this job require keeping or regaining your balance?
Exposed to Whole Body Vibration	How often does this job require exposure to whole body vibration (e.g., operate a jackhammer)?
Spend Time Climbing Ladders, Scaffolds, or Poles	How much does this job require climbing ladders, scaffolds, or poles?
In an Open Vehicle or Equipment	How often does this job require working in an open vehicle or equipment (e.g., tractor)?
Exposed to High Places	How often does this job require exposure to high places?

Work_Styles	**Work_Styles Definitions**
Dependability	Job requires being reliable, responsible, and dependable, and fulfilling obligations.
Attention to Detail	Job requires being careful about detail and thorough in completing work tasks.
Integrity	Job requires being honest and ethical.
Cooperation	Job requires being pleasant with others on the job and displaying a good-natured, cooperative attitude.
Self Control	Job requires maintaining composure, keeping emotions in check, controlling anger, and avoiding aggressive behavior, even in very difficult situations.

Concern for Others	Job requires being sensitive to others' needs and feelings and being understanding and helpful on the job.
Initiative	Job requires a willingness to take on responsibilities and challenges.
Stress Tolerance	Job requires accepting criticism and dealing calmly and effectively with high stress situations.
Adaptability/Flexibility	Job requires being open to change (positive or negative) and to considerable variety in the workplace.
Persistence	Job requires persistence in the face of obstacles.
Social Orientation	Job requires preferring to work with others rather than alone, and being personally connected with others on the job.
Independence	Job requires developing one's own ways of doing things, guiding oneself with little or no supervision, and depending on oneself to get things done.
Innovation	Job requires creativity and alternative thinking to develop new ideas for and answers to work-related problems.
Analytical Thinking	Job requires analyzing information and using logic to address work-related issues and problems.
Achievement/Effort	Job requires establishing and maintaining personally challenging achievement goals and exerting effort toward mastering tasks.
Leadership	Job requires a willingness to lead, take charge, and offer opinions and direction.

Job Zone Component	Job Zone Component Definitions
Title	Job Zone Three: Medium Preparation Needed
Overall Experience	Previous work-related skill, knowledge, or experience is required for these occupations. For example, an electrician must have completed three or four years of apprenticeship or several years of vocational training, and often must have passed a licensing exam, in order to perform the job.
Job Training	Employees in these occupations usually need one or two years of training involving both on-the-job experience and informal training with experienced workers.
Job Zone Examples	These occupations usually involve using communication and organizational skills to coordinate, supervise, manage, or train others to accomplish goals. Examples include dental assistants, electricians, fish and game wardens, legal secretaries, personnel recruiters, and recreation workers.
SVP Range	(6.0 to < 7.0)
Education	Most occupations in this zone require training in vocational schools, related on-the-job experience, or an associate's degree. Some may require a bachelor's degree.

29-2034.02 - Radiologic Technicians

Maintain and use equipment and supplies necessary to demonstrate portions the human body on X-ray film or fluoroscopic screen for diagnostic purposes.

Tasks

1) Operate mobile x-ray equipment in operating room, emergency room, or at patient's bedside.

2) Explain procedures to patients to reduce anxieties and obtain cooperation.

3) Determine patients' x-ray needs by reading requests or instructions from physicians.

4) Coordinate work of other technicians or technologists when procedures require more than one person.

5) Position x-ray equipment and adjust controls to set exposure factors, such as time and distance.

6) Provide assistance in radiopharmaceutical administration, monitoring patients' vital signs and notifying the radiologist of any relevant changes.

7) Make exposures necessary for the requested procedures, rejecting and repeating work that does not meet established standards.

8) Process exposed radiographs using film processors or computer generated methods.

9) Monitor equipment operation and report malfunctioning equipment to supervisor.

10) Use beam-restrictive devices and patient-shielding techniques to minimize radiation exposure to patient and staff.

11) Maintain records of patients examined, examinations performed, views taken, and technical factors used.

12) Assure that sterile supplies, contrast materials, catheters, and other required equipment are present and in working order, requisitioning materials as necessary.

13) Maintain a current file of examination protocols.

14) Prepare contrast material, radiopharmaceuticals and anesthetic or antispasmodic drugs under the direction of a radiologist.

15) Operate digital picture archiving communications systems.

16) Perform procedures such as linear tomography, mammography, sonograms, joint and cyst aspirations, routine contrast studies, routine fluoroscopy and examinations of the head, trunk, and extremities under supervision of physician.

17) Position patient on examining table and set up and adjust equipment to obtain optimum view of specific body area as requested by physician.

18) Prepare and set up x-ray room for patient.

19) Assist with on-the-job training of new employees and students, and provide input to supervisors regarding training performance.

20) Provide students and other technologists with suggestions of additional views, alternate positioning or improved techniques to ensure the images produced are of the highest quality.

29-2041.00 - Emergency Medical Technicians and Paramedics

Assess injuries, administer emergency medical care, and extricate trapped individuals. Transport injured or sick persons to medical facilities.

Tasks

1) Coordinate work with other emergency medical team members and police and fire department personnel.

2) Maintain vehicles and medical and communication equipment, and replenish first-aid equipment and supplies.

3) Operate equipment such as EKGs, external defibrillators and bag-valve mask resuscitators in advanced life-support environments.

4) Communicate with dispatchers and treatment center personnel to provide information about situation, to arrange reception of victims, and to receive instructions for further treatment.

5) Coordinate with treatment center personnel to obtain patients' vital statistics and medical history, to determine the circumstances of the emergency, and to administer emergency treatment.

6) Observe, record, and report to physician the patient's condition or injury, the treatment provided, and reactions to drugs and treatment.

7) Administer drugs, orally or by injection, and perform intravenous procedures under a physician's direction.

8) Perform emergency diagnostic and treatment procedures, such as stomach suction, airway management and heart monitoring, during ambulance ride.

9) Decontaminate ambulance interior following treatment of patient with infectious disease and report case to proper authorities.

10) Drive mobile intensive care unit to specified location, following instructions from emergency medical dispatcher.

11) Administer first-aid treatment and life-support care to sick or injured persons in prehospital setting.

12) Assess nature and extent of illness or injury to establish and prioritize medical procedures.

13) Comfort and reassure patients.

Knowledge	Knowledge Definitions
Customer and Personal Service	Knowledge of principles and processes for providing customer and personal services. This includes customer needs assessment, meeting quality standards for services, and evaluation of customer satisfaction.
Medicine and Dentistry	Knowledge of the information and techniques needed to diagnose and treat human injuries, diseases, and deformities. This includes symptoms, treatment alternatives, drug properties and interactions, and preventive health-care measures.
Public Safety and Security	Knowledge of relevant equipment, policies, procedures, and strategies to promote effective local, state, or national security operations for the protection of people, data, property, and institutions.
Education and Training	Knowledge of principles and methods for curriculum and training design, teaching and instruction for individuals and groups, and the measurement of training effects.
Chemistry	Knowledge of the chemical composition, structure, and properties of substances and of the chemical processes and transformations that they undergo. This includes uses of chemicals and their interactions, danger signs, production techniques, and disposal methods.
Mathematics	Knowledge of arithmetic, algebra, geometry, calculus, statistics, and their applications.
English Language	Knowledge of the structure and content of the English language including the meaning and spelling of words, rules of composition, and grammar.
Psychology	Knowledge of human behavior and performance; individual differences in ability, personality, and interests; learning and motivation; psychological research methods; and the assessment and treatment of behavioral and affective disorders.

Administration and Management	Knowledge of business and management principles involved in strategic planning, resource allocation, human resources modeling, leadership technique, production methods, and coordination of people and resources.
Personnel and Human Resources	Knowledge of principles and procedures for personnel recruitment, selection, training, compensation and benefits, labor relations and negotiation, and personnel information systems.
Biology	Knowledge of plant and animal organisms, their tissues, cells, functions, interdependencies, and interactions with each other and the environment.
Law and Government	Knowledge of laws, legal codes, court procedures, precedents, government regulations, executive orders, agency rules, and the democratic political process.
Transportation	Knowledge of principles and methods for moving people or goods by air, rail, sea, or road, including the relative costs and benefits.
Therapy and Counseling	Knowledge of principles, methods, and procedures for diagnosis, treatment, and rehabilitation of physical and mental dysfunctions, and for career counseling and guidance.
Mechanical	Knowledge of machines and tools, including their designs, uses, repair, and maintenance.
Physics	Knowledge and prediction of physical principles, laws, their interrelationships, and applications to understanding fluid, material, and atmospheric dynamics, and mechanical, electrical, atomic and sub-atomic structures and processes.
Telecommunications	Knowledge of transmission, broadcasting, switching, control, and operation of telecommunications systems.
Communications and Media	Knowledge of media production, communication, and dissemination techniques and methods. This includes alternative ways to inform and entertain via written, oral, and visual media.
Computers and Electronics	Knowledge of circuit boards, processors, chips, electronic equipment, and computer hardware and software, including applications and programming.
Building and Construction	Knowledge of materials, methods, and the tools involved in the construction or repair of houses, buildings, or other structures such as highways and roads.
Clerical	Knowledge of administrative and clerical procedures and systems such as word processing, managing files and records, stenography and transcription, designing forms, and other office procedures and terminology.
Geography	Knowledge of principles and methods for describing the features of land, sea, and air masses, including their physical characteristics, locations, interrelationships, and distribution of plant, animal, and human life.
Engineering and Technology	Knowledge of the practical application of engineering science and technology. This includes applying principles, techniques, procedures, and equipment to the design and production of various goods and services.
Sociology and Anthropology	Knowledge of group behavior and dynamics, societal trends and influences, human migrations, ethnicity, cultures and their history and origins.
Foreign Language	Knowledge of the structure and content of a foreign (non-English) language including the meaning and spelling of words, rules of composition and grammar, and pronunciation.
Economics and Accounting	Knowledge of economic and accounting principles and practices, the financial markets, banking and the analysis and reporting of financial data.
Philosophy and Theology	Knowledge of different philosophical systems and religions. This includes their basic principles, values, ethics, ways of thinking, customs, practices, and their impact on human culture.
Production and Processing	Knowledge of raw materials, production processes, quality control, costs, and other techniques for maximizing the effective manufacture and distribution of goods.
Design	Knowledge of design techniques, tools, and principles involved in production of precision technical plans, blueprints, drawings, and models.
Sales and Marketing	Knowledge of principles and methods for showing, promoting, and selling products or services. This includes marketing strategy and tactics, product demonstration, sales techniques, and sales control systems.
History and Archeology	Knowledge of historical events and their causes, indicators, and effects on civilizations and cultures.
Food Production	Knowledge of techniques and equipment for planting, growing, and harvesting food products (both plant and animal) for consumption, including storage/handling techniques.
Fine Arts	Knowledge of the theory and techniques required to compose, produce, and perform works of music, dance, visual arts, drama, and sculpture.

Skills	**Skills Definitions**
Active Listening	Giving full attention to what other people are saying, taking time to understand the points being made, asking questions as appropriate, and not interrupting at inappropriate times.

Critical Thinking	Using logic and reasoning to identify the strengths and weaknesses of alternative solutions, conclusions or approaches to problems.
Speaking	Talking to others to convey information effectively.
Coordination	Adjusting actions in relation to others' actions.
Equipment Maintenance	Performing routine maintenance on equipment and determining when and what kind of maintenance is needed.
Reading Comprehension	Understanding written sentences and paragraphs in work related documents.
Writing	Communicating effectively in writing as appropriate for the needs of the audience.
Learning Strategies	Selecting and using training/instructional methods and procedures appropriate for the situation when learning or teaching new things.
Active Learning	Understanding the implications of new information for both current and future problem-solving and decision-making.
Instructing	Teaching others how to do something.
Social Perceptiveness	Being aware of others' reactions and understanding why they react as they do.
Monitoring	Monitoring/Assessing performance of yourself, other individuals, or organizations to make improvements or take corrective action.
Judgment and Decision Making	Considering the relative costs and benefits of potential actions to choose the most appropriate one.
Service Orientation	Actively looking for ways to help people.
Complex Problem Solving	Identifying complex problems and reviewing related information to develop and evaluate options and implement solutions.
Equipment Selection	Determining the kind of tools and equipment needed to do a job.
Mathematics	Using mathematics to solve problems.
Time Management	Managing one's own time and the time of others.
Troubleshooting	Determining causes of operating errors and deciding what to do about it.
Persuasion	Persuading others to change their minds or behavior.
Negotiation	Bringing others together and trying to reconcile differences.
Operation and Control	Controlling operations of equipment or systems.
Management of Personnel Resources	Motivating, developing, and directing people as they work, identifying the best people for the job.
Operation Monitoring	Watching gauges, dials, or other indicators to make sure a machine is working properly.
Quality Control Analysis	Conducting tests and inspections of products, services, or processes to evaluate quality or performance.
Science	Using scientific rules and methods to solve problems.
Management of Material Resources	Obtaining and seeing to the appropriate use of equipment, facilities, and materials needed to do certain work.
Operations Analysis	Analyzing needs and product requirements to create a design.
Repairing	Repairing machines or systems using the needed tools.
Technology Design	Generating or adapting equipment and technology to serve user needs.
Systems Analysis	Determining how a system should work and how changes in conditions, operations, and the environment will affect outcomes.
Systems Evaluation	Identifying measures or indicators of system performance and the actions needed to improve or correct performance, relative to the goals of the system.
Installation	Installing equipment, machines, wiring, or programs to meet specifications.
Management of Financial Resources	Determining how money will be spent to get the work done, and accounting for these expenditures.
Programming	Writing computer programs for various purposes.

Ability	**Ability Definitions**
Oral Comprehension	The ability to listen to and understand information and ideas presented through spoken words and sentences.
Problem Sensitivity	The ability to tell when something is wrong or is likely to go wrong. It does not involve solving the problem, only recognizing there is a problem.
Oral Expression	The ability to communicate information and ideas in speaking so others will understand.
Deductive Reasoning	The ability to apply general rules to specific problems to produce answers that make sense.
Inductive Reasoning	The ability to combine pieces of information to form general rules or conclusions (includes finding a relationship among seemingly unrelated events).
Response Orientation	The ability to choose quickly between two or more movements in response to two or more different signals (lights, sounds, pictures). It includes the speed with which the correct response is started with the hand, foot, or other body part.
Static Strength	The ability to exert maximum muscle force to lift, push, pull, or carry objects.
Extent Flexibility	The ability to bend, stretch, twist, or reach with your body, arms, and/or legs.
Arm-Hand Steadiness	The ability to keep your hand and arm steady while moving your arm or while holding your arm and hand in one position.

Far Vision	The ability to see details at a distance.
Speed of Closure	The ability to quickly make sense of, combine, and organize information into meaningful patterns.
Speech Recognition	The ability to identify and understand the speech of another person.
Speech Clarity	The ability to speak clearly so others can understand you.
Information Ordering	The ability to arrange things or actions in a certain order or pattern according to a specific rule or set of rules (e.g., patterns of numbers, letters, words, pictures, mathematical operations).
Control Precision	The ability to quickly and repeatedly adjust the controls of a machine or a vehicle to exact positions.
Manual Dexterity	The ability to quickly move your hand, your hand together with your arm, or your two hands to grasp, manipulate, or assemble objects.
Multilimb Coordination	The ability to coordinate two or more limbs (for example, two arms, two legs, or one leg and one arm) while sitting, standing, or lying down. It does not involve performing the activities while the whole body is in motion.
Glare Sensitivity	The ability to see objects in the presence of glare or bright lighting.
Time Sharing	The ability to shift back and forth between two or more activities or sources of information (such as speech, sounds, touch, or other sources).
Reaction Time	The ability to quickly respond (with the hand, finger, or foot) to a signal (sound, light, picture) when it appears.
Near Vision	The ability to see details at close range (within a few feet of the observer).
Perceptual Speed	The ability to quickly and accurately compare similarities and differences among sets of letters, numbers, objects, pictures, or patterns. The things to be compared may be presented at the same time or one after the other. This ability also includes comparing a presented object with a remembered object.
Selective Attention	The ability to concentrate on a task over a period of time without being distracted.
Flexibility of Closure	The ability to identify or detect a known pattern (a figure, object, word, or sound) that is hidden in other distracting material.
Spatial Orientation	The ability to know your location in relation to the environment or to know where other objects are in relation to you.
Gross Body Coordination	The ability to coordinate the movement of your arms, legs, and torso together when the whole body is in motion.
Finger Dexterity	The ability to make precisely coordinated movements of the fingers of one or both hands to grasp, manipulate, or assemble very small objects.
Stamina	The ability to exert yourself physically over long periods of time without getting winded or out of breath.
Written Expression	The ability to communicate information and ideas in writing so others will understand.
Depth Perception	The ability to judge which of several objects is closer or farther away from you, or to judge the distance between you and an object.
Rate Control	The ability to time your movements or the movement of a piece of equipment in anticipation of changes in the speed and/or direction of a moving object or scene.
Written Comprehension	The ability to read and understand information and ideas presented in writing.
Hearing Sensitivity	The ability to detect or tell the differences between sounds that vary in pitch and loudness.
Speed of Limb Movement	The ability to quickly move the arms and legs.
Category Flexibility	The ability to generate or use different sets of rules for combining or grouping things in different ways.
Trunk Strength	The ability to use your abdominal and lower back muscles to support part of the body repeatedly or continuously over time without 'giving out' or fatiguing.
Visualization	The ability to imagine how something will look after it is moved around or when its parts are moved or rearranged.
Auditory Attention	The ability to focus on a single source of sound in the presence of other distracting sounds.
Visual Color Discrimination	The ability to match or detect differences between colors, including shades of color and brightness.
Night Vision	The ability to see under low light conditions.
Gross Body Equilibrium	The ability to keep or regain your body balance or stay upright when in an unstable position.
Memorization	The ability to remember information such as words, numbers, pictures, and procedures.
Explosive Strength	The ability to use short bursts of muscle force to propel oneself (as in jumping or sprinting), or to throw an object.
Originality	The ability to come up with unusual or clever ideas about a given topic or situation, or to develop creative ways to solve a problem.
Dynamic Strength	The ability to exert muscle force repeatedly or continuously over time. This involves muscular endurance and resistance to muscle fatigue.
Wrist-Finger Speed	The ability to make fast, simple, repeated movements of the fingers, hands, and wrists.

Fluency of Ideas	The ability to come up with a number of ideas about a topic (the number of ideas is important, not their quality, correctness, or creativity).
Peripheral Vision	The ability to see objects or movement of objects to one's side when the eyes are looking ahead.
Sound Localization	The ability to tell the direction from which a sound originated.
Mathematical Reasoning	The ability to choose the right mathematical methods or formulas to solve a problem.
Number Facility	The ability to add, subtract, multiply, or divide quickly and correctly.
Dynamic Flexibility	The ability to quickly and repeatedly bend, stretch, twist, or reach out with your body, arms, and/or legs.

Work_Activity	**Work_Activity Definitions**
Making Decisions and Solving Problems	Analyzing information and evaluating results to choose the best solution and solve problems.
Assisting and Caring for Others	Providing personal assistance, medical attention, emotional support, or other personal care to others such as coworkers, customers, or patients.
Getting Information	Observing, receiving, and otherwise obtaining information from all relevant sources.
Operating Vehicles, Mechanized Devices, or Equipme	Running, maneuvering, navigating, or driving vehicles or mechanized equipment, such as forklifts, passenger vehicles, aircraft, or water craft.
Performing General Physical Activities	Performing physical activities that require considerable use of your arms and legs and moving your whole body, such as climbing, lifting, balancing, walking, stooping, and handling of materials.
Documenting/Recording Information	Entering, transcribing, recording, storing, or maintaining information in written or electronic/magnetic form.
Performing for or Working Directly with the Public	Performing for people or dealing directly with the public. This includes serving customers in restaurants and stores, and receiving clients or guests.
Communicating with Supervisors, Peers, or Subordin	Providing information to supervisors, co-workers, and subordinates by telephone, in written form, e-mail, or in person.
Identifying Objects, Actions, and Events	Identifying information by categorizing, estimating, recognizing differences or similarities, and detecting changes in circumstances or events.
Updating and Using Relevant Knowledge	Keeping up-to-date technically and applying new knowledge to your job.
Inspecting Equipment, Structures, or Material	Inspecting equipment, structures, or materials to identify the cause of errors or other problems or defects.
Processing Information	Compiling, coding, categorizing, calculating, tabulating, auditing, or verifying information or data.
Training and Teaching Others	Identifying the educational needs of others, developing formal educational or training programs or classes, and teaching or instructing others.
Handling and Moving Objects	Using hands and arms in handling, installing, positioning, and moving materials, and manipulating things.
Establishing and Maintaining Interpersonal Relatio	Developing constructive and cooperative working relationships with others, and maintaining them over time.
Communicating with Persons Outside Organization	Communicating with people outside the organization, representing the organization to customers, the public, government, and other external sources. This information can be exchanged in person, in writing, or by telephone or e-mail.
Monitor Processes, Materials, or Surroundings	Monitoring and reviewing information from materials, events, or the environment, to detect or assess problems.
Developing and Building Teams	Encouraging and building mutual trust, respect, and cooperation among team members.
Coaching and Developing Others	Identifying the developmental needs of others and coaching, mentoring, or otherwise helping others to improve their knowledge or skills.
Judging the Qualities of Things, Services, or Peop	Assessing the value, importance, or quality of things or people.
Guiding, Directing, and Motivating Subordinates	Providing guidance and direction to subordinates, including setting performance standards and monitoring performance.
Organizing, Planning, and Prioritizing Work	Developing specific goals and plans to prioritize, organize, and accomplish your work.
Analyzing Data or Information	Identifying the underlying principles, reasons, or facts of information by breaking down information or data into separate parts.
Evaluating Information to Determine Compliance wit	Using relevant information and individual judgment to determine whether events or processes comply with laws, regulations, or standards.
Resolving Conflicts and Negotiating with Others	Handling complaints, settling disputes, and resolving grievances and conflicts, or otherwise negotiating with others.
Thinking Creatively	Developing, designing, or creating new applications, ideas, relationships, systems, or products, including artistic contributions.
Coordinating the Work and Activities of Others	Getting members of a group to work together to accomplish tasks.

Estimating the Quantifiable Characteristics of Pro	Estimating sizes, distances, and quantities; or determining time, costs, resources, or materials needed to perform a work activity.
Scheduling Work and Activities	Scheduling events, programs, and activities, as well as the work of others.
Provide Consultation and Advice to Others	Providing guidance and expert advice to management or other groups on technical, systems-, or process-related topics.
Controlling Machines and Processes	Using either control mechanisms or direct physical activity to operate machines or processes (not including computers or vehicles).
Interpreting the Meaning of Information for Others	Translating or explaining what information means and how it can be used.
Performing Administrative Activities	Performing day-to-day administrative tasks such as maintaining information files and processing paperwork.
Interacting With Computers	Using computers and computer systems (including hardware and software) to program, write software, set up functions, enter data, or process information.
Developing Objectives and Strategies	Establishing long-range objectives and specifying the strategies and actions to achieve them.
Repairing and Maintaining Mechanical Equipment	Servicing, repairing, adjusting, and testing machines, devices, moving parts, and equipment that operate primarily on the basis of mechanical (not electronic) principles.
Monitoring and Controlling Resources	Monitoring and controlling resources and overseeing the spending of money.
Selling or Influencing Others	Convincing others to buy merchandise/goods or to otherwise change their minds or actions.
Repairing and Maintaining Electronic Equipment	Servicing, repairing, calibrating, regulating, fine-tuning, or testing machines, devices, and equipment that operate primarily on the basis of electrical or electronic (not mechanical) principles.
Staffing Organizational Units	Recruiting, interviewing, selecting, hiring, and promoting employees in an organization.
Drafting, Laying Out, and Specifying Technical Dev	Providing documentation, detailed instructions, drawings, or specifications to tell others about how devices, parts, equipment, or structures are to be fabricated, constructed, assembled, modified, or used.

Work_Content	Work_Content Definitions
Face-to-Face Discussions	How often do you have to have face-to-face discussions with individuals or teams in this job?
Physical Proximity	To what extent does this job require the worker to perform job tasks in close physical proximity to other people?
Exposed to Disease or Infections	How often does this job require exposure to disease/infections?
Contact With Others	How much does this job require the worker to be in contact with others (face-to-face, by telephone, or otherwise) in order to perform it?
Work With Work Group or Team	How important is it to work with others in a group or team in this job?
Deal With External Customers	How important is it to work with external customers or the public in this job?
Frequency of Decision Making	How frequently is the worker required to make decisions that affect other people, the financial resources, and/or the image and reputation of the organization?
Extremely Bright or Inadequate Lighting	How often does this job require working in extremely bright or inadequate lighting conditions?
Impact of Decisions on Co-workers or Company Resul	How do the decisions an employee makes impact the results of co-workers, clients or the company?
Outdoors, Exposed to Weather	How often does this job require working outdoors, exposed to all weather conditions?
Sounds, Noise Levels Are Distracting or Uncomforta	How often does this job require working exposed to sounds and noise levels that are distracting or uncomfortable?
Importance of Being Exact or Accurate	How important is being very exact or highly accurate in performing this job?
Consequence of Error	How serious would the result usually be if the worker made a mistake that was not readily correctable?
In an Enclosed Vehicle or Equipment	How often does this job require working in a closed vehicle or equipment (e.g., car)?
Telephone	How often do you have telephone conversations in this job?
Wear Common Protective or Safety Equipment such as	How much does this job require wearing common protective or safety equipment such as safety shoes, glasses, gloves, hard hats or live jackets?
Responsible for Others' Health and Safety	How much responsibility is there for the health and safety of others in this job?
Cramped Work Space, Awkward Positions	How often does this job require working in cramped work spaces that requires getting into awkward positions?
Coordinate or Lead Others	How important is it to coordinate or lead others in accomplishing work activities in this job?
Exposed to Contaminants	How often does this job require working exposed to contaminants (such as pollutants, gases, dust or odors)?
Very Hot or Cold Temperatures	How often does this job require working in very hot (above 90 F degrees) or very cold (below 32 F degrees) temperatures?
Exposed to Hazardous Equipment	How often does this job require exposure to hazardous equipment?

Deal With Unpleasant or Angry People	How frequently does the worker have to deal with unpleasant, angry, or discourteous individuals as part of the job requirements?
Exposed to Minor Burns, Cuts, Bites, or Stings	How often does this job require exposure to minor burns, cuts, bites, or stings?
Freedom to Make Decisions	How much decision making freedom, without supervision, does the job offer?
Responsibility for Outcomes and Results	How responsible is the worker for work outcomes and results of other workers?
Time Pressure	How often does this job require the worker to meet strict deadlines?
Spend Time Using Your Hands to Handle, Control, or	How much does this job require using your hands to handle, control, or feel objects, tools or controls?
Deal With Physically Aggressive People	How frequently does this job require the worker to deal with physical aggression of violent individuals?
Structured versus Unstructured Work	To what extent is this job structured for the worker, rather than allowing the worker to determine tasks, priorities, and goals?
Importance of Repeating Same Tasks	How important is repeating the same physical activities (e.g., key entry) or mental activities (e.g., checking entries in a ledger) over and over, without stopping, to performing this job?
Indoors, Environmentally Controlled	How often does this job require working indoors in environmentally controlled conditions?
Frequency of Conflict Situations	How often are there conflict situations the employee has to face in this job?
Exposed to Hazardous Conditions	How often does this job require exposure to hazardous conditions?
Spend Time Walking and Running	How much does this job require walking and running?
Indoors, Not Environmentally Controlled	How often does this job require working indoors in non-controlled environmental conditions (e.g., warehouse without heat)?
Spend Time Making Repetitive Motions	How much does this job require making repetitive motions?
Spend Time Standing	How much does this job require standing?
Letters and Memos	How often does the job require written letters and memos?
Spend Time Bending or Twisting the Body	How much does this job require bending or twisting your body?
Spend Time Kneeling, Crouching, Stooping, or Crawl	How much does this job require kneeling, crouching, stooping or crawling?
Wear Specialized Protective or Safety Equipment su	How much does this job require wearing specialized protective or safety equipment such as breathing apparatus, safety harness, full protection suits, or radiation protection?
Level of Competition	To what extent does this job require the worker to compete or to be aware of competitive pressures?
Exposed to High Places	How often does this job require exposure to high places?
Spend Time Sitting	How much does this job require sitting?
In an Open Vehicle or Equipment	How often does this job require working in an open vehicle or equipment (e.g., tractor)?
Spend Time Keeping or Regaining Balance	How much does this job require keeping or regaining your balance?
Pace Determined by Speed of Equipment	How important is it to this job that the pace is determined by the speed of equipment or machinery? (This does not refer to keeping busy at all times on this job.)
Outdoors, Under Cover	How often does this job require working outdoors, under cover (e.g., structure with roof but no walls)?
Public Speaking	How often do you have to perform public speaking in this job?
Degree of Automation	How automated is the job?
Exposed to Radiation	How often does this job require exposure to radiation?
Spend Time Climbing Ladders, Scaffolds, or Poles	How much does this job require climbing ladders, scaffolds, or poles?
Electronic Mail	How often do you use electronic mail in this job?
Exposed to Whole Body Vibration	How often does this job require exposure to whole body vibration (e.g., operate a jackhammer)?

Work_Styles	Work_Styles Definitions
Stress Tolerance	Job requires accepting criticism and dealing calmly and effectively with high stress situations.
Dependability	Job requires being reliable, responsible, and dependable, and fulfilling obligations.
Attention to Detail	Job requires being careful about detail and thorough in completing work tasks.
Self Control	Job requires maintaining composure, keeping emotions in check, controlling anger, and avoiding aggressive behavior, even in very difficult situations.
Adaptability/Flexibility	Job requires being open to change (positive or negative) and to considerable variety in the workplace.
Integrity	Job requires being honest and ethical.
Concern for Others	Job requires being sensitive to others' needs and feelings and being understanding and helpful on the job.
Cooperation	Job requires being pleasant with others on the job and displaying a good-natured, cooperative attitude.

Initiative	Job requires a willingness to take on responsibilities and challenges.
Social Orientation	Job requires preferring to work with others rather than alone, and being personally connected with others on the job.
Persistence	Job requires persistence in the face of obstacles.
Analytical Thinking	Job requires analyzing information and using logic to address work-related issues and problems.
Innovation	Job requires creativity and alternative thinking to develop new ideas for and answers to work-related problems.
Leadership	Job requires a willingness to lead, take charge, and offer opinions and direction.
Achievement/Effort	Job requires establishing and maintaining personally challenging achievement goals and exerting effort toward mastering tasks.
Independence	Job requires developing one's own ways of doing things, guiding oneself with little or no supervision, and depending on oneself to get things done.

Job Zone Component	Job Zone Component Definitions
Title	Job Zone Two: Some Preparation Needed
Overall Experience	Some previous work-related skill, knowledge, or experience may be helpful in these occupations, but usually is not needed. For example, a drywall installer might benefit from experience installing drywall, but an inexperienced person could still learn to be an installer with little difficulty.
Job Training	Employees in these occupations need anywhere from a few months to one year of working with experienced employees.
Job Zone Examples	These occupations often involve using your knowledge and skills to help others. Examples include drywall installers, fire inspectors, flight attendants, pharmacy technicians, salespersons (retail), and tellers.
SVP Range	(4.0 to < 6.0)
Education	These occupations usually require a high school diploma and may require some vocational training or job-related course work. In some cases, an associate's or bachelor's degree could be needed.

29-2051.00 - Dietetic Technicians

Assist dietitians in the provision of food service and nutritional programs. Under the supervision of dietitians, may plan and produce meals based on established guidelines, teach principles of food and nutrition, or counsel individuals.

Tasks

1) Analyze menus and recipes, standardize recipes and test new products.

2) Observe patient food intake and report progress and dietary problems to dietician.

3) Obtain and evaluate dietary histories of individuals to plan nutritional programs.

4) Plan menus and diets or guide individuals and families in food selection, preparation, and menu planning, based upon nutritional needs and established guidelines.

5) Prepare a major meal, following recipes and determining group food quantities.

6) Provide dietitians with assistance researching food, nutrition and food service systems.

7) Supervise food production and service, or assist dietitians and nutritionists in food service supervision and planning.

8) Develop job specifications, job descriptions, and work schedules.

9) Select, schedule, and conduct orientation and in-service education programs.

10) Determine food and beverage costs and assist in implementing cost control procedures.

11) Refer patients to other relevant services to provide continuity of care.

29-2052.00 - Pharmacy Technicians

Prepare medications under the direction of a pharmacist. May measure, mix, count out, label, and record amounts and dosages of medications.

Tasks

1) Supply and monitor robotic machines that dispense medicine into containers, and label the containers.

2) Answer telephones, responding to questions or requests.

3) Price and file prescriptions that have been filled.

4) Compute charges for medication and equipment dispensed to hospital patients, and enter data in computer.

5) Prepare and process medical insurance claim forms and records.

6) Fill bottles with prescribed medications and type and affix labels.

7) Assist customers by answering simple questions, locating items or referring them to the pharmacist for medication information.

8) Add measured drugs or nutrients to intravenous solutions under sterile conditions to prepare intravenous (IV) packs under pharmacist supervision.

9) Receive and store incoming supplies, verify quantities against invoices, and inform supervisors of stock needs and shortages.

10) Clean, and help maintain, equipment and work areas, and sterilize glassware according to prescribed methods.

11) Maintain and merchandise home health-care products and services.

12) Price stock and mark items for sale.

13) Operate cash registers to accept payment from customers.

14) Maintain proper storage and security conditions for drugs.

15) Deliver medications and pharmaceutical supplies to patients, nursing stations or surgery.

16) Establish and maintain patient profiles, including lists of medications taken by individual patients.

17) Receive written prescription or refill requests and verify that information is complete and accurate.

18) Order, label, and count stock of medications, chemicals, and supplies, and enter inventory data into computer.

19) Mix pharmaceutical preparations according to written prescriptions.

29-2053.00 - Psychiatric Technicians

Care for mentally impaired or emotionally disturbed individuals, following physician instructions and hospital procedures. Monitor patients' physical and emotional well-being and report to medical staff. May participate in rehabilitation and treatment programs, help with personal hygiene, and administer oral medications and hypodermic injections.

Tasks

1) Collaborate with and assist doctors, psychologists, and rehabilitation therapists working with mentally ill, emotionally disturbed, or developmentally disabled patients in order to treat, rehabilitate, and return patients to the community.

2) Aid patients in performing tasks such as bathing and keeping beds, clothing and living areas clean.

3) Administer oral medications and hypodermic injections, following physician's prescriptions and hospital procedures.

4) Observe and influence patients' behavior, communicating and interacting with them and teaching, counseling and befriending them.

5) Encourage patients to develop work skills and to participate in social, recreational, and other therapeutic activities that enhance interpersonal skills and develop social relationships.

6) Provide nursing, psychiatric and personal care to mentally ill, emotionally disturbed or mentally retarded patients.

7) Develop and teach strategies to promote client wellness and independence.

8) Issue medications from dispensary and maintain records in accordance with specified procedures.

9) Restrain violent, potentially violent, or suicidal patients by verbal or physical means as required.

10) Take and record measures of patients' physical condition, using devices such as thermometers and blood pressure gauges.

11) Monitor patients' physical and emotional well-being and report unusual behavior or physical ailments to medical staff.

12) Interview new patients to complete admission forms, to assess their mental health status and to obtain their mental health and treatment history.

13) Lead prescribed individual or group therapy sessions as part of specific therapeutic procedures.

29-2054.00 - Respiratory Therapy Technicians

Provide specific, well defined respiratory care procedures under the direction of respiratory therapists and physicians.

Tasks

1) Administer breathing and oxygen procedures such as intermittent positive pressure breathing treatments, ultrasonic nebulizer treatments and incentive spirometer treatments.

2) Follow and enforce safety rules applying to equipment.

3) Perform diagnostic procedures to assess the severity of respiratory dysfunction in patients.

4) Clean, sterilize, check and maintain respiratory therapy equipment.

5) Teach patients how to use respiratory equipment at home.

6) Use ventilators and various oxygen devices and aerosol and breathing treatments in the provision of respiratory therapy.

7) Interview and examine patients to collect clinical data.

8) Prepare and test devices such as mechanical ventilators, therapeutic gas administration apparatus, environmental control systems, aerosol generators and EKG machines.

9) Monitor patients during treatment and report any unusual reactions to the respiratory therapist.

10) Provide respiratory care involving the application of well-defined therapeutic techniques under the supervision of a respiratory therapist and a physician.

11) Teach or oversee other workers who provide respiratory care services.

12) Recommend and review bedside procedures, x-rays, and laboratory tests.

13) Assess patients' response to treatments and modify treatments according to protocol if necessary.

14) Explain treatment procedures to patients.

15) Set equipment controls to regulate the flow of oxygen, gases, mists, or aerosols.

16) Keep records of patients' therapy, completing all necessary forms.

17) Read and evaluate physicians' orders and patients' chart information to determine patients' condition and treatment protocols.

Knowledge	Knowledge Definitions
Medicine and Dentistry	Knowledge of the information and techniques needed to diagnose and treat human injuries, diseases, and deformities. This includes symptoms, treatment alternatives, drug properties and interactions, and preventive health-care measures.
Customer and Personal Service	Knowledge of principles and processes for providing customer and personal services. This includes customer needs assessment, meeting quality standards for services, and evaluation of customer satisfaction.
Chemistry	Knowledge of the chemical composition, structure, and properties of substances and of the chemical processes and transformations that they undergo. This includes uses of chemicals and their interactions, danger signs, production techniques, and disposal methods.
Psychology	Knowledge of human behavior and performance; individual differences in ability, personality, and interests; learning and motivation; psychological research methods; and the assessment and treatment of behavioral and affective disorders.
English Language	Knowledge of the structure and content of the English language including the meaning and spelling of words, rules of composition, and grammar.
Mathematics	Knowledge of arithmetic, algebra, geometry, calculus, statistics, and their applications.
Education and Training	Knowledge of principles and methods for curriculum and training design, teaching and instruction for individuals and groups, and the measurement of training effects.
Public Safety and Security	Knowledge of relevant equipment, policies, procedures, and strategies to promote effective local, state, or national security operations for the protection of people, data, property, and institutions.
Biology	Knowledge of plant and animal organisms, their tissues, cells, functions, interdependencies, and interactions with each other and the environment.
Physics	Knowledge and prediction of physical principles, laws, their interrelationships, and applications to understanding fluid, material, and atmospheric dynamics, and mechanical, electrical, atomic and sub- atomic structures and processes.
Computers and Electronics	Knowledge of circuit boards, processors, chips, electronic equipment, and computer hardware and software, including applications and programming.
Mechanical	Knowledge of machines and tools, including their designs, uses, repair, and maintenance.
Therapy and Counseling	Knowledge of principles, methods, and procedures for diagnosis, treatment, and rehabilitation of physical and mental dysfunctions, and for career counseling and guidance.
Law and Government	Knowledge of laws, legal codes, court procedures, precedents, government regulations, executive orders, agency rules, and the democratic political process.
Clerical	Knowledge of administrative and clerical procedures and systems such as word processing, managing files and records, stenography and transcription, designing forms, and other office procedures and terminology.
Administration and Management	Knowledge of business and management principles involved in strategic planning, resource allocation, human resources modeling, leadership technique, production methods, and coordination of people and resources.
Engineering and Technology	Knowledge of the practical application of engineering science and technology. This includes applying principles, techniques, procedures, and equipment to the design and production of various goods and services.
Sociology and Anthropology	Knowledge of group behavior and dynamics, societal trends and influences, human migrations, ethnicity, cultures and their history and origins.
Philosophy and Theology	Knowledge of different philosophical systems and religions. This includes their basic principles, values, ethics, ways of thinking, customs, practices, and their impact on human culture.
Personnel and Human Resources	Knowledge of principles and procedures for personnel recruitment, selection, training, compensation and benefits, labor relations and negotiation, and personnel information systems.
Economics and Accounting	Knowledge of economic and accounting principles and practices, the financial markets, banking and the analysis and reporting of financial data.
Foreign Language	Knowledge of the structure and content of a foreign (non-English) language including the meaning and spelling of words, rules of composition and grammar, and pronunciation.
Communications and Media	Knowledge of media production, communication, and dissemination techniques and methods. This includes alternative ways to inform and entertain via written, oral, and visual media.
Production and Processing	Knowledge of raw materials, production processes, quality control, costs, and other techniques for maximizing the effective manufacture and distribution of goods.
Telecommunications	Knowledge of transmission, broadcasting, switching, control, and operation of telecommunications systems.
Sales and Marketing	Knowledge of principles and methods for showing, promoting, and selling products or services. This includes marketing strategy and tactics, product demonstration, sales techniques, and sales control systems.
Geography	Knowledge of principles and methods for describing the features of land, sea, and air masses, including their physical characteristics, locations, interrelationships, and distribution of plant, animal, and human life.
Design	Knowledge of design techniques, tools, and principles involved in production of precision technical plans, blueprints, drawings, and models.
History and Archeology	Knowledge of historical events and their causes, indicators, and effects on civilizations and cultures.
Transportation	Knowledge of principles and methods for moving people or goods by air, rail, sea, or road, including the relative costs and benefits.
Building and Construction	Knowledge of materials, methods, and the tools involved in the construction or repair of houses, buildings, or other structures such as highways and roads.
Food Production	Knowledge of techniques and equipment for planting, growing, and harvesting food products (both plant and animal) for consumption, including storage/handling techniques.
Fine Arts	Knowledge of the theory and techniques required to compose, produce, and perform works of music, dance, visual arts, drama, and sculpture.

Skills	Skills Definitions
Time Management	Managing one's own time and the time of others.
Critical Thinking	Using logic and reasoning to identify the strengths and weaknesses of alternative solutions, conclusions or approaches to problems.
Reading Comprehension	Understanding written sentences and paragraphs in work related documents.
Troubleshooting	Determining causes of operating errors and deciding what to do about it.
Active Listening	Giving full attention to what other people are saying, taking time to understand the points being made, asking questions as appropriate, and not interrupting at inappropriate times.
Instructing	Teaching others how to do something.
Operation Monitoring	Watching gauges, dials, or other indicators to make sure a machine is working properly.
Judgment and Decision Making	Considering the relative costs and benefits of potential actions to choose the most appropriate one.
Speaking	Talking to others to convey information effectively
Service Orientation	Actively looking for ways to help people.
Operation and Control	Controlling operations of equipment or systems.
Active Learning	Understanding the implications of new information for both current and future problem-solving and decision-making.

Equipment Maintenance	Performing routine maintenance on equipment and determining when and what kind of maintenance is needed.
Monitoring	Monitoring/Assessing performance of yourself, other individuals, or organizations to make improvements or take corrective action.
Learning Strategies	Selecting and using training/instructional methods and procedures appropriate for the situation when learning or teaching new things.
Equipment Selection	Determining the kind of tools and equipment needed to do a job.
Writing	Communicating effectively in writing as appropriate for the needs of the audience.
Science	Using scientific rules and methods to solve problems.
Mathematics	Using mathematics to solve problems.
Quality Control Analysis	Conducting tests and inspections of products, services, or processes to evaluate quality or performance.
Social Perceptiveness	Being aware of others' reactions and understanding why they react as they do.
Management of Material Resources	Obtaining and seeing to the appropriate use of equipment, facilities, and materials needed to do certain work.
Complex Problem Solving	Identifying complex problems and reviewing related information to develop and evaluate options and implement solutions.
Management of Personnel Resources	Motivating, developing, and directing people as they work, identifying the best people for the job.
Persuasion	Persuading others to change their minds or behavior.
Technology Design	Generating or adapting equipment and technology to serve user needs.
Coordination	Adjusting actions in relation to others' actions.
Operations Analysis	Analyzing needs and product requirements to create a design.
Systems Analysis	Determining how a system should work and how changes in conditions, operations, and the environment will affect outcomes.
Systems Evaluation	Identifying measures or indicators of system performance and the actions needed to improve or correct performance, relative to the goals of the system.
Negotiation	Bringing others together and trying to reconcile differences.
Repairing	Repairing machines or systems using the needed tools.
Installation	Installing equipment, machines, wiring, or programs to meet specifications.
Management of Financial Resources	Determining how money will be spent to get the work done, and accounting for these expenditures.
Programming	Writing computer programs for various purposes.

Ability	Ability Definitions
Oral Expression	The ability to communicate information and ideas in speaking so others will understand.
Problem Sensitivity	The ability to tell when something is wrong or is likely to go wrong. It does not involve solving the problem, only recognizing there is a problem.
Oral Comprehension	The ability to listen to and understand information and ideas presented through spoken words and sentences.
Written Comprehension	The ability to read and understand information and ideas presented in writing.
Speech Recognition	The ability to identify and understand the speech of another person.
Information Ordering	The ability to arrange things or actions in a certain order or pattern according to a specific rule or set of rules (e.g., patterns of numbers, letters, words, pictures, mathematical operations).
Near Vision	The ability to see details at close range (within a few feet of the observer).
Speech Clarity	The ability to speak clearly so others can understand you.
Inductive Reasoning	The ability to combine pieces of information to form general rules or conclusions (includes finding a relationship among seemingly unrelated events).
Deductive Reasoning	The ability to apply general rules to specific problems to produce answers that make sense.
Written Expression	The ability to communicate information and ideas in writing so others will understand.
Category Flexibility	The ability to generate or use different sets of rules for combining or grouping things in different ways.
Control Precision	The ability to quickly and repeatedly adjust the controls of a machine or a vehicle to exact positions.
Selective Attention	The ability to concentrate on a task over a period of time without being distracted.
Perceptual Speed	The ability to quickly and accurately compare similarities and differences among sets of letters, numbers, objects, pictures, or patterns. The things to be compared may be presented at the same time or one after the other. This ability also includes comparing a presented object with a remembered object.
Finger Dexterity	The ability to make precisely coordinated movements of the fingers of one or both hands to grasp, manipulate, or assemble very small objects.

Originality	The ability to come up with unusual or clever ideas about a given topic or situation, or to develop creative ways to solve a problem.
Flexibility of Closure	The ability to identify or detect a known pattern (a figure, object, word, or sound) that is hidden in other distracting material.
Time Sharing	The ability to shift back and forth between two or more activities or sources of information (such as speech, sounds, touch, or other sources).
Arm-Hand Steadiness	The ability to keep your hand and arm steady while moving your arm or while holding your arm and hand in one position.
Fluency of Ideas	The ability to come up with a number of ideas about a topic (the number of ideas is important, not their quality, correctness, or creativity).
Trunk Strength	The ability to use your abdominal and lower back muscles to support part of the body repeatedly or continuously over time without 'giving out' or fatiguing.
Extent Flexibility	The ability to bend, stretch, twist, or reach with your body, arms, and/or legs.
Auditory Attention	The ability to focus on a single source of sound in the presence of other distracting sounds.
Speed of Closure	The ability to quickly make sense of, combine, and organize information into meaningful patterns.
Memorization	The ability to remember information such as words, numbers, pictures, and procedures.
Hearing Sensitivity	The ability to detect or tell the differences between sounds that vary in pitch and loudness.
Manual Dexterity	The ability to quickly move your hand, your hand together with your arm, or your two hands to grasp, manipulate, or assemble objects.
Multilimb Coordination	The ability to coordinate two or more limbs (for example, two arms, two legs, or one leg and one arm) while sitting, standing, or lying down. It does not involve performing the activities while the whole body is in motion.
Stamina	The ability to exert yourself physically over long periods of time without getting winded or out of breath.
Static Strength	The ability to exert maximum muscle force to lift, push, pull, or carry objects.
Gross Body Coordination	The ability to coordinate the movement of your arms, legs, and torso together when the whole body is in motion.
Response Orientation	The ability to choose quickly between two or more movements in response to two or more different signals (lights, sounds, pictures). It includes the speed with which the correct response is started with the hand, foot, or other body part.
Speed of Limb Movement	The ability to quickly move the arms and legs.
Visual Color Discrimination	The ability to match or detect differences between colors, including shades of color and brightness.
Reaction Time	The ability to quickly respond (with the hand, finger, or foot) to a signal (sound, light, picture) when it appears.
Visualization	The ability to imagine how something will look after it is moved around or when its parts are moved or rearranged.
Depth Perception	The ability to judge which of several objects is closer or farther away from you, or to judge the distance between you and an object.
Far Vision	The ability to see details at a distance.
Mathematical Reasoning	The ability to choose the right mathematical methods or formulas to solve a problem.
Number Facility	The ability to add, subtract, multiply, or divide quickly and correctly.
Wrist-Finger Speed	The ability to make fast, simple, repeated movements of the fingers, hands, and wrists.
Rate Control	The ability to time your movements or the movement of a piece of equipment in anticipation of changes in the speed and/or direction of a moving object or scene.
Gross Body Equilibrium	The ability to keep or regain your body balance or stay upright when in an unstable position.
Dynamic Strength	The ability to exert muscle force repeatedly or continuously over time. This involves muscular endurance and resistance to muscle fatigue.
Explosive Strength	The ability to use short bursts of muscle force to propel oneself (as in jumping or sprinting), or to throw an object.
Spatial Orientation	The ability to know your location in relation to the environment or to know where other objects are in relation to you.
Sound Localization	The ability to tell the direction from which a sound originated.
Night Vision	The ability to see under low light conditions.
Glare Sensitivity	The ability to see objects in the presence of glare or bright lighting.
Dynamic Flexibility	The ability to quickly and repeatedly bend, stretch, twist, or reach out with your body, arms, and/or legs.
Peripheral Vision	The ability to see objects or movement of objects to one's side when the eyes are looking ahead.

Work_Activity	Work_Activity Definitions

Assisting and Caring for Others	Providing personal assistance, medical attention, emotional support, or other personal care to others such as coworkers, customers, or patients.
Inspecting Equipment, Structures, or Material	Inspecting equipment, structures, or materials to identify the cause of errors or other problems or defects.
Performing for or Working Directly with the Public	Performing for people or dealing directly with the public. This includes serving customers in restaurants and stores, and receiving clients or guests.
Communicating with Supervisors, Peers, or Subordin	Providing information to supervisors, co-workers, and subordinates by telephone, in written form, e-mail, or in person.
Identifying Objects, Actions, and Events	Identifying information by categorizing, estimating, recognizing differences or similarities, and detecting changes in circumstances or events.
Making Decisions and Solving Problems	Analyzing information and evaluating results to choose the best solution and solve problems.
Updating and Using Relevant Knowledge	Keeping up-to-date technically and applying new knowledge to your job.
Getting Information	Observing, receiving, and otherwise obtaining information from all relevant sources.
Establishing and Maintaining Interpersonal Relatio	Developing constructive and cooperative working relationships with others, and maintaining them over time.
Organizing, Planning, and Prioritizing Work	Developing specific goals and plans to prioritize, organize, and accomplish your work.
Evaluating Information to Determine Compliance wit	Using relevant information and individual judgment to determine whether events or processes comply with laws, regulations, or standards.
Interpreting the Meaning of Information for Others	Translating or explaining what information means and how it can be used.
Controlling Machines and Processes	Using either control mechanisms or direct physical activity to operate machines or processes (not including computers or vehicles).
Training and Teaching Others	Identifying the educational needs of others, developing formal educational or training programs or classes, and teaching or instructing others.
Processing Information	Compiling, coding, categorizing, calculating, tabulating, auditing, or verifying information or data.
Documenting/Recording Information	Entering, transcribing, recording, storing, or maintaining information in written or electronic/magnetic form.
Developing Objectives and Strategies	Establishing long-range objectives and specifying the strategies and actions to achieve them.
Monitor Processes, Materials, or Surroundings	Monitoring and reviewing information from materials, events, or the environment, to detect or assess problems.
Judging the Qualities of Things, Services, or Peop	Assessing the value, importance, or quality of things or people.
Coordinating the Work and Activities of Others	Getting members of a group to work together to accomplish tasks.
Thinking Creatively	Developing, designing, or creating new applications, ideas, relationships, systems, or products, including artistic contributions.
Provide Consultation and Advice to Others	Providing guidance and expert advice to management or other groups on technical, systems-, or process-related topics.
Developing and Building Teams	Encouraging and building mutual trust, respect, and cooperation among team members.
Analyzing Data or Information	Identifying the underlying principles, reasons, or facts of information by breaking down information or data into separate parts.
Performing General Physical Activities	Performing physical activities that require considerable use of your arms and legs and moving your whole body, such as climbing, lifting, balancing, walking, stooping, and handling of materials.
Communicating with Persons Outside Organization	Communicating with people outside the organization, representing the organization to customers, the public, government, and other external sources. This information can be exchanged in person, in writing, or by telephone or e-mail.
Guiding, Directing, and Motivating Subordinates	Providing guidance and direction to subordinates, including setting performance standards and monitoring performance.
Interacting With Computers	Using computers and computer systems (including hardware and software) to program, write software, set up functions, enter data, or process information.
Selling or Influencing Others	Convincing others to buy merchandise/goods or to otherwise change their minds or actions.
Handling and Moving Objects	Using hands and arms in handling, installing, positioning, and moving materials, and manipulating things.
Resolving Conflicts and Negotiating with Others	Handling complaints, settling disputes, and resolving grievances and conflicts, or otherwise negotiating with others.
Scheduling Work and Activities	Scheduling events, programs, and activities, as well as the work of others.
Estimating the Quantifiable Characteristics of Pro	Estimating sizes, distances, and quantities; or determining time, costs, resources, or materials needed to perform a work activity.
Performing Administrative Activities	Performing day-to-day administrative tasks such as maintaining information files and processing paperwork.

Coaching and Developing Others	Identifying the developmental needs of others and coaching, mentoring, or otherwise helping others to improve their knowledge or skills.
Repairing and Maintaining Electronic Equipment	Servicing, repairing, calibrating, regulating, fine-tuning, or testing machines, devices, and equipment that operate primarily on the basis of electrical or electronic (not mechanical) principles.
Staffing Organizational Units	Recruiting, interviewing, selecting, hiring, and promoting employees in an organization.
Monitoring and Controlling Resources	Monitoring and controlling resources and overseeing the spending of money.
Repairing and Maintaining Mechanical Equipment	Servicing, repairing, adjusting, and testing machines, devices, moving parts, and equipment that operate primarily on the basis of mechanical (not electronic) principles.
Drafting, Laying Out, and Specifying Technical Dev	Providing documentation, detailed instructions, drawings, or specifications to tell others about how devices, parts, equipment, or structures are to be fabricated, constructed, assembled, modified, maintained, or used.
Operating Vehicles, Mechanized Devices, or Equipme	Running, maneuvering, navigating, or driving vehicles or mechanized equipment, such as forklifts, passenger vehicles, aircraft, or water craft.

Work_Content	Work_Content Definitions
Contact With Others	How much does this job require the worker to be in contact with others (face-to-face, by telephone, or otherwise) in order to perform it?
Face-to-Face Discussions	How often do you have to have face-to-face discussions with individuals or teams in this job?
Indoors, Environmentally Controlled	How often does this job require working indoors in environmentally controlled conditions?
Exposed to Disease or Infections	How often does this job require exposure to disease/infections?
Telephone	How often do you have telephone conversations in this job?
Structured versus Unstructured Work	To what extent is this job structured for the worker, rather than allowing the worker to determine tasks, priorities, and goals?
Physical Proximity	To what extent does this job require the worker to perform job tasks in close physical proximity to other people?
Consequence of Error	How serious would the result usually be if the worker made a mistake that was not readily correctable?
Work With Work Group or Team	How important is it to work with others in a group or team in this job?
Frequency of Decision Making	How frequently is the worker required to make decisions that affect other people, the financial resources, and/or the image and reputation of the organization?
Freedom to Make Decisions	How much decision making freedom, without supervision, does the job offer?
Spend Time Using Your Hands to Handle, Control, or	How much does this job require using your hands to handle, control, or feel objects, tools or controls?
Exposed to Contaminants	How often does this job require working exposed to contaminants (such as pollutants, gases, dust or odors)?
Wear Common Protective or Safety Equipment such as	How much does this job require wearing common protective or safety equipment such as safety shoes, glasses, gloves, hard hats or live jackets?
Importance of Being Exact or Accurate	How important is being very exact or highly accurate in performing this job?
Deal With Unpleasant or Angry People	How frequently does the worker have to deal with unpleasant, angry, or discourteous individuals as part of the job requirements?
Spend Time Walking and Running	How much does this job require walking and running?
Spend Time Standing	How much does this job require standing?
Time Pressure	How often does this job require the worker to meet strict deadlines?
Impact of Decisions on Co-workers or Company Resul	How do the decisions an employee makes impact the results of co-workers, clients or the company?
Responsible for Others' Health and Safety	How much responsibility is there for the health and safety of others in this job?
Sounds, Noise Levels Are Distracting or Uncomforta	How often does this job require working exposed to sounds and noise levels that are distracting or uncomfortable?
Cramped Work Space, Awkward Positions	How often does this job require working in cramped work spaces that requires getting into awkward positions?
Exposed to Radiation	How often does this job require exposure to radiation?
Deal With External Customers	How important is it to work with external customers or the public in this job?
Responsibility for Outcomes and Results	How responsible is the worker for work outcomes and results of other workers?
Importance of Repeating Same Tasks	How important is repeating the same physical activities (e.g., key entry) or mental activities (e.g., checking entries in a ledger) over and over, without stopping, to performing this job?
Coordinate or Lead Others	How important is it to coordinate or lead others in accomplishing work activities in this job?
Spend Time Making Repetitive Motions	How much does this job require making repetitive motions?

187

Frequency of Conflict Situations	How often are there conflict situations the employee has to face in this job?
Spend Time Bending or Twisting the Body	How much does this job require bending or twisting your body?
Level of Competition	To what extent does this job require the worker to compete or to be aware of competitive pressures?
Letters and Memos	How often does the job require written letters and memos?
Deal With Physically Aggressive People	How frequently does this job require the worker to deal with physical aggression of violent individuals?
Spend Time Kneeling, Crouching, Stooping, or Crawl	How much does this job require kneeling, crouching, stooping or crawling?
Wear Specialized Protective or Safety Equipment su	How much does this job require wearing specialized protective or safety equipment such as breathing apparatus, safety harness, full protection suits, or radiation protection?
Spend Time Sitting	How much does this job require sitting?
Extremely Bright or Inadequate Lighting	How often does this job require working in extremely bright or inadequate lighting conditions?
Electronic Mail	How often do you use electronic mail in this job?
Public Speaking	How often do you have to perform public speaking in this job?
Exposed to Hazardous Conditions	How often does this job require exposure to hazardous conditions?
Exposed to Minor Burns, Cuts, Bites, or Stings	How often does this job require exposure to minor burns, cuts, bites, or stings?
Degree of Automation	How automated is the job?
Spend Time Keeping or Regaining Balance	How much does this job require keeping or regaining your balance?
Pace Determined by Speed of Equipment	How important is it to this job that the pace is determined by the speed of equipment or machinery? (This does not refer to keeping busy at all times on this job.)
In an Enclosed Vehicle or Equipment	How often does this job require working in a closed vehicle or equipment (e.g., car)?
Exposed to Hazardous Equipment	How often does this job require exposure to hazardous equipment?
Indoors, Not Environmentally Controlled	How often does this job require working indoors in non-controlled environmental conditions (e.g., warehouse without heat)?
Outdoors, Exposed to Weather	How often does this job require working outdoors, exposed to all weather conditions?
Very Hot or Cold Temperatures	How often does this job require working in very hot (above 90 F degrees) or very cold (below 32 F degrees) temperatures?
In an Open Vehicle or Equipment	How often does this job require working in an open vehicle or equipment (e.g., tractor)?
Outdoors, Under Cover	How often does this job require working outdoors, under cover (e.g., structure with roof but no walls)?
Exposed to High Places	How often does this job require exposure to high places?
Spend Time Climbing Ladders, Scaffolds, or Poles	How much does this job require climbing ladders, scaffolds, or poles?
Exposed to Whole Body Vibration	How often does this job require exposure to whole body vibration (e.g., operate a jackhammer)?

Work_Styles	Work_Styles Definitions
Dependability	Job requires being reliable, responsible, and dependable, and fulfilling obligations.
Integrity	Job requires being honest and ethical.
Attention to Detail	Job requires being careful about detail and thorough in completing work tasks.
Concern for Others	Job requires being sensitive to others' needs and feelings and being understanding and helpful on the job.
Cooperation	Job requires being pleasant with others on the job and displaying a good-natured, cooperative attitude.
Self Control	Job requires maintaining composure, keeping emotions in check, controlling anger, and avoiding aggressive behavior, even in very difficult situations.
Stress Tolerance	Job requires accepting criticism and dealing calmly and effectively with high stress situations.
Independence	Job requires developing one's own ways of doing things, guiding oneself with little or no supervision, and depending on oneself to get things done.
Adaptability/Flexibility	Job requires being open to change (positive or negative) and to considerable variety in the workplace.
Social Orientation	Job requires preferring to work with others rather than alone, and being personally connected with others on the job.
Initiative	Job requires a willingness to take on responsibilities and challenges.
Achievement/Effort	Job requires establishing and maintaining personally challenging achievement goals and exerting effort toward mastering tasks.
Analytical Thinking	Job requires analyzing information and using logic to address work-related issues and problems.
Persistence	Job requires persistence in the face of obstacles.
Leadership	Job requires a willingness to lead, take charge, and offer opinions and direction.

Innovation	Job requires creativity and alternative thinking to develop new ideas for and answers to work-related problems.

Job Zone Component	Job Zone Component Definitions
Title	Job Zone Three: Medium Preparation Needed
Overall Experience	Previous work-related skill, knowledge, or experience is required for these occupations. For example, an electrician must have completed three or four years of apprenticeship or several years of vocational training, and often must have passed a licensing exam, in order to perform the job.
Job Training	Employees in these occupations usually need one or two years of training involving both on-the-job experience and informal training with experienced workers.
Job Zone Examples	These occupations usually involve using communication and organizational skills to coordinate, supervise, manage, or train others to accomplish goals. Examples include dental assistants, electricians, fish and game wardens, legal secretaries, personnel recruiters, and recreation workers.
SVP Range	(6.0 to < 7.0)
Education	Most occupations in this zone require training in vocational schools, related on-the-job experience, or an associate's degree. Some may require a bachelor's degree.

29-2055.00 - Surgical Technologists

Assist in operations, under the supervision of surgeons, registered nurses, or other surgical personnel. May help set up operating room, prepare and transport patients for surgery, adjust lights and equipment, pass instruments and other supplies to surgeons and surgeon's assistants, hold retractors, cut sutures, and help count sponges, needles, supplies, and instruments.

Tasks

1) Observe patients' vital signs to assess physical condition.

2) Clean and restock the operating room, placing equipment and supplies and arranging instruments according to instruction.

3) Hand instruments and supplies to surgeons and surgeons' assistants, hold retractors and cut sutures, and perform other tasks as directed by surgeon during operation.

4) Provide technical assistance to surgeons, surgical nurses and anesthesiologists.

5) Monitor and continually assess operating room conditions, including patient and surgical team needs.

6) Position patients on the operating table and cover them with sterile surgical drapes to prevent exposure.

7) Scrub arms and hands and assist the surgical team to scrub and put on gloves, masks, and surgical clothing.

8) Maintain files and records of surgical procedures.

9) Prepare, care for and dispose of tissue specimens taken for laboratory analysis.

10) Prepare dressings or bandages and apply or assist with their application following surgery.

11) Wash and sterilize equipment using germicides and sterilizers

12) Operate, assemble, adjust, or monitor sterilizers, lights, suction machines, and diagnostic equipment to ensure proper operation.

13) Count sponges, needles, and instruments before and after operation.

29-2056.00 - Veterinary Technologists and Technicians

Perform medical tests in a laboratory environment for use in the treatment and diagnosis of diseases in animals. Prepare vaccines and serums for prevention of diseases. Prepare tissue samples, take blood samples, and execute laboratory tests, such as urinalysis and blood counts. Clean and sterilize instruments and materials and maintain equipment and machines.

Tasks

1) Provide information and counseling regarding issues such as animal health care, behavior problems, and nutrition.

2) Conduct specialized procedures such as animal branding or tattooing, and hoof trimming.

3) Prepare treatment rooms for surgery.

4) Collect, prepare, and label samples for laboratory testing, culture, or microscopic examination.

5) Care for and monitor the condition of animals recovering from surgery.

6) Take and develop diagnostic radiographs, using x-ray equipment.

7) Prepare and administer medications, vaccines, serums, and treatments, as prescribed by

veterinarians.

8) Perform laboratory tests on blood, urine, and feces, such as urinalyses and blood counts, to assist in the diagnosis and treatment of animal health problems.

9) Maintain laboratory, research, and treatment records, as well as inventories of pharmaceuticals, equipment, and supplies.

10) Maintain instruments, equipment, and machinery to ensure proper working condition.

11) Clean and sterilize instruments, equipment, and materials.

12) Administer emergency first aid, such as performing emergency resuscitation or other life saving procedures.

13) Clean kennels, animal holding areas, surgery suites, examination rooms, and animal loading/unloading facilities to control the spread of disease.

14) Bathe animals, clip nails or claws, and brush and cut animals' hair.

15) Administer anesthesia to animals, under the direction of a veterinarian, and monitor animals' responses to anesthetics so that dosages can be adjusted.

16) Perform dental work such as cleaning, polishing, and extracting teeth.

17) Fill prescriptions, measuring medications and labeling containers.

18) Dress and suture wounds, and apply splints and other protective devices.

19) Provide assistance with animal euthanasia and the disposal of remains.

20) Observe the behavior and condition of animals, and monitor their clinical symptoms.

21) Take animals into treatment areas, and assist with physical examinations by performing such duties as obtaining temperature, pulse, and respiration data.

22) Perform a variety of office, clerical, and accounting duties, such as reception, billing, bookkeeping, and/or selling products.

23) Give enemas and perform catheterizations, ear flushes, intravenous feedings, and gavages.

24) Prepare animals for surgery, performing such tasks as shaving surgical areas.

29-2061.00 - Licensed Practical and Licensed Vocational Nurses

Care for ill, injured, convalescent, or disabled persons in hospitals, nursing homes, clinics, private homes, group homes, and similar institutions. May work under the supervision of a registered nurse. Licensing required.

Tasks

1) Measure and record patients' vital signs, such as height, weight, temperature, blood pressure, pulse and respiration.

2) Answer patients' calls and determine how to assist them.

3) Prepare patients for examinations, tests and treatments and explain procedures.

4) Provide basic patient care and treatments, such as taking temperatures and blood pressure, dressing wounds, treating bedsores, giving enemas, douches, alcohol rubs, and massages, or performing catheterizations.

5) Apply compresses, ice bags, and hot water bottles.

6) Evaluate nursing intervention outcomes, conferring with other health-care team members as necessary.

7) Work as part of a health care team to assess patient needs, plan and modify care and implement interventions.

8) Supervise nurses' aides and assistants.

9) Assemble and use equipment such as catheters, tracheotomy tubes, and oxygen suppliers.

10) Help patients with bathing, dressing, personal hygiene, moving in bed, and standing and walking.

11) Record food and fluid intake and output.

12) Collect samples such as blood, urine and sputum from patients, and perform routine laboratory tests on samples.

13) Inventory and requisition supplies and instruments.

14) Prepare food trays and examine them for conformance to prescribed diet.

15) Clean rooms and make beds.

16) Set up equipment and prepare medical treatment rooms.

17) Wash and dress bodies of deceased persons.

18) Make appointments, keep records and perform other clerical duties in doctors' offices and clinics.

19) Sterilize equipment and supplies, using germicides, sterilizer, or autoclave.

20) Assist in delivery, care, and feeding of infants.

21) Provide medical treatment and personal care to patients in private home settings, such as

cooking, keeping rooms orderly, seeing that patients are comfortable and in good spirits, and instructing family members in simple nursing tasks.

22) Observe patients, charting and reporting changes in patients' conditions, such as adverse reactions to medication or treatment, and taking any necessary action.

Knowledge	Knowledge Definitions
English Language	Knowledge of the structure and content of the English language including the meaning and spelling of words, rules of composition, and grammar.
Medicine and Dentistry	Knowledge of the information and techniques needed to diagnose and treat human injuries, diseases, and deformities. This includes symptoms, treatment alternatives, drug properties and interactions, and preventive health-care measures.
Customer and Personal Service	Knowledge of principles and processes for providing customer and personal services. This includes customer needs assessment, meeting quality standards for services, and evaluation of customer satisfaction.
Therapy and Counseling	Knowledge of principles, methods, and procedures for diagnosis, treatment, and rehabilitation of physical and mental dysfunctions, and for career counseling and guidance.
Education and Training	Knowledge of principles and methods for curriculum and training design, teaching and instruction for individuals and groups, and the measurement of training effects.
Psychology	Knowledge of human behavior and performance; individual differences in ability, personality, and interests; learning and motivation; psychological research methods; and the assessment and treatment of behavioral and affective disorders.
Mathematics	Knowledge of arithmetic, algebra, geometry, calculus, statistics, and their applications.
Public Safety and Security	Knowledge of relevant equipment, policies, procedures, and strategies to promote effective local, state, or national security operations for the protection of people, data, property, and institutions.
Administration and Management	Knowledge of business and management principles involved in strategic planning, resource allocation, human resources modeling, leadership technique, production methods, and coordination of people and resources.
Chemistry	Knowledge of the chemical composition, structure, and properties of substances and of the chemical processes and transformations that they undergo. This includes uses of chemicals and their interactions, danger signs, production techniques, and disposal methods.
Personnel and Human Resources	Knowledge of principles and procedures for personnel recruitment, selection, training, compensation and benefits, labor relations and negotiation, and personnel information systems.
Sociology and Anthropology	Knowledge of group behavior and dynamics, societal trends and influences, human migrations, ethnicity, cultures and their history and origins.
Biology	Knowledge of plant and animal organisms, their tissues, cells, functions, interdependencies, and interactions with each other and the environment.
Law and Government	Knowledge of laws, legal codes, court procedures, precedents, government regulations, executive orders, agency rules, and the democratic political process.
Telecommunications	Knowledge of transmission, broadcasting, switching, control, and operation of telecommunications systems.
Clerical	Knowledge of administrative and clerical procedures and systems such as word processing, managing files and records, stenography and transcription, designing forms, and other office procedures and terminology.
Transportation	Knowledge of principles and methods for moving people or goods by air, rail, sea, or road, including the relative costs and benefits.
Philosophy and Theology	Knowledge of different philosophical systems and religions. This includes their basic principles, values, ethics, ways of thinking, customs, practices, and their impact on human culture.
Communications and Media	Knowledge of media production, communication, and dissemination techniques and methods. This includes alternative ways to inform and entertain via written, oral, and visual media.
Foreign Language	Knowledge of the structure and content of a foreign (non-English) language including the meaning and spelling of words, rules of composition and grammar, and pronunciation.
Computers and Electronics	Knowledge of circuit boards, processors, chips, electronic equipment, and computer hardware and software, including applications and programming.
Production and Processing	Knowledge of raw materials, production processes, quality control, costs, and other techniques for maximizing the effective manufacture and distribution of goods.
Food Production	Knowledge of techniques and equipment for planting, growing, and harvesting food products (both plant and animal) for consumption, including storage/handling techniques.
Mechanical	Knowledge of machines and tools, including their designs, uses, repair, and maintenance.

Physics	Knowledge and prediction of physical principles, laws, their interrelationships, and applications to understanding fluid, material, and atmospheric dynamics, and mechanical, electrical, atomic and sub- atomic structures and processes.
Engineering and Technology	Knowledge of the practical application of engineering science and technology. This includes applying principles, techniques, procedures, and equipment to the design and production of various goods and services.
History and Archeology	Knowledge of historical events and their causes, indicators, and effects on civilizations and cultures.
Geography	Knowledge of principles and methods for describing the features of land, sea, and air masses, including their physical characteristics, locations, interrelationships, and distribution of plant, animal, and human life.
Economics and Accounting	Knowledge of economic and accounting principles and practices, the financial markets, banking and the analysis and reporting of financial data.
Sales and Marketing	Knowledge of principles and methods for showing, promoting, and selling products or services. This includes marketing strategy and tactics, product demonstration, sales techniques, and sales control systems.
Fine Arts	Knowledge of the theory and techniques required to compose, produce, and perform works of music, dance, visual arts, drama, and sculpture.
Design	Knowledge of design techniques, tools, and principles involved in production of precision technical plans, blueprints, drawings, and models.
Building and Construction	Knowledge of materials, methods, and the tools involved in the construction or repair of houses, buildings, or other structures such as highways and roads.

Skills	Skills Definitions
Active Listening	Giving full attention to what other people are saying, taking time to understand the points being made, asking questions as appropriate, and not interrupting at inappropriate times.
Reading Comprehension	Understanding written sentences and paragraphs in work related documents.
Time Management	Managing one's own time and the time of others.
Writing	Communicating effectively in writing as appropriate for the needs of the audience.
Monitoring	Monitoring/Assessing performance of yourself, other individuals, or organizations to make improvements or take corrective action.
Critical Thinking	Using logic and reasoning to identify the strengths and weaknesses of alternative solutions, conclusions or approaches to problems.
Speaking	Talking to others to convey information effectively.
Service Orientation	Actively looking for ways to help people.
Judgment and Decision Making	Considering the relative costs and benefits of potential actions to choose the most appropriate one.
Active Learning	Understanding the implications of new information for both current and future problem-solving and decision-making.
Instructing	Teaching others how to do something.
Learning Strategies	Selecting and using training/instructional methods and procedures appropriate for the situation when learning or teaching new things.
Complex Problem Solving	Identifying complex problems and reviewing related information to develop and evaluate options and implement solutions.
Coordination	Adjusting actions in relation to others' actions.
Troubleshooting	Determining causes of operating errors and deciding what to do about it.
Science	Using scientific rules and methods to solve problems.
Operation Monitoring	Watching gauges, dials, or other indicators to make sure a machine is working properly.
Social Perceptiveness	Being aware of others' reactions and understanding why they react as they do.
Mathematics	Using mathematics to solve problems.
Management of Personnel Resources	Motivating, developing, and directing people as they work, identifying the best people for the job.
Equipment Maintenance	Performing routine maintenance on equipment and determining when and what kind of maintenance is needed.
Persuasion	Persuading others to change their minds or behavior.
Repairing	Repairing machines or systems using the needed tools.
Equipment Selection	Determining the kind of tools and equipment needed to do a job.
Operation and Control	Controlling operations of equipment or systems.
Systems Evaluation	Identifying measures or indicators of system performance and the actions needed to improve or correct performance, relative to the goals of the system.
Systems Analysis	Determining how a system should work and how changes in conditions, operations, and the environment will affect outcomes.
Management of Material Resources	Obtaining and seeing to the appropriate use of equipment, facilities, and materials needed to do certain work.

Quality Control Analysis	Conducting tests and inspections of products, services, or processes to evaluate quality or performance.
Technology Design	Generating or adapting equipment and technology to serve user needs.
Negotiation	Bringing others together and trying to reconcile differences.
Installation	Installing equipment, machines, wiring, or programs to meet specifications.
Operations Analysis	Analyzing needs and product requirements to create a design.
Management of Financial Resources	Determining how money will be spent to get the work done, and accounting for these expenditures.
Programming	Writing computer programs for various purposes.

Ability	Ability Definitions
Oral Comprehension	The ability to listen to and understand information and ideas presented through spoken words and sentences.
Problem Sensitivity	The ability to tell when something is wrong or is likely to go wrong. It does not involve solving the problem, only recognizing there is a problem.
Oral Expression	The ability to communicate information and ideas in speaking so others will understand.
Deductive Reasoning	The ability to apply general rules to specific problems to produce answers that make sense.
Inductive Reasoning	The ability to combine pieces of information to form general rules or conclusions (includes finding a relationship among seemingly unrelated events).
Information Ordering	The ability to arrange things or actions in a certain order or pattern according to a specific rule or set of rules (e.g., patterns of numbers, letters, words, pictures, mathematical operations).
Written Expression	The ability to communicate information and ideas in writing so others will understand.
Near Vision	The ability to see details at close range (within a few feet of the observer).
Speech Recognition	The ability to identify and understand the speech of another person.
Speech Clarity	The ability to speak clearly so others can understand you.
Written Comprehension	The ability to read and understand information and ideas presented in writing.
Selective Attention	The ability to concentrate on a task over a period of time without being distracted.
Time Sharing	The ability to shift back and forth between two or more activities or sources of information (such as speech, sounds, touch, or other sources).
Category Flexibility	The ability to generate or use different sets of rules for combining or grouping things in different ways.
Speed of Closure	The ability to quickly make sense of, combine, and organize information into meaningful patterns.
Finger Dexterity	The ability to make precisely coordinated movements of the fingers of one or both hands to grasp, manipulate, or assemble very small objects.
Perceptual Speed	The ability to quickly and accurately compare similarities and differences among sets of letters, numbers, objects, pictures, or patterns. The things to be compared may be presented at the same time or one after the other. This ability also includes comparing a presented object with a remembered object.
Arm-Hand Steadiness	The ability to keep your hand and arm steady while moving your arm or while holding your arm and hand in one position.
Flexibility of Closure	The ability to identify or detect a known pattern (a figure, object, word, or sound) that is hidden in other distracting material.
Hearing Sensitivity	The ability to detect or tell the differences between sounds that vary in pitch and loudness.
Memorization	The ability to remember information such as words, numbers, pictures, and procedures.
Originality	The ability to come up with unusual or clever ideas about a given topic or situation, or to develop creative ways to solve a problem.
Manual Dexterity	The ability to quickly move your hand, your hand together with your arm, or your two hands to grasp, manipulate, or assemble objects.
Gross Body Coordination	The ability to coordinate the movement of your arms, legs, and torso together when the whole body is in motion.
Stamina	The ability to exert yourself physically over long periods of time without getting winded or out of breath.
Far Vision	The ability to see details at a distance.
Visual Color Discrimination	The ability to match or detect differences between colors, including shades of color and brightness.
Number Facility	The ability to add, subtract, multiply, or divide quickly and correctly.
Trunk Strength	The ability to use your abdominal and lower back muscles to support part of the body repeatedly or continuously over time without 'giving out' or fatiguing.
Auditory Attention	The ability to focus on a single source of sound in the presence of other distracting sounds.

Fluency of Ideas	The ability to come up with a number of ideas about a topic (the number of ideas is important, not their quality, correctness, or creativity).
Extent Flexibility	The ability to bend, stretch, twist, or reach with your body, arms, and/or legs.
Depth Perception	The ability to judge which of several objects is closer or farther away from you, or to judge the distance between you and an object.
Mathematical Reasoning	The ability to choose the right mathematical methods or formulas to solve a problem.
Static Strength	The ability to exert maximum muscle force to lift, push, pull, or carry objects.
Multilimb Coordination	The ability to coordinate two or more limbs (for example, two arms, two legs, or one leg and one arm) while sitting, standing, or lying down. It does not involve performing the activities while the whole body is in motion.
Control Precision	The ability to quickly and repeatedly adjust the controls of a machine or a vehicle to exact positions.
Visualization	The ability to imagine how something will look after it is moved around or when its parts are moved or rearranged.
Reaction Time	The ability to quickly respond (with the hand, finger, or foot) to a signal (sound, light, picture) when it appears.
Speed of Limb Movement	The ability to quickly move the arms and legs.
Response Orientation	The ability to choose quickly between two or more movements in response to two or more different signals (lights, sounds, pictures). It includes the speed with which the correct response is started with the hand, foot, or other body part.
Dynamic Strength	The ability to exert muscle force repeatedly or continuously over time. This involves muscular endurance and resistance to muscle fatigue.
Gross Body Equilibrium	The ability to keep or regain your body balance or stay upright when in an unstable position.
Rate Control	The ability to time your movements or the movement of a piece of equipment in anticipation of changes in the speed and/or direction of a moving object or scene.
Sound Localization	The ability to tell the direction from which a sound originated.
Peripheral Vision	The ability to see objects or movement of objects to one's side when the eyes are looking ahead.
Spatial Orientation	The ability to know your location in relation to the environment or to know where other objects are in relation to you.
Night Vision	The ability to see under low light conditions.
Glare Sensitivity	The ability to see objects in the presence of glare or bright lighting.
Dynamic Flexibility	The ability to quickly and repeatedly bend, stretch, twist, or reach out with your body, arms, and/or legs.
Explosive Strength	The ability to use short bursts of muscle force to propel oneself (as in jumping or sprinting), or to throw an object.
Wrist-Finger Speed	The ability to make fast, simple, repeated movements of the fingers, hands, and wrists.

Work_Activity	Work_Activity Definitions
Documenting/Recording Information	Entering, transcribing, recording, storing, or maintaining information in written or electronic/magnetic form.
Assisting and Caring for Others	Providing personal assistance, medical attention, emotional support, or other personal care to others such as coworkers, customers, or patients.
Making Decisions and Solving Problems	Analyzing information and evaluating results to choose the best solution and solve problems.
Updating and Using Relevant Knowledge	Keeping up-to-date technically and applying new knowledge to your job.
Getting Information	Observing, receiving, and otherwise obtaining information from all relevant sources.
Organizing, Planning, and Prioritizing Work	Developing specific goals and plans to prioritize, organize, and accomplish your work.
Communicating with Supervisors, Peers, or Subordin	Providing information to supervisors, co-workers, and subordinates by telephone, in written form, e-mail, or in person.
Monitor Processes, Materials, or Surroundings	Monitoring and reviewing information from materials, events, or the environment, to detect or assess problems.
Evaluating Information to Determine Compliance wit	Using relevant information and individual judgment to determine whether events or processes comply with laws, regulations, or standards.
Identifying Objects, Actions, and Events	Identifying information by categorizing, estimating, recognizing differences or similarities, and detecting changes in circumstances or events.
Interpreting the Meaning of Information for Others	Translating or explaining what information means and how it can be used.
Establishing and Maintaining Interpersonal Relatio	Developing constructive and cooperative working relationships with others, and maintaining them over time.
Training and Teaching Others	Identifying the educational needs of others, developing formal educational or training programs or classes, and teaching or instructing others.

Scheduling Work and Activities	Scheduling events, programs, and activities, as well as the work of others.
Judging the Qualities of Things, Services, or Peop	Assessing the value, importance, or quality of things or people.
Developing and Building Teams	Encouraging and building mutual trust, respect, and cooperation among team members.
Performing Administrative Activities	Performing day-to-day administrative tasks such as maintaining information files and processing paperwork.
Performing for or Working Directly with the Public	Performing for people or dealing directly with the public. This includes serving customers in restaurants and stores, and receiving clients or guests.
Performing General Physical Activities	Performing physical activities that require considerable use of your arms and legs and moving your whole body, such as climbing, lifting, balancing, walking, stooping, and handling of materials.
Repairing and Maintaining Electronic Equipment	Servicing, repairing, calibrating, regulating, fine-tuning, or testing machines, devices, and equipment that operate primarily on the basis of electrical or electronic (not mechanical) principles.
Estimating the Quantifiable Characteristics of Pro	Estimating sizes, distances, and quantities; or determining time, costs, resources, or materials needed to perform a work activity.
Resolving Conflicts and Negotiating with Others	Handling complaints, settling disputes, and resolving grievances and conflicts, or otherwise negotiating with others.
Developing Objectives and Strategies	Establishing long-range objectives and specifying the strategies and actions to achieve them.
Inspecting Equipment, Structures, or Material	Inspecting equipment, structures, or materials to identify the cause of errors or other problems or defects.
Processing Information	Compiling, coding, categorizing, calculating, tabulating, auditing, or verifying information or data.
Analyzing Data or Information	Identifying the underlying principles, reasons, or facts of information by breaking down information or data into separate parts.
Provide Consultation and Advice to Others	Providing guidance and expert advice to management or other groups on technical, systems-, or process-related topics.
Communicating with Persons Outside Organization	Communicating with people outside the organization, representing the organization to customers, the public, government, and other external sources. This information can be exchanged in person, in writing, or by telephone or e-mail.
Coordinating the Work and Activities of Others	Getting members of a group to work together to accomplish tasks.
Coaching and Developing Others	Identifying the developmental needs of others and coaching, mentoring, or otherwise helping others to improve their knowledge or skills.
Interacting With Computers	Using computers and computer systems (including hardware and software) to program, write software, set up functions, enter data, or process information.
Handling and Moving Objects	Using hands and arms in handling, installing, positioning, and moving materials, and manipulating things.
Guiding, Directing, and Motivating Subordinates	Providing guidance and direction to subordinates, including setting performance standards and monitoring performance.
Thinking Creatively	Developing, designing, or creating new applications, ideas, relationships, systems, or products, including artistic contributions.
Controlling Machines and Processes	Using either control mechanisms or direct physical activity to operate machines or processes (not including computers or vehicles).
Repairing and Maintaining Mechanical Equipment	Servicing, repairing, adjusting, and testing machines, devices, moving parts, and equipment that operate primarily on the basis of mechanical (not electronic) principles.
Staffing Organizational Units	Recruiting, interviewing, selecting, hiring, and promoting employees in an organization.
Selling or Influencing Others	Convincing others to buy merchandise/goods or to otherwise change their minds or actions.
Monitoring and Controlling Resources	Monitoring and controlling resources and overseeing the spending of money.
Operating Vehicles, Mechanized Devices, or Equipme	Running, maneuvering, navigating, or driving vehicles or mechanized equipment, such as forklifts, passenger vehicles, aircraft, or water craft.
Drafting, Laying Out, and Specifying Technical Dev	Providing documentation, detailed instructions, drawings, or specifications to tell others about how devices, parts, equipment, or structures are to be fabricated, constructed, assembled, modified, maintained, or used.

Work_Content	Work_Content Definitions
Contact With Others	How much does this job require the worker to be in contact with others (face-to-face, by telephone, or otherwise) in order to perform it?
Telephone	How often do you have telephone conversations in this job?
Face-to-Face Discussions	How often do you have to have face-to-face discussions with individuals or teams in this job?
Structured versus Unstructured Work	To what extent is this job structured for the worker, rather than allowing the worker to determine tasks, priorities, and goals?
Work With Work Group or Team	How important is it to work with others in a group or team in this job?

Coordinate or Lead Others	How important is it to coordinate or lead others in accomplishing work activities in this job?
Deal With External Customers	How important is it to work with external customers or the public in this job?
Exposed to Disease or Infections	How often does this job require exposure to disease/infections?
Importance of Being Exact or Accurate	How important is being very exact or highly accurate in performing this job?
Time Pressure	How often does this job require the worker to meet strict deadlines?
Impact of Decisions on Co-workers or Company Resul	How do the decisions an employee makes impact the results of co-workers, clients or the company?
Frequency of Decision Making	How frequently is the worker required to make decisions that affect other people, the financial resources, and/or the image and reputation of the organization?
Indoors, Environmentally Controlled	How often does this job require working indoors in environmentally controlled conditions?
Freedom to Make Decisions	How much decision making freedom, without supervision, does the job offer?
Consequence of Error	How serious would the result usually be if the worker made a mistake that was not readily correctable?
Physical Proximity	To what extent does this job require the worker to perform job tasks in close physical proximity to other people?
Deal With Unpleasant or Angry People	How frequently does the worker have to deal with unpleasant, angry, or discourteous individuals as part of the job requirements?
Responsibility for Outcomes and Results	How responsible is the worker for work outcomes and results of other workers?
Responsible for Others' Health and Safety	How much responsibility is there for the health and safety of others in this job?
Letters and Memos	How often does the job require written letters and memos?
Frequency of Conflict Situations	How often are there conflict situations the employee has to face in this job?
Importance of Repeating Same Tasks	How important is repeating the same physical activities (e.g., key entry) or mental activities (e.g., checking entries in a ledger) over and over, without stopping, to performing this job?
Spend Time Walking and Running	How much does this job require walking and running?
Spend Time Standing	How much does this job require standing?
Wear Common Protective or Safety Equipment such as	How much does this job require wearing common protective or safety equipment such as safety shoes, glasses, gloves, hard hats or live jackets?
Electronic Mail	How often do you use electronic mail in this job?
Level of Competition	To what extent does this job require the worker to compete or to be aware of competitive pressures?
Sounds, Noise Levels Are Distracting or Uncomforta	How often does this job require working exposed to sounds and noise levels that are distracting or uncomfortable?
Spend Time Sitting	How much does this job require sitting?
Deal With Physically Aggressive People	How frequently does this job require the worker to deal with physical aggression of violent individuals?
Spend Time Bending or Twisting the Body	How much does this job require bending or twisting your body?
Public Speaking	How often do you have to perform public speaking in this job?
In an Enclosed Vehicle or Equipment	How often does this job require working in a closed vehicle or equipment (e.g., car)?
Spend Time Making Repetitive Motions	How much does this job require making repetitive motions?
Spend Time Using Your Hands to Handle, Control, or	How much does this job require using your hands to handle, control, or feel objects, tools or controls?
Degree of Automation	How automated is the job?
Exposed to Contaminants	How often does this job require working exposed to contaminants (such as pollutants, gases, dust or odors)?
Spend Time Kneeling, Crouching, Stooping, or Crawl	How much does this job require kneeling, crouching, stooping or crawling?
Cramped Work Space, Awkward Positions	How often does this job require working in cramped work spaces that requires getting into awkward positions?
Spend Time Keeping or Regaining Balance	How much does this job require keeping or regaining your balance?
Wear Specialized Protective or Safety Equipment su	How much does this job require wearing specialized protective or safety equipment such as breathing apparatus, safety harness, full protection suits, or radiation protection?
Exposed to Hazardous Conditions	How often does this job require exposure to hazardous conditions?
Indoors, Not Environmentally Controlled	How often does this job require working indoors in non-controlled environmental conditions (e.g., warehouse without heat)?
Exposed to Minor Burns, Cuts, Bites, or Stings	How often does this job require exposure to minor burns, cuts, bites, or stings?
Very Hot or Cold Temperatures	How often does this job require working in very hot (above 90 F degrees) or very cold (below 32 F degrees) temperatures?
Extremely Bright or Inadequate Lighting	How often does this job require working in extremely bright or inadequate lighting conditions?
Exposed to Radiation	How often does this job require exposure to radiation?

Outdoors, Under Cover	How often does this job require working outdoors, under cover (e.g., structure with roof but no walls)?
Pace Determined by Speed of Equipment	How important is it to this job that the pace is determined by the speed of equipment or machinery? (This does not refer to keeping busy at all times on this job.)
Outdoors, Exposed to Weather	How often does this job require working outdoors, exposed to all weather conditions?
Exposed to High Places	How often does this job require exposure to high places?
In an Open Vehicle or Equipment	How often does this job require working in an open vehicle or equipment (e.g., tractor)?
Exposed to Whole Body Vibration	How often does this job require exposure to whole body vibration (e.g., operate a jackhammer)?
Spend Time Climbing Ladders, Scaffolds, or Poles	How much does this job require climbing ladders, scaffolds, or poles?
Exposed to Hazardous Equipment	How often does this job require exposure to hazardous equipment?

Work_Styles	Work_Styles Definitions
Concern for Others	Job requires being sensitive to others' needs and feelings and being understanding and helpful on the job.
Stress Tolerance	Job requires accepting criticism and dealing calmly and effectively with high stress situations.
Dependability	Job requires being reliable, responsible, and dependable, and fulfilling obligations.
Attention to Detail	Job requires being careful about detail and thorough in completing work tasks.
Self Control	Job requires maintaining composure, keeping emotions in check, controlling anger, and avoiding aggressive behavior, even in very difficult situations.
Cooperation	Job requires being pleasant with others on the job and displaying a good-natured, cooperative attitude.
Integrity	Job requires being honest and ethical.
Adaptability/Flexibility	Job requires being open to change (positive or negative) and to considerable variety in the workplace.
Leadership	Job requires a willingness to lead, take charge, and offer opinions and direction.
Achievement/Effort	Job requires establishing and maintaining personally challenging achievement goals and exerting effort toward mastering tasks.
Initiative	Job requires a willingness to take on responsibilities and challenges.
Social Orientation	Job requires preferring to work with others rather than alone, and being personally connected with others on the job.
Persistence	Job requires persistence in the face of obstacles.
Analytical Thinking	Job requires analyzing information and using logic to address work-related issues and problems.
Independence	Job requires developing one's own ways of doing things, guiding oneself with little or no supervision, and depending on oneself to get things done.
Innovation	Job requires creativity and alternative thinking to develop new ideas for and answers to work-related problems.

Job Zone Component	Job Zone Component Definitions
Title	Job Zone Three: Medium Preparation Needed
Overall Experience	Previous work-related skill, knowledge, or experience is required for these occupations. For example, an electrician must have completed three or four years of apprenticeship or several years of vocational training, and often must have passed a licensing exam, in order to perform the job.
Job Training	Employees in these occupations usually need one or two years of training involving both on-the-job experience and informal training with experienced workers.
Job Zone Examples	These occupations usually involve using communication and organizational skills to coordinate, supervise, manage, or train others to accomplish goals. Examples include dental assistants, electricians, fish and game wardens, legal secretaries, personnel recruiters, and recreation workers.
SVP Range	(6.0 to < 7.0)
Education	Most occupations in this zone require training in vocational schools, related on-the-job experience, or an associate's degree. Some may require a bachelor's degree.

29-2071.00 - Medical Records and Health Information Technicians

Compile, process, and maintain medical records of hospital and clinic patients in a manner consistent with medical, administrative, ethical, legal, and regulatory requirements of the health care system. Process, maintain, compile, and report patient information for health requirements and standards.

Tasks

1) Release information to persons and agencies according to regulations.

2) Review records for completeness, accuracy and compliance with regulations.

3) Plan, develop, maintain and operate a variety of health record indexes and storage and retrieval systems to collect, classify, store and analyze information.

4) Compile and maintain patients' medical records to document condition and treatment and to provide data for research or cost control and care improvement efforts.

5) Process patient admission and discharge documents.

6) Enter data, such as demographic characteristics, history and extent of disease, diagnostic procedures and treatment into computer.

7) Train medical records staff.

8) Manage the department and supervise clerical workers, directing and controlling activities of personnel in the medical records department.

9) Resolve/clarify codes and diagnoses with conflicting, missing, or unclear information by consulting with doctors or others to get additional information and by participating in the coding team's regular meetings.

10) Identify, compile, abstract and code patient data, using standard classification systems.

11) Process and prepare business and government forms.

12) Transcribe medical reports.

13) Develop in-service educational materials.

14) Assign the patient to one of several hundred diagnosis-related groups, or DRGs, using appropriate computer software.

15) Consult classification manuals to locate information about disease processes.

16) Prepare statistical reports, narrative reports and graphic presentations of information such as tumor registry data for use by hospital staff, researchers, and other users.

17) Post medical insurance billings.

18) Compile medical care and census data for statistical reports on diseases treated, surgery performed, and use of hospital beds.

19) Contact discharged patients, their families, and physicians to maintain registry with follow-up information, such as quality of life and length of survival of cancer patients.

Knowledge	Knowledge Definitions
Clerical	Knowledge of administrative and clerical procedures and systems such as word processing, managing files and records, stenography and transcription, designing forms, and other office procedures and terminology.
Customer and Personal Service	Knowledge of principles and processes for providing customer and personal services. This includes customer needs assessment, meeting quality standards for services, and evaluation of customer satisfaction.
English Language	Knowledge of the structure and content of the English language including the meaning and spelling of words, rules of composition, and grammar.
Computers and Electronics	Knowledge of circuit boards, processors, chips, electronic equipment, and computer hardware and software, including applications and programming.
Administration and Management	Knowledge of business and management principles involved in strategic planning, resource allocation, human resources modeling, leadership technique, production methods, and coordination of people and resources.
Foreign Language	Knowledge of the structure and content of a foreign (non-English) language including the meaning and spelling of words, rules of composition and grammar, and pronunciation.
Mathematics	Knowledge of arithmetic, algebra, geometry, calculus, statistics, and their applications.
Personnel and Human Resources	Knowledge of principles and procedures for personnel recruitment, selection, training, compensation and benefits, labor relations and negotiation, and personnel information systems.
Telecommunications	Knowledge of transmission, broadcasting, switching, control, and operation of telecommunications systems.
Education and Training	Knowledge of principles and methods for curriculum and training design, teaching and instruction for individuals and groups, and the measurement of training effects.
Medicine and Dentistry	Knowledge of the information and techniques needed to diagnose and treat human injuries, diseases, and deformities. This includes symptoms, treatment alternatives, drug properties and interactions, and preventive health-care measures.
Public Safety and Security	Knowledge of relevant equipment, policies, procedures, and strategies to promote effective local, state, or national security operations for the protection of people, data, property, and institutions.
Communications and Media	Knowledge of media production, communication, and dissemination techniques and methods. This includes alternative ways to inform and entertain via written, oral, and visual media.

Law and Government	Knowledge of laws, legal codes, court procedures, precedents, government regulations, executive orders, agency rules, and the democratic political process.
Sales and Marketing	Knowledge of principles and methods for showing, promoting, and selling products or services. This includes marketing strategy and tactics, product demonstration, sales techniques, and sales control systems.
Philosophy and Theology	Knowledge of different philosophical systems and religions. This includes their basic principles, values, ethics, ways of thinking, customs, practices, and their impact on human culture.
Psychology	Knowledge of human behavior and performance; individual differences in ability, personality, and interests; learning and motivation; psychological research methods; and the assessment and treatment of behavioral and affective disorders.
Economics and Accounting	Knowledge of economic and accounting principles and practices, the financial markets, banking and the analysis and reporting of financial data.
Production and Processing	Knowledge of raw materials, production processes, quality control, costs, and other techniques for maximizing the effective manufacture and distribution of goods.
Biology	Knowledge of plant and animal organisms, their tissues, cells, functions, interdependencies, and interactions with each other and the environment.
Therapy and Counseling	Knowledge of principles, methods, and procedures for diagnosis, treatment, and rehabilitation of physical and mental dysfunctions, and for career counseling and guidance.
Transportation	Knowledge of principles and methods for moving people or goods by air, rail, sea, or road, including the relative costs and benefits.
Sociology and Anthropology	Knowledge of group behavior and dynamics, societal trends and influences, human migrations, ethnicity, cultures and their history and origins.
Geography	Knowledge of principles and methods for describing the features of land, sea, and air masses, including their physical characteristics, locations, interrelationships, and distribution of plant, animal, and human life.
Engineering and Technology	Knowledge of the practical application of engineering science and technology. This includes applying principles, techniques, procedures, and equipment to the design and production of various goods and services.
Mechanical	Knowledge of machines and tools, including their designs, uses, repair, and maintenance.
Design	Knowledge of design techniques, tools, and principles involved in production of precision technical plans, blueprints, drawings, and models.
Physics	Knowledge and prediction of physical principles, laws, their interrelationships, and applications to understanding fluid, material, and atmospheric dynamics, and mechanical, electrical, atomic and sub-atomic structures and processes.
Chemistry	Knowledge of the chemical composition, structure, and properties of substances and of the chemical processes and transformations that they undergo. This includes uses of chemicals and their interactions, danger signs, production techniques, and disposal methods.
History and Archeology	Knowledge of historical events and their causes, indicators, and effects on civilizations and cultures.
Building and Construction	Knowledge of materials, methods, and the tools involved in the construction or repair of houses, buildings, or other structures such as highways and roads.
Fine Arts	Knowledge of the theory and techniques required to compose, produce, and perform works of music, dance, visual arts, drama, and sculpture.
Food Production	Knowledge of techniques and equipment for planting, growing, and harvesting food products (both plant and animal) for consumption, including storage/handling techniques.

Skills	Skills Definitions
Active Listening	Giving full attention to what other people are saying, taking time to understand the points being made, asking questions as appropriate, and not interrupting at inappropriate times.
Reading Comprehension	Understanding written sentences and paragraphs in work related documents.
Time Management	Managing one's own time and the time of others.
Speaking	Talking to others to convey information effectively.
Writing	Communicating effectively in writing as appropriate for the needs of the audience.
Instructing	Teaching others how to do something.
Active Learning	Understanding the implications of new information for both current and future problem-solving and decision-making.
Critical Thinking	Using logic and reasoning to identify the strengths and weaknesses of alternative solutions, conclusions or approaches to problems.
Social Perceptiveness	Being aware of others' reactions and understanding why they react as they do.

Judgment and Decision Making	Considering the relative costs and benefits of potential actions to choose the most appropriate one.
Learning Strategies	Selecting and using training/instructional methods and procedures appropriate for the situation when learning or teaching new things.
Service Orientation	Actively looking for ways to help people.
Monitoring	Monitoring/Assessing performance of yourself, other individuals, or organizations to make improvements or take corrective action.
Systems Evaluation	Identifying measures or indicators of system performance and the actions needed to improve or correct performance, relative to the goals of the system.
Complex Problem Solving	Identifying complex problems and reviewing related information to develop and evaluate options and implement solutions.
Quality Control Analysis	Conducting tests and inspections of products, services, or processes to evaluate quality or performance.
Coordination	Adjusting actions in relation to others' actions.
Negotiation	Bringing others together and trying to reconcile differences.
Operation and Control	Controlling operations of equipment or systems.
Equipment Selection	Determining the kind of tools and equipment needed to do a job.
Management of Personnel Resources	Motivating, developing, and directing people as they work, identifying the best people for the job.
Troubleshooting	Determining causes of operating errors and deciding what to do about it.
Systems Analysis	Determining how a system should work and how changes in conditions, operations, and the environment will affect outcomes.
Persuasion	Persuading others to change their minds or behavior.
Operations Analysis	Analyzing needs and product requirements to create a design.
Management of Material Resources	Obtaining and seeing to the appropriate use of equipment, facilities, and materials needed to do certain work.
Mathematics	Using mathematics to solve problems.
Management of Financial Resources	Determining how money will be spent to get the work done, and accounting for these expenditures.
Operation Monitoring	Watching gauges, dials, or other indicators to make sure a machine is working properly.
Science	Using scientific rules and methods to solve problems.
Equipment Maintenance	Performing routine maintenance on equipment and determining when and what kind of maintenance is needed.
Programming	Writing computer programs for various purposes.
Installation	Installing equipment, machines, wiring, or programs to meet specifications.
Technology Design	Generating or adapting equipment and technology to serve user needs.
Repairing	Repairing machines or systems using the needed tools.

Ability	Ability Definitions
Oral Comprehension	The ability to listen to and understand information and ideas presented through spoken words and sentences.
Written Comprehension	The ability to read and understand information and ideas presented in writing.
Information Ordering	The ability to arrange things or actions in a certain order or pattern according to a specific rule or set of rules (e.g., patterns of numbers, letters, words, pictures, mathematical operations).
Oral Expression	The ability to communicate information and ideas in speaking so others will understand.
Near Vision	The ability to see details at close range (within a few feet of the observer).
Speech Clarity	The ability to speak clearly so others can understand you.
Speech Recognition	The ability to identify and understand the speech of another person.
Category Flexibility	The ability to generate or use different sets of rules for combining or grouping things in different ways.
Written Expression	The ability to communicate information and ideas in writing so others will understand.
Deductive Reasoning	The ability to apply general rules to specific problems to produce answers that make sense.
Problem Sensitivity	The ability to tell when something is wrong or is likely to go wrong. It does not involve solving the problem, only recognizing there is a problem.
Selective Attention	The ability to concentrate on a task over a period of time without being distracted.
Inductive Reasoning	The ability to combine pieces of information to form general rules or conclusions (includes finding a relationship among seemingly unrelated events).
Finger Dexterity	The ability to make precisely coordinated movements of the fingers of one or both hands to grasp, manipulate, or assemble very small objects.
Perceptual Speed	The ability to quickly and accurately compare similarities and differences among sets of letters, numbers, objects, pictures, or patterns. The things to be compared may be presented at the same time or one after the other. This ability also includes comparing a presented object with a remembered object.

Flexibility of Closure	The ability to identify or detect a known pattern (a figure, object, word, or sound) that is hidden in other distracting material.
Manual Dexterity	The ability to quickly move your hand, your hand together with your arm, or your two hands to grasp, manipulate, or assemble objects.
Originality	The ability to come up with unusual or clever ideas about a given topic or situation, or to develop creative ways to solve a problem.
Memorization	The ability to remember information such as words, numbers, pictures, and procedures.
Static Strength	The ability to exert maximum muscle force to lift, push, pull, or carry objects.
Auditory Attention	The ability to focus on a single source of sound in the presence of other distracting sounds.
Time Sharing	The ability to shift back and forth between two or more activities or sources of information (such as speech, sounds, touch, or other sources).
Mathematical Reasoning	The ability to choose the right mathematical methods or formulas to solve a problem.
Arm-Hand Steadiness	The ability to keep your hand and arm steady while moving your arm or while holding your arm and hand in one position.
Speed of Closure	The ability to quickly make sense of, combine, and organize information into meaningful patterns.
Number Facility	The ability to add, subtract, multiply, or divide quickly and correctly.
Trunk Strength	The ability to use your abdominal and lower back muscles to support part of the body repeatedly or continuously over time without 'giving out' or fatiguing.
Fluency of Ideas	The ability to come up with a number of ideas about a topic (the number of ideas is important, not their quality, correctness, or creativity).
Multilimb Coordination	The ability to coordinate two or more limbs (for example, two arms, two legs, or one leg and one arm) while sitting, standing, or lying down. It does not involve performing the activities while the whole body is in motion.
Wrist-Finger Speed	The ability to make fast, simple, repeated movements of the fingers, hands, and wrists.
Far Vision	The ability to see details at a distance.
Visual Color Discrimination	The ability to match or detect differences between colors, including shades of color and brightness.
Visualization	The ability to imagine how something will look after it is moved around or when its parts are moved or rearranged.
Gross Body Coordination	The ability to coordinate the movement of your arms, legs, and torso together when the whole body is in motion.
Extent Flexibility	The ability to bend, stretch, twist, or reach with your body, arms, and/or legs.
Dynamic Strength	The ability to exert muscle force repeatedly or continuously over time. This involves muscular endurance and resistance to muscle fatigue.
Control Precision	The ability to quickly and repeatedly adjust the controls of a machine or a vehicle to exact positions.
Hearing Sensitivity	The ability to detect or tell the differences between sounds that vary in pitch and loudness.
Stamina	The ability to exert yourself physically over long periods of time without getting winded or out of breath.
Gross Body Equilibrium	The ability to keep or regain your body balance or stay upright when in an unstable position.
Sound Localization	The ability to tell the direction from which a sound originated.
Reaction Time	The ability to quickly respond (with the hand, finger, or foot) to a signal (sound, light, picture) when it appears.
Response Orientation	The ability to choose quickly between two or more movements in response to two or more different signals (lights, sounds, pictures). It includes the speed with which the correct response is started with the hand, foot, or other body part.
Spatial Orientation	The ability to know your location in relation to the environment or to know where other objects are in relation to you.
Explosive Strength	The ability to use short bursts of muscle force to propel oneself (as in jumping or sprinting), or to throw an object.
Night Vision	The ability to see under low light conditions.
Peripheral Vision	The ability to see objects or movement of objects to one's side when the eyes are looking ahead.
Depth Perception	The ability to judge which of several objects is closer or farther away from you, or to judge the distance between you and an object.
Speed of Limb Movement	The ability to quickly move the arms and legs.
Rate Control	The ability to time your movements or the movement of a piece of equipment in anticipation of changes in the speed and/or direction of a moving object or scene.
Dynamic Flexibility	The ability to quickly and repeatedly bend, stretch, twist, or reach out with your body, arms, and/or legs.
Glare Sensitivity	The ability to see objects in the presence of glare or bright lighting.

Work_Activity	Work_Activity Definitions
Getting Information	Observing, receiving, and otherwise obtaining information from all relevant sources.
Interacting With Computers	Using computers and computer systems (including hardware and software) to program, write software, set up functions, enter data, or process information.
Communicating with Supervisors, Peers, or Subordin	Providing information to supervisors, co-workers, and subordinates by telephone, in written form, e-mail, or in person.
Performing Administrative Activities	Performing day-to-day administrative tasks such as maintaining information files and processing paperwork.
Updating and Using Relevant Knowledge	Keeping up-to-date technically and applying new knowledge to your job.
Evaluating Information to Determine Compliance wit	Using relevant information and individual judgment to determine whether events or processes comply with laws, regulations, or standards.
Documenting/Recording Information	Entering, transcribing, recording, storing, or maintaining information in written or electronic/magnetic form.
Establishing and Maintaining Interpersonal Relatio	Developing constructive and cooperative working relationships with others, and maintaining them over time.
Handling and Moving Objects	Using hands and arms in handling, installing, positioning, and moving materials, and manipulating things.
Organizing, Planning, and Prioritizing Work	Developing specific goals and plans to prioritize, organize, and accomplish your work.
Processing Information	Compiling, coding, categorizing, calculating, tabulating, auditing, or verifying information or data.
Interpreting the Meaning of Information for Others	Translating or explaining what information means and how it can be used.
Making Decisions and Solving Problems	Analyzing information and evaluating results to choose the best solution and solve problems.
Performing General Physical Activities	Performing physical activities that require considerable use of your arms and legs and moving your whole body, such as climbing, lifting, balancing, walking, stooping, and handling of materials.
Identifying Objects, Actions, and Events	Identifying information by categorizing, estimating, recognizing differences or similarities, and detecting changes in circumstances or events.
Communicating with Persons Outside Organization	Communicating with people outside the organization, representing the organization to customers, the public, government, and other external sources. This information can be exchanged in person, in writing, or by telephone or e-mail.
Training and Teaching Others	Identifying the educational needs of others, developing formal educational or training programs or classes, and teaching or instructing others.
Coordinating the Work and Activities of Others	Getting members of a group to work together to accomplish tasks.
Analyzing Data or Information	Identifying the underlying principles, reasons, or facts of information by breaking down information or data into separate parts.
Monitor Processes, Materials, or Surroundings	Monitoring and reviewing information from materials, events, or the environment, to detect or assess problems.
Provide Consultation and Advice to Others	Providing guidance and expert advice to management or other groups on technical, systems-, or process-related topics.
Assisting and Caring for Others	Providing personal assistance, medical attention, emotional support, or other personal care to others such as coworkers, customers, or patients.
Coaching and Developing Others	Identifying the developmental needs of others and coaching, mentoring, or otherwise helping others to improve their knowledge or skills.
Performing for or Working Directly with the Public	Performing for people or dealing directly with the public. This includes serving customers in restaurants and stores, and receiving clients or guests.
Thinking Creatively	Developing, designing, or creating new applications, ideas, relationships, systems, or products, including artistic contributions.
Guiding, Directing, and Motivating Subordinates	Providing guidance and direction to subordinates, including setting performance standards and monitoring performance.
Developing Objectives and Strategies	Establishing long-range objectives and specifying the strategies and actions to achieve them.
Scheduling Work and Activities	Scheduling events, programs, and activities, as well as the work of others.
Developing and Building Teams	Encouraging and building mutual trust, respect, and cooperation among team members.
Inspecting Equipment, Structures, or Material	Inspecting equipment, structures, or materials to identify the cause of errors or other problems or defects.
Estimating the Quantifiable Characteristics of Pro	Estimating sizes, distances, and quantities; or determining time, costs, resources, or materials needed to perform a work activity.
Resolving Conflicts and Negotiating with Others	Handling complaints, settling disputes, and resolving grievances and conflicts, or otherwise negotiating with others.
Controlling Machines and Processes	Using either control mechanisms or direct physical activity to operate machines or processes (not including computers or vehicles).

Judging the Qualities of Things, Services, or Peop	Assessing the value, importance, or quality of things or people.
Repairing and Maintaining Electronic Equipment	Servicing, repairing, calibrating, regulating, fine-tuning, or testing machines, devices, and equipment that operate primarily on the basis of electrical or electronic (not mechanical) principles.
Selling or Influencing Others	Convincing others to buy merchandise/goods or to otherwise change their minds or actions.
Monitoring and Controlling Resources	Monitoring and controlling resources and overseeing the spending of money.
Staffing Organizational Units	Recruiting, interviewing, selecting, hiring, and promoting employees in an organization.
Repairing and Maintaining Mechanical Equipment	Servicing, repairing, adjusting, and testing machines, devices, moving parts, and equipment that operate primarily on the basis of mechanical (not electronic) principles.
Drafting, Laying Out, and Specifying Technical Dev	Providing documentation, detailed instructions, drawings, or specifications to tell others about how devices, parts, equipment, or structures are to be fabricated, constructed, assembled, modified, maintained, or used.
Operating Vehicles, Mechanized Devices, or Equipme	Running, maneuvering, navigating, or driving vehicles or mechanized equipment, such as forklifts, passenger vehicles, aircraft, or water craft.

Work_Content	Work_Content Definitions
Telephone	How often do you have telephone conversations in this job?
Face-to-Face Discussions	How often do you have to have face-to-face discussions with individuals or teams in this job?
Contact With Others	How much does this job require the worker to be in contact with others (face-to-face, by telephone, or otherwise) in order to perform it?
Importance of Being Exact or Accurate	How important is being very exact or highly accurate in performing this job?
Indoors, Environmentally Controlled	How often does this job require working indoors in environmentally controlled conditions?
Letters and Memos	How often does the job require written letters and memos?
Importance of Repeating Same Tasks	How important is repeating the same physical activities (e.g., key entry) or mental activities (e.g., checking entries in a ledger) over and over, without stopping, to performing this job?
Freedom to Make Decisions	How much decision making freedom, without supervision, does the job offer?
Structured versus Unstructured Work	To what extent is this job structured for the worker, rather than allowing the worker to determine tasks, priorities, and goals?
Physical Proximity	To what extent does this job require the worker to perform job tasks in close physical proximity to other people?
Work With Work Group or Team	How important is it to work with others in a group or team in this job?
Spend Time Sitting	How much does this job require sitting?
Frequency of Decision Making	How frequently is the worker required to make decisions that affect other people, the financial resources, and/or the image and reputation of the organization?
Time Pressure	How often does this job require the worker to meet strict deadlines?
Impact of Decisions on Co-workers or Company Resul	How do the decisions an employee makes impact the results of co-workers, clients or the company?
Deal With External Customers	How important is it to work with external customers or the public in this job?
Coordinate or Lead Others	How important is it to coordinate or lead others in accomplishing work activities in this job?
Spend Time Making Repetitive Motions	How much does this job require making repetitive motions?
Spend Time Using Your Hands to Handle, Control, or	How much does this job require using your hands to handle, control, or feel objects, tools or controls?
Sounds, Noise Levels Are Distracting or Uncomforta	How often does this job require working exposed to sounds and noise levels that are distracting or uncomfortable?
Frequency of Conflict Situations	How often are there conflict situations the employee has to face in this job?
Degree of Automation	How automated is the job?
Responsibility for Outcomes and Results	How responsible is the worker for work outcomes and results of other workers?
Deal With Unpleasant or Angry People	How frequently does the worker have to deal with unpleasant, angry, or discourteous individuals as part of the job requirements?
Electronic Mail	How often do you use electronic mail in this job?
Level of Competition	To what extent does this job require the worker to compete or to be aware of competitive pressures?
Exposed to Contaminants	How often does this job require working exposed to contaminants (such as pollutants, gases, dust or odors)?
Pace Determined by Speed of Equipment	How important is it to this job that the pace is determined by the speed of equipment or machinery? (This does not refer to keeping busy at all times on this job.)
Cramped Work Space, Awkward Positions	How often does this job require working in cramped work spaces that requires getting into awkward positions?
Spend Time Standing	How much does this job require standing?

Spend Time Bending or Twisting the Body	How much does this job require bending or twisting your body?
Exposed to Disease or Infections	How often does this job require exposure to disease/infections?
Spend Time Walking and Running	How much does this job require walking and running?
Consequence of Error	How serious would the result usually be if the worker made a mistake that was not readily correctable?
Responsible for Others' Health and Safety	How much responsibility is there for the health and safety of others in this job?
Spend Time Kneeling, Crouching, Stooping, or Crawl	How much does this job require kneeling, crouching, stooping or crawling?
Exposed to Minor Burns. Cuts, Bites, or Stings	How often does this job require exposure to minor burns, cuts, bites, or stings?
Extremely Bright or Inadequate Lighting	How often does this job require working in extremely bright or inadequate lighting conditions?
Wear Common Protective or Safety Equipment such as	How much does this job require wearing common protective or safety equipment such as safety shoes, glasses, gloves, hard hats or live jackets?
Spend Time Keeping or Regaining Balance	How much does this job require keeping or regaining your balance?
Public Speaking	How often do you have to perform public speaking in this job?
Deal With Physically Aggressive People	How frequently does this job require the worker to deal with physical aggression of violent individuals?
Very Hot or Cold Temperatures	How often does this job require working in very hot (above 90 F degrees) or very cold (below 32 F degrees) temperatures?
Exposed to Hazardous Conditions	How often does this job require exposure to hazardous conditions?
Spend Time Climbing Ladders, Scaffolds, or Poles	How much does this job require climbing ladders, scaffolds, or poles?
Exposed to Radiation	How often does this job require exposure to radiation?
Wear Specialized Protective or Safety Equipment su	How much does this job require wearing specialized protective or safety equipment such as breathing apparatus, safety harness, full protection suits, or radiation protection?
Indoors, Not Environmentally Controlled	How often does this job require working indoors in non-controlled environmental conditions (e.g., warehouse without heat)?
Outdoors, Under Cover	How often does this job require working outdoors, under cover (e.g., structure with roof but no walls)?
In an Enclosed Vehicle or Equipment	How often does this job require working in a closed vehicle or equipment (e.g., car)?
In an Open Vehicle or Equipment	How often does this job require working in an open vehicle or equipment (e.g., tractor)?
Outdoors, Exposed to Weather	How often does this job require working outdoors, exposed to all weather conditions?
Exposed to High Places	How often does this job require exposure to high places?
Exposed to Whole Body Vibration	How often does this job require exposure to whole body vibration (e.g., operate a jackhammer)?
Exposed to Hazardous Equipment	How often does this job require exposure to hazardous equipment?

Work_Styles	Work_Styles Definitions
Cooperation	Job requires being pleasant with others on the job and displaying a good-natured, cooperative attitude.
Stress Tolerance	Job requires accepting criticism and dealing calmly and effectively with high stress situations.
Integrity	Job requires being honest and ethical.
Dependability	Job requires being reliable, responsible, and dependable, and fulfilling obligations.
Attention to Detail	Job requires being careful about detail and thorough in completing work tasks.
Concern for Others	Job requires being sensitive to others' needs and feelings and being understanding and helpful on the job.
Independence	Job requires developing one's own ways of doing things, guiding oneself with little or no supervision, and depending on oneself to get things done.
Adaptability/Flexibility	Job requires being open to change (positive or negative) and to considerable variety in the workplace.
Initiative	Job requires a willingness to take on responsibilities and challenges.
Self Control	Job requires maintaining composure, keeping emotions in check, controlling anger, and avoiding aggressive behavior, even in very difficult situations.
Persistence	Job requires persistence in the face of obstacles.
Achievement/Effort	Job requires establishing and maintaining personally challenging achievement goals and exerting effort toward mastering tasks.
Analytical Thinking	Job requires analyzing information and using logic to address work-related issues and problems.
Innovation	Job requires creativity and alternative thinking to develop new ideas for and answers to work-related problems.
Social Orientation	Job requires preferring to work with others rather than alone, and being personally connected with others on the job.

Leadership	Job requires a willingness to lead, take charge, and offer opinions and direction.

Job Zone Component	Job Zone Component Definitions
Title	Job Zone Three: Medium Preparation Needed
Overall Experience	Previous work-related skill, knowledge, or experience is required for these occupations. For example, an electrician must have completed three or four years of apprenticeship or several years of vocational training, and often must have passed a licensing exam, in order to perform the job.
Job Training	Employees in these occupations usually need one or two years of training involving both on-the-job experience and informal training with experienced workers.
Job Zone Examples	These occupations usually involve using communication and organizational skills to coordinate, supervise, manage, or train others to accomplish goals. Examples include dental assistants, electricians, fish and game wardens, legal secretaries, personnel recruiters, and recreation workers.
SVP Range	(6.0 to < 7.0)
Education	Most occupations in this zone require training in vocational schools, related on-the-job experience, or an associate's degree. Some may require a bachelor's degree.

29-2081.00 - Opticians, Dispensing

Design, measure, fit, and adapt lenses and frames for client according to written optical prescription or specification. Assist client with selecting frames. Measure customer for size of eyeglasses and coordinate frames with facial and eye measurements and optical prescription. Prepare work order for optical laboratory containing instructions for grinding and mounting lenses in frames. Verify exactness of finished lens spectacles. Adjust frame and lens position to fit client. May shape or reshape frames.

Tasks

1) Supervise the training of student opticians.

2) Recommend specific lenses, lens coatings, and frames to suit client needs.

3) Repair damaged frames.

4) Evaluate prescriptions in conjunction with clients' vocational and avocational visual requirements.

5) Assist clients in selecting frames according to style and color, and ensure that frames are coordinated with facial and eye measurements and optical prescriptions.

6) Determine clients' current lens prescriptions, when necessary, using lensometers or lens analyzers and clients' eyeglasses.

7) Show customers how to insert, remove, and care for their contact lenses.

8) Prepare work orders and instructions for grinding lenses and fabricating eyeglasses.

9) Fabricate lenses to meet prescription specifications.

10) Measure clients' bridge and eye size, temple length, vertex distance, pupillary distance, and optical centers of eyes, using measuring devices.

11) Assemble eyeglasses by cutting and edging lenses, then fitting the lenses into frames.

12) Grind lens edges, or apply coatings to lenses.

13) Verify that finished lenses are ground to specifications.

14) Arrange and maintain displays of optical merchandise.

15) Obtain a customer's previous record, or verify a prescription with the examining optometrist or ophthalmologist.

16) Fit contact lenses by measuring the shape and size of the eye, using various measuring instruments.

17) Maintain records of customer prescriptions, work orders, and payments.

18) Instruct clients in how to wear and care for eyeglasses.

19) Perform administrative duties such as tracking inventory and sales, submitting patient insurance information, and performing simple bookkeeping.

20) Sell goods such as contact lenses, spectacles, sunglasses, and other goods related to eyes in general.

29-2091.00 - Orthotists and Prosthetists

Assist patients with disabling conditions of limbs and spine or with partial or total absence of limb by fitting and preparing orthopedic braces or prostheses.

Tasks

1) Repair, rebuild, and modify prosthetic and orthopedic appliances.

2) Construct and fabricate appliances or supervise others who are constructing the appliances.

3) Design orthopedic and prosthetic devices. based on physicians' prescriptions, and examination and measurement of patients.

4) Examine, interview, and measure patients in order to determine their appliance needs, and to identify factors that could affect appliance fit.

5) Update skills and knowledge by attending conferences and seminars.

6) Make and modify plaster casts of areas that will be fitted with prostheses or orthoses, for use in the device construction process.

7) Publish research findings, and present them at conferences and seminars.

8) Research new ways to construct and use orthopedic and prosthetic devices.

9) Show and explain orthopedic and prosthetic appliances to healthcare workers.

10) Train and supervise orthopedic and prosthetic assistants and technicians, and other support staff.

11) Confer with physicians in order to formulate specifications and prescriptions for orthopedic and/or prosthetic devices.

12) Instruct patients in the use and care of orthoses and prostheses.

13) Fit, test, and evaluate devices on patients. and make adjustments for proper fit, function, and comfort.

14) Maintain patients' records.

29-9091.00 - Athletic Trainers

Evaluate, advise, and treat athletes to assist recovery from injury, avoid injury, or maintain peak physical fitness.

Tasks

1) Perform team-support duties such as running errands, maintaining equipment, and stocking supplies.

2) Lead stretching exercises for team members prior to games and practices.

3) Instruct coaches, athletes, parents, medical personnel, and community members in the care and prevention of athletic injuries.

4) Travel with athletic teams in order to be available at sporting events.

5) Evaluate athletes' readiness to play, and provide participation clearances when necessary and warranted.

6) Assess and report the progress of recovering athletes to coaches and physicians.

7) Inspect playing fields in order to locate any items that could injure players.

8) Confer with coaches in order to select protective equipment.

9) Recommend special diets in order to improve athletes' health, increase their stamina, and/or alter their weight.

10) Accompany injured athletes to hospitals.

11) Collaborate with physicians in order to develop and implement comprehensive rehabilitation programs for athletic injuries.

12) Conduct an initial assessment of an athlete's injury or illness in order to provide emergency or continued care, and to determine whether they should be referred to physicians for definitive diagnosis and treatment.

13) Develop training programs and routines designed to improve athletic performance.

14) Massage body parts in order to relieve soreness, strains, and bruises.

15) Conduct research and provide instruction on subject matter related to athletic training or sports medicine.

16) Advise athletes on the proper use of equipment.

17) Apply protective or injury preventive devices such as tape, bandages, or braces to body parts such as ankles, fingers, or wrists.

18) Care for athletic injuries using physical therapy equipment, techniques, and medication.

31-1011.00 - Home Health Aides

Provide routine, personal healthcare, such as bathing, dressing, or grooming, to elderly, convalescent, or disabled persons in the home of patients or in a residential care facility.

Tasks

1) Check patients' pulse. temperature and respiration.

2) Direct patients in simple prescribed exercises and in the use of braces or artificial limbs.

3) Maintain records of patient care, condition, progress, and problems in order to report and discuss observations with a supervisor or case manager.

4) Massage patients and apply preparations and treatments, such as liniment. alcohol rubs. and heat-lamp stimulation.

5) Administer prescribed oral medications under written direction of physician or as directed by home care nurse and aide.

6) Change bed linens, wash and iron patients' laundry, and clean patients' quarters.

7) Entertain, converse with, or read aloud to patients to keep them mentally healthy and alert.

8) Perform a variety of duties as requested by client, such as obtaining household supplies and running errands.

9) Plan, purchase, prepare, and serve meals to patients and other family members. according to prescribed diets.

10) Provide patients and families with emotional support and instruction in areas such as infant care, preparing healthy meals, independent living, and adaptation to disability or illness.

11) Accompany clients to doctors' offices and on other trips outside the home, providing transportation. assistance and companionship.

12) Provide patients with help moving in and out of beds, baths, wheelchairs or automobiles. and with dressing and grooming.

13) Care for children who are disabled or who have sick or disabled parents.

31-1012.00 - Nursing Aides, Orderlies, and Attendants

Provide basic patient care under direction of nursing staff. Perform duties, such as feed, bathe, dress, groom, or move patients, or change linens.

Tasks

1) Set up equipment such as oxygen tents, portable x-ray machines, and overhead irrigation bottles.

2) Collect specimens such as urine, feces, or sputum.

3) Deliver messages, documents and specimens.

4) Explain medical instructions to patients and family members.

5) Maintain inventory by storing, preparing, sterilizing, and issuing supplies such as dressing packs and treatment trays.

6) Observe patients' conditions, measuring and recording food and liquid intake and output and vital signs, and report changes to professional staff.

7) Perform clerical duties such as processing documents and scheduling appointments.

8) Restrain patients if necessary.

9) Clean rooms and change linens.

10) Administer medications and treatments, such as catheterizations, suppositories, irrigations, enemas, massages, and douches, as directed by a physician or nurse.

11) Turn and re-position bedridden patients, alone or with assistance, to prevent bedsores.

12) Bathe, groom, shave, dress, and/or drape patients to prepare them for surgery, treatment, or examination.

13) Answer patients' call signals.

14) Work as part of a medical team that examines and treats clinic outpatients.

15) Feed patients who are unable to feed themselves.

16) Prepare, serve, and collect food trays.

17) Provide patient care by supplying and emptying bed pans, applying dressings and supervising exercise routines.

18) Provide patients with help walking, exercising, and moving in and out of bed.

19) Transport patients to treatment units, using a wheelchair or stretcher.

31-1013.00 - Psychiatric Aides

Assist mentally impaired or emotionally disturbed patients, working under direction of nursing and medical staff.

Tasks

1) Aid patients in becoming accustomed to hospital routine.

2) Maintain patients' restrictions to assigned areas.

3) Participate in recreational activities with patients, including card games, sports, or television viewing.

4) Organize, supervise, and encourage patient participation in social, educational, and recreational activities.

5) Record and maintain records of patient condition and activity, including vital signs, eating habits, and behavior.

6) Accompany patients to and from wards for medical and dental treatments, shopping trips, and religious and recreational events.

7) Clean and disinfect rooms and furnishings to maintain a safe and orderly environment.

8) Provide patients with assistance in bathing, dressing, and grooming, demonstrating these skills as necessary.

9) Restrain or aid patients as necessary to prevent injury.

10) Serve meals, and feed patients needing assistance or persuasion.

11) Interview patients upon admission and record information.

12) Provide mentally impaired or emotionally disturbed patients with routine physical, emotional, psychological or rehabilitation care under the direction of nursing and medical staff.

13) Work as part of a team that may include psychiatrists, psychologists, psychiatric nurses and social workers.

14) Monitor patients in order to detect unusual behavior, and report observations to professional staff.

31-2011.00 - Occupational Therapist Assistants

Assist occupational therapists in providing occupational therapy treatments and procedures. May, in accordance with State laws, assist in development of treatment plans, carry out routine functions, direct activity programs, and document the progress of treatments. Generally requires formal training.

Tasks

1) Work under the direction of occupational therapists to plan, implement and administer educational, vocational, and recreational programs that restore and enhance performance in individuals with functional impairments.

2) Maintain and promote a positive attitude toward clients and their treatment programs.

3) Order any needed educational or treatment supplies.

4) Perform clerical duties such as scheduling appointments, collecting data, and documenting health insurance billings.

5) Aid patients in dressing and grooming themselves.

6) Assist educational specialists or clinical psychologists in administering situational or diagnostic tests to measure client's abilities or progress.

7) Assemble, clean, and maintain equipment and materials for patient use.

8) Transport patients to and from the occupational therapy work area.

9) Monitor patients' performance in therapy activities, providing encouragement.

10) Instruct, or assist in instructing, patients and families in home programs, basic living skills, and the care and use of adaptive equipment.

11) Implement, or assist occupational therapists with implementing, treatment plans designed to help clients function independently.

12) Evaluate the daily living skills and capacities of physically, developmentally or emotionally disabled clients.

13) Demonstrate therapy techniques, such as manual and creative arts, and games.

14) Alter treatment programs to obtain better results if treatment is not having the intended effect.

15) Observe and record patients' progress, attitudes, and behavior, and maintain this information in client records.

16) Teach patients how to deal constructively with their emotions.

17) Report to supervisors, verbally or in writing, on patients' progress, attitudes and behavior.

18) Design, fabricate, and repair assistive devices and make adaptive changes to equipment and environments.

31-2012.00 - Occupational Therapist Aides

Under close supervision of an occupational therapist or occupational therapy assistant, perform only delegated, selected, or routine tasks in specific situations. These duties include preparing patient and treatment room.

Tasks

1) Observe patients' attendance, progress, attitudes, and accomplishments, and record and maintain information in client records.

2) Instruct patients and families in work, social, and living skills, the care and use of adaptive equipment and other skills to facilitate home and work adjustment to disability.

3) Manage intra-departmental infection control and equipment security.

4) Evaluate the living skills and capacities of physically, developmentally, or emotionally disabled clients.

5) Assist educational specialists or clinical psychologists in administering situational or diagnostic tests to measure client's abilities or progress.

6) Assist occupational therapists in planning, implementing, and administering therapy programs to restore, reinforce, and enhance performance, using selected activities and special equipment..

7) Encourage patients and attend to their physical needs to facilitate the attainment of therapeutic goals.

8) Transport patients to and from the occupational therapy work area.

9) Adjust and repair assistive devices and make adaptive changes to other equipment and to environments.

10) Supervise patients in choosing and completing work details or arts and crafts projects.

11) Report to supervisors or therapists, verbally or in writing, on patients' progress, attitudes, attendance and accomplishments.

12) Prepare and maintain work area, materials, and equipment, and maintain inventory of treatment and educational supplies.

13) Perform clerical, administrative and secretarial duties such as answering phones, restocking and ordering supplies, filling out paperwork and scheduling appointments.

14) Demonstrate therapy techniques, such as manual and creative arts, and games.

31-2021.00 - Physical Therapist Assistants

Assist physical therapists in providing physical therapy treatments and procedures. May, in accordance with State laws, assist in the development of treatment plans, carry out routine functions, document the progress of treatment, and modify specific treatments in accordance with patient status and within the scope of treatment plans established by a physical therapist. Generally requires formal training.

Tasks

1) Transport patients to and from treatment areas, lifting and transferring them according to positioning requirements.

2) Administer active and passive manual therapeutic exercises, therapeutic massage, and heat, light, sound, water, and electrical modality treatments, such as ultrasound.

3) Administer traction to relieve neck and back pain, using intermittent and static traction equipment.

4) Assist patients to dress, undress, and put on and remove supportive devices, such as braces, splints, and slings.

5) Confer with physical therapy staff and others to discuss and evaluate patient information for planning, modifying, and coordinating treatment.

6) Fit patients for orthopedic braces, prostheses, and supportive devices, such as crutches.

7) Instruct, motivate, safeguard and assist patients as they practice exercises and functional activities.

8) Monitor operation of equipment and record use of equipment and administration of treatment.

9) Secure patients into or onto therapy equipment.

10) Clean work area and check and store equipment after treatment.

11) Perform clerical duties, such as taking inventory, ordering supplies, answering telephone, taking messages, and filling out forms.

12) Perform postural drainage, percussions and vibrations, and teach deep breathing exercises to treat respiratory conditions.

13) Prepare treatment areas and electrotherapy equipment for use by physiotherapists.

14) Observe patients during treatments to compile and evaluate data on patients' responses and progress, and report to physical therapist.

15) Measure patients' range-of-joint motion, body parts, and vital signs to determine effects of treatments or for patient evaluations.

31-2022.00 - Physical Therapist Aides

Under close supervision of a physical therapist or physical therapy assistant, perform only delegated, selected, or routine tasks in specific situations. These duties include preparing the patient and the treatment area.

Tasks

1) Participate in patient care tasks, such as assisting with passing food trays and feeding residents, and bathing residents on bed rest.

2) Arrange treatment supplies to keep them in order.

3) Assist patients to dress, undress, and put on and remove supportive devices, such as braces, splints, and slings.

4) Clean and organize work area and disinfect equipment after treatment.

5) Instruct, motivate, safeguard and assist patients practicing exercises and functional activities, under direction of medical staff.

6) Maintain equipment and furniture to keep it in good working condition, including performing the assembly and disassembly of equipment and accessories.

7) Administer active and passive manual therapeutic exercises, therapeutic massage, and heat, light, sound, water, and electrical modality treatments, such as ultrasound.

8) Secure patients into or onto therapy equipment.

9) Record treatment given and equipment used.

10) Train patients to use orthopedic braces, prostheses and supportive devices.

11) Fit patients for orthopedic braces, prostheses, and supportive devices, adjusting fit as needed.

12) Confer with physical therapy staff and others to discuss and evaluate patient information for planning, modifying, and coordinating treatment.

13) Change linens, such as bed sheets and pillow cases.

14) Administer traction to relieve neck and back pain, using intermittent and static traction equipment.

15) Transport patients to and from treatment areas, using wheelchairs or providing standing support.

16) Perform clerical duties, such as taking inventory, ordering supplies, answering telephone, taking messages, and filling out forms.

17) Observe patients during treatment to compile and evaluate data on patients' responses and progress, and report to physical therapist.

31-9011.00 - Massage Therapists

Massage customers for hygienic or remedial purposes.

Tasks

1) Massage and knead the muscles and soft tissues of the human body in order to provide courses of treatment for medical conditions and injuries or wellness maintenance.

2) Refer clients to other types of therapists when necessary.

3) Maintain treatment records.

4) Treat clients in own offices, or travel to clients' offices and homes.

5) Develop and propose client treatment plans that specify which types of massage are to be used.

6) Confer with clients about their medical histories and any problems with stress and/or pain in order to determine whether massage would be helpful.

7) Assess clients' soft tissue condition, joint quality and function, muscle strength, and range of motion.

8) Apply finger and hand pressure to specific points of the body.

9) Consult with other health care professionals such as physiotherapists, chiropractors, physicians and psychologists in order to develop treatment plans for clients.

10) Prepare and blend oils, and apply the blends to clients' skin.

11) Use complementary aids, such as infrared lamps, wet compresses, ice, and whirlpool baths in order to promote clients' recovery, relaxation and well-being.

31-9091.00 - Dental Assistants

Assist dentist, set up patient and equipment, and keep records.

Tasks

1) Expose dental diagnostic x-rays.

2) Assist dentist in management of medical and dental emergencies.

3) Instruct patients in oral hygiene and plaque control programs.

4) Make preliminary impressions for study casts and occlusal registrations for mounting study casts.

5) Record treatment information in patient records.

6) Pour, trim, and polish study casts.

7) Clean and polish removable appliances.

8) Take and record medical and dental histories and vital signs of patients.

9) Schedule appointments, prepare bills and receive payment for dental services, complete insurance forms, and maintain records, manually or using computer.

10) Apply protective coating of fluoride to teeth.

11) Fabricate temporary restorations and custom impressions from preliminary impressions.

12) Clean teeth, using dental instruments.

13) Prepare patient, sterilize and disinfect instruments, set up instrument trays, prepare materials, and assist dentist during dental procedures.

Knowledge	Knowledge Definitions
Medicine and Dentistry	Knowledge of the information and techniques needed to diagnose and treat human injuries, diseases, and deformities. This includes symptoms, treatment alternatives, drug properties and interactions, and preventive health-care measures.
Customer and Personal Service	Knowledge of principles and processes for providing customer and personal services. This includes customer needs assessment, meeting quality standards for services, and evaluation of customer satisfaction.
English Language	Knowledge of the structure and content of the English language including the meaning and spelling of words, rules of composition, and grammar.
Clerical	Knowledge of administrative and clerical procedures and systems such as word processing, managing files and records, stenography and transcription, designing forms, and other office procedures and terminology.
Chemistry	Knowledge of the chemical composition, structure, and properties of substances and of the chemical processes and transformations that they undergo. This includes uses of chemicals and their interactions, danger signs, production techniques, and disposal methods.
Computers and Electronics	Knowledge of circuit boards, processors, chips, electronic equipment, and computer hardware and software, including applications and programming.
Psychology	Knowledge of human behavior and performance; individual differences in ability, personality, and interests; learning and motivation; psychological research methods; and the assessment and treatment of behavioral and affective disorders.
Public Safety and Security	Knowledge of relevant equipment, policies, procedures, and strategies to promote effective local, state, or national security operations for the protection of people, data, property, and institutions.
Mechanical	Knowledge of machines and tools, including their designs, uses, repair, and maintenance.
Communications and Media	Knowledge of media production, communication, and dissemination techniques and methods. This includes alternative ways to inform and entertain via written, oral, and visual media.
Administration and Management	Knowledge of business and management principles involved in strategic planning, resource allocation, human resources modeling, leadership technique, production methods, and coordination of people and resources.
Production and Processing	Knowledge of raw materials, production processes, quality control, costs, and other techniques for maximizing the effective manufacture and distribution of goods.
Economics and Accounting	Knowledge of economic and accounting principles and practices, the financial markets, banking and the analysis and reporting of financial data.
Education and Training	Knowledge of principles and methods for curriculum and training design, teaching and instruction for individuals and groups, and the measurement of training effects.
Biology	Knowledge of plant and animal organisms, their tissues, cells, functions, interdependencies, and interactions with each other and the environment.
Law and Government	Knowledge of laws, legal codes, court procedures, precedents, government regulations, executive orders, agency rules, and the democratic political process.
Sales and Marketing	Knowledge of principles and methods for showing, promoting, and selling products or services. This includes marketing strategy and tactics, product demonstration, sales techniques, and sales control systems.

Engineering and Technology	Knowledge of the practical application of engineering science and technology. This includes applying principles, techniques, procedures, and equipment to the design and production of various goods and services.
Mathematics	Knowledge of arithmetic, algebra, geometry, calculus, statistics, and their applications.
Design	Knowledge of design techniques, tools, and principles involved in production of precision technical plans, blueprints, drawings, and models.
Foreign Language	Knowledge of the structure and content of a foreign (non-English) language including the meaning and spelling of words, rules of composition and grammar, and pronunciation.
Sociology and Anthropology	Knowledge of group behavior and dynamics, societal trends and influences, human migrations, ethnicity, cultures and their history and origins.
Philosophy and Theology	Knowledge of different philosophical systems and religions. This includes their basic principles, values, ethics, ways of thinking, customs, practices, and their impact on human culture.
Telecommunications	Knowledge of transmission, broadcasting, switching, control, and operation of telecommunications systems.
Personnel and Human Resources	Knowledge of principles and procedures for personnel recruitment, selection, training, compensation and benefits, labor relations and negotiation, and personnel information systems.
Therapy and Counseling	Knowledge of principles, methods, and procedures for diagnosis, treatment, and rehabilitation of physical and mental dysfunctions, and for career counseling and guidance.
Transportation	Knowledge of principles and methods for moving people or goods by air, rail, sea, or road, including the relative costs and benefits.
Physics	Knowledge and prediction of physical principles, laws, their interrelationships, and applications to understanding fluid, material, and atmospheric dynamics, and mechanical, electrical, atomic and sub- atomic structures and processes.
History and Archeology	Knowledge of historical events and their causes, indicators, and effects on civilizations and cultures.
Geography	Knowledge of principles and methods for describing the features of land, sea, and air masses, including their physical characteristics, locations, interrelationships, and distribution of plant, animal, and human life.
Building and Construction	Knowledge of materials, methods, and the tools involved in the construction or repair of houses, buildings, or other structures such as highways and roads.
Fine Arts	Knowledge of the theory and techniques required to compose, produce, and perform works of music, dance, visual arts, drama, and sculpture.
Food Production	Knowledge of techniques and equipment for planting, growing, and harvesting food products (both plant and animal) for consumption, including storage/handling techniques.

Skills	Skills Definitions
Active Listening	Giving full attention to what other people are saying, taking time to understand the points being made, asking questions as appropriate, and not interrupting at inappropriate times.
Reading Comprehension	Understanding written sentences and paragraphs in work related documents.
Speaking	Talking to others to convey information effectively.
Coordination	Adjusting actions in relation to others' actions.
Social Perceptiveness	Being aware of others' reactions and understanding why they react as they do.
Equipment Maintenance	Performing routine maintenance on equipment and determining when and what kind of maintenance is needed.
Active Learning	Understanding the implications of new information for both current and future problem-solving and decision-making.
Time Management	Managing one's own time and the time of others.
Instructing	Teaching others how to do something.
Equipment Selection	Determining the kind of tools and equipment needed to do a job.
Writing	Communicating effectively in writing as appropriate for the needs of the audience.
Learning Strategies	Selecting and using training/instructional methods and procedures appropriate for the situation when learning or teaching new things.
Management of Material Resources	Obtaining and seeing to the appropriate use of equipment, facilities, and materials needed to do certain work.
Troubleshooting	Determining causes of operating errors and deciding what to do about it.
Monitoring	Monitoring/Assessing performance of yourself, other individuals, or organizations to make improvements or take corrective action.
Service Orientation	Actively looking for ways to help people.
Judgment and Decision Making	Considering the relative costs and benefits of potential actions to choose the most appropriate one.

Critical Thinking	Using logic and reasoning to identify the strengths and weaknesses of alternative solutions, conclusions or approaches to problems.
Operation and Control	Controlling operations of equipment or systems.
Persuasion	Persuading others to change their minds or behavior.
Operation Monitoring	Watching gauges, dials, or other indicators to make sure a machine is working properly.
Complex Problem Solving	Identifying complex problems and reviewing related information to develop and evaluate options and implement solutions.
Repairing	Repairing machines or systems using the needed tools.
Operations Analysis	Analyzing needs and product requirements to create a design.
Installation	Installing equipment, machines, wiring, or programs to meet specifications.
Quality Control Analysis	Conducting tests and inspections of products, services, or processes to evaluate quality or performance.
Science	Using scientific rules and methods to solve problems.
Technology Design	Generating or adapting equipment and technology to serve user needs.
Negotiation	Bringing others together and trying to reconcile differences.
Mathematics	Using mathematics to solve problems.
Management of Personnel Resources	Motivating, developing, and directing people as they work, identifying the best people for the job.
Management of Financial Resources	Determining how money will be spent to get the work done, and accounting for these expenditures.
Systems Evaluation	Identifying measures or indicators of system performance and the actions needed to improve or correct performance, relative to the goals of the system.
Systems Analysis	Determining how a system should work and how changes in conditions, operations, and the environment will affect outcomes.
Programming	Writing computer programs for various purposes.

Ability	Ability Definitions
Oral Expression	The ability to communicate information and ideas in speaking so others will understand.
Oral Comprehension	The ability to listen to and understand information and ideas presented through spoken words and sentences.
Near Vision	The ability to see details at close range (within a few feet of the observer).
Written Expression	The ability to communicate information and ideas in writing so others will understand.
Information Ordering	The ability to arrange things or actions in a certain order or pattern according to a specific rule or set of rules (e.g., patterns of numbers, letters, words, pictures, mathematical operations).
Speech Clarity	The ability to speak clearly so others can understand you.
Arm-Hand Steadiness	The ability to keep your hand and arm steady while moving your arm or while holding your arm and hand in one position.
Speech Recognition	The ability to identify and understand the speech of another person.
Selective Attention	The ability to concentrate on a task over a period of time without being distracted.
Finger Dexterity	The ability to make precisely coordinated movements of the fingers of one or both hands to grasp, manipulate, or assemble very small objects.
Written Comprehension	The ability to read and understand information and ideas presented in writing.
Problem Sensitivity	The ability to tell when something is wrong or is likely to go wrong. It does not involve solving the problem, only recognizing there is a problem.
Manual Dexterity	The ability to quickly move your hand, your hand together with your arm, or your two hands to grasp, manipulate, or assemble objects.
Time Sharing	The ability to shift back and forth between two or more activities or sources of information (such as speech, sounds, touch, or other sources).
Flexibility of Closure	The ability to identify or detect a known pattern (a figure, object, word, or sound) that is hidden in other distracting material.
Deductive Reasoning	The ability to apply general rules to specific problems to produce answers that make sense.
Inductive Reasoning	The ability to combine pieces of information to form general rules or conclusions (includes finding a relationship among seemingly unrelated events).
Category Flexibility	The ability to generate or use different sets of rules for combining or grouping things in different ways.
Control Precision	The ability to quickly and repeatedly adjust the controls of a machine or a vehicle to exact positions.
Extent Flexibility	The ability to bend, stretch, twist, or reach with your body, arms, and/or legs.
Memorization	The ability to remember information such as words, numbers, pictures, and procedures.
Far Vision	The ability to see details at a distance.

Perceptual Speed	The ability to quickly and accurately compare similarities and differences among sets of letters, numbers, objects. pictures, or patterns. The things to be compared may be presented at the same time or one after the other. This ability also includes comparing a presented object with a remembered object.
Depth Perception	The ability to judge which of several objects is closer or farther away from you, or to judge the distance between you and an object.
Multilimb Coordination	The ability to coordinate two or more limbs (for example, two arms. two legs, or one leg and one arm) while sitting. standing. or lying down. It does not involve performing the activities while the whole body is in motion.
Trunk Strength	The ability to use your abdominal and lower back muscles to support part of the body repeatedly or continuously over time without 'giving out' or fatiguing.
Mathematical Reasoning	The ability to choose the right mathematical methods or formulas to solve a problem.
Visualization	The ability to imagine how something will look after it is moved around or when its parts are moved or rearranged.
Visual Color Discrimination	The ability to match or detect differences between colors, including shades of color and brightness.
Auditory Attention	The ability to focus on a single source of sound in the presence of other distracting sounds.
Originality	The ability to come up with unusual or clever ideas about a given topic or situation, or to develop creative ways to solve a problem.
Speed of Closure	The ability to quickly make sense of, combine, and organize information into meaningful patterns.
Hearing Sensitivity	The ability to detect or tell the differences between sounds that vary in pitch and loudness.
Number Facility	The ability to add, subtract, multiply, or divide quickly and correctly.
Fluency of Ideas	The ability to come up with a number of ideas about a topic (the number of ideas is important, not their quality, correctness, or creativity).
Wrist-Finger Speed	The ability to make fast, simple, repeated movements of the fingers, hands, and wrists.
Rate Control	The ability to time your movements or the movement of a piece of equipment in anticipation of changes in the speed and/or direction of a moving object or scene.
Static Strength	The ability to exert maximum muscle force to lift, push, pull, or carry objects.
Stamina	The ability to exert yourself physically over long periods of time without getting winded or out of breath.
Response Orientation	The ability to choose quickly between two or more movements in response to two or more different signals (lights, sounds, pictures). It includes the speed with which the correct response is started with the hand, foot, or other body part.
Glare Sensitivity	The ability to see objects in the presence of glare or bright lighting.
Dynamic Strength	The ability to exert muscle force repeatedly or continuously over time. This involves muscular endurance and resistance to muscle fatigue.
Gross Body Coordination	The ability to coordinate the movement of your arms, legs, and torso together when the whole body is in motion.
Speed of Limb Movement	The ability to quickly move the arms and legs.
Reaction Time	The ability to quickly respond (with the hand, finger, or foot) to a signal (sound, light, picture) when it appears.
Gross Body Equilibrium	The ability to keep or regain your body balance or stay upright when in an unstable position.
Dynamic Flexibility	The ability to quickly and repeatedly bend, stretch. twist, or reach out with your body, arms, and/or legs.
Night Vision	The ability to see under low light conditions.
Spatial Orientation	The ability to know your location in relation to the environment or to know where other objects are in relation to you.
Sound Localization	The ability to tell the direction from which a sound originated.
Peripheral Vision	The ability to see objects or movement of objects to one's side when the eyes are looking ahead.
Explosive Strength	The ability to use short bursts of muscle force to propel oneself (as in jumping or sprinting), or to throw an object.

Work_Activity	**Work_Activity Definitions**
Assisting and Caring for Others	Providing personal assistance, medical attention, emotional support, or other personal care to others such as coworkers, customers, or patients.
Communicating with Supervisors, Peers, or Subordin	Providing information to supervisors, co-workers, and subordinates by telephone, in written form, e-mail, or in person.
Documenting/Recording Information	Entering, transcribing, recording, storing, or maintaining information in written or electronic/magnetic form.
Developing and Building Teams	Encouraging and building mutual trust, respect, and cooperation among team members.
Getting Information	Observing, receiving, and otherwise obtaining information from all relevant sources.

Training and Teaching Others	Identifying the educational needs of others. developing formal educational or training programs or classes. and teaching or instructing others.
Performing for or Working Directly with the Public	Performing for people or dealing directly with the public. This includes serving customers in restaurants and stores, and receiving clients or guests.
Coordinating the Work and Activities of Others	Getting members of a group to work together to accomplish tasks.
Identifying Objects, Actions, and Events	Identifying information by categorizing, estimating. recognizing differences or similarities. and detecting changes in circumstances or events.
Interpreting the Meaning of Information for Others	Translating or explaining what information means and how it can be used.
Processing Information	Compiling, coding. categorizing, calculating, tabulating, auditing, or verifying information or data.
Monitor Processes, Materials, or Surroundings	Monitoring and reviewing information from materials, events, or the environment, to detect or assess problems.
Organizing, Planning, and Prioritizing Work	Developing specific goals and plans to prioritize, organize, and accomplish your work.
Communicating with Persons Outside Organization	Communicating with people outside the organization, representing the organization to customers, the public, government, and other external sources. This information can be exchanged in person, in writing, or by telephone or e-mail.
Resolving Conflicts and Negotiating with Others	Handling complaints, settling disputes, and resolving grievances and conflicts, or otherwise negotiating with others.
Performing Administrative Activities	Performing day-to-day administrative tasks such as maintaining information files and processing paperwork.
Updating and Using Relevant Knowledge	Keeping up-to-date technically and applying new knowledge to your job.
Handling and Moving Objects	Using hands and arms in handling, installing, positioning, and moving materials, and manipulating things.
Inspecting Equipment, Structures, or Material	Inspecting equipment, structures, or materials to identify the cause of errors or other problems or defects.
Establishing and Maintaining Interpersonal Relatio	Developing constructive and cooperative working relationships with others, and maintaining them over time.
Making Decisions and Solving Problems	Analyzing information and evaluating results to choose the best solution and solve problems.
Evaluating Information to Determine Compliance wit	Using relevant information and individual judgment to determine whether events or processes comply with laws, regulations, or standards.
Provide Consultation and Advice to Others	Providing guidance and expert advice to management or other groups on technical, systems-, or process-related topics.
Scheduling Work and Activities	Scheduling events, programs, and activities, as well as the work of others.
Interacting With Computers	Using computers and computer systems (including hardware and software) to program, write software, set up functions, enter data, or process information.
Guiding, Directing, and Motivating Subordinates	Providing guidance and direction to subordinates, including setting performance standards and monitoring performance.
Judging the Qualities of Things, Services, or Peop	Assessing the value, importance, or quality of things or people.
Thinking Creatively	Developing, designing, or creating new applications, ideas, relationships, systems, or products, including artistic contributions.
Controlling Machines and Processes	Using either control mechanisms or direct physical activity to operate machines or processes (not including computers or vehicles).
Estimating the Quantifiable Characteristics of Pro	Estimating sizes, distances, and quantities; or determining time, costs, resources, or materials needed to perform a work activity.
Coaching and Developing Others	Identifying the developmental needs of others and coaching, mentoring, or otherwise helping others to improve their knowledge or skills.
Selling or Influencing Others	Convincing others to buy merchandise/goods or to otherwise change their minds or actions.
Analyzing Data or Information	Identifying the underlying principles, reasons, or facts of information by breaking down information or data into separate parts.
Performing General Physical Activities	Performing physical activities that require considerable use of your arms and legs and moving your whole body, such as climbing, lifting, balancing, walking, stooping, and handling of materials.
Monitoring and Controlling Resources	Monitoring and controlling resources and overseeing the spending of money.
Developing Objectives and Strategies	Establishing long-range objectives and specifying the strategies and actions to achieve them.
Staffing Organizational Units	Recruiting, interviewing, selecting, hiring, and promoting employees in an organization.
Repairing and Maintaining Electronic Equipment	Servicing, repairing, calibrating, regulating, fine-tuning, or testing machines, devices, and equipment that operate primarily on the basis of electrical or electronic (not mechanical) principles.

Repairing and Maintaining Mechanical Equipment	Servicing. repairing. adjusting. and testing machines. devices. moving parts, and equipment that operate primarily on the basis of mechanical (not electronic) principles.
Drafting, Laying Out, and Specifying Technical Dev	Providing documentation, detailed instructions, drawings, or specifications to tell others about how devices, parts. equipment, or structures are to be fabricated, constructed, assembled, modified, maintained, or used.
Operating Vehicles, Mechanized Devices, or Equipme	Running, maneuvering, navigating, or driving vehicles or mechanized equipment, such as forklifts, passenger vehicles, aircraft, or water craft.

Work_Content	**Work_Content Definitions**
Contact With Others	How much does this job require the worker to be in contact with others (face-to-face, by telephone, or otherwise) in order to perform it?
Physical Proximity	To what extent does this job require the worker to perform job tasks in close physical proximity to other people?
Wear Common Protective or Safety Equipment such as	How much does this job require wearing common protective or safety equipment such as safety shoes, glasses, gloves, hard hats or live jackets?
Spend Time Using Your Hands to Handle, Control, or	How much does this job require using your hands to handle, control, or feel objects, tools or controls?
Indoors, Environmentally Controlled	How often does this job require working indoors in environmentally controlled conditions?
Work With Work Group or Team	How important is it to work with others in a group or team in this job?
Exposed to Disease or Infections	How often does this job require exposure to disease/infections?
Face-to-Face Discussions	How often do you have to have face-to-face discussions with individuals or teams in this job?
Importance of Being Exact or Accurate	How important is being very exact or highly accurate in performing this job?
Spend Time Making Repetitive Motions	How much does this job require making repetitive motions?
Telephone	How often do you have telephone conversations in this job?
Frequency of Decision Making	How frequently is the worker required to make decisions that affect other people, the financial resources, and/or the image and reputation of the organization?
Exposed to Contaminants	How often does this job require working exposed to contaminants (such as pollutants, gases, dust or odors)?
Deal With External Customers	How important is it to work with external customers or the public in this job?
Structured versus Unstructured Work	To what extent is this job structured for the worker, rather than allowing the worker to determine tasks, priorities, and goals?
Responsible for Others' Health and Safety	How much responsibility is there for the health and safety of others in this job?
Time Pressure	How often does this job require the worker to meet strict deadlines?
Spend Time Bending or Twisting the Body	How much does this job require bending or twisting your body?
Freedom to Make Decisions	How much decision making freedom, without supervision, does the job offer?
Impact of Decisions on Co-workers or Company Resul	How do the decisions an employee makes impact the results of co-workers, clients or the company?
Exposed to Radiation	How often does this job require exposure to radiation?
Spend Time Sitting	How much does this job require sitting?
Importance of Repeating Same Tasks	How important is repeating the same physical activities (e.g., key entry) or mental activities (e.g., checking entries in a ledger) over and over, without stopping, to performing this job?
Sounds, Noise Levels Are Distracting or Uncomforta	How often does this job require working exposed to sounds and noise levels that are distracting or uncomfortable?
Spend Time Standing	How much does this job require standing?
Deal With Unpleasant or Angry People	How frequently does the worker have to deal with unpleasant, angry, or discourteous individuals as part of the job requirements?
Coordinate or Lead Others	How important is it to coordinate or lead others in accomplishing work activities in this job?
Cramped Work Space, Awkward Positions	How often does this job require working in cramped work spaces that requires getting into awkward positions?
Level of Competition	To what extent does this job require the worker to compete or to be aware of competitive pressures?
Spend Time Walking and Running	How much does this job require walking and running?
Extremely Bright or Inadequate Lighting	How often does this job require working in extremely bright or inadequate lighting conditions?
Frequency of Conflict Situations	How often are there conflict situations the employee has to face in this job?
Responsibility for Outcomes and Results	How responsible is the worker for work outcomes and results of other workers?
Letters and Memos	How often does the job require written letters and memos?
Exposed to Minor Burns, Cuts, Bites, or Stings	How often does this job require exposure to minor burns, cuts, bites, or stings?

Exposed to Hazardous Conditions	How often does this job require exposure to hazardous conditions?
Degree of Automation	How automated is the job?
Consequence of Error	How serious would the result usually be if the worker made a mistake that was not readily correctable?
Exposed to Hazardous Equipment	How often does this job require exposure to hazardous equipment?
Spend Time Keeping or Regaining Balance	How much does this job require keeping or regaining your balance?
Spend Time Kneeling, Crouching, Stooping, or Crawl	How much does this job require kneeling, crouching, stooping or crawling?
Deal With Physically Aggressive People	How frequently does this job require the worker to deal with physical aggression of violent individuals?
Very Hot or Cold Temperatures	How often does this job require working in very hot (above 90 F degrees) or very cold (below 32 F degrees) temperatures?
Pace Determined by Speed of Equipment	How important is it to this job that the pace is determined by the speed of equipment or machinery? (This does not refer to keeping busy at all times on this job.)
Public Speaking	How often do you have to perform public speaking in this job?
Wear Specialized Protective or Safety Equipment su	How much does this job require wearing specialized protective or safety equipment such as breathing apparatus, safety harness, full protection suits, or radiation protection?
Electronic Mail	How often do you use electronic mail in this job?
Spend Time Climbing Ladders, Scaffolds, or Poles	How much does this job require climbing ladders, scaffolds, or poles?
Exposed to Whole Body Vibration	How often does this job require exposure to whole body vibration (e.g., operate a jackhammer)?
Indoors, Not Environmentally Controlled	How often does this job require working indoors in non-controlled environmental conditions (e.g., warehouse without heat)?
Outdoors, Exposed to Weather	How often does this job require working outdoors, exposed to all weather conditions?
Outdoors, Under Cover	How often does this job require working outdoors, under cover (e.g., structure with roof but no walls)?
In an Open Vehicle or Equipment	How often does this job require working in an open vehicle or equipment (e.g., tractor)?
Exposed to High Places	How often does this job require exposure to high places?
In an Enclosed Vehicle or Equipment	How often does this job require working in a closed vehicle or equipment (e.g., car)?

Work_Styles	**Work_Styles Definitions**
Attention to Detail	Job requires being careful about detail and thorough in completing work tasks.
Dependability	Job requires being reliable, responsible, and dependable, and fulfilling obligations.
Self Control	Job requires maintaining composure, keeping emotions in check, controlling anger, and avoiding aggressive behavior, even in very difficult situations.
Cooperation	Job requires being pleasant with others on the job and displaying a good-natured, cooperative attitude.
Social Orientation	Job requires preferring to work with others rather than alone, and being personally connected with others on the job.
Concern for Others	Job requires being sensitive to others' needs and feelings and being understanding and helpful on the job.
Integrity	Job requires being honest and ethical.
Initiative	Job requires a willingness to take on responsibilities and challenges.
Adaptability/Flexibility	Job requires being open to change (positive or negative) and to considerable variety in the workplace.
Stress Tolerance	Job requires accepting criticism and dealing calmly and effectively with high stress situations.
Independence	Job requires developing one's own ways of doing things, guiding oneself with little or no supervision, and depending on oneself to get things done.
Leadership	Job requires a willingness to lead, take charge, and offer opinions and direction.
Achievement/Effort	Job requires establishing and maintaining personally challenging achievement goals and exerting effort toward mastering tasks.
Persistence	Job requires persistence in the face of obstacles.
Innovation	Job requires creativity and alternative thinking to develop new ideas for and answers to work-related problems.
Analytical Thinking	Job requires analyzing information and using logic to address work-related issues and problems.

Job Zone Component	**Job Zone Component Definitions**
Title	Job Zone Two: Some Preparation Needed Some previous work-related skill, knowledge, or experience may be helpful in these occupations, but usually is not needed.
Overall Experience	For example, a drywall installer might benefit from experience installing drywall, but an inexperienced person could still learn to be an installer with little difficulty.

Job Training	Employees in these occupations need anywhere from a few months to one year of working with experienced employees. These occupations often involve using your knowledge and skills to help others. Examples include drywall installers, fire inspectors, flight attendants, pharmacy technicians, salespersons (retail), and tellers.
Job Zone Examples	
SVP Range	(4.0 to < 6.0)
Education	These occupations usually require a high school diploma and may require some vocational training or job-related course work. In some cases, an associate's or bachelor's degree could be needed.

31-9092.00 - Medical Assistants

Perform administrative and certain clinical duties under the direction of physician. Administrative duties may include scheduling appointments, maintaining medical records, billing, and coding for insurance purposes. Clinical duties may include taking and recording vital signs and medical histories, preparing patients for examination, drawing blood, and administering medications as directed by physician.

Tasks

1) Set up medical laboratory equipment.

2) Operate x-ray, electrocardiogram (EKG), and other equipment to administer routine diagnostic tests.

3) Give physiotherapy treatments, such as diathermy, galvanics, and hydrotherapy.

4) Explain treatment procedures, medications, diets and physicians' instructions to patients.

5) Clean and sterilize instruments and dispose of contaminated supplies.

6) Change dressings on wounds.

7) Prepare bodies for release to funeral home by cleaning and sewing as necessary.

8) Show patients to examination rooms and prepare them for the physician.

9) Assist ophthalmologists with fitting contact lenses or performing office surgery.

10) Inventory and order medical, lab, and office supplies and equipment.

11) Authorize drug refills and provide prescription information to pharmacies.

12) Contact medical facilities or departments to schedule patients for tests and/or admission.

13) Help physicians examine and treat patients, handing them instruments and materials or performing such tasks as giving injections and removing sutures.

14) Greet and log in patients arriving at office or clinic.

15) Prepare and administer medications as directed by a physician.

16) Collect blood, tissue or other laboratory specimens, log the specimens, and prepare them for testing.

17) Keep financial records and perform other bookkeeping duties, such as handling credit and collections and mailing monthly statements to patients.

18) Perform general office duties such as answering telephones, taking dictation and completing insurance forms.

19) Record patients' medical history, vital statistics and information such as test results in medical records.

20) Schedule appointments for patients.

21) Perform routine laboratory tests and sample analyses.

22) Prepare treatment rooms for patient examinations, keeping the rooms neat and clean.

31-9093.00 - Medical Equipment Preparers

Prepare, sterilize, install, or clean laboratory or healthcare equipment. May perform routine laboratory tasks and operate or inspect equipment.

Tasks

1) Purge wastes from equipment by connecting equipment to water sources and flushing water through systems.

2) Clean instruments in order to prepare them for sterilization.

3) Disinfect and sterilize equipment such as respirators, hospital beds, and oxygen and dialysis equipment, using sterilizers, aerators, and washers.

4) Operate and maintain steam autoclaves, keeping records of loads completed, items in loads, and maintenance procedures performed.

5) Install and set up medical equipment using hand tools.

6) Check sterile supplies to ensure that they are not outdated.

7) Start equipment and observe gauges and equipment operation, in order to detect malfunctions and to ensure equipment is operating to prescribed standards.

8) Attend hospital in-service programs related to areas of work specialization.

9) Deliver equipment to specified hospital locations or to patients' residences.

10) Maintain records of inventory and equipment usage.

11) Record sterilizer test results.

12) Assist hospital staff with patient care duties such as providing transportation and setting up traction.

13) Report defective equipment to appropriate supervisors or staff.

14) Examine equipment to detect leaks, worn or loose parts, or other indications of disrepair.

31-9095.00 - Pharmacy Aides

Record drugs delivered to the pharmacy, store incoming merchandise, and inform the supervisor of stock needs. May operate cash register and accept prescriptions for filling.

Tasks

1) Compound, package and label pharmaceutical products under direction of pharmacist.

2) Deliver medication to treatment areas, living units, residences and clinics, using various means of transportation.

3) Maintain and clean equipment, work areas and shelves.

4) Operate capsule and tablet counting machine that automatically distributes a certain number of capsules or tablets into smaller containers.

5) Prepare solid and liquid dosage medications for dispensing into bottles and unit dose packaging.

6) Process medical insurance claims, posting bill amounts and calculating co-payments.

7) Prepare prescription labels by typing and/or operating a computer and printer.

8) Calculate anticipated drug usage for a prescribed period.

9) Greet customers and help them locate merchandise.

10) Provide customers with information about the uses and effects of drugs.

11) Restock storage areas, replenishing items on shelves.

12) Operate cash register to process cash and credit sales.

13) Accept prescriptions for filling, gathering and processing necessary information.

14) Unpack, sort, count and label incoming merchandise, including items requiring special handling or refrigeration.

15) Perform clerical tasks such as filing, compiling and maintaining prescription records, and composing letters.

16) Answer telephone inquiries, referring callers to pharmacist when necessary.

17) Receive, store and inventory pharmaceutical supplies, notifying pharmacist when levels are low.

31-9096.00 - Veterinary Assistants and Laboratory Animal Caretakers

Feed, water, and examine pets and other nonfarm animals for signs of illness, disease, or injury in laboratories and animal hospitals and clinics. Clean and disinfect cages and work areas, and sterilize laboratory and surgical equipment. May provide routine post-operative care, administer medication orally or topically, or prepare samples for laboratory examination under the supervision of veterinary or laboratory animal technologists or technicians, veterinarians, or scientists.

Tasks

1) Teach pet owners in obedience classes to train dogs to obey commands and perform specific tasks in response to signals.

2) Fill medication prescriptions.

3) Sell pet food and supplies to customers.

4) Provide assistance with euthanasia of animals and disposal of corpses.

5) Assist professional personnel with research projects in commercial, public health, or research laboratories.

6) Educate and advise clients on animal health care, nutrition, and behavior problems.

7) Dust, spray, or bathe animals to control insect pests.

8) Groom, trim, or clip animals' coats.

9) Provide emergency first aid to sick or injured animals.

10) Exercise animals, and provide them with companionship.

11) Write reports, maintain research information, and perform clerical duties.

12) Perform accounting duties, including bookkeeping, billing customers for services, and maintaining inventories.

13) Administer anesthetics during surgery and monitor the effects on animals.

14) Monitor animals' recovering from surgery and notify veterinarians of any unusual changes or symptoms.

15) Prepare surgical equipment, and pass instruments and materials to veterinarians during surgical procedures.

16) Clean and maintain kennels, animal holding areas, examination and operating rooms, and animal loading/unloading facilities to control the spread of disease.

17) Assist veterinarians in examining animals to determine the nature of illnesses or injuries.

18) Clean, maintain, and sterilize instruments and equipment.

19) Collect laboratory specimens such as blood, urine, and feces for testing.

20) Hold or restrain animals during veterinary procedures.

21) Perform enemas, catheterization, ear flushes, intravenous feedings, and gavages.

22) Perform hygiene-related duties such as clipping animals' claws, and cleaning and polishing teeth.

23) Perform routine laboratory tests or diagnostic tests such as taking and developing x-rays.

24) Prepare examination or treatment rooms by stocking them with appropriate supplies.

25) Administer medication, immunizations, and blood plasma to animals as prescribed by veterinarians.

26) Record information relating to animal genealogy, feeding schedules, appearance, behavior, and breeding.

27) Examine animals to detect behavioral changes or clinical symptoms that could indicate illness or injury.

28) Prepare feed for animals according to specific instructions such as diet lists and schedules.

33-1012.00 - First-Line Supervisors/Managers of Police and Detectives

Supervise and coordinate activities of members of police force.

Tasks

1) Inspect facilities, supplies, vehicles, and equipment to ensure conformance to standards.

2) Prepare work schedules and assign duties to subordinates.

3) Investigate and resolve personnel problems within organization and charges of misconduct against staff.

4) Train staff in proper police work procedures.

5) Maintain logs, prepare reports, and direct the preparation, handling, and maintenance of departmental records.

6) Cooperate with court personnel and officials from other law enforcement agencies and testify in court as necessary.

7) Discipline staff for violation of department rules and regulations.

8) Supervise and coordinate the investigation of criminal cases, offering guidance and expertise to investigators, and ensuring that procedures are conducted in accordance with laws and regulations.

9) Monitor and evaluate the job performance of subordinates, and authorize promotions and transfers.

10) Develop, implement and revise departmental policies and procedures.

11) Review contents of written orders to ensure adherence to legal requirements.

12) Requisition and issue equipment and supplies.

13) Meet with civic, educational, and community groups to develop community programs and events, and to discuss law enforcement subjects.

14) Conduct raids and order detention of witnesses and suspects for questioning.

15) Direct collection, preparation, and handling of evidence and personal property of prisoners.

16) Prepare news releases and respond to police correspondence.

17) Prepare budgets and manage expenditures of department funds.

18) Direct release or transfer of prisoners.

19) Inform personnel of changes in regulations and policies, implications of new or amended laws, and new techniques of police work.

Knowledge	Knowledge Definitions
Law and Government	Knowledge of laws, legal codes, court procedures, precedents, government regulations, executive orders, agency rules, and the democratic political process.
Public Safety and Security	Knowledge of relevant equipment, policies, procedures, and strategies to promote effective local, state, or national security operations for the protection of people, data, property, and institutions.
English Language	Knowledge of the structure and content of the English language including the meaning and spelling of words, rules of composition, and grammar.
Education and Training	Knowledge of principles and methods for curriculum and training design, teaching and instruction for individuals and groups, and the measurement of training effects.
Administration and Management	Knowledge of business and management principles involved in strategic planning, resource allocation, human resources modeling, leadership technique, production methods, and coordination of people and resources.
Psychology	Knowledge of human behavior and performance; individual differences in ability, personality, and interests; learning and motivation; psychological research methods; and the assessment and treatment of behavioral and affective disorders.
Customer and Personal Service	Knowledge of principles and processes for providing customer and personal services. This includes customer needs assessment, meeting quality standards for services, and evaluation of customer satisfaction.
Personnel and Human Resources	Knowledge of principles and procedures for personnel recruitment, selection, training, compensation and benefits, labor relations and negotiation, and personnel information systems.
Telecommunications	Knowledge of transmission, broadcasting, switching, control, and operation of telecommunications systems.
Computers and Electronics	Knowledge of circuit boards, processors, chips, electronic equipment, and computer hardware and software, including applications and programming.
Communications and Media	Knowledge of media production, communication, and dissemination techniques and methods. This includes alternative ways to inform and entertain via written, oral, and visual media.
Clerical	Knowledge of administrative and clerical procedures and systems such as word processing, managing files and records, stenography and transcription, designing forms, and other office procedures and terminology.
Sociology and Anthropology	Knowledge of group behavior and dynamics, societal trends and influences, human migrations, ethnicity, cultures and their history and origins.
Therapy and Counseling	Knowledge of principles, methods, and procedures for diagnosis, treatment, and rehabilitation of physical and mental dysfunctions, and for career counseling and guidance.
Mathematics	Knowledge of arithmetic, algebra, geometry, calculus, statistics, and their applications.
Geography	Knowledge of principles and methods for describing the features of land, sea, and air masses, including their physical characteristics, locations, interrelationships, and distribution of plant, animal, and human life.
Transportation	Knowledge of principles and methods for moving people or goods by air, rail, sea, or road, including the relative costs and benefits.
Philosophy and Theology	Knowledge of different philosophical systems and religions. This includes their basic principles, values, ethics, ways of thinking, customs, practices, and their impact on human culture.
Medicine and Dentistry	Knowledge of the information and techniques needed to diagnose and treat human injuries, diseases, and deformities. This includes symptoms, treatment alternatives, drug properties and interactions, and preventive health-care measures.
Physics	Knowledge and prediction of physical principles, laws, their interrelationships, and applications to understanding fluid, material, and atmospheric dynamics, and mechanical, electrical, atomic and sub- atomic structures and processes.
Foreign Language	Knowledge of the structure and content of a foreign (non-English) language including the meaning and spelling of words, rules of composition and grammar, and pronunciation.
Economics and Accounting	Knowledge of economic and accounting principles and practices, the financial markets, banking and the analysis and reporting of financial data.
History and Archeology	Knowledge of historical events and their causes, indicators, and effects on civilizations and cultures.
Chemistry	Knowledge of the chemical composition, structure, and properties of substances and of the chemical processes and transformations that they undergo. This includes uses of chemicals and their interactions, danger signs, production techniques, and disposal methods.
Mechanical	Knowledge of machines and tools, including their designs, uses, repair, and maintenance.

Sales and Marketing	Knowledge of principles and methods for showing, promoting, and selling products or services. This includes marketing strategy and tactics, product demonstration. sales techniques, and sales control systems.
Biology	Knowledge of plant and animal organisms. their tissues, cells, functions, interdependencies. and interactions with each other and the environment.
Design	Knowledge of design techniques, tools, and principles involved in production of precision technical plans, blueprints, drawings, and models.
Engineering and Technology	Knowledge of the practical application of engineering science and technology. This includes applying principles. techniques, procedures, and equipment to the design and production of various goods and services.
Production and Processing	Knowledge of raw materials, production processes, quality control, costs, and other techniques for maximizing the effective manufacture and distribution of goods.
Building and Construction	Knowledge of materials, methods. and the tools involved in the construction or repair of houses, buildings, or other structures such as highways and roads.
Fine Arts	Knowledge of the theory and techniques required to compose, produce, and perform works of music, dance, visual arts, drama, and sculpture.
Food Production	Knowledge of techniques and equipment for planting, growing, and harvesting food products (both plant and animal) for consumption, including storage/handling techniques.

Skills	Skills Definitions
Judgment and Decision Making	Considering the relative costs and benefits of potential actions to choose the most appropriate one.
Active Listening	Giving full attention to what other people are saying, taking time to understand the points being made, asking questions as appropriate, and not interrupting at inappropriate times.
Management of Personnel Resources	Motivating, developing, and directing people as they work, identifying the best people for the job.
Critical Thinking	Using logic and reasoning to identify the strengths and weaknesses of alternative solutions, conclusions or approaches to problems.
Speaking	Talking to others to convey information effectively.
Writing	Communicating effectively in writing as appropriate for the needs of the audience.
Reading Comprehension	Understanding written sentences and paragraphs in work related documents.
Coordination	Adjusting actions in relation to others' actions.
Time Management	Managing one's own time and the time of others.
Negotiation	Bringing others together and trying to reconcile differences.
Persuasion	Persuading others to change their minds or behavior.
Social Perceptiveness	Being aware of others' reactions and understanding why they react as they do.
Active Learning	Understanding the implications of new information for both current and future problem-solving and decision-making.
Instructing	Teaching others how to do something.
Monitoring	Monitoring/Assessing performance of yourself, other individuals, or organizations to make improvements or take corrective action.
Service Orientation	Actively looking for ways to help people.
Learning Strategies	Selecting and using training/instructional methods and procedures appropriate for the situation when learning or teaching new things.
Complex Problem Solving	Identifying complex problems and reviewing related information to develop and evaluate options and implement solutions.
Equipment Selection	Determining the kind of tools and equipment needed to do a job.
Management of Material Resources	Obtaining and seeing to the appropriate use of equipment, facilities, and materials needed to do certain work.
Systems Evaluation	Identifying measures or indicators of system performance and the actions needed to improve or correct performance, relative to the goals of the system.
Equipment Maintenance	Performing routine maintenance on equipment and determining when and what kind of maintenance is needed.
Operations Analysis	Analyzing needs and product requirements to create a design.
Troubleshooting	Determining causes of operating errors and deciding what to do about it.
Quality Control Analysis	Conducting tests and inspections of products, services, or processes to evaluate quality or performance.
Operation and Control	Controlling operations of equipment or systems.
Management of Financial Resources	Determining how money will be spent to get the work done, and accounting for these expenditures.
Mathematics	Using mathematics to solve problems.
Systems Analysis	Determining how a system should work and how changes in conditions, operations, and the environment will affect outcomes.
Technology Design	Generating or adapting equipment and technology to serve user needs.

Science	Using scientific rules and methods to solve problems.
Operation Monitoring	Watching gauges, dials, or other indicators to make sure a machine is working properly.
Installation	Installing equipment, machines, wiring, or programs to meet specifications.
Repairing	Repairing machines or systems using the needed tools.
Programming	Writing computer programs for various purposes.

Ability	Ability Definitions
Oral Expression	The ability to communicate information and ideas in speaking so others will understand.
Inductive Reasoning	The ability to combine pieces of information to form general rules or conclusions (includes finding a relationship among seemingly unrelated events).
Oral Comprehension	The ability to listen to and understand information and ideas presented through spoken words and sentences.
Problem Sensitivity	The ability to tell when something is wrong or is likely to go wrong. It does not involve solving the problem, only recognizing there is a problem.
Deductive Reasoning	The ability to apply general rules to specific problems to produce answers that make sense.
Speech Clarity	The ability to speak clearly so others can understand you.
Written Comprehension	The ability to read and understand information and ideas presented in writing.
Speech Recognition	The ability to identify and understand the speech of another person.
Information Ordering	The ability to arrange things or actions in a certain order or pattern according to a specific rule or set of rules (e.g., patterns of numbers, letters, words, pictures, mathematical operations).
Written Expression	The ability to communicate information and ideas in writing so others will understand.
Time Sharing	The ability to shift back and forth between two or more activities or sources of information (such as speech, sounds, touch, or other sources).
Near Vision	The ability to see details at close range (within a few feet of the observer).
Reaction Time	The ability to quickly respond (with the hand, finger, or foot) to a signal (sound, light, picture) when it appears.
Selective Attention	The ability to concentrate on a task over a period of time without being distracted.
Far Vision	The ability to see details at a distance.
Flexibility of Closure	The ability to identify or detect a known pattern (a figure, object, word, or sound) that is hidden in other distracting material.
Category Flexibility	The ability to generate or use different sets of rules for combining or grouping things in different ways.
Multilimb Coordination	The ability to coordinate two or more limbs (for example, two arms, two legs, or one leg and one arm) while sitting, standing, or lying down. It does not involve performing the activities while the whole body is in motion.
Speed of Closure	The ability to quickly make sense of, combine, and organize information into meaningful patterns.
Control Precision	The ability to quickly and repeatedly adjust the controls of a machine or a vehicle to exact positions.
Response Orientation	The ability to choose quickly between two or more movements in response to two or more different signals (lights, sounds, pictures). It includes the speed with which the correct response is started with the hand, foot, or other body part.
Fluency of Ideas	The ability to come up with a number of ideas about a topic (the number of ideas is important, not their quality, correctness, or creativity).
Depth Perception	The ability to judge which of several objects is closer or farther away from you, or to judge the distance between you and an object.
Perceptual Speed	The ability to quickly and accurately compare similarities and differences among sets of letters, numbers, objects, pictures, or patterns. The things to be compared may be presented at the same time or one after the other. This ability also includes comparing a presented object with a remembered object.
Memorization	The ability to remember information such as words, numbers, pictures, and procedures.
Arm-Hand Steadiness	The ability to keep your hand and arm steady while moving your arm or while holding your arm and hand in one position.
Stamina	The ability to exert yourself physically over long periods of time without getting winded or out of breath.
Spatial Orientation	The ability to know your location in relation to the environment or to know where other objects are in relation to you.
Originality	The ability to come up with unusual or clever ideas about a given topic or situation, or to develop creative ways to solve a problem.
Static Strength	The ability to exert maximum muscle force to lift, push, pull, or carry objects.
Finger Dexterity	The ability to make precisely coordinated movements of the fingers of one or both hands to grasp, manipulate, or assemble very small objects.

Rate Control	The ability to time your movements or the movement of a piece of equipment in anticipation of changes in the speed and/or direction of a moving object or scene.
Glare Sensitivity	The ability to see objects in the presence of glare or bright lighting.
Visual Color Discrimination	The ability to match or detect differences between colors, including shades of color and brightness.
Manual Dexterity	The ability to quickly move your hand, your hand together with your arm, or your two hands to grasp, manipulate, or assemble objects.
Hearing Sensitivity	The ability to detect or tell the differences between sounds that vary in pitch and loudness.
Auditory Attention	The ability to focus on a single source of sound in the presence of other distracting sounds.
Gross Body Coordination	The ability to coordinate the movement of your arms, legs, and torso together when the whole body is in motion.
Visualization	The ability to imagine how something will look after it is moved around or when its parts are moved or rearranged.
Trunk Strength	The ability to use your abdominal and lower back muscles to support part of the body repeatedly or continuously over time without 'giving out' or fatiguing.
Number Facility	The ability to add, subtract, multiply, or divide quickly and correctly.
Peripheral Vision	The ability to see objects or movement of objects to one's side when the eyes are looking ahead.
Night Vision	The ability to see under low light conditions.
Extent Flexibility	The ability to bend, stretch, twist, or reach with your body, arms, and/or legs.
Mathematical Reasoning	The ability to choose the right mathematical methods or formulas to solve a problem.
Sound Localization	The ability to tell the direction from which a sound originated.
Speed of Limb Movement	The ability to quickly move the arms and legs.
Gross Body Equilibrium	The ability to keep or regain your body balance or stay upright when in an unstable position.
Explosive Strength	The ability to use short bursts of muscle force to propel oneself (as in jumping or sprinting), or to throw an object.
Dynamic Strength	The ability to exert muscle force repeatedly or continuously over time. This involves muscular endurance and resistance to muscle fatigue.
Wrist-Finger Speed	The ability to make fast, simple, repeated movements of the fingers, hands, and wrists.
Dynamic Flexibility	The ability to quickly and repeatedly bend, stretch, twist, or reach out with your body, arms, and/or legs.

Work_Activity	Work_Activity Definitions
Making Decisions and Solving Problems	Analyzing information and evaluating results to choose the best solution and solve problems.
Communicating with Supervisors, Peers, or Subordin	Providing information to supervisors, co-workers, and subordinates by telephone, in written form, e-mail, or in person.
Performing for or Working Directly with the Public	Performing for people or dealing directly with the public. This includes serving customers in restaurants and stores, and receiving clients or guests.
Operating Vehicles, Mechanized Devices, or Equipme	Running, maneuvering, navigating, or driving vehicles or mechanized equipment, such as forklifts, passenger vehicles, aircraft, or water craft.
Guiding, Directing, and Motivating Subordinates	Providing guidance and direction to subordinates, including setting performance standards and monitoring performance.
Resolving Conflicts and Negotiating with Others	Handling complaints, settling disputes, and resolving grievances and conflicts, or otherwise negotiating with others.
Documenting/Recording Information	Entering, transcribing, recording, storing, or maintaining information in written or electronic/magnetic form.
Getting Information	Observing, receiving, and otherwise obtaining information from all relevant sources.
Training and Teaching Others	Identifying the educational needs of others, developing formal educational or training programs or classes, and teaching or instructing others.
Coaching and Developing Others	Identifying the developmental needs of others and coaching, mentoring, or otherwise helping others to improve their knowledge or skills.
Updating and Using Relevant Knowledge	Keeping up-to-date technically and applying new knowledge to your job.
Communicating with Persons Outside Organization	Communicating with people outside the organization, representing the organization to customers, the public, government, and other external sources. This information can be exchanged in person, in writing, or by telephone or e-mail.
Identifying Objects, Actions, and Events	Identifying information by categorizing, estimating, recognizing differences or similarities, and detecting changes in circumstances or events.
Coordinating the Work and Activities of Others	Getting members of a group to work together to accomplish tasks.
Establishing and Maintaining Interpersonal Relatio	Developing constructive and cooperative working relationships with others, and maintaining them over time.

Assisting and Caring for Others	Providing personal assistance, medical attention, emotional support, or other personal care to others such as coworkers, customers, or patients.
Evaluating Information to Determine Compliance wit	Using relevant information and individual judgment to determine whether events or processes comply with laws, regulations, or standards.
Scheduling Work and Activities	Scheduling events, programs, and activities, as well as the work of others.
Performing General Physical Activities	Performing physical activities that require considerable use of your arms and legs and moving your whole body, such as climbing, lifting, balancing, walking, stooping, and handling of materials.
Organizing, Planning, and Prioritizing Work	Developing specific goals and plans to prioritize, organize, and accomplish your work.
Performing Administrative Activities	Performing day-to-day administrative tasks such as maintaining information files and processing paperwork.
Monitor Processes, Materials, or Surroundings	Monitoring and reviewing information from materials, events, or the environment, to detect or assess problems.
Interacting With Computers	Using computers and computer systems (including hardware and software) to program, write software, set up functions, enter data, or process information.
Developing and Building Teams	Encouraging and building mutual trust, respect, and cooperation among team members.
Analyzing Data or Information	Identifying the underlying principles, reasons, or facts of information by breaking down information or data into separate parts.
Processing Information	Compiling, coding, categorizing, calculating, tabulating, auditing, or verifying information or data.
Interpreting the Meaning of Information for Others	Translating or explaining what information means and how it can be used.
Judging the Qualities of Things, Services, or Peop	Assessing the value, importance, or quality of things or people.
Thinking Creatively	Developing, designing, or creating new applications, ideas, relationships, systems, or products, including artistic contributions.
Developing Objectives and Strategies	Establishing long-range objectives and specifying the strategies and actions to achieve them.
Provide Consultation and Advice to Others	Providing guidance and expert advice to management or other groups on technical, systems-, or process-related topics.
Staffing Organizational Units	Recruiting, interviewing, selecting, hiring, and promoting employees in an organization.
Estimating the Quantifiable Characteristics of Pro	Estimating sizes, distances, and quantities; or determining time, costs, resources, or materials needed to perform a work activity.
Handling and Moving Objects	Using hands and arms in handling, installing, positioning, and moving materials, and manipulating things.
Inspecting Equipment, Structures, or Material	Inspecting equipment, structures, or materials to identify the cause of errors or other problems or defects.
Monitoring and Controlling Resources	Monitoring and controlling resources and overseeing the spending of money.
Controlling Machines and Processes	Using either control mechanisms or direct physical activity to operate machines or processes (not including computers or vehicles).
Selling or Influencing Others	Convincing others to buy merchandise/goods or to otherwise change their minds or actions.
Repairing and Maintaining Mechanical Equipment	Servicing, repairing, adjusting, and testing machines, devices, moving parts, and equipment that operate primarily on the basis of mechanical (not electronic) principles.
Repairing and Maintaining Electronic Equipment	Servicing, repairing, calibrating, regulating, fine-tuning, or testing machines, devices, and equipment that operate primarily on the basis of electrical or electronic (not mechanical) principles.
Drafting, Laying Out, and Specifying Technical Dev	Providing documentation, detailed instructions, drawings, or specifications to tell others about how devices, parts, equipment, or structures are to be fabricated, constructed, assembled, modified, maintained, or used.

Work_Content	Work_Content Definitions
Telephone	How often do you have telephone conversations in this job?
In an Enclosed Vehicle or Equipment	How often does this job require working in a closed vehicle or equipment (e.g., car)?
Face-to-Face Discussions	How often do you have to have face-to-face discussions with individuals or teams in this job?
Frequency of Decision Making	How frequently is the worker required to make decisions that affect other people, the financial resources, and/or the image and reputation of the organization?
Outdoors, Exposed to Weather	How often does this job require working outdoors, exposed to all weather conditions?
Deal With External Customers	How important is it to work with external customers or the public in this job?
Impact of Decisions on Co-workers or Company Resul	How do the decisions an employee makes impact the results of co-workers, clients or the company?

Importance of Being Exact or Accurate	How important is being very exact or highly accurate in performing this job?
Contact With Others	How much does this job require the worker to be in contact with others (face-to-face, by telephone, or otherwise) in order to perform it?
Responsible for Others' Health and Safety	How much responsibility is there for the health and safety of others in this job?
Work With Work Group or Team	How important is it to work with others in a group or team in this job?
Frequency of Conflict Situations	How often are there conflict situations the employee has to face in this job?
Responsibility for Outcomes and Results	How responsible is the worker for work outcomes and results of other workers?
Freedom to Make Decisions	How much decision making freedom, without supervision, does the job offer?
Consequence of Error	How serious would the result usually be if the worker made a mistake that was not readily correctable?
Deal With Unpleasant or Angry People	How frequently does the worker have to deal with unpleasant, angry, or discourteous individuals as part of the job requirements?
Coordinate or Lead Others	How important is it to coordinate or lead others in accomplishing work activities in this job?
Very Hot or Cold Temperatures	How often does this job require working in very hot (above 90 F degrees) or very cold (below 32 F degrees) temperatures?
Physical Proximity	To what extent does this job require the worker to perform job tasks in close physical proximity to other people?
Electronic Mail	How often do you use electronic mail in this job?
Indoors, Environmentally Controlled	How often does this job require working indoors in environmentally controlled conditions?
Structured versus Unstructured Work	To what extent is this job structured for the worker, rather than allowing the worker to determine tasks, priorities, and goals?
Exposed to Hazardous Equipment	How often does this job require exposure to hazardous equipment?
Time Pressure	How often does this job require the worker to meet strict deadlines?
Deal With Physically Aggressive People	How frequently does this job require the worker to deal with physical aggression of violent individuals?
Extremely Bright or Inadequate Lighting	How often does this job require working in extremely bright or inadequate lighting conditions?
Letters and Memos	How often does the job require written letters and memos?
Wear Common Protective or Safety Equipment such as	How much does this job require wearing common protective or safety equipment such as safety shoes, glasses, gloves, hard hats or live jackets?
Spend Time Sitting	How much does this job require sitting?
Importance of Repeating Same Tasks	How important is repeating the same physical activities (e.g., key entry) or mental activities (e.g., checking entries in a ledger) over and over, without stopping, to performing this job?
Exposed to Disease or Infections	How often does this job require exposure to disease/infections?
Exposed to Contaminants	How often does this job require working exposed to contaminants (such as pollutants, gases, dust or odors)?
Exposed to Minor Burns, Cuts, Bites, or Stings	How often does this job require exposure to minor burns, cuts, bites, or stings?
Sounds, Noise Levels Are Distracting or Uncomfortable	How often does this job require working exposed to sounds and noise levels that are distracting or uncomfortable?
Public Speaking	How often do you have to perform public speaking in this job?
Spend Time Using Your Hands to Handle, Control, or	How much does this job require using your hands to handle, control, or feel objects, tools or controls?
Level of Competition	To what extent does this job require the worker to compete or to be aware of competitive pressures?
Exposed to Hazardous Conditions	How often does this job require exposure to hazardous conditions?
Indoors, Not Environmentally Controlled	How often does this job require working indoors in non-controlled environmental conditions (e.g., warehouse without heat)?
Cramped Work Space, Awkward Positions	How often does this job require working in cramped work spaces that requires getting into awkward positions?
Spend Time Standing	How much does this job require standing?
Degree of Automation	How automated is the job?
Wear Specialized Protective or Safety Equipment su	How much does this job require wearing specialized protective or safety equipment such as breathing apparatus, safety harness, full protection suits, or radiation protection?
Spend Time Making Repetitive Motions	How much does this job require making repetitive motions?
Spend Time Walking and Running	How much does this job require walking and running?
Outdoors, Under Cover	How often does this job require working outdoors, under cover (e.g., structure with roof but no walls)?
Spend Time Bending or Twisting the Body	How much does this job require bending or twisting your body?
In an Open Vehicle or Equipment	How often does this job require working in an open vehicle or equipment (e.g., tractor)?
Spend Time Keeping or Regaining Balance	How much does this job require keeping or regaining your balance?
Exposed to High Places	How often does this job require exposure to high places?

Spend Time Kneeling, Crouching, Stooping, or Crawl	How much does this job require kneeling, crouching, stooping or crawling?
Pace Determined by Speed of Equipment	How important is it to this job that the pace is determined by the speed of equipment or machinery? (This does not refer to keeping busy at all times on this job.)
Exposed to Radiation	How often does this job require exposure to radiation?
Spend Time Climbing Ladders, Scaffolds, or Poles	How much does this job require climbing ladders, scaffolds, or poles?
Exposed to Whole Body Vibration	How often does this job require exposure to whole body vibration (e.g., operate a jackhammer)?

Work_Styles	Work_Styles Definitions
Integrity	Job requires being honest and ethical.
Stress Tolerance	Job requires accepting criticism and dealing calmly and effectively with high stress situations.
Dependability	Job requires being reliable, responsible, and dependable, and fulfilling obligations.
Self Control	Job requires maintaining composure, keeping emotions in check, controlling anger, and avoiding aggressive behavior, even in very difficult situations.
Leadership	Job requires a willingness to lead, take charge, and offer opinions and direction.
Adaptability/Flexibility	Job requires being open to change (positive or negative) and to considerable variety in the workplace.
Attention to Detail	Job requires being careful about detail and thorough in completing work tasks.
Initiative	Job requires a willingness to take on responsibilities and challenges.
Cooperation	Job requires being pleasant with others on the job and displaying a good-natured, cooperative attitude.
Independence	Job requires developing one's own ways of doing things, guiding oneself with little or no supervision, and depending on oneself to get things done.
Analytical Thinking	Job requires analyzing information and using logic to address work-related issues and problems.
Concern for Others	Job requires being sensitive to others' needs and feelings and being understanding and helpful on the job.
Persistence	Job requires persistence in the face of obstacles.
Innovation	Job requires creativity and alternative thinking to develop new ideas for and answers to work-related problems.
Social Orientation	Job requires preferring to work with others rather than alone, and being personally connected with others on the job.
Achievement/Effort	Job requires establishing and maintaining personally challenging achievement goals and exerting effort toward mastering tasks.

Job Zone Component	Job Zone Component Definitions
Title	Job Zone Four: Considerable Preparation Needed
Overall Experience	A minimum of two to four years of work-related skill, knowledge, or experience is needed for these occupations. For example, an accountant must complete four years of college and work for several years in accounting to be considered qualified.
Job Training	Employees in these occupations usually need several years of work-related experience, on-the-job training, and/or vocational training.
Job Zone Examples	Many of these occupations involve coordinating, supervising, managing, or training others. Examples include accountants, chefs and head cooks, computer programmers, historians, pharmacists, and police detectives.
SVP Range	(7.0 to < 8.0)
Education	Most of these occupations require a four - year bachelor's degree, but some do not.

33-1021.01 - Municipal Fire Fighting and Prevention Supervisors

Supervise fire fighters who control and extinguish municipal fires, protect life and property, and conduct rescue efforts.

Tasks

1) Identify corrective actions needed to bring properties into compliance with applicable fire codes and ordinances and conduct follow-up inspections to see if corrective actions have been taken.

2) Coordinate the distribution of fire prevention promotional materials.

3) Develop or review building fire exit plans.

4) Direct firefighters in station maintenance duties, and participate in these duties.

5) Direct investigation of cases of suspected arson, hazards, and false alarms and submit reports outlining findings.

6) Recommend to proper authorities possible fire code revisions, additions, and deletions.

7) Inspect and test new and existing fire protection systems, fire detection systems, and fire safety equipment in order to ensure that they are operating properly.

8) Maintain required maps and records.

9) Instruct and drill fire department personnel in assigned duties, including firefighting, medical care, hazardous materials response, fire prevention, and related subjects.

10) Supervise and participate in the inspection of properties in order to ensure that they are in compliance with applicable fire codes, ordinances, laws, regulations, and standards.

11) Recommend personnel actions related to disciplinary procedures, performance, leaves of absence, and grievances.

12) Provide emergency medical services as required, and perform light to heavy rescue functions at emergencies.

13) Prepare activity reports listing fire call locations, actions taken, fire types and probable causes, damage estimates, and situation dispositions.

14) Participate in creating fire safety guidelines and evacuation schemes for non-residential buildings.

15) Oversee review of new building plans to ensure compliance with laws, ordinances, and administrative rules for public fire safety.

16) Compile and maintain equipment and personnel records, including accident reports.

17) Present and interpret fire prevention and fire code information to citizens' groups, organizations, contractors, engineers, and developers.

18) Evaluate the performance of assigned firefighting personnel.

19) Evaluate fire station procedures in order to ensure efficiency and enforcement of departmental regulations.

20) Direct the training of firefighters, assigning of instructors to training classes, and providing of supervisors with reports on training progress and status.

21) Assign firefighters to jobs at strategic locations in order to facilitate rescue of persons and maximize application of extinguishing agents.

22) Attend in-service training classes to remain current in knowledge of codes, laws, ordinances, and regulations.

23) Study and interpret fire safety codes to establish procedures for issuing permits regulating storage or use of hazardous or flammable substances.

24) Document efforts taken to bring property owners into compliance with laws, codes, regulations, ordinances, and standards.

25) Write and submit proposals for repair, modification, or replacement of firefighting equipment.

26) Assess nature and extent of fire, condition of building, danger to adjacent buildings, and water supply status in order to determine crew or company requirements.

27) Report and issue citations for fire code violations found during inspections, testifying in court about violations when required to do so.

33-1021.02 - Forest Fire Fighting and Prevention Supervisors

Supervise fire fighters who control and suppress fires in forests or vacant public land.

Tasks

1) Maintain knowledge of forest fire laws and fire prevention techniques and tactics.

2) Train workers in such skills as parachute jumping, fire suppression, aerial observation, and radio communication, both in the classroom and on the job.

3) Appraise damage caused by fires in order to prepare damage reports.

4) Operate wildland fire engines and hoselays.

5) Direct and supervise prescribed burn projects, and prepare post-burn reports analyzing burn conditions and results.

6) Drive crew carriers in order to transport firefighters to fire sites.

7) Educate the public about forest fire prevention by participating in activities such as exhibits and presentations, and by distributing promotional materials.

8) Inspect all stations, uniforms, equipment, and recreation areas in order to ensure compliance with safety standards, taking corrective action as necessary.

9) Monitor fire suppression expenditures in order to ensure that they are necessary and reasonable.

10) Parachute to major fire locations in order to direct fire containment and suppression activities.

11) Evaluate size, location, and condition of forest fires in order to request and dispatch crews and position equipment so fires can be contained safely and effectively.

12) Perform administrative duties such as compiling and maintaining records, completing forms, preparing reports, and composing correspondence.

13) Lead work crews in the maintenance of structures and access roads in forest areas.

14) Review and evaluate employee performance.

15) Serve as working leader of an engine-, hand-, helicopter-, or prescribed fire crew of three or more firefighters.

16) Recruit and hire forest fire-fighting personnel.

17) Recommend equipment modifications or new equipment purchases.

18) Maintain fire suppression equipment in good condition, checking equipment periodically in order to ensure that it is ready for use.

19) Schedule employee work assignments, and set work priorities.

20) Direct the loading of fire suppression equipment into aircraft and the parachuting of equipment to crews on the ground.

21) Communicate fire details to superiors, subordinates, and interagency dispatch centers, using two-way radios.

22) Identify staff training and development needs in order to ensure that appropriate training can be arranged.

23) Direct investigations of suspected arsons in wildfires, working closely with other investigating agencies.

24) Observe fires and crews from air to determine fire-fighting force requirements and to note changing conditions that will affect fire-fighting efforts.

25) Monitor prescribed burns to ensure that they are conducted safely and effectively.

26) Regulate open burning by issuing burning permits, inspecting problem sites, issuing citations for violations of laws and ordinances, and educating the public in proper burning practices.

33-2011.01 - Municipal Fire Fighters

Control and extinguish municipal fires, protect life and property and conduct rescue efforts.

Tasks

1) Select and attach hose nozzles, depending on fire type, and direct streams of water or chemicals onto fires.

2) Assess fires and situations and report conditions to superiors in order to receive instructions, using two-way radios.

3) Take action to contain hazardous chemicals that might catch fire, leak, or spill.

4) Salvage property by removing broken glass, pumping out water, and ventilating buildings to remove smoke.

5) Create openings in buildings for ventilation or entrance, using axes, chisels, crowbars, electric saws, or core cutters.

6) Collaborate with police to respond to accidents, disasters, and arson investigation calls.

7) Search burning buildings to locate fire victims.

8) Operate pumps connected to high-pressure hoses.

9) Inform and educate the public on fire prevention.

10) Position and climb ladders in order to gain access to upper levels of buildings, or to rescue individuals from burning structures.

11) Lay hose lines and connect them to water supplies.

12) Respond to fire alarms and other calls for assistance, such as automobile and industrial accidents.

13) Rescue victims from burning buildings and accident sites.

14) Inspect fire sites after flames have been extinguished in order to ensure that there is no further danger.

15) Drive and operate fire fighting vehicles and equipment.

16) Move toward the source of a fire using knowledge of types of fires, construction design, building materials, and physical layout of properties.

17) Dress with equipment such as fire resistant clothing and breathing apparatus.

18) Administer first aid and cardiopulmonary resuscitation to injured persons.

19) Protect property from water and smoke using waterproof salvage covers, smoke ejectors, and deodorants.

20) Spray foam onto runways, extinguish fires, and rescue aircraft crew and passengers in air-crash emergencies.

21) Clean and maintain fire stations and fire fighting equipment and apparatus.

22) Establish firelines to prevent unauthorized persons from entering areas near fires.

23) Inspect buildings for fire hazards and compliance with fire prevention ordinances, testing

and checking smoke alarms and fire suppression equipment as necessary.

24) Participate in courses, seminars and conferences, and study fire science literature, in order to learn firefighting techniques.

25) Participate in fire drills and demonstrations of fire fighting techniques.

26) Prepare written reports that detail specifics of fire incidents.

33-2011.02 - Forest Fire Fighters

Control and suppress fires in forests or vacant public land.

Tasks

1) Serve as fully trained lead helicopter crewmember and as helispot manager.

2) Participate in fire prevention and inspection programs.

3) Maintain knowledge of current firefighting practices by participating in drills and by attending seminars, conventions, and conferences.

4) Transport personnel and cargo to and from fire areas.

5) Take action to contain any hazardous chemicals that could catch fire, leak, or spill.

6) Rescue fire victims, and administer emergency medical aid.

7) Perform forest maintenance and improvement tasks such as cutting brush, planting trees, building trails and marking timber.

8) Drop weighted paper streamers from aircraft to determine the speed and direction of the wind at fire sites.

9) Inform and educate the public about fire prevention.

10) Parachute from aircraft into remote areas for initial attack on wildland fires.

11) Fell trees, cut and clear brush, and dig trenches in order to create firelines, using axes, chainsaws or shovels.

12) Observe forest areas from fire lookout towers in order to spot potential problems.

13) Maintain fire equipment and firehouse living quarters.

14) Collaborate with other firefighters as a member of a firefighting crew.

15) Extinguish flames and embers to suppress fires, using shovels, or engine- or hand-driven water or chemical pumps.

16) Operate pumps connected to high-pressure hoses.

17) Orient self in relation to fire, using compass and map, and collect supplies and equipment dropped by parachute.

18) Participate in physical training in order to maintain high levels of physical fitness.

19) Patrol burned areas after fires to locate and eliminate hot spots that may restart fires.

20) Test and maintain tools, equipment, jump gear and parachutes in order to ensure readiness for fire suppression activities.

21) Establish water supplies, connect hoses, and direct water onto fires.

22) Maintain contact with fire dispatchers at all times in order to notify them of the need for additional firefighters and supplies, or to detail any difficulties encountered.

33-2021.01 - Fire Inspectors

Inspect buildings and equipment to detect fire hazards and enforce state and local regulations.

Tasks

1) Attend training classes in order to maintain current knowledge of fire prevention, safety, and firefighting procedures.

2) Inspect liquefied petroleum installations, storage containers, and transportation and delivery systems for compliance with fire laws.

3) Identify corrective actions necessary to bring properties into compliance with applicable fire codes, laws, regulations, and standards, and explain these measures to property owners or their representatives.

4) Develop or review fire exit plans.

5) Conduct inspections and acceptance testing of newly installed fire protection systems.

6) Review blueprints and plans for new or remodeled buildings in order to ensure the structures meet fire safety codes.

7) Issue permits for public assemblies.

8) Write detailed reports of fire inspections performed, fire code violations observed, and corrective recommendations offered.

9) Investigate causes of fires, collecting and preparing evidence and presenting it in court when necessary.

10) Present and explain fire code requirements and fire prevention information to architects, contractors, attorneys, engineers, developers, fire service personnel, and the general public.

11) Recommend changes to fire prevention, inspection, and fire code endorsement procedures.

12) Arrange for the replacement of defective fire fighting equipment and for repair of fire alarm and sprinkler systems, making minor repairs such as servicing fire extinguishers when feasible.

13) Search for clues as to the cause of a fire, once the fire is completely extinguished.

14) Collect fees for permits and licenses.

15) Supervise staff, training them, planning their work, and evaluating their performance.

16) Inspect buildings to locate hazardous conditions and fire code violations such as accumulations of combustible material, electrical wiring problems, and inadequate or non-functional fire exits.

17) Serve court appearance summonses and/or condemnation notices on parties responsible for violations of fire codes, laws, and ordinances.

18) Conduct fire code compliance follow-ups to ensure that corrective actions have been taken in cases where violations were found.

19) Inspect properties that store, handle, and use hazardous materials to ensure compliance with laws, codes, and regulations, and issue hazardous materials permits to facilities found in compliance.

20) Develop and coordinate fire prevention programs such as false alarm billing, fire inspection reporting, and hazardous materials management.

21) Testify in court regarding fire code and fire safety issues.

22) Conduct fire exit drills to monitor and evaluate evacuation procedures.

33-2021.02 - Fire Investigators

Conduct investigations to determine causes of fires and explosions.

Tasks

1) Testify in court cases involving fires, suspected arson, and false alarms.

2) Photograph damage and evidence related to causes of fires or explosions in order to document investigation findings.

3) Package collected pieces of evidence in securely closed containers such as bags, crates, or boxes, in order to protect them.

4) Instruct children about the dangers of fire.

5) Examine fire sites and collect evidence such as glass, metal fragments, charred wood, and accelerant residue for use in determining the cause of a fire.

6) Swear out warrants, and arrest and process suspected arsonists.

7) Test sites and materials to establish facts, such as burn patterns and flash points of materials, using test equipment.

8) Subpoena and interview witnesses, property owners, and building occupants to obtain information and sworn testimony.

9) Analyze evidence and other information to determine probable cause of fire or explosion.

10) Prepare and maintain reports of investigation results, and records of convicted arsonists and arson suspects.

11) Conduct internal investigation to determine negligence and violation of laws and regulations by fire department employees.

33-2022.00 - Forest Fire Inspectors and Prevention Specialists

Enforce fire regulations and inspect for forest fire hazards. Report forest fires and weather conditions.

Tasks

1) Locate forest fires on area maps, using azimuth sighters and known landmarks.

2) Estimate sizes and characteristics of fires, and report findings to base camps by radio or telephone.

3) Inspect forest tracts and logging areas for fire hazards such as accumulated wastes or mishandling of combustibles, and recommend appropriate fire prevention measures.

4) Administer regulations regarding sanitation, fire prevention, violation corrections, and related forest regulations.

209

5) Inspect camp sites to ensure that campers are in compliance with forest use regulations.

6) Relay messages about emergencies, accidents, locations of crew and personnel, and fire hazard conditions.

7) Maintain records and logbooks.

8) Examine a. d inventory firefighting equipment such as axes, fire hoses, shovels, pumps, buckets, and fire extinguishers in order to determine amount and condition.

9) Direct crews working on firelines during forest fires.

10) Patrol assigned areas, looking for forest fires, hazardous conditions, and weather phenomena.

11) Compile and report meteorological data, such as temperature, relative humidity, wind direction and velocity, and types of cloud formations.

12) Direct maintenance and repair of firefighting equipment, or requisition new equipment.

13) Extinguish smaller fires with portable extinguishers, shovels, and axes.

33-3011.00 - Bailiffs

Maintain order in courts of law.

Tasks

1) Report need for police or medical assistance to sheriff's office.

2) Check courtroom for security and cleanliness and assure availability of sundry supplies for use of judge.

3) Stop people from entering courtroom while judge charges jury.

4) Announce entrance of judge.

5) Maintain order in courtroom during trial and guard jury from outside contact.

6) Enforce courtroom rules of behavior and warn persons not to smoke or disturb court procedure.

7) Guard lodging of sequestered jury.

8) Collect and retain unauthorized firearms from persons entering courtroom.

33-3012.00 - Correctional Officers and Jailers

Guard inmates in penal or rehabilitative institution in accordance with established regulations and procedures. May guard prisoners in transit between jail, courtroom, prison, or other point. Includes deputy sheriffs and police who spend the majority of their time guarding prisoners in correctional institutions.

Tasks

1) Monitor conduct of prisoners, according to established policies, regulations, and procedures, in order to prevent escape or violence.

2) Issue clothing, tools, and other authorized items to inmates.

3) Inspect mail for the presence of contraband.

4) Investigate crimes that have occurred within an institution, or assist police in their investigations of crimes and inmates.

5) Conduct fire, safety, and sanitation inspections.

6) Serve meals and distribute commissary items to prisoners.

7) Inspect conditions of locks, window bars, grills, doors, and gates at correctional facilities, in order to ensure that they will prevent escapes.

8) Settle disputes between inmates.

9) Record information, such as prisoner identification, charges, and incidences of inmate disturbance.

10) Search for and recapture escapees.

11) Sponsor inmate recreational activities such as newspapers and self-help groups.

12) Maintain records of prisoners' identification and charges.

13) Drive passenger vehicles and trucks used to transport inmates to other institutions, courtrooms, hospitals, and work sites.

14) Arrange daily schedules for prisoners including library visits, work assignments, family visits, and counseling appointments.

15) Use weapons, handcuffs, and physical force to maintain discipline and order among prisoners.

16) Take prisoners into custody and escort to locations within and outside of facility, such as visiting room, courtroom, or airport.

17) Assign duties to inmates, providing instructions as needed.

18) Provide to supervisors oral and written reports of the quality and quantity of work performed by inmates, inmate disturbances and rule violations, and unusual occurrences.

19) Search prisoners, cells, and vehicles for weapons, valuables, or drugs.

20) Guard facility entrances in order to screen visitors.

33-3021.01 - Police Detectives

Conduct investigations to prevent crimes or solve criminal cases.

Tasks

1) Analyze completed police reports to determine what additional information and investigative work is needed.

2) Provide testimony as a witness in court.

3) Prepare and serve search and arrest warrants.

4) Obtain evidence from suspects.

5) Obtain facts or statements from complainants, witnesses, and accused persons and record interviews, using recording device.

6) Maintain surveillance of establishments to obtain identifying information on suspects.

7) Record progress of investigation, maintain informational files on suspects, and submit reports to commanding officer or magistrate to authorize warrants.

8) Prepare charges or responses to charges, or information for court cases, according to formalized procedures.

9) Notify command of situation and request assistance.

10) Participate or assist in raids and arrests.

11) Question individuals or observe persons and establishments to confirm information given to patrol officers.

12) Block or rope off scene and check perimeter to ensure that entire scene is secured.

13) Note relevant details upon arrival at scene, such as time of day and weather conditions.

14) Coordinate with outside agencies and serve on interagency task forces to combat specific types of crime.

15) Provide information to lab personnel concerning the source of an item of evidence and tests to be performed.

16) Obtain summary of incident from officer in charge at crime scene, taking care to avoid disturbing evidence.

17) Examine crime scenes to obtain clues and evidence, such as loose hairs, fibers, clothing, or weapons.

18) Note, mark, and photograph location of objects found, such as footprints, tire tracks, bullets and bloodstains, and take measurements of the scene.

19) Organize scene search, assigning specific tasks and areas of search to individual officers and obtaining adequate lighting as necessary.

20) Notify, or request notification of, medical examiner or district attorney representative.

21) Preserve, process, and analyze items of evidence obtained from crime scenes and suspects, placing them in proper containers and destroying evidence no longer needed.

22) Schedule polygraph tests for consenting parties and record results of test interpretations for presentation with findings.

23) Take photographs from all angles of relevant parts of a crime scene, including entrance and exit routes and streets and intersections.

24) Monitor conditions of victims who are unconscious so that arrangements can be made to take statements if consciousness is regained.

25) Secure persons at scene, keeping witnesses from conversing or leaving the scene before investigators arrive.

26) Summon medical help for injured individuals and alert medical personnel to take statements from them.

27) Videotape scenes where possible, including collection of evidence, examination of victim at scene, and defendants and witnesses.

28) Secure deceased body and obtain evidence from it, preventing bystanders from tampering with it prior to medical examiner's arrival.

29) Check victims for signs of life, such as breathing and pulse.

30) Observe and photograph narcotic purchase transactions to compile evidence and protect undercover investigators.

Knowledge	Knowledge Definitions

Law and Government	Knowledge of laws, legal codes, court procedures, precedents, government regulations, executive orders, agency rules, and the democratic political process.
Public Safety and Security	Knowledge of relevant equipment, policies, procedures, and strategies to promote effective local, state, or national security operations for the protection of people, data, property, and institutions.
English Language	Knowledge of the structure and content of the English language including the meaning and spelling of words, rules of composition, and grammar.
Psychology	Knowledge of human behavior and performance; individual differences in ability, personality, and interests; learning and motivation; psychological research methods; and the assessment and treatment of behavioral and affective disorders.
Administration and Management	Knowledge of business and management principles involved in strategic planning, resource allocation, human resources modeling, leadership technique, production methods, and coordination of people and resources.
Education and Training	Knowledge of principles and methods for curriculum and training design, teaching and instruction for individuals and groups, and the measurement of training effects.
Customer and Personal Service	Knowledge of principles and processes for providing customer and personal services. This includes customer needs assessment, meeting quality standards for services, and evaluation of customer satisfaction.
Computers and Electronics	Knowledge of circuit boards, processors, chips, electronic equipment, and computer hardware and software, including applications and programming.
Communications and Media	Knowledge of media production, communication, and dissemination techniques and methods. This includes alternative ways to inform and entertain via written, oral, and visual media.
Telecommunications	Knowledge of transmission, broadcasting, switching, control, and operation of telecommunications systems.
Clerical	Knowledge of administrative and clerical procedures and systems such as word processing, managing files and records, stenography and transcription, designing forms, and other office procedures and terminology.
Therapy and Counseling	Knowledge of principles, methods, and procedures for diagnosis, treatment, and rehabilitation of physical and mental dysfunctions, and for career counseling and guidance.
Sociology and Anthropology	Knowledge of group behavior and dynamics, societal trends and influences, human migrations, ethnicity, cultures and their history and origins.
Transportation	Knowledge of principles and methods for moving people or goods by air, rail, sea, or road, including the relative costs and benefits.
Personnel and Human Resources	Knowledge of principles and procedures for personnel recruitment, selection, training, compensation and benefits, labor relations and negotiation, and personnel information systems.
Mathematics	Knowledge of arithmetic, algebra, geometry, calculus, statistics, and their applications.
Philosophy and Theology	Knowledge of different philosophical systems and religions. This includes their basic principles, values, ethics, ways of thinking, customs, practices, and their impact on human culture.
Foreign Language	Knowledge of the structure and content of a foreign (non-English) language including the meaning and spelling of words, rules of composition and grammar, and pronunciation.
Geography	Knowledge of principles and methods for describing the features of land, sea, and air masses, including their physical characteristics, locations, interrelationships, and distribution of plant, animal, and human life.
Medicine and Dentistry	Knowledge of the information and techniques needed to diagnose and treat human injuries, diseases, and deformities. This includes symptoms, treatment alternatives, drug properties and interactions, and preventive health-care measures.
Engineering and Technology	Knowledge of the practical application of engineering science and technology. This includes applying principles, techniques, procedures, and equipment to the design and production of various goods and services.
Economics and Accounting	Knowledge of economic and accounting principles and practices, the financial markets, banking and the analysis and reporting of financial data.
Design	Knowledge of design techniques, tools, and principles involved in production of precision technical plans, blueprints, drawings, and models.
Chemistry	Knowledge of the chemical composition, structure, and properties of substances and of the chemical processes and transformations that they undergo. This includes uses of chemicals and their interactions, danger signs, production techniques, and disposal methods.
Production and Processing	Knowledge of raw materials, production processes, quality control, costs, and other techniques for maximizing the effective manufacture and distribution of goods.
Mechanical	Knowledge of machines and tools, including their designs, uses, repair, and maintenance.
Biology	Knowledge of plant and animal organisms, their tissues, cells, functions, interdependencies, and interactions with each other and the environment.
Physics	Knowledge and prediction of physical principles, laws, their interrelationships, and applications to understanding fluid, material, and atmospheric dynamics, and mechanical, electrical, atomic and sub-atomic structures and processes.
History and Archeology	Knowledge of historical events and their causes, indicators, and effects on civilizations and cultures.
Building and Construction	Knowledge of materials, methods, and the tools involved in the construction or repair of houses, buildings, or other structures such as highways and roads.
Sales and Marketing	Knowledge of principles and methods for showing, promoting, and selling products or services. This includes marketing strategy and tactics, product demonstration, sales techniques, and sales control systems.
Fine Arts	Knowledge of the theory and techniques required to compose, produce, and perform works of music, dance, visual arts, drama, and sculpture.
Food Production	Knowledge of techniques and equipment for planting, growing, and harvesting food products (both plant and animal) for consumption, including storage/handling techniques.

Skills	Skills Definitions
Active Listening	Giving full attention to what other people are saying, taking time to understand the points being made, asking questions as appropriate, and not interrupting at inappropriate times.
Writing	Communicating effectively in writing as appropriate for the needs of the audience.
Reading Comprehension	Understanding written sentences and paragraphs in work related documents.
Critical Thinking	Using logic and reasoning to identify the strengths and weaknesses of alternative solutions, conclusions or approaches to problems.
Speaking	Talking to others to convey information effectively.
Coordination	Adjusting actions in relation to others' actions.
Social Perceptiveness	Being aware of others' reactions and understanding why they react as they do.
Active Learning	Understanding the implications of new information for both current and future problem-solving and decision-making.
Persuasion	Persuading others to change their minds or behavior.
Time Management	Managing one's own time and the time of others.
Judgment and Decision Making	Considering the relative costs and benefits of potential actions to choose the most appropriate one.
Negotiation	Bringing others together and trying to reconcile differences.
Learning Strategies	Selecting and using training/instructional methods and procedures appropriate for the situation when learning or teaching new things.
Complex Problem Solving	Identifying complex problems and reviewing related information to develop and evaluate options and implement solutions.
Service Orientation	Actively looking for ways to help people.
Instructing	Teaching others how to do something.
Monitoring	Monitoring/Assessing performance of yourself, other individuals, or organizations to make improvements or take corrective action.
Equipment Selection	Determining the kind of tools and equipment needed to do a job.
Science	Using scientific rules and methods to solve problems.
Management of Personnel Resources	Motivating, developing, and directing people as they work, identifying the best people for the job.
Mathematics	Using mathematics to solve problems.
Equipment Maintenance	Performing routine maintenance on equipment and determining when and what kind of maintenance is needed.
Operations Analysis	Analyzing needs and product requirements to create a design.
Troubleshooting	Determining causes of operating errors and deciding what to do about it.
Technology Design	Generating or adapting equipment and technology to serve user needs.
Management of Material Resources	Obtaining and seeing to the appropriate use of equipment, facilities, and materials needed to do certain work.
Systems Evaluation	Identifying measures or indicators of system performance and the actions needed to improve or correct performance, relative to the goals of the system.
Management of Financial Resources	Determining how money will be spent to get the work done, and accounting for these expenditures.
Systems Analysis	Determining how a system should work and how changes in conditions, operations, and the environment will affect outcomes.
Operation and Control	Controlling operations of equipment or systems.
Quality Control Analysis	Conducting tests and inspections of products, services, or processes to evaluate quality or performance.

Operation Monitoring	Watching gauges, dials, or other indicators to make sure a machine is working properly.
Repairing	Repairing machines or systems using the needed tools.
Installation	Installing equipment, machines, wiring, or programs to meet specifications.
Programming	Writing computer programs for various purposes.

Ability	**Ability Definitions**
Inductive Reasoning	The ability to combine pieces of information to form general rules or conclusions (includes finding a relationship among seemingly unrelated events).
Oral Comprehension	The ability to listen to and understand information and ideas presented through spoken words and sentences.
Oral Expression	The ability to communicate information and ideas in speaking so others will understand.
Speech Recognition	The ability to identify and understand the speech of another person.
Information Ordering	The ability to arrange things or actions in a certain order or pattern according to a specific rule or set of rules (e.g., patterns of numbers, letters, words, pictures, mathematical operations).
Near Vision	The ability to see details at close range (within a few feet of the observer).
Deductive Reasoning	The ability to apply general rules to specific problems to produce answers that make sense.
Problem Sensitivity	The ability to tell when something is wrong or is likely to go wrong. It does not involve solving the problem, only recognizing there is a problem.
Speech Clarity	The ability to speak clearly so others can understand you.
Flexibility of Closure	The ability to identify or detect a known pattern (a figure, object, word, or sound) that is hidden in other distracting material.
Speed of Closure	The ability to quickly make sense of, combine, and organize information into meaningful patterns.
Written Comprehension	The ability to read and understand information and ideas presented in writing.
Written Expression	The ability to communicate information and ideas in writing so others will understand.
Selective Attention	The ability to concentrate on a task over a period of time without being distracted.
Originality	The ability to come up with unusual or clever ideas about a given topic or situation, or to develop creative ways to solve a problem.
Far Vision	The ability to see details at a distance.
Multilimb Coordination	The ability to coordinate two or more limbs (for example, two arms, two legs, or one leg and one arm) while sitting, standing, or lying down. It does not involve performing the activities while the whole body is in motion.
Fluency of Ideas	The ability to come up with a number of ideas about a topic (the number of ideas is important, not their quality, correctness, or creativity).
Time Sharing	The ability to shift back and forth between two or more activities or sources of information (such as speech, sounds, touch, or other sources).
Category Flexibility	The ability to generate or use different sets of rules for combining or grouping things in different ways.
Control Precision	The ability to quickly and repeatedly adjust the controls of a machine or a vehicle to exact positions.
Depth Perception	The ability to judge which of several objects is closer or farther away from you, or to judge the distance between you and an object.
Memorization	The ability to remember information such as words, numbers, pictures, and procedures.
Perceptual Speed	The ability to quickly and accurately compare similarities and differences among sets of letters, numbers, objects, pictures, or patterns. The things to be compared may be presented at the same time or one after the other. This ability also includes comparing a presented object with a remembered object.
Visualization	The ability to imagine how something will look after it is moved around or when its parts are moved or rearranged.
Reaction Time	The ability to quickly respond (with the hand, finger, or foot) to a signal (sound, light, picture) when it appears.
Finger Dexterity	The ability to make precisely coordinated movements of the fingers of one or both hands to grasp, manipulate, or assemble very small objects.
Arm-Hand Steadiness	The ability to keep your hand and arm steady while moving your arm or while holding your arm and hand in one position.
Visual Color Discrimination	The ability to match or detect differences between colors, including shades of color and brightness.
Response Orientation	The ability to choose quickly between two or more movements in response to two or more different signals (lights, sounds, pictures). It includes the speed with which the correct response is started with the hand, foot, or other body part.
Auditory Attention	The ability to focus on a single source of sound in the presence of other distracting sounds.

Static Strength	The ability to exert maximum muscle force to lift, push, pull, or carry objects.
Manual Dexterity	The ability to quickly move your hand, your hand together with your arm, or your two hands to grasp, manipulate, or assemble objects.
Spatial Orientation	The ability to know your location in relation to the environment or to know where other objects are in relation to you.
Stamina	The ability to exert yourself physically over long periods of time without getting winded or out of breath.
Gross Body Coordination	The ability to coordinate the movement of your arms, legs, and torso together when the whole body is in motion.
Explosive Strength	The ability to use short bursts of muscle force to propel oneself (as in jumping or sprinting), or to throw an object.
Rate Control	The ability to time your movements or the movement of a piece of equipment in anticipation of changes in the speed and/or direction of a moving object or scene.
Extent Flexibility	The ability to bend, stretch, twist, or reach with your body, arms, and/or legs.
Dynamic Strength	The ability to exert muscle force repeatedly or continuously over time. This involves muscular endurance and resistance to muscle fatigue.
Trunk Strength	The ability to use your abdominal and lower back muscles to support part of the body repeatedly or continuously over time without 'giving out' or fatiguing.
Night Vision	The ability to see under low light conditions.
Peripheral Vision	The ability to see objects or movement of objects to one's side when the eyes are looking ahead.
Speed of Limb Movement	The ability to quickly move the arms and legs.
Number Facility	The ability to add, subtract, multiply, or divide quickly and correctly.
Glare Sensitivity	The ability to see objects in the presence of glare or bright lighting.
Hearing Sensitivity	The ability to detect or tell the differences between sounds that vary in pitch and loudness.
Mathematical Reasoning	The ability to choose the right mathematical methods or formulas to solve a problem.
Gross Body Equilibrium	The ability to keep or regain your body balance or stay upright when in an unstable position.
Sound Localization	The ability to tell the direction from which a sound originated.
Wrist-Finger Speed	The ability to make fast, simple, repeated movements of the fingers, hands, and wrists.
Dynamic Flexibility	The ability to quickly and repeatedly bend, stretch, twist, or reach out with your body, arms, and/or legs.

Work_Activity	**Work_Activity Definitions**
Getting Information	Observing, receiving, and otherwise obtaining information from all relevant sources.
Identifying Objects, Actions, and Events	Identifying information by categorizing, estimating, recognizing differences or similarities, and detecting changes in circumstances or events.
Documenting/Recording Information	Entering, transcribing, recording, storing, or maintaining information in written or electronic/magnetic form.
Making Decisions and Solving Problems	Analyzing information and evaluating results to choose the best solution and solve problems.
Updating and Using Relevant Knowledge	Keeping up-to-date technically and applying new knowledge to your job.
Performing for or Working Directly with the Public	Performing for people or dealing directly with the public. This includes serving customers in restaurants and stores, and receiving clients or guests.
Communicating with Supervisors, Peers, or Subordin	Providing information to supervisors, co-workers, and subordinates by telephone, in written form, e-mail, or in person.
Processing Information	Compiling, coding, categorizing, calculating, tabulating, auditing, or verifying information or data.
Organizing, Planning, and Prioritizing Work	Developing specific goals and plans to prioritize, organize, and accomplish your work.
Interacting With Computers	Using computers and computer systems (including hardware and software) to program, write software, set up functions, enter data, or process information.
Communicating with Persons Outside Organization	Communicating with people outside the organization, representing the organization to customers, the public, government, and other external sources. This information can be exchanged in person, in writing, or by telephone or e-mail.
Analyzing Data or Information	Identifying the underlying principles, reasons, or facts of information by breaking down information or data into separate parts.
Establishing and Maintaining Interpersonal Relatio	Developing constructive and cooperative working relationships with others, and maintaining them over time.
Operating Vehicles, Mechanized Devices, or Equipme	Running, maneuvering, navigating, or driving vehicles or mechanized equipment, such as forklifts, passenger vehicles, aircraft, or water craft.
Evaluating Information to Determine Compliance wit	Using relevant information and individual judgment to determine whether events or processes comply with laws, regulations, or standards.

Monitor Processes, Materials, or Surroundings	Monitoring and reviewing information from materials, events, or the environment, to detect or assess problems.
Performing General Physical Activities	Performing physical activities that require considerable use of your arms and legs and moving your whole body, such as climbing, lifting, balancing, walking, stooping, and handling of materials.
Resolving Conflicts and Negotiating with Others	Handling complaints, settling disputes, and resolving grievances and conflicts, or otherwise negotiating with others.
Assisting and Caring for Others	Providing personal assistance, medical attention, emotional support, or other personal care to others such as coworkers, customers, or patients.
Training and Teaching Others	Identifying the educational needs of others, developing formal educational or training programs or classes, and teaching or instructing others.
Thinking Creatively	Developing, designing, or creating new applications, ideas, relationships, systems, or products, including artistic contributions.
Developing Objectives and Strategies	Establishing long-range objectives and specifying the strategies and actions to achieve them.
Interpreting the Meaning of Information for Others	Translating or explaining what information means and how it can be used.
Scheduling Work and Activities	Scheduling events, programs, and activities, as well as the work of others.
Judging the Qualities of Things, Services, or Peop	Assessing the value, importance, or quality of things or people.
Coordinating the Work and Activities of Others	Getting members of a group to work together to accomplish tasks.
Performing Administrative Activities	Performing day-to-day administrative tasks such as maintaining information files and processing paperwork.
Provide Consultation and Advice to Others	Providing guidance and expert advice to management or other groups on technical, systems-, or process-related topics.
Developing and Building Teams	Encouraging and building mutual trust, respect, and cooperation among team members.
Guiding, Directing, and Motivating Subordinates	Providing guidance and direction to subordinates, including setting performance standards and monitoring performance.
Inspecting Equipment, Structures, or Material	Inspecting equipment, structures, or materials to identify the cause of errors or other problems or defects.
Coaching and Developing Others	Identifying the developmental needs of others and coaching, mentoring, or otherwise helping others to improve their knowledge or skills.
Estimating the Quantifiable Characteristics of Pro	Estimating sizes, distances, and quantities; or determining time, costs, resources, or materials needed to perform a work activity.
Handling and Moving Objects	Using hands and arms in handling, installing, positioning, and moving materials, and manipulating things.
Monitoring and Controlling Resources	Monitoring and controlling resources and overseeing the spending of money.
Selling or Influencing Others	Convincing others to buy merchandise/goods or to otherwise change their minds or actions.
Controlling Machines and Processes	Using either control mechanisms or direct physical activity to operate machines or processes (not including computers or vehicles).
Staffing Organizational Units	Recruiting, interviewing, selecting, hiring, and promoting employees in an organization.
Repairing and Maintaining Electronic Equipment	Servicing, repairing, calibrating, regulating, fine-tuning, or testing machines, devices, and equipment that operate primarily on the basis of electrical or electronic (not mechanical) principles.
Drafting, Laying Out, and Specifying Technical Dev	Providing documentation, detailed instructions, drawings, or specifications to tell others about how devices, parts, equipment, or structures are to be fabricated, constructed, assembled, modified, maintained, or used.
Repairing and Maintaining Mechanical Equipment	Servicing, repairing, adjusting, and testing machines, devices, moving parts, and equipment that operate primarily on the basis of mechanical (not electronic) principles.

Work_Content	Work_Content Definitions
Telephone	How often do you have telephone conversations in this job?
In an Enclosed Vehicle or Equipment	How often does this job require working in a closed vehicle or equipment (e.g., car)?
Face-to-Face Discussions	How often do you have to have face-to-face discussions with individuals or teams in this job?
Contact With Others	How much does this job require the worker to be in contact with others (face-to-face, by telephone, or otherwise) in order to perform it?
Impact of Decisions on Co-workers or Company Resul	How do the decisions an employee makes impact the results of co-workers, clients or the company?
Freedom to Make Decisions	How much decision making freedom, without supervision, does the job offer?
Indoors, Environmentally Controlled	How often does this job require working indoors in environmentally controlled conditions?
Structured versus Unstructured Work	To what extent is this job structured for the worker, rather than allowing the worker to determine tasks, priorities, and goals?

Deal With External Customers	How important is it to work with external customers or the public in this job?
Importance of Being Exact or Accurate	How important is being very exact or highly accurate in performing this job?
Deal With Unpleasant or Angry People	How frequently does the worker have to deal with unpleasant, angry, or discourteous individuals as part of the job requirements?
Work With Work Group or Team	How important is it to work with others in a group or team in this job?
Letters and Memos	How often does the job require written letters and memos?
Frequency of Decision Making	How frequently is the worker required to make decisions that affect other people, the financial resources, and/or the image and reputation of the organization?
Consequence of Error	How serious would the result usually be if the worker made a mistake that was not readily correctable?
Outdoors, Exposed to Weather	How often does this job require working outdoors, exposed to all weather conditions?
Frequency of Conflict Situations	How often are there conflict situations the employee has to face in this job?
Coordinate or Lead Others	How important is it to coordinate or lead others in accomplishing work activities in this job?
Physical Proximity	To what extent does this job require the worker to perform job tasks in close physical proximity to other people?
Indoors, Not Environmentally Controlled	How often does this job require working indoors in non-controlled environmental conditions (e.g., warehouse without heat)?
Responsible for Others' Health and Safety	How much responsibility is there for the health and safety of others in this job?
Deal With Physically Aggressive People	How frequently does this job require the worker to deal with physical aggression of violent individuals?
Very Hot or Cold Temperatures	How often does this job require working in very hot (above 90 F degrees) or very cold (below 32 F degrees) temperatures?
Spend Time Sitting	How much does this job require sitting?
Electronic Mail	How often do you use electronic mail in this job?
Time Pressure	How often does this job require the worker to meet strict deadlines?
Importance of Repeating Same Tasks	How important is repeating the same physical activities (e.g., key entry) or mental activities (e.g., checking entries in a ledger) over and over, without stopping, to performing this job?
Outdoors, Under Cover	How often does this job require working outdoors, under cover (e.g., structure with roof but no walls)?
Level of Competition	To what extent does this job require the worker to compete or to be aware of competitive pressures?
Extremely Bright or Inadequate Lighting	How often does this job require working in extremely bright or inadequate lighting conditions?
Exposed to Hazardous Equipment	How often does this job require exposure to hazardous equipment?
Sounds, Noise Levels Are Distracting or Uncomforta	How often does this job require working exposed to sounds and noise levels that are distracting or uncomfortable?
Exposed to Contaminants	How often does this job require working exposed to contaminants (such as pollutants, gases, dust or odors)?
Exposed to Disease or Infections	How often does this job require exposure to disease/infections?
Responsibility for Outcomes and Results	How responsible is the worker for work outcomes and results of other workers?
Wear Common Protective or Safety Equipment such as	How much does this job require wearing common protective or safety equipment such as safety shoes, glasses, gloves, hard hats or live jackets?
Spend Time Standing	How much does this job require standing?
Public Speaking	How often do you have to perform public speaking in this job?
Degree of Automation	How automated is the job?
Spend Time Using Your Hands to Handle, Control, or	How much does this job require using your hands to handle, control, or feel objects, tools or controls?
Spend Time Walking and Running	How much does this job require walking and running?
Exposed to Hazardous Conditions	How often does this job require exposure to hazardous conditions?
Spend Time Making Repetitive Motions	How much does this job require making repetitive motions?
Spend Time Bending or Twisting the Body	How much does this job require bending or twisting your body?
Wear Specialized Protective or Safety Equipment su	How much does this job require wearing specialized protective or safety equipment such as breathing apparatus, safety harness, full protection suits, or radiation protection?
Exposed to Minor Burns, Cuts, Bites, or Stings	How often does this job require exposure to minor burns, cuts, bites, or stings?
Cramped Work Space, Awkward Positions	How often does this job require working in cramped work spaces that requires getting into awkward positions?
Spend Time Kneeling, Crouching, Stooping, or Crawl	How much does this job require kneeling, crouching, stooping or crawling?
Exposed to High Places	How often does this job require exposure to high places?
Spend Time Keeping or Regaining Balance	How much does this job require keeping or regaining your balance?

Pace Determined by Speed of Equipment	How important is it to this job that the pace is determined by the speed of equipment or machinery? (This does not refer to keeping busy at all times on this job.)
Spend Time Climbing Ladders, Scaffolds, or Poles	How much does this job require climbing ladders, scaffolds, or poles?
In an Open Vehicle or Equipment	How often does this job require working in an open vehicle or equipment (e.g., tractor)?
Exposed to Radiation	How often does this job require exposure to radiation?
Exposed to Whole Body Vibration	How often does this job require exposure to whole body vibration (e.g., operate a jackhammer)?

Work_Styles	**Work_Styles Definitions**
Integrity	Job requires being honest and ethical.
Self Control	Job requires maintaining composure, keeping emotions in check, controlling anger, and avoiding aggressive behavior, even in very difficult situations.
Dependability	Job requires being reliable, responsible, and dependable, and fulfilling obligations.
Attention to Detail	Job requires being careful about detail and thorough in completing work tasks.
Stress Tolerance	Job requires accepting criticism and dealing calmly and effectively with high stress situations.
Initiative	Job requires a willingness to take on responsibilities and challenges.
Adaptability/Flexibility	Job requires being open to change (positive or negative) and to considerable variety in the workplace.
Cooperation	Job requires being pleasant with others on the job and displaying a good-natured, cooperative attitude.
Persistence	Job requires persistence in the face of obstacles.
Analytical Thinking	Job requires analyzing information and using logic to address work-related issues and problems.
Independence	Job requires developing one's own ways of doing things, guiding oneself with little or no supervision, and depending on oneself to get things done.
Concern for Others	Job requires being sensitive to others' needs and feelings and being understanding and helpful on the job.
Leadership	Job requires a willingness to lead, take charge, and offer opinions and direction.
Achievement/Effort	Job requires establishing and maintaining personally challenging achievement goals and exerting effort toward mastering tasks.
Innovation	Job requires creativity and alternative thinking to develop new ideas for and answers to work-related problems.
Social Orientation	Job requires preferring to work with others rather than alone, and being personally connected with others on the job.

Job Zone Component	**Job Zone Component Definitions**
Title	Job Zone Four: Considerable Preparation Needed
Overall Experience	A minimum of two to four years of work-related skill, knowledge, or experience is needed for these occupations. For example, an accountant must complete four years of college and work for several years in accounting to be considered qualified.
Job Training	Employees in these occupations usually need several years of work-related experience, on-the-job training, and/or vocational training.
Job Zone Examples	Many of these occupations involve coordinating, supervising, managing, or training others. Examples include accountants, chefs and head cooks, computer programmers, historians, pharmacists, and police detectives.
SVP Range	(7.0 to < 8.0)
Education	Most of these occupations require a four - year bachelor's degree, but some do not.

33-3021.02 - Police Identification and Records Officers

Collect evidence at crime scene, classify and identify fingerprints, and photograph evidence for use in criminal and civil cases.

Tasks

1) Process film and prints from crime or accident scenes.

2) Testify in court and present evidence.

3) Submit evidence to supervisors.

4) Photograph crime or accident scenes for evidence records.

5) Package, store and retrieve evidence.

6) Look for trace evidence, such as fingerprints, hairs, fibers, or shoe impressions, using alternative light sources when necessary.

7) Identify, classify, and file fingerprints, using systems such as the Henry Classification

system.

8) Analyze and process evidence at crime scenes and in the laboratory, wearing protective equipment and using powders and chemicals.

9) Serve as technical advisor and coordinate with other law enforcement workers to exchange information on crime scene collection activities.

10) Dust selected areas of crime scene and lift latent fingerprints, adhering to proper preservation procedures.

33-3021.03 - Criminal Investigators and Special Agents

Investigate alleged or suspected criminal violations of Federal, state, or local laws to determine if evidence is sufficient to recommend prosecution.

Tasks

1) Perform undercover assignments and maintain surveillance, including monitoring authorized wiretaps.

2) Develop relationships with informants in order to obtain information related to cases.

3) Collaborate with other authorities on activities such as surveillance, transcription and research.

4) Manage security programs designed to protect personnel, facilities, and information.

5) Prepare reports that detail investigation findings.

6) Collect and record physical information about arrested suspects, including fingerprints, height and weight measurements, and photographs.

7) Obtain and verify evidence by interviewing and observing suspects and witnesses, or by analyzing records.

8) Obtain and use search and arrest warrants.

9) Examine records in order to locate links in chains of evidence or information.

10) Collaborate with other offices and agencies in order to exchange information and coordinate activities.

11) Determine scope, timing, and direction of investigations.

12) Administer counter-terrorism and counter-narcotics reward programs.

13) Analyze evidence in laboratories, or in the field.

14) Search for and collect evidence such as fingerprints, using investigative equipment.

15) Issue security clearances.

16) Testify before grand juries concerning criminal activity investigations.

17) Serve subpoenas or other official papers.

18) Record evidence and documents, using equipment such as cameras and photocopy machines.

19) Investigate organized crime, public corruption, financial crime, copyright infringement, civil rights violations, bank robbery, extortion, kidnapping, and other violations of federal or state statutes.

20) Compare crime scene fingerprints with those from suspects or fingerprint files to identify perpetrators, using computers.

21) Identify case issues and evidence needed, based on analysis of charges, complaints, or allegations of law violations.

22) Provide protection for individuals such as government leaders, political candidates and visiting foreign dignitaries.

33-3021.05 - Immigration and Customs Inspectors

Investigate and inspect persons, common carriers, goods, and merchandise, arriving in or departing from the United States or between states to detect violations of immigration and customs laws and regulations.

Tasks

1) Determine duty and taxes to be paid on goods.

2) Locate and seize contraband, undeclared merchandise, and vehicles, aircraft, or boats that contain such merchandise.

3) Investigate applications for duty refunds, and petition for remission or mitigation of penalties when warranted.

4) Detain persons found to be in violation of customs or immigration laws, and arrange for legal action such as deportation.

5) Examine immigration applications, visas, and passports, and interview persons in order to

determine eligibility for admission, residence, and travel in U.S.

6) Inspect cargo, baggage, and personal articles entering or leaving U.S. for compliance with revenue laws and U.S. Customs Service regulations.

7) Record and report job-related activities, findings, transactions, violations, discrepancies, and decisions.

8) Institute civil and criminal prosecutions, and cooperate with other law enforcement agencies in the investigation and prosecution of those in violation of immigration or customs laws.

9) Interpret and explain laws and regulations to travelers, prospective immigrants, shippers, and manufacturers.

10) Collect samples of merchandise for examination, appraisal, or testing.

33-3041.00 - Parking Enforcement Workers

Patrol assigned area, such as public parking lot or section of city to issue tickets to overtime parking violators and illegally parked vehicles.

Tasks

1) Assign and review the work of subordinates.

2) Mark tires of parked vehicles with chalk and record time of marking, and return at regular intervals to ensure that parking time limits are not exceeded.

3) Remove handbills within patrol areas.

4) Enter and retrieve information pertaining to vehicle registration, identification, and status, using handheld computers.

5) Deliver money to be used as change at attended parking facilities.

6) Collect coins deposited in meters.

7) Appear in court at hearings regarding contested traffic citations.

8) Train new or temporary staff.

9) Perform traffic control duties such as setting up barricades and temporary signs, placing bags on parking meters to limit their use, or directing traffic.

10) Identify vehicles in violation of parking codes, checking with dispatchers when necessary to confirm identities or to determine whether vehicles need to be booted or towed.

11) Prepare and maintain required records, including logs of parking enforcement activities, and records of contested citations.

12) Investigate and answer complaints regarding contested parking citations, determining their validity and routing them appropriately.

13) Maintain close communications with dispatching personnel, using two-way radios or cell phones.

14) Locate lost, stolen, and counterfeit parking permits, and take necessary enforcement action.

15) Respond to and make radio dispatch calls regarding parking violations and complaints.

16) Maintain assigned equipment and supplies such as handheld citation computers, citation books, rain gear, tire-marking chalk, and street cones.

17) Provide information to the public regarding parking regulations and facilities, and the location of streets, buildings and points of interest.

18) Provide assistance to motorists needing help with problems, such as flat tires, keys locked in cars, or dead batteries.

19) Wind parking meter clocks.

20) Perform simple vehicle maintenance procedures such as checking oil and gas, and report mechanical problems to supervisors.

21) Observe and report hazardous conditions such as missing traffic signals or signs, and street markings that need to be repainted.

22) Make arrangements for illegally parked or abandoned vehicles to be towed, and direct tow-truck drivers to the correct vehicles.

23) Write warnings and citations for illegally parked vehicles.

33-3051.01 - Police Patrol Officers

Patrol assigned area to enforce laws and ordinances, regulate traffic, control crowds, prevent crime, and arrest violators.

Tasks

1) Record facts to prepare reports that document incidents and activities.

2) Issue citations or warnings to violators of motor vehicle ordinances.

3) Testify in court to present evidence or act as witness in traffic and criminal cases.

4) Review facts of incidents to determine if criminal act or statute violations were involved.

5) Monitor traffic to ensure motorists observe traffic regulations and exhibit safe driving procedures.

6) Direct traffic flow and reroute traffic in case of emergencies.

7) Photograph or draw diagrams of crime or accident scenes and interview principals and eyewitnesses.

8) Investigate traffic accidents and other accidents to determine causes and to determine if a crime has been committed.

9) Provide road information to assist motorists.

10) Render aid to accident victims and other persons requiring first aid for physical injuries.

11) Patrol specific area on foot, horseback, or motorized conveyance, responding promptly to calls for assistance.

12) Inform citizens of community services and recommend options to facilitate longer-term problem resolution.

13) Relay complaint and emergency-request information to appropriate agency dispatchers.

14) Evaluate complaint and emergency-request information to determine response requirements.

15) Act as official escorts, such as when leading funeral processions or firefighters.

16) Inspect public establishments to ensure compliance with rules and regulations.

17) Process prisoners, and prepare and maintain records of prisoner bookings and prisoner status during booking and pre-trial process.

18) Identify, pursue, and arrest suspects and perpetrators of criminal acts.

19) Provide for public safety by maintaining order, responding to emergencies, protecting people and property, enforcing motor vehicle and criminal laws, and promoting good community relations.

Knowledge	Knowledge Definitions
Law and Government	Knowledge of laws, legal codes, court procedures, precedents, government regulations, executive orders, agency rules, and the democratic political process.
Public Safety and Security	Knowledge of relevant equipment, policies, procedures, and strategies to promote effective local, state, or national security operations for the protection of people, data, property, and institutions.
English Language	Knowledge of the structure and content of the English language including the meaning and spelling of words, rules of composition, and grammar.
Customer and Personal Service	Knowledge of principles and processes for providing customer and personal services. This includes customer needs assessment, meeting quality standards for services, and evaluation of customer satisfaction.
Education and Training	Knowledge of principles and methods for curriculum and training design, teaching and instruction for individuals and groups, and the measurement of training effects.
Psychology	Knowledge of human behavior and performance; individual differences in ability, personality, and interests; learning and motivation; psychological research methods; and the assessment and treatment of behavioral and affective disorders.
Administration and Management	Knowledge of business and management principles involved in strategic planning, resource allocation, human resources modeling, leadership technique, production methods, and coordination of people and resources.
Telecommunications	Knowledge of transmission, broadcasting, switching, control, and operation of telecommunications systems.
Transportation	Knowledge of principles and methods for moving people or goods by air, rail, sea, or road, including the relative costs and benefits.
Clerical	Knowledge of administrative and clerical procedures and systems such as word processing, managing files and records, stenography and transcription, designing forms, and other office procedures and terminology.
Sociology and Anthropology	Knowledge of group behavior and dynamics, societal trends and influences, human migrations, ethnicity, cultures and their history and origins.
Computers and Electronics	Knowledge of circuit boards, processors, chips, electronic equipment, and computer hardware and software, including applications and programming.
Mathematics	Knowledge of arithmetic, algebra, geometry, calculus, statistics, and their applications.
Geography	Knowledge of principles and methods for describing the features of land, sea, and air masses, including their physical characteristics, locations, interrelationships, and distribution of plant, animal, and human life.

Communications and Media	Knowledge of media production, communication, and dissemination techniques and methods. This includes alternative ways to inform and entertain via written, oral, and visual media.
Therapy and Counseling	Knowledge of principles, methods, and procedures for diagnosis, treatment, and rehabilitation of physical and mental dysfunctions, and for career counseling and guidance.
Personnel and Human Resources	Knowledge of principles and procedures for personnel recruitment, selection, training, compensation and benefits, labor relations and negotiation, and personnel information systems.
Philosophy and Theology	Knowledge of different philosophical systems and religions. This includes their basic principles, values, ethics, ways of thinking, customs, practices, and their impact on human culture.
Foreign Language	Knowledge of the structure and content of a foreign (non-English) language including the meaning and spelling of words, rules of composition and grammar, and pronunciation.
Medicine and Dentistry	Knowledge of the information and techniques needed to diagnose and treat human injuries, diseases, and deformities. This includes symptoms, treatment alternatives, drug properties and interactions, and preventive health-care measures.
Chemistry	Knowledge of the chemical composition, structure, and properties of substances and of the chemical processes and transformations that they undergo. This includes uses of chemicals and their interactions, danger signs, production techniques, and disposal methods.
Physics	Knowledge and prediction of physical principles, laws, their interrelationships, and applications to understanding fluid, material, and atmospheric dynamics, and mechanical, electrical, atomic and sub-atomic structures and processes.
History and Archeology	Knowledge of historical events and their causes, indicators, and effects on civilizations and cultures.
Economics and Accounting	Knowledge of economic and accounting principles and practices, the financial markets, banking and the analysis and reporting of financial data.
Mechanical	Knowledge of machines and tools, including their designs, uses, repair, and maintenance.
Biology	Knowledge of plant and animal organisms, their tissues, cells, functions, interdependencies, and interactions with each other and the environment.
Design	Knowledge of design techniques, tools, and principles involved in production of precision technical plans, blueprints, drawings, and models.
Building and Construction	Knowledge of materials, methods, and the tools involved in the construction or repair of houses, buildings, or other structures such as highways and roads.
Engineering and Technology	Knowledge of the practical application of engineering science and technology. This includes applying principles, techniques, procedures, and equipment to the design and production of various goods and services.
Production and Processing	Knowledge of raw materials, production processes, quality control, costs, and other techniques for maximizing the effective manufacture and distribution of goods.
Sales and Marketing	Knowledge of principles and methods for showing, promoting, and selling products or services. This includes marketing strategy and tactics, product demonstration, sales techniques, and sales control systems.
Fine Arts	Knowledge of the theory and techniques required to compose, produce, and perform works of music, dance, visual arts, drama, and sculpture.
Food Production	Knowledge of techniques and equipment for planting, growing, and harvesting food products (both plant and animal) for consumption, including storage/handling techniques.

Skills	Skills Definitions
Judgment and Decision Making	Considering the relative costs and benefits of potential actions to choose the most appropriate one.
Active Listening	Giving full attention to what other people are saying, taking time to understand the points being made, asking questions as appropriate, and not interrupting at inappropriate times.
Critical Thinking	Using logic and reasoning to identify the strengths and weaknesses of alternative solutions, conclusions or approaches to problems.
Writing	Communicating effectively in writing as appropriate for the needs of the audience.
Speaking	Talking to others to convey information effectively.
Social Perceptiveness	Being aware of others' reactions and understanding why they react as they do.
Reading Comprehension	Understanding written sentences and paragraphs in work related documents.
Negotiation	Bringing others together and trying to reconcile differences.
Persuasion	Persuading others to change their minds or behavior.
Active Learning	Understanding the implications of new information for both current and future problem-solving and decision-making.
Coordination	Adjusting actions in relation to others' actions.

Complex Problem Solving	Identifying complex problems and reviewing related information to develop and evaluate options and implement solutions.
Service Orientation	Actively looking for ways to help people.
Time Management	Managing one's own time and the time of others.
Learning Strategies	Selecting and using training/instructional methods and procedures appropriate for the situation when learning or teaching new things.
Instructing	Teaching others how to do something.
Monitoring	Monitoring/Assessing performance of yourself, other individuals, or organizations to make improvements or take corrective action.
Equipment Selection	Determining the kind of tools and equipment needed to do a job.
Equipment Maintenance	Performing routine maintenance on equipment and determining when and what kind of maintenance is needed.
Management of Personnel Resources	Motivating, developing, and directing people as they work, identifying the best people for the job.
Troubleshooting	Determining causes of operating errors and deciding what to do about it.
Operations Analysis	Analyzing needs and product requirements to create a design.
Operation and Control	Controlling operations of equipment or systems.
Mathematics	Using mathematics to solve problems.
Operation Monitoring	Watching gauges, dials, or other indicators to make sure a machine is working properly.
Technology Design	Generating or adapting equipment and technology to serve user needs.
Quality Control Analysis	Conducting tests and inspections of products, services, or processes to evaluate quality or performance.
Science	Using scientific rules and methods to solve problems.
Systems Evaluation	Identifying measures or indicators of system performance and the actions needed to improve or correct performance, relative to the goals of the system.
Management of Material Resources	Obtaining and seeing to the appropriate use of equipment, facilities, and materials needed to do certain work.
Systems Analysis	Determining how a system should work and how changes in conditions, operations, and the environment will affect outcomes.
Repairing	Repairing machines or systems using the needed tools.
Installation	Installing equipment, machines, wiring, or programs to meet specifications.
Management of Financial Resources	Determining how money will be spent to get the work done, and accounting for these expenditures.
Programming	Writing computer programs for various purposes.

Ability	Ability Definitions
Inductive Reasoning	The ability to combine pieces of information to form general rules or conclusions (includes finding a relationship among seemingly unrelated events).
Oral Comprehension	The ability to listen to and understand information and ideas presented through spoken words and sentences.
Near Vision	The ability to see details at close range (within a few feet of the observer).
Oral Expression	The ability to communicate information and ideas in speaking so others will understand.
Far Vision	The ability to see details at a distance.
Speech Clarity	The ability to speak clearly so others can understand you.
Problem Sensitivity	The ability to tell when something is wrong or is likely to go wrong. It does not involve solving the problem, only recognizing there is a problem.
Deductive Reasoning	The ability to apply general rules to specific problems to produce answers that make sense.
Speech Recognition	The ability to identify and understand the speech of another person.
Reaction Time	The ability to quickly respond (with the hand, finger, or foot) to a signal (sound, light, picture) when it appears.
Flexibility of Closure	The ability to identify or detect a known pattern (a figure, object, word, or sound) that is hidden in other distracting material.
Response Orientation	The ability to choose quickly between two or more movements in response to two or more different signals (lights, sounds, pictures). It includes the speed with which the correct response is started with the hand, foot, or other body part.
Speed of Closure	The ability to quickly make sense of, combine, and organize information into meaningful patterns.
Time Sharing	The ability to shift back and forth between two or more activities or sources of information (such as speech, sounds, touch, or other sources).
Selective Attention	The ability to concentrate on a task over a period of time without being distracted.
Information Ordering	The ability to arrange things or actions in a certain order or pattern according to a specific rule or set of rules (e.g., patterns of numbers, letters, words, pictures, mathematical operations).
Control Precision	The ability to quickly and repeatedly adjust the controls of a machine or a vehicle to exact positions.

Multilimb Coordination	The ability to coordinate two or more limbs (for example, two arms, two legs, or one leg and one arm) while sitting, standing, or lying down. It does not involve performing the activities while the whole body is in motion.
Written Comprehension	The ability to read and understand information and ideas presented in writing.
Written Expression	The ability to communicate information and ideas in writing so others will understand.
Rate Control	The ability to time your movements or the movement of a piece of equipment in anticipation of changes in the speed and/or direction of a moving object or scene.
Perceptual Speed	The ability to quickly and accurately compare similarities and differences among sets of letters, numbers, objects, pictures, or patterns. The things to be compared may be presented at the same time or one after the other. This ability also includes comparing a presented object with a remembered object.
Spatial Orientation	The ability to know your location in relation to the environment or to know where other objects are in relation to you.
Depth Perception	The ability to judge which of several objects is closer or farther away from you, or to judge the distance between you and an object.
Category Flexibility	The ability to generate or use different sets of rules for combining or grouping things in different ways.
Speed of Limb Movement	The ability to quickly move the arms and legs.
Night Vision	The ability to see under low light conditions.
Peripheral Vision	The ability to see objects or movement of objects to one's side when the eyes are looking ahead.
Static Strength	The ability to exert maximum muscle force to lift, push, pull, or carry objects.
Stamina	The ability to exert yourself physically over long periods of time without getting winded or out of breath.
Arm-Hand Steadiness	The ability to keep your hand and arm steady while moving your arm or while holding your arm and hand in one position.
Gross Body Coordination	The ability to coordinate the movement of your arms, legs, and torso together when the whole body is in motion.
Gross Body Equilibrium	The ability to keep or regain your body balance or stay upright when in an unstable position.
Visualization	The ability to imagine how something will look after it is moved around or when its parts are moved or rearranged.
Finger Dexterity	The ability to make precisely coordinated movements of the fingers of one or both hands to grasp, manipulate, or assemble very small objects.
Explosive Strength	The ability to use short bursts of muscle force to propel oneself (as in jumping or sprinting), or to throw an object.
Glare Sensitivity	The ability to see objects in the presence of glare or bright lighting.
Manual Dexterity	The ability to quickly move your hand, your hand together with your arm, or your two hands to grasp, manipulate, or assemble objects.
Auditory Attention	The ability to focus on a single source of sound in the presence of other distracting sounds.
Memorization	The ability to remember information such as words, numbers, pictures, and procedures.
Originality	The ability to come up with unusual or clever ideas about a given topic or situation, or to develop creative ways to solve a problem.
Fluency of Ideas	The ability to come up with a number of ideas about a topic (the number of ideas is important, not their quality, correctness, or creativity).
Visual Color Discrimination	The ability to match or detect differences between colors, including shades of color and brightness.
Trunk Strength	The ability to use your abdominal and lower back muscles to support part of the body repeatedly or continuously over time without 'giving out' or fatiguing.
Dynamic Strength	The ability to exert muscle force repeatedly or continuously over time. This involves muscular endurance and resistance to muscle fatigue.
Sound Localization	The ability to tell the direction from which a sound originated.
Hearing Sensitivity	The ability to detect or tell the differences between sounds that vary in pitch and loudness.
Extent Flexibility	The ability to bend, stretch, twist, or reach with your body, arms, and/or legs.
Mathematical Reasoning	The ability to choose the right mathematical methods or formulas to solve a problem.
Number Facility	The ability to add, subtract, multiply, or divide quickly and correctly.
Wrist-Finger Speed	The ability to make fast, simple, repeated movements of the fingers, hands, and wrists.
Dynamic Flexibility	The ability to quickly and repeatedly bend, stretch, twist, or reach out with your body, arms, and/or legs.

Work_Activity	Work_Activity Definitions
Getting Information	Observing, receiving, and otherwise obtaining information from all relevant sources.

Performing for or Working Directly with the Public	Performing for people or dealing directly with the public. This includes serving customers in restaurants and stores, and receiving clients or guests.
Operating Vehicles, Mechanized Devices, or Equipme	Running, maneuvering, navigating, or driving vehicles or mechanized equipment, such as forklifts, passenger vehicles, aircraft, or water craft.
Resolving Conflicts and Negotiating with Others	Handling complaints, settling disputes, and resolving grievances and conflicts, or otherwise negotiating with others.
Identifying Objects, Actions, and Events	Identifying information by categorizing, estimating, recognizing differences or similarities, and detecting changes in circumstances or events.
Making Decisions and Solving Problems	Analyzing information and evaluating results to choose the best solution and solve problems.
Communicating with Supervisors, Peers, or Subordin	Providing information to supervisors, co-workers, and subordinates by telephone, in written form, e-mail, or in person.
Communicating with Persons Outside Organization	Communicating with people outside the organization, representing the organization to customers, the public, government, and other external sources. This information can be exchanged in person, in writing, or by telephone or e-mail.
Evaluating Information to Determine Compliance wit	Using relevant information and individual judgment to determine whether events or processes comply with laws, regulations, or standards.
Documenting/Recording Information	Entering, transcribing, recording, storing, or maintaining information in written or electronic/magnetic form.
Monitor Processes, Materials, or Surroundings	Monitoring and reviewing information from materials, events, or the environment, to detect or assess problems.
Performing General Physical Activities	Performing physical activities that require considerable use of your arms and legs and moving your whole body, such as climbing, lifting, balancing, walking, stooping, and handling of materials.
Establishing and Maintaining Interpersonal Relatio	Developing constructive and cooperative working relationships with others, and maintaining them over time.
Assisting and Caring for Others	Providing personal assistance, medical attention, emotional support, or other personal care to others such as coworkers, customers, or patients.
Updating and Using Relevant Knowledge	Keeping up-to-date technically and applying new knowledge to your job.
Analyzing Data or Information	Identifying the underlying principles, reasons, or facts of information by breaking down information or data into separate parts.
Training and Teaching Others	Identifying the educational needs of others, developing formal educational or training programs or classes, and teaching or instructing others.
Processing Information	Compiling, coding, categorizing, calculating, tabulating, auditing, or verifying information or data.
Inspecting Equipment, Structures, or Material	Inspecting equipment, structures, or materials to identify the cause of errors or other problems or defects.
Interacting With Computers	Using computers and computer systems (including hardware and software) to program, write software, set up functions, enter data, or process information.
Judging the Qualities of Things, Services, or Peop	Assessing the value, importance, or quality of things or people.
Interpreting the Meaning of Information for Others	Translating or explaining what information means and how it can be used.
Organizing, Planning, and Prioritizing Work	Developing specific goals and plans to prioritize, organize, and accomplish your work.
Performing Administrative Activities	Performing day-to-day administrative tasks such as maintaining information files and processing paperwork.
Thinking Creatively	Developing, designing, or creating new applications, ideas, relationships, systems, or products, including artistic contributions.
Developing and Building Teams	Encouraging and building mutual trust, respect, and cooperation among team members.
Coaching and Developing Others	Identifying the developmental needs of others and coaching, mentoring, or otherwise helping others to improve their knowledge or skills.
Handling and Moving Objects	Using hands and arms in handling, installing, positioning, and moving materials, and manipulating things.
Scheduling Work and Activities	Scheduling events, programs, and activities, as well as the work of others.
Guiding, Directing, and Motivating Subordinates	Providing guidance and direction to subordinates, including setting performance standards and monitoring performance.
Estimating the Quantifiable Characteristics of Pro	Estimating sizes, distances, and quantities; or determining time, costs, resources, or materials needed to perform a work activity.
Coordinating the Work and Activities of Others	Getting members of a group to work together to accomplish tasks.
Selling or Influencing Others	Convincing others to buy merchandise/goods or to otherwise change their minds or actions.
Developing Objectives and Strategies	Establishing long-range objectives and specifying the strategies and actions to achieve them.
Provide Consultation and Advice to Others	Providing guidance and expert advice to management or other groups on technical, systems-, or process-related topics.

Controlling Machines and Processes	Using either control mechanisms or direct physical activity to operate machines or processes (not including computers or vehicles).
Monitoring and Controlling Resources	Monitoring and controlling resources and overseeing the spending of money.
Staffing Organizational Units	Recruiting, interviewing, selecting, hiring, and promoting employees in an organization.
Repairing and Maintaining Electronic Equipment	Servicing, repairing, calibrating, regulating, fine-tuning, or testing machines, devices, and equipment that operate primarily on the basis of electrical or electronic (not mechanical) principles.
Drafting, Laying Out, and Specifying Technical Dev	Providing documentation, detailed instructions, drawings, or specifications to tell others about how devices, parts, equipment, or structures are to be fabricated, constructed, assembled, modified, maintained, or used.
Repairing and Maintaining Mechanical Equipment	Servicing, repairing, adjusting, and testing machines, devices, moving parts, and equipment that operate primarily on the basis of mechanical (not electronic) principles.

Work_Content	Work_Content Definitions
In an Enclosed Vehicle or Equipment	How often does this job require working in a closed vehicle or equipment (e.g., car)?
Face-to-Face Discussions	How often do you have to have face-to-face discussions with individuals or teams in this job?
Deal With External Customers	How important is it to work with external customers or the public in this job?
Contact With Others	How much does this job require the worker to be in contact with others (face-to-face, by telephone, or otherwise) in order to perform it?
Freedom to Make Decisions	How much decision making freedom, without supervision, does the job offer?
Frequency of Conflict Situations	How often are there conflict situations the employee has to face in this job?
Frequency of Decision Making	How frequently is the worker required to make decisions that affect other people, the financial resources, and/or the image and reputation of the organization?
Work With Work Group or Team	How important is it to work with others in a group or team in this job?
Deal With Unpleasant or Angry People	How frequently does the worker have to deal with unpleasant, angry, or discourteous individuals as part of the job requirements?
Outdoors, Exposed to Weather	How often does this job require working outdoors, exposed to all weather conditions?
Impact of Decisions on Co-workers or Company Resul	How do the decisions an employee makes impact the results of co-workers, clients or the company?
Importance of Being Exact or Accurate	How important is being very exact or highly accurate in performing this job?
Structured versus Unstructured Work	To what extent is this job structured for the worker, rather than allowing the worker to determine tasks, priorities, and goals?
Telephone	How often do you have telephone conversations in this job?
Exposed to Contaminants	How often does this job require working exposed to contaminants (such as pollutants, gases, dust or odors)?
Letters and Memos	How often does the job require written letters and memos?
Exposed to Hazardous Equipment	How often does this job require exposure to hazardous equipment?
Consequence of Error	How serious would the result usually be if the worker made a mistake that was not readily correctable?
Physical Proximity	To what extent does this job require the worker to perform job tasks in close physical proximity to other people?
Wear Common Protective or Safety Equipment such as	How much does this job require wearing common protective or safety equipment such as safety shoes, glasses, gloves, hard hats or live jackets?
Responsible for Others' Health and Safety	How much responsibility is there for the health and safety of others in this job?
Sounds, Noise Levels Are Distracting or Uncomforta	How often does this job require working exposed to sounds and noise levels that are distracting or uncomfortable?
Deal With Physically Aggressive People	How frequently does this job require the worker to deal with physical aggression of violent individuals?
Coordinate or Lead Others	How important is it to coordinate or lead others in accomplishing work activities in this job?
Spend Time Using Your Hands to Handle, Control, or	How much does this job require using your hands to handle, control, or feel objects, tools or controls?
Time Pressure	How often does this job require the worker to meet strict deadlines?
Very Hot or Cold Temperatures	How often does this job require working in very hot (above 90 F degrees) or very cold (below 32 F degrees) temperatures?
Exposed to Disease or Infections	How often does this job require exposure to disease/infections?
Importance of Repeating Same Tasks	How important is repeating the same physical activities (e.g., key entry) or mental activities (e.g., checking entries in a ledger) over and over, without stopping, to performing this job?
Electronic Mail	How often do you use electronic mail in this job?

Extremely Bright or Inadequate Lighting	How often does this job require working in extremely bright or inadequate lighting conditions?
Wear Specialized Protective or Safety Equipment su	How much does this job require wearing specialized protective or safety equipment such as breathing apparatus, safety harness, full protection suits, or radiation protection?
Spend Time Sitting	How much does this job require sitting?
Level of Competition	To what extent does this job require the worker to compete or to be aware of competitive pressures?
Exposed to Hazardous Conditions	How often does this job require exposure to hazardous conditions?
Responsibility for Outcomes and Results	How responsible is the worker for work outcomes and results of other workers?
Spend Time Making Repetitive Motions	How much does this job require making repetitive motions?
Spend Time Standing	How much does this job require standing?
Indoors, Not Environmentally Controlled	How often does this job require working indoors in non-controlled environmental conditions (e.g., warehouse without heat)?
Exposed to Minor Burns, Cuts, Bites, or Stings	How often does this job require exposure to minor burns, cuts, bites, or stings?
Indoors, Environmentally Controlled	How often does this job require working indoors in environmentally controlled conditions?
Public Speaking	How often do you have to perform public speaking in this job?
Degree of Automation	How automated is the job?
Spend Time Walking and Running	How much does this job require walking and running?
Spend Time Bending or Twisting the Body	How much does this job require bending or twisting your body?
Outdoors, Under Cover	How often does this job require working outdoors, under cover (e.g., structure with roof but no walls)?
Cramped Work Space, Awkward Positions	How often does this job require working in cramped work spaces that requires getting into awkward positions?
Exposed to High Places	How often does this job require exposure to high places?
Spend Time Keeping or Regaining Balance	How much does this job require keeping or regaining your balance?
Spend Time Kneeling, Crouching, Stooping, or Crawl	How much does this job require kneeling, crouching, stooping or crawling?
Spend Time Climbing Ladders, Scaffolds, or Poles	How much does this job require climbing ladders, scaffolds, or poles?
Exposed to Radiation	How often does this job require exposure to radiation?
Pace Determined by Speed of Equipment	How important is it to this job that the pace is determined by the speed of equipment or machinery? (This does not refer to keeping busy at all times on this job.)
In an Open Vehicle or Equipment	How often does this job require working in an open vehicle or equipment (e.g., tractor)?
Exposed to Whole Body Vibration	How often does this job require exposure to whole body vibration (e.g., operate a jackhammer)?

Work_Styles	Work_Styles Definitions
Self Control	Job requires maintaining composure, keeping emotions in check, controlling anger, and avoiding aggressive behavior, even in very difficult situations.
Integrity	Job requires being honest and ethical.
Stress Tolerance	Job requires accepting criticism and dealing calmly and effectively with high stress situations.
Attention to Detail	Job requires being careful about detail and thorough in completing work tasks.
Dependability	Job requires being reliable, responsible, and dependable, and fulfilling obligations.
Concern for Others	Job requires being sensitive to others' needs and feelings and being understanding and helpful on the job.
Independence	Job requires developing one's own ways of doing things, guiding oneself with little or no supervision, and depending on oneself to get things done.
Initiative	Job requires a willingness to take on responsibilities and challenges.
Cooperation	Job requires being pleasant with others on the job and displaying a good-natured, cooperative attitude.
Adaptability/Flexibility	Job requires being open to change (positive or negative) and to considerable variety in the workplace.
Leadership	Job requires a willingness to lead, take charge, and offer opinions and direction.
Persistence	Job requires persistence in the face of obstacles.
Analytical Thinking	Job requires analyzing information and using logic to address work-related issues and problems.
Social Orientation	Job requires preferring to work with others rather than alone, and being personally connected with others on the job.
Achievement/Effort	Job requires establishing and maintaining personally challenging achievement goals and exerting effort toward mastering tasks.
Innovation	Job requires creativity and alternative thinking to develop new ideas for and answers to work-related problems.

Job Zone Component	Job Zone Component Definitions
Title	Job Zone Three: Medium Preparation Needed
Overall Experience	Previous work-related skill, knowledge, or experience is required for these occupations. For example, an electrician must have completed three or four years of apprenticeship or several years of vocational training, and often must have passed a licensing exam, in order to perform the job.
Job Training	Employees in these occupations usually need one or two years of training involving both on-the-job experience and informal training with experienced workers.
Job Zone Examples	These occupations usually involve using communication and organizational skills to coordinate, supervise, manage, or train others to accomplish goals. Examples include dental assistants, electricians, fish and game wardens, legal secretaries, personnel recruiters, and recreation workers.
SVP Range	(6.0 to < 7.0)
Education	Most occupations in this zone require training in vocational schools, related on-the-job experience, or an associate's degree. Some may require a bachelor's degree.

33-3052.00 - Transit and Railroad Police

Protect and police railroad and transit property, employees, or passengers.

Tasks

1) Investigate or direct investigations of freight theft, suspicious damage or loss of passengers' valuables, and other crimes on railroad property.

2) Apprehend or remove trespassers or thieves from railroad property, or coordinate with law enforcement agencies in apprehensions and removals.

3) Direct and coordinate the daily activities and training of security staff.

4) Examine credentials of unauthorized persons attempting to enter secured areas.

5) Patrol railroad yards, cars, stations, and other facilities in order to protect company property and shipments, and to maintain order.

6) Record and verify seal numbers from boxcars containing frequently pilfered items, such as cigarettes and liquor, in order to detect tampering.

7) Plan and implement special safety and preventive programs, such as fire and accident prevention.

8) Interview neighbors, associates, and former employers of job applicants in order to verify personal references and to obtain work history data.

9) Direct security activities at derailments, fires, floods, and strikes involving railroad property.

10) Prepare reports documenting investigation activities and results.

33-9011.00 - Animal Control Workers

Handle animals for the purpose of investigations of mistreatment, or control of abandoned, dangerous, or unattended animals.

Tasks

1) Examine animals for injuries or malnutrition, and arrange for any necessary medical treatment.

2) Remove captured animals from animal-control service vehicles and place animals in shelter cages or other enclosures.

3) Answer inquiries from the public concerning animal control operations.

4) Capture and remove stray, uncontrolled, or abused animals from undesirable conditions, using nets, nooses, or tranquilizer darts as necessary.

5) Examine animal licenses, and inspect establishments housing animals for compliance with laws.

6) Investigate reports of animal attacks or animal cruelty, interviewing witnesses, collecting evidence, and writing reports.

7) Train police officers in dog handling and training techniques for tracking, crowd control, and narcotics and bomb detection.

8) Supply animals with food, water, and personal care.

9) Clean facilities and equipment such as dog pens and animal control trucks.

10) Prepare for prosecutions related to animal treatment, and give evidence in court.

11) Contact animal owners to inform them that their pets are at animal holding facilities.

12) Educate the public about animal welfare, and animal control laws and regulations.

13) Organize the adoption of unclaimed animals.

14) Euthanize rabid, unclaimed, or severely injured animals.

15) Write reports of activities, and maintain files of impoundments and dispositions of animals.

33-9031.00 - Gaming Surveillance Officers and Gaming Investigators

Act as oversight and security agent for management and customers. Observe casino or casino hotel operation for irregular activities such as cheating or theft by either employees or patrons. May utilize one-way mirrors above the casino floor, cashier's cage, and from desk. Use of audio/video equipment is also common to observe operation of the business. Usually required to provide verbal and written reports of all violations and suspicious behavior to supervisor.

Tasks

1) Observe casino or casino hotel operations for irregular activities such as cheating or theft by employees or patrons, using audio/video equipment and one-way mirrors.

2) Report all violations and suspicious behaviors to supervisors, verbally or in writing.

3) Act as oversight and security agents for management and customers.

4) Monitor establishment activities to ensure adherence to all state gaming regulations and company policies and procedures.

33-9032.00 - Security Guards

Guard, patrol, or monitor premises to prevent theft, violence, or infractions of rules.

Tasks

1) Circulate among visitors, patrons, and employees to preserve order and protect property.

2) Answer telephone calls to take messages, answer questions, and provide information during non- business hours or when switchboard is closed.

3) Patrol industrial and commercial premises to prevent and detect signs of intrusion and ensure security of doors, windows, and gates.

4) Answer alarms and investigate disturbances.

5) Monitor and authorize entrance and departure of employees, visitors, and other persons to guard against theft and maintain security of premises.

6) Drive and guard armored vehicle to transport money and valuables to prevent theft and ensure safe delivery.

7) Monitor and adjust controls that regulate building systems, such as air conditioning, furnace, or boiler.

8) Inspect and adjust security systems, equipment, and machinery to ensure operational use and to detect evidence of tampering.

9) Warn persons of rule infractions or violations, and apprehend or evict violators from premises, using force when necessary.

10) Call police or fire departments in cases of emergency, such as fire or presence of unauthorized persons.

11) Escort or drive motor vehicle to transport individuals to specified locations and to provide personal protection.

12) Write reports of daily activities and irregularities, such as equipment or property damage, theft, presence of unauthorized persons, or unusual occurrences.

33-9091.00 - Crossing Guards

Guide or control vehicular or pedestrian traffic at such places as streets, schools, railroad crossings, or construction sites.

Tasks

1) Distribute traffic control signs and markers at designated points.

2) Direct or escort pedestrians across streets, stopping traffic as necessary.

3) Stop speeding vehicles to warn drivers of traffic laws.

4) Report unsafe behavior of children to school officials.

5) Record license numbers of vehicles disregarding traffic signals, and report infractions to appropriate authorities.

6) Activate railroad warning signal lights, lower crossing gates until trains pass, and raise

219

gates when crossings are clear.

7) Learn the location and purpose of street traffic signs within assigned patrol areas.

8) Direct traffic movement or warn of hazards, using signs, flags, lanterns, and hand signals.

9) Guide or control vehicular or pedestrian traffic at such places as street and railroad crossings and construction sites.

10) Communicate traffic and crossing rules and other information to students and adults.

11) Inform drivers of detour routes through construction sites.

12) Monitor traffic flow to locate safe gaps through which pedestrians can cross streets.

33-9092.00 - Lifeguards, Ski Patrol, and Other Recreational Protective Service Workers

Monitor recreational areas, such as pools, beaches, or ski slopes to provide assistance and protection to participants.

Tasks

1) Examine injured persons, and administer first aid or cardiopulmonary resuscitation if necessary, utilizing training and medical supplies and equipment.

2) Complete and maintain records of weather and beach conditions, emergency medical treatments performed, and other relevant incident information.

3) Contact emergency medical personnel in case of serious injury.

4) Observe activities in assigned areas, using binoculars in order to detect hazards, disturbances, or safety infractions.

5) Patrol or monitor recreational areas such as trails, slopes, and swimming areas, on foot, in vehicles, or from towers.

6) Provide assistance in the safe use of equipment such as ski lifts.

7) Instruct participants in skiing, swimming, or other recreational activities, and provide safety precaution information.

8) Provide assistance with staff selection, training, and supervision.

9) Drive a four-wheel drive vehicle equipped for major emergencies such as beached boats or cliff accidents.

10) Participate in recreational demonstrations to entertain resort guests.

11) Operate underwater recovery units.

12) Inspect recreational equipment, such as rope tows, T-bars, J-bars, and chair lifts, for safety hazards and damage or wear.

13) Rescue distressed persons, using rescue techniques and equipment.

14) Warn recreational participants of inclement weather, unsafe areas, or illegal conduct.

35-1011.00 - Chefs and Head Cooks

Direct the preparation, seasoning, and cooking of salads, soups, fish, meats, vegetables, desserts, or other foods. May plan and price menu items, order supplies, and keep records and accounts. May participate in cooking.

Tasks

1) Determine production schedules and staff requirements necessary to ensure timely delivery of services.

2) Meet with sales representatives in order to negotiate prices and order supplies.

3) Recruit and hire staff, including cooks and other kitchen workers.

4) Plan, direct, and supervise the food preparation and cooking activities of multiple kitchens or restaurants in an establishment such as a restaurant chain, hospital, or hotel.

5) Order or requisition food and other supplies needed to ensure efficient operation.

6) Record production and operational data on specified forms.

7) Meet with customers to discuss menus for special occasions such as weddings, parties, and banquets.

8) Arrange for equipment purchases and repairs.

9) Supervise and coordinate activities of cooks and workers engaged in food preparation.

10) Coordinate planning, budgeting, and purchasing for all the food operations within establishments such as clubs, hotels, or restaurant chains.

11) Demonstrate new cooking techniques and equipment to staff.

12) Collaborate with other personnel to plan and develop recipes and menus, taking into account such factors as seasonal availability of ingredients and the likely number of

customers.

13) Check the quality of raw and cooked food products to ensure that standards are met.

14) Prepare and cook foods of all types, either on a regular basis or for special guests or functions.

15) Check the quantity and quality of received products.

16) Determine how food should be presented, and create decorative food displays.

17) Estimate amounts and costs of required supplies, such as food and ingredients.

18) Inspect supplies, equipment, and work areas to ensure conformance to established standards.

19) Instruct cooks and other workers in the preparation, cooking, garnishing, and presentation of food.

20) Analyze recipes to assign prices to menu items, based on food, labor, and overhead costs.

35-1012.00 - First-Line Supervisors/Managers of Food Preparation and Serving Workers

Supervise workers engaged in preparing and serving food.

Tasks

1) Forecast staff, equipment, and supply requirements based on a master menu.

2) Assign duties, responsibilities, and work stations to employees in accordance with work requirements.

3) Collaborate with other personnel in order to plan menus, serving arrangements, and related details.

4) Analyze operational problems, such as theft and wastage, and establish procedures to alleviate these problems.

5) Train workers in food preparation, and in service, sanitation, and safety procedures.

6) Control inventories of food, equipment, smallware, and liquor, and report shortages to designated personnel.

7) Compile and balance cash receipts at the end of the day or shift.

8) Supervise and check the assembly of regular and special diet trays and the delivery of food trolleys to hospital patients.

9) Greet and seat guests, and present menus and wine lists.

10) Perform personnel actions such as hiring and firing staff, consulting with other managers as necessary.

11) Resolve customer complaints regarding food service.

12) Observe and evaluate workers and work procedures in order to ensure quality standards and service.

13) Schedule parties and take reservations.

14) Develop departmental objectives, budgets, policies, procedures, and strategies.

15) Present bills and accept payments.

16) Perform serving duties such as carving meat, preparing flambe dishes, or serving wine and liquor.

17) Evaluate new products for usefulness and suitability.

18) Record production and operational data on specified forms.

19) Purchase or requisition supplies and equipment needed to ensure quality and timely delivery of services.

20) Estimate ingredients and supplies required to prepare a recipe.

21) Develop equipment maintenance schedules and arrange for repairs.

22) Specify food portions and courses, production and time sequences, and workstation and equipment arrangements.

23) Inspect supplies, equipment, and work areas in order to ensure efficient service and conformance to standards.

35-2011.00 - Cooks, Fast Food

Prepare and cook food in a fast food restaurant with a limited menu. Duties of the cooks are limited to preparation of a few basic items and normally involve operating large-volume single-purpose cooking equipment.

Tasks

1) Measure ingredients required for specific food items being prepared.

220

2) Read food order slips or receive verbal instructions as to food required by patron, and prepare and cook food according to instructions.

3) Wash, cut, and prepare foods designated for cooking.

4) Prepare and serve beverages such as coffee and fountain drinks.

5) Prepare dough, following recipe.

6) Maintain sanitation, health, and safety standards in work areas.

7) Clean food preparation areas, cooking surfaces, and utensils.

8) Mix ingredients such as pancake or waffle batters.

9) Operate large-volume cooking equipment such as grills, deep-fat fryers, or griddles.

10) Take food and drink orders and receive payment from customers.

11) Cook the exact number of items ordered by each customer, working on several different orders simultaneously.

12) Order and take delivery of supplies.

13) Pre-cook items such as bacon, in order to prepare them for later use.

14) Prepare specialty foods such as pizzas, fish and chips, sandwiches, and tacos, following specific methods that usually require short preparation time.

15) Clean, stock, and restock workstations and display cases.

16) Serve orders to customers at windows, counters, or tables.

17) Cook and package batches of food, such as hamburgers and fried chicken, which are prepared to order or kept warm until sold.

18) Verify that prepared food meets requirements for quality and quantity.

35-2012.00 - Cooks, Institution and Cafeteria

Prepare and cook large quantities of food for institutions, such as schools, hospitals, or cafeterias.

Tasks

1) Monitor menus and spending in order to ensure that meals are prepared economically.

2) Determine meal prices based on calculations of ingredient prices.

3) Apportion and serve food to facility residents, employees, or patrons.

4) Requisition food supplies, kitchen equipment, and appliances, based on estimates of future needs.

5) Train new employees.

6) Plan menus that are varied, nutritionally balanced, and appetizing, taking advantage of foods in season and local availability.

7) Monitor use of government food commodities to ensure that proper procedures are followed.

8) Wash pots, pans, dishes, utensils, and other cooking equipment.

9) Bake breads, rolls, and other pastries.

10) Cook foodstuffs according to menus, special dietary or nutritional restrictions, and numbers of portions to be served.

11) Clean and inspect galley equipment, kitchen appliances, and work areas in order to ensure cleanliness and functional operation.

12) Direct activities of one or more workers who assist in preparing and serving meals.

13) Clean, cut, and cook meat, fish, and poultry.

14) Compile and maintain records of food use and expenditures.

35-2014.00 - Cooks, Restaurant

Prepare, season, and cook soups, meats, vegetables, desserts, or other foodstuffs in restaurants. May order supplies, keep records and accounts, price items on menu, or plan menu.

Tasks

1) Season and cook food according to recipes or personal judgment and experience.

2) Prepare relishes and hors d'oeuvres.

3) Bake breads, rolls, cakes, and pastries.

4) Bake, roast, broil, and steam meats, fish, vegetables, and other foods.

5) Carve and trim meats such as beef, veal, ham, pork, and lamb for hot or cold service, or for sandwiches.

6) Coordinate and supervise work of kitchen staff.

7) Estimate expected food consumption; then requisition or purchase supplies, or procure food from storage.

8) Wash, peel, cut, and seed fruits and vegetables to prepare them for consumption.

9) Substitute for or assist other cooks during emergencies or rush periods.

10) Weigh, measure, and mix ingredients according to recipes or personal judgment, using various kitchen utensils and equipment.

11) Observe and test foods to determine if they have been cooked sufficiently, using methods such as tasting, smelling, or piercing them with utensils.

12) Plan and price menu items.

13) Turn or stir foods to ensure even cooking.

14) Inspect food preparation and serving areas to ensure observance of safe, sanitary food-handling practices.

15) Consult with supervisory staff to plan menus, taking into consideration factors such as costs and special event needs.

16) Butcher and dress animals, fowl, or shellfish, or cut and bone meat prior to cooking.

17) Portion, arrange, and garnish food, and serve food to waiters or patrons.

18) Keep records and accounts.

35-2015.00 - Cooks, Short Order

Prepare and cook to order a variety of foods that require only a short preparation time. May take orders from customers and serve patrons at counters or tables.

Tasks

1) Perform simple food preparation tasks such as making sandwiches, carving meats, and brewing coffee.

2) Clean food preparation equipment, work areas, and counters or tables.

3) Grill, cook, and fry foods such as french fries, eggs, and pancakes.

4) Accept payments, and make change or write charge slips as necessary.

5) Order supplies and stock them on shelves.

6) Take orders from customers and cook foods requiring short preparation times, according to customer requirements.

7) Plan work on orders so that items served together are finished at the same time.

8) Grill and garnish hamburgers or other meats such as steaks and chops.

35-2021.00 - Food Preparation Workers

Perform a variety of food preparation duties other than cooking, such as preparing cold foods and shellfish, slicing meat, and brewing coffee or tea.

Tasks

1) Clean work areas, equipment, utensils, dishes, and silverware.

2) Assist cooks and kitchen staff with various tasks as needed, and provide cooks with needed items.

3) Scrape leftovers from dishes into garbage containers.

4) Wash, peel and/or cut various foods to prepare for cooking or serving.

5) Distribute menus to hospital patients, collect diet sheets, and deliver food trays and snacks to nursing units or directly to patients.

6) Stir and strain soups and sauces.

7) Carry food supplies, equipment, and utensils to and from storage and work areas.

8) Mix ingredients for green salads, molded fruit salads, vegetable salads, and pasta salads.

9) Work on assembly lines adding cutlery, napkins, food, and other items to trays in hospitals, cafeterias, airline kitchens, and similar establishments.

10) Receive and store food supplies, equipment, and utensils in refrigerators, cupboards, and other storage areas.

11) Place food trays over food warmers for immediate service, or store them in refrigerated storage cabinets.

12) Weigh or measure ingredients.

13) Make special dressings and sauces as condiments for sandwiches.

14) Load dishes, glasses, and tableware into dishwashing machines.

15) Inform supervisors when supplies are getting low or equipment is not working properly.

16) Butcher and clean fowl, fish, poultry, and shellfish to prepare for cooking or serving.

17) Remove trash and clean kitchen garbage containers.

18) Keep records of the quantities of food used.

19) Portion and wrap the food, or place it directly on plates for service to patrons.

20) Prepare a variety of foods according to customers' orders or supervisors' instructions, following approved procedures.

21) Distribute food to waiters and waitresses to serve to customers.

22) Stock cupboards and refrigerators, and tend salad bars and buffet meals.

23) Use manual and/or electric appliances to clean, peel, slice, and trim foods.

24) Package take-out foods and/or serve food to customers.

25) Store food in designated containers and storage areas to prevent spoilage.

26) Prepare and serve a variety of beverages such as coffee, tea, and soft drinks.

35-3011.00 - Bartenders

Mix and serve drinks to patrons, directly or through waitstaff.

Tasks

1) Slice and pit fruit for garnishing drinks.

2) Clean glasses, utensils, and bar equipment.

3) Ask customers who become loud and obnoxious to leave, or physically remove them.

4) Mix ingredients, such as liquor, soda, water, sugar, and bitters, in order to prepare cocktails and other drinks.

5) Plan, organize, and control the operations of a cocktail lounge or bar.

6) Order or requisition liquors and supplies.

7) Balance cash receipts.

8) Serve snacks or food items to customers seated at the bar.

9) Collect money for drinks served.

10) Plan bar menus.

11) Serve wine, and bottled or draft beer.

12) Clean bars, work areas, and tables.

13) Check identification of customers in order to verify age requirements for purchase of alcohol.

14) Supervise the work of bar staff and other bartenders.

15) Take beverage orders from serving staff or directly from patrons.

16) Attempt to limit problems and liability related to customers' excessive drinking by taking steps such as persuading customers to stop drinking, or ordering taxis or other transportation for intoxicated patrons.

17) Prepare appetizers, such as pickles, cheese, and cold meats.

18) Arrange bottles and glasses to make attractive displays.

35-3021.00 - Combined Food Preparation and Serving Workers, Including Fast Food

Perform duties which combine both food preparation and food service.

Tasks

1) Notify kitchen personnel of shortages or special orders.

2) Prepare simple foods and beverages such as sandwiches, salads, and coffee.

3) Accept payment from customers, and make change as necessary.

4) Select food items from serving or storage areas and place them in dishes, on serving trays, or in takeout bags.

5) Prepare and serve cold drinks, or frozen milk drinks or desserts, using drink-dispensing, milkshake, or frozen custard machines.

6) Request and record customer orders, and compute bills using cash registers, multicounting machines, or pencil and paper.

7) Clean and organize eating and service areas.

8) Wash dishes, glassware, and silverware after meals.

9) Serve customers in eating places that specialize in fast service and inexpensive carry-out food.

10) Serve food and beverages to guests at banquets or other social functions.

11) Provide caterers with assistance in food preparation or service.

12) Pack food, dishes, utensils, tablecloths, and accessories for transportation from catering or food preparation establishments to locations designated by customers.

13) Collect and return dirty dishes to the kitchen for washing.

14) Relay food orders to cooks.

15) Cook or re-heat food items such as french fries.

16) Arrange tables and decorations according to instructions.

35-3022.00 - Counter Attendants, Cafeteria, Food Concession, and Coffee Shop

Serve food to diners at counter or from a steam table.

Tasks

1) Wrap menu item such as sandwiches, hot entrees, and desserts for serving or for takeout.

2) Deliver orders to kitchens, and pick up and serve food when it is ready.

3) Prepare food such as sandwiches, salads, and ice cream dishes, using standard formulas or following directions.

4) Arrange reservations for patrons of dining establishments.

5) Serve salads, vegetables, meat, breads, and cocktails; ladle soups and sauces; portion desserts; and fill beverage cups and glasses.

6) Set up dining areas for meals and clear them following meals.

7) Serve food, beverages, or desserts to customers in such settings as take-out counters of restaurants or lunchrooms, business or industrial establishments, hotel rooms, and cars.

8) Order items needed to replenish supplies.

9) Brew coffee and tea, and fill containers with requested beverages.

10) Carve meat.

11) Scrub and polish counters, steam tables, and other equipment, and clean glasses, dishes, and fountain equipment.

12) Prepare bills for food, using cash registers, calculators, or adding machines; and accept payment and make change.

13) Balance receipts and payments in cash registers.

14) Take customers' orders and write ordered items on tickets, giving ticket stubs to customers when needed to identify filled orders.

15) Replenish foods at serving stations.

35-3031.00 - Waiters and Waitresses

Take orders and serve food and beverages to patrons at tables in dining establishment.

Tasks

1) Serve food and/or beverages to patrons; prepare and serve specialty dishes at tables as required.

2) Prepare tables for meals, including setting up items such as linens, silverware, and glassware.

3) Perform food preparation duties such as preparing salads, appetizers, and cold dishes, portioning desserts, and brewing coffee.

4) Collect payments from customers.

5) Describe and recommend wines to customers.

6) Clean tables and/or counters after patrons have finished dining.

7) Bring wine selections to tables with appropriate glasses, and pour the wines for customers.

8) Write patrons' food orders on order slips, memorize orders, or enter orders into computers for transmittal to kitchen staff.

9) Garnish and decorate dishes in preparation for serving.

10) Stock service areas with supplies such as coffee, food, tableware, and linens.

11) Escort customers to their tables.

12) Check with customers to ensure that they are enjoying their meals and take action to correct any problems.

222

13) Present menus to patrons and answer questions about menu items, making recommendations upon request.

14) Prepare checks that itemize and total meal costs and sales taxes.

15) Inform customers of daily specials.

16) Explain how various menu items are prepared, describing ingredients and cooking methods.

17) Remove dishes and glasses from tables or counters, and take them to kitchen for cleaning.

18) Prepare hot, cold, and mixed drinks for patrons, and chill bottles of wine.

19) Check patrons' identification in order to ensure that they meet minimum age requirements for consumption of alcoholic beverages.

20) Take orders from patrons for food or beverages.

35-3041.00 - Food Servers, Nonrestaurant

Serve food to patrons outside of a restaurant environment, such as in hotels, hospital rooms, or cars.

Tasks

1) Load trays with accessories such as eating utensils, napkins, and condiments.

2) Examine trays to ensure that they contain required items.

3) Prepare food items such as sandwiches, salads, soups, and beverages.

4) Monitor food distribution, ensuring that meals are delivered to the correct recipients and that guidelines such as those for special diets are followed.

5) Remove trays and stack dishes for return to kitchen after meals are finished.

6) Carry food, silverware, and/or linen on trays, or use carts to carry trays.

7) Take food orders and relay orders to kitchens or serving counters so they can be filled.

8) Total checks, present them to customers, and accept payment for services.

9) Record amounts and types of special food items served to customers.

10) Monitor food preparation and serving techniques to ensure that proper procedures are followed.

11) Clean and sterilize dishes, kitchen utensils, equipment, and facilities.

12) Stock service stations with items such as ice, napkins, and straws.

13) Determine where patients or patrons would like to eat their meals and help them get situated.

35-9011.00 - Dining Room and Cafeteria Attendants and Bartender Helpers

Facilitate food service. Clean tables, carry dirty dishes, replace soiled table linens; set tables; replenish supply of clean linens, silverware, glassware, and dishes; supply service bar with food, and serve water, butter, and coffee to patrons.

Tasks

1) Carry food, dishes, trays, and silverware from kitchens and supply departments to serving counters.

2) Set tables with clean linens, condiments, and other supplies.

3) Replenish supplies of food and equipment at steam tables and service bars.

4) Scrape and stack dirty dishes, and carry dishes and other tableware to kitchens for cleaning.

5) Slice and pit fruit used to garnish drinks.

6) Serve food to customers when waiters and waitresses need assistance.

7) Maintain adequate supplies of items such as clean linens, silverware, glassware, dishes, and trays.

8) Serve ice water, coffee, rolls, and butter to patrons.

9) Clean and polish counters, shelves, walls, furniture, and equipment in food service areas and other areas of restaurants, and mop and vacuum floors.

10) Run cash registers.

11) Carry linens to and from laundry areas.

12) Mix and prepare flavors for mixed drinks.

13) Carry trays from food counters to tables for cafeteria patrons.

14) Locate items requested by customers.

15) Fill beverage and ice dispensers.

16) Wash glasses and other serving equipment at bars.

17) Stock refrigerating units with wines and bottled beer, and replace empty beer kegs.

18) Perform serving, cleaning, and stocking duties in establishments such as cafeterias or dining rooms in order to facilitate customer service.

19) Clean up spilled food, drink and broken dishes, and remove empty bottles and trash.

20) Stock cabinets and serving areas with condiments, and refill condiment containers as necessary.

21) Stock vending machines with food.

22) Wipe tables and seats with dampened cloths, and replace dirty tablecloths.

35-9021.00 - Dishwashers

Clean dishes, kitchen, food preparation equipment, or utensils.

Tasks

1) Load or unload trucks that deliver or pick up food and supplies.

2) Set up banquet tables.

3) Stock supplies such as food and utensils in serving stations, cupboards, refrigerators, and salad bars.

4) Clean garbage cans with water or steam.

5) Maintain kitchen work areas, equipment, and utensils in clean and orderly condition.

6) Sweep and scrub floors.

7) Transfer supplies and equipment between storage and work areas, by hand or using hand trucks.

8) Receive and store supplies.

9) Place clean dishes, utensils, and cooking equipment in storage areas.

10) Sort and remove trash, placing it in designated pickup areas.

11) Wash dishes, glassware, flatware, pots, and/or pans using dishwashers or by hand.

12) Prepare and package individual place settings.

35-9031.00 - Hosts and Hostesses, Restaurant, Lounge, and Coffee Shop

Welcome patrons, seat them at tables or in lounge, and help ensure quality of facilities and service.

Tasks

1) Supervise and coordinate activities of dining room staff to ensure that patrons receive prompt and courteous service.

2) Provide guests with menus.

3) Inform patrons of establishment specialties and features.

4) Direct patrons to coatrooms and waiting areas such as lounges.

5) Operate cash registers to accept payments for food and beverages.

6) Receive and record patrons' dining reservations.

7) Greet guests and seat them at tables or in waiting areas.

8) Perform marketing and advertising services.

9) Speak with patrons to ensure satisfaction with food and service, and to respond to complaints.

10) Prepare staff work schedules.

11) Prepare cash receipts after establishments close, and make bank deposits.

12) Confer with other staff to help plan establishments' menus.

13) Order or requisition supplies and equipment for tables and serving stations.

14) Hire, train, and supervise food and beverage service staff.

15) Assign patrons to tables suitable for their needs.

16) Maintain records of time worked by staff, and prepare payrolls.

17) Inspect dining and serving areas to ensure cleanliness and proper setup.

18) Plan parties or other special events and services.

37-2011.00 - Janitors and Cleaners, Except Maids and

Housekeeping Cleaners

Keep buildings in clean and orderly condition. Perform heavy cleaning duties, such as cleaning floors, shampooing rugs, washing walls and glass, and removing rubbish. Duties may include tending furnace and boiler, performing routine maintenance activities, notifying management of need for repairs, and cleaning snow or debris from sidewalk.

Tasks

1) Clean chimneys, flues, and connecting pipes, using power and hand tools.

2) Follow procedures for the use of chemical cleaners and power equipment, in order to prevent damage to floors and fixtures.

3) Monitor building security and safety by performing such tasks as locking doors after operating hours and checking electrical appliance use to ensure that hazards are not created.

4) Mow and trim lawns and shrubbery, using mowers and hand and power trimmers, and clear debris from grounds.

5) Remove snow from sidewalks, driveways, and parking areas, using snowplows, snow blowers, and snow shovels, and spread snow melting chemicals.

6) Notify managers concerning the need for major repairs or additions to building operating systems.

7) Clean laboratory equipment, such as glassware and metal instruments, using solvents, brushes, rags, and power cleaning equipment.

8) Steam-clean or shampoo carpets.

9) Set up, arrange, and remove decorations, tables, chairs, ladders, and scaffolding to prepare facilities for events such as banquets and meetings.

10) Clean building floors by sweeping, mopping, scrubbing, or vacuuming them.

11) Clean windows, glass partitions, and mirrors, using soapy water or other cleaners, sponges, and squeegees.

12) Gather and empty trash.

13) Make adjustments and minor repairs to heating, cooling, ventilating, plumbing, and electrical systems.

14) Dust furniture, walls, machines, and equipment.

15) Move heavy furniture, equipment, and supplies, either manually or by using hand trucks.

16) Clean and polish furniture and fixtures.

17) Requisition supplies and equipment needed for cleaning and maintenance duties.

18) Mix water and detergents or acids in containers to prepare cleaning solutions, according to specifications.

19) Clean and restore building interiors damaged by fire, smoke, or water, using commercial cleaning equipment.

20) Service, clean, and supply restrooms.

21) Spray insecticides and fumigants to prevent insect and rodent infestation.

22) Strip, seal, finish, and polish floors.

37-2012.00 - Maids and Housekeeping Cleaners

Perform any combination of light cleaning duties to maintain private households or commercial establishments, such as hotels, restaurants, and hospitals, in a clean and orderly manner. Duties include making beds, replenishing linens, cleaning rooms and halls, and vacuuming.

Tasks

1) Remove debris from driveways, garages, and swimming pool areas.

2) Polish silver accessories and metalwork such as fixtures and fittings.

3) Wash windows, walls, ceilings, and woodwork, waxing and polishing as necessary.

4) Sweep, scrub, wax, and/or polish floors, using brooms, mops, and/or powered scrubbing and waxing machines.

5) Prepare rooms for meetings, and arrange decorations, media equipment, and furniture for social or business functions.

6) Sort, count, and mark clean linens, and store them in linen closets.

7) Sort clothing and other articles, load washing machines, and iron and fold dried items.

8) Replenish supplies such as drinking glasses, linens, writing supplies, and bathroom items.

9) Replace light bulbs.

10) Empty wastebaskets, empty and clean ashtrays, and transport other trash and waste to disposal areas.

11) Dust and polish furniture and equipment.

12) Assign duties to other staff and give instructions regarding work methods and routines.

13) Request repair services and wait for repair workers to arrive.

14) Keep storage areas and carts well-stocked, clean, and tidy.

15) Take care of pets by grooming, exercising, and/or feeding them.

16) Disinfect equipment and supplies, using germicides or steam-operated sterilizers.

17) Hang draperies, and dust window blinds.

18) Observe precautions required to protect hotel and guest property, and report damage, theft, and found articles to supervisors.

19) Run errands such as taking laundry to the cleaners and buying groceries.

20) Purchase or order groceries and household supplies to keep kitchens stocked, and record expenditures.

21) Carry linens, towels, toilet items, and cleaning supplies, using wheeled carts.

22) Care for children and/or elderly persons by overseeing their activities, providing companionship, and assisting them with dressing, bathing, eating, and other needs.

23) Wash dishes and clean kitchens, cooking utensils, and silverware.

24) Deliver television sets, ironing boards, baby cribs, and rollaway beds to guests' rooms.

25) Clean rooms, hallways, lobbies, lounges, restrooms, corridors, elevators, stairways, locker rooms and other work areas so that health standards are met.

26) Move and arrange furniture, and turn mattresses.

27) Plan menus, and cook and serve meals and refreshments following employer's instructions or own methods.

28) Answer telephones and doorbells.

37-2021.00 - Pest Control Workers

Spray or release chemical solutions or toxic gases and set traps to kill pests and vermin, such as mice, termites, and roaches, that infest buildings and surrounding areas.

Tasks

1) Inspect premises to identify infestation source and extent of damage to property, wall and roof porosity, and access to infested locations.

2) Post warning signs and lock building doors to secure area to be fumigated.

3) Position and fasten edges of tarpaulins over building and tape vents to ensure air-tight environment and check for leaks.

4) Measure area dimensions requiring treatment, using rule, calculate fumigant requirements, and estimate cost for service.

5) Cut or bore openings in building or surrounding concrete, access infested areas, insert nozzle, and inject pesticide to impregnate ground.

6) Record work activities performed.

7) Set mechanical traps and place poisonous paste or bait in sewers, burrows, and ditches.

8) Spray or dust chemical solutions, powders, or gases into rooms, onto clothing, furnishings or wood, and over marshlands, ditches, and catch-basins.

9) Clean work site after completion of job.

10) Dig up and burn, or spray weeds with herbicides.

11) Study preliminary reports and diagrams of infested area and determine treatment type required to eliminate and prevent recurrence of infestation.

12) Drive truck equipped with power spraying equipment.

13) Direct and/or assist other workers in treatment and extermination processes to eliminate and control rodents, insects, and weeds.

37-3011.00 - Landscaping and Groundskeeping Workers

Landscape or maintain grounds of property using hand or power tools or equipment. Workers typically perform a variety of tasks, which may include any combination of the following: sod laying, mowing, trimming, planting, watering, fertilizing, digging, raking, sprinkler installation, and installation of mortarless segmental concrete masonry wall units.

Tasks

1) Trim and pick flowers, and clean flower beds.

2) Install rock gardens, ponds, decks, drainage systems, irrigation systems, retaining walls, fences, planters, and/or playground equipment.

3) Maintain and repair tools, equipment, and structures such as buildings, greenhouses, fences, and benches, using hand and power tools.

4) Provide proper upkeep of sidewalks, driveways, parking lots, fountains, planters, burial sites, and other grounds features.

5) Shovel snow from walks, driveways, and parking lots, and spread salt in those areas.

6) Use irrigation methods to adjust the amount of water consumption and to prevent waste.

7) Care for natural turf fields, making sure the underlying soil has the required composition to allow proper drainage and to support the grasses used on the fields.

8) Advise customers on plant selection and care.

9) Operate powered equipment such as mowers, tractors, twin-axle vehicles, snow blowers, chain-saws, electric clippers, sod cutters, and pruning saws.

10) Water lawns, trees, and plants, using portable sprinkler systems, hoses, or watering cans.

11) Gather and remove litter.

12) Mix and spray or spread fertilizers, herbicides, or insecticides onto grass, shrubs, and trees, using hand or automatic sprayers or spreaders.

13) Mow and edge lawns, using power mowers and edgers.

14) Build forms, and mix and pour cement to form garden borders.

15) Attach wires from planted trees to support stakes.

16) Mark design boundaries, and paint natural and artificial turf fields with team logos and names before events.

17) Decorate gardens with stones and plants.

18) Rake, mulch, and compost leaves.

19) Prune and trim trees, shrubs, and hedges, using shears, pruners, or chain saws.

20) Plan and cultivate lawns and gardens.

21) Maintain irrigation systems, including winterizing the systems and starting them up in spring.

22) Haul or spread topsoil, and spread straw over seeded soil to hold soil in place.

23) Care for established lawns by mulching, aerating, weeding, grubbing and removing thatch, and trimming and edging around flower beds, walks, and walls.

24) Plant seeds, bulbs, foliage, flowering plants, grass, ground covers, trees, and shrubs, and apply mulch for protection, using gardening tools.

25) Care for artificial turf fields, periodically removing the turf and replacing cushioning pads, and vacuuming and disinfecting the turf after use to prevent the growth of harmful bacteria.

26) Follow planned landscaping designs to determine where to lay sod, sow grass, or plant flowers and foliage.

39-1011.00 - Gaming Supervisors

Supervise gaming operations and personnel in an assigned area. Circulate among tables and observe operations. Ensure that stations and games are covered for each shift. May explain and interpret operating rules of house to patrons. May plan and organize activities and create friendly atmosphere for guests in hotels/casinos. May adjust service complaints.

Tasks

1) Monitor game operations to ensure that house rules are followed, that tribal, state, and federal regulations are adhered to, and that employees provide prompt and courteous service.

2) Monitor stations and games, and move dealers from game to game to ensure adequate staffing.

3) Perform paperwork required for monetary transactions.

4) Resolve customer and employee complaints.

5) Greet customers and ask about the quality of service they are receiving.

6) Establish policies on types of gambling offered, odds, and extension of credit.

7) Explain and interpret house rules, such as game rules and betting limits, for patrons.

8) Record, issue receipts for, and pay off bets.

9) Provide fire protection and first-aid assistance when necessary.

10) Interview, hire, and train workers.

11) Supervise the distribution of complimentary meals, hotel rooms, discounts, and other items given to players based on length of play and amount bet.

12) Review operational expenses, budget estimates, betting accounts, and collection reports for accuracy.

13) Direct workers compiling summary sheets for each race or event to record amounts wagered and amounts to be paid to winners.

14) Evaluate workers' performance and prepare written performance evaluations.

15) Establish and maintain banks and table limits for each game.

16) Determine how many gaming tables to open each day and schedule staff accordingly.

17) Maintain familiarity with the games at a facility, and with strategies and tricks used by cheaters at such games.

18) Monitor patrons for signs of compulsive gambling, offering assistance if necessary.

19) Report customer-related incidents occurring in gaming areas to supervisors.

20) Monitor and verify the counting, wrapping, weighing, and distribution of currency and coins.

39-1012.00 - Slot Key Persons

Coordinate/supervise functions of slot department workers to provide service to patrons. Handle and settle complaints of players. Verify and payoff jackpots. Reset slot machines after payoffs. Make minor repairs or adjustments to slot machines. Recommend removal of slot machines for repair. Report hazards and enforces safety rules.

Tasks

1) Respond to and resolve patrons' complaints.

2) Answer patrons' questions about gaming machine functions and payouts.

3) Coordinate and oversee the work of slot department workers, including change runners and slot technicians.

4) Monitor functioning of slot machine coin dispensers and fill coin hoppers when necessary.

5) Monitor payment of hand-delivered jackpots to ensure promptness.

6) Patrol assigned areas to ensure that players are following rules and that machines are functioning correctly.

7) Perform minor repairs or make adjustments to slot machines, resolving problems such as machine tilts and coin jams.

8) Reset slot machines after payoffs.

9) Exchange currency for customers, converting currency into requested combinations of bills and coins.

10) Record the specifics of malfunctioning machines and document malfunctions needing repair.

11) Attach out of order signs to malfunctioning machines, and notify technicians when machines need to be repaired or removed.

39-2011.00 - Animal Trainers

Train animals for riding, harness, security, performance, or obedience, or assisting persons with disabilities. Accustom animals to human voice and contact; and condition animals to respond to commands. Train animals according to prescribed standards for show or competition. May train animals to carry pack loads or work as part of pack team.

Tasks

1) Train and rehearse animals, according to scripts, for motion picture, television, film, stage, or circus performances.

2) Evaluate animals in order to determine their temperaments, abilities, and aptitude for training.

3) Retrain horses to break bad habits, such as kicking, bolting, and resisting bridling and grooming.

4) Place tack or harnesses on horses in order to accustom horses to the feel of equipment.

5) Keep records documenting animal health, diet, and behavior.

6) Arrange for mating of stallions and mares, and assist mares during foaling.

7) Cue or signal animals during performances.

8) Instruct jockeys in handling specific horses during races.

9) Conduct training programs in order to develop and maintain desired animal behaviors for competition, entertainment, obedience, security, riding and related areas.

10) Organize and conduct animal shows.

11) Feed and exercise animals, and provide other general care such as cleaning and maintaining holding and performance areas.

12) Use oral, spur, rein, and/or hand commands in order to condition horses to carry riders or to pull horse-drawn equipment.

13) Advise animal owners regarding the purchase of specific animals.

14) Administer prescribed medications to animals.

15) Train horses or other equines for riding, harness, show, racing, or other work, using knowledge of breed characteristics, training methods, performance standards, and the peculiarities of each animal.

16) Train dogs in human-assistance or property protection duties.

17) Observe animals' physical conditions in order to detect illness or unhealthy conditions requiring medical care.

39-2021.00 - Nonfarm Animal Caretakers

Feed, water, groom, bathe, exercise, or otherwise care for pets and other nonfarm animals, such as dogs, cats, ornamental fish or birds, zoo animals, and mice. Work in settings such as kennels, animal shelters, zoos, circuses, and aquariums. May keep records of feedings, treatments, and animals received or discharged. May clean, disinfect, and repair cages, pens, or fish tanks.

Tasks

1) Perform animal grooming duties such as washing, brushing, clipping, and trimming coats, cutting nails, and cleaning ears.

2) Discuss with clients their pets' grooming needs.

3) Feed and water animals according to schedules and feeding instructions.

4) Install, maintain, and repair animal care facility equipment such as infrared lights, feeding devices, and cages.

5) Clean, organize, and disinfect animal quarters such as pens, stables, cages, and yards, and animal equipment such as saddles and bridles.

6) Saddle and shoe animals.

7) Teach obedience classes.

8) Sell pet food and supplies.

9) Transfer animals between enclosures in order to facilitate breeding, birthing, shipping, or rearrangement of exhibits.

10) Respond to questions from patrons, and provide information about animals, such as behavior, habitat, breeding habits, or facility activities.

11) Examine and observe animals in order to detect signs of illness, disease, or injury.

12) Mix food, liquid formulas, medications, or food supplements according to instructions, prescriptions, and knowledge of animal species.

13) Find homes for stray or unwanted animals.

14) Anesthetize and inoculate animals, according to instructions.

15) Administer laboratory tests to experimental animals, and keep records of responses.

16) Provide treatment to sick or injured animals, or contact veterinarians in order to secure treatment.

17) Adjust controls to regulate specified temperature and humidity of animal quarters, nurseries, or exhibit areas.

18) Clean and disinfect surgical equipment.

19) Collect and record animal information such as weight, size, physical condition, treatments received, medications given, and food intake.

20) Order, unload, and store feed and supplies.

21) Exercise animals in order to maintain their physical and mental health.

22) Observe and caution children petting and feeding animals in designated areas in order to ensure the safety of humans and animals.

23) Answer telephones and schedule appointments.

39-3011.00 - Gaming Dealers

Operate table games. Stand or sit behind table and operate games of chance by dispensing the appropriate number of cards or blocks to players, or operating other gaming equipment. Compare the house's hand against players' hands and payoff or collect players' money or chips.

Tasks

1) Check to ensure that all players have placed bets before play begins.

2) Compute amounts of players' wins or losses, or scan winning tickets presented by patrons to calculate the amount of money won.

3) Refer patrons to gaming cashiers to collect winnings.

4) Pay winnings or collect losing bets as established by the rules and procedures of a specific game.

5) Conduct gambling games such as dice, roulette, cards, or keno, following all applicable rules and regulations.

6) Open and close cash floats and game tables.

7) Receive, verify, and record patrons' cash wagers.

8) Deal cards to house hands, and compare these with players' hands to determine winners, as in black jack.

9) Inspect cards and equipment to be used in games to ensure that they are in good condition.

10) Stand behind a gaming table and deal the appropriate number of cards to each player.

11) Apply rule variations to card games such as poker, in which players bet on the value of their hands.

12) Start and control games and gaming equipment, and announce winning numbers or colors.

13) Exchange paper currency for playing chips or coin money.

14) Monitor gambling tables and supervise staff.

15) Participate in games for gambling establishments in order to provide the minimum complement of players at a table.

16) Train new dealers.

17) Seat patrons at gaming tables.

18) Work as part of a team of dealers in games such as baccarat or craps.

19) Sell food, beverages, and tobacco to players.

20) Prepare collection reports for submission to supervisors.

39-3012.00 - Gaming and Sports Book Writers and Runners

Assist in the operation of games such as keno and bingo. Scan winning tickets presented by patrons, calculate amount of winnings and pay patrons. May operate keno and bingo equipment. May start gaming equipment that randomly selects numbers. May announce number selected until total numbers specified for each game are selected. May pick up tickets from players, collect bets, receive, verify and record patrons' cash wages.

Tasks

1) Answer questions about game rules and casino policies.

2) Collect bets in the form of cash or chips, verifying and recording amounts.

3) Collect cards or tickets from players.

4) Compare the house hand with players' hands in order to determine the winner.

5) Conduct gambling tables or games, such as dice, roulette, cards, or keno, and ensure that game rules are followed.

6) Compute and verify amounts won and lost, then pay out winnings or refer patrons to workers such as gaming cashiers so that winnings can be collected.

7) Operate games in which players bet that a ball will come to rest in a particular slot on a rotating wheel, performing actions such as spinning the wheel and releasing the ball.

8) Pay off or move bets as established by game rules and procedures.

9) Sell food, beverages, and tobacco to players.

10) Inspect cards and equipment to be used in games to ensure they are in proper condition.

11) Start gaming equipment that randomly selects numbered balls, and announce winning numbers and colors.

12) Record the number of tickets cashed and the amount paid out after each race or event.

13) Check to ensure that all players have placed their bets before play begins.

14) Seat patrons at gaming tables.

15) Take the house percentage from each pot.

16) Deliver tickets, cards, and money to bingo callers.

17) Exchange paper currency for playing chips or coins.

18) Supervise staff and games, and mediate disputes.

19) Prepare collection reports for submission to supervisors.

20) Push dice to shooters and retrieve thrown dice.

21) Participate in games for gambling establishments in order to provide the minimum complement of players at a table.

39-3021.00 - Motion Picture Projectionists

Set up and operate motion picture projection and related sound reproduction equipment.

Tasks

1) Observe projector operation in order to anticipate need to transfer operations from one projector to another.

2) Inspect movie films to ensure that they are complete and in good condition.

3) Inspect projection equipment prior to operation in order to ensure proper working order.

4) Monitor operations to ensure that standards for sound and image projection quality are met.

5) Remove full take-up reels and run film through rewinding machines to rewind projected films so they may be shown again.

6) Operate equipment in order to show films in a number of theaters simultaneously.

7) Perform minor repairs such as replacing worn sprockets, or notify maintenance personnel of the need for major repairs.

8) Perform regular maintenance tasks such as rotating or replacing xenon bulbs, cleaning lenses, lubricating machinery, and keeping electrical contacts clean and tight.

9) Splice and rewind film onto reels automatically, or by hand, to repair faulty or broken sections of film.

10) Splice separate film reels, advertisements, and movie trailers together to form a feature-length presentation on one continuous reel.

11) Set up and inspect curtain and screen controls.

12) Install and connect auxiliary equipment, such as microphones, amplifiers, disc playback machines, and lights.

13) Set up and adjust picture projectors and screens to achieve proper size, illumination, and focus of images, and proper volume and tone of sound.

14) Start projectors and open shutters to project images onto screens.

15) Coordinate equipment operation with presentation of supplemental material, such as music, oral commentaries, or sound effects.

16) Project motion pictures onto back screens for inclusion in scenes within film or stage productions.

17) Operate special-effects equipment, such as stereopticons, to project pictures onto screens.

18) Insert film into top magazine reel, or thread film through a series of sprockets and guide rollers, attaching the end to a take-up reel.

19) Remove film splicing in order to prepare films for shipment after showings, and return films to their sources.

20) Prepare film inspection reports, attendance sheets, and log books.

39-3031.00 - Ushers, Lobby Attendants, and Ticket Takers

Assist patrons at entertainment events by performing duties, such as collecting admission tickets and passes from patrons, assisting in finding seats, searching for lost articles, and locating such facilities as rest rooms and telephones.

Tasks

1) Manage informational kiosk and display of event signs and posters.

2) Direct patrons to restrooms, concession stands and telephones.

3) Count and record number of tickets collected.

4) Assist patrons in finding seats, lighting the way with flashlights if necessary.

5) Schedule and manage volunteer usher corps.

6) Maintain order and ensure adherence to safety rules.

7) Page individuals wanted at the box office.

8) Guide patrons to exits or provide other instructions or assistance in case of emergency.

9) Verify credentials of patrons desiring entrance into press-box and permit only authorized persons to enter.

10) Settle seating disputes and help solve other customer concerns.

11) Manage inventory and sale of artist merchandise.

12) Operate refreshment stands during intermission or obtain refreshments for press box patrons during performances.

13) Search for lost articles or for parents of lost children.

14) Distribute programs to patrons.

15) Examine tickets or passes to verify authenticity, using criteria such as color and date issued.

16) Greet patrons attending entertainment events.

17) Refuse admittance to undesirable persons or persons without tickets or passes.

18) Give door checks to patrons who are temporarily leaving establishments.

19) Sell and collect admission tickets and passes from patrons at entertainment events.

20) Provide assistance with patrons' special needs, such as helping those with wheelchairs.

39-3091.00 - Amusement and Recreation Attendants

Perform variety of attending duties at amusement or recreation facility. May schedule use of recreation facilities, maintain and provide equipment to participants of sporting events or recreational pursuits, or operate amusement concessions and rides.

Tasks

1) Provide information about facilities, entertainment options, and rules and regulations.

2) Provide assistance to patrons entering or exiting amusement rides, boats, or ski lifts, or mounting or dismounting animals.

3) Operate, drive, or explain the use of mechanical riding devices or other automatic equipment in amusement parks, carnivals, or recreation areas.

4) Monitor activities to ensure adherence to rules and safety procedures, and arrange for the removal of unruly patrons.

5) Fasten safety devices for patrons, or provide them with directions for fastening devices.

6) Direct patrons to rides, seats, or attractions.

7) Maintain inventories of equipment, storing and retrieving items and assembling and disassembling equipment as necessary.

8) Sell and serve refreshments to customers.

9) Schedule the use of recreation facilities such as golf courses, tennis courts, bowling alleys, and softball diamonds.

10) Announce and describe amusement park attractions to patrons in order to entice customers to games and other entertainment.

11) Tend amusement booths in parks, carnivals, or stadiums, performing duties such as conducting games, photographing patrons, and awarding prizes.

12) Operate and demonstrate the use of boats, such as rowboats, canoes, and motorboats.

13) Rent, sell, or issue sporting equipment and supplies such as bowling shoes, golf balls, swimming suits, and beach chairs.

14) Verify, collect, or punch tickets before admitting patrons to venues such as amusement parks and rides.

15) Keep informed of shut-down and emergency evacuation procedures.

16) Tend animals, performing such tasks as harnessing, saddling, feeding, watering, and grooming; and drive horse-drawn vehicles for entertainment or advertising purposes.

17) Record details of attendance, sales, receipts, reservations, and repair activities.

18) Operate machines to clean, smooth, and prepare the ice surfaces of rinks for activities such as skating, hockey, and curling.

19) Clean sporting equipment, vehicles, rides, booths, facilities, and grounds.

20) Inspect equipment to detect wear and damage and perform minor repairs, adjustments and maintenance tasks such as oiling parts.

21) Sell tickets and collect fees from customers.

39-3092.00 - Costume Attendants

Select, fit, and take care of costumes for cast members, and aid entertainers.

Tasks

1) Provide assistance to cast members in wearing costumes, or assign cast dressers to assist specific cast members with costume changes.

2) Monitor, maintain, and secure inventories of costumes, wigs, and makeup, providing keys or access to assigned directors, costume designers, and wardrobe mistresses/masters.

3) Inventory stock in order to determine types and conditions of available costuming.

4) Examine costume fit on cast members, and sketch or write notes for alterations.

5) Distribute costumes and related equipment, and keep records of item status.

6) Create worksheets for dressing lists, show notes, and costume checks.

7) Collaborate with production designers, costume designers, and other production staff in order to discuss and execute costume design details.

8) Clean and press costumes before and after performances, and perform any minor repairs.

9) Design and construct costumes or send them to tailors for construction, major repairs, or alterations.

10) Care for non-clothing items such as flags, table skirts, and draperies.

227

11) Review scripts or other production information in order to determine a story's locale and period, as well as the number of characters and required costumes.

12) Assign lockers to employees, and maintain locker rooms, dressing rooms, wig rooms, and costume storage and laundry areas.

13) Check the appearance of costumes on-stage and under lights in order to determine whether desired effects are being achieved.

14) Return borrowed or rented items when productions are complete and return other items to storage.

15) Direct the work of wardrobe crews during dress rehearsals and performances.

16) Participate in the hiring, training, scheduling, and supervision of alteration workers.

17) Provide managers with budget recommendations, and take responsibility for budgetary line items related to costumes, storage, and makeup needs.

18) Purchase, rent, or requisition costumes and other wardrobe necessities.

19) Recommend vendors and monitor their work.

20) Arrange costumes in order of use to facilitate quick-change procedures for performances.

39-3093.00 - Locker Room, Coatroom, and Dressing Room Attendants

Provide personal items to patrons or customers in locker rooms, dressing rooms, or coatrooms.

Tasks

1) Operate controls that regulate temperatures or room environments.

2) Provide or arrange for services such as clothes pressing, cleaning, and repair.

3) Assign dressing room facilities, locker space, or clothing containers to patrons of athletic or bathing establishments.

4) Bathe or massage customers in tubs or steam rooms, using water, brushes, mitts, sponges, and towels.

5) Activate emergency action plans and administer first aid, as necessary.

6) Provide towels and sheets to clients in public baths, steam rooms, and restrooms.

7) Monitor patrons' facility use in order to ensure that rules and regulations are followed, and safety and order are maintained.

8) Collect soiled linen or clothing for laundering.

9) Clean and polish footwear, using brushes, sponges, cleaning fluid, polishes, waxes, liquid or sole dressing, and daubers.

10) Check supplies to ensure adequate availability, and order new supplies when necessary.

11) Issue gym clothes, uniforms, towels, athletic equipment, and special athletic apparel.

12) Procure beverages, food, and other items as requested.

13) Store personal possessions for patrons, issue claim checks for articles stored, and return articles on receipt of checks.

14) Operate washing machines and dryers in order to clean soiled apparel and towels.

15) Stencil identifying information on equipment.

16) Provide assistance to patrons by performing duties such as opening doors and carrying bags.

17) Refer guest problems or complaints to supervisors.

18) Set up various apparatus or athletic equipment.

19) Attend to needs of athletic teams in clubhouses.

20) Answer customer inquiries; and explain cost, availability, policies, and procedures of facilities.

21) Maintain a lost-and-found collection.

22) Maintain inventories of clothing or uniforms, accessories, equipment, and/or linens.

39-4011.00 - Embalmers

Prepare bodies for interment in conformity with legal requirements.

Tasks

1) Apply cosmetics to impart lifelike appearance to the deceased.

2) Reshape or reconstruct disfigured or maimed bodies when necessary, using derma-surgery techniques and materials such as clay, cotton, plaster of paris, and wax.

3) Close incisions, using needles and sutures.

4) Conform to laws of health and sanitation, and ensure that legal requirements concerning embalming are met.

5) Dress bodies and place them in caskets.

6) Incise stomach and abdominal walls and probe internal organs, using trocar, to withdraw blood and waste matter from organs.

7) Pack body orifices with cotton saturated with embalming fluid to prevent escape of gases or waste matter.

8) Join lips, using needles and thread or wire.

9) Maintain records such as itemized lists of clothing or valuables delivered with body and names of persons embalmed.

10) Wash and dry bodies, using germicidal soap and towels or hot air dryers.

11) Insert convex celluloid or cotton between eyeballs and eyelids to prevent slipping and sinking of eyelids.

12) Assist coroners at death scenes or at autopsies, file police reports, and testify at inquests or in court, if employed by a coroner.

13) Serve as pallbearers, attend visiting rooms, and provide other assistance to the bereaved.

14) Arrange funeral home equipment and perform general maintenance.

15) Arrange for transporting the deceased to another state for interment.

16) Attach trocar to pump-tube, start pump, and repeat probing to force embalming fluid into organs.

17) Supervise funeral attendants and other funeral home staff.

18) Assist with placing caskets in hearses, and organize cemetery processions.

19) Conduct interviews to arrange for the preparation of obituary notices, to assist with the selection of caskets or urns, and to determine the location and time of burials or cremations.

20) Perform the duties of funeral directors, including coordinating funeral activities.

21) Press diaphragm to evacuate air from lungs.

22) Direct casket and floral display placement and arrange guest seating.

23) Perform special procedures necessary for remains that are to be transported to other states or overseas, or where death was caused by infectious disease.

39-4021.00 - Funeral Attendants

Perform variety of tasks during funeral, such as placing casket in parlor or chapel prior to service; arranging floral offerings or lights around casket; directing or escorting mourners; closing casket; and issuing and storing funeral equipment.

Tasks

1) Obtain burial permits and register deaths.

2) Act as pallbearers.

3) Arrange floral offerings or lights around caskets.

4) Carry flowers to hearses or limousines for transportation to places of interment.

5) Clean and drive funeral vehicles such as cars or hearses in funeral processions.

6) Greet people at the funeral home.

7) Place caskets in parlors or chapels prior to wakes or funerals.

8) Perform a variety of tasks during funerals to assist funeral directors and to ensure that services run smoothly and as planned.

9) Provide advice to mourners on how to make charitable donations in honor of the deceased.

10) Direct or escort mourners to parlors or chapels in which wakes or funerals are being held.

11) Offer assistance to mourners as they enter or exit limousines.

12) Transfer the deceased to funeral homes.

13) Issue and store funeral equipment.

14) Perform general maintenance duties for funeral homes.

15) Clean funeral parlors and chapels.

16) Close caskets at appropriate point in services.

39-5011.00 - Barbers

Provide barbering services, such as cutting, trimming, shampooing, and styling hair, trimming beards, or giving shaves.

Tasks

1) Recommend and sell lotions, tonics, or other cosmetic supplies.

2) Provide skin care and nail treatments.

3) Shape and trim beards and moustaches, using scissors.

4) Identify hair problems, using microscopes and testing devices, or by sending clients' hair samples out to independent laboratories for analysis.

5) Clean work stations and sweep floors.

6) Apply lather; and shave beards, or neck and temple hair contours, using razors.

7) Clean and sterilize scissors, combs, clippers, and other instruments.

8) Provide face, neck, and scalp massages.

9) Cut and trim hair according to clients' instructions and/or current hairstyles, using clippers, combs, hand-held blow driers, and scissors.

10) Drape and pin protective cloths around customers' shoulders.

11) Question patrons regarding desired services and haircut styles.

12) Record services provided on cashiers' tickets or receive payment from customers.

13) Shampoo hair.

14) Suggest treatments to alleviate hair problems.

15) Order supplies.

16) Measure, fit, and groom hairpieces.

17) Keep card files on clientele, recording notes of work done, products used and fees charged after each visit.

18) Stay informed of the latest styles and hair care techniques.

19) Perform clerical and administrative duties such as keeping records, paying bills, and hiring and supervising personnel.

39-5012.00 - Hairdressers, Hairstylists, and Cosmetologists

Provide beauty services, such as shampooing, cutting, coloring, and styling hair, and massaging and treating scalp. May also apply makeup, dress wigs, perform hair removal, and provide nail and skin care services.

Tasks

1) Keep work stations clean and sanitize tools such as scissors and combs.

2) Apply water, setting, straightening or waving solutions to hair and use curlers, rollers, hot combs and curling irons to press and curl hair.

3) Shampoo, rinse, condition and dry hair and scalp or hairpieces with water, liquid soap, or other solutions.

4) Cut, trim and shape hair or hairpieces, based on customers' instructions, hair type and facial features, using clippers, scissors, trimmers and razors.

5) Develop new styles and techniques.

6) Demonstrate and sell hair care products and cosmetics.

7) Shave, trim and shape beards and moustaches.

8) Schedule client appointments.

9) Comb, brush, and spray hair or wigs to set style.

10) Massage and treat scalp for hygienic and remedial purposes, using hands, fingers, or vibrating equipment.

11) Shape eyebrows and remove facial hair, using depilatory cream, tweezers, electrolysis or wax.

12) Administer therapeutic medication and advise patron to seek medical treatment for chronic or contagious scalp conditions.

13) Operate cash registers to receive payments from patrons.

14) Attach wigs or hairpieces to model heads and dress wigs and hairpieces according to instructions, samples, sketches or photographs.

15) Train or supervise other hairstylists, hairdressers and assistants.

16) Recommend and explain the use of cosmetics, lotions, and creams to soften and lubricate skin and enhance and restore natural appearance.

17) Clean, shape, and polish fingernails and toenails using files and nail polish.

18) Apply artificial fingernails.

19) Give facials to patrons, using special compounds such as lotions and creams.

20) Analyze patrons' hair and other physical features to determine and recommend beauty treatment or suggest hair styles.

21) Bleach, dye, or tint hair, using applicator or brush.

Knowledge	Knowledge Definitions
Customer and Personal Service	Knowledge of principles and processes for providing customer and personal services. This includes customer needs assessment, meeting quality standards for services, and evaluation of customer satisfaction.
English Language	Knowledge of the structure and content of the English language including the meaning and spelling of words, rules of composition, and grammar.
Chemistry	Knowledge of the chemical composition, structure, and properties of substances and of the chemical processes and transformations that they undergo. This includes uses of chemicals and their interactions, danger signs, production techniques, and disposal methods.
Administration and Management	Knowledge of business and management principles involved in strategic planning, resource allocation, human resources modeling, leadership technique, production methods, and coordination of people and resources.
Education and Training	Knowledge of principles and methods for curriculum and training design, teaching and instruction for individuals and groups, and the measurement of training effects.
Sales and Marketing	Knowledge of principles and methods for showing, promoting, and selling products or services. This includes marketing strategy and tactics, product demonstration, sales techniques, and sales control systems.
Mathematics	Knowledge of arithmetic, algebra, geometry, calculus, statistics, and their applications.
Psychology	Knowledge of human behavior and performance; individual differences in ability, personality, and interests; learning and motivation; psychological research methods; and the assessment and treatment of behavioral and affective disorders.
Communications and Media	Knowledge of media production, communication, and dissemination techniques and methods. This includes alternative ways to inform and entertain via written, oral, and visual media.
Law and Government	Knowledge of laws, legal codes, court procedures, precedents, government regulations, executive orders, agency rules, and the democratic political process.
Public Safety and Security	Knowledge of relevant equipment, policies, procedures, and strategies to promote effective local, state, or national security operations for the protection of people, data, property, and institutions.
Clerical	Knowledge of administrative and clerical procedures and systems such as word processing, managing files and records, stenography and transcription, designing forms, and other office procedures and terminology.
Personnel and Human Resources	Knowledge of principles and procedures for personnel recruitment, selection, training, compensation and benefits, labor relations and negotiation, and personnel information systems.
Economics and Accounting	Knowledge of economic and accounting principles and practices, the financial markets, banking and the analysis and reporting of financial data.
Biology	Knowledge of plant and animal organisms, their tissues, cells, functions, interdependencies, and interactions with each other and the environment.
Telecommunications	Knowledge of transmission, broadcasting, switching, control, and operation of telecommunications systems.
Production and Processing	Knowledge of raw materials, production processes, quality control, costs, and other techniques for maximizing the effective manufacture and distribution of goods.
Physics	Knowledge and prediction of physical principles, laws, their interrelationships, and applications to understanding fluid, material, and atmospheric dynamics, and mechanical, electrical, atomic and sub- atomic structures and processes.
Therapy and Counseling	Knowledge of principles, methods, and procedures for diagnosis, treatment, and rehabilitation of physical and mental dysfunctions, and for career counseling and guidance.
Design	Knowledge of design techniques, tools, and principles involved in production of precision technical plans, blueprints, drawings, and models.
Philosophy and Theology	Knowledge of different philosophical systems and religions. This includes their basic principles, values, ethics, ways of thinking, customs, practices, and their impact on human culture.
Computers and Electronics	Knowledge of circuit boards, processors, chips, electronic equipment, and computer hardware and software, including applications and programming.
Engineering and Technology	Knowledge of the practical application of engineering science and technology. This includes applying principles, techniques, procedures, and equipment to the design and production of various goods and services.
Medicine and Dentistry	Knowledge of the information and techniques needed to diagnose and treat human injuries, diseases, and deformities. This includes symptoms, treatment alternatives, drug properties and interactions, and preventive health-care measures.
Mechanical	Knowledge of machines and tools, including their designs, uses, repair, and maintenance.

History and Archeology	Knowledge of historical events and their causes, indicators, and effects on civilizations and cultures.
Sociology and Anthropology	Knowledge of group behavior and dynamics, societal trends and influences, human migrations, ethnicity, cultures and their history and origins.
Transportation	Knowledge of principles and methods for moving people or goods by air, rail, sea, or road, including the relative costs and benefits.
Foreign Language	Knowledge of the structure and content of a foreign (non-English) language including the meaning and spelling of words, rules of composition and grammar, and pronunciation.
Fine Arts	Knowledge of the theory and techniques required to compose, produce, and perform works of music, dance, visual arts, drama, and sculpture.
Geography	Knowledge of principles and methods for describing the features of land, sea, and air masses, including their physical characteristics, locations, interrelationships, and distribution of plant, animal, and human life.
Food Production	Knowledge of techniques and equipment for planting, growing, and harvesting food products (both plant and animal) for consumption, including storage/handling techniques.
Building and Construction	Knowledge of materials, methods, and the tools involved in the construction or repair of houses, buildings, or other structures such as highways and roads.

Skills	**Skills Definitions**
Active Listening	Giving full attention to what other people are saying, taking time to understand the points being made, asking questions as appropriate, and not interrupting at inappropriate times.
Speaking	Talking to others to convey information effectively.
Time Management	Managing one's own time and the time of others.
Coordination	Adjusting actions in relation to others' actions.
Social Perceptiveness	Being aware of others' reactions and understanding why they react as they do.
Reading Comprehension	Understanding written sentences and paragraphs in work related documents.
Learning Strategies	Selecting and using training/instructional methods and procedures appropriate for the situation when learning or teaching new things.
Active Learning	Understanding the implications of new information for both current and future problem-solving and decision-making.
Equipment Selection	Determining the kind of tools and equipment needed to do a job.
Critical Thinking	Using logic and reasoning to identify the strengths and weaknesses of alternative solutions, conclusions or approaches to problems.
Service Orientation	Actively looking for ways to help people.
Monitoring	Monitoring/Assessing performance of yourself, other individuals, or organizations to make improvements or take corrective action.
Operations Analysis	Analyzing needs and product requirements to create a design.
Judgment and Decision Making	Considering the relative costs and benefits of potential actions to choose the most appropriate one.
Writing	Communicating effectively in writing as appropriate for the needs of the audience.
Management of Material Resources	Obtaining and seeing to the appropriate use of equipment, facilities, and materials needed to do certain work.
Equipment Maintenance	Performing routine maintenance on equipment and determining when and what kind of maintenance is needed.
Instructing	Teaching others how to do something.
Complex Problem Solving	Identifying complex problems and reviewing related information to develop and evaluate options and implement solutions.
Persuasion	Persuading others to change their minds or behavior.
Mathematics	Using mathematics to solve problems.
Science	Using scientific rules and methods to solve problems.
Negotiation	Bringing others together and trying to reconcile differences.
Management of Personnel Resources	Motivating, developing, and directing people as they work, identifying the best people for the job.
Management of Financial Resources	Determining how money will be spent to get the work done, and accounting for these expenditures.
Troubleshooting	Determining causes of operating errors and deciding what to do about it.
Technology Design	Generating or adapting equipment and technology to serve user needs.
Quality Control Analysis	Conducting tests and inspections of products, services, or processes to evaluate quality or performance.
Installation	Installing equipment, machines, wiring, or programs to meet specifications.
Repairing	Repairing machines or systems using the needed tools.
Operation and Control	Controlling operations of equipment or systems.
Systems Evaluation	Identifying measures or indicators of system performance and the actions needed to improve or correct performance, relative to the goals of the system.
Programming	Writing computer programs for various purposes.

Systems Analysis	Determining how a system should work and how changes in conditions, operations, and the environment will affect outcomes.
Operation Monitoring	Watching gauges, dials, or other indicators to make sure a machine is working properly.

Ability	**Ability Definitions**
Arm-Hand Steadiness	The ability to keep your hand and arm steady while moving your arm or while holding your arm and hand in one position.
Manual Dexterity	The ability to quickly move your hand, your hand together with your arm, or your two hands to grasp, manipulate, or assemble objects.
Finger Dexterity	The ability to make precisely coordinated movements of the fingers of one or both hands to grasp, manipulate, or assemble very small objects.
Oral Comprehension	The ability to listen to and understand information and ideas presented through spoken words and sentences.
Near Vision	The ability to see details at close range (within a few feet of the observer).
Originality	The ability to come up with unusual or clever ideas about a given topic or situation, or to develop creative ways to solve a problem.
Oral Expression	The ability to communicate information and ideas in speaking so others will understand.
Speech Recognition	The ability to identify and understand the speech of another person.
Visualization	The ability to imagine how something will look after it is moved around or when its parts are moved or rearranged.
Speech Clarity	The ability to speak clearly so others can understand you.
Trunk Strength	The ability to use your abdominal and lower back muscles to support part of the body repeatedly or continuously over time without 'giving out' or fatiguing.
Fluency of Ideas	The ability to come up with a number of ideas about a topic (the number of ideas is important, not their quality, correctness, or creativity).
Problem Sensitivity	The ability to tell when something is wrong or is likely to go wrong. It does not involve solving the problem, only recognizing there is a problem.
Visual Color Discrimination	The ability to match or detect differences between colors, including shades of color and brightness.
Multilimb Coordination	The ability to coordinate two or more limbs (for example, two arms, two legs, or one leg and one arm) while sitting, standing, or lying down. It does not involve performing the activities while the whole body is in motion.
Selective Attention	The ability to concentrate on a task over a period of time without being distracted.
Deductive Reasoning	The ability to apply general rules to specific problems to produce answers that make sense.
Inductive Reasoning	The ability to combine pieces of information to form general rules or conclusions (includes finding a relationship among seemingly unrelated events).
Extent Flexibility	The ability to bend, stretch, twist, or reach with your body, arms, and/or legs.
Flexibility of Closure	The ability to identify or detect a known pattern (a figure, object, word, or sound) that is hidden in other distracting material.
Written Comprehension	The ability to read and understand information and ideas presented in writing.
Time Sharing	The ability to shift back and forth between two or more activities or sources of information (such as speech, sounds, touch, or other sources).
Information Ordering	The ability to arrange things or actions in a certain order or pattern according to a specific rule or set of rules (e.g., patterns of numbers, letters, words, pictures, mathematical operations).
Written Expression	The ability to communicate information and ideas in writing so others will understand.
Category Flexibility	The ability to generate or use different sets of rules for combining or grouping things in different ways.
Control Precision	The ability to quickly and repeatedly adjust the controls of a machine or a vehicle to exact positions.
Auditory Attention	The ability to focus on a single source of sound in the presence of other distracting sounds.
Perceptual Speed	The ability to quickly and accurately compare similarities and differences among sets of letters, numbers, objects, pictures, or patterns. The things to be compared may be presented at the same time or one after the other. This ability also includes comparing a presented object with a remembered object.
Mathematical Reasoning	The ability to choose the right mathematical methods or formulas to solve a problem.
Far Vision	The ability to see details at a distance.
Stamina	The ability to exert yourself physically over long periods of time without getting winded or out of breath.
Depth Perception	The ability to judge which of several objects is closer or farther away from you, or to judge the distance between you and an object.

Speed of Closure	The ability to quickly make sense of, combine, and organize information into meaningful patterns.
Dynamic Strength	The ability to exert muscle force repeatedly or continuously over time. This involves muscular endurance and resistance to muscle fatigue.
Number Facility	The ability to add, subtract, multiply, or divide quickly and correctly.
Wrist-Finger Speed	The ability to make fast, simple, repeated movements of the fingers, hands, and wrists.
Memorization	The ability to remember information such as words, numbers, pictures, and procedures.
Static Strength	The ability to exert maximum muscle force to lift, push, pull, or carry objects.
Hearing Sensitivity	The ability to detect or tell the differences between sounds that vary in pitch and loudness.
Gross Body Coordination	The ability to coordinate the movement of your arms, legs, and torso together when the whole body is in motion.
Gross Body Equilibrium	The ability to keep or regain your body balance or stay upright when in an unstable position.
Speed of Limb Movement	The ability to quickly move the arms and legs.
Glare Sensitivity	The ability to see objects in the presence of glare or bright lighting.
Reaction Time	The ability to quickly respond (with the hand, finger, or foot) to a signal (sound, light, picture) when it appears.
Explosive Strength	The ability to use short bursts of muscle force to propel oneself (as in jumping or sprinting), or to throw an object.
Rate Control	The ability to time your movements or the movement of a piece of equipment in anticipation of changes in the speed and/or direction of a moving object or scene.
Response Orientation	The ability to choose quickly between two or more movements in response to two or more different signals (lights, sounds, pictures). It includes the speed with which the correct response is started with the hand, foot, or other body part.
Dynamic Flexibility	The ability to quickly and repeatedly bend, stretch, twist, or reach out with your body, arms, and/or legs.
Peripheral Vision	The ability to see objects or movement of objects to one's side when the eyes are looking ahead.
Sound Localization	The ability to tell the direction from which a sound originated.
Spatial Orientation	The ability to know your location in relation to the environment or to know where other objects are in relation to you.
Night Vision	The ability to see under low light conditions.

Work_Activity	**Work_Activity Definitions**
Performing for or Working Directly with the Public	Performing for people or dealing directly with the public. This includes serving customers in restaurants and stores, and receiving clients or guests.
Thinking Creatively	Developing, designing, or creating new applications, ideas, relationships, systems, or products, including artistic contributions.
Updating and Using Relevant Knowledge	Keeping up-to-date technically and applying new knowledge to your job.
Assisting and Caring for Others	Providing personal assistance, medical attention, emotional support, or other personal care to others such as coworkers, customers, or patients.
Getting Information	Observing, receiving, and otherwise obtaining information from all relevant sources.
Establishing and Maintaining Interpersonal Relatio	Developing constructive and cooperative working relationships with others, and maintaining them over time.
Performing General Physical Activities	Performing physical activities that require considerable use of your arms and legs and moving your whole body, such as climbing, lifting, balancing, walking, stooping, and handling of materials.
Provide Consultation and Advice to Others	Providing guidance and expert advice to management or other groups on technical, systems-, or process-related topics.
Making Decisions and Solving Problems	Analyzing information and evaluating results to choose the best solution and solve problems.
Handling and Moving Objects	Using hands and arms in handling, installing, positioning, and moving materials, and manipulating things.
Resolving Conflicts and Negotiating with Others	Handling complaints, settling disputes, and resolving grievances and conflicts, or otherwise negotiating with others.
Judging the Qualities of Things, Services, or Peop	Assessing the value, importance, or quality of things or people.
Communicating with Persons Outside Organization	Communicating with people outside the organization, representing the organization to customers, the public, government, and other external sources. This information can be exchanged in person, in writing, or by telephone or e-mail.
Selling or Influencing Others	Convincing others to buy merchandise/goods or to otherwise change their minds or actions.
Estimating the Quantifiable Characteristics of Pro	Estimating sizes, distances, and quantities; or determining time, costs, resources, or materials needed to perform a work activity.
Communicating with Supervisors, Peers, or Subordin	Providing information to supervisors, co-workers, and subordinates by telephone, in written form, e-mail, or in person.

Inspecting Equipment, Structures, or Material	Inspecting equipment, structures, or materials to identify the cause of errors or other problems or defects.
Monitor Processes, Materials, or Surroundings	Monitoring and reviewing information from materials, events, or the environment, to detect or assess problems.
Organizing, Planning, and Prioritizing Work	Developing specific goals and plans to prioritize, organize, and accomplish your work.
Documenting/Recording Information	Entering, transcribing, recording, storing, or maintaining information in written or electronic/magnetic form.
Evaluating Information to Determine Compliance wit	Using relevant information and individual judgment to determine whether events or processes comply with laws, regulations, or standards.
Developing Objectives and Strategies	Establishing long-range objectives and specifying the strategies and actions to achieve them.
Identifying Objects, Actions, and Events	Identifying information by categorizing, estimating, recognizing differences or similarities, and detecting changes in circumstances or events.
Scheduling Work and Activities	Scheduling events, programs, and activities, as well as the work of others.
Interpreting the Meaning of Information for Others	Translating or explaining what information means and how it can be used.
Analyzing Data or Information	Identifying the underlying principles, reasons, or facts of information by breaking down information or data into separate parts.
Developing and Building Teams	Encouraging and building mutual trust, respect, and cooperation among team members.
Coaching and Developing Others	Identifying the developmental needs of others and coaching, mentoring, or otherwise helping others to improve their knowledge or skills.
Training and Teaching Others	Identifying the educational needs of others, developing formal educational or training programs or classes, and teaching or instructing others.
Guiding, Directing, and Motivating Subordinates	Providing guidance and direction to subordinates, including setting performance standards and monitoring performance.
Performing Administrative Activities	Performing day-to-day administrative tasks such as maintaining information files and processing paperwork.
Processing Information	Compiling, coding, categorizing, calculating, tabulating, auditing, or verifying information or data.
Coordinating the Work and Activities of Others	Getting members of a group to work together to accomplish tasks.
Controlling Machines and Processes	Using either control mechanisms or direct physical activity to operate machines or processes (not including computers or vehicles).
Monitoring and Controlling Resources	Monitoring and controlling resources and overseeing the spending of money.
Repairing and Maintaining Mechanical Equipment	Servicing, repairing, adjusting, and testing machines, devices, moving parts, and equipment that operate primarily on the basis of mechanical (not electronic) principles.
Interacting With Computers	Using computers and computer systems (including hardware and software) to program, write software, set up functions, enter data, or process information.
Staffing Organizational Units	Recruiting, interviewing, selecting, hiring, and promoting employees in an organization.
Repairing and Maintaining Electronic Equipment	Servicing, repairing, calibrating, regulating, fine-tuning, or testing machines, devices, and equipment that operate primarily on the basis of electrical or electronic (not mechanical) principles.
Operating Vehicles, Mechanized Devices, or Equipme	Running, maneuvering, navigating, or driving vehicles or mechanized equipment, such as forklifts, passenger vehicles, aircraft, or water craft.
Drafting, Laying Out, and Specifying Technical Dev	Providing documentation, detailed instructions, drawings, or specifications to tell others about how devices, parts, equipment, or structures are to be fabricated, constructed, assembled, modified, maintained, or used.

Work_Content	**Work_Content Definitions**
Freedom to Make Decisions	How much decision making freedom, without supervision, does the job offer?
Structured versus Unstructured Work	To what extent is this job structured for the worker, rather than allowing the worker to determine tasks, priorities, and goals?
Face-to-Face Discussions	How often do you have to have face-to-face discussions with individuals or teams in this job?
Telephone	How often do you have telephone conversations in this job?
Spend Time Standing	How much does this job require standing?
Contact With Others	How much does this job require the worker to be in contact with others (face-to-face, by telephone, or otherwise) in order to perform it?
Spend Time Making Repetitive Motions	How much does this job require making repetitive motions?
Spend Time Using Your Hands to Handle, Control, or	How much does this job require using your hands to handle, control, or feel objects, tools or controls?
Deal With External Customers	How important is it to work with external customers or the public in this job?

Exposed to Contaminants	How often does this job require working exposed to contaminants (such as pollutants, gases, dust or odors)?
Indoors, Environmentally Controlled	How often does this job require working indoors in environmentally controlled conditions?
Frequency of Decision Making	How frequently is the worker required to make decisions that affect other people, the financial resources, and/or the image and reputation of the organization?
Work With Work Group or Team	How important is it to work with others in a group or team in this job?
Importance of Being Exact or Accurate	How important is being very exact or highly accurate in performing this job?
Exposed to Minor Burns, Cuts, Bites, or Stings	How often does this job require exposure to minor burns, cuts, bites, or stings?
Physical Proximity	To what extent does this job require the worker to perform job tasks in close physical proximity to other people?
Spend Time Bending or Twisting the Body	How much does this job require bending or twisting your body?
Impact of Decisions on Co-workers or Company Resul	How do the decisions an employee makes impact the results of co-workers, clients or the company?
Importance of Repeating Same Tasks	How important is repeating the same physical activities (e.g., key entry) or mental activities (e.g., checking entries in a ledger) over and over, without stopping, to performing this job?
Level of Competition	To what extent does this job require the worker to compete or to be aware of competitive pressures?
Wear Common Protective or Safety Equipment such as	How much does this job require wearing common protective or safety equipment such as safety shoes, glasses, gloves, hard hats or live jackets?
Exposed to Hazardous Conditions	How often does this job require exposure to hazardous conditions?
Time Pressure	How often does this job require the worker to meet strict deadlines?
Deal With Unpleasant or Angry People	How frequently does the worker have to deal with unpleasant, angry, or discourteous individuals as part of the job requirements?
Sounds, Noise Levels Are Distracting or Uncomforta	How often does this job require working exposed to sounds and noise levels that are distracting or uncomfortable?
Exposed to Disease or Infections	How often does this job require exposure to disease/infections?
Coordinate or Lead Others	How important is it to coordinate or lead others in accomplishing work activities in this job?
Frequency of Conflict Situations	How often are there conflict situations the employee has to face in this job?
Letters and Memos	How often does the job require written letters and memos?
Spend Time Walking and Running	How much does this job require walking and running?
Public Speaking	How often do you have to perform public speaking in this job?
Consequence of Error	How serious would the result usually be if the worker made a mistake that was not readily correctable?
Responsible for Others' Health and Safety	How much responsibility is there for the health and safety of others in this job?
Responsibility for Outcomes and Results	How responsible is the worker for work outcomes and results of other workers?
Spend Time Kneeling, Crouching, Stooping, or Crawl	How much does this job require kneeling, crouching, stooping or crawling?
Electronic Mail	How often do you use electronic mail in this job?
Extremely Bright or Inadequate Lighting	How often does this job require working in extremely bright or inadequate lighting conditions?
Cramped Work Space, Awkward Positions	How often does this job require working in cramped work spaces that requires getting into awkward positions?
Deal With Physically Aggressive People	How frequently does this job require the worker to deal with physical aggression of violent individuals?
Degree of Automation	How automated is the job?
Spend Time Sitting	How much does this job require sitting?
Spend Time Keeping or Regaining Balance	How much does this job require keeping or regaining your balance?
Very Hot or Cold Temperatures	How often does this job require working in very hot (above 90 F degrees) or very cold (below 32 F degrees) temperatures?
Wear Specialized Protective or Safety Equipment su	How much does this job require wearing specialized protective or safety equipment such as breathing apparatus, safety harness, full protection suits, or radiation protection?
Pace Determined by Speed of Equipment	How important is it to this job that the pace is determined by the speed of equipment or machinery? (This does not refer to keeping busy at all times on this job).
Indoors, Not Environmentally Controlled	How often does this job require working indoors in non-controlled environmental conditions (e.g., warehouse without heat)?
Exposed to Hazardous Equipment	How often does this job require exposure to hazardous equipment?
In an Enclosed Vehicle or Equipment	How often does this job require working in a closed vehicle or equipment (e.g., car)?
Outdoors, Exposed to Weather	How often does this job require working outdoors, exposed to all weather conditions?
Outdoors, Under Cover	How often does this job require working outdoors, under cover (e.g., structure with roof but no walls)?

Spend Time Climbing Ladders, Scaffolds, or Poles	How much does this job require climbing ladders, scaffolds, or poles?
Exposed to High Places	How often does this job require exposure to high places?
Exposed to Radiation	How often does this job require exposure to radiation?
In an Open Vehicle or Equipment	How often does this job require working in an open vehicle or equipment (e.g., tractor)?
Exposed to Whole Body Vibration	How often does this job require exposure to whole body vibration (e.g., operate a jackhammer)?

Work_Styles	Work_Styles Definitions
Cooperation	Job requires being pleasant with others on the job and displaying a good-natured, cooperative attitude.
Self Control	Job requires maintaining composure, keeping emotions in check, controlling anger, and avoiding aggressive behavior, even in very difficult situations.
Attention to Detail	Job requires being careful about detail and thorough in completing work tasks.
Integrity	Job requires being honest and ethical.
Dependability	Job requires being reliable, responsible, and dependable, and fulfilling obligations.
Innovation	Job requires creativity and alternative thinking to develop new ideas for and answers to work-related problems.
Concern for Others	Job requires being sensitive to others' needs and feelings and being understanding and helpful on the job.
Social Orientation	Job requires preferring to work with others rather than alone, and being personally connected with others on the job.
Independence	Job requires developing one's own ways of doing things, guiding oneself with little or no supervision, and depending on oneself to get things done.
Initiative	Job requires a willingness to take on responsibilities and challenges.
Achievement/Effort	Job requires establishing and maintaining personally challenging achievement goals and exerting effort toward mastering tasks.
Persistence	Job requires persistence in the face of obstacles.
Stress Tolerance	Job requires accepting criticism and dealing calmly and effectively with high stress situations.
Adaptability/Flexibility	Job requires being open to change (positive or negative) and to considerable variety in the workplace.
Leadership	Job requires a willingness to lead, take charge, and offer opinions and direction.
Analytical Thinking	Job requires analyzing information and using logic to address work-related issues and problems.

Job Zone Component	Job Zone Component Definitions
Title	Job Zone Three: Medium Preparation Needed
Overall Experience	Previous work-related skill, knowledge, or experience is required for these occupations. For example, an electrician must have completed three or four years of apprenticeship or several years of vocational training, and often must have passed a licensing exam, in order to perform the job.
Job Training	Employees in these occupations usually need one or two years of training involving both on-the-job experience and informal training with experienced workers.
Job Zone Examples	These occupations usually involve using communication and organizational skills to coordinate, supervise, manage, or train others to accomplish goals. Examples include dental assistants, electricians, fish and game wardens, legal secretaries, personnel recruiters, and recreation workers.
SVP Range	(6.0 to < 7.0)
Education	Most occupations in this zone require training in vocational schools, related on-the-job experience, or an associate's degree. Some may require a bachelor's degree.

39-5091.00 - Makeup Artists, Theatrical and Performance

Apply makeup to performers to reflect period, setting, and situation of their role.

Tasks

1) Advise hairdressers on the hairstyles required for character parts.

2) Requisition or acquire needed materials for special effects, including wigs, beards, and special cosmetics.

3) Create character drawings or models, based upon independent research, in order to augment period production files.

4) Evaluate environmental characteristics such as venue size and lighting plans in order to determine makeup requirements.

5) Wash and reset wigs.

6) Establish budgets, and work within budgetary limits.

7) Demonstrate products to clients, and provide instruction in makeup application.

8) Alter or maintain makeup during productions as necessary to compensate for lighting changes or to achieve continuity of effect.

9) Duplicate work precisely in order to replicate characters' appearances on a daily basis.

10) Provide performers with makeup removal assistance after performances have been completed.

11) Write makeup sheets and take photos in order to document specific looks and the products that were used to achieve the looks.

12) Study production information, such as character descriptions, period settings, and situations in order to determine makeup requirements.

13) Examine sketches, photographs, and plaster models in order to obtain desired character image depiction.

14) Apply makeup to enhance, and/or alter the appearance of people appearing in productions such as movies.

15) Confer with stage or motion picture officials and performers in order to determine desired effects.

16) Analyze a script, noting events that affect each character's appearance, so that plans can be made for each scene.

17) Assess performers' skin-type in order to ensure that make-up will not cause break-outs or skin irritations.

18) Attach prostheses to performers and apply makeup in order to create special features or effects such as scars, aging, or illness.

19) Cleanse and tone the skin in order to prepare it for makeup application.

20) Select desired makeup shades from stock, or mix oil, grease, and coloring in order to achieve specific color effects.

39-5092.00 - Manicurists and Pedicurists

Clean and shape customers' fingernails and toenails. May polish or decorate nails.

Tasks

1) Promote and sell nail care products.

2) Polish nails, using powdered polish and buffer.

3) Apply undercoat and clear or colored polish onto nails with brush.

4) Attach paper forms to tips of customers' fingers to support and shape artificial nails.

5) Roughen surfaces of fingernails, using abrasive wheel.

6) Shape and smooth ends of nails, using scissors, files, and emery boards.

7) Soften nail cuticles with water and oil, push back cuticles, using cuticle knife, and trim cuticles, using scissors or nippers.

8) Schedule client appointments and accept payments.

9) Whiten underside of nails with white paste or pencil.

10) Advise clients on nail care and use of products and colors.

11) Assess the condition of clients' hands, remove dead skin from the hands and massage them.

12) Maintain supply inventories and records of client services.

13) Brush powder and solvent onto nails and paper forms to maintain nail appearance and to extend nails, then remove forms and shape and smooth nail edges using rotary abrasive wheel.

14) Treat nails to repair or improve strength and resilience by wrapping, or provide treatment to nail biters.

15) Clean and sanitize tools and work environment.

16) Decorate clients' nails by piercing them or attaching ornaments or designs.

17) Remove previously applied nail polish, using liquid remover and swabs.

39-5093.00 - Shampooers

Shampoo and rinse customers' hair.

Tasks

1) Treat scalp conditions and hair loss, using specialized lotions, shampoos, or equipment such as infrared lamps or vibrating equipment.

2) Maintain treatment records.

3) Advise patrons with chronic or potentially contagious scalp conditions to seek medical treatment.

39-5094.00 - Skin Care Specialists

Provide skin care treatments to face and body to enhance an individual's appearance.

Tasks

1) Remove body and facial hair by applying wax.

2) Apply chemical peels in order to reduce fine lines and age spots.

3) Cleanse clients' skin with water, creams and/or lotions.

4) Determine which products or colors will improve clients' skin quality and appearance.

5) Keep records of client needs and preferences, and the services provided.

6) Perform simple extractions to remove blackheads.

7) Advise clients about colors and types of makeup, and instruct them in makeup application techniques.

8) Give manicures and pedicures, and apply artificial nails.

9) Sterilize equipment, and clean work areas.

10) Demonstrate how to clean and care for skin properly, and recommend skin-care regimens.

11) Provide facial and body massages.

12) Refer clients to medical personnel for treatment of serious skin problems.

13) Sell makeup to clients.

14) Tint eyelashes and eyebrows.

15) Treat the facial skin to maintain and improve its appearance, using specialized techniques and products such as peels and masks.

16) Select and apply cosmetic products such as creams, lotions, and tonics.

17) Examine clients' skin, using magnifying lamps or visors when necessary, in order to evaluate skin condition and appearance.

39-6011.00 - Baggage Porters and Bellhops

Handle baggage for travelers at transportation terminals or for guests at hotels or similar establishments.

Tasks

1) Inspect guests' rooms to ensure that they are adequately stocked, orderly, and comfortable.

2) Pick up and return items for laundry and valet service.

3) Set up conference rooms, display tables, racks, or shelves, and arrange merchandise displays for sales personnel.

4) Supply guests or travelers with directions, travel information, and other information such as available services and points of interest.

5) Transport guests about premises and local areas, or arrange for transportation.

6) Page guests in hotel lobbies, dining rooms, or other areas.

7) Complete baggage insurance forms.

8) Greet incoming guests and escort them to their rooms.

9) Act as part of the security team at transportation terminals, hotels, or similar establishments.

10) Transfer luggage, trunks, and packages to and from rooms, loading areas, vehicles, or transportation terminals, by hand or using baggage carts.

11) Arrange for shipments of baggage, express mail, and parcels by providing weighing and billing services.

12) Receive and mark baggage by completing and attaching claim checks.

13) Assist physically challenged travelers and other guests with special needs.

14) Deliver messages and room service orders, and run errands for guests.

15) Explain the operation of room features such as locks, ventilation systems, and televisions.

16) Compute and complete charge slips for services rendered and maintain records.

39-6012.00 - Concierges

Assist patrons at hotel, apartment or office building with personal services. May take messages, arrange or give advice on transportation, business services or entertainment, or monitor guest requests for housekeeping and maintenance.

Tasks

1) Pick up and deliver items, or run errands for guests.

2) Receive, store, and deliver luggage and mail.

3) Arrange for the replacement of items lost by travelers.

4) Make dining and other reservations for patrons, and obtain tickets for events.

5) Make travel arrangements for sightseeing and other tours.

6) Provide information about local features such as shopping, dining, nightlife, and recreational destinations.

7) Arrange for interpreters or translators when patrons require such services.

8) Perform office duties on a temporary basis when needed.

9) Plan special events, parties, and meetings, which may include booking musicians or celebrities to appear.

39-6021.00 - Tour Guides and Escorts

Escort individuals or groups on sightseeing tours or through places of interest, such as industrial establishments, public buildings, and art galleries.

Tasks

1) Escort individuals or groups on cruises, sightseeing tours, or through places of interest such as industrial establishments, public buildings, and art galleries.

2) Distribute brochures, show audiovisual presentations, and explain establishment processes and operations at tour sites.

3) Describe tour points of interest to group members, and respond to questions.

4) Greet and register visitors, and issue any required identification badges and/or safety devices.

5) Provide directions and other pertinent information to visitors.

6) Solicit tour patronage and sell souvenirs.

7) Collect fees and tickets from group members.

8) Plan rest stops and meals, preparing meals or teaching clients how to prepare meals on such trips as hunting expeditions.

9) Select travel routes and sites to be visited based on knowledge of specific areas.

10) Conduct educational activities for school children.

11) Carry equipment and luggage for visitors, and provide errand service.

12) Assemble and check the required supplies and equipment prior to departure.

13) Monitor visitors' activities in order to ensure compliance with establishment or tour regulations and safety practices.

14) Drive motor vehicles in order to transport visitors to establishments and tour site locations.

15) Speak foreign languages in order to communicate with foreign visitors.

16) Set up camp on overnight outdoors expeditions, and prepare base camps for longer expeditions.

17) Teach skills, such as proper climbing methods, and demonstrate and advise on the use of equipment.

18) Provide for physical safety of groups, performing such activities as providing first aid and directing emergency evacuations.

19) Perform clerical duties such as filing, typing, operating switchboards, and routing mail and messages.

20) Research environmental conditions and clients' skill and ability levels in order to plan expeditions, instruction, and commentary that are appropriate.

21) Provide information about wildlife varieties and habitats, as well as any relevant regulations, such as those pertaining to hunting and fishing.

22) Plan and conduct itineraries and activities on specialized trips such as mountain expeditions, rafting trips, hunting trips, fishing trips, photo safaris, nature study expeditions, and trail rides.

23) Secure any equipment required by a specific type of expedition, such as camping or climbing equipment.

24) Select and care for any animals required on an expedition, such as horses or dogs.

39-9011.00 - Child Care Workers

Attend to children at schools, businesses, private households, and child care institutions. Perform a variety of tasks, such as dressing, feeding, bathing, and overseeing play.

Tasks

1) Sterilize bottles and prepare formulas.

2) Organize and participate in recreational activities, such as games.

3) Place or hoist children into baths or pools.

4) Instruct children in health and personal habits such as eating, resting, and toilet habits.

5) Read to children, and teach them simple painting, drawing, handicrafts, and songs.

6) Wheel handicapped children to classes or other areas of facility, secure in equipment, such as chairs and slings.

7) Monitor children on life-support equipment to detect malfunctioning of equipment, and call for medical assistance when needed.

8) Accompany children to and from school, on outings, and to medical appointments.

9) Care for children in institutional setting, such as group homes, nursery schools, private businesses, or schools for the handicapped.

10) Keep records on individual children, including daily observations and information about activities, meals served, and medications administered.

11) Sanitize toys and play equipment.

12) Assist in preparing food for children and serve meals and refreshments to children and regulate rest periods.

13) Organize and store toys and materials to ensure order in activity areas.

14) Operate in-house daycare centers within businesses.

15) Observe and monitor children's play activities.

16) Provide counseling or therapy to mentally disturbed, delinquent, or handicapped children.

17) Help children with homework and school work.

18) Identify signs of emotional or developmental problems in children and bring them to parents' or guardians' attention.

19) Discipline children and recommend or initiate other measures to control behavior, such as caring for own clothing and picking up toys and books.

20) Support children's emotional and social development, encouraging understanding of others and positive self-concepts.

21) Perform housekeeping duties such as laundry, cleaning, dishwashing, and changing of linens.

39-9021.00 - Personal and Home Care Aides

Assist elderly or disabled adults with daily living activities at the person's home or in a daytime non-residential facility. Duties performed at a place of residence may include keeping house (making beds, doing laundry, washing dishes) and preparing meals. May provide meals and supervised activities at non-residential care facilities. May advise families, the elderly, and disabled on such things as nutrition, cleanliness, and household utilities.

Tasks

1) Instruct and advise clients on issues such as household cleanliness, utilities, hygiene, nutrition and infant care.

2) Administer bedside and personal care, such as ambulation and personal hygiene assistance.

3) Care for individuals and families during periods of incapacitation, family disruption or convalescence, providing companionship, personal care and help in adjusting to new lifestyles.

4) Plan, shop for, and prepare meals, including special diets, and assist families in planning, shopping for, and preparing nutritious meals.

5) Participate in case reviews, consulting with the team caring for the client, to evaluate the client's needs and plan for continuing services.

6) Transport clients to locations outside the home, such as to physicians' offices or on outings, using a motor vehicle.

7) Prepare and maintain records of client progress and services performed, reporting changes in client condition to manager or supervisor.

8) Perform housekeeping duties, such as cooking, cleaning, washing clothes and dishes, and running errands.

9) Perform health-care related tasks, such as monitoring vital signs and medication, under the direction of registered nurses and physiotherapists.

10) Provide clients with communication assistance, typing their correspondence and obtaining information for them.

11) Assist in training children, such as by helping to establish good study habits and by assigning duties according to children's capabilities.

39-9031.00 - Fitness Trainers and Aerobics Instructors

Instruct or coach groups or individuals in exercise activities and the fundamentals of sports. Demonstrate techniques and methods of participation. Observe participants and inform them of corrective measures necessary to improve their skills. Those required to hold teaching degrees should be reported in the appropriate teaching category.

Tasks

1) Plan physical education programs to promote development of participants' physical attributes and social skills.

2) Organize, lead, and referee indoor and outdoor games such as volleyball, baseball, and basketball.

3) Offer alternatives during classes to accommodate different levels of fitness.

4) Monitor participants' progress and adapt programs as needed.

5) Explain and enforce safety rules and regulations governing sports, recreational activities, and the use of exercise equipment.

6) Teach and demonstrate use of gymnastic and training equipment such as trampolines and weights.

7) Teach individual and team sports to participants through instruction and demonstration, utilizing knowledge of sports techniques and of participants' physical capabilities.

8) Conduct therapeutic, recreational, or athletic activities.

9) Promote health clubs through membership sales, and record member information.

10) Evaluate individuals' abilities, needs, and physical conditions, and develop suitable training programs to meet any special requirements.

11) Advise clients about proper clothing and shoes.

12) Maintain fitness equipment.

13) Plan routines, choose appropriate music, and choose different movements for each set of muscles, depending on participants' capabilities and limitations.

14) Advise participants in use of heat or ultraviolet treatments and hot baths.

15) Massage body parts to relieve soreness, strains, and bruises.

16) Administer emergency first aid, wrap injuries, treat minor chronic disabilities, or refer injured persons to physicians.

17) Organize and conduct competitions and tournaments.

18) Instruct participants in maintaining exertion levels in order to maximize benefits from exercise routines.

19) Provide students with information and resources regarding nutrition, weight control, and lifestyle issues.

20) Wrap ankles, fingers, wrists, or other body parts with synthetic skin, gauze, or adhesive tape, in order to support muscles and ligaments.

21) Teach proper breathing techniques used during physical exertion.

22) Maintain equipment inventories; and select, store, and issue equipment as needed.

39-9032.00 - Recreation Workers

Conduct recreation activities with groups in public, private, or volunteer agencies or recreation facilities. Organize and promote activities, such as arts and crafts, sports, games, music, dramatics, social recreation, camping, and hobbies, taking into account the needs and interests of individual members.

Tasks

1) Schedule maintenance and use of facilities.

2) Provide for entertainment and set up related decorations and equipment.

3) Organize, lead, and promote interest in recreational activities such as arts, crafts, sports, games, camping, and hobbies.

4) Greet new arrivals to activities, introducing them to other participants, explaining facility rules, and encouraging their participation.

5) Manage the daily operations of recreational facilities.

6) Serve as liaison between park or recreation administrators and activity instructors.

7) Enforce rules and regulations of recreational facilities in order to maintain discipline and ensure safety.

8) Explain principles, techniques, and safety procedures to participants in recreational activities, and demonstrate use of materials and equipment.

9) Complete and maintain time and attendance forms and inventory lists.

10) Supervise and coordinate the work activities of personnel, such as training staff members and assigning work duties.

11) Evaluate staff performance, recording evaluations on appropriate forms.

12) Oversee the purchase, planning, design, construction, and upkeep of recreation facilities and areas.

13) Evaluate recreation areas, facilities, and services in order to determine if they are producing desired results.

14) Encourage participants to develop their own activities and leadership skills through group discussions.

15) Direct special activities or events such as aquatics, gymnastics, or performing arts.

16) Confer with management in order to discuss and resolve participant complaints.

17) Administer first aid according to prescribed procedures, and notify emergency medical personnel when necessary.

18) Meet and collaborate with agency personnel, community organizations, and other professional personnel to plan balanced recreational programs for participants.

19) Meet with staff to discuss rules, regulations, and work-related problems.

39-9041.00 - Residential Advisors

Coordinate activities for residents of boarding schools, college fraternities or sororities, college dormitories, or similar establishments. Order supplies and determine need for maintenance, repairs, and furnishings. May maintain household records and assign rooms. May refer residents to counseling resources if needed.

Tasks

1) Supervise participants in work-study programs.

2) Plan meal menus for establishment residents.

3) Supervise the activities of housekeeping personnel.

4) Provide requested information on students' progress and the development of case plans.

5) Provide transportation and/or escort for expeditions such as shopping trips or visits to doctors or dentists.

6) Sort and distribute mail.

7) Supervise students' housekeeping work to ensure that it is done properly.

8) Collaborate with counselors to develop counseling programs that address the needs of individual students.

9) Answer telephones, and route calls or deliver messages.

10) Accompany and supervise students during meals.

11) Order supplies for facilities.

12) Mediate interpersonal problems between residents.

13) Provide emergency first aid and summon medical assistance when necessary.

14) Hold regular meetings with each assigned unit.

15) Develop program plans for individuals or assist in plan development.

16) Chaperone group-sponsored trips and social functions.

17) Counsel students in the handling of issues such as family, financial, and educational problems.

18) Inventory, pack, and remove items left behind by former residents.

19) Collect laundry and send it to be cleaned.

20) Process contract cancellations for students who are unable to follow residence hall policies and procedures.

21) Observe students in order to detect and report unusual behavior.

22) Confer with medical personnel to better understand the backgrounds and needs of individual residents.

23) Administer, coordinate, or recommend disciplinary and corrective actions.

24) Communicate with other staff to resolve problems with individual students.

25) Make regular rounds to ensure that residents and areas are safe and secure.

26) Assign rooms to students.

27) Determine the need for facility maintenance and repair, and notify appropriate personnel.

28) Direct and participate in on- and off-campus recreational activities for residents of institutions, boarding schools, fraternities or sororities, children's homes, or similar establishments.

29) Enforce rules and regulations to ensure the smooth and orderly operation of dormitory programs.

41-1011.00 - First-Line Supervisors/Managers of Retail Sales Workers

Directly supervise sales workers in a retail establishment or department. Duties may include management functions, such as purchasing, budgeting, accounting, and personnel work, in addition to supervisory duties.

Tasks

1) Enforce safety, health, and security rules.

2) Monitor sales activities to ensure that customers receive satisfactory service and quality goods.

3) Perform work activities of subordinates, such as cleaning and organizing shelves and displays and selling merchandise.

4) Examine products purchased for resale or received for storage to assess the condition of each product or item.

5) Direct and supervise employees engaged in sales, inventory-taking, reconciling cash receipts, or in performing services for customers.

6) Instruct staff on how to handle difficult and complicated sales.

7) Inventory stock and reorder when inventory drops to a specified level.

8) Establish and implement policies, goals, objectives, and procedures for their department.

9) Keep records of purchases, sales, and requisitions.

10) Hire, train, and evaluate personnel in sales or marketing establishments, promoting or firing workers when appropriate.

11) Confer with company officials to develop methods and procedures to increase sales, expand markets, and promote business.

12) Plan and prepare work schedules and keep records of employees' work schedules and time cards.

13) Examine merchandise to ensure that it is correctly priced and displayed and that it functions as advertised.

14) Estimate consumer demand and determine the types and amounts of goods to be sold.

15) Establish credit policies and operating procedures.

16) Review inventory and sales records to prepare reports for management and budget departments.

17) Plan budgets and authorize payments and merchandise returns.

18) Formulate pricing policies for merchandise, according to profitability requirements.

19) Plan and coordinate advertising campaigns and sales promotions, and prepare merchandise displays and advertising copy.

20) Provide customer service by greeting and assisting customers, and responding to customer inquiries and complaints.

Knowledge	Knowledge Definitions
Customer and Personal Service	Knowledge of principles and processes for providing customer and personal services. This includes customer needs assessment, meeting quality standards for services, and evaluation of customer satisfaction.
Administration and Management	Knowledge of business and management principles involved in strategic planning, resource allocation, human resources modeling, leadership technique, production methods, and coordination of people and resources.
English Language	Knowledge of the structure and content of the English language including the meaning and spelling of words, rules of composition, and grammar.
Mathematics	Knowledge of arithmetic, algebra, geometry, calculus, statistics, and their applications.
Personnel and Human Resources	Knowledge of principles and procedures for personnel recruitment, selection, training, compensation and benefits, labor relations and negotiation, and personnel information systems.
Food Production	Knowledge of techniques and equipment for planting, growing, and harvesting food products (both plant and animal) for consumption, including storage/handling techniques.
Sales and Marketing	Knowledge of principles and methods for showing, promoting, and selling products or services. This includes marketing strategy and tactics, product demonstration, sales techniques, and sales control systems.

Public Safety and Security	Knowledge of relevant equipment, policies, procedures, and strategies to promote effective local, state, or national security operations for the protection of people, data, property, and institutions.
Education and Training	Knowledge of principles and methods for curriculum and training design, teaching and instruction for individuals and groups, and the measurement of training effects.
Economics and Accounting	Knowledge of economic and accounting principles and practices, the financial markets, banking and the analysis and reporting of financial data.
Clerical	Knowledge of administrative and clerical procedures and systems such as word processing, managing files and records, stenography and transcription, designing forms, and other office procedures and terminology.
Mechanical	Knowledge of machines and tools, including their designs, uses, repair, and maintenance.
Computers and Electronics	Knowledge of circuit boards, processors, chips, electronic equipment, and computer hardware and software, including applications and programming.
Production and Processing	Knowledge of raw materials, production processes, quality control, costs, and other techniques for maximizing the effective manufacture and distribution of goods.
Communications and Media	Knowledge of media production, communication, and dissemination techniques and methods. This includes alternative ways to inform and entertain via written, oral, and visual media.
Telecommunications	Knowledge of transmission, broadcasting, switching, control, and operation of telecommunications systems.
Law and Government	Knowledge of laws, legal codes, court procedures, precedents, government regulations, executive orders, agency rules, and the democratic political process.
Psychology	Knowledge of human behavior and performance; individual differences in ability, personality, and interests; learning and motivation; psychological research methods; and the assessment and treatment of behavioral and affective disorders.
Engineering and Technology	Knowledge of the practical application of engineering science and technology. This includes applying principles, techniques, procedures, and equipment to the design and production of various goods and services.
Building and Construction	Knowledge of materials, methods, and the tools involved in the construction or repair of houses, buildings, or other structures such as highways and roads.
Therapy and Counseling	Knowledge of principles, methods, and procedures for diagnosis, treatment, and rehabilitation of physical and mental dysfunctions, and for career counseling and guidance.
Transportation	Knowledge of principles and methods for moving people or goods by air, rail, sea, or road, including the relative costs and benefits.
Physics	Knowledge and prediction of physical principles, laws, their interrelationships, and applications to understanding fluid, material, and atmospheric dynamics, and mechanical, electrical, atomic and sub- atomic structures and processes.
Foreign Language	Knowledge of the structure and content of a foreign (non-English) language including the meaning and spelling of words, rules of composition and grammar, and pronunciation.
Chemistry	Knowledge of the chemical composition, structure, and properties of substances and of the chemical processes and transformations that they undergo. This includes uses of chemicals and their interactions, danger signs, production techniques, and disposal methods.
Geography	Knowledge of principles and methods for describing the features of land, sea, and air masses, including their physical characteristics, locations, interrelationships, and distribution of plant, animal, and human life.
Sociology and Anthropology	Knowledge of group behavior and dynamics, societal trends and influences, human migrations, ethnicity, cultures and their history and origins.
Medicine and Dentistry	Knowledge of the information and techniques needed to diagnose and treat human injuries, diseases, and deformities. This includes symptoms, treatment alternatives, drug properties and interactions, and preventive health-care measures.
Design	Knowledge of design techniques, tools, and principles involved in production of precision technical plans, blueprints, drawings, and models.
Philosophy and Theology	Knowledge of different philosophical systems and religions. This includes their basic principles, values, ethics, ways of thinking, customs, practices, and their impact on human culture.
History and Archeology	Knowledge of historical events and their causes, indicators, and effects on civilizations and cultures.
Fine Arts	Knowledge of the theory and techniques required to compose, produce, and perform works of music, dance, visual arts, drama, and sculpture.
Biology	Knowledge of plant and animal organisms, their tissues, cells, functions, interdependencies, and interactions with each other and the environment.

Skills	Skills Definitions
Management of Personnel Resources	Motivating, developing, and directing people as they work, identifying the best people for the job.
Active Listening	Giving full attention to what other people are saying, taking time to understand the points being made, asking questions as appropriate, and not interrupting at inappropriate times.
Service Orientation	Actively looking for ways to help people.
Time Management	Managing one's own time and the time of others.
Instructing	Teaching others how to do something.
Monitoring	Monitoring/Assessing performance of yourself, other individuals, or organizations to make improvements or take corrective action.
Reading Comprehension	Understanding written sentences and paragraphs in work related documents.
Judgment and Decision Making	Considering the relative costs and benefits of potential actions to choose the most appropriate one.
Critical Thinking	Using logic and reasoning to identify the strengths and weaknesses of alternative solutions, conclusions or approaches to problems.
Active Learning	Understanding the implications of new information for both current and future problem-solving and decision-making.
Speaking	Talking to others to convey information effectively.
Mathematics	Using mathematics to solve problems.
Social Perceptiveness	Being aware of others' reactions and understanding why they react as they do.
Persuasion	Persuading others to change their minds or behavior.
Troubleshooting	Determining causes of operating errors and deciding what to do about it.
Equipment Maintenance	Performing routine maintenance on equipment and determining when and what kind of maintenance is needed.
Learning Strategies	Selecting and using training/instructional methods and procedures appropriate for the situation when learning or teaching new things.
Writing	Communicating effectively in writing as appropriate for the needs of the audience.
Complex Problem Solving	Identifying complex problems and reviewing related information to develop and evaluate options and implement solutions.
Negotiation	Bringing others together and trying to reconcile differences.
Coordination	Adjusting actions in relation to others' actions.
Quality Control Analysis	Conducting tests and inspections of products, services, or processes to evaluate quality or performance.
Operation and Control	Controlling operations of equipment or systems.
Equipment Selection	Determining the kind of tools and equipment needed to do a job.
Management of Financial Resources	Determining how money will be spent to get the work done, and accounting for these expenditures.
Operation Monitoring	Watching gauges, dials, or other indicators to make sure a machine is working properly.
Operations Analysis	Analyzing needs and product requirements to create a design.
Repairing	Repairing machines or systems using the needed tools.
Systems Analysis	Determining how a system should work and how changes in conditions, operations, and the environment will affect outcomes.
Management of Material Resources	Obtaining and seeing to the appropriate use of equipment, facilities, and materials needed to do certain work.
Systems Evaluation	Identifying measures or indicators of system performance and the actions needed to improve or correct performance, relative to the goals of the system.
Science	Using scientific rules and methods to solve problems.
Installation	Installing equipment, machines, wiring, or programs to meet specifications.
Programming	Writing computer programs for various purposes.
Technology Design	Generating or adapting equipment and technology to serve user needs.

Ability	Ability Definitions
Oral Comprehension	The ability to listen to and understand information and ideas presented through spoken words and sentences.
Oral Expression	The ability to communicate information and ideas in speaking so others will understand.
Speech Clarity	The ability to speak clearly so others can understand you.
Deductive Reasoning	The ability to apply general rules to specific problems to produce answers that make sense.
Speech Recognition	The ability to identify and understand the speech of another person.
Inductive Reasoning	The ability to combine pieces of information to form general rules or conclusions (includes finding a relationship among seemingly unrelated events).
Problem Sensitivity	The ability to tell when something is wrong or is likely to go wrong. It does not involve solving the problem, only recognizing there is a problem.

Information Ordering	The ability to arrange things or actions in a certain order or pattern according to a specific rule or set of rules (e.g., patterns of numbers, letters, words, pictures, mathematical operations).
Originality	The ability to come up with unusual or clever ideas about a given topic or situation, or to develop creative ways to solve a problem.
Written Expression	The ability to communicate information and ideas in writing so others will understand.
Time Sharing	The ability to shift back and forth between two or more activities or sources of information (such as speech, sounds, touch, or other sources).
Fluency of Ideas	The ability to come up with a number of ideas about a topic (the number of ideas is important, not their quality, correctness, or creativity).
Category Flexibility	The ability to generate or use different sets of rules for combining or grouping things in different ways.
Mathematical Reasoning	The ability to choose the right mathematical methods or formulas to solve a problem.
Written Comprehension	The ability to read and understand information and ideas presented in writing.
Near Vision	The ability to see details at close range (within a few feet of the observer).
Number Facility	The ability to add, subtract, multiply, or divide quickly and correctly.
Memorization	The ability to remember information such as words, numbers, pictures, and procedures.
Trunk Strength	The ability to use your abdominal and lower back muscles to support part of the body repeatedly or continuously over time without 'giving out' or fatiguing.
Selective Attention	The ability to concentrate on a task over a period of time without being distracted.
Static Strength	The ability to exert maximum muscle force to lift, push, pull, or carry objects.
Extent Flexibility	The ability to bend, stretch, twist, or reach with your body, arms, and/or legs.
Finger Dexterity	The ability to make precisely coordinated movements of the fingers of one or both hands to grasp, manipulate, or assemble very small objects.
Stamina	The ability to exert yourself physically over long periods of time without getting winded or out of breath.
Far Vision	The ability to see details at a distance.
Flexibility of Closure	The ability to identify or detect a known pattern (a figure, object, word, or sound) that is hidden in other distracting material.
Perceptual Speed	The ability to quickly and accurately compare similarities and differences among sets of letters, numbers, objects, pictures, or patterns. The things to be compared may be presented at the same time or one after the other. This ability also includes comparing a presented object with a remembered object.
Manual Dexterity	The ability to quickly move your hand, your hand together with your arm, or your two hands to grasp, manipulate, or assemble objects.
Visualization	The ability to imagine how something will look after it is moved around or when its parts are moved or rearranged.
Speed of Limb Movement	The ability to quickly move the arms and legs.
Speed of Closure	The ability to quickly make sense of, combine, and organize information into meaningful patterns.
Multilimb Coordination	The ability to coordinate two or more limbs (for example, two arms, two legs, or one leg and one arm) while sitting, standing, or lying down. It does not involve performing the activities while the whole body is in motion.
Auditory Attention	The ability to focus on a single source of sound in the presence of other distracting sounds.
Visual Color Discrimination	The ability to match or detect differences between colors, including shades of color and brightness.
Gross Body Coordination	The ability to coordinate the movement of your arms, legs, and torso together when the whole body is in motion.
Arm-Hand Steadiness	The ability to keep your hand and arm steady while moving your arm or while holding your arm and hand in one position.
Hearing Sensitivity	The ability to detect or tell the differences between sounds that vary in pitch and loudness.
Gross Body Equilibrium	The ability to keep or regain your body balance or stay upright when in an unstable position.
Dynamic Strength	The ability to exert muscle force repeatedly or continuously over time. This involves muscular endurance and resistance to muscle fatigue.
Reaction Time	The ability to quickly respond (with the hand, finger, or foot) to a signal (sound, light, picture) when it appears.
Control Precision	The ability to quickly and repeatedly adjust the controls of a machine or a vehicle to exact positions.
Depth Perception	The ability to judge which of several objects is closer or farther away from you, or to judge the distance between you and an object.
Wrist-Finger Speed	The ability to make fast, simple, repeated movements of the fingers, hands, and wrists.
Sound Localization	The ability to tell the direction from which a sound originated.

Night Vision	The ability to see under low light conditions.
Peripheral Vision	The ability to see objects or movement of objects to one's side when the eyes are looking ahead.
Glare Sensitivity	The ability to see objects in the presence of glare or bright lighting.
Rate Control	The ability to time your movements or the movement of a piece of equipment in anticipation of changes in the speed and/or direction of a moving object or scene.
Dynamic Flexibility	The ability to quickly and repeatedly bend, stretch, twist, or reach out with your body, arms, and/or legs.
Response Orientation	The ability to choose quickly between two or more movements in response to two or more different signals (lights, sounds, pictures). It includes the speed with which the correct response is started with the hand, foot, or other body part.
Spatial Orientation	The ability to know your location in relation to the environment or to know where other objects are in relation to you.
Explosive Strength	The ability to use short bursts of muscle force to propel oneself (as in jumping or sprinting), or to throw an object.

Work_Activity	**Work_Activity Definitions**
Performing for or Working Directly with the Public	Performing for people or dealing directly with the public. This includes serving customers in restaurants and stores, and receiving clients or guests.
Organizing, Planning, and Prioritizing Work	Developing specific goals and plans to prioritize, organize, and accomplish your work.
Establishing and Maintaining Interpersonal Relatio	Developing constructive and cooperative working relationships with others, and maintaining them over time.
Communicating with Persons Outside Organization	Communicating with people outside the organization, representing the organization to customers, the public, government, and other external sources. This information can be exchanged in person, in writing, or by telephone or e-mail.
Communicating with Supervisors, Peers, or Subordin	Providing information to supervisors, co-workers, and subordinates by telephone, in written form, e-mail, or in person.
Coaching and Developing Others	Identifying the developmental needs of others and coaching, mentoring, or otherwise helping others to improve their knowledge or skills.
Coordinating the Work and Activities of Others	Getting members of a group to work together to accomplish tasks.
Guiding, Directing, and Motivating Subordinates	Providing guidance and direction to subordinates, including setting performance standards and monitoring performance.
Thinking Creatively	Developing, designing, or creating new applications, ideas, relationships, systems, or products, including artistic contributions.
Making Decisions and Solving Problems	Analyzing information and evaluating results to choose the best solution and solve problems.
Performing General Physical Activities	Performing physical activities that require considerable use of your arms and legs and moving your whole body, such as climbing, lifting, balancing, walking, stooping, and handling of materials.
Resolving Conflicts and Negotiating with Others	Handling complaints, settling disputes, and resolving grievances and conflicts, or otherwise negotiating with others.
Training and Teaching Others	Identifying the educational needs of others, developing formal educational or training programs or classes, and teaching or instructing others.
Documenting/Recording Information	Entering, transcribing, recording, storing, or maintaining information in written or electronic/magnetic form.
Developing and Building Teams	Encouraging and building mutual trust, respect, and cooperation among team members.
Scheduling Work and Activities	Scheduling events, programs, and activities, as well as the work of others.
Getting Information	Observing, receiving, and otherwise obtaining information from all relevant sources.
Selling or Influencing Others	Convincing others to buy merchandise/goods or to otherwise change their minds or actions.
Handling and Moving Objects	Using hands and arms in handling, installing, positioning, and moving materials, and manipulating things.
Updating and Using Relevant Knowledge	Keeping up-to-date technically and applying new knowledge to your job.
Interacting With Computers	Using computers and computer systems (including hardware and software) to program, write software, set up functions, enter data, or process information.
Evaluating Information to Determine Compliance wit	Using relevant information and individual judgment to determine whether events or processes comply with laws, regulations, or standards.
Inspecting Equipment, Structures, or Material	Inspecting equipment, structures, or materials to identify the cause of errors or other problems or defects.
Monitor Processes, Materials, or Surroundings	Monitoring and reviewing information from materials, events, or the environment, to detect or assess problems.
Assisting and Caring for Others	Providing personal assistance, medical attention, emotional support, or other personal care to others such as coworkers, customers, or patients.

Staffing Organizational Units	Recruiting, interviewing, selecting, hiring, and promoting employees in an organization.
Performing Administrative Activities	Performing day-to-day administrative tasks such as maintaining information files and processing paperwork.
Processing Information	Compiling, coding, categorizing, calculating, tabulating, auditing, or verifying information or data.
Judging the Qualities of Things, Services, or Peop	Assessing the value, importance, or quality of things or people.
Provide Consultation and Advice to Others	Providing guidance and expert advice to management or other groups on technical, systems-, or process-related topics.
Identifying Objects, Actions, and Events	Identifying information by categorizing, estimating, recognizing differences or similarities, and detecting changes in circumstances or events.
Monitoring and Controlling Resources	Monitoring and controlling resources and overseeing the spending of money.
Developing Objectives and Strategies	Establishing long-range objectives and specifying the strategies and actions to achieve them.
Analyzing Data or Information	Identifying the underlying principles, reasons, or facts of information by breaking down information or data into separate parts.
Controlling Machines and Processes	Using either control mechanisms or direct physical activity to operate machines or processes (not including computers or vehicles).
Estimating the Quantifiable Characteristics of Pro	Estimating sizes, distances, and quantities; or determining time, costs, resources, or materials needed to perform a work activity.
Repairing and Maintaining Mechanical Equipment	Servicing, repairing, adjusting, and testing machines, devices, moving parts, and equipment that operate primarily on the basis of mechanical (not electronic) principles.
Repairing and Maintaining Electronic Equipment	Servicing, repairing, calibrating, regulating, fine-tuning, or testing machines, devices, and equipment that operate primarily on the basis of electrical or electronic (not mechanical) principles.
Operating Vehicles, Mechanized Devices, or Equipme	Running, maneuvering, navigating, or driving vehicles or mechanized equipment, such as forklifts, passenger vehicles, aircraft, or water craft.
Interpreting the Meaning of Information for Others	Translating or explaining what information means and how it can be used.
Drafting, Laying Out, and Specifying Technical Dev	Providing documentation, detailed instructions, drawings, or specifications to tell others about how devices, parts, equipment, or structures are to be fabricated, constructed, assembled, modified, maintained, or used.

Work_Content	**Work_Content Definitions**
Frequency of Decision Making	How frequently is the worker required to make decisions that affect other people, the financial resources, and/or the image and reputation of the organization?
Deal With External Customers	How important is it to work with external customers or the public in this job?
Indoors, Environmentally Controlled	How often does this job require working indoors in environmentally controlled conditions?
Contact With Others	How much does this job require the worker to be in contact with others (face-to-face, by telephone, or otherwise) in order to perform it?
Telephone	How often do you have telephone conversations in this job?
Spend Time Standing	How much does this job require standing?
Coordinate or Lead Others	How important is it to coordinate or lead others in accomplishing work activities in this job?
Responsibility for Outcomes and Results	How responsible is the worker for work outcomes and results of other workers?
Work With Work Group or Team	How important is it to work with others in a group or team in this job?
Face-to-Face Discussions	How often do you have to have face-to-face discussions with individuals or teams in this job?
Freedom to Make Decisions	How much decision making freedom, without supervision, does the job offer?
Physical Proximity	To what extent does this job require the worker to perform job tasks in close physical proximity to other people?
Time Pressure	How often does this job require the worker to meet strict deadlines?
Impact of Decisions on Co-workers or Company Resul	How do the decisions an employee makes impact the results of co-workers, clients or the company?
Spend Time Walking and Running	How much does this job require walking and running?
Structured versus Unstructured Work	To what extent is this job structured for the worker, rather than allowing the worker to determine tasks, priorities, and goals?
Responsible for Others' Health and Safety	How much responsibility is there for the health and safety of others in this job?
Deal With Unpleasant or Angry People	How frequently does the worker have to deal with unpleasant, angry, or discourteous individuals as part of the job requirements?
Letters and Memos	How often does the job require written letters and memos?
Level of Competition	To what extent does this job require the worker to compete or to be aware of competitive pressures?

Importance of Being Exact or Accurate	How important is being very exact or highly accurate in performing this job?
Spend Time Using Your Hands to Handle, Control, or	How much does this job require using your hands to handle, control, or feel objects, tools or controls?
Exposed to Hazardous Equipment	How often does this job require exposure to hazardous equipment?
Frequency of Conflict Situations	How often are there conflict situations the employee has to face in this job?
Wear Common Protective or Safety Equipment such as	How much does this job require wearing common protective or safety equipment such as safety shoes, glasses, gloves, hard hats or life jackets?
Exposed to Minor Burns, Cuts, Bites, or Stings	How often does this job require exposure to minor burns, cuts, bites, or stings?
Importance of Repeating Same Tasks	How important is repeating the same physical activities (e.g., key entry) or mental activities (e.g., checking entries in a ledger) over and over, without stopping, to performing this job?
Consequence of Error	How serious would the result usually be if the worker made a mistake that was not readily correctable?
Sounds, Noise Levels Are Distracting or Uncomforta	How often does this job require working exposed to sounds and noise levels that are distracting or uncomfortable?
Deal With Physically Aggressive People	How frequently does this job require the worker to deal with physical aggression of violent individuals?
Cramped Work Space, Awkward Positions	How often does this job require working in cramped work spaces that requires getting into awkward positions?
Spend Time Making Repetitive Motions	How much does this job require making repetitive motions?
Degree of Automation	How automated is the job?
Pace Determined by Speed of Equipment	How important is it to this job that the pace is determined by the speed of equipment or machinery? (This does not refer to keeping busy at all times on this job.)
In an Enclosed Vehicle or Equipment	How often does this job require working in a closed vehicle or equipment (e.g., car)?
Spend Time Sitting	How much does this job require sitting?
Electronic Mail	How often do you use electronic mail in this job?
Spend Time Bending or Twisting the Body	How much does this job require bending or twisting your body?
Public Speaking	How often do you have to perform public speaking in this job?
Very Hot or Cold Temperatures	How often does this job require working in very hot (above 90 F degrees) or very cold (below 32 F degrees) temperatures?
Indoors, Not Environmentally Controlled	How often does this job require working indoors in non-controlled environmental conditions (e.g., warehouse without heat)?
Outdoors, Exposed to Weather	How often does this job require working outdoors, exposed to all weather conditions?
Extremely Bright or Inadequate Lighting	How often does this job require working in extremely bright or inadequate lighting conditions?
Spend Time Kneeling, Crouching, Stooping, or Crawl	How much does this job require kneeling, crouching, stooping or crawling?
Outdoors, Under Cover	How often does this job require working outdoors, under cover (e.g., structure with roof but no walls)?
Exposed to Contaminants	How often does this job require working exposed to contaminants (such as pollutants, gases, dust or odors)?
Spend Time Keeping or Regaining Balance	How much does this job require keeping or regaining your balance?
Exposed to Hazardous Conditions	How often does this job require exposure to hazardous conditions?
Exposed to Disease or Infections	How often does this job require exposure to disease/infections?
Exposed to High Places	How often does this job require exposure to high places?
Spend Time Climbing Ladders, Scaffolds, or Poles	How much does this job require climbing ladders, scaffolds, or poles?
In an Open Vehicle or Equipment	How often does this job require working in an open vehicle or equipment (e.g., tractor)?
Exposed to Whole Body Vibration	How often does this job require exposure to whole body vibration (e.g., operate a jackhammer)?
Wear Specialized Protective or Safety Equipment su	How much does this job require wearing specialized protective or safety equipment such as breathing apparatus, safety harness, full protection suits, or radiation protection?
Exposed to Radiation	How often does this job require exposure to radiation?

Work_Styles	Work_Styles Definitions
Stress Tolerance	Job requires accepting criticism and dealing calmly and effectively with high stress situations.
Dependability	Job requires being reliable, responsible, and dependable, and fulfilling obligations.
Integrity	Job requires being honest and ethical.
Self Control	Job requires maintaining composure, keeping emotions in check, controlling anger, and avoiding aggressive behavior, even in very difficult situations.
Adaptability/Flexibility	Job requires being open to change (positive or negative) and to considerable variety in the workplace.

Leadership	Job requires a willingness to lead, take charge, and offer opinions and direction.
Attention to Detail	Job requires being careful about detail and thorough in completing work tasks.
Cooperation	Job requires being pleasant with others on the job and displaying a good-natured, cooperative attitude.
Achievement/Effort	Job requires establishing and maintaining personally challenging achievement goals and exerting effort toward mastering tasks.
Independence	Job requires developing one's own ways of doing things, guiding oneself with little or no supervision, and depending on oneself to get things done.
Concern for Others	Job requires being sensitive to others' needs and feelings and being understanding and helpful on the job.
Persistence	Job requires persistence in the face of obstacles.
Initiative	Job requires a willingness to take on responsibilities and challenges.
Social Orientation	Job requires preferring to work with others rather than alone, and being personally connected with others on the job.
Analytical Thinking	Job requires analyzing information and using logic to address work-related issues and problems.
Innovation	Job requires creativity and alternative thinking to develop new ideas for and answers to work-related problems.

Job Zone Component	Job Zone Component Definitions
Title	Job Zone Two: Some Preparation Needed
Overall Experience	Some previous work-related skill, knowledge, or experience may be helpful in these occupations, but usually is not needed. For example, a drywall installer might benefit from experience installing drywall, but an inexperienced person could still learn to be an installer with little difficulty.
Job Training	Employees in these occupations need anywhere from a few months to one year of working with experienced employees.
Job Zone Examples	These occupations often involve using your knowledge and skills to help others. Examples include drywall installers, fire inspectors, flight attendants, pharmacy technicians, salespersons (retail), and tellers.
SVP Range	(4.0 to < 6.0)
Education	These occupations usually require a high school diploma and may require some vocational training or job-related course work. In some cases, an associate's or bachelor's degree could be needed.

41-2011.00 - Cashiers

Receive and disburse money in establishments other than financial institutions. Usually involves use of electronic scanners, cash registers, or related equipment. Often involved in processing credit or debit card transactions and validating checks.

Tasks

1) Compile and maintain non-monetary reports and records.

2) Accept reservations or requests for take-out orders.

3) Weigh items sold by weight in order to determine prices.

4) Resolve customer complaints.

5) Sort, count, and wrap currency and coins.

6) Post charges against guests' or patients' accounts.

7) Cash checks for customers.

8) Issue trading stamps, and redeem food stamps and coupons.

9) Maintain clean and orderly checkout areas.

10) Process merchandise returns and exchanges.

11) Keep periodic balance sheets of amounts and numbers of transactions.

12) Compute and record totals of transactions.

13) Greet customers entering establishments.

14) Offer customers carry-out service at the completion of transactions.

15) Count money in cash drawers at the beginning of shifts to ensure that amounts are correct and that there is adequate change.

16) Bag, box, wrap, or gift-wrap merchandise, and prepare packages for shipment.

17) Answer customers' questions, and provide information on procedures or policies.

18) Receive payment by cash, check, credit cards, vouchers, or automatic debits.

19) Stock shelves, and mark prices on shelves and items.

20) Request information or assistance using paging systems.

21) Pay company bills by cash, vouchers, or checks.

22) Sell tickets and other items to customers.

23) Monitor checkout stations to ensure that they have adequate cash available and that they are staffed appropriately.

24) Issue receipts, refunds, credits, or change due to customers.

25) Establish or identify prices of goods, services or admission, and tabulate bills using calculators, cash registers, or optical price scanners.

41-2012.00 - Gaming Change Persons and Booth Cashiers

Exchange coins and tokens for patrons' money. May issue payoffs and obtain customer's signature on receipt when winnings exceed the amount held in the slot machine. May operate a booth in the slot machine area and furnish change persons with money bank at the start of the shift, or count and audit money in drawers.

Tasks

1) Count money and audit money drawers.

2) Exchange money, credit, and casino chips, and make change for customers.

3) Obtain customers' signatures on receipts when winnings exceed the amount held in a slot machine.

4) Calculate the value of chips won or lost by players.

5) Listen for jackpot alarm bells and issue payoffs to winners.

6) Work in and monitor an assigned area on the casino floor where slot machines are located.

7) Reconcile daily summaries of transactions to balance books.

8) Maintain cage security according to rules.

9) Furnish change persons with a money bank at the start of each shift.

10) Accept credit applications and verify credit references in order to provide check-cashing authorization or to establish house credit accounts.

11) Sell gambling chips, tokens, or tickets to patrons, or to other workers for resale to patrons.

41-2021.00 - Counter and Rental Clerks

Receive orders for repairs, rentals, and services. May describe available options, compute cost, and accept payment.

Tasks

1) Answer telephones to provide information and receive orders.

2) Prepare merchandise for display, or for purchase or rental.

3) Recommend and provide advice on a wide variety of products and services.

4) Greet customers and discuss the type, quality and quantity of merchandise sought for rental.

5) Advise customers on use and care of merchandise.

6) Inspect and adjust rental items to meet needs of customer.

7) Receive orders for services, such as rentals, repairs, dry cleaning, and storage.

8) Keep records of transactions, and of the number of customers entering an establishment.

9) Explain rental fees, policies and procedures.

10) Provide information about rental items, such as availability, operation or description.

11) Receive, examine, and tag articles to be altered, cleaned, stored, or repaired.

12) Reserve items for requested times and keep records of items rented.

13) Prepare rental forms, obtaining customer signature and other information, such as required licenses.

14) Rent items, arrange for provision of services to customers and accept returns.

15) Allocate equipment to participants in sporting events or recreational activities.

Knowledge	Knowledge Definitions
English Language	Knowledge of the structure and content of the English language including the meaning and spelling of words, rules of composition, and grammar.
Customer and Personal Service	Knowledge of principles and processes for providing customer and personal services. This includes customer needs assessment, meeting quality standards for services, and evaluation of customer satisfaction.
Administration and Management	Knowledge of business and management principles involved in strategic planning, resource allocation, human resources modeling, leadership technique, production methods, and coordination of people and resources.
Mathematics	Knowledge of arithmetic, algebra, geometry, calculus, statistics, and their applications.
Sales and Marketing	Knowledge of principles and methods for showing, promoting, and selling products or services. This includes marketing strategy and tactics, product demonstration, sales techniques, and sales control systems.
Economics and Accounting	Knowledge of economic and accounting principles and practices, the financial markets, banking and the analysis and reporting of financial data.
Transportation	Knowledge of principles and methods for moving people or goods by air, rail, sea, or road, including the relative costs and benefits.
Clerical	Knowledge of administrative and clerical procedures and systems such as word processing, managing files and records, stenography and transcription, designing forms, and other office procedures and terminology.
Food Production	Knowledge of techniques and equipment for planting, growing, and harvesting food products (both plant and animal) for consumption, including storage/handling techniques.
Production and Processing	Knowledge of raw materials, production processes, quality control, costs, and other techniques for maximizing the effective manufacture and distribution of goods.
Personnel and Human Resources	Knowledge of principles and procedures for personnel recruitment, selection, training, compensation and benefits, labor relations and negotiation, and personnel information systems.
Computers and Electronics	Knowledge of circuit boards, processors, chips, electronic equipment, and computer hardware and software, including applications and programming.
Public Safety and Security	Knowledge of relevant equipment, policies, procedures, and strategies to promote effective local, state, or national security operations for the protection of people, data, property, and institutions.
Law and Government	Knowledge of laws, legal codes, court procedures, precedents, government regulations, executive orders, agency rules, and the democratic political process.
Chemistry	Knowledge of the chemical composition, structure, and properties of substances and of the chemical processes and transformations that they undergo. This includes uses of chemicals and their interactions, danger signs, production techniques, and disposal methods.
Education and Training	Knowledge of principles and methods for curriculum and training design, teaching and instruction for individuals and groups, and the measurement of training effects.
Medicine and Dentistry	Knowledge of the information and techniques needed to diagnose and treat human injuries, diseases, and deformities. This includes symptoms, treatment alternatives, drug properties and interactions, and preventive health-care measures.
Foreign Language	Knowledge of the structure and content of a foreign (non-English) language including the meaning and spelling of words, rules of composition and grammar, and pronunciation.
Communications and Media	Knowledge of media production, communication, and dissemination techniques and methods. This includes alternative ways to inform and entertain via written, oral, and visual media.
Design	Knowledge of design techniques, tools, and principles involved in production of precision technical plans, blueprints, drawings, and models.
Telecommunications	Knowledge of transmission, broadcasting, switching, control, and operation of telecommunications systems.
Psychology	Knowledge of human behavior and performance; individual differences in ability, personality, and interests; learning and motivation; psychological research methods; and the assessment and treatment of behavioral and affective disorders.
Engineering and Technology	Knowledge of the practical application of engineering science and technology. This includes applying principles, techniques, procedures, and equipment to the design and production of various goods and services.
Physics	Knowledge and prediction of physical principles, laws, their interrelationships, and applications to understanding fluid, material, and atmospheric dynamics, and mechanical, electrical, atomic and sub-atomic structures and processes.
Biology	Knowledge of plant and animal organisms, their tissues, cells, functions, interdependencies, and interactions with each other and the environment.
Mechanical	Knowledge of machines and tools, including their designs, uses, repair, and maintenance.
Building and Construction	Knowledge of materials, methods, and the tools involved in the construction or repair of houses, buildings, or other structures such as highways and roads.
Therapy and Counseling	Knowledge of principles, methods, and procedures for diagnosis, treatment, and rehabilitation of physical and mental dysfunctions, and for career counseling and guidance.

History and Archeology	Knowledge of historical events and their causes, indicators, and effects on civilizations and cultures.
Geography	Knowledge of principles and methods for describing the features of land, sea, and air masses, including their physical characteristics, locations, interrelationships, and distribution of plant, animal, and human life.
Philosophy and Theology	Knowledge of different philosophical systems and religions. This includes their basic principles, values, ethics, ways of thinking, customs, practices, and their impact on human culture.
Sociology and Anthropology	Knowledge of group behavior and dynamics, societal trends and influences, human migrations, ethnicity, cultures and their history and origins.
Fine Arts	Knowledge of the theory and techniques required to compose, produce, and perform works of music, dance, visual arts, drama, and sculpture.

Skills	Skills Definitions
Active Listening	Giving full attention to what other people are saying, taking time to understand the points being made, asking questions as appropriate, and not interrupting at inappropriate times.
Reading Comprehension	Understanding written sentences and paragraphs in work related documents.
Speaking	Talking to others to convey information effectively.
Mathematics	Using mathematics to solve problems.
Service Orientation	Actively looking for ways to help people.
Social Perceptiveness	Being aware of others' reactions and understanding why they react as they do.
Monitoring	Monitoring/Assessing performance of yourself, other individuals, or organizations to make improvements or take corrective action.
Time Management	Managing one's own time and the time of others.
Instructing	Teaching others how to do something.
Critical Thinking	Using logic and reasoning to identify the strengths and weaknesses of alternative solutions, conclusions or approaches to problems.
Negotiation	Bringing others together and trying to reconcile differences.
Active Learning	Understanding the implications of new information for both current and future problem-solving and decision-making.
Writing	Communicating effectively in writing as appropriate for the needs of the audience.
Operation and Control	Controlling operations of equipment or systems.
Judgment and Decision Making	Considering the relative costs and benefits of potential actions to choose the most appropriate one.
Equipment Maintenance	Performing routine maintenance on equipment and determining when and what kind of maintenance is needed.
Repairing	Repairing machines or systems using the needed tools.
Learning Strategies	Selecting and using training/instructional methods and procedures appropriate for the situation when learning or teaching new things.
Troubleshooting	Determining causes of operating errors and deciding what to do about it.
Systems Evaluation	Identifying measures or indicators of system performance and the actions needed to improve or correct performance, relative to the goals of the system.
Persuasion	Persuading others to change their minds or behavior.
Coordination	Adjusting actions in relation to others' actions.
Equipment Selection	Determining the kind of tools and equipment needed to do a job.
Management of Material Resources	Obtaining and seeing to the appropriate use of equipment, facilities, and materials needed to do certain work.
Systems Analysis	Determining how a system should work and how changes in conditions, operations, and the environment will affect outcomes.
Management of Personnel Resources	Motivating, developing, and directing people as they work, identifying the best people for the job.
Complex Problem Solving	Identifying complex problems and reviewing related information to develop and evaluate options and implement solutions.
Operations Analysis	Analyzing needs and product requirements to create a design.
Quality Control Analysis	Conducting tests and inspections of products, services, or processes to evaluate quality or performance.
Management of Financial Resources	Determining how money will be spent to get the work done, and accounting for these expenditures.
Science	Using scientific rules and methods to solve problems.
Installation	Installing equipment, machines, wiring, or programs to meet specifications.
Operation Monitoring	Watching gauges, dials, or other indicators to make sure a machine is working properly.
Programming	Writing computer programs for various purposes.
Technology Design	Generating or adapting equipment and technology to serve user needs.

Ability	Ability Definitions

Oral Comprehension	The ability to listen to and understand information and ideas presented through spoken words and sentences.
Oral Expression	The ability to communicate information and ideas in speaking so others will understand.
Speech Clarity	The ability to speak clearly so others can understand you.
Speech Recognition	The ability to identify and understand the speech of another person.
Near Vision	The ability to see details at close range (within a few feet of the observer).
Trunk Strength	The ability to use your abdominal and lower back muscles to support part of the body repeatedly or continuously over time without 'giving out' or fatiguing.
Information Ordering	The ability to arrange things or actions in a certain order or pattern according to a specific rule or set of rules (e.g., patterns of numbers, letters, words, pictures, mathematical operations).
Problem Sensitivity	The ability to tell when something is wrong or is likely to go wrong. It does not involve solving the problem, only recognizing there is a problem.
Selective Attention	The ability to concentrate on a task over a period of time without being distracted.
Deductive Reasoning	The ability to apply general rules to specific problems to produce answers that make sense.
Category Flexibility	The ability to generate or use different sets of rules for combining or grouping things in different ways.
Inductive Reasoning	The ability to combine pieces of information to form general rules or conclusions (includes finding a relationship among seemingly unrelated events).
Number Facility	The ability to add, subtract, multiply, or divide quickly and correctly.
Written Expression	The ability to communicate information and ideas in writing so others will understand.
Mathematical Reasoning	The ability to choose the right mathematical methods or formulas to solve a problem.
Written Comprehension	The ability to read and understand information and ideas presented in writing.
Manual Dexterity	The ability to quickly move your hand, your hand together with your arm, or your two hands to grasp, manipulate, or assemble objects.
Auditory Attention	The ability to focus on a single source of sound in the presence of other distracting sounds.
Time Sharing	The ability to shift back and forth between two or more activities or sources of information (such as speech, sounds, touch, or other sources).
Originality	The ability to come up with unusual or clever ideas about a given topic or situation, or to develop creative ways to solve a problem.
Arm-Hand Steadiness	The ability to keep your hand and arm steady while moving your arm or while holding your arm and hand in one position.
Far Vision	The ability to see details at a distance.
Stamina	The ability to exert yourself physically over long periods of time without getting winded or out of breath.
Gross Body Coordination	The ability to coordinate the movement of your arms, legs, and torso together when the whole body is in motion.
Extent Flexibility	The ability to bend, stretch, twist, or reach with your body, arms, and/or legs.
Finger Dexterity	The ability to make precisely coordinated movements of the fingers of one or both hands to grasp, manipulate, or assemble very small objects.
Fluency of Ideas	The ability to come up with a number of ideas about a topic (the number of ideas is important, not their quality, correctness, or creativity).
Memorization	The ability to remember information such as words, numbers, pictures, and procedures.
Visual Color Discrimination	The ability to match or detect differences between colors, including shades of color and brightness.
Flexibility of Closure	The ability to identify or detect a known pattern (a figure, object, word, or sound) that is hidden in other distracting material.
Perceptual Speed	The ability to quickly and accurately compare similarities and differences among sets of letters, numbers, objects, pictures, or patterns. The things to be compared may be presented at the same time or one after the other. This ability also includes comparing a presented object with a remembered object.
Visualization	The ability to imagine how something will look after it is moved around or when its parts are moved or rearranged.
Speed of Closure	The ability to quickly make sense of, combine, and organize information into meaningful patterns.
Speed of Limb Movement	The ability to quickly move the arms and legs.
Hearing Sensitivity	The ability to detect or tell the differences between sounds that vary in pitch and loudness.
Static Strength	The ability to exert maximum muscle force to lift, push, pull, or carry objects.
Depth Perception	The ability to judge which of several objects is closer or farther away from you, or to judge the distance between you and an object.

241

Reaction Time	The ability to quickly respond (with the hand, finger. or foot) to a signal (sound, light, picture) when it appears.
Control Precision	The ability to quickly and repeatedly adjust the controls of a machine or a vehicle to exact positions.
Sound Localization	The ability to tell the direction from which a sound originated.
Multilimb Coordination	The ability to coordinate two or more limbs (for example, two arms, two legs, or one leg and one arm) while sitting, standing, or lying down. It does not involve performing the activities while the whole body is in motion.
Glare Sensitivity	The ability to see objects in the presence of glare or bright lighting.
Night Vision	The ability to see under low light conditions.
Wrist-Finger Speed	The ability to make fast, simple, repeated movements of the fingers, hands, and wrists.
Dynamic Flexibility	The ability to quickly and repeatedly bend, stretch, twist, or reach out with your body, arms, and/or legs.
Spatial Orientation	The ability to know your location in relation to the environment or to know where other objects are in relation to you.
Explosive Strength	The ability to use short bursts of muscle force to propel oneself (as in jumping or sprinting), or to throw an object.
Gross Body Equilibrium	The ability to keep or regain your body balance or stay upright when in an unstable position.
Rate Control	The ability to time your movements or the movement of a piece of equipment in anticipation of changes in the speed and/or direction of a moving object or scene.
Peripheral Vision	The ability to see objects or movement of objects to one's side when the eyes are looking ahead.
Dynamic Strength	The ability to exert muscle force repeatedly or continuously over time. This involves muscular endurance and resistance to muscle fatigue.
Response Orientation	The ability to choose quickly between two or more movements in response to two or more different signals (lights, sounds, pictures). It includes the speed with which the correct response is started with the hand, foot, or other body part.

Work_Activity	**Work_Activity Definitions**
Performing for or Working Directly with the Public	Performing for people or dealing directly with the public. This includes serving customers in restaurants and stores, and receiving clients or guests.
Getting Information	Observing, receiving, and otherwise obtaining information from all relevant sources.
Identifying Objects, Actions, and Events	Identifying information by categorizing, estimating, recognizing differences or similarities, and detecting changes in circumstances or events.
Developing and Building Teams	Encouraging and building mutual trust, respect, and cooperation among team members.
Establishing and Maintaining Interpersonal Relatio	Developing constructive and cooperative working relationships with others, and maintaining them over time.
Making Decisions and Solving Problems	Analyzing information and evaluating results to choose the best solution and solve problems.
Updating and Using Relevant Knowledge	Keeping up-to-date technically and applying new knowledge to your job.
Evaluating Information to Determine Compliance wit	Using relevant information and individual judgment to determine whether events or processes comply with laws, regulations, or standards.
Judging the Qualities of Things, Services, or Peop	Assessing the value, importance, or quality of things or people.
Assisting and Caring for Others	Providing personal assistance, medical attention, emotional support, or other personal care to others such as coworkers, customers, or patients.
Monitor Processes, Materials, or Surroundings	Monitoring and reviewing information from materials, events, or the environment, to detect or assess problems.
Resolving Conflicts and Negotiating with Others	Handling complaints, settling disputes, and resolving grievances and conflicts, or otherwise negotiating with others.
Estimating the Quantifiable Characteristics of Pro	Estimating sizes, distances, and quantities; or determining time, costs, resources, or materials needed to perform a work activity.
Organizing, Planning, and Prioritizing Work	Developing specific goals and plans to prioritize, organize, and accomplish your work.
Performing Administrative Activities	Performing day-to-day administrative tasks such as maintaining information files and processing paperwork.
Communicating with Persons Outside Organization	Communicating with people outside the organization, representing the organization to customers, the public, government, and other external sources. This information can be exchanged in person, in writing, or by telephone or e-mail.
Performing General Physical Activities	Performing physical activities that require considerable use of your arms and legs and moving your whole body, such as climbing, lifting, balancing, walking, stooping, and handling of materials.
Coaching and Developing Others	Identifying the developmental needs of others and coaching, mentoring, or otherwise helping others to improve their knowledge or skills.

Selling or Influencing Others	Convincing others to buy merchandise/goods or to otherwise change their minds or actions.
Interacting With Computers	Using computers and computer systems (including hardware and software) to program, write software, set up functions, enter data, or process information.
Provide Consultation and Advice to Others	Providing guidance and expert advice to management or other groups on technical, systems-, or process-related topics.
Communicating with Supervisors, Peers, or Subordin	Providing information to supervisors, co-workers, and subordinates by telephone, in written form, e-mail, or in person.
Handling and Moving Objects	Using hands and arms in handling, installing, positioning, and moving materials, and manipulating things.
Inspecting Equipment, Structures, or Material	Inspecting equipment, structures, or materials to identify the cause of errors or other problems or defects.
Documenting/Recording Information	Entering, transcribing, recording, storing, or maintaining information in written or electronic/magnetic form.
Interpreting the Meaning of Information for Others	Translating or explaining what information means and how it can be used.
Coordinating the Work and Activities of Others	Getting members of a group to work together to accomplish tasks.
Processing Information	Compiling, coding, categorizing, calculating, tabulating, auditing, or verifying information or data.
Training and Teaching Others	Identifying the educational needs of others, developing formal educational or training programs or classes, and teaching or instructing others.
Thinking Creatively	Developing, designing, or creating new applications, ideas, relationships, systems, or products, including artistic contributions.
Guiding, Directing, and Motivating Subordinates	Providing guidance and direction to subordinates, including setting performance standards and monitoring performance.
Scheduling Work and Activities	Scheduling events, programs, and activities, as well as the work of others.
Analyzing Data or Information	Identifying the underlying principles, reasons, or facts of information by breaking down information or data into separate parts.
Controlling Machines and Processes	Using either control mechanisms or direct physical activity to operate machines or processes (not including computers or vehicles).
Monitoring and Controlling Resources	Monitoring and controlling resources and overseeing the spending of money.
Repairing and Maintaining Mechanical Equipment	Servicing, repairing, adjusting, and testing machines, devices, moving parts, and equipment that operate primarily on the basis of mechanical (not electronic) principles.
Staffing Organizational Units	Recruiting, interviewing, selecting, hiring, and promoting employees in an organization.
Operating Vehicles, Mechanized Devices, or Equipme	Running, maneuvering, navigating, or driving vehicles or mechanized equipment, such as forklifts, passenger vehicles, aircraft, or water craft.
Developing Objectives and Strategies	Establishing long-range objectives and specifying the strategies and actions to achieve them.
Repairing and Maintaining Electronic Equipment	Servicing, repairing, calibrating, regulating, fine-tuning, or testing machines, devices, and equipment that operate primarily on the basis of electrical or electronic (not mechanical) principles.
Drafting, Laying Out, and Specifying Technical Dev	Providing documentation, detailed instructions, drawings, or specifications to tell others about how devices, parts, equipment, or structures are to be fabricated, constructed, assembled, modified, maintained, or used.

Work_Content	**Work_Content Definitions**
Contact With Others	How much does this job require the worker to be in contact with others (face-to-face, by telephone, or otherwise) in order to perform it?
Deal With External Customers	How important is it to work with external customers or the public in this job?
Spend Time Standing	How much does this job require standing?
Face-to-Face Discussions	How often do you have to have face-to-face discussions with individuals or teams in this job?
Indoors, Environmentally Controlled	How often does this job require working indoors in environmentally controlled conditions?
Physical Proximity	To what extent does this job require the worker to perform job tasks in close physical proximity to other people?
Freedom to Make Decisions	How much decision making freedom, without supervision, does the job offer?
Work With Work Group or Team	How important is it to work with others in a group or team in this job?
Coordinate or Lead Others	How important is it to coordinate or lead others in accomplishing work activities in this job?
Frequency of Decision Making	How frequently is the worker required to make decisions that affect other people, the financial resources, and/or the image and reputation of the organization?
Structured versus Unstructured Work	To what extent is this job structured for the worker, rather than allowing the worker to determine tasks, priorities, and goals?
Importance of Being Exact or Accurate	How important is being very exact or highly accurate in performing this job?

242

Level of Competition	To what extent does this job require the worker to compete or to be aware of competitive pressures?
Spend Time Using Your Hands to Handle, Control, or	How much does this job require using your hands to handle, control, or feel objects, tools or controls?
Spend Time Walking and Running	How much does this job require walking and running?
Impact of Decisions on Co-workers or Company Resul	How do the decisions an employee makes impact the results of co-workers, clients or the company?
Importance of Repeating Same Tasks	How important is repeating the same physical activities (e.g., key entry) or mental activities (e.g., checking entries in a ledger) over and over, without stopping, to performing this job?
Deal With Unpleasant or Angry People	How frequently does the worker have to deal with unpleasant, angry, or discourteous individuals as part of the job requirements?
Sounds, Noise Levels Are Distracting or Uncomforta	How often does this job require working exposed to sounds and noise levels that are distracting or uncomfortable?
Frequency of Conflict Situations	How often are there conflict situations the employee has to face in this job?
Public Speaking	How often do you have to perform public speaking in this job?
Telephone	How often do you have telephone conversations in this job?
Exposed to Hazardous Equipment	How often does this job require exposure to hazardous equipment?
Exposed to Minor Burns, Cuts, Bites, or Stings	How often does this job require exposure to minor burns, cuts, bites, or stings?
Exposed to Contaminants	How often does this job require working exposed to contaminants (such as pollutants, gases, dust or odors)?
Responsibility for Outcomes and Results	How responsible is the worker for work outcomes and results of other workers?
Degree of Automation	How automated is the job?
Spend Time Kneeling, Crouching, Stooping, or Crawl	How much does this job require kneeling, crouching, stooping or crawling?
Responsible for Others' Health and Safety	How much responsibility is there for the health and safety of others in this job?
Letters and Memos	How often does the job require written letters and memos?
Pace Determined by Speed of Equipment	How important is it to this job that the pace is determined by the speed of equipment or machinery? (This does not refer to keeping busy at all times on this job.)
Time Pressure	How often does this job require the worker to meet strict deadlines?
Spend Time Making Repetitive Motions	How much does this job require making repetitive motions?
Consequence of Error	How serious would the result usually be if the worker made a mistake that was not readily correctable?
Spend Time Sitting	How much does this job require sitting?
Deal With Physically Aggressive People	How frequently does this job require the worker to deal with physical aggression of violent individuals?
Spend Time Bending or Twisting the Body	How much does this job require bending or twisting your body?
Indoors, Not Environmentally Controlled	How often does this job require working indoors in non-controlled environmental conditions (e.g., warehouse without heat)?
Extremely Bright or Inadequate Lighting	How often does this job require working in extremely bright or inadequate lighting conditions?
Very Hot or Cold Temperatures	How often does this job require working in very hot (above 90 F degrees) or very cold (below 32 F degrees) temperatures?
In an Enclosed Vehicle or Equipment	How often does this job require working in a closed vehicle or equipment (e.g., car)?
Exposed to Hazardous Conditions	How often does this job require exposure to hazardous conditions?
Electronic Mail	How often do you use electronic mail in this job?
Spend Time Keeping or Regaining Balance	How much does this job require keeping or regaining your balance?
Cramped Work Space, Awkward Positions	How often does this job require working in cramped work spaces that requires getting into awkward positions?
In an Open Vehicle or Equipment	How often does this job require working in an open vehicle or equipment (e.g., tractor)?
Wear Common Protective or Safety Equipment such as	How much does this job require wearing common protective or safety equipment such as safety shoes, glasses, gloves, hard hats or live jackets?
Exposed to High Places	How often does this job require exposure to high places?
Outdoors, Exposed to Weather	How often does this job require working outdoors, exposed to all weather conditions?
Exposed to Disease or Infections	How often does this job require exposure to disease/infections?
Exposed to Radiation	How often does this job require exposure to radiation?
Spend Time Climbing Ladders, Scaffolds, or Poles	How much does this job require climbing ladders, scaffolds, or poles?
Outdoors, Under Cover	How often does this job require working outdoors, under cover (e.g., structure with roof but no walls)?
Exposed to Whole Body Vibration	How often does this job require exposure to whole body vibration (e.g., operate a jackhammer)?

Wear Specialized Protective or Safety Equipment su	How much does this job require wearing specialized protective or safety equipment such as breathing apparatus, safety harness, full protection suits, or radiation protection?

Work_Styles	Work_Styles Definitions
Integrity	Job requires being honest and ethical.
Dependability	Job requires being reliable, responsible, and dependable, and fulfilling obligations.
Self Control	Job requires maintaining composure, keeping emotions in check, controlling anger, and avoiding aggressive behavior, even in very difficult situations.
Attention to Detail	Job requires being careful about detail and thorough in completing work tasks.
Adaptability/Flexibility	Job requires being open to change (positive or negative) and to considerable variety in the workplace.
Cooperation	Job requires being pleasant with others on the job and displaying a good-natured, cooperative attitude.
Stress Tolerance	Job requires accepting criticism and dealing calmly and effectively with high stress situations.
Leadership	Job requires a willingness to lead, take charge, and offer opinions and direction.
Concern for Others	Job requires being sensitive to others' needs and feelings and being understanding and helpful on the job.
Achievement/Effort	Job requires establishing and maintaining personally challenging achievement goals and exerting effort toward mastering tasks.
Independence	Job requires developing one's own ways of doing things, guiding oneself with little or no supervision, and depending on oneself to get things done.
Social Orientation	Job requires preferring to work with others rather than alone, and being personally connected with others on the job.
Initiative	Job requires a willingness to take on responsibilities and challenges.
Persistence	Job requires persistence in the face of obstacles.
Innovation	Job requires creativity and alternative thinking to develop new ideas for and answers to work-related problems.
Analytical Thinking	Job requires analyzing information and using logic to address work-related issues and problems.

Job Zone Component	Job Zone Component Definitions
Title	Job Zone One: Little or No Preparation Needed
Overall Experience	No previous work-related skill, knowledge, or experience is needed for these occupations. For example, a person can become a general office clerk even if he/she has never worked in an office before.
Job Training	Employees in these occupations need anywhere from a few days to a few months of training. Usually, an experienced worker could show you how to do the job.
Job Zone Examples	These occupations involve following instructions and helping others. Examples include bus drivers, forest and conservation workers, general office clerks, home health aides, and waiters/waitresses.
SVP Range	(Below 4.0)
Education	These occupations may require a high school diploma or GED certificate. Some may require a formal training course to obtain a license.

41-2022.00 - Parts Salespersons

Sell spare and replacement parts and equipment in repair shop or parts store.

Tasks

1) Examine returned parts for defects, and exchange defective parts or refund money.

2) Determine replacement parts required, according to inspections of old parts, customer requests, or customers' descriptions of malfunctions.

3) Read catalogs, microfiche viewers, or computer displays in order to determine replacement part stock numbers and prices.

4) Advise customers on substitution or modification of parts when identical replacements are not available.

5) Prepare sales slips or sales contracts.

6) Discuss use and features of various parts, based on knowledge of machines or equipment.

7) Measure parts, using precision measuring instruments, in order to determine whether similar parts may be machined to required sizes.

8) Repair parts or equipment.

9) Place new merchandise on display.

10) Mark and store parts in stockrooms according to prearranged systems.

11) Take inventory of stock.

12) Demonstrate equipment to customers and explain functioning of equipment.

13) Fill customer orders from stock.

14) Receive payment or obtain credit authorization.

41-2031.00 - Retail Salespersons

Sell merchandise, such as furniture, motor vehicles, appliances, or apparel in a retail establishment.

Tasks

1) Greet customers and ascertain what each customer wants or needs.

2) Recommend, select, and help locate or obtain merchandise based on customer needs and desires.

3) Clean shelves, counters, and tables.

4) Maintain knowledge of current sales and promotions, policies regarding payment and exchanges, and security practices.

5) Ticket, arrange and display merchandise to promote sales.

6) Compute sales prices, total purchases and receive and process cash or credit payment.

7) Watch for and recognize security risks and thefts, and know how to prevent or handle these situations.

8) Describe merchandise and explain use, operation, and care of merchandise to customers.

9) Bag or package purchases, and wrap gifts.

10) Exchange merchandise for customers and accept returns.

11) Open and close cash registers, performing tasks such as counting money, separating charge slips, coupons, and vouchers, balancing cash drawers, and making deposits.

12) Demonstrate use or operation of merchandise.

13) Maintain records related to sales.

14) Prepare sales slips or sales contracts.

15) Place special orders or call other stores to find desired items.

16) Inventory stock and requisition new stock.

17) Prepare merchandise for purchase or rental.

18) Help customers try on or fit merchandise.

19) Sell or arrange for delivery, insurance, financing, or service contracts for merchandise.

20) Estimate cost of repair or alteration of merchandise.

21) Estimate quantity and cost of merchandise required, such as paint or floor covering.

22) Estimate and quote trade-in allowances.

23) Rent merchandise to customers.

Knowledge	Knowledge Definitions
Customer and Personal Service	Knowledge of principles and processes for providing customer and personal services. This includes customer needs assessment, meeting quality standards for services, and evaluation of customer satisfaction.
Sales and Marketing	Knowledge of principles and methods for showing, promoting, and selling products or services. This includes marketing strategy and tactics, product demonstration, sales techniques, and sales control systems.
Administration and Management	Knowledge of business and management principles involved in strategic planning, resource allocation, human resources modeling, leadership technique, production methods, and coordination of people and resources.
Education and Training	Knowledge of principles and methods for curriculum and training design, teaching and instruction for individuals and groups, and the measurement of training effects.
Mathematics	Knowledge of arithmetic, algebra, geometry, calculus, statistics, and their applications.
English Language	Knowledge of the structure and content of the English language including the meaning and spelling of words, rules of composition, and grammar.
Public Safety and Security	Knowledge of relevant equipment, policies, procedures, and strategies to promote effective local, state, or national security operations for the protection of people, data, property, and institutions.
Personnel and Human Resources	Knowledge of principles and procedures for personnel recruitment, selection, training, compensation and benefits, labor relations and negotiation, and personnel information systems.
Clerical	Knowledge of administrative and clerical procedures and systems such as word processing, managing files and records, stenography and transcription, designing forms, and other office procedures and terminology.
Economics and Accounting	Knowledge of economic and accounting principles and practices, the financial markets, banking and the analysis and reporting of financial data.
Psychology	Knowledge of human behavior and performance; individual differences in ability, personality, and interests; learning and motivation; psychological research methods; and the assessment and treatment of behavioral and affective disorders.
Telecommunications	Knowledge of transmission, broadcasting, switching, control, and operation of telecommunications systems.
Law and Government	Knowledge of laws, legal codes, court procedures, precedents, government regulations, executive orders, agency rules, and the democratic political process.
Computers and Electronics	Knowledge of circuit boards, processors, chips, electronic equipment, and computer hardware and software, including applications and programming.
Transportation	Knowledge of principles and methods for moving people or goods by air, rail, sea, or road, including the relative costs and benefits.
Production and Processing	Knowledge of raw materials, production processes, quality control, costs, and other techniques for maximizing the effective manufacture and distribution of goods.
Communications and Media	Knowledge of media production, communication, and dissemination techniques and methods. This includes alternative ways to inform and entertain via written, oral, and visual media.
Sociology and Anthropology	Knowledge of group behavior and dynamics, societal trends and influences, human migrations, ethnicity, cultures and their history and origins.
Mechanical	Knowledge of machines and tools, including their designs, uses, repair, and maintenance.
Foreign Language	Knowledge of the structure and content of a foreign (non-English) language including the meaning and spelling of words, rules of composition and grammar, and pronunciation.
Geography	Knowledge of principles and methods for describing the features of land, sea, and air masses, including their physical characteristics, locations, interrelationships, and distribution of plant, animal, and human life.
Therapy and Counseling	Knowledge of principles, methods, and procedures for diagnosis, treatment, and rehabilitation of physical and mental dysfunctions, and for career counseling and guidance.
Medicine and Dentistry	Knowledge of the information and techniques needed to diagnose and treat human injuries, diseases, and deformities. This includes symptoms, treatment alternatives, drug properties and interactions, and preventive health-care measures.
Design	Knowledge of design techniques, tools, and principles involved in production of precision technical plans, blueprints, drawings, and models.
Engineering and Technology	Knowledge of the practical application of engineering science and technology. This includes applying principles, techniques, procedures, and equipment to the design and production of various goods and services.
Chemistry	Knowledge of the chemical composition, structure, and properties of substances and of the chemical processes and transformations that they undergo. This includes uses of chemicals and their interactions, danger signs, production techniques, and disposal methods.
Food Production	Knowledge of techniques and equipment for planting, growing, and harvesting food products (both plant and animal) for consumption, including storage/handling techniques.
Fine Arts	Knowledge of the theory and techniques required to compose, produce, and perform works of music, dance, visual arts, drama, and sculpture.
Biology	Knowledge of plant and animal organisms, their tissues, cells, functions, interdependencies, and interactions with each other and the environment.
Physics	Knowledge and prediction of physical principles, laws, their interrelationships, and applications to understanding fluid, material, and atmospheric dynamics, and mechanical, electrical, atomic and sub-atomic structures and processes.
Philosophy and Theology	Knowledge of different philosophical systems and religions. This includes their basic principles, values, ethics, ways of thinking, customs, practices, and their impact on human culture.
History and Archeology	Knowledge of historical events and their causes, indicators, and effects on civilizations and cultures.
Building and Construction	Knowledge of materials, methods, and the tools involved in construction or repair of houses, buildings, or other structures such as highways and roads.

Skills	Skills Definitions
Active Listening	Giving full attention to what other people are saying, taking time to understand the points being made, asking questions as appropriate, and not interrupting at inappropriate times.

Mathematics	Using mathematics to solve problems.
Speaking	Talking to others to convey information effectively.
Social Perceptiveness	Being aware of others' reactions and understanding why they react as they do.
Critical Thinking	Using logic and reasoning to identify the strengths and weaknesses of alternative solutions, conclusions or approaches to problems.
Writing	Communicating effectively in writing as appropriate for the needs of the audience.
Judgment and Decision Making	Considering the relative costs and benefits of potential actions to choose the most appropriate one.
Instructing	Teaching others how to do something.
Reading Comprehension	Understanding written sentences and paragraphs in work related documents.
Time Management	Managing one's own time and the time of others.
Negotiation	Bringing others together and trying to reconcile differences.
Learning Strategies	Selecting and using training/instructional methods and procedures appropriate for the situation when learning or teaching new things.
Active Learning	Understanding the implications of new information for both current and future problem-solving and decision-making.
Service Orientation	Actively looking for ways to help people.
Operation and Control	Controlling operations of equipment or systems.
Management of Personnel Resources	Motivating, developing, and directing people as they work, identifying the best people for the job.
Coordination	Adjusting actions in relation to others' actions.
Systems Analysis	Determining how a system should work and how changes in conditions, operations, and the environment will affect outcomes.
Systems Evaluation	Identifying measures or indicators of system performance and the actions needed to improve or correct performance, relative to the goals of the system.
Monitoring	Monitoring/Assessing performance of yourself, other individuals, or organizations to make improvements or take corrective action.
Persuasion	Persuading others to change their minds or behavior.
Operations Analysis	Analyzing needs and product requirements to create a design.
Complex Problem Solving	Identifying complex problems and reviewing related information to develop and evaluate options and implement solutions.
Equipment Maintenance	Performing routine maintenance on equipment and determining when and what kind of maintenance is needed.
Troubleshooting	Determining causes of operating errors and deciding what to do about it.
Management of Financial Resources	Determining how money will be spent to get the work done, and accounting for these expenditures.
Equipment Selection	Determining the kind of tools and equipment needed to do a job.
Operation Monitoring	Watching gauges, dials, or other indicators to make sure a machine is working properly.
Repairing	Repairing machines or systems using the needed tools.
Quality Control Analysis	Conducting tests and inspections of products, services, or processes to evaluate quality or performance.
Management of Material Resources	Obtaining and seeing to the appropriate use of equipment, facilities, and materials needed to do certain work.
Programming	Writing computer programs for various purposes.
Technology Design	Generating or adapting equipment and technology to serve user needs.
Installation	Installing equipment, machines, wiring, or programs to meet specifications.
Science	Using scientific rules and methods to solve problems.

Ability	Ability Definitions
Oral Comprehension	The ability to listen to and understand information and ideas presented through spoken words and sentences.
Oral Expression	The ability to communicate information and ideas in speaking so others will understand.
Trunk Strength	The ability to use your abdominal and lower back muscles to support part of the body repeatedly or continuously over time without 'giving out' or fatiguing.
Speech Clarity	The ability to speak clearly so others can understand you.
Speech Recognition	The ability to identify and understand the speech of another person.
Information Ordering	The ability to arrange things or actions in a certain order or pattern according to a specific rule or set of rules (e.g., patterns of numbers, letters, words, pictures, mathematical operations).
Problem Sensitivity	The ability to tell when something is wrong or is likely to go wrong. It does not involve solving the problem, only recognizing there is a problem.
Number Facility	The ability to add, subtract, multiply, or divide quickly and correctly.
Inductive Reasoning	The ability to combine pieces of information to form general rules or conclusions (includes finding a relationship among seemingly unrelated events).

Deductive Reasoning	The ability to apply general rules to specific problems to produce answers that make sense.
Manual Dexterity	The ability to quickly move your hand, your hand together with your arm, or your two hands to grasp, manipulate, or assemble objects.
Near Vision	The ability to see details at close range (within a few feet of the observer).
Finger Dexterity	The ability to make precisely coordinated movements of the fingers of one or both hands to grasp, manipulate, or assemble very small objects.
Time Sharing	The ability to shift back and forth between two or more activities or sources of information (such as speech, sounds, touch, or other sources).
Category Flexibility	The ability to generate or use different sets of rules for combining or grouping things in different ways.
Selective Attention	The ability to concentrate on a task over a period of time without being distracted.
Written Comprehension	The ability to read and understand information and ideas presented in writing.
Mathematical Reasoning	The ability to choose the right mathematical methods or formulas to solve a problem.
Perceptual Speed	The ability to quickly and accurately compare similarities and differences among sets of letters, numbers, objects, pictures, or patterns. The things to be compared may be presented at the same time or one after the other. This ability also includes comparing a presented object with a remembered object.
Memorization	The ability to remember information such as words, numbers, pictures, and procedures.
Multilimb Coordination	The ability to coordinate two or more limbs (for example, two arms, two legs, or one leg and one arm) while sitting, standing, or lying down. It does not involve performing the activities while the whole body is in motion.
Written Expression	The ability to communicate information and ideas in writing so others will understand.
Visual Color Discrimination	The ability to match or detect differences between colors, including shades of color and brightness.
Far Vision	The ability to see details at a distance.
Fluency of Ideas	The ability to come up with a number of ideas about a topic (the number of ideas is important, not their quality, correctness, or creativity).
Static Strength	The ability to exert maximum muscle force to lift, push, pull, or carry objects.
Originality	The ability to come up with unusual or clever ideas about a given topic or situation, or to develop creative ways to solve a problem.
Extent Flexibility	The ability to bend, stretch, twist, or reach with your body, arms, and/or legs.
Stamina	The ability to exert yourself physically over long periods of time without getting winded or out of breath.
Arm-Hand Steadiness	The ability to keep your hand and arm steady while moving your arm or while holding your arm and hand in one position.
Visualization	The ability to imagine how something will look after it is moved around or when its parts are moved or rearranged.
Gross Body Coordination	The ability to coordinate the movement of your arms, legs, and torso together when the whole body is in motion.
Flexibility of Closure	The ability to identify or detect a known pattern (a figure, object, word, or sound) that is hidden in other distracting material.
Speed of Closure	The ability to quickly make sense of, combine, and organize information into meaningful patterns.
Gross Body Equilibrium	The ability to keep or regain your body balance or stay upright when in an unstable position.
Speed of Limb Movement	The ability to quickly move the arms and legs.
Control Precision	The ability to quickly and repeatedly adjust the controls of a machine or a vehicle to exact positions.
Wrist-Finger Speed	The ability to make fast, simple, repeated movements of the fingers, hands, and wrists.
Spatial Orientation	The ability to know your location in relation to the environment or to know where other objects are in relation to you.
Hearing Sensitivity	The ability to detect or tell the differences between sounds that vary in pitch and loudness.
Dynamic Strength	The ability to exert muscle force repeatedly or continuously over time. This involves muscular endurance and resistance to muscle fatigue.
Auditory Attention	The ability to focus on a single source of sound in the presence of other distracting sounds.
Peripheral Vision	The ability to see objects or movement of objects to one's side when the eyes are looking ahead.
Explosive Strength	The ability to use short bursts of muscle force to propel oneself (as in jumping or sprinting), or to throw an object.
Reaction Time	The ability to quickly respond (with the hand, finger, or foot) to a signal (sound, light, picture) when it appears.
Sound Localization	The ability to tell the direction from which a sound originated.
Dynamic Flexibility	The ability to quickly and repeatedly bend, stretch, twist, or reach out with your body, arms, and/or legs.

Glare Sensitivity	The ability to see objects in the presence of glare or bright lighting.
Depth Perception	The ability to judge which of several objects is closer or farther away from you, or to judge the distance between you and an object.
Night Vision	The ability to see under low light conditions.
Response Orientation	The ability to choose quickly between two or more movements in response to two or more different signals (lights. sounds, pictures). It includes the speed with which the correct response is started with the hand. foot. or other body part.
Rate Control	The ability to time your movements or the movement of a piece of equipment in anticipation of changes in the speed and/or direction of a moving object or scene.

Work_Activity	**Work_Activity Definitions**
Performing for or Working Directly with the Public	Performing for people or dealing directly with the public. This includes serving customers in restaurants and stores, and receiving clients or guests.
Selling or Influencing Others	Convincing others to buy merchandise/goods or to otherwise change their minds or actions.
Getting Information	Observing, receiving, and otherwise obtaining information from all relevant sources.
Establishing and Maintaining Interpersonal Relatio	Developing constructive and cooperative working relationships with others, and maintaining them over time.
Communicating with Supervisors, Peers, or Subordin	Providing information to supervisors, co-workers, and subordinates by telephone, in written form, e-mail, or in person.
Updating and Using Relevant Knowledge	Keeping up-to-date technically and applying new knowledge to your job.
Resolving Conflicts and Negotiating with Others	Handling complaints, settling disputes, and resolving grievances and conflicts, or otherwise negotiating with others.
Training and Teaching Others	Identifying the educational needs of others, developing formal educational or training programs or classes, and teaching or instructing others.
Communicating with Persons Outside Organization	Communicating with people outside the organization, representing the organization to customers, the public, government, and other external sources. This information can be exchanged in person, in writing, or by telephone or e-mail.
Assisting and Caring for Others	Providing personal assistance, medical attention, emotional support, or other personal care to others such as coworkers, customers, or patients.
Handling and Moving Objects	Using hands and arms in handling, installing, positioning, and moving materials, and manipulating things.
Making Decisions and Solving Problems	Analyzing information and evaluating results to choose the best solution and solve problems.
Documenting/Recording Information	Entering, transcribing, recording, storing, or maintaining information in written or electronic/magnetic form.
Identifying Objects, Actions, and Events	Identifying information by categorizing, estimating, recognizing differences or similarities, and detecting changes in circumstances or events.
Performing General Physical Activities	Performing physical activities that require considerable use of your arms and legs and moving your whole body, such as climbing, lifting, balancing, walking, stooping, and handling of materials.
Interacting With Computers	Using computers and computer systems (including hardware and software) to program, write software, set up functions, enter data, or process information.
Thinking Creatively	Developing, designing, or creating new applications, ideas, relationships, systems, or products, including artistic contributions.
Performing Administrative Activities	Performing day-to-day administrative tasks such as maintaining information files and processing paperwork.
Processing Information	Compiling, coding, categorizing, calculating, tabulating, auditing, or verifying information or data.
Organizing, Planning, and Prioritizing Work	Developing specific goals and plans to prioritize, organize, and accomplish your work.
Judging the Qualities of Things, Services, or Peop	Assessing the value, importance, or quality of things or people.
Monitor Processes, Materials, or Surroundings	Monitoring and reviewing information from materials, events, or the environment, to detect or assess problems.
Interpreting the Meaning of Information for Others	Translating or explaining what information means and how it can be used.
Scheduling Work and Activities	Scheduling events, programs, and activities, as well as the work of others.
Developing and Building Teams	Encouraging and building mutual trust, respect, and cooperation among team members.
Analyzing Data or Information	Identifying the underlying principles, reasons, or facts of information by breaking down information or data into separate parts.
Estimating the Quantifiable Characteristics of Pro	Estimating sizes, distances, and quantities; or determining time, costs, resources, or materials needed to perform a work activity.

Controlling Machines and Processes	Using either control mechanisms or direct physical activity to operate machines or processes (not including computers or vehicles).
Inspecting Equipment, Structures, or Material	Inspecting equipment, structures, or materials to identify the cause of errors or other problems or defects.
Coordinating the Work and Activities of Others	Getting members of a group to work together to accomplish tasks.
Coaching and Developing Others	Identifying the developmental needs of others and coaching. mentoring, or otherwise helping others to improve their knowledge or skills.
Evaluating Information to Determine Compliance wit	Using relevant information and individual judgment to determine whether events or processes comply with laws, regulations, or standards.
Provide Consultation and Advice to Others	Providing guidance and expert advice to management or other groups on technical, systems-, or process-related topics.
Developing Objectives and Strategies	Establishing long-range objectives and specifying the strategies and actions to achieve them.
Operating Vehicles. Mechanized Devices, or Equipme	Running, maneuvering, navigating, or driving vehicles or mechanized equipment, such as forklifts, passenger vehicles, aircraft, or water craft.
Guiding, Directing, and Motivating Subordinates	Providing guidance and direction to subordinates, including setting performance standards and monitoring performance.
Monitoring and Controlling Resources	Monitoring and controlling resources and overseeing the spending of money.
Repairing and Maintaining Mechanical Equipment	Servicing. repairing, adjusting, and testing machines, devices, moving parts, and equipment that operate primarily on the basis of mechanical (not electronic) principles.
Repairing and Maintaining Electronic Equipment	Servicing, repairing, calibrating, regulating, fine-tuning, or testing machines, devices, and equipment that operate primarily on the basis of electrical or electronic (not mechanical) principles.
Staffing Organizational Units	Recruiting, interviewing, selecting, hiring, and promoting employees in an organization.
Drafting, Laying Out, and Specifying Technical Dev	Providing documentation, detailed instructions, drawings, or specifications to tell others about how devices, parts, equipment, or structures are to be fabricated, constructed, assembled, modified, maintained, or used.

Work_Content	**Work_Content Definitions**
Spend Time Standing	How much does this job require standing?
Deal With External Customers	How important is it to work with external customers or the public in this job?
Telephone	How often do you have telephone conversations in this job?
Contact With Others	How much does this job require the worker to be in contact with others (face-to-face, by telephone, or otherwise) in order to perform it?
Face-to-Face Discussions	How often do you have to have face-to-face discussions with individuals or teams in this job?
Indoors, Environmentally Controlled	How often does this job require working indoors in environmentally controlled conditions?
Frequency of Decision Making	How frequently is the worker required to make decisions that affect other people, the financial resources, and/or the image and reputation of the organization?
Work With Work Group or Team	How important is it to work with others in a group or team in this job?
Physical Proximity	To what extent does this job require the worker to perform job tasks in close physical proximity to other people?
Structured versus Unstructured Work	To what extent is this job structured for the worker, rather than allowing the worker to determine tasks, priorities, and goals?
Time Pressure	How often does this job require the worker to meet strict deadlines?
Freedom to Make Decisions	How much decision making freedom, without supervision, does the job offer?
Impact of Decisions on Co-workers or Company Resul	How do the decisions an employee makes impact the results of co-workers, clients or the company?
Coordinate or Lead Others	How important is it to coordinate or lead others in accomplishing work activities in this job?
Deal With Unpleasant or Angry People	How frequently does the worker have to deal with unpleasant, angry, or discourteous individuals as part of the job requirements?
Importance of Being Exact or Accurate	How important is being very exact or highly accurate in performing this job?
Level of Competition	To what extent does this job require the worker to compete or to be aware of competitive pressures?
Spend Time Walking and Running	How much does this job require walking and running?
Spend Time Making Repetitive Motions	How much does this job require making repetitive motions?
Responsible for Others' Health and Safety	How much responsibility is there for the health and safety of others in this job?
Frequency of Conflict Situations	How often are there conflict situations the employee has to face in this job?

Spend Time Using Your Hands to Handle, Control, or	How much does this job require using your hands to handle. control, or feel objects, tools or controls?
Responsibility for Outcomes and Results	How responsible is the worker for work outcomes and results of other workers?
Importance of Repeating Same Tasks	How important is repeating the same physical activities (e.g.. key entry) or mental activities (e.g., checking entries in a ledger) over and over, without stopping, to performing this job?
Letters and Memos	How often does the job require written letters and memos?
Sounds, Noise Levels Are Distracting or Uncomforta	How often does this job require working exposed to sounds and noise levels that are distracting or uncomfortable?
Degree of Automation	How automated is the job?
Spend Time Kneeling, Crouching, Stooping, or Crawl	How much does this job require kneeling, crouching, stooping or crawling?
Exposed to Contaminants	How often does this job require working exposed to contaminants (such as pollutants, gases, dust or odors)?
Exposed to Minor Burns, Cuts, Bites, or Stings	How often does this job require exposure to minor burns. cuts, bites, or stings?
Very Hot or Cold Temperatures	How often does this job require working in very hot (above 90 F degrees) or very cold (below 32 F degrees) temperatures?
Spend Time Bending or Twisting the Body	How much does this job require bending or twisting your body?
Spend Time Sitting	How much does this job require sitting?
Consequence of Error	How serious would the result usually be if the worker made a mistake that was not readily correctable?
Spend Time Keeping or Regaining Balance	How much does this job require keeping or regaining your balance?
Electronic Mail	How often do you use electronic mail in this job?
Cramped Work Space, Awkward Positions	How often does this job require working in cramped work spaces that requires getting into awkward positions?
Extremely Bright or Inadequate Lighting	How often does this job require working in extremely bright or inadequate lighting conditions?
Outdoors, Exposed to Weather	How often does this job require working outdoors, exposed to all weather conditions?
Deal With Physically Aggressive People	How frequently does this job require the worker to deal with physical aggression of violent individuals?
Wear Common Protective or Safety Equipment such as	How much does this job require wearing common protective or safety equipment such as safety shoes, glasses, gloves, hard hats or live jackets?
Public Speaking	How often do you have to perform public speaking in this job?
Exposed to Hazardous Equipment	How often does this job require exposure to hazardous equipment?
Pace Determined by Speed of Equipment	How important is it to this job that the pace is determined by the speed of equipment or machinery? (This does not refer to keeping busy at all times on this job.)
Spend Time Climbing Ladders, Scaffolds, or Poles	How much does this job require climbing ladders, scaffolds, or poles?
Exposed to Hazardous Conditions	How often does this job require exposure to hazardous conditions?
Indoors, Not Environmentally Controlled	How often does this job require working indoors in non-controlled environmental conditions (e.g., warehouse without heat)?
Exposed to High Places	How often does this job require exposure to high places?
In an Enclosed Vehicle or Equipment	How often does this job require working in a closed vehicle or equipment (e.g., car)?
In an Open Vehicle or Equipment	How often does this job require working in an open vehicle or equipment (e.g., tractor)?
Outdoors, Under Cover	How often does this job require working outdoors, under cover (e.g., structure with roof but no walls)?
Exposed to Disease or Infections	How often does this job require exposure to disease/infections?
Exposed to Whole Body Vibration	How often does this job require exposure to whole body vibration (e.g., operate a jackhammer)?
Wear Specialized Protective or Safety Equipment su	How much does this job require wearing specialized protective or safety equipment such as breathing apparatus, safety harness, full protection suits, or radiation protection?
Exposed to Radiation	How often does this job require exposure to radiation?

Work_Styles	Work_Styles Definitions
Dependability	Job requires being reliable, responsible, and dependable, and fulfilling obligations.
Cooperation	Job requires being pleasant with others on the job and displaying a good-natured, cooperative attitude.
Self Control	Job requires maintaining composure, keeping emotions in check, controlling anger, and avoiding aggressive behavior, even in very difficult situations.
Integrity	Job requires being honest and ethical.
Adaptability/Flexibility	Job requires being open to change (positive or negative) and to considerable variety in the workplace.
Concern for Others	Job requires being sensitive to others' needs and feelings and being understanding and helpful on the job.
Stress Tolerance	Job requires accepting criticism and dealing calmly and effectively with high stress situations.

Attention to Detail	Job requires being careful about detail and thorough in completing work tasks.
Initiative	Job requires a willingness to take on responsibilities and challenges.
Persistence	Job requires persistence in the face of obstacles.
Achievement/Effort	Job requires establishing and maintaining personally challenging achievement goals and exerting effort toward mastering tasks.
Leadership	Job requires a willingness to lead. take charge, and offer opinions and direction.
Independence	Job requires developing one's own ways of doing things, guiding oneself with little or no supervision, and depending on oneself to get things done.
Social Orientation	Job requires preferring to work with others rather than alone, and being personally connected with others on the job.
Innovation	Job requires creativity and alternative thinking to develop new ideas for and answers to work-related problems.
Analytical Thinking	Job requires analyzing information and using logic to address work-related issues and problems.

Job Zone Component	Job Zone Component Definitions
Title	Job Zone Two: Some Preparation Needed
Overall Experience	Some previous work-related skill, knowledge, or experience may be helpful in these occupations, but usually is not needed. For example, a drywall installer might benefit from experience installing drywall, but an inexperienced person could still learn to be an installer with little difficulty.
Job Training	Employees in these occupations need anywhere from a few months to one year of working with experienced employees.
Job Zone Examples	These occupations often involve using your knowledge and skills to help others. Examples include drywall installers, fire inspectors, flight attendants, pharmacy technicians, salespersons (retail), and tellers.
SVP Range	(4.0 to < 6.0)
Education	These occupations usually require a high school diploma and may require some vocational training or job-related course work. In some cases, an associate's or bachelor's degree could be needed.

41-3011.00 - Advertising Sales Agents

Sell or solicit advertising, including graphic art, advertising space in publications, custom made signs, or TV and radio advertising time. May obtain leases for outdoor advertising sites or persuade retailer to use sales promotion display items.

Tasks

1) Process all correspondence and paperwork related to accounts.

2) Consult with company officials, sales departments, and advertising agencies in order to develop promotional plans.

3) Deliver advertising or illustration proofs to customers for approval.

4) Draw up contracts for advertising work, and collect payments due.

5) Determine advertising medium to be used, and prepare sample advertisements within the selected medium for presentation to customers.

6) Explain to customers how specific types of advertising will help promote their products or services in the most effective way possible.

7) Identify new advertising markets, and propose products to serve them.

8) Maintain assigned account bases while developing new accounts.

9) Obtain and study information about clients' products, needs, problems, advertising history, and business practices in order to offer effective sales presentations and appropriate product assistance.

10) Prepare promotional plans, sales literature, media kits, and sales contracts, using computer.

11) Gather all relevant material for bid processes, and coordinate bidding and contract approval.

12) Provide clients with estimates of the costs of advertising products or services.

13) Write sales outlines for use by staff.

14) Inform customers of available options for advertisement artwork, and provide samples.

15) Attend sales meetings, industry trade shows, and training seminars in order to gather information, promote products, expand network of contacts, and increase knowledge.

16) Arrange for commercial taping sessions, and accompany clients to sessions.

17) Recommend appropriate sizes and formats for advertising, depending on medium being used.

18) Write copy as part of layout.

19) Locate and contact potential clients in order to offer advertising services.

41-3021.00 - Insurance Sales Agents

Sell life, property, casualty, health, automotive, or other types of insurance. May refer clients to independent brokers, work as independent broker, or be employed by an insurance company.

Tasks

1) Interview prospective clients to obtain data about their financial resources and needs, the physical condition of the person or property to be insured, and to discuss any existing coverage.

2) Call on policyholders to deliver and explain policy, to analyze insurance program and suggest additions or changes, or to change beneficiaries.

3) Explain features, advantages and disadvantages of various policies to promote sale of insurance plans.

4) Customize insurance programs to suit individual customers, often covering a variety of risks.

5) Perform administrative tasks, such as maintaining records and handling policy renewals.

6) Contact underwriter and submit forms to obtain binder coverage.

7) Confer with clients to obtain and provide information when claims are made on a policy.

8) Ensure that policy requirements are fulfilled, including any necessary medical examinations and the completion of appropriate forms.

9) Seek out new clients and develop clientele by networking to find new customers and generate lists of prospective clients.

10) Sell various types of insurance policies to businesses and individuals on behalf of insurance companies, including automobile, fire, life, property, medical and dental insurance or specialized policies such as marine, farm/crop, and medical malpractice.

11) Develop marketing strategies to compete with other individuals or companies who sell insurance.

12) Monitor insurance claims to ensure they are settled equitably for both the client and the insurer.

13) Select company that offers type of coverage requested by client to underwrite policy.

14) Inspect property, examining its general condition, type of construction, age, and other characteristics, to decide if it is a good insurance risk.

15) Explain necessary bookkeeping requirements for customer to implement and provide group insurance program.

16) Plan and oversee incorporation of insurance program into bookkeeping system of company.

17) Install bookkeeping systems and resolve system problems.

18) Attend meetings, seminars and programs to learn about new products and services, learn new skills, and receive technical assistance in developing new accounts.

Knowledge	Knowledge Definitions
Customer and Personal Service	Knowledge of principles and processes for providing customer and personal services. This includes customer needs assessment, meeting quality standards for services, and evaluation of customer satisfaction.
Sales and Marketing	Knowledge of principles and methods for showing, promoting, and selling products or services. This includes marketing strategy and tactics, product demonstration, sales techniques, and sales control systems.
English Language	Knowledge of the structure and content of the English language including the meaning and spelling of words, rules of composition, and grammar.
Computers and Electronics	Knowledge of circuit boards, processors, chips, electronic equipment, and computer hardware and software, including applications and programming.
Administration and Management	Knowledge of business and management principles involved in strategic planning, resource allocation, human resources modeling, leadership technique, production methods, and coordination of people and resources.
Clerical	Knowledge of administrative and clerical procedures and systems such as word processing, managing files and records, stenography and transcription, designing forms, and other office procedures and terminology.
Economics and Accounting	Knowledge of economic and accounting principles and practices, the financial markets, banking and the analysis and reporting of financial data.
Mathematics	Knowledge of arithmetic, algebra, geometry, calculus, statistics, and their applications.
Personnel and Human Resources	Knowledge of principles and procedures for personnel recruitment, selection, training, compensation and benefits, labor relations and negotiation, and personnel information systems.
Education and Training	Knowledge of principles and methods for curriculum and training design, teaching and instruction for individuals and groups, and the measurement of training effects.
Law and Government	Knowledge of laws, legal codes, court procedures, precedents, government regulations, executive orders, agency rules, and the democratic political process.
Communications and Media	Knowledge of media production, communication, and dissemination techniques and methods. This includes alternative ways to inform and entertain via written, oral, and visual media.
Psychology	Knowledge of human behavior and performance; individual differences in ability, personality, and interests; learning and motivation; psychological research methods; and the assessment and treatment of behavioral and affective disorders.
Production and Processing	Knowledge of raw materials, production processes, quality control, costs, and other techniques for maximizing the effective manufacture and distribution of goods.
Telecommunications	Knowledge of transmission, broadcasting, switching, control, and operation of telecommunications systems.
Transportation	Knowledge of principles and methods for moving people or goods by air, rail, sea, or road, including the relative costs and benefits.
Public Safety and Security	Knowledge of relevant equipment, policies, procedures, and strategies to promote effective local, state, or national security operations for the protection of people, data, property, and institutions.
Geography	Knowledge of principles and methods for describing the features of land, sea, and air masses, including their physical characteristics, locations, interrelationships, and distribution of plant, animal, and human life.
Therapy and Counseling	Knowledge of principles, methods, and procedures for diagnosis, treatment, and rehabilitation of physical and mental dysfunctions, and for career counseling and guidance.
Sociology and Anthropology	Knowledge of group behavior and dynamics, societal trends and influences, human migrations, ethnicity, cultures and their history and origins.
Philosophy and Theology	Knowledge of different philosophical systems and religions. This includes their basic principles, values, ethics, ways of thinking, customs, practices, and their impact on human culture.
Building and Construction	Knowledge of materials, methods, and the tools involved in the construction or repair of houses, buildings, or other structures such as highways and roads.
Foreign Language	Knowledge of the structure and content of a foreign (non-English) language including the meaning and spelling of words, rules of composition and grammar, and pronunciation.
Engineering and Technology	Knowledge of the practical application of engineering science and technology. This includes applying principles, techniques, procedures, and equipment to the design and production of various goods and services.
History and Archeology	Knowledge of historical events and their causes, indicators, and effects on civilizations and cultures.
Design	Knowledge of design techniques, tools, and principles involved in production of precision technical plans, blueprints, drawings, and models.
Fine Arts	Knowledge of the theory and techniques required to compose, produce, and perform works of music, dance, visual arts, drama, and sculpture.
Mechanical	Knowledge of machines and tools, including their designs, uses, repair, and maintenance.
Medicine and Dentistry	Knowledge of the information and techniques needed to diagnose and treat human injuries, diseases, and deformities. This includes symptoms, treatment alternatives, drug properties and interactions, and preventive health-care measures.
Physics	Knowledge and prediction of physical principles, laws, their interrelationships, and applications to understanding fluid, material, and atmospheric dynamics, and mechanical, electrical, atomic and sub-atomic structures and processes.
Food Production	Knowledge of techniques and equipment for planting, growing, and harvesting food products (both plant and animal) for consumption, including storage/handling techniques.
Biology	Knowledge of plant and animal organisms, their tissues, cells, functions, interdependencies, and interactions with each other and the environment.
Chemistry	Knowledge of the chemical composition, structure, and properties of substances and of the chemical processes and transformations that they undergo. This includes uses of chemicals and their interactions, danger signs, production techniques, and disposal methods.
Skills	**Skills Definitions**

Active Listening	Giving full attention to what other people are saying, taking time to understand the points being made, asking questions as appropriate, and not interrupting at inappropriate times.
Speaking	Talking to others to convey information effectively.
Time Management	Managing one's own time and the time of others.
Reading Comprehension	Understanding written sentences and paragraphs in work related documents.
Persuasion	Persuading others to change their minds or behavior.
Service Orientation	Actively looking for ways to help people.
Social Perceptiveness	Being aware of others' reactions and understanding why they react as they do.
Active Learning	Understanding the implications of new information for both current and future problem-solving and decision-making.
Judgment and Decision Making	Considering the relative costs and benefits of potential actions to choose the most appropriate one.
Critical Thinking	Using logic and reasoning to identify the strengths and weaknesses of alternative solutions, conclusions or approaches to problems.
Writing	Communicating effectively in writing as appropriate for the needs of the audience.
Mathematics	Using mathematics to solve problems.
Negotiation	Bringing others together and trying to reconcile differences.
Complex Problem Solving	Identifying complex problems and reviewing related information to develop and evaluate options and implement solutions.
Coordination	Adjusting actions in relation to others' actions.
Learning Strategies	Selecting and using training/instructional methods and procedures appropriate for the situation when learning or teaching new things.
Monitoring	Monitoring/Assessing performance of yourself, other individuals, or organizations to make improvements or take corrective action.
Instructing	Teaching others how to do something.
Management of Personnel Resources	Motivating, developing, and directing people as they work, identifying the best people for the job.
Management of Financial Resources	Determining how money will be spent to get the work done, and accounting for these expenditures.
Operations Analysis	Analyzing needs and product requirements to create a design.
Troubleshooting	Determining causes of operating errors and deciding what to do about it.
Management of Material Resources	Obtaining and seeing to the appropriate use of equipment, facilities, and materials needed to do certain work.
Equipment Selection	Determining the kind of tools and equipment needed to do a job.
Systems Evaluation	Identifying measures or indicators of system performance and the actions needed to improve or correct performance, relative to the goals of the system.
Quality Control Analysis	Conducting tests and inspections of products, services, or processes to evaluate quality or performance.
Technology Design	Generating or adapting equipment and technology to serve user needs.
Operation and Control	Controlling operations of equipment or systems.
Operation Monitoring	Watching gauges, dials, or other indicators to make sure a machine is working properly.
Installation	Installing equipment, machines, wiring, or programs to meet specifications.
Equipment Maintenance	Performing routine maintenance on equipment and determining when and what kind of maintenance is needed.
Programming	Writing computer programs for various purposes.
Systems Analysis	Determining how a system should work and how changes in conditions, operations, and the environment will affect outcomes.
Repairing	Repairing machines or systems using the needed tools.
Science	Using scientific rules and methods to solve problems.

Ability	Ability Definitions
Oral Expression	The ability to communicate information and ideas in speaking so others will understand.
Oral Comprehension	The ability to listen to and understand information and ideas presented through spoken words and sentences.
Written Comprehension	The ability to read and understand information and ideas presented in writing.
Speech Recognition	The ability to identify and understand the speech of another person.
Speech Clarity	The ability to speak clearly so others can understand you.
Deductive Reasoning	The ability to apply general rules to specific problems to produce answers that make sense.
Written Expression	The ability to communicate information and ideas in writing so others will understand.
Near Vision	The ability to see details at close range (within a few feet of the observer).
Problem Sensitivity	The ability to tell when something is wrong or is likely to go wrong. It does not involve solving the problem, only recognizing there is a problem.

Category Flexibility	The ability to generate or use different sets of rules for combining or grouping things in different ways.
Inductive Reasoning	The ability to combine pieces of information to form general rules or conclusions (includes finding a relationship among seemingly unrelated events).
Selective Attention	The ability to concentrate on a task over a period of time without being distracted.
Information Ordering	The ability to arrange things or actions in a certain order or pattern according to a specific rule or set of rules (e.g., patterns of numbers, letters, words, pictures, mathematical operations).
Fluency of Ideas	The ability to come up with a number of ideas about a topic (the number of ideas is important, not their quality, correctness, or creativity).
Mathematical Reasoning	The ability to choose the right mathematical methods or formulas to solve a problem.
Originality	The ability to come up with unusual or clever ideas about a given topic or situation, or to develop creative ways to solve a problem.
Speed of Closure	The ability to quickly make sense of, combine, and organize information into meaningful patterns.
Number Facility	The ability to add, subtract, multiply, or divide quickly and correctly.
Far Vision	The ability to see details at a distance.
Flexibility of Closure	The ability to identify or detect a known pattern (a figure, object, word, or sound) that is hidden in other distracting material.
Finger Dexterity	The ability to make precisely coordinated movements of the fingers of one or both hands to grasp, manipulate, or assemble very small objects.
Time Sharing	The ability to shift back and forth between two or more activities or sources of information (such as speech, sounds, touch, or other sources).
Memorization	The ability to remember information such as words, numbers, pictures, and procedures.
Perceptual Speed	The ability to quickly and accurately compare similarities and differences among sets of letters, numbers, objects, pictures, or patterns. The things to be compared may be presented at the same time or one after the other. This ability also includes comparing a presented object with a remembered object.
Visualization	The ability to imagine how something will look after it is moved around or when its parts are moved or rearranged.
Depth Perception	The ability to judge which of several objects is closer or farther away from you, or to judge the distance between you and an object.
Multilimb Coordination	The ability to coordinate two or more limbs (for example, two arms, two legs, or one leg and one arm) while sitting, standing, or lying down. It does not involve performing the activities while the whole body is in motion.
Control Precision	The ability to quickly and repeatedly adjust the controls of a machine or a vehicle to exact positions.
Visual Color Discrimination	The ability to match or detect differences between colors, including shades of color and brightness.
Hearing Sensitivity	The ability to detect or tell the differences between sounds that vary in pitch and loudness.
Auditory Attention	The ability to focus on a single source of sound in the presence of other distracting sounds.
Trunk Strength	The ability to use your abdominal and lower back muscles to support part of the body repeatedly or continuously over time without 'giving out' or fatiguing.
Extent Flexibility	The ability to bend, stretch, twist, or reach with your body, arms, and/or legs.
Manual Dexterity	The ability to quickly move your hand, your hand together with your arm, or your two hands to grasp, manipulate, or assemble objects.
Gross Body Coordination	The ability to coordinate the movement of your arms, legs, and torso together when the whole body is in motion.
Rate Control	The ability to time your movements or the movement of a piece of equipment in anticipation of changes in the speed and/or direction of a moving object or scene.
Reaction Time	The ability to quickly respond (with the hand, finger, or foot) to a signal (sound, light, picture) when it appears.
Response Orientation	The ability to choose quickly between two or more movements in response to two or more different signals (lights, sounds, pictures). It includes the speed with which the correct response is started with the hand, foot, or other body part.
Stamina	The ability to exert yourself physically over long periods of time without getting winded or out of breath.
Arm-Hand Steadiness	The ability to keep your hand and arm steady while moving your arm or while holding your arm and hand in one position.
Wrist-Finger Speed	The ability to make fast, simple, repeated movements of the fingers, hands, and wrists.
Speed of Limb Movement	The ability to quickly move the arms and legs.
Static Strength	The ability to exert maximum muscle force to lift, push, pull, or carry objects.
Spatial Orientation	The ability to know your location in relation to the environment or to know where other objects are in relation to you.

Dynamic Strength	The ability to exert muscle force repeatedly or continuously over time. This involves muscular endurance and resistance to muscle fatigue.
Gross Body Equilibrium	The ability to keep or regain your body balance or stay upright when in an unstable position.
Sound Localization	The ability to tell the direction from which a sound originated.
Peripheral Vision	The ability to see objects or movement of objects to one's side when the eyes are looking ahead.
Glare Sensitivity	The ability to see objects in the presence of glare or bright lighting.
Night Vision	The ability to see under low light conditions.
Explosive Strength	The ability to use short bursts of muscle force to propel oneself (as in jumping or sprinting), or to throw an object.
Dynamic Flexibility	The ability to quickly and repeatedly bend, stretch, twist, or reach out with your body, arms, and/or legs.

Work_Activity	Work_Activity Definitions
Getting Information	Observing, receiving, and otherwise obtaining information from all relevant sources.
Establishing and Maintaining Interpersonal Relatio	Developing constructive and cooperative working relationships with others, and maintaining them over time.
Making Decisions and Solving Problems	Analyzing information and evaluating results to choose the best solution and solve problems.
Processing Information	Compiling, coding, categorizing, calculating, tabulating, auditing, or verifying information or data.
Interacting With Computers	Using computers and computer systems (including hardware and software) to program, write software, set up functions, enter data, or process information.
Evaluating Information to Determine Compliance wit	Using relevant information and individual judgment to determine whether events or processes comply with laws, regulations, or standards.
Communicating with Supervisors, Peers, or Subordin	Providing information to supervisors, co-workers, and subordinates by telephone, in written form, e-mail, or in person.
Identifying Objects, Actions, and Events	Identifying information by categorizing, estimating, recognizing differences or similarities, and detecting changes in circumstances or events.
Selling or Influencing Others	Convincing others to buy merchandise/goods or to otherwise change their minds or actions.
Resolving Conflicts and Negotiating with Others	Handling complaints, settling disputes, and resolving grievances and conflicts, or otherwise negotiating with others.
Communicating with Persons Outside Organization	Communicating with people outside the organization, representing the organization to customers, the public, government, and other external sources. This information can be exchanged in person, in writing, or by telephone or e-mail.
Performing for or Working Directly with the Public	Performing for people or dealing directly with the public. This includes serving customers in restaurants and stores, and receiving clients or guests.
Thinking Creatively	Developing, designing, or creating new applications, ideas, relationships, systems, or products, including artistic contributions.
Developing Objectives and Strategies	Establishing long-range objectives and specifying the strategies and actions to achieve them.
Documenting/Recording Information	Entering, transcribing, recording, storing, or maintaining information in written or electronic/magnetic form.
Performing Administrative Activities	Performing day-to-day administrative tasks such as maintaining information files and processing paperwork.
Analyzing Data or Information	Identifying the underlying principles, reasons, or facts of information by breaking down information or data into separate parts.
Updating and Using Relevant Knowledge	Keeping up-to-date technically and applying new knowledge to your job.
Judging the Qualities of Things, Services, or Peop	Assessing the value, importance, or quality of things or people.
Interpreting the Meaning of Information for Others	Translating or explaining what information means and how it can be used.
Organizing, Planning, and Prioritizing Work	Developing specific goals and plans to prioritize, organize, and accomplish your work.
Coaching and Developing Others	Identifying the developmental needs of others and coaching, mentoring, or otherwise helping others to improve their knowledge or skills.
Developing and Building Teams	Encouraging and building mutual trust, respect, and cooperation among team members.
Training and Teaching Others	Identifying the educational needs of others, developing formal educational or training programs or classes, and teaching or instructing others.
Assisting and Caring for Others	Providing personal assistance, medical attention, emotional support, or other personal care to others such as coworkers, customers, or patients.
Scheduling Work and Activities	Scheduling events, programs, and activities, as well as the work of others.
Monitor Processes, Materials, or Surroundings	Monitoring and reviewing information from materials, events, or the environment, to detect or assess problems.

Coordinating the Work and Activities of Others	Getting members of a group to work together to accomplish tasks.
Estimating the Quantifiable Characteristics of Pro	Estimating sizes, distances, and quantities; or determining time, costs, resources, or materials needed to perform a work activity.
Provide Consultation and Advice to Others	Providing guidance and expert advice to management or other groups on technical, systems-, or process-related topics.
Monitoring and Controlling Resources	Monitoring and controlling resources and overseeing the spending of money.
Guiding, Directing, and Motivating Subordinates	Providing guidance and direction to subordinates, including setting performance standards and monitoring performance.
Performing General Physical Activities	Performing physical activities that require considerable use of your arms and legs and moving your whole body, such as climbing, lifting, balancing, walking, stooping, and handling of materials.
Inspecting Equipment, Structures, or Material	Inspecting equipment, structures, or materials to identify the cause of errors or other problems or defects.
Operating Vehicles, Mechanized Devices, or Equipme	Running, maneuvering, navigating, or driving vehicles or mechanized equipment, such as forklifts, passenger vehicles, aircraft, or water craft.
Controlling Machines and Processes	Using either control mechanisms or direct physical activity to operate machines or processes (not including computers or vehicles).
Handling and Moving Objects	Using hands and arms in handling, installing, positioning, and moving materials, and manipulating things.
Staffing Organizational Units	Recruiting, interviewing, selecting, hiring, and promoting employees in an organization.
Repairing and Maintaining Electronic Equipment	Servicing, repairing, calibrating, regulating, fine-tuning, or testing machines, devices, and equipment that operate primarily on the basis of electrical or electronic (not mechanical) principles.
Repairing and Maintaining Mechanical Equipment	Servicing, repairing, adjusting, and testing machines, devices, moving parts, and equipment that operate primarily on the basis of mechanical (not electronic) principles.
Drafting, Laying Out, and Specifying Technical Dev	Providing documentation, detailed instructions, drawings, or specifications to tell others about how devices, parts, equipment, or structures are to be fabricated, constructed, assembled, modified, maintained, or used.

Work_Content	Work_Content Definitions
Telephone	How often do you have telephone conversations in this job?
Letters and Memos	How often does the job require written letters and memos?
Level of Competition	To what extent does this job require the worker to compete or to be aware of competitive pressures?
Structured versus Unstructured Work	To what extent is this job structured for the worker, rather than allowing the worker to determine tasks, priorities, and goals?
Contact With Others	How much does this job require the worker to be in contact with others (face-to-face, by telephone, or otherwise) in order to perform it?
Face-to-Face Discussions	How often do you have to have face-to-face discussions with individuals or teams in this job?
Freedom to Make Decisions	How much decision making freedom, without supervision, does the job offer?
Frequency of Decision Making	How frequently is the worker required to make decisions that affect other people, the financial resources, and/or the image and reputation of the organization?
Spend Time Sitting	How much does this job require sitting?
Importance of Being Exact or Accurate	How important is being very exact or highly accurate in performing this job?
Deal With External Customers	How important is it to work with external customers or the public in this job?
Impact of Decisions on Co-workers or Company Resul	How do the decisions an employee makes impact the results of co-workers, clients or the company?
Indoors, Environmentally Controlled	How often does this job require working indoors in environmentally controlled conditions?
Importance of Repeating Same Tasks	How important is repeating the same physical activities (e.g., key entry) or mental activities (e.g., checking entries in a ledger) over and over, without stopping, to performing this job?
Work With Work Group or Team	How important is it to work with others in a group or team in this job?
Time Pressure	How often does this job require the worker to meet strict deadlines?
Electronic Mail	How often do you use electronic mail in this job?
Physical Proximity	To what extent does this job require the worker to perform job tasks in close physical proximity to other people?
Deal With Unpleasant or Angry People	How frequently does the worker have to deal with unpleasant, angry, or discourteous individuals as part of the job requirements?
In an Enclosed Vehicle or Equipment	How often does this job require working in a closed vehicle or equipment (e.g., car)?
Frequency of Conflict Situations	How often are there conflict situations the employee has to face in this job?
Degree of Automation	How automated is the job?

Coordinate or Lead Others	How important is it to coordinate or lead others in accomplishing work activities in this job?
Sounds, Noise Levels Are Distracting or Uncomforta	How often does this job require working exposed to sounds and noise levels that are distracting or uncomfortable?
Spend Time Making Repetitive Motions	How much does this job require making repetitive motions?
Consequence of Error	How serious would the result usually be if the worker made a mistake that was not readily correctable?
Public Speaking	How often do you have to perform public speaking in this job?
Responsibility for Outcomes and Results	How responsible is the worker for work outcomes and results of other workers?
Indoors, Not Environmentally Controlled	How often does this job require working indoors in non-controlled environmental conditions (e.g., warehouse without heat)?
Extremely Bright or Inadequate Lighting	How often does this job require working in extremely bright or inadequate lighting conditions?
Outdoors, Exposed to Weather	How often does this job require working outdoors, exposed to all weather conditions?
Spend Time Standing	How much does this job require standing?
Exposed to Contaminants	How often does this job require working exposed to contaminants (such as pollutants, gases, dust or odors)?
Responsible for Others' Health and Safety	How much responsibility is there for the health and safety of others in this job?
Spend Time Walking and Running	How much does this job require walking and running?
Very Hot or Cold Temperatures	How often does this job require working in very hot (above 90 F degrees) or very cold (below 32 F degrees) temperatures?
Spend Time Using Your Hands to Handle, Control, or	How much does this job require using your hands to handle, control, or feel objects, tools or controls?
Spend Time Bending or Twisting the Body	How much does this job require bending or twisting your body?
Spend Time Kneeling, Crouching, Stooping, or Crawl	How much does this job require kneeling, crouching, stooping or crawling?
Outdoors, Under Cover	How often does this job require working outdoors, under cover (e.g., structure with roof but no walls)?
Cramped Work Space, Awkward Positions	How often does this job require working in cramped work spaces that requires getting into awkward positions?
Pace Determined by Speed of Equipment	How important is it to this job that the pace is determined by the speed of equipment or machinery? (This does not refer to keeping busy at all times on this job.)
Deal With Physically Aggressive People	How frequently does this job require the worker to deal with physical aggression of violent individuals?
Exposed to Hazardous Conditions	How often does this job require exposure to hazardous conditions?
Exposed to Minor Burns, Cuts, Bites, or Stings	How often does this job require exposure to minor burns, cuts, bites, or stings?
Wear Common Protective or Safety Equipment such as	How much does this job require wearing common protective or safety equipment such as safety shoes, glasses, gloves, hard hats or live jackets?
In an Open Vehicle or Equipment	How often does this job require working in an open vehicle or equipment (e.g., tractor)?
Exposed to Disease or Infections	How often does this job require exposure to disease/infections?
Exposed to Whole Body Vibration	How often does this job require exposure to whole body vibration (e.g., operate a jackhammer)?
Spend Time Climbing Ladders, Scaffolds, or Poles	How much does this job require climbing ladders, scaffolds, or poles?
Spend Time Keeping or Regaining Balance	How much does this job require keeping or regaining your balance?
Exposed to Radiation	How often does this job require exposure to radiation?
Exposed to Hazardous Equipment	How often does this job require exposure to hazardous equipment?
Wear Specialized Protective or Safety Equipment su	How much does this job require wearing specialized protective or safety equipment such as breathing apparatus, safety harness, full protection suits, or radiation protection?
Exposed to High Places	How often does this job require exposure to high places?

Work_Styles	Work_Styles Definitions
Integrity	Job requires being honest and ethical.
Dependability	Job requires being reliable, responsible, and dependable, and fulfilling obligations.
Attention to Detail	Job requires being careful about detail and thorough in completing work tasks.
Self Control	Job requires maintaining composure, keeping emotions in check, controlling anger, and avoiding aggressive behavior, even in very difficult situations.
Initiative	Job requires a willingness to take on responsibilities and challenges.
Persistence	Job requires persistence in the face of obstacles.
Stress Tolerance	Job requires accepting criticism and dealing calmly and effectively with high stress situations.

Cooperation	Job requires being pleasant with others on the job and displaying a good-natured, cooperative attitude.
Concern for Others	Job requires being sensitive to others' needs and feelings and being understanding and helpful on the job.
Independence	Job requires developing one's own ways of doing things, guiding oneself with little or no supervision, and depending on oneself to get things done.
Achievement/Effort	Job requires establishing and maintaining personally challenging achievement goals and exerting effort toward mastering tasks.
Adaptability/Flexibility	Job requires being open to change (positive or negative) and to considerable variety in the workplace.
Social Orientation	Job requires preferring to work with others rather than alone, and being personally connected with others on the job.
Leadership	Job requires a willingness to lead, take charge, and offer opinions and direction.
Analytical Thinking	Job requires analyzing information and using logic to address work-related issues and problems.

Job Zone Component	Job Zone Component Definitions
Title	Job Zone Three: Medium Preparation Needed
Overall Experience	Previous work-related skill, knowledge, or experience is required for these occupations. For example, an electrician must have completed three or four years of apprenticeship or several years of vocational training, and often must have passed a licensing exam, in order to perform the job.
Job Training	Employees in these occupations usually need one or two years of training involving both on-the-job experience and informal training with experienced workers.
Job Zone Examples	These occupations usually involve using communication and organizational skills to coordinate, supervise, manage, or train others to accomplish goals. Examples include dental assistants, electricians, fish and game wardens, legal secretaries, personnel recruiters, and recreation workers.
SVP Range	(6.0 to < 7.0)
Education	Most occupations in this zone require training in vocational schools, related on-the-job experience, or an associate's degree. Some may require a bachelor's degree.

41-3031.01 - Sales Agents, Securities and Commodities

Buy and sell securities in investment and trading firms and develop and implement financial plans for individuals, businesses, and organizations.

Tasks

1) Complete sales order tickets and submit for processing of client requested transactions.

2) Review financial periodicals, stock and bond reports, business publications and other material in order to identify potential investments for clients and to keep abreast of trends affecting market conditions.

3) Develop financial plans based on analysis of clients' financial status, and discuss financial options with clients.

4) Relay buy or sell orders to securities exchanges or to firm trading departments.

5) Record transactions accurately, and keep clients informed about transactions.

6) Analyze market conditions in order to determine optimum times to execute securities transactions.

7) Read corporate reports and calculate ratios to determine best prospects for profit on stock purchases and to monitor client accounts.

8) Prepare financial reports to monitor client or corporate finances.

9) Identify potential clients, using advertising campaigns, mailing lists, and personal contacts.

10) Contact prospective customers to determine customer needs, present information, and explain available services.

11) Explain stock market terms and trading practices to clients.

12) Offer advice on the purchase or sale of particular securities.

13) Supply the latest price quotes on any security, as well as information on the activities and financial positions of the corporations issuing these securities.

14) Calculate costs for billings and commissions purposes.

15) Review all securities transactions to ensure accuracy of information and that trades conform to regulations of governing agencies.

16) Prepare documents needed to implement plans selected by clients.

17) Interview clients to determine clients' assets, liabilities, cash flow, insurance coverage, tax status, and financial objectives.

41-3031.02 - Sales Agents, Financial Services

Sell financial services, such as loan, tax, and securities counseling to customers of financial institutions and business establishments.

Tasks

1) Prepare forms or agreements to complete sales.

2) Make presentations on financial services to groups in order to attract new clients.

3) Contact prospective customers in order to present information and explain available services.

4) Determine customers' financial services needs, and prepare proposals to sell services that address these needs.

5) Evaluate costs and revenue of agreements in order to determine continued profitability.

6) Sell services and equipment, such as trusts, investments, and check processing services.

7) Develop prospects from current commercial customers, referral leads, and sales and trade meetings.

41-3041.00 - Travel Agents

Plan and sell transportation and accommodations for travel agency customers. Determine destination, modes of transportation, travel dates, costs, and accommodations required.

Tasks

1) Book transportation and hotel reservations, using computer terminal or telephone.

2) Print or request transportation carrier tickets, using computer printer system or system link to travel carrier.

3) Plan, describe, arrange, and sell itinerary tour packages and promotional travel incentives offered by various travel carriers.

4) Converse with customer to determine destination, mode of transportation, travel dates, financial considerations, and accommodations required.

5) Provide customer with brochures and publications containing travel information, such as local customs, points of interest, or foreign country regulations.

6) Compute cost of travel and accommodations, using calculator, computer, carrier tariff books, and hotel rate books, or quote package tour's costs.

Knowledge	Knowledge Definitions
Customer and Personal Service	Knowledge of principles and processes for providing customer and personal services. This includes customer needs assessment, meeting quality standards for services, and evaluation of customer satisfaction.
Geography	Knowledge of principles and methods for describing the features of land, sea, and air masses, including their physical characteristics, locations, interrelationships, and distribution of plant, animal, and human life.
Sales and Marketing	Knowledge of principles and methods for showing, promoting, and selling products or services. This includes marketing strategy and tactics, product demonstration, sales techniques, and sales control systems.
Transportation	Knowledge of principles and methods for moving people or goods by air, rail, sea, or road, including the relative costs and benefits.
English Language	Knowledge of the structure and content of the English language including the meaning and spelling of words, rules of composition, and grammar.
Clerical	Knowledge of administrative and clerical procedures and systems such as word processing, managing files and records, stenography and transcription, designing forms, and other office procedures and terminology.
Computers and Electronics	Knowledge of circuit boards, processors, chips, electronic equipment, and computer hardware and software, including applications and programming.
Economics and Accounting	Knowledge of economic and accounting principles and practices, the financial markets, banking and the analysis and reporting of financial data.
Administration and Management	Knowledge of business and management principles involved in strategic planning, resource allocation, human resources modeling, leadership technique, production methods, and coordination of people and resources.
Mathematics	Knowledge of arithmetic, algebra, geometry, calculus, statistics, and their applications.
Education and Training	Knowledge of principles and methods for curriculum and training design, teaching and instruction for individuals and groups, and the measurement of training effects.
Foreign Language	Knowledge of the structure and content of a foreign (non-English) language including the meaning and spelling of words, rules of composition and grammar, and pronunciation.
Law and Government	Knowledge of laws, legal codes, court procedures, precedents, government regulations, executive orders, agency rules, and the democratic political process.
Communications and Media	Knowledge of media production, communication, and dissemination techniques and methods. This includes alternative ways to inform and entertain via written, oral, and visual media.
Telecommunications	Knowledge of transmission, broadcasting, switching, control, and operation of telecommunications systems.
History and Archeology	Knowledge of historical events and their causes, indicators, and effects on civilizations and cultures.
Psychology	Knowledge of human behavior and performance; individual differences in ability, personality, and interests; learning and motivation; psychological research methods; and the assessment and treatment of behavioral and affective disorders.
Personnel and Human Resources	Knowledge of principles and procedures for personnel recruitment, selection, training, compensation and benefits, labor relations and negotiation, and personnel information systems.
Public Safety and Security	Knowledge of relevant equipment, policies, procedures, and strategies to promote effective local, state, or national security operations for the protection of people, data, property, and institutions.
Sociology and Anthropology	Knowledge of group behavior and dynamics, societal trends and influences, human migrations, ethnicity, cultures and their history and origins.
Production and Processing	Knowledge of raw materials, production processes, quality control, costs, and other techniques for maximizing the effective manufacture and distribution of goods.
Mechanical	Knowledge of machines and tools, including their designs, uses, repair, and maintenance.
Design	Knowledge of design techniques, tools, and principles involved in production of precision technical plans, blueprints, drawings, and models.
Philosophy and Theology	Knowledge of different philosophical systems and religions. This includes their basic principles, values, ethics, ways of thinking, customs, practices, and their impact on human culture.
Engineering and Technology	Knowledge of the practical application of engineering science and technology. This includes applying principles, techniques, procedures, and equipment to the design and production of various goods and services.
Therapy and Counseling	Knowledge of principles, methods, and procedures for diagnosis, treatment, and rehabilitation of physical and mental dysfunctions, and for career counseling and guidance.
Fine Arts	Knowledge of the theory and techniques required to compose, produce, and perform works of music, dance, visual arts, drama, and sculpture.
Medicine and Dentistry	Knowledge of the information and techniques needed to diagnose and treat human injuries, diseases, and deformities. This includes symptoms, treatment alternatives, drug properties and interactions, and preventive health-care measures.
Food Production	Knowledge of techniques and equipment for planting, growing, and harvesting food products (both plant and animal) for consumption, including storage/handling techniques.
Physics	Knowledge and prediction of physical principles, laws, their interrelationships, and applications to understanding fluid, material, and atmospheric dynamics, and mechanical, electrical, atomic and sub- atomic structures and processes.
Building and Construction	Knowledge of materials, methods, and the tools involved in the construction or repair of houses, buildings, or other structures such as highways and roads.
Chemistry	Knowledge of the chemical composition, structure, and properties of substances and of the chemical processes and transformations that they undergo. This includes uses of chemicals and their interactions, danger signs, production techniques, and disposal methods.
Biology	Knowledge of plant and animal organisms, their tissues, cells, functions, interdependencies, and interactions with each other and the environment.

Skills	Skills Definitions
Active Listening	Giving full attention to what other people are saying, taking time to understand the points being made, asking questions as appropriate, and not interrupting at inappropriate times.
Service Orientation	Actively looking for ways to help people.
Reading Comprehension	Understanding written sentences and paragraphs in work related documents.
Speaking	Talking to others to convey information effectively.
Time Management	Managing one's own time and the time of others.
Social Perceptiveness	Being aware of others' reactions and understanding why they react as they do.
Coordination	Adjusting actions in relation to others' actions.

252

Active Learning	Understanding the implications of new information for both current and future problem-solving and decision-making.
Mathematics	Using mathematics to solve problems.
Writing	Communicating effectively in writing as appropriate for the needs of the audience.
Persuasion	Persuading others to change their minds or behavior.
Learning Strategies	Selecting and using training/instructional methods and procedures appropriate for the situation when learning or teaching new things.
Critical Thinking	Using logic and reasoning to identify the strengths and weaknesses of alternative solutions, conclusions or approaches to problems.
Judgment and Decision Making	Considering the relative costs and benefits of potential actions to choose the most appropriate one.
Monitoring	Monitoring/Assessing performance of yourself, other individuals, or organizations to make improvements or take corrective action.
Instructing	Teaching others how to do something.
Management of Personnel Resources	Motivating, developing, and directing people as they work, identifying the best people for the job.
Complex Problem Solving	Identifying complex problems and reviewing related information to develop and evaluate options and implement solutions.
Negotiation	Bringing others together and trying to reconcile differences.
Technology Design	Generating or adapting equipment and technology to serve user needs.
Operation and Control	Controlling operations of equipment or systems.
Quality Control Analysis	Conducting tests and inspections of products, services, or processes to evaluate quality or performance.
Operations Analysis	Analyzing needs and product requirements to create a design.
Equipment Selection	Determining the kind of tools and equipment needed to do a job.
Management of Financial Resources	Determining how money will be spent to get the work done, and accounting for these expenditures.
Systems Evaluation	Identifying measures or indicators of system performance and the actions needed to improve or correct performance, relative to the goals of the system.
Equipment Maintenance	Performing routine maintenance on equipment and determining when and what kind of maintenance is needed.
Troubleshooting	Determining causes of operating errors and deciding what to do about it.
Operation Monitoring	Watching gauges, dials, or other indicators to make sure a machine is working properly.
Management of Material Resources	Obtaining and seeing to the appropriate use of equipment, facilities, and materials needed to do certain work.
Systems Analysis	Determining how a system should work and how changes in conditions, operations, and the environment will affect outcomes.
Repairing	Repairing machines or systems using the needed tools.
Installation	Installing equipment, machines, wiring, or programs to meet specifications.
Programming	Writing computer programs for various purposes.
Science	Using scientific rules and methods to solve problems.

Ability	**Ability Definitions**
Oral Comprehension	The ability to listen to and understand information and ideas presented through spoken words and sentences.
Oral Expression	The ability to communicate information and ideas in speaking so others will understand.
Speech Clarity	The ability to speak clearly so others can understand you.
Speech Recognition	The ability to identify and understand the speech of another person.
Written Comprehension	The ability to read and understand information and ideas presented in writing.
Near Vision	The ability to see details at close range (within a few feet of the observer).
Problem Sensitivity	The ability to tell when something is wrong or is likely to go wrong. It does not involve solving the problem, only recognizing there is a problem.
Selective Attention	The ability to concentrate on a task over a period of time without getting distracted.
Information Ordering	The ability to arrange things or actions in a certain order or pattern according to a specific rule or set of rules (e.g., patterns of numbers, letters, words, pictures, mathematical operations).
Number Facility	The ability to add, subtract, multiply, or divide quickly and correctly.
Deductive Reasoning	The ability to apply general rules to specific problems to produce answers that make sense.
Category Flexibility	The ability to generate or use different sets of rules for combining or grouping things in different ways.
Fluency of Ideas	The ability to come up with a number of ideas about a topic (the number of ideas is important, not their quality, correctness, or creativity).

Time Sharing	The ability to shift back and forth between two or more activities or sources of information (such as speech, sounds. touch, or other sources).
Inductive Reasoning	The ability to combine pieces of information to form general rules or conclusions (includes finding a relationship among seemingly unrelated events).
Written Expression	The ability to communicate information and ideas in writing so others will understand.
Originality	The ability to come up with unusual or clever ideas about a given topic or situation, or to develop creative ways to solve a problem.
Memorization	The ability to remember information such as words, numbers, pictures, and procedures.
Mathematical Reasoning	The ability to choose the right mathematical methods or formulas to solve a problem.
Finger Dexterity	The ability to make precisely coordinated movements of the fingers of one or both hands to grasp, manipulate, or assemble very small objects.
Auditory Attention	The ability to focus on a single source of sound in the presence of other distracting sounds.
Flexibility of Closure	The ability to identify or detect a known pattern (a figure. object, word, or sound) that is hidden in other distracting material.
Visualization	The ability to imagine how something will look after it is moved around or when its parts are moved or rearranged.
Perceptual Speed	The ability to quickly and accurately compare similarities and differences among sets of letters, numbers, objects, pictures, or patterns. The things to be compared may be presented at the same time or one after the other. This ability also includes comparing a presented object with a remembered object.
Wrist-Finger Speed	The ability to make fast, simple, repeated movements of the fingers, hands, and wrists.
Speed of Closure	The ability to quickly make sense of, combine, and organize information into meaningful patterns.
Far Vision	The ability to see details at a distance.
Hearing Sensitivity	The ability to detect or tell the differences between sounds that vary in pitch and loudness.
Visual Color Discrimination	The ability to match or detect differences between colors, including shades of color and brightness.
Trunk Strength	The ability to use your abdominal and lower back muscles to support part of the body repeatedly or continuously over time without 'giving out' or fatiguing.
Depth Perception	The ability to judge which of several objects is closer or farther away from you, or to judge the distance between you and an object.
Manual Dexterity	The ability to quickly move your hand, your hand together with your arm, or your two hands to grasp, manipulate, or assemble objects.
Multilimb Coordination	The ability to coordinate two or more limbs (for example, two arms, two legs, or one leg and one arm) while sitting, standing, or lying down. It does not involve performing the activities while the whole body is in motion.
Arm-Hand Steadiness	The ability to keep your hand and arm steady while moving your arm or while holding your arm and hand in one position.
Glare Sensitivity	The ability to see objects in the presence of glare or bright lighting.
Static Strength	The ability to exert maximum muscle force to lift, push, pull, or carry objects.
Extent Flexibility	The ability to bend, stretch, twist, or reach with your body, arms, and/or legs.
Spatial Orientation	The ability to know your location in relation to the environment or to know where other objects are in relation to you.
Sound Localization	The ability to tell the direction from which a sound originated.
Dynamic Strength	The ability to exert muscle force repeatedly or continuously over time. This involves muscular endurance and resistance to muscle fatigue.
Control Precision	The ability to quickly and repeatedly adjust the controls of a machine or a vehicle to exact positions.
Gross Body Coordination	The ability to coordinate the movement of your arms, legs, and torso together when the whole body is in motion.
Stamina	The ability to exert yourself physically over long periods of time without getting winded or out of breath.
Explosive Strength	The ability to use short bursts of muscle force to propel oneself (as in jumping or sprinting), or to throw an object.
Speed of Limb Movement	The ability to quickly move the arms and legs.
Response Orientation	The ability to choose quickly between two or more movements in response to two or more different signals (lights, sounds, pictures). It includes the speed with which the correct response is started with the hand, foot, or other body part.
Peripheral Vision	The ability to see objects or movement of objects to one's side when the eyes are looking ahead.
Gross Body Equilibrium	The ability to keep or regain your body balance or stay upright when in an unstable position.
Rate Control	The ability to time your movements or the movement of a piece of equipment in anticipation of changes in the speed and/or direction of a moving object or scene.

253

Night Vision	The ability to see under low light conditions.
Reaction Tim.	The ability to quickly respond (with the hand, finger, or foot) to a signal (sound, light, picture) when it appears.
Dynamic Flexibility	The ability to quickly and repeatedly bend, stretch, twist, or reach out with your body, arms, and/or legs.

Work_Activity	Work_Activity Definitions
Performing for or Working Directly with the Public	Performing for people or dealing directly with the public. This includes serving customers in restaurants and stores, and receiving clients or guests.
Getting Information	Observing, receiving, and otherwise obtaining information from all relevant sources.
Interacting With Computers	Using computers and computer systems (including hardware and software) to program, write software, set up functions, enter data, or process information.
Selling or Influencing Others	Convincing others to buy merchandise/goods or to otherwise change their minds or actions.
Communicating with Persons Outside Organization	Communicating with people outside the organization, representing the organization to customers, the public, government, and other external sources. This information can be exchanged in person, in writing, or by telephone or e-mail.
Updating and Using Relevant Knowledge	Keeping up-to-date technically and applying new knowledge to your job.
Establishing and Maintaining Interpersonal Relatio	Developing constructive and cooperative working relationships with others, and maintaining them over time.
Organizing, Planning, and Prioritizing Work	Developing specific goals and plans to prioritize, organize, and accomplish your work.
Communicating with Supervisors, Peers, or Subordin	Providing information to supervisors, co-workers, and subordinates by telephone, in written form, e-mail, or in person.
Documenting/Recording Information	Entering, transcribing, recording, storing, or maintaining information in written or electronic/magnetic form.
Making Decisions and Solving Problems	Analyzing information and evaluating results to choose the best solution and solve problems.
Interpreting the Meaning of Information for Others	Translating or explaining what information means and how it can be used.
Resolving Conflicts and Negotiating with Others	Handling complaints, settling disputes, and resolving grievances and conflicts, or otherwise negotiating with others.
Performing Administrative Activities	Performing day-to-day administrative tasks such as maintaining information files and processing paperwork.
Judging the Qualities of Things, Services, or Peop	Assessing the value, importance, or quality of things or people.
Processing Information	Compiling, coding, categorizing, calculating, tabulating, auditing, or verifying information or data.
Thinking Creatively	Developing, designing, or creating new applications, ideas, relationships, systems, or products, including artistic contributions.
Analyzing Data or Information	Identifying the underlying principles, reasons, or facts of information by breaking down information or data into separate parts.
Assisting and Caring for Others	Providing personal assistance, medical attention, emotional support, or other personal care to others such as coworkers, customers, or patients.
Coordinating the Work and Activities of Others	Getting members of a group to work together to accomplish tasks.
Scheduling Work and Activities	Scheduling events, programs, and activities, as well as the work of others.
Monitoring and Controlling Resources	Monitoring and controlling resources and overseeing the spending of money.
Training and Teaching Others	Identifying the educational needs of others, developing formal educational or training programs or classes, and teaching or instructing others.
Developing Objectives and Strategies	Establishing long-range objectives and specifying the strategies and actions to achieve them.
Identifying Objects, Actions, and Events	Identifying information by categorizing, estimating, recognizing differences or similarities, and detecting changes in circumstances or events.
Estimating the Quantifiable Characteristics of Pro	Estimating sizes, distances, and quantities; or determining time, costs, resources, or materials needed to perform a work activity.
Provide Consultation and Advice to Others	Providing guidance and expert advice to management or other groups on technical, systems-, or process-related topics.
Developing and Building Teams	Encouraging and building mutual trust, respect, and cooperation among team members.
Coaching and Developing Others	Identifying the developmental needs of others and coaching, mentoring, or otherwise helping others to improve their knowledge or skills.
Monitor Processes, Materials, or Surroundings	Monitoring and reviewing information from materials, events, or the environment, to detect or assess problems.
Evaluating Information to Determine Compliance wit	Using relevant information and individual judgment to determine whether events or processes comply with laws, regulations, or standards.

Guiding, Directing, and Motivating Subordinates	Providing guidance and direction to subordinates, including setting performance standards and monitoring performance.
Staffing Organizational Units	Recruiting, interviewing, selecting, hiring, and promoting employees in an organization.
Handling and Moving Objects	Using hands and arms in handling, installing, positioning, and moving materials, and manipulating things.
Controlling Machines and Processes	Using either control mechanisms or direct physical activity to operate machines or processes (not including computers or vehicles).
Performing General Physical Activities	Performing physical activities that require considerable use of your arms and legs and moving your whole body, such as climbing, lifting, balancing, walking, stooping, and handling of materials.
Inspecting Equipment, Structures, or Material	Inspecting equipment, structures, or materials to identify the cause of errors or other problems or defects.
Drafting, Laying Out, and Specifying Technical Dev	Providing documentation, detailed instructions, drawings, or specifications to tell others about how devices, parts, equipment, or structures are to be fabricated, constructed, assembled, modified, maintained, or used.
Repairing and Maintaining Electronic Equipment	Servicing, repairing, calibrating, regulating, fine-tuning, or testing machines, devices, and equipment that operate primarily on the basis of electrical or electronic (not mechanical) principles.
Repairing and Maintaining Mechanical Equipment	Servicing, repairing, adjusting, and testing machines, devices, moving parts, and equipment that operate primarily on the basis of mechanical (not electronic) principles.
Operating Vehicles, Mechanized Devices, or Equipme	Running, maneuvering, navigating, or driving vehicles or mechanized equipment, such as forklifts, passenger vehicles, aircraft, or water craft.

Work_Content	Work_Content Definitions
Contact With Others	How much does this job require the worker to be in contact with others (face-to-face, by telephone, or otherwise) in order to perform it?
Telephone	How often do you have telephone conversations in this job?
Electronic Mail	How often do you use electronic mail in this job?
Spend Time Sitting	How much does this job require sitting?
Face-to-Face Discussions	How often do you have to have face-to-face discussions with individuals or teams in this job?
Deal With External Customers	How important is it to work with external customers or the public in this job?
Importance of Being Exact or Accurate	How important is being very exact or highly accurate in performing this job?
Freedom to Make Decisions	How much decision making freedom, without supervision, does the job offer?
Letters and Memos	How often does the job require written letters and memos?
Level of Competition	To what extent does this job require the worker to compete or to be aware of competitive pressures?
Impact of Decisions on Co-workers or Company Resul	How do the decisions an employee makes impact the results of co-workers, clients or the company?
Structured versus Unstructured Work	To what extent is this job structured for the worker, rather than allowing the worker to determine tasks, priorities, and goals?
Indoors, Environmentally Controlled	How often does this job require working indoors in environmentally controlled conditions?
Degree of Automation	How automated is the job?
Time Pressure	How often does this job require the worker to meet strict deadlines?
Consequence of Error	How serious would the result usually be if the worker made a mistake that was not readily correctable?
Work With Work Group or Team	How important is it to work with others in a group or team in this job?
Frequency of Decision Making	How frequently is the worker required to make decisions that affect other people, the financial resources, and/or the image and reputation of the organization?
Importance of Repeating Same Tasks	How important is repeating the same physical activities (e.g., key entry) or mental activities (e.g., checking entries in a ledger) over and over, without stopping, to performing this job?
Deal With Unpleasant or Angry People	How frequently does the worker have to deal with unpleasant, angry, or discourteous individuals as part of the job requirements?
Physical Proximity	To what extent does this job require the worker to perform job tasks in close physical proximity to other people?
Frequency of Conflict Situations	How often are there conflict situations the employee has to face in this job?
Sounds, Noise Levels Are Distracting or Uncomforta	How often does this job require working exposed to sounds and noise levels that are distracting or uncomfortable?
Spend Time Making Repetitive Motions	How much does this job require making repetitive motions?
Responsibility for Outcomes and Results	How responsible is the worker for work outcomes and results of other workers?
Spend Time Using Your Hands to Handle, Control, or	How much does this job require using your hands to handle, control, or feel objects, tools or controls?

Responsible for Others' Health and Safety — How much responsibility is there for the health and safety of others in this job?

Public Speaking — How often do you have to perform public speaking in this job?

Coordinate or Lead Others — How important is it to coordinate or lead others in accomplishing work activities in this job?

Spend Time Bending or Twisting the Body — How much does this job require bending or twisting your body?

Spend Time Standing — How much does this job require standing?

In an Enclosed Vehicle or Equipment — How much does this job require working in a closed vehicle or equipment (e.g., car)?

Pace Determined by Speed of Equipment — How important is it to this job that the pace is determined by the speed of equipment or machinery? (This does not refer to keeping busy at all times on this job.)

Spend Time Walking and Running — How much does this job require walking and running?

Exposed to Contaminants — How often does this job require working exposed to contaminants (such as pollutants, gases, dust or odors)?

Indoors, Not Environmentally Controlled — How often does this job require working indoors in non-controlled environmental conditions (e.g., warehouse without heat)?

Outdoors, Exposed to Weather — How often does this job require working outdoors, exposed to all weather conditions?

Cramped Work Space, Awkward Positions — How often does this job require working in cramped work spaces that requires getting into awkward positions?

Deal With Physically Aggressive People — How frequently does this job require the worker to deal with physical aggression of violent individuals?

Outdoors, Under Cover — How often does this job require working outdoors, under cover (e.g., structure with roof but no walls)?

In an Open Vehicle or Equipment — How often does this job require working in an open vehicle or equipment (e.g., tractor)?

Extremely Bright or Inadequate Lighting — How often does this job require working in extremely bright or inadequate lighting conditions?

Spend Time Kneeling, Crouching, Stooping, or Crawl — How much does this job require kneeling, crouching, stooping or crawling?

Spend Time Keeping or Regaining Balance — How much does this job require keeping or regaining your balance?

Very Hot or Cold Temperatures — How often does this job require working in very hot (above 90 F degrees) or very cold (below 32 F degrees) temperatures?

Exposed to Whole Body Vibration — How often does this job require exposure to whole body vibration (e.g., operate a jackhammer)?

Exposed to Hazardous Equipment — How often does this job require exposure to hazardous equipment?

Exposed to Minor Burns, Cuts, Bites, or Stings — How often does this job require exposure to minor burns, cuts, bites, or stings?

Wear Specialized Protective or Safety Equipment su — How much does this job require wearing specialized protective or safety equipment such as breathing apparatus, safety harness, full protection suits, or radiation protection?

Exposed to Disease or Infections — How often does this job require exposure to disease/infections?

Exposed to High Places — How often does this job require exposure to high places?

Exposed to Hazardous Conditions — How often does this job require exposure to hazardous conditions?

Spend Time Climbing Ladders, Scaffolds, or Poles — How much does this job require climbing ladders, scaffolds, or poles?

Exposed to Radiation — How often does this job require exposure to radiation?

Wear Common Protective or Safety Equipment such as — How much does this job require wearing common protective or safety equipment such as safety shoes, glasses, gloves, hard hats or live jackets?

Work_Styles	Work_Styles Definitions
Attention to Detail	Job requires being careful about detail and thorough in completing work tasks.
Dependability	Job requires being reliable, responsible, and dependable, and fulfilling obligations.
Integrity	Job requires being honest and ethical.
Cooperation	Job requires being pleasant with others on the job and displaying a good-natured, cooperative attitude.
Self Control	Job requires maintaining composure, keeping emotions in check, controlling anger, and avoiding aggressive behavior, even in very difficult situations.
Independence	Job requires developing one's own ways of doing things, guiding oneself with little or no supervision, and depending on oneself to get things done.
Initiative	Job requires a willingness to take on responsibilities and challenges.
Stress Tolerance	Job requires accepting criticism and dealing calmly and effectively with high stress situations.
Concern for Others	Job requires being sensitive to others' needs and feelings and being understanding and helpful on the job.
Leadership	Job requires a willingness to lead, take charge, and offer opinions and direction.
Adaptability/Flexibility	Job requires being open to change (positive or negative) and to considerable variety in the workplace.

Persistence — Job requires persistence in the face of obstacles.

Achievement/Effort — Job requires establishing and maintaining personally challenging achievement goals and exerting effort toward mastering tasks.

Social Orientation — Job requires preferring to work with others rather than alone, and being personally connected with others on the job.

Analytical Thinking — Job requires analyzing information and using logic to address work-related issues and problems.

Innovation — Job requires creativity and alternative thinking to develop new ideas for and approaches to work-related problems.

Job Zone Component	Job Zone Component Definitions
Title	Job Zone Three: Medium Preparation Needed
Overall Experience	Previous work-related skill, knowledge, or experience is required for these occupations. For example, an electrician must have completed three or four years of apprenticeship or several years of vocational training, and often must have passed a licensing exam, in order to perform the job.
Job Training	Employees in these occupations usually need one or two years of training involving both on-the-job experience and informal training with experienced workers.
Job Zone Examples	These occupations usually involve using communication and organizational skills to coordinate, supervise, manage, or train others to accomplish goals. Examples include dental assistants, electricians, fish and game wardens, legal secretaries, personnel recruiters, and recreation workers.
SVP Range	(6.0 to < 7.0)
Education	Most occupations in this zone require training in vocational schools, related on-the-job experience, or an associate's degree. Some may require a bachelor's degree.

41-9021.00 - Real Estate Brokers

Operate real estate office, or work for commercial real estate firm, overseeing real estate transactions. Other duties usually include selling real estate or renting properties and arranging loans.

Tasks

1) Sell, for a fee, real estate owned by others.

2) Maintain awareness of current income tax regulations, local zoning, building and tax laws, and growth possibilities of the area where a property is located.

3) Compare a property with similar properties that have recently sold, in order to determine its competitive market price.

4) Supervise agents who handle real estate transactions.

5) Act as an intermediary in negotiations between buyers and sellers over property prices and settlement details, and during the closing of sales.

6) Check work completed by loan officers, attorneys, and other professionals to ensure that it is performed properly.

7) Manage and operate real estate offices, handling associated business details.

8) Generate lists of properties for sale, their locations and descriptions, and available financing options, using computers.

9) Monitor fulfillment of purchase contract terms to ensure that they are handled in a timely manner.

10) Arrange for title searches of properties being sold.

11) Arrange for financing of property purchases.

12) Develop, sell, or lease property used for industry or manufacturing.

13) Review property details to ensure that environmental regulations are met.

14) Give buyers virtual tours of properties in which they are interested, using computers.

15) Maintain working knowledge of various factors that determine a farm's capacity to produce, including agricultural variables and proximity to market centers and transportation facilities.

16) Rent properties or manage rental properties.

17) Obtain agreements from property owners to place properties for sale with real estate firms.

18) Maintain knowledge of real estate law, local economies, fair housing laws, and types of available mortgages, financing options and government programs.

41-9022.00 - Real Estate Sales Agents

Rent, buy, or sell property for clients. Perform duties, such as study property listings.

interview prospective clients, accompany clients to property site. discuss conditions of sale, and draw up real estate contracts. Includes agents who represent buyer.

Tasks

1) Act as an intermediary in negotiations between buyers and sellers, generally representing one or the other.

2) Accompany buyers during visits to and inspections of property, advising them on the suitability and value of the homes they are visiting.

3) Coordinate appointments to show homes to prospective buyers.

4) Locate and appraise undeveloped areas for building sites, based on evaluations of area market conditions.

5) Appraise properties to determine loan values.

6) Advise clients on market conditions, prices, mortgages, legal requirements and related matters.

7) Secure construction or purchase financing with own firm or mortgage company.

8) Develop networks of attorneys, mortgage lenders, and contractors to whom clients may be referred.

9) Investigate clients' financial and credit status in order to determine eligibility for financing.

10) Inspect condition of premises, and arrange for necessary maintenance or notify owners of maintenance needs.

11) Evaluate mortgage options to help clients obtain financing at the best prevailing rates and terms.

12) Solicit and compile listings of available rental properties.

13) Contact utility companies for service hookups to clients' property.

14) Confer with escrow companies, lenders, home inspectors, and pest control operators to ensure that terms and conditions of purchase agreements are met before closing dates.

15) Coordinate property closings, overseeing signing of documents and disbursement of funds.

16) Interview clients to determine what kinds of properties they are seeking.

17) Conduct seminars and training sessions for sales agents in order to improve sales techniques.

18) Review property listings, trade journals, and relevant literature, and attend conventions, seminars, and staff and association meetings in order to remain knowledgeable about real estate markets.

19) Review plans for new construction with clients, enumerating and recommending available options and features.

20) Promote sales of properties through advertisements, open houses, and participation in multiple listing services.

21) Advise sellers on how to make homes more appealing to potential buyers.

22) Prepare documents such as representation contracts, purchase agreements, closing statements, deeds and leases.

23) Display commercial, industrial, agricultural, and residential properties to clients and explain their features.

24) Visit properties to assess them before showing them to clients.

25) Contact property owners and advertise services in order to solicit property sales listings.

26) Generate lists of properties that are compatible with buyers' needs and financial resources.

27) Compare a property with similar properties that have recently sold in order to determine its competitive market price.

28) Arrange meetings between buyers and sellers when details of transactions need to be negotiated.

29) Arrange for title searches to determine whether clients have clear property titles.

30) Answer clients' questions regarding construction work, financing, maintenance, repairs, and appraisals.

31) Present purchase offers to sellers for consideration.

41-9041.00 - Telemarketers

Solicit orders for goods or services over the telephone.

Tasks

1) Explain products or services and prices, and answer questions from customers.

2) Obtain names and telephone numbers of potential customers from sources such as telephone directories, magazine reply cards, and lists purchased from other organizations.

3) Adjust sales scripts to better target the needs and interests of specific individuals.

4) Answer telephone calls from potential customers who have been solicited through advertisements.

5) Obtain customer information such as name, address, and payment method, and enter orders into computers.

6) Record names, addresses, purchases, and reactions of prospects contacted.

7) Conduct client or market surveys in order to obtain information about potential customers.

8) Maintain records of contacts, accounts, and orders.

9) Schedule appointments for sales representatives to meet with prospective customers or for customers to attend sales presentations.

10) Deliver prepared sales talks, reading from scripts that describe products or services, in order to persuade potential customers to purchase a product or service or to make a donation.

11) Contact businesses or private individuals by telephone in order to solicit sales for goods or services, or to request donations for charitable causes.

43-2011.00 - Switchboard Operators, Including Answering Service

Operate telephone business systems equipment or switchboards to relay incoming, outgoing, and interoffice calls. May supply information to callers and record messages.

Tasks

1) Stamp messages with time and date, and file them appropriately.

2) Answer simple questions about clients' businesses, using reference files.

3) Keep records of calls placed and charges incurred.

4) Operate communication systems, such as telephone, switchboard, intercom, two-way radio, or public address.

5) Page individuals to inform them of telephone calls, using paging and interoffice communication equipment.

6) Place telephone calls or arrange conference calls as instructed.

7) Record messages, suggesting rewording for clarity and conciseness.

8) Complete forms for sales orders.

9) Contact security staff members when necessary, using radio-telephones.

10) Monitor alarm systems in order to ensure that secure conditions are maintained.

11) Perform clerical duties, such as typing, proofreading, accepting orders, scheduling appointments, and sorting mail.

12) Relay and route written and verbal messages.

13) Route emergency calls appropriately.

43-3011.00 - Bill and Account Collectors

Locate and notify customers of delinquent accounts by mail, telephone, or personal visit to solicit payment. Duties include receiving payment and posting amount to customer's account; preparing statements to credit department if customer fails to respond; initiating repossession proceedings or service disconnection; keeping records of collection and status of accounts.

Tasks

1) Arrange for debt repayment or establish repayment schedules, based on customers' financial situations.

2) Negotiate credit extensions when necessary.

3) Perform various administrative functions for assigned accounts, such as recording address changes and purging the records of deceased customers.

4) Persuade customers to pay amounts due on credit accounts, damage claims, or nonpayable checks, or to return merchandise.

5) Confer with customers by telephone or in person to determine reasons for overdue payments and to review the terms of sales, service, or credit contracts.

6) Locate and notify customers of delinquent accounts by mail, telephone, or personal visits in order to solicit payment.

7) Notify credit departments, order merchandise repossession or service disconnection, and turn over account records to attorneys when customers fail to respond to collection attempts.

8) Receive payments and post amounts paid to customer accounts.

9) Record information about financial status of customers and status of collection efforts.

10) Trace delinquent customers to new addresses by inquiring at post offices, telephone companies, credit bureaus, or through the questioning of neighbors.

11) Drive vehicles to visit customers, return merchandise to creditors, or deliver bills.

12) Advise customers of necessary actions and strategies for debt repayment.

13) Sort and file correspondence, and perform miscellaneous clerical duties such as answering correspondence and writing reports.

43-3021.01 - Statement Clerks

Prepare and distribute bank statements to customers, answer inquiries, and reconcile discrepancies in records and accounts.

Tasks

1) Route statements for mailing or over-the-counter delivery to customers.

2) Compare previously prepared bank statements with canceled checks, and reconcile discrepancies.

3) Encode and cancel checks, using bank machines.

4) Load machines with statements, cancelled checks, and envelopes in order to prepare statements for distribution to customers, or stuff envelopes by hand.

5) Maintain files of canceled checks and customers' signatures.

6) Match statements with batches of canceled checks by account numbers.

7) Verify signatures and required information on checks.

8) Fix minor problems, such as equipment jams, and notify repair personnel of major equipment problems.

9) Post stop-payment notices in order to prevent payment of protested checks.

10) Take orders for imprinted checks.

11) Monitor equipment in order to ensure proper operation.

12) Retrieve checks returned to customers in error, adjusting customer accounts and answering inquiries about errors as necessary.

43-3021.02 - Billing, Cost, and Rate Clerks

Compile data, compute fees and charges, and prepare invoices for billing purposes. Duties include computing costs and calculating rates for goods, services, and shipment of goods; posting data; and keeping other relevant records. May involve use of computer or typewriter, calculator, and adding and bookkeeping machines.

Tasks

1) Review documents such as purchase orders, sales tickets, charge slips, or hospital records in order to compute fees and charges due.

2) Answer mail and telephone inquiries regarding rates, routing, and procedures.

3) Compile reports of cost factors, such as labor, production, storage, and equipment.

4) Compute credit terms, discounts, shipment charges, and rates for goods and services in order to complete billing documents.

5) Consult sources such as rate books, manuals, and insurance company representatives in order to determine specific charges and information such as rules, regulations, and government tax and tariff information.

6) Operate typing, adding, calculating, and billing machines.

7) Track accumulated hours and dollar amounts charged to each client job in order to calculate client fees for professional services such as legal and accounting services.

8) Perform bookkeeping work, including posting data and keeping other records concerning costs of goods and services and the shipment of goods.

9) Resolve discrepancies in accounting records.

10) Review compiled data on operating costs and revenues in order to set rates.

11) Type billing documents, shipping labels, credit memorandums, and credit forms, using typewriters or computers.

12) Update manuals when rates, rules, or regulations are amended.

13) Keep records of invoices and support documents.

14) Contact customers in order to obtain or relay account information.

15) Prepare itemized statements, bills, or invoices; and record amounts due for items purchased or services rendered.

16) Estimate market value of products or services.

43-3021.03 - Billing, Posting, and Calculating Machine

Operators

Operate machines that automatically perform mathematical processes, such as addition, subtraction, multiplication, and division, to calculate and record billing, accounting, statistical, and other numerical data. Duties include operating special billing machines to prepare statements, bills, and invoices, and operating bookkeeping machines to copy and post data, make computations, and compile records of transactions.

Tasks

1) Verify completeness and accuracy of original documents such as business property statements, tax rolls, invoices, bonds and coupons, and redemption certificates.

2) Compute payroll and retirement amounts, applying knowledge of payroll deductions, actuarial tables, disability factors, and survivor allowances.

3) Enter into machines all information needed for bill generation.

4) Observe operation of sorters to locate documents that machines cannot read, and manually record amounts of these documents.

5) Reconcile and post receipts for cash received by various departments.

6) Send completed bills to billing clerks for information verification.

7) Compute monies due on personal and real property, inventories, redemption payments and other amounts, applying specialized knowledge of tax rates, formulas, interest rates, and other relevant information.

8) Transcribe data from office records, using specified forms, billing machines, and transcribing machines.

9) Train other calculating machine operators, and review their work.

10) Balance and reconcile batch control totals with source documents or computer listings in order to locate errors, encode correct amounts, or prepare correction records.

11) Sort and microfilm transaction documents, such as checks, using sorting machines.

12) Encode and add amounts of transaction documents, such as checks or money orders, using encoding machines.

13) Verify and post to ledgers purchase orders, reports of goods received, invoices, paid vouchers, and other information.

14) Operate special billing machines to prepare statements, bills, and invoices.

15) Sort and list items for proof or collection.

16) Prepare transmittal reports for changes to assessment and tax rolls, redemption file changes, and for warrants, deposits, and invoices.

17) Maintain ledgers and registers, posting charges and refunds to individual funds, and computing and verifying balances.

18) Compute and record inventory data from audio transcription, using transcribing machines and calculators.

19) Compile, code, and verify requisition, production, statistical, mileage, and other reports which require specialized knowledge in selecting the totals used.

20) Clean machines, and replace ribbons, film, and tape.

21) Bundle sorted documents to prepare those drawn on other banks for collection.

22) Operate bookkeeping machines to copy and post data, make computations, and compile records of transactions.

23) Assign purchase order numbers to invoices, requisitions, and formal and informal bids.

43-3031.00 - Bookkeeping, Accounting, and Auditing Clerks

Compute, classify, and record numerical data to keep financial records complete. Perform any combination of routine calculating, posting, and verifying duties to obtain primary financial data for use in maintaining accounting records. May also check the accuracy of figures, calculations, and postings pertaining to business transactions recorded by other workers.

Tasks

1) Check figures, postings, and documents for correct entry, mathematical accuracy, and proper codes.

2) Perform personal bookkeeping services.

3) Calculate, prepare, and issue bills, invoices, account statements, and other financial statements according to established procedures.

4) Prepare purchase orders and expense reports.

5) Prepare bank deposits by compiling data from cashiers, verifying and balancing receipts, and sending cash, checks, or other forms of payment to banks.

6) Perform financial calculations such as amounts due, interest charges, balances, discounts, equity, and principal.

7) Operate computers programmed with accounting software to record. store, and analyze information.

8) Monitor status of loans and accounts to ensure that payments are up to date.

9) Debit, credit, and total accounts on computer spreadsheets and databases. using specialized accounting software.

10) Complete and submit tax forms and returns, workers' compensation forms. pension contribution forms, and other government documents.

11) Compare computer printouts to manually maintained journals in o der to determine if they match.

12) Calculate and prepare checks for utilities, taxes, and other payments.

13) Compute deductions for income and social security taxes.

14) Classify, record, and summarize numerical and financial data in order to compile and keep financial records, using journals and ledgers or computers.

15) Transfer details from separate journals to general ledgers and/or data processing sheets.

16) Code documents according to company procedures.

17) Reconcile or note and report discrepancies found in records.

18) Prepare trial balances of books.

19) Access computerized financial information to answer general questions as well as those related to specific accounts.

20) Perform general office duties such as filing, answering telephones, and handling routine correspondence.

21) Compile statistical, financial, accounting or auditing reports and tables pertaining to such matters as cash receipts, expenditures, accounts payable and receivable, and profits and losses.

22) Compile budget data and documents, based on estimated revenues and expenses and previous budgets.

23) Comply with federal, state, and company policies, procedures, and regulations.

24) Maintain inventory records.

25) Match order forms with invoices, and record the necessary information.

26) Operate 10-key calculators, typewriters, and copy machines to perform calculations and produce documents.

27) Receive, record, and bank cash, checks, and vouchers.

28) Reconcile records of bank transactions.

43-3041.00 - Gaming Cage Workers

In a gaming establishment, conduct financial transactions for patrons. May reconcile daily summaries of transactions to balance books. Accept patron's credit application and verify credit references to provide check-cashing authorization or to establish house credit accounts. May sell gambling chips, tokens, or tickets to patrons, or to other workers for resale to patrons. May convert gaming chips, tokens, or tickets to currency upon patron's request. May use a cash register or computer to record transaction.

Tasks

1) Perform removal and rotation of cash, coin, and chip inventories as necessary.

2) Record casino exchange transactions, using cash registers.

3) Provide customers with information about casino operations.

4) Follow all gaming regulations.

5) Cash checks and process credit card advances for patrons.

6) Determine cash requirements for windows, and order all necessary currency, coins, and chips.

7) Convert gaming checks, coupons, tokens, and coins to currency for gaming patrons.

8) Prepare bank deposits, balancing assigned funds as necessary.

9) Supply currency, coins, chips, and gaming checks to other departments as needed.

10) Count funds and reconcile daily summaries of transactions to balance books.

11) Establish new computer accounts.

12) Maintain confidentiality of customers' transactions.

13) Provide assistance in the training and orientation of new cashiers.

14) Prepare reports, including assignment of company funds and recording of department revenues.

15) Maintain cage security.

16) Verify accuracy of reports such as authorization forms, transaction reconciliations, and exchange summary reports.

43-3051.00 - Payroll and Timekeeping Clerks

Compile and post employee time and payroll data. May compute employees' time worked, production. and commission. May compute and post wages and deductions. May prepare paychecks.

Tasks

1) Compile statistical reports, statements, and summaries related to pay and benefits accounts, and submit them to appropriate departments.

2) Review time sheets, work charts, wage computation, and other information in order to detect and reconcile payroll discrepancies.

3) Complete time sheets showing employees' arrival and departure times.

4) Complete, verify, and process forms and documentation for administration of benefits such as pension plans, and unemployment and medical insurance.

5) Compute wages and deductions, and enter data into computers.

6) Issue and record adjustments to pay related to previous errors or retroactive increases.

7) Post relevant work hours to client files in order to bill clients properly.

8) Compile employee time, production, and payroll data from time sheets and other records.

9) Verify attendance, hours worked, and pay adjustments, and post information onto designated records.

10) Coordinate special programs, such as United Way campaigns, that involve payroll deductions.

11) Distribute and collect timecards each pay period.

12) Keep informed about changes in tax and deduction laws that apply to the payroll process.

13) Process and issue employee paychecks and statements of earnings and deductions.

14) Provide information to employees and managers on payroll matters, tax issues, benefit plans, and collective agreement provisions.

15) Prepare and balance period-end reports, and reconcile issued payrolls to bank statements.

43-3061.00 - Procurement Clerks

Compile information and records to draw up purchase orders for procurement of materials and services.

Tasks

1) Monitor contractor performance, recommending contract modifications when necessary.

2) Approve bills for payment.

3) Prepare, maintain, and review purchasing files, reports and price lists.

4) Calculate costs of orders, and charge or forward invoices to appropriate accounts.

5) Monitor in-house inventory movement and complete inventory transfer forms for bookkeeping purposes.

6) Review requisition orders in order to verify accuracy, terminology, and specifications.

7) Maintain knowledge of all organizational and governmental rules affecting purchases, and provide information about these rules to organization staff members and to vendors.

8) Track the status of requisitions, contracts, and orders.

9) Prepare invitation-of-bid forms, and mail forms to supplier firms or distribute forms for public posting.

10) Respond to customer and supplier inquiries about order status, changes, or cancellations.

11) Contact suppliers in order to schedule or expedite deliveries and to resolve shortages, missed or late deliveries, and other problems.

12) Compare suppliers' bills with bids and purchase orders in order to verify accuracy.

13) Compare prices, specifications, and delivery dates in order to determine the best bid among potential suppliers.

14) Check shipments when they arrive to ensure that orders have been filled correctly and that goods meet specifications.

15) Perform buying duties when necessary.

16) Locate suppliers, using sources such as catalogs and the internet, and interview them to gather information about products to be ordered.

17) Determine if inventory quantities are sufficient for needs, ordering more materials when necessary.

43-3071.00 - Tellers

Receive and pay out money. Keep records of money and negotiable instruments involved in a financial institution's various transactions.

Tasks

1) Identify transaction mistakes when debits and credits do not balance.

2) Receive and count daily inventories of cash, drafts, and travelers' checks.

3) Compose, type, and mail customer statements and other correspondence related to issues such as discrepancies and outstanding unpaid items.

4) Explain, promote, or sell products or services such as travelers' checks, savings bonds, money orders, and cashier's checks, using computerized information about customers to tailor recommendations.

5) Count, verify, and post armored car deposits.

6) Enter customers' transactions into computers in order to record transactions and issue computer-generated receipts.

7) Examine checks for endorsements and to verify other information such as dates, bank names, identification of the persons receiving payments and the legality of the documents.

8) Order a supply of cash to meet daily needs.

9) Prepare and verify cashier's checks.

10) Count currency, coins, and checks received, by hand or using currency-counting machine, in order to prepare them for deposit or shipment to branch banks or the Federal Reserve Bank.

11) Quote unit exchange rates, following daily international rate sheets or computer displays.

12) Inform customers about foreign currency regulations, and compute transaction fees for currency exchanges.

13) Process transactions such as term deposits, retirement savings plan contributions, automated teller transactions, night deposits, and mail deposits.

14) Resolve problems or discrepancies concerning customers' accounts.

15) Issue checks to bond owners in settlement of transactions.

16) Carry out special services for customers, such as ordering bank cards and checks.

17) Obtain and process information required for the provision of services, such as opening accounts, savings plans, and purchasing bonds.

18) Monitor bank vaults to ensure cash balances are correct.

19) Receive mortgage, loan, or public utility bill payments, verifying payment dates and amounts due.

20) Receive checks and cash for deposit, verify amounts, and check accuracy of deposit slips.

21) Prepare work schedules for staff.

22) Process and maintain records of customer loans.

23) Cash checks and pay out money after verifying that signatures are correct, that written and numerical amounts agree, and that accounts have sufficient funds.

24) Compute financial fees, interest, and service charges.

25) Sort and file deposit slips and checks.

26) Balance currency, coin, and checks in cash drawers at ends of shifts, and calculate daily transactions using computers, calculators, or adding machines.

27) Perform clerical tasks such as typing, filing, and microfilm photography.

43-4011.00 - Brokerage Clerks

Perform clerical duties involving the purchase or sale of securities. Duties include writing orders for stock purchases and sales, computing transfer taxes, verifying stock transactions, accepting and delivering securities, tracking stock price fluctuations, computing equity, distributing dividends, and keeping records of daily transactions and holdings.

Tasks

1) File, type, and operate standard office machines.

2) Verify ownership and transaction information and dividend distribution instructions to ensure conformance with governmental regulations, using stock records and reports.

3) Monitor daily stock prices, and compute fluctuations in order to determine the need for additional collateral to secure loans.

4) Schedule and coordinate transfer and delivery of security certificates between companies, departments, and customers.

5) Correspond with customers and confer with coworkers in order to answer inquiries, discuss market fluctuations, and resolve account problems.

6) Prepare forms, such as receipts, withdrawal orders, transmittal papers, and transfer confirmations, based on transaction requests from stockholders.

7) Prepare reports summarizing daily transactions and earnings for individual customer

accounts.

8) Record and document security transactions, such as purchases, sales, conversions, redemptions, and payments, using computers, accounting ledgers, and certificate records.

43-4021.00 - Correspondence Clerks

Compose letters in reply to requests for merchandise, damage claims, credit and other information, delinquent accounts, incorrect billings, or unsatisfactory services. Duties may include gathering data to formulate reply and typing correspondence.

Tasks

1) Complete form letters in response to requests or problems identified by correspondence.

2) Prepare records for shipment by certified mail.

3) Route correspondence to other departments for reply.

4) Present clear and concise explanations of governing rules and regulations.

5) Read incoming correspondence to ascertain nature of writers' concerns and to determine disposition of correspondence.

6) Submit completed documents to typists for typing in final form, and instruct typists in matters such as format, addresses, addressees, and the necessary number of copies.

7) Maintain files and control records to show correspondence activities.

8) Compose correspondence requesting medical information and records.

9) Gather records pertinent to specific problems, review them for completeness and accuracy, and attach records to correspondence as necessary.

10) Review correspondence for format and typographical accuracy, assemble the information into a prescribed form with the correct number of copies, and submit it to an authorized official for signature.

11) Compile data from records to prepare periodic reports.

12) Type acknowledgment letters to persons sending correspondence.

13) Compute costs of records furnished to requesters, and write letters to obtain payment.

14) Respond to internal and external requests for the release of information contained in medical records, copying medical records, and selective extracts in accordance with laws and regulations.

15) Process orders for goods requested in correspondence.

16) Obtain written authorization to access required medical information.

17) Ensure that money collected is properly recorded and secured.

18) Confer with company personnel regarding feasibility of complying with writers' requests.

19) Compile data pertinent to manufacture of special products for customers.

20) Compose letters in reply to correspondence concerning such items as requests for merchandise, damage claims, credit information requests, delinquent accounts, incorrect billing, or unsatisfactory service.

43-4031.01 - Court Clerks

Perform clerical duties in court of law; prepare docket of cases to be called; secure information for judges; and contact witnesses, attorneys, and litigants to obtain information for court.

Tasks

1) Amend indictments when necessary, and endorse indictments with pertinent information.

2) Prepare and mark all applicable court exhibits and evidence.

3) Record court proceedings, using recording equipment, or record minutes of court proceedings using stenotype machines or shorthand.

4) Meet with judges, lawyers, parole officers, police, and social agency officials in order to coordinate the functions of the court.

5) Search files, and contact witnesses, attorneys, and litigants, in order to obtain information for the court.

6) Examine legal documents submitted to courts for adherence to laws or court procedures.

7) Prepare and issue orders of the court, including probation orders, release documentation, sentencing information, and summonses.

8) Read charges and related information to the court and, if necessary, record defendants' pleas.

9) Instruct parties about timing of court appearances.

10) Direct support staff in handling of paperwork processed by clerks' offices.

11) Open courts, calling them to order and announcing judges.

12) Prepare dockets or calendars of cases to be called, using typewriters or computers.

13) Follow procedures to secure courtrooms and exhibits such as money, drugs, and weapons.

14) Collect court fees or fines, and record amounts collected.

15) Arrange transportation and accommodation for witnesses and jurors, if required.

16) Answer inquiries from the general public regarding judicial procedures, court appearances, trial dates, adjournments, outstanding warrants, summonses, subpoenas, witness fees, and payment of fines.

17) Conduct roll calls, and poll jurors.

18) Record case dispositions, court orders, and arrangements made for payment of court fees.

19) Explain procedures or forms to parties in cases or to the general public.

20) Prepare documents recording the outcomes of court proceedings.

21) Swear in jury members, interpreters, witnesses and defendants.

43-4031.02 - Municipal Clerks

Draft agendas and bylaws for town or city council; record minutes of council meetings; answer official correspondence; keep fiscal records and accounts; and prepare reports on civic needs.

Tasks

1) Respond to requests for information from the public, other municipalities, state officials, and state and federal legislative offices.

2) Provide assistance to persons with disabilities in reaching less accessible areas of municipal facilities.

3) Develop and conduct orientation programs for candidates for political office.

4) Serve as a notary of the public.

5) Represent municipalities at community events, and serve as liaisons on community committees.

6) Prepare reports on civic needs.

7) Perform contract administration duties, assisting with bid openings and the awarding of contracts.

8) Issue various permits and licenses, including marriage, fishing, hunting, and dog licenses, and collect appropriate fees.

9) Maintain and update documents such as municipal codes and city charters.

10) Process claims against the municipality, maintaining files and log of claims, and coordinate claim response and handling with municipal claims administrators.

11) Collaborate with other staff to assist in the development and implementation of goals, objectives, policies, and priorities.

12) Issue public notification of all official activities and meetings.

13) Record and edit the minutes of meetings, then distribute them to appropriate officials and staff members.

14) Prepare ordinances, resolutions, and proclamations so that they can be executed, recorded, archived, and distributed.

15) Prepare meeting agendas and packets of related information.

16) Plan and direct the maintenance, filing, safekeeping, and computerization of all municipal documents.

17) Perform general office duties such as taking and transcribing dictation, typing and proofreading correspondence, distributing and filing official forms, and scheduling appointments.

18) Maintain fiscal records and accounts.

19) Perform budgeting duties, including assisting in budget preparation, expenditure review, and budget administration.

20) Participate in the administration of municipal elections, including preparation and distribution of ballots, appointment and training of election officers, and tabulation and certification of results.

21) Provide assistance with events such as police department auctions of abandoned automobiles.

22) Coordinate and maintain office-tracking systems for correspondence and follow-up actions.

43-4031.03 - License Clerks

Issue licenses or permits to qualified applicants. Obtain necessary information; record data; advise applicants on requirements; collect fees; and issue licenses. May conduct oral, written, visual, or performance testing.

Tasks

1) Enforce canine licensing regulations, contacting non-compliant owners in person or by mail to inform them of the required regulations and potential enforcement actions.

2) Prepare bank deposits, and take them to banks.

3) Conduct and score oral, visual, written, or performance tests to determine applicant qualifications, and notify applicants of their scores.

4) Provide assistance in the preparation of insurance examinations covering a variety of types of insurance.

5) Send by mail drivers' licenses to out-of-county or out-of-state applicants.

6) Question applicants to obtain required information, such as name, address, and age, and record data on prescribed forms.

7) Answer questions and provide advice to the public regarding licensing policies, procedures, and regulations.

8) Collect prescribed fees for licenses.

9) Evaluate information on applications to verify completeness and accuracy and to determine whether applicants are qualified to obtain desired licenses.

10) Instruct customers in the completion of drivers' license application forms and other forms such as voter registration cards and organ donor forms.

11) Maintain records of applications made and licensing fees collected.

12) Perform routine data entry and other office support activities including creating, sorting, photocopying, distributing, and filing documents.

13) Prepare lists of overdue accounts, license suspensions and issuances.

14) Stock counters with adequate supplies of forms, film, licenses, and other required materials.

15) Update operational records and licensing information, using computer terminals.

16) Code information on license applications for entry into computers.

17) Inform customers by mail or telephone of additional steps they need to take to obtain licenses.

18) Perform record checks on past and current licensees, as required by investigations.

19) Perform driver education program enrollments for participating schools.

20) Operate specialized photographic equipment in order to obtain photographs for drivers' licenses and photo identification cards.

21) Train other workers, and coordinate their work as necessary.

22) Respond to correspondence from insurance companies regarding the licensure of agents, brokers and adjusters.

43-4041.01 - Credit Authorizers

Authorize credit charges against customers' accounts.

Tasks

1) Prepare credit cards or charge account plates.

2) File sales slips in customers' ledgers for billing purposes.

3) Receive charge slips or credit applications by mail, or receive information from salespeople or merchants by telephone.

4) Keep records of customers' charges and payments.

5) Mail charge statements to customers.

43-4041.02 - Credit Checkers

Investigate history and credit standing of individuals or business establishments applying for credit. Telephone or write to credit departments of business and service establishments to obtain information about applicant's credit standing.

Tasks

1) Compile and analyze credit information gathered by investigation.

2) Contact former employers and other acquaintances to verify applicants' references, employment, health history, and social behavior.

3) Interview credit applicants by telephone or in person in order to obtain personal and financial data needed to complete credit report.

4) Prepare reports of findings and recommendations, using typewriters or computers.

5) Relay credit report information to subscribers by mail or by telephone.

6) Examine city directories and public records in order to verify residence property ownership, bankruptcies, liens, arrest record, or unpaid taxes of applicants.

43-4051.00 - Customer Service Representatives

Interact with customers to provide information in response to inquiries about products and services and to handle and resolve complaints.

Tasks

1) Complete contract forms, prepare change of address records, and issue service discontinuance orders, using computers.

2) Confer with customers by telephone or in person in order to provide information about products and services, to take orders or cancel accounts, or to obtain details of complaints.

3) Contact customers in order to respond to inquiries or to notify them of claim investigation results and any planned adjustments.

4) Determine charges for services requested, collect deposits or payments, and/or arrange for billing.

5) Obtain and examine all relevant information in order to assess validity of complaints and to determine possible causes, such as extreme weather conditions that could increase utility bills.

6) Refer unresolved customer grievances to designated departments for further investigation.

7) Check to ensure that appropriate changes were made to resolve customers' problems.

8) Review insurance policy terms in order to determine whether a particular loss is covered by insurance.

9) Review claims adjustments with dealers, examining parts claimed to be defective and approving or disapproving dealers' claims.

10) Solicit sale of new or additional services or products.

11) Resolve customers' service or billing complaints by performing activities such as exchanging merchandise, refunding money, and adjusting bills.

12) Compare disputed merchandise with original requisitions and information from invoices, and prepare invoices for returned goods.

13) Keep records of customer interactions and transactions, recording details of inquiries, complaints, and comments, as well as actions taken.

14) Recommend improvements in products, packaging, shipping, service, or billing methods and procedures in order to prevent future problems.

43-4071.00 - File Clerks

File correspondence, cards, invoices, receipts, and other records in alphabetical or numerical order or according to the filing system used. Locate and remove material from file when requested.

Tasks

1) Track materials removed from files in order to ensure that borrowed files are returned.

2) Eliminate outdated or unnecessary materials, destroying them or transferring them to inactive storage according to file maintenance guidelines and/or legal requirements.

3) Enter document identification codes into systems in order to determine locations of documents to be retrieved.

4) Keep records of materials filed or removed, using logbooks or computers.

5) Perform periodic inspections of materials or files in order to ensure correct placement, legibility, and proper condition.

6) Scan or read incoming materials in order to determine how and where they should be classified or filed.

7) Place materials into storage receptacles, such as file cabinets, boxes, bins, or drawers, according to classification and identification information.

8) Find and retrieve information from files in response to requests from authorized users.

9) Convert documents to films for storage on microforms such as microfilm or microfiche.

10) Design forms related to filing systems.

11) Assign and record or stamp identification numbers or codes in order to index materials for filing.

12) Gather materials to be filed from departments and employees.

13) Operate mechanized files that rotate to bring needed records to a particular location.

14) Perform general office duties such as typing, operating office machines, and sorting mail.

15) Retrieve documents stored in microfilm or microfiche and place them in viewers for reading.

16) Add new material to file records, and create new records as necessary.

17) Answer questions about records and files.

18) Modify and improve filing systems, or implement new filing systems.

43-4081.00 - Hotel, Motel, and Resort Desk Clerks

Accommodate hotel, motel, and resort patrons by registering and assigning rooms to guests, issuing room keys, transmitting and receiving messages, keeping records of occupied rooms and guests' accounts, making and confirming reservations, and presenting statements to and collecting payments from departing guests.

Tasks

1) Advise housekeeping staff when rooms have been vacated and are ready for cleaning.

2) Date-stamp, sort, and rack incoming mail and messages.

3) Post charges, such those for rooms, food, liquor, or telephone calls, to ledgers manually, or by using computers.

4) Greet, register, and assign rooms to guests of hotels or motels.

5) Keep records of room availability and guests' accounts, manually or using computers.

6) Compute bills, collect payments, and make change for guests.

7) Make and confirm reservations.

8) Verify customers' credit, and establish how the customer will pay for the accommodation.

9) Issue room keys and escort instructions to bellhops.

10) Review accounts and charges with guests during the check out process.

11) Deposit guests' valuables in hotel safes or safe-deposit boxes.

12) Arrange tours, taxis, and restaurants for customers.

13) Contact housekeeping or maintenance staff when guests report problems.

14) Perform simple bookkeeping activities, such as balancing cash accounts.

15) Answer inquiries pertaining to hotel services, registration of guests, and shopping, dining, entertainment, and travel directions.

16) Transmit and receive messages, using telephones or telephone switchboards.

43-4111.00 - Interviewers, Except Eligibility and Loan

Interview persons by telephone, mail, in person, or by other means for the purpose of completing forms, applications, or questionnaires. Ask specific questions, record answers, and assist persons with completing form. May sort, classify, and file forms.

Tasks

1) Identify and resolve inconsistencies in interviewees' responses by means of appropriate questioning and/or explanation.

2) Explain survey objectives and procedures to interviewees, and interpret survey questions to help interviewees' comprehension.

3) Compile, record and code results and data from interview or survey, using computer or specified form.

4) Meet with supervisor daily to submit completed assignments and discuss progress.

5) Prepare reports to provide answers in response to specific problems.

6) Review data obtained from interview for completeness and accuracy.

7) Ask questions in accordance with instructions to obtain various specified information, such as person's name, address, age, religious preference, and state of residency.

8) Locate and list addresses and households.

9) Collect and analyze data, such as studying old records, tallying the number of outpatients entering each day or week, or participating in federal, state, or local population surveys as a Census Enumerator.

10) Identify and report problems in obtaining valid data.

11) Perform other office duties as needed, such as telemarketing and customer service inquiries, billing patients and receiving payments.

12) Perform patient services, such as answering the telephone and assisting patients with financial and medical questions.

13) Contact individuals to be interviewed at home, place of business, or field location, by telephone, mail, or in person.

14) Ensure payment for services by verifying benefits with the person's insurance provider or working out financing options.

43-4121.00 - Library Assistants, Clerical

Compile records, sort and shelve books, and issue and receive library materials such as pictures, cards, slides and microfilm. Locate library materials for loan and replace material in shelving area, stacks, or files according to identification number and title. Register patrons to permit them to borrow books, periodicals, and other library materials.

Tasks

1) Register new patrons and issue borrower identification cards that permit patrons to borrow books and other materials.

2) Enter and update patrons' records on computers.

3) Maintain records of items received, stored, issued, and returned, and file catalog cards according to system used.

4) Operate and maintain audiovisual equipment.

5) Operate small branch libraries, under the direction of off-site librarian supervisors.

6) Take action to deal with disruptive or problem patrons.

7) Select substitute titles when requested materials are unavailable following criteria such as age, education, and interests.

8) Lend and collect books, periodicals, videotapes, and other materials at circulation desks.

9) Send out notices and accept fine payments for lost or overdue books.

10) Assist in the preparation of book displays.

11) Review records, such as microfilm and issue cards, in order to identify titles of overdue materials and delinquent borrowers.

12) Repair books, using mending tape, paste, and brushes.

13) Provide assistance to librarians in the maintenance of collections of books, periodicals, magazines, newspapers, and audiovisual and other materials.

14) Place books in mailing containers, affix address labels, and secure containers with straps for mailing to blind library patrons.

15) Perform clerical activities such as filing, typing, word processing, photocopying and mailing out material, and mail sorting.

16) Schedule and supervise clerical workers, volunteers, and student assistants.

17) Process new materials including books, audiovisual materials, and computer software.

18) Facilitate the acquisition of books, pamphlets, periodicals, and audiovisual materials by checking prices, figuring costs, and preparing appropriate order forms.

19) Answer routine inquiries, and refer patrons in need of professional assistance to librarians.

20) Sort books, publications, and other items according to established procedure and return them to shelves, files, or other designated storage areas.

21) Classify and catalog items according to content and purpose.

22) Drive bookmobiles to specified off-site locations following library service schedules, and to garages for preventive maintenance and repairs.

23) Inspect returned books for condition and due-date status, and compute any applicable fines.

24) Deliver and retrieve items to and from departments by hand or using push carts.

25) Instruct patrons on how to use reference sources, card catalogs, and automated information systems.

26) Locate library materials for patrons, including books, periodicals, tape cassettes, Braille volumes, and pictures.

43-4131.00 - Loan Interviewers and Clerks

Interview loan applicants to elicit information; investigate applicants' backgrounds and verify references; prepare loan request papers; and forward findings, reports, and documents to appraisal department. Review loan papers to ensure completeness, and complete transactions between loan establishment, borrowers, and sellers upon approval of loan.

Tasks

1) Submit loan applications with recommendation for underwriting approval.

2) Establish credit limits and grant extensions of credit on overdue accounts.

3) Contact credit bureaus, employers, and other sources in order to check applicants' credit and personal references.

4) Review customer accounts in order to determine whether payments are made on time and that other loan terms are being followed.

5) Calculate, review, and correct errors on interest, principal, payment, and closing costs, using computers or calculators.

6) Answer questions and advise customers regarding loans and transactions.

7) Check value of customer collateral to be held as loan security.

8) File and maintain loan records.

9) Interview loan applicants in order to obtain personal and financial data, and to assist in completing applications.

10) Accept payment on accounts.

11) Assemble and compile documents for loan closings, such as title abstracts, insurance forms, loan forms, and tax receipts.

12) Record applications for loan and credit, loan information, and disbursements of funds, using computers.

13) Schedule and conduct closings of mortgage transactions.

14) Verify and examine information and accuracy of loan application and closing documents.

15) Prepare and type loan applications, closing documents, legal documents, letters, forms, government notices, and checks, using computers.

16) Present loan and repayment schedules to customers.

17) Contact customers by mail, telephone, or in person concerning acceptance or rejection of applications.

43-4141.00 - New Accounts Clerks

Interview persons desiring to open bank accounts. Explain banking services available to prospective customers and assist them in preparing application form.

Tasks

1) Issue initial and replacement safe-deposit keys to customers, and admit customers to vaults.

2) Refer customers to appropriate bank personnel in order to meet their financial needs.

3) Perform foreign currency transactions and sell traveler's checks.

4) Schedule repairs for locks on safe-deposit boxes.

5) Perform teller duties as required.

6) Investigate and correct errors upon customers' request, according to customer and bank records.

7) Interview customers in order to obtain information needed for opening accounts or renting safe-deposit boxes.

8) Inform customers of procedures for applying for services such as ATM cards, direct deposit of checks, and certificates of deposit.

9) Collect and record customer deposits and fees, and issue receipts using computers.

10) Answer customers' questions, and explain available services such as deposit accounts, bonds, and securities.

11) Execute wire transfers of funds.

12) Compile information about new accounts, enter account information into computers, and file related forms or other documents.

13) Obtain credit records from reporting agencies.

43-4151.00 - Order Clerks

Receive and process incoming orders for materials, merchandise, classified ads, or services such as repairs, installations, or rental of facilities. Duties include informing customers of receipt, prices, shipping dates, and delays; preparing contracts; and handling complaints.

Tasks

1) Check inventory records to determine availability of requested merchandise.

2) Notify departments when supplies of specific items are low, or when orders would deplete available supplies.

3) Inspect outgoing work for compliance with customers' specifications.

4) Confer with production, sales, shipping, warehouse, or common carrier personnel in order to expedite or trace shipments.

5) Collect payment for merchandise, record transactions, and send items such as checks or money orders for further processing.

6) Recommend type of packing or labeling needed on order.

7) Direct specified departments or units to prepare and ship orders to designated locations.

8) Calculate and compile order-related statistics, and prepare reports for management.

9) Verify customer and order information for correctness, checking it against previously obtained information as necessary.

10) Adjust inventory records to reflect product movement.

11) Receive and respond to customer complaints.

12) Review orders for completeness according to reporting procedures and forward incomplete orders for further processing.

13) Prepare invoices, shipping documents, and contracts.

14) Obtain customers' names, addresses, and billing information, product numbers, and specifications of items to be purchased, and enter this information on order forms.

15) Inform customers by mail or telephone of order information, such as unit prices, shipping dates, and any anticipated delays.

16) File copies of orders received, or post orders on records.

17) Recommend merchandise or services that will meet customers' needs.

18) Attempt to sell additional merchandise or services to prospective or current customers by telephone or through visits.

43-4161.00 - Human Resources Assistants, Except Payroll and Timekeeping

Compile and keep personnel records. Record data for each employee, such as address, weekly earnings, absences, amount of sales or production, supervisory reports on ability, and date of and reason for termination. Compile and type reports from employment records. File employment records. Search employee files and furnish information to authorized persons.

Tasks

1) Select applicants meeting specified job requirements and refer them to hiring personnel.

2) Answer questions regarding examinations, eligibility, salaries, benefits, and other pertinent information.

3) Search employee files in order to obtain information for authorized persons and organizations, such as credit bureaus and finance companies.

4) Arrange for in-house and external training activities.

5) Process, verify, and maintain documentation relating to personnel activities such as staffing, recruitment, training, grievances, performance evaluations, and classifications.

6) Administer and score applicant and employee aptitude, personality, and interest assessment instruments.

7) Gather personnel records from other departments and/or employees.

8) Prepare badges, passes, and identification cards, and perform other security-related duties.

9) Arrange for advertising or posting of job vacancies, and notify eligible workers of position availability.

10) Request information from law enforcement officials, previous employers, and other references in order to determine applicants' employment acceptability.

11) Process and review employment applications in order to evaluate qualifications or eligibility of applicants.

12) Provide assistance in administering employee benefit programs and worker's compensation plans.

13) Record data for each employee, including such information as addresses, weekly earnings, absences, amount of sales or production, supervisory reports on performance, and dates of and reasons for terminations.

14) Examine employee files to answer inquiries and provide information for personnel actions.

15) Explain company personnel policies, benefits, and procedures to employees or job applicants.

16) Inform job applicants of their acceptance or rejection of employment.

17) Compile and prepare reports and documents pertaining to personnel activities.

43-4171.00 - Receptionists and Information Clerks

Answer inquiries and obtain information for general public, customers, visitors, and other interested parties. Provide information regarding activities conducted at establishment;

location of departments, offices, and employees within organization.

Tasks

1) Greet persons entering establishment, determine nature and purpose of visit, and direct or escort them to specific destinations.

2) File and maintain records.

3) Collect, sort, distribute and prepare mail, messages and courier deliveries.

4) Provide information about establishment, such as location of departments or offices, employees within the organization, or services provided.

5) Transmit information or documents to customers, using computer, mail, or facsimile machine.

6) Perform administrative support tasks such as proofreading, transcribing handwritten information, and operating calculators or computers to work with pay records, invoices, balance sheets and other documents.

7) Hear and resolve complaints from customers and public.

8) Receive payment and record receipts for services.

9) Perform duties such as taking care of plants and straightening magazines to maintain lobby or reception area.

10) Keep a current record of staff members' whereabouts and availability.

11) Analyze data to determine answers to questions from customers or members of the public.

12) Schedule appointments, and maintain and update appointment calendars.

13) Process and prepare memos, correspondence, travel vouchers, or other documents.

14) Take orders for merchandise or materials and send them to the proper departments to be filled.

15) Schedule space and equipment for special programs and prepare lists of participants.

16) Enroll individuals to participate in programs and notify them of their acceptance.

17) Calculate and quote rates for tours, stocks, insurance policies, and other products and services.

18) Conduct tours or deliver talks describing features of public facility, such as historic site or national park.

Knowledge	Knowledge Definitions
Customer and Personal Service	Knowledge of principles and processes for providing customer and personal services. This includes customer needs assessment, meeting quality standards for services, and evaluation of customer satisfaction.
Clerical	Knowledge of administrative and clerical procedures and systems such as word processing, managing files and records, stenography and transcription, designing forms, and other office procedures and terminology.
English Language	Knowledge of the structure and content of the English language including the meaning and spelling of words, rules of composition, and grammar.
Computers and Electronics	Knowledge of circuit boards, processors, chips, electronic equipment, and computer hardware and software, including applications and programming.
Mathematics	Knowledge of arithmetic, algebra, geometry, calculus, statistics, and their applications.
Administration and Management	Knowledge of business and management principles involved in strategic planning, resource allocation, human resources modeling, leadership technique, production methods, and coordination of people and resources.
Transportation	Knowledge of principles and methods for moving people or goods by air, rail, sea, or road, including the relative costs and benefits.
Psychology	Knowledge of human behavior and performance; individual differences in ability, personality, and interests; learning and motivation; psychological research methods; and the assessment and treatment of behavioral and affective disorders.
Telecommunications	Knowledge of transmission, broadcasting, switching, control, and operation of telecommunications systems.
Sales and Marketing	Knowledge of principles and methods for showing, promoting, and selling products or services. This includes marketing strategy and tactics, product demonstration, sales techniques, and sales control systems.
Economics and Accounting	Knowledge of economic and accounting principles and practices, the financial markets, banking and the analysis and reporting of financial data.
Education and Training	Knowledge of principles and methods for curriculum and training design, teaching and instruction for individuals and groups, and the measurement of training effects.
Public Safety and Security	Knowledge of relevant equipment, policies, procedures, and strategies to promote effective local, state, or national security operations for the protection of people, data, property, and institutions.

Geography	Knowledge of principles and methods for describing the features of land, sea, and air masses, including their physical characteristics, locations, interrelationships, and distribution of plant, animal, and human life.
Personnel and Human Resources	Knowledge of principles and procedures for personnel recruitment, selection, training, compensation and benefits, labor relations and negotiation, and personnel information systems.
Sociology and Anthropology	Knowledge of group behavior and dynamics, societal trends and influences, human migrations, ethnicity, cultures and their history and origins.
Communications and Media	Knowledge of media production, communication, and dissemination techniques and methods. This includes alternative ways to inform and entertain via written, oral, and visual media.
Foreign Language	Knowledge of the structure and content of a foreign (non-English) language including the meaning and spelling of words, rules of composition and grammar, and pronunciation.
Law and Government	Knowledge of laws, legal codes, court procedures, precedents, government regulations, executive orders, agency rules, and the democratic political process.
Production and Processing	Knowledge of raw materials, production processes, quality control, costs, and other techniques for maximizing the effective manufacture and distribution of goods.
Philosophy and Theology	Knowledge of different philosophical systems and religions. This includes their basic principles, values, ethics, ways of thinking, customs, practices, and their impact on human culture.
Therapy and Counseling	Knowledge of principles, methods, and procedures for diagnosis, treatment, and rehabilitation of physical and mental dysfunctions, and for career counseling and guidance.
Medicine and Dentistry	Knowledge of the information and techniques needed to diagnose and treat human injuries, diseases, and deformities. This includes symptoms, treatment alternatives, drug properties and interactions, and preventive health-care measures.
Mechanical	Knowledge of machines and tools, including their designs, uses, repair, and maintenance.
Engineering and Technology	Knowledge of the practical application of engineering science and technology. This includes applying principles, techniques, procedures, and equipment to the design and production of various goods and services.
Design	Knowledge of design techniques, tools, and principles involved in production of precision technical plans, blueprints, drawings, and models.
Chemistry	Knowledge of the chemical composition, structure, and properties of substances and of the chemical processes and transformations that they undergo. This includes uses of chemicals and their interactions, danger signs, production techniques, and disposal methods.
Building and Construction	Knowledge of materials, methods, and the tools involved in the construction or repair of houses, buildings, or other structures such as highways and roads.
Biology	Knowledge of plant and animal organisms, their tissues, cells, functions, interdependencies, and interactions with each other and the environment.
Physics	Knowledge and prediction of physical principles, laws, their interrelationships, and applications to understanding fluid, material, and atmospheric dynamics, and mechanical, electrical, atomic and sub- atomic structures and processes.
History and Archeology	Knowledge of historical events and their causes, indicators, and effects on civilizations and cultures.
Fine Arts	Knowledge of the theory and techniques required to compose, produce, and perform works of music, dance, visual arts, drama, and sculpture.
Food Production	Knowledge of techniques and equipment for planting, growing, and harvesting food products (both plant and animal) for consumption, including storage/handling techniques.

Skills	Skills Definitions
Active Listening	Giving full attention to what other people are saying, taking time to understand the points being made, asking questions as appropriate, and not interrupting at inappropriate times.
Speaking	Talking to others to convey information effectively.
Reading Comprehension	Understanding written sentences and paragraphs in work related documents.
Writing	Communicating effectively in writing as appropriate for the needs of the audience.
Service Orientation	Actively looking for ways to help people.
Learning Strategies	Selecting and using training/instructional methods and procedures appropriate for the situation when learning or teaching new things.
Social Perceptiveness	Being aware of others' reactions and understanding why they react as they do.
Critical Thinking	Using logic and reasoning to identify the strengths and weaknesses of alternative solutions, conclusions or approaches to problems.
Time Management	Managing one's own time and the time of others.

Active Learning	Understanding the implications of new information for both current and future problem-solving and decision-making.
Judgment and Decision Making	Considering the relative costs and benefits of potential actions to choose the most appropriate one.
Coordination	Adjusting actions in relation to others' actions.
Mathematics	Using mathematics to solve problems.
Negotiation	Bringing others together and trying to reconcile differences.
Instructing	Teaching others how to do something.
Persuasion	Persuading others to change their minds or behavior.
Monitoring	Monitoring/Assessing performance of yourself, other individuals, or organizations to make improvements or take corrective action.
Complex Problem Solving	Identifying complex problems and reviewing related information to develop and evaluate options and implement solutions.
Management of Personnel Resources	Motivating, developing, and directing people as they work, identifying the best people for the job.
Equipment Selection	Determining the kind of tools and equipment needed to do a job.
Management of Financial Resources	Determining how money will be spent to get the work done, and accounting for these expenditures.
Operations Analysis	Analyzing needs and product requirements to create a design.
Systems Analysis	Determining how a system should work and how changes in conditions, operations, and the environment will affect outcomes.
Technology Design	Generating or adapting equipment and technology to serve user needs.
Equipment Maintenance	Performing routine maintenance on equipment and determining when and what kind of maintenance is needed.
Quality Control Analysis	Conducting tests and inspections of products, services, or processes to evaluate quality or performance.
Operation and Control	Controlling operations of equipment or systems.
Programming	Writing computer programs for various purposes.
Installation	Installing equipment, machines, wiring, or programs to meet specifications.
Management of Material Resources	Obtaining and seeing to the appropriate use of equipment, facilities, and materials needed to do certain work.
Troubleshooting	Determining causes of operating errors and deciding what to do about it.
Science	Using scientific rules and methods to solve problems.
Systems Evaluation	Identifying measures or indicators of system performance and the actions needed to improve or correct performance, relative to the goals of the system.
Repairing	Repairing machines or systems using the needed tools.
Operation Monitoring	Watching gauges, dials, or other indicators to make sure a machine is working properly.

Ability	Ability Definitions
Oral Expression	The ability to communicate information and ideas in speaking so others will understand.
Oral Comprehension	The ability to listen to and understand information and ideas presented through spoken words and sentences.
Speech Recognition	The ability to identify and understand the speech of another person.
Speech Clarity	The ability to speak clearly so others can understand you.
Written Comprehension	The ability to read and understand information and ideas presented in writing.
Near Vision	The ability to see details at close range (within a few feet of the observer).
Information Ordering	The ability to arrange things or actions in a certain order or pattern according to a specific rule or set of rules (e.g., patterns of numbers, letters, words, pictures, mathematical operations).
Selective Attention	The ability to concentrate on a task over a period of time without being distracted.
Written Expression	The ability to communicate information and ideas in writing so others will understand.
Deductive Reasoning	The ability to apply general rules to specific problems to produce answers that make sense.
Inductive Reasoning	The ability to combine pieces of information to form general rules or conclusions (includes finding a relationship among seemingly unrelated events).
Category Flexibility	The ability to generate or use different sets of rules for combining or grouping things in different ways.
Mathematical Reasoning	The ability to choose the right mathematical methods or formulas to solve a problem.
Problem Sensitivity	The ability to tell when something is wrong or is likely to go wrong. It does not involve solving the problem, only recognizing there is a problem.
Number Facility	The ability to add, subtract, multiply, or divide quickly and correctly.
Finger Dexterity	The ability to make precisely coordinated movements of the fingers of one or both hands to grasp, manipulate, or assemble very small objects.

Time Sharing	The ability to shift back and forth between two or more activities or sources of information (such as speech, sounds, touch, or other sources).
Memorization	The ability to remember information such as words, numbers, pictures, and procedures.
Originality	The ability to come up with unusual or clever ideas about a given topic or situation, or to develop creative ways to solve a problem.
Flexibility of Closure	The ability to identify or detect a known pattern (a figure, object, word, or sound) that is hidden in other distracting material.
Fluency of Ideas	The ability to come up with a number of ideas about a topic (the number of ideas is important, not their quality, correctness, or creativity).
Far Vision	The ability to see details at a distance.
Perceptual Speed	The ability to quickly and accurately compare similarities and differences among sets of letters, numbers, objects, pictures, or patterns. The things to be compared may be presented at the same time or one after the other. This ability also includes comparing a presented object with a remembered object.
Manual Dexterity	The ability to quickly move your hand, your hand together with your arm, or your two hands to grasp, manipulate, or assemble objects.
Speed of Closure	The ability to quickly make sense of, combine, and organize information into meaningful patterns.
Arm-Hand Steadiness	The ability to keep your hand and arm steady while moving your arm or while holding your arm and hand in one position.
Visualization	The ability to imagine how something will look after it is moved around or when its parts are moved or rearranged.
Control Precision	The ability to quickly and repeatedly adjust the controls of a machine or a vehicle to exact positions.
Multilimb Coordination	The ability to coordinate two or more limbs (for example, two arms, two legs, or one leg and one arm) while sitting, standing, or lying down. It does not involve performing the activities while the whole body is in motion.
Static Strength	The ability to exert maximum muscle force to lift, push, pull, or carry objects.
Response Orientation	The ability to choose quickly between two or more movements in response to two or more different signals (lights, sounds, pictures). It includes the speed with which the correct response is started with the hand, foot, or other body part.
Hearing Sensitivity	The ability to detect or tell the differences between sounds that vary in pitch and loudness.
Wrist-Finger Speed	The ability to make fast, simple, repeated movements of the fingers, hands, and wrists.
Spatial Orientation	The ability to know your location in relation to the environment or to know where other objects are in relation to you.
Auditory Attention	The ability to focus on a single source of sound in the presence of other distracting sounds.
Visual Color Discrimination	The ability to match or detect differences between colors, including shades of color and brightness.
Extent Flexibility	The ability to bend, stretch, twist, or reach with your body, arms, and/or legs.
Trunk Strength	The ability to use your abdominal and lower back muscles to support part of the body repeatedly or continuously over time without 'giving out' or fatiguing.
Reaction Time	The ability to quickly respond (with the hand, finger, or foot) to a signal (sound, light, picture) when it appears.
Night Vision	The ability to see under low light conditions.
Gross Body Coordination	The ability to coordinate the movement of your arms, legs, and torso together when the whole body is in motion.
Dynamic Flexibility	The ability to quickly and repeatedly bend, stretch, twist, or reach out with your body, arms, and/or legs.
Stamina	The ability to exert yourself physically over long periods of time without getting winded or out of breath.
Dynamic Strength	The ability to exert muscle force repeatedly or continuously over time. This involves muscular endurance and resistance to muscle fatigue.
Explosive Strength	The ability to use short bursts of muscle force to propel oneself (as in jumping or sprinting), or to throw an object.
Speed of Limb Movement	The ability to quickly move the arms and legs.
Gross Body Equilibrium	The ability to keep or regain your body balance or stay upright when in an unstable position.
Sound Localization	The ability to tell the direction from which a sound originated.
Rate Control	The ability to time your movements or the movement of a piece of equipment in anticipation of changes in the speed and/or direction of a moving object or scene.
Depth Perception	The ability to judge which of several objects is closer or farther away from you, or to judge the distance between you and an object.
Glare Sensitivity	The ability to see objects in the presence of glare or bright lighting.
Peripheral Vision	The ability to see objects or movement of objects to one's side when the eyes are looking ahead.

Work_Activity	Work_Activity Definitions
Interacting With Computers	Using computers and computer systems (including hardware and software) to program, write software, set up functions, enter data, or process information.
Getting Information	Observing, receiving, and otherwise obtaining information from all relevant sources.
Performing Administrative Activities	Performing day-to-day administrative tasks such as maintaining information files and processing paperwork.
Communicating with Supervisors, Peers, or Subordin	Providing information to supervisors, co-workers, and subordinates by telephone, in written form, e-mail, or in person.
Communicating with Persons Outside Organization	Communicating with people outside the organization, representing the organization to customers, the public, government, and other external sources. This information can be exchanged in person, in writing, or by telephone or e-mail.
Organizing, Planning, and Prioritizing Work	Developing specific goals and plans to prioritize, organize, and accomplish your work.
Documenting/Recording Information	Entering, transcribing, recording, storing, or maintaining information in written or electronic/magnetic form.
Establishing and Maintaining Interpersonal Relatio	Developing constructive and cooperative working relationships with others, and maintaining them over time.
Assisting and Caring for Others	Providing personal assistance, medical attention, emotional support, or other personal care to others such as coworkers, customers, or patients.
Performing for or Working Directly with the Public	Performing for people or dealing directly with the public. This includes serving customers in restaurants and stores, and receiving clients or guests.
Processing Information	Compiling, coding, categorizing, calculating, tabulating, auditing, or verifying information or data.
Updating and Using Relevant Knowledge	Keeping up-to-date technically and applying new knowledge to your job.
Making Decisions and Solving Problems	Analyzing information and evaluating results to choose the best solution and solve problems.
Resolving Conflicts and Negotiating with Others	Handling complaints, settling disputes, and resolving grievances and conflicts, or otherwise negotiating with others.
Thinking Creatively	Developing, designing, or creating new applications, ideas, relationships, systems, or products, including artistic contributions.
Scheduling Work and Activities	Scheduling events, programs, and activities, as well as the work of others.
Handling and Moving Objects	Using hands and arms in handling, installing, positioning, and moving materials, and manipulating things.
Interpreting the Meaning of Information for Others	Translating or explaining what information means and how it can be used.
Monitor Processes, Materials, or Surroundings	Monitoring and reviewing information from materials, events, or the environment, to detect or assess problems.
Monitoring and Controlling Resources	Monitoring and controlling resources and overseeing the spending of money.
Identifying Objects, Actions, and Events	Identifying information by categorizing, estimating, recognizing differences or similarities, and detecting changes in circumstances or events.
Analyzing Data or Information	Identifying the underlying principles, reasons, or facts of information by breaking down information or data into separate parts.
Training and Teaching Others	Identifying the educational needs of others, developing formal educational or training programs or classes, and teaching or instructing others.
Evaluating Information to Determine Compliance wit	Using relevant information and individual judgment to determine whether events or processes comply with laws, regulations, or standards.
Selling or Influencing Others	Convincing others to buy merchandise/goods or to otherwise change their minds or actions.
Coaching and Developing Others	Identifying the developmental needs of others and coaching, mentoring, or otherwise helping others to improve their knowledge or skills.
Judging the Qualities of Things, Services, or Peop	Assessing the value, importance, or quality of things or people.
Performing General Physical Activities	Performing physical activities that require considerable use of your arms and legs and moving your whole body, such as climbing, lifting, balancing, walking, stooping, and handling of materials.
Coordinating the Work and Activities of Others	Getting members of a group to work together to accomplish tasks.
Guiding, Directing, and Motivating Subordinates	Providing guidance and direction to subordinates, including setting performance standards and monitoring performance.
Developing and Building Teams	Encouraging and building mutual trust, respect, and cooperation among team members.
Provide Consultation and Advice to Others	Providing guidance and expert advice to management or other groups on technical, systems-, or process-related topics.
Controlling Machines and Processes	Using either control mechanisms or direct physical activity to operate machines or processes (not including computers or vehicles).

Staffing Organizational Units	Recruiting, interviewing, selecting, hiring, and promoting employees in an organization.
Developing Objectives and Strategies	Establishing long-range objectives and specifying the strategies and actions to achieve them.
Inspecting Equipment, Structures, or Material	Inspecting equipment, structures, or materials to identify the cause of errors or other problems or defects.
Estimating the Quantifiable Characteristics of Pro	Estimating sizes, distances, and quantities; or determining time. costs, resources, or materials needed to perform a work activity.
Repairing and Maintaining Electronic Equipment	Servicing, repairing, calibrating, regulating, fine-tuning. or testing machines, devices, and equipment that operate primarily on the basis of electrical or electronic (not mechanical) principles.
Drafting, Laying Out, and Specifying Technical Dev	Providing documentation, detailed instructions, drawings, or specifications to tell others about how devices, parts, equipment, or structures are to be fabricated, constructed, assembled, modified, maintained, or used.
Operating Vehicles, Mechanized Devices, or Equipme	Running, maneuvering, navigating, or driving vehicles or mechanized equipment, such as forklifts, passenger vehicles. aircraft, or water craft.
Repairing and Maintaining Mechanical Equipment	Servicing, repairing, adjusting, and testing machines, devices. moving parts, and equipment that operate primarily on the basis of mechanical (not electronic) principles.

Work_Content	**Work_Content Definitions**
Telephone	How often do you have telephone conversations in this job?
Contact With Others	How much does this job require the worker to be in contact with others (face-to-face, by telephone, or otherwise) in order to perform it?
Face-to-Face Discussions	How often do you have to have face-to-face discussions with individuals or teams in this job?
Structured versus Unstructured Work	To what extent is this job structured for the worker, rather than allowing the worker to determine tasks, priorities, and goals?
Importance of Being Exact or Accurate	How important is being very exact or highly accurate in performing this job?
Spend Time Sitting	How much does this job require sitting?
Work With Work Group or Team	How important is it to work with others in a group or team in this job?
Importance of Repeating Same Tasks	How important is repeating the same physical activities (e.g., key entry) or mental activities (e.g., checking entries in a ledger) over and over, without stopping, to performing this job?
Letters and Memos	How often does the job require written letters and memos?
Indoors, Environmentally Controlled	How often does this job require working indoors in environmentally controlled conditions?
Freedom to Make Decisions	How much decision making freedom, without supervision, does the job offer?
Deal With External Customers	How important is it to work with external customers or the public in this job?
Frequency of Decision Making	How frequently is the worker required to make decisions that affect other people, the financial resources, and/or the image and reputation of the organization?
Time Pressure	How often does this job require the worker to meet strict deadlines?
Physical Proximity	To what extent does this job require the worker to perform job tasks in close physical proximity to other people?
Impact of Decisions on Co-workers or Company Resul	How do the decisions an employee makes impact the results of co-workers, clients or the company?
Electronic Mail	How often do you use electronic mail in this job?
Deal With Unpleasant or Angry People	How frequently does the worker have to deal with unpleasant, angry, or discourteous individuals as part of the job requirements?
Spend Time Making Repetitive Motions	How much does this job require making repetitive motions?
Coordinate or Lead Others	How important is it to coordinate or lead others in accomplishing work activities in this job?
Spend Time Using Your Hands to Handle, Control, or	How much does this job require using your hands to handle, control, or feel objects, tools or controls?
Frequency of Conflict Situations	How often are there conflict situations the employee has to face in this job?
Sounds, Noise Levels Are Distracting or Uncomforta	How often does this job require working exposed to sounds and noise levels that are distracting or uncomfortable?
Exposed to Contaminants	How often does this job require working exposed to contaminants (such as pollutants, gases, dust or odors)?
Responsibility for Outcomes and Results	How responsible is the worker for work outcomes and results of other workers?
Consequence of Error	How serious would the result usually be if the worker made a mistake that was not readily correctable?
Spend Time Standing	How much does this job require standing?
Degree of Automation	How automated is the job?
Indoors, Not Environmentally Controlled	How often does this job require working indoors in non-controlled environmental conditions (e.g., warehouse without heat)?

Level of Competition	To what extent does this job require the worker to compete or to be aware of competitive pressures?
Spend Time Walking and Running	How much does this job require walking and running?
Extremely Bright or Inadequate Lighting	How often does this job require working in extremely bright or inadequate lighting conditions?
Responsible for Others' Health and Safety	How much responsibility is there for the health and safety of others in this job?
Spend Time Bending or Twisting the Body	How much does this job require bending or twisting your body?
Exposed to Disease or Infections	How often does this job require exposure to disease/infections?
Pace Determined by Speed of Equipment	How important is it to this job that the pace is determined by the speed of equipment or machinery? (This does not refer to keeping busy at all times on this job.)
Spend Time Kneeling, Crouching, Stooping, or Crawl	How much does this job require kneeling, crouching, stooping or crawling?
Exposed to Minor Burns, Cuts, Bites, or Stings	How often does this job require exposure to minor burns, cuts, bites, or stings?
Deal With Physically Aggressive People	How frequently does this job require the worker to deal with physical aggression of violent individuals?
In an Enclosed Vehicle or Equipment	How often does this job require working in a closed vehicle or equipment (e.g., car)?
Public Speaking	How often do you have to perform public speaking in this job?
Very Hot or Cold Temperatures	How often does this job require working in very hot (above 90 F degrees) or very cold (below 32 F degrees) temperatures?
Cramped Work Space, Awkward Positions	How often does this job require working in cramped work spaces that requires getting into awkward positions?
Wear Common Protective or Safety Equipment such as	How much does this job require wearing common protective or safety equipment such as safety shoes, glasses, gloves, hard hats or live jackets?
Spend Time Keeping or Regaining Balance	How much does this job require keeping or regaining your balance?
Exposed to Radiation	How often does this job require exposure to radiation?
Exposed to High Places	How often does this job require exposure to high places?
Outdoors, Under Cover	How often does this job require working outdoors, under cover (e.g., structure with roof but no walls)?
Exposed to Hazardous Equipment	How often does this job require exposure to hazardous equipment?
Outdoors, Exposed to Weather	How often does this job require working outdoors, exposed to all weather conditions?
Exposed to Hazardous Conditions	How often does this job require exposure to hazardous conditions?
In an Open Vehicle or Equipment	How often does this job require working in an open vehicle or equipment (e.g., tractor)?
Wear Specialized Protective or Safety Equipment su	How much does this job require wearing specialized protective or safety equipment such as breathing apparatus, safety harness, full protection suits, or radiation protection?
Exposed to Whole Body Vibration	How often does this job require exposure to whole body vibration (e.g., operate a jackhammer)?
Spend Time Climbing Ladders, Scaffolds, or Poles	How much does this job require climbing ladders, scaffolds, or poles?

Work_Styles	**Work_Styles Definitions**
Cooperation	Job requires being pleasant with others on the job and displaying a good-natured, cooperative attitude.
Dependability	Job requires being reliable, responsible, and dependable, and fulfilling obligations.
Integrity	Job requires being honest and ethical.
Stress Tolerance	Job requires accepting criticism and dealing calmly and effectively with high stress situations.
Self Control	Job requires maintaining composure, keeping emotions in check, controlling anger, and avoiding aggressive behavior, even in very difficult situations.
Concern for Others	Job requires being sensitive to others' needs and feelings and being understanding and helpful on the job.
Attention to Detail	Job requires being careful about detail and thorough in completing work tasks.
Independence	Job requires developing one's own ways of doing things, guiding oneself with little or no supervision, and depending on oneself to get things done.
Social Orientation	Job requires preferring to work with others rather than alone, and being personally connected with others on the job.
Initiative	Job requires a willingness to take on responsibilities and challenges.
Adaptability/Flexibility	Job requires being open to change (positive or negative) and to considerable variety in the workplace.
Persistence	Job requires persistence in the face of obstacles.
Achievement/Effort	Job requires establishing and maintaining personally challenging achievement goals and exerting effort toward mastering tasks.
Leadership	Job requires a willingness to lead, take charge, and offer opinions and direction.

Innovation	Job requires creativity and alternative thinking to develop new ideas for and answers to work-related problems.
Analytical Thinking	Job requires analyzing information and using logic to address work-related issues and problems.

Job Zone Component	Job Zone Component Definitions
Title	Job Zone Two: Some Preparation Needed
Overall Experience	Some previous work-related skill, knowledge, or experience may be helpful in these occupations, but usually is not needed. For example, a drywall installer might benefit from experience installing drywall, but an inexperienced person could still learn to be an installer with little difficulty.
Job Training	Employees in these occupations need anywhere from a few months to one year of working with experienced employees.
Job Zone Examples	These occupations often involve using your knowledge and skills to help others. Examples include drywall installers, fire inspectors, flight attendants, pharmacy technicians, salespersons (retail), and tellers.
SVP Range	(4.0 to < 6.0)
Education	These occupations usually require a high school diploma and may require some vocational training or job-related course work. In some cases, an associate's or bachelor's degree could be needed.

43-5011.00 - Cargo and Freight Agents

Expedite and route movement of incoming and outgoing cargo and freight shipments in airline, train, and trucking terminals, and shipping docks. Take orders from customers and arrange pickup of freight and cargo for delivery to loading platform. Prepare and examine bills of lading to determine shipping charges and tariffs.

Tasks

1) Install straps, braces, and padding to loads in order to prevent shifting or damage during shipment.

2) Route received goods to first available flight or to appropriate storage areas or departments, using forklifts, handtrucks, or other equipment.

3) Estimate freight or postal rates, and record shipment costs and weights.

4) Inspect trucks and vans to ensure cleanliness when shipping such items as grain, flour, and milk.

5) Maintain a supply of packing materials.

6) Coordinate and supervise activities of workers engaged in packing and shipping merchandise.

7) Retrieve stored items and trace lost shipments as necessary.

8) Notify consignees, passengers, or customers of the arrival of freight or baggage, and arrange for delivery.

9) Negotiate and arrange transport of goods with shipping or freight companies.

10) Keep records of all goods shipped, received, and stored.

11) Inspect and count items received and check them against invoices or other documents, recording shortages and rejecting damaged goods.

12) Determine method of shipment, and prepare bills of lading, invoices, and other shipping documents.

13) Pack goods for shipping, using tools such as staplers, strapping machines, and hammers.

14) Remove ramps after airplane loading is complete, and signal pilots that personnel and equipment are clear of plane.

15) Arrange insurance coverage for goods.

16) Contact vendors and/or claims adjustment departments in order to resolve problems with shipments, or contact service depots to arrange for repairs.

17) Open cargo containers and unwrap contents, using steel cutters, crowbars, or other hand tools.

18) Direct delivery trucks to shipping doors or designated marshalling areas, and help load and unload goods safely.

19) Attach address labels, identification codes, and shipping instructions to containers.

20) Enter shipping information into a computer by hand or by using a hand-held scanner that reads bar codes on goods.

21) Position ramps for loading of airplanes.

22) Prepare manifests showing baggage, mail, and freight weights, and number of passengers on airplanes, and transmit data to destinations.

23) Shovel loose materials into machine hoppers or into vehicles and containers.

24) Force conditioned air into interiors of planes prior to departure, using mobile aircraft-air-conditioning-units.

25) Send samples of merchandise to quality control units for inspection.

26) Advise clients on transportation and payment methods.

27) Obtain flight numbers, airplane numbers, and names of crew members from dispatchers, and record data on airplane flight papers.

28) Direct or participate in cargo loading in order to ensure completeness of load and even distribution of weight.

29) Assemble containers and crates used to transport items such as machines or vehicles.

43-5021.00 - Couriers and Messengers

Pick up and carry messages, documents, packages, and other items between offices or departments within an establishment or to other business concerns, traveling by foot, bicycle, motorcycle, automobile, or public conveyance.

Tasks

1) Record information, such as items received and delivered and recipients' responses to messages.

2) Unload and sort items collected along delivery routes.

3) Obtain signatures and payments, or arrange for recipients to make payments.

4) Deliver messages and items, such as newspapers, documents, and packages, between establishment departments, and to other establishments and private homes.

5) Receive messages or materials to be delivered, and information on recipients, such as names, addresses, telephone numbers, and delivery instructions, communicated via telephone, two-way radio, or in person.

6) Sort items to be delivered according to the delivery route.

7) Perform general office or clerical work such as filing materials, operating duplicating machines, or running errands.

8) Call by telephone in order to deliver verbal messages.

9) Collect, seal, and stamp outgoing mail, using postage meters and envelope sealers.

10) Load vehicles with listed goods, ensuring goods are loaded correctly and taking precautions with hazardous goods.

11) Open, sort, and distribute incoming mail.

12) Perform routine maintenance on delivery vehicles, such as monitoring fluid levels and replenishing fuel.

13) Walk, ride bicycles, drive vehicles, or use public conveyances in order to reach destinations to deliver messages or materials.

14) Check with home offices after completed deliveries, in order to confirm deliveries and collections and to receive instructions for other deliveries.

15) Unload goods from large trucks, and load them onto smaller delivery vehicles.

43-5031.00 - Police, Fire, and Ambulance Dispatchers

Receive complaints from public concerning crimes and police emergencies. Broadcast orders to police patrol units in vicinity of complaint to investigate. Operate radio, telephone, or computer equipment to receive reports of fires and medical emergencies and relay information or orders to proper officials.

Tasks

1) Question callers to determine their locations, and the nature of their problems in order to determine type of response needed.

2) Provide emergency medical instructions to callers.

3) Receive incoming telephone or alarm system calls regarding emergency and non-emergency police and fire service, emergency ambulance service, information and after hours calls for departments within a city.

4) Relay information and messages to and from emergency sites, to law enforcement agencies, and to all other individuals or groups requiring notification.

5) Determine response requirements and relative priorities of situations, and dispatch units in accordance with established procedures.

6) Operate and maintain mobile dispatch vehicles and equipment.

7) Test and adjust communication and alarm systems, and report malfunctions to maintenance units.

8) Monitor various radio frequencies such as those used by public works departments, school security, and civil defense in order to keep apprised of developing situations.

9) Maintain files of information relating to emergency calls such as personnel rosters, and

emergency call-out and pager files.

10) Scan status charts and computer screens, and contact emergency response field units in order to determine emergency units available for dispatch.

11) Maintain access to, and security of, highly sensitive materials.

12) Monitor alarm systems to detect emergencies such as fires and illegal entry into establishments.

13) Enter, update, and retrieve information from teletype networks and computerized data systems regarding such things as wanted persons, stolen property, vehicle registration, and stolen vehicles.

14) Learn material and pass required tests for certification.

15) Record details of calls, dispatches, and messages.

16) Answer routine inquiries, and refer calls not requiring dispatches to appropriate departments and agencies.

17) Read and effectively interpret small-scale maps and information from a computer screen in order to determine locations and provide directions.

43-5032.00 - Dispatchers, Except Police, Fire, and Ambulance

Schedule and dispatch workers, work crews, equipment, or service vehicles for conveyance of materials, freight, or passengers, or for normal installation, service, or emergency repairs rendered outside the place of business. Duties may include using radio, telephone, or computer to transmit assignments and compiling statistics and reports on work progress.

Tasks

1) Determine types or amounts of equipment, vehicles, materials, or personnel required according to work orders or specifications.

2) Order supplies and equipment, and issue them to personnel.

3) Oversee all communications within specifically assigned territories.

4) Prepare daily work and run schedules.

5) Receive or prepare work orders.

6) Record and maintain files and records of customer requests, work or services performed, charges, expenses, inventory, and other dispatch information.

7) Relay work orders, messages, and information to or from work crews, supervisors, and field inspectors using telephones or two-way radios.

8) Advise personnel about traffic problems such as construction areas, accidents, congestion, weather conditions, and other hazards.

9) Ensure timely and efficient movement of trains according to train orders and schedules.

10) Monitor personnel and/or equipment locations and utilization in order to coordinate service and schedules.

11) Arrange for necessary repairs in order to restore service and schedules.

12) Schedule and dispatch workers, work crews, equipment, or service vehicles to appropriate locations according to customer requests, specifications, or needs, using radios or telephones.

43-5051.00 - Postal Service Clerks

Perform any combination of tasks in a post office, such as receive letters and parcels; sell postage and revenue stamps, postal cards, and stamped envelopes; fill out and sell money orders; place mail in pigeon holes of mail rack or in bags according to State, address, or other scheme; and examine mail for correct postage.

Tasks

1) Provide customers with assistance in filing claims for mail theft, or lost or damaged mail.

2) Obtain signatures from recipients of registered or special delivery mail.

3) Keep money drawers in order, and record and balance daily transactions.

4) Feed mail into postage canceling devices or hand stamp mail to cancel postage.

5) Complete forms regarding changes of address, or theft or loss of mail, or for special services such as registered or priority mail.

6) Receive letters and parcels, and place mail into bags.

7) Answer questions regarding mail regulations and procedures, postage rates, and post office boxes.

8) Rent post office boxes to customers.

9) Check mail in order to ensure correct postage and that packages and letters are in proper condition for mailing.

10) Put undelivered parcels away, retrieve them when customers come to claim them, and complete any related documentation.

11) Post announcements or government information on public bulletin boards.

12) Set postage meters, and calibrate them to ensure correct operation.

13) Provide assistance to the public in complying with federal regulations of Postal Service and other federal agencies.

14) Cash money orders.

15) Weigh letters and parcels; compute mailing costs based on type, weight, and destination; and affix correct postage.

16) Sort incoming and outgoing mail, according to type and destination, by hand or by operating electronic mail-sorting and scanning devices.

17) Sell and collect payment for products such as stamps, prepaid mail envelopes, and money orders.

18) Respond to complaints regarding mail theft, delivery problems, and lost or damaged mail, filling out forms and making appropriate referrals for investigation.

19) Transport mail from one work station to another.

43-5052.00 - Postal Service Mail Carriers

Sort mail for delivery. Deliver mail on established route by vehicle or on foot.

Tasks

1) Return to the post office with mail collected from homes, businesses, and public mailboxes.

2) Report any unusual circumstances concerning mail delivery, including the condition of street letter boxes.

3) Register, certify, and insure parcels and letters.

4) Provide customers with change of address cards and other forms.

5) Obtain signed receipts for registered, certified, and insured mail; collect associated charges; and complete any necessary paperwork.

6) Complete forms that notify publishers of address changes.

7) Answer customers' questions about postal services and regulations.

8) Sort mail for delivery, arranging it in delivery sequence.

9) Travel to post offices to pick up the mail for routes and/or pick up mail from postal relay boxes.

10) Sign for cash-on-delivery and registered mail before leaving the post office.

11) Bundle mail in preparation for delivery or transportation to relay boxes.

12) Record address changes and redirect mail for those addresses.

13) Meet schedules for the collection and return of mail.

14) Maintain accurate records of deliveries.

15) Leave notices telling patrons where to collect mail that could not be delivered.

16) Hold mail for customers who are away from delivery locations.

17) Enter change of address orders into computers that process forwarding address stickers.

18) Return incorrectly addressed mail to senders.

19) Turn in money and receipts collected along mail routes.

20) Deliver mail to residences and business establishments along specified routes by walking and/or driving, using a combination of satchels, carts, cars, and small trucks.

43-5053.00 - Postal Service Mail Sorters, Processors, and Processing Machine Operators

Prepare incoming and outgoing mail for distribution. Examine, sort, and route mail by State, type of mail, or other scheme. Load, operate, and occasionally adjust and repair mail processing, sorting, and canceling machinery. Keep records of shipments, pouches, and sacks; and other duties related to mail handling within the postal service. Must complete a competitive exam.

Tasks

1) Remove envelopes or tape from postmarking machines.

2) Operate various types of equipment, such as computer scanning equipment, addressographs, mimeographs, optical character readers, and bar-code sorters.

3) Operate machines that seal envelopes and print postage and postmarks.

4) Open and label mail containers.

5) Move containers of mail, using equipment such as forklifts and automated trains.

6) Load and unload mail trucks, sometimes lifting containers of mail onto equipment that transports items to sorting stations.

7) Distribute incoming mail into the correct boxes or pigeonholes.

8) Sort odd-sized mail by hand, sort mail that other workers have been unable to sort, and segregate items requiring special handling.

9) Rewrap soiled or broken parcels.

10) Weigh articles to determine required postage.

11) Serve the public at counters or windows, such as by selling stamps and weighing parcels.

12) Train new workers.

13) Direct items according to established routing schemes, using computer controlled keyboards or voice recognition equipment.

14) Check items to ensure that addresses are legible and correct, that sufficient postage has been paid or the appropriate documentation is attached, and that items are in a suitable condition for processing.

15) Cancel letter or parcel post stamps by hand.

16) Bundle, label, and route sorted mail to designated areas depending on destinations and according to established procedures and deadlines.

17) Accept and check containers of mail from large volume mailers, couriers, and contractors.

18) Supervise other mail sorters.

19) Dump sacks of mail onto conveyors for culling and sorting.

20) Clear jams in sorting equipment.

43-5071.00 - Shipping, Receiving, and Traffic Clerks

Verify and keep records on incoming and outgoing shipments. Prepare items for shipment. Duties include assembling, addressing, stamping, and shipping merchandise or material; receiving, unpacking, verifying and recording incoming merchandise or material; and arranging for the transportation of products.

Tasks

1) Examine contents and compare with records, such as manifests, invoices, or orders, to verify accuracy of incoming or outgoing shipment.

2) Prepare documents, such as work orders, bills of lading, and shipping orders to route materials.

3) Requisition and store shipping materials and supplies to maintain inventory of stock.

4) Deliver or route materials to departments, using work devices, such as handtruck, conveyor, or sorting bins.

5) Pack, seal, label, and affix postage to prepare materials for shipping, using work devices such as hand tools, power tools, and postage meter.

6) Contact carrier representative to make arrangements and to issue instructions for shipping and delivery of materials.

7) Record shipment data, such as weight, charges, space availability, and damages and discrepancies, for reporting, accounting, and record keeping purposes.

8) Compute amounts, such as space available, and shipping, storage, and demurrage charges, using calculator or price list.

9) Confer and correspond with establishment representatives to rectify problems, such as damages, shortages, and nonconformance to specifications.

43-5081.01 - Stock Clerks, Sales Floor

Receive, store, and issue sales floor merchandise. Stock shelves, racks, cases, bins, and tables with merchandise and arrange merchandise displays to attract customers. May periodically take physical count of stock or check and mark merchandise.

Tasks

1) Stock shelves, racks, cases, bins, and tables with new or transferred merchandise.

2) Stamp, attach, or change price tags on merchandise, referring to price list.

3) Receive, open, unpack and issue sales floor merchandise.

4) Answer customers' questions about merchandise and advise customers on merchandise selection.

5) Transport packages to customers' vehicles.

6) Design and set up advertising signs and displays of merchandise on shelves, counters, or tables to attract customers and promote sales.

7) Cut lumber, screening, glass, and related materials to size requested by customer.

8) Take inventory or examine merchandise to identify items to be reordered or replenished.

9) Clean display cases, shelves, and aisles.

10) Itemize and total customer merchandise selection at checkout counter, using cash register, and accept cash or charge card for purchases.

11) Pack customer purchases in bags or cartons.

12) Compare merchandise invoices to items actually received to ensure that shipments are correct.

43-5081.02 - Marking Clerks

Print and attach price tickets to articles of merchandise using one or several methods, such as marking price on tickets by hand or using ticket-printing machine.

Tasks

1) Put price information on tickets, marking by hand or using ticket-printing machine.

2) Keep records of production, returned goods, and related transactions.

3) Change the price of books in a warehouse.

4) Record price, buyer, and grade of product on tickets attached to products auctioned.

5) Record number and types of articles marked and pack articles in boxes.

6) Mark selling price by hand on boxes containing merchandise.

7) Compare printed price tickets with entries on purchase orders to verify accuracy and notify supervisor of discrepancies.

8) Pin, paste, sew, tie, or staple tickets, tags, or labels to article.

43-5081.03 - Stock Clerks- Stockroom, Warehouse, or Storage Yard

Receive, store, and issue materials, equipment, and other items from stockroom, warehouse, or storage yard. Keep records and compile stock reports.

Tasks

1) Keep records on the use and/or damage of stock or stock handling equipment.

2) Pack and unpack items to be stocked on shelves in stockrooms, warehouses, or storage yards.

3) Prepare and maintain records and reports of inventories, price lists, shortages, shipments, expenditures, and goods used or issued.

4) Prepare products, supplies, equipment, or other items for use by adjusting, repairing or assembling them as necessary.

5) Issue or distribute materials, products, parts, and supplies to customers or coworkers, based on information from incoming requisitions.

6) Receive and count stock items, and record data manually or using computer.

7) Advise retail customers or internal users on the appropriateness of parts, supplies, or materials requested.

8) Examine and inspect stock items for wear or defects, reporting any damage to supervisors.

9) Provide assistance or direction to other stockroom, warehouse, or storage yard workers.

10) Confer with engineering and purchasing personnel and vendors regarding stock procurement and availability.

11) Store items in an orderly and accessible manner in warehouses, tool rooms, supply rooms, or other areas.

12) Sell materials, equipment, and other items from stock in retail settings.

13) Recommend disposal of excess, defective, or obsolete stock.

14) Purchase new or additional stock, or prepare documents that provide for such purchases.

15) Drive trucks in order to pick up incoming stock or to deliver parts to designated locations.

16) Dispose of damaged or defective items, or return them to vendors.

17) Determine sequence and release of back orders according to stock availability.

18) Mark stock items using identification tags, stamps, electric marking tools, or other labeling equipment.

19) Verify inventory computations by comparing them to physical counts of stock, and investigate discrepancies or adjust errors.

20) Clean and maintain supplies, tools, equipment, and storage areas in order to ensure compliance with safety regulations.

21) Compile, review, and maintain data from contracts, purchase orders, requisitions, and other documents in order to assess supply needs.

43-5081.04 - Order Fillers, Wholesale and Retail Sales

Fill customers' mail and telephone orders from stored merchandise in accordance with specifications on sales slips or order forms. Duties include computing prices of items, completing order receipts, keeping records of out-going orders, and requisitioning additional materials, supplies, and equipment.

Tasks

1) Keep records of out-going orders.

2) Complete order receipts.

3) Place merchandise on conveyors leading to wrapping areas.

4) Compute prices of items or groups of items.

5) Read orders to ascertain catalog numbers, sizes, colors, and quantities of merchandise.

6) Requisition additional materials, supplies, and equipment.

43-6011.00 - Executive Secretaries and Administrative Assistants

Provide high-level administrative support by conducting research, preparing statistical reports, handling information requests, and performing clerical functions such as preparing correspondence, receiving visitors, arranging conference calls, and scheduling meetings. May also train and supervise lower-level clerical staff.

Tasks

1) Prepare responses to correspondence containing routine inquiries.

2) Perform general office duties such as ordering supplies, maintaining records management systems, and performing basic bookkeeping work.

3) Meet with individuals, special interest groups and others on behalf of executives, committees and boards of directors.

4) Interpret administrative and operating policies and procedures for employees.

5) Conduct research, compile data, and prepare papers for consideration and presentation by executives, committees and boards of directors.

6) Supervise and train other clerical staff.

7) Read and analyze incoming memos, submissions, and reports in order to determine their significance and plan their distribution.

8) Open, sort, and distribute incoming correspondence, including faxes and email.

9) Prepare invoices, reports, memos, letters, financial statements and other documents, using word processing, spreadsheet, database, and/or presentation software.

10) File and retrieve corporate documents, records, and reports.

11) Set up and oversee administrative policies and procedures for offices and/or organizations.

12) Compile, transcribe, and distribute minutes of meetings.

13) Review operating practices and procedures in order to determine whether improvements can be made in areas such as workflow, reporting procedures, or expenditures.

14) Coordinate and direct office services, such as records and budget preparation, personnel, and housekeeping, in order to aid executives.

15) Attend meetings in order to record minutes.

16) Prepare agendas and make arrangements for committee, board, and other meetings.

17) Manage and maintain executives' schedules.

18) Greet visitors and determine whether they should be given access to specific individuals.

43-6012.00 - Legal Secretaries

Perform secretarial duties utilizing legal terminology, procedures, and documents. Prepare legal papers and correspondence, such as summonses, complaints, motions, and subpoenas. May also assist with legal research.

Tasks

1) Mail, fax, or arrange for delivery of legal correspondence to clients, witnesses, and court officials.

2) Prepare and process legal documents and papers, such as summonses, subpoenas, complaints, appeals, motions, and pretrial agreements.

3) Make photocopies of correspondence, document, and other printed matter.

4) Schedule and make appointments.

5) Assist attorneys in collecting information such as employment, medical, and other records.

6) Draft and type office memos.

7) Organize and maintain law libraries and document and case files.

8) Attend legal meetings, such as client interviews, hearings, or depositions, and take notes.

9) Complete various forms, such as accident reports, trial and courtroom requests, and applications for clients.

10) Submit articles and information from searches to attorneys for review and approval for use.

11) Review legal publications and perform data base searches to identify laws and court decisions relevant to pending cases.

Knowledge	Knowledge Definitions
Clerical	Knowledge of administrative and clerical procedures and systems such as word processing, managing files and records, stenography and transcription, designing forms, and other office procedures and terminology.
Law and Government	Knowledge of laws, legal codes, court procedures, precedents, government regulations, executive orders, agency rules, and the democratic political process.
English Language	Knowledge of the structure and content of the English language including the meaning and spelling of words, rules of composition, and grammar.
Customer and Personal Service	Knowledge of principles and processes for providing customer and personal services. This includes customer needs assessment, meeting quality standards for services, and evaluation of customer satisfaction.
Economics and Accounting	Knowledge of economic and accounting principles and practices, the financial markets, banking and the analysis and reporting of financial data.
Computers and Electronics	Knowledge of circuit boards, processors, chips, electronic equipment, and computer hardware and software, including applications and programming.
Administration and Management	Knowledge of business and management principles involved in strategic planning, resource allocation, human resources modeling, leadership technique, production methods, and coordination of people and resources.
Mathematics	Knowledge of arithmetic, algebra, geometry, calculus, statistics, and their applications.
Communications and Media	Knowledge of media production, communication, and dissemination techniques and methods. This includes alternative ways to inform and entertain via written, oral, and visual media.
Geography	Knowledge of principles and methods for describing the features of land, sea, and air masses, including their physical characteristics, locations, interrelationships, and distribution of plant, animal, and human life.
Personnel and Human Resources	Knowledge of principles and procedures for personnel recruitment, selection, training, compensation and benefits, labor relations and negotiation, and personnel information systems.
Psychology	Knowledge of human behavior and performance; individual differences in ability, personality, and interests; learning and motivation; psychological research methods; and the assessment and treatment of behavioral and affective disorders.
Sales and Marketing	Knowledge of principles and methods for showing, promoting, and selling products or services. This includes marketing strategy and tactics, product demonstration, sales techniques, and sales control systems.
Sociology and Anthropology	Knowledge of group behavior and dynamics, societal trends and influences, human migrations, ethnicity, cultures and their history and origins.
Education and Training	Knowledge of principles and methods for curriculum and training design, teaching and instruction for individuals and groups, and the measurement of training effects.
History and Archeology	Knowledge of historical events and their causes, indicators, and effects on civilizations and cultures.
Telecommunications	Knowledge of transmission, broadcasting, switching, control, and operation of telecommunications systems.
Public Safety and Security	Knowledge of relevant equipment, policies, procedures, and strategies to promote effective local, state, or national security operations for the protection of people, data, property, and institutions.

Foreign Language	Knowledge of the structure and content of a foreign (non-English) language including the meaning and spelling of words, rules of composition and grammar, and pronunciation.
Philosophy and Theology	Knowledge of different philosophical systems and religions. This includes their basic principles, values, ethics, ways of thinking, customs, practices, and their impact on human culture.
Mechanical	Knowledge of machines and tools, including their designs, uses, repair, and maintenance.
Transportation	Knowledge of principles and methods for moving people or goods by air, rail, sea, or road, including the relative costs and benefits.
Production and Processing	Knowledge of raw materials, production processes, quality control, costs, and other techniques for maximizing the effective manufacture and distribution of goods.
Therapy and Counseling	Knowledge of principles, methods, and procedures for diagnosis, treatment, and rehabilitation of physical and mental dysfunctions, and for career counseling and guidance.
Engineering and Technology	Knowledge of the practical application of engineering science and technology. This includes applying principles, techniques, procedures, and equipment to the design and production of various goods and services.
Medicine and Dentistry	Knowledge of the information and techniques needed to diagnose and treat human injuries, diseases, and deformities. This includes symptoms, treatment alternatives, drug properties and interactions, and preventive health-care measures.
Design	Knowledge of design techniques, tools, and principles involved in production of precision technical plans, blueprints, drawings, and models.
Physics	Knowledge and prediction of physical principles, laws, their interrelationships, and applications to understanding fluid, material, and atmospheric dynamics, and mechanical, electrical, atomic and sub- atomic structures and processes.
Biology	Knowledge of plant and animal organisms, their tissues, cells, functions, interdependencies, and interactions with each other and the environment.
Fine Arts	Knowledge of the theory and techniques required to compose, produce, and perform works of music, dance, visual arts, drama, and sculpture.
Building and Construction	Knowledge of materials, methods, and the tools involved in the construction or repair of houses, buildings, or other structures such as highways and roads.
Chemistry	Knowledge of the chemical composition, structure, and properties of substances and of the chemical processes and transformations that they undergo. This includes uses of chemicals and their interactions, danger signs, production techniques, and disposal methods.
Food Production	Knowledge of techniques and equipment for planting, growing, and harvesting food products (both plant and animal) for consumption, including storage/handling techniques.

Skills	Skills Definitions
Reading Comprehension	Understanding written sentences and paragraphs in work related documents.
Active Listening	Giving full attention to what other people are saying, taking time to understand the points being made, asking questions as appropriate, and not interrupting at inappropriate times.
Time Management	Managing one's own time and the time of others.
Writing	Communicating effectively in writing as appropriate for the needs of the audience.
Active Learning	Understanding the implications of new information for both current and future problem-solving and decision-making.
Speaking	Talking to others to convey information effectively.
Learning Strategies	Selecting and using training/instructional methods and procedures appropriate for the situation when learning or teaching new things.
Judgment and Decision Making	Considering the relative costs and benefits of potential actions to choose the most appropriate one.
Coordination	Adjusting actions in relation to others' actions.
Critical Thinking	Using logic and reasoning to identify the strengths and weaknesses of alternative solutions, conclusions or approaches to problems.
Social Perceptiveness	Being aware of others' reactions and understanding why they react as they do.
Complex Problem Solving	Identifying complex problems and reviewing related information to develop and evaluate options and implement solutions.
Service Orientation	Actively looking for ways to help people.
Monitoring	Monitoring/Assessing performance of yourself, other individuals, or organizations to make improvements or take corrective action.
Instructing	Teaching others how to do something.
Mathematics	Using mathematics to solve problems.
Persuasion	Persuading others to change their minds or behavior.
Operation and Control	Controlling operations of equipment or systems.

Quality Control Analysis	Conducting tests and inspections of products, services, or processes to evaluate quality or performance.
Negotiation	Bringing others together and trying to reconcile differences.
Equipment Selection	Determining the kind of tools and equipment needed to do a job.
Management of Personnel Resources	Motivating, developing, and directing people as they work, identifying the best people for the job.
Technology Design	Generating or adapting equipment and technology to serve user needs.
Management of Financial Resources	Determining how money will be spent to get the work done, and accounting for these expenditures.
Troubleshooting	Determining causes of operating errors and deciding what to do about it.
Equipment Maintenance	Performing routine maintenance on equipment and determining when and what kind of maintenance is needed.
Management of Material Resources	Obtaining and seeing to the appropriate use of equipment, facilities, and materials needed to do certain work.
Operations Analysis	Analyzing needs and product requirements to create a design.
Systems Evaluation	Identifying measures or indicators of system performance and the actions needed to improve or correct performance, relative to the goals of the system.
Installation	Installing equipment, machines, wiring, or programs to meet specifications.
Operation Monitoring	Watching gauges, dials, or other indicators to make sure a machine is working properly.
Systems Analysis	Determining how a system should work and how changes in conditions, operations, and the environment will affect outcomes.
Repairing	Repairing machines or systems using the needed tools.
Programming	Writing computer programs for various purposes.
Science	Using scientific rules and methods to solve problems.

Ability	Ability Definitions
Oral Comprehension	The ability to listen to and understand information and ideas presented through spoken words and sentences.
Oral Expression	The ability to communicate information and ideas in speaking so others will understand.
Speech Recognition	The ability to identify and understand the speech of another person.
Speech Clarity	The ability to speak clearly so others can understand you.
Information Ordering	The ability to arrange things or actions in a certain order or pattern according to a specific rule or set of rules (e.g., patterns of numbers, letters, words, pictures, mathematical operations).
Written Comprehension	The ability to read and understand information and ideas presented in writing.
Near Vision	The ability to see details at close range (within a few feet of the observer).
Written Expression	The ability to communicate information and ideas in writing so others will understand.
Problem Sensitivity	The ability to tell when something is wrong or is likely to go wrong. It does not involve solving the problem, only recognizing there is a problem.
Selective Attention	The ability to concentrate on a task over a period of time without being distracted.
Deductive Reasoning	The ability to apply general rules to specific problems to produce answers that make sense.
Category Flexibility	The ability to generate or use different sets of rules for combining or grouping things in different ways.
Inductive Reasoning	The ability to combine pieces of information to form general rules or conclusions (includes finding a relationship among seemingly unrelated events).
Time Sharing	The ability to shift back and forth between two or more activities or sources of information (such as speech, sounds, touch, or other sources).
Flexibility of Closure	The ability to identify or detect a known pattern (a figure, object, word, or sound) that is hidden in other distracting material.
Speed of Closure	The ability to quickly make sense of, combine, and organize information into meaningful patterns.
Originality	The ability to come up with unusual or clever ideas about a given topic or situation, or to develop creative ways to solve a problem.
Wrist-Finger Speed	The ability to make fast, simple, repeated movements of the fingers, hands, and wrists.
Finger Dexterity	The ability to make precisely coordinated movements of the fingers of one or both hands to grasp, manipulate, or assemble very small objects.
Manual Dexterity	The ability to quickly move your hand, your hand together with your arm, or your two hands to grasp, manipulate, or assemble objects.
Fluency of Ideas	The ability to come up with a number of ideas about a topic (the number of ideas is important, not their quality, correctness, or creativity).
Far Vision	The ability to see details at a distance.

Memorization	The ability to remember information such as words. numbers, pictures, and procedures.
Number Facility	The ability to add, subtract, multiply, or divide quickly and correctly.
Auditory Attention	The ability to focus on a single source of sound in the presence of other distracting sounds.
Arm-Hand Steadiness	The ability to keep your hand and arm steady while moving your arm or while holding your arm and hand in one position.
Perceptual Speed	The ability to quickly and accurately compare similarities and differences among sets of letters, numbers, objects, pictures, or patterns. The things to be compared may be presented at the same time or one after the other. This ability also includes comparing a presented object with a remembered object.
Control Precision	The ability to quickly and repeatedly adjust the controls of a machine or a vehicle to exact positions.
Mathematical Reasoning	The ability to choose the right mathematical methods or formulas to solve a problem.
Visualization	The ability to imagine how something will look after it is moved around or when its parts are moved or rearranged.
Trunk Strength	The ability to use your abdominal and lower back muscles to support part of the body repeatedly or continuously over time without 'giving out' or fatiguing.
Sound Localization	The ability to tell the direction from which a sound originated.
Extent Flexibility	The ability to bend, stretch, twist, or reach with your body, arms, and/or legs.
Night Vision	The ability to see under low light conditions.
Static Strength	The ability to exert maximum muscle force to lift, push, pull, or carry objects.
Reaction Time	The ability to quickly respond (with the hand, finger, or foot) to a signal (sound, light, picture) when it appears.
Hearing Sensitivity	The ability to detect or tell the differences between sounds that vary in pitch and loudness.
Multilimb Coordination	The ability to coordinate two or more limbs (for example, two arms, two legs, or one leg and one arm) while sitting, standing, or lying down. It does not involve performing the activities while the whole body is in motion.
Response Orientation	The ability to choose quickly between two or more movements in response to two or more different signals (lights, sounds, pictures). It includes the speed with which the correct response is started with the hand, foot, or other body part.
Spatial Orientation	The ability to know your location in relation to the environment or to know where other objects are in relation to you.
Gross Body Coordination	The ability to coordinate the movement of your arms, legs, and torso together when the whole body is in motion.
Dynamic Flexibility	The ability to quickly and repeatedly bend, stretch, twist, or reach out with your body, arms, and/or legs.
Stamina	The ability to exert yourself physically over long periods of time without getting winded or out of breath.
Dynamic Strength	The ability to exert muscle force repeatedly or continuously over time. This involves muscular endurance and resistance to muscle fatigue.
Speed of Limb Movement	The ability to quickly move the arms and legs.
Gross Body Equilibrium	The ability to keep or regain your body balance or stay upright when in an unstable position.
Glare Sensitivity	The ability to see objects in the presence of glare or bright lighting.
Rate Control	The ability to time your movements or the movement of a piece of equipment in anticipation of changes in the speed and/or direction of a moving object or scene.
Visual Color Discrimination	The ability to match or detect differences between colors, including shades of color and brightness.
Peripheral Vision	The ability to see objects or movement of objects to one's side when the eyes are looking ahead.
Depth Perception	The ability to judge which of several objects is closer or farther away from you, or to judge the distance between you and an object.
Explosive Strength	The ability to use short bursts of muscle force to propel oneself (as in jumping or sprinting), or to throw an object.

Work_Activity	Work_Activity Definitions
Interacting With Computers	Using computers and computer systems (including hardware and software) to program, write software, set up functions, enter data, or process information.
Performing Administrative Activities	Performing day-to-day administrative tasks such as maintaining information files and processing paperwork.
Getting Information	Observing, receiving, and otherwise obtaining information from all relevant sources.
Communicating with Persons Outside Organization	Communicating with people outside the organization, representing the organization to customers, the public, government, and other external sources. This information can be exchanged in person, in writing, or by telephone or e-mail.
Communicating with Supervisors, Peers, or Subordin	Providing information to supervisors, co-workers, and subordinates by telephone, in written form, e-mail, or in person.

Organizing, Planning, and Prioritizing Work	Developing specific goals and plans to prioritize, organize, and accomplish your work.
Documenting/Recording Information	Entering, transcribing, recording, storing, or maintaining information in written or electronic/magnetic form.
Performing for or Working Directly with the Public	Performing for people or dealing directly with the public. This includes serving customers in restaurants and stores, and receiving clients or guests.
Monitoring and Controlling Resources	Monitoring and controlling resources and overseeing the spending of money.
Processing Information	Compiling, coding, categorizing, calculating, tabulating, auditing, or verifying information or data.
Updating and Using Relevant Knowledge	Keeping up-to-date technically and applying new knowledge to your job.
Establishing and Maintaining Interpersonal Relatio	Developing constructive and cooperative working relationships with others, and maintaining them over time.
Scheduling Work and Activities	Scheduling events, programs, and activities, as well as the work of others.
Making Decisions and Solving Problems	Analyzing information and evaluating results to choose the best solution and solve problems.
Resolving Conflicts and Negotiating with Others	Handling complaints, settling disputes, and resolving grievances and conflicts, or otherwise negotiating with others.
Interpreting the Meaning of Information for Others	Translating or explaining what information means and how it can be used.
Monitor Processes, Materials, or Surroundings	Monitoring and reviewing information from materials, events, or the environment, to detect or assess problems.
Coordinating the Work and Activities of Others	Getting members of a group to work together to accomplish tasks.
Identifying Objects, Actions, and Events	Identifying information by categorizing, estimating, recognizing differences or similarities, and detecting changes in circumstances or events.
Evaluating Information to Determine Compliance wit	Using relevant information and individual judgment to determine whether events or processes comply with laws, regulations, or standards.
Assisting and Caring for Others	Providing personal assistance, medical attention, emotional support, or other personal care to others such as coworkers, customers, or patients.
Analyzing Data or Information	Identifying the underlying principles, reasons, or facts of information by breaking down information or data into separate parts.
Developing Objectives and Strategies	Establishing long-range objectives and specifying the strategies and actions to achieve them.
Developing and Building Teams	Encouraging and building mutual trust, respect, and cooperation among team members.
Thinking Creatively	Developing, designing, or creating new applications, ideas, relationships, systems, or products, including artistic contributions.
Judging the Qualities of Things, Services, or Peop	Assessing the value, importance, or quality of things or people.
Coaching and Developing Others	Identifying the developmental needs of others and coaching, mentoring, or otherwise helping others to improve their knowledge or skills.
Training and Teaching Others	Identifying the educational needs of others, developing formal educational or training programs or classes, and teaching or instructing others.
Controlling Machines and Processes	Using either control mechanisms or direct physical activity to operate machines or processes (not including computers or vehicles).
Handling and Moving Objects	Using hands and arms in handling, installing, positioning, and moving materials, and manipulating things.
Performing General Physical Activities	Performing physical activities that require considerable use of your arms and legs and moving your whole body, such as climbing, lifting, balancing, walking, stooping, and handling of materials.
Inspecting Equipment, Structures, or Material	Inspecting equipment, structures, or materials to identify the cause of errors or other problems or defects.
Provide Consultation and Advice to Others	Providing guidance and expert advice to management or other groups on technical, systems-, or process-related topics.
Selling or Influencing Others	Convincing others to buy merchandise/goods or to otherwise change their minds or actions.
Guiding, Directing, and Motivating Subordinates	Providing guidance and direction to subordinates, including setting performance standards and monitoring performance.
Estimating the Quantifiable Characteristics of Pro	Estimating sizes, distances, and quantities; or determining time, costs, resources, or materials needed to perform a work activity.
Repairing and Maintaining Electronic Equipment	Servicing, repairing, calibrating, regulating, fine-tuning, or testing machines, devices, and equipment that operate primarily on the basis of electrical or electronic (not mechanical) principles.
Staffing Organizational Units	Recruiting, interviewing, selecting, hiring, and promoting employees in an organization.
Operating Vehicles, Mechanized Devices, or Equipme	Running, maneuvering, navigating, or driving vehicles or mechanized equipment, such as forklifts, passenger vehicles, aircraft, or water craft.

Repairing and Maintaining Mechanical Equipment	Servicing, repairing, adjusting, and testing machines, devices, moving parts, and equipment that operate primarily on the basis of mechanical (not electronic) principles.
Drafting, Laying Out, and Specifying Technical Dev	Providing documentation, detailed instructions, drawings, or specifications to tell others about how devices, parts, equipment, or structures are to be fabricated, constructed, assembled, modified, maintained, or used.

Work_Content	Work_Content Definitions
Letters and Memos	How often does the job require written letters and memos?
Telephone	How often do you have telephone conversations in this job?
Importance of Being Exact or Accurate	How important is being very exact or highly accurate in performing this job?
Contact With Others	How much does this job require the worker to be in contact with others (face-to-face, by telephone, or otherwise) in order to perform it?
Face-to-Face Discussions	How often do you have to have face-to-face discussions with individuals or teams in this job?
Importance of Repeating Same Tasks	How important is repeating the same physical activities (e.g., key entry) or mental activities (e.g., checking entries in a ledger) over and over, without stopping, to performing this job?
Time Pressure	How often does this job require the worker to meet strict deadlines?
Spend Time Sitting	How much does this job require sitting?
Structured versus Unstructured Work	To what extent is this job structured for the worker, rather than allowing the worker to determine tasks, priorities, and goals?
Indoors, Environmentally Controlled	How often does this job require working indoors in environmentally controlled conditions?
Frequency of Decision Making	How frequently is the worker required to make decisions that affect other people, the financial resources, and/or the image and reputation of the organization?
Spend Time Making Repetitive Motions	How much does this job require making repetitive motions?
Impact of Decisions on Co-workers or Company Resul	How do the decisions an employee makes impact the results of co-workers, clients or the company?
Electronic Mail	How often do you use electronic mail in this job?
Freedom to Make Decisions	How much decision making freedom, without supervision, does the job offer?
Deal With Unpleasant or Angry People	How frequently does the worker have to deal with unpleasant, angry, or discourteous individuals as part of the job requirements?
Deal With External Customers	How important is it to work with external customers or the public in this job?
Consequence of Error	How serious would the result usually be if the worker made a mistake that was not readily correctable?
Level of Competition	To what extent does this job require the worker to compete or to be aware of competitive pressures?
Spend Time Using Your Hands to Handle, Control, or	How much does this job require using your hands to handle, control, or feel objects, tools or controls?
Physical Proximity	To what extent does this job require the worker to perform job tasks in close physical proximity to other people?
Work With Work Group or Team	How important is it to work with others in a group or team in this job?
Coordinate or Lead Others	How important is it to coordinate or lead others in accomplishing work activities in this job?
Spend Time Standing	How much does this job require standing?
Frequency of Conflict Situations	How often are there conflict situations the employee has to face in this job?
Spend Time Walking and Running	How much does this job require walking and running?
Degree of Automation	How automated is the job?
Public Speaking	How often do you have to perform public speaking in this job?
Sounds, Noise Levels Are Distracting or Uncomforta	How often does this job require working exposed to sounds and noise levels that are distracting or uncomfortable?
Pace Determined by Speed of Equipment	How important is it to this job that the pace is determined by the speed of equipment or machinery? (This does not refer to keeping busy at all times on this job.)
In an Enclosed Vehicle or Equipment	How often does this job require working in a closed vehicle or equipment (e.g., car)?
Responsibility for Outcomes and Results	How responsible is the worker for work outcomes and results of other workers?
Responsible for Others' Health and Safety	How much responsibility is there for the health and safety of others in this job?
Spend Time Bending or Twisting the Body	How much does this job require bending or twisting your body?
Extremely Bright or Inadequate Lighting	How often does this job require working in extremely bright or inadequate lighting conditions?
Deal With Physically Aggressive People	How frequently does this job require the worker to deal with physical aggression of violent individuals?
Spend Time Kneeling, Crouching, Stooping, or Crawl	How much does this job require kneeling, crouching, stooping, or crawling?

Exposed to Contaminants	How often does this job require working exposed to contaminants (such as pollutants, gases, dust or odors)?
Cramped Work Space, Awkward Positions	How often does this job require working in cramped work spaces that requires getting into awkward positions?
Outdoors, Exposed to Weather	How often does this job require working outdoors, exposed to all weather conditions?
Exposed to Minor Burns, Cuts, Bites, or Stings	How often does this job require exposure to minor burns, cuts, bites, or stings?
Spend Time Keeping or Regaining Balance	How much does this job require keeping or regaining your balance?
Outdoors, Under Cover	How often does this job require working outdoors, under cover (e.g., structure with roof but no walls)?
Exposed to Radiation	How often does this job require exposure to radiation?
Exposed to Hazardous Conditions	How often does this job require exposure to hazardous conditions?
Wear Common Protective or Safety Equipment such as	How much does this job require wearing common protective or safety equipment such as safety shoes, glasses, gloves, hard hats or life jackets?
Exposed to Hazardous Equipment	How often does this job require exposure to hazardous equipment?
Exposed to High Places	How often does this job require exposure to high places?
Exposed to Disease or Infections	How often does this job require exposure to disease/infections?
Exposed to Whole Body Vibration	How often does this job require exposure to whole body vibration (e.g., operate a jackhammer)?
In an Open Vehicle or Equipment	How often does this job require working in an open vehicle or equipment (e.g., tractor)?
Indoors, Not Environmentally Controlled	How often does this job require working indoors in non-controlled environmental conditions (e.g., warehouse without heat)?
Spend Time Climbing Ladders, Scaffolds, or Poles	How much does this job require climbing ladders, scaffolds, or poles?
Very Hot or Cold Temperatures	How often does this job require working in very hot (above 90 F degrees) or very cold (below 32 F degrees) temperatures?
Wear Specialized Protective or Safety Equipment su	How much does this job require wearing specialized protective or safety equipment such as breathing apparatus, safety harness, full protection suits, or radiation protection?

Work_Styles	Work_Styles Definitions
Attention to Detail	Job requires being careful about detail and thorough in completing work tasks.
Integrity	Job requires being honest and ethical.
Dependability	Job requires being reliable, responsible, and dependable, and fulfilling obligations.
Cooperation	Job requires being pleasant with others on the job and displaying a good-natured, cooperative attitude.
Independence	Job requires developing one's own ways of doing things, guiding oneself with little or no supervision, and depending on oneself to get things done.
Stress Tolerance	Job requires accepting criticism and dealing calmly and effectively with high stress situations.
Initiative	Job requires a willingness to take on responsibilities and challenges.
Self Control	Job requires maintaining composure, keeping emotions in check, controlling anger, and avoiding aggressive behavior, even in very difficult situations.
Achievement/Effort	Job requires establishing and maintaining personally challenging achievement goals and exerting effort toward mastering tasks.
Persistence	Job requires persistence in the face of obstacles.
Adaptability/Flexibility	Job requires being open to change (positive or negative) and to considerable variety in the workplace.
Concern for Others	Job requires being sensitive to others' needs and feelings and being understanding and helpful on the job.
Leadership	Job requires a willingness to lead, take charge, and offer opinions and direction.
Innovation	Job requires creativity and alternative thinking to develop new ideas for and answers to work-related problems.
Analytical Thinking	Job requires analyzing information and using logic to address work-related issues and problems.
Social Orientation	Job requires preferring to work with others rather than alone, and being personally connected with others on the job.

Job Zone Component	Job Zone Component Definitions
Title	Job Zone Three: Medium Preparation Needed
Overall Experience	Previous work-related skill, knowledge, or experience is required for these occupations. For example, an electrician must have completed three or four years of apprenticeship or several years of vocational training, and often must have passed a licensing exam, in order to perform the job.
Job Training	Employees in these occupations usually need one or two years of training involving both on-the-job experience and informal training with experienced workers.

Job Zone Examples	These occupations usually involve using communication and organizational skills to coordinate, supervise, manage, or train others to accomplish goals. Examples include dental assistants, electricians, fish and game wardens, legal secretaries, personnel recruiters, and recreation workers.
SVP Range	(6.0 to < 7.0)
Education	Most occupations in this zone require training in vocational schools, related on-the-job experience, or an associate's degree. Some may require a bachelor's degree.

43-6013.00 - Medical Secretaries

Perform secretarial duties utilizing specific knowledge of medical terminology and hospital, clinic, or laboratory procedures. Duties include scheduling appointments, billing patients, and compiling and recording medical charts, reports, and correspondence.

Tasks

1) Greet visitors, ascertain purpose of visit, and direct them to appropriate staff.

2) Compile and record medical charts, reports, and correspondence, using typewriter or personal computer.

3) Transmit correspondence and medical records by mail, e-mail, or fax.

4) Perform various clerical and administrative functions, such as ordering and maintaining an inventory of supplies.

5) Maintain medical records, technical library and correspondence files.

6) Operate office equipment such as voice mail messaging systems, and use word processing, spreadsheet, and other software applications to prepare reports, invoices, financial statements, letters, case histories and medical records.

7) Schedule and confirm patient diagnostic appointments, surgeries and medical consultations.

8) Interview patients in order to complete documents, case histories, and forms such as intake and insurance forms.

9) Complete insurance and other claim forms.

10) Transcribe recorded messages and practitioners' diagnoses and recommendations into patients' medical records.

11) Perform bookkeeping duties, such as credits and collections, preparing and sending financial statements and bills, and keeping financial records.

12) Prepare correspondence and assist physicians or medical scientists with preparation of reports, speeches, articles and conference proceedings.

13) Arrange hospital admissions for patients.

14) Answer telephones, and direct calls to appropriate staff.

Knowledge	Knowledge Definitions
Customer and Personal Service	Knowledge of principles and processes for providing customer and personal services. This includes customer needs assessment, meeting quality standards for services, and evaluation of customer satisfaction.
Clerical	Knowledge of administrative and clerical procedures and systems such as word processing, managing files and records, stenography and transcription, designing forms, and other office procedures and terminology.
English Language	Knowledge of the structure and content of the English language including the meaning and spelling of words, rules of composition, and grammar.
Computers and Electronics	Knowledge of circuit boards, processors, chips, electronic equipment, and computer hardware and software, including applications and programming.
Telecommunications	Knowledge of transmission, broadcasting, switching, control, and operation of telecommunications systems.
Communications and Media	Knowledge of media production, communication, and dissemination techniques and methods. This includes alternative ways to inform and entertain via written, oral, and visual media.
Education and Training	Knowledge of principles and methods for curriculum and training design, teaching and instruction for individuals and groups, and the measurement of training effects.
Mathematics	Knowledge of arithmetic, algebra, geometry, calculus, statistics, and their applications.
Administration and Management	Knowledge of business and management principles involved in strategic planning, resource allocation, human resources modeling, leadership technique, production methods, and coordination of people and resources.
Transportation	Knowledge of principles and methods for moving people or goods by air, rail, sea, or road, including the relative costs and benefits.

Public Safety and Security	Knowledge of relevant equipment, policies, procedures, and strategies to promote effective local, state, or national security operations for the protection of people, data, property, and institutions.
Medicine and Dentistry	Knowledge of the information and techniques needed to diagnose and treat human injuries, diseases, and deformities. This includes symptoms, treatment alternatives, drug properties and interactions, and preventive health-care measures.
Philosophy and Theology	Knowledge of different philosophical systems and religions. This includes their basic principles, values, ethics, ways of thinking, customs, practices, and their impact on human culture.
Food Production	Knowledge of techniques and equipment for planting, growing, and harvesting food products (both plant and animal) for consumption, including storage/handling techniques.
Economics and Accounting	Knowledge of economic and accounting principles and practices, the financial markets, banking and the analysis and reporting of financial data.
Law and Government	Knowledge of laws, legal codes, court procedures, precedents, government regulations, executive orders, agency rules, and the democratic political process.
Sociology and Anthropology	Knowledge of group behavior and dynamics, societal trends and influences, human migrations, ethnicity, cultures and their history and origins.
Personnel and Human Resources	Knowledge of principles and procedures for personnel recruitment, selection, training, compensation and benefits, labor relations and negotiation, and personnel information systems.
Production and Processing	Knowledge of raw materials, production processes, quality control, costs, and other techniques for maximizing the effective manufacture and distribution of goods.
Psychology	Knowledge of human behavior and performance; individual differences in ability, personality, and interests; learning and motivation; psychological research methods; and the assessment and treatment of behavioral and affective disorders.
Mechanical	Knowledge of machines and tools, including their designs, uses, repair, and maintenance.
Therapy and Counseling	Knowledge of principles, methods, and procedures for diagnosis, treatment, and rehabilitation of physical and mental dysfunctions, and for career counseling and guidance.
Geography	Knowledge of principles and methods for describing the features of land, sea, and air masses, including their physical characteristics, locations, interrelationships, and distribution of plant, animal, and human life.
Foreign Language	Knowledge of the structure and content of a foreign (non-English) language including the meaning and spelling of words, rules of composition and grammar, and pronunciation.
Biology	Knowledge of plant and animal organisms, their tissues, cells, functions, interdependencies, and interactions with each other and the environment.
Sales and Marketing	Knowledge of principles and methods for showing, promoting, and selling products or services. This includes marketing strategy and tactics, product demonstration, sales techniques, and sales control systems.
Engineering and Technology	Knowledge of the practical application of engineering science and technology. This includes applying principles, techniques, procedures, and equipment to the design and production of various goods and services.
Chemistry	Knowledge of the chemical composition, structure, and properties of substances and of the chemical processes and transformations that they undergo. This includes uses of chemicals and their interactions, danger signs, production techniques, and disposal methods.
History and Archeology	Knowledge of historical events and their causes, indicators, and effects on civilizations and cultures.
Design	Knowledge of design techniques, tools, and principles involved in production of precision technical plans, blueprints, drawings, and models.
Fine Arts	Knowledge of the theory and techniques required to compose, produce, and perform works of music, dance, visual arts, drama, and sculpture.
Physics	Knowledge and prediction of physical principles, laws, their interrelationships, and applications to understanding fluid, material, and atmospheric dynamics, and mechanical, electrical, atomic and sub- atomic structures and processes.
Building and Construction	Knowledge of materials, methods, and the tools involved in the construction or repair of houses, buildings, or other structures such as highways and roads.

Skills	Skills Definitions
Active Listening	Giving full attention to what other people are saying, taking time to understand the points being made, asking questions as appropriate, and not interrupting at inappropriate times.
Reading Comprehension	Understanding written sentences and paragraphs in work related documents.
Speaking	Talking to others to convey information effectively.

274

Coordination	Adjusting actions in relation to others' actions.
Active Learning	Understanding the implications of new information for both current and future problem-solving and decision-making.
Time Management	Managing one's own time and the time of others.
Instructing	Teaching others how to do something.
Writing	Communicating effectively in writing as appropriate for the needs of the audience.
Service Orientation	Actively looking for ways to help people.
Learning Strategies	Selecting and using training/instructional methods and procedures appropriate for the situation when learning or teaching new things.
Social Perceptiveness	Being aware of others' reactions and understanding why they react as they do.
Management of Material Resources	Obtaining and seeing to the appropriate use of equipment, facilities, and materials needed to do certain work.
Operation and Control	Controlling operations of equipment or systems.
Monitoring	Monitoring/Assessing performance of yourself, other individuals, or organizations to make improvements or take corrective action.
Judgment and Decision Making	Considering the relative costs and benefits of potential actions to choose the most appropriate one.
Equipment Selection	Determining the kind of tools and equipment needed to do a job.
Critical Thinking	Using logic and reasoning to identify the strengths and weaknesses of alternative solutions, conclusions or approaches to problems.
Negotiation	Bringing others together and trying to reconcile differences.
Management of Personnel Resources	Motivating, developing, and directing people as they work, identifying the best people for the job.
Mathematics	Using mathematics to solve problems.
Systems Evaluation	Identifying measures or indicators of system performance and the actions needed to improve or correct performance, relative to the goals of the system.
Persuasion	Persuading others to change their minds or behavior.
Quality Control Analysis	Conducting tests and inspections of products, services, or processes to evaluate quality or performance.
Equipment Maintenance	Performing routine maintenance on equipment and determining when and what kind of maintenance is needed.
Complex Problem Solving	Identifying complex problems and reviewing related information to develop and evaluate options and implement solutions.
Technology Design	Generating or adapting equipment and technology to serve user needs.
Troubleshooting	Determining causes of operating errors and deciding what to do about it.
Operations Analysis	Analyzing needs and product requirements to create a design.
Repairing	Repairing machines or systems using the needed tools.
Management of Financial Resources	Determining how money will be spent to get the work done, and accounting for these expenditures.
Installation	Installing equipment, machines, wiring, or programs to meet specifications.
Operation Monitoring	Watching gauges, dials, or other indicators to make sure a machine is working properly.
Science	Using scientific rules and methods to solve problems.
Systems Analysis	Determining how a system should work and how changes in conditions, operations, and the environment will affect outcomes.
Programming	Writing computer programs for various purposes.

Ability	Ability Definitions
Oral Comprehension	The ability to listen to and understand information and ideas presented through spoken words and sentences.
Oral Expression	The ability to communicate information and ideas in speaking so others will understand.
Speech Clarity	The ability to speak clearly so others can understand you.
Near Vision	The ability to see details at close range (within a few feet of the observer).
Information Ordering	The ability to arrange things or actions in a certain order or pattern according to a specific rule or set of rules (e.g., patterns of numbers, letters, words, pictures, mathematical operations).
Speech Recognition	The ability to identify and understand the speech of another person.
Written Comprehension	The ability to read and understand information and ideas presented in writing.
Time Sharing	The ability to shift back and forth between two or more activities or sources of information (such as speech, sounds, touch, or other sources).
Selective Attention	The ability to concentrate on a task over a period of time without being distracted.
Problem Sensitivity	The ability to tell when something is wrong or is likely to go wrong. It does not involve solving the problem, only recognizing there is a problem.
Written Expression	The ability to communicate information and ideas in writing so others will understand.

Category Flexibility	The ability to generate or use different sets of rules for combining or grouping things in different ways.
Inductive Reasoning	The ability to combine pieces of information to form general rules or conclusions (includes finding a relationship among seemingly unrelated events).
Deductive Reasoning	The ability to apply general rules to specific problems to produce answers that make sense.
Finger Dexterity	The ability to make precisely coordinated movements of the fingers of one or both hands to grasp, manipulate, or assemble very small objects.
Perceptual Speed	The ability to quickly and accurately compare similarities and differences among sets of letters, numbers, objects, pictures, or patterns. The things to be compared may be presented at the same time or one after the other. This ability also includes comparing a presented object with a remembered object.
Mathematical Reasoning	The ability to choose the right mathematical methods or formulas to solve a problem.
Originality	The ability to come up with unusual or clever ideas about a given topic or situation, or to develop creative ways to solve a problem.
Fluency of Ideas	The ability to come up with a number of ideas about a topic (the number of ideas is important, not their quality, correctness, or creativity).
Arm-Hand Steadiness	The ability to keep your hand and arm steady while moving your arm or while holding your arm and hand in one position.
Auditory Attention	The ability to focus on a single source of sound in the presence of other distracting sounds.
Number Facility	The ability to add, subtract, multiply, or divide quickly and correctly.
Memorization	The ability to remember information such as words, numbers, pictures, and procedures.
Trunk Strength	The ability to use your abdominal and lower back muscles to support part of the body repeatedly or continuously over time without 'giving out' or fatiguing.
Manual Dexterity	The ability to quickly move your hand, your hand together with your arm, or your two hands to grasp, manipulate, or assemble objects.
Flexibility of Closure	The ability to identify or detect a known pattern (a figure, object, word, or sound) that is hidden in other distracting material.
Speed of Closure	The ability to quickly make sense of, combine, and organize information into meaningful patterns.
Gross Body Coordination	The ability to coordinate the movement of your arms, legs, and torso together when the whole body is in motion.
Static Strength	The ability to exert maximum muscle force to lift, push, pull, or carry objects.
Multilimb Coordination	The ability to coordinate two or more limbs (for example, two arms, two legs, or one leg and one arm) while sitting, standing, or lying down. It does not involve performing the activities while the whole body is in motion.
Control Precision	The ability to quickly and repeatedly adjust the controls of a machine or a vehicle to exact positions.
Stamina	The ability to exert yourself physically over long periods of time without getting winded or out of breath.
Far Vision	The ability to see details at a distance.
Speed of Limb Movement	The ability to quickly move the arms and legs.
Hearing Sensitivity	The ability to detect or tell the differences between sounds that vary in pitch and loudness.
Visual Color Discrimination	The ability to match or detect differences between colors, including shades of color and brightness.
Wrist-Finger Speed	The ability to make fast, simple, repeated movements of the fingers, hands, and wrists.
Visualization	The ability to imagine how something will look after it is moved around or when its parts are moved or rearranged.
Depth Perception	The ability to judge which of several objects is closer or farther away from you, or to judge the distance between you and an object.
Reaction Time	The ability to quickly respond (with the hand, finger, or foot) to a signal (sound, light, picture) when it appears.
Response Orientation	The ability to choose quickly between two or more movements in response to two or more different signals (lights, sounds, pictures). It includes the speed with which the correct response is started with the hand, foot, or other body part.
Sound Localization	The ability to tell the direction from which a sound originated.
Extent Flexibility	The ability to bend, stretch, twist, or reach with your body, arms, and/or legs.
Gross Body Equilibrium	The ability to keep or regain your body balance or stay upright when in an unstable position.
Night Vision	The ability to see under low light conditions.
Peripheral Vision	The ability to see objects or movement of objects to one's side when the eyes are looking ahead.
Explosive Strength	The ability to use short bursts of muscle force to propel oneself (as in jumping or sprinting), or to throw an object.
Dynamic Flexibility	The ability to quickly and repeatedly bend, stretch, twist, or reach out with your body, arms, and/or legs.

Rate Control — The ability to time your movements or the movement of a piece of equipment in anticipation of changes in the speed and/or direction of a moving object or scene.

Spatial Orientation — The ability to know your location in relation to the environment or to know where other objects are in relation to you.

Glare Sensitivity — The ability to see objects in the presence of glare or bright lighting.

Dynamic Strength — The ability to exert muscle force repeatedly or continuously over time. This involves muscular endurance and resistance to muscle fatigue.

Work_Activity	Work_Activity Definitions
Getting Information	Observing, receiving, and otherwise obtaining information from all relevant sources.
Communicating with Supervisors, Peers, or Subordin	Providing information to supervisors, co-workers, and subordinates by telephone, in written form, e-mail, or in person.
Communicating with Persons Outside Organization	Communicating with people outside the organization, representing the organization to customers, the public, government, and other external sources. This information can be exchanged in person, in writing, or by telephone or e-mail.
Interacting With Computers	Using computers and computer systems (including hardware and software) to program, write software, set up functions, enter data, or process information.
Establishing and Maintaining Interpersonal Relatio	Developing constructive and cooperative working relationships with others, and maintaining them over time.
Assisting and Caring for Others	Providing personal assistance, medical attention, emotional support, or other personal care to others such as coworkers, customers, or patients.
Documenting/Recording Information	Entering, transcribing, recording, storing, or maintaining information in written or electronic/magnetic form.
Organizing, Planning, and Prioritizing Work	Developing specific goals and plans to prioritize, organize, and accomplish your work.
Performing Administrative Activities	Performing day-to-day administrative tasks such as maintaining information files and processing paperwork.
Processing Information	Compiling, coding, categorizing, calculating, tabulating, auditing, or verifying information or data.
Performing for or Working Directly with the Public	Performing for people or dealing directly with the public. This includes serving customers in restaurants and stores, and receiving clients or guests.
Making Decisions and Solving Problems	Analyzing information and evaluating results to choose the best solution and solve problems.
Updating and Using Relevant Knowledge	Keeping up-to-date technically and applying new knowledge to your job.
Monitor Processes, Materials, or Surroundings	Monitoring and reviewing information from materials, events, or the environment, to detect or assess problems.
Scheduling Work and Activities	Scheduling events, programs, and activities, as well as the work of others.
Interpreting the Meaning of Information for Others	Translating or explaining what information means and how it can be used.
Coordinating the Work and Activities of Others	Getting members of a group to work together to accomplish tasks.
Resolving Conflicts and Negotiating with Others	Handling complaints, settling disputes, and resolving grievances and conflicts, or otherwise negotiating with others.
Evaluating Information to Determine Compliance wit	Using relevant information and individual judgment to determine whether events or processes comply with laws, regulations, or standards.
Identifying Objects, Actions, and Events	Identifying information by categorizing, estimating, recognizing differences or similarities, and detecting changes in circumstances or events.
Developing and Building Teams	Encouraging and building mutual trust, respect, and cooperation among team members.
Estimating the Quantifiable Characteristics of Pro	Estimating sizes, distances, and quantities; or determining time, costs, resources, or materials needed to perform a work activity.
Thinking Creatively	Developing, designing, or creating new applications, ideas, relationships, systems, or products, including artistic contributions.
Provide Consultation and Advice to Others	Providing guidance and expert advice to management or other groups on technical, systems-, or process-related topics.
Handling and Moving Objects	Using hands and arms in handling, installing, positioning, and moving materials, and manipulating things.
Coaching and Developing Others	Identifying the developmental needs of others and coaching, mentoring, or otherwise helping others to improve their knowledge or skills.
Analyzing Data or Information	Identifying the underlying principles, reasons, or facts of information by breaking down information or data into separate parts.
Developing Objectives and Strategies	Establishing long-range objectives and specifying the strategies and actions to achieve them.
Judging the Qualities of Things, Services, or Peop	Assessing the value, importance, or quality of things or people.

Selling or Influencing Others — Convincing others to buy merchandise/goods or to otherwise change their minds or actions.

Performing General Physical Activities — Performing physical activities that require considerable use of your arms and legs and moving your whole body, such as climbing, lifting, balancing, walking, stooping, and handling of materials.

Monitoring and Controlling Resources — Monitoring and controlling resources and overseeing the spending of money.

Inspecting Equipment, Structures, or Material — Inspecting equipment, structures, or materials to identify the cause of errors or other problems or defects.

Controlling Machines and Processes — Using either control mechanisms or direct physical activity to operate machines or processes (not including computers or vehicles).

Training and Teaching Others — Identifying the educational needs of others, developing formal educational or training programs or classes, and teaching or instructing others.

Guiding, Directing, and Motivating Subordinates — Providing guidance and direction to subordinates, including setting performance standards and monitoring performance.

Staffing Organizational Units — Recruiting, interviewing, selecting, hiring, and promoting employees in an organization.

Repairing and Maintaining Mechanical Equipment — Servicing, repairing, adjusting, and testing machines, devices, moving parts, and equipment that operate primarily on the basis of mechanical (not electronic) principles.

Repairing and Maintaining Electronic Equipment — Servicing, repairing, calibrating, regulating, fine-tuning, or testing machines, devices, and equipment that operate primarily on the basis of electrical or electronic (not mechanical) principles.

Drafting, Laying Out, and Specifying Technical Dev — Providing documentation, detailed instructions, drawings, or specifications to tell others about how devices, parts, equipment, or structures are to be fabricated, constructed, assembled, modified, maintained, or used.

Operating Vehicles, Mechanized Devices, or Equipme — Running, maneuvering, navigating, or driving vehicles or mechanized equipment, such as forklifts, passenger vehicles, aircraft, or water craft.

Work_Content	Work_Content Definitions
Telephone	How often do you have telephone conversations in this job?
Contact With Others	How much does this job require the worker to be in contact with others (face-to-face, by telephone, or otherwise) in order to perform it?
Face-to-Face Discussions	How often do you have to have face-to-face discussions with individuals or teams in this job?
Work With Work Group or Team	How important is it to work with others in a group or team in this job?
Spend Time Using Your Hands to Handle, Control, or	How much does this job require using your hands to handle, control, or feel objects, tools or controls?
Structured versus Unstructured Work	To what extent is this job structured for the worker, rather than allowing the worker to determine tasks, priorities, and goals?
Importance of Being Exact or Accurate	How important is being very exact or highly accurate in performing this job?
Frequency of Decision Making	How frequently is the worker required to make decisions that affect other people, the financial resources, and/or the image and reputation of the organization?
Time Pressure	How often does this job require the worker to meet strict deadlines?
Deal With Unpleasant or Angry People	How frequently does the worker have to deal with unpleasant, angry, or discourteous individuals as part of the job requirements?
Deal With External Customers	How important is it to work with external customers or the public in this job?
Exposed to Disease or Infections	How often does this job require exposure to disease/infections?
Frequency of Conflict Situations	How often are there conflict situations the employee has to face in this job?
Impact of Decisions on Co-workers or Company Resul	How do the decisions an employee makes impact the results of co-workers, clients or the company?
Coordinate or Lead Others	How important is it to coordinate or lead others in accomplishing work activities in this job?
Physical Proximity	To what extent does this job require the worker to perform job tasks in close physical proximity to other people?
Sounds, Noise Levels Are Distracting or Uncomforta	How often does this job require working exposed to sounds and noise levels that are distracting or uncomfortable?
Freedom to Make Decisions	How much decision making freedom, without supervision, does the job offer?
Spend Time Sitting	How much does this job require sitting?
Consequence of Error	How serious would the result usually be if the worker made a mistake that was not readily correctable?
Letters and Memos	How often does the job require written letters and memos?
Importance of Repeating Same Tasks	How important is repeating the same physical activities (e.g., key entry) or mental activities (e.g., checking entries in a ledger) over and over, without stopping, to performing this job?
Spend Time Making Repetitive Motions	How much does this job require making repetitive motions?

Indoors, Environmentally Controlled	How often does this job require working indoors in environmentally controlled conditions?
Responsibility for Outcomes and Results	How responsible is the worker for work outcomes and results of other workers?
Electronic Mail	How often do you use electronic mail in this job?
Spend Time Walking and Running	How much does this job require walking and running?
Level of Competition	To what extent does this job require the worker to compete or to be aware of competitive pressures?
Degree of Automation	How automated is the job?
Responsible for Others' Health and Safety	How much responsibility is there for the health and safety of others in this job?
Spend Time Standing	How much does this job require standing?
Cramped Work Space, Awkward Positions	How often does this job require working in cramped work spaces that requires getting into awkward positions?
Exposed to Radiation	How often does this job require exposure to radiation?
Spend Time Bending or Twisting the Body	How much does this job require bending or twisting your body?
Wear Common Protective or Safety Equipment such as	How much does this job require wearing common protective or safety equipment such as safety shoes, glasses, gloves, hard hats or live jackets?
Spend Time Kneeling, Crouching, Stooping, or Crawl	How much does this job require kneeling, crouching, stooping, or crawling?
Pace Determined by Speed of Equipment	How important is it to this job that the pace is determined by the speed of equipment or machinery? (This does not refer to keeping busy at all times on this job.)
Deal With Physically Aggressive People	How frequently does this job require the worker to deal with physical aggression of violent individuals?
Extremely Bright or Inadequate Lighting	How often does this job require working in extremely bright or inadequate lighting conditions?
Public Speaking	How often do you have to perform public speaking in this job?
Indoors, Not Environmentally Controlled	How often does this job require working indoors in non-controlled environmental conditions (e.g., warehouse without heat)?
Exposed to Minor Burns, Cuts, Bites, or Stings	How often does this job require exposure to minor burns, cuts, bites, or stings?
Exposed to Contaminants	How often does this job require working exposed to contaminants (such as pollutants, gases, dust or odors)?
Spend Time Climbing Ladders, Scaffolds, or Poles	How much does this job require climbing ladders, scaffolds, or poles?
Very Hot or Cold Temperatures	How often does this job require working in very hot (above 90 F degrees) or very cold (below 32 F degrees) temperatures?
Exposed to Hazardous Equipment	How often does this job require exposure to hazardous equipment?
Exposed to Hazardous Conditions	How often does this job require exposure to hazardous conditions?
Wear Specialized Protective or Safety Equipment su	How much does this job require wearing specialized protective or safety equipment such as breathing apparatus, safety harness, full protection suits, or radiation protection?
Exposed to High Places	How often does this job require exposure to high places?
Exposed to Whole Body Vibration	How often does this job require exposure to whole body vibration (e.g., operate a jackhammer)?
In an Enclosed Vehicle or Equipment	How often does this job require working in a closed vehicle or equipment (e.g., car)?
Spend Time Keeping or Regaining Balance	How much does this job require keeping or regaining your balance?
Outdoors, Under Cover	How often does this job require working outdoors, under cover (e.g., structure with roof but no walls)?
Outdoors, Exposed to Weather	How often does this job require working outdoors, exposed to all weather conditions?
In an Open Vehicle or Equipment	How often does this job require working in an open vehicle or equipment (e.g., tractor)?

Work_Styles	Work_Styles Definitions
Cooperation	Job requires being pleasant with others on the job and displaying a good-natured, cooperative attitude.
Dependability	Job requires being reliable, responsible, and dependable, and fulfilling obligations.
Attention to Detail	Job requires being careful about detail and thorough in completing work tasks.
Self Control	Job requires maintaining composure, keeping emotions in check, controlling anger, and avoiding aggressive behavior, even in very difficult situations.
Adaptability/Flexibility	Job requires being open to change (positive or negative) and to considerable variety in the workplace.
Stress Tolerance	Job requires accepting criticism and dealing calmly and effectively with high stress situations.
Integrity	Job requires being honest and ethical.
Concern for Others	Job requires being sensitive to others' needs and feelings and being understanding and helpful on the job.
Independence	Job requires developing one's own ways of doing things, guiding oneself with little or no supervision, and depending on oneself to get things done.

Initiative	Job requires a willingness to take on responsibilities and challenges.
Social Orientation	Job requires preferring to work with others rather than alone, and being personally connected with others on the job.
Achievement/Effort	Job requires establishing and maintaining personally challenging achievement goals and exerting effort toward mastering tasks.
Persistence	Job requires persistence in the face of obstacles.
Innovation	Job requires creativity and alternative thinking to develop new ideas for and answers to work-related problems.
Leadership	Job requires a willingness to lead, take charge, and offer opinions and direction.
Analytical Thinking	Job requires analyzing information and using logic to address work-related issues and problems.

Job Zone Component	Job Zone Component Definitions
Title	Job Zone Two: Some Preparation Needed
Overall Experience	Some previous work-related skill, knowledge, or experience may be helpful in these occupations, but usually is not needed. For example, a drywall installer might benefit from experience installing drywall, but an inexperienced person could still learn to be an installer with little difficulty.
Job Training	Employees in these occupations need anywhere from a few months to one year of working with experienced employees.
Job Zone Examples	These occupations often involve using your knowledge and skills to help others. Examples include drywall installers, fire inspectors, flight attendants, pharmacy technicians, salespersons (retail), and tellers.
SVP Range	(4.0 to < 6.0)
Education	These occupations usually require a high school diploma and may require some vocational training or job-related course work. In some cases, an associate's or bachelor's degree could be needed.

43-6014.00 - Secretaries, Except Legal, Medical, and Executive

Perform routine clerical and administrative functions such as drafting correspondence, scheduling appointments, organizing and maintaining paper and electronic files, or providing information to callers.

Tasks

1) Order and dispense supplies.

2) Prepare and mail checks.

3) Provide services to customers, such as order placement and account information.

4) Review work done by others to check for correct spelling and grammar, ensure that company format policies are followed, and recommend revisions.

5) Supervise other clerical staff, and provide training and orientation to new staff.

6) Coordinate conferences and meetings.

7) Mail newsletters, promotional material, and other information.

8) Operate office equipment such as fax machines, copiers, and phone systems, and use computers for spreadsheet, word processing, database management, and other applications.

9) Complete forms in accordance with company procedures.

10) Operate electronic mail systems and coordinate the flow of information both internally and with other organizations.

11) Arrange conferences, meetings, and travel reservations for office personnel.

12) Answer telephones and give information to callers, take messages, or transfer calls to appropriate individuals.

13) Maintain scheduling and event calendars.

14) Locate and attach appropriate files to incoming correspondence requiring replies.

15) Greet visitors and callers, handle their inquiries, and direct them to the appropriate persons according to their needs.

16) Take dictation in shorthand or by machine, and transcribe information.

17) Collect and disburse funds from cash accounts, and keep records of collections and disbursements.

18) Open, read, route, and distribute incoming mail and other material, and prepare answers to routine letters.

19) Schedule and confirm appointments for clients, customers, or supervisors.

20) Manage projects, and contribute to committee and team work.

21) Conduct searches to find needed information, using such sources as the Internet.

22) Make copies of correspondence and other printed material.

23) Establish work procedures and schedules, and keep track of the daily work of clerical

staff.

24) Compose, type, and distribute meeting notes, routine correspondence, and reports.

25) Learn to operate new office technologies as they are developed and implemented.

43-9011.00 - Computer Operators

Monitor and control electronic computer and peripheral electronic data processing equipment to process business, scientific, engineering, and other data according to operating instructions. May enter commands at a computer terminal and set controls on computer and peripheral devices. Monitor and respond to operating and error messages.

Tasks

1) Respond to program error messages by finding and correcting problems or terminating the program.

2) Retrieve, separate and sort program output as needed, and send data to specified users.

3) Load peripheral equipment with selected materials for operating runs, or oversee loading of peripheral equipment by peripheral equipment operators.

4) Read job set-up instructions to determine equipment to be used, order of use, material such as disks and paper to be loaded, and control settings.

5) Record information such as computer operating time, problems that occurred, and actions taken.

6) Answer telephone calls to assist computer users encountering problems.

7) Oversee the operation of computer hardware systems, including coordinating and scheduling the use of computer terminals and networks to ensure efficient use.

8) Monitor the system for equipment failure or errors in performance.

9) Type command on keyboard to transfer encoded data from memory unit to magnetic tape and assist in labeling, classifying, cataloging and maintaining tapes.

10) Operate spreadsheet programs and other types of software to load and manipulate data and to produce reports.

11) Help programmers and systems analysts test and debug new programs.

12) Operate encoding machine to trace coordinates on documents such as maps or drawings, and to encode document points into computer.

13) Clear equipment at end of operating run and review schedule to determine next assignment.

14) Supervise and train peripheral equipment operators and computer operator trainees.

15) Enter commands, using computer terminal, and activate controls on computer and peripheral equipment to integrate and operate equipment.

43-9022.00 - Word Processors and Typists

Use word processor/computer or typewriter to type letters, reports, forms, or other material from rough draft, corrected copy, or voice recording. May perform other clerical duties as assigned.

Tasks

1) Perform other clerical duties such as answering telephone, sorting and distributing mail, running errands or sending faxes.

2) Type correspondence, reports, text and other written material from rough drafts, corrected copies, voice recordings, dictation or previous versions, using a computer, word processor, or typewriter.

3) Address envelopes or prepare envelope labels, using typewriter or computer.

4) Adjust settings for format, page layout, line spacing, and other style requirements.

5) File and store completed documents on computer hard drive or disk, and/or maintain a computer filing system to store, retrieve, update and delete documents.

6) Collate pages of reports and other documents prepared.

7) Check completed work for spelling, grammar, punctuation, and format.

8) Operate and resupply printers and computers, changing print wheels or fluid cartridges, adding paper, and loading blank tapes, cards, or disks into equipment.

9) Electronically sort and compile text and numerical data, retrieving, updating, and merging documents as required.

10) Reformat documents, moving paragraphs and/or columns.

11) Gather, register, and arrange the material to be typed, following instructions.

12) Search for specific sets of stored, typed characters in order to make changes.

13) Compute and verify totals on report forms, requisitions, or bills, using adding machine or calculator.

14) Keep records of work performed.

15) Transmit work electronically to other locations.

16) Work with technical material, preparing statistical reports, planning and typing statistical tables, and combining and rearranging material from different sources.

17) Use data entry devices, such as optical scanners, to input data into computers for revision or editing.

18) Transcribe stenotyped notes of court proceedings.

Knowledge	Knowledge Definitions
Clerical	Knowledge of administrative and clerical procedures and systems such as word processing, managing files and records, stenography and transcription, designing forms, and other office procedures and terminology.
English Language	Knowledge of the structure and content of the English language including the meaning and spelling of words, rules of composition, and grammar.
Customer and Personal Service	Knowledge of principles and processes for providing customer and personal services. This includes customer needs assessment, meeting quality standards for services, and evaluation of customer satisfaction.
Computers and Electronics	Knowledge of circuit boards, processors, chips, electronic equipment, and computer hardware and software, including applications and programming.
Administration and Management	Knowledge of business and management principles involved in strategic planning, resource allocation, human resources modeling, leadership technique, production methods, and coordination of people and resources.
Mathematics	Knowledge of arithmetic, algebra, geometry, calculus, statistics, and their applications.
Sales and Marketing	Knowledge of principles and methods for showing, promoting, and selling products or services. This includes marketing strategy and tactics, product demonstration, sales techniques, and sales control systems.
Economics and Accounting	Knowledge of economic and accounting principles and practices, the financial markets, banking and the analysis and reporting of financial data.
Personnel and Human Resources	Knowledge of principles and procedures for personnel recruitment, selection, training, compensation and benefits, labor relations and negotiation, and personnel information systems.
Psychology	Knowledge of human behavior and performance; individual differences in ability, personality, and interests; learning and motivation; psychological research methods; and the assessment and treatment of behavioral and affective disorders.
Law and Government	Knowledge of laws, legal codes, court procedures, precedents, government regulations, executive orders, agency rules, and the democratic political process.
Production and Processing	Knowledge of raw materials, production processes, quality control, costs, and other techniques for maximizing the effective manufacture and distribution of goods.
Communications and Media	Knowledge of media production, communication, and dissemination techniques and methods. This includes alternative ways to inform and entertain via written, oral, and visual media.
Telecommunications	Knowledge of transmission, broadcasting, switching, control, and operation of telecommunications systems.
Transportation	Knowledge of principles and methods for moving people or goods by air, rail, sea, or road, including the relative costs and benefits.
Education and Training	Knowledge of principles and methods for curriculum and training design, teaching and instruction for individuals and groups, and the measurement of training effects.
Public Safety and Security	Knowledge of relevant equipment, policies, procedures, and strategies to promote effective local, state, or national security operations for the protection of people, data, property, and institutions.
Therapy and Counseling	Knowledge of principles, methods, and procedures for diagnosis, treatment, and rehabilitation of physical and mental dysfunctions, and for career counseling and guidance.
Foreign Language	Knowledge of the structure and content of a foreign (non-English) language including the meaning and spelling of words, rules of composition and grammar, and pronunciation.
Philosophy and Theology	Knowledge of different philosophical systems and religions. This includes their basic principles, values, ethics, ways of thinking, customs, practices, and their impact on human culture.
Geography	Knowledge of principles and methods for describing the features of land, sea, and air masses, including their physical characteristics, locations, interrelationships, and distribution of plant, animal, and human life.
History and Archeology	Knowledge of historical events and their causes, indicators, and effects on civilizations and cultures.

Sociology and Anthropology	Knowledge of group behavior and dynamics, societal trends and influences, human migrations, ethnicity, cultures and their history and origins.
Mechanical	Knowledge of machines and tools, including their designs, uses, repair, and maintenance.
Engineering and Technology	Knowledge of the practical application of engineering science and technology. This includes applying principles, techniques, procedures, and equipment to the design and production of various goods and services.
Building and Construction	Knowledge of materials, methods, and the tools involved in the construction or repair of houses, buildings, or other structures such as highways and roads.
Medicine and Dentistry	Knowledge of the information and techniques needed to diagnose and treat human injuries, diseases, and deformities. This includes symptoms, treatment alternatives, drug properties and interactions, and preventive health-care measures.
Food Production	Knowledge of techniques and equipment for planting, growing, and harvesting food products (both plant and animal) for consumption, including storage/handling techniques.
Chemistry	Knowledge of the chemical composition, structure, and properties of substances and of the chemical processes and transformations that they undergo. This includes uses of chemicals and their interactions, danger signs, production techniques, and disposal methods.
Physics	Knowledge and prediction of physical principles, laws, their interrelationships, and applications to understanding fluid, material, and atmospheric dynamics, and mechanical, electrical, atomic and sub-atomic structures and processes.
Design	Knowledge of design techniques, tools, and principles involved in production of precision technical plans, blueprints, drawings, and models.
Biology	Knowledge of plant and animal organisms, their tissues, cells, functions, interdependencies, and interactions with each other and the environment.
Fine Arts	Knowledge of the theory and techniques required to compose, produce, and perform works of music, dance, visual arts, drama, and sculpture.

Skills	Skills Definitions
Writing	Communicating effectively in writing as appropriate for the needs of the audience.
Active Listening	Giving full attention to what other people are saying, taking time to understand the points being made, asking questions as appropriate, and not interrupting at inappropriate times.
Time Management	Managing one's own time and the time of others.
Reading Comprehension	Understanding written sentences and paragraphs in work related documents.
Speaking	Talking to others to convey information effectively.
Mathematics	Using mathematics to solve problems.
Critical Thinking	Using logic and reasoning to identify the strengths and weaknesses of alternative solutions, conclusions or approaches to problems.
Learning Strategies	Selecting and using training/instructional methods and procedures appropriate for the situation when learning or teaching new things.
Coordination	Adjusting actions in relation to others' actions.
Judgment and Decision Making	Considering the relative costs and benefits of potential actions to choose the most appropriate one.
Instructing	Teaching others how to do something.
Social Perceptiveness	Being aware of others' reactions and understanding why they react as they do.
Active Learning	Understanding the implications of new information for both current and future problem-solving and decision-making.
Service Orientation	Actively looking for ways to help people.
Troubleshooting	Determining causes of operating errors and deciding what to do about it.
Equipment Selection	Determining the kind of tools and equipment needed to do a job.
Complex Problem Solving	Identifying complex problems and reviewing related information to develop and evaluate options and implement solutions.
Negotiation	Bringing others together and trying to reconcile differences.
Operation Monitoring	Watching gauges, dials, or other indicators to make sure a machine is working properly.
Equipment Maintenance	Performing routine maintenance on equipment and determining when and what kind of maintenance is needed.
Monitoring	Monitoring/Assessing performance of yourself, other individuals, or organizations to make improvements or take corrective action.
Installation	Installing equipment, machines, wiring, or programs to meet specifications.
Persuasion	Persuading others to change their minds or behavior.
Systems Evaluation	Identifying measures or indicators of system performance and the actions needed to improve or correct performance, relative to the goals of the system.

Management of Financial Resources	Determining how money will be spent to get the work done, and accounting for these expenditures.
Systems Analysis	Determining how a system should work and how changes in conditions, operations, and the environment will affect outcomes.
Repairing	Repairing machines or systems using the needed tools.
Operation and Control	Controlling operations of equipment or systems.
Management of Personnel Resources	Motivating, developing, and directing people as they work, identifying the best people for the job.
Operations Analysis	Analyzing needs and product requirements to create a design.
Technology Design	Generating or adapting equipment and technology to serve user needs.
Programming	Writing computer programs for various purposes.
Quality Control Analysis	Conducting tests and inspections of products, services, or processes to evaluate quality or performance.
Management of Material Resources	Obtaining and seeing to the appropriate use of equipment, facilities, and materials needed to do certain work.
Science	Using scientific rules and methods to solve problems.

Ability	Ability Definitions
Near Vision	The ability to see details at close range (within a few feet of the observer).
Written Comprehension	The ability to read and understand information and ideas presented in writing.
Oral Comprehension	The ability to listen to and understand information and ideas presented through spoken words and sentences.
Speech Recognition	The ability to identify and understand the speech of another person.
Information Ordering	The ability to arrange things or actions in a certain order or pattern according to a specific rule or set of rules (e.g., patterns of numbers, letters, words, pictures, mathematical operations).
Speech Clarity	The ability to speak clearly so others can understand you.
Perceptual Speed	The ability to quickly and accurately compare similarities and differences among sets of letters, numbers, objects, pictures, or patterns. The things to be compared may be presented at the same time or one after the other. This ability also includes comparing a presented object with a remembered object.
Oral Expression	The ability to communicate information and ideas in speaking so others will understand.
Category Flexibility	The ability to generate or use different sets of rules for combining or grouping things in different ways.
Finger Dexterity	The ability to make precisely coordinated movements of the fingers of one or both hands to grasp, manipulate, or assemble very small objects.
Written Expression	The ability to communicate information and ideas in writing so others will understand.
Wrist-Finger Speed	The ability to make fast, simple, repeated movements of the fingers, hands, and wrists.
Problem Sensitivity	The ability to tell when something is wrong or is likely to go wrong. It does not involve solving the problem, only recognizing there is a problem.
Deductive Reasoning	The ability to apply general rules to specific problems to produce answers that make sense.
Selective Attention	The ability to concentrate on a task over a period of time without being distracted.
Time Sharing	The ability to shift back and forth between two or more activities or sources of information (such as speech, sounds, touch, or other sources).
Mathematical Reasoning	The ability to choose the right mathematical methods or formulas to solve a problem.
Inductive Reasoning	The ability to combine pieces of information to form general rules or conclusions (includes finding a relationship among seemingly unrelated events).
Visualization	The ability to imagine how something will look after it is moved around or when its parts are moved or rearranged.
Number Facility	The ability to add, subtract, multiply, or divide quickly and correctly.
Auditory Attention	The ability to focus on a single source of sound in the presence of other distracting sounds.
Flexibility of Closure	The ability to identify or detect a known pattern (a figure, object, word, or sound) that is hidden in other distracting material.
Fluency of Ideas	The ability to come up with a number of ideas about a topic (the number of ideas is important, not their quality, correctness, or creativity).
Originality	The ability to come up with unusual or clever ideas about a given topic or situation, or to develop creative ways to solve a problem.
Manual Dexterity	The ability to quickly move your hand, your hand together with your arm, or your two hands to grasp, manipulate, or assemble objects.
Memorization	The ability to remember information such as words, numbers, pictures, and procedures.
Visual Color Discrimination	The ability to match or detect differences between colors, including shades of color and brightness.

Far Vision	The ability to see details at a distance.
Speed of Closure	The ability to quickly make sense of, combine, and organize information into meaningful patterns.
Hearing Sensitivity	The ability to detect or tell the differences between sounds that vary in pitch and loudness.
Control Precision	The ability to quickly and repeatedly adjust the controls of a machine or a vehicle to exact positions.
Arm-Hand Steadiness	The ability to keep your hand and arm steady while moving your arm or while holding your arm and hand in one position.
Trunk Strength	The ability to use your abdominal and lower back muscles to support part of the body repeatedly or continuously over time without 'giving out' or fatiguing.
Multilimb Coordination	The ability to coordinate two or more limbs (for example, two arms, two legs, or one leg and one arm) while sitting, standing, or lying down. It does not involve performing the activities while the whole body is in motion.
Response Orientation	The ability to choose quickly between two or more movements in response to two or more different signals (lights, sounds, pictures). It includes the speed with which the correct response is started with the hand, foot, or other body part.
Reaction Time	The ability to quickly respond (with the hand, finger, or foot) to a signal (sound, light, picture) when it appears.
Speed of Limb Movement	The ability to quickly move the arms and legs.
Extent Flexibility	The ability to bend, stretch, twist, or reach with your body, arms, and/or legs.
Peripheral Vision	The ability to see objects or movement of objects to one's side when the eyes are looking ahead.
Gross Body Equilibrium	The ability to keep or regain your body balance or stay upright when in an unstable position.
Depth Perception	The ability to judge which of several objects is closer or farther away from you, or to judge the distance between you and an object.
Spatial Orientation	The ability to know your location in relation to the environment or to know where other objects are in relation to you.
Explosive Strength	The ability to use short bursts of muscle force to propel oneself (as in jumping or sprinting), or to throw an object.
Rate Control	The ability to time your movements or the movement of a piece of equipment in anticipation of changes in the speed and/or direction of a moving object or scene.
Static Strength	The ability to exert maximum muscle force to lift, push, pull, or carry objects.
Stamina	The ability to exert yourself physically over long periods of time without getting winded or out of breath.
Dynamic Flexibility	The ability to quickly and repeatedly bend, stretch, twist, or reach out with your body, arms, and/or legs.
Gross Body Coordination	The ability to coordinate the movement of your arms, legs, and torso together when the whole body is in motion.
Night Vision	The ability to see under low light conditions.
Sound Localization	The ability to tell the direction from which a sound originated.
Glare Sensitivity	The ability to see objects in the presence of glare or bright lighting.
Dynamic Strength	The ability to exert muscle force repeatedly or continuously over time. This involves muscular endurance and resistance to muscle fatigue.

Work_Activity	**Work_Activity Definitions**
Getting Information	Observing, receiving, and otherwise obtaining information from all relevant sources.
Interacting With Computers	Using computers and computer systems (including hardware and software) to program, write software, set up functions, enter data, or process information.
Communicating with Supervisors, Peers, or Subordin	Providing information to supervisors, co-workers, and subordinates by telephone, in written form, e-mail, or in person.
Performing Administrative Activities	Performing day-to-day administrative tasks such as maintaining information files and processing paperwork.
Establishing and Maintaining Interpersonal Relatio	Developing constructive and cooperative working relationships with others, and maintaining them over time.
Organizing, Planning, and Prioritizing Work	Developing specific goals and plans to prioritize, organize, and accomplish your work.
Processing Information	Compiling, coding, categorizing, calculating, tabulating, auditing, or verifying information or data.
Thinking Creatively	Developing, designing, or creating new applications, ideas, relationships, systems, or products, including artistic contributions.
Communicating with Persons Outside Organization	Communicating with people outside the organization, representing the organization to customers, the public, government, and other external sources. This information can be exchanged in person, in writing, or by telephone or e-mail.
Documenting/Recording Information	Entering, transcribing, recording, storing, or maintaining information in written or electronic/magnetic form.
Updating and Using Relevant Knowledge	Keeping up-to-date technically and applying new knowledge to your job.

Identifying Objects, Actions, and Events	Identifying information by categorizing, estimating, recognizing differences or similarities, and detecting changes in circumstances or events.
Scheduling Work and Activities	Scheduling events, programs, and activities, as well as the work of others.
Assisting and Caring for Others	Providing personal assistance, medical attention, emotional support, or other personal care to others such as coworkers, customers, or patients.
Making Decisions and Solving Problems	Analyzing information and evaluating results to choose the best solution and solve problems.
Performing for or Working Directly with the Public	Performing for people or dealing directly with the public. This includes serving customers in restaurants and stores, and receiving clients or guests.
Interpreting the Meaning of Information for Others	Translating or explaining what information means and how it can be used.
Developing and Building Teams	Encouraging and building mutual trust, respect, and cooperation among team members.
Judging the Qualities of Things, Services, or Peop	Assessing the value, importance, or quality of things or people.
Monitor Processes, Materials, or Surroundings	Monitoring and reviewing information from materials, events, or the environment, to detect or assess problems.
Coordinating the Work and Activities of Others	Getting members of a group to work together to accomplish tasks.
Developing Objectives and Strategies	Establishing long-range objectives and specifying the strategies and actions to achieve them.
Analyzing Data or Information	Identifying the underlying principles, reasons, or facts of information by breaking down information or data into separate parts.
Evaluating Information to Determine Compliance wit	Using relevant information and individual judgment to determine whether events or processes comply with laws, regulations, or standards.
Resolving Conflicts and Negotiating with Others	Handling complaints, settling disputes, and resolving grievances and conflicts, or otherwise negotiating with others.
Coaching and Developing Others	Identifying the developmental needs of others and coaching, mentoring, or otherwise helping others to improve their knowledge or skills.
Training and Teaching Others	Identifying the educational needs of others, developing formal educational or training programs or classes, and teaching or instructing others.
Inspecting Equipment, Structures, or Material	Inspecting equipment, structures, or materials to identify the cause of errors or other problems or defects.
Monitoring and Controlling Resources	Monitoring and controlling resources and overseeing the spending of money.
Handling and Moving Objects	Using hands and arms in handling, installing, positioning, and moving materials, and manipulating things.
Estimating the Quantifiable Characteristics of Pro	Estimating sizes, distances, and quantities; or determining time, costs, resources, or materials needed to perform a work activity.
Provide Consultation and Advice to Others	Providing guidance and expert advice to management or other groups on technical, systems-, or process-related topics.
Performing General Physical Activities	Performing physical activities that require considerable use of your arms and legs and moving your whole body, such as climbing, lifting, balancing, walking, stooping, and handling of materials.
Guiding, Directing, and Motivating Subordinates	Providing guidance and direction to subordinates, including setting performance standards and monitoring performance.
Controlling Machines and Processes	Using either control mechanisms or direct physical activity to operate machines or processes (not including computers or vehicles).
Repairing and Maintaining Electronic Equipment	Servicing, repairing, calibrating, regulating, fine-tuning, or testing machines, devices, and equipment that operate primarily on the basis of electrical or electronic (not mechanical) principles.
Staffing Organizational Units	Recruiting, interviewing, selecting, hiring, and promoting employees in an organization.
Operating Vehicles, Mechanized Devices, or Equipme	Running, maneuvering, navigating, or driving vehicles or mechanized equipment, such as forklifts, passenger vehicles, aircraft, or water craft.
Selling or Influencing Others	Convincing others to buy merchandise/goods or to otherwise change their minds or actions.
Repairing and Maintaining Mechanical Equipment	Servicing, repairing, adjusting, and testing machines, devices, moving parts, and equipment that operate primarily on the basis of mechanical (not electronic) principles.
Drafting, Laying Out, and Specifying Technical Dev	Providing documentation, detailed instructions, drawings, or specifications to tell others about how devices, parts, equipment, or structures are to be fabricated, constructed, assembled, modified, maintained, or used.

Work_Content	**Work_Content Definitions**
Face-to-Face Discussions	How often do you have to have face-to-face discussions with individuals or teams in this job?
Spend Time Sitting	How much does this job require sitting?
Importance of Being Exact or Accurate	How important is being very exact or highly accurate in performing this job?

Telephone	How often do you have telephone conversations in this job?
Structured versus Unstructured Work	To what extent is this job structured for the worker, rather than allowing the worker to determine tasks, priorities, and goals?
Indoors, Environmentally Controlled	How often does this job require working indoors in environmentally controlled conditions?
Letters and Memos	How often does the job require written letters and memos?
Work With Work Group or Team	How important is it to work with others in a group or team in this job?
Contact With Others	How much does this job require the worker to be in contact with others (face-to-face, by telephone, or otherwise) in order to perform it?
Electronic Mail	How often do you use electronic mail in this job?
Freedom to Make Decisions	How much decision making freedom, without supervision, does the job offer?
Time Pressure	How often does this job require the worker to meet strict deadlines?
Importance of Repeating Same Tasks	How important is repeating the same physical activities (e.g., key entry) or mental activities (e.g., checking entries in a ledger) over and over, without stopping, to performing this job?
Deal With External Customers	How important is it to work with external customers or the public in this job?
Coordinate or Lead Others	How important is it to coordinate or lead others in accomplishing work activities in this job?
Impact of Decisions on Co-workers or Company Resul	How do the decisions an employee makes impact the results of co-workers, clients or the company?
Frequency of Decision Making	How frequently is the worker required to make decisions that affect other people, the financial resources, and/or the image and reputation of the organization?
Physical Proximity	To what extent does this job require the worker to perform job tasks in close physical proximity to other people?
Level of Competition	To what extent does this job require the worker to compete or to be aware of competitive pressures?
Frequency of Conflict Situations	How often are there conflict situations the employee has to face in this job?
Degree of Automation	How automated is the job?
Spend Time Using Your Hands to Handle, Control, or	How much does this job require using your hands to handle, control, or feel objects, tools or controls?
Sounds, Noise Levels Are Distracting or Uncomforta	How often does this job require working exposed to sounds and noise levels that are distracting or uncomfortable?
Spend Time Making Repetitive Motions	How much does this job require making repetitive motions?
Responsibility for Outcomes and Results	How responsible is the worker for work outcomes and results of other workers?
Deal With Unpleasant or Angry People	How frequently does the worker have to deal with unpleasant, angry, or discourteous individuals as part of the job requirements?
Consequence of Error	How serious would the result usually be if the worker made a mistake that was not readily correctable?
Spend Time Standing	How much does this job require standing?
Pace Determined by Speed of Equipment	How important is it to this job that the pace is determined by the speed of equipment or machinery? (This does not refer to keeping busy at all times on this job.)
Spend Time Walking and Running	How much does this job require walking and running?
Public Speaking	How often do you have to perform public speaking in this job?
Responsible for Others' Health and Safety	How much responsibility is there for the health and safety of others in this job?
Spend Time Bending or Twisting the Body	How much does this job require bending or twisting your body?
Exposed to Contaminants	How often does this job require working exposed to contaminants (such as pollutants, gases, dust or odors)?
Cramped Work Space, Awkward Positions	How often does this job require working in cramped work spaces that requires getting into awkward positions?
Very Hot or Cold Temperatures	How often does this job require working in very hot (above 90 F degrees) or very cold (below 32 F degrees) temperatures?
Outdoors, Exposed to Weather	How often does this job require working outdoors, exposed to all weather conditions?
Indoors, Not Environmentally Controlled	How often does this job require working indoors in non-controlled environmental conditions (e.g., warehouse without heat)?
Deal With Physically Aggressive People	How frequently does this job require the worker to deal with physical aggression of violent individuals?
Extremely Bright or Inadequate Lighting	How often does this job require working in extremely bright or inadequate lighting conditions?
In an Enclosed Vehicle or Equipment	How often does this job require working in a closed vehicle or equipment (e.g., car)?
Exposed to Disease or Infections	How often does this job require exposure to disease/infections?
In an Open Vehicle or Equipment	How often does this job require working in an open vehicle or equipment (e.g., tractor)?
Spend Time Keeping or Regaining Balance	How much does this job require keeping or regaining your balance?
Spend Time Kneeling, Crouching, Stooping, or Crawl	How much does this job require kneeling, crouching, stooping or crawling?
Exposed to Radiation	How often does this job require exposure to radiation?
Exposed to Minor Burns, Cuts, Bites, or Stings	How often does this job require exposure to minor burns, cuts, bites, or stings?
Spend Time Climbing Ladders, Scaffolds, or Poles	How much does this job require climbing ladders, scaffolds, or poles?
Wear Common Protective or Safety Equipment such as	How much does this job require wearing common protective or safety equipment such as safety shoes, glasses, gloves, hard hats or live jackets?
Exposed to Hazardous Conditions	How often does this job require exposure to hazardous conditions?
Exposed to High Places	How often does this job require exposure to high places?
Exposed to Whole Body Vibration	How often does this job require exposure to whole body vibration (e.g., operate a jackhammer)?
Outdoors, Under Cover	How often does this job require working outdoors, under cover (e.g., structure with roof but no walls)?
Exposed to Hazardous Equipment	How often does this job require exposure to hazardous equipment?
Wear Specialized Protective or Safety Equipment su	How much does this job require wearing specialized protective or safety equipment such as breathing apparatus, safety harness, full protection suits, or radiation protection?

Work_Styles

Work_Styles	Work_Styles Definitions
Attention to Detail	Job requires being careful about detail and thorough in completing work tasks.
Integrity	Job requires being honest and ethical.
Dependability	Job requires being reliable, responsible, and dependable, and fulfilling obligations.
Cooperation	Job requires being pleasant with others on the job and displaying a good-natured, cooperative attitude.
Concern for Others	Job requires being sensitive to others' needs and feelings and being understanding and helpful on the job.
Self Control	Job requires maintaining composure, keeping emotions in check, controlling anger, and avoiding aggressive behavior, even in very difficult situations.
Social Orientation	Job requires preferring to work with others rather than alone, and being personally connected with others on the job.
Initiative	Job requires a willingness to take on responsibilities and challenges.
Independence	Job requires developing one's own ways of doing things, guiding oneself with little or no supervision, and depending on oneself to get things done.
Achievement/Effort	Job requires establishing and maintaining personally challenging achievement goals and exerting effort toward mastering tasks.
Persistence	Job requires persistence in the face of obstacles.
Adaptability/Flexibility	Job requires being open to change (positive or negative) and to considerable variety in the workplace.
Stress Tolerance	Job requires accepting criticism and dealing calmly and effectively with high stress situations.
Innovation	Job requires creativity and alternative thinking to develop new ideas for and answers to work-related problems.
Analytical Thinking	Job requires analyzing information and using logic to address work-related issues and problems.
Leadership	Job requires a willingness to lead, take charge, and offer opinions and direction.

Job Zone Component

Job Zone Component	Job Zone Component Definitions
Title	Job Zone Two: Some Preparation Needed
Overall Experience	Some previous work-related skill, knowledge, or experience may be helpful in these occupations, but usually is not needed. For example, a drywall installer might benefit from experience installing drywall, but an inexperienced person could still learn to be an installer with little difficulty.
Job Training	Employees in these occupations need anywhere from a few months to one year of working with experienced employees.
Job Zone Examples	These occupations often involve using your knowledge and skills to help others. Examples include drywall installers, fire inspectors, flight attendants, pharmacy technicians, salespersons (retail), and tellers.
SVP Range	(4.0 to < 6.0)
Education	These occupations usually require a high school diploma and may require some vocational training or job-related course work. In some cases, an associate's or bachelor's degree could be needed.

43-9031.00 - Desktop Publishers

Format typescript and graphic elements using computer software to produce publication-ready material.

Tasks

1) Enter digitized data into electronic prepress system computer memory, using scanner, camera, keyboard, or mouse.

2) View monitors for visual representation of work in progress and for instructions and feedback throughout process, making modifications as necessary.

3) Transmit, deliver or mail publication master to printer for production into film and plates.

4) Study layout or other design instructions to determine work to be done and sequence of operations.

5) Select number of colors and determine color separations.

6) Prepare sample layouts for approval, using computer software.

7) Position text and art elements from a variety of databases in a visually appealing way in order to design print or web pages, using knowledge of type styles and size and layout patterns.

8) Convert various types of files for printing or for the Internet, using computer software.

9) Operate desktop publishing software and equipment to design, lay out, and produce camera-ready copy.

10) Import text and art elements such as electronic clip-art or electronic files from photographs that have been scanned or produced with a digital camera, using computer software.

11) Create special effects such as vignettes, mosaics, and image combining, and add elements such as sound and animation to electronic publications.

12) Enter data, such as coordinates of images and color specifications, into system to retouch and make color corrections.

13) Edit graphics and photos using pixel or bitmap editing, airbrushing, masking, or image retouching.

14) Check preliminary and final proofs for errors and make necessary corrections.

15) Collaborate with graphic artists, editors and writers to produce master copies according to design specifications.

16) Store copies of publications on paper, magnetic tape, film or diskette

17) Load floppy disks or tapes containing information into system.

43-9041.01 - Insurance Claims Clerks

Obtain information from insured or designated persons for purpose of settling claim with insurance carrier.

Tasks

1) Contact insured or other involved persons to obtain missing information.

2) Prepare and review insurance-claim forms and related documents for completeness.

3) Provide customer service, such as giving limited instructions on how to proceed with claims or providing referrals to auto repair facilities or local contractors.

4) Apply insurance rating systems.

5) Calculate amount of claim.

6) Review insurance policy to determine coverage.

7) Transmit claims for payment or further investigation.

8) Pay small claims.

9) Organize and work with detailed office or warehouse records, using computers to enter, access, search and retrieve data.

43-9041.02 - Insurance Policy Processing Clerks

Process applications for, changes to, reinstatement of, and cancellation of insurance policies. Duties include reviewing insurance applications to ensure that all questions have been answered, compiling data on insurance policy changes, changing policy records to conform to insured party's specifications, compiling data on lapsed insurance policies to determine automatic reinstatement according to company policies, canceling insurance policies as requested by agents, and verifying the accuracy of insurance company records.

Tasks

1) Examine letters from policyholders or agents, original insurance applications, and other company documents to determine if changes are needed and effects of changes.

2) Process and record new insurance policies and claims.

3) Modify, update, and process existing policies and claims to reflect any change in beneficiary, amount of coverage, or type of insurance.

4) Organize and work with detailed office or warehouse records, maintaining files for each policyholder, including policies that are to be reinstated or cancelled.

5) Review and verify data, such as age, name, address, and principal sum and value of property on insurance applications and policies.

6) Notify insurance agent and accounting department of policy cancellation.

7) Transcribe data to worksheets and enter data into computer for use in preparing documents and adjusting accounts.

8) Collect initial premiums and issue receipts.

9) Calculate premiums, refunds, commissions, adjustments, and new reserve requirements, using insurance rate standards.

10) Interview clients and take their calls in order to provide customer service and obtain information on claims.

11) Compare information from application to criteria for policy reinstatement and approve reinstatement when criteria are met.

12) Compose business correspondence for supervisors, managers and professionals.

13) Obtain computer printout of policy cancellations or retrieve cancellation cards from file.

14) Process, prepare, and submit business or government forms, such as submitting applications for coverage to insurance carriers.

15) Check computations of interest accrued, premiums due, and settlement surrender on loan values.

Knowledge	Knowledge Definitions
Customer and Personal Service	Knowledge of principles and processes for providing customer and personal services. This includes customer needs assessment, meeting quality standards for services, and evaluation of customer satisfaction.
Clerical	Knowledge of administrative and clerical procedures and systems such as word processing, managing files and records, stenography and transcription, designing forms, and other office procedures and terminology.
English Language	Knowledge of the structure and content of the English language including the meaning and spelling of words, rules of composition, and grammar.
Computers and Electronics	Knowledge of circuit boards, processors, chips, electronic equipment, and computer hardware and software, including applications and programming.
Mathematics	Knowledge of arithmetic, algebra, geometry, calculus, statistics, and their applications.
Administration and Management	Knowledge of business and management principles involved in strategic planning, resource allocation, human resources modeling, leadership technique, production methods, and coordination of people and resources.
Sales and Marketing	Knowledge of principles and methods for showing, promoting, and selling products or services. This includes marketing strategy and tactics, product demonstration, sales techniques, and sales control systems.
Production and Processing	Knowledge of raw materials, production processes, quality control, costs, and other techniques for maximizing the effective manufacture and distribution of goods.
Economics and Accounting	Knowledge of economic and accounting principles and practices, the financial markets, banking and the analysis and reporting of financial data.
Communications and Media	Knowledge of media production, communication, and dissemination techniques and methods. This includes alternative ways to inform and entertain via written, oral, and visual media.
Telecommunications	Knowledge of transmission, broadcasting, switching, control, and operation of telecommunications systems.
Education and Training	Knowledge of principles and methods for curriculum and training design, teaching and instruction for individuals and groups, and the measurement of training effects.
Law and Government	Knowledge of laws, legal codes, court procedures, precedents, government regulations, executive orders, agency rules, and the democratic political process.
Personnel and Human Resources	Knowledge of principles and procedures for personnel recruitment, selection, training, compensation and benefits, labor relations and negotiation, and personnel information systems.
Public Safety and Security	Knowledge of relevant equipment, policies, procedures, and strategies to promote effective local, state, or national security operations for the protection of people, data, property, and institutions.
Transportation	Knowledge of principles and methods for moving people or goods by air, rail, sea, or road, including the relative costs and benefits.

Geography	Knowledge of principles and methods for describing the features of land, sea, and air masses, including their physical characteristics, locations, interrelationships, and distribution of plant, animal, and human life.
Psychology	Knowledge of human behavior and performance; individual differences in ability, personality, and interests; learning and motivation; psychological research methods; and the assessment and treatment of behavioral and affective disorders.
Engineering and Technology	Knowledge of the practical application of engineering science and technology. This includes applying principles, techniques, procedures, and equipment to the design and production of various goods and services.
Medicine and Dentistry	Knowledge of the information and techniques needed to diagnose and treat human injuries, diseases, and deformities. This includes symptoms, treatment alternatives, drug properties and interactions, and preventive health-care measures.
Foreign Language	Knowledge of the structure and content of a foreign (non-English) language including the meaning and spelling of words, rules of composition and grammar, and pronunciation.
Building and Construction	Knowledge of materials, methods, and the tools involved in the construction or repair of houses, buildings, or other structures such as highways and roads.
Philosophy and Theology	Knowledge of different philosophical systems and religions. This includes their basic principles, values, ethics, ways of thinking, customs, practices, and their impact on human culture.
Mechanical	Knowledge of machines and tools, including their designs, uses, repair, and maintenance.
Design	Knowledge of design techniques, tools, and principles involved in production of precision technical plans, blueprints, drawings, and models.
Sociology and Anthropology	Knowledge of group behavior and dynamics, societal trends and influences, human migrations, ethnicity, cultures and their history and origins.
Therapy and Counseling	Knowledge of principles, methods, and procedures for diagnosis, treatment, and rehabilitation of physical and mental dysfunctions, and for career counseling and guidance.
Chemistry	Knowledge of the chemical composition, structure, and properties of substances and of the chemical processes and transformations that they undergo. This includes uses of chemicals and their interactions, danger signs, production techniques, and disposal methods.
Biology	Knowledge of plant and animal organisms, their tissues, cells, functions, interdependencies, and interactions with each other and the environment.
Fine Arts	Knowledge of the theory and techniques required to compose, produce, and perform works of music, dance, visual arts, drama, and sculpture.
Food Production	Knowledge of techniques and equipment for planting, growing, and harvesting food products (both plant and animal) for consumption, including storage/handling techniques.
History and Archeology	Knowledge of historical events and their causes, indicators, and effects on civilizations and cultures.
Physics	Knowledge and prediction of physical principles, laws, their interrelationships, and applications to understanding fluid, material, and atmospheric dynamics, and mechanical, electrical, atomic and sub- atomic structures and processes.

Skills	Skills Definitions
Active Listening	Giving full attention to what other people are saying, taking time to understand the points being made, asking questions as appropriate, and not interrupting at inappropriate times.
Speaking	Talking to others to convey information effectively.
Reading Comprehension	Understanding written sentences and paragraphs in work related documents.
Critical Thinking	Using logic and reasoning to identify the strengths and weaknesses of alternative solutions, conclusions or approaches to problems.
Active Learning	Understanding the implications of new information for both current and future problem-solving and decision-making.
Mathematics	Using mathematics to solve problems.
Time Management	Managing one's own time and the time of others.
Complex Problem Solving	Identifying complex problems and reviewing related information to develop and evaluate options and implement solutions.
Coordination	Adjusting actions in relation to others' actions.
Service Orientation	Actively looking for ways to help people.
Writing	Communicating effectively in writing as appropriate for the needs of the audience.
Social Perceptiveness	Being aware of others' reactions and understanding why they react as they do.
Instructing	Teaching others how to do something.
Learning Strategies	Selecting and using training/instructional methods and procedures appropriate for the situation when learning or teaching new things.

Judgment and Decision Making	Considering the relative costs and benefits of potential actions to choose the most appropriate one.
Monitoring	Monitoring/Assessing performance of yourself, other individuals, or organizations to make improvements or take corrective action.
Persuasion	Persuading others to change their minds or behavior.
Negotiation	Bringing others together and trying to reconcile differences.
Quality Control Analysis	Conducting tests and inspections of products, services, or processes to evaluate quality or performance.
Management of Personnel Resources	Motivating, developing, and directing people as they work, identifying the best people for the job.
Troubleshooting	Determining causes of operating errors and deciding what to do about it.
Operations Analysis	Analyzing needs and product requirements to create a design.
Technology Design	Generating or adapting equipment and technology to serve user needs.
Equipment Selection	Determining the kind of tools and equipment needed to do a job.
Operation and Control	Controlling operations of equipment or systems.
Systems Evaluation	Identifying measures or indicators of system performance and the actions needed to improve or correct performance, relative to the goals of the system.
Equipment Maintenance	Performing routine maintenance on equipment and determining when and what kind of maintenance is needed.
Management of Material Resources	Obtaining and seeing to the appropriate use of equipment, facilities, and materials needed to do certain work.
Operation Monitoring	Watching gauges, dials, or other indicators to make sure a machine is working properly.
Science	Using scientific rules and methods to solve problems.
Systems Analysis	Determining how a system should work and how changes in conditions, operations, and the environment will affect outcomes.
Management of Financial Resources	Determining how money will be spent to get the work done, and accounting for these expenditures.
Repairing	Repairing machines or systems using the needed tools.
Installation	Installing equipment, machines, wiring, or programs to meet specifications.
Programming	Writing computer programs for various purposes.

Ability	Ability Definitions
Written Comprehension	The ability to read and understand information and ideas presented in writing.
Information Ordering	The ability to arrange things or actions in a certain order or pattern according to a specific rule or set of rules (e.g., patterns of numbers, letters, words, pictures, mathematical operations).
Speech Clarity	The ability to speak clearly so others can understand you.
Near Vision	The ability to see details at close range (within a few feet of the observer).
Problem Sensitivity	The ability to tell when something is wrong or is likely to go wrong. It does not involve solving the problem, only recognizing there is a problem.
Written Expression	The ability to communicate information and ideas in writing so others will understand.
Oral Comprehension	The ability to listen to and understand information and ideas presented through spoken words and sentences.
Speech Recognition	The ability to identify and understand the speech of another person.
Oral Expression	The ability to communicate information and ideas in speaking so others will understand.
Deductive Reasoning	The ability to apply general rules to specific problems to produce answers that make sense.
Inductive Reasoning	The ability to combine pieces of information to form general rules or conclusions (includes finding a relationship among seemingly unrelated events).
Selective Attention	The ability to concentrate on a task over a period of time without being distracted.
Category Flexibility	The ability to generate or use different sets of rules for combining or grouping things in different ways.
Finger Dexterity	The ability to make precisely coordinated movements of the fingers of one or both hands to grasp, manipulate, or assemble very small objects.
Number Facility	The ability to add, subtract, multiply, or divide quickly and correctly.
Mathematical Reasoning	The ability to choose the right mathematical methods or formulas to solve a problem.
Perceptual Speed	The ability to quickly and accurately compare similarities and differences among sets of letters, numbers, objects, pictures, or patterns. The things to be compared may be presented at the same time or one after the other. This ability also includes comparing a presented object with a remembered object.
Speed of Closure	The ability to quickly make sense of, combine, and organize information into meaningful patterns.
Flexibility of Closure	The ability to identify or detect a known pattern (a figure, object, word, or sound) that is hidden in other distracting material.

Time Sharing	The ability to shift back and forth between two or more activities or sources of information (such as speech, sounds, touch, or other sources).
Originality	The ability to come up with unusual or clever ideas about a given topic or situation, or to develop creative ways to solve a problem.
Memorization	The ability to remember information such as words, numbers, pictures, and procedures.
Fluency of Ideas	The ability to come up with a number of ideas about a topic (the number of ideas is important, not their q ality, correctness, or creativity).
Auditory Attention	The ability to focus on a single source of sound in the presence of other distracting sounds.
Far Vision	The ability to see details at a distance.
Visualization	The ability to imagine how something will look after it is moved around or when its parts are moved or rearranged.
Wrist-Finger Speed	The ability to make fast, simple, repeated movements of the fingers, hands, and wrists.
Hearing Sensitivity	The ability to detect or tell the differences between sounds that vary in pitch and loudness.
Trunk Strength	The ability to use your abdominal and lower back muscles to support part of the body repeatedly or continuously over time without 'giving out' or fatiguing.
Manual Dexterity	The ability to quickly move your hand, your hand together with your arm, or your two hands to grasp, manipulate, or assemble objects.
Visual Color Discrimination	The ability to match or detect differences between colors, including shades of color and brightness.
Reaction Time	The ability to quickly respond (with the hand, finger, or foot) to a signal (sound, light, picture) when it appears.
Multilimb Coordination	The ability to coordinate two or more limbs (for example, two arms, two legs, or one leg and one arm) while sitting, standing, or lying down. It does not involve performing the activities while the whole body is in motion.
Extent Flexibility	The ability to bend, stretch, twist, or reach with your body, arms, and/or legs.
Stamina	The ability to exert yourself physically over long periods of time without getting winded or out of breath.
Rate Control	The ability to time your movements or the movement of a piece of equipment in anticipation of changes in the speed and/or direction of a moving object or scene.
Dynamic Strength	The ability to exert muscle force repeatedly or continuously over time. This involves muscular endurance and resistance to muscle fatigue.
Explosive Strength	The ability to use short bursts of muscle force to propel oneself (as in jumping or sprinting), or to throw an object.
Static Strength	The ability to exert maximum muscle force to lift, push, pull, or carry objects.
Response Orientation	The ability to choose quickly between two or more movements in response to two or more different signals (lights, sounds, pictures). It includes the speed with which the correct response is started with the hand, foot, or other body part.
Gross Body Equilibrium	The ability to keep or regain your body balance or stay upright when in an unstable position.
Speed of Limb Movement	The ability to quickly move the arms and legs.
Sound Localization	The ability to tell the direction from which a sound originated.
Dynamic Flexibility	The ability to quickly and repeatedly bend, stretch, twist, or reach out with your body, arms, and/or legs.
Spatial Orientation	The ability to know your location in relation to the environment or to know where other objects are in relation to you.
Gross Body Coordination	The ability to coordinate the movement of your arms, legs, and torso together when the whole body is in motion.
Control Precision	The ability to quickly and repeatedly adjust the controls of a machine or a vehicle to exact positions.
Arm-Hand Steadiness	The ability to keep your hand and arm steady while moving your arm or while holding your arm and hand in one position.
Glare Sensitivity	The ability to see objects in the presence of glare or bright lighting.
Depth Perception	The ability to judge which of several objects is closer or farther away from you, or to judge the distance between you and an object.
Peripheral Vision	The ability to see objects or movement of objects to one's side when the eyes are looking ahead.
Night Vision	The ability to see objects under low light conditions.

Work_Activity	**Work_Activity Definitions**
Getting Information	Observing, receiving, and otherwise obtaining information from all relevant sources.
Interacting With Computers	Using computers and computer systems (including hardware and software) to program, write software, set up functions, enter data, or process information.
Communicating with Supervisors, Peers, or Subordin	Providing information to supervisors, co-workers, and subordinates by telephone, in written form, e-mail, or in person.

Updating and Using Relevant Knowledge	Keeping up-to-date technically and applying new knowledge to your job.
Organizing, Planning, and Prioritizing Work	Developing specific goals and plans to prioritize, organize, and accomplish your work.
Making Decisions and Solving Problems	Analyzing information and evaluating results to choose the best solution and solve problems.
Evaluating Information to Determine Compliance wit	Using relevant information and individual judgment to determine whether events or processes comply with laws, regulations, or standards.
Communicating with Persons Outside Organization	Communicating with people outside the organization, representing the organization to customers, the public, government, and other external sources. This information can be exchanged in person, in writing, or by telephone or e-mail.
Performing for or Working Directly with the Public	Performing for people or dealing directly with the public. This includes serving customers in restaurants and stores, and receiving clients or guests.
Processing Information	Compiling, coding, categorizing, calculating, tabulating, auditing, or verifying information or data.
Identifying Objects, Actions, and Events	Identifying information by categorizing, estimating, recognizing differences or similarities, and detecting changes in circumstances or events.
Analyzing Data or Information	Identifying the underlying principles, reasons, or facts of information by breaking down information or data into separate parts.
Establishing and Maintaining Interpersonal Relatio	Developing constructive and cooperative working relationships with others, and maintaining them over time.
Performing Administrative Activities	Performing day-to-day administrative tasks such as maintaining information files and processing paperwork.
Documenting/Recording Information	Entering, transcribing, recording, storing, or maintaining information in written or electronic/magnetic form.
Monitor Processes, Materials, or Surroundings	Monitoring and reviewing information from materials, events, or the environment, to detect or assess problems.
Resolving Conflicts and Negotiating with Others	Handling complaints, settling disputes, and resolving grievances and conflicts, or otherwise negotiating with others.
Selling or Influencing Others	Convincing others to buy merchandise/goods or to otherwise change their minds or actions.
Judging the Qualities of Things, Services, or Peop	Assessing the value, importance, or quality of things or people.
Developing Objectives and Strategies	Establishing long-range objectives and specifying the strategies and actions to achieve them.
Interpreting the Meaning of Information for Others	Translating or explaining what information means and how it can be used.
Thinking Creatively	Developing, designing, or creating new applications, ideas, relationships, systems, or products, including artistic contributions.
Assisting and Caring for Others	Providing personal assistance, medical attention, emotional support, or other personal care to others such as coworkers, customers, or patients.
Scheduling Work and Activities	Scheduling events, programs, and activities, as well as the work of others.
Performing General Physical Activities	Performing physical activities that require considerable use of your arms and legs and moving your whole body, such as climbing, lifting, balancing, walking, stooping, and handling of materials.
Provide Consultation and Advice to Others	Providing guidance and expert advice to management or other groups on technical, systems-, or process-related topics.
Handling and Moving Objects	Using hands and arms in handling, installing, positioning, and moving materials, and manipulating things.
Estimating the Quantifiable Characteristics of Pro	Estimating sizes, distances, and quantities; or determining time, costs, resources, or materials needed to perform a work activity.
Coordinating the Work and Activities of Others	Getting members of a group to work together to accomplish tasks.
Training and Teaching Others	Identifying the educational needs of others, developing formal educational or training programs or classes, and teaching or instructing others.
Guiding, Directing, and Motivating Subordinates	Providing guidance and direction to subordinates, including setting performance standards and monitoring performance.
Coaching and Developing Others	Identifying the developmental needs of others and coaching, mentoring, or otherwise helping others to improve their knowledge or skills.
Developing and Building Teams	Encouraging and building mutual trust, respect, and cooperation among team members.
Inspecting Equipment, Structures, or Material	Inspecting equipment, structures, or materials to identify the cause of errors or other problems or defects.
Controlling Machines and Processes	Using either control mechanisms or direct physical activity to operate machines or processes (not including computers or vehicles).
Operating Vehicles, Mechanized Devices, or Equipme	Running, maneuvering, navigating, or driving vehicles or mechanized equipment, such as forklifts, passenger vehicles, aircraft, or water craft.
Staffing Organizational Units	Recruiting, interviewing, selecting, hiring, and promoting employees in an organization.

Monitoring and Controlling Resources	Monitoring and controlling resources and overseeing the spending of money.
Drafting, Laying Out, and Specifying Technical Dev	Providing documentation, detailed instructions, drawings, or specifications to tell others about how devices, parts, equipment, or structures are to be fabricated, constructed, assembled, modified, maintained, or used.
Repairing and Maintaining Electronic Equipment	Servicing, repairing, calibrating, regulating, fine-tuning, or testing machines, devices, and equipment that operate primarily on the basis of electrical or electronic (not mechanical) principles.
Repairing and Maintaining Mechanical Equipment	Servicing, repairing, adjusting, and testing machines, devices, moving parts, and equipment that operate primarily on the basis of mechanical (not electronic) principles.

Work_Content	Work_Content Definitions
Importance of Being Exact or Accurate	How important is being very exact or highly accurate in performing this job?
Structured versus Unstructured Work	To what extent is this job structured for the worker, rather than allowing the worker to determine tasks, priorities, and goals?
Freedom to Make Decisions	How much decision making freedom, without supervision, does the job offer?
Telephone	How often do you have telephone conversations in this job?
Importance of Repeating Same Tasks	How important is repeating the same physical activities (e.g., key entry) or mental activities (e.g., checking entries in a ledger) over and over, without stopping, to performing this job?
Spend Time Sitting	How much does this job require sitting?
Face-to-Face Discussions	How often do you have to have face-to-face discussions with individuals or teams in this job?
Contact With Others	How much does this job require the worker to be in contact with others (face-to-face, by telephone, or otherwise) in order to perform it?
Time Pressure	How often does this job require the worker to meet strict deadlines?
Deal With External Customers	How important is it to work with external customers or the public in this job?
Frequency of Decision Making	How frequently is the worker required to make decisions that affect other people, the financial resources, and/or the image and reputation of the organization?
Electronic Mail	How often do you use electronic mail in this job?
Impact of Decisions on Co-workers or Company Resul	How do the decisions an employee makes impact the results of co-workers, clients or the company?
Letters and Memos	How often does the job require written letters and memos?
Work With Work Group or Team	How important is it to work with others in a group or team in this job?
Coordinate or Lead Others	How important is it to coordinate or lead others in accomplishing work activities in this job?
Degree of Automation	How automated is the job?
Deal With Unpleasant or Angry People	How frequently does the worker have to deal with unpleasant, angry, or discourteous individuals as part of the job requirements?
Spend Time Making Repetitive Motions	How much does this job require making repetitive motions?
Physical Proximity	To what extent does this job require the worker to perform job tasks in close physical proximity to other people?
Responsibility for Outcomes and Results	How responsible is the worker for work outcomes and results of other workers?
Indoors, Environmentally Controlled	How often does this job require working indoors in environmentally controlled conditions?
Frequency of Conflict Situations	How often are there conflict situations the employee has to face in this job?
Consequence of Error	How serious would the result usually be if the worker made a mistake that was not readily correctable?
Level of Competition	To what extent does this job require the worker to compete or to be aware of competitive pressures?
Spend Time Using Your Hands to Handle, Control, or	How much does this job require using your hands to handle, control, or feel objects, tools or controls?
Spend Time Standing	How much does this job require standing?
Sounds, Noise Levels Are Distracting or Uncomforta	How often does this job require working exposed to sounds and noise levels that are distracting or uncomfortable?
Responsible for Others' Health and Safety	How much responsibility is there for the health and safety of others in this job?
Spend Time Walking and Running	How much does this job require walking and running?
Deal With Physically Aggressive People	How frequently does this job require the worker to deal with physical aggression of violent individuals?
Pace Determined by Speed of Equipment	How important is it to this job that the pace is determined by the speed of equipment or machinery? (This does not refer to keeping busy at all times on this job.)
In an Enclosed Vehicle or Equipment	How often does this job require working in a closed vehicle or equipment (e.g., car)?
Extremely Bright or Inadequate Lighting	How often does this job require working in extremely bright or inadequate lighting conditions?

Exposed to Contaminants	How often does this job require working exposed to contaminants (such as pollutants, gases, dust or odors)?
Spend Time Bending or Twisting the Body	How much does this job require bending or twisting your body?
Public Speaking	How often do you have to perform public speaking in this job?
Very Hot or Cold Temperatures	How often does this job require working in very hot (above 90 F degrees) or very cold (below 32 F degrees) temperatures?
Cramped Work Space, Awkward Positions	How often does this job require working in cramped work spaces that requires getting into awkward positions?
Exposed to Disease or Infections	How often does this job require exposure to disease/infections?
Exposed to Minor Burns, Cuts, Bites, or Stings	How often does this job require exposure to minor burns, cuts, bites, or stings?
Spend Time Kneeling, Crouching, Stooping, or Crawl	How much does this job require kneeling, crouching, stooping, or crawling?
Spend Time Climbing Ladders, Scaffolds, or Poles	How much does this job require climbing ladders, scaffolds, or poles?
Spend Time Keeping or Regaining Balance	How much does this job require keeping or regaining your balance?
In an Open Vehicle or Equipment	How often does this job require working in an open vehicle or equipment (e.g., tractor)?
Exposed to High Places	How often does this job require exposure to high places?
Exposed to Hazardous Conditions	How often does this job require exposure to hazardous conditions?
Wear Specialized Protective or Safety Equipment su	How much does this job require wearing specialized protective or safety equipment such as breathing apparatus, safety harness, full protection suits, or radiation protection?
Wear Common Protective or Safety Equipment such as	How much does this job require wearing common protective or safety equipment such as safety shoes, glasses, gloves, hard hats or live jackets?
Exposed to Whole Body Vibration	How often does this job require exposure to whole body vibration (e.g., operate a jackhammer)?
Exposed to Radiation	How often does this job require exposure to radiation?
Outdoors, Exposed to Weather	How often does this job require working outdoors, exposed to all weather conditions?
Indoors, Not Environmentally Controlled	How often does this job require working indoors in non-controlled environmental conditions (e.g., warehouse without heat)?
Outdoors, Under Cover	How often does this job require working outdoors, under cover (e.g., structure with roof but no walls)?
Exposed to Hazardous Equipment	How often does this job require exposure to hazardous equipment?

Work_Styles	Work_Styles Definitions
Attention to Detail	Job requires being careful about detail and thorough in completing work tasks.
Integrity	Job requires being honest and ethical.
Cooperation	Job requires being pleasant with others on the job and displaying a good-natured, cooperative attitude.
Dependability	Job requires being reliable, responsible, and dependable, and fulfilling obligations.
Achievement/Effort	Job requires establishing and maintaining personally challenging achievement goals and exerting effort toward mastering tasks.
Initiative	Job requires a willingness to take on responsibilities and challenges.
Concern for Others	Job requires being sensitive to others' needs and feelings and being understanding and helpful on the job.
Stress Tolerance	Job requires accepting criticism and dealing calmly and effectively with high stress situations.
Self Control	Job requires maintaining composure, keeping emotions in check, controlling anger, and avoiding aggressive behavior, even in very difficult situations.
Adaptability/Flexibility	Job requires being open to change (positive or negative) and to considerable variety in the workplace.
Independence	Job requires developing one's own ways of doing things, guiding oneself with little or no supervision, and depending on oneself to get things done.
Social Orientation	Job requires preferring to work with others rather than alone, and being personally connected with others on the job.
Persistence	Job requires persistence in the face of obstacles.
Analytical Thinking	Job requires analyzing information and using logic to address work-related issues and problems.
Leadership	Job requires a willingness to lead, take charge, and offer opinions and direction.
Innovation	Job requires creativity and alternative thinking to develop new ideas for and answers to work-related problems.

Job Zone Component	Job Zone Component Definitions
Title	Job Zone Two: Some Preparation Needed

Overall Experience	Some previous work-related skill, knowledge. or experience may be helpful in these occupations. but usually is not needed. For example, a drywall installer might benefit from experience installing drywall, but an inexperienced person could still learn to be an installer with little difficulty.
Job Training	Employees in these occupations need anywhere from a few months to one year of working with experienced employees. These occupations often involve using your knowledge and skills to help others. Examples include drywall installers, fire inspectors, flight attendants, pharmacy technicians. salespersons (retail), and tellers.
Job Zone Examples	
SVP Range	(4.0 to < 6.0)
Education	These occupations usually require a high school diploma and may require some vocational training or job-related course work. In some cases, an associate's or bachelor's degree could be needed.

43-9061.00 - Office Clerks, General

Perform duties too varied and diverse to be classified in any specific office clerical occupation, requiring limited knowledge of office management systems and procedures. Clerical duties may be assigned in accordance with the office procedures of individual establishments and may include a combination of answering telephones, bookkeeping, typing or word processing, stenography, office machine operation, and filing.

Tasks

1) Answer telephones, direct calls and take messages.

2) Operate office machines, such as photocopiers and scanners, facsimile machines, voice mail systems and personal computers.

3) Compile, copy, sort, and file records of office activities, business transactions, and other activities.

4) Maintain and update filing, inventory, mailing, and database systems, either manually or using a computer.

5) Compute, record, and proofread data and other information, such as records or reports.

6) Open, sort and route incoming mail, answer correspondence, and prepare outgoing mail.

7) Deliver messages and run errands.

8) Inventory and order materials, supplies, and services.

9) Complete and mail bills, contracts, policies, invoices, or checks.

10) Collect, count, and disburse money, do basic bookkeeping and complete banking transactions.

11) Review files, records, and other documents to obtain information to respond to requests.

12) Complete work schedules, manage calendars and arrange appointments.

13) Type, format, proofread and edit correspondence and other documents, from notes or dictating machines, using computers or typewriters.

14) Train other staff members to perform work activities, such as using computer applications.

15) Troubleshoot problems involving office equipment, such as computer hardware and software.

16) Process and prepare documents, such as business or government forms and expense reports.

17) Prepare meeting agendas, attend meetings, and record and transcribe minutes.

18) Count, weigh, measure, and/or organize materials.

19) Monitor and direct the work of lower-level clerks.

20) Make travel arrangements for office personnel.

Knowledge	Knowledge Definitions
Customer and Personal Service	Knowledge of principles and processes for providing customer and personal services. This includes customer needs assessment, meeting quality standards for services, and evaluation of customer satisfaction.
Clerical	Knowledge of administrative and clerical procedures and systems such as word processing, managing files and records, stenography and transcription, designing forms, and other office procedures and terminology.
English Language	Knowledge of the structure and content of the English language including the meaning and spelling of words, rules of composition, and grammar.
Mathematics	Knowledge of arithmetic, algebra, geometry, calculus, statistics, and their applications.
Economics and Accounting	Knowledge of economic and accounting principles and practices, the financial markets, banking and the analysis and reporting of financial data.

Computers and Electronics	Knowledge of circuit boards, processors, chips, electronic equipment, and computer hardware and software, including applications and programming.
Administration and Management	Knowledge of business and management principles involved in strategic planning, resource allocation, human resources modeling, leadership technique, production methods, and coordination of people and resources.
Personnel and Human Resources	Knowledge of principles and procedures for personnel recruitment, selection, training, compensation and benefits. labor relations and negotiation, and personnel information systems.
Communications and Media	Knowledge of media production, communication, and dissemination techniques and methods. This includes alternative ways to inform and entertain via written, oral, and visual media.
Education and Training	Knowledge of principles and methods for curriculum and training design, teaching and instruction for individuals and groups, and the measurement of training effects.
Telecommunications	Knowledge of transmission, broadcasting, switching, control, and operation of telecommunications systems.
Law and Government	Knowledge of laws, legal codes, court procedures, precedents, government regulations, executive orders, agency rules, and the democratic political process.
Psychology	Knowledge of human behavior and performance; individual differences in ability, personality, and interests; learning and motivation; psychological research methods; and the assessment and treatment of behavioral and affective disorders.
Sales and Marketing	Knowledge of principles and methods for showing, promoting, and selling products or services. This includes marketing strategy and tactics, product demonstration, sales techniques, and sales control systems.
Public Safety and Security	Knowledge of relevant equipment, policies, procedures, and strategies to promote effective local, state, or national security operations for the protection of people, data, property, and institutions.
Transportation	Knowledge of principles and methods for moving people or goods by air, rail, sea, or road, including the relative costs and benefits.
Mechanical	Knowledge of machines and tools, including their designs, uses, repair, and maintenance.
Production and Processing	Knowledge of raw materials, production processes, quality control, costs, and other techniques for maximizing the effective manufacture and distribution of goods.
Chemistry	Knowledge of the chemical composition, structure, and properties of substances and of the chemical processes and transformations that they undergo. This includes uses of chemicals and their interactions, danger signs, production techniques, and disposal methods.
Foreign Language	Knowledge of the structure and content of a foreign (non-English) language including the meaning and spelling of words, rules of composition and grammar, and pronunciation.
Design	Knowledge of design techniques, tools, and principles involved in production of precision technical plans, blueprints, drawings, and models.
Geography	Knowledge of principles and methods for describing the features of land, sea, and air masses, including their physical characteristics, locations, interrelationships, and distribution of plant, animal, and human life.
Therapy and Counseling	Knowledge of principles, methods, and procedures for diagnosis, treatment, and rehabilitation of physical and mental dysfunctions, and for career counseling and guidance.
Philosophy and Theology	Knowledge of different philosophical systems and religions. This includes their basic principles, values, ethics, ways of thinking, customs, practices, and their impact on human culture.
Medicine and Dentistry	Knowledge of the information and techniques needed to diagnose and treat human injuries, diseases, and deformities. This includes symptoms, treatment alternatives, drug properties and interactions, and preventive health-care measures.
Sociology and Anthropology	Knowledge of group behavior and dynamics, societal trends and influences, human migrations, ethnicity, cultures and their history and origins.
Fine Arts	Knowledge of the theory and techniques required to compose, produce, and perform works of music, dance, visual arts, drama, and sculpture.
Physics	Knowledge and prediction of physical principles, laws, their interrelationships, and applications to understanding fluid, material, and atmospheric dynamics, and mechanical, electrical, atomic and sub- atomic structures and processes.
Building and Construction	Knowledge of materials, methods, and the tools involved in the construction or repair of houses, buildings, or other structures such as highways and roads.
History and Archeology	Knowledge of historical events and their causes, indicators, and effects on civilizations and cultures.
Engineering and Technology	Knowledge of the practical application of engineering science and technology. This includes applying principles, techniques, procedures, and equipment to the design and production of various goods and services.

Food Production	Knowledge of techniques and equipment for planting, growing, and harvesting food products (both plant and animal) for consumption, including storage/handling techniques.
Biology	Knowledge of plant and animal organisms, their tissues, cells, functions, interdependencies, and interactions with each other and the environment.

Skills	**Skills Definitions**
Active Listening	Giving full attention to what other people are saying, taking time to understand the points being made, asking questions as appropriate, and not interrupting at inappropriate times.
Reading Comprehension	Understanding written sentences and paragraphs in work related documents.
Speaking	Talking to others to convey information effectively.
Writing	Communicating effectively in writing as appropriate for the needs of the audience.
Social Perceptiveness	Being aware of others' reactions and understanding why they react as they do.
Mathematics	Using mathematics to solve problems.
Learning Strategies	Selecting and using training/instructional methods and procedures appropriate for the situation when learning or teaching new things.
Service Orientation	Actively looking for ways to help people.
Critical Thinking	Using logic and reasoning to identify the strengths and weaknesses of alternative solutions, conclusions or approaches to problems.
Time Management	Managing one's own time and the time of others.
Coordination	Adjusting actions in relation to others' actions.
Active Learning	Understanding the implications of new information for both current and future problem-solving and decision-making.
Instructing	Teaching others how to do something.
Judgment and Decision Making	Considering the relative costs and benefits of potential actions to choose the most appropriate one.
Monitoring	Monitoring/Assessing performance of yourself, other individuals, or organizations to make improvements or take corrective action.
Persuasion	Persuading others to change their minds or behavior.
Negotiation	Bringing others together and trying to reconcile differences.
Equipment Selection	Determining the kind of tools and equipment needed to do a job.
Operation and Control	Controlling operations of equipment or systems.
Complex Problem Solving	Identifying complex problems and reviewing related information to develop and evaluate options and implement solutions.
Management of Personnel Resources	Motivating, developing, and directing people as they work, identifying the best people for the job.
Troubleshooting	Determining causes of operating errors and deciding what to do about it.
Management of Financial Resources	Determining how money will be spent to get the work done, and accounting for these expenditures.
Operations Analysis	Analyzing needs and product requirements to create a design.
Quality Control Analysis	Conducting tests and inspections of products, services, or processes to evaluate quality or performance.
Management of Material Resources	Obtaining and seeing to the appropriate use of equipment, facilities, and materials needed to do certain work.
Technology Design	Generating or adapting equipment and technology to serve user needs.
Equipment Maintenance	Performing routine maintenance on equipment and determining when and what kind of maintenance is needed.
Systems Evaluation	Identifying measures or indicators of system performance and the actions needed to improve or correct performance, relative to the goals of the system.
Operation Monitoring	Watching gauges, dials, or other indicators to make sure a machine is working properly.
Systems Analysis	Determining how a system should work and how changes in conditions, operations, and the environment will affect outcomes.
Installation	Installing equipment, machines, wiring, or programs to meet specifications.
Repairing	Repairing machines or systems using the needed tools.
Science	Using scientific rules and methods to solve problems.
Programming	Writing computer programs for various purposes.

Ability	**Ability Definitions**
Oral Comprehension	The ability to listen to and understand information and ideas presented through spoken words and sentences.
Oral Expression	The ability to communicate information and ideas in speaking so others will understand.
Speech Recognition	The ability to identify and understand the speech of another person.
Speech Clarity	The ability to speak clearly so others can understand you.
Written Comprehension	The ability to read and understand information and ideas presented in writing.

Near Vision	The ability to see details at close range (within a few feet of the observer).
Information Ordering	The ability to arrange things or actions in a certain order or pattern according to a specific rule or set of rules (e.g., patterns of numbers, letters, words, pictures, mathematical operations).
Number Facility	The ability to add, subtract, multiply, or divide quickly and correctly.
Mathematical Reasoning	The ability to choose the right mathematical methods or formulas to solve a problem.
Selective Attention	The ability to concentrate on a task over a period of time without being distracted.
Perceptual Speed	The ability to quickly and accurately compare similarities and differences among sets of letters, numbers, objects, pictures, or patterns. The things to be compared may be presented at the same time or one after the other. This ability also includes comparing a presented object with a remembered object.
Problem Sensitivity	The ability to tell when something is wrong or is likely to go wrong. It does not involve solving the problem, only recognizing there is a problem.
Written Expression	The ability to communicate information and ideas in writing so others will understand.
Category Flexibility	The ability to generate or use different sets of rules for combining or grouping things in different ways.
Inductive Reasoning	The ability to combine pieces of information to form general rules or conclusions (includes finding a relationship among seemingly unrelated events).
Deductive Reasoning	The ability to apply general rules to specific problems to produce answers that make sense.
Finger Dexterity	The ability to make precisely coordinated movements of the fingers of one or both hands to grasp, manipulate, or assemble very small objects.
Time Sharing	The ability to shift back and forth between two or more activities or sources of information (such as speech, sounds, touch, or other sources).
Wrist-Finger Speed	The ability to make fast, simple, repeated movements of the fingers, hands, and wrists.
Manual Dexterity	The ability to quickly move your hand, your hand together with your arm, or your two hands to grasp, manipulate, or assemble objects.
Far Vision	The ability to see details at a distance.
Arm-Hand Steadiness	The ability to keep your hand and arm steady while moving your arm or while holding your arm and hand in one position.
Flexibility of Closure	The ability to identify or detect a known pattern (a figure, object, word, or sound) that is hidden in other distracting material.
Speed of Closure	The ability to quickly make sense of, combine, and organize information into meaningful patterns.
Fluency of Ideas	The ability to come up with a number of ideas about a topic (the number of ideas is important, not their quality, correctness, or creativity).
Originality	The ability to come up with unusual or clever ideas about a given topic or situation, or to develop creative ways to solve a problem.
Visualization	The ability to imagine how something will look after it is moved around or when its parts are moved or rearranged.
Control Precision	The ability to quickly and repeatedly adjust the controls of a machine or a vehicle to exact positions.
Auditory Attention	The ability to focus on a single source of sound in the presence of other distracting sounds.
Memorization	The ability to remember information such as words, numbers, pictures, and procedures.
Visual Color Discrimination	The ability to match or detect differences between colors, including shades of color and brightness.
Hearing Sensitivity	The ability to detect or tell the differences between sounds that vary in pitch and loudness.
Trunk Strength	The ability to use your abdominal and lower back muscles to support part of the body repeatedly or continuously over time without 'giving out' or fatiguing.
Extent Flexibility	The ability to bend, stretch, twist, or reach with your body, arms, and/or legs.
Gross Body Coordination	The ability to coordinate the movement of your arms, legs, and torso together when the whole body is in motion.
Static Strength	The ability to exert maximum muscle force to lift, push, pull, or carry objects.
Depth Perception	The ability to judge which of several objects is closer or farther away from you, or to judge the distance between you and an object.
Multilimb Coordination	The ability to coordinate two or more limbs (for example, two arms, two legs, or one leg and one arm) while sitting, standing, or lying down. It does not involve performing the activities while the whole body is in motion.
Gross Body Equilibrium	The ability to keep or regain your body balance or stay upright when in an unstable position.
Dynamic Flexibility	The ability to quickly and repeatedly bend, stretch, twist, or reach out with your body, arms, and/or legs.

Spatial Orientation	The ability to know your location in relation to the environment or to know where other objects are in relation to you.
Dynamic Strength	The ability to exert muscle force repeatedly or continuously over time. This involves muscular endurance and resistance to muscle fatigue.
Reaction Time	The ability to quickly respond (with the hand, finger, or foot) to a signal (sound, light, picture) when it appears.
Speed of Limb Movement	The ability to quickly move the arms and legs.
Explosive Strength	The ability to use short bursts of muscle force to propel oneself (as in jumping or sprinting), or to throw an object.
Response Orientation	The ability to choose quickly between two or more movements in response to two or more different signals (lights, sounds, pictures). It includes the speed with which the correct response is started with the hand, foot, or other body part.
Glare Sensitivity	The ability to see objects in the presence of glare or bright lighting.
Sound Localization	The ability to tell the direction from which a sound originated.
Peripheral Vision	The ability to see objects or movement of objects to one's side when the eyes are looking ahead.
Night Vision	The ability to see under low light conditions.
Stamina	The ability to exert yourself physically over long periods of time without getting winded or out of breath.
Rate Control	The ability to time your movements or the movement of a piece of equipment in anticipation of changes in the speed and/or direction of a moving object or scene.

Work_Activity	Work_Activity Definitions
Interacting With Computers	Using computers and computer systems (including hardware and software) to program, write software, set up functions, enter data, or process information.
Getting Information	Observing, receiving, and otherwise obtaining information from all relevant sources.
Communicating with Supervisors, Peers, or Subordin	Providing information to supervisors, co-workers, and subordinates by telephone, in written form, e-mail, or in person.
Performing Administrative Activities	Performing day-to-day administrative tasks such as maintaining information files and processing paperwork.
Processing Information	Compiling, coding, categorizing, calculating, tabulating, auditing, or verifying information or data.
Establishing and Maintaining Interpersonal Relatio	Developing constructive and cooperative working relationships with others, and maintaining them over time.
Documenting/Recording Information	Entering, transcribing, recording, storing, or maintaining information in written or electronic/magnetic form.
Organizing, Planning, and Prioritizing Work	Developing specific goals and plans to prioritize, organize, and accomplish your work.
Performing for or Working Directly with the Public	Performing for people or dealing directly with the public. This includes serving customers in restaurants and stores, and receiving clients or guests.
Making Decisions and Solving Problems	Analyzing information and evaluating results to choose the best solution and solve problems.
Identifying Objects, Actions, and Events	Identifying information by categorizing, estimating, recognizing differences or similarities, and detecting changes in circumstances or events.
Communicating with Persons Outside Organization	Communicating with people outside the organization, representing the organization to customers, the public, government, and other external sources. This information can be exchanged in person, in writing, or by telephone or e-mail.
Updating and Using Relevant Knowledge	Keeping up-to-date technically and applying new knowledge to your job.
Monitor Processes, Materials, or Surroundings	Monitoring and reviewing information from materials, events, or the environment, to detect or assess problems.
Analyzing Data or Information	Identifying the underlying principles, reasons, or facts of information by breaking down information or data into separate parts.
Evaluating Information to Determine Compliance wit	Using relevant information and individual judgment to determine whether events or processes comply with laws, regulations, or standards.
Coordinating the Work and Activities of Others	Getting members of a group to work together to accomplish tasks.
Resolving Conflicts and Negotiating with Others	Handling complaints, settling disputes, and resolving grievances and conflicts, or otherwise negotiating with others.
Scheduling Work and Activities	Scheduling events, programs, and activities, as well as the work of others.
Assisting and Caring for Others	Providing personal assistance, medical attention, emotional support, or other personal care to others such as coworkers, customers, or patients.
Thinking Creatively	Developing, designing, or creating new applications, ideas, relationships, systems, or products, including artistic contributions.
Interpreting the Meaning of Information for Others	Translating or explaining what information means and how it can be used.

Training and Teaching Others	Identifying the educational needs of others, developing formal educational or training programs or classes, and teaching or instructing others.
Coaching and Developing Others	Identifying the developmental needs of others and coaching, mentoring, or otherwise helping others to improve their knowledge or skills.
Estimating the Quantifiable Characteristics of Pro	Estimating sizes, distances, and quantities; or determining time, costs, resources, or materials needed to perform a work activity.
Judging the Qualities of Things, Services, or Peop	Assessing the value, importance, or quality of things or people.
Developing and Building Teams	Encouraging and building mutual trust, respect, and cooperation among team members.
Inspecting Equipment, Structures, or Material	Inspecting equipment, structures, or materials to identify the cause of errors or other problems or defects.
Developing Objectives and Strategies	Establishing long-range objectives and specifying the strategies and actions to achieve them.
Provide Consultation and Advice to Others	Providing guidance and expert advice to management or other groups on technical, systems-, or process-related topics.
Guiding, Directing, and Motivating Subordinates	Providing guidance and direction to subordinates, including setting performance standards and monitoring performance.
Monitoring and Controlling Resources	Monitoring and controlling resources and overseeing the spending of money.
Handling and Moving Objects	Using hands and arms in handling, installing, positioning, and moving materials, and manipulating things.
Controlling Machines and Processes	Using either control mechanisms or direct physical activity to operate machines or processes (not including computers or vehicles).
Selling or Influencing Others	Convincing others to buy merchandise/goods or to otherwise change their minds or actions.
Performing General Physical Activities	Performing physical activities that require considerable use of your arms and legs and moving your whole body, such as climbing, lifting, balancing, walking, stooping, and handling of materials.
Staffing Organizational Units	Recruiting, interviewing, selecting, hiring, and promoting employees in an organization.
Repairing and Maintaining Electronic Equipment	Servicing, repairing, calibrating, regulating, fine-tuning, or testing machines, devices, and equipment that operate primarily on the basis of electrical or electronic (not mechanical) principles.
Operating Vehicles, Mechanized Devices, or Equipme	Running, maneuvering, navigating, or driving vehicles or mechanized equipment, such as forklifts, passenger vehicles, aircraft, or water craft.
Repairing and Maintaining Mechanical Equipment	Servicing, repairing, adjusting, and testing machines, devices, moving parts, and equipment that operate primarily on the basis of mechanical (not electronic) principles.
Drafting, Laying Out, and Specifying Technical Dev	Providing documentation, detailed instructions, drawings, or specifications to tell others about how devices, parts, equipment, or structures are to be fabricated, constructed, assembled, modified, maintained, or used.

Work_Content	Work_Content Definitions
Telephone	How often do you have telephone conversations in this job?
Contact With Others	How much does this job require the worker to be in contact with others (face-to-face, by telephone, or otherwise) in order to perform it?
Face-to-Face Discussions	How often do you have to have face-to-face discussions with individuals or teams in this job?
Importance of Being Exact or Accurate	How important is being very exact or highly accurate in performing this job?
Spend Time Sitting	How much does this job require sitting?
Structured versus Unstructured Work	To what extent is this job structured for the worker, rather than allowing the worker to determine tasks, priorities, and goals?
Importance of Repeating Same Tasks	How important is repeating the same physical activities (e.g., key entry) or mental activities (e.g., checking entries in a ledger) over and over, without stopping, to performing this job?
Indoors, Environmentally Controlled	How often does this job require working indoors in environmentally controlled conditions?
Electronic Mail	How often do you use electronic mail in this job?
Work With Work Group or Team	How important is it to work with others in a group or team in this job?
Deal With External Customers	How important is it to work with external customers or the public in this job?
Freedom to Make Decisions	How much decision making freedom, without supervision, does the job offer?
Impact of Decisions on Co-workers or Company Resul	How do the decisions an employee makes impact the results of co-workers, clients or the company?
Time Pressure	How often does this job require the worker to meet strict deadlines?
Frequency of Decision Making	How frequently is the worker required to make decisions that affect other people, the financial resources, and/or the image and reputation of the organization?

Deal With Unpleasant or Angry People	How frequently does the worker have to deal with unpleasant. angry, or discourteous individuals as part of the job requirements?
Letters and Memos	How often does the job require written letters and memos?
Physical Proximity	To what extent does this job require the worker to perform job tasks in close physical proximity to other people?
Spend Time Using Your Hands to Handle. Control, or	How much does this job require using your hands to handle. control, or feel objects, tools or controls?
Coordinate or Lead Others	How important is it to coordinate or lead others in accomplishing work activities in this job?
Frequency of Conflict Situations	How often are there conflict situations the employee has to face in this job?
Spend Time Making Repetitive Motions	How much does this job require making repetitive motions?
Responsibility for Outcomes and Results	How responsible is the worker for work outcomes and results of other workers?
Sounds, Noise Levels Are Distracting or Uncomforta	How often does this job require working exposed to sounds and noise levels that are distracting or uncomfortable?
Degree of Automation	How automated is the job?
Spend Time Standing	How much does this job require standing?
Consequence of Error	How serious would the result usually be if the worker made a mistake that was not readily correctable?
Level of Competition	To what extent does this job require the worker to compete or to be aware of competitive pressures?
Responsible for Others' Health and Safety	How much responsibility is there for the health and safety of others in this job?
Cramped Work Space, Awkward Positions	How often does this job require working in cramped work spaces that requires getting into awkward positions?
Spend Time Walking and Running	How much does this job require walking and running?
Pace Determined by Speed of Equipment	How important is it to this job that the pace is determined by the speed of equipment or machinery? (This does not refer to keeping busy at all times on this job.)
In an Enclosed Vehicle or Equipment	How often does this job require working in a closed vehicle or equipment (e.g., car)?
Spend Time Bending or Twisting the Body	How much does this job require bending or twisting your body?
Exposed to Disease or Infections	How often does this job require exposure to disease/infections?
Wear Common Protective or Safety Equipment such as	How much does this job require wearing common protective or safety equipment such as safety shoes, glasses, gloves, hard hats or live jackets?
Deal With Physically Aggressive People	How frequently does this job require the worker to deal with physical aggression of violent individuals?
Spend Time Kneeling, Crouching, Stooping, or Crawl	How much does this job require kneeling, crouching, stooping or crawling?
Exposed to Contaminants	How often does this job require working exposed to contaminants (such as pollutants, gases, dust or odors)?
Indoors, Not Environmentally Controlled	How often does this job require working indoors in non-controlled environmental conditions (e.g., warehouse without heat)?
Public Speaking	How often do you have to perform public speaking in this job?
Exposed to Minor Burns, Cuts, Bites, or Stings	How often does this job require exposure to minor burns, cuts, bites, or stings?
Spend Time Keeping or Regaining Balance	How much does this job require keeping or regaining your balance?
Exposed to Hazardous Equipment	How often does this job require exposure to hazardous equipment?
Extremely Bright or Inadequate Lighting	How often does this job require working in extremely bright or inadequate lighting conditions?
Exposed to Hazardous Conditions	How often does this job require exposure to hazardous conditions?
Outdoors, Exposed to Weather	How often does this job require working outdoors, exposed to all weather conditions?
Exposed to High Places	How often does this job require exposure to high places?
Wear Specialized Protective or Safety Equipment su	How much does this job require wearing specialized protective or safety equipment such as breathing apparatus, safety harness, full protection suits, or radiation protection?
Outdoors, Under Cover	How often does this job require working outdoors, under cover (e.g., structure with roof but no walls)?
Spend Time Climbing Ladders, Scaffolds, or Poles	How often does this job require climbing ladders, scaffolds, or poles?
Very Hot or Cold Temperatures	How often does this job require working in very hot (above 90 F degrees) or very cold (below 32 F degrees) temperatures?
Exposed to Radiation	How often does this job require exposure to radiation?
Exposed to Whole Body Vibration	How often does this job require exposure to whole body vibration (e.g., operate a jackhammer)?
In an Open Vehicle or Equipment	How often does this job require working in an open vehicle or equipment (e.g., tractor)?
Work_Styles	**Work_Styles Definitions**

Cooperation	Job requires being pleasant with others on the job and displaying a good-natured. cooperative attitude.
Dependability	Job requires being reliable, responsible, and dependable, and fulfilling obligations.
Integrity	Job requires being honest and ethical.
Attention to Detail	Job requires being careful about detail and thorough in completing work tasks.
Concern for Others	Job requires being sensitive to others' needs and feelings and being understanding and helpful on the job.
Independence	Job requires developing one's own ways of doing things, guiding oneself with little or no supervision, and depending on oneself to get things done.
Self Control	Job requires maintaining composure, keeping emotions in check, controlling anger, and avoiding aggressive behavior, even in very difficult situations.
Stress Tolerance	Job requires accepting criticism and dealing calmly and effectively with high stress situations.
Initiative	Job requires a willingness to take on responsibilities and challenges.
Social Orientation	Job requires preferring to work with others rather than alone, and being personally connected with others on the job.
Adaptability/Flexibility	Job requires being open to change (positive or negative) and to considerable variety in the workplace.
Persistence	Job requires persistence in the face of obstacles.
Leadership	Job requires a willingness to lead, take charge, and offer opinions and direction.
Achievement/Effort	Job requires establishing and maintaining personally challenging achievement goals and exerting effort toward mastering tasks.
Analytical Thinking	Job requires analyzing information and using logic to address work-related issues and problems.
Innovation	Job requires creativity and alternative thinking to develop new ideas for and answers to work-related problems.

Job Zone Component	**Job Zone Component Definitions**
Title	Job Zone Two: Some Preparation Needed
Overall Experience	Some previous work-related skill, knowledge, or experience may be helpful in these occupations, but usually is not needed. For example, a drywall installer might benefit from experience installing drywall, but an inexperienced person could still learn to be an installer with little difficulty.
Job Training	Employees in these occupations need anywhere from a few months to one year of working with experienced employees.
Job Zone Examples	These occupations often involve using your knowledge and skills to help others. Examples include drywall installers, fire inspectors, flight attendants, pharmacy technicians, salespersons (retail), and tellers.
SVP Range	(4.0 to < 6.0)
Education	These occupations usually require a high school diploma and may require some vocational training or job-related course work. In some cases, an associate's or bachelor's degree could be needed.

43-9081.00 - Proofreaders and Copy Markers

Read transcript or proof type setup to detect and mark for correction any grammatical, typographical, or compositional errors.

Tasks

1) Mark copy to indicate and correct errors in type, arrangement, grammar, punctuation, or spelling, using standard printers' marks.

2) Measure dimensions, spacing, and positioning of page elements (copy and illustrations) in order to verify conformance to specifications, using printer's ruler.

3) Correct or record omissions, errors, or inconsistencies found.

4) Consult reference books or secure aid of readers to check references with rules of grammar and composition.

5) Compare information or figures on one record against same data on other records, or with original copy, to detect errors.

6) Route proofs with marked corrections to authors, editors, typists, or typesetters for correction and/or reprinting.

7) Read proof sheets aloud, calling out punctuation marks and spelling unusual words and proper names.

43-9111.00 - Statistical Assistants

289

Compile and compute data according to statistical formulas for use in statistical studies. May perform actuarial computations and compile charts and graphs for use by actuaries. Includes actuarial clerks.

Tasks

1) Check source data in order to verify its completeness and accuracy.

2) Check survey responses for errors such as the use of pens instead of pencils, and set aside response forms that cannot be used.

3) Code data as necessary prior to computer entry, using lists of codes.

4) Compile reports, charts, and graphs that describe and interpret findings of analyses.

5) Compile statistics from source materials, such as production and sales records, quality-control and test records, time sheets, and survey sheets.

6) Compute and analyze data, using statistical formulas and computers or calculators.

7) Enter data into computers for use in analyses and reports.

8) File data and related information, and maintain and update databases.

9) Organize paperwork such as survey forms and reports for distribution and for analysis.

10) Discuss data presentation requirements with clients.

11) Participate in the publication of data and information.

12) Send out surveys.

13) Select statistical tests for analyzing data.

14) Feed response sheets through optical scanners that read responses and store data in a format that computers can read.

45-2021.00 - Animal Breeders

Breed animals, including cattle, goats, horses, sheep, swine, poultry, dogs, cats, or pet birds. Select and breed animals according to their genealogy, characteristics, and offspring. May require a knowledge of artificial insemination techniques and equipment use. May involve keeping records on heats, birth intervals, or pedigree.

Tasks

1) Prepare containers of semen for freezing and storage or shipment, placing them in dry ice or liquid nitrogen.

2) Adjust controls in order to maintain specific building temperatures required for animals' health and safety.

3) Confine roosters (pinioning) in order to collect semen in vial.

4) Examine animals in order to detect symptoms of illness or injury.

5) Examine semen microscopically in order to assess and record density and motility of gametes, and dilute semen with prescribed diluents according to formulas.

6) Kill animals, remove their pelts, and arrange for sale of pelts.

7) Package and label semen to be used for artificial insemination, recording information such as the date, source, quality, and concentration.

8) Clip or shear hair on animals.

9) Inject semen into hens' oviducts or through holes in egg shells.

10) Incubate eggs to induce hatching.

11) Record animal characteristics such as weights, growth patterns, and diets.

12) Milk cows and goats.

13) Treat minor injuries and ailments, and contact veterinarians in order to obtain treatment for animals with serious illnesses or injuries.

14) Perform procedures such as animal dehorning or castration.

15) Exhibit animals at shows.

16) Build hutches, pens, and fenced yards.

17) Brand, tattoo, or tag animals in order to allow animal identification.

18) Arrange for sale of animals and eggs to hospitals, research centers, pet shops, and food processing plants.

19) Select animals to be bred, and semen specimens to be used, according to knowledge of animals, genealogies, traits, and desired offspring characteristics.

20) Maintain logs of semen specimens used and animals bred.

21) Place vaccines in drinking water, inject vaccines, or dust air with vaccine powder, in order to protect animals from diseases.

22) Feed and water animals, and clean and disinfect pens, cages, yards, and hutches.

23) Observe animals in heat in order to detect approach of estrus, and exercise animals to induce or hasten estrus, if necessary.

24) Inject prepared animal semen into female animals for breeding purposes, by inserting nozzle of syringe into vagina and depressing syringe plunger.

25) Measure specified amounts of semen into calibrated syringes, and insert syringes into inseminating guns.

45-4011.00 - Forest and Conservation Workers

Under supervision, perform manual labor necessary to develop, maintain, or protect forest, forested areas, and woodlands through such activities as raising and transporting tree seedlings; combating insects, pests, and diseases harmful to trees; and building erosion and water control structures and leaching of forest soil. Includes forester aides, seedling pullers, and tree planters.

Tasks

1) Examine and grade trees according to standard charts, and staple color-coded grade tags to limbs.

2) Sort and separate tree seedlings, discarding substandard seedlings, according to standard charts and verbal instructions.

3) Select tree seedlings, prepare the ground, and plant the trees in reforestation areas, using manual planting tools.

4) Drag cut trees from cutting areas and load trees onto trucks.

5) Check equipment to ensure that it is operating properly.

6) Prune or shear tree tops and limbs in order to control growth, increase density, and improve shape.

7) Identify diseased or undesirable trees, and remove them, using power saws or hand saws.

8) Fight forest fires or perform prescribed burning tasks under the direction of fire suppression officers or forestry technicians.

9) Spray or inject vegetation with insecticides to kill insects and to protect against disease, and with herbicides to reduce competing vegetation.

10) Maintain tallies of trees examined and counted during tree marking and measuring efforts.

11) Explain and enforce regulations regarding camping, vehicle use, fires, use of building and sanitation.

12) Select and cut trees according to markings or sizes, types, and grades.

13) Sow and harvest cover crops such as alfalfa.

14) Confer with other workers to discuss issues such as safety, cutting heights, and work needs.

15) Maintain campsites and recreational areas, replenishing firewood and other supplies, and cleaning kitchens and restrooms.

16) Operate a skidder, bulldozer or other prime mover to pull a variety of scarification or site preparation equipment over areas to be regenerated.

17) Provide assistance to forest survey crews by clearing site-lines, holding measuring tools, and setting stakes.

18) Gather, package, and deliver forest products to buyers.

19) Thin and space trees, using power thinning saws.

20) Erect signs and fences, using posthole diggers, shovels, or other hand tools.

47-2021.00 - Brickmasons and Blockmasons

Lay and bind building materials, such as brick, structural tile, concrete block, cinder block, glass block, and terra-cotta block, with mortar and other substances to construct or repair walls, partitions, arches, sewers, and other structures.

Tasks

1) Interpret blueprints and drawings to determine specifications and to calculate the materials required.

2) Remove excess mortar with trowels and hand tools, and finish mortar joints with jointing tools, for a sealed, uniform appearance.

3) Remove burned or damaged brick or mortar, using sledgehammer, crowbar, chipping gun, or chisel.

4) Mix specified amounts of sand, clay, dirt, or mortar powder with water to form refractory mixtures.

5) Measure distance from reference points and mark guidelines to lay out work, using plumb bobs and levels.

6) Clean working surface to remove scale, dust, soot, or chips of brick and mortar, using broom, wire brush, or scraper.

7) Construct corners by fastening in plumb position a corner pole or building a corner pyramid of bricks, then filling in between the corners using a line from corner to corner to guide each course, or layer, of brick.

8) Calculate angles and courses and determine vertical and horizontal alignment of courses.

9) Break or cut bricks, tiles, or blocks to size, using trowel edge, hammer, or power saw.

10) Apply and smooth mortar or other mixture over work surface.

11) Fasten or fuse brick or other building material to structure with wire clamps, anchor holes, torch, or cement.

12) Spray or spread refractory material over brickwork to protect against deterioration.

13) Lay and align bricks, blocks, or tiles to build or repair structures or high temperature equipment, such as cupola, kilns, ovens, or furnaces.

47-2022.00 - Stonemasons

Build stone structures, such as piers, walls, and abutments. Lay walks, curbstones, or special types of masonry for vats, tanks, and floors.

Tasks

1) Clean excess mortar or grout from surface of marble, stone, or monument, using sponge, brush, water, or acid.

2) Smooth, polish, and bevel surfaces, using hand tools and power tools.

3) Lay out wall patterns or foundations, using straight edge, rule, or staked lines.

4) Dig trench for foundation of monument, using pick and shovel.

5) Mix mortar or grout and pour or spread mortar or grout on marble slabs, stone, or foundation.

6) Remove wedges, fill joints between stones, finish joints between stones, using a trowel, and smooth the mortar to an attractive finish, using a tuck pointer.

7) Set stone or marble in place, according to layout or pattern.

8) Shape, trim, face and cut marble or stone preparatory to setting, using power saws, cutting equipment, and hand tools.

9) Repair cracked or chipped areas of stone or marble, using blowtorch and mastic, and remove rough or defective spots from concrete, using power grinder or chisel and hammer.

10) Line interiors of molds with treated paper and fill molds with composition-stone mixture.

11) Position mold along guidelines of wall, press mold in place, and remove mold and paper from wall.

12) Construct and install prefabricated masonry units.

13) Lay brick to build shells of chimneys and smokestacks or to line or reline industrial furnaces, kilns, boilers and similar installations.

14) Set vertical and horizontal alignment of structures, using plumb bob, gauge line, and level.

15) Replace broken or missing masonry units in walls or floors.

16) Drill holes in marble or ornamental stone and anchor brackets in holes.

47-2031.01 - Construction Carpenters

Construct, erect, install, and repair structures and fixtures of wood, plywood, and wallboard, using carpenter's hand tools and power tools.

Tasks

1) Measure and mark cutting lines on materials, using ruler, pencil, chalk, and marking gauge.

2) Follow established safety rules and regulations and maintain a safe and clean environment.

3) Build or repair cabinets, doors, frameworks, floors, and other wooden fixtures used in buildings, using woodworking machines, carpenter's hand tools, and power tools.

4) Study specifications in blueprints, sketches or building plans to prepare project layout and determine dimensions and materials required.

5) Verify trueness of structure, using plumb bob and level.

6) Install structures and fixtures, such as windows, frames, floorings, and trim, or hardware, using carpenter's hand and power tools.

7) Remove damaged or defective parts or sections of structures and repair or replace, using hand tools.

8) Erect scaffolding and ladders for assembling structures above ground level.

9) Select and order lumber and other required materials.

10) Maintain records, document actions and present written progress reports.

11) Apply shock-absorbing, sound-deadening, and decorative paneling to ceilings and walls.

12) Perform minor plumbing, welding and/or concrete mixing work.

13) Inspect ceiling or floor tile, wall coverings, siding, glass, or woodwork to detect broken or damaged structures.

14) Finish surfaces of woodwork or wallboard in houses and buildings, using paint, hand tools, and paneling.

15) Fill cracks and other defects in plaster or plasterboard and sand patch, using patching plaster, trowel, and sanding tool.

16) Cover subfloors with building paper to keep out moisture and lay hardwood, parquet, and wood-strip-block floors by nailing floors to subfloor or cementing them to mastic or asphalt base.

17) Construct forms and chutes for pouring concrete.

18) Arrange for subcontractors to deal with special areas such as heating and electrical wiring work.

19) Prepare cost estimates for clients or employers.

20) Work with and/or remove hazardous material.

21) Assemble and fasten materials to make framework or props, using hand tools and wood screws, nails, dowel pins, or glue.

Knowledge	Knowledge Definitions
Building and Construction	Knowledge of materials, methods, and the tools involved in the construction or repair of houses, buildings, or other structures such as highways and roads.
Mathematics	Knowledge of arithmetic, algebra, geometry, calculus, statistics, and their applications.
Design	Knowledge of design techniques, tools, and principles involved in production of precision technical plans, blueprints, drawings, and models.
Production and Processing	Knowledge of raw materials, production processes, quality control, costs, and other techniques for maximizing the effective manufacture and distribution of goods.
Engineering and Technology	Knowledge of the practical application of engineering science and technology. This includes applying principles, techniques, procedures, and equipment to the design and production of various goods and services.
Mechanical	Knowledge of machines and tools, including their designs, uses, repair, and maintenance.
Public Safety and Security	Knowledge of relevant equipment, policies, procedures, and strategies to promote effective local, state, or national security operations for the protection of people, data, property, and institutions.
Law and Government	Knowledge of laws, legal codes, court procedures, precedents, government regulations, executive orders, agency rules, and the democratic political process.
Customer and Personal Service	Knowledge of principles and processes for providing customer and personal services. This includes customer needs assessment, meeting quality standards for services, and evaluation of customer satisfaction.
English Language	Knowledge of the structure and content of the English language including the meaning and spelling of words, rules of composition, and grammar.
Transportation	Knowledge of principles and methods for moving people or goods by air, rail, sea, or road, including the relative costs and benefits.
Psychology	Knowledge of human behavior and performance; individual differences in ability, personality, and interests; learning and motivation; psychological research methods; and the assessment and treatment of behavioral and affective disorders.
Education and Training	Knowledge of principles and methods for curriculum and training design, teaching and instruction for individuals and groups, and the measurement of training effects.
Administration and Management	Knowledge of business and management principles involved in strategic planning, resource allocation, human resources modeling, leadership technique, production methods, and coordination of people and resources.
Physics	Knowledge and prediction of physical principles, laws, their interrelationships, and applications to understanding fluid, material, and atmospheric dynamics, and mechanical, electrical, atomic and sub-atomic structures and processes.
Personnel and Human Resources	Knowledge of principles and procedures for personnel recruitment, selection, training, compensation and benefits, labor relations and negotiation, and personnel information systems.
Computers and Electronics	Knowledge of circuit boards, processors, chips, electronic equipment, and computer hardware and software, including applications and programming.
Telecommunications	Knowledge of transmission, broadcasting, switching, control, and operation of telecommunications systems.

Clerical	Knowledge of administrative and clerical procedures and systems such as word processing, managing files and records, stenography and transcription, designing forms, and other office procedures and terminology.
Communications and Media	Knowledge of media production, communication, and dissemination techniques and methods. This includes alternative ways to inform and entertain via written, oral, and visual media.
Economics and Accounting	Knowledge of economic and accounting principles and practices, the financial markets, banking and the analysis and reporting of financial data.
Sales and Marketing	Knowledge of principles and methods for showing, promoting, and selling products or services. This includes marketing strategy and tactics, product demonstration, sales techniques, and sales control systems.
Chemistry	Knowledge of the chemical composition, structure, and properties of substances and of the chemical processes and transformations that they undergo. This includes uses of chemicals and their interactions, danger signs, production techniques, and disposal methods.
Geography	Knowledge of principles and methods for describing the features of land, sea, and air masses, including their physical characteristics, locations, interrelationships, and distribution of plant, animal, and human life.
Medicine and Dentistry	Knowledge of the information and techniques needed to diagnose and treat human injuries, diseases, and deformities. This includes symptoms, treatment alternatives, drug properties and interactions, and preventive health-care measures.
History and Archeology	Knowledge of historical events and their causes, indicators, and effects on civilizations and cultures.
Foreign Language	Knowledge of the structure and content of a foreign (non-English) language including the meaning and spelling of words, rules of composition and grammar, and pronunciation.
Therapy and Counseling	Knowledge of principles, methods, and procedures for diagnosis, treatment, and rehabilitation of physical and mental dysfunctions, and for career counseling and guidance.
Fine Arts	Knowledge of the theory and techniques required to compose, produce, and perform works of music, dance, visual arts, drama, and sculpture.
Biology	Knowledge of plant and animal organisms, their tissues, cells, functions, interdependencies, and interactions with each other and the environment.
Philosophy and Theology	Knowledge of different philosophical systems and religions. This includes their basic principles, values, ethics, ways of thinking, customs, practices, and their impact on human culture.
Sociology and Anthropology	Knowledge of group behavior and dynamics, societal trends and influences, human migrations, ethnicity, cultures and their history and origins.
Food Production	Knowledge of techniques and equipment for planting, growing, and harvesting food products (both plant and animal) for consumption, including storage/handling techniques.

Skills	Skills Definitions
Mathematics	Using mathematics to solve problems.
Time Management	Managing one's own time and the time of others.
Critical Thinking	Using logic and reasoning to identify the strengths and weaknesses of alternative solutions, conclusions or approaches to problems.
Active Listening	Giving full attention to what other people are saying, taking time to understand the points being made, asking questions as appropriate, and not interrupting at inappropriate times.
Judgment and Decision Making	Considering the relative costs and benefits of potential actions to choose the most appropriate one.
Quality Control Analysis	Conducting tests and inspections of products, services, or processes to evaluate quality or performance.
Management of Material Resources	Obtaining and seeing to the appropriate use of equipment, facilities, and materials needed to do certain work.
Active Learning	Understanding the implications of new information for both current and future problem-solving and decision-making.
Installation	Installing equipment, machines, wiring, or programs to meet specifications.
Management of Financial Resources	Determining how money will be spent to get the work done, and accounting for these expenditures.
Equipment Maintenance	Performing routine maintenance on equipment and determining when and what kind of maintenance is needed.
Management of Personnel Resources	Motivating, developing, and directing people as they work, identifying the best people for the job.
Speaking	Talking to others to convey information effectively.
Service Orientation	Actively looking for ways to help people.
Complex Problem Solving	Identifying complex problems and reviewing related information to develop and evaluate options and implement solutions.
Monitoring	Monitoring/Assessing performance of yourself, other individuals, or organizations to make improvements or take corrective action.

Equipment Selection	Determining the kind of tools and equipment needed to do a job.
Instructing	Teaching others how to do something.
Coordination	Adjusting actions in relation to others' actions.
Repairing	Repairing machines or systems using the needed tools.
Learning Strategies	Selecting and using training/instructional methods and procedures appropriate for the situation when learning or teaching new things.
Troubleshooting	Determining causes of operating errors and deciding what to do about it.
Reading Comprehension	Understanding written sentences and paragraphs in work related documents.
Technology Design	Generating or adapting equipment and technology to serve user needs.
Operation and Control	Controlling operations of equipment or systems.
Social Perceptiveness	Being aware of others' reactions and understanding why they react as they do.
Persuasion	Persuading others to change their minds or behavior.
Operations Analysis	Analyzing needs and product requirements to create a design.
Operation Monitoring	Watching gauges, dials, or other indicators to make sure a machine is working properly.
Negotiation	Bringing others together and trying to reconcile differences.
Science	Using scientific rules and methods to solve problems.
Systems Evaluation	Identifying measures or indicators of system performance and the actions needed to improve or correct performance, relative to the goals of the system.
Writing	Communicating effectively in writing as appropriate for the needs of the audience.
Systems Analysis	Determining how a system should work and how changes in conditions, operations, and the environment will affect outcomes.
Programming	Writing computer programs for various purposes.

Ability	Ability Definitions
Arm-Hand Steadiness	The ability to keep your hand and arm steady while moving your arm or while holding your arm and hand in one position.
Multilimb Coordination	The ability to coordinate two or more limbs (for example, two arms, two legs, or one leg and one arm) while sitting, standing, or lying down. It does not involve performing the activities while the whole body is in motion.
Trunk Strength	The ability to use your abdominal and lower back muscles to support part of the body repeatedly or continuously over time without 'giving out' or fatiguing.
Near Vision	The ability to see details at close range (within a few feet of the observer).
Information Ordering	The ability to arrange things or actions in a certain order or pattern according to a specific rule or set of rules (e.g., patterns of numbers, letters, words, pictures, mathematical operations).
Manual Dexterity	The ability to quickly move your hand, your hand together with your arm, or your two hands to grasp, manipulate, or assemble objects.
Visualization	The ability to imagine how something will look after it is moved around or when its parts are moved or rearranged.
Problem Sensitivity	The ability to tell when something is wrong or is likely to go wrong. It does not involve solving the problem, only recognizing there is a problem.
Deductive Reasoning	The ability to apply general rules to specific problems to produce answers that make sense.
Oral Comprehension	The ability to listen to and understand information and ideas presented through spoken words and sentences.
Speech Recognition	The ability to identify and understand the speech of another person.
Static Strength	The ability to exert maximum muscle force to lift, push, pull, or carry objects.
Dynamic Strength	The ability to exert muscle force repeatedly or continuously over time. This involves muscular endurance and resistance to muscle fatigue.
Originality	The ability to come up with unusual or clever ideas about a given topic or situation, or to develop creative ways to solve a problem.
Finger Dexterity	The ability to make precisely coordinated movements of the fingers of one or both hands to grasp, manipulate, or assemble very small objects.
Speech Clarity	The ability to speak clearly so others can understand you.
Oral Expression	The ability to communicate information and ideas in speaking so others will understand.
Control Precision	The ability to quickly and repeatedly adjust the controls of a machine or a vehicle to exact positions.
Selective Attention	The ability to concentrate on a task over a period of time without being distracted.
Far Vision	The ability to see details at a distance.
Extent Flexibility	The ability to bend, stretch, twist, or reach with your body, arms, and/or legs.
Stamina	The ability to exert yourself physically over long periods of time without getting winded or out of breath.

Depth Perception	The ability to judge which of several objects is closer or farther away from you, or to judge the distance between you and an object.
Written Comprehension	The ability to read and understand information and ideas presented in writing.
Gross Body Coordination	The ability to coordinate the movement of your arms, legs, and torso together when the whole body is in motion.
Category Flexibility	The ability to generate or use different sets of rules for combining or grouping things in different ways.
Inductive Reasoning	The ability to combine pieces of information to form general rules or conclusions (includes finding a relationship among seemingly unrelated events).
Gross Body Equilibrium	The ability to keep or regain your body balance or stay upright when in an unstable position.
Perceptual Speed	The ability to quickly and accurately compare similarities and differences among sets of letters, numbers, objects, pictures, or patterns. The things to be compared may be presented at the same time or one after the other. This ability also includes comparing a presented object with a remembered object.
Flexibility of Closure	The ability to identify or detect a known pattern (a figure, object, word, or sound) that is hidden in other distracting material.
Reaction Time	The ability to quickly respond (with the hand, finger, or foot) to a signal (sound, light, picture) when it appears.
Speed of Limb Movement	The ability to quickly move the arms and legs.
Auditory Attention	The ability to focus on a single source of sound in the presence of other distracting sounds.
Fluency of Ideas	The ability to come up with a number of ideas about a topic (the number of ideas is important, not their quality, correctness, or creativity).
Written Expression	The ability to communicate information and ideas in writing so others will understand.
Visual Color Discrimination	The ability to match or detect differences between colors, including shades of color and brightness.
Wrist-Finger Speed	The ability to make fast, simple, repeated movements of the fingers, hands, and wrists.
Spatial Orientation	The ability to know your location in relation to the environment or to know where other objects are in relation to you.
Memorization	The ability to remember information such as words, numbers, pictures, and procedures.
Explosive Strength	The ability to use short bursts of muscle force to propel oneself (as in jumping or sprinting), or to throw an object.
Response Orientation	The ability to choose quickly between two or more movements in response to two or more different signals (lights, sounds, pictures). It includes the speed with which the correct response is started with the hand, foot, or other body part.
Mathematical Reasoning	The ability to choose the right mathematical methods or formulas to solve a problem.
Glare Sensitivity	The ability to see objects in the presence of glare or bright lighting.
Hearing Sensitivity	The ability to detect or tell the differences between sounds that vary in pitch and loudness.
Speed of Closure	The ability to quickly make sense of, combine, and organize information into meaningful patterns.
Time Sharing	The ability to shift back and forth between two or more activities or sources of information (such as speech, sounds, touch, or other sources).
Rate Control	The ability to time your movements or the movement of a piece of equipment in anticipation of changes in the speed and/or direction of a moving object or scene.
Peripheral Vision	The ability to see objects or movement of objects to one's side when the eyes are looking ahead.
Number Facility	The ability to add, subtract, multiply, or divide quickly and correctly.
Night Vision	The ability to see under low light conditions.
Sound Localization	The ability to tell the direction from which a sound originated.
Dynamic Flexibility	The ability to quickly and repeatedly bend, stretch, twist, or reach out with your body, arms, and/or legs.

Work_Activity	Work_Activity Definitions
Controlling Machines and Processes	Using either control mechanisms or direct physical activity to operate machines or processes (not including computers or vehicles).
Judging the Qualities of Things, Services, or Peop	Assessing the value, importance, or quality of things or people.
Monitor Processes, Materials, or Surroundings	Monitoring and reviewing information from materials, events, or the environment, to detect or assess problems.
Communicating with Supervisors, Peers, or Subordin	Providing information to supervisors, co-workers, and subordinates by telephone, in written form, e-mail, or in person.
Coordinating the Work and Activities of Others	Getting members of a group to work together to accomplish tasks.

Performing General Physical Activities	Performing physical activities that require considerable use of your arms and legs and moving your whole body, such as climbing, lifting, balancing, walking, stooping, and handling of materials.
Scheduling Work and Activities	Scheduling events, programs, and activities, as well as the work of others.
Getting Information	Observing, receiving, and otherwise obtaining information from all relevant sources.
Communicating with Persons Outside Organization	Communicating with people outside the organization, representing the organization to customers, the public, government, and other external sources. This information can be exchanged in person, in writing, or by telephone or e-mail.
Making Decisions and Solving Problems	Analyzing information and evaluating results to choose the best solution and solve problems.
Organizing, Planning, and Prioritizing Work	Developing specific goals and plans to prioritize, organize, and accomplish your work.
Training and Teaching Others	Identifying the educational needs of others, developing formal educational or training programs or classes, and teaching or instructing others.
Inspecting Equipment, Structures, or Material	Inspecting equipment, structures, or materials to identify the cause of errors or other problems or defects.
Thinking Creatively	Developing, designing, or creating new applications, ideas, relationships, systems, or products, including artistic contributions.
Handling and Moving Objects	Using hands and arms in handling, installing, positioning, and moving materials, and manipulating things.
Identifying Objects, Actions, and Events	Identifying information by categorizing, estimating, recognizing differences or similarities, and detecting changes in circumstances or events.
Operating Vehicles, Mechanized Devices, or Equipme	Running, maneuvering, navigating, or driving vehicles or mechanized equipment, such as forklifts, passenger vehicles, aircraft, or water craft.
Updating and Using Relevant Knowledge	Keeping up-to-date technically and applying new knowledge to your job.
Guiding, Directing, and Motivating Subordinates	Providing guidance and direction to subordinates, including setting performance standards and monitoring performance.
Evaluating Information to Determine Compliance wit	Using relevant information and individual judgment to determine whether events or processes comply with laws, regulations, or standards.
Estimating the Quantifiable Characteristics of Pro	Estimating sizes, distances, and quantities; or determining time, costs, resources, or materials needed to perform a work activity.
Repairing and Maintaining Mechanical Equipment	Servicing, repairing, adjusting, and testing machines, devices, moving parts, and equipment that operate primarily on the basis of mechanical (not electronic) principles.
Establishing and Maintaining Interpersonal Relatio	Developing constructive and cooperative working relationships with others, and maintaining them over time.
Developing Objectives and Strategies	Establishing long-range objectives and specifying the strategies and actions to achieve them.
Developing and Building Teams	Encouraging and building mutual trust, respect, and cooperation among team members.
Analyzing Data or Information	Identifying the underlying principles, reasons, or facts of information by breaking down information or data into separate parts.
Interpreting the Meaning of Information for Others	Translating or explaining what information means and how it can be used.
Drafting, Laying Out, and Specifying Technical Dev	Providing documentation, detailed instructions, drawings, or specifications to tell others about how devices, parts, equipment, or structures are to be fabricated, constructed, assembled, modified, maintained, or used.
Documenting/Recording Information	Entering, transcribing, recording, storing, or maintaining information in written or electronic/magnetic form.
Processing Information	Compiling, coding, categorizing, calculating, tabulating, auditing, or verifying information or data.
Coaching and Developing Others	Identifying the developmental needs of others and coaching, mentoring, or otherwise helping others to improve their knowledge or skills.
Resolving Conflicts and Negotiating with Others	Handling complaints, settling disputes, and resolving grievances and conflicts, or otherwise negotiating with others.
Performing for or Working Directly with the Public	Performing for people or dealing directly with the public. This includes serving customers in restaurants and stores, and receiving clients or guests.
Provide Consultation and Advice to Others	Providing guidance and expert advice to management or other groups on technical, systems-, or process-related topics.
Assisting and Caring for Others	Providing personal assistance, medical attention, emotional support, or other personal care to others such as coworkers, customers, or patients.
Repairing and Maintaining Electronic Equipment	Servicing, repairing, calibrating, regulating, fine-tuning, or testing machines, devices, and equipment that operate primarily on the basis of electrical or electronic (not mechanical) principles.
Performing Administrative Activities	Performing day-to-day administrative tasks such as maintaining information files and processing paperwork.

293

Interacting With Computers	Using computers and computer systems (including hardware and software) to program, write software, set up functions, enter data, or process information.
Selling or Influencing Others	Convincing others to buy merchandise/goods or to otherwise change their minds or actions.
Staffing Organizational Units	Recruiting, interviewing, selecting, hiring, and promoting employees in an organization.
Monitoring and Controlling Resources	Monitoring and controlling resources and overseeing the spending of money.

Work_Content	Work_Content Definitions
Spend Time Standing	How much does this job require standing?
Spend Time Using Your Hands to Handle, Control, or	How much does this job require using your hands to handle, control, or feel objects, tools or controls?
Wear Common Protective or Safety Equipment such as	How much does this job require wearing common protective or safety equipment such as safety shoes, glasses, gloves, hard hats or live jackets?
Face-to-Face Discussions	How often do you have to have face-to-face discussions with individuals or teams in this job?
Exposed to Hazardous Equipment	How often does this job require exposure to hazardous equipment?
Sounds, Noise Levels Are Distracting or Uncomforta	How often does this job require working exposed to sounds and noise levels that are distracting or uncomfortable?
Importance of Being Exact or Accurate	How important is being very exact or highly accurate in performing this job?
Freedom to Make Decisions	How much decision making freedom, without supervision, does the job offer?
Outdoors, Exposed to Weather	How often does this job require working outdoors, exposed to all weather conditions?
Telephone	How often do you have telephone conversations in this job?
Work With Work Group or Team	How important is it to work with others in a group or team in this job?
Structured versus Unstructured Work	To what extent is this job structured for the worker, rather than allowing the worker to determine tasks, priorities, and goals?
Frequency of Decision Making	How frequently is the worker required to make decisions that affect other people, the financial resources, and/or the image and reputation of the organization?
Physical Proximity	To what extent does this job require the worker to perform job tasks in close physical proximity to other people?
Contact With Others	How much does this job require the worker to be in contact with others (face-to-face, by telephone, or otherwise) in order to perform it?
Impact of Decisions on Co-workers or Company Resul	How do the decisions an employee makes impact the results of co-workers, clients or the company?
Level of Competition	To what extent does this job require the worker to compete or to be aware of competitive pressures?
Coordinate or Lead Others	How important is it to coordinate or lead others in accomplishing work activities in this job?
Spend Time Walking and Running	How much does this job require walking and running?
Exposed to Contaminants	How often does this job require working exposed to contaminants (such as pollutants, gases, dust or odors)?
Exposed to Minor Burns, Cuts, Bites, or Stings	How often does this job require exposure to minor burns, cuts, bites, or stings?
Time Pressure	How often does this job require the worker to meet strict deadlines?
Responsibility for Outcomes and Results	How responsible is the worker for work outcomes and results of other workers?
Very Hot or Cold Temperatures	How often does this job require working in very hot (above 90 F degrees) or very cold (below 32 F degrees) temperatures?
Exposed to High Places	How often does this job require exposure to high places?
Responsible for Others' Health and Safety	How much responsibility is there for the health and safety of others in this job?
Spend Time Bending or Twisting the Body	How much does this job require bending or twisting your body?
Spend Time Making Repetitive Motions	How much does this job require making repetitive motions?
Spend Time Kneeling, Crouching, Stooping, or Crawl	How much does this job require kneeling, crouching, stooping or crawling?
Outdoors, Under Cover	How often does this job require working outdoors, under cover (e.g., structure with roof but no walls)?
Deal With External Customers	How important is it to work with external customers or the public in this job?
Indoors, Not Environmentally Controlled	How often does this job require working indoors in non-controlled environmental conditions (e.g., warehouse without heat)?
Cramped Work Space, Awkward Positions	How often does this job require working in cramped work spaces that requires getting into awkward positions?
Extremely Bright or Inadequate Lighting	How often does this job require working in extremely bright or inadequate lighting conditions?
In an Enclosed Vehicle or Equipment	How often does this job require working in a closed vehicle or equipment (e.g., car)?

Spend Time Climbing Ladders, Scaffolds, or Poles	How much does this job require climbing ladders, scaffolds, or poles?
In an Open Vehicle or Equipment	How often does this job require working in an open vehicle or equipment (e.g., tractor)?
Letters and Memos	How often does the job require written letters and memos?
Importance of Repeating Same Tasks	How important is repeating the same physical activities (e.g., key entry) or mental activities (e.g., checking entries in a ledger) over and over, without stopping, to performing this job?
Frequency of Conflict Situations	How often are there conflict situations the employee has to face in this job?
Spend Time Keeping or Regaining Balance	How much does this job require keeping or regaining your balance?
Deal With Unpleasant or Angry People	How frequently does the worker have to deal with unpleasant, angry, or discourteous individuals as part of the job requirements?
Indoors, Environmentally Controlled	How often does this job require working indoors in environmentally controlled conditions?
Wear Specialized Protective or Safety Equipment su	How much does this job require wearing specialized protective or safety equipment such as breathing apparatus, safety harness, full protection suits, or radiation protection?
Consequence of Error	How serious would the result usually be if the worker made a mistake that was not readily correctable?
Pace Determined by Speed of Equipment	How important is it to this job that the pace is determined by the speed of equipment or machinery? (This does not refer to keeping busy at all times on this job.)
Degree of Automation	How automated is this job?
Public Speaking	How often do you have to perform public speaking in this job?
Electronic Mail	How often do you use electronic mail in this job?
Exposed to Disease or Infections	How often does this job require exposure to disease/infections?
Exposed to Whole Body Vibration	How often does this job require exposure to whole body vibration (e.g., operate a jackhammer)?
Deal With Physically Aggressive People	How frequently does this job require the worker to deal with physical aggression of violent individuals?
Spend Time Sitting	How much does this job require sitting?
Exposed to Hazardous Conditions	How often does this job require exposure to hazardous conditions?
Exposed to Radiation	How often does this job require exposure to radiation?

Work_Styles	Work_Styles Definitions
Attention to Detail	Job requires being careful about detail and thorough in completing work tasks.
Dependability	Job requires being reliable, responsible, and dependable, and fulfilling obligations.
Persistence	Job requires persistence in the face of obstacles.
Cooperation	Job requires being pleasant with others on the job and displaying a good-natured, cooperative attitude.
Integrity	Job requires being honest and ethical.
Adaptability/Flexibility	Job requires being open to change (positive or negative) and to considerable variety in the workplace.
Analytical Thinking	Job requires analyzing information and using logic to address work-related issues and problems.
Innovation	Job requires creativity and alternative thinking to develop new ideas for and answers to work-related problems.
Self Control	Job requires maintaining composure, keeping emotions in check, controlling anger, and avoiding aggressive behavior, even in very difficult situations.
Initiative	Job requires a willingness to take on responsibilities and challenges.
Independence	Job requires developing one's own ways of doing things, guiding oneself with little or no supervision, and depending on oneself to get things done.
Stress Tolerance	Job requires accepting criticism and dealing calmly and effectively with high stress situations.
Achievement/Effort	Job requires establishing and maintaining personally challenging achievement goals and exerting effort toward mastering tasks.
Concern for Others	Job requires being sensitive to others' needs and feelings and being understanding and helpful on the job.
Leadership	Job requires a willingness to lead, take charge, and offer opinions and direction.
Social Orientation	Job requires preferring to work with others rather than alone, and being personally connected with others on the job.

Job Zone Component	Job Zone Component Definitions
Title	Job Zone Three: Medium Preparation Needed
Overall Experience	Previous work-related skill, knowledge, or experience is required for these occupations. For example, an electrician must have completed three or four years of apprenticeship or several years of vocational training, and often must have passed a licensing exam, in order to perform the job.

Job Training	Employees in these occupations usually need one or two years of training involving both on-the-job experience and informal training with experienced workers.
Job Zone Examples	These occupations usually involve using communication and organizational skills to coordinate, supervise, manage, or train others to accomplish goals. Examples include dental assistants, electricians, fish and game wardens, legal secretaries, personnel recruiters, and recreation workers.
SVP Range	(6.0 to < 7.0)
Education	Most occupations in this zone require training in vocational schools, related on-the-job experience, or an associate's degree. Some may require a bachelor's degree.

47-2031.02 - Rough Carpenters

Build rough wooden structures, such as concrete forms, scaffolds, tunnel, bridge, or sewer supports, billboard signs, and temporary frame shelters, according to sketches, blueprints, or oral instructions.

Tasks

1) Cut or saw boards, timbers, or plywood to required size, using handsaw, power saw, or woodworking machine.

2) Measure materials or distances, using square, measuring tape, or rule to lay out work.

3) Anchor and brace forms and other structures in place, using nails, bolts, anchor rods, steel cables, planks, wedges, and timbers.

4) Bore boltholes in timber, masonry or concrete walls, using power drill.

5) Install rough door and window frames, subflooring, fixtures, or temporary supports in structures undergoing construction or repair.

6) Dig or direct digging of post holes and set poles to support structures.

7) Build sleds from logs and timbers for use in hauling camp buildings and machinery through wooded areas.

8) Examine structural timbers and supports to detect decay, and replace timbers as required, using hand tools, nuts, and bolts.

9) Fabricate parts, using woodworking and metalworking machines.

10) Assemble and fasten material together to construct wood or metal framework of structure, using bolts, nails, or screws.

11) Mark cutting lines on materials, using pencil and scriber.

12) Study blueprints and diagrams to determine dimensions of structure or form to be constructed.

13) Erect forms, framework, scaffolds, hoists, roof supports, or chutes, using hand tools, plumb rule, and level.

47-2041.00 - Carpet Installers

Lay and install carpet from rolls or blocks on floors. Install padding and trim flooring materials.

Tasks

1) Cut and trim carpet to fit along wall edges, openings, and projections, finishing the edges with a wall trimmer.

2) Stretch carpet to align with walls and ensure a smooth surface, and press carpet in place over tack strips or use staples, tape, tacks or glue to hold carpet in place.

3) Plan the layout of the carpet, allowing for expected traffic patterns and placing seams for best appearance and longest wear.

4) Measure, cut and install tackless strips along the baseboard or wall.

5) Draw building diagrams and record dimensions.

6) Cut and bind material.

7) Take measurements and study floor sketches to calculate the area to be carpeted and the amount of material needed.

8) Roll out, measure, mark, and cut carpeting to size with a carpet knife, following floor sketches and allowing extra carpet for final fitting.

9) Nail tack strips around area to be carpeted or use old strips to attach edges of new carpet.

10) Install carpet on some floors using adhesive, following prescribed method.

11) Inspect the surface to be covered to determine its condition, and correct any imperfections that might show through carpet or cause carpet to wear unevenly.

12) Fasten metal treads across door openings or where carpet meets flooring to hold carpet in place.

13) Cut carpet padding to size and install padding, following prescribed method.

14) Move furniture from area to be carpeted and remove old carpet and padding.

47-2042.00 - Floor Layers, Except Carpet, Wood, and Hard Tiles

Apply blocks, strips, or sheets of shock-absorbing, sound-deadening, or decorative coverings to floors.

Tasks

1) Heat and soften floor covering materials to patch cracks or fit floor coverings around irregular surfaces, using blowtorch.

2) Lay out, position, and apply shock-absorbing, sound-deadening, or decorative coverings to floors, walls, and cabinets, following guidelines to keep courses straight and create designs.

3) Cut covering and foundation materials, according to blueprints and sketches.

4) Cut flooring material to fit around obstructions.

5) Determine traffic areas and decide location of seams.

6) Form a smooth foundation by stapling plywood or Masonite over the floor or by brushing waterproof compound onto surface and filling cracks with plaster, putty, or grout to seal pores.

7) Remove excess cement to clean finished surface.

8) Sweep, scrape, sand, or chip dirt and irregularities to clean base surfaces, correcting imperfections that may show through the covering.

9) Disconnect and remove appliances, light fixtures, and worn floor and wall covering from floors, walls, and cabinets.

10) Apply adhesive cement to floor or wall material to join and adhere foundation material.

11) Measure and mark guidelines on surfaces or foundations, using chalk lines and dividers.

12) Inspect surface to be covered to ensure that it is firm and dry.

13) Roll and press sheet wall and floor covering into cement base to smooth and finish surface, using hand roller.

47-2044.00 - Tile and Marble Setters

Apply hard tile, marble, and wood tile to walls, floors, ceilings, and roof decks.

Tasks

1) Mix and apply mortar or cement to edges and ends of drain tiles to seal halves and joints.

2) Remove and replace cracked or damaged tile.

3) Prepare cost and labor estimates based on calculations of time and materials needed for project.

4) Level concrete and allow to dry.

5) Cut, surface, polish and install marble and granite and/or install pre-cast terrazzo, granite or marble units.

6) Brush glue onto manila paper on which design has been drawn and position tiles finished side down onto paper.

7) Mix, apply, and spread plaster, concrete, mortar, cement, mastic, glue or other adhesives to form a bed for the tiles, using brush, trowel and screed.

8) Remove any old tile, grout and adhesive using chisels and scrapers and clean the surface carefully.

9) Study blueprints and examine surface to be covered to determine amount of material needed.

10) Lay and set mosaic tiles to create decorative wall, mural and floor designs.

11) Select and order tile and other items to be installed, such as bathroom accessories, walls, panels, and cabinets, according to specifications.

12) Prepare surfaces for tiling by attaching lath or waterproof paper, or by applying a cement mortar coat onto a metal screen.

13) Measure and cut metal lath to size for walls and ceilings, using tin snips.

14) Install and anchor fixtures in designated positions, using hand tools.

15) Finish and dress the joints and wipe excess grout from between tiles, using damp sponge.

16) Cut tile backing to required size, using shears.

17) Cut and shape tile to fit around obstacles and into odd spaces and corners, using hand and

power cutting tools.

18) Measure and mark surfaces to be tiled, following blueprints.

19) Apply a sealer to make grout stain- and water-resistant.

20) Assist customers in selection of tile and grout.

21) Align and straighten tile using levels, squares and straightedges.

22) Build underbeds and install anchor bolts, wires and brackets.

23) Determine and implement the best layout to achieve a desired pattern.

24) Apply mortar to tile back, position the tile and press or tap with trowel handle to affix tile to base.

47-2051.00 - Cement Masons and Concrete Finishers

Smooth and finish surfaces of poured concrete, such as floors, walks, sidewalks, roads, or curbs using a variety of hand and power tools. Align forms for sidewalks, curbs, or gutters; patch voids; use saws to cut expansion joints.

Tasks

1) Chip, scrape, and grind high spots, ridges, and rough projections to finish concrete, using pneumatic chisels, power grinders, or hand tools.

2) Apply hardening and sealing compounds to cure surface of concrete, and waterproof or restore surface.

3) Mix cement, sand, and water to produce concrete, grout, or slurry, using hoe, trowel, tamper, scraper, or concrete-mixing machine.

4) Mold expansion joints and edges, using edging tools, jointers, and straightedge.

5) Check the forms that hold the concrete to see that they are properly constructed.

6) Monitor how the wind, heat, or cold affect the curing of the concrete throughout the entire process.

7) Spread, level, and smooth concrete, using rake, shovel, hand or power trowel, hand or power screed, and float.

8) Wet concrete surface, and rub with stone to smooth surface and obtain specified finish.

9) Wet surface to prepare for bonding, fill holes and cracks with grout or slurry, and smooth, using trowel.

10) Polish surface, using polishing or surfacing machine.

11) Set the forms that hold concrete to the desired pitch and depth, and align them.

12) Apply muriatic acid to clean surface, and rinse with water.

13) Spread roofing paper on surface of foundation, and spread concrete onto roofing paper with trowel to form terrazzo base.

14) Clean chipped area, using wire brush, and feel and observe surface to determine if it is rough or uneven.

15) Signal truck driver to position truck to facilitate pouring concrete, and move chute to direct concrete on forms.

16) Build wooden molds, and clamp molds around area to be repaired, using hand tools.

17) Fabricate concrete beams, columns, and panels.

18) Produce rough concrete surface, using broom.

19) Install anchor bolts, steel plates, door sills and other fixtures in freshly poured concrete and/or pattern or stamp the surface to provide a decorative finish.

20) Direct the casting of the concrete and supervise laborers who use shovels or special tools to spread it.

21) Cut out damaged areas, drill holes for reinforcing rods, and position reinforcing rods to repair concrete, using power saw and drill.

22) Cut metal division strips, and press them into terrazzo base so that top edges form desired design or pattern.

23) Push roller over surface to embed chips in surface.

24) Operate power vibrator to compact concrete.

25) Sprinkle colored marble or stone chips, powdered steel, or coloring powder over surface to produce prescribed finish.

47-2053.00 - Terrazzo Workers and Finishers

Apply a mixture of cement, sand, pigment, or marble chips to floors, stairways, and cabinet fixtures to fashion durable and decorative surfaces.

Tasks

1) Chip, scrape, and grind high spots, ridges, and rough projections to finish concrete, using pneumatic chisel, hand chisel, or other hand tools.

2) Clean chipped area, using wire brush, and feel and observe surface to determine if it is rough or uneven.

3) Clean installation site, mixing and storage areas, tools, machines, and equipment, and store materials and equipment.

4) Cut out damaged areas, drill holes for reinforcing rods, and position reinforcing rods to repair concrete, using power saw and drill.

5) Move terrazzo installation materials, tools, machines, and work devices to work areas, manually or using wheelbarrow.

6) Produce rough concrete surface, using broom.

7) Remove frames once the foundation is dry.

8) Wet surface to prepare for bonding, fill holes and cracks with grout or slurry, and smooth, using trowel.

9) Wet concrete surface, and rub with stone to smooth surface and obtain specified finish.

10) Fill slight depressions left by grinding with a matching grout material, and then hand trowel for a smooth, uniform surface.

11) Build wooden molds, clamping molds around areas to be repaired, and setting up frames to the proper depth and alignment.

12) Cut metal division strips and press them into the terrazzo base wherever there is to be a joint or change of color, to form desired designs or patterns, and to help prevent cracks.

13) Mold expansion joints and edges, using edging tools, jointers, and straightedges.

14) Wash polished terrazzo surface, using cleaner and water, and apply sealer and curing agent according to manufacturer's specifications, using brush or sprayer.

15) Blend marble chip mixtures and place into panels, then push a roller over the surface to embed the chips.

16) Grind curved surfaces and areas inaccessible to surfacing machine, such as stairways and cabinet tops, with portable hand grinder.

17) Grind surfaces with a power grinder and polish surfaces with polishing or surfacing machines.

18) Measure designated amounts of ingredients for terrazzo or grout according to standard formulas and specifications, using graduated containers and scale, and load ingredients into portable mixer.

19) Modify mixing, grouting, grinding, and cleaning procedures according to type of installation or material used.

20) Position and secure moisture membrane and wire mesh prior to pouring base materials for terrazzo installation.

21) Spread roofing paper on surface of foundation, and spread concrete onto roofing paper with trowel to form terrazzo base.

22) Mix cement, sand, and water to produce concrete, grout, or slurry, using hoe, trowel, tamper, scraper, or concrete-mixing machine.

23) Spread, level, and smooth concrete and terrazzo mixtures to form bases and finished surfaces, using rakes, shovels, hand or power trowels, hand or power screeds, and floats.

24) Signal truck driver to position truck to facilitate pouring concrete, and move chute to direct concrete on forms.

25) Sprinkle colored marble or stone chips, powdered steel, or coloring powder over surface to produce prescribed finish.

47-2071.00 - Paving, Surfacing, and Tamping Equipment Operators

Operate equipment used for applying concrete, asphalt, or other materials to road beds, parking lots, or airport runways and taxiways, or equipment used for tamping gravel, dirt, or other materials. Includes concrete and asphalt paving machine operators, form tampers, tamping machine operators, and stone spreader operators.

Tasks

1) Coordinate truck dumping.

2) Cut or break up pavement and drive guardrail posts, using machines equipped with interchangeable hammers.

3) Drive machines onto truck trailers, and drive trucks to transport machines and material to and from job sites.

4) Shovel blacktop.

5) Operate oil distributors, loaders, chip spreaders, dump trucks, and snow plows.

6) Operate machines that clean or cut expansion joints in concrete or asphalt and that rout out

cracks in pavement.

7) Set up forms and lay out guidelines for curbs, according to written specifications, using string, spray paint, and concrete/water mixes.

8) Observe distribution of paving material in order to adjust machine settings or material flow, and indicate low spots for workers to add material.

9) Start machine, engage clutch, and push and move levers to guide machine along forms or guidelines and to control the operation of machine attachments.

10) Light burners or start heating units of machines, and regulate screed temperatures and asphalt flow rates.

11) Install dies, cutters, and extensions to screeds onto machines, using hand tools.

12) Fill tanks, hoppers, or machines with paving materials.

13) Drive and operate curbing machines to extrude concrete or asphalt curbing.

14) Control paving machines to push dump trucks and to maintain a constant flow of asphalt or other material into hoppers or screeds.

15) Set up and tear down equipment.

16) Place strips of material such as cork, asphalt, or steel into joints, or place rolls of expansion-joint material on machines that automatically insert material.

17) Operate tamping machines or manually roll surfaces to compact earth fills, foundation forms, and finished road materials, according to grade specifications.

18) Inspect, clean, maintain, and repair equipment, using mechanics' hand tools, or report malfunctions to supervisors.

47-2111.00 - Electricians

Install, maintain, and repair electrical wiring, equipment, and fixtures. Ensure that work is in accordance with relevant codes. May install or service street lights, intercom systems, or electrical control systems.

Tasks

1) Advise management on whether continued operation of equipment could be hazardous.

2) Perform business management duties such as maintaining records and files, preparing reports and ordering supplies and equipment.

3) Perform physically demanding tasks, such as digging trenches to lay conduit and moving and lifting heavy objects.

4) Provide assistance during emergencies by operating floodlights and generators, placing flares, and driving needed vehicles.

5) Provide preliminary sketches and cost estimates for materials and services.

6) Use a variety of tools and equipment such as power construction equipment, measuring devices, power tools, and testing equipment including oscilloscopes, ammeters, and test lamps.

7) Test electrical systems and continuity of circuits in electrical wiring, equipment, and fixtures, using testing devices such as ohmmeters, voltmeters, and oscilloscopes, to ensure compatibility and safety of system.

8) Work from ladders, scaffolds, and roofs to install, maintain or repair electrical wiring, equipment, and fixtures.

9) Construct and fabricate parts, using hand tools and specifications.

10) Diagnose malfunctioning systems, apparatus, and components, using test equipment and hand tools, to locate the cause of a breakdown and correct the problem.

11) Fasten small metal or plastic boxes to walls to house electrical switches or outlets.

12) Connect wires to circuit breakers, transformers, or other components.

13) Prepare sketches or follow blueprints to determine the location of wiring and equipment and to ensure conformance to building and safety codes.

14) Inspect electrical systems, equipment, and components to identify hazards, defects, and the need for adjustment or repair, and to ensure compliance with codes.

15) Plan layout and installation of electrical wiring, equipment and fixtures, based on job specifications and local codes.

16) Place conduit (pipes or tubing) inside designated partitions, walls, or other concealed areas, and pull insulated wires or cables through the conduit to complete circuits between boxes.

17) Maintain current electrician's license or identification card to meet governmental regulations.

18) Direct and train workers to install, maintain, or repair electrical wiring, equipment, and fixtures.

19) Install ground leads and connect power cables to equipment, such as motors.

20) Assemble, install, test, and maintain electrical or electronic wiring, equipment, appliances, apparatus, and fixtures, using hand tools and power tools.

47-2152.01 - Pipe Fitters

Lay out, assemble, install, and maintain pipe systems, pipe supports, and related hydraulic and pneumatic equipment for steam, hot water, heating, cooling, lubricating, sprinkling, and industrial production and processing systems.

Tasks

1) Inspect, examine, and test installed systems and pipe lines, using pressure gauge, hydrostatic testing, observation, or other methods.

2) Dip nonferrous piping materials in a mixture of molten tin and lead to obtain a coating that prevents erosion or galvanic and electrolytic action.

3) Lay out full scale drawings of pipe systems, supports, and related equipment, following blueprints.

4) Modify, clean, and maintain pipe systems, units, fittings, and related machines and equipment, following specifications and using hand and power tools.

5) Cut, thread, and hammer pipe to specifications, using tools such as saws, cutting torches, and pipe threaders and benders.

6) Cut and bore holes in structures, such as bulkheads, decks, walls, and mains, prior to pipe installation, using hand and power tools.

7) Assemble and secure pipes, tubes, fittings, and related equipment, according to specifications, by welding, brazing, cementing, soldering, and threading joints.

8) Plan pipe system layout, installation, or repair according to specifications.

9) Attach pipes to walls, structures and fixtures, such as radiators or tanks, using brackets, clamps, tools or welding equipment.

10) Operate motorized pumps to remove water from flooded manholes, basements, or facility floors.

11) Remove and replace worn components.

12) Turn valves to shut off steam, water, or other gases or liquids from pipe sections, using valve keys or wrenches.

13) Select pipe sizes and types and related materials, such as supports, hangers, and hydraulic cylinders, according to specifications.

14) Measure and mark pipes for cutting and threading.

15) Inspect work sites for obstructions and to ensure that holes will not cause structural weakness.

16) Install automatic controls used to regulate pipe systems.

47-2152.02 - Plumbers

Assemble, install, and repair pipes, fittings, and fixtures of heating, water, and drainage systems, according to specifications and plumbing codes.

Tasks

1) Hang steel supports from ceiling joists to hold pipes in place.

2) Install pipe assemblies, fittings, valves, appliances such as dishwashers and water heaters, and fixtures such as sinks and toilets, using hand and power tools.

3) Install underground storm, sanitary and water piping systems and extend piping to connect fixtures and plumbing to these systems.

4) Study building plans and inspect structures to assess material and equipment needs, to establish the sequence of pipe installations, and to plan installation around obstructions such as electrical wiring.

5) Measure, cut, thread, and bend pipe to required angle, using hand and power tools or machines such as pipe cutters, pipe-threading machines, and pipe-bending machines.

6) Assemble pipe sections, tubing and fittings, using couplings, clamps, screws, bolts, cement, plastic solvent, caulking, or soldering, brazing and welding equipment.

7) Cut openings in structures to accommodate pipes and pipe fittings, using hand and power tools.

8) Use specialized techniques, equipment, or materials, such as performing computer-assisted welding of small pipes, or working with the special piping used in microchip fabrication.

9) Fill pipes or plumbing fixtures with water or air and observe pressure gauges to detect and locate leaks.

10) Clear away debris in a renovation.

11) Direct workers engaged in pipe cutting and preassembly and installation of plumbing systems and components.

12) Keep records of assignments and produce detailed work reports.

13) Perform complex calculations and planning for special or very large jobs.

297

14) Prepare written work cost estimates and negotiate contracts.

15) Install oxygen and medical gas in hospitals.

16) Review blueprints and building codes and specifications to determine work details and procedures.

17) Locate and mark the position of pipe installations, connections, passage holes, and fixtures in structures, using measuring instruments such as rulers and levels.

47-2152.03 - Pipelaying Fitters

Align pipeline section in preparation of welding. Signal tractor driver for placement of pipeline sections in proper alignment. Insert steel spacer.

Tasks

1) Correct misalignments of pipe, using a sledge hammer.

2) Inspect joints to ensure uniform spacing and proper alignment of pipe surfaces.

3) Insert spacers between pipe ends.

47-2161.00 - Plasterers and Stucco Masons

Apply interior or exterior plaster, cement, stucco, or similar materials. May also set ornamental plaster.

Tasks

1) Cure freshly plastered surfaces.

2) Mold and install ornamental plaster pieces, panels, and trim.

3) Apply insulation to building exteriors by installing prefabricated insulation systems over existing walls or by covering the outer wall with insulation board, reinforcing mesh, and a base coat.

4) Spray acoustic materials or texture finish over walls and ceilings.

5) Apply coats of plaster or stucco to walls, ceilings, or partitions of buildings, using trowels, brushes, or spray guns.

6) Clean and prepare surfaces for applications of plaster, cement, stucco, or similar materials, such as by drywall taping.

7) Rough the undercoat surface with a scratcher so the finish coat will adhere.

8) Mix mortar and plaster to desired consistency or direct workers who perform mixing.

9) Create decorative textures in finish coat, using brushes or trowels, sand, pebbles, or stones.

10) Install guidewires on exterior surfaces of buildings to indicate thickness of plaster or stucco, and nail wire mesh, lath, or similar materials to the outside surface to hold stucco in place.

47-2211.00 - Sheet Metal Workers

Fabricate, assemble, install, and repair sheet metal products and equipment, such as ducts, control boxes, drainpipes, and furnace casings. Work may involve any of the following: setting up and operating fabricating machines to cut, bend, and straighten sheet metal; shaping metal over anvils, blocks, or forms using hammer operating soldering and welding equipment to join sheet metal parts inspecting, assembling, and smoothing seams and joints of burred surfaces.

Tasks

1) Convert blueprints into shop drawings to be followed in the construction and assembly of sheet metal products.

2) Drill and punch holes in metal, for screws, bolts, and rivets.

3) Transport prefabricated parts to construction sites for assembly and installation.

4) Trim, file, grind, deburr, buff, and smooth surfaces, seams, and joints of assembled parts, using hand tools and portable power tools.

5) Shape metal material over anvils, blocks, or other forms, using hand tools.

6) Select gauges and types of sheet metal or non-metallic material, according to product specifications.

7) Lay out, measure, and mark dimensions and reference lines on material, such as roofing panels, according to drawings or templates, using calculators, scribes, dividers, squares, and rulers.

8) Install assemblies, such as flashing, pipes, tubes, heating and air conditioning ducts, furnace casings, rain gutters, and down spouts, in supportive frameworks.

9) Finish parts, using hacksaws, and hand, rotary, or squaring shears.

10) Inspect individual parts, assemblies, and installations for conformance to specifications and building codes, using measuring instruments such as calipers, scales, and micrometers.

11) Maintain equipment, making repairs and modifications when necessary.

12) Determine project requirements, including scope, assembly sequences, and required methods and materials, according to blueprints, drawings, and written or verbal instructions.

13) Maneuver completed units into position for installation, and anchor the units.

14) Develop and lay out patterns that use materials most efficiently, using computerized metalworking equipment to experiment with different layouts.

15) Fasten roof panel edges and machine-made molding to structures, nailing or welding pieces into place.

16) Fabricate or alter parts at construction sites, using shears, hammers, punches, and drills.

17) Secure metal roof panels in place, then interlock and fasten grooved panel edges.

47-3012.00 - Helpers--Carpenters

Help carpenters by performing duties of lesser skill. Duties include using, supplying or holding materials or tools, and cleaning work area and equipment.

Tasks

1) Cut timbers, lumber and/or paneling to specified dimensions, and drill holes in timbers or lumber.

2) Cover surfaces with laminated plastic covering material.

3) Secure stakes to grids for constructions of footings, nail scabs to footing forms, and vibrate and float concrete.

4) Hold plumb bobs, sighting rods, and other equipment, to aid in establishing reference points and lines.

5) Position and hold timbers, lumber, and paneling in place for fastening or cutting.

6) Select tools, equipment, and materials from storage and transport items to work site.

7) Fasten timbers and/or lumber with glue, screws, pegs, or nails, and install hardware.

8) Align, straighten, plumb and square forms for installation.

9) Construct forms, then assist in raising them to the required elevation.

10) Perform tie spacing layout, then measure, mark, drill and/or cut.

11) Smooth and sand surfaces to remove ridges, tool marks, glue, or caulking.

12) Cut tile or linoleum to fit, and spread adhesives on flooring to install tile or linoleum.

13) Erect scaffolding, shoring, and braces.

14) Install handrails under the direction of a carpenter.

15) Cut and install insulating or sound-absorbing material.

16) Glue and clamp edges or joints of assembled parts.

47-3013.00 - Helpers--Electricians

Help electricians by performing duties of lesser skill. Duties include using, supplying or holding materials or tools, and cleaning work area and equipment.

Tasks

1) Transport tools, materials, equipment, and supplies to work site by hand, handtruck, or heavy, motorized truck.

2) Perform semi-skilled and unskilled laboring duties related to the installation, maintenance and repair of a wide variety of electrical systems and equipment.

3) Trace out short circuits in wiring, using test meter.

4) Break up concrete, using airhammer, to facilitate installation, construction, or repair of equipment.

5) Clean work area and wash parts.

6) Dig trenches or holes for installation of conduit or supports.

7) Install copper-clad ground rods, using a manual post driver.

8) Operate cutting torches and welding equipment, while working with conduit and metal components to construct devices associated with electrical functions.

9) Paint a variety of objects related to electrical functions.

10) Trim trees and clear undergrowth along right-of-way.

11) Thread conduit ends, connect couplings, and fabricate and secure conduit support brackets, using hand tools.

12) Disassemble defective electrical equipment, replace defective or worn parts, and reassemble equipment, using hand tools.

13) Raise, lower, or position equipment, tools, and materials, using hoist, hand line, or block and tackle.

14) Requisition materials, using warehouse requisition or release forms.

15) String transmission lines or cables through ducts or conduits, under the ground, through equipment, or to towers.

16) Solder electrical connections, using soldering iron.

17) Measure, cut, and bend wire and conduit, using measuring instruments and hand tools.

18) Examine electrical units for loose connections and broken insulation and tighten connections, using hand tools.

19) Drill holes and pull or push wiring through openings, using hand and power tools.

20) Strip insulation from wire ends, using wire stripping pliers, and attach wires to terminals for subsequent soldering.

21) Bolt component parts together to form tower assemblies, using hand tools.

22) Erect electrical system components and barricades, and rig scaffolds, hoists, and shoring.

23) Construct controllers and panels, using power drills, drill presses, taps, saws and punches.

47-3015.00 - Helpers--Pipelayers, Plumbers, Pipefitters, and Steamfitters

Help plumbers, pipefitters, steamfitters, or pipelayers by performing duties of lesser skill. Duties include using, supplying or holding materials or tools, and cleaning work area and equipment.

Tasks

1) Assist pipefitters in the layout, assembly, and installation of piping for air, ammonia, gas, and water systems.

2) Clean shop, work area, and machines, using solvent and rags.

3) Disassemble and remove damaged or worn pipe.

4) Excavate and grade ditches, and lay and join pipe for water and sewer service.

5) Fill pipes with sand or resin to prevent distortion, and hold pipes during bending and installation.

6) Assist plumbers by performing rough-ins, repairing and replacing fixtures, and locating and repairing leaking or broken pipes.

7) Requisition tools and equipment, select type and size of pipe, and collect and transport materials and equipment to work site.

8) Cut pipe and lift up to fitters.

9) Measure, cut, thread and assemble new pipe, placing the assembled pipe in hangers or other supports.

10) Mount brackets and hangers on walls and ceilings to hold pipes, and set sleeves or inserts to provide support for pipes.

11) Immerse pipe in chemical solution to remove dirt, oil, and scale.

12) Fit or assist in fitting valves, couplings, or assemblies to tanks, pumps, or systems, using hand tools.

13) Cut or drill holes in walls or floors to accommodate the passage of pipes.

14) Install gas burners to convert furnaces from wood, coal, or oil.

47-4011.00 - Construction and Building Inspectors

Inspect structures using engineering skills to determine structural soundness and compliance with specifications, building codes, and other regulations. Inspections may be general in nature or may be limited to a specific area, such as electrical systems or plumbing.

Tasks

1) Inspect bridges, dams, highways, buildings, wiring, plumbing, electrical circuits, sewers, heating systems, and foundations during and after construction for structural quality, general safety and conformance to specifications and codes.

2) Review and interpret plans, blueprints, site layouts, specifications, and construction methods to ensure compliance to legal requirements and safety regulations.

3) Use survey instruments, metering devices, tape measures, and test equipment, such as concrete strength measurers, to perform inspections.

47-3015.00 - Helpers--Pipelayers, Plumbers, Pipefitters, and Steamfitters

4) Inspect and monitor construction sites to ensure adherence to safety standards, building codes, and specifications.

5) Measure dimensions and verify level, alignment, and elevation of structures and fixtures to ensure compliance to building plans and codes.

6) Issue violation notices and stop-work orders, conferring with owners, violators, and authorities to explain regulations and recommend rectifications.

7) Train, direct and supervise other construction inspectors.

8) Approve and sign plans that meet required specifications.

9) Monitor installation of plumbing, wiring, equipment, and appliances to ensure that installation is performed properly and is in compliance with applicable regulations.

10) Compute estimates of work completed or of needed renovations or upgrades, and approve payment for contractors.

11) Evaluate premises for cleanliness, including proper garbage disposal and lack of vermin infestation.

12) Issue permits for construction, relocation, demolition and occupancy.

13) Examine lifting and conveying devices, such as elevators, escalators, moving sidewalks, lifts and hoists, inclined railways, ski lifts, and amusement rides to ensure safety and proper functioning.

Knowledge	Knowledge Definitions
Building and Construction	Knowledge of materials, methods, and the tools involved in the construction or repair of houses, buildings, or other structures such as highways and roads.
Engineering and Technology	Knowledge of the practical application of engineering science and technology. This includes applying principles, techniques, procedures, and equipment to the design and production of various goods and services.
Customer and Personal Service	Knowledge of principles and processes for providing customer and personal services. This includes customer needs assessment, meeting quality standards for services, and evaluation of customer satisfaction.
Public Safety and Security	Knowledge of relevant equipment, policies, procedures, and strategies to promote effective local, state, or national security operations for the protection of people, data, property, and institutions.
Design	Knowledge of design techniques, tools, and principles involved in production of precision technical plans, blueprints, drawings, and models.
English Language	Knowledge of the structure and content of the English language including the meaning and spelling of words, rules of composition, and grammar.
Mathematics	Knowledge of arithmetic, algebra, geometry, calculus, statistics, and their applications.
Administration and Management	Knowledge of business and management principles involved in strategic planning, resource allocation, human resources modeling, leadership technique, production methods, and coordination of people and resources.
Computers and Electronics	Knowledge of circuit boards, processors, chips, electronic equipment, and computer hardware and software, including applications and programming.
Clerical	Knowledge of administrative and clerical procedures and systems such as word processing, managing files and records, stenography and transcription, designing forms, and other office procedures and terminology.
Education and Training	Knowledge of principles and methods for curriculum and training design, teaching and instruction for individuals and groups, and the measurement of training effects.
Mechanical	Knowledge of machines and tools, including their designs, uses, repair, and maintenance.
Geography	Knowledge of principles and methods for describing the features of land, sea, and air masses, including their physical characteristics, locations, interrelationships, and distribution of plant, animal, and human life.
Personnel and Human Resources	Knowledge of principles and procedures for personnel recruitment, selection, training, compensation and benefits, labor relations and negotiation, and personnel information systems.
Telecommunications	Knowledge of transmission, broadcasting, switching, control, and operation of telecommunications systems.
Communications and Media	Knowledge of media production, communication, and dissemination techniques and methods. This includes alternative ways to inform and entertain via written, oral, and visual media.
Transportation	Knowledge of principles and methods for moving people or goods by air, rail, sea, or road, including the relative costs and benefits.
Physics	Knowledge and prediction of physical principles, laws, their interrelationships, and applications to understanding fluid, material, and atmospheric dynamics, and mechanical, electrical, atomic and sub-atomic structures and processes.

Production and Processing	Knowledge of raw materials, production processes, quality control, costs. and other techniques for maximizing the effective manufacture and distribution of goods.
Sales and Marketing	Knowledge of principles and methods for showing, promoting, and selling products or services. This includes marketing strategy and tactics, product demonstration, sales techniques, and sales control systems.
Law and Government	Knowledge of laws. legal codes. court procedures, precedents. government regulations. executive orders. agency rules, and the democratic political process.
Economics and Accounting	Knowledge of economic and accounting principles and practices, the financial markets, banking and the analysis and reporting of financial data.
Psychology	Knowledge of human behavior and performance; individual differences in ability, personality, and interests; learning and motivation; psychological research methods; and the assessment and treatment of behavioral and affective disorders.
Chemistry	Knowledge of the chemical composition, structure, and properties of substances and of the chemical processes and transformations that they undergo. This includes uses of chemicals and their interactions, danger signs, production techniques, and disposal methods.
Biology	Knowledge of plant and animal organisms, their tissues, cells, functions, interdependencies. and interactions with each other and the environment.
Sociology and Anthropology	Knowledge of group behavior and dynamics, societal trends and influences, human migrations, ethnicity, cultures and their history and origins.
Food Production	Knowledge of techniques and equipment for planting, growing, and harvesting food products (both plant and animal) for consumption, including storage/handling techniques.
Fine Arts	Knowledge of the theory and techniques required to compose, produce, and perform works of music, dance, visual arts, drama, and sculpture.
History and Archeology	Knowledge of historical events and their causes, indicators, and effects on civilizations and cultures.
Foreign Language	Knowledge of the structure and content of a foreign (non-English) language including the meaning and spelling of words, rules of composition and grammar, and pronunciation.
Philosophy and Theology	Knowledge of different philosophical systems and religions. This includes their basic principles, values, ethics, ways of thinking, customs, practices, and their impact on human culture.
Therapy and Counseling	Knowledge of principles, methods, and procedures for diagnosis, treatment, and rehabilitation of physical and mental dysfunctions, and for career counseling and guidance.
Medicine and Dentistry	Knowledge of the information and techniques needed to diagnose and treat human injuries, diseases, and deformities. This includes symptoms, treatment alternatives, drug properties and interactions, and preventive health-care measures.

Skills	**Skills Definitions**
Reading Comprehension	Understanding written sentences and paragraphs in work related documents.
Active Listening	Giving full attention to what other people are saying, taking time to understand the points being made, asking questions as appropriate, and not interrupting at inappropriate times.
Mathematics	Using mathematics to solve problems.
Critical Thinking	Using logic and reasoning to identify the strengths and weaknesses of alternative solutions, conclusions or approaches to problems.
Active Learning	Understanding the implications of new information for both current and future problem-solving and decision-making.
Time Management	Managing one's own time and the time of others.
Writing	Communicating effectively in writing as appropriate for the needs of the audience.
Coordination	Adjusting actions in relation to others' actions.
Social Perceptiveness	Being aware of others' reactions and understanding why they react as they do.
Quality Control Analysis	Conducting tests and inspections of products, services, or processes to evaluate quality or performance.
Complex Problem Solving	Identifying complex problems and reviewing related information to develop and evaluate options and implement solutions.
Speaking	Talking to others to convey information effectively.
Judgment and Decision Making	Considering the relative costs and benefits of potential actions to choose the most appropriate one.
Instructing	Teaching others how to do something.
Learning Strategies	Selecting and using training/instructional methods and procedures appropriate for the situation when learning or teaching new things.
Persuasion	Persuading others to change their minds or behavior.
Monitoring	Monitoring/Assessing performance of yourself, other individuals, or organizations to make improvements or take corrective action.

Troubleshooting	Determining causes of operating errors and deciding what to do about it.
Science	Using scientific rules and methods to solve problems.
Service Orientation	Actively looking for ways to help people.
Negotiation	Bringing others together and trying to reconcile differences.
Equipment Selection	Determining the kind of tools and equipment needed to do a job.
Equipment Maintenance	Performing routine maintenance on equipment and determining when and what kind of maintenance is needed.
Operation Monitoring	Watching gauges, dials, or other indicators to make sure a machine is working properly.
Installation	Installing equipment, machines, wiring, or programs to meet specifications.
Operations Analysis	Analyzing needs and product requirements to create a design.
Technology Design	Generating or adapting equipment and technology to serve user needs.
Operation and Control	Controlling operations of equipment or systems.
Management of Material Resources	Obtaining and seeing to the appropriate use of equipment, facilities, and materials needed to do certain work.
Systems Analysis	Determining how a system should work and how changes in conditions, operations, and the environment will affect outcomes.
Systems Evaluation	Identifying measures or indicators of system performance and the actions needed to improve or correct performance, relative to the goals of the system.
Management of Personnel Resources	Motivating, developing, and directing people as they work, identifying the best people for the job.
Management of Financial Resources	Determining how money will be spent to get the work done, and accounting for these expenditures.
Programming	Writing computer programs for various purposes.
Repairing	Repairing machines or systems using the needed tools.

Ability	**Ability Definitions**
Problem Sensitivity	The ability to tell when something is wrong or is likely to go wrong. It does not involve solving the problem, only recognizing there is a problem.
Oral Expression	The ability to communicate information and ideas in speaking so others will understand.
Oral Comprehension	The ability to listen to and understand information and ideas presented through spoken words and sentences.
Inductive Reasoning	The ability to combine pieces of information to form general rules or conclusions (includes finding a relationship among seemingly unrelated events).
Near Vision	The ability to see details at close range (within a few feet of the observer).
Speech Clarity	The ability to speak clearly so others can understand you.
Deductive Reasoning	The ability to apply general rules to specific problems to produce answers that make sense.
Written Comprehension	The ability to read and understand information and ideas presented in writing.
Speech Recognition	The ability to identify and understand the speech of another person.
Information Ordering	The ability to arrange things or actions in a certain order or pattern according to a specific rule or set of rules (e.g., patterns of numbers, letters, words, pictures, mathematical operations).
Flexibility of Closure	The ability to identify or detect a known pattern (a figure, object, word, or sound) that is hidden in other distracting material.
Written Expression	The ability to communicate information and ideas in writing so others will understand.
Visualization	The ability to imagine how something will look after it is moved around or when its parts are moved or rearranged.
Selective Attention	The ability to concentrate on a task over a period of time without being distracted.
Far Vision	The ability to see details at a distance.
Arm-Hand Steadiness	The ability to keep your hand and arm steady while moving your arm or while holding your arm and hand in one position.
Perceptual Speed	The ability to quickly and accurately compare similarities and differences among sets of letters, numbers, objects, pictures, or patterns. The things to be compared may be presented at the same time or one after the other. This ability also includes comparing a presented object with a remembered object.
Visual Color Discrimination	The ability to match or detect differences between colors, including shades of color and brightness.
Depth Perception	The ability to judge which of several objects is closer or farther away from you, or to judge the distance between you and an object.
Speed of Closure	The ability to quickly make sense of, combine, and organize information into meaningful patterns.
Time Sharing	The ability to shift back and forth between two or more activities or sources of information (such as speech, sounds, touch, or other sources).
Auditory Attention	The ability to focus on a single source of sound in the presence of other distracting sounds.

Control Precision	The ability to quickly and repeatedly adjust the controls of a machine or a vehicle to exact positions.
Finger Dexterity	The ability to make precisely coordinated movements of the fingers of one or both hands to grasp, manipulate, or assemble very small objects.
Number Facility	The ability to add, subtract, multiply, or divide quickly and correctly.
Mathematical Reasoning	The ability to choose the right mathematical methods or formulas to solve a problem.
Category Flexibility	The ability to generate or use different sets of rules for combining or grouping things in different ways.
Gross Body Coordination	The ability to coordinate the movement of your arms, legs, and torso together when the whole body is in motion.
Multilimb Coordination	The ability to coordinate two or more limbs (for example, two arms, two legs, or one leg and one arm) while sitting, standing, or lying down. It does not involve performing the activities while the whole body is in motion.
Originality	The ability to come up with unusual or clever ideas about a given topic or situation, or to develop creative ways to solve a problem.
Spatial Orientation	The ability to know your location in relation to the environment or to know where other objects are in relation to you.
Memorization	The ability to remember information such as words, numbers, pictures, and procedures.
Trunk Strength	The ability to use your abdominal and lower back muscles to support part of the body repeatedly or continuously over time without 'giving out' or fatiguing.
Extent Flexibility	The ability to bend, stretch, twist, or reach with your body, arms, and/or legs.
Manual Dexterity	The ability to quickly move your hand, your hand together with your arm, or your two hands to grasp, manipulate, or assemble objects.
Reaction Time	The ability to quickly respond (with the hand, finger, or foot) to a signal (sound, light, picture) when it appears.
Gross Body Equilibrium	The ability to keep or regain your body balance or stay upright when in an unstable position.
Fluency of Ideas	The ability to come up with a number of ideas about a topic (the number of ideas is important, not their quality, correctness, or creativity).
Glare Sensitivity	The ability to see objects in the presence of glare or bright lighting.
Peripheral Vision	The ability to see objects or movement of objects to one's side when the eyes are looking ahead.
Static Strength	The ability to exert maximum muscle force to lift, push, pull, or carry objects.
Stamina	The ability to exert yourself physically over long periods of time without getting winded or out of breath.
Hearing Sensitivity	The ability to detect or tell the differences between sounds that vary in pitch and loudness.
Rate Control	The ability to time your movements or the movement of a piece of equipment in anticipation of changes in the speed and/or direction of a moving object or scene.
Sound Localization	The ability to tell the direction from which a sound originated.
Speed of Limb Movement	The ability to quickly move the arms and legs.
Response Orientation	The ability to choose quickly between two or more movements in response to two or more different signals (lights, sounds, pictures). It includes the speed with which the correct response is started with the hand, foot, or other body part.
Wrist-Finger Speed	The ability to make fast, simple, repeated movements of the fingers, hands, and wrists.
Night Vision	The ability to see under low light conditions.
Dynamic Strength	The ability to exert muscle force repeatedly or continuously over time. This involves muscular endurance and resistance to muscle fatigue.
Dynamic Flexibility	The ability to quickly and repeatedly bend, stretch, twist, or reach out with your body, arms, and/or legs.
Explosive Strength	The ability to use short bursts of muscle force to propel oneself (as in jumping or sprinting), or to throw an object.

Work_Activity	Work_Activity Definitions
Inspecting Equipment, Structures, or Material	Inspecting equipment, structures, or materials to identify the cause of errors or other problems or defects.
Evaluating Information to Determine Compliance wit	Using relevant information and individual judgment to determine whether events or processes comply with laws, regulations, or standards.
Getting Information	Observing, receiving, and otherwise obtaining information from all relevant sources.
Monitor Processes, Materials, or Surroundings	Monitoring and reviewing information from materials, events, or the environment, to detect or assess problems.
Identifying Objects, Actions, and Events	Identifying information by categorizing, estimating, recognizing differences or similarities, and detecting changes in circumstances or events.
Documenting/Recording Information	Entering, transcribing, recording, storing, or maintaining information in written or electronic/magnetic form.

Communicating with Supervisors, Peers, or Subordin	Providing information to supervisors, co-workers, and subordinates by telephone, in written form, e-mail, or in person.
Communicating with Persons Outside Organization	Communicating with people outside the organization, representing the organization to customers, the public, government, and other external sources. This information can be exchanged in person, in writing, or by telephone or e-mail.
Making Decisions and Solving Problems	Analyzing information and evaluating results to choose the best solution and solve problems.
Processing Information	Compiling, coding, categorizing, calculating, tabulating, auditing, or verifying information or data.
Resolving Conflicts and Negotiating with Others	Handling complaints, settling disputes, and resolving grievances and conflicts, or otherwise negotiating with others.
Establishing and Maintaining Interpersonal Relatio	Developing constructive and cooperative working relationships with others, and maintaining them over time.
Performing Administrative Activities	Performing day-to-day administrative tasks such as maintaining information files and processing paperwork.
Analyzing Data or Information	Identifying the underlying principles, reasons, or facts of information by breaking down information or data into separate parts.
Performing for or Working Directly with the Public	Performing for people or dealing directly with the public. This includes serving customers in restaurants and stores, and receiving clients or guests.
Estimating the Quantifiable Characteristics of Pro	Estimating sizes, distances, and quantities; or determining time, costs, resources, or materials needed to perform a work activity.
Interacting With Computers	Using computers and computer systems (including hardware and software) to program, write software, set up functions, enter data, or process information.
Organizing, Planning, and Prioritizing Work	Developing specific goals and plans to prioritize, organize, and accomplish your work.
Interpreting the Meaning of Information for Others	Translating or explaining what information means and how it can be used.
Updating and Using Relevant Knowledge	Keeping up-to-date technically and applying new knowledge to your job.
Scheduling Work and Activities	Scheduling events, programs, and activities, as well as the work of others.
Judging the Qualities of Things, Services, or Peop	Assessing the value, importance, or quality of things or people.
Monitoring and Controlling Resources	Monitoring and controlling resources and overseeing the spending of money.
Drafting, Laying Out, and Specifying Technical Dev	Providing documentation, detailed instructions, drawings, or specifications to tell others about how devices, parts, equipment, or structures are to be fabricated, constructed, assembled, modified, maintained, or used.
Thinking Creatively	Developing, designing, or creating new applications, ideas, relationships, systems, or products, including artistic contributions.
Performing General Physical Activities	Performing physical activities that require considerable use of your arms and legs and moving your whole body, such as climbing, lifting, balancing, walking, stooping, and handling of materials.
Provide Consultation and Advice to Others	Providing guidance and expert advice to management or other groups on technical, systems-, or process-related topics.
Controlling Machines and Processes	Using either control mechanisms or direct physical activity to operate machines or processes (not including computers or vehicles).
Operating Vehicles, Mechanized Devices, or Equipme	Running, maneuvering, navigating, or driving vehicles or mechanized equipment, such as forklifts, passenger vehicles, aircraft, or water craft.
Developing and Building Teams	Encouraging and building mutual trust, respect, and cooperation among team members.
Developing Objectives and Strategies	Establishing long-range objectives and specifying the strategies and actions to achieve them.
Coordinating the Work and Activities of Others	Getting members of a group to work together to accomplish tasks.
Handling and Moving Objects	Using hands and arms in handling, installing, positioning, and moving materials, and manipulating things.
Coaching and Developing Others	Identifying the developmental needs of others and coaching, mentoring, or otherwise helping others to improve their knowledge or skills.
Training and Teaching Others	Identifying the educational needs of others, developing formal educational or training programs or classes, and teaching or instructing others.
Assisting and Caring for Others	Providing personal assistance, medical attention, emotional support, or other personal care to others such as coworkers, customers, or patients.
Repairing and Maintaining Electronic Equipment	Servicing, repairing, calibrating, regulating, fine-tuning, or testing machines, devices, and equipment that operate primarily on the basis of electrical or electronic (not mechanical) principles.
Repairing and Maintaining Mechanical Equipment	Servicing, repairing, adjusting, and testing machines, devices, moving parts, and equipment that operate primarily on the basis of mechanical (not electronic) principles.

Guiding. Directing. and Motivating Subordinates	Providing guidance and direction to subordinates, including setting performance standards and monitoring performance.
Selling or Influencing Others	Convincing others to buy merchandise/goods or to otherwise change their minds or actions.
Staffing Organizational Units	Recruiting, interviewing, selecting, hiring, and promoting employees in an organization.

Work_Content	**Work_Content Definitions**
Face-to-Face Discussions	How often do you have to have face-to-face discussions with individuals or teams in this job?
Telephone	How often do you have telephone conversations in this job?
Contact With Others	How much does this job require the worker to be in contact with others (face-to-face, by telephone, or otherwise) in order to perform it?
Frequency of Decision Making	How frequently is the worker required to make decisions that affect other people, the financial resources, and/or the image and reputation of the organization?
Freedom to Make Decisions	How much decision making freedom, without supervision, does the job offer?
Outdoors. Exposed to Weather	How often does this job require working outdoors, exposed to all weather conditions?
In an Enclosed Vehicle or Equipment	How often does this job require working in a closed vehicle or equipment (e.g., car)?
Letters and Memos	How often does the job require written letters and memos?
Structured versus Unstructured Work	To what extent is this job structured for the worker, rather than allowing the worker to determine tasks, priorities, and goals?
Time Pressure	How often does this job require the worker to meet strict deadlines?
Importance of Being Exact or Accurate	How important is being very exact or highly accurate in performing this job?
Work With Work Group or Team	How important is it to work with others in a group or team in this job?
Sounds. Noise Levels Are Distracting or Uncomforta	How often does this job require working exposed to sounds and noise levels that are distracting or uncomfortable?
Impact of Decisions on Co-workers or Company Resul	How do the decisions an employee makes impact the results of co-workers, clients or the company?
Frequency of Conflict Situations	How often are there conflict situations the employee has to face in this job?
Exposed to Hazardous Equipment	How often does this job require exposure to hazardous equipment?
Wear Common Protective or Safety Equipment such as	How much does this job require wearing common protective or safety equipment such as safety shoes, glasses, gloves, hard hats or live jackets?
Deal With Unpleasant or Angry People	How frequently does the worker have to deal with unpleasant, angry, or discourteous individuals as part of the job requirements?
Exposed to Contaminants	How often does this job require working exposed to contaminants (such as pollutants, gases, dust or odors)?
Physical Proximity	To what extent does this job require the worker to perform job tasks in close physical proximity to other people?
Indoors, Environmentally Controlled	How often does this job require working indoors in environmentally controlled conditions?
Responsibility for Outcomes and Results	How responsible is the worker for work outcomes and results of other workers?
Spend Time Standing	How much does this job require standing?
Coordinate or Lead Others·	How important is it to coordinate or lead others in accomplishing work activities in this job?
Very Hot or Cold Temperatures	How often does this job require working in very hot (above 90 F degrees) or very cold (below 32 F degrees) temperatures?
Extremely Bright or Inadequate Lighting	How often does this job require working in extremely bright or inadequate lighting conditions?
Importance of Repeating Same Tasks	How important is repeating the same physical activities (e.g., key entry) or mental activities (e.g., checking entries in a ledger) over and over, without stopping, to performing this job?
Cramped Work Space, Awkward Positions	How often does this job require working in cramped work spaces that requires getting into awkward positions?
Exposed to Minor Burns, Cuts, Bites, or Stings	How often does this job require exposure to minor burns, cuts, bites, or stings?
Deal With External Customers	How important is it to work with external customers or the public in this job?
Spend Time Walking and Running	How much does this job require walking and running?
Responsible for Others' Health and Safety	How much responsibility is there for the health and safety of others in this job?
Electronic Mail	How often do you use electronic mail in this job?
Spend Time Sitting	How much does this job require sitting?
Consequence of Error	How serious would the result usually be if the worker made a mistake that was not readily correctable?
Indoors, Not Environmentally Controlled	How often does this job require working indoors in non-controlled environmental conditions (e.g., warehouse without heat)?
Exposed to Radiation	How often does this job require exposure to radiation?
Exposed to High Places	How often does this job require exposure to high places?

Spend Time Using Your Hands to Handle. Control. or	How much does this job require using your hands to handle, control, or feel objects, tools or controls?
Spend Time Making Repetitive Motions	How much does this job require making repetitive motions?
Pace Determined by Speed of Equipment	How important is it to this job that the pace is determined by the speed of equipment or machinery? (This does not refer to keeping busy at all times on this job.)
Level of Competition	To what extent does this job require the worker to compete or to be aware of competitive pressures?
Degree of Automation	How automated is the job?
Spend Time Bending or Twisting the Body	How much does this job require bending or twisting your body?
Spend Time Kneeling. Crouching, Stooping, or Crawl	How much does this job require kneeling, crouching, stooping or crawling?
Exposed to Whole Body Vibration	How often does this job require exposure to whole body vibration (e.g., operate a jackhammer)?
Wear Specialized Protective or Safety Equipment su	How much does this job require wearing specialized protective or safety equipment such as breathing apparatus, safety harness, full protection suits, or radiation protection?
Exposed to Hazardous Conditions	How often does this job require exposure to hazardous conditions?
Spend Time Climbing Ladders, Scaffolds, or Poles	How much does this job require climbing ladders, scaffolds, or poles?
Spend Time Keeping or Regaining Balance	How much does this job require keeping or regaining your balance?
Outdoors, Under Cover	How often does this job require working outdoors, under cover (e.g., structure with roof but no walls)?
Public Speaking	How often do you have to perform public speaking in this job?
Exposed to Disease or Infections	How often does this job require exposure to disease/infections?
Deal With Physically Aggressive People	How frequently does this job require the worker to deal with physical aggression of violent individuals?
In an Open Vehicle or Equipment	How often does this job require working in an open vehicle or equipment (e.g., tractor)?

Work_Styles	**Work_Styles Definitions**
Dependability	Job requires being reliable, responsible, and dependable, and fulfilling obligations.
Integrity	Job requires being honest and ethical.
Attention to Detail	Job requires being careful about detail and thorough in completing work tasks.
Cooperation	Job requires being pleasant with others on the job and displaying a good-natured, cooperative attitude.
Stress Tolerance	Job requires accepting criticism and dealing calmly and effectively with high stress situations.
Self Control	Job requires maintaining composure, keeping emotions in check, controlling anger, and avoiding aggressive behavior, even in very difficult situations.
Adaptability/Flexibility	Job requires being open to change (positive or negative) and to considerable variety in the workplace.
Independence	Job requires developing one's own ways of doing things, guiding oneself with little or no supervision, and depending on oneself to get things done.
Leadership	Job requires a willingness to lead, take charge, and offer opinions and direction.
Initiative	Job requires a willingness to take on responsibilities and challenges.
Innovation	Job requires creativity and alternative thinking to develop new ideas for and answers to work-related problems.
Concern for Others	Job requires being sensitive to others' needs and feelings and being understanding and helpful on the job.
Social Orientation	Job requires preferring to work with others rather than alone, and being personally connected with others on the job.
Persistence	Job requires persistence in the face of obstacles.
Analytical Thinking	Job requires analyzing information and using logic to address work-related issues and problems.
Achievement/Effort	Job requires establishing and maintaining personally challenging achievement goals and exerting effort toward mastering tasks.

Job Zone Component	**Job Zone Component Definitions**
Title	Job Zone Three: Medium Preparation Needed
Overall Experience	Previous work-related skill, knowledge, or experience is required for these occupations. For example, an electrician must have completed three or four years of apprenticeship or several years of vocational training, and often must have passed a licensing exam, in order to perform the job.
Job Training	Employees in these occupations usually need one or two years of training involving both on-the-job experience and informal training with experienced workers.

Job Zone Examples	These occupations usually involve using communication and organizational skills to coordinate, supervise, manage, or train others to accomplish goals. Examples include dental assistants, electricians, fish and game wardens, legal secretaries, personnel recruiters, and recreation workers.
SVP Range	(6.0 to · 7.0)
Education	Most occupations in this zone require training in vocational schools, related on-the-job experience, or an associate's degree. Some may require a bachelor's degree.

47-4051.00 - Highway Maintenance Workers

Maintain highways, municipal and rural roads, airport runways, and rights-of-way. Duties include patching broken or eroded pavement, repairing guard rails, highway markers, and snow fences. May also mow or clear brush from along road or plow snow from roadway.

Tasks

1) Blend compounds to form adhesive mixtures used for marker installation.

2) Set out signs and cones around work areas to divert traffic.

3) Remove litter and debris from roadways, including debris from rock and mud slides.

4) Place and remove snow fences used to prevent the accumulation of drifting snow on highways.

5) Perform roadside landscaping work, such as clearing weeds and brush, and planting and trimming trees.

6) Haul and spread sand, gravel, and clay to fill washouts and repair road shoulders.

7) Erect, install, or repair guardrails, road shoulders, berms, highway markers, warning signals, and highway lighting, using hand tools and power tools.

8) Dump, spread, and tamp asphalt, using pneumatic tampers, to repair joints and patch broken pavement.

9) Drive trucks or tractors with adjustable attachments to sweep debris from paved surfaces, mow grass and weeds, and remove snow and ice.

10) Clean and clear debris from culverts, catch basins, drop inlets, ditches, and other drain structures.

11) Apply poisons along roadsides and in animal burrows to eliminate unwanted roadside vegetation and rodents.

12) Apply oil to road surfaces, using sprayers.

13) Flag motorists to warn them of obstacles or repair work ahead.

14) Measure and mark locations for installation of markers, using tape, string, or chalk.

15) Inspect, clean, and repair drainage systems, bridges, tunnels, and other structures.

16) Drive trucks to transport crews and equipment to work sites.

17) Inspect markers to verify accurate installation.

47-4091.00 - Segmental Pavers

Lay out, cut, and paste segmental paving units. Includes installers of bedding and restraining materials for the paving units.

Tasks

1) Discuss the design with the client.

2) Sweep sand into the joints and compact pavement until the joints are full.

3) Supply and place base materials, edge restraints, bedding sand and jointing sand.

4) Design paver installation layout pattern and create markings for directional references of joints and stringlines.

5) Screed sand level to an even thickness, and recheck sand exposed to elements, raking and rescreeding if necessary.

6) Set pavers, aligning and spacing them correctly.

7) Resurface an outside area with cobblestones, terracotta tiles, concrete or other materials.

8) Compact bedding sand and pavers to finish the paved area, using a plate compactor.

9) Cut paving stones to size and for edges, using a splitter and a masonry saw.

10) Prepare base for installation by removing unstable or unsuitable materials, compacting and grading the soil, draining or stabilizing weak or saturated soils and taking measures to prevent water penetration and migration of bedding sand.

11) Cement the edges of the paved area.

47-5011.00 - Derrick Operators, Oil and Gas

Rig derrick equipment and operate pumps to circulate mud through drill hole.

Tasks

1) Start pumps that circulate mud through drill pipes and boreholes to cool drill bits and flush out drill-cuttings.

2) Clamp holding fixtures on ends of hoisting cables.

3) Control the viscosity and weight of the drilling fluid.

4) Guide lengths of pipe into and out of elevators.

5) Inspect derricks for flaws, and clean and oil derricks in order to maintain proper working conditions.

6) Position and align derrick elements, using harnesses and platform climbing devices.

7) Listen to mud pumps and check regularly for vibration and other problems, in order to ensure that rig pumps and drilling mud systems are working properly.

8) Weigh clay, and mix with water and chemicals in order to make drilling mud, using portable mixers.

9) Steady pipes during connection to or disconnection from drill or casing strings.

10) String cables through pulleys and blocks.

11) Prepare mud reports, and instruct crews about the handling of any chemical additives.

12) Repair pumps, mud tanks, and related equipment.

13) Supervise crew members, and provide assistance in training them.

14) Inspect derricks, or order their inspection, prior to being raised or lowered.

47-5012.00 - Rotary Drill Operators, Oil and Gas

Set up or operate a variety of drills to remove petroleum products from the earth and to find and remove core samples for testing during oil and gas exploration.

Tasks

1) Push levers and brake pedals in order to control gasoline, diesel, electric, or steam draw works that lower and raise drill pipes and casings in and out of wells.

2) Remove core samples during drilling in order to determine the nature of the strata being drilled.

3) Cap wells with packers, or turn valves, in order to regulate outflow of oil from wells.

4) Monitor progress of drilling operations, and select and change drill bits according to the nature of strata, using hand tools.

5) Lower and explode charges in boreholes in order to start flow of oil from wells.

6) Line drilled holes with pipes, and install all necessary hardware, in order to prepare new wells.

7) Direct rig crews in drilling and other activities, such as setting up rigs and completing or servicing wells.

8) Count sections of drill rod in order to determine depths of boreholes.

9) Clean and oil pulleys, blocks, and cables.

10) Start and examine operation of slush pumps in order to ensure circulation and consistency of drilling fluid or mud in well.

11) Observe pressure gauge and move throttles and levers in order to control the speed of rotary tables, and to regulate pressure of tools at bottoms of boreholes.

12) Weigh clay, and mix with water and chemicals to make drilling mud.

13) Plug observation wells, and restore sites.

14) Repair or replace defective parts of machinery, such as rotary drill rigs, water trucks, air compressors, and pumps, using hand tools.

15) Train crews, and introduce procedures to make drill work more safe and effective.

16) Position and prepare truck-mounted derricks at drilling areas that are specified on field maps.

17) Maintain records of footage drilled, location and nature of strata penetrated, materials and tools used, services rendered, and time required.

18) Maintain and adjust machinery in order to ensure proper performance.

19) Connect sections of drill pipe, using hand tools and powered wrenches and tongs.

20) Bolt together pump and engine parts, and connect tanks and flow lines.

21) Dig holes, set forms, and mix and pour concrete, for foundations of steel or wooden derricks.

47-5013.00 - Service Unit Operators, Oil, Gas, and Mining

Operate equipment to increase oil flow from producing wells or to remove stuck pipe, casing, tools, or other obstructions from drilling wells. May also perform similar services in mining exploration operations.

Tasks

1) Analyze conditions of unserviceable wells in order to determine actions to be taken to improve well conditions.

2) Quote prices to customers; and prepare reports of services rendered, tools used, and time required so that bills can be produced.

3) Perforate well casings or sidewalls of boreholes with explosive charges.

4) Operate controls that raise derricks and level rigs.

5) Install pressure-control devices onto well heads.

6) Drive truck-mounted units to well sites.

7) Observe load variations on strain gauges, mud pumps, and motor pressure indicators; and listen to engines, rotary chains, and other equipment in order to detect faulty operations or unusual well conditions.

8) Thread cables through pulleys in derricks and connect hydraulic lines, using hand tools.

9) Confer with other personnel in order to gather information regarding pipe and tool sizes, and borehole conditions in wells.

10) Direct lowering of specialized equipment to point of obstruction, and push switches or pull levers in order to back-off or sever pipes by chemical or explosive action.

11) Direct drilling crews performing such activities as assembling and connecting pipe, applying weights to drill pipes, and drilling around lodged obstacles.

12) Assemble and operate sound-wave generating and detecting mechanisms in order to determine well fluid levels.

13) Plan fishing methods and select tools for removing obstacles, such as liners, broken casing, screens, and drill pipe, from wells.

14) Start pumps that circulate water, oil, or other fluids through wells, in order to remove sand and other materials obstructing the free flow of oil.

15) Close and seal wells no longer in use.

16) Assemble and lower detection instruments into wells with obstructions.

47-5042.00 - Mine Cutting and Channeling Machine Operators

Operate machinery--such as longwall shears, plows, and cutting machines--to cut or channel along the face or seams of coal mines, stone quarries, or other mining surfaces to facilitate blasting, separating, or removing minerals or materials from mines or from the earth's surface.

Tasks

1) Signal truck drivers to position their vehicles for receiving shale from planer hoppers.

2) Free jams in planer hoppers, using metal pinch bars.

3) Guide and assist crews in laying track for machines and resetting planer rails, supports, and blocking, using jacks, shovels, sledges, picks, and pinch bars.

4) Position jacks, timbers, or roof supports, and install casings, in order to prevent cave-ins.

5) Press buttons to activate conveyor belts, and push or pull chain handles to regulate conveyor movement so that material can be moved or loaded into dinkey cars or dump trucks.

6) Replace worn or broken tools and machine bits and parts, using wrenches, pry bars, and other hand tools, and lubricate machines, using grease guns.

7) Cut entries between rooms and haulage-ways.

8) Signal crewmembers to adjust the speed of equipment to the rate of installation of roof supports, and to adjust the speed of conveyors to the volume of coal.

9) Signal that machine plow blades are properly positioned, using electronic buzzers or two-way radios.

10) Reposition machines and move controls in order to make additional holes or cuts.

11) Move planer levers to control and adjust the movement of equipment, the speed, height, and depth of cuts, and to rotate swivel cutting booms.

12) Move controls to start and position drill cutters or torches, and to advance tools into mines or quarry faces in order to complete horizontal or vertical cuts.

13) Drive mobile, truck-mounted, or track-mounted drilling or cutting machine in mines and quarries or on construction sites.

14) Determine locations, boundaries, and depths of holes or channels to be cut.

15) Cut slots along working faces of coal, salt, or other non-metal deposits in order to

facilitate blasting, by moving levers to start the machine and to control the vertical reciprocating drills.

16) Advance plow blades through coal strata by remote control, according to electronic or radio signals from the tailer.

17) Charge and set off explosives in blasting holes.

18) Cut and move shale from open pits.

19) Remove debris such as loose shale from channels and planer travel areas.

20) Monitor movement of shale along conveyors from hoppers to trucks or railcars.

47-5061.00 - Roof Bolters, Mining

Operate machinery to install roof support bolts in underground mine.

Tasks

1) Drill bolt holes into roofs at specified distances from ribs or adjacent bolts.

2) Position safety jacks to support underground mine roofs until bolts can be installed.

3) Remove drill bits from chucks after drilling holes, then insert bolts into chucks.

4) Rotate chucks to turn bolts and open expansion heads against rock formations.

5) Test bolts for specified tension, using torque wrenches.

6) Tighten ends of anchored truss bolts, using turnbuckles.

7) Force bolts into holes, using hydraulic mechanisms of self-propelled bolting machines.

8) Position bolting machines, and insert drill bits into chucks.

47-5071.00 - Roustabouts, Oil and Gas

Assemble or repair oil field equipment using hand and power tools. Perform other tasks as needed.

Tasks

1) Bolt or nail together wood or steel framework in order to erect derricks.

2) Clean up spilled oil by bailing it into barrels.

3) Move pipes to and from trucks, using truck winches and motorized lifts, or by hand.

4) Bolt together pump and engine parts.

5) Dig holes, set forms, and mix and pour concrete into forms in order to make foundations for wood or steel derricks.

6) Dismantle and repair oil field machinery, boilers, and steam engine parts, using hand tools and power tools.

7) Unscrew or tighten pipes, casing, tubing, and pump rods, using hand and power wrenches and tongs.

8) Dig drainage ditches around wells and storage tanks.

9) Supply equipment to rig floors as requested, and provide assistance to roughnecks.

10) Guide cranes to move loads about decks.

11) Cut down and remove trees and brush to clear drill sites, in order to reduce fire hazards, and to make way for roads to sites.

12) Keep pipe deck and main deck areas clean and tidy.

47-5081.00 - Helpers--Extraction Workers

Help extraction craft workers, such as earth drillers, blasters and explosives workers, derrick operators, and mining machine operators, by performing duties of lesser skill. Duties include supplying equipment or cleaning work area.

Tasks

1) Collect and examine geological matter, using hand tools and testing devices.

2) Set up and adjust equipment used to excavate geological materials.

3) Dig trenches.

4) Organize materials in order to prepare for use.

5) Repair and maintain automotive and drilling equipment, using hand tools.

6) Provide assistance to extraction craft workers such as earth drillers and derrick operators.

7) Unload materials. devices and machine parts, using hand tools.

8) Clean and prepare sites for excavation or boring.

9) Clean up work areas and remove debris after extraction activities are complete.

10) Dismantle extracting and boring equipment used for excavation, using hand tools.

11) Drive moving equipment in order to transport materials and parts to excavation sites.

12) Load materials into well holes or into equipment, using hand tools.

13) Observe and monitor equipment operation during the extraction process in order to detect any problems.

49-1011.00 - First-Line Supervisors/Managers of Mechanics, Installers, and Repairers

Supervise and coordinate the activities of mechanics, installers, and repairers.

Tasks

1) Investigate accidents and injuries, and prepare reports of findings.

2) Meet with vendors and suppliers in order to discuss products used in repair work.

3) Conduct or arrange for worker training in safety, repair, and maintenance techniques; operational procedures; and equipment use.

4) Counsel employees about work-related issues and assist employees to correct job-skill deficiencies.

5) Determine schedules, sequences, and assignments for work activities, based on work priority, quantity of equipment and skill of personnel.

6) Monitor employees' work levels and review work performance.

7) Develop, implement, and evaluate maintenance policies and procedures.

8) Interpret specifications, blueprints, and job orders in order to construct templates and lay out reference points for workers.

9) Patrol and monitor work areas and examine tools and equipment in order to detect unsafe conditions or violations of procedures or safety rules.

10) Compile operational and personnel records, such as time and production records, inventory data, repair and maintenance statistics, and test results.

11) Requisition materials and supplies, such as tools, equipment, and replacement parts.

12) Perform skilled repair and maintenance operations, using equipment such as hand and power tools, hydraulic presses and shears, and welding equipment.

13) Design equipment configurations to meet personnel needs.

14) Monitor tool inventories and the condition and maintenance of shops in order to ensure adequate working conditions.

15) Examine objects, systems, or facilities; and analyze information to determine needed installations, services, or repairs.

16) Develop and implement electronic maintenance programs and computer information management systems.

17) Confer with personnel, such as management, engineering, quality control, customer, and union workers' representatives, in order to coordinate work activities, resolve employee grievances, and identify and review resource needs.

18) Inspect, test, and measure completed work, using devices such as hand tools and gauges to verify conformance to standards and repair requirements.

19) Compute estimates and actual costs of factors such as materials, labor, and outside contractors.

20) Participate in budget preparation and administration, coordinating purchasing and documentation, and monitoring departmental expenditures.

49-2094.00 - Electrical and Electronics Repairers, Commercial and Industrial Equipment

Repair, test, adjust, or install electronic equipment, such as industrial controls, transmitters, and antennas.

Tasks

1) Operate equipment to demonstrate proper use and to analyze malfunctions.

2) Perform scheduled preventive maintenance tasks, such as checking, cleaning, and repairing equipment, to detect and prevent problems.

3) Examine work orders and converse with equipment operators to detect equipment problems and to ascertain whether mechanical or human errors contributed to the problems.

49-1011.00 - First-Line Supervisors/Managers of Mechanics, Installers, and Repairers

4) Test faulty equipment to diagnose malfunctions, using test equipment and software, and applying knowledge of the functional operation of electronic units and systems.

5) Repair and adjust equipment, machines, and defective components, replacing worn parts such as gaskets and seals in watertight electrical equipment.

6) Inspect components of industrial equipment for accurate assembly and installation and for defects such as loose connections and frayed wires.

7) Coordinate efforts with other workers involved in installing and maintaining equipment or components.

8) Consult with customers, supervisors, and engineers to plan layout of equipment and to resolve problems in system operation and maintenance.

9) Calibrate testing instruments and installed or repaired equipment to prescribed specifications.

10) Set up and test industrial equipment to ensure that it functions properly.

11) Maintain equipment logs that record performance problems, repairs, calibrations, and tests.

12) Advise management regarding customer satisfaction, product performance, and suggestions for product improvements.

13) Send defective units to the manufacturer or to a specialized repair shop for repair.

14) Maintain inventory of spare parts.

15) Install repaired equipment in various settings, such as industrial or military establishments.

16) Determine feasibility of using standardized equipment, and develop specifications for equipment required to perform additional functions.

17) Develop or modify industrial electronic devices, circuits, and equipment according to available specifications.

18) Enter information into computer to copy program or to draw, modify, or store schematics, applying knowledge of software package used.

19) Sign overhaul documents for equipment replaced or repaired.

Knowledge	Knowledge Definitions
Mechanical	Knowledge of machines and tools, including their designs, uses, repair, and maintenance.
Computers and Electronics	Knowledge of circuit boards, processors, chips, electronic equipment, and computer hardware and software, including applications and programming.
Engineering and Technology	Knowledge of the practical application of engineering science and technology. This includes applying principles, techniques, procedures, and equipment to the design and production of various goods and services.
Telecommunications	Knowledge of transmission, broadcasting, switching, control, and operation of telecommunications systems.
Customer and Personal Service	Knowledge of principles and processes for providing customer and personal services. This includes customer needs assessment, meeting quality standards for services, and evaluation of customer satisfaction.
Mathematics	Knowledge of arithmetic, algebra, geometry, calculus, statistics, and their applications.
Production and Processing	Knowledge of raw materials, production processes, quality control, costs, and other techniques for maximizing the effective manufacture and distribution of goods.
English Language	Knowledge of the structure and content of the English language including the meaning and spelling of words, rules of composition, and grammar.
Design	Knowledge of design techniques, tools, and principles involved in production of precision technical plans, blueprints, drawings, and models.
Communications and Media	Knowledge of media production, communication, and dissemination techniques and methods. This includes alternative ways to inform and entertain via written, oral, and visual media.
Transportation	Knowledge of principles and methods for moving people or goods by air, rail, sea, or road, including the relative costs and benefits.
Administration and Management	Knowledge of business and management principles involved in strategic planning, resource allocation, human resources modeling, leadership technique, production methods, and coordination of people and resources.
Public Safety and Security	Knowledge of relevant equipment, policies, procedures, and strategies to promote effective local, state, or national security operations for the protection of people, data, property, and institutions.
Building and Construction	Knowledge of materials, methods, and the tools involved in the construction or repair of houses, buildings, or other structures such as highways and roads.
Education and Training	Knowledge of principles and methods for curriculum and training design, teaching and instruction for individuals and groups, and the measurement of training effects.

305

Clerical	Knowledge of administrative and clerical procedures and systems such as word processing, managing files and records, stenography and transcription, designing forms, and other office procedures and terminology.
Physics	Knowledge and prediction of physical principles, laws, their interrelationships, and applications to understanding fluid, material, and atmospheric dynamics, and mechanical, electrical, atomic and sub- atomic structures and processes.
Sales and Marketing	Knowledge of principles and methods for showing, promoting, and selling products or services. This includes marketing strategy and tactics, product demonstration, sales techniques, and sales control systems.
Chemistry	Knowledge of the chemical composition, structure, and properties of substances and of the chemical processes and transformations that they undergo. This includes uses of chemicals and their interactions, danger signs, production techniques, and disposal methods.
Law and Government	Knowledge of laws, legal codes, court procedures, precedents, government regulations, executive orders, agency rules, and the democratic political process.
Personnel and Human Resources	Knowledge of principles and procedures for personnel recruitment, selection, training, compensation and benefits, labor relations and negotiation, and personnel information systems.
Economics and Accounting	Knowledge of economic and accounting principles and practices, the financial markets, banking and the analysis and reporting of financial data.
Psychology	Knowledge of human behavior and performance; individual differences in ability, personality, and interests; learning and motivation; psychological research methods; and the assessment and treatment of behavioral and affective disorders.
Geography	Knowledge of principles and methods for describing the features of land, sea, and air masses, including their physical characteristics, locations, interrelationships, and distribution of plant, animal, and human life.
Biology	Knowledge of plant and animal organisms, their tissues, cells, functions, interdependencies, and interactions with each other and the environment.
Food Production	Knowledge of techniques and equipment for planting, growing, and harvesting food products (both plant and animal) for consumption, including storage/handling techniques.
Therapy and Counseling	Knowledge of principles, methods, and procedures for diagnosis, treatment, and rehabilitation of physical and mental dysfunctions, and for career counseling and guidance.
Philosophy and Theology	Knowledge of different philosophical systems and religions. This includes their basic principles, values, ethics, ways of thinking, customs, practices, and their impact on human culture.
Medicine and Dentistry	Knowledge of the information and techniques needed to diagnose and treat human injuries, diseases, and deformities. This includes symptoms, treatment alternatives, drug properties and interactions, and preventive health-care measures.
History and Archeology	Knowledge of historical events and their causes, indicators, and effects on civilizations and cultures.
Sociology and Anthropology	Knowledge of group behavior and dynamics, societal trends and influences, human migrations, ethnicity, cultures and their history and origins.
Fine Arts	Knowledge of the theory and techniques required to compose, produce, and perform works of music, dance, visual arts, drama, and sculpture.
Foreign Language	Knowledge of the structure and content of a foreign (non-English) language including the meaning and spelling of words, rules of composition and grammar, and pronunciation.

Skills	**Skills Definitions**
Troubleshooting	Determining causes of operating errors and deciding what to do about it.
Repairing	Repairing machines or systems using the needed tools.
Reading Comprehension	Understanding written sentences and paragraphs in work related documents.
Installation	Installing equipment, machines, wiring, or programs to meet specifications.
Active Listening	Giving full attention to what other people are saying, taking time to understand the points being made, asking questions as appropriate, and not interrupting at inappropriate times.
Operation Monitoring	Watching gauges, dials, or other indicators to make sure a machine is working properly.
Equipment Maintenance	Performing routine maintenance on equipment and determining when and what kind of maintenance is needed.
Coordination	Adjusting actions in relation to others' actions.
Critical Thinking	Using logic and reasoning to identify the strengths and weaknesses of alternative solutions, conclusions or approaches to problems.
Active Learning	Understanding the implications of new information for both current and future problem-solving and decision-making.

Equipment Selection	Determining the kind of tools and equipment needed to do a job.
Operation and Control	Controlling operations of equipment or systems.
Learning Strategies	Selecting and using training/instructional methods and procedures appropriate for the situation when learning or teaching new things.
Writing	Communicating effectively in writing as appropriate for the needs of the audience.
Complex Problem Solving	Identifying complex problems and reviewing related information to develop and evaluate options and implement solutions.
Judgment and Decision Making	Considering the relative costs and benefits of potential actions to choose the most appropriate one.
Instructing	Teaching others how to do something.
Time Management	Managing one's own time and the time of others.
Speaking	Talking to others to convey information effectively.
Monitoring	Monitoring/Assessing performance of yourself, other individuals, or organizations to make improvements or take corrective action.
Mathematics	Using mathematics to solve problems.
Systems Analysis	Determining how a system should work and how changes in conditions, operations, and the environment will affect outcomes.
Technology Design	Generating or adapting equipment and technology to serve user needs.
Social Perceptiveness	Being aware of others' reactions and understanding why they react as they do.
Systems Evaluation	Identifying measures or indicators of system performance and the actions needed to improve or correct performance, relative to the goals of the system.
Service Orientation	Actively looking for ways to help people.
Quality Control Analysis	Conducting tests and inspections of products, services, or processes to evaluate quality or performance.
Persuasion	Persuading others to change their minds or behavior.
Negotiation	Bringing others together and trying to reconcile differences.
Science	Using scientific rules and methods to solve problems.
Operations Analysis	Analyzing needs and product requirements to create a design.
Management of Personnel Resources	Motivating, developing, and directing people as they work, identifying the best people for the job.
Management of Material Resources	Obtaining and seeing to the appropriate use of equipment, facilities, and materials needed to do certain work.
Programming	Writing computer programs for various purposes.
Management of Financial Resources	Determining how money will be spent to get the work done, and accounting for these expenditures.

Ability	**Ability Definitions**
Problem Sensitivity	The ability to tell when something is wrong or is likely to go wrong. It does not involve solving the problem, only recognizing there is a problem.
Near Vision	The ability to see details at close range (within a few feet of the observer).
Deductive Reasoning	The ability to apply general rules to specific problems to produce answers that make sense.
Oral Expression	The ability to communicate information and ideas in speaking so others will understand.
Oral Comprehension	The ability to listen to and understand information and ideas presented through spoken words and sentences.
Selective Attention	The ability to concentrate on a task over a period of time without being distracted.
Written Comprehension	The ability to read and understand information and ideas presented in writing.
Arm-Hand Steadiness	The ability to keep your hand and arm steady while moving your arm or while holding your arm and hand in one position.
Information Ordering	The ability to arrange things or actions in a certain order or pattern according to a specific rule or set of rules (e.g., patterns of numbers, letters, words, pictures, mathematical operations).
Speech Clarity	The ability to speak clearly so others can understand you.
Control Precision	The ability to quickly and repeatedly adjust the controls of a machine or a vehicle to exact positions.
Inductive Reasoning	The ability to combine pieces of information to form general rules or conclusions (includes finding a relationship among seemingly unrelated events).
Speech Recognition	The ability to identify and understand the speech of another person.
Visual Color Discrimination	The ability to match or detect differences between colors, including shades of color and brightness.
Extent Flexibility	The ability to bend, stretch, twist, or reach with your body, arms, and/or legs.
Finger Dexterity	The ability to make precisely coordinated movements of the fingers of one or both hands to grasp, manipulate, or assemble very small objects.
Manual Dexterity	The ability to quickly move your hand, your hand together with your arm, or your two hands to grasp, manipulate, or assemble objects.

Multilimb Coordination	The ability to coordinate two or more limbs (for example. two arms. two legs. or one leg and one arm) while sitting. standing. or lying down. It does not involve performing the activities while the whole body is in motion.
Memorization	The ability to remember information such as words. numbers. pictures, and procedures.
Written Expression	The ability to communicate information and ideas in writing so others will understand.
Visualization	The ability to imagine how something will look after it is moved around or when its parts are moved or rearranged.
Trunk Strength	The ability to use your abdominal and lower back muscles to support part of the body repeatedly or continuously over time without 'giving out' or fatiguing.
Perceptual Speed	The ability to quickly and accurately compare similarities and differences among sets of letters, numbers, objects, pictures. or patterns. The things to be compared may be presented at the same time or one after the other. This ability also includes comparing a presented object with a remembered object.
Flexibility of Closure	The ability to identify or detect a known pattern (a figure, object, word, or sound) that is hidden in other distracting material.
Category Flexibility	The ability to generate or use different sets of rules for combining or grouping things in different ways.
Time Sharing	The ability to shift back and forth between two or more activities or sources of information (such as speech, sounds. touch, or other sources).
Auditory Attention	The ability to focus on a single source of sound in the presence of other distracting sounds.
Gross Body Coordination	The ability to coordinate the movement of your arms, legs, and torso together when the whole body is in motion.
Hearing Sensitivity	The ability to detect or tell the differences between sounds that vary in pitch and loudness.
Far Vision	The ability to see details at a distance.
Fluency of Ideas	The ability to come up with a number of ideas about a topic (the number of ideas is important, not their quality, correctness, or creativity).
Static Strength	The ability to exert maximum muscle force to lift, push, pull, or carry objects.
Depth Perception	The ability to judge which of several objects is closer or farther away from you, or to judge the distance between you and an object.
Stamina	The ability to exert yourself physically over long periods of time without getting winded or out of breath.
Speed of Closure	The ability to quickly make sense of, combine, and organize information into meaningful patterns.
Originality	The ability to come up with unusual or clever ideas about a given topic or situation, or to develop creative ways to solve a problem.
Reaction Time	The ability to quickly respond (with the hand, finger, or foot) to a signal (sound, light, picture) when it appears.
Mathematical Reasoning	The ability to choose the right mathematical methods or formulas to solve a problem.
Number Facility	The ability to add, subtract, multiply, or divide quickly and correctly.
Peripheral Vision	The ability to see objects or movement of objects to one's side when the eyes are looking ahead.
Response Orientation	The ability to choose quickly between two or more movements in response to two or more different signals (lights, sounds, pictures). It includes the speed with which the correct response is started with the hand, foot, or other body part.
Spatial Orientation	The ability to know your location in relation to the environment or to know where other objects are in relation to you.
Speed of Limb Movement	The ability to quickly move the arms and legs.
Dynamic Strength	The ability to exert muscle force repeatedly or continuously over time. This involves muscular endurance and resistance to muscle fatigue.
Sound Localization	The ability to tell the direction from which a sound originated.
Glare Sensitivity	The ability to see objects in the presence of glare or bright lighting.
Gross Body Equilibrium	The ability to keep or regain your body balance or stay upright when in an unstable position.
Rate Control	The ability to time your movements or the movement of a piece of equipment in anticipation of changes in the speed and/or direction of a moving object or scene.
Night Vision	The ability to see under low light conditions.
Wrist-Finger Speed	The ability to make fast, simple, repeated movements of the fingers, hands, and wrists.
Dynamic Flexibility	The ability to quickly and repeatedly bend, stretch, twist, or reach out with your body, arms, and/or legs.
Explosive Strength	The ability to use short bursts of muscle force to propel oneself (as in jumping or sprinting), or to throw an object.

Work_Activity	Work_Activity Definitions
Making Decisions and Solving Problems	Analyzing information and evaluating results to choose the best solution and solve problems.

Repairing and Maintaining Electronic Equipment	Servicing, repairing. calibrating. regulating. fine-tuning, or testing machines. devices. and equipment that operate primarily on the basis of electrical or electronic (not mechanical) principles.
Communicating with Supervisors, Peers, or Subordin	Providing information to supervisors. co-workers, and subordinates by telephone. in written form. e-mail, or in person.
Getting Information	Observing. receiving. and otherwise obtaining information from all relevant sources.
Interacting With Computers	Using computers and computer systems (including hardware and software) to program. write software, set up functions, enter data, or process information.
Establishing and Maintaining Interpersonal Relatio	Developing constructive and cooperative working relationships with others, and maintaining them over time.
Updating and Using Relevant Knowledge	Keeping up-to-date technically and applying new knowledge to your job.
Interpreting the Meaning of Information for Others	Translating or explaining what information means and how it can be used.
Communicating with Persons Outside Organization	Communicating with people outside the organization, representing the organization to customers, the public, government, and other external sources. This information can be exchanged in person, in writing. or by telephone or e-mail.
Inspecting Equipment, Structures, or Material	Inspecting equipment, structures. or materials to identify the cause of errors or other problems or defects.
Identifying Objects, Actions, and Events	Identifying information by categorizing, estimating, recognizing differences or similarities. and detecting changes in circumstances or events.
Evaluating Information to Determine Compliance wit	Using relevant information and individual judgment to determine whether events or processes comply with laws, regulations, or standards.
Handling and Moving Objects	Using hands and arms in handling, installing, positioning, and moving materials, and manipulating things.
Monitor Processes, Materials, or Surroundings	Monitoring and reviewing information from materials, events, or the environment, to detect or assess problems.
Training and Teaching Others	Identifying the educational needs of others, developing formal educational or training programs or classes, and teaching or instructing others.
Organizing, Planning, and Prioritizing Work	Developing specific goals and plans to prioritize, organize, and accomplish your work.
Performing General Physical Activities	Performing physical activities that require considerable use of your arms and legs and moving your whole body, such as climbing, lifting, balancing, walking, stooping, and handling of materials.
Documenting/Recording Information	Entering, transcribing, recording, storing, or maintaining information in written or electronic/magnetic form.
Operating Vehicles, Mechanized Devices, or Equipme	Running, maneuvering, navigating, or operating vehicles or mechanized equipment, such as forklifts, passenger vehicles, aircraft, or water craft.
Repairing and Maintaining Mechanical Equipment	Servicing, repairing, adjusting, and testing machines, devices, moving parts, and equipment that operate primarily on the basis of mechanical (not electronic) principles.
Scheduling Work and Activities	Scheduling events, programs, and activities, as well as the work of others.
Provide Consultation and Advice to Others	Providing guidance and expert advice to management or other groups on technical, systems-, or process-related topics.
Analyzing Data or Information	Identifying the underlying principles, reasons, or facts of information by breaking down information or data into separate parts.
Judging the Qualities of Things, Services, or Peop	Assessing the value, importance, or quality of things or people.
Assisting and Caring for Others	Providing personal assistance. medical attention, emotional support, or other personal care to others such as coworkers, customers, or patients.
Processing Information	Compiling, coding, categorizing, calculating, tabulating, auditing, or verifying information or data.
Performing Administrative Activities	Performing day-to-day administrative tasks such as maintaining information files and processing paperwork.
Thinking Creatively	Developing, designing, or creating new applications, ideas, relationships, systems. or products, including artistic contributions.
Coordinating the Work and Activities of Others	Getting members of a group to work together to accomplish tasks.
Controlling Machines and Processes	Using either control mechanisms or direct physical activity to operate machines or processes (not including computers or vehicles).
Performing for or Working Directly with the Public	Performing for people or dealing directly with the public. This includes serving customers in restaurants and stores, and receiving clients or guests.
Estimating the Quantifiable Characteristics of Pro	Estimating sizes, distances, and quantities; or determining time, costs, resources, or materials needed to perform a work activity.
Coaching and Developing Others	Identifying the developmental needs of others and coaching, mentoring, or otherwise helping others to improve their knowledge or skills.

Drafting, Laying Out, and Specifying Technical Dev	Providing documentation, detailed instructions, drawings, or specifications to tell others about how devices, parts, equipment, or structures are to be fabricated, constructed, assembled, modified, maintained, or used.
Developing and Building Teams	Encouraging and building mutual trust, respect, and cooperation among team members.
Developing Objectives and Strategies	Establishing long-range objectives and specifying the strategies and actions to achieve them.
Guiding, Directing, and Motivating Subordinates	Providing guidance and direction to subordinates, including setting performance standards and monitoring performance.
Resolving Conflicts and Negotiating with Others	Handling complaints, settling disputes, and resolving grievances and conflicts, or otherwise negotiating with others.
Monitoring and Controlling Resources	Monitoring and controlling resources and overseeing the spending of money.
Staffing Organizational Units	Recruiting, interviewing, selecting, hiring, and promoting employees in an organization.
Selling or Influencing Others	Convincing others to buy merchandise/goods or to otherwise change their minds or actions.

Work_Content	Work_Content Definitions
Face-to-Face Discussions	How often do you have to have face-to-face discussions with individuals or teams in this job?
Importance of Being Exact or Accurate	How important is being very exact or highly accurate in performing this job?
Contact With Others	How much does this job require the worker to be in contact with others (face-to-face, by telephone, or otherwise) in order to perform it?
Telephone	How often do you have telephone conversations in this job?
Indoors, Environmentally Controlled	How often does this job require working indoors in environmentally controlled conditions?
Spend Time Using Your Hands to Handle, Control, or	How much does this job require using your hands to handle, control, or feel objects, tools or controls?
Structured versus Unstructured Work	To what extent is this job structured for the worker, rather than allowing the worker to determine tasks, priorities, and goals?
Freedom to Make Decisions	How much decision making freedom, without supervision, does the job offer?
Time Pressure	How often does this job require the worker to meet strict deadlines?
Wear Common Protective or Safety Equipment such as	How much does this job require wearing common protective or safety equipment such as safety shoes, glasses, gloves, hard hats or live jackets?
Cramped Work Space, Awkward Positions	How often does this job require working in cramped work spaces that requires getting into awkward positions?
Physical Proximity	To what extent does this job require the worker to perform job tasks in close physical proximity to other people?
Sounds, Noise Levels Are Distracting or Uncomforta	How often does this job require working exposed to sounds and noise levels that are distracting or uncomfortable?
Work With Work Group or Team	How important is it to work with others in a group or team in this job?
Indoors, Not Environmentally Controlled	How often does this job require working indoors in non-controlled environmental conditions (e.g., warehouse without heat)?
Frequency of Decision Making	How frequently is the worker required to make decisions that affect other people, the financial resources, and/or the image and reputation of the organization?
Impact of Decisions on Co-workers or Company Resul	How do the decisions an employee makes impact the results of co-workers, clients or the company?
Exposed to Hazardous Conditions	How often does this job require exposure to hazardous conditions?
Spend Time Standing	How much does this job require standing?
Consequence of Error	How serious would the result usually be if the worker made a mistake that was not readily correctable?
Responsible for Others' Health and Safety	How much responsibility is there for the health and safety of others in this job?
Coordinate or Lead Others	How important is it to coordinate or lead others in accomplishing work activities in this job?
Electronic Mail	How often do you use electronic mail in this job?
Exposed to Contaminants	How often does this job require working exposed to contaminants (such as pollutants, gases, dust or odors)?
Level of Competition	To what extent does this job require the worker to compete or to be aware of competitive pressures?
Deal With External Customers	How important is it to work with external customers or the public in this job?
Letters and Memos	How often does the job require written letters and memos?
Spend Time Bending or Twisting the Body	How much does this job require bending or twisting your body?
Very Hot or Cold Temperatures	How often does this job require working in very hot (above 90 F degrees) or very cold (below 32 F degrees) temperatures?
Spend Time Walking and Running	How much does this job require walking and running?
Spend Time Kneeling, Crouching, Stooping, or Crawl	How much does this job require kneeling, crouching, stooping or crawling?

In an Enclosed Vehicle or Equipment	How often does this job require working in a closed vehicle or equipment (e.g., car)?
Frequency of Conflict Situations	How often are there conflict situations the employee has to face in this job?
Importance of Repeating Same Tasks	How important is repeating the same physical activities (e.g., key entry) or mental activities (e.g., checking entries in a ledger) over and over, without stopping, to performing this job?
Deal With Unpleasant or Angry People	How frequently does the worker have to deal with unpleasant, angry, or discourteous individuals as part of the job requirements?
Exposed to Hazardous Equipment	How often does this job require exposure to hazardous equipment?
Exposed to Minor Burns, Cuts, Bites, or Stings	How often does this job require exposure to minor burns, cuts, bites, or stings?
Spend Time Sitting	How much does this job require sitting?
Outdoors, Exposed to Weather	How often does this job require working outdoors, exposed to all weather conditions?
Spend Time Making Repetitive Motions	How much does this job require making repetitive motions?
Responsibility for Outcomes and Results	How responsible is the worker for work outcomes and results of other workers?
Extremely Bright or Inadequate Lighting	How often does this job require working in extremely bright or inadequate lighting conditions?
Wear Specialized Protective or Safety Equipment su	How much does this job require wearing specialized protective or safety equipment such as breathing apparatus, safety harness, full protection suits, or radiation protection?
Exposed to High Places	How often does this job require exposure to high places?
Pace Determined by Speed of Equipment	How important is it to this job that the pace is determined by the speed of equipment or machinery? (This does not refer to keeping busy at all times on this job.)
Outdoors, Under Cover	How often does this job require working outdoors, under cover (e.g., structure with roof but no walls)?
Degree of Automation	How automated is the job?
Spend Time Climbing Ladders, Scaffolds, or Poles	How much does this job require climbing ladders, scaffolds, or poles?
Spend Time Keeping or Regaining Balance	How much does this job require keeping or regaining your balance?
Exposed to Whole Body Vibration	How often does this job require exposure to whole body vibration (e.g., operate a jackhammer)?
Exposed to Radiation	How often does this job require exposure to radiation?
In an Open Vehicle or Equipment	How often does this job require working in an open vehicle or equipment (e.g., tractor)?
Public Speaking	How often do you have to perform public speaking in this job?
Exposed to Disease or Infections	How often does this job require exposure to disease/infections?
Deal With Physically Aggressive People	How frequently does this job require the worker to deal with physical aggression of violent individuals?

Work_Styles	Work_Styles Definitions
Attention to Detail	Job requires being careful about detail and thorough in completing work tasks.
Dependability	Job requires being reliable, responsible, and dependable, and fulfilling obligations.
Initiative	Job requires a willingness to take on responsibilities and challenges.
Persistence	Job requires persistence in the face of obstacles.
Stress Tolerance	Job requires accepting criticism and dealing calmly and effectively with high stress situations.
Self Control	Job requires maintaining composure, keeping emotions in check, controlling anger, and avoiding aggressive behavior, even in very difficult situations.
Cooperation	Job requires being pleasant with others on the job and displaying a good-natured, cooperative attitude.
Integrity	Job requires being honest and ethical.
Independence	Job requires developing one's own ways of doing things, guiding oneself with little or no supervision, and depending on oneself to get things done.
Analytical Thinking	Job requires analyzing information and using logic to address work-related issues and problems.
Innovation	Job requires creativity and alternative thinking to develop new ideas for and answers to work-related problems.
Achievement/Effort	Job requires establishing and maintaining personally challenging achievement goals and exerting effort toward mastering tasks.
Leadership	Job requires a willingness to lead, take charge, and offer opinions and direction.
Adaptability/Flexibility	Job requires being open to change (positive or negative) and to considerable variety in the workplace.
Concern for Others	Job requires being sensitive to others' needs and feelings and being understanding and helpful on the job.
Social Orientation	Job requires preferring to work with others rather than alone, and being personally connected with others on the job.

Job Zone Component	Job Zone Component Definitions
Title	Job Zone Three: Medium Preparation Needed
Overall Experience	Previous work-related skill, knowledge, or experience is required for these occupations. For example, an electrician must have completed three or four years of apprenticeship or several years of vocational training, and often must have passed a licensing exam, in order to perform the job.
Job Training	Employees in these occupations usually need one or two years of training involving both on-the-job experience and informal training with experienced workers.
Job Zone Examples	These occupations usually involve using communication and organizational skills to coordinate, supervise, manage, or train others to accomplish goals. Examples include dental assistants, electricians, fish and game wardens, legal secretaries, personnel recruiters, and recreation workers.
SVP Range	(6.0 to < 7.0)
Education	Most occupations in this zone require training in vocational schools, related on-the-job experience, or an associate's degree. Some may require a bachelor's degree.

49-3021.00 - Automotive Body and Related Repairers

Repair and refinish automotive vehicle bodies and straighten vehicle frames.

Tasks

1) Measure and mark vinyl material and cut material to size for roof installation, using rules, straightedges, and hand shears.

2) Remove damaged sections of vehicles using metal-cutting guns, air grinders and wrenches, and install replacement parts using wrenches or welding equipment.

3) Replace damaged glass on vehicles.

4) Apply heat to plastic panels, using hot-air welding guns or immersion in hot water, and press the softened panels back into shape by hand.

5) Sand body areas to be painted and cover bumpers, windows, and trim with masking tape or paper to protect them from the paint.

6) Fill small dents that cannot be worked out with plastic or solder.

7) File, grind, sand and smooth filled or repaired surfaces, using power tools and hand tools.

8) Adjust or align headlights, wheels, and brake systems.

9) Remove small pits and dimples in body metal using pick hammers and punches.

10) Position dolly blocks against surfaces of dented areas and beat opposite surfaces to remove dents, using hammers.

11) Remove upholstery, accessories, electrical window-and-seat-operating equipment, and trim in order to gain access to vehicle bodies and fenders.

12) Follow supervisors' instructions as to which parts to restore or replace and how much time the job should take.

13) Inspect repaired vehicles for dimensional accuracy and test drive them to ensure proper alignment and handling.

14) Cut and tape plastic separating film to outside repair areas in order to avoid damaging surrounding surfaces during repair procedure, and remove tape and wash surfaces after repairs are complete.

15) Clean work areas, using air hoses, in order to remove damaged material and discarded fiberglass strips used in repair procedures.

16) Fit and secure windows, vinyl roofs, and metal trim to vehicle bodies, using caulking guns, adhesive brushes, and mallets.

17) Fit and weld replacement parts into place, using wrenches and welding equipment, and grind down welds to smooth them, using power grinders and other tools.

18) Prime and paint repaired surfaces, using paint sprayguns and motorized sanders.

19) Review damage reports, prepare or review repair cost estimates, and plan work to be performed.

20) Remove damaged panels, and identify the family and properties of the plastic used on a vehicle.

21) Mix polyester resins and hardeners to be used in restoring damaged areas.

22) Read specifications or confer with customers in order to determine the desired custom modifications for altering the appearance of vehicles.

23) Soak fiberglass matting in resin mixtures, and apply layers of matting over repair areas to specified thickness.

24) Cut openings in vehicle bodies for the installation of customized windows, using templates and power shears or chisels.

49-3022.00 - Automotive Glass Installers and Repairers

Replace or repair broken windshields and window glass in motor vehicles.

Tasks

1) Apply a bead of urethane around the perimeter of each pinchweld, and dress the remaining urethane on the pinchwelds so that it is of uniform level and thickness all the way around.

2) Cut flat safety glass according to specified patterns, or perform precision pattern-making and glass-cutting to custom-fit replacement windows.

3) Install replacement glass in vehicles after old glass has been removed and all necessary preparations have been made.

4) Remove all moldings, clips, windshield wipers, screws, bolts, and inside A-pillar moldings; then lower headliners prior to beginning installation or repair work.

5) Install, repair, and replace safety glass and related materials, such as backglass heating-elements, on vehicles and equipment.

6) Obtain windshields or windows for specific automobile makes and models from stock, and examine them for defects prior to installation.

7) Replace or adjust motorized or manual window-raising mechanisms.

8) Replace all moldings, clips, windshield wipers, and any other parts that were removed prior to glass replacement or repair.

9) Remove broken or damaged glass windshields or window-glass from motor vehicles, using hand tools to remove screws from frames holding glass.

10) Install rubber-channeling strips around edges of glass or frames in order to weatherproof windows or to prevent rattling.

11) Check for moisture or contamination in damaged areas, dry out any moisture prior to making repairs, and keep damaged areas dry until repairs are complete.

12) Allow all glass parts installed with urethane ample time to cure, taking temperature and humidity into account.

13) Install new foam dams on pinchwelds if required.

14) Hold cut or uneven edges of glass against automated abrasive belts in order to shape or smooth edges.

15) Cool or warm glass in the event of temperature extremes.

16) Select appropriate tools, safety equipment, and parts according to job requirements.

17) Prime all scratches on pinchwelds with primer, and allow primed scratches to dry.

49-3023.01 - Automotive Master Mechanics

Repair automobiles, trucks, buses, and other vehicles. Master mechanics repair virtually any part on the vehicle or specialize in the transmission system.

Tasks

1) Repair and service air conditioning, heating, engine-cooling, and electrical systems.

2) Repair manual and automatic transmissions.

3) Align vehicles' front ends.

4) Repair or replace shock absorbers.

5) Repair radiator leaks.

6) Repair, reline, replace, and adjust brakes.

7) Replace and adjust headlights.

8) Rewire ignition systems, lights, and instrument panels.

9) Tear down, repair, and rebuild faulty assemblies such as power systems, steering systems, and linkages.

10) Follow checklists to ensure all important parts are examined, including belts, hoses, steering systems, spark plugs, brake and fuel systems, wheel bearings, and other potentially troublesome areas.

11) Test and adjust repaired systems to meet manufacturers' performance specifications.

12) Test drive vehicles, and test components and systems, using equipment such as infrared engine analyzers, compression gauges, and computerized diagnostic devices.

13) Disassemble units and inspect parts for wear, using micrometers, calipers, and gauges.

14) Repair damaged automobile bodies.

15) Confer with customers to obtain descriptions of vehicle problems, and to discuss work to be performed and future repair requirements.

16) Rebuild parts such as crankshafts and cylinder blocks.

17) Plan work procedures, using charts, technical manuals, and experience.

18) Perform routine and scheduled maintenance services such as oil changes, lubrications, and tune-ups.

19) Overhaul or replace carburetors, blowers, generators, distributors, starters, and pumps.

20) Install and repair accessories such as radios, heaters, mirrors, and windshield wipers.

21) Examine vehicles to determine extent of damage or malfunctions.

22) Repair or replace parts such as pistons, rods, gears, valves, and bearings.

49-3023.02 - Automotive Specialty Technicians

Repair only one system or component on a vehicle, such as brakes, suspension, or radiator.

Tasks

1) Test electronic computer components in automobiles to ensure that they are working properly.

2) Repair, replace, and adjust defective carburetor parts and gasoline filters.

3) Repair, overhaul, and adjust automobile brake systems.

4) Examine vehicles, compile estimates of repair costs, and secure customers' approval to perform repairs.

5) Repair and replace automobile leaf springs.

6) Tune automobile engines to ensure proper and efficient functioning.

7) Install and repair air conditioners, and service components such as compressors, condensers, and controls.

8) Convert vehicle fuel systems from gasoline to butane gas operations, and repair and service operating butane fuel units.

9) Inspect and test new vehicles for damage, then record findings so that necessary repairs can be made.

10) Repair, install, and adjust hydraulic and electromagnetic automatic lift mechanisms used to raise and lower automobile windows, seats, and tops.

11) Repair and replace defective balljoint suspensions, brakeshoes, and wheelbearings.

12) Rebuild, repair, and test automotive fuel injection units.

13) Use electronic test equipment to locate and correct malfunctions in fuel, ignition, and emissions control systems.

14) Remove and replace defective mufflers and tailpipes.

15) Repair and rebuild clutch systems.

49-3031.00 - Bus and Truck Mechanics and Diesel Engine Specialists

Diagnose, adjust, repair, or overhaul trucks, buses, and all types of diesel engines. Includes mechanics working primarily with automobile diesel engines.

Tasks

1) Raise trucks, buses, and heavy parts or equipment using hydraulic jacks or hoists.

2) Attach test instruments to equipment, and read dials and gauges in order to diagnose malfunctions.

3) Specialize in repairing and maintaining parts of the engine, such as fuel injection systems.

4) Disassemble and overhaul internal combustion engines, pumps, generators, transmissions, clutches, and differential units.

5) Examine and adjust protective guards, loose bolts, and specified safety devices.

6) Operate valve-grinding machines to grind and reset valves.

7) Inspect, repair, and maintain automotive and mechanical equipment and machinery such as pumps and compressors.

8) Test drive trucks and buses to diagnose malfunctions or to ensure that they are working properly.

9) Repair and adjust seats, doors, and windows, and install and repair accessories.

10) Recondition and replace parts, pistons, bearings, gears, and valves.

11) Rebuild gas and/or diesel engines.

12) Inspect and verify dimensions and clearances of parts to ensure conformance to factory specifications.

13) Perform routine maintenance such as changing oil, checking batteries, and lubricating equipment and machinery.

14) Align front ends and suspension systems.

15) Inspect brake systems, steering mechanisms, wheel bearings, and other important parts to ensure that they are in proper operating condition.

16) Inspect, test, and listen to defective equipment to diagnose malfunctions, using test instruments such as handheld computers, motor analyzers, chassis charts, and pressure gauges.

17) Adjust and reline brakes, align wheels, tighten bolts and screws, and reassemble equipment.

18) Use handtools such as screwdrivers, pliers, wrenches, pressure gauges, and precision instruments, as well as power tools such as pneumatic wrenches, lathes, welding equipment, and jacks and hoists.

49-3042.00 - Mobile Heavy Equipment Mechanics, Except Engines

Diagnose, adjust, repair, or overhaul mobile mechanical, hydraulic, and pneumatic equipment, such as cranes, bulldozers, graders, and conveyors, used in construction, logging, and surface mining.

Tasks

1) Weld or solder broken parts and structural members, using electric or gas welders and soldering tools.

2) Direct workers who are assembling or disassembling equipment or cleaning parts.

3) Fabricate needed parts or items from sheet metal.

4) Schedule maintenance for industrial machines and equipment, and keep equipment service records.

5) Repair and replace damaged or worn parts.

6) Overhaul and test machines or equipment to ensure operating efficiency.

7) Fit bearings to adjust, repair, or overhaul mobile mechanical, hydraulic, and pneumatic equipment.

8) Adjust and maintain industrial machinery, using control and regulating devices.

9) Examine parts for damage or excessive wear, using micrometers and gauges.

10) Assemble gear systems, and align frames and gears.

11) Diagnose faults or malfunctions to determine required repairs, using engine diagnostic equipment such as computerized test equipment and calibration devices.

12) Clean, lubricate, and perform other routine maintenance work on equipment and vehicles.

13) Clean parts by spraying them with grease solvent or immersing them in tanks of solvent.

14) Adjust, maintain, and repair or replace subassemblies, such as transmissions and crawler heads, using hand tools, jacks, and cranes.

15) Operate and inspect machines or heavy equipment in order to diagnose defects.

16) Test mechanical products and equipment after repair or assembly to ensure proper performance and compliance with manufacturers' specifications.

17) Read and understand operating manuals, blueprints, and technical drawings.

49-3052.00 - Motorcycle Mechanics

Diagnose, adjust, repair, or overhaul motorcycles, scooters, mopeds, dirt bikes, or similar motorized vehicles.

Tasks

1) Connect test panels to engines and measure generator output, ignition timing, and other engine performance indicators.

2) Listen to engines, examine vehicle frames, and confer with customers in order to determine nature and extent of malfunction or damage.

3) Disassemble subassembly units and examine condition, movement or alignment of parts visually or using gauges.

4) Hammer out dents and bends in frames, weld tears and breaks; then reassemble frames and reinstall engines.

5) Dismantle engines and repair or replace defective parts, such as magnetos, carburetors, and generators.

6) Reassemble and test subassembly units.

7) Repair or replace other parts, such as headlights, horns, handlebar controls, gasoline and oil tanks, starters, and mufflers.

8) Repair and adjust motorcycle subassemblies such as forks, transmissions, brakes, and drive chains, according to specifications.

9) Replace defective parts, using hand tools, arbor presses, flexible power presses, or power tools.

49-3091.00 - Bicycle Repairers

Repair and service bicycles.

Tasks

1) Weld broken or cracked frames together, using oxyacetylene torches and welding rods.

2) Install, repair, and replace equipment or accessories, such as handlebars, stands, lights, and seats.

3) Align wheels.

4) Disassemble axles in order to repair, adjust, and replace defective parts, using hand tools.

5) Install and adjust speed and gear mechanisms.

6) Paint bicycle frames, using spray guns or brushes.

7) Shape replacement parts, using bench grinders.

8) Repair holes in tire tubes, using scrapers and patches.

49-3093.00 - Tire Repairers and Changers

Repair and replace tires.

Tasks

1) Clean sides of whitewall tires.

2) Remount wheels onto vehicles.

3) Order replacements for tires and tubes.

4) Patch tubes with adhesive rubber patches, or seal rubber patches to tubes using hot vulcanizing plates.

5) Identify and inflate tires correctly for the size and ply.

6) Rotate tires to different positions on vehicles, using hand tools.

7) Replace valve stems and remove puncturing objects.

8) Inspect tire casings for defects, such as holes and tears.

9) Prepare rims and wheel drums for reassembly by scraping, grinding, or sandblasting.

10) Place casing-camelback assemblies in tire molds for the vulcanization process, and exert pressure on the camelbacks to ensure good adhesion.

11) Locate punctures in tubeless tires by visual inspection or by immersing inflated tires in water baths and observing air bubbles.

12) Inflate inner tubes and immerse them in water to locate leaks.

13) Hammer required counterweights onto rims of wheels.

14) Glue boots (tire patches) over ruptures in tire casings, using rubber cement.

15) Separate tubed tires from wheels, using rubber mallets and metal bars, or mechanical tire changers.

16) Place wheels on balancing machines to determine counterweights required to balance wheels.

17) Seal punctures in tubeless tires by inserting adhesive material and expanding rubber plugs into punctures, using hand tools.

18) Buff defective areas of inner tubes, using scrapers.

19) Roll new rubber treads, known as camelbacks, over tire casings, and mold the semi-raw rubber treads onto the buffed casings.

20) Assist mechanics and perform other duties as directed.

21) Reassemble tires onto wheels.

22) Unbolt wheels from vehicles and remove them, using lug wrenches and other hand and power tools.

23) Apply rubber cement to buffed tire casings prior to vulcanization process.

24) Raise vehicles using hydraulic jacks.

49-9011.00 - Mechanical Door Repairers

Install, service, or repair opening and closing mechanisms of automatic doors and hydraulic door closers. Includes garage door mechanics.

Tasks

1) Install door frames, rails, steel rolling curtains, electronic-eye mechanisms, and electric door openers and closers, using power tools, hand tools, and electronic test equipment.

2) Repair or replace worn or broken door parts, using hand tools.

3) Install dock seals, bumpers, and shelters.

4) Fasten angle iron back-hangers to ceilings and tracks, using fasteners or welding equipment.

5) Cover treadles with carpeting or other floor covering materials and test systems by operating treadles.

6) Assemble and fasten tracks to structures or bucks, using impact wrenches or welding equipment.

7) Carry springs to tops of doors, using ladders or scaffolding, and attach springs to tracks in order to install spring systems.

8) Adjust doors to open or close with the correct amount of effort, and make simple adjustments to electric openers.

9) Order replacement springs, sections, and slats.

10) Apply hardware to door sections, such as drilling holes to install locks.

11) Clean door closer parts, using caustic soda, rotary brushes, and grinding wheels.

12) Fabricate replacements for worn or broken parts, using welders, lathes, drill presses, and shaping and milling machines.

13) Lubricate door closer oil chambers and pack spindles with leather washers.

14) Remove or disassemble defective automatic mechanical door closers, using hand tools.

15) Operate lifts, winches, or chain falls in order to move heavy curtain doors.

16) Complete required paperwork, such as work orders, according to services performed or required.

17) Collect payment upon job completion.

18) Wind large springs with upward motion of arm.

19) Study blueprints and schematic diagrams in order to determine appropriate methods of installing and repairing automated door openers.

20) Set in and secure floor treadles for door activating mechanisms; then connect power packs and electrical panelboards to treadles.

21) Run low voltage wiring on ceiling surfaces, using insulated staples.

22) Inspect job sites, assessing headroom, side room, and other conditions in order to determine appropriateness of door for a given location.

23) Set doors into place or stack hardware sections into openings after rail or track installation.

24) Cut door stops and angle irons to fit openings.

49-9021.01 - Heating and Air Conditioning Mechanics

Install, service, and repair heating and air conditioning systems in residences and commercial establishments.

Tasks

1) Test pipe or tubing joints and connections for leaks, using pressure gauge or soap-and-water solution.

2) Test electrical circuits and components for continuity, using electrical test equipment.

3) Install, connect, and adjust thermostats, humidistats and timers, using hand tools.

4) Discuss heating-cooling system malfunctions with users to isolate problems or to verify that malfunctions have been corrected.

5) Recommend, develop, and perform preventive and general maintenance procedures such as cleaning, power-washing and vacuuming equipment, oiling parts, and changing filters.

6) Lay out and connect electrical wiring between controls and equipment according to wiring diagram, using electrician's hand tools.

7) Install auxiliary components to heating-cooling equipment, such as expansion and discharge valves, air ducts, pipes, blowers, dampers, flues and stokers, following blueprints.

8) Adjust system controls to setting recommended by manufacturer to balance system, using hand tools.

9) Record and report all faults, deficiencies, and other unusual occurrences, as well as the time and materials expended on work orders.

10) Cut and drill holes in floors, walls, and roof to install equipment, using power saws and drills.

11) Join pipes or tubing to equipment and to fuel, water, or refrigerant source, to form complete circuit.

12) Inspect and test system to verify system compliance with plans and specifications and to detect and locate malfunctions.

13) Obtain and maintain required certification(s).

14) Study blueprints, design specifications, and manufacturers! recommendations to ascertain the configuration of heating or cooling equipment components and to ensure the proper installation of components.

15) Reassemble and test equipment following repairs.

16) Assemble, position and mount heating or cooling equipment, following blueprints.

17) Measure, cut, thread, and bend pipe or tubing, using pipefitter's tools.

18) Assist with other work in coordination with repair and maintenance teams.

19) Wrap pipes in insulation, securing it in place with cement or wire bands.

20) Generate work orders that address deficiencies in need of correction.

21) Fabricate, assemble and install duct work and chassis parts, using portable metal-working tools and welding equipment.

22) Comply with all applicable standards, policies, and procedures, including safety procedures and the maintenance of a clean work area.

Knowledge	Knowledge Definitions
Mechanical	Knowledge of machines and tools, including their designs, uses, repair, and maintenance.
Customer and Personal Service	Knowledge of principles and processes for providing customer and personal services. This includes customer needs assessment, meeting quality standards for services, and evaluation of customer satisfaction.
Engineering and Technology	Knowledge of the practical application of engineering science and technology. This includes applying principles, techniques, procedures, and equipment to the design and production of various goods and services.
Design	Knowledge of design techniques, tools, and principles involved in production of precision technical plans, blueprints, drawings, and models.
English Language	Knowledge of the structure and content of the English language including the meaning and spelling of words, rules of composition, and grammar.
Building and Construction	Knowledge of materials, methods, and the tools involved in the construction or repair of houses, buildings, or other structures such as highways and roads.
Mathematics	Knowledge of arithmetic, algebra, geometry, calculus, statistics, and their applications.
Sales and Marketing	Knowledge of principles and methods for showing, promoting, and selling products or services. This includes marketing strategy and tactics, product demonstration, sales techniques, and sales control systems.
Computers and Electronics	Knowledge of circuit boards, processors, chips, electronic equipment, and computer hardware and software, including applications and programming.
Physics	Knowledge and prediction of physical principles, laws, their interrelationships, and applications to understanding fluid, material, and atmospheric dynamics, and mechanical, electrical, atomic and sub- atomic structures and processes.
Education and Training	Knowledge of principles and methods for curriculum and training design, teaching and instruction for individuals and groups, and the measurement of training effects.
Public Safety and Security	Knowledge of relevant equipment, policies, procedures, and strategies to promote effective local, state, or national security operations for the protection of people, data, property, and institutions.
Administration and Management	Knowledge of business and management principles involved in strategic planning, resource allocation, human resources modeling, leadership technique, production methods, and coordination of people and resources.
Law and Government	Knowledge of laws, legal codes, court procedures, precedents, government regulations, executive orders, agency rules, and the democratic political process.
Chemistry	Knowledge of the chemical composition, structure, and properties of substances and of the chemical processes and transformations that they undergo. This includes uses of chemicals and their interactions, danger signs, production techniques, and disposal methods.
Production and Processing	Knowledge of raw materials, production processes, quality control, costs, and other techniques for maximizing the effective manufacture and distribution of goods.
Economics and Accounting	Knowledge of economic and accounting principles and practices, the financial markets, banking and the analysis and reporting of financial data.
Clerical	Knowledge of administrative and clerical procedures and systems such as word processing, managing files and records, stenography and transcription, designing forms, and other office procedures and terminology.

Transportation	Knowledge of principles and methods for moving people or goods by air, rail, sea, or road, including the relative costs and benefits.
Personnel and Human Resources	Knowledge of principles and procedures for personnel recruitment, selection, training, compensation and benefits, labor relations and negotiation, and personnel information systems.
Psychology	Knowledge of human behavior and performance; individual differences in ability, personality, and interests; learning and motivation; psychological research methods; and the assessment and treatment of behavioral and affective disorders.
Communications and Media	Knowledge of media production, communication, and dissemination techniques and methods. This includes alternative ways to inform and entertain via written, oral, and visual media.
Telecommunications	Knowledge of transmission, broadcasting, switching, control, and operation of telecommunications systems.
Biology	Knowledge of plant and animal organisms, their tissues, cells, functions, interdependencies, and interactions with each other and the environment.
Therapy and Counseling	Knowledge of principles, methods, and procedures for diagnosis, treatment, and rehabilitation of physical and mental dysfunctions, and for career counseling and guidance.
Geography	Knowledge of principles and methods for describing the features of land, sea, and air masses, including their physical characteristics, locations, interrelationships, and distribution of plant, animal, and human life.
Medicine and Dentistry	Knowledge of the information and techniques needed to diagnose and treat human injuries, diseases, and deformities. This includes symptoms, treatment alternatives, drug properties and interactions, and preventive health-care measures.
Food Production	Knowledge of techniques and equipment for planting, growing, and harvesting food products (both plant and animal) for consumption, including storage/handling techniques.
Sociology and Anthropology	Knowledge of group behavior and dynamics, societal trends and influences, human migrations, ethnicity, cultures and their history and origins.
Foreign Language	Knowledge of the structure and content of a foreign (non-English) language including the meaning and spelling of words, rules of composition and grammar, and pronunciation.
Philosophy and Theology	Knowledge of different philosophical systems and religions. This includes their basic principles, values, ethics, ways of thinking, customs, practices, and their impact on human culture.
History and Archeology	Knowledge of historical events and their causes, indicators, and effects on civilizations and cultures.
Fine Arts	Knowledge of the theory and techniques required to compose, produce, and perform works of music, dance, visual arts, drama, and sculpture.

Skills	Skills Definitions
Troubleshooting	Determining causes of operating errors and deciding what to do about it.
Repairing	Repairing machines or systems using the needed tools.
Active Listening	Giving full attention to what other people are saying, taking time to understand the points being made, asking questions as appropriate, and not interrupting at inappropriate times.
Equipment Maintenance	Performing routine maintenance on equipment and determining when and what kind of maintenance is needed.
Installation	Installing equipment, machines, wiring, or programs to meet specifications.
Social Perceptiveness	Being aware of others' reactions and understanding why they react as they do.
Critical Thinking	Using logic and reasoning to identify the strengths and weaknesses of alternative solutions, conclusions or approaches to problems.
Active Learning	Understanding the implications of new information for both current and future problem-solving and decision-making.
Coordination	Adjusting actions in relation to others' actions.
Reading Comprehension	Understanding written sentences and paragraphs in work related documents.
Time Management	Managing one's own time and the time of others.
Learning Strategies	Selecting and using training/instructional methods and procedures appropriate for the situation when learning or teaching new things.
Speaking	Talking to others to convey information effectively.
Operation Monitoring	Watching gauges, dials, or other indicators to make sure a machine is working properly.
Complex Problem Solving	Identifying complex problems and reviewing related information to develop and evaluate options and implement solutions.
Equipment Selection	Determining the kind of tools and equipment needed to do a job.
Science	Using scientific rules and methods to solve problems.
Systems Evaluation	Identifying measures or indicators of system performance and the actions needed to improve or correct performance, relative to the goals of the system.

Persuasion	Persuading others to change their minds or behavior.
Systems Analysis	Determining how a system should work and how changes in conditions, operations, and the environment will affect outcomes.
Mathematics	Using mathematics to solve problems.
Monitoring	Monitoring/Assessing performance of yourself, other individuals. or organizations to make improvements or take corrective action.
Instructing	Teaching others how to do something.
Negotiation	Bringing others together and trying to reconcile differences.
Service Orientation	Actively looking for ways to help people.
Judgment and Decision Making	Considering the relative costs and benefits of potential actions to choose the most appropriate one.
Writing	Communicating effectively in writing as appropriate for the needs of the audience.
Quality Control Analysis	Conducting tests and inspections of products, services, or processes to evaluate quality or performance.
Operations Analysis	Analyzing needs and product requirements to create a design.
Management of Material Resources	Obtaining and seeing to the appropriate use of equipment, facilities, and materials needed to do certain work.
Technology Design	Generating or adapting equipment and technology to serve user needs.
Operation and Control	Controlling operations of equipment or systems.
Management of Personnel Resources	Motivating. developing, and directing people as they work, identifying the best people for the job.
Management of Financial Resources	Determining how money will be spent to get the work done, and accounting for these expenditures.
Programming	Writing computer programs for various purposes.

Ability	Ability Definitions
Extent Flexibility	The ability to bend, stretch, twist, or reach with your body, arms, and/or legs.
Manual Dexterity	The ability to quickly move your hand, your hand together with your arm, or your two hands to grasp, manipulate, or assemble objects.
Finger Dexterity	The ability to make precisely coordinated movements of the fingers of one or both hands to grasp, manipulate, or assemble very small objects.
Problem Sensitivity	The ability to tell when something is wrong or is likely to go wrong. It does not involve solving the problem, only recognizing there is a problem.
Inductive Reasoning	The ability to combine pieces of information to form general rules or conclusions (includes finding a relationship among seemingly unrelated events).
Trunk Strength	The ability to use your abdominal and lower back muscles to support part of the body repeatedly or continuously over time without 'giving out' or fatiguing.
Arm-Hand Steadiness	The ability to keep your hand and arm steady while moving your arm or while holding your arm and hand in one position.
Deductive Reasoning	The ability to apply general rules to specific problems to produce answers that make sense.
Oral Comprehension	The ability to listen to and understand information and ideas presented through spoken words and sentences.
Information Ordering	The ability to arrange things or actions in a certain order or pattern according to a specific rule or set of rules (e.g., patterns of numbers, letters, words, pictures, mathematical operations).
Control Precision	The ability to quickly and repeatedly adjust the controls of a machine or a vehicle to exact positions.
Oral Expression	The ability to communicate information and ideas in speaking so others will understand.
Multilimb Coordination	The ability to coordinate two or more limbs (for example, two arms, two legs, or one leg and one arm) while sitting, standing, or lying down. It does not involve performing the activities while the whole body is in motion.
Near Vision	The ability to see details at close range (within a few feet of the observer).
Static Strength	The ability to exert maximum muscle force to lift, push, pull, or carry objects.
Selective Attention	The ability to concentrate on a task over a period of time without being distracted.
Gross Body Coordination	The ability to coordinate the movement of your arms, legs, and torso together when the whole body is in motion.
Speech Clarity	The ability to speak clearly so others can understand you.
Visualization	The ability to imagine how something will look after it is moved around or when its parts are moved or rearranged.
Gross Body Equilibrium	The ability to keep or regain your body balance or stay upright when in an unstable position.
Hearing Sensitivity	The ability to detect or tell the differences between sounds that vary in pitch and loudness.
Visual Color Discrimination	The ability to match or detect differences between colors, including shades of color and brightness.
Written Comprehension	The ability to read and understand information and ideas presented in writing.
Stamina	The ability to exert yourself physically over long periods of time without getting winded or out of breath.

Reaction Time	The ability to quickly respond (with the hand. finger. or foot) to a signal (sound, light, picture) when it appears.
Speed of Limb Movement	The ability to quickly move the arms and legs.
Speech Recognition	The ability to identify and understand the speech of another person.
Perceptual Speed	The ability to quickly and accurately compare similarities and differences among sets of letters, numbers, objects. pictures, or patterns. The things to be compared may be presented at the same time or one after the other. This ability also includes comparing a presented object with a remembered object.
Auditory Attention	The ability to focus on a single source of sound in the presence of other distracting sounds.
Flexibility of Closure	The ability to identify or detect a known pattern (a figure, object. word, or sound) that is hidden in other distracting material.
Speed of Closure	The ability to quickly make sense of, combine. and organize information into meaningful patterns.
Category Flexibility	The ability to generate or use different sets of rules for combining or grouping things in different ways.
Written Expression	The ability to communicate information and ideas in writing so others will understand.
Far Vision	The ability to see details at a distance.
Depth Perception	The ability to judge which of several objects is closer or farther away from you, or to judge the distance between you and an object.
Originality	The ability to come up with unusual or clever ideas about a given topic or situation, or to develop creative ways to solve a problem.
Wrist-Finger Speed	The ability to make fast, simple, repeated movements of the fingers, hands, and wrists.
Dynamic Strength	The ability to exert muscle force repeatedly or continuously over time. This involves muscular endurance and resistance to muscle fatigue.
Fluency of Ideas	The ability to come up with a number of ideas about a topic (the number of ideas is important, not their quality, correctness, or creativity).
Memorization	The ability to remember information such as words. numbers, pictures, and procedures.
Glare Sensitivity	The ability to see objects in the presence of glare or bright lighting.
Time Sharing	The ability to shift back and forth between two or more activities or sources of information (such as speech, sounds, touch, or other sources).
Sound Localization	The ability to tell the direction from which a sound originated.
Spatial Orientation	The ability to know your location in relation to the environment or to know where other objects are in relation to you.
Response Orientation	The ability to choose quickly between two or more movements in response to two or more different signals (lights, sounds, pictures). It includes the speed with which the correct response is started with the hand, foot, or other body part.
Night Vision	The ability to see under low light conditions.
Rate Control	The ability to time your movements or the movement of a piece of equipment in anticipation of changes in the speed and/or direction of a moving object or scene.
Peripheral Vision	The ability to see objects or movement of objects to one's side when the eyes are looking ahead.
Mathematical Reasoning	The ability to choose the right mathematical methods or formulas to solve a problem.
Number Facility	The ability to add, subtract, multiply, or divide quickly and correctly.
Explosive Strength	The ability to use short bursts of muscle force to propel oneself (as in jumping or sprinting), or to throw an object.
Dynamic Flexibility	The ability to quickly and repeatedly bend, stretch, twist, or reach out with your body, arms, and/or legs.

Work_Activity	Work_Activity Definitions
Performing General Physical Activities	Performing physical activities that require considerable use of your arms and legs and moving your whole body, such as climbing, lifting, balancing, walking, stooping, and handling of materials.
Repairing and Maintaining Mechanical Equipment	Servicing, repairing, adjusting, and testing machines, devices, moving parts, and equipment that operate primarily on the basis of mechanical (not electronic) principles.
Handling and Moving Objects	Using hands and arms in handling, installing, positioning, and moving materials, and manipulating things.
Getting Information	Observing, receiving, and otherwise obtaining information from all relevant sources.
Operating Vehicles, Mechanized Devices, or Equipme	Running, maneuvering, navigating, or driving vehicles or mechanized equipment, such as forklifts, passenger vehicles, aircraft, or water craft.
Performing for or Working Directly with the Public	Performing for people or dealing directly with the public. This includes serving customers in restaurants and stores, and receiving clients or guests.
Making Decisions and Solving Problems	Analyzing information and evaluating results to choose the best solution and solve problems.

Communicating with Persons Outside Organization	Communicating with people outside the organization, representing the organization to customers, the public, government, and other external sources. This information can be exchanged in person, in writing, or by telephone or e-mail.
Inspecting Equipment, Structures, or Material	Inspecting equipment, structures, or materials to identify the cause of errors or other problems or defects.
Communicating with Supervisors, Peers, or Subordin	Providing information to supervisors, co-workers, and subordinates by telephone, in written form, e-mail, or in person.
Thinking Creatively	Developing, designing, or creating new applications, ideas, relationships, systems, or products, including artistic contributions.
Organizing, Planning, and Prioritizing Work	Developing specific goals and plans to prioritize, organize, and accomplish your work.
Updating and Using Relevant Knowledge	Keeping up-to-date technically and applying new knowledge to your job.
Establishing and Maintaining Interpersonal Relatio	Developing constructive and cooperative working relationships with others, and maintaining them over time.
Coordinating the Work and Activities of Others	Getting members of a group to work together to accomplish tasks.
Repairing and Maintaining Electronic Equipment	Servicing, repairing, calibrating, regulating, fine-tuning, or testing machines, devices, and equipment that operate primarily on the basis of electrical or electronic (not mechanical) principles.
Selling or Influencing Others	Convincing others to buy merchandise/goods or to otherwise change their minds or actions.
Identifying Objects, Actions, and Events	Identifying information by categorizing, estimating, recognizing differences or similarities, and detecting changes in circumstances or events.
Controlling Machines and Processes	Using either control mechanisms or direct physical activity to operate machines or processes (not including computers or vehicles).
Drafting, Laying Out, and Specifying Technical Dev	Providing documentation, detailed instructions, drawings, or specifications to tell others about how devices, parts, equipment, or structures are to be fabricated, constructed, assembled, modified, maintained, or used.
Training and Teaching Others	Identifying the educational needs of others, developing formal educational or training programs or classes, and teaching or instructing others.
Estimating the Quantifiable Characteristics of Pro	Estimating sizes, distances, and quantities; or determining time, costs, resources, or materials needed to perform a work activity.
Judging the Qualities of Things, Services, or Peop	Assessing the value, importance, or quality of things or people.
Developing and Building Teams	Encouraging and building mutual trust, respect, and cooperation among team members.
Coaching and Developing Others	Identifying the developmental needs of others and coaching, mentoring, or otherwise helping others to improve their knowledge or skills.
Evaluating Information to Determine Compliance wit	Using relevant information and individual judgment to determine whether events or processes comply with laws, regulations, or standards.
Documenting/Recording Information	Entering, transcribing, recording, storing, or maintaining information in written or electronic/magnetic form.
Developing Objectives and Strategies	Establishing long-range objectives and specifying the strategies and actions to achieve them.
Resolving Conflicts and Negotiating with Others	Handling complaints, settling disputes, and resolving grievances and conflicts, or otherwise negotiating with others.
Provide Consultation and Advice to Others	Providing guidance and expert advice to management or other groups on technical, systems-, or process-related topics.
Guiding, Directing, and Motivating Subordinates	Providing guidance and direction to subordinates, including setting performance standards and monitoring performance.
Analyzing Data or Information	Identifying the underlying principles, reasons, or facts of information by breaking down information or data into separate parts.
Monitor Processes, Materials, or Surroundings	Monitoring and reviewing information from materials, events, or the environment, to detect or assess problems.
Interpreting the Meaning of Information for Others	Translating or explaining what information means and how it can be used.
Processing Information	Compiling, coding, categorizing, calculating, tabulating, auditing, or verifying information or data.
Assisting and Caring for Others	Providing personal assistance, medical attention, emotional support, or other personal care to others such as coworkers, customers, or patients.
Scheduling Work and Activities	Scheduling events, programs, and activities, as well as the work of others.
Performing Administrative Activities	Performing day-to-day administrative tasks such as maintaining information files and processing paperwork.
Interacting With Computers	Using computers and computer systems (including hardware and software) to program, write software, set up functions, enter data, or process information.
Monitoring and Controlling Resources	Monitoring and controlling resources and overseeing the spending of money.

Staffing Organizational Units	Recruiting, interviewing, selecting, hiring, and promoting employees in an organization.

Work_Content	Work_Content Definitions
Face-to-Face Discussions	How often do you have to have face-to-face discussions with individuals or teams in this job?
Telephone	How often do you have telephone conversations in this job?
Freedom to Make Decisions	How much decision making freedom, without supervision, does the job offer?
Contact With Others	How much does this job require the worker to be in contact with others (face-to-face, by telephone, or otherwise) in order to perform it?
Exposed to Hazardous Conditions	How often does this job require exposure to hazardous conditions?
Exposed to Contaminants	How often does this job require working exposed to contaminants (such as pollutants, gases, dust or odors)?
Structured versus Unstructured Work	To what extent is this job structured for the worker, rather than allowing the worker to determine tasks, priorities, and goals?
In an Enclosed Vehicle or Equipment	How often does this job require working in a closed vehicle or equipment (e.g., car)?
Spend Time Using Your Hands to Handle, Control, or	How much does this job require using your hands to handle, control, or feel objects, tools or controls?
Outdoors, Exposed to Weather	How often does this job require working outdoors, exposed to all weather conditions?
Exposed to Minor Burns, Cuts, Bites, or Stings	How often does this job require exposure to minor burns, cuts, bites, or stings?
Impact of Decisions on Co-workers or Company Resul	How do the decisions an employee makes impact the results of co-workers, clients or the company?
Very Hot or Cold Temperatures	How often does this job require working in very hot (above 90 F degrees) or very cold (below 32 F degrees) temperatures?
Spend Time Standing	How much does this job require standing?
Sounds, Noise Levels Are Distracting or Uncomforta	How often does this job require working exposed to sounds and noise levels that are distracting or uncomfortable?
Cramped Work Space, Awkward Positions	How often does this job require working in cramped work spaces that requires getting into awkward positions?
Exposed to High Places	How often does this job require exposure to high places?
Frequency of Decision Making	How frequently is the worker required to make decisions that affect other people, the financial resources, and/or the image and reputation of the organization?
Spend Time Bending or Twisting the Body	How much does this job require bending or twisting your body?
Exposed to Hazardous Equipment	How often does this job require exposure to hazardous equipment?
Wear Common Protective or Safety Equipment such as	How much does this job require wearing common protective or safety equipment such as safety shoes, glasses, gloves, hard hats or live jackets?
Time Pressure	How often does this job require the worker to meet strict deadlines?
Indoors, Not Environmentally Controlled	How often does this job require working indoors in non-controlled environmental conditions (e.g., warehouse without heat)?
Level of Competition	To what extent does this job require the worker to compete or to be aware of competitive pressures?
Consequence of Error	How serious would the result usually be if the worker made a mistake that was not readily correctable?
Deal With External Customers	How important is it to work with external customers or the public in this job?
Responsibility for Outcomes and Results	How responsible is the worker for work outcomes and results of other workers?
Spend Time Kneeling, Crouching, Stooping, or Crawl	How much does this job require kneeling, crouching, stooping or crawling?
Indoors, Environmentally Controlled	How often does this job require working indoors in environmentally controlled conditions?
Importance of Being Exact or Accurate	How important is being very exact or highly accurate in performing this job?
Spend Time Climbing Ladders, Scaffolds, or Poles	How much does this job require climbing ladders, scaffolds, or poles?
Physical Proximity	To what extent does this job require the worker to perform job tasks in close physical proximity to other people?
Spend Time Making Repetitive Motions	How much does this job require making repetitive motions?
Spend Time Walking and Running	How much does this job require walking and running?
Extremely Bright or Inadequate Lighting	How often does this job require working in extremely bright or inadequate lighting conditions?
Work With Work Group or Team	How important is it to work with others in a group or team in this job?
Outdoors, Under Cover	How often does this job require working outdoors, under cover (e.g., structure with roof but no walls)?
Letters and Memos	How often does the job require written letters and memos?

314

Spend Time Keeping or Regaining Balance	How much does this job require keeping or regaining your balance?
Coordinate or Lead Others	How important is it to coordinate or lead others in accomplishing work activities in this job?
Frequency of Conflict Situations	How often are there conflict situations the employee has to face in this job?
Responsible for Others' Health and Safety	How much responsibility is there for the health and safety of others in this job?
Deal With Unpleasant or Angry People	How frequently does the worker have to deal with unpleasant, angry, or discourteous individuals as part of the job requirements?
Wear Specialized Protective or Safety Equipment su	How much does this job require wearing specialized protective or safety equipment such as breathing apparatus, safety harness, full protection suits, or radiation protection?
Exposed to Whole Body Vibration	How often does this job require exposure to whole body vibration (e.g., operate a jackhammer)?
Importance of Repeating Same Tasks	How important is repeating the same physical activities (e.g., key entry) or mental activities (e.g., checking entries in a ledger) over and over, without stopping, to performing this job?
Pace Determined by Speed of Equipment	How important is it to this job that the pace is determined by the speed of equipment or machinery? (This does not refer to keeping busy at all times on this job.)
Degree of Automation	How automated is the job?
In an Open Vehicle or Equipment	How often does this job require working in an open vehicle or equipment (e.g., tractor)?
Exposed to Disease or Infections	How often does this job require exposure to disease/infections?
Spend Time Sitting	How much does this job require sitting?
Electronic Mail	How often do you use electronic mail in this job?
Public Speaking	How often do you have to perform public speaking in this job?
Exposed to Radiation	How often does this job require exposure to radiation?
Deal With Physically Aggressive People	How frequently does this job require the worker to deal with physical aggression of violent individuals?

Work_Styles	Work_Styles Definitions
Dependability	Job requires being reliable, responsible, and dependable, and fulfilling obligations.
Integrity	Job requires being honest and ethical.
Cooperation	Job requires being pleasant with others on the job and displaying a good-natured, cooperative attitude.
Stress Tolerance	Job requires accepting criticism and dealing calmly and effectively with high stress situations.
Attention to Detail	Job requires being careful about detail and thorough in completing work tasks.
Initiative	Job requires a willingness to take on responsibilities and challenges.
Self Control	Job requires maintaining composure, keeping emotions in check, controlling anger, and avoiding aggressive behavior, even in very difficult situations.
Persistence	Job requires persistence in the face of obstacles.
Independence	Job requires developing one's own ways of doing things, guiding oneself with little or no supervision, and depending on oneself to get things done.
Leadership	Job requires a willingness to lead, take charge, and offer opinions and direction.
Analytical Thinking	Job requires analyzing information and using logic to address work-related issues and problems.
Achievement/Effort	Job requires establishing and maintaining personally challenging achievement goals and exerting effort toward mastering tasks.
Adaptability/Flexibility	Job requires being open to change (positive or negative) and to considerable variety in the workplace.
Concern for Others	Job requires being sensitive to others' needs and feelings and being understanding and helpful on the job.
Innovation	Job requires creativity and alternative thinking to develop new ideas for and answers to work-related problems.
Social Orientation	Job requires preferring to work with others rather than alone, and being personally connected with others on the job.

Job Zone Component	Job Zone Component Definitions
Title	Job Zone Three: Medium Preparation Needed
Overall Experience	Previous work-related skill, knowledge, or experience is required for these occupations. For example, an electrician must have completed three or four years of apprenticeship or several years of vocational training, and often must have passed a licensing exam, in order to perform the job.
Job Training	Employees in these occupations usually need one or two years of training involving both on-the-job experience and informal training with experienced workers.
Job Zone Examples	These occupations usually involve using communication and organizational skills to coordinate, supervise, manage, or train others to accomplish goals. Examples include dental assistants, electricians, fish and game wardens, legal secretaries, personnel recruiters, and recreation workers.

SVP Range	(6.0 to < 7.0)
Education	Most occupations in this zone require training in vocational schools, related on-the-job experience, or an associate's degree. Some may require a bachelor's degree.

49-9021.02 - Refrigeration Mechanics

Install and repair industrial and commercial refrigerating systems.

Tasks

1) Observe and test system operation, using gauges and instruments.

2) Read blueprints to determine location, size, capacity, and type of components needed to build refrigeration system.

3) Test lines, components, and connections for leaks.

4) Estimate, order, pick up, deliver, and install materials and supplies needed to maintain equipment in good working condition.

5) Insulate shells and cabinets of systems.

6) Keep records of repairs and replacements made and causes of malfunctions.

7) Lift and align components into position, using hoist or block and tackle.

8) Supervise and instruct assistants.

9) Mount compressor, condenser, and other components in specified locations on frames, using hand tools and acetylene welding equipment.

10) Drill holes and install mounting brackets and hangers into floor and walls of building.

11) Adjust or replace worn or defective mechanisms and parts, and reassemble repaired systems.

12) Lay out reference points for installation of structural and functional components, using measuring instruments.

13) Braze or solder parts to repair defective joints and leaks.

14) Cut, bend, thread, and connect pipe to functional components and water, power, or refrigeration system.

15) Dismantle malfunctioning systems and test components, using electrical, mechanical, and pneumatic testing equipment.

16) Fabricate and assemble structural and functional components of refrigeration system, using hand tools, power tools, and welding equipment.

17) Install expansion and control valves, using acetylene torches and wrenches.

18) Install wiring to connect components to an electric power source.

19) Schedule work with customers and initiate work orders, house requisitions and orders from stock.

20) Adjust valves according to specifications and charge system with proper type of refrigerant by pumping the specified gas or fluid into the system.

49-9042.00 - Maintenance and Repair Workers, General

Perform work involving the skills of two or more maintenance or craft occupations to keep machines, mechanical equipment, or the structure of an establishment in repair. Duties may involve pipe fitting; boiler making; insulating; welding; machining; carpentry; repairing electrical or mechanical equipment; installing, aligning, and balancing new equipment; and repairing buildings, floors, or stairs.

Tasks

1) Maintain and repair specialized equipment and machinery found in cafeterias, laundries, hospitals, stores, offices, and factories.

2) Lay brick to repair and maintain buildings, walls, arches and other structures.

3) Inspect, operate, and test machinery and equipment in order to diagnose machine malfunctions.

4) Dismantle devices to gain access to and remove defective parts, using hoists, cranes, hand tools, and power tools.

5) Diagnose mechanical problems and determine how to correct them, checking blueprints, repair manuals, and parts catalogs as necessary.

6) Perform routine preventive maintenance to ensure that machines continue to run smoothly, building systems operate efficiently, and the physical condition of buildings does not deteriorate.

7) Plan and lay out repair work using diagrams, drawings, blueprints, maintenance manuals, and schematic diagrams.

8) Inspect drives, motors, and belts, check fluid levels, replace filters, and perform other

maintenance actions, following checklists.

9) Assemble, install and/or repair wiring, electrical and electronic components, pipe systems and plumbing, machinery, and equipment.

10) Clean and lubricate shafts, bearings, gears, and other parts of machinery.

11) Align and balance new equipment after installation.

12) Order parts, supplies, and equipment from catalogs and suppliers, or obtain them from storerooms.

13) Adjust functional parts of devices and control instruments, using hand tools, levels, plumb bobs, and straightedges.

14) Record maintenance and repair work performed and the costs of the work.

15) Inspect used parts to determine changes in dimensional requirements, using rules, calipers, micrometers, and other measuring instruments.

16) Grind and reseat valves, using valve-grinding machines.

17) Fabricate and repair counters, benches, partitions, and other wooden structures such as sheds and outbuildings.

18) Estimate repair costs.

19) Operate cutting torches or welding equipment to cut or join metal parts.

20) Use tools ranging from common hand and power tools, such as hammers, hoists, saws, drills, and wrenches, to precision measuring instruments and electrical and electronic testing devices.

21) Set up and operate machine tools to repair or fabricate machine parts, jigs and fixtures, and tools.

22) Repair or replace defective equipment parts using hand tools and power tools, and reassemble equipment.

49-9044.00 - Millwrights

Install, dismantle, or move machinery and heavy equipment according to layout plans, blueprints, or other drawings.

Tasks

1) Install robot and modify its program, using teach pendant.

2) Construct foundation for machines, using hand tools and building materials such as wood, cement, and steel.

3) Dismantle machinery and equipment for shipment to installation site, usually performing installation and maintenance work as part of team.

4) Move machinery and equipment, using hoists, dollies, rollers, and trucks.

5) Dismantle machines, using hammers, wrenches, crowbars, and other hand tools.

6) Connect power unit to machines or steam piping to equipment, and test unit to evaluate its mechanical operation.

7) Assemble machines, and bolt, weld, rivet, or otherwise fasten them to foundation or other structures, using hand tools and power tools.

8) Insert shims, adjust tension on nuts and bolts, or position parts, using hand tools and measuring instruments, to set specified clearances between moving and stationary parts.

9) Position steel beams to support bedplates of machines and equipment, using blueprints and schematic drawings, to determine work procedures.

10) Attach moving parts and subassemblies to basic assembly unit, using hand tools and power tools.

11) Align machines and equipment, using hoists, jacks, hand tools, squares, rules, micrometers, and plumb bobs.

12) Repair and lubricate machines and equipment.

13) Operate engine lathe to grind, file, and turn machine parts to dimensional specifications.

14) Bolt parts, such as side and deck plates, jaw plates, and journals, to basic assembly unit.

15) Replace defective parts of machine or adjust clearances and alignment of moving parts.

16) Signal crane operator to lower basic assembly units to bedplate, and align unit to centerline.

17) Lay out mounting holes, using measuring instruments, and drill holes with power drill.

18) Level bedplate and establish centerline, using straightedge, levels, and transit.

19) Shrink-fit bushings, sleeves, rings, liners, gears, and wheels to specified items, using portable gas heating equipment.

49-9061.00 - Camera and Photographic Equipment Repairers

Repair and adjust cameras and photographic equipment, including commercial video and motion picture camera equipment.

Tasks

1) Install film in aircraft camera and electrical assemblies and wiring in camera housing, following blueprints, using hand tools and soldering equipment.

2) Lay out reference points and dimensions on parts and metal stock to be machined, using precision measuring instruments.

3) Test equipment performance, focus of lens system, alignment of diaphragm, lens mounts, and film transport, using precision gauges.

4) Fabricate or modify defective electronic, electrical, and mechanical components, using bench lathe, milling machine, shaper, grinder, and precision hand tools according to specifications.

5) Recommend design changes or upgrades of micro-filming, film-developing, and photographic equipment.

6) Requisition parts and materials.

7) Measure parts to verify specified dimensions/settings, such as camera shutter speed and light meter reading accuracy, using measuring instruments.

8) Examine cameras, equipment, processed film, and laboratory reports to diagnose malfunction, using work aids and specifications.

9) Disassemble equipment to gain access to defect, using hand tools.

10) Adjust cameras, photographic mechanisms, and equipment, such as range and view finders, shutters, light meters, and lens systems, using hand tools.

11) Calibrate and verify accuracy of light meters, shutter diaphragm operation, and lens carriers, using timing instruments.

12) Clean and lubricate cameras and polish camera lenses, using cleaning materials and work aids.

13) Record test data and document fabrication techniques on reports.

14) Assemble aircraft cameras, still and motion picture cameras, photographic equipment, and frames, using diagrams, blueprints, bench machines, hand tools, and power tools.

49-9062.00 - Medical Equipment Repairers

Test, adjust, or repair biomedical or electromedical equipment.

Tasks

1) Fabricate, dress down, or substitute parts or major new items to modify equipment to meet unique operational or research needs, working from job orders, sketches, modification orders, samples or discussions with operating officials.

2) Research catalogs and repair part lists to locate sources for repair parts, requisitioning parts and recording their receipt.

3) Supervise and advise subordinate personnel.

4) Test, evaluate, and classify excess or in-use medical equipment and determine serviceability, condition, and disposition in accordance with regulations.

5) Explain and demonstrate correct operation and preventive maintenance of medical equipment to personnel.

6) Test and calibrate components and equipment following manufacturers' manuals and troubleshooting techniques, using hand tools, power tools and measuring devices.

7) Contribute expertise to develop medical maintenance standard operating procedures.

8) Solder loose connections, using soldering iron.

9) Evaluate technical specifications to identify equipment and systems best suited for intended use and possible purchase based on specifications, user needs and technical requirements.

10) Perform preventive maintenance or service such as cleaning, lubricating and adjusting equipment.

11) Compute power and space requirements for installing medical, dental or related equipment and install units to manufacturers' specifications.

12) Inspect and test malfunctioning medical and related equipment following manufacturers' specifications, using test and analysis instruments.

13) Examine medical equipment and facility's structural environment and check for proper use of equipment, to protect patients and staff from electrical or mechanical hazards and to ensure compliance with safety regulations.

14) Disassemble malfunctioning equipment and remove, repair and replace defective parts such as motors, clutches or transformers.

15) Study technical manuals and attend training sessions provided by equipment manufacturers to maintain current knowledge.

16) Keep records of maintenance, repair, and required updates of equipment.

17) Repair shop equipment, metal furniture, and hospital equipment, including welding broken parts and replacing missing parts, or bring item into local shop for major repairs.

18) Make computations relating to load requirements of wiring and equipment, using algebraic expressions and standard formulas.

49-9094.00 - Locksmiths and Safe Repairers

Repair and open locks; make keys; change locks and safe combinations; and install and repair safes.

Tasks

1) Keep records of company locks and keys.

2) Open safe locks by drilling.

3) Cut new or duplicate keys, using keycutting machines.

4) Insert new or repaired tumblers into locks in order to change combinations.

5) Disassemble mechanical or electrical locking devices, and repair or replace worn tumblers, springs, and other parts, using hand tools.

6) Install safes, vault doors, and deposit boxes according to blueprints, using equipment such as powered drills, taps, dies, truck cranes, and dollies.

7) Move picklocks in cylinders in order to open door locks without keys.

8) Remove interior and exterior finishes on safes and vaults, and spray on new finishes.

49-9098.00 - Helpers--Installation, Maintenance, and Repair Workers

Help installation, maintenance, and repair workers in maintenance, parts replacement, and repair of vehicles, industrial machinery, and electrical and electronic equipment. Perform duties, such as furnishing tools, materials, and supplies to other workers; cleaning work area, machines, and tools; and holding materials or tools for other workers.

Tasks

1) Adjust, connect, or disconnect wiring, piping, tubing, and other parts, using hand tools or power tools.

2) Clean or lubricate vehicles, machinery, equipment, instruments, tools, work areas, and other objects, using hand tools, power tools, and cleaning equipment.

3) Transfer tools, parts, equipment, and supplies to and from work stations and other areas.

4) Apply protective materials to equipment, components, and parts in order to prevent defects and corrosion.

5) Provide assistance to more skilled workers involved in the adjustment, maintenance, part replacement, and repair of tools, equipment, and machines.

6) Prepare work stations so mechanics and repairers can conduct work.

7) Position vehicles, machinery, equipment, physical structures, and other objects for assembly or installation, using hand tools, power tools, and moving equipment.

8) Hold or supply tools, parts, equipment, and supplies for other workers.

9) Disassemble broken or defective equipment in order to facilitate repair; reassemble equipment when repairs are complete.

10) Assemble and maintain physical structures, using hand tools or power tools.

11) Tend and observe equipment and machinery in order to verify efficient and safe operation.

12) Install or replace machinery, equipment, and new or replacement parts and instruments, using hand tools or power tools.

51-3021.00 - Butchers and Meat Cutters

Cut, trim, or prepare consumer-sized portions of meat for use or sale in retail establishments.

Tasks

1) Shape, lace, and tie roasts, using boning knife, skewer, and twine.

2) Estimate requirements and order or requisition meat supplies to maintain inventories.

3) Cure, smoke, tenderize and preserve meat.

4) Cut, trim, bone, tie, and grind meats, such as beef, pork, poultry, and fish, to prepare meat in cooking form.

5) Prepare and place meat cuts and products in display counter, so they will appear attractive and catch the shopper's eye.

6) Wrap, weigh, label and price cuts of meat.

7) Prepare special cuts of meat ordered by customers.

8) Record quantity of meat received and issued to cooks and/or keep records of meat sales.

9) Supervise other butchers or meat cutters.

10) Total sales, and collect money from customers.

11) Negotiate with representatives from supply companies to determine order details.

51-3022.00 - Meat, Poultry, and Fish Cutters and Trimmers

Use hand tools to perform routine cutting and trimming of meat, poultry, and fish.

Tasks

1) Use knives, cleavers, meat saws, bandsaws, or other equipment to perform meat cutting and trimming.

2) Separate meats and byproducts into specified containers and seal containers.

3) Inspect meat products for defects, bruises or blemishes and remove them along with any excess fat.

4) Clean, trim, slice, and section carcasses for future processing.

5) Cut and trim meat to prepare for packing.

6) Prepare sausages, luncheon meats, hot dogs, and other fabricated meat products, using meat trimmings and hamburger meat.

7) Obtain and distribute specified meat or carcass.

8) Process primal parts into cuts that are ready for retail use.

9) Produce hamburger meat and meat trimmings.

10) Weigh meats and tag containers for weight and contents.

11) Clean and salt hides.

12) Prepare ready-to-heat foods by filleting meat or fish or cutting it into bite-sized pieces, preparing and adding vegetables or applying sauces or breading.

13) Remove parts, such as skin, feathers, scales or bones, from carcass.

51-3091.00 - Food and Tobacco Roasting, Baking, and Drying Machine Operators and Tenders

Operate or tend food or tobacco roasting, baking, or drying equipment, including hearth ovens, kiln driers, roasters, char kilns, and vacuum drying equipment.

Tasks

1) Lift racks of fish from washing tanks and place racks in smoke chambers.

2) Weigh or measure products, using scale hoppers or scale conveyors.

3) Clear or dislodge blockages in bins, screens, or other equipment, using poles, brushes, or mallets.

4) Dump sugar dust from collectors into melting tanks and add water, in order to reclaim sugar lost during processing.

5) Take product samples during and/or after processing for laboratory analyses.

6) Start conveyors to move roasted grain to cooling pans and agitate grain with rakes as blowers force air through perforated bottoms of pans.

7) Fill or remove product from trays, carts, hoppers, or equipment, using scoops, peels, or shovels, or by hand.

8) Set temperature and time controls; light ovens, burners, driers, or roasters; and start equipment, such as conveyors, cylinders, blowers, driers, or pumps.

9) Clean equipment with steam, hot water, and hoses.

10) Smooth out products in bins, pans, trays, or conveyors, using rakes or shovels.

11) Observe temperature, humidity, pressure gauges, and product samples, and adjust controls, such as thermostats and valves, in order to maintain prescribed operating conditions for specific stages.

12) Remove salt-cured fish from barrels, hang fish on racks, and place racks in washing tank, turning valves to regulate fresh water flow.

13) Test products for moisture content, using moisture meters.

14) Observe flow of materials and listen for machine malfunctions, such as jamming or spillage, and notify supervisors if corrective actions fail.

15) Signal coworkers in order to synchronize flow of materials.

16) Read work orders in order to determine quantities and types of products to be baked, dried, or roasted.

17) Push racks or carts in order to transfer products to storage, cooling stations, or the next stage of processing.

18) Operate or tend equipment that roasts, bakes, dries, or cures food items such as cocoa and coffee beans, grains, nuts, and bakery products.

19) Open valves, gates, or chutes, or use shovels in order to load or remove products from ovens or other equipment.

20) Observe, feel, taste, or otherwise examine products during and after processing, in order to ensure conformance to standards.

21) Record production data, such as weight and amount of product processed, type of product, and time and temperature of processing.

51-3092.00 - Food Batchmakers

Set up and operate equipment that mixes or blends ingredients used in the manufacturing of food products. Includes candy makers and cheese makers.

Tasks

1) Determine mixing sequences, based on knowledge of temperature effects and of the solubility of specific ingredients.

2) Press switches and turn knobs to start, adjust, and regulate equipment such as beaters, extruders, discharge pipes, and salt pumps.

3) Examine, feel, and taste product samples during production in order to evaluate quality, color, texture, flavor, and bouquet, and document the results.

4) Fill processing or cooking containers, such as kettles, rotating cookers, pressure cookers, or vats, with ingredients, by opening valves, by starting pumps or injectors, or by hand.

5) Follow recipes to produce food products of specified flavor, texture, clarity, bouquet, and/or color.

6) Manipulate products, by hand or using machines, in order to separate, spread, knead, spin, cast, cut, pull, or roll products.

7) Homogenize or pasteurize material to prevent separation or to obtain prescribed butterfat content, using a homogenizing device.

8) Modify cooking and forming operations based on the results of sampling processes, adjusting time cycles and ingredients in order to achieve desired qualities, such as firmness or texture.

9) Grade food products according to government regulations or according to type, color, bouquet, and moisture content.

10) Formulate and/or modify recipes for specific kinds of food products.

11) Clean and sterilize vats and factory processing areas.

12) Place products on carts or conveyors in order to transfer them to the next stage of processing.

13) Inspect vats after cleaning in order to ensure that fermentable residue has been removed.

14) Turn valve controls to start equipment and to adjust operation in order to maintain product quality.

15) Give directions to other workers who are assisting in the batchmaking process.

16) Set up, operate, and tend equipment that cooks, mixes, blends, or processes ingredients in the manufacturing of food products, according to formulas or recipes.

17) Operate refining machines in order to reduce the particle size of cooked batches.

18) Record production and test data for each food product batch, such as the ingredients used, temperature, test results, and time cycle.

19) Test food product samples for moisture content, acidity level, specific gravity, and/or butter-fat content, and continue processing until desired levels are reached.

20) Cool food product batches on slabs or in water-cooled kettles.

21) Mix or blend ingredients, according to recipes, using a paddle or an agitator, or by controlling vats that heat and mix ingredients.

22) Inspect and pack the final product.

23) Observe gauges and thermometers to determine if the mixing chamber temperature is within specified limits, and turn valves to control the temperature.

24) Select and measure or weigh ingredients, using English or metric measures and balance scales.

51-3093.00 - Food Cooking Machine Operators and Tenders

Operate or tend cooking equipment, such as steam cooking vats, deep fry cookers, pressure cookers, kettles, and boilers, to prepare food products.

Tasks

1) Set temperature, pressure, and time controls; and start conveyers, machines, or pumps.

2) Place products on conveyors or carts, and monitor product flow.

3) Operate auxiliary machines and equipment, such as grinders, canners, and molding presses, in order to prepare or further process products.

4) Notify or signal other workers to operate equipment or when processing is complete.

5) Listen for malfunction alarms, and shut down equipment and notify supervisors when necessary.

6) Clean, wash, and sterilize equipment and cooking area, using water hoses, cleaning or sterilizing solutions, or rinses.

7) Record production and test data, such as processing steps, temperature and steam readings, cooking time, batches processed, and test results.

8) Tend or operate and control equipment such as kettles, cookers, vats and tanks, and boilers, in order to cook ingredients or prepare products for further processing.

9) Turn valves or start pumps to add ingredients or drain products from equipment and to transfer products for storage, cooling, or further processing.

10) Remove cooked material or products from equipment.

11) Measure or weigh ingredients, using scales or measuring containers.

12) Observe gauges, dials, and product characteristics, and adjust controls in order to maintain appropriate temperature, pressure, and flow of ingredients.

13) Pour, dump, or load prescribed quantities of ingredients or products into cooking equipment, manually or using a hoist.

14) Read work orders, recipes, or formulas in order to determine cooking times and temperatures, and ingredient specifications.

15) Activate agitators and paddles in order to mix or stir ingredients, stopping machines when ingredients are thoroughly mixed.

16) Collect and examine product samples during production in order to test them for quality, color, content, consistency, viscosity, acidity, and/or specific gravity.

51-4041.00 - Machinists

Set up and operate a variety of machine tools to produce precision parts and instruments. Includes precision instrument makers who fabricate, modify, or repair mechanical instruments. May also fabricate and modify parts to make or repair machine tools or maintain industrial machines, applying knowledge of mechanics, shop mathematics, metal properties, layout, and machining procedures.

Tasks

1) Evaluate experimental procedures, and recommend changes or modifications for improved efficiency and adaptability to setup and production.

2) Install experimental parts and assemblies such as hydraulic systems, electrical wiring, lubricants, and batteries into machines and mechanisms.

3) Prepare working sketches for the illustration of product appearance.

4) Test experimental models under simulated operating conditions for such purposes as development, standardization, and feasibility of design.

5) Support metalworking projects from planning and fabrication through assembly, inspection, and testing, using knowledge of machine functions, metal properties and mathematics.

6) Align and secure holding fixtures, cutting tools, attachments, accessories, and materials onto machines.

7) Advise clients about the materials being used for finished products.

8) Clean and lubricate machines, tools, and equipment in order to remove grease, rust, stains, and foreign matter.

9) Set up and operate metalworking, brazing, heat-treating, welding, and cutting equipment.

10) Maintain industrial machines, applying knowledge of mechanics, shop mathematics, metal properties, layout, and machining procedures.

11) Establish work procedures for fabricating new structural products, using a variety of metalworking machines.

12) Dismantle machines or equipment, using hand tools and power tools, in order to examine parts for defects and replace defective parts where needed.

13) Observe and listen to operating machines or equipment in order to diagnose machine malfunctions and to determine need for adjustments or repairs.

14) Check workpieces to ensure that they are properly lubricated and cooled.

15) Machine parts to specifications using machine tools such as lathes, milling machines, shapers, or grinders.

16) Study sample parts, blueprints, drawings, and engineering information in order to determine methods and sequences of operations needed to fabricate products, and determine product dimensions and tolerances.

17) Measure, examine, and test completed units in order to detect defects and ensure conformance to specifications, using precision instruments such as micrometers.

18) Monitor the feed and speed of machines during the machining process.

19) Operate equipment to verify operational efficiency.

20) Position and fasten workpieces.

21) Select the appropriate tools, machines, and materials to be used in preparation of machinery work.

22) Set controls to regulate machining, or enter commands to retrieve, input, or edit computerized machine control media.

23) Set up, adjust, and operate all of the basic machine tools and many specialized or advanced variation tools in order to perform precision machining operations.

24) Lay out, measure, and mark metal stock in order to display placement of cuts.

25) Calculate dimensions and tolerances using knowledge of mathematics and instruments such as micrometers and vernier calipers.

26) Confer with numerical control programmers in order to check and ensure that new programs or machinery will function properly, and that output will meet specifications.

27) Install repaired parts into equipment, or install new equipment.

28) Confer with engineering, supervisory, and manufacturing personnel in order to exchange technical information.

29) Program computers and electronic instruments such as numerically controlled machine tools.

30) Design fixtures, tooling, and experimental parts to meet special engineering needs.

51-8031.00 - Water and Liquid Waste Treatment Plant and System Operators

Operate or control an entire process or system of machines, often through the use of control boards, to transfer or treat water or liquid waste.

Tasks

1) Record operational data, personnel attendance, and meter and gauge readings on specified forms.

2) Operate and adjust controls on equipment to purify and clarify water, process or dispose of sewage, and generate power.

3) Collect and test water and sewage samples, using test equipment and color analysis standards.

4) Maintain, repair, and lubricate equipment, using hand tools and power tools.

5) Clean and maintain tanks and filter beds, using hand tools and power tools.

6) Direct and coordinate plant workers engaged in routine operations and maintenance activities.

7) Inspect equipment and monitor operating conditions, meters, and gauges to determine load requirements and detect malfunctions.

Knowledge	Knowledge Definitions
Biology	Knowledge of plant and animal organisms, their tissues, cells, functions, interdependencies, and interactions with each other and the environment.
Chemistry	Knowledge of the chemical composition, structure, and properties of substances and of the chemical processes and transformations that they undergo. This includes uses of chemicals and their interactions, danger signs, production techniques, and disposal methods.
Public Safety and Security	Knowledge of relevant equipment, policies, procedures, and strategies to promote effective local, state, or national security operations for the protection of people, data, property, and institutions.
Mathematics	Knowledge of arithmetic, algebra, geometry, calculus, statistics, and their applications.
English Language	Knowledge of the structure and content of the English language including the meaning and spelling of words, rules of composition, and grammar.
Mechanical	Knowledge of machines and tools, including their designs, uses, repair, and maintenance.

51-8031.00 - Water and Liquid Waste Treatment Plant and System Operators

Physics	Knowledge and prediction of physical principles, laws, their interrelationships, and applications to understanding fluid, material, and atmospheric dynamics, and mechanical, electrical, atomic and sub- atomic structures and processes.
Law and Government	Knowledge of laws, legal codes, court procedures, precedents, government regulations, executive orders, agency rules, and the democratic political process.
Computers and Electronics	Knowledge of circuit boards, processors, chips, electronic equipment, and computer hardware and software, including applications and programming.
Customer and Personal Service	Knowledge of principles and processes for providing customer and personal services. This includes customer needs assessment, meeting quality standards for services, and evaluation of customer satisfaction.
Administration and Management	Knowledge of business and management principles involved in strategic planning, resource allocation, human resources modeling, leadership technique, production methods, and coordination of people and resources.
Engineering and Technology	Knowledge of the practical application of engineering science and technology. This includes applying principles, techniques, procedures, and equipment to the design and production of various goods and services.
Education and Training	Knowledge of principles and methods for curriculum and training design, teaching and instruction for individuals and groups, and the measurement of training effects.
Production and Processing	Knowledge of raw materials, production processes, quality control, costs, and other techniques for maximizing the effective manufacture and distribution of goods.
Clerical	Knowledge of administrative and clerical procedures and systems such as word processing, managing files and records, stenography and transcription, designing forms, and other office procedures and terminology.
Building and Construction	Knowledge of materials, methods, and the tools involved in the construction or repair of houses, buildings, or other structures such as highways and roads.
Geography	Knowledge of principles and methods for describing the features of land, sea, and air masses, including their physical characteristics, locations, interrelationships, and distribution of plant, animal, and human life.
Telecommunications	Knowledge of transmission, broadcasting, switching, control, and operation of telecommunications systems.
Personnel and Human Resources	Knowledge of principles and procedures for personnel recruitment, selection, training, compensation and benefits, labor relations and negotiation, and personnel information systems.
Communications and Media	Knowledge of media production, communication, and dissemination techniques and methods. This includes alternative ways to inform and entertain via written, oral, and visual media.
Design	Knowledge of design techniques, tools, and principles involved in production of precision technical plans, blueprints, drawings, and models.
Medicine and Dentistry	Knowledge of the information and techniques needed to diagnose and treat human injuries, diseases, and deformities. This includes symptoms, treatment alternatives, drug properties and interactions, and preventive health-care measures.
Transportation	Knowledge of principles and methods for moving people or goods by air, rail, sea, or road, including the relative costs and benefits.
Psychology	Knowledge of human behavior and performance; individual differences in ability, personality, and interests; learning and motivation; psychological research methods; and the assessment and treatment of behavioral and affective disorders.
Economics and Accounting	Knowledge of economic and accounting principles and practices, the financial markets, banking and the analysis and reporting of financial data.
Sociology and Anthropology	Knowledge of group behavior and dynamics, societal trends and influences, human migrations, ethnicity, cultures and their history and origins.
History and Archeology	Knowledge of historical events and their causes, indicators, and effects on civilizations and cultures.
Therapy and Counseling	Knowledge of principles, methods, and procedures for diagnosis, treatment, and rehabilitation of physical and mental dysfunctions, and for career counseling and guidance.
Philosophy and Theology	Knowledge of different philosophical systems and religions. This includes their basic principles, values, ethics, ways of thinking, customs, practices, and their impact on human culture.
Foreign Language	Knowledge of the structure and content of a foreign (non-English) language including the meaning and spelling of words, rules of composition and grammar, and pronunciation.
Food Production	Knowledge of techniques and equipment for planting, growing, and harvesting food products (both plant and animal) for consumption, including storage/handling techniques.
Sales and Marketing	Knowledge of principles and methods for showing, promoting, and selling products or services. This includes marketing strategy and tactics, product demonstration, sales techniques, and sales control systems.

| Fine Arts | Knowledge of the theory and techniques required to compose, produce, and perform works of music, dance, visual arts, drama, and sculpture. |

Skills	**Skills Definitions**
Reading Comprehension	Understanding written sentences and paragraphs in work related documents.
Operation and Control	Controlling operations of equipment or systems.
Troubleshooting	Determining causes of operating errors and deciding what to do about it.
Active Listening	Giving full attention to what other people are saying, taking time to understand the points being made, asking questions as appropriate, and not interrupting at inappropriate times.
Monitoring	Monitoring/Assessing performance of yourself, other individuals, or organizations to make improvements or take corrective action.
Operation Monitoring	Watching gauges, dials, or other indicators to make sure a machine is working properly.
Equipment Maintenance	Performing routine maintenance on equipment and determining when and what kind of maintenance is needed.
Learning Strategies	Selecting and using training/instructional methods and procedures appropriate for the situation when learning or teaching new things.
Critical Thinking	Using logic and reasoning to identify the strengths and weaknesses of alternative solutions, conclusions or approaches to problems.
Mathematics	Using mathematics to solve problems.
Writing	Communicating effectively in writing as appropriate for the needs of the audience.
Active Learning	Understanding the implications of new information for both current and future problem-solving and decision-making.
Judgment and Decision Making	Considering the relative costs and benefits of potential actions to choose the most appropriate one.
Installation	Installing equipment, machines, wiring, or programs to meet specifications.
Speaking	Talking to others to convey information effectively.
Coordination	Adjusting actions in relation to others' actions.
Management of Material Resources	Obtaining and seeing to the appropriate use of equipment, facilities, and materials needed to do certain work.
Instructing	Teaching others how to do something.
Quality Control Analysis	Conducting tests and inspections of products, services, or processes to evaluate quality or performance.
Complex Problem Solving	Identifying complex problems and reviewing related information to develop and evaluate options and implement solutions.
Management of Personnel Resources	Motivating, developing, and directing people as they work, identifying the best people for the job.
Repairing	Repairing machines or systems using the needed tools.
Systems Evaluation	Identifying measures or indicators of system performance and the actions needed to improve or correct performance, relative to the goals of the system.
Systems Analysis	Determining how a system should work and how changes in conditions, operations, and the environment will affect outcomes.
Operations Analysis	Analyzing needs and product requirements to create a design.
Equipment Selection	Determining the kind of tools and equipment needed to do a job.
Technology Design	Generating or adapting equipment and technology to serve user needs.
Social Perceptiveness	Being aware of others' reactions and understanding why they react as they do.
Time Management	Managing one's own time and the time of others.
Science	Using scientific rules and methods to solve problems.
Service Orientation	Actively looking for ways to help people.
Programming	Writing computer programs for various purposes.
Negotiation	Bringing others together and trying to reconcile differences.
Management of Financial Resources	Determining how money will be spent to get the work done, and accounting for these expenditures.
Persuasion	Persuading others to change their minds or behavior.

Ability	**Ability Definitions**
Near Vision	The ability to see details at close range (within a few feet of the observer).
Problem Sensitivity	The ability to tell when something is wrong or is likely to go wrong. It does not involve solving the problem, only recognizing there is a problem.
Control Precision	The ability to quickly and repeatedly adjust the controls of a machine or a vehicle to exact positions.
Deductive Reasoning	The ability to apply general rules to specific problems to produce answers that make sense.
Information Ordering	The ability to arrange things or actions in a certain order or pattern according to a specific rule or set of rules (e.g., patterns of numbers, letters, words, pictures, mathematical operations).

Arm-Hand Steadiness	The ability to keep your hand and arm steady while moving your arm or while holding your arm and hand in one position.
Multilimb Coordination	The ability to coordinate two or more limbs (for example, two arms, two legs, or one leg and one arm) while sitting, standing, or lying down. It does not involve performing the activities while the whole body is in motion.
Oral Comprehension	The ability to listen to and understand information and ideas presented through spoken words and sentences.
Inductive Reasoning	The ability to combine pieces of information to form general rules or conclusions (includes finding a relationship among seemingly unrelated events).
Oral Expression	The ability to communicate information and ideas in speaking so others will understand.
Manual Dexterity	The ability to quickly move your hand, your hand together with your arm, or your two hands to grasp, manipulate, or assemble objects.
Selective Attention	The ability to concentrate on a task over a period of time without being distracted.
Far Vision	The ability to see details at a distance.
Speech Clarity	The ability to speak clearly so others can understand you.
Trunk Strength	The ability to use your abdominal and lower back muscles to support part of the body repeatedly or continuously over time without 'giving out' or fatiguing.
Category Flexibility	The ability to generate or use different sets of rules for combining or grouping things in different ways.
Speech Recognition	The ability to identify and understand the speech of another person.
Depth Perception	The ability to judge which of several objects is closer or farther away from you, or to judge the distance between you and an object.
Visual Color Discrimination	The ability to match or detect differences between colors, including shades of color and brightness.
Perceptual Speed	The ability to quickly and accurately compare similarities and differences among sets of letters, numbers, objects, pictures, or patterns. The things to be compared may be presented at the same time or one after the other. This ability also includes comparing a presented object with a remembered object.
Flexibility of Closure	The ability to identify or detect a known pattern (a figure, object, word, or sound) that is hidden in other distracting material.
Written Comprehension	The ability to read and understand information and ideas presented in writing.
Spatial Orientation	The ability to know your location in relation to the environment or to know where other objects are in relation to you.
Written Expression	The ability to communicate information and ideas in writing so others will understand.
Reaction Time	The ability to quickly respond (with the hand, finger, or foot) to a signal (sound, light, picture) when it appears.
Finger Dexterity	The ability to make precisely coordinated movements of the fingers of one or both hands to grasp, manipulate, or assemble very small objects.
Extent Flexibility	The ability to bend, stretch, twist, or reach with your body, arms, and/or legs.
Static Strength	The ability to exert maximum muscle force to lift, push, pull, or carry objects.
Time Sharing	The ability to shift back and forth between two or more activities or sources of information (such as speech, sounds, touch, or other sources).
Visualization	The ability to imagine how something will look after it is moved around or when its parts are moved or rearranged.
Rate Control	The ability to time your movements or the movement of a piece of equipment in anticipation of changes in the speed and/or direction of a moving object or scene.
Hearing Sensitivity	The ability to detect or tell the differences between sounds that vary in pitch and loudness.
Auditory Attention	The ability to focus on a single source of sound in the presence of other distracting sounds.
Originality	The ability to come up with unusual or clever ideas about a given topic or situation, or to develop creative ways to solve a problem.
Response Orientation	The ability to choose quickly between two or more movements in response to two or more different signals (lights, sounds, pictures). It includes the speed with which the correct response is started with the hand, foot, or other body part.
Glare Sensitivity	The ability to see objects in the presence of glare or bright lighting.
Gross Body Coordination	The ability to coordinate the movement of your arms, legs, and torso together when the whole body is in motion.
Memorization	The ability to remember information such as words, numbers, pictures, and procedures.
Speed of Closure	The ability to quickly make sense of, combine, and organize information into meaningful patterns.
Sound Localization	The ability to tell the direction from which a sound originated.
Dynamic Strength	The ability to exert muscle force repeatedly or continuously over time. This involves muscular endurance and resistance to muscle fatigue.

Stamina	The ability to exert yourself physically over long periods of time without getting winded or out of breath.
Peripheral Vision	The ability to see objects or movement of objects to one's side when the eyes are looking ahead.
Number Facility	The ability to add, subtract, multiply, or divide quickly and correctly.
Gross Body Equilibrium	The ability to keep or regain your body balance or stay upright when in an unstable position.
Speed of Limb Movement	The ability to quickly move the arms and legs.
Fluency of Ideas	The ability to come up with a number of ideas about a topic (the number of ideas is important, not their quality, correctness, or creativity).
Wrist-Finger Speed	The ability to make fast, simple, repeated movements of the fingers, hands, and wrists.
Mathematical Reasoning	The ability to choose the right mathematical methods or formulas to solve a problem.
Night Vision	The ability to see under low light conditions.
Explosive Strength	The ability to use short bursts of muscle force to propel oneself (as in jumping or sprinting), or to throw an object.
Dynamic Flexibility	The ability to quickly and repeatedly bend, stretch, twist, or reach out with your body, arms, and/or legs.

Work_Activity	Work_Activity Definitions
Monitor Processes, Materials, or Surroundings	Monitoring and reviewing information from materials, events, or the environment, to detect or assess problems.
Performing General Physical Activities	Performing physical activities that require considerable use of your arms and legs and moving your whole body, such as climbing, lifting, balancing, walking, stooping, and handling of materials.
Inspecting Equipment, Structures, or Material	Inspecting equipment, structures, or materials to identify the cause of errors or other problems or defects.
Evaluating Information to Determine Compliance wit	Using relevant information and individual judgment to determine whether events or processes comply with laws, regulations, or standards.
Handling and Moving Objects	Using hands and arms in handling, installing, positioning, and moving materials, and manipulating things.
Updating and Using Relevant Knowledge	Keeping up-to-date technically and applying new knowledge to your job.
Making Decisions and Solving Problems	Analyzing information and evaluating results to choose the best solution and solve problems.
Identifying Objects, Actions, and Events	Identifying information by categorizing, estimating, recognizing differences or similarities, and detecting changes in circumstances or events.
Documenting/Recording Information	Entering, transcribing, recording, storing, or maintaining information in written or electronic/magnetic form.
Getting Information	Observing, receiving, and otherwise obtaining information from all relevant sources.
Communicating with Supervisors, Peers, or Subordin	Providing information to supervisors, co-workers, and subordinates by telephone, in written form, e-mail, or in person.
Operating Vehicles, Mechanized Devices, or Equipme	Running, maneuvering, navigating, or driving vehicles or mechanized equipment, such as forklifts, passenger vehicles, aircraft, or water craft.
Controlling Machines and Processes	Using either control mechanisms or direct physical activity to operate machines or processes (not including computers or vehicles).
Organizing, Planning, and Prioritizing Work	Developing specific goals and plans to prioritize, organize, and accomplish your work.
Analyzing Data or Information	Identifying the underlying principles, reasons, or facts of information by breaking down information or data into separate parts.
Processing Information	Compiling, coding, categorizing, calculating, tabulating, auditing, or verifying information or data.
Monitoring and Controlling Resources	Monitoring and controlling resources and overseeing the spending of money.
Thinking Creatively	Developing, designing, or creating new applications, ideas, relationships, systems, or products, including artistic contributions.
Performing for or Working Directly with the Public	Performing for people or dealing directly with the public. This includes serving customers in restaurants and stores, and receiving clients or guests.
Establishing and Maintaining Interpersonal Relatio	Developing constructive and cooperative working relationships with others, and maintaining them over time.
Developing Objectives and Strategies	Establishing long-range objectives and specifying the strategies and actions to achieve them.
Communicating with Persons Outside Organization	Communicating with people outside the organization, representing the organization to customers, the public, government, and other external sources. This information can be exchanged in person, in writing, or by telephone or e-mail.
Repairing and Maintaining Mechanical Equipment	Servicing, repairing, adjusting, and testing machines, devices, moving parts, and equipment that operate primarily on the basis of mechanical (not electronic) principles.
Repairing and Maintaining Electronic Equipment	Servicing, repairing, calibrating, regulating, fine-tuning, or testing machines, devices, and equipment that operate primarily on the basis of electrical or electronic (not mechanical) principles.
Estimating the Quantifiable Characteristics of Pro	Estimating sizes, distances, and quantities; or determining time, costs, resources, or materials needed to perform a work activity.
Resolving Conflicts and Negotiating with Others	Handling complaints, settling disputes, and resolving grievances and conflicts, or otherwise negotiating with others.
Scheduling Work and Activities	Scheduling events, programs, and activities, as well as the work of others.
Training and Teaching Others	Identifying the educational needs of others, developing formal educational or training programs or classes, and teaching or instructing others.
Interpreting the Meaning of Information for Others	Translating or explaining what information means and how it can be used.
Interacting With Computers	Using computers and computer systems (including hardware and software) to program, write software, set up functions, enter data, or process information.
Judging the Qualities of Things, Services, or Peop	Assessing the value, importance, or quality of things or people.
Guiding, Directing, and Motivating Subordinates	Providing guidance and direction to subordinates, including setting performance standards and monitoring performance.
Assisting and Caring for Others	Providing personal assistance, medical attention, emotional support, or other personal care to others such as coworkers, customers, or patients.
Coaching and Developing Others	Identifying the developmental needs of others and coaching, mentoring, or otherwise helping others to improve their knowledge or skills.
Coordinating the Work and Activities of Others	Getting members of a group to work together to accomplish tasks.
Provide Consultation and Advice to Others	Providing guidance and expert advice to management or other groups on technical, systems-, or process-related topics.
Performing Administrative Activities	Performing day-to-day administrative tasks such as maintaining information files and processing paperwork.
Developing and Building Teams	Encouraging and building mutual trust, respect, and cooperation among team members.
Selling or Influencing Others	Convincing others to buy merchandise/goods or to otherwise change their minds or actions.
Drafting, Laying Out, and Specifying Technical Dev	Providing documentation, detailed instructions, drawings, or specifications to tell others about how devices, parts, equipment, or structures are to be fabricated, constructed, assembled, modified, maintained, or used.
Staffing Organizational Units	Recruiting, interviewing, selecting, hiring, and promoting employees in an organization.

Work_Content	Work_Content Definitions
Outdoors, Exposed to Weather	How often does this job require working outdoors, exposed to all weather conditions?
Freedom to Make Decisions	How much decision making freedom, without supervision, does the job offer?
In an Enclosed Vehicle or Equipment	How often does this job require working in a closed vehicle or equipment (e.g., car)?
Wear Common Protective or Safety Equipment such as	How much does this job require wearing common protective or safety equipment such as safety shoes, glasses, gloves, hard hats or live jackets?
Structured versus Unstructured Work	To what extent is this job structured for the worker, rather than allowing the worker to determine tasks, priorities, and goals?
Frequency of Decision Making	How frequently is the worker required to make decisions that affect other people, the financial resources, and/or the image and reputation of the organization?
Impact of Decisions on Co-workers or Company Resul	How do the decisions an employee makes impact the results of co-workers, clients or the company?
Face-to-Face Discussions	How often do you have to have face-to-face discussions with individuals or teams in this job?
Indoors, Environmentally Controlled	How often does this job require working indoors in environmentally controlled conditions?
Exposed to Contaminants	How often does this job require working exposed to contaminants (such as pollutants, gases, dust or odors)?
Importance of Being Exact or Accurate	How important is being very exact or highly accurate in performing this job?
Sounds, Noise Levels Are Distracting or Uncomforta	How often does this job require working exposed to sounds and noise levels that are distracting or uncomfortable?
Telephone	How often do you have telephone conversations in this job?
Indoors, Not Environmentally Controlled	How often does this job require working indoors in non-controlled environmental conditions (e.g., warehouse without heat)?
Consequence of Error	How serious would the result usually be if the worker made a mistake that was not readily correctable?
Responsibility for Outcomes and Results	How responsible is the worker for work outcomes and results of other workers?
Very Hot or Cold Temperatures	How often does this job require working in very hot (above 90 F degrees) or very cold (below 32 F degrees) temperatures?

Exposed to Minor Burns. Cuts. Bites, or Stings	How often does this job require exposure to minor burns. cuts. bites, or stings?
Responsible for Others' Health and Safety	How much responsibility is there for the health and safety of others in this job?
Spend Time Standing	How much does this job require standing?
Exposed to Hazardous Equipment	How often does this job require exposure to hazardous equipment?
Exposed to Hazardous Conditions	How often does this job require exposure to hazardous conditions?
Spend Time Using Your Hands to Handle, Control, or	How much does this job require using your hands to handle. control, or feel objects, tools or controls?
Work With Work Group or Team	How important is it to work with others in a group or team in this job?
Importance of Repeating Same Tasks	How important is repeating the same physical activities (e.g., key entry) or mental activities (e.g., checking entries in a ledger) over and over, without stopping, to performing this job?
Exposed to Disease or Infections	How often does this job require exposure to disease/infections?
Time Pressure	How often does this job require the worker to meet strict deadlines?
Exposed to High Places	How often does this job require exposure to high places?
Contact With Others	How much does this job require the worker to be in contact with others (face-to-face, by telephone, or otherwise) in order to perform it?
Spend Time Walking and Running	How much does this job require walking and running?
Coordinate or Lead Others	How important is it to coordinate or lead others in accomplishing work activities in this job?
Degree of Automation	How automated is the job?
Outdoors, Under Cover	How often does this job require working outdoors, under cover (e.g., structure with roof but no walls)?
Letters and Memos	How often does the job require written letters and memos?
Cramped Work Space, Awkward Positions	How often does this job require working in cramped work spaces that requires getting into awkward positions?
Deal With External Customers	How important is it to work with external customers or the public in this job?
Pace Determined by Speed of Equipment	How important is it to this job that the pace is determined by the speed of equipment or machinery? (This does not refer to keeping busy at all times on this job.)
Extremely Bright or Inadequate Lighting	How often does this job require working in extremely bright or inadequate lighting conditions?
Spend Time Sitting	How often does this job require sitting?
Electronic Mail	How often do you use electronic mail in this job?
Deal With Unpleasant or Angry People	How frequently does the worker have to deal with unpleasant, angry, or discourteous individuals as part of the job requirements?
Physical Proximity	To what extent does this job require the worker to perform job tasks in close physical proximity to other people?
Spend Time Making Repetitive Motions	How much does this job require making repetitive motions?
Spend Time Climbing Ladders, Scaffolds, or Poles	How much does this job require climbing ladders, scaffolds, or poles?
Frequency of Conflict Situations	How often are there conflict situations the employee has to face in this job?
Level of Competition	To what extent does this job require the worker to compete or to be aware of competitive pressures?
Spend Time Bending or Twisting the Body	How much does this job require bending or twisting your body?
In an Open Vehicle or Equipment	How often does this job require working in an open vehicle or equipment (e.g., tractor)?
Wear Specialized Protective or Safety Equipment su	How much does this job require wearing specialized protective or safety equipment such as breathing apparatus, safety harness, full protection suits, or radiation protection?
Spend Time Keeping or Regaining Balance	How much does this job require keeping or regaining your balance?
Exposed to Whole Body Vibration	How often does this job require exposure to whole body vibration (e.g., operate a jackhammer)?
Spend Time Kneeling, Crouching, Stooping, or Crawl	How much does this job require kneeling, crouching, stooping, or crawling?
Public Speaking	How often do you have to perform public speaking in this job?
Deal With Physically Aggressive People	How frequently does this job require the worker to deal with physical aggression of violent individuals?
Exposed to Radiation	How often does this job require exposure to radiation?

Work_Styles

Work_Styles	Work_Styles Definitions
Dependability	Job requires being reliable, responsible, and dependable, and fulfilling obligations.
Attention to Detail	Job requires being careful about detail and thorough in completing work tasks.
Cooperation	Job requires being pleasant with others on the job and displaying a good-natured, cooperative attitude.
Self Control	Job requires maintaining composure, keeping emotions in check, controlling anger, and avoiding aggressive behavior, even in very difficult situations.
Analytical Thinking	Job requires analyzing information and using logic to address work-related issues and problems.
Integrity	Job requires being honest and ethical.
Initiative	Job requires a willingness to take on responsibilities and challenges.
Leadership	Job requires a willingness to lead, take charge, and offer opinions and direction.
Adaptability/Flexibility	Job requires being open to change (positive or negative) and to considerable variety in the workplace.
Independence	Job requires developing one's own ways of doing things, guiding oneself with little or no supervision, and depending on oneself to get things done.
Persistence	Job requires persistence in the face of obstacles.
Stress Tolerance	Job requires accepting criticism and dealing calmly and effectively with high stress situations.
Achievement/Effort	Job requires establishing and maintaining personally challenging achievement goals and exerting effort toward mastering tasks.
Concern for Others	Job requires being sensitive to others' needs and feelings and being understanding and helpful on the job.
Innovation	Job requires creativity and alternative thinking to develop new ideas for and answers to work-related problems.
Social Orientation	Job requires preferring to work with others rather than alone, and being personally connected with others on the job.

Job Zone Component	Job Zone Component Definitions
Title	Job Zone Three: Medium Preparation Needed
Overall Experience	Previous work-related skill, knowledge, or experience is required for these occupations. For example, an electrician must have completed three or four years of apprenticeship or several years of vocational training, and often must have passed a licensing exam, in order to perform the job.
Job Training	Employees in these occupations usually need one or two years of training involving both on-the-job experience and informal training with experienced workers.
Job Zone Examples	These occupations usually involve using communication and organizational skills to coordinate, supervise, manage, or train others to accomplish goals. Examples include dental assistants, electricians, fish and game wardens, legal secretaries, personnel recruiters, and recreation workers.
SVP Range	(6.0 to < 7.0)
Education	Most occupations in this zone require training in vocational schools, related on-the-job experience, or an associate's degree. Some may require a bachelor's degree.

51-9051.00 - Furnace, Kiln, Oven, Drier, and Kettle Operators and Tenders

Operate or tend heating equipment other than basic metal, plastic, or food processing equipment. Includes activities, such as annealing glass, drying lumber, curing rubber, removing moisture from materials, or boiling soap.

Tasks

1) Weigh or measure specified amounts of ingredients or materials for processing, using devices such as scales and calipers.

2) Stop equipment and clear blockages or jams, using fingers, wire, or hand tools.

3) Remove products from equipment, manually or using hoists, and prepare them for storage, shipment, or additional processing.

4) Read and interpret work orders and instructions in order to determine work assignments, process specifications, and production schedules.

5) Press and adjust controls in order to activate, set, and regulate equipment according to specifications.

6) Calculate amounts of materials to be loaded into furnaces, adjusting amounts as necessary for specific conditions.

7) Load equipment receptacles or conveyors with material to be processed, by hand or using hoists.

8) Direct crane operators and crew members to load vessels with materials to be processed.

9) Transport materials and products to and from work areas, manually or using carts, handtrucks, or hoists.

10) Confer with supervisors or other equipment operators in order to report equipment malfunctions or to resolve production problems.

11) Clean, lubricate, and adjust equipment, using scrapers, solvents, air hoses, oil, and hand tools.

12) Examine or test samples of processed substances, or collect samples for laboratory testing, in order to ensure conformance to specifications.

13) Sprinkle chemicals on the surface of molten metal in order to bring impurities to surface and remove impurities, using strainers.

14) Replace worn or defective equipment parts, using hand tools.

15) Record gauge readings, test results, and shift production in log books.

16) Feed fuel, such as coal and coke, into fireboxes or onto conveyors, and remove ashes from furnaces, using shovels and buckets.

17) Monitor equipment operation, gauges, and panel lights in order to detect deviations from standards.

51-9081.00 - Dental Laboratory Technicians

Construct and repair full or partial dentures or dental appliances.

Tasks

1) Rebuild or replace linings, wire sections, and missing teeth in order to repair dentures.

2) Mold wax over denture set-ups in order to form the full contours of artificial gums.

3) Melt metals or mix plaster, porcelain, or acrylic pastes; and pour materials into molds or over frameworks in order to form dental prostheses or apparatus.

4) Load newly constructed teeth into porcelain furnaces in order to bake the porcelain onto the metal framework.

5) Fill chipped or low spots in surfaces of devices, using acrylic resins.

6) Fabricate, alter, and repair dental devices such as dentures, crowns, bridges, inlays, and appliances for straightening teeth.

7) Apply porcelain paste or wax over prosthesis frameworks or setups, using brushes and spatulas.

8) Place tooth models on apparatus that mimics bite and movement of patient's jaw to evaluate functionality of model.

9) Train and supervise other dental technicians or dental laboratory bench workers.

10) Read prescriptions or specifications, and examine models and impressions, in order to determine the design of dental products to be constructed.

11) Remove excess metal or porcelain, and polish surfaces of prostheses or frameworks, using polishing machines.

12) Test appliances for conformance to specifications and accuracy of occlusion, using articulators and micrometers.

13) Create a model of patient's mouth by pouring plaster into a dental impression and allowing plaster to set.

14) Prepare wax bite-blocks and impression trays for use.

15) Prepare metal surfaces for bonding with porcelain to create artificial teeth, using small hand tools.

16) Build and shape wax teeth, using small hand instruments and information from observations or dentists' specifications.

51-9082.00 - Medical Appliance Technicians

Construct, fit, maintain, or repair medical supportive devices, such as braces, artificial limbs, joints, arch supports, and other surgical and medical appliances.

Tasks

1) Polish artificial limbs, braces, and supports, using grinding and buffing wheels.

2) Bend, form, and shape fabric or material so that it conforms to prescribed contours needed to fabricate structural components.

3) Construct or receive casts or impressions of patients' torsos or limbs for use as cutting and fabrication patterns.

4) Cover or pad metal or plastic structures and devices, using coverings such as rubber, leather, felt, plastic, or fiberglass.

5) Drill and tap holes for rivets, and glue, weld, bolt, and rivet parts together in order to form prosthetic or orthotic devices.

6) Instruct patients in use of prosthetic or orthotic devices.

7) Read prescriptions or specifications in order to determine the type of product or device to be fabricated, and the materials and tools that will be required.

8) Repair, modify, and maintain medical supportive devices, such as artificial limbs, braces, and surgical supports, according to specifications.

9) Test medical supportive devices for proper alignment, movement, and biomechanical stability, using meters and alignment fixtures.

10) Service and repair machinery used in the fabrication of appliances.

11) Mix pigments to match patients' skin coloring, according to formulas, and apply mixtures to orthotic or prosthetic devices.

12) Make orthotic/prosthetic devices using materials such as thermoplastic and thermosetting materials, metal alloys and leather, and hand and power tools.

13) Take patients' body or limb measurements for use in device construction.

14) Fit appliances onto patients, and make any necessary adjustments.

51-9083.01 - Precision Lens Grinders and Polishers

Set up and operate variety of machines and equipment to grind and polish lens and other optical elements.

Tasks

1) Adjust lenses and frames in order to correct alignment.

2) Clean finished lenses and eyeglasses, using cloths and solvents.

3) Control equipment that coats lenses to alter their reflective qualities.

4) Mount, secure, and align finished lenses in frames or optical assemblies, using precision hand tools.

5) Inspect lens blanks in order to detect flaws, verify smoothness of surface, and ensure thickness of coating on lenses.

6) Lay out lenses and trace lens outlines on glass, using templates.

7) Inspect, weigh, and measure mounted or unmounted lenses after completion in order to verify alignment and conformance to specifications, using precision instruments.

8) Shape lenses appropriately so that they can be inserted into frames.

9) Mount and secure lens blanks or optical lenses in holding tools or chucks of cutting, polishing, grinding, or coating machines.

10) Select lens blanks, molds, tools, and polishing or grinding wheels, according to production specifications.

11) Position and adjust cutting tools to specified curvature, dimensions, and depth of cut.

12) Remove lenses from molds, and separate lenses in containers for further processing or storage.

13) Examine prescriptions, work orders, or broken or used eyeglasses in order to determine specifications for lenses, contact lenses, and other optical elements.

14) Set dials and start machines to polish lenses, or hold lenses against rotating wheels in order to polish them manually.

15) Set up machines to polish, bevel, edge, and grind lenses, flats, blanks, and other precision optical elements.

16) Assemble eyeglass frames and attach shields, nose pads, and temple pieces, using pliers, screwdrivers, and drills.

17) Immerse eyeglass frames in solutions in order to harden, soften, or dye frames.

18) Repair broken parts, using precision hand tools and soldering irons.

51-9083.02 - Optical Instrument Assemblers

Assemble optical instruments, such as telescopes, level-transits, and gunsights.

Tasks

1) Position targets in darkroom tunnels, and connect optical instruments to test devices, such as oscilloscopes and collimators.

2) Measure and mark dimensions and reference points, and lay out stock for machining.

3) Insert and screw locking rings into housings in order to hold elements in place; apply cement to locking rings in order to prevent loosening.

4) Grind and polish optics, using hand tools and polishing cloths.

5) Fill instrument housings with nitrogen gas in order to minimize corrosive effects on internal optical surfaces, using vacuum pumps.

6) Coat optical elements according to specifications, using coating equipment.

7) Measure elements and instrument parts in order to verify dimensional specifications, using precision measuring instruments.

8) Mix holding compounds, and mount workpieces or optical elements on holding fixtures.

9) Set up and operate machines in order to assemble structural, mechanical, and optical parts of instruments.

10) Sight instruments on targets, and read dials in order to determine optical centers of instrument lenses and to verify compliance to focusing power specifications.

11) Study work orders, blueprints, and sketches in order to formulate plans and sequences for fabricating optical elements, instruments, and systems.

12) Compute sighting instrument distances, using trigonometric formulas.

13) Paint parts, using brushes and spray guns.

14) Record production, inspection, and test data in logs.

15) Pick up elements, using vacuum-holding devices, and position elements in mounting seats of instrument housings.

16) Cement multiple lens assemblies together.

51-9111.00 - Packaging and Filling Machine Operators and Tenders

Operate or tend machines to prepare industrial or consumer products for storage or shipment. Includes cannery workers who pack food products.

Tasks

1) Adjust machine components and machine tension and pressure according to size or processing angle of product.

2) Start machine by engaging controls.

3) Remove finished packaged items from machine and separate rejected items.

4) Regulate machine flow, speed, or temperature.

5) Package the product in the form in which it will be sent out, for example, filling bags with flour from a chute or spout.

6) Monitor the production line, watching for problems such as pile-ups, jams, or glue that isn't sticking properly.

7) Observe machine operations to ensure quality and conformity of filled or packaged products to standards.

8) Clean and remove damaged or otherwise inferior materials to prepare raw products for processing.

9) Supply materials to spindles, conveyors, hoppers, or other feeding devices and unload packaged product.

10) Attach identification labels to finished packaged items, or cut stencils and stencil information on containers, such as lot numbers or shipping destinations.

11) Clean, oil, and make minor adjustments or repairs to machinery and equipment, such as opening valves or setting guides.

12) Clean packaging containers, line and pad crates, and/or assemble cartons to prepare for product packing.

13) Count and record finished and rejected packaged items.

14) Secure finished packaged items by hand tying, sewing, gluing, stapling, or attaching fastener.

15) Sort, grade, weigh, and inspect products, verifying and adjusting product weight or measurement to meet specifications.

16) Tend or operate machine that packages product.

17) Inspect and remove defective products and packaging material.

18) Stack finished packaged items, or wrap protective material around each item and pack the items in cartons or containers.

19) Stop or reset machines when malfunctions occur, clear machine jams, and report malfunctions to a supervisor.

51-9122.00 - Painters, Transportation Equipment

Operate or tend painting machines to paint surfaces of transportation equipment, such as automobiles, buses, trucks, trains, boats, and airplanes.

Tasks

1) Apply designs, lettering, or other identifying or decorative items to finished products, using paint brushes or paint sprayers.

2) Adjust controls on infrared ovens, heat lamps, portable ventilators, and exhaust units in order to speed the drying of vehicles between coats.

3) Apply rust-resistant undercoats, and caulk and seal seams.

4) Buff and wax the finished paintwork.

5) Fill small dents and scratches with body fillers, and smooth surfaces in order to prepare vehicles for painting.

6) Lay out logos, symbols, or designs on painted surfaces, according to blueprint specifications, using measuring instruments, stencils, and patterns.

7) Paint by hand areas that cannot be reached with a spray gun, or those that need retouching, using brushes.

8) Monitor painting operations in order to identify flaws such as blisters and streaks so that their causes can be corrected.

9) Select the correct spray gun system for the material being applied.

10) Mix paints to match color specifications or vehicles' original colors, then stir and thin the paints, using spatulas or power mixing equipment.

11) Sand the final finish, and apply sealer once a vehicle has dried properly.

12) Apply primer over any repairs made to vehicle surfaces.

13) Disassemble, clean, and reassemble sprayers and power equipment, using solvents, wire brushes, and cloths for cleaning duties.

14) Pour paint into spray guns, and adjust nozzles and paint mixes in order to get the proper paint flow and coating thickness.

15) Allow the sprayed product to dry, and then touch up any spots that may have been missed.

16) Select paint according to company requirements, and match colors of paint following specified color charts.

17) Sand vehicle surfaces between coats of paint and/or primer in order to remove flaws and enhance adhesion for subsequent coats.

18) Remove grease, dirt, paint, and rust from vehicle surfaces in preparation for paint application, using abrasives, solvents, brushes, blowtorches, washing tanks, or sandblasters.

19) Verify paint consistency, using a viscosity meter.

20) Remove accessories from vehicles, such as chrome or mirrors, and mask other surfaces with tape or paper in order to protect them from paint.

21) Dispose of hazardous waste in an appropriate manner.

22) Spray prepared surfaces with specified amounts of primers and decorative or finish coatings.

23) Set up portable equipment such as ventilators, exhaust units, ladders, and scaffolding.

51-9141.00 - Semiconductor Processors

Perform any or all of the following functions in the manufacture of electronic semiconductors: load semiconductor material into furnace; saw formed ingots into segments; load individual segment into crystal growing chamber and monitor controls; locate crystal axis in ingot using x-ray equipment and saw ingots into wafers; clean, polish, and load wafers into series of special purpose furnaces, chemical baths, and equipment used to form circuitry and change conductive properties.

Tasks

1) Monitor operation and adjust controls of processing machines and equipment to produce compositions with specific electronic properties, using computer terminals.

2) Measure and weigh amounts of crystal growing materials, mix and grind materials, load materials into container, and monitor processing procedures to help identify crystal growing problems.

3) Manipulate valves, switches, and buttons, or key commands into control panels to start semiconductor processing cycles.

4) Load semiconductor material into furnace.

5) Etch, lap, polish, or grind wafers or ingots to form circuitry and change conductive properties, using etching, lapping, polishing, or grinding equipment.

6) Calculate etching time based on thickness of material to be removed from wafers or crystals.

7) Align photo mask pattern on photoresist layer, expose pattern to ultraviolet light, and develop pattern, using specialized equipment.

8) Count, sort, and weigh processed items.

9) Mount crystal ingots or wafers on blocks or plastic laminate, using special mounting devices, to facilitate their positioning in the holding fixtures of sawing, drilling, grinding or sanding equipment.

10) Attach ampoule to diffusion pump to remove air from ampoule, and seal ampoule, using blowtorch.

11) Inspect materials, components, or products for surface defects and measure circuitry, using electronic test equipment, precision measuring instruments, microscope, and standard procedures.

12) Locate crystal axis of ingot, and draw orientation lines on ingot, using x-ray equipment,

drill, and sanding machine.

13) Maintain processing, production, and inspection information and reports.

14) Operate saw to cut remelt into sections of specified size or to cut ingots into wafers.

15) Inspect equipment for leaks, diagnose malfunctions, and request repairs.

16) Connect reactor to computer, using hand tools and power tools.

17) Study work orders, instructions, formulas, and processing charts to determine specifications and sequence of operations.

18) Stamp, etch, or scribe identifying information on finished component according to specifications.

19) Set, adjust, and readjust computerized or mechanical equipment controls to regulate power level, temperature, vacuum, and rotation speed of furnace, according to crystal growing specifications.

20) Scribe or separate wafers into dice.

21) Place semiconductor wafers in processing containers or equipment holders, using vacuum wand or tweezers.

22) Clean semiconductor wafers using cleaning equipment, such as chemical baths, automatic wafer cleaners, or blow-off wands.

23) Load and unload equipment chambers and transport finished product to storage or to area for further processing.

51-9192.00 - Cleaning, Washing, and Metal Pickling Equipment Operators and Tenders

Operate or tend machines to wash or clean products, such as barrels or kegs, glass items, tin plate, food, pulp, coal, plastic, or rubber, to remove impurities.

Tasks

1) Adjust, clean, and lubricate mechanical parts of machines, using hand tools and grease guns.

2) Draw samples for laboratory analysis, or test solutions for conformance to specifications, such as acidity or specific gravity.

3) Add specified amounts of chemicals to equipment at required times to maintain solution levels and concentrations.

4) Drain, clean, and refill machines or tanks at designated intervals, using cleaning solutions or water.

5) Measure, weigh, or mix cleaning solutions, using measuring tanks, calibrated rods or suction tubes.

6) Set controls to regulate temperature and length of cycles, and start conveyors, pumps, agitators, and machines.

7) Examine and inspect machines to detect malfunctions.

8) Operate or tend machines to wash and remove impurities from items such as barrels or kegs, glass products, tin plate surfaces, dried fruit, pulp, animal stock, coal, manufactured articles, plastic, or rubber.

9) Record gauge readings, materials used, processing times, and/or test results in production logs.

10) Load machines with objects to be processed, then unload objects after cleaning and place them on conveyors or racks.

51-9193.00 - Cooling and Freezing Equipment Operators and Tenders

Operate or tend equipment, such as cooling and freezing units, refrigerators, batch freezers, and freezing tunnels, to cool or freeze products, food, blood plasma, and chemicals.

Tasks

1) Monitor pressure gauges, ammeters, flowmeters, thermometers, or products, and adjust controls to maintain specified conditions, such as feed rate, product consistency, temperature, air pressure, and machine speed.

2) Insert forming fixtures, and start machines that cut frozen products into measured portions or specified shapes.

3) Correct machinery malfunctions by performing actions such as removing jams, and inform supervisors of malfunctions as necessary.

4) Adjust machine or freezer speed and air intake in order to obtain desired consistency and amount of product.

5) Inspect and flush lines with solutions or steam, and spray equipment with sterilizing

solutions.

6) Place or position containers into equipment, and remove containers after completion of cooling or freezing processes.

7) Position molds on conveyors, and measure and adjust level of fill, using depth gauges.

8) Sample and test product characteristics such as specific gravity, acidity, and sugar content, using hydrometers, pH meters, or refractometers.

9) Record temperatures, amounts of materials processed, and/or test results on report forms.

10) Scrape, dislodge, or break excess frost, ice, or frozen product from equipment in order to prevent accumulation, using hands and hand tools.

11) Start agitators to blend contents, or start beater, scraper, and expeller blades to mix contents with air and prevent sticking.

12) Start machinery such as pumps, feeders, or conveyors, and turn valves in order to heat, admit, or transfer products, refrigerants, or mixes.

13) Stir material with spoons or paddles in order to mix ingredients or allow even cooling and prevent coagulation.

14) Weigh packages and adjust freezer air valves or switches on filler heads in order to obtain specified amounts of product in each container.

15) Activate mechanical rakes in order to regulate flow of ice from storage bins to vats.

16) Measure or weigh specified amounts of ingredients or materials, and load them into tanks, vats, hoppers, or other equipment.

17) Read dials and gauges on panel control boards in order to ascertain temperatures, alkalinities, and densities of mixtures, and turn valves in order to obtain specified mixtures.

18) Load and position wrapping paper, sticks, bags, or cartons into dispensing machines.

53-3011.00 - Ambulance Drivers and Attendants, Except Emergency Medical Technicians

Drive ambulance or assist ambulance driver in transporting sick, injured, or convalescent persons. Assist in lifting patients.

Tasks

1) Report facts concerning accidents or emergencies to hospital personnel or law enforcement officials.

2) Accompany and assist emergency medical technicians on calls.

3) Administer first aid such as bandaging, splinting, and administering oxygen.

4) Drive ambulances or assist ambulance drivers in transporting sick, injured, or convalescent persons.

5) Replace supplies and disposable items on ambulances.

6) Restrain or shackle violent patients.

7) Remove and replace soiled linens and equipment in order to maintain sanitary conditions.

8) Place patients on stretchers, and load stretchers into ambulances, usually with assistance from other attendants.

53-3021.00 - Bus Drivers, Transit and Intercity

Drive bus or motor coach, including regular route operations, charters, and private carriage. May assist passengers with baggage. May collect fares or tickets.

Tasks

1) Load and unload baggage in baggage compartments.

2) Assist passengers with baggage and collect tickets or cash fares.

3) Regulate heating, lighting, and ventilating systems for passenger comfort.

4) Inspect vehicles, and check gas, oil, and water levels prior to departure.

5) Report delays or accidents.

6) Drive vehicles over specified routes or to specified destinations according to time schedules in order to transport passengers, complying with traffic regulations.

7) Make minor repairs to vehicle and change tires.

8) Record cash receipts and ticket fares.

9) Park vehicles at loading areas so that passengers can board.

53-3022.00 - Bus Drivers, School

Transport students or special clients, such as the elderly or persons with disabilities. Ensure adherence to safety rules. May assist passengers in boarding or exiting.

Tasks

1) Comply with traffic regulations in order to operate vehicles in a safe and courteous manner.

2) Prepare and submit reports that may include the number of passengers or trips, hours worked, mileage, fuel consumption, and/or fares received.

3) Maintain order among pupils during trips, in order to ensure safety.

4) Maintain knowledge of first-aid procedures.

5) Keep bus interiors clean for passengers.

6) Escort small children across roads and highways.

7) Regulate heating, lighting, and ventilation systems for passenger comfort.

8) Read maps, and follow written and verbal geographic directions.

9) Drive gasoline, diesel, or electrically powered multi-passenger vehicles to transport students between neighborhoods, schools, and school activities.

10) Follow safety rules as students are boarding and exiting buses, and as they cross streets near bus stops.

11) Check the condition of a vehicle's tires, brakes, windshield wipers, lights, oil, fuel, water, and safety equipment to ensure that everything is in working order.

12) Report delays, accidents, or other traffic and transportation situations, using telephones or mobile two-way radios.

13) Pick up and drop off students at regularly scheduled neighborhood locations, following strict time schedules.

14) Report any bus malfunctions or needed repairs.

53-3031.00 - Driver/Sales Workers

Drive truck or other vehicle over established routes or within an established territory and sell goods, such as food products, including restaurant take-out items, or pick up and deliver items, such as laundry. May also take orders and collect payments. Includes newspaper delivery drivers.

Tasks

1) Record sales or delivery information on daily sales or delivery record.

2) Listen to and resolve customers' complaints regarding products or services.

3) Collect coins from vending machines, refill machines, and remove aged merchandise.

4) Collect money from customers, make change, and record transactions on customer receipts.

5) Call on prospective customers in order to explain company services and to solicit new business.

6) Write customer orders and sales contracts according to company guidelines.

7) Maintain trucks and food-dispensing equipment and clean inside of machines that dispense food or beverages.

8) Arrange merchandise and sales promotion displays, or issue sales promotion materials to customers.

9) Review lists of dealers, customers, or station drops and load trucks.

10) Inform regular customers of new products or services and price changes.

11) Sell food specialties, such as sandwiches and beverages, to office workers and patrons of sports events.

53-3033.00 - Truck Drivers, Light or Delivery Services

Drive a truck or van with a capacity of under 26,000 GVW, primarily to deliver or pick up merchandise or to deliver packages within a specified area. May require use of automatic routing or location software. May load and unload truck.

Tasks

1) Read maps, and follow written and verbal geographic directions.

2) Report delays, accidents, or other traffic and transportation situations to bases or other vehicles, using telephones or mobile two-way radios.

3) Maintain records such as vehicle logs, records of cargo, or billing statements in accordance with regulations.

4) Drive vehicles with capacities under three tons in order to transport materials to and from specified destinations such as railroad stations, plants, residences and offices, or within industrial yards.

5) Inspect and maintain vehicle supplies and equipment, such as gas, oil, water, tires, lights, and brakes in order to ensure that vehicles are in proper working condition.

6) Load and unload trucks, vans, or automobiles.

7) Obey traffic laws, and follow established traffic and transportation procedures.

8) Perform emergency repairs such as changing tires or installing light bulbs, fuses, tire chains, and spark plugs.

9) Turn in receipts and money received from deliveries.

10) Sell and keep records of sales for products from truck inventory.

11) Use and maintain the tools and equipment found on commercial vehicles, such as weighing and measuring devices.

12) Verify the contents of inventory loads against shipping papers.

13) Report any mechanical problems encountered with vehicles.

14) Present bills and receipts, and collect payments for goods delivered or loaded.

53-3041.00 - Taxi Drivers and Chauffeurs

Drive automobiles, vans, or limousines to transport passengers. May occasionally carry cargo.

Tasks

1) Arrange to pick up particular customers or groups on a regular schedule.

2) Drive taxicabs, limousines, company cars, or privately owned vehicles in order to transport passengers.

3) Notify dispatchers or company mechanics of vehicle problems.

4) Perform routine vehicle maintenance, such as regulating tire pressure and adding gasoline, oil, and water.

5) Pick up or meet employers according to requests, appointments, or schedules.

6) Pick up passengers at prearranged locations, at taxi stands, or by cruising streets in high traffic areas.

7) Collect fares or vouchers from passengers; and make change and/or issue receipts, as necessary.

8) Determine fares based on trip distances and times, using taximeters and fee schedules, and announce fares to passengers.

9) Provide passengers with information about the local area and points of interest, and/or give advice on hotels and restaurants.

10) Communicate with dispatchers by radio, telephone, or computer in order to exchange information and receive requests for passenger service.

11) Provide passengers with assistance entering and exiting vehicles, and help them with any luggage.

12) Perform minor vehicle repairs such as cleaning spark plugs, or take vehicles to mechanics for servicing.

13) Follow regulations governing taxi operation and ensure that passengers follow safety regulations.

14) Test vehicle equipment such as lights, brakes, horns, and windshield wipers, in order to ensure proper operation.

15) Vacuum and clean interiors, and wash and polish exteriors of automobiles.

16) Perform errands for customers or employers, such as delivering or picking up mail and packages.

17) Report to taxicab services or garages in order to receive vehicle assignments.

18) Deliver automobiles to customers from rental agencies, car dealerships, or repair shops.

19) Operate vans with special equipment, such as wheelchair lifts to transport people with special needs.

20) Turn the taximeter on when passengers enter the cab, and turn it off when they reach the final destination.

21) Drive automobiles in order to escort vehicles carrying wide loads.

22) Complete accident reports when necessary.

53-4041.00 - Subway and Streetcar Operators

Operate subway or elevated suburban train with no separate locomotive, or electric-powered streetcar to transport passengers. May handle fares.

Tasks

1) Complete reports, including shift summaries and incident or accident reports.

2) Drive and control rail-guided public transportation, such as subways, elevated trains, and electric-powered streetcars, trams, or trolleys, in order to transport passengers.

3) Make announcements to passengers, such as notifications of upcoming stops or schedule delays.

4) Operate controls to open and close transit vehicle doors.

5) Report delays, mechanical problems, and emergencies to supervisors or dispatchers, using radios.

6) Collect fares from passengers, and issue change and transfers.

7) Direct emergency evacuation procedures.

8) Greet passengers, provide information, and answer questions concerning fares, schedules, transfers, and routings.

9) Record transactions and coin receptor readings in order to verify the amount of money collected.

10) Regulate vehicle speed and the time spent at each stop, in order to maintain schedules.

11) Attend meetings on driver and passenger safety in order to learn ways in which job performance might be affected.

53-5022.00 - Motorboat Operators

Operate small motor-driven boats to carry passengers and freight between ships, or ship to shore. May patrol harbors and beach areas. May assist in navigational activities.

Tasks

1) Clean boats and repair hulls and superstructures, using hand tools, paint, and brushes.

2) Follow safety procedures in order to ensure the protection of passengers, cargo, and vessels.

3) Issue directions for loading, unloading, and seating in boats.

4) Secure boats to docks with mooring lines, and cast off lines to enable departure.

5) Maintain desired courses, using compasses or electronic navigational aids.

6) Perform general labor duties such as repairing booms.

7) Operate engine throttles and steering mechanisms in order to guide boats on desired courses.

8) Oversee operation of vessels used for carrying passengers, motor vehicles, or goods across rivers, harbors, lakes, and coastal waters.

9) Organize and direct the activities of crew members.

10) Report any observed navigational hazards to authorities.

11) Tow, push, or guide other boats, barges, logs, or rafts.

12) Position booms around docked ships.

13) Take depth soundings in turning basins.

14) Arrange repairs, fuel, and supplies for vessels.

15) Maintain equipment such as range markers, fire extinguishers, boat fenders, lines, pumps, and fittings.

16) Service motors by performing tasks such as changing oil and lubricating parts.

53-6021.00 - Parking Lot Attendants

Park automobiles or issue tickets for customers in a parking lot or garage. May collect fee.

Tasks

1) Greet customers and open their car doors.

2) Calculate parking charges, and collect fees from customers.

3) Direct motorists to parking areas or parking spaces, using hand signals or flashlights as necessary.

4) Issue ticket stubs, or place numbered tags on windshields, and give customers matching tags for locating parked vehicles.

5) Lift, position, and remove barricades in order to open or close parking areas.

6) Escort customers to their vehicles in order to ensure their safety.

7) Keep parking areas clean and orderly to ensure that space usage is maximized.

8) Patrol parking areas in order to prevent vehicle damage and vehicle or property thefts.

9) Perform maintenance on cars in storage in order to protect tires, batteries, and exteriors from deterioration.

10) Review motorists' identification before allowing them to enter parking facilities.

11) Service vehicles with gas, oil, and water.

12) Take numbered tags from customers, locate vehicles, and deliver vehicles, or provide customers with instructions for locating vehicles.

13) Park and retrieve automobiles for customers in parking lots, storage garages, or new car lots.

53-6031.00 - Service Station Attendants

Service automobiles, buses, trucks, boats, and other automotive or marine vehicles with fuel, lubricants, and accessories. Collect payment for services and supplies. May lubricate vehicle, change motor oil, install antifreeze, or replace lights or other accessories, such as windshield wiper blades or fan belts. May repair or replace tires.

Tasks

1) Prepare daily reports of fuel, oil, and accessory sales.

2) Check air pressure in vehicle tires; and levels of fuel, motor oil, transmission, radiator, battery, and other fluids; and add air, oil, water, or other fluids, as required.

3) Clean parking areas, offices, restrooms, and equipment, and remove trash.

4) Clean windshields, and/or wash and wax vehicles.

5) Collect cash payments from customers and make change, or charge purchases to customers' credit cards and provide customers with receipts.

6) Activate fuel pumps and fill fuel tanks of vehicles with gasoline or diesel fuel to specified levels.

7) Order stock, and price and shelve incoming goods.

8) Maintain customer records and follow up periodically with telephone, mail, or personal reminders of service due.

9) Grease and lubricate vehicles or specified units, such as springs, universal joints, and steering knuckles, using grease guns or spray lubricants.

10) Test and charge batteries.

11) Sell prepared food, groceries, and related items.

12) Sell and install accessories, such as batteries, windshield wiper blades, fan belts, bulbs and headlamps.

13) Rotate, test, and repair or replace tires.

14) Perform minor repairs such as adjusting brakes, replacing spark plugs, and changing engine oil and filters.

15) Operate car washes.

53-6041.00 - Traffic Technicians

Conduct field studies to determine traffic volume, speed, effectiveness of signals, adequacy of lighting, and other factors influencing traffic conditions, under direction of traffic engineer.

Tasks

1) Study factors affecting traffic conditions, such as lighting, and sign and marking visibility, in order to assess their effectiveness.

2) Visit development and work sites in order to determine projects' effect on traffic and the adequacy of plans to control traffic and maintain safety, and to suggest traffic control measures.

3) Develop plans and long-range strategies for providing adequate parking space.

4) Provide technical supervision regarding traffic control devices to other traffic technicians and laborers.

5) Interact with the public in order to answer traffic-related questions, respond to complaints and requests, or to discuss traffic control ordinances, plans, policies, and procedures.

6) Prepare work orders for repair, maintenance, and changes in traffic systems.

7) Prepare drawings of proposed signal installations or other control devices, using drafting instruments or computer automated drafting equipment.

8) Plan, design, and improve components of traffic control systems in order to accommodate current and projected traffic, and to increase usability and efficiency.

9) Monitor street and utility projects for compliance to traffic control permit conditions.

10) Interview motorists about specific intersections or highways in order to secure information regarding roadway conditions for use in planning.

53-7041.00 - Hoist and Winch Operators

11) Prepare graphs, charts, diagrams, and other aids in order to illustrate observations and conclusions.

12) Compute time settings for traffic signals and speed restrictions, using standard formulas.

13) Analyze data related to traffic flow, accident rate data, and proposed development in order to determine the most efficient methods to expedite traffic flow.

14) Time stoplights or other delays, using stopwatches.

15) Establish procedures for street closures and for repair or construction projects.

16) Lay out pavement markings for striping crews.

17) Maintain and make minor adjustments and field repairs to equipment used in surveys, including the replacement of parts on traffic data gathering devices.

18) Measure and record the speed of vehicular traffic, using electrical timing devices or radar equipment.

19) Operate counters and record data in order to assess the volume, type, and movement of vehicular and pedestrian traffic at specified times.

20) Place and secure automatic counters, using power tools, and retrieve counters after counting periods end.

21) Study traffic delays by noting times of delays, the numbers of vehicles affected, and vehicle speed through the delay area.

22) Gather and compile data from hand count sheets, machine count tapes, and radar speed checks, and code data for computer input.

53-7041.00 - Hoist and Winch Operators

Operate or tend hoists or winches to lift and pull loads using power-operated cable equipment.

Tasks

1) Signal and assist other workers loading or unloading materials.

2) Climb ladders in order to position and setup vehicle-mounted derricks.

3) Start engines of hoists or winches and use levers and pedals to wind or unwind cable on drums.

4) Move levers, pedals, and throttles in order to stop, start, and regulate speeds of hoist or winch drums in response to hand, bell, buzzer, telephone, loud-speaker, or whistle signals, or by observing dial indicators or cable marks.

5) Attach, fasten, and disconnect cables or lines to loads, materials, and equipment, using hand tools.

6) Move or reposition hoists, winches, loads and materials, manually or using equipment and machines such as trucks, cars, and hand trucks.

7) Observe equipment gauges and indicators and hand signals of other workers in order to verify load positions and/or depths.

8) Operate compressed air, diesel, electric, gasoline, or steam-driven hoists or winches in order to control movement of cableways, cages, derricks, draglines, loaders, railcars, or skips.

9) Select loads or materials according to weight and size specifications.

10) Fire boilers on steam hoists.

11) Oil winch drums so that cables will wind smoothly.

12) Repair, maintain, and adjust equipment, using hand tools.

13) Tend auxiliary equipment such as jacks, slings, cables, or stop blocks, in order to facilitate moving items or materials for further processing.

53-7051.00 - Industrial Truck and Tractor Operators

Operate industrial trucks or tractors equipped to move materials around a warehouse, storage yard, factory, construction site, or similar location.

Tasks

1) Weigh materials or products, and record weight and other production data on tags or labels.

2) Signal workers to discharge, dump, or level materials.

3) Operate or tend automatic stacking, loading, packaging, or cutting machines.

4) Perform routine maintenance on vehicles and auxiliary equipment, such as cleaning, lubricating, recharging batteries, fueling, or replacing liquefied-gas tank.

5) Hook tow trucks to trailer hitches and fasten attachments, such as graders, plows, rollers, and winch cables to tractors, using hitchpins.

6) Position lifting devices under, over, or around loaded pallets, skids, and boxes, and secure material or products for transport to designated areas.

7) Move controls to drive gasoline- or electric-powered trucks, cars, or tractors and transport materials between loading, processing, and storage areas.

8) Turn valves and open chutes in order to dump, spray, or release materials from dump cars or storage bins into hoppers.

9) Manually load or unload materials onto or off pallets, skids, platforms, cars, or lifting devices.

53-7061.00 - Cleaners of Vehicles and Equipment

Wash or otherwise clean vehicles, machinery, and other equipment. Use such materials as water, cleaning agents, brushes, cloths, and hoses.

Tasks

1) Mix cleaning solutions, abrasive compositions, and other compounds, according to formulas.

2) Collect and test samples of cleaning solutions and vapors.

3) Clean the plastic work inside cars, using paintbrushes.

4) Transport materials, equipment, or supplies to and from work areas, using carts or hoists.

5) Clean and polish vehicle windows.

6) Drive vehicles to and from workshops and/or customers' workplaces or homes.

7) Connect hoses and lines to pumps and other equipment.

8) Inspect parts, equipment, and vehicles for cleanliness, damage, and compliance with standards or regulations.

9) Maintain inventories of supplies.

10) Turn valves or disconnect hoses in order to eliminate water, cleaning solutions, or vapors from machinery or tanks.

11) Fit boot spoilers, side skirts, and mud flaps to cars.

12) Monitor operation of cleaning machines, and stop machines or notify supervisors when malfunctions occur.

13) Apply paints, dyes, polishes, reconditioners, waxes, and masking materials to vehicles in order to preserve, protect, or restore color and condition.

14) Disassemble and reassemble machines or equipment; or remove and reattach vehicle parts and trim, using hand tools.

15) Sweep, shovel, or vacuum loose debris and salvageable scrap into containers; and remove containers from work areas.

16) Scrub, scrape, or spray machine parts, equipment, or vehicles, using scrapers, brushes, clothes, cleaners, disinfectants, insecticides, acid, abrasives, vacuums, and hoses.

17) Rinse objects and place them on drying racks; or use cloth, squeegees, or air compressors to dry surfaces.

18) Press buttons to activate cleaning equipment or machines.

19) Pre-soak or rinse machine parts, equipment, or vehicles by immersing objects in cleaning solutions or water, manually or using hoists.

20) Lubricate machinery, vehicles, and equipment, and perform minor repairs and adjustments, using hand tools.

53-7064.00 - Packers and Packagers, Hand

Pack or package by hand a wide variety of products and materials.

Tasks

1) Clean containers, materials, supplies, or work areas, using cleaning solutions and hand tools.

2) Obtain, move, and sort products, materials, containers, and orders, using hand tools.

3) Transport packages to customers' vehicles.

4) Load materials and products into package processing equipment.

5) Seal containers or materials, using glues, fasteners, nails, and hand tools.

6) Mark and label containers, container tags, or products, using marking tools.

7) Place or pour products or materials into containers, using hand tools and equipment, or fill containers from spouts or chutes.

8) Remove completed or defective products or materials, placing them on moving equipment such as conveyors or in specified areas such as loading docks.

9) Assemble, line, and pad cartons, crates, and containers, using hand tools.